EXPERIENCING
THE LIFESPAN

EXPERIENCING THE LIFESPAN

Janet Belsky

Middle Tennessee State University

Worth Publishers

Grateful acknowledgment is made for permission to use the images on the following pages:
Pages 2, 34—Jupiter Images; pages 72, 452—Larry Williams/zefa/Corbis; pages 2, 106, 452—Corbis; pages 2, 138, 452—Simon Marcus/CORBIS; pages 172, 452—Jupiter Images; pages 2, 204—Christina Kennedy/Getty Images; pages 238, 452—Medioimages/Getty Images; pages 2, 268—Maria Teijeiro/Getty Images; pages 2, 301, 452—Seth Joel/Getty Images; pages 334, 452—Ranald Mackechnie/Getty Images; pages 2, 364, 452—Marc Romanelli/Getty Images; pages 2, 396, 452—Derek Shapton/Masterfile; pages 2, 422—Big Cheese Photo/Jupiter Images

Publisher: Catherine Woods

Executive Editor: Jessica Bayne

Executive Marketing Manager: Katherine Nurre

Developmental Editors: Cecilia Gardner, Nancy Fleming, Randee Falk

Media Editor: Sharon Merritt

Photo Editor: Bianca Moscatelli

Photo Researcher: Nicole Villamora

Art Director, Cover Designer: Babs Reingold

Text Designer: Charles Yuen

Layout Designer: Lee Ann Mahler

Chapter-opening Layouts: Lyndall Culbertson

Project Editor: Anthony Calcara

Illustrations: Northeastern Graphic, Dragonfly Media Group, Christy Krames

Illustration Coordinators: Susan Timmins, Bill Page

Production Manager: Sarah Segal

Composition: Northeastern Graphic

Printing and Binding: RR Donnelley

Cover: Shinichi Imanaka/Getty Images

ISBN-13: 978-0-7167-5130-4
ISBN-10: 0-7167-5130-5

Printed in the United States of America

First printing

Worth Publishers
41 Madison Avenue
New York, NY 10010
www.worthpublishers.com

To Jessica and the Worth Team—the best possible collaborators

For the students

Born in New York City, JANET BELSKY always wanted to be a writer but was also very interested in people. After receiving her undergraduate degree from the University of Pennsylvania, she deferred to her more practical and people-loving side and got her Ph.D. in clinical psychology at the University of Chicago. After years in New York teaching at Lehman College in the Bronx and doing clinical work in nursing homes and city hospitals, she migrated to Tennessee in 1991 to teach full time. In between teaching three sections of lifespan development every semester, she found the time to write a few textbooks in adult development and aging and one trade book, *Here Tomorrow: Making the Most of Life After 50* (which netted her several spots on the Today show and CNN). Her son Thomas is now an emerging adult working at Universal Studios. Janet lives in Murfreesboro, Tennessee, with her husband David, to whom she has been married for more than 27 years. In writing *Experiencing the Lifespan*, she's finally been able to merge her three passions—writing, teaching undergraduates about the lifespan, and interviewing people from age 3 to 103.

BRIEF CONTENTS

CONTENTS

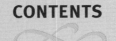

I've spent most of my adult life writing textbooks on adult development. I've spent the past thirty years (more than half of my life!) teaching this course. *Experiencing the Lifespan* represents the embodiment of my life dream. This book is the culmination of my writing and teaching careers.

It goes without saying that, being a first-edition textbook, *Experiencing the Lifespan* offers the most up-to-date research. In these pages you will find more than 1,500 21st-century citations, spanning everything from the latest neuroscience findings relating to brain development to provocative social policy critiques. But my goal is to do more than explore the science of development in its myriad magnificent forms. I've been striving to write a book that is *qualitatively* different, one that advances the art of textbook writing in our field. Here are some features that I hope will make *Experiencing the Lifespan* an experience that delights readers—and, ideally, changes students' lives.

What makes this book special?

Experiencing the Lifespan **is written to unfold like a story.** The main feature that distinguishes my book relates to the writing style. *Experiencing the Lifespan* reads like a personal conversation rather than a traditional text. Each chapter begins with a vignette constructed to highlight the material I will be discussing. I've designed my narrative to flow from topic to topic; and I've planned every chapter to interconnect. In this text, the main themes that undergird developmental science flow throughout the *entire* book. I want to give people the sense of reading an exciting, ongoing story. Most important, I want them to feel that they are learning about a coherent, *organized* field.

For this grandmother, mother, and daughter, getting dressed up to visit this Shinto family shrine and pay their respects to their ancestors is an important ritual. It is one way that the lesson "honor your elders" is taught to children living in collectivist societies such as Japan from an early age.

Experiencing the Lifespan **is uniquely organized to highlight development.** A second mission that has been driving my writing is to highlight lives evolving. How can I convey *exactly* what makes an 8-year-old different from a 4-year-old, or a 60-year-old different from a person of 85? In order to emphasize how children develop, I made the decision to cover all of childhood in a single three-chapter part. This strategy has allowed me to fully explore the magic of Piaget's preoperational and concrete operational stages. It has given me the chance to trace the evolution of aggression, childhood friendships, and gender-stereotyped play. It permits me to show *concretely* how the ability to think through their actions changes as children travel from preschool through elementary school. I decided to put early and middle adulthood in one unit (Part IV) for similar reasons: It simply made logical sense to discuss centrally important topics that transcend a single life stage, such as marriage, parenting, and work (Chapter 11, Relationships and Roles) and adult personality and cognitive development (Chapter 12, Midlife), together in the same place.

The birth of a Down syndrome child has a life-changing effect on every family member. Will this big sister become a more caring, sensitive adult through having grown up with this younger sibling?

In fact, I've designed this *whole* text to highlight development. I follow the characters in the chapter-opening vignettes throughout each several-chapter unit. I've planned each life stage segment to flow in a developmental way. In the first infancy chapter (Chapter 3, Infancy: Physical and Cognitive Development) I begin with a discussion of newborn states. The second chapter in this sequence (Infancy: Socioemotional Development) ends with a discussion of toddlerhood. My three-chapter unit devoted to adolescence and emerging adulthood starts with an exploration of puberty (Chapter 8, Physical Development) and culminates with a chapter devoted to the challenges of the early twenties (Chapter 10, Constructing an Adult Life). In Part VI, Later Life, I reverse this sequence. This section begins with a chapter devoted to topics such as retirement that typically take place during the young-old years. Then I focus on physical aging (Chapter 14, The Physical Challenges of Old Age) because sensory-motor impairments, dementing diseases, and interventions for late-life frailty become focal concerns mainly in the eighties and beyond. Yes, this textbook does—for the most part—move through the lifespan chronologically, stage by stage. However, it's targeted to highlight the aspects of development (such as physical change during early adolescence) that become salient at particular times of life. I believe that my textbook captures the best features of the chronological and topical approaches.

Families come in many forms, and the love you have for an adopted child is no different than if you gave birth. Take it from me as an adoptive mom!

This new member of the Efé people of central Africa will be lovingly cared for by the whole community, males as well as females, from his first minutes of life. Because he sleeps with his mother, however, at the "right" age he will develop his primary attachment to her.

Experiencing the Lifespan **is both shorter and more in-depth.** Adopting this flexible, development-friendly organization has the advantage of making for a more manageable, teacher-friendly book. With 15 chapters and at 475 pages, this textbook *really* can be mastered in a one-semester course! But not being locked into covering each stage of life in tiny slices gives me the freedom to focus on what is most important in special depth. As you will discover as you read my unusually comprehensive discussions of focal topics in our field, such as attachment, parenting, puberty, and adult personality consistency and change, omitting superficial coverage of "everything" allows ample time for students to reflect on the core issues in developmental science in a deeper, more thoughtful way.

Experiencing the Lifespan **actively fosters critical thinking.** Guiding students to reflect more deeply on what they are reading is actually another of my major writing goals. One great advantage of writing a text that reads like a personal dialogue is that I am able to embed critical thinking within the narrative itself. On a more academic level, this means that as I move from discussing Piaget's ideas on cognition to Vygotsky's theory to the information-processing approach in Chapter 5, I can point up the gaps in each perspective and highlight *why* each approach offers a unique contribution to understanding children's intellectual growth. On a policy-oriented level, after discussing the research relating to day care or teenage storm and stress, I can ask readers to think critically about how to improve the way our society cares for children or to devise strategies for making the wider world more user-friendly for the teenage brain.

Experiencing the Lifespan **has an international focus.** Intrinsic to getting students to think more critically about our own practices is the need to spell out different societal perspectives on our developing life. Therefore, *Experiencing the Lifespan* is a *truly* global book. This global orientation is evident in the very first chapter, when I introduce the concept of collectivist and individualistic cultures and spell out the differences between the developed and developing worlds. It is front and center in the introductory "Setting the Context" sections that often offer a cultural perspective on the material in each chapter. It is part and parcel of the ongoing discussion. In the childhood section, when discussing topics such as parenting, elementary school friendships, or constructing a self, I have full sections devoted to cultural differences. In the adulthood chapters, I offer snapshots of marriage in different cultures, look at how other societies treat the frail elderly, and explore different cultural practices and attitudes toward death. (In fact, "How do other societies handle this?" is a question that crops up when I talk about practically every topic in the book!) Moreover, by framing my cultural comparisons in terms of the collectivism–individualism dimension, I provide an overarching framework for understanding the many societal practices that are explored, rather than simply saying, "They do *this* here." (The table on pages xxxii–xxxiii offers a guide to this text's extensive cross-cultural coverage.)

Experiencing the Lifespan **highlights the multiple forces that shape development.** Given my emphasis on the cultural context, it should come as no surprise that the guiding framework that pervades my writing is the need to adopt a developmental systems approach. In *every* chapter, I emphasize the fact that relationships are bidirectional (or multidirectional). I explore the many different influences that interact to predict diverse developmental science phenomena—from the onset of puberty to childhood externalizing problems to late-life IQ. Erikson's stages, attachment theory, behavioral genetics, evolutionary theory, self-efficacy, and, especially, the importance of looking at nature *and* nurture and providing the best person–environment fit—all are concepts that I introduce in the first chapter and return to stress as the book unfolds. Another basic theme that runs through this text is the impact of socioeconomic status, both internationally and in the United States, on everything from breast-feeding practices to the rate at which we age and die. Moreover, because of my background in gerontology, I feel that it is crucial to bring home the message that our human lifespan is an evolving work in progress. Therefore, in the "Setting the Context" sections that introduce each chapter, I often offer a historical perspective on the topics we will be discussing. For example, I trace how adolescence became a life stage during the 1930s in Chapter 9. In Chapter 15, I begin by discussing how our attitudes toward death have changed over the centuries, and explore how the process of dying was transformed by the early-20th-century conquest of infectious disease.

Experiencing the Lifespan **is applications-oriented.** Because of my background as a clinical psychologist, my other passion is to bring home how the scientific findings translate into practice. So *each* topic in this text ends with an "Interventions" section spelling out practical implications of the research. With its varied Interventions, such as "How Can You Get Babies to Sleep Through the Night?" in Chapter 3 or "Using Piaget's Theory at Home and at Work" in Chapter 5, and its regular summary tables offering practical recaps of the research, such as "How to Flourish During Adulthood" in Chapter 12, *Experiencing the Lifespan* demonstrates graphically how students (and society) can use the scientific insights to personally improve lives.

Experiencing the Lifespan **is a person-centered, hands-on textbook.** My mission is also to make the developmental science findings come alive for students in a riveting, personal way. So in "Experiencing the Lifespan" boxes in each chapter, I report on interviews I've conducted with people ranging from a 15-year-old socialist in the making to a 70-year-old man with Alzheimer's disease. Because I want to teach students to empathize with the challenges of every life stage, I continually ask readers to "Imagine you are a toddler" or "a sleep-deprived mother" or "an older person struggling with the challenges of driving in later life."

Another person-centered feature of my writing is regular questionnaires (based on the research) that students can fill out to think more deeply about their *own* lives: The checklist to identify their parenting priorities in Chapter 7, reproduced here; a scale for "using selective optimization with compensation at home and work" in Chapter 12; surveys for "evaluating your relationships" in Chapters 10 and 11; true/false quizzes at the beginning of my chapters on adolescence (Chapter 9) and adult roles (Chapter 11) that provide a hands-on preview of the content and entice students into reading the chapter so that they can assess the scientific accuracy of their ideas.

In fact, I've devised a *wealth* of hands-on exercises designed to make the content of this course come alive. For instance, in Chapters 3 and 5, I offer step-by-step instructions to test for the A-not-B error in an infant or for the presence of theory of mind in a 4-year-old. In Chapter 6 I ask readers to visit a playground to see in action how the play styles of girls and boys differ. In Chapter 14, I have students think up creative alternatives to nursing homes or come up with ways of changing the driving environment in their community to make it user-friendly for older adults.

Experiencing the Lifespan **is designed to get students to learn the material while they read.** The chapter-opening vignettes, the applications sections with their regular summary tables, the hands-on exercises, and the end-of-section questionnaires (such as "A Research-based Guide for Evaluating Your Relationship" in Chapter 10) are components of an overall pedagogical plan. As I explain in my introductory letter to students on page 1, I want this to be a textbook you don't really have to study from much—one that will assist you to *naturally* cement the concepts in mind. The centerpiece of this effort is the "Tying It All Together" quizzes, which follow each major section. These mini-tests, involving multiple-choice, essay, and critical thinking questions, enable students to test themselves on what they have absorbed. (This semester we've been having a lot of fun going over the Tying It All Together quizzes as a class.) I've also planned the photo program in *Experiencing the Lifespan* to directly illustrate the major terms and concepts. As you page through the text, you may notice how the pictures and their captions feel organically connected to the writing. They function as visual extensions of the narrative itself. When it's important for students to learn a series of terms or related concepts, I provide a summary series of vivid photos. You can see examples in the photographs illustrating the different infant and adult attachment styles on pages 113 and 326; in Table 3.6 on page 95, outlining Jean Piaget's circular reactions; and in Figure 7.2 on page 207, where I visually illustrate each of Diana Baumrind's parenting styles.

TABLE 7.1: Checklist for Identifying Your Parenting Priorities

Rank the following goals in order of their importance to you, from 1 (for highest priority) to 8 (for lowest priority). It's OK to use the same number twice if two goals are equally important to you.

_____ Producing an obedient, well-behaved child

_____ Producing a caring, prosocial child

_____ Producing an independent, self-sufficient child

_____ Producing a child who is extremely close to you

_____ Producing an intelligent, creative thinker

_____ Producing a well-rounded child

_____ Producing a happy, emotionally secure child

_____ Producing a spiritual (religious) child

What do your rankings reveal about the qualities you most admire in human beings?

Does a girl this age have the memory capacity and self-regulation skills necessary to take proper care of a dog? This is the kind of question that an information-processing perspective on cognition can answer.

Steve Lyne / Getty Images

Gianni Giansanti / Corbis

Many Italian men in their late twenties are still living with their parents because they cannot afford to leave the nest. If you were in this situation, how would you react?

As you scan this book, you will notice a variety of other special features: Frequently Asked Questions (labeled "FAQ" in the margins), solicited from undergraduates around the nation, offer questions students really want to know about lifespan development. "How do we know . . . ?" boxes delve more deeply into particular research programs. "Focus on a Topic" features embedded in the chapter discussions showcase "hot topics," such as ADHD and driving in later life. Timelines pull everything together at the end of some complex sections (such as the chart summarizing the landmarks of pregnancy and prenatal development on pages 58–59). Master timelines at the beginning of each part of the book provide a detailed developmental overview of the life stage(s) I'll be discussing and alert readers to the specific landmarks and terms that I will cover in that unit.

What will make this text a pleasure to teach from? How can I make this book a joy to read? These are questions I have been grappling with as I've been glued to my computer—often seven days a week—to produce this eight-year-long labor of love.

What makes each chapter special?

Now that I've spelled out my major missions in writing this book, here are a few highlights of each chapter.

PART I: Foundations

CHAPTER 1: THE PEOPLE AND THE FIELD

- Outlines the basic contexts of development: social class, culture, and cohort.

- Traces the evolution of the lifespan over the centuries and the twentieth-century evolution of the developmental science theories that have shaped our understanding of life.

- Spells out the concepts, the perspectives, and the research strategies I will be exploring in each chapter of the book.

CHAPTER 2: PRENATAL DEVELOPMENT, PREGNANCY, AND BIRTH

- Discusses pregnancy rituals and superstitions around the world.

- Highlights the latest research on how the fetal brain develops.

- Explores the experience of pregnancy from the mother's and father's points of view.

- Looks at the experience of birth historically and discusses policy issues relating to pregnancy and birth in the United States and around the world.

PART II: Infancy

CHAPTER 3: INFANCY: PHYSICAL AND COGNITIVE DEVELOPMENT

- Covers the latest research on early brain development.

- Focuses in depth on basic infant states such as eating, crying, and sleep.

- Offers a global perspective on breast-feeding and undernutrition.

- Offers an in-depth, personal, and practice-oriented look at infant motor milestones, Piaget's sensorimotor stage, and developing language.

CHAPTER 4: INFANCY: SOCIOEMOTIONAL DEVELOPMENT

- Provides unusually in-depth coverage of attachment theory.

- Explores day care and early childhood poverty.

- Highlights exuberant and shy toddler temperaments and stresses the need to promote the right temperament–environment fit.

PART III: Childhood

CHAPTER 5: PHYSICAL AND COGNITIVE DEVELOPMENT

◼ Begins by exploring why we have childhood, illustrating what makes human beings qualitatively different from other species.

◼ Covers motor development and childhood obesity.

◼ Offers extensive coverage of Piaget's, Vygotsky's, and the information-processing models of childhood cognition—with examples that help bring the material to life and stress the practical implications of these landmark perspectives for parents and people who work with children.

◼ Explores the latest research on ADHD.

CHAPTER 6: SOCIOEMOTIONAL DEVELOPMENT

◼ Discusses the development of self-understanding, prosocial behavior, aggression (including relational aggression), and fantasy play, and explores popularity in middle childhood.

◼ Clearly spells out the developmental pathway to becoming an aggressive child.

◼ Highlights the challenge of emotion regulation and focuses on internalizing and externalizing disorders.

◼ Offers extensive coverage of bullying.

CHAPTER 7: SETTINGS FOR DEVELOPMENT: HOME AND SCHOOL

◼ This final childhood chapter shifts from the process of development to the major settings for development—home and school—and tackles important controversies in the field, such as the influence of parents versus peers versus genetics in shaping development and the pros and cons of intelligence testing.

◼ Offers extensive discussions of cultural variations in parenting styles and of the latest research on how to stimulate intrinsic motivation.

◼ Showcases schools that beat the odds and targets the core qualities involved in effective teaching.

This photograph shows the reality of motherhood today. Young working mothers are spending much *more* time teaching their children than their own, stay-at-home mothers did in the past!

PART IV: Adolescence and Emerging Adulthood

CHAPTER 8: PHYSICAL DEVELOPMENT

◼ Examines the multiple forces that program the timing of puberty and looks at historical and cultural variations in puberty timetables.

◼ Explores the emotional experience of puberty (an "insider's" view) and the emotional impact of maturing early for girls.

◼ Offers up-to-date coverage of teenage sexuality.

CHAPTER 9: COGNITIVE AND SOCIOEMOTIONAL DEVELOPMENT

◼ Covers the latest developmental science research on teenage brain development and various facets of adolescent "storm and stress."

◼ Spells out the forces that enable teenagers to thrive and explains what society can do.

◼ Explores parent–child relationships and discusses teenage peer groups.

CHAPTER 10: CONSTRUCTING AN ADULT LIFE

◼ Devotes a whole chapter to the concerns of emerging adulthood.

◼ Offers extensive coverage of cross-national variations in this life stage.

◼ Gives students tips for succeeding in college as well as spelling out career issues for non-college graduates.

◼ Introduces career-relevant topics, such as the concept of "flow," and offers extensive coverage of adult attachment styles.

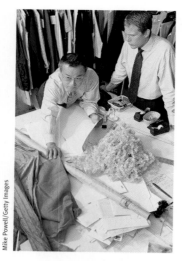

Mike Powell/Getty Images

Is the middle-aged fashion designer on the left at his creative peak? According to the research, the answer is yes. How proficient will this young man watching ultimately be at designing suits? For answers, we would want to look at this person's creative talents right now.

PART V: Early and Middle Adulthood

CHAPTER 11: RELATIONSHIPS AND ROLES

■ Focuses directly on the core issues of adult life: work and family.

■ Provides an extensive discussion of the research relating to how to have happy, enduring relationships, the challenges of parenting, and women's and men's changing work and family roles.

■ Looks at marriage, parenthood, and work in their cultural and historical contexts.

■ Offers research-based tips for having a satisfying marriage and career.

CHAPTER 12: MIDLIFE

■ Describes the complexities of measuring adult personality development, and organizes the discussion according to the "we don't change" and "we do change" points of view.

■ Anchors the research on adult intellectual change (the fluid and crystallized distinctions) to lifespan changes in creativity and careers.

■ Offers thorough coverage of the latest research on generativity.

■ Provides research-based advice for constructing a fulfilling adult life.

■ Covers age-related changes in sexuality, menopause, grandparenthood, and parent care.

PART VI: Later Life

CHAPTER 13: COGNITIVE AND SOCIOEMOTIONAL DEVELOPMENT

■ Offers an extensive discussion of Carstensen's socioemotional selectivity theory.

■ Helps decode the core qualities that make for a happy or unsatisfying old age.

■ Describes the latest research on aging memory, with special focus on making this information relevant to everyone's daily life.

■ Provides a thorough look at retirement and widowhood, including an exploration of how these transitions occur around the world.

■ Looks at later life developmentally by tracing changes from the young-old to the old-old years.

CHAPTER 14: THE PHYSICAL CHALLENGES OF OLD AGE

■ Offers a clear developmental look at how normal aging shades into chronic disease and ADL impairments, and looks at the impact of gender and socioeconomic status on physical aging.

■ Focuses on how to change the environment to compensate for sensorimotor declines.

■ Provides an in-depth look at dementia, accompanied by compelling firsthand descriptions of their inner experience by people with Alzheimer's disease.

■ Explores alternatives to institutionalization and provides a full description of nursing home care.

■ Strives to provide a realistic, honest, and yet action-oriented and uplifting portrait of the physical frailties of advanced old age.

CHAPTER 15: ENDINGS: DEATH AND DYING

■ Explores cross-cultural variations in dying and offers a historical look at death practices from the Middle Ages to today.

■ Discusses the pros and cons of the hospice movement, with its focus on dying at home.

■ Hits hard on the fact that attachment issues loom large in the experience of dying.

■ Offers a look at the pros and cons of different types of advance directives and explores controversial topics such as physician-assisted suicide.

What comes along with this book?

When you decide to use this book, you're adopting far more than just this text. You have access to an incredible learning system—everything from tests to video clips that bring the material to life. The Worth team and several dozen dedicated instructors have worked to provide an array of supplements to my text, to foster student learning and make this course a memorable one: Video clips convey the magic of prenatal development, clarify Piaget's tasks, highlight child undernutrition, and showcase the life stories of active and healthy people in their ninth and tenth decades of life; pre-built PowerPoint slides and clicker questions make class sessions more visual and interactive; student CDs allow students to learn the material at their own pace. My publisher has amassed a rich archive of developmental science materials. For additional information, please contact your Worth Publishers sales consultant or look at the Worth Web site at www.worthpublishers.com/belsky. Here are descriptions of the supplements:

Although his main goal is to greet this woman in a warm, personal way, in order to remember his new friend's name, this elderly man might want to step back and use the mnemonic strategy of forming a mental image, thinking, "I'll remember it's Mrs. Silver because of her hair."

Exploring Human Development: A Media Tool Kit

Written by a talented cast of instructors—including Carol E. Bailey, Rochester Community and Technical College; Elaine Cassal, Marymount University and Lord Fairfax Community College; Sheridan Dewolf, Grossmont College; Robin Eliason, Piedmont Virginia Community College; Lisa Huffman, Ball State University; Tom E. Ludwig, Hope College; Cathleen Erin McGreal, Michigan State University; Amy Obegi, Grossmont College; Barbara Brennan Peraino, Houston Community College; Jean Raniseski, Alvin Community College; Tanya Renner, Kapiolani Community College; Catherine F. Robertson, Grossmont College; Michael S. Swett, University of California, Berkeley Extension Online; and S. Stavros Valenti, Hofstra University—this archive of animations, videos, and PowerPoint slides offers students an interactive learning experience and gives them a huge array of electronic resources. *For instructors*, the Tool Kit is available as a set of three CD-ROMs, four VHS cassettes, or three DVDs with more than 300 video clips. Each CD includes lecture, outline, art, and video PowerPoint presentation slides and text-related figures. *For students*, the Tool Kit is a set of two CD-ROMs with more than 40 interactive video and animation-based activities, each designed to hone observational skills and bring research to life. Each activity includes a quiz that students can e-mail or print out and hand in. Also featured are quizzes and interactive flashcards for every chapter of *Experiencing the Lifespan*.

The Companion Web Site At www.worthpublishers.com/belsky

My Web site provides students with a *virtual study guide, 24 hours a day, seven days a week*. Best of all, these resources are free and do not require any special access codes or passwords. The tools on the site include: *chapter previews* highlighting key points within each chapter; *annotated Web links* related to the study of development, updated regularly to provide students with the chance to explore key topics in more depth; *online quizzes* offering multiple-choice practice tests (for every chapter) that allow students to test their knowledge of chapter concepts; *Internet exercises* asking students to expand their knowledge of core concepts with Web-based research; *interactive flashcards* that tutor students on all chapter terminology and allow them to then quiz themselves on the terms; and *frequently asked questions about developmental psychology* that permit students to think critically about lifespan development and that explore such topics as how understanding human development can help students in their careers and lives and how to pursue an advanced degree in developmental psychology.

Password-Protected Instructor's Web Site

Offers a full array of teaching resources, including PowerPoint slides, an online quiz grade book, and links to additional tools (Faculty Guides, WebCT, Blackboard, the Image and Lecture Gallery).

PowerPoint Presentation Slides

There are two prebuilt slide sets for each chapter of *Experiencing the Lifespan* (one featuring a full chapter lecture, the other featuring all chapter art and illustrations). In addition, Video PowerPoint Presentation Slides provide an easy way to integrate the Instructor's Media Tool

Kit video clips into these PowerPoint slide sets. For every video clip, PowerPoint slides tie chapter concepts to the selected clip, present explanatory slides introducing each segment, and then follow each clip with discussion questions designed to promote critical thinking and foster the student discussion that is so critical to making this course a success.

Video/DVD Resources

Journey Through the Lifespan Developmental Video Series. *Journey Through the Lifespan* illustrates the story of human growth and development from birth to old age in nine narrated segments. It includes vivid footage of people of all ages from around the world (North America, Europe, Africa, Asia, South America) in their normal environments (homes, hospitals, schools, office buildings) and at major life transitions (birth, marriage, divorce, becoming grandparents). More than one hour of unedited video footage helps students sharpen their observational skills. Interviews with prominent developmentalists, including Charles Nelson, Ann Peterson, Steven Pinker, and Barbara Rogoff, are integrated throughout this video to help show students exactly how researchers approach questions. Interviews with social workers, teachers, and nurses who work with children, adults, and older adults offer students insights into the challenges and rewards of these human service careers.

The *Scientific American Frontiers* Video Collection for Developmental Psychology. You can use these short videos, featuring 17 segments of approximately 15 minutes each, to enrich your classroom lectures, to expand on topics in the text, or even to focus on topics not covered in my book. Topics here include gene therapy, infant motor skill development, language development across the stages of child development, the nature/nurture debate, dyslexia, and memory.

Assessment

Printed Test Bank. Prepared by Kathleen Ratican, Santa Fe Community College, and Pamela Manners, Troy State University, this Test Bank includes more than 75 multiple-choice and over 60 fill-in, true-false, and essay questions for each chapter of *Experiencing the Lifespan*. Each question is keyed to the textbook by topic, page number, and level of difficulty.

Diploma Computerized Test Bank (Windows and Macintosh on one CD-ROM). This CD-ROM offers an easy-to-use test-generation system that guides you through the process of creating tests. The CD allows you to add an unlimited number of questions, edit questions, format a test, scramble questions, and include pictures, equations, or multimedia links. The accompanying gradebook enables you to record students' grades throughout a course, and it includes the capacity to sort student records and view detailed analyses of test items, curve tests, generate reports, add weights to grades, and much more. The CD-ROM is also the access point for Diploma Online Testing, and Blackboard- and WebCT-formatted versions of the Test Bank.

Diploma Online Testing. With Diploma, you can easily create and administer exams over a network and over the Internet, with questions that incorporate multimedia and interactive exercises. The program allows you to restrict tests to specific computers or time blocks, and it includes an impressive suite of gradebook and result-analysis features. For more information on Diploma, visit www.brownstone.net.

On-line Quizzing at www.worthpublishers.com/belsky. Prepared by Laura Gruntmeir, Redlands Community College, and Barry Stennet, Gainesville College. Using Worth Publishers' online quizzing engine, you can easily and securely quiz students on-line using prewritten multiple-choice questions (not from the Test Bank) for each text chapter. Students receive instant feedback and can take the quizzes multiple times. You can view results by quiz, student, or question and get weekly results via e-mail.

Course Management

Worth's E-Packs for Blackboard and WebCT provide you with cutting-edge on-line materials that facilitate critical thinking and learning. Best of all, this material is preprogrammed and fully functional in your course management system. Prebuilt materials based on my text eliminate hours of work and offer you significant support as you develop on-line courses. This package includes course outlines, preprogrammed quizzes, links, activities, interactive flashcards, and a wide array of other materials.

Instructor's Resources. Prepared by Barbara Nicoll, University of LaVerne, and Jean Raniseski, Alvin Community College, the Instructor's Resources include chapter outlines, chapter objectives, springboard topics for discussion and debate, handouts for student projects, ideas for term projects, and a guide to integrating audiovisual material and software into the course. They also include our **Teaching Tips Booklet to Accompany** *Experiencing the Lifespan.* The Worth team has canvassed instructors around the nation to gather innovative classroom practices in teaching this course and put them in one place, in a convenient format that allows for easy copying and dissemination. Most of the creative activities in this booklet involve worksheets, classroom or small-group discussions, or writing assignments.

Study Guide. Prepared by Rodger Rossman, College of the Albemarle. Each chapter includes a review of key concepts, guided study questions, and section reviews that encourage students' active participation in their learning. Two practice tests and a challenge test help students assess their mastery of the material.

This 100-year-old Chinese man showing off his calligraphy skills is a testament to the fact that people can remain extremely intellectually sharp in their areas of special expertise well into advanced old age.

Claro Cortes IV / Reuters

Who made this book possible?

This book was a completely collaborative endeavor. And the reason that I've dedicated the book to Jessica Bayne (and the exceptional Worth team) is that Jessica, my primary editor, masterminded this book from day one. Jessica encouraged me to make this book international. She was the inspiration for the Tying It All Together quizzes. She helped select the photos and selected the cover illustration. She has meticulously gone over the manuscript line by line, many, many, many, many different times. She has calmed my outbursts and kept this book on track. Jessica—let's be honest—is really the co-author of this book.

Thanks also go to Nancy Fleming, my original developmental editor, for many creative contributions and numerous helpful tips. Randee Falk and Cele Gardner offered meticulous critiques of the narrative. Cele, who coordinated the tables and figures, also deserves congratulations for her laser-sharp editor's eye. My copyeditors, Lisa Story and Emilia Westney, helped make my sentences real sentences. Tom Chao saved me hundreds of frustrating hours ferreting out references. Amanda Cotton helped me collate the references in earlier incarnations of this book.

Now we move on to the production team. Project editor Anthony Calcara coordinated the heroic task of pulling this book together—from manuscript copyediting to galleys to page proof—with aplomb. Associate managing editor Tracey Kuehn has been another unflappable guiding hand. Production manager Sarah Segal pushed everyone to get the book out on time.

Then there are the talented people who have made *Experiencing the Lifespan* look like a breathtaking work of art. As you delight in looking at the fabulous pictures, you can thank Nicole Villamora for her outstanding photo research and Bianca Moscatelli for coordinating the photo program. I have been blessed to have a brilliant layout designer, Lee Mahler, to magically manipulate the hundreds of tables and figures and photographs so that everything came together beautifully on exactly the right page. Babs Reingold, Worth's resident artistic genius, was responsible for planning the gorgeous design and layout of the book. Shinichi Imanaka is the artist who made the beautiful drawings.

Mainly off-screen, from my author's perspective, at least, are the Worth staff who coordinated the supplements and helped to develop the media package: thanks to Sharon Merritt; Andrea Musick (good luck with the baby, Andrea!), and Elaine Epstein. Elizabeth Bayne, Robin Freyberg, and Estelle Mayhew helped with the research. Kudos to my supplements authors: Rodger Rossman for the student Study Guide; Barbara Nicoll and Jean Raniseski for the Instructor's Resources; and Kathy Ratican and Pam Manners for developing the Test Bank questions in addition to providing ongoing, thorough critiques of this book.

You might think that a marketing department could not be a pivotal force in helping me with the writing. You would be wrong. Steve Rigolosi, our marketing guru, has literally kept me going through his heroic work. Steve solicited several dozen instructors to class-test a chapter. He scoured the country for instructors who offered the suggestions in the Teaching Tips booklet that accompanies the text. He was instrumental in setting up the surveys that produced the FAQs that dot the margins of the pages. He was cheering this book on for years before it actually arrived in the world. Now that I have Kate Nurre in charge of marketing, I know I am in the best possible hands. I also want to thank the sales reps, especially Tom Kling, for their valuable comments and hard work.

I am grateful to the students who *actually* came up with the FAQs that they wanted answered about lifespan development, as well as to their instructors. I feel enormously gratified to have the Teaching Tips booklet that will help this course really come alive. The thousands of students and dozens of professors who class-tested Chapter 10, 'Constructing an Adult Life,' in the spring of 2005 were a lifeline. They not only sharpened my writing but gave me courage to feel I might be on the right track.

Then there are the many reviewers who made the book what it is. Special credit goes to Suzy Horton for alerting me to the fact that attachment needed to be a main theme of this book. Kathy Ratican is responsible for suggesting my chapter on midlife and for encouraging me to put in the crucially important section on toddlerhood. Thanks also to Barry Stennett, Tom Frangigetto, James W. Collins, and Pam Manners for their inspiration and for reviewing large segments of this book. At the beginning of this process, I was fortunate to have Dave Bjorklund to help me with the chapter on childhood cognition. At the end, Denise Simonsen alerted me to some last-minute errors as she pioneered the book with her class. I'm also incredibly grateful to my other advance adopters for believing in this book and taking it on faith without really knowing if there really *would be* a book: Maria Chavira, Suzanne Cox, Heather Hill, Susie Horton, Duane Lundy, Pam Manners, Gayla Presser, and Susan Shapiro.

Here are the names of *all* the class testers, survey participants, teaching tips contributors, and the many additional reviewers who offered their insightful comments over these eight long years:

Dana Van Abbema, *St. Mary's College of Maryland*

Daisuke Akiba, *Queens College*

Cecilia Alvarez, *San Antonio College*

Emilie Aubert, *Marquette University*

Tracy Babcock, *Montana State University*

Harriet Bachner, *Northeastern State University*

Carol Bailey, *Rochester Community and Technical College*

Thomas Bailey, *University of Baltimore*

Shelly Ball, *Western Kentucky University*

Mary Ballard, *Appalachian State University*

Lacy Barnes-Mileham, *Reedley College*

Kay Bartosz, *Eastern Kentucky University*

Laura Barwegen, *Wheaton College*

Don Beach, *Tarleton State University*

Lori Beasley, *University of Central Oklahoma*

Martha-Ann Bell, *Virginia Tech*

Daniel Bellack, *Trident Technical College*

Karen Bendersky, *Georgia College and State University*

Keisha Bentley, *University of La Verne*

Robert Billingham, *Indiana University*

Jim Blonsky, *University of Tulsa*

Cheryl Bluestone, *Queensborough Community College, CUNY*

Greg Bonanno, *Teachers College, Columbia University*

Aviva Bower, *College of St. Rose*

Tom Brian, *University of Tulsa*

Marlys Bratteli, *North Dakota State University*

Bonnie Breitmayer, *University of Illinois, Chicago*

Jennifer Brennom, *Kirkwood Community College*

Adam Brown, *St. Bonaventure University*

Donna Browning, *Mississippi State University*

Janine Buckner, *Seton Hall University*

Ted Bulling, *Nebraska Wesleyan University*

Holly Bunje, *University of Minnesota, Twin Cities*

Barbara Burns, *University of Louisville*

Marilyn Burns, *Modesto Junior College*

Norma Caltagirone, *Hillsborough Community College, Ybor City*

Debb Campbell, *College of Sequoias*

Lee H. Campbell, *Edison Community College*

Robin Campbell, *Brevard Community College*

Peter Carson, *South Florida Community College*

Michael Casey, *College of Wooster*

Kimberly Chapman, *Blue River Community College*

Tom Chiaromonte, *Fullerton College*

Toni Christopherson, *California State University, Dominguez Hills*

Yiling Chow, *North Island College, Port Albernia*

Wanda Clark, *South Plains College*

Judy Collmer, *Cedar Valley College*

David Conner, *Truman State University*

Deborah Conway, *University of Virginia*

Diana Cooper, *Purdue University*

Ellen Cotter, *Georgia Southwestern State University*

Deborah M. Cox, *Madisonville Community College*

Kim B. Cragin, *Snow College*

Karen Curran, *Mt. San Antonio College*

Antonio Cutolo-Ring, *Kansas City (KS) Community College*

Nancy Darling, *Bard College*

Paul Dawson, *Weber State University*

Lynda De Dee, *University of Wisconsin, Oshkosh*

Charles Dickel, *Creighton University*

Darryl Dietrich, *College of St. Scholastica*

Benjamin Dobrin, *Virginia Wesleyan College*

Delores Doench, *Southwestern Community College*

Sundi Donovan, *Liberty University*

Lana Dryden, *Sir Sanford Fleming College*

Gwenden Dueker, *Grand Valley State University*

Bryan Duke, *University of Central Oklahoma*

Robin Eliason, *Piedmont Virginia Community College*

Frank Ellis, *University of Maine, Augusta*

Kelley Eltzroth, *Mid Michigan Community College*

Marya Endriga, *California State University, Stanislaus*

Kathryn Fagan, *California Baptist University*

Daniel Fasko, *Bowling Green State University*

Gary Felt, *City University of New York*

Martha Fewell, *Barat College*

John Foley, *Hagerstown Community College*

James Foster, *George Fox University*

Geri Fox, *University of Illinois, Chicago*

Thomas Francigetto, *Northampton Community College*

James Francis, *San Jacinto College*

Doug Friedrich, *University of West Florida*

Lynn Garrioch, *Colby-Sawyer College*

Bill Garris, *Cumberland College*

C. Ray Gentry, *Lenoir-Rhyne College*

Carol George, *Mills College*

Elizabeth Gersten, *Victor Valley College*

Linde Getahun, *Bethel University*

Afshin Gharib, *California State University, East Bay*

Nada Glick, *Yeshiva University*

Arthur Gonchar, *University of La Verne*

Helen Gore-Laird, *University of Houston, University Park*

Tyhesha N. Goss, *University of Pennsylvania*

Dan Grangaard, *Austin Community College, Rio Grande*

Julie Graul, *St. Louis Community College, Florissant Valley*

Elizabeth Gray, *North Park University*

Stefanie Gray Greiner, *Mississippi University for Women*

Dale D. Grubb, *Baldwin-Wallace College*

Laura Gruntmeir, *Redlands Community College*

Lisa Hager, *Spring Hill College*

Michael Hall, *Iowa Western Community College*

Laura Hanish, *Arizona State University*

Richard Harland, *West Texas A&M University*

Gregory Harris, *Polk Community College*

Virginia Harvey, *University of Massachusetts, Boston*

Robert Hansson, *University of Tulsa*

Gertrude Henry, *Hampton University*

Rod Hetzel, *Baylor University*

Heather Hill, *University of Texas, San Antonio*

Elaine Hogan, *University of North Carolina, Wilmington*

Judith Holland, *Hawaii Pacific University*

Debra Hollister, *Valencia Community College*

Heather Holmes-Lonergan, *Metropolitan State College of Denver*

Rosemary Hornak, *Meredith College*

Rebecca Hoss, *College of Saint Mary*

Cynthia Hudley, *University of California, Santa Barbara*

David P. Hurford, *Pittsburg State University*

Margaret Hellie Huyck, *Illinois Institute of Technology*

Elaine Ironsmith, *East Carolina University*

Sabra Jacobs, *Big Sandy Community and Technical College*

Nina Lyon Jenkins, *University of Maryland, Eastern Shore*

David Johnson, *John Brown University*

Emilie Johnson, *Lindenwood University*

Mary Johnson, *Loras College*

Peggy Jordan, *Oklahoma City Community College*

Lisa Judd, *Western Wisconsin Technical College*

Elaine Justice, *Old Dominion University*

Steve Kaatz, *Bethel University*

Chi-Ming Kam, *City College of New York, CUNY*

Skip Keith, *Delaware Technical and Community College*

Michelle L. Kelley, *Old Dominion University*

Richie Kelley, *Baptist Bible College and Seminary*

Robert Kelley, *Mira Costa College*

Jeff Kellogg, *Marian College*

Colleen Kennedy, *Roosevelt University*

Sarah Kern, *The College of New Jersey*

Marcia Killien, *University of Washington*

Kenyon Knapp, *Troy State University*

Cynthia Koenig, *Mt. St. Mary's College of Maryland*

Steve Kohn, *Valdosta State University*

Holly Krogh, *Mississippi University for Women*

Martha Kuehn, *Central Lakes College*

Alvin Kuest, *Great Lakes Christian College*

Rich Lanthier, *George Washington University*

Peggy Lauria, *Central Connecticut State University*

Melisa Layne, *Danville Community College*

John LeChapitaine, *University of Wisconsin, River Falls*

Barbara Lehmann, *Augsburg College*

Rhinehart Lintonen, *Gateway Technical College*

Nancey Lobb, *Alvin Community College*

Carol Ludders, *University of St. Francis*

Vickie Luttrell, *Dury University*

Marlowe Manger, *Stanly Community College*

Christine Malecki, *Northern Illinois University*

Pamela Manners, *Troy State University*

Kathy Manuel, *Bossier Parish Community College*

Jayne D. B. Marsh, *University of Southern Maine, Lewiston Auburn College*

Esther Martin, *California State University, Dominguez Hills*

Jan Mast, *Miami Dade College, North Campus*

Pan Maxson, *Duke University*

Nancy Mazurek, *Long Beach City College*

Christine McCormick, *Eastern Illinois University*

Jim McDonald, *California State University, Fresno*

Christy Miller, *Coker College*

Clark McKinney, *Southwest Tennessee Community College*

Al Montgomery, *Our Lady of Holy Cross College*

Robin Montvilo, *Rhode Island College*

Peggy Moody, *St. Louis Community College*

Michelle Moriarty, *Johnson County Community College*

Ken Mumm, *University of Nebraska, Kearney*

Joyce Munsch, *Texas Tech University*

Jeannette Murphey, *Meridian Community College*

Lori Myers, *Louisiana Tech University*

Lana Nenide, *University of Wisconsin, Madison*

Margaret Nettles, *Alliant University*

Gregory Newton, *Diablo Valley College*

Barbara Nicoll, *University of La Verne*

Nancy Nolan, *Nashville State Community College*

Harriett Nordstrom, *University of Michigan, Flint*

Elizabeth O'Connor, *St. Mary's College*

Susan O'Donnell, *George Fox University*

Shirley Ogletree, *Texas State University*

Claudius Oni, *South Piedmont Community College*

Randall E. Osborne, *Texas State University, San Marcos*

John Otey, *Southern Arkansas University*

Carol Ott, *University of Wisconsin, Milwaukee*

Patti Owen-Smith, *Oxford College*

Heidi Pasek, *Montana State University*

Margaret Patton, *University of North Carolina, Charlotte*

Julie Hicks Patrick, *West Virginia University*

Evelyn Payne, *Albany State University*

Carole Penner-Faje, *Molloy College*

Michelle L. Pilati, *Rio Hondo College*

Shannon M. Pruden, *Temple University*

Meril Posy, *Touro College, Brooklyn*

Ellery Pullman, *Briarcrest Bible College*

Samuel Putnam, *Bowdoin College*

Jeanne Quarles, *Oregon Coast Community College*

Mark Rafter, *College of the Canyons*

Cynthia Rand-Johnson, *Albany State University*

Janet Rangel, *Palo Alto College*

Jean Raniseski, *Alvin Community College*

Celinda Reese, *Oklahoma State University*

Ethan Remmel, *Western Washington University*

Paul Rhoads, *Williams Baptist College*

Jeanne Rivers, *Finger Lakes Community College*

Mark Rittman, *Cuyahoga Community College*

Wendy Robertson, *Western Michigan University*

Richard Robins, *University of California, Davis*

Melanie Domenech Rodriguez, *Utah State University*

Millie Roqueta, *Miami Dade College*

June Rosenberg, *Lyndon State College*

Christopher Rosnick, *University of South Florida*

Rodger Rossman, *College of the Albemarle*

Stephanie Rowley, *University of Michigan, Ann Arbor*

Lisa Routh, *Pikes Peak Community College*

Randall Russac, *University of North Florida*

Dawn Ella Rust, *Stephen F. Austin State University*

Tara Saathoff-Wells, *Central Michigan University*

Douglas Sauber, *Arcadia University*

Chris Saxild, *Wisconsin Indianhead Technical College*

Barbara Schaudt, *California State University, Bakersfield*

Pamela Schuetze, *SUNY College at Buffalo*

Donna Seagle, *Chattanooga State Technical Community College*

Bonnie Seegmiller, *Hunter College, CUNY*

Chris Seifert, *Montana State University*

Susan Shapiro, *Indiana University, East*

Elliot Sharpe, *Maryville University*

Lawrence Shelton, *University of Vermont*

Shamani Shikwambi, *University of Northern Iowa*

Denise Simonsen, *Fort Lewis College*

Penny Skemp, *Mira Costa College*

Peggy Skinner, *South Plains College*

Barbara Smith, *Westminster College*

Valerie Smith, *Collin County Community College*

Edward Sofranko, *University of Rio Grande*

Joan Spiegel, *West Los Angeles College*

Carolyn I. Spies, *Bloomfield College*

Scott Stein, *Southern Vermont College*

Stephanie Stein, *Central Washington University*

Sheila Steiner, *Jamestown College*

Jacqueline Stewart, *Seminole State College*

Robert Stewart, Jr., *Oakland University*

Cynthia Suarez, *Wofford College*

Joshua Susskind, *University of Northern Iowa*

Josephine Swalloway, *Curry College*

Emily Sweitzer, *California University of Pennsylvania*

Chuck Talor, *Valdosta State University*

Jamie Tanner, *South Georgia College*

Norma Tedder, *Edison Community College*

George Thatcher, *Texas Tech University*

Shannon Thomas, *Wallace Community College*

Donna Thompson, *Midland College*

Vicki Tinsley, *Brescia University*

Eugene Tootle, *Barry University*

David Tracer, *University of Colorado, Denver*

Stephen Truhon, *Austin Peay Centre, Fort Campbell*

Mary Vandendorpe, *Lewis University*

Janice Vidic, *University of Rio Grande*

Steven Voss, *Moberly Area Community College*

William Walkup, *Southwest Baptist University*

Anne Weiher, *Metropolitan State College of Denver*

Robert Weis, *University of Wisconsin, Stevens Point*

Lori Werdenschlag, *Lydon State College*

Noel Wescombe, *Whitworth College*

Andrea White, *Ithaca College*

Meade Whorton, *Louisiana Delta Community College*

Wanda A. Willard, *Monroe Community College*

Joylynne Wills, *Howard University*

Steffen Wilson, *Eastern Kentucky University*

Bernadette Wise, *Iowa Lakes Community College*

Steve Wisecarver, *Lord Fairfax Community College*

Alex Wiseman, *University of Tulsa*

Stephanie Wright, *Georgetown University*

Nanci Woods, *Austin Peay State University*

David Yarbrough, *Texas State University*

Nikki Yonts, *Lyon College*

Ling-Yi Zhou, *University of St. Francis*

On the home front, I am indebted to my students at Middle Tennessee State University. As any teacher will tell you, I learn as much—or more—from you each semester as you do from me. I want to thank my interviewees for sharing their lives and thereby making this book really come alive. My department deserves my gratitude for patiently listening to my frustrations with grace and for being such a special group of people that it's a joy to come to Jones Hall at 7 a.m. Thanks go to Jules Seeman, for masterfully guiding me through the minefields of life and—at a young 92—for showing me that development is the main theme of living at *every* age. I want to thank my life love, David, for making my life happy and putting this book and my happiness center stage. Thanks also to my baby, Thomas, whom you will meet throughout this book, for being born and growing up to be such a wonderful person; and for teaching me what living and being human is really all about.

Janet Belsky
October 2006

A Guide to Cross-Cultural Coverage in *Experiencing the Lifespan*

Part I

The Foundation

This two-chapter unit will give you the foundations for understanding the life-span journey. In fact, Chapter 1 introduces all the major concepts and themes in this course. Here, in "The People and the Field" you will learn our basic terminology and get advice about how to study and get the most out of this class. It will provide a bird's-eye view of our evolving lifespan, offer a framework for how to think about our world cultures, and highlight some new twenty-first-century life stages. Most important, in this chapter you will learn about the major theories, research strategies, and ideas that have shaped our field. Bottom line: Chapter 1 gives you the basic tools you will need for approaching the rest of this book.

Chapter 2, "Prenatal Development, Pregnancy, and Birth," lays out the foundation for our developing lives. Here you will learn about how a baby develops from a tiny clump of cells and get insights into the experience of pregnancy from the point of view of mothers- (and fathers-) to-be. This chapter describes pregnancy rituals in different cultures, discusses problems (including infertility) that may lie on the prenatal pathway, and offers an in-depth look at the miracle of birth.

CHAPTER 1

Dear Students,

Welcome to lifespan development! This course is about your past, your future, and who you are now. It's about your parents and grandparents, friends and colleagues, the children you have or expect to have. If you plan to work with children, adults, or older people, this course will give you an important foundation for your career. This semester, starting with the first minutes in the womb, you will get a motion picture of human life.

As we travel through the lifespan, I urge you to look outward to the wider world. While reading the infancy chapters, notice babies at restaurants. In the sections on childhood and adolescence, pay attention to boys and girls at a playground, spend an afternoon with a 4-year-old, watch pre-teens at the mall. Then observe married couples. Interview a middle-aged relative. Talk to a 60-year-old about to retire or an 85-year-old coping with the physical challenges of old age. The purpose of this class is to widen your horizons, to enable you to look at each stage of life in a more empathic way.

How can you fully enjoy the scenery on this semester-long trip and still get a great grade in this course? Following the principle that the more emotionally engaged we are, the more we learn, once again: Make it relevant; make it personal; see the concepts come alive in the world. To help you, I've begun each chapter with a vignette. Enjoy the vignette. It's been constructed to alert you to the major chapter themes. Look at the photos, charts, and the summary tables. Complete each hands-on activity. They also are planned to help you effortlessly solidify the key concepts in mind. My goal is to have you reach the end of each chapter and realize, "I don't really have to study at all (or all that much)." But most important, I want you to think: "I loved this reading. This isn't like a traditional textbook!"

Now that you know my main agendas (stay tuned for more scholarly ones later), let's get started. This chapter introduces all of the basic themes in the course. We begin by introducing the characters that you will be meeting in the introductory vignettes.

Janet Belsky

The People and the Field

It's Sadie and Saul's fiftieth anniversary, and they are having a party. They've been spending a fabulous retirement traveling and meeting different types of people. Now it's time to get their friends together for "our celebration of twenty-first-century American life."

One invitation is for Maria and baby Manuel, whom Saul and Sadie met on their Las Vegas trip five years ago. What will that precious child be like now that he's in third grade?

Sam gets another invitation, because that peppy kid has (finally) stopped floating around the world. But Sam hasn't returned to college, and he's already 26. Saul enlisted to go to Korea at age 16. He married the love of his life at 21. What's wrong with the younger generation? Will that kid ever grow up?

Still, Saul is aware how much life has changed today. Think of Kevin and Mary, that couple Sadie bumped into (literally) at the water slide at Disney World last summer. Given their hectic work schedules, and this being an interracial marriage, it's a miracle that these new friends have stayed blissfully happy for 15 years!

A final invitation goes to Kim and her daughter Elissa. With Elissa there's always catching up to do. Every week is a milestone when you are turning one. Sadie's kept up with everyone by e-mail, and everyone's coming. Now it's time to really reconnect.

First let's go to the children. Kim reports that since Elissa started walking, she does not slow down for a second. Actually, it's kind of depressing. Elissa used to go to Sadie with a smile. Now all she wants is Mom. The changes in Manuel are equally astonishing. At age 8, that child can talk to you like an adult. Still, Sadie sees the same boy she first fell in love with: sunny, kind, and just as gifted mechanically as he was at age 3!

Sam tells Sadie that he's moved in with a wonderful woman. He's thinking about getting engaged. But with his divorced parents he's anxious. Can Sadie give him clues as to whether this relationship might last?

Mary also wants advice from her "second mom." She just turned 52. This is her last chance to fulfill her dream of becoming a social worker. Can she make it in the classroom at her age?

Sadie and Saul (knock wood) are still feeling okay, but they also have worries. There's the slowness, Sadie's vision problems, and Saul's heart disease. It's lovely for them to see these young people flowering. The last act has definitely been the best. This celebration is a bit bittersweet. Their eighties won't be like the seventies. There isn't much time left.

What does Saul mean that the eighties won't be like the seventies? If you met Sadie and Saul at age 30 or 50, would they be the same vibrant, outgoing people as they are today? Is Sam's late start on his career normal, and what challenges is he facing as he makes the transition into adult life? What qualities allow couples, such as Kevin and Mary, to stay together happily; and what can you do to help ensure that you have a happy married life? Why do 1-year-olds like Elissa get clingy just as they begin walking, and can we pinpoint the mental leaps that make children of 8, such as Manuel, seem so adult?

Developmentalists or **developmental scientists**—researchers who study the lifespan—are about to answer these questions and hundreds of others about our unfolding life.

developmentalists (developmental scientists) Researchers and practitioners whose professional interest lies in the study of some aspect of human development.

Who We Are and What We Study

lifespan development The scientific field covering all of human development.

child development The scientific study of development from birth through adolescence.

gerontology The scientific study of the aging process and older adults.

adult development The scientific study of the developing adult.

Lifespan development, the scientific study of the human lifespan, is a hybrid late-comer to psychology. Its roots lie in **child development,** one of psychology's oldest specialties. Child development traces its origins back more than a century. In 1877, Charles Darwin published an article based on notes he had made about his baby during the first years of life. In the 1890s, a pioneering psychologist named G. Stanley Hall established the first institute in the United States devoted to scientifically studying the child. The field of child development began to take off between World Wars I and II (Lerner, 1998). It remains the passion of thousands of developmental scientists working in every corner of the globe.

Gerontology, the scientific study of aging—the other core discipline in lifespan development—had a slower start. Researchers began to really study the aging process only after World War II (Birren & Birren, 1990). Gerontology and its related field, **adult development,** underwent their phenomenal growth spurt during the final third of the twentieth century.

Lifespan development puts it all together. It synthesizes what researchers know about our developing life. Who works in this mammoth mega-discipline, and what passions do developmentalists have?

- **Lifespan development is multidisciplinary.** It draws on fields as diverse as neuroscience and nursing, psychology and social policy to understand every topic relating to human development. A biologically oriented developmentalist interested in day care might examine toddlers' output of salivary cortisol (a stress hormone) when they first arrive at day care in the morning. His anthropologist colleague might look at cultural values relating to the day-care choice. A social policy expert might explore the impact of offering universal government-funded day care in nations such as Finland and France. A researcher interested in the physiology of Alzheimer's disease might focus on examining the development of the plaques and tangles that ravage the brain. A nurse might head an innovative Alzheimer's unit. A research-oriented psychologist might construct a scale to measure the behavioral impairments produced by this devastating disease.

Chris Hondros / Getty Images

This woman working with youth in Palestine is one of thousands of developmental scientists whose mission it is to help children around the world.

- **Lifespan development explores the predictable milestones on our human journey,** from walking to working, to Elissa's sudden shyness and attachment to her mother. Is Mary right to worry about her learning abilities in her fifties? What is physical aging, or puberty, or menopause all about? Are there specific emotions we feel as we approach that final universal milestone, death?

- **Lifespan development focuses on the individual differences that give spice to human life,** from Manuel's mechanical talents to Sadie's outgoing personality. Can we really see the person we will be at age 8 (or 83) by age 3? How much does personality or intelligence change as we travel through life? Developmentalists want to understand what *causes* the striking individual differences we see in temperament, talents, and traits. They are interested in exploring individual differences in the *timing of* developmental milestones, too; examining, for instance, why people reach puberty earlier or later or age more quickly or slowly than their peers.

normative transitions Predictable life changes that occur during development.

non-normative transitions Unpredictable or atypical life changes that occur during development.

- **Lifespan development explores the impact of life transitions and practices.** It deals with **normative,** or predictable, **transitions,** such as Sadie and Saul's retirement, becoming parents, or beginning middle school. It focuses on **non-normative,** or atypical, **transitions,** such as divorce or the death of a child, or how the events of September 11 affected how we approach the world. It explores more enduring life practices, such as smoking, spanking, or sleeping in the same bed with your child.

Developmentalists realize that life transitions that we consider normative, such as retiring or starting middle school, are products of living in a particular time in history. They understand that life practices such as smoking or spanking or sleeping in bed with a child vary, depending on our social class and cultural background. They know that our travels through the lifespan are affected by several very basic markers, or overall conditions of life.

Our cultural background is one force that affects every aspect of development. So, culturally oriented researchers in our field might study how this South Asian wedding ceremony is designed to express this society's messages about how family life should go.

Setting the Context: Basic Markers That Shape the Lifespan

How does being born in a particular historical time affect our journey through life? What about our social class, cultural background, or that basic biological difference, being female or male? Now it's time to introduce these basic **contexts of development,** or broad general influences, which we will be continually discussing throughout this book.

The Impact of Cohort

Cohort refers to our birth group, the age group with whom we travel through life. Turn back to the vignette and you can immediately see the heavy role our cohort plays in influencing adult life. Saul reached his late teens in the 1950s, when men expected to go into the service, married young, and typically stayed married for life. Sam, who is coming of age a half-century later, faces a dazzling array of lifestyle choices, when adults regularly change careers (and often marriage partners!) and young people are especially sensitive to the problems with having relationships that last. Mary and Kevin, as an interracial couple, might have been run out of town if they'd gotten married in the 1950s or even in 1975! Being in their fifties, they are in an especially interesting cohort. They are members of the famous baby boom.

The **baby boom cohort,** defined as people born from 1946 to 1964, is leaving an indelible imprint on the Western world as it moves through society (Morgan, 1998). The reason lies in size. When soldiers returned from serving in the Second World War to get married, the average family size ballooned to almost four children. When this huge group was growing up during the 1950s, families were traditional, with the two-parent, stay-at-home-mother family being our national ideal (Coontz, 1991). Then, as rebellious adolescents during the 1960s and 1970s, the baby boomers helped engineer a radical transformation in these attitudes and roles (more about this lifestyle revolution soon). Society is bracing for an explosion of senior citizens as the baby boom cohort enters its retirement years.

The cohorts inhabiting the early twenty-first century are part of an endless march of cohorts stretching back thousands of years. Let's now take a brief historical tour, to get a sense of the dramatic changes in childhood, old age, and adulthood during just the past few centuries, and pinpoint what our lifespan looks like today.

contexts of development Fundamental markers, including cohort, socioeconomic status, culture, and gender, that shape how we develop throughout the lifespan.

cohort The age group with whom we travel through life.

baby boom cohort The huge age group born between 1946 and 1964.

Changing Conceptions of Childhood

At age ten he began his work life helping his father manufacture candles and soap. He hated dipping wicks into wax and wanted to go to sea, but his father refused and apprenticed him to a master printer. At age 17 he ran away from Boston to Philadelphia to search for work.

His father died when he was 11, and he left school. At 17 he was appointed official surveyor for Culpeper County in Virginia. By age 20 he was in charge of managing his family's plantation. (Mintz, 2004)

Library of Congress, Prints & Photographs Division, National Child Labor Committee Collection

In the nineteenth century, if you visited factories such as this cannery, you would see many young children at work—showing how far we have come over the past century in our attitudes about childhood.

[**FAQ:** Are the stages of life rigid?]

emerging adulthood The phase of life that begins after high school, tapers off toward the late twenties, and is devoted to constructing an adult life.

This twenty-something adult, who dropped out of college, went to work, and returned to a community college for practical training, is struggling with the challenges of *emerging adulthood*—that extended new life phase when we try out different options on the way to constructing an adult life.

Ulli Seit / The New York Times

Who were these boys? Their names were Benjamin Franklin and George Washington.

Imagine you were born in Colonial times. In addition to reaching adulthood at a much younger age, your chance of having *any* lifespan would have been far from secure. In seventeenth-century Paris, roughly 1 in every 3 babies died in early infancy (Ariès, 1962; Hrdy, 1999). As late as 1900, almost 3 of every 10 U.S. children did not live beyond age 5 (Mintz, 2004).

The astronomical childhood mortality rates, plus the dire poverty, may have explained why child-rearing practices that we would see as abusive today used to be routine. In eighteenth- and nineteenth-century Europe, middle-class babies were farmed out to be nursed by country women. They were separated from their parents during the first two years of life. Child abandonment was common, especially among the poor. In the early 1800s in Paris, about 1 in 5 newborns were "exposed"—placed in the doorways of churches, or simply left outside to survive or die. In cities such as St. Petersburg and Milan during the same era, the proportion might have been as high as 1 in 2 (Ariès, 1962; Hrdy, 1999).

In addition, for most of human history, historians believe that people did not have the same sense of childhood as a special stage of life (Ariès,1962; Mintz, 2004). Children, as you saw above, entered their work lives as young as age 9 or 10. During the industrial revolution, in British and U.S. mills, impoverished boys and girls made up more than a third of the labor force. They worked from dawn till dark (Mintz, 2004).

In the seventeenth and eighteenth centuries, philosophers such as John Locke and Jean Jacques Rousseau had spelled out a different vision of childhood. Locke believed that human beings are born a *tabula rasa*, a blank slate on which anything could be written, and that the way we treat children shapes their adult lives. Rousseau argued that babies enter life totally innocent and felt we should shower these dependent creatures with love. However, this message could fully penetrate society only when the scientific advances of the early twentieth century dramatically improved living standards, and we entered our modern age.

One crucial force producing our new view of childhood was universal education. During the late nineteenth century in Western Europe and much of the United States, attendance at primary school became mandatory (Ariès, 1962). School kept children from working and insulated these years as a protected, dependent life phase. Still, as late as 1915, only 1 in 10 U.S. children attended high school; most entered the work world after seventh or eighth grade (Mintz, 2004).

At the beginning of the twentieth century, the developmentalist G. Stanley Hall (1904/1969) had identified a stage of "storm and stress," located between childhood and adulthood, which he named *adolescence*. However, the person who did the most to make the teenage years into a life stage was not a psychologist but a U.S. president. During the Great Depression, faced with roaming bands of out-of-work youth, President Franklin Roosevelt signed a bill making high school attendance mandatory (Mintz, 2004). The famous adolescent culture has existed for only 60 or 70 years!

Today, with so many of us going to college and sometimes graduate school, and the fact that it typically takes at least 6 years to get a B.A. (National Center for Education Statistics, 2004), we have pushed the beginning of adulthood to an older age. Developmentalists (for example, Arnett, 2000, 2004) have recently identified a new in-between stage of life in affluent countries. **Emerging adulthood,** lasting from age 18 to roughly the late twenties, is devoted to exploring our place in the world. One reason that young people such as Sam feel perfectly comfortable about postponing marriage or settling down to a career is that we now can expect to live for an amazingly long time.

Changing Conceptions of Later Life

In every culture, a few people always lived to "old age." However, for most of history, largely due to the high rates of infant and childhood mortality, **average life expectancy,** our fifty-fifty chance at birth of living to a given age, was shockingly low. In the New England colonies, average life expectancy was about age 30. In Maryland during Colonial times, it was *under age 20,* for both masters and their slaves (Fischer, 1977).

Toward the end of the nineteenth century, life expectancy in the United States rapidly improved. By 1900 it was 46. Then, during the next century, it shot up to 76.7. Over the twentieth century, life expectancy in North America and Western Europe increased by almost 30 years! (See Kinsella & Velkoff, 2001; Sahyoun & others, 2001.)

The **twentieth-century life expectancy revolution** is perhaps the most important milestone that has occurred in the history of our species. The most dramatic increases in longevity occurred during the early decades of the previous century. During this time, medical advances, such as antibiotics, wiped out deaths from many *infectious diseases.* Since these illnesses, such as diphtheria, killed both the young and old, their conquest allowed us to live past mid-life. In the last 50 years, our progress has been slower because we are waging war against another category of disease. The illnesses we now typically die from, called *chronic diseases*—such as heart disease, cancer, and stroke—are tied to the aging process itself.

The outcome is that today life expectancies have zoomed into the upper seventies in North America, Western Europe, New Zealand, Australia, and Japan. As you can see in Figure 1.1, a baby born in the most affluent parts of the world, especially if that child is female, has a good chance of making it close to our **maximum lifespan,** the biological limit of human life (about age 105) (Kinsella & Velkoff, 2001).

This extension of the lifespan has changed how we think of *every* life stage. It has moved grandparenthood, once a sign of being "old," down into middle age. If you become a grandparent in your late forties, expect to be called grandma or grandpa for roughly half of your life! People such as Mary can start new careers in their fifties, given that they can expect to live about 30 more years. For well-off retirees, such as Saul and Sadie, retirement is now as long a life stage as childhood and adolescence combined (Clark & Quinn, 2002; Hardy, 2002). Most important, we have moved the entry point of old age beyond age 65.

Today, most often people in their sixties and seventies are active and healthy. But as we approach our eighties, our chance of being disabled by disease increases dramatically. Because of this, developmentalists make a distinction between two age groups of older adults. The **young-old,** defined as people in their sixties and seventies, often look and feel middle-aged. They reject the idea that they are old (Lachman, 2004; Palmore, 1990). The **old-old,** people in their eighties and beyond, seem in a different class. Since they are more likely to have physical and mental disabilities, they are more prone to fit the stereotype of the frail, dependent older adult. In sum, Saul is right: Today the eighties are a very different stage of life!

Changing Conceptions of Adult Life

If the medical advances of the early twentieth century made it possible for us to make it to old age, during the last third of the previous century a revolution in lifestyles transformed the way we live our adult lives. This change in society, which started in Western countries and is spreading to many other regions of the globe, occurred when the baby boomers moved into their teenage years.

average life expectancy A person's fifty-fifty chance at birth of living to a given age.

twentieth-century life expectancy revolution The dramatic increase in average life expectancy that occurred during the first half of the twentieth century in the developed world.

maximum lifespan The biological limit of human life (about 105 years).

young-old People in their sixties and seventies.

old-old People age 80 and older.

FIGURE 1.1: Average life expectancy of men and women in some affluent nations: Women today can expect to live close to the maximum lifespan in affluent countries. Notice, for instance, the astonishingly high life expectancy for women in Japan. *Source:* Kinsella & Velkoff (2001).

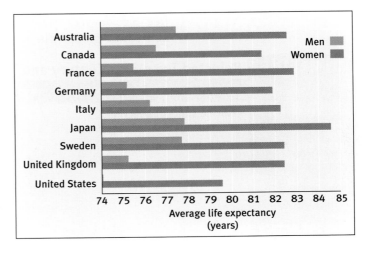

The healthy, active couple in their 60s *(left)* have little in common with the disabled 90-year-old man living in a nursing home *(right)*—showing why developmentalists divide the elderly into the *young-old* and the *old-old*.

George Shellye / Masterfile

Myrleen Ferguson Cate / Photo Edit, Inc.

The 1960s "Decade of Protest" included the civil rights and women's movements, the sexual revolution, and the "counterculture" movement that emphasized liberation in every area of life (Bengtson, 1989). People could have sex without being married. Women were free to fulfill themselves in a career. We encouraged men to share the housework and child care equally with their wives. Divorce became an acceptable alternative to living unhappily in a marriage. To have a baby, women no longer needed to be married at all (Cherlin, 2004; Furstenberg & Cherlin, 2002).

Today, with women making up roughly half the labor force, only a minority of couples fit the traditional 1950s roles of breadwinner husband and homemaker wife. Today, with roughly one out of two U.S. marriages ending in divorce (Waite & Gallagher, 2000), we can no longer be confident of following the traditional path of marrying for life. While divorce rates have stabilized and may even be declining a bit, the trend toward having children without being married continues to rise. In northern European nations, such as Sweden, today one of every two babies is born to a single mom (Kiernan, 2002, 2004).

The accompanying timeline illustrates these two twentieth-century changes. It charts the progress of the mammoth baby boom as it moves through society and highlights the emergence of our new life stages. In this book, in addition to dividing the lifespan into its standard categories—infancy, childhood, adolescence, adulthood, and old age—we will specifically focus on emerging adulthood and the old-old years. We will trace how the later-twentieth-century changes in adult lifestyles are transforming every other stage of life—from infancy to adolescence to old age.

What do you think of these changes? Have they been a benefit or not? On the positive side, we have a much more open society where anything is possible at any time of life. Mary can go back to school in her fifties. Sadie and Saul feel perfectly free to go down the water slide at Disney World and to make good friends of every age and ethnic group. The downside of the lifestyle revolution, at least in the United

TIMELINE	Selected Twentieth-Century and New Twenty-First-Century Milestones													
	1900	**1910**	**1920**	**1930**	**1940**	**1950**	**1960**	**1970**	**1980**	**1990**	**2000**	**2010**	**2020**	**2030**
LIFE EXPECTANCY TAKES OFF	Medicine shifts deaths from infectious to chronic diseases.													
LIFESTYLE REVOLUTION								Women's revolution/rise in divorce and single parenthood/more lifestyle freedom						
BABY BOOM COHORT						Born					Young-old			→
							Teenagers						Old-old	→
NEW LIFE STAGES				Adolescence					Old-old		Emerging adulthood			

States, relates to economics. Imagine the challenges of supporting a family alone, and you will understand why the rise in single parenthood and higher child poverty rates have gone hand in hand (McLanahan, 2004; Musick & Mare, 2004; Proctor & Dalaker, 2003; Song & Lu, 2002).

The Impact of Socioeconomic Status

Socioeconomic status (SES) is a term referring to our education and, especially, our income. As we will see throughout this book, living in poverty, in particular, sets people up for a cascade of problems—from being born less healthy to going to lower-quality schools; from living in more dangerous neighborhoods to dying at a younger age. In fact, adults who live under the poverty line in the United States—with an average life expectancy in the mid-sixties—may not even survive to reach later life! (See Adler and others, 1999.) Not only do developmentalists rank people by socioeconomic status, but they rank countries too.

Developed world nations are characterized by their affluence, or high median per-person incomes. In these countries—the United States, Canada, Australia, New Zealand, and Japan, as well as every Western European nation—life expectancy is high. Technology is advanced. People have widespread access to higher education and social services. They can fully enjoy the latest advances of twenty-first-century life.

Developing world countries are at the opposite end of the spectrum. Here poverty is rampant, and life can be a struggle to survive. In the least-developed nations, much of the population may not have cars, indoor plumbing, clean running water, or access to adequate education and medical care (see Figure 1.2).

Living in poverty has widespread consequences on development. How do you think the educational experiences, health, and life chances of these girls will differ from those of children growing up with affluent parents, given that they are being raised by this poor single mom?

Peter Blakely / Corbis

socioeconomic status (SES) A basic marker referring to status on the educational and—especially—income rungs.

developed world The most affluent countries in the world.

developing world The more impoverished countries of the world.

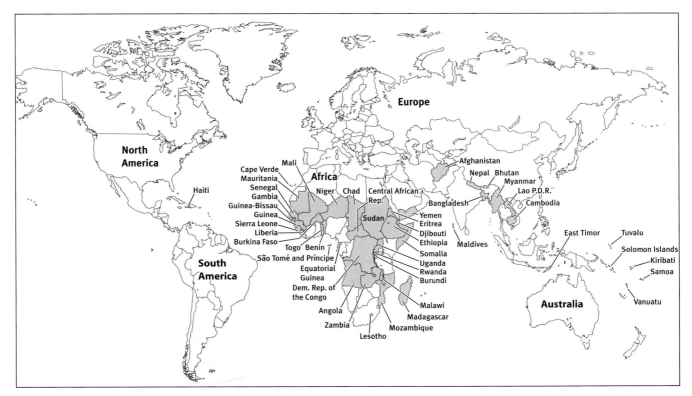

FIGURE 1.2: **Least-developed countries:** Here you can see the world's *least-developed* countries (LDCs). The criteria for this label are: low per-capita income; weak human resources (inadequate calorie intake, high rates of infant mortality, low adult literacy); and lack of economic diversification (meaning a country relies on just a few crops or industries). Africa has the most LDCs. The entire Western Hemisphere has just one—Haiti.

TABLE 1.1: Health, Wealth, and Lifestyle Gaps Between a Few of the Most- and Least-Developed Nations

	Per Capita Income (average wages per year in U.S. dollars)	Deaths of Children Under Age 5 (per 1,000)	Adult Literacy (percent) (2001)	Cell Phones (per 1,000 people)
Most-Developed Nations				
Ireland	$32,570	7	99+	774
Norway	$35,533	4	99+	815
United States	$36,056	9	99+	451
Least-Developed Nations				
Burundi	$518	196	49	4
Haiti	$1,093	123	50	11
Ethiopia	$366	177	40	0

The lifestyle, health, and educational disparities between the world's least- and most-developed countries are astonishing.

Source: World Health Organization (2005).

Table 1.1 illustrates the dramatic health and wealth gaps between a few of the most- and least-developed countries. Imagine living in a part of the world where infectious diseases such as malaria are common, many of your neighbors are unable to read or write, and you have less than a fifty-fifty chance of living beyond middle age. Babies born in the most impoverished regions of the globe face a twenty-first-century lifespan that has striking similarities to the one poor developed-world children faced several centuries ago.

The Impact of Culture

[FAQ: How does culture affect development?

Residents of developing world nations, especially those living outside of urban areas, tend not to have experienced the late-twentieth-century changes in men's and women's roles. Gender roles are often more rigid. Divorce may be against the law. Arranged marriages still occur, with parents deciding whom their children should wed. Still, if you visited these countries, you might be struck by the stong shared sense of community and family commitment that we might not often find in the West. Is there a way of categorizing cultures according to their basic values? Developmentalists who study culture answer yes.

collectivist cultures Societies that prize social harmony, obedience, and close family connectedness over individual achievement.

Collectivist cultures value social harmony over individual achievement. The family generations expect to live together, even as adults. Children are taught to obey their elders and to subordinate their needs to the good of the wider group.

individualistic cultures Societies that prize independence, competition, and personal success.

Individualistic cultures emphasize independence, competition, and personal success. Children are encouraged to openly express their feelings and to become self-sufficient, independent adults. Traditionally, Western nations score high on indexes of individualism. Nations in Asia, Africa, and South America rank higher on collectivism scales (Hofstede, 1981, 2001; Triandis, 1995).

Imagine how your perspective on life might differ if becoming independent from your parents or honestly sharing your feelings was not seen as the appropriate way to behave. How would you raise your children, choose a career, or select a spouse? What concerns would you have as you were facing death?

In this book, we will regularly make the distinction between collectivist and more individualistic societies. We will contrast the values of European Americans with more collectivist-oriented U.S. ethnic groups, such as Hispanic Americans, Asian

Americans, Native Americans, and African Americans. However, we need to make these distinctions cautiously. People of *every* nationality and ethnicity have a mix of collectivist and individualistic worldviews (Green, Deschamps, & Paez, 2005; Oishi and others, 2005). Just as people change, so do societies. The winds of the individualistic 1960s social revolution are now sweeping through nations that have traditionally been ranked highest in collectivist attitudes, such as China, Korea, and Japan.

In the top-ranking individualistic nation—no surprise, it's the United States—cultural values differ greatly. True, as nations become more affluent they tend to develop more individualistic attitudes. Still, we don't know what will happen in the future. At least there is one difference between people that will definitely endure. It's called being female or male.

For this grandmother, mother, and daughter, getting dressed up to visit this Shinto family shrine and pay their respects to their ancestors is an important ritual. It is one way that the lesson "honor your elders" is taught to children living in collectivist societies such as Japan from an early age.

The Impact of Gender

Obviously, our culture's values shape our life path as males and females. Are you living in a society or at a time in history when men are encouraged to be househusbands and women to be corporate CEOs? Biology, however, looms large in driving at least one fundamental in the pathways of women and men: Females outlive males by roughly 5 to 10 years throughout the developed world (2004 *World Population Data Sheet*, http:www.prb/org, retrieved November 19, 2005). Because they must survive childbearing and because they carry an extra X chromosome, women are the physiologically hardier sex.

Are boys more aggressive than girls? When we see sex differences in caregiving, in career interests, and in childhood play styles, are they mainly due to the environment (societal pressures or the way we are brought up) or to inborn, biological forces? Throughout this book we will examine these questions as we explore the scientific truth of our gender stereotypes and learn some interesting facts about sex differences, too. To set you up for this ongoing conversation, you might want to take the "Is it males or females?" quiz in Table 1.2. Keep a copy handy. As we travel through the lifespan, you can check the accuracy of each of your ideas.

TABLE 1.2: Is It Males or Females?

1. Who is more likely to survive the hazards of prenatal development, male or female fetuses? (You will find the answer in Chapter 2.)

2. Who is more vulnerable to experiencing high levels of stress when sent to day care, male or female toddlers? (You will find the answer in Chapter 4.)

3. Who is more aggressive, boys or girls? (You will find the answer in Chapter 6.)

4. Who is more likely to be diagnosed with learning disabilities in school, boys or girls? (You will find the answer in Chapter 7.)

5. Who, when they reach puberty at an earlier-than-typical age, is more at risk of developing problems, boys or girls? (You will find the answer in Chapter 8.)

6. Who is likely to stay in the "nest" (at home) longer during the emerging-adult years, men or women? (You will find the answer in Chapter 10.)

7. Who is more at risk of having enduring emotional problems after being widowed, men or women? (You will find the answer in Chapter 13.)

8. Who lives longer in the face of serious age-related disabilities, men or women? (You will find the answer in Chapter 14.)

9. Who cares more about being closely attached, males or females—or both sexes? (You will find the answer throughout this book.)

Now that we've laid out the framework and highlighted the fundamental developmental science principle that our lifespan is a continuing work in progress that varies across cultures and historical times, let's get to the science. After you complete this section's Tying It All Together review quiz, we will introduce the theories, research methods, concepts, and scientific terms that we will be repeatedly drawing on in the chapters to come.

 TYING IT ALL TOGETHER

1. Raymond, a historian, is arguing that during the twentieth century, conditions for children changed dramatically in very positive ways. He should mention all of the following examples *except* (check the statement that is *false*):

    a. Child mortality used to be high. Today, it is low in the developed world.
    b. Poor infants often used to be abandoned. Today, this practice would be severely condemned.
    c. Children used to start their work lives at a young age. Today, childhood extends through (and even beyond) the adolescent years.
    d. Children used to be the poorest segment of the population. Today, they are the most affluent group.

2. Maria just became a grandmother; Sara just retired from her job; Rosa just entered a nursing home. If these women live in the United States and are middle class, roughly how old are they likely to be?

3. Jim and Joe are arguing about the impact of the 1960s lifestyle revolution. Jim believes that life is much better today. Joe says that life was better in the 1950s. Argue Jim's position, then Joe's, backing up your points by using the information in this section.

4. Pablo says, "I would never think of leaving my parents or living far from my brothers and sisters. A person must take care of the wider family before satisfying his own needs." Peter says, "My primary commitment is to my wife and children. A person needs, above all, to make an independent life." Pablo has a(n) _____ worldview, while Peter's worldview is more _____.

Answers to the Tying It All Together questions can be found in the answers section of the book.

[FAQ: How do theories of development help to explain overall development?]

Lenses for Looking at the Lifespan: Theories

Sam is searching for his identity. Manuel's mechanical talents must be hereditary. If Elissa's mother gives her a lot of love during her first years of life, she will grow up to be a loving, secure adult. If any of these thoughts entered your mind while reading about the people in the opening vignette, you were using a major theory that developmentalists use to understand human life.

Theories offer insights into that crucial *why* question. They attempt to explain what causes us to act as we do. They may allow us to predict the future. Ideally, they give us information about how to improve the quality of life. Theories in developmental science may offer broad general explanations of behavior that apply to people at every age. Or they may go stage by stage through the lifespan, describing specific changes that occur at particular ages. This section provides a preview of both kinds of theories.

Let's begin by outlining some very broad theories (one is actually a research discipline) that offer general explanations of behavior. We'll organize our discussion according to how each theory approaches that fundamental question mentioned earlier: Is it the environment, or the wider world, that determines how we develop? Are our personalities, talents, and traits shaped mainly by biological or genetic forces? This is the famous **nature** (biology) versus **nurture** (environment) question.

theory Any perspective explaining why people act the way they do. Theories allow us to predict behavior and also suggest how to intervene to improve behavior.

nature Biological or genetic causes of development.

nurture Environmental causes of development.

Behaviorism: The Original Blockbuster "Nurture" Theory

Give me a dozen healthy infants . . . and I'll guarantee to take any one at random and train him to be any specialist I might select—doctor, lawyer, artist, merchant-chief, and yes, even beggar man and thief.

(Watson, 1930, p. 104)

So proclaimed the early-twentieth-century psychologist John Watson as he spelled out the nurture-is-all-important position of **traditional behaviorism.** Intoxicated by the scientific advances that were transforming society and allowing most people to live to old age, Watson and his fellow behaviorist B. F. Skinner (1960, 1974) dreamed of a science of human behavior that would mimic physics. These pioneering behaviorists believed that it was not appropriate to study feelings and thoughts, because inner experiences could not be observed. To be a real science, it was vital that psychology confine itself to studying measurable, observable responses. Moreover, according to these theorists, a few general laws of learning explain behavior in every age group and every life situation.

B.F. Skinner Foundation

This photo shows B. F. Skinner with his favorite research subject for exploring operant conditioning—the pigeon. By charting how often pigeons pecked to get reinforced by food and varying the patterns of reinforcement, this famous behaviorist was able to tell us a good deal about how humans act.

Exploring Reinforcement

According to Skinner, the general law of learning that explains each voluntary action, from forming our first words to mastering higher math, is **operant conditioning.** Responses that are rewarded, or **reinforced,** will be learned. Responses that are not reinforced will go away or *extinguish.* What, then, accounts for Watson's beggar men and thieves, the out-of-control kids, all of the marriages that start out so loving and then fall apart? According to Skinner, the reinforcements are operating as they should. The problem is that instead of reinforcing positive behavior, we often reinforce the wrong things.

One excellent place to see Skinner's point in action is to take a trip to your local Wal-Mart or restaurant. Notice how, when children begin to act up at the store, parents often buy them a toy to quiet them down. At a restaurant, as long as a toddler is playing quietly, adults ignore her. When she starts to hurl objects off the table or spill her milk, they pick her up, kiss her, and take her outside. Then they complain about their child's difficult personality, not realizing that its source is really them. Their *own* reinforcements have produced these responses!

One of Skinner's most interesting concepts, derived from his work with pigeons, relates to the impact of variable reinforcement schedules. This is the type of reinforcement that typically occurs in daily life: We get reinforced at unpredictable intervals, so we learn to keep responding, realizing that if we continue, *at some point* we will be reinforced. Readers with children will appreciate just how difficult it is to follow the basic behavioral principle, to be consistent or not let a negative variable schedule unfold. At Wal-Mart, even though you vow, "I won't give in to bad behavior!" as your toddler's tantrums continue, you end up caving in. It simply is more reinforcing to you to avoid the shoppers' disapproving stares. Unfortunately, your child has learned a valuable lesson: "If I keep whining, *eventually* I'll get what I want."

Reinforcement (and its opposite process, extinction) is a powerful developmental phenomenon for both good and bad. It explains why, if a child starts out succeeding early in elementary school (being reinforced by receiving As), he's likely to continue to study and become more connected to academics. If a kindergartener begins failing socially (does not get

traditional behaviorism A behavioral worldview that focuses on charting and modifying only "objective," externally visible behaviors.

operant conditioning According to the traditional behavioral perspective, the law of learning that determines any voluntary response. Specifically, we act the way we do because we are reinforced for acting in that way.

reinforcement Behavioral term for reward.

Cindy Charles / Photo Edit, Inc.

When this boy spills his milk, behaviorists believe he may immediately be reinforced for his bad behavior by getting an adult's full attention. How often have you seen parents inadvertently reinforce their children for these kinds of actions?

positive reinforcement from her peers), she is at risk for developing a social phobia or even a serious problem with aggression in third or fourth grade (see Chapter 6). When you are not being reinforced in one area, wouldn't you stop trying and look for rewards in less appropriate areas of life?

Behaviorism makes sense of why, after starting out so loving, marriages can end in divorce court. As newlyweds, couples are continually reinforcing each other with expressions of love. Then, over time, they tend to ignore the good parts of their partner and pay more attention when there is something wrong. One psychologist you will read about in Chapter 11 has found that he can predict which marriages will break up, simply by charting the ratio of positive to negative comments spouses make while discussing an issue in their lives.

Behaviorism even offers an optimistic environmental explanation for the physical and mental impairments of old age. If you were in a nursing home and weren't being reinforced for remembering or walking, wouldn't your memory or physical abilities decline? The key to producing well-behaved children, enduring, loving marriages, and fewer old-age disabilities (see the Experiencing the Lifespan box) is simple. According to traditional behaviorists, we merely need to reinforce the right things.

However, things are not quite that simple. Human beings *do* think and reason. People do not need to be personally reinforced to actually learn.

Taking a Different Perspective: Exploring Cognitions

Enter **cognitive behaviorism (social learning theory)**, launched by Albert Bandura (1977; 1986) and his colleagues in the 1970s in a series of studies demonstrating the powerful influence of **modeling**, or learning by watching and imitating what other people do.

cognitive behaviorism (social learning theory) A behavioral worldview that emphasizes that people learn by watching others and that our thoughts about the reinforcers determine our behavior. Cognitive behaviorists focus on charting and modifying people's thoughts.

modeling Learning by watching and imitating others.

EXPERIENCING THE LIFESPAN: A BEHAVIORIST IN THE NURSING HOME

How are behavioral principles used with disabled older adults? What are some issues psychologists face in using these strategies in settings such as nursing homes? For insights, consider this interview that I conducted with a geriatric psychologist.

I decided to be a clinical psychologist because I wanted to help people. Behavioral approaches, because they are so well documented, were attractive to me. I liked the precision of behaviorism, the idea that by changing the reinforcements you could make a difference in people's lives.

My interest is in the iatrogenic effects of institutional care—that means the effect that the environment has on residents even when, quote, "good care" is being provided. As my definition of the environment includes the social world, my main focus is the staff. I became interested in care in nursing homes. When you do applied research, you pick a problem that the staff is interested in. I was more interested in deteriorating cognition as a function of being in the institution, but the staff was concerned about incontinence. So, I ran a project to determine the reinforcers controlling incontinence. I was convinced that residents were being incontinent in order to receive attention from the staff, because if you looked at the staff–resident interactions, most social contact was occurring around dressing and changing the person.

My colleague and I set up a procedure whereby residents would be regularly given the chance to go to the toilet, and attention would be applied as a consequence of requesting assistance and withheld when the person was wet. An aide went into residents' rooms every hour asking if the person wanted to go the bathroom. Residents were only taken to the toilet if they requested to go. The purpose of this strategy, which we called "prompted voiding," was to put control back in the hands of the residents so they would get assistance only when they wanted it. Over half—and I emphasize, half—of the incidents of incontinence are eradicated within two days if you do that. Incontinence is a multibillion-dollar problem, and our idea was that if you could reduce incontinent episodes, you could significantly reduce nursing home costs.

The problem, we found, was that the staff was actually being reinforced for not taking residents to the toilet. When you have 10 or 15 people in your care, changing a soiled bed is simply easier than taking the 30 or 40 minutes to get the person to the toilet and back. So the pressures were actually working against continence, and the staff were producing the very problem that worried them the most!

Courtesy Albert Bandura, Stanford University

In Bandura's classic study, children who watched a film of an adult kicking and hitting a Bobo doll *(top row)* later modeled her actions *(bottom row)*.

Because we are a social species, Bandura argued, modeling is actually the major way we learn. Given that we are continually modeling everything, from the expressions of the person we are talking with to the latest hairstyle, whom are we most likely to model as we travel through life?

Bandura's (1986) studies suggest that we tend to model people who are nurturant, or more involved with us. (The good news here is that being a loving, hands-on parent is the best way to naturally embed your values and ideas.) We model people whom we categorize as being like us. At age 2, you probably modeled anything from the vacuum cleaner to the behavior of the family dog. As we grow older, we tailor our modeling selectively, based on our understanding of who we are.

Modeling similar people partly explains why, after children understand their gender label (girl or boy) at about age 2 1/2, they begin to separate into sex-segregated play groups and prefer to play with their "own group." It accounts for why teenagers gravitate to the Goths or druggies, and then model the leader who most embodies these group norms. While we will be drawing on the principles of modeling to explain everything from preschool sex role behavior to predicting whether a given adolescent is having sex, another cognitive behavioral concept developed by Bandura is even more influential in developmental science today. It's called self-efficacy.

Self-efficacy refers to our belief in our competence, our sense that we can be successful at a given task. According to Bandura (1989, 1992, 1997), self-efficacy determines the goals we set. It predicts which activities we engage in as we travel through life. When self-efficacy is low, we decide not to tackle that difficult math problem. We choose not to ask a beautiful stranger for a date. When self-efficacy is high, we not only take action but continue to act long after the traditional behavioral approach suggests that extinction should occur.

Let's illustrate by returning to the example of Mary, who wants to go back to school. If Mary has extremely poor self-efficacy with regard to academics, she won't enroll in the social work program. Furthermore, by exploring her efficacy feelings ("How competent intellectually do I feel?"), we can predict what will happen if Mary has trouble with tests in her first semester. If her academic self-efficacy is relatively low, this test-taking trouble might cause extinction—and she will drop out of college. If her academic self-efficacy is high, Mary will work even harder, spending more hours in the library than before: "I can do it . . . I just need to work harder to succeed!"

How does low self-efficacy unfold during our early school years? How can we enhance self-efficacy during childhood and at any time of life? These are the kinds of questions we will be exploring as we examine the vital role that efficacy feelings play from elementary school to old age.

By now you may be impressed with how behaviorism's simple, action-oriented concepts can help us improve the quality of life: Be consistent. Don't reinforce

Joseph Marzullo / Retina Ltd.

Oprah Winfrey's triumphant success after having grown up in an abusive family can only be explained by her intense sense of self-efficacy. Cognitive behaviorists, such as Bandura, believe that by exploring efficacy feelings we can predict a good deal about the lives of people, such as Oprah, who triumph against the odds.

self-efficacy According to cognitive behaviorism, an internal belief in our competence that predicts whether we initiate activities or persist in the face of failures, and predicts the goals we set.

TABLE 1.3: Traditional Behavioral Principles Applied to Childrearing: A Summary and an Additional Suggestion

1. **Take care to reinforce appropriate behavior.** Pay attention to a child when she engages in positive behaviors, not negative ones.

2. **Be consistent.** Never give in to negative behavior.

3. **To cement in the behavior you want, build in a few experiences of failure.** Then your child won't immediately give up when she isn't immediately reinforced.

negative behavior. Reinforce positive things (from traditional behaviorism; see also Table 1.3). Draw on the principles of modeling and stimulate efficacy feelings to help children and adults succeed (from cognitive behaviorism).

Still, many developmentalists, even when they believe that nurture is vitally important, find behaviorism unsatisfying. Aren't we more than just a collection of efficacy feelings or reinforced responses? Isn't there a basic core to our personality, and aren't the lessons we learn in early childhood especially important in adult life?

Notice that behaviorism doesn't address that core question: What *really* tends to motivate us as human beings? To illustrate the problems that we run into when we don't consider basic human needs and motivations, let's listen to John Watson (1924/1998) lashing out at what he calls pathological "love conditioning" destined to produce a whiny, dependent adult: "The child is alone putting blocks together and the mother comes in. . . . The child crawls . . . to the mother . . . climbs into her lap, puts its arms around her neck. The mother fondles her child, kisses it and holds it" (p. 78). Wait a second! Isn't that the way parents and children are supposed to behave?

Attachment Theory: Focus on Nurture, Nature, and Love

According to **attachment theory,** the answer is yes. Attachment theory, formulated by British psychiatrist John Bowlby during the mid-twentieth century, has the same premise as traditional Freudian psychoanalytic theory. (Bowlby was actually trained as a psychoanalyst and worked with Freud's daughter, Anna.) According to Freud and his followers, the way our parents treat us during the first years of life either gives us the foundation for being loving, successful adults or causes lasting emotional scars. Bowlby shared the psychoanalytic view that our early life experiences with caregivers shape our lifelong ability to love, but he focused specifically on what he called the *attachment response.*

Bowlby believes that the intense, loving bond between this father and his infant son will set the baby up for a fulfilling life. Do you agree with this basic principle of attachment theory?

attachment theory Theory, formulated by John Bowlby, centering on the crucial importance to our species' survival of being closely connected with a caregiver during early childhood and being attached to a significant other during all of life.

In observing young children separated from their mothers, Bowlby noticed that, as with Elissa, infants need to be physically close to a caregiver during the time when they are beginning to walk (Bowlby, 1969, 1973; Karen, 1998). Disruptions in this biologically programmed attachment response, he argued, if prolonged, cause serious problems later in life. Moreover, our impulse to be close to a "significant other" is a basic human need during every stage of life.

How does the attachment response develop during infancy? Was Bowlby right that the quality of our early attachments determines our adult mental health? How can we draw on the principles of attachment theory to understand everything from adult love relationships to widowhood to our concerns as we approach death? Stay tuned for answers as we highlight the principles of this influential theory throughout this book.

Today, attachment theory is in the mainstream of developmental science. But when Bowlby first spelled out his ideas, he was shunned by his psychoanalytic colleagues. Ironically, the psychoanalysts rejected attachment theory for the very reason

Bowlby's ideas have such appeal today (Fonagy, 2001; Karen, 1998). Yes, Bowlby did believe that our upbringing (nurture) was important; but he also firmly believed in heredity (nature). Bowlby (1969, 1973, 1980) felt that the attachment response is biologically programmed into our species to promote survival. As it turns out, Bowlby was an early evolutionary psychologist.

Evolutionary Psychology: Theorizing About the Nature of Human Similarities

Evolutionary psychologists are the mirror image of behaviorists. They look to nature, or biological predispositions that have evolved to promote survival, to explain why people act the way they do. Why do pregnant women develop morning sickness just as the fetal organs are being formed, and why do newborns prefer to look at attractive faces rather than ugly ones? (That's actually true!) According to evolutionary psychologists, these reactions cannot be changed by modifying the reinforcers. They are based in the human genetic code that we all share.

Evolutionary psychology lacks the practical, action-oriented approach of behaviorism, although it does alert us to the fact that we need to pay very close attention to basic human needs. Still, this "look to built-in biology" explanation of behavior is very popular in developmental science today (Bjorklund & Pellegrini, 2001; Buller, 2005). The reason is that during the final decades of the twentieth century, most developmentalists changed their perspective about what motivates human beings. They rejected the behaviorist and traditional Freudian idea that nurture, or outside world experiences, are all-important. They realized that genetics does matter—often a great deal—in determining the person we will become. Research in an exploding field brought this message home.

evolutionary psychology
Theory or worldview highlighting the role that inborn, species-specific behaviors play in human development and life.

Behavioral Genetics: Scientifically Exploring the "Nature" of Human Differences

"I have a genetic tendency to become alcoholic/to develop bipolar disorder/to bite my nails." Have you ever wondered about the scientific basis of these kinds of statements? They come from research in **behavioral genetics**—a field devoted to studying the role genetics plays in understanding why people vary in their personalities or any other human trait. To study the genetic contribution to human differences, behavioral geneticists use twin and adoption studies as their main research tools (Bouchard, 1994; McClearn, 1993; Plomin & McClearn, 1993; Plomin and others, 2003b).

In **twin studies**, researchers typically compare identical (monozygotic) twins and fraternal (dizygotic) twins on a particular trait of interest—be it motor speed, math talents, or mental health. Identical twins develop from the same fertilized egg (it splits after the one-cell stage) and are genetic clones. Fraternal twins, like any brother or

behavioral genetics Field devoted to scientifically determining the role that hereditary forces play in determining individual differences in behavior.

twin study Behavioral genetic research strategy, designed to determine the genetic contribution of a given trait, that involves comparing identical twins with fraternal twins (or with other people).

Grace / Zefa /Corbis

John-Francis Bourke / Getty Images

How "genetic" are these children's friendly personalities? To answer this question, researchers compare identical twins, such these two girls (left), with fraternal twins, like this girl and boy (right). If the identicals (who share exactly the same DNA) are much more similar to each other than the fraternals in their friendliness scores, friendliness is defined as a highly heritable trait.

adoption study Behavioral genetic research strategy, designed to determine the genetic contribution to a given trait, that involves comparing adopted children with their biological and adoptive parents.

twin/adoption studies Behavioral genetic research strategy that involves comparing the similarities of identical twin pairs adopted into different families, to determine the genetic contribution to a given trait.

[FAQ: How influential are innate, biological factors vs. environmental factors in development?]

Imagine how you (and other people) would respond to this grumpy boy versus a sunny, upbeat child and you will understand how evocative influences work to make us more like ourselves genetically and why all human relationships are *bidirectional*.

sister, develop from separate conceptions and so, on average, share 50 percent of their genes. The idea is that if a given trait is highly influenced by genetics, identical twins should be much more alike in that quality than fraternal twins. Specifically, behavioral geneticists use a statistic called *heritability* (which ranges from 1 = totally genetic, to 0 = no genetic contribution) to summarize the extent to which a given behavior is shaped by genetic forces.

For instance, suppose you decided to conduct a twin study to determine the heritability of Manuel's mechanical talents. First you would select a large group of identical and fraternal twins and give both sets of twins various tests of mechanical skills. You would then compare the strength of the test score relationships you found for each twin group. Let's say the identical twins' scores tended to be incredibly similar—almost like the same person taking the tests twice—and the fraternal twins' test scores tended to vary much more from each other. Your heritability statistic would be high, and you then would conclude: "Mechanical talents such as Manuel's are highly genetically determined traits."

In **adoption studies,** researchers compare adopted children with their biological and adoptive parents. Here, too, they evaluate the impact of heredity on a trait by looking at how closely these children resemble their birth parents (with whom they share only genes) and their adoptive parents (with whom they share only environments).

Twin studies of children growing up in the same family and simple adoption studies are not difficult to carry out. The most striking evidence for the power of genetics comes from the rare **twin/adoption studies,** in which identical twins are separated in childhood and reunited in adult life. If Joe and James, who have exactly the same genetic endowments, have very similar abilities, traits, and personalities even though they grew up in *different families*, this would be strong evidence that genetics plays a crucial role in making us who we are.

Consider, for instance, the Swedish Twin Adoption Study of Aging. Developmental scientists combed national registries to find identical and fraternal twins adopted into different families in that country—where birth records of every adoptee are kept. Then they reunited these children in late middle age and gave the twins an extensive battery of tests (Finkel & Pedersen, 2004; Kato, & Pedersen, 2005; Pedersen, 1996).

While genetic forces influenced a wide range of behaviors, specific qualities varied in their heritabilities. The most genetically determined quality, interestingly, was overall IQ (Pedersen, 1996). In fact, if one twin took the standard intelligence test, statistically speaking we could predict that his brother (or her sister) would have an almost identical IQ despite living apart for an entire life!

Behavioral genetic studies such as these have opened our eyes to the often incredible impact of nature. Even qualities that we thought *must* be due to how our parents raised us, such as our political attitudes, our child-rearing styles, and our chance of getting divorced, are somewhat influenced by genetic forces (Plomin & others, 2003b).

These studies have given us equally tantalizing insights into the meaning of nurture. It's tempting to assume that children growing up in the same family share the same nurture, or environment. But as you can see in the How Do We Know research, that assumption is wrong. We inhabit very different life spaces than our brothers and sisters, even when we eat at the same dinner table and share the same room. These environments are shaped in part by our genes (Rowe, 2003).

The bottom line is that there is no such thing as nature *or* nurture. To really understand human development, we need to explore how nature *and* nurture combine. That is exactly how developmental scientists conceptualize and study the lifespan today.

Nature and Nurture Combined

Now let's look at two nature-plus-nurture principles that we will be drawing on again and again in this book.

Our Nature Shapes Our Nurture

Developmentalists now understand that it doesn't make sense to separate nature and nurture into independent entities (Rowe, 2003; Scarr, 1992, 1997). Our genetic tendencies mold and shape our life experiences in two distinctive ways.

Evocative forces refer to the fact that our inborn talents and temperamental tendencies naturally evoke, or produce, certain responses from the human world. A joyous child elicits smiles from everyone. A child who is temperamentally irritable, is hard to handle, or has trouble sitting still is apt to get the kind of harsh parenting she least needs to succeed. Human relationships are **bidirectional.** Just as you get grumpy when with a grumpy person, fight with your difficult neighbor, or shy away from your colleague who is paralyzingly shy, who we are as people causes others to react to us in specific ways, propelling our development for the good and the bad.

Active forces refer to the fact that we *actively select* our environments based on our genetic tendencies. A child who is talented at reading will gravitate toward devouring books, and so become an even better reader. His brother who is exceptionally well coordinated may play baseball three hours a day and become a star athlete in his teenage years. Because we tailor our activities to fit our biological predilections and skills, what start out as minor differences in early childhood tend to snowball over time—ultimately producing huge gaps in talents and traits. The unusually high heritabilities for IQ in the Swedish Twin Adoption Study are consistently lower in similar behavioral genetic studies conducted during childhood (Plomin, 2003; Plomin &

[FAQ: How does genetics influence lifestyle choices?]

evocative forces The nature-interacts-with-nurture principle that our genetic temperamental tendencies and predispositions evoke, or produce, certain responses from other people.

bidirectionality The crucial principle that people affect one another, or that interpersonal influences flow in both directions.

active forces The nature-interacts-with-nurture principle that our genetic temperamental tendencies and predispositions cause us to actively choose to put ourselves into specific environments.

✿ HOW DO WE KNOW . . .

that our nature affects our upbringing?

For most of the twentieth century, developmentalists assumed that parents treated all of their children the same way. We could classify mothers as either nurturing or rejecting, caring or cold. Then the Swedish Twin/Adoption Study turned these basic parenting assumptions upside down (Plomin, 1994).

Researchers asked middle-aged identical twins who had been adopted into different families as babies to rate their parents along dimensions such as caring, acceptance, and discipline styles. They were astonished to find similarities in the ratings, even though the twins were evaluating different families!

What was happening here? The answer, the researchers concluded, was that the genetic similarities in the twins' personalities *created* similar family environments. If Joe and Jim were both easy, kind, and caring, they evoked more loving parenting. If they were both temperamentally difficult, they caused their adoptive parents to react in more rejecting, less nurturant ways.

This principle—that a child's genetics drives how parents act—does not just apply to personality, but to cognitive stimulation, too, as I vividly saw in my own life. Because my adopted son has dyslexia and is very physically active, in our house we ended up doing active things like sports. As Thomas didn't like to sit still for story time, I probably would have been rated as a "less than optimally stimulating" parent had some psychologist come into my home to rate how much I read to my child.

And now the plot thickens. When I met Thomas's biological mother, I found out that she also has dyslexia. She's tremendously energetic and peppy. It's one thing to see the impact of nature in my son and his mother revealed. But I can't help wondering. . . . Maureen is a very different kind of person than me (although we have a terrific time together—traveling and doing active things). Would Thomas have had the *same* kind of upbringing (at least partly) that I gave my son if he had *not* been adopted—and had grown up with his biological mom?

Because this musically talented girl is choosing to spend hours playing the piano, she is likely to become even more talented as she gets older, illustrating the fact that we actively shape our environment to fit our genetic tendencies and talents.

Nicole Katano / PictureQuest

Could this African boy have grown up to be a scientist, a writer, or a genius painter? We won't know because the accident of being born into an impoverished environment will make it impossible for him to show his genetic gifts.

Peter Magubane / Time Life Pictures / Getty Images

person–environment fit The extent to which the environment is tailored to our biological tendencies and talents. In developmental science, fostering this fit between our talents and the wider world is an important goal.

Piaget's cognitive developmental theory Jean Piaget's principle that from infancy to adolescence, children progress through four qualitatively different stages of intellectual growth.

This autistic boy is using a specially designed tire swing his family set up in the basement that helps to orient him and calm him down. When a child's problem is biological or genetic, providing nurturing parenting and the best possible environment is more important than ever.

Suzanne Krieter / The Boston Globe

Spinath, 2004). The reason is that, like heat-seeking missiles, our nature causes us to gravitate toward specific life experiences, so we literally become *more like ourselves* genetically as we travel into adult life.

We Need the Right Nurture to Express Our Nature

Developmentalists understand that even if a specific trait or quality is 100 percent genetic, its expression is 100 percent dependent on the outside world. Let's illustrate by returning to the incredibly high heritabilities for overall intelligence. Suppose you were living in an impoverished developing world country, malnourished, and forced to work as a laborer in a field. In this environment, having a genius-level IQ might be irrelevant, as there would be little chance to demonstrate your hereditary gifts.

Extending this principle to real life, a basic goal of developmental science is to foster the correct **person–environment fit.** We need to try to select the environment that is right for our talents and skills (Lawton, 1977; Lerner & Lerner, 1994). How can we use our understanding of our species-specific biology (evolutionary theory) and our unique personal biology (advances in genetics) to provide the right person–environment fit for children, working moms and dads, and older adults? This is the basic challenge we face as we move into the twenty-first century.

Actually, far from making what we do—as parents, teachers, and health-care professionals—irrelevant, our understanding of the importance of genetics makes the environment we provide even *more* crucial. As researchers conduct more sophisticated nature-plus-nurture studies, the message "The environment really matters" comes through loud and clear (Plomin & others, 2003b). From the research showing that loving mothers can lessen the negative biological impact of being born extremely premature, to the discovery of a genetic marker that predisposes some people to get seriously depressed, but only under conditions of extreme life stress (see Chapter 7), the real impact of the nature revolution is to allow us to intervene to change the environment in order to enhance the quality of life.

Emphasis on Age-Linked Theories

Now that we have the basic "Nature combines with nurture" perspective that guides how we need to view overall development, let's look at two theories that will guide us as we travel through the lifespan stage by stage.

Piaget's Cognitive Developmental Theory

A 3-year-old tells you that "Mr. Sun goes to bed because it's time for me to go to sleep." A toddler is obsessed with flushing different-sized wads of paper down the toilet and can't resist touching everything she sees. Do you ever wish you could get into the minds of young children and understand how they view the world? If so, you share the passion of the number-one genius in child psychology, Jean Piaget.

Piaget, born in 1894 in Switzerland, was a childhood prodigy himself. As the author of several dozen published articles on mollusks, by age 20 he was well on his way to becoming a well-known expert in that field (Wadsworth, 1996; Flavell, 1963). Piaget's interests quickly shifted to studying children, however, when he went to work with Alfred Binet, a French psychologist who was devising the original intelligence test. Rather than focusing on ranking children according to how much they knew, Piaget became fascinated by the characteristics of children's *incorrect* responses. He spent the next 60 years meticulously devising tasks to map the minds of these mysterious creatures in our midst.

Piaget believed that as they travel from birth through adolescence, children progress through *qualitatively different* stages of cognitive growth (see Table 1.4). The term *qualitative* means that rather than simply knowing less or more (on the kind of scale we can rank from 1 to 10), infants, preschoolers, elementary-school-age children, and teenagers conceptualize the world in *completely* different ways. However, Piaget also believed that there was a basic continuity to cognitive development. Human beings have a built-in hunger to learn and mentally grow. Mental growth occurs through **assimilation**: We fit the world to our capacities or existing cognitive structures (which Piaget calls *schemas*). And then **accommodation** occurs. We naturally change our thinking to fit the world (Piaget, 1971).

Let's illustrate these two basic concepts by reflecting on your own mental processes while you were reading the previous section. Before beginning this chapter, you probably had a certain set of ideas about heredity and environment. In Piaget's terminology, let's call them your "heredity/environment schemas." Perhaps you felt that if a trait is highly genetic, changing the environment doesn't matter; or you may have believed that genetics and environment were totally separate. While fitting (assimilating) your reading into these existing ideas, you entered a state of disequilibrium—"Hey, this contradicts what I've always believed"—and were forced to accommodate. The result was that your "nature/nurture" schemas became more complex and you developed a more advanced (intelligent) way of perceiving the world! From a newborn who assimilates each object, from a rattle to a pacifier, to his "sucking" schema, to a neuroscientist who incorporates every new discovery into her complex knowledge base, while assimilating everything to what we know, we need to continually accommodate, and so—inch by inch—we cognitively advance.

Piaget was a great believer in hands-on experiences. He felt that we learn by acting on or physically operating in the world. Rather than using an adult-centered framework, he had the revolutionary idea that we need to understand how children

Jean Piaget, in his masterful studies spanning much of the twentieth century, transformed the way we think about children's thinking.

assimilation In Jean Piaget's theory, the first step promoting mental growth, involving fitting environmental input to our existing mental capacities.

accommodation In Piaget's theory, enlarging our mental capacities to fit input from the wider world.

TABLE 1.4: Piaget's Stages of Development

Age	Name of Stage	Description
0–2	Sensorimotor	The baby manipulates objects to pin down the basics of physical reality. This stage, ending with the development of language, will be described in Chapter 3.
2–7	Preoperations	Children's perceptions are captured by their immediate appearances. "What they see is what is real." They believe, among other things, that inanimate objects are really alive and that if the appearance of a quantity of liquid changes (for instance, if it is poured from a short, wide glass into a tall, thin one), the amount actually becomes different. You will learn about all of these perceptions in Chapter 5.
8–12	Concrete operations	Children have a realistic understanding of the world. Their thinking is really on the same wavelength as adults'. While they can reason conceptually about concrete objects, however, they cannot think abstractly in a scientific way.
12+	Formal operations	Reasoning is at its pinnacle: hypothetical, scientific, flexible, fully adult. Our full cognitive human potential has been reached. We will explore this stage in Chapter 9.

Ted Streshinsky / Time Life Pictures / Getty Images

With his powerful writings on identity and especially his concept of age-related psychosocial tasks, Erik Erikson (shown here with his wife, Joan) has become a father of our field.

experience life *from their own point of view.* Since the main purpose of this book is to make this material personal and experiential, and to look at life from the perspective of people ranging from age 2 to 92, how can we go beyond cognition and childhood to understand the qualitatively different agendas we have at *every* stage of life? Erik Erikson offered us this basic road map.

Erik Erikson's Psychosocial Tasks

Erik Erikson, born in Germany in 1904—a few years after Piaget—was a psychoanalyst who disagreed with Freud in a few specific respects. Still, Erikson qualifies as the father of lifespan development because he had a simple idea. Unlike Bowlby or the traditional psychoanalysts, who believed our personality is basically formed in early childhood and then doesn't change, Erikson felt that we continue to develop throughout life. He set out to chart the developmental tasks we face at each stage of life.

Erikson (1963), as Table 1.5 illustrates, spelled out a particular **psychosocial task,** or challenge, that we face during each of eight life stages. These tasks, he argued, build on one another because we cannot master the issue of a later stage unless we have accomplished the developmental milestones of the previous ones.

TABLE 1.5: Erikson's Psychosocial Stages

Life Stage	Primary Task
Infancy (birth to 1 year)	Basic trust versus mistrust
Toddlerhood (1 to 2 years)	Autonomy versus shame and doubt
Early childhood ((3 to 6 years)	Initiative versus guilt
Middle childhood (6 years to puberty)	Industry versus inferiority
Adolescence (tens into twenties)	Identity versus role confusion
Young adulthood (twenties to early forties)	Intimacy versus isolation
Middle adulthood (forties to sixties)	Generativity versus stagnation
Late adulthood (late sixties and beyond)	Integrity versus despair

Notice how adults are continually kissing infants and you will understand why Erikson identified *basic trust* (the belief that the human world is caring) as our fundamental mission in the first year of life. Erikson's second psychosocial task, *autonomy*, makes perfect sense of the infamous *"no stage"* and "terrible twos." It tells us that we need to *celebrate* this not-so-pleasant toddler behavior as the beginning of a separate self! Think back to elementary school, and you may realize why Erikson used the term *industry*, or learning to work—at friendships, sports, academics—as our basic challenge during our school years, from age 6 to 12.

Erikson's adolescent task, the search for *identity*, has now become a household word. Erikson was particularly interested in issues related to constructing an adult identity. As a young person, he wandered around Europe for some time, thinking he wanted to be an artist before finding his life path as a teacher and psychoanalyst. Then he witnessed firsthand the pain of identity issues when he worked as a psychotherapist in a psychiatric hospital for troubled teens (Coles, 1970).

How have developmentalists elaborated on Erikson's task of identity? Is Erikson right that nurturing the next generation, or *generativity*, is the key to a fulfilling adult life? These are some of the questions we will be exploring as we draw on many of Erikson's psychosocial tasks to help us think more deeply about the challenges we face at each life stage.

Erikson's psychosocial tasks In Erik Erikson's theory, each challenge that we face as we travel through the eight stages of the lifespan.

TABLE 1.6: Summary of the Major Theories in Lifespan Development

	Nature vs. Nurture Emphasis and Ages of Interest	Representative Questions
Behaviorism	Nurture (all ages)	What reinforcers are shaping this behavior? Who is this person modeling? How can I stimulate self-efficacy?
Attachment theory	Nature and nurture (infancy, but also all ages)	How does attachment response unfold in infancy? What conditions evoke this biologically programmed response at every life stage?
Behavioral genetics	Nature (all ages)	To what degree are the differences I see in people due to genetics?
Evolutionary theory	Nature (all ages)	How might this behavior be built into the human genetic code?
Piaget's theory	Children	How does this child understand the world? What is his thinking like?
Erikson's theory	(all ages)	Is this baby experiencing basic trust? Where is this teenager in terms of identity? Has this middle-aged person reached generativity?

By now you may be overwhelmed by all these theories and terms. But take heart. You already have the fundamental concepts you will need for understanding this whole semester well in hand! (For a summary of the various theories, see Table 1.6.)

The Developmental Systems Perspective

The **developmental systems perspective** is not really a specific theory. It is an overall approach to understanding development that has the following basic themes (Baltes, 1987; Baltes, Featherman, & Lerner, 1988; Baltes, Reese, & Lipsitt, 1980; Bronfenbrenner, 2005; Ford & Lerner, 1992; Lerner, 1998; Lerner, Dowling, & Roth, 2003):

- **Developmental systems theory emphasizes the need to use many different perspectives.** There are *many* valid ways of looking at behavior. Our actions *do* have many different causes. To fully understand development, we need to draw on the principles of behaviorism, attachment theory, evolutionary psychology, and Piaget. We need the input from nurses and neuroscientists, psychologists and social policy experts. We must look outward to explore our culture and inward to focus on our DNA. We need every level of analysis, and the input from every perspective, to understand human life.

- **Developmental systems theory highlights the interactions of processes.** We also need to understand that every system and level of development dynamically interrelates. Our genetic tendencies influence the cultures we construct; the cultures we live in affect the expression of our genes. In the same way that our body systems and processes are in constant communication, continual back-and-forth influences are what human development is all about.

For example, let's consider that basic contextual marker discussed earlier: poverty (Lerner, 2003). Growing up in poverty might affect your attachment relationships. You are less likely to get attention from your parents, because they are under stress. You might not get adequate nutrition. Your neighborhood could be a frightening place to live. Each stress might combine to overload your body, activating negative genetic tendencies and setting you up physiologically for emotional problems.

developmental systems perspective An all-encompassing outlook on development that stresses the need to embrace a variety of theories, and the idea that all systems and processes interrelate.

[FAQ: What is the most all-encompassing theory of human development?**]**

But some children, because of their genetics, their cultural background, or their relationships at home and school, might be insulated from the negative effects of growing up poor. Others might actually thrive. In a classic study tracing the lives of children growing up during the Great Depression, developmentalists discovered that if this major historical event occurred at the right time in the life cycle (adolescence), having experienced severe economic hardship made for an enduring sense of self-efficacy. It produced a more competent, resilient adult (Elder & Caspi, 1988).

In sum, development occurs in surprising directions for good and for bad. Diversity of change processes and individual differences are the spice of human life.

 TYING IT ALL TOGETHER

1. Hernando, a third grader, is very physically active and is having trouble sitting still and paying attention in class. When Hernando's parents consult developmentalists about the origin and possible treatments for their son's problem, pick out the comments that might be made by: (1) a traditional behaviorist; (2) a cognitive behaviorist; (3) an evolutionary psychologist; (4) a behavioral geneticist; (5) an Eriksonian; (6) an advocate of developmental systems theory.

    a. Hernando may have low self-efficacy in academics. Let's focus on improving his feelings of competence at school.
    b. Hernando, like other boys, is biologically programmed to run around. If the class had regular gym time, Hernando's ability to focus on his classwork might improve.
    c. Hernando is being reinforced for this behavior by getting attention from the teacher and his classmates. Let's shift the reinforcements to reward appropriate classroom behavior.
    d. Did you or your husband also have trouble focusing and sitting still at this age? Perhaps your son's difficulties are hereditary.
    e. Hernando's behavior may be partly genetic; it could be promoted by peer influences, his home life, or the physical environment at school. Let's explore these multiple conditions and how they interact, and perhaps intervene at any point to make positive changes.
    f. Hernando is having trouble mastering the developmental task of industry and is at risk of feeling inferior. Let's explore ways to promote the ability to work that is so crucially important at this life stage.

2. In the above question, which suggestion involves providing an appropriate person–environment fit?

3. Billy, a 1-year-old, mouths everything—pencils, his favorite toy, DVDs—changing his mouthing to fit the object that he is "sampling" at that moment. According to Piaget, the act of mouthing everything refers to _____, while the process of changing the mouthing behavior to fit the different objects refers to _____.

4. Samantha, a vehement behaviorist, is arguing for her worldview, while Sally, acting as the devil's advocate, is pointing up behaviorism's fatal flaws. First take Samantha's position, arguing for the virtues of behaviorism, and then discuss some limitations of the theory.

Answers to the Tying It All Together questions can be found in the answers section of the book.

The Tools of the Trade: Research Methods

Theories give us the lenses or framework for understanding behavior. *Research* is the way we find out the scientific truth. We already touched on the specialized research technique designed to determine the genetic contributions to behavior. Now we sketch out the general research strategies that developmental scientists use.

Two Standard Research Strategies: Experiments and Correlations

What impact does poverty have on relationships, personality, or physical health? What forces cause children to model certain people? Does a particular intervention to help memory or improve self-efficacy really work? To answer any question about the impact one condition or entity (called a *variable*) has on another, developmental scientists use two basic kinds of research designs: correlational studies and true experiments.

In a **correlational study**, researchers chart the relationships between the dimensions they are interested in exploring as they naturally occur. Let's say you want to test the hypothesis that providing a more cognitively stimulating environment at home—for instance, by extensively teaching or reading to your children—leads to better school performance. Your overall game plan is simple: Get a group of children by going to a class. Relate their academic skills to the amount of reading and teaching activities their parents provide.

Immediately, however, you are faced with decisions about choosing your participants. Are you going to look at first or second graders, explore the practices of both parents or of mothers alone, solicit your group from a public or private school? You would need to get permission from the school system. You would need to get the parents to volunteer. Are you choosing a **representative sample**—meaning a group that reflects the characteristics of the overall population about whom you want to generalize?

Then you would face your most important challenge. This is the need to measure your variables in an accurate way. Just as a broken thermometer can't tell us if we have a fever, if we don't have adequate indexes of the concepts we are measuring, we can't conclude anything at all.

With regard to the adult dimension, one possibility might be to directly observe parents with their children. This technique, called **naturalistic observation**, is appealing because it is very concrete. You are actually seeing the behavior as it occurs in "nature," or real life. However, a minute's thought suggests this approach presents a huge practical challenge: the need to travel to each home to observe each family on many occasions for an extended time. Plus, when we watch parent–child interactions, or any socially desirable activity, people try to act their best. Wouldn't you be on good behavior if a psychologist arrived at your house to monitor your behavior with your child?

The most cost-effective strategy would be to give the parents a questionnaire with items such as: "How often do you read to your child?" or "How often do you go to museums?" This **self-report strategy**, in which people evaluate their own behavior and ideas anonymously by filling out scales, is the main approach researchers use with adults. Still, it's subject to its own biases. Do you think that people can report accurately on their activities? Is there a natural human tendency to magnify our positive behaviors and minimize our negative ones?

Turning to measuring the child side of your question, a reasonable way to assess academic skills would be to give standard tests assessing abilities in areas such as reading or math (more about these measures, called *achievement tests,* in Chapter 7). Another strategy might be to ask the teacher to evaluate students' skills. Assessments from knowledgeable others, such as teachers or parents, are a very common approach that developmentalists use to measure behavior during the childhood years.

Table 1.7 spells out the uses, and the pluses and minuses, of these four frequently used measurement strategies: naturalistic observation, self-reports, ability measures, and observer reports. Now, returning to our study, suppose you found a relationship, or correlation, between the amount of cognitive stimulation at home and school performance. Could you infer that what parents do *causes* children to perform better in school? The answer is no!

correlational study A research strategy that involves relating two or more variables.

representative sample A group that reflects the characteristics of the overall population.

naturalistic observation A measurement strategy that involves directly watching and coding behaviors.

self-report strategy A measurement strategy that involves having people report on their feelings and activities through questionnaires.

TABLE 1.7: Common Measurement Strategies in Lifespan Development

Type	Strategy	Commonly Used Ages	Pluses and Problems
Naturalistic observation	Observes behavior directly; codes specific actions, often by rating the behavior as either present or not	Typically during childhood but also sometimes used with adults; can, for instance, be used in hospitals and nursing homes to chart staff behaviors toward residents or residents' behaviors themselves	**Pluses:** Gets direct, unfiltered record of behavior **Problems:** Very time-intensive; subject to bias if people act differently while being watched
Self-reports	Questionnaires in which people report on their feelings, interests, attitudes, and thoughts	Adults and older children	**Pluses:** Easy to administer, can get large amount of data in short time **Problems:** Subject to bias if person is reporting on socially desirable activities
Ability tests	Measures evaluating mental (or physical) skills	Children and adults	**Pluses:** Offers an objective record of performance **Problems:** Subject to bias if the test-taker is frightened or ill; also need to have measures that accurately reflect the ability in the real world
Observer reports	Knowledgeable person such as a parent, teacher, or trained observer completes scales evaluating the individual	Typically during childhood; also is occasionally used during adulthood, especially when the person is mentally or physically impaired	**Pluses:** Easy to administer (must be used for people who are incapable of reporting on their own behavior) **Problems:** Observers have their own biases

- **With correlations we may be mixing up the result with the cause.** Given that parent–child relationships are bidirectional, does parental cognitive stimulation really *cause* superior school performance, or do academically talented children provoke parents to act in more cognitively stimulating ways: "Mom, please read to me," "I want go to the science museum"? (Remember the How Do We Know story about my son and his reading disability.) This chicken-or-egg argument applies to far more than child–parent relationships, cognition, and personality. Does exercising promote health in later life, or are older adults likely to become physically active because they are *already* in good health?

If this committed skier is unusually healthy, is it just because he exercises or because he probably also takes care of his health in other ways? Or maybe he has the stamina for this sport because he is already in exceptionally good health? These questions show how difficult it is to make conclusions about causes from observing correlational relationships.

- **With correlations, there may be another variable that explains the results.** In view of our discussion of the heritability of intelligence, with regard to the cognitive stimulation study, the immediate third-force candidate that comes to mind is genetics. Wouldn't parents who are genetically academically inclined provide a more intellectually enriching home environment and also have children who are more genetically talented in school? In the exercise example above, older adults who go to the gym or ski regularly are probably also watching their diet, visiting the doctor for checkups, and generally interested in their health. Given that these other activities should naturally be associated with keeping physically fit, can we conclude that exercise *alone* accounts for the association we find?

The solution is to conduct a **true experiment** (see Figure 1.3). Researchers take active steps to isolate their variable of interest by manipulating that condition (called the *independent variable*), then

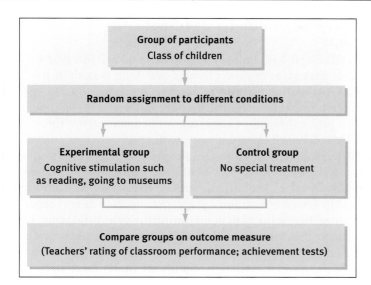

FIGURE 1.3: How an experiment looks: By randomly assigning our children to different groups and then giving an intervention, we know that our treatment (cognitive stimulation) *caused* better school skills.

randomly assign people to either receive that treatment or another, *control* intervention. The strategy of *random assignment* ensures that any pre-existing selection differences between participants "wash out." If the group exposed to the treatment does differ as predicted, then it can be concluded that the intervention *caused* the particular result.

The problem is that we could never randomly assign children to cognitively stimulating parents! If a developmentalist decided to give some cognitively stimulating intervention to one group of children and withhold it from another, he could run into serious ethical problems. Would it be fair to deprive the control group of that treatment? In the name of science, is it right to take the risk of doing people genuine harm? Experiments are ideal for addressing important developmental science questions. But to tackle many of the most compelling questions about human development, correlational studies are often required.

Given that researchers need to take such care to "do no harm," we might think the scientific community would be attuned to the hazards of prescribing treatments based on correlational findings. We would be wrong. During the 1990s, U.S. physicians strongly advocated that every older woman take postmenopausal hormone replacement therapy (HRT). HRT was touted as a magic intervention to stave off everything from cancer to heart attacks to Alzheimer's disease. But there was a problem. This advice was based on studies comparing the health of women who chose to take these supplements with that of the overall population. And who do you think these women were likely to be? You guessed it! They were a self-selected, upper-middle-class, health-aware group.

Once researchers at the National Institutes of Health conducted a genuine clinical trial—an experiment in which they randomly assigned women to take hormones or not—the study had to be stopped midway. Women taking HRT actually had a *higher* risk of developing breast cancer, blood clots, and heart disease. Furthermore, the therapy *increased* the risk of Alzheimer's disease! (See Alzheimer's Disease Education and Referral [ADEAR] Center, 2004; and Healthlink Medical College of Wisconsin, 2002.)

true experiments The only research strategy that can determine that something causes something else; involves randomly assigning people to different treatments and then looking at the outcome.

Designs for Studying Development: Cross-Sectional and Longitudinal Studies

Experiments and correlational studies are standard, all-purpose research strategies. In developmental science, however, we have a special interest: "How do people change with age?" To answer this all-important question, we also use two research techniques—cross-sectional and longitudinal studies.

Cross-Sectional Studies: Getting a One-Shot Snapshot of Groups

Because cross-sectional research is relatively easy to carry out, developmentalists typically use this research strategy to explore changes over long periods of the lifespan (Hertzog, 1996). In a **cross-sectional study**, researchers compare *different age groups at the same time* on the trait or characteristic they are interested in, be it political attitudes, personality, or physical health. Consider a study that used the Internet to answer the question: "How does self-esteem change with age?"

Developmentalists got an incredible 326,461 people of different ages to answer the online question: "I see myself as a very self-confident person" on a five-point scale from "very true" to "totally false" (Robins and others, 2002). Notice from Figure 1.4 that self-esteem was at its lowest ebb in the age group from 18 to 22 and began to rise dramatically in the forties, to reach a high point during the young-old years. Does this heartening finding mean that emerging-adult readers should expect to feel much more self-confident as they travel into midlife?

Not necessarily. Perhaps today's emerging adults are under more stress than the baby boomers or Sadie and Saul's cohort were at that age. After all, job prospects may not be as good for recent college grads today as they were during the 1950s or 1970s. Emerging adults are coming of age in the era of divorce. If we had polled midlife and older people in their early twenties, they might have reported feeling just as self-confident as they do today. The bottom line message is that cross-sectional studies do tell us about differences between cohorts or age groups; but they don't necessarily tell us about true *changes that occur with age*.

Cross-sectional studies have a more basic problem. Because they measure only *group differences*, they can't reveal anything about the individual differences that give spice to life. Are people like Sadie and Saul, who are outgoing and vibrant in their seventies, likely to have also been outgoing at age 30 or 55? If you have very low self-esteem compared to the typical 20-year-old, will you *personally* become more self-confident as you grow older? To answer these critically important questions about how *individual people* develop, as well as to look at what forces make for specific kinds of changes (for example, what childhood influences produce high or low self-esteem), we need to be on the scene to measure what is going on. This means doing longitudinal research.

cross-sectional study A developmental research strategy that involves testing different age groups at the same time.

FIGURE 1.4: Self-esteem ratings at different ages in a cross-sectional Internet poll: In this online survey, people rated their self-confidence on a scale from 1 to 5 (with 5 representing highly self-confident). Notice that ratings are highest for those in their 60s. As an aside, you also might notice that women's ratings are generally much lower than men's.

Source: Robins and others (2002), Figure 1.

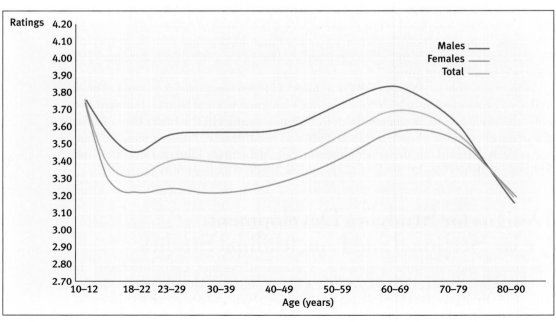

Longitudinal Studies: The Gold-Standard Developmental Science Research Design

In **longitudinal studies,** researchers typically select a group of a particular age and periodically test those people over years (the operative word here is *long*).

Consider the Dunedin Multidisciplinary and Development Study: An international team of researchers descended on Dunedin, a city in New Zealand, to follow more than 1,000 children born between April 1972 and March 1973, examining them at two-year intervals from age 3 into adult life (Caspi, 2000; Caspi & Silva, 1995; Caspi and others, 1995, 1997, 2003). At each evaluation, they examined the participants' personalities. They looked at parenting practices and life events. They last gave each person a comprehensive evaluation at age 26. As of this writing, they are poised to give the age 32 test.

The outcome has been an incredible array of findings, especially relating to psychological problems. Can we predict adult emotional difficulties as early as age 3? Do sleep problems in elementary school foreshadow excessive anxiety in adulthood (Gregory and others, 2005)? If you smoke marijuana, would you want to know if you have a genetic vulnerability that puts you at an elevated risk of developing schizophrenic symptoms (Caspi and others, 2005)?

Because the researchers are using cutting-edge technology to examine participants' DNA, they can tackle these vital nature-plus-nurture questions. Plus, like other longitudinal research, this study offers a crystal ball into those questions at the heart of our field: "How will I change as I get older?" "When should we worry about children, and when should we *not* be concerned?"

Longitudinal studies are tremendously exciting, but they have their own problems. For one thing, they involve a tremendous amount of time, effort, and expense. Imagine the resources involved in planning this particular study. Think of the hassles involved in searching out the participants and getting them to return again and again to take the tests. The researchers must fly the overseas Dunedin volunteers back for each evaluation. They need to reimburse people for their time and lost wages. These logistical and cost problems become more serious the longer a study continues. For this reason, we do have a good deal of longitudinal research covering infancy and short phases of childhood, but mammoth longitudinal studies that follow people from birth into adult life or trace development during long periods of adult life are rare.

The difficulty with getting people to return to be tested presents more than just practical hurdles. It leads to an important bias. Participating in a longitudinal study requires a special commitment. Therefore, people who agree to come back to be tested, particularly during adult life, tend to be highly motivated. Think of which classmates are going to come back to your high school reunion. Aren't they apt to be the people who are succeeding, versus those who have made a mess of their lives? Adults who stay in longitudinal studies, especially for the long haul, are an elite, much better than average group. While longitudinal studies offer us unparalleled information about life, these gold-standard studies have their biases, too.

longitudinal study A developmental research strategy that involves testing an age group repeatedly over many years.

Critiquing the Research

So, remembering our discussion, how would you go about being a good consumer of the research? When you are evaluating the findings in our field, here are some key points to keep in mind:

- Consider the study's participants. How were they selected? Ask yourself, "To what extent can I generalize from this population to the wider world?"

- Examine the study's measures. Are they accurate indexes of the behavior the researcher wants to assess? What biases and problems might they have?

- In looking at correlational studies, be alert to competing causal possibilities. What other forces might be responsible for the associations this researcher finds?

- With cross-sectional findings, beware of making assumptions that this is the way people *really* change with age.

- Look for longitudinal studies and welcome their insights. However, understand—especially during adult life—that these investigations are probably tracing the lives of the best and brightest people rather than the average adult.

Emerging Research Trends

Today, developmental scientists are attuned to these issues. In conducting correlational studies, they use sophisticated statistical techniques to disentangle confounding influences that might bias their results (Fried, 1997). They may use several measures, such as teacher ratings and parent input, as well as direct observations, to make sure they are measuring their concepts accurately. They sometimes make special efforts to travel to different cultures to check out whether their findings are limited to a particular society or apply to all human beings. Still, along with the emphasis on conducting better-designed, bigger, more global studies, there is an emerging trend. Developmentalists are getting up close and personal, too.

Quantitative research techniques—the strategies we have been describing, using groups of people and statistical tests—are the main approach that developmentalists use to study human behavior. In order to make general predictions about people, we need to examine the behavior of different individuals. We need to pin down our concepts by using scales or ratings with numerical values that can be tallied and compared. Researchers who conduct **qualitative research** are not interested in making numerical comparisons. They want to understand the unique life of the individual person by conducting in-depth interviews. In this book we will focus mainly on quantitative research, because that is how we find out the scientific "truth." But we will also highlight the growing number of qualitative, interview studies, to put a human face on our exploraion of developing life.

quantitative research Standard developmental science data-collection strategy that involves testing groups of people and using numerical scales and statistics.

qualitative research Occasional developmental science data-collection strategy that involves interviewing people to obtain information that cannot be quantified on a numerical scale.

✿ TYING IT ALL TOGETHER

1. Craig and Jessica are taking a course in research methods at their university and want to test the hypothesis that children who eat excessive sugar at breakfast do more poorly at school—but each student decides to tackle this question differently. Craig's plan is to go into children's homes to directly record their sugar consumption at breakfast, and relate these data to scores on math and reading tests. Jessica decides to randomly assign one group of children to eat a sugary breakfast (for example, Froot Loops, Cap'n Crunch) and another to eat a low-sugar alternative (for example, Wheaties), then have the first-grade teacher rate the math and reading skills of each group. Which student is conducting a correlational study, and which student is conducting a true experiment?

2. In the question above, which student, Craig or Jessica:
   a. will run into real ethical problems conducting the study?
   b. is employing naturalistic observation?
   c. is using expert observer ratings?
   d. will be able to prove that excess sugar consumption *causes* children to do more poorly at school?
   e. may run into the danger of people acting differently because they are being watched?
   f. is conducting a study that—although ethically acceptable—poses enormous practical hurdles in terms of actually carrying out the research?

3. Cecila and Jamel both want to test the hypothesis that people get wiser with age—but each decides to use a different research strategy. Cecila gives young adults, middle-aged people, and older adults a wisdom questionnaire and compares their scores. Jamel solicits a large group of 20-year-olds, gives them the wisdom questionnaire, and then has them return every five years to take the test again. Which student is conducting a cross-sectional study, and which student is conducting a longitudinal study?

4. Plan a longitudinal study to test a developmental science question that interests you. Describe how you would select your participants, how your study would proceed, what measures you would use, and what practical problems and biases your study would have.

Answers to the Tying It All Together questions can be found in the answers section of the book.

Final Thoughts

This brings me back to the letter that begins this chapter and my promise to let you in on my other agendas in writing this text. Because I want to teach you to critically evaluate the research, in the following pages I'll be analyzing individual studies and — in the "How Do We Know?" features that appear in some chapters — I will focus on research-related questions and issues in more depth. To bring home the personal experience of the lifespan, I've filled each chapter with quotations and vignettes, and — in the "Experiencing the Lifespan" boxes — I've interviewed people myself. To bring home the basic principle that our human lifespan is a continuing work in progress, I'll be starting each chapter by setting the historical and cultural context before moving on to explore the research. To emphasize the power of the developmental science research to improve lives, I've concluded many sections by spelling out interventions that improve the quality of life.

This book is designed to be read like an unfolding story, with each subsequent chapter building on concepts and terms mentioned in the previous ones. It's planned to emphasize how what developmentalists know about each earlier life stage relates to other times of life. I will be discussing three major aspects of development — physical development, cognitive development, and personality and social relationships (psychosocial development) — separately. However, I'll be continually stressing how each aspect of development connects. After all, we are not just bodies, minds, and personalities, but whole human beings!

Now, beginning with prenatal development and infancy (Chapters 2, 3, and 4); then moving on to childhood (Chapters 5, 6, and 7); adolescence and emerging adulthood (Chapters 8, 9, and 10); early and middle adulthood (Chapters 11 and 12); later life (Chapters 13 and 14); and, finally, that last milestone, death (Chapter 15), welcome to the lifespan and to the rest of this book! ▪

▌ SUMMARY

Who We Are and What We Study

Lifespan development is a huge mega-discipline encompassing **child development, gerontology,** and **adult development. Developmental scientists,** or **developmentalists,** chart the universal changes we undergo from birth to old age, explore individual differences in development, study the impact of **normative** and **nonnormative** life transitions, and explore every other topic relevant to our unfolding life.

Several major **contexts of development** shape our lives. The first is our **cohort,** or the time in history in which we live. The huge **baby boom cohort,** born in the years following World War II, has dramatically affected society as it passes through the lifespan. Cohorts of babies born before the twentieth century faced a shorter, harsher childhood, and many did not survive. As life got easier and education got longer, we first extended the growing-up phase of life to include adolescence and, in recent years, with a new life stage called **emerging adulthood,** have extended the start date of full adulthood to our late twenties.

The early-**twentieth-century life expectancy revolution,** with its dramatic advances in curing *infectious disease* and shift to deaths from *chronic illnesses,* allowed us to survive to later life. Today, **average life expectancy** is within striking distance of the **maximum lifespan** in the most affluent parts of the world, and we distinguish between two groups of elderly, the healthy **young-old** (people in their sixties and seventies) and the frail **old-old** (people in and over their eighties). The second major twentieth-century lifespan change occurred in the 1960s with the sexual revolution, the women's movement, and the counterculture movement. Today, we have enormous freedom to engineer our own lives the way we want. However, with single parenthood so common, child poverty levels are higher than before.

Socioeconomic status also greatly affects our lifespan — with people who live in poverty in the United States facing a harsher, more stressful, shorter life. The gaps between **developed world** countries and **developing world** countries are even more dramatic, with the least-developed countries lagging well behind in terms of health, wealth, and technology.

Our cultural background also determines how we develop. Scientists distinguish between **collectivist cultures,** which place a premium on social harmony and close extended-family relationships, and **individualistic cultures,** which value independence and personal achievement. Although Western nations traditionally rank high on individualism, cultures are continually evolving, and residents in every nation have a mix of individualistic and collectivist worldviews. Finally, our gender dramatically influences our travels through life. Women, for instance, outlive men by at least 5 to 10 years in the developed world.

Lenses for Looking at the Lifespan: Theories

Theories offer explanations about what causes people to act the way they do. The main theories in developmental science offering general explanations of behavior vary in their position on the fundamental **nature** versus **nurture** question. Behaviorists believe nurture is all-important. According to **traditional behaviorists,** in particular B. F. Skinner, **operant conditioning** and **reinforcement** determine all voluntary behaviors. According to **cognitive behaviorism/social learning theory, modeling** and **self-efficacy**—our internal sense that we can competently perform given tasks—predict how we act.

John Bowlby's **attachment theory** emphasizes both nature and nurture. According to Bowlby, the biological attachment response that develops during early childhood is genetically programmed to promote human survival, and the quality of our attachment relationships in our earliest years is crucial to later mental health. **Evolutionary psychologists** adopt a nature perspective, viewing human behaviors as genetically programmed into evolution to promote survival. **Behavioral genetics** research—in particular, **twin studies, adoption studies,** and occasionally **twin/adoption studies**—have convinced developmental scientists of the real-world power of nature, revealing genetic contributions to individual differences in virtually every trait.

Developmental scientists today, however, have gone beyond the nature *or* nurture question to explore how nature *and* nurture combine. Due to **evocative** and **active forces,** we shape our environments to go along with our genetic tendencies, and human relationships are **bidirectional**—that is our temperamental qualities and actions influence the responses of others, just as their actions influence us. A basic developmental science challenge is to foster an appropriate **person–environment fit.** We need to match our biologically based talents and abilities to the right environment. Advances in understanding genetics allow us to better arrange the environment to promote an optimal life.

According to Jean Piaget's **cognitive developmental theory,** children progress through four qualitatively different stages of intellectual development, and all learning occurs though **assimilation and accommodation.** The other most influential stage theorist of the lifespan, Erik Erikson, spells out eight **psychosocial tasks,** or challenges, that we must master as we travel from birth to old age.

Most developmental scientists today adopt the **developmental systems perspective.** They welcome input from every theory. They realize that systems dynamically relate. They understand that diversity among people and change processes is the essence of development.

The two main research strategies scientists use are **correlational studies,** which relate naturally occurring variations among people, and **true experiments,** in which researchers take action to manipulate their variables of interest and randomly assign people to receive a given treatment or not. With correlational studies, there are always competing possibilities for the relationships we find. While experiments do isolate causes, they are often unethical and impractical to carry out. In conducting research, it's best to strive for a **representative sample,** and it's essential to have accurate measures. **Naturalistic observation, self-reports,** tests of abilities, and expert observer evaluations are the main measurement strategies developmental scientists use.

The Tools of the Trade: Research Methods

The two major designs for studying development are longitudinal and cross-sectional research. **Cross-sectional studies,** which involve testing people of different age groups at the same time, are very easy to carry out. However, they may confuse differences between age groups with true changes that occur as people age, and they can't tell us about individual differences in development. **Longitudinal studies** are at the heart of our field because they do answer vital questions about how people develop. However, this "gold-standard" developmental research—following people over years—is difficult to carry out and often involves atypical, elite volunteers.

Today our studies are getting more global and statistically sophisticated. **Quantitative research**—studies involving groups of participants, and using statistical tests—is still the standard way we learn the scientific truth. But developmentalists are now occasionally conducting **qualitative research**—interviewing people in depth.

▮ KEY TERMS

▌ RECOMMENDED RESOURCES

THE CONTEXT

Mintz, S. (2004). *Huck's raft: A history of American childhood.* Cambridge, MA: Harvard University Press.

In this fascinating book touring American childhood—from the Colonial era to the current era—you will get a full picture of the transformations we have undergone in our ideas about children. You also might want to read Mark Twain's *Huckleberry Finn;* it offers a fabulous look at nineteenth-century life!

THEORIES

Bandura, A. (1997). *Self-efficacy: The exercise of control.* New York: W. H. Freeman.

In this book, Bandura summarizes the decades of research linking self-efficacy to everything from health to societal change.

Erikson, E. H. (1963). *Childhood and society.* New York: Norton.

Erikson's classic account of the eight stages of man (and woman) is in this book.

Karen, R. (1998). *Becoming attached: First relationships and how they shape our capacity to love.* London: Oxford University Press.

This combination biography of Bowlby and exploration of the latest research devoted to attachment theory is beautifully written.

Plomin, R., DeFreis, J. C., and McClearn, G. E. (1980). *Behavioral genetics: A primer.* San Francisco: W. H. Freeman.

Plomin, R., and McClearn, G. E. (Eds.) (1993). *Nature, nurture and psychology.* Washington, DC: American Psychological Association.

The two books above describe the findings and the basic approach of behavioral geneticists. The first is written for students without much background in the field.

Wadsworth, B. (1989). *Piaget's theory of cognitive and affective development.* New York: Longman.

This is a simple illustrated primer spelling out the essentials of Piaget's theory.

Watson, J. (1928/1972). *Psychological care of the infant and child.* New York: Arno Press.

Watson's early-twentieth-century childrearing guide reveals (inadvertently) the serious limitations of the behavioral model. Check it out for some horrifying advice relating to how to raise children according to the latest "scientific" behavioral principles.

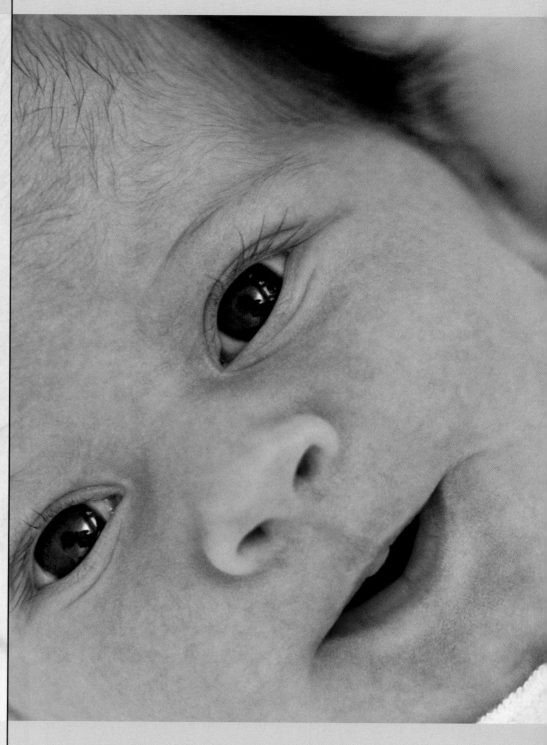

CHAPTER 2

Prenatal Development, Pregnancy, and Birth

It's hard to explain, different from anything that's happened before, says Kim. Your whole self shifts. You are all about two people now. When you wake up, shop for groceries, or plan meals, this other person is always with you. You are always thinking, "What will be good for the baby? What will be best for the two of us?"

Feeling the first kick—like little feathers brushing inside me—was amazing. It was as if she woke up to tell me, "I'm there, Mommy." Another incredible thing was seeing the ultrasound. It's frightening when you go for that test. You wonder, "Will there be something wrong?" But when I saw her shape and heart, the feeling was unbelievable. At first I felt like I could never explain this to my husband. But Jeff is wonderful. I think he really gets it. So I feel very lucky. I can't imagine what this experience would be like if I was going through these nine months completely alone.

Now that it's the twenty-seventh week and I know that my little girl can survive, there is another shift. I am suddenly mentally at that moment: "Can I really do this? Will she be born healthy?"

The main downside has always been the anxieties—fears that she will be born with some problem. I keep going back to the beginning. Did I do something that could have caused harm before the nausea and tiredness hit, which made me realize that I was pregnant? Could my baby have a birth defect?

The other downside is that, until recently, I still felt really nauseous and tired. Some days, I could barely make it to work. (Everything they told you about morning sickness only lasting through the first trimester is wrong—at least for me!)

But most amazing is what happens with strangers, when I'm at the store or walking around the mall. People light up and grin, wish me good luck, or give me advice. It's like the world is watching out for me, rooting for me, cherishing me.

In this traditional southern Indian ceremony performed at the sixth or eighth month of pregnancy, family members and friends gather around to protect the woman and fetus from "the evil eyes." Rituals such as this one are common around the world and embody our fears about this special time of life.

Setting the Context: Superstitions About Life Before Birth

The concern and awe Kim is getting from the wider world may be built into our humanity. Many societies see pregnancy as a special time of life. Pregnant women are often pampered, kept calm and happy. Their desires and cravings are satisfied. But we also see pregnancy as a uniquely vulnerable time. In some cultures, pregnant women are shielded from funerals and sad events. Rituals—such as the nine-day Navajo Blessing Way ceremony—may be performed to ensure that all goes well. In previous eras and in some regions of the world today, people use good luck charms to keep evil spirits away—a pregnancy girdle in medieval England, a bell placed between the breasts in Brazil, a small sack of garlic worn in Guatemala (Aldred, 1997; Von Raffler-Engel, 1994), a cotton pregnancy sash in Japan (Ito & Sharts-Hopko, 2002).

We have the same uneasy feelings in the twenty-first-century developed West. Many couples are reluctant to announce the news until after the first three months. Perhaps you have friends who refuse to buy baby items before the birth: "It's a sign of bad luck." In traditional societies, the message—better hold off on celebrating—has been built into formal rituals. In Bulgaria, the first kick is the signal for a woman to bake bread and take it to the church. In Bali, at the seventh month, a formal prayer ceremony takes place to recognize that there is now, finally, a real person inside whom the spirits need to protect from harm (Kitzinger, 2000; Von Raffler-Engel, 1994).

As these practices reveal, pregnancy stands out as one of the most exciting and frightening times of life. There can be wonderfully uplifting emotions, when women are totally absorbed with the baby and with their physical state. At the same time, there is a sense of impending danger and fear about the hazards that lie on the journey ahead. Let's keep these two very different feelings in mind as we turn to explore the science of what happens during the baby's nine months in the womb.

In the first part of this chapter we trace prenatal development, describing what happens, stage by stage, as the baby grows. Then we shift focus to the mother-to-be, examining the inner experience of being pregnant, stage by stage. Next we tackle the anxieties related to the baby, describing the external and internal threats to fetal development that, thankfully, only infrequently occur. Finally, we look at the event that Kim is anxiously awaiting: birth. What is this amazing experience really like? What were labor and delivery like in previous centuries, and what birth options do women in the developed world have today? We conclude this chapter by describing the newborn and exploring the major threats after birth—arriving in the world too soon and/or too small, and infant mortality.

The First Step: Fertilization

Before embarking on this chapter-long journey, however, we need to understand the starting point. What are the structures involved in reproduction? What is the physiological process involved in conceiving a child? What is taking place at the genetic level when a sperm and an egg unite to form a new human being?

The Reproductive Systems

The female and male reproductive systems are shown in Figure 2.1. As you can see, the female system has several basic parts:

- Center stage is the **uterus,** the pear-shaped muscular organ that will carry the baby to term. The uterus is lined with a velvety tissue, the *endometrium*, which thickens

uterus The pear-shaped muscular organ in a woman's abdomen that house the developing baby.

in preparation for becoming pregnant and, if that event does not occur, is shed at the end of the monthly cycle, during menstruation.

- The lower section of the uterus, protruding into the vagina, is the **cervix**. During pregnancy, this thick uterine neck must perform an amazing feat: Be strong enough to stay intact for nine months under the pressure of the expanding uterus; be flexible enough to open fully at birth.

- Branching from the upper ends of the uterus are the **fallopian tubes**. These slim, pipelike structures serve as conduits to the uterus.

- The feathery ends of the fallopian tubes surround the **ovaries**, the almond-shaped organs where the **ova**, the mother's egg cells, reside.

The Process of Fertilization

The pathway that results in **fertilization**—the union of sperm and egg—begins at **ovulation**. This is the moment, typically around day 14 of a woman's cycle, when a mature ovum erupts from the ovary wall. **Hormones**—chemical substances released into the bloodstream that target certain tissues and body processes and cause them to change—orchestrate the process of ovulation as well as the other events that program pregnancy.

At the moment of ovulation, the feathery ends of the fallopian tube, reacting to signals showing the site of the rupture, move to that location. As they suction the ovum in, the fallopian tube begins vigorous contractions that launch the ovum on its three-day journey toward the uterus.

Now the male's contribution to forming a new life makes its entrance. In contrast to females, whose ova are all mainly formed at birth or early in life, the **testes**—the male structures comparable to the ovaries—are continually manufacturing sperm. An adult male typically produces several hundred million sperm a day. During sexual intercourse, these millions of cells, released at ejaculation, are expelled into the vagina, where a small proportion enter the body of the uterus and wend their way up the fallopian tubes.

cervix The neck, or narrow lower portion, of the uterus.

fallopian tube One of a pair of slim, pipelike structures that connect the ovaries with the uterus.

ovary One of a pair of almond-shaped organs that contain a woman's ova, or eggs.

ovum An egg cell containing the genetic material contributed by the mother to the baby.

fertilization The union of sperm and egg.

ovulation The moment during a woman's monthly cycle when an ovum is expelled from the ovary.

hormones Chemical substances released in the bloodstream that target and change organs and tissues.

testes Male organs that manufacture sperm.

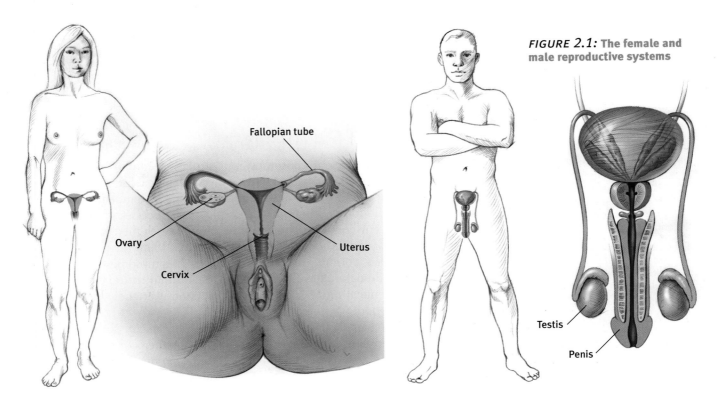

Fallopian tube

Ovary

Cervix

Uterus

Testis

Penis

FIGURE 2.1: The female and male reproductive systems

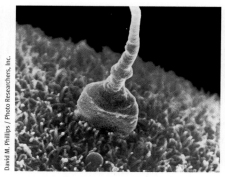

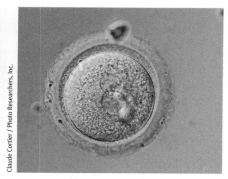

The sperm surround the ovum.

One sperm burrows in (notice the large head).

The nuclei of the two cells fuse. The watershed event called fertilization has occurred.

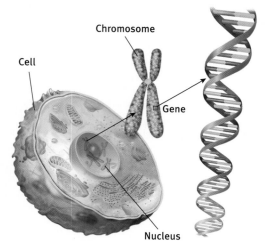

Cell

Chromosome

Gene

Nucleus

FIGURE 2.2: **The human building blocks:** The nucleus of every human cell contains chromosomes, each of which is made up of two strands of DNA connected in a double helix.

chromosome A threadlike strand of DNA located in the nucleus of every cell that carries the genes, which transmit hereditary information.

DNA (deoxyribonucleic acid) The material that makes up genes, which bear our hereditary characteristics.

gene A segment of DNA that contains a chemical blueprint for manufacturing a particular protein.

To promote pregnancy, the best time to have intercourse is right around ovulation. (Readers not interested in becoming pregnant, be forewarned: The hormones triggering ovulation are sensitive to erotic cues. So this event may occur in response to intense sexual arousal—at erratic times of the month.) The ovum is receptive for about 24 hours while in the tube's wide outer part. Sperm take a few hours to journey from the cervix to the tube. However, sperm can live almost a week in the recesses of the uterus and cervix, which means that intercourse several days prior to ovulation may also result in fertilization (Marieb, 2004).

Although the ovum emits chemical signals as to its location, the tiny tadpole-shaped travelers cannot easily locate the single cell or make the perilous journey upward into the tubes. So, of the estimated several hundred million sperm expelled at ejaculation, only 200 to 300 reach their destination, find their target, and begin to burrow in.

What happens now is a team assault. The sperm drill into the ovum, piercing its outer layers and penetrating through toward the center. Suddenly one reaches the innermost part. Then the chemical composition of the ovum wall changes, shutting out the other sperm. The head of this sperm, containing its genetic blueprint, lies inside the nucleus of the ovum. The nuclei of the male and female cells move slowly together. When they meld into one cell, the landmark event called fertilization has occurred. What exactly happens genetically when the sperm and egg combine?

The Genetics of Fertilization

The answer lies in looking at **chromosomes**, ropy structures composed of long ladder-like strands of the genetic material **DNA**. Arrayed along each chromosome are segments of DNA called **genes**, each of which functions as the template for creating the proteins responsible for carrying out all the physical processes of life (see Figure 2.2). Every cell in our body contains 46 chromosomes, with the exception of the sperm and ova, each of which has half this number, or 23. When the nuclei of these two cells, called *gametes*, combine at fertilization, their chromosomes align in pairs to again comprise 46. So nature has a marvelous mechanism to ensure that each new human life has an identical number of chromosomes and every new human being gets half of its genetic heritage from the parent of each sex.

You can see the 46 paired chromosomes of a male in Figure 2.3. Notice that each chromosome pair (one member of which we get from our mother and one from our father) is a perfect match, with one exception—the sex chromosomes (X and Y). The X is far longer and heavier than the Y. Because each ovum carries an X chromosome, our father's contribution to fertilization determines our sex. If a lighter, faster-swimming, Y-carrying sperm fertilizes the ovum, we get a boy (XY). If the victor is a more resilient, slower-moving X, we get a girl (XX).

In the race to fertilization, the Ys are statistically more successful; scientists estimate that 20 percent more male than female babies are conceived. But the prenatal period is particularly hard on developing males. If a family member learns that she is pregnant, the odds still favor her having a boy; but because more males die in the uterus, only 5 percent more boys than girls make it to birth (Werth, 2002). And throughout life, males continue to be the less hardy sex, dying off at higher rates at every age. Recall from our discussion in Chapter 1 that women outlive men by at least five years throughout the developed world.

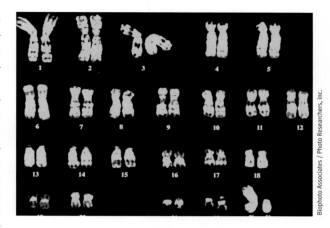

FIGURE 2.3: **A map of human chromosomes:** This magnified grid, called a karyotype, shows the 46 chromosomes in their matched pairs. The final pair, with its X and Y, shows that this person is a male. Also notice the huge size of the X chromosome compared to the Y.

 TYING IT ALL TOGETHER

1. Sketch the female reproductive system and label the uterus, fallopian tubes, cervix, and ovaries.

2. What is the parallel structure to the ovary in the male reproductive system?

3. Tiffany feels certain that if she has intercourse at the right time, she will get pregnant—but asks you, "What is the right time?" Give Tiffany your answer carefully, referring to the text discussion, and then tell her the chain of events that lead from ovulation to fertilization.

4. If your aunt is pregnant, statistically speaking she is going to have a _____, and _____ is responsible for the child's sex.

   a. boy; your aunt
   b. girl; your uncle
   c. boy; your uncle
   d. girl; your aunt

Answers to the Tying It All Together questions can be found in the answers section of the book.

Prenatal Development

Now that we have an overview of the starting point, we turn to the process of prenatal development, tracing how the microscopic fertilized ovum divides millions of times and differentiates into a living, breathing child. This miraculous transformation takes place in three distinct stages.

[FAQ: What stages does the unborn baby go through during prenatal development?]

First Two Weeks: The Germinal Stage

The first approximately two weeks after fertilization—the time when the cell mass has not yet fully attached to the wall of the uterus—is called the **germinal stage** (see Figure 2.4 on page 40). Within 36 hours, the fertilized ovum, now a single cell called the **zygote,** makes its first cell division. Then the tiny cluster of cells continues to divide every 12 to 15 hours as it wends its way on a roughly three-day trip down the fallopian tube.

When the mass of cells passes into the uterine cavity, it sheds its outer wall and differentiates into layers. Now called a **blastocyst,** the rapidly dividing cells form a hollow ball of roughly 100 cells. The next major challenge is **implantation**—the several-day process of embedding into the uterine wall.

germinal stage The first 14 days of prenatal development, from fertilization to full implantation.

zygote A fertilized ovum.

blastocyst The hollow sphere of cells formed during the germinal stage in preparation for implantation.

implantation The process in which a blastocyst becomes embedded in the uterine wall.

FIGURE 2.4: **The events of the germinal stage:** The fertilized ovum divides on its trip to the uterus, then becomes a hollow ball called a blastocyst, and finally fully implants in the wall of the uterus at about 14 days after fertilization.

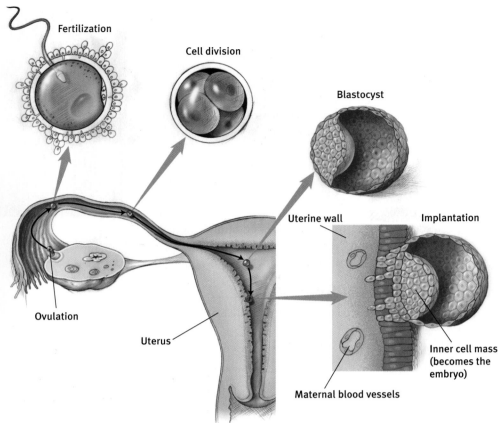

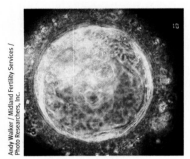

This is a photo of the blastocyst, the roughly 100-cell ball, soon to attach itself to the uterine wall. When implantation occurs, this event will signal the end of the germinal phase.

placenta The structure projecting from the wall of the uterus during pregnancy through which the developing baby absorbs nutrients.

embryonic stage The second stage of prenatal development, lasting from week 3 through week 8.

neural tube A cylindrical structure that forms along the back of the embryo and develops into the brain and spinal cord.

neuron A nerve cell.

The blastocyst seeks an ideal landing site on an upper section of the uterus. Meanwhile, hormones have prepared the uterus to receive the cell mass. The outer layer of the blastocyst develops projections. At about day 9, these tentacles burrow in. From this landing zone, blood vessels proliferate that will eventually make up the **placenta,** the lifeline that passes nutrients from the mother's system to the developing baby. After implantation, the next stage of prenatal development begins. This is the all-important embryonic phase.

Week 3 to Week 8: The Embryonic Stage

Although the **embryonic stage** lasts roughly only six weeks, it is the fasted-paced period of development. During this brief time, all the major organs are constructed! By the end of the embryonic stage, what began as an ill-defined clump of cells now looks like a clearly recognizable human being.

One early task after implantation is to form the mechanism that makes all future development possible. After the baby is hooked up to the maternal bloodstream—which will nourish it as it grows—nutrients must be pumped to each of its rapidly differentiating cells. So by the third week after fertilization, the circulatory system (our body's transport system) forms, and its pump, the heart, starts to beat.

At around the same time, the rudiments of the nervous system appear. Between 21 and 24 days after fertilization, an indentation forms along the back of the embryo and soon closes up to become the **neural tube** (see Figure 2.5). The uppermost part of this cylindrical structure will become the brain. Its lower part will form the spinal cord. Almost all of the **neurons,** or nerve cells, that enable us to think, to respond, and to process information from the outside world are formed from cells that originated in the neural tube during our first few months in the womb (Huttenlocher, 2002).

Meanwhile, the body is developing at an astounding rate. At day 26, arm buds form; by day 28, swellings appear where the legs will form. The embryo now has the outlines of eyes and indentations for ears. At day 37, rudimentary feet start to develop.

By day 41, elbows, wrist curves, and the precursors of fingers can be seen. Several days later, ray-like structures that will turn into toes emerge. By about week 8, the embryo is only about the length of a thumb, but its internal organs are all in place. What started out looking like a curved stalk or twisted dinner napkin, then a strange outer-space alien, now appears like a distinctly *human* being.

Principles of Prenatal Development

Imagine that you wanted to spell out some guiding principles related to the sequence of development just described. In looking at the photographs of the developing embryo on this page, can you identify three basic patterns that underlie this rapid transformation to a fully formed human being?

- You might notice that from a core cylindrical shape, the arms and legs grow outward and then (not unexpectedly) the fingers and toes protrude. So the first principle is that growth follows the **proximodistal sequence,** from the most interior (proximal) part of the body to the outer (distal) sides.

- You might also notice that from the initial swelling that makes the embryo look mainly like a mammoth head, the arms emerge and the legs sprout. So development takes place according to the **cephalocaudal sequence,** meaning from top (*cephalo* = head) to bottom (*caudal* = tail).

- Finally, just as in constructing a sculpture, development begins with the basic building blocks and then fills in details. A head is formed before eyes and ears are carved in; legs are constructed before feet and toes are chiseled. So the **mass-to-specific sequence,** or gross (large) structures before smaller refinements, is the third basic principle of body growth.

Keep these principles in mind. As you will see when we discuss physical development in infancy and childhood, the same patterns apply to growth and to our unfolding motor abilities *after* the baby leaves the womb.

Week 9 to Birth: The Fetal Stage

During the embryonic stage, basic body structures sprout almost day by day. In the final period of prenatal growth—the **fetal stage**—development occurs at a more leisurely pace. From the eyebrows, fingernails, and hair follicles that develop from

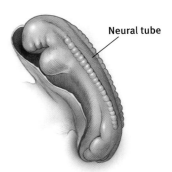

FIGURE 2.5: The neural tube: This structure is one of the first to form after implantation. The brain and spinal cord will develop from it.

proximodistal sequence The developmental principle that growth occurs from the most interior parts of the body outward.

cephalocaudal sequence The developmental principle that growth occurs in a sequence from head to toe.

mass-to-specific sequence The developmental principle that large structures (and movements) precede increasingly detailed refinements.

fetal stage The final period of prenatal development, lasting seven months, characterized by physical refinements, massive growth, and the development of the brain.

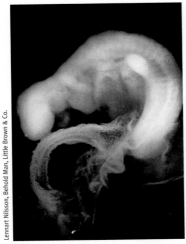

At about week 3, the embryo (the upside-down U across the top) looks like a curved stalk.

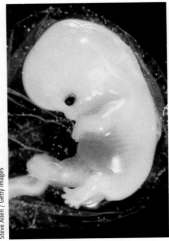

At week 4, you can see the indentations for eyes and the arms and legs beginning to sprout.

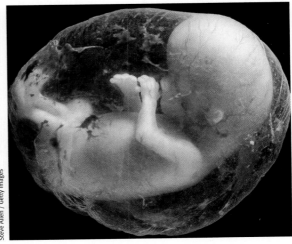

At week 9, the baby-to-be has fingers, toes, and ears. All the major organs have developed and the fetal stage has begun!

FIGURE 2.6: **Forming a brain: climbing neurons:** During the earlier part of the fetal period, the neurons destined to make up the brain ascend these ladderlike filaments to reach the uppermost part of what had been the neural tube.
Source: Huttenlocher (2002).

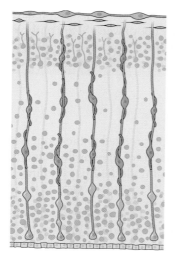

weeks 9 to 12 to the cushion of fat that accumulates during the final weeks before birth, it takes a full seven months to transform the fully formed embryo into a resilient baby ready to embrace life.

Why does our species need this prolonged period of refining and elaborating lasting for so many months? One reason is to allow time for the neurons composing that masterpiece organ—the human brain—to align themselves into place. Let's now pause to look at this crucial process of making a brain.

During the late embryonic stage, a mass of cells starts to form within the neural tube that will eventually produce the billions of neurons that compose our brain. From this zone, the new neurons begin to steadily migrate to a region just under the top of the differentiating tube (Huttenlocher, 2002). This intense period of cell formation and migration, diagrammed in Figure 2.6, concludes when all of the neurons assemble in their "staging area" by the middle of the fetal period, or week 25. Then they are poised to rapidly differentiate into their mature form. The cells lengthen and develop their characteristic branches. They start to interlink. This vital process of interconnecting—which is responsible for every human thought and action—will continue until almost our final day of life.

Figure 2.7 shows the mushrooming brain during the phase of fetal development. Notice that the brain almost doubles in size from month 4 to month 7. By now, the brain has already assumed the wrinkled structure of an adult.

This massive growth has a profound effect. At around month 6, the fetus shows signs of consciousness. It reacts to sound (Crade & Lovett, 1988). Its heart beats faster in response to loud noises. If a doctor shines a light inside the uterus, it tries to shield its face (Kisilevsky, Muir, & Low, 1992). And—provided the lungs are mature enough to take in oxygen and expel carbon dioxide—around this time, a few babies can even be born and survive. Today, the **age of viability**, or earliest date at which babies can survive, has dropped to a remarkable 22 weeks—almost halving the 38 weeks the fetus would normally spend in the womb. By week 25, babies have a fifty-fifty chance of surviving (Werth, 2002). But this statistic applies only to infants born in affluent areas of the globe, who have access to top-notch medical interventions and world-class care during their many hazardous months after birth.

Week by week the chances of survival increase. Still, it is vitally important that the fetus stay in the uterus as long as possible. As you will see later in this chapter,

age of viability The earliest point at which a baby can survive outside the womb.

[FAQ: At what moment does the fetus become viable?**]**

FIGURE 2.7: **The expanding brain:** The brain grows dramatically month by month during the fetal period. During the final months, it develops its characteristic folds.

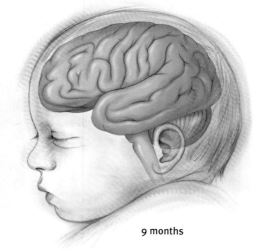

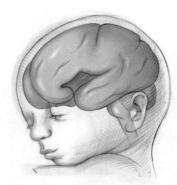

4 months

7 months

9 months

being born too early (and too small) makes a tremendous difference in terms of health. In fact, in the last two months of fetal development alone, in addition to maturing neurologically and in many other ways, the baby gains almost five pounds.

Figure 2.8 shows the fetus during the final month of pregnancy, when its prenatal nest becomes cramped and birth is looming on the horizon. Notice the major support structures the developing baby requires: the placenta, projecting from the uterine wall, which supplies nutrients from the mother to the fetus; the **umbilical cord,** protruding from what will be the baby's bellybutton, the conduit through which nutrients flow; and the **amniotic sac,** the fluid-filled chamber within which the baby floats. This tough, encasing membrane provides vital insulation from infection and harm.

At this stage of prenatal development, first-time mothers and fathers may be running around, buying the crib or shopping for baby clothes. Especially in developed world countries, middle-class women, such as Kim, may be marveling at the array of items their precious son or daughter "requires": "a pacifier, a receiving blanket, a bassinet . . . and what else!" As you saw in the vignette, parents-to-be are anxiously focusing on that upcoming event: birth. What is happening physically and emotionally during *all* nine months from the mother's—and father's—point of view?

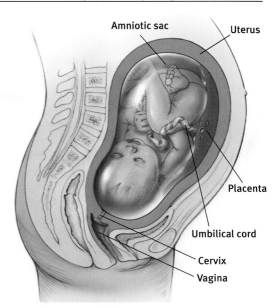

FIGURE 2.8: *Poised to be born:* This diagram shows the fetus inside the woman's uterus late in pregnancy. Notice the placenta, amniotic sac, and umbilical cord.

 TYING IT ALL TOGETHER

1. Rapid organ formation; neural migration to the top of the brain; the blastocyst: Match each term or process to the appropriate prenatal stage.

   a. embryonic, fetal, germinal
   b. germinal, fetal, embryonic
   c. fetal, germinal, embryonic
   d. germinal, fetal, embryonic

2. A pregnant friend asks you, "How does my baby's brain develop?" Describe the process of neural migration, when it occurs, and when it is complete.

3. Give a concrete example of (a) the cephalocaudal sequence, (b) the proximodistal sequence, and (c) the mass-to-specific sequence.

Answers to the Tying It All Together questions can be found in the answers section of the book.

Pregnancy

The 266- to 277-day **gestation** period (or pregnancy) is divided into three segments. These phases, called **trimesters,** comprise roughly three months each. (Because it is difficult to know exactly when fertilization occurs, nurses, doctors, and midwives date the duration of pregnancy from the woman's last menstrual period.)

Pregnancy differs, however, from the carefully patterned process of prenatal development just described. Although there are some classic symptoms, there really is no universal pregnancy experience at all.

To bring this point home, ask a few mothers to describe their pregnancies. One person might complain about being violently ill for the entire nine months; another might rave about feeling physically better than ever. Some women adore looking pregnant and joyously look forward to the baby; others despise their expanding body (Bondas & Eriksson, 2001) and feel demoralized and depressed. With the strong caution that variability—from person to person (and child to child)—is the norm, let's offer a trimester-by-trimester overview of what pregnancy *can* be like.

umbilical cord The structure that attaches the placenta to the fetus, through which nutrients are passed and fetal wastes are removed.

amniotic sac A bag-shaped, fluid-filled membrane that contains and insulates the fetus.

gestation The period of pregnancy.

trimester One of the 3-month-long segments into which pregnancy is divided.

First Trimester: Often Feeling Tired and Ill

[FAQ: How soon does a woman know she is pregnant?]

After the blastocyst implants in the uterus—a few days before the woman first misses her period—pregnancy often signals its presence through some unpleasant symptoms. Many women feel faint. (Yes, fainting can be an early sign of pregnancy!) They may get headaches or have to urinate frequently. Like Kim in the vignette, they may feel incredibly tired. Their breasts become tender, painful to the touch. So, many women do not need that definite tip-off—a missed menstrual period—to realize they are carrying a child.

The trigger for these varied symptoms is a flood of hormones. After implantation, the production of *progesterone* (literally *pro*, or "for," *gestation*)—the hormone responsible for maintaining the pregnancy—surges. The placenta produces its own unique hormone, *human chorionic gonadotropin (HCG)*, thought to prevent the woman's body from rejecting the "foreign" embryo. It is the presence of this hormone that is picked up by the classic over-the-counter pregnancy test.

Given the high levels of circulating hormones, the massive physiological changes that are taking place, and the fact that the blood supply is being diverted to the uterus, the tiredness, dizziness, and headaches make perfect sense. What about that classic symptom mentioned in the chapter-opening vignette—morning sickness?

Morning sickness—waves of nausea and sometimes vomiting—affects at least two out of every three women during the first trimester (Aldred, 1997; Beckmann and others, 2002). This well-known pregnancy symptom is not just confined to the morning. Many women feel queasy on and off all day. A few get so violently ill that they cannot keep any food down (Aldred, 1997; Beckmann and others, 2002). And men can sometimes develop morning sickness along with their wives! (See Bogren, 1983.) This phenomenon even has its own name: *couvade.*

But this symptom seems senseless. The developing embryo needs all the nourishment it can get. Can you think of why it might be adaptive to our species' survival, if evolution built in a mechanism—especially during the first months of pregnancy—that caused women to feel revolted at the sight and smell of particular foods?

Consider these clues: The queasiness is at its height during the period of intense organ formation, and, like magic, one day toward the end of the first trimester, usually (but not always) disappears. Munching on crackers or bread products is helpful. Strong odors make many women gag. Evolutionary psychologists theorize that, in the days before refrigeration, morning sickness may have evolved as a way of protecting the developing embryo if the mother ate spoiled meat or toxic plants, which could be particularly dangerous to the baby while its basic body structures were being formed (Bjorklund & Pellegrini, 2002; Profet, 1997).

In support of this theory, crackers—the traditional treatment for morning sickness—do not spoil. To alleviate mothers' distress, health-care professionals advise eating more frequently and consuming smaller (less potentially toxic) quantities of food. If you have a friend who is struggling with morning sickness, you can tell her that ginger root and acupressure bands may provide some relief (Profet, 1997). You can also give her this heartening information: Some research suggests that women who experience morning sickness are more likely to carry their babies to term.

This brings up the topic of pregnancy anxieties. There is a logical reason why many women are reluctant to announce the news that they are pregnant until after the first three months. During the first trimester, roughly 1 in 10 confirmed pregnancies are destined to end in **miscarriage.** For women in their late thirties, the chance of miscarrying during the first 12 weeks escalates to roughly 1 in 5. Many of these miscarriages are inevitable. They are caused by profound genetic problems in the developing embryo that are incompatible with life.

miscarriage The naturally occurring loss of a pregnancy and death of the fetus.

Second Trimester: Feeling Much Better and Connecting Emotionally

Another reason that the first three months of pregnancy have a tentative quality is that mothers-to-be still don't feel the baby inside. During the second trimester, the fetus makes its presence physically known.

By week 14, the uterus is dramatically expanding, often creating a need to shop for maternity clothes. The wider world may begin to notice the woman's expanding body: "Are you really pregnant?" "How wonderful!" "Take my seat."

Around week 18, an event called **quickening**—a sensation like bubbles that signals the baby kicking in the womb—appears. As Kim described in the vignette, and as you can see below, the woman feels viscerally connected to a growing human being:

> When I felt him move, I found myself fantasizing about this new person, visualizing what he would look like—seeing him growing up, getting married, becoming a wonderful human being. That's when the magic really kicked in.

quickening A pregnant woman's first feeling of the fetus moving inside her body.

This mystical sense of attachment varies from woman to woman. Some mothers-to-be are intensely bonded to their babies from the minute they learn they are pregnant (Mikulincer & Florian, 1999). For many, the sense of connection intensifies during the second trimester when they experience some watershed event such as feeling the baby move (Mikulincer & Florian, 1999; Righetti and others, 2005; Salisbury and others, 2003).

Whenever it occurs, this feeling is vital. Women who continually think about their babies, dream about them, and talk to them tend to take exceptional care of their health. Conversely, as one longitudinal study showed, women who felt negative about impending motherhood and their babies had infants who developed more slowly during their first two years of life (Deave, 2005). With the caution that caregiver–infant love can blossom at any point, being strongly bonded to the baby during pregnancy is linked to being a loving, caring mother after the child enters the world (Salisbury and others, 2003).

Another landmark event that alters the emotional experience of pregnancy occurs toward the end of the second trimester, when, as you saw in the vignette with Kim, the woman realizes that she is finally able to give birth to a living child. This important late-pregnancy marker explains why some societies build in celebrations at month 6 or 7 to welcome the baby to the human community.

Third Trimester: Getting Very Large and Anxiously Waiting for Birth

Look at a pregnant woman struggling upstairs and you'll get a sense of her feelings during the third trimester: backaches (think of carrying a bowling ball); leg cramps; numbness and tingling as the uterus presses against the nerves of the lower limbs; heartburn, insomnia, anticipation, and anxiety as focus shifts to the birth ("When will this baby ever arrive!"); uterine contractions occurring irregularly as the baby sinks into the birth canal and delivery draws very near.

Although many women are able to work right up to the day of delivery, health-care professionals advise taking time off to rest, take naps, and rely on caring family members and friends for help with cooking and household chores during the final months. Actually, having a caring social network looms large in the emotional experience of being pregnant for *all* nine months.

Pregnancy Emotions and the Wider Social World

I don't know what it's like for you and your partner to hear the baby's heartbeat, or see the ultrasound together, or feel the first kick. I lived through nine months of pregnancy by myself. No one understood how lonely I felt. I thought this was supposed to be the happiest time of your life. I found myself losing weight instead of gaining and being depressed most of the time.

When I told my husband I was pregnant, he got furious and told me we can't afford this baby. I'm frightened. All I know is that God is the provider of life and abortion is a sin.

Rolf Bruderer / Masterfile

Keith Dannemiller / Corbis

Women with loving partners are likely to see pregnancy as a joyous event. Women undergoing this experience alone are more likely to be anxious and ambivalent about the child. Imagine, like the woman in the photograph at right, being pregnant and alone. How would you feel?

As you can see in these quotations, pregnancy takes on a very different emotional flavor depending on what is happening in the wider world. What forces can turn this joyous time of life into nine months of distress?

One influence, as suggested above, lies in economic concerns. Low-income pregnant women, in both the developed and developing worlds, are more likely to feel demoralized and depressed (Rahman, Iqbal, & Harrington, 2003; Rubertsson and others, 2005; Zayas, Jankowski, & McKee, 2003). Women who report serious financial worries tend, not unexpectedly, to be more anxious and ambivalent about their pregnancies (Lewis, 2003; Rubertsson and others, 2005). In one tantalizing longitudinal study tracing a national sample of thousands of U.S. pregnant women, researchers found evidence that economic stress can even physically affect the developing child. The women who were laid off from their jobs during the course of their pregnancies tended to have lighter-than-average babies at birth (Dooley & Prause, 2005).

The main force, however, that determines the emotional quality of pregnancy applies to both affluent and economically deprived women alike—feeling cared about and loved. Women with an unsupportive social network have special trouble coping (Besser, Priel, & Wiznitzer, 2002; Glazier and others, 2004; Rahman, Iqbal, & Harrington, 2003; Rubertsson, Waldenström, & Wickberg, 2003; Zayas, Jankowski, & McKee, 2003; Zelkowitz and others, 2004). As you can see in the quotation above, the absence of a caring partner causes special pain (Dimitrovsky, Levy-Shiff, & Schattner-Zanany, 2002). However, it is not necessary to be married or in a committed relationship to feel supported and loved; having nurturing family members or close friends is often enough (Logsdon & Davis, 2003). Moreover, even going for regular prenatal care—which 99 percent of women in affluent regions of the world now do (AbouZahr & Wardlaw, 2003)—can also make an emotional difference (in addition to being vital to ensuring the fetus's health). There is nothing like the close bond that develops, month by month, when a woman is being watched over by a compassionate health-care provider during this intimate journey of life.

Feeling cared for during pregnancy is like money in the bank. In one longitudinal study tracing low-income women from their third trimester through their children's first year of life, social support was one force that predicted the quality of mother–infant attachment at age one (Huth-Bocks and others, 2004). Imagine being an impoverished, isolated single mother. Or, like the woman quoted at the beginning of the section, suppose your partner was actively hostile to your pregnant state. Could you feel free to fully devote your love to your baby once it was born?

What About Dads?

This brings up the experience of the partner in the pregnancy and childrearing journey—dads. Given all of the attention we lavish on pregnant women throughout history and in every culture, it should come as no surprise that fathers have been relatively ignored in the developmental science research exploring this major transition of life. But fathers are also bonded to their babies-to-be. They can feel just as devastated when a pregnancy doesn't work out. Here are some heartrending stories about miscarriage, taken from a rare study exploring this event from the perspective of men (McCreight, 2004).

> I had to be strong for Kate. I had to let her cry on me and then I would . . . drive up into the hills and cry to myself. I was trying to support her even though I felt my whole life had just caved in, you know, my whole life just ended then and there.
>
> (quoted in McCreight, 2004, p. 337)

One father in this study had scanned the ultrasound image of the baby onto his screen saver and took enormous pleasure in looking at it. Three weeks later, when the fetus died in the womb, he could not bear to let the image go, even though every sight of the photo evoked waves of intense grief. Although the men in this study complained that their emotions were often marginalized (one angrily reported having friends call to ask only: "How is your wife doing?"), losing a child—particularly late in pregnancy—can be an unforgettable life trauma for men.

Is pregnancy *normally* a stressful time for men? The answer is maybe. Developmentalists asked several hundred first-time fathers to report on their psychological symptoms during mid-pregnancy and at various points after the baby's birth (Condon, Boyce, & Corkindale, 2004). Men reported that pregnancy was more stressful than the exhausting first few months after birth!

Put yourself in the place of a father-to-be. Perhaps you wonder: "Will the baby take away from my relationship with my wife?" "Can I be an involved father and support the family?" "Will I *really* be able to handle these two demanding roles?"

Men usually don't have the safety valve of discussing their worries with friends and family. As you saw in the quotation above, our culture expects them to be strong on their own. And pregnancy—especially late pregnancy—puts a serious damper on sexual life. Women report having less interest in having sex as pregnancy advances (Gokyildiz & Beji, 2005).

So, by returning to the beginning of the chapter, we now know that the widespread cultural practice of pampering and cherishing pregnant women makes excellent psychological sense—for both the mother *and* her child (Logsdon & Davis, 2003; Salisbury and others, 2003). But we also need to understand that expectant fathers need cherishing, too!

Table 2.1 summarizes our discussion and expands on it slightly in a "determining the risk of depression during pregnancy" questionnaire. Now let's return to the baby and tackle that fear in the vignette: "Will my baby be healthy?"

TABLE 2.1: Determining the Risk of Depression (and Possible Bonding Issues): A Questionnaire for Measuring Life Stress in Parents-to-Be

---

1. Does this family (or person) have serious financial troubles?

2. Has the mother (or father) recently been laid off from work, or are there serious fears about losing a job?

3. Is the woman having marital problems, and does her husband want this baby?

4. Is the woman a single mother? If so, does she have a supportive network of friends and family members, or is she socially isolated?

5. Was the pregnancy "unexpected"? While parents can get attached to the developing baby even if they initially did not want a child, a surprise, unwelcome pregnancy may predict depression and less intense bonding with the baby.

TYING IT ALL TOGETHER

1. Your friend Samantha just learned she is pregnant. Describe how she is likely to feel during each trimester.

2. Which trimester is most likely to be the best time for Samantha, physically and emotionally?

3. As a nurse-practitioner, you want to be on the alert for signs of depression in your patients. List two *wider world* forces—mentioned in the text—that will tip you off that a woman may need special help coping with pregnancy.

4. As a clinic director, you are concerned about the fact that men are often left out of the pregnancy experience. Design a few innovative interventions to make your clinic responsive to the needs of fathers-to-be.

Answers to the Tying It All Together questions can be found in the answers section of the book.

Threats to the Developing Baby

birth defect A physical or neurological problem that occurs prenatally or at birth.

In this section, we explore the prenatal reasons for **birth defects,** or health problems at birth. In reading this "what can possibly go wrong" catalogue, keep these encouraging thoughts in mind: The vast majority of babies are born healthy. Only 4 percent have a birth defect of any kind. While some birth defects are indeed very disabling, many are treatable or very mild. Many birth defects result from a complex nature-plus-nurture interaction. Fetal genetic vulnerabilities combine with often unknown environmental hazards in the womb. However, in this section we separate the causes of these problems into two categories: toxins that flow through the placenta to impair the baby's development and genetic diseases.

Threats from Outside: Teratogens

[FAQ: What are teratogens, and what are their effects on pregnancy?]

The universal fears about the growing baby are expressed in mountains of cultural prohibitions: "Don't use scissors or your baby will have cut lips" (a cleft palate) (Afghanistan); "Avoid looking at monkeys [Indonesia] or gossiping [China] or your baby will be deformed." The rules are particularly rigid surrounding what to eat. In Sicily, iced drinks are supposed to make the fetus shiver. Some societies forbid specific foods, such as pineapples, strawberries, or potatoes with spots. Or the off-limit items might be spicy meats or even all "hot foods" (Von Raffler-Engel, 1994).

If you think these practices are strange, consider the standard mid-twentieth-century medical pregnancy advice. Physicians put women in the United States on a strict diet if they gained over 15 pounds. (The recommended weight gain now is 25 to 35 pounds.) They encouraged mothers-to-be to drink two beers each night to relax. They routinely prescribed medications to combat miscarriage or nausea, especially during the first trimester (Von Raffler-Engel, 1994; Wertz & Wertz, 1989). Today, these once "up-to-date" medical pronouncements would qualify as a form of fetal abuse! What *can* hurt the developing baby? At what times during prenatal development is damage most apt to occur?

teratogen A substance that crosses the placenta and harms the fetus.

A **teratogen** (from the Greek word *teras,* "monster," and *gen,* "creating") is the name for any substance that crosses the placenta to harm the fetus. A teratogen may be an infectious disease; a medication; a recreational drug; environmental hazards, such as radiation or pollution; or even the hormones produced by a pregnant woman who is under extreme stress. Table 2.2 describes potential teratogens in each of these categories.

TABLE 2.2: Examples of Known Teratogens and the Damage They Can Do

Teratogen	Consequences of Exposure
Infectious Diseases	
Rubella (German measles)	If a pregnant woman contracted rubella during the embryonic stage, the consequence was, not infrequently, mental retardation, blindness, or eye, ear, and heart abnormalities in the baby—depending on the week the virus entered the bloodstream. Luckily, women of childbearing age are now routinely immunized for this typically minor adult disease.
Cytomegalovirus	About 25% of babies infected with this virus develop vision or hearing loss; 10% develop neurological problems.
AIDS	HIV-infected women can transmit the virus to their babies prenatally through the placenta, during delivery (when blood is exchanged between the mother and child), or after birth (through breast milk). Rates of transmission are much lower if infected mothers take the anti-AIDS drug AZT or if newborns are given a new drug that blocks the transmission of HIV at birth. If a mother takes these precautions, does not breast-feed, and delivers her baby by c-section, the infection rate falls to less than 1%. While mother-to-child transmission of HIV has declined dramatically in the developed world, it remains a devastating problem in sub-Saharan Africa and other impoverished regions of the globe (Avert, 2005).
Herpes	This familiar sexually transmitted disease can cause miscarriage, growth retardation, and eye abnormalities in affected fetuses. Doctors recommend that pregnant women with active genital herpes undergo c-sections to avoid infecting their babies during delivery.
Toxoplasmosis	This disease, caused by a parasite found in raw meat and cat feces, can lead to blindness, deafness, and mental retardation in infants. Pregnant women should avoid handling raw meat and cat litter.
Medications	
Antibiotics	Streptomycin has been linked to hearing loss; tetracycline to stained infant tooth enamel.
Thalidomide	This drug, prescribed in 1960s Europe to prevent nausea during the first trimester, prevented the baby's arms and legs from developing if taken during the embryonic period.
Anti-seizure drugs	These medications have been linked to nasal abnormalities and learning and behavior problems in the fetus.
Antidepressants	Although typically safe, third-trimester exposure to selective serotonin reuptake inhibitors and tricyclic antidepressants has been linked to temporary jitteriness and excessive crying and to eating and sleeping difficulties in newborns. Rarely, these drugs can produce a serious syndrome involving seizures and dehydration (Keltner & Hall, 2005; Moses-Kolko and others, 2005).
Recreational Drugs	
Cocaine	This drug is linked to miscarriage, growth retardation, and learning and behavior problems.
Methamphetamines	This drug may cause miscarriage and growth retardation.
Chemicals	
Radiation	Japanese children who had been exposed to radiation from the atomic bomb during the second trimester had extremely high rates of severe mental retardation. Miscarriages were virtually universal among pregnant women living within 5 miles of the blast. Pregnant women are also advised to avoid clinical doses of radiation such as those used in X-rays (and especially cancer treatment radiation).
Lead	Babies with high levels of lead in the umbilical cord may show impairments in cognitive functioning (Bellinger and others, 1987). Maternal exposure to lead is associated with miscarriage.
Mercury and PCBs	These pollutants are linked to learning and behavior problems.
Stress	High stress levels during pregnancy have been linked to lower infant mental and motor milestone scores and to miscarriage and premature delivery. But as women experiencing severe stress are less likely to take care of their health, the direct physiological impact of stress hormones on the fetus is unclear.
Vitamin Deficiencies	Every woman of childbearing age should take folic acid supplements. This vitamin, part of the B complex, protects against the incomplete closure of the neural tube during the first month of development—an event that may produce *spina bifida* (paralysis in the body below the region of the spine that has not completely closed) or *anencephaly* (failure of the brain to develop—and certain death) if the gap occurs toward the top of the developing tube.

General sources: Huizink, Mulder, & Buitelaar, 2004; Huttenlocher, 2002.

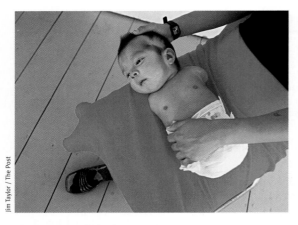

Jim Taylor / The Post

This Honduran baby is a testament to the horrible damage
teratogens can potentially cause
during the embryonic period, as
his condition was believed to be
due to his mother's exposure to
pesticides during early pregnancy.

sensitive period The time
when a certain develop-
mental process is occurring
or a body structure is most
vulnerable to damage by a
teratogen.

developmental disorders
Learning impairments and
behavioral problems during
infancy and childhood.

[**FAQ:** When is the fetus vulnerable to certain types of
teratogens, including medicines, drugs, and infectious
diseases?]

Basic Teratogenic Principles

Teratogens typically exert their damage during the **sensitive period**
for the development of a particular organ or system. For example,
the infectious disease called rubella (German measles) often damaged a baby's heart or ears, depending on the time during the first
trimester when a mother contracted the disease. The sedative
Thalidomide, prescribed in Europe during the late 1950s to prevent morning sickness, impaired limb formation, depending on
which day after fertilization the drug was imbibed. In general, with
regard to teratogens, the following principles apply:

1. **Teratogens are most likely to cause major structural damage
   during the embryonic stage.** Before implantation, teratogens
   have an all-or-nothing impact. They either inhibit implantation
   and cause death, or they leave the not-yet-attached blastocyst unscathed. It is
   during the time of organ formation (after implantation through week 8) that
   major body structures are most likely to be affected. This is why—unless
   expectant mothers have a chronic disease that demands they continue this
   practice—physicians strongly advise women not to take any medications during the first trimester (American Academy of Pediatrics [AAP], Committee on
   Drugs, 2000).

2. **Teratogens can affect the developing brain throughout pregnancy.** As you
   saw earlier, because the brain is forming well into the second and third
   trimesters, the potential for neurological damage extends for all nine months.
   Japanese fetuses exposed to that incredibly severe teratogen, radiation from the
   atomic bomb, during the second trimester were born with microcephaly (a
   small brain) and severe mental retardation (Huttenlocher, 2002). Typically,
   however, during the second and third trimesters, exposure to teratogens
   increases the risk of **developmental disorders**. This umbrella term refers to a
   host of conditions that compromise normal development—from delays in
   reaching basic milestones, such as walking or talking, to serious learning problems and hyperactivity.

3. **Teratogens operate in a dose-response fashion.** With toxic substances there is
   often a threshold level above which damage occurs. For instance, women who
   use caffeine to excess (drinking more than four cups of coffee a day) throughout pregnancy have a slightly higher risk of miscarriage; but drinking an occasional Diet Coke is perfectly fine (Fernandes and others, 1998; Gilbert-
   Barness, 2000).

4. **Teratogens exert their damage unpredictably, depending on fetal and
   maternal vulnerabilities.** Still, mothers-to-be metabolize potential toxins differently, and babies differ genetically in susceptibility. So the damaging effects
   of a particular toxin can vary. On the plus side, you may know a child in your
   local school's gifted program whose mother drank heavily during pregnancy.
   On the negative side, we do not know where the teratogenic threshold lies in
   any particular case. Therefore, during pregnancy, erring on the side of caution
   is best.

Finally, while the damaging impact of a teratogen typically shows up during infancy or childhood, it can appear decades later. An unfortunate example of this teratogenic time bomb took place in my own life. My mother was given a drug called
diethylstilbestrol (DES) while she was pregnant with me. (DES was routinely prescribed in the 1950s and 1960s to prevent miscarriage.) During my early twenties, I developed cancerous cells in my cervix—and, after surgery, had three miscarriages
before ultimately being blessed by adopting my son.

The Teratogenic Impact of Medicines and Recreational Drugs

The fact that certain medications are teratogenic can present dilemmas for women who have some chronic diseases (Gilbert & Harmon, 1998; Jain & Lacy, 2005; Kaaja, Kaaja, & Hiilesmaa, 2003; Keltner & Hall, 2005; Moses-Kolko and others, 2005; Robinson, 2005).

My daughter has epilepsy and has gone off her meds—as she knows these drugs can harm the baby. But what if my heroic child has a seizure and endangers her own and the baby's life?

As this quotation illustrates, with medications and pregnancy it can be a difficult balancing act. Sometimes there are no perfect choices.

With all recreational drugs, the choice is clear. Each substance is potentially teratogenic. So just say *no!*

Because tobacco and alcohol are woven into the fabric of daily life, let's now focus on these widely used teratogens. What really *can* happen to the baby when pregnant women smoke and drink?

SMOKING Each time she reads the information on a cigarette pack, a pregnant woman gets a reminder that she may be doing her baby harm. Still, according to various national surveys, roughly one out of every nine pregnant women in the United States continues to smoke (Martin and others, 2003). As more developing-world women than ever now have this addiction, the dangers smoking poses to the fetus are becoming a global public health concern (Islam & Gerdtham, 2006).

The main danger with smoking is giving birth to a smaller-than-normal baby—an event that, as you will see later, in extreme cases, may result in developmental disorders (Brennan and others, 2002; Kotimaa and others, 2003; Leitner and others, 2000; Thapar and others, 2003; Behrman & Butler, 2006). Nicotine constricts the mother's blood vessels, reducing the blood flow to the developing fetus and so not allowing as many nutrients to reach the child.

Given this risk, why do pregnant women smoke? The answer—as any smoker knows well—is that this addiction is hard to shake (Abrahamsson and others, 2005; Haslam & Lawrence, 2004). Surveys suggest that one in four U.S. pregnant smokers take the difficult step of quitting for the health of their baby, and almost all cut down—although even six cigarettes a day can raise the risk of giving birth to a small child (LeClere & Wilson, 1997).

ALCOHOL As you saw earlier, it used to be standard practice to encourage pregnant women to have a nightcap to relieve stress. In Italy, drinking red wine during pregnancy was supposed to produce a healthy, rosy-cheeked child! (See Von Raffler-Engel, 1994.) During the 1970s, as evidence mounted for a disorder called **fetal alcohol syndrome (FAS)**, these prescriptions were quickly revised. Whenever you hear the word *syndrome*, it is a signal that the condition has a constellation of features that are present to varying degrees. The defining qualities of fetal alcohol syndrome include a far-smaller-than-normal birth weight; an abnormally small cranium, or brain; various facial abnormalities (such as a flattened face); and, most important, developmental disorders ranging from serious mental retardation to seizures and hyperactivity (Gilbert & Harmon, 1998).

Women who binge-drink (have more than five drinks at a time) or who regularly consume several drinks throughout all nine months are at highest risk of giving birth to a baby with fetal alcohol syndrome (Jacobson & Jacobson, 1994;

Ellen B. Senisi / The Image Works

fetal alcohol syndrome (FAS) A cluster of birth defects caused by the mother's alcohol consumption during pregnancy.

This boy has some of the facial features characteristic of fetal alcohol syndrome. He also has serious learning problems.

[**FAQ:** How much alcohol is too much during pregnancy? What types of fetal brain damage can drinking cause?]

Streissguth and others, 1994). How dangerous is occasional social drinking? What about having one glass of wine a day?

Every U.S. public health organization, from the American Academy of Pediatrics to the U.S. Centers for Disease Control, recommends no drinking during pregnancy (CDC, n.d.). Interestingly, however, our European counterparts, such as the British Royal College of Obstetricians and Gynaecologists, take a much more permissive stance: "One drink per day is perfectly acceptable" (RCOG, 1999). Still, as fetal alcohol syndrome ranks as the number-one preventable birth defect in the United States—affecting roughly 1 out of every 650 newborns (MMWR, May 24, 2002)—when someone offers a pregnant woman a glass of wine, it's wise for her to just say no.

Measurement Issues

Why is there *any* controversy about the minimum safe level to smoke or drink? For answers, imagine the challenges you would face as a researcher exploring the impact of these teratogens on the developing child. You would have to ask thousands of pregnant women to estimate how often they indulged in these "unacceptable" behaviors. Could you trust these *self-reports* of, say, one beer per night or just five cigarettes a day? You would then have to track the children for decades, looking for learning and behavior problems that might appear as late as the teenage years. Then there is the reality that, because your study is correlational, any problems you found might actually be due to a variety of influences. Wouldn't women who drink during pregnancy be more apt to smoke, and to be under considerable stress? Might they not be more ambivalent about their babies and, possibly, less bonded to their children once they arrive? (See, for example, Sood and others, 2005.)

Then there is the confounding effect of shared genetics. Women who are genetically prone to engage in "acting-out" behaviors, such as smoking and drinking during pregnancy, might have children who are genetically predisposed to have their own acting-out behavior problems. Could you really isolate the difficulties you found years later to just your substance of interest—given these multiple "at-risk" forces?

When we see a pregnant woman smoking or drinking, we have all sorts of vengeful emotions: "She is doing terrible damage to her child!" With the diseases we turn to now, there is no person to blame, no question of how much of which substance was too much. The child's fate was sealed at conception. Still, the emotional issues can be even more wrenching: "Should I terminate this pregnancy?" "What will happen to my child?"

Threats from Within: Chromosomal and Genetic Disorders

When a birth defect is classified as "genetic," there are two main causes. The child might have an unusual number of chromosomes, or the problem might be caused by a specific faulty gene (or set of genes).

Chromosomal Problems

As we know, the normal human chromosomal complement is 46. However, sometimes a baby with a missing or extra chromosome is conceived. The vast majority of these fertilizations end in first-trimester miscarriages, as the mass of cells cannot differentiate much past the blastocyst stage.

Still, babies can be born with an abnormal number of sex chromosomes (such as an extra X or two, an extra Y, or a single X) and survive. In this case, although the symptoms vary, the result is often learning impairments and sometimes infertility.

Survival is also potentially possible when a child is born with an extra chromosome on a specific other pair. The most common example—happening in roughly

1 in every 2,000 births (Eurocat, 2004; Martin and others, 2003; *MMWR*, 1994)—produces a baby with Down syndrome.

Down syndrome typically occurs because a cell-division error, called non-disjunction, in the egg or sperm causes an extra chromosome or piece of that copy to adhere to chromosome pair 21. (Notice, if you turn back to Figure 2.3 on page 39, that this is the smallest matching set.) The child is born with 47 chromosomes instead of the normal human complement of 46.

This extra chromosome produces familiar physical features: a flat facial profile, an upward slant to the eyes, a stocky appearance, and an enlarged tongue. Babies born with Down syndrome are at high risk for heart defects and childhood leukemia. Here, too, there is a lifespan time-bomb impact. During midlife, many adults with Down syndrome develop Alzheimer's disease (Schupf and others, 2003). The most well-known problem with this familiar disorder, however, is mild to moderate mental retardation.

A century ago, Down syndrome children rarely lived to adulthood. They were shunted to institutions to live out their severely shortened lives. Today, due to modern medical advances, infants with this condition in the United States now have an average life expectancy of 58 (Bellenir, 2004; Wynbrandt & Ludman, 2000). Ironically, this dramatic longevity gain can be a double-edged sword. Elderly parent caregivers may worry what will happen to their middle-aged child when they die or become physically impaired (Gath, 1993).

This is not to say that every baby with Down syndrome is destined to be dependent on a caregiver's help. These children can sometimes learn to read and write (Turner & Alborz, 2003). They can live independently, hold down jobs, marry, and have children. They can construct richly fulfilling lives (Bellenir, 2004; Wynbrandt & Ludman, 2000). Do you know an adult with Down syndrome—such as my cousin Norma—who is the light of her loving extended family's life?

Although women of any age can give birth to babies with this condition (my aunt was in her early twenties when she gave birth to Norma), the risk rises exponentially among older mothers. Over age 40, the chance of having a Down syndrome birth is 1 in 100; over age 45, it is 1 in 25 (Bellenir, 2004). The reason is that, with more time "in storage," older ova are more apt to develop chromosomal faults.

Down syndrome is typically caused by a random event. A spontaneous genetic mistake has occurred in one ovum or, more rarely (in an estimated 5 percent of cases), in one sperm (Massimini, 2000). Now let's look at a different category of genetic disorder—those passed down in the parents' DNA to potentially affect *every* child.

Down syndrome The most common chromosomal abnormality, causing mental retardation, susceptibility to heart disease, and other health problems; and distinctive physical characteristics, such as slanted eyes and stocky build.

The birth of a Down syndrome child has a life-changing effect on every family member. Will this big sister become a more caring, sensitive adult through having grown up with this younger sibling?

Genetic Disorders

Most illnesses—from cancer to heart disease to schizophrenia—are caused by complex nature-plus-nurture interactions. They result from several, often unknown genes acting in conjunction with often unknown environmental forces (Plomin and others, 2003a). The conditions we turn to now are different: These illnesses are caused by a *single*, known gene.

Single-gene disorders are passed down according to three modes of inheritance: They may be *dominant*, *recessive*, or *sex-linked*. To understand these patterns, you might want to look back at the paired arrangement of the chromosomes in Figure 2.3 (page 39) and remember that we get one copy of each gene from our mother and one from our father. Also, in understanding these illnesses, it is important to know that one member of each gene pair can be dominant. This means that the quality will always show up in real life. If both members of the gene pair are not

single-gene disorder An illness caused by a single gene.

dominant (that is, if they are recessive), the illness will manifest itself only if the child inherits two of the faulty genes.

Dominant disorders are in the first category. A person who inherits one copy of the faulty gene always gets the disease. In this case, if one parent harbors the problem gene (and so has the illness), each child the couple gives birth to has a fifty-fifty chance of also getting ill.

Recessive disorders are in the second category. Unless a person gets two copies of the gene, one from the father and one from the mother, that child is disease free. In this case, the odds of a baby born to two carriers—that is, parents who each have one copy of that gene—having the illness are 1 in 4.

The mode of transmission for **sex-linked single-gene disorders** is more compli-cated. Most often, the woman is carrying a recessive (non-expressed in real life) gene for the illness on *one* of her two X chromosomes. Since her daughters have another X from their father (who doesn't carry the illness), the female side of the family is typ-ically disease free. Her sons, however—having just one X chromosome and a Y chro-mosome that is "silent"—have a fifty-fifty chance of getting ill, depending on whether they get the normal or abnormal version of their mother's X.

Because their silent Y leaves them vulnerable, sex-linked disorders typically affect males. But as an intellectual exercise, you might now want to figure out under what rare conditions females can get this type of disease. If you guessed that it's when the mother is a carrier (having one faulty X) and the dad has the disorder (having the gene on his single X), you are right!

Table 2.3 visually decodes these different modes of inheritance and describes a few of the best-known single-gene diseases. In scanning the first illness on the chart, Huntington's disease, imagine your emotional burden as a genetically at-risk child. People with Huntington's develop an incurable dementia in the prime of life. As a child you would probably have watched a beloved parent slowly lose his memory and bodily functions, and then slowly die. You would know that your odds of suffering the same fate are 1 in 2. (Although babies born with lethal dominant genetic disorders typ-ically die before they can have children, Huntington's disease has remained in the population because it, too, operates as an internal time bomb, showing up during the prime reproductive years.)

With the other illnesses in the table—programmed by recessive genes—the fears relate to bearing a child. If both you and your partner have the Tay-Sachs carrier gene, you may have suffered the trauma of seeing a child die in infancy. With cystic fibro-sis, your affected child would be subject to recurrent medical crises as his lungs filled up with fluid and would face a dramatically shortened life. Would you want to take the 1-in-4 chance of having this experience again?

The good news, as the table shows, is that the prognoses for some very serious single-gene disorders are no longer as dire. With hemophilia, the life-threatening episodes of uncontrolled bleeding can be avoided by supplying the missing blood fac-tor through transfusions (Bellenir, 2004). While cystic fibrosis used to be a childhood death sentence, babies born with this disorder can now expect to live to early adult-hood (CysticFibrosis.com, n.d.). Still, with Tay-Sachs or Huntington's disease, there is *nothing* medically that can be done.

In sum, the answer to the question "Can single-gene disorders be treated and cured?" is "It depends." Although people still have the faulty gene—and so are not "cured" in the traditional sense—through advances in nurture (or changing the envi-ronment), we have made remarkable progress in treating what used to be uniformly fatal diseases.

Our most dramatic progress, however, lies in advances in **genetic testing.** Through a simple blood test, people can now find out whether they carry the gene for these (and other) illnesses.

These diagnostic breakthroughs, however, bring up difficult issues (Plomin and others, 2003a). Would you want to know whether you have the gene for Huntington's

---

dominant disorder An illness that a child gets by inherit-ing one copy of the abnor-mal gene that causes the disorder.

recessive disorder An illness that a child gets by inherit-ing two copies of the abnor-mal gene that causes the disorder.

sex-linked single-gene dis-order An illness, carried on the mother's X chromo-some, that typically leaves the female offspring unaf-fected but has a fifty-fifty chance of striking each male child.

[FAQ: How can I reduce possible negative genetic effects on my children?]

genetic testing A blood test to determine whether a person carries the gene for a given genetic disorder.

TABLE 2.3: Some Examples of Dominant, Recessive, and Sex-Linked Single-Gene Disorders

Dominant Disorders

- **Huntington's disease (HD)** This fatal nervous system disorder is characterized by uncontrollable jerky movements and irreversible intellectual impairment (dementia). Symptoms usually appear around age 35, although the illness can occasionally erupt in childhood and in old age. There is no treatment for this disease.

Recessive Disorders

- **Cystic fibrosis (CF)** This most common single-gene disorder in the United States is typically identified at birth by the salty character of the sweat. The child's body produces mucus that clogs the lungs and pancreas, interfering with breathing and digestion and causing repeated medical crises. As the hairlike cells in the lungs are destroyed, these vital organs degenerate and eventually cause premature death. Advances in treatment have extended the average life expectancy for people with CF to the early thirties. One in 28 U.S. Caucasians is a carrier for this disease.*

- **Sickle cell anemia** This blood disorder takes its name from the characteristic sickle shape of the red blood cells. The blood cells collapse and clump together, causing oxygen deprivation and organ damage. The symptoms of sickle cell anemia are fatigue, pain, growth retardation, ulcers, stroke, and, ultimately, a shortened life. Treatments include transfusions and medications for infection and pain. One in 10 African Americans is a carrier of this disease.*

- **Tay-Sachs disease** In this universally fatal infant nervous system disorder, the child appears healthy at birth, but then fatty material accumulates in the neurons and, at 6 months, symptoms such as blindness, mental retardation, and paralysis occur and the baby dies. Tay-Sachs is found primarily among Jewish people of Eastern European ancestry. An estimated 1 in 25 U.S. Jews is a carrier.†

Sex-Linked Disorders

- **Hemophilia** These blood-clotting disorders typically affect males. The most serious forms of hemophilia (A and B) produce severe episodes of uncontrolled joint bleeding and pain. In the past, these episodes often resulted in death during childhood. Today, with transfusions of the missing clotting factors, affected children can have a fairly normal life expectancy.

*Sickle cell anemia may have remained in the population because having the trait (one copy of the gene) conferred an evolutionary advantage: It protected against malaria in Africa. Scientists also speculate that the cystic fibrosis trait may have conferred immunity to typhoid fever.

†Due to a vigorous public awareness program in the Jewish community, potential carriers are routinely screened and the rate of Tay-Sachs disease has declined dramatically.

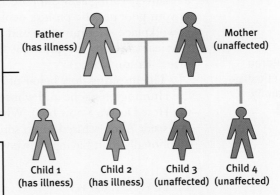

Here the gene is dominant, and there is a 1-in-2 chance that each child of an affected parent will have the disease.

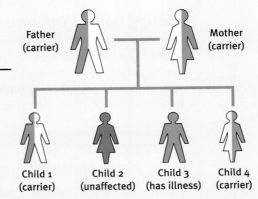

Here both parents are carriers, and each child has a 1-in-4 chance of having the disease.

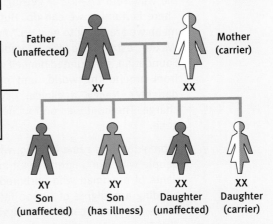

Here the mother has the faulty gene on her X chromosome, so the daughters are typically disease-free, but each son has a 1-in-2 chance of getting ill.

or possess a genetic marker that puts you at high risk of getting Alzheimer's disease at a relatively young age? Suppose an employer got hold of your test results and, in view of your poor genetic profile, denied you a job? Because of the potential for this kind of workplace discrimination and because people have a right *not* to know their future physical fate, some people argue that Congress should ban genetic testing in the workplace (Krumm, 2002).

The inspiring story below of Nancy Wexler, the psychologist who helped discover the Huntington's gene and whose mother died of the disease, is instructive here (see the How Do We Know box). While Nancy will not say whether she has been tested, her sister Alice refused to be screened because she felt being uncertain was better emotionally than having to live with a positive result.

[FAQ: Will my children inherit . . . (a genetic disease that other family members have)?]

Interventions

The pluses of genetic testing are clearer when the issue relates to having a child. Let's imagine you and your spouse have been tested and know you are carriers of the gene for cystic fibrosis or another serious genetic disorder. If you are contemplating having children, what should you do?

Sorting Out the Options: Genetic Counseling

genetic counselor A professional who counsels parents-to-be about their own or their children's risk of developing genetic disorders, as well as about available treatments.

Your first step would be to consult a **genetic counselor,** a professional skilled in both genetics and counseling, to help you think through your choices. Genetic counselors are experts in risk assessment. In addition to laying out the odds, they describe advances in treatment. For example, they would inform couples who are carriers for cystic fibrosis about life-prolonging strategies on the horizon, such as gene therapy. They

---

✕ HOW DO WE KNOW . . .

about the gene for Huntington's disease?

Nancy Wexler and her sister got the devastating news from their physician father, Milton, more than 30 years ago: "Your mother has a fatal illness. She will die of dementia in a horrible way. Your chance of getting it is fifty-fifty. There is nothing we can do. But that doesn't mean we are going to give up." In 1969, Milton Wexler established the Hereditary Disease Foundation, surrounded himself with scientists from around the world, and put his young daughter, Nancy, a clinical psychologist, in charge. The hunt was on for the Huntington's gene.

Courtesy of Nancy Wexler, http://www.hdfoundation.org/

A breakthrough came in 1979, when Nancy learned that the world's largest group of people with Huntington's lived in a small, inbred community in Venezuela—descendants of a woman who harbored the gene mutation that caused the disease. After building a pedigree of 18,000 family members, collecting blood samples from thousands more, and carefully analyzing the DNA for differences, the researchers hit pay dirt. They isolated the Huntington's gene.

Having this diagnostic marker is the first step to eventually finding a cure. So far the cure is elusive, but the hunt continues. Nancy still serves as the head of the foundation, vigorously agitating for research on the illness that killed her mother. She works full time as a professor in Columbia University's Neurology and Psychiatry Department. But every year, she comes back to the village in Venezuela to counsel and just visit with her families—her relatives in blood.

would also highlight the interpersonal and economic costs of having a child with this disease. But they are trained never to offer specific advice. Their goal is to permit couples to make a *mutual decision* on their own (Bodenhorn & Lawson, 2003).

Now suppose that, armed with this information, you and your partner go ahead and conceive. Let's briefly scan the major tests that are available to every woman carrying a child.

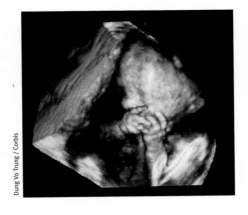

In this ultrasound photo, you can clearly see the baby's head, arms, hands, and fingers. Now imagine the emotional impact on parents upon seeing this image when they go for this standard test.

Dung Vo Trung / Corbis

Tools of Discovery: Prenatal Tests

Blood tests performed during the first trimester are now able to show (with reasonable accuracy) various chromosomal conditions, such as Down syndrome (ACOG Practice Bulletin, 2001). Perhaps the best-known test for assessing the fetus was highlighted in our introductory vignette: the **ultrasound.**

Ultrasounds, which provide an image of the baby in the womb, are used to date the pregnancy and assess the fetus's growth, in addition to revealing various structural abnormalities and confirming the results of blood tests suggesting that the child might have a particular disorder such as Down syndrome (Wapner and others, 2003).

As you saw in the vignette, this famous test has an interesting side benefit. By making the baby visually real, the ultrasound visits have become emotional landmarks on the pregnancy journey itself (Righetti and others, 2005). Have you ever had a friend proudly display a precious photograph of her baby's ultrasound? If you are a parent, perhaps you have shown your own child this priceless image of what he looked like before entering the world.

Because these tests are noninvasive, advances in ultrasound technology and maternal blood testing will probably be the wave of the future in testing for fetal problems (Benn and others, 2004). The two procedures we turn to now, while usually safe, are a bit more risky, as they require actually entering the womb.

During the first trimester, **chorionic villus sampling (CVS)** can diagnose a variety of chromosomal and genetic diseases. A physician inserts a catheter into the woman's abdomen or vagina and withdraws a piece of the developing placenta for analysis. As this test carries a 5 percent risk of miscarriage, and a chance of limb impairments, CVS is recommended only for couples at high risk of carrying a child with a particular disease.

During the second trimester, a safer test, called **amniocentesis,** can be used to determine the fetus's genetic fate. Aided by an ultrasound, the doctor inserts a syringe into the woman's uterus and extracts a sample of amniotic fluid. The cells can reveal a host of genetic and chromosomal conditions, as well as the sex of the fetus.

Amniocentesis is carefully timed for a gestational age (typically week 14) when there is enough fluid to safely siphon out and ample time to decide whether or not to carry the baby to term. However, it, too, carries a small chance of infection and miscarriage, depending on the skill of the doctor performing the test (March of Dimes Birth Defects Foundation, 2005). Moreover, as culturing the cells for analysis takes several weeks, by the time the results of the "amnio" arrive, quickening may have occurred. The woman must endure the trauma of a full labor should she decide to terminate the pregnancy at this late stage.

The summary timeline on pages 58–59 illustrates these tools of discovery, the threat zones for problems, and the landmarks of pregnancy from both the maternal and fetal points of view. Now that we have a good understanding of what normally occurs and what can go wrong, let's pause to look at what happens when the pregnancy journey is unfulfilled.

ultrasound In pregnancy, an image of the fetus in the womb that helps to date the pregnancy, assess the fetus's growth, and identify abnormalities.

chorionic villus sampling (CVS) A relatively risky first-trimester pregnancy test for fetal genetic disorders.

amniocentesis A second-trimester procedure that involves inserting a syringe into a woman's uterus to extract a sample of amniotic fluid, which is tested for a variety of genetic and chromosomal conditions.

Infertility

Been riding an emotional and financial roller coaster for the past five years. Had uterine surgery—Dr. took a cyst out. Had artificial insemination with my husband's sperm. Dr. gave me Clomid [a fertility drug], but I'm still not pregnant. All of my friends have babies. I know I was meant to be a mother. Why is this happening to me?

Some societies view a woman's ability to bear children as vital to the well-being of the whole community. When women are pregnant, the spirits will provide a bountiful harvest. Many cultures view bearing children as critical to the success of a marital bond. In fact, the practice of throwing rice at a just-married couple is actually a fertility rite (Kitzinger, 2000). And, as you can see in the fertility chat-line quotation above, many people view having a child as critical to their *own* well-being.

infertility The inability to conceive after a year of unprotected sex. (Includes the inability to carry a child to term.)

Infertility, defined as the inability to conceive a child after a year of unprotected intercourse, affects an estimated 1 in 6 U.S. couples (Turkington & Alper, 2001; Ulbrich, Coyle, & Llabre, 1990). Stress on a marriage is common. Jealously witnessing other couples drifting effortlessly into pregnancy causes special pain (Strauss, 2002).

Infertility can affect women (and men) of every age. However, just as with miscarriage and Down syndrome, female infertility rates tilt upward at older ages. Within the first six months of trying, roughly 3 out of 4 women in their twenties are able to conceive. At age 40, only 1 out of 5 achieves that goal (Turkington & Alper, 2001). Because of their more complicated anatomy, we tend to assume infertility is usually a "female" problem. We would be wrong. Male issues are *equally* likely to be involved when a couple cannot conceive (Turkington & Alper, 2001). And yes, just as with women, male infertility is more common at older ages.

[FAQ: What is involved in assisted reproductive technology?**]**

To attack the multiple reasons for infertility, we have a twenty-first-century medical arsenal. To demonstrate the need for multiple weapons, Figure 2.9 offers another look at the female reproductive system, showing some places on the complex chain from ovulation to implantation where problems may arise.

assisted reproductive technology (ART) Any infertility treatment in which the egg is fertilized outside the womb.

in vitro fertilization An infertility treatment in which conception occurs outside the womb; the developing cell mass is then inserted into the woman's uterus so that pregnancy can occur.

INTERVENTIONS: Assisted Reproductive Technology

Each problem on the chain has its treatment—from fertility drugs to stimulate ovulation, to hormonal supplements to foster implantation; from surgery to help clean out the uterus and the fallopian tubes, to artificial insemination (inserting the sperm into the woman's uterus through a syringe). Then some couples turn to that ultimate medical weapon: **assisted reproductive technology (ART).**

Assisted reproductive technology refers to any strategy in which the egg is fertilized outside the womb. The most widely used ART procedure is **in vitro fertilization (IVF).** After the woman has been given fertility drugs (which stimulate multiple ovulations), her

TIMELINE	Prenatal Development, Pregnancy, Prenatal Threats, Tools of Discovery		
	Germinal Stage (weeks 1 and 2)	**Embryonic stage** (weeks 3–8)	**Fetal stage** (weeks 9–38)
PRENATAL DEVELOPMENT	Zygote →blastocyst, which implants in uterus.	All major organs and structures form.	Massive growth and refinements; brain develops; live birth is possible at 22–24 weeks.
THREATS	At fertilization: chromosomal and single-gene diseases.	Teratogens can cause basic structural abnormalities.	Teratogens can impair growth, affect the brain, and so cause developmental disorders. They can also produce miscarriage or premature labor.

eggs are harvested and put in a laboratory dish, along with the partner's sperm, to be fertilized. A few days later, the fertilized eggs are inserted into the uterus. Then the couple anxiously waits to find out if the cells have implanted in the uterine wall.

In vitro fertilization, which was initially developed to bypass blocked fallopian tubes, has spawned amazing variations. The sperm may be placed directly in the woman's fallopian tube or injected into the ova. The fertilized eggs may be inserted into a "carrier womb"—a surrogate mother, who carries the couple's genetic offspring to term (Turkington & Alper, 2001). In view of these modifications, you may be wondering: Can babies conceived this way be normal? One study suggests that the risk of birth defects with in vitro conceptions is roughly double the normal rate—about 9 percent (Hansen and others, 2002). But most couples willingly accept these odds in their desperate quest to have a child.

The real problem lies in the daunting commitment of time and money. There is the day-by-day monitoring and the invasive procedures to harvest and insert the eggs. Some couples may need to relocate to a city with a major medical center that offers treatment. And despite all this effort, success is far from assured. In 2003, according to the Centers for Disease Control, the odds of a couple getting pregnant after a round of U.S. in vitro treatments was less than 1 in 3. In that same year, the average U.S. cost for just one cycle of interventions was $7,500 (CDC, 2004).

The final insult is that some of these conceptions are doomed to end in miscarriage. Inserting several fertilized eggs into a woman's uterus increases the odds that one will implant. However, if all "take," there is the possibility that none of the tiny babies will survive at birth.

What happens when *any* woman gives birth? The answer brings us to the final stop on the pregnancy pathway—labor and birth.

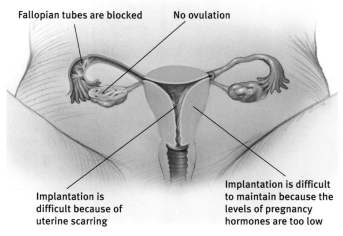

Fallopian tubes are blocked **No ovulation**

Implantation is difficult because of uterine scarring

Implantation is difficult to maintain because the levels of pregnancy hormones are too low

FIGURE 2.9: **Some possible missteps on the path to reproduction:** In this diagram you can see some problems that may cause infertility in women. You can also use it to review the ovulation-to-implantation sequence.

 TYING IT ALL TOGETHER

1. Teratogen A caused limb malformations. Teratogen B caused developmental disorders. Teratogen A wreaked its damage during the _____ stage of prenatal development and was taken during the _____ trimester of pregnancy, while teratogen B probably did its damage during the _____ stage and was taken during the _____ trimester.

	First trimester (month 1–month 3)	Second trimester (month 4–month 6)	Third trimester (month 7 –month 9)
PREGNANCY	Morning sickness, tiredness, and other unpleasant symptoms may occur; miscarriage is a worry.	Woman looks pregnant. Quickening occurs (around week 18). Mother can feel intensely bonded to baby.	Woman gets very large and anxiously waits for birth.
TOOLS OF DISCOVERY	Ultrasound Blood tests Chorionic villus sampling (CVS) around week 10	Ultrasound Amniocentesis (around week 15)	Ultrasound

2. Michelle's and Brandon's mothers contracted rubella (German measles) during different weeks in their first trimester of pregnancy. Michelle has heart problems; Brandon has hearing problems. Which teratogenic principle is illustrated here?

3. Your friend Monique is planning to become pregnant and asks you if it will be OK for her to have a glass of wine with dinner each night. What should your answer be?

   a. Go for it! Teratogens operate in a dose-response fashion, and this is definitely too low a dose to do harm.
   b. Go for it! The stress-reducing benefits of a glass of wine would outweigh any harm.
   c. Absolutely not. Even one glass of wine per night is certain to harm the fetus.
   d. Don't press your luck. One glass of wine *should* be perfectly OK, but as your fetus may be especially vulnerable, it's best to avoid alcohol completely.

4. Latasha gives birth to a child with Down syndrome, while Jennifer gives birth to a child with cystic fibrosis. Which woman should be more worried about having another child with that condition, and why?

5. To a friend who is thinking of choosing between chorionic villus sampling (CVS) and amniocentesis, mention the advantages and disadvantages of each procedure.

6. Devise a checklist to help infertile couples determine whether in vitro fertilization might be an appropriate strategy.

Answers to the Tying It All Together questions can be found in the answers section of the book.

FIGURE 2.10: **Labor and childbirth:** In the first stage of labor, the cervix dilates; then in the second stage, the baby's head emerges and the baby is born.

Dilation

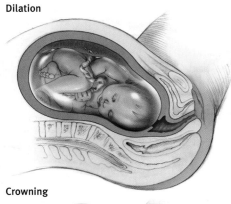

Crowning

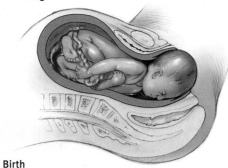

Birth

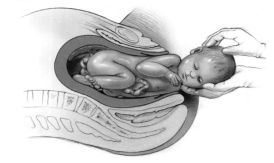

Birth

During the last weeks of pregnancy, the fetus's head drops lower into the uterus. On her weekly visits to the health-care provider, the woman may be told, "It should be any minute now." Her uterus begins to contract as it prepares for birth. Her cervix thins out and softens under the weight of the child. Anticipation builds . . . and then—she waits!

I am 39 weeks and desperate for some sign that labor is near, but so far NOTHING—no softening of the cervix, no contractions, and the baby has not dropped—the idea of two more weeks makes me want to SCREAM!!!

What sets off labor? One hypothesis is that the trigger is a hormonal signal that the fetus sends to the mother's brain. Whatever the case, a complex chain of chemical messages signals the process to begin (López Bernal, 2001). Once it's officially under way, labor proceeds through three stages.

Stage 1: Dilation and Effacement

This first stage of labor is the most arduous. The thick, protective cervix, which has held in the expanding fetus for so long, has finished its job. Now it must *efface*, or thin out, and *dilate*, or widen from a tiny gap about the size of a dime to the width of a coffee mug or a medium bowl of soup. This dramatic transformation is accomplished by *contractions*—muscular, wavelike batterings against the uterine floor. The uterus is far stronger than a boxer's biceps. Even at the beginning of labor, the contractions put about 30 pounds of pressure on the cervix to expand to its cuplike shape.

The contractions start out slowly, perhaps 20 to 30 minutes apart. They become more frequent and painful as the cervix more rapidly opens up. Sweating, nausea, and intense pain can accompany the final phase—as the closely spaced contractions reach a crescendo, and the baby is poised for the miracle of birth (see Figure 2.10).

Stage Two: Birth

The fetus descends through the uterus and enters the vagina, or birth canal. Then, as the baby's scalp appears (an event called *crowning*), parents get their first exciting glimpse of this new life. The shoulders rotate; the baby slowly slithers out, to be captured and joyously cradled as it enters the world. The prenatal journey has ended; the journey of life is about to begin.

Stage Three: The Expulsion of the Placenta

In the ecstasy of the birth, the final event is almost unnoticed. The placenta and other supporting structures must be pushed out. Fully expelling these materials is essential to avoid infection and to help the uterus return to its pre-pregnant state.

Threats at Birth

Just as with pregnancy, a variety of missteps may happen during this landmark passage into life: problems with the contraction mechanism; the inability of the cervix to fully dilate; deviations from the normal head-down position as the fetus descends and positions itself for birth (this atypical positioning, with feet, buttocks, or knees first, is called a *breech birth*); difficulties stemming from the position of the placenta or the umbilical cord as the baby makes its way into the world. Today, these in-transit troubles are often surmounted through various obstetrical techniques. This was not true in the past.

Birth Options, Past and Present

For most of human history, pregnancy was a grim nine-month march to an uncertain end (Kitzinger, 2000; Leavitt, 1986; Wertz & Wertz, 1989). The eighteenth-century New England preacher Cotton Mather captured the emotions of his era perfectly when, on learning that a woman in his parish was pregnant, he darkly thundered, "Your death has entered into you!" Not only were there the hazards involved in getting the baby to emerge from the womb, but a raging infection called childbed fever could quickly set in and kill a new mother (and her child) within days.

Women had only one another or lay midwives to rely on during this frightening time. So birth was a social event. Friends and relatives flocked around, perhaps traveling miles to offer comfort when the woman's due date drew near. Doctors were called to the scene in emergencies, but they were of little help. Because this age of modesty made it impossible to view the female anatomy directly, the training in "male midwifery" schools was all academic. In fact, due to their clumsiness (using primitive forceps to yank the baby out) and their tendency to unknowingly spread childbed fever by failing to wash their hands, eighteenth- and nineteenth-century doctors often made the situation worse (Wertz & Wertz, 1989).

Public domain. In "Richard W. Wertz and Dorothy C. Wertz, Lying-In: A History of Childbirth in America, 1977, p. 78"

This classic nineteenth-century illustration shows just why early doctors were clueless about how to help pregnant women. They could not actually view the relevant body parts!

Techniques gradually improved toward the end of the nineteenth century, but few wealthy women dared enter hospitals to deliver, as these institutions were hotbeds of contagious disease. Then, with the early-twentieth-century conquest of many infectious diseases, it became fashionable for affluent middle-class women to have a "modern" hospital birth. By the late 1930s, the science of obstetrics gained the upper hand, fetal mortality plummeted, and birth became genuinely safe for the first time (Leavitt, 1986). Today, in the developed world, this conquest is virtually complete. In 1997, there were only 329 pregnancy-related maternal deaths in the United States (Miniño and others, 2002).

Today, women have a variety of birth choices in the developed world. The woman in the top photo is having a traditional hospital delivery. The woman in the bottom photo is having a water birth.

natural childbirth A general term for labor and birth without medical interventions.

cesarean section (c-section) A method of delivering a baby surgically by extracting the baby through incisions in the woman's abdominal wall and in the uterus.

This watershed medical victory was accompanied by discontent. The natural process of birth had become an impersonal event. Women began to protest the assembly-line hospital procedures; for example, the fact that they were strapped down and sedated in order to give birth. They eagerly devoured books describing the new Lamaze technique, which taught controlled breathing, allowed partner involvement, and promised undrugged birth without pain. During the women's movement of the 1960s and early 1970s, the natural-childbirth movement fully arrived (Wertz & Wertz, 1989).

Natural Childbirth

Natural childbirth, a vague label for returning the birth experience to its "true" natural state, is now firmly embedded in the array of labor and birth choices available to women today. To avoid the medical atmosphere of a traditional maternity ward, some women choose to deliver in homelike birthing centers. They may use certified midwives rather than doctors in their quest for a less medical birth. They may avoid the routine epidural in order to ease their pain, and draw on the help of a *doula*, a nonmedical pregnancy and labor coach. At the most daring end of the spectrum, some women choose to give birth in their own homes. (Table 2.4 describes some natural- birth options, as well as some commonly used medical procedures.)

While women in North America have been more reluctant to shed the traditional medical procedures, European women have enthusiastically embraced all aspects of natural birth. In Britain, more than 2 out of every 3 babies are delivered by a midwife. In the United States, the number is less than 1 in 10 (Martin and others, 2003). In Holland, almost 1 in 3 women give birth at home. In the United States—because many people see this alternative as unacceptably dangerous—less than one percent choose home birth (Wiegers and others, 1996).

At the medical end of the spectrum, as Table 2.4 shows, lies the arsenal of physician interventions designed to promote a less painful and safer birth. Let's now pause for a minute to look at the last procedure listed in the table: the cesarean section.

The Cesarean Section

A **cesarean section** (or **c-section**), in which a surgeon makes incisions in the woman's abdominal wall and in the uterus to remove the baby, is often the final solution for problems that occur during labor and delivery. This operation exploded in popularity during the 1970s, rising from 5 to 16 percent of all U.S. births (Wertz & Wertz, 1989). Since then, the rate has continued to steadily escalate. C-sections accounted for roughly 29 percent of U.S. deliveries in 2004 (Martin and others, 2005).

Controversy about c-sections both within the medical community and outside is intense (www.acog.org, retrieved September 15, 2005). Is this common operation being overused? Critics cite the differences in c-section rates from physician to physician and argue that women are sometimes given this procedure when labor is not progressing according to an arbitrary, doctor-determined schedule (Kitzinger, 2000; Strong, 2000). Natural-childbirth advocates argue that physicians sometimes take this path both because of their fears of legal liability and, possibly, even their desire for higher reimbursement rates (Kitzinger, 2000). While typically very safe, c-sections are more costly because they are operations that require a hospital stay.

In the United States, most women do not choose to have a c-section unless problems prevent a normal vaginal delivery. This is not the case in other areas of the globe. In Brazil, more than 1 in 3 babies is delivered by c-section. In private hospitals catering to affluent women, the rate is almost 9 in 10 (Behague, Victora, & Barros, 2002). Upper-class Brazilian women prefer this type of birth because they see it as safer and more painless—and middle-class women save up for their c-section in advance (Behague, Victora, & Barros, 2002). As one woman commented, "All you have to do is to say you want a cesarean, that you don't want to suffer. Pay, and it's done" (quoted in Behague, Victora, & Barros, 2002, p. 3).

TABLE 2.4: The Major Players and Interventions in Labor and Birth

Natural-Birth Providers and Options

Certified midwife: Certified by the American College of Nurse Midwives, this health-care professional is trained to handle *low-risk* deliveries, with obstetrical backup should complications arise.

- *Plus:* Offers a birth experience with fewer medical interventions and more humanistic care.
- *Minus:* If the delivery suddenly becomes high risk, an obstetrician may be needed on the scene.

Doula: Mirroring the "old style" female experience, this person provides loving emotional and physical support during labor, offering massage and help in breathing and relaxation, but not performing actual health-care tasks, such as vaginal exams. (Doulas have no medical training.)

- *Plus:* Provides caring support from an advocate.
- *Minus:* Drives up the birth expense.

Lamaze method: Developed by the French physician Ferdinand Lamaze, this popular method prepares women for childbirth by teaching pain management through relaxation and breathing exercises.

- *Plus:* Offers a shared experience with a partner (who acts as the coach) and the sense of approaching the birth experience with greater control.
- *Minus:* Doesn't necessarily work for pain control "as advertised"!

Bradley method: Developed by Robert Bradley in the 1940s, this technique is designed for women interested in having a completely natural, nonmedicated birth. It stresses good diet and exercise, partner coaching, and deep relaxation.

- *Plus:* Tailored for women firmly committed to forgoing any medical interventions.
- *Minus:* May set women up for disappointment if things don't go as planned and they need those interventions.

Medical Interventions

Episiotomy: The cutting of the perineum or vagina to widen that opening and allow the fetus to emerge (not recommended unless there is a problem delivery).*

- *Plus:* May prevent a fistula, a vaginal tear into the rectal opening, which produces chronic incontinence and pain.
- *Minus:* May increase the risk of infection after delivery and hinder healing.

Epidural: This most popular type of anesthesia used during labor involves injecting a painkilling medication into a small space outside the spinal cord to numb the woman's body below the waist. Epidurals are now used during the active stage of labor—effectively dulling much of the pain—and during c-sections, so that the woman is awake to see her child during the first moments after birth.

- *Plus:* Combines optimum pain control with awareness; because the dose can be varied, the woman can see everything, and she has enough feeling to push during vaginal deliveries.
- *Minus:* Can slow the progress of labor in vaginal deliveries, can result in headaches, and is subject to errors if the needle is improperly inserted. Concerns also center on the fact that the newborn may emerge "groggy."

Electronic fetal monitor: This device is used to monitor the fetus's heart rate and alert the doctor to distress. With an external monitor, the woman wears two belts around her abdomen. With an internal monitor, an electrode is inserted through the cervix to record the heart rate through the fetal scalp.

- *Plus:* Shown to be useful in high-risk pregnancies.
- *Minus:* Can give false readings, leading to a premature c-section. Also, its superiority over the lower-tech method of listening to the baby's heartbeat with a stethoscope has not been demonstrated.

C-section: The doctor makes an incision in the abdominal wall and the uterus and removes the fetus manually.

- *Plus:* Is life-saving to the mother and baby when a vaginal delivery cannot occur (as when the baby is too big to emerge or the placenta is obstructing the cervix). Also is needed when the mother has certain health problems or when the fetus is in serious distress.
- *Minus:* As a surgical procedure, it is more expensive than vaginal delivery and can have complications.

*Late-twentieth-century research has suggested that the once-common U.S. practice of routinely performing episiotomies had no advantages and actually hindered recovery from birth. Therefore, the episiotomy rate in the United States declined from 2 out of 3 women in the mid-1980s to 1 in 3 by the turn of the century (Goldberg and others, 2002).

In China, where government policy limits each couple to one child, prospective parents frantic to have a perfect baby also often request this procedure. Today, an amazing 1 out of every 2 (47 percent) Chinese babies arrives in the world by the c-section route (Mazurkewich, 2004).

So, in the United States, we actually straddle a middle ground with regard to medical technologies and birth. We are especially leery about the most completely natural option, home birth, but are often unwilling to have the ultimate medical procedure, a c-section, unless it is required. Here is a testimonial that highlights the negative emotions that can accompany the need for a c-section and the types of labor problems that can make this procedure necessary:

> It all started on Sunday, April twenty-first. I arrived with my doula and was feeling contractions. Twelve hours later, my cervix had only dilated 1/2 centimeter, and I was given a Pitocin drip [a labor-stimulating drug]. Terrible, terrible contractions. But I only dilated to 4 centimeters by the next morning—and the doctor said that if things didn't change by 3 P.M. I needed a c-section. I freaked, as for months I had been planning a vaginal birth. Then the moment of my section, I saw the most beautiful sight in the world emerge—and forgot everything else.

As a final comment, the vast majority of mothers do not have the luxury of making *any* choice. Their fear remains more basic—surviving their child's birth. Complications from pregnancy and childbirth are a leading cause of death for women in the developing world. The reason is poor access to health care and poor health—that is, women suffering from infectious diseases like malaria, anemia, and HIV (Islam & Gerdtham, 2006). So yes, we should rejoice in our landmark twentieth-century strides toward conquering maternal mortality and our rich menu of possible birth choices—but let's also understand that the conquest over death during pregnancy and delivery still has very far to go.

TYING IT ALL TOGETHER

1. Melissa says that her contractions are coming every 10 minutes now. Margo has just seen her baby's scalp emerge. In which stages of labor are Melissa and Margo?

2. "Maternal mortality is very low, and a relatively high fraction of women give birth at home." "Maternal mortality is high, and most women give birth at home." "Many women get c-sections on demand." Link the eras and countries to each statement.

   a. Nineteenth-century United States
   b. Twenty-first-century Holland
   c. Twenty-first-century Brazil

3. Lo Sue is a great advocate of c-sections; Sara is vehement about the overuse of this operation. First make Lo Sue's pro-cesarean case and then make Sara's anti-cesarean case.

Answers to the Tying It All Together questions can be found in the answers section of the book.

This baby has an excellent Apgar score. Notice his healthy, robust appearance.

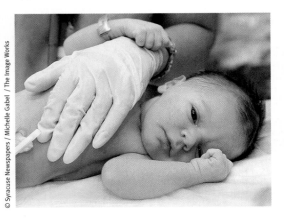

© Syracuse Newspapers / Michelle Gabel / The Image Works

The Newborn

Now that we have examined the process by which the baby arrives, we turn our attention to that tiny arrival. What happens after the baby is born? What are the main dangers that babies face after birth?

Tools of Discovery: Testing Newborns

The first step after the newborn enters the world is to evaluate its health in the delivery room with a checklist called the **Apgar scale.** The child's heart rate, muscle tone, respiration, reflex response, and color are rated on a scale of 0 to 2 at one minute and then again at five minutes after birth. Newborns with five-minute Apgar scores over 7 are usually in excellent shape. However, if the score stays below 7, the child must be monitored or resuscitated and kept in the hospital for awhile. Then health-care personnel take a drop of blood from the baby's heel to test for certain genetic disorders, such as the metabolic defect called *PKU*, that require early intervention to stave off death (Beasley, 1997; U.S. GAO, March 2003).

Threats to Development Just After Birth

After their babies have been checked out medically, most mothers and fathers are eagerly poised to leave the hospital and take their robust, full-term baby home. But other parents must hover at the hospital and anxiously wait. The reason, most often, is that their child has arrived in the world too small and/or too soon.

Born Too Small and Too Soon

In 2004, one out of every eight U.S. babies were *preterm*, or premature—they arrived in the world more than three weeks early. In 2004, about one in every eleven U.S. babies were categorized as having **low birth weight.** They entered the world weighing less than 5 1/2 pounds (Martin and others, 2005). Babies can be designated low birth weight because they either arrived before their due date or did not grow sufficiently in the womb. Earlier in this chapter we highlighted poor health practices, such as maternal smoking, as risk factors for low birth weight. But often, uncontrollable influences—such as an infection that prematurely ruptures the amniotic sac, or a cervix that cannot withstand the pressure of the growing baby's weight—cause this too-early or excessively small arrival into life.

Most low-birth-weight babies are fine. The truly vulnerable newborns are the 1.4 percent classified as **very low birth weight,** babies weighing less than 3 1/4 pounds (Martin and others, 2005). When these frail babies are delivered, often *very* prematurely, they are immediately rushed to a major medical center to enter a special hospital unit for frail newborns—the **neonatal intensive care unit.**

> At 24 weeks my water broke, and I was put in the hospital and given drugs to stop the labor. I hung on, and then, at week 26, gave birth. Peter was sent by ambulance to Children's Hospital. When I first saw my son, he had needles in every point of his body and was wrapped in plastic to keep his skin from drying out. Peter's intestines had a hole in them, and the doctor had to perform an emergency operation. But Peter made it! A week later another surgery was needed to close a valve in Peter's heart. Now it's four months later, and my husband and I are about to bring our miracle baby home.

Is this survival story purchased at the price of a life of pain? Developmental disabilities and enduring health problems are a serious risk with newborns such as Peter, born far too soon and excessively small (Samson & de Groot, 2001). The intellectual abilities of these babies often lag behind those of their peers well into the older childhood years (Anderson and others, 2003). And what about the costs? Astronomical sums are required to keep critically ill babies such as Peter alive—expenses that can bankrupt families and are often borne by society as a whole (Caplan, Blank, & Merrick, 1992).

However, there is no question that with babies such as Peter, we must vigorously intervene. It is difficult to make predictions about how these tiniest babies will fare (Caplan, Blank, & Merrick, 1992). Developmental lags during infancy are virtually guaranteed. But many very-low-birth-weight babies outgrow their early problems with special care (Dezoete, MacArthur, & Tuck, 2003; Lawrence & Blair, 2003; Ment and others, 2003). Even with enduring disabilities, some of these miracle babies can have a full life. Sitting before me in her wheelchair every day this semester as I teach this course is Marcia, whose 15-ounce body at birth would have easily fit in the palm of your hand—and whom no doctor believed was capable of surviving. My student, as the Experiencing the Lifespan box describes, is partially deaf, is blind in one eye, and suffers from the disorder cerebral palsy. But rarely have I met someone so upbeat, joyous, and fully engaged in life.

Apgar scale A quick test used to assess a just-delivered baby's condition by measuring heart rate, muscle tone, respiration, reflex response, and color.

low birth weight (LBW) A body weight at birth of less than 5 1/2 pounds.

very low birth weight (VLBW) A body weight at birth of less than 3 1/4 pounds.

neonatal intensive care unit (NICU) A special hospital unit that treats at-risk newborns, such as low-birth-weight and very-low-birth-weight babies.

In this neonatal intensive care unit, health-care personnel use the latest technology to help very small babies survive the perilous first months of life.

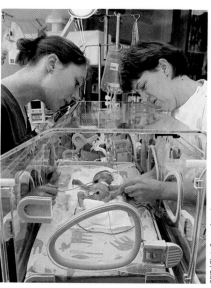

BSIP / Photo Researchers, Inc.

The service elevator at Peck Hall takes forever to get there, then moves in extra-slow motion up to the third floor. If, as sometimes happens, it's out of service, you are out of luck. It's about a 30-minute drive from my dorm in the motorized wheelchair, including the ramps. When it rains, there's the muck—slowing you up—keeping you wet. So I try to leave at least an hour to get to class.

My goal is to be at least five minutes early so I don't disrupt everything as I move the chair, back and forth, back and forth, to be positioned right in front. Because my bad eye wanders to the side, you may not think I can read the board. That's no problem, although it takes me weeks to get through a chapter in your book! The CP [cerebral palsy], as you know, affects my vocal cords, making it hard to get a sentence out. But I won't be ashamed. I am determined to participate in class. I have my note-taker. I have my hearing amplifier turned up to catch every sound. My mind is on full alert. I'm set to go.

I usually can take about two courses each semester—sometimes one. I'm careful to screen my teachers to make sure they will work with me. I'm almost 30 and still only a junior, but I'm determined to get my degree. I'd like to be a counselor and work with CP kids. I know all about it—the troubles, the physical pain, what people are like. I've got tons of experience starting from day one.

I'm not sure exactly what week I was born, but it wasn't really all that early; maybe two months at the most. My problem was being incredibly small. They think my mom might have gotten an infection that made me born less than one pound. The doctors were sure I'd never make it. They told Mom and Dad to prepare for the fact that I would die. But I proved everyone wrong. Once I got out of the ICU and, at about eight months, went into convulsions, and then had a stroke, everyone thought that would be the end again. They were wrong. I want to keep proving them wrong as long as I live.

I've had tons of physical therapy, and a few surgeries; so I can get up from a chair and walk around a room. But it took me until about age five to begin to speak or take my first step. The worst time of my life was elementary school—the kids who make fun of you; call you a freak. The parents were the meanest. When someone did invite me to their house, the answer was often, "You can't let that cripple come." In high school, and especially here at MTSU, things are much better. I've made close friends, both in the disability community and outside. Actually, I'm a well-known figure, especially since I've been here so long! Everyone on campus greets me with a smile as I scoot around.

In my future? I'd love to get married and adopt a kid. OK, I know that's going to be hard. Because of my speech problem, I know you're thinking it's going to be hard to be a counselor, too. But I'm determined to keep trying, and take every day as a blessing. Life is very special. I've always been living on borrowed time.

The Unthinkable: Infant Mortality

infant mortality Death during the first year of life.

Some babies are not as lucky as Peter or Marcia. Premature deliveries and low birth weight rank as the most common causes of **infant mortality**, the label for deaths occurring within the first year of life. In the least developed regions of the globe, where infant mortality rates are highest, infants may die soon after birth due to labor and delivery traumas. Or they may succumb to infectious diseases such as pneumonia and diarrhea (Islam & Gerdtham, 2006). In the developed world—where infant morality is generally very low (see Figure 2.11)—babies who do not make it beyond their first year tend to have other health conditions, such as serious genetic disorders like Tay-Sachs disease.

The good news is that U.S. infant mortality is at a low ebb. Out of every 1,000 births, roughly only 7 babies die before age 1. The bad news is our dismal standing compared to many other industrialized countries. Why does the United States rank a humiliating twenty-fifth (Miniño and others, 2002) in this basic marker of a society's health? The main cause lies in socioeconomic inequalities, poor health practices, and unequal access to high-quality prenatal care.

The ethnic disparities in infant mortality are particularly troubling. In 2002, for instance, African American infant mortality rates stood at 13.9 deaths per 1,000 live births—more than double the 5.8 figure for Whites (Martin and others, 2005). African American women are less likely to see a health-care provider in their first trimester (Freid and others, 2003). They may be more susceptible to health conditions such as high blood pressure or pregnancy-induced diabetes, both of which require careful monitoring and are associated with premature births. The main issue, however, relates to socioeconomic status. Low-income women of every ethnic group are at far higher risk of suffering the trauma of having their baby die before age 1.

The bottom line is that economics shapes every aspect of the pregnancy journey—from the emotions of the mother to the anxieties of the father to the health of the child. This same message, "Socioeconomic status matters," will be a continual theme as we explore the baby's journey through life.

TYING IT ALL TOGETHER

1. Baby David gets a two-minute Apgar score of 8; at five minutes, his score is 9. What does this mean?

2. Bill says, "Pregnancy and birth are very safe today." George says, "Hey, you are very wrong!" Who is right?

    a. Bill, because worldwide maternal mortality is now very low.
    b. George, because birth is still unsafe around the world.
    c. Both are partly correct: Birth is typically very safe in the developed world, but maternal and infant mortality remain unacceptably high in the poorest regions of the globe.

3. If Latisha goes into labor at 26 weeks and has a very-low-birth-weight baby, what can you predict about this child's development?

    a. Due to medical advances, the baby will have no developmental problems.
    b. The baby will probably have developmental lags and *possibly* more enduring problems.
    c. The baby will almost certainly have severe impairments throughout life.

4. Sally brags about the U.S. infant mortality rate, while Samantha is horrified by it. First make Sally's case and then Samantha's, referring to the chapter points.

5. You want to set up a program in the African American community to reduce infant mortality. List some steps that you might take.

Answers to the Tying It All Together questions can be found in the answers section of the book.

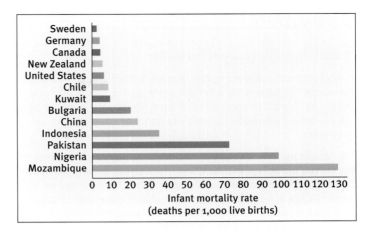

FIGURE 2.11: Infant mortality rates in selected countries, 2005 (est.): Infant mortality rates vary tremendously around the globe. Notice the incredible disparities between the most affluent and least-developed countries.

Source: Central Intelligence Agency, (2005).

Final Thoughts: Biological Parenthood and Early Bonding

Before we move on to our lifespan journey, a final comment is required. In this chapter, you learned a good deal about the bonding experience that begins before the baby emerges from the womb. During the early 1970s, as the natural-childbirth movement was gaining steam, advocates suggested that to fully bond with your baby it was important to hold that child right after birth. This premise left out not only every adoptive parent but also the millions of women whose babies needed to stay in the hospital for their first months of life.

This "up-to-date" pronouncement, as it turned out, was another example of misplaced scientific advice. Parent–child love, or attachment, does not lock in according to a rigid timetable. To bond with a baby, you don't need to personally carry that child inside (or share the same set of genes). So just a small reminder is needed for later chapters when we scan the beautiful mosaic of families on our landscape today: The bottom-line blessing is being a parent, not being pregnant. Parenting is far different from personally giving birth!

In Chapter 3, we begin by catching up with Kim and her baby girl, Elissa, who is now about 4 months old. ▮

Families come in many forms, and the love you have for an adopted child is no different than if you gave birth. Take it from me as an adoptive mom!

AP Photo / Seth Perlman

∎ SUMMARY

The First Step: Fertilization

Every culture cherishes pregnant women. Some build in rituals to announce the baby after a certain point during pregnancy, and many use charms to ward off fetal harm. Pregnancy is a time of intense mixed emotions—joyous expectations coupled with uneasy fears.

The female reproductive system includes the **uterus** and its neck, the **cervix;** the **fallopian tubes;** and the **ovaries,** housing the **ova.** To promote **fertilization** the optimum time for intercourse is when the egg is released. **Ovulation** and all of the events of pregnancy are programmed by **hormones.** At intercourse, hundreds of millions of sperm, produced in the **testes,** are ejaculated, but only a small fraction make their way to the fallopian tubes to reach the ovum. When the single victorious sperm penetrates the ovum, the two 23 **chromosome** cells (composed of **DNA,** segmented into **genes**) unite to regain the normal complement of 46 that form every body cell.

Prenatal Development

During the first stage of pregnancy, the two-week-long **germinal phase,** the rapidly dividing **zygote** travels to the uterus, becomes a **blastocyst,** and faces the next challenge—**implantation.** The second stage of pregnancy, the **embryonic stage,** begins after implantation and ends around week 8. During this intense six-week period, the **neural tube** forms and all the major body structures are constructed—according to the **proximodistal, cephalocaudal,** and **mass-to-specific** principles of development.

During the third stage of pregnancy, the **fetal stage,** development is slower paced. The hallmarks of this stage are enormous body growth and construction of the brain as the **neurons** migrate to the top of the tube and differentiate. Another defining landmark of this seven-month phase occurs around week 22, when the fetus can possibly be **viable,** that is, survive outside the womb if born.

Pregnancy

The nine months of **gestation,** or pregnancy, are divided into **trimesters.** The first trimester is often characterized by unpleasant symptoms, such as morning sickness, and a relatively high risk of **miscarriage.** The landmarks of the second trimester are looking clearly pregnant, experiencing **quickening,** and often feeling more intensely emotionally connected to the child. During the third trimester, the woman's uterus gets very large, and she anxiously awaits the birth.

The emotional experience of pregnancy varies dramatically, depending on socioeconomic status and, most important, social support. A woman needs to feel cared about by other people during this intimate life journey—to feel good about being pregnant and about her child. Fathers, the neglected pregnancy partners, also feel intensely bonded to their babies, and often find that pregnancy is a stressful time.

Threats to the Developing Baby

About 4 percent of babies are born with a **birth defect.** One cause is **teratogens,** toxins from the outside that exert their damage during the **sensitive period** for the development of a particular body part. In general, the embryonic stage is the time of greatest vulnerability, although toxins can affect the developing brain during the second and third trimesters also, producing **developmental disorders.** While there is typically a threshold level beyond which damage can occur, teratogens have unpredictable effects, depending on the vulnerabilities of the baby and mother and other forces. Damage may not show up until decades later.

Any recreational drug is potentially teratogenic. Smoking during pregnancy is a risk factor for having a smaller-than-optimal-size baby. Drinking excessively during pregnancy can produce **fetal alcohol syndrome.** Conducting studies that explore the causal impact of small amounts of alcohol (or any recreational drug) on the baby is difficult, as so many forces are correlated with engaging in these problematic health practices. However, the best advice to women is to avoid all recreational drugs when carrying a child.

The second major cause of birth defects is internal—chromosomal problems and single-gene diseases. **Down syndrome** is one of the few disorders in which babies born with an abnormal number of chromosomes survive. Although Down syndrome, caused by having an extra chromosome on pair 21, produces mental retardation and other health problems, people with this condition do live fulfilling lives.

With **single-gene disorders,** a specific gene passed down from one's parents causes the disease. In **dominant disorders,** a person who harbors a single copy of the gene gets ill, and each child born to this couple (one of whom has the disease) has a fifty-fifty chance of developing the condition. If the disorder is **recessive,** both parents carry a single copy of the "problem gene" that is not expressed in real life, but they have a 1-in-4 chance of giving birth to a child with that disease (that is, a son or daughter with two copies of the gene). With **sex-linked disorders,** the problem gene is recessive and lies on the X chromosome. If a mother carries a single copy of the gene, her daughters are spared (because they have two Xs), but each male baby has a fifty-fifty risk of getting the disease. Through advances in **genetic testing,** couples (and individuals) can find out if they harbor the genes for many diseases. Genetic testing poses difficult issues with regard to workplace discrimination, and whether people want to find out if they have incurable adult-onset diseases.

Couples at high risk for having a baby with a single-gene disorder (or any couple) may undergo **genetic counseling** to decide whether they should try to have a child. During pregnancy, blood tests, an **ultrasound,** and more invasive tests such as **chorionic villus sampling** (during the first trimester) and **amniocentesis** (during the second trimester) allow us to determine the baby's genetic fate.

Infertility is tackled by a variety of treatments, including **assisted reproductive technologies (ART),** such as **in vitro fertilization (IVF).** IVF, in which the egg is fertilized outside of the womb, is arduous and expensive and offers no guarantee that a baby will result.

Birth

Labor and birth consist of three stages. During the first stage of labor, contractions cause the cervix to efface and fully dilate. During the second stage, birth, the baby emerges. During the third stage, the placenta and supporting structures are expelled.

For most of human history, childbirth was life-threatening to both the mother and the child. During the first third of the twentieth century, birth became much safer. This victory set the stage for the later-twentieth-century **natural childbirth** movement. Today women in the developed world can choose from a variety of birth possibilities. Women in Europe tend to tilt toward more natural options. Women in Brazil and China, unlike American women, often actively choose **cesarean sections.** Most women in the developing world do not have this luxury. Their main concern is surviving their baby's birth.

The Newborn

After birth, the **Apgar scale** and other tests are used to assess the baby's health. While most babies are healthy, **low birth weight** can compromise development. Most vulnerable are **very-low-birth-weight** infants. While some of these most fragile babies have serious enduring problems, others outgrow their difficulties, although they typically need monitoring in the **neonatal intensive care unit** during their early weeks or months of life.

Infant mortality is a serious concern in the developing world. While rates of infant mortality are generally very low in developed-world countries, the United States has a comparatively dismal standing compared to other affluent countries on this basic health parameter. African American women—and low-income mothers in the United States—are at higher risk than affluent women of having a baby die before age 1. Economics looms large in the prenatal and pregnancy experience and every other experience of our developing life.

∎ KEY TERMS

uterus, p. 36
cervix, p. 37
fallopian tube, p. 37
ovary, p. 37
ovum, p. 37
fertilization, p. 37
ovulation, p. 37
hormones, p. 37
testes, p. 37
chromosome, p. 38
DNA, p. 38
gene, p. 38
germinal stage, p. 39
zygote, p. 39
blastocyst, p. 39
implantation, p. 39

placenta, p. 40
embryonic stage, p. 40
neural tube, p. 40
neuron, p. 40
proximodistal sequence, p. 41
cephalocaudal sequence, p. 41
mass-to-specific sequence, p. 41
fetal stage, p. 41
age of viability, p. 42
umbilical cord, p. 43
amniotic sac, p. 43
gestation, p. 43
trimester, p. 43
miscarriage, p. 44

quickening, p. 45
birth defect, p. 48
teratogen, p. 48
sensitive period, p. 50
developmental disorders, p. 50
fetal alcohol syndrome (FAS), p. 51
Down syndrome, p. 53
single-gene disorder, p. 53
dominant disorder, p. 54
recessive disorder, p. 54
sex-linked single-gene disorder, p. 54
genetic testing, p. 54
genetic counselor, p. 56
ultrasound, p. 57

chorionic villus sampling (CVS), p. 57
amniocentesis, p. 57
infertility, p. 58
assisted reproductive technology (ART), p. 58
in vitro fertilization (IVF), p. 58
natural childbirth, p. 62
cesarean section (c-section), p. 62
Apgar scale, p. 64
low birth weight (LBW), p. 65
very low birth weight (VLBW), p. 65
neonatal intensive care unit (NICU), p. 65
infant mortality, p. 66

∎ RECOMMENDED RESOURCES

BEAUTIFUL PHOTOGRAPHS

Kitzinger, S. (2000). *Rediscovering birth.* New York: Pocket Books.
Photographs and artworks from different cultures illustrate this book describing birth across time and in different areas of the world. The author's thesis is that birth should be a natural, spiritual experience.

Nilsson, L. (1990). *A child is born.* New York: Delacorte Press.
This classic book beautifully outlines the journey from conception to birth via photographs, a selection of which appears in this chapter.

REFERENCE WORK

Wynbrandt, J., and Ludman, M. (2000). *The encyclopedia of genetic disorders and birth defects.* New York: Facts on File Library of Health and Living.
This book offers capsule descriptions of every rare single-gene disease.

HISTORIES AND CROSS-CULTURAL WORKS

Von Raffler-Engel, W. (1994). *The perception of the unborn in cultures around the world.* Seattle: Hogrefe and Huber.

This book scans pregnancy folklore, exploring pre-pregnancy instructions and charms. Particularly interesting are the diverse cultural opinions as to when the fetus is considered alive.

Wertz, R., and Wertz, D. (1989). *Lying-in: A history of childbirth in America.* New Haven, CT: Yale University Press.
This book offers a fascinating history of birth from Colonial times to the modern era.

FIRST-PERSON POPULAR ACCOUNT

Dorris, M. (1989). *The broken cord.* New York: Harper.
This book offers the author's account of what it is like to raise a child with fetal alcohol syndrome.

WEB SITE

www.visembryo.com
This terrific Web site has photographs of the developing baby virtually every day through week 8 and at regular intervals afterward, going into detail about each aspect of development.

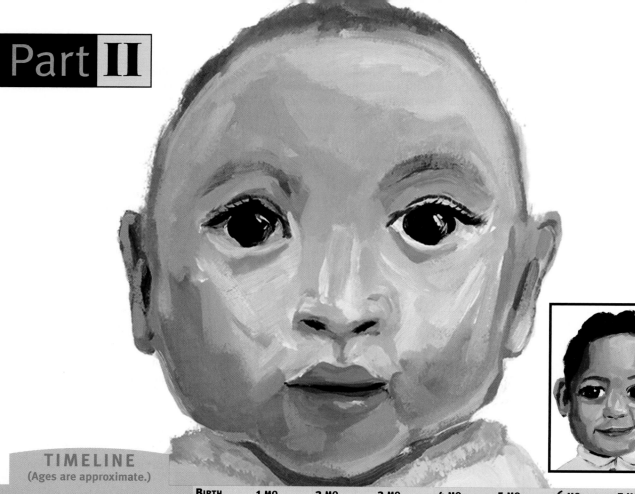

Part II

TIMELINE
(Ages are approximate.)

	BIRTH	1 MO.	2 MO.	3 MO.	4 MO.	5 MO.	6 MO.	7 MO.
PHYSICAL DEVELOPMENT								
BRAIN	Newborn reflexes			Blossoming of cortex				
EATING	Breast milk alone						Weaning	
CRYING	Reflex crying (possible colic) (Crying at life peak)			Cries in response to external stimuli				
SLEEPING	Signaling (wakes every 3 hours)						Self-soothing (puts self back to sleep at night)	
VISION	Preferential looking (at faces, mother, etc.); sizes, shape constancy						Depth perception	
MOTOR SKILLS						Turns over	Sits without support Cruises (discipline and baby-proofing begin)	
COGNITIVE DEVELOPMENT								
SENSORIMOTOR INTELLIGENCE	Primary circular reactions			Secondary circular reactions				
					Onset of object permanence			
LANGUAGE				Cooing				
SOCIOEMOTIONAL DEVELOPMENT (ATTACHMENT)								
			Social smile	Attachment in the making				

Infancy

This two-chapter unit is devoted to infancy and toddlerhood (the period from birth through age 2). How does a helpless newborn change into a walking, talking, loving child?

In Chapter 3, "Infancy: Physical and Cognitive Development," we start by examining the basic newborn states: feeding, crying, and sleeping. Then we turn to sensory and motor development: What exactly do babies see? How do newborns develop from lying helplessly to being able to walk? What can caregivers do to keep babies safe as they travel into the world? Finally, we chart evolving cognition and babies' first steps toward language, the capacity that allows us to really enter the human community.

Chapter 4, "Infancy: Socioemotional Development," looks directly at what makes us human: our relationships. First, we explore the attachment relationship between caregiver and child in depth. Then, we examine poverty and day care during the first years of life. Finally, we focus on the last phase of infancy, toddlerhood—the age from roughly 1 to 2½. Toddlers are intensely attached to their caregivers and desperate to be independent. During this watershed time of life, when we are walking and beginning to talk, we first learn the rules of the human world.

The timeline below alerts you to some milestons we will be exploring during this packed phase of life.

8 MO.	9 MO.	10 MO.	11 MO.	12 MO.	18 MO.	2 YEARS	3 YEARS
						Brain reaches ¾ adult size	
				Picky eating			
				2 naps		1 nap	Occasional naps
				Adultlike visual capacities			
	Crawls			Toddles			
				Tertiary circular reactions ("little scientist" behavior)			
					Full object permanence		
A-not-B error					Deferred imitation; onset of make-believe play		
	Means–end behavior						
Babbling				Single words	Explosion of language		Multi-word sentences
Clear-cut attachment (stranger anxiety, separation anxiety)							Working model
					Onset of self-awareness (shame)		
			Exuberant/inhibited toddler				
				Serious discipline begins			

CHAPTER 3

Infancy: Physical and Cognitive Development

In Chapter 2 we talked to Kim at the beginning of the third trimester, anxiously waiting for her child's birth. Now let's pay her a visit in the first months of new motherhood and meet Elissa, her baby girl.

She's been here for less than four months—fifteen weeks and two days, to be exact—and I feel like she's been here forever. For me, it was total love at first sight and, of course, the same for Jeff. But the real thrill is watching a wonderful new person emerge day by day. Take what's happening now. At first, she couldn't care less, but since a few days ago, it's like, "Wow, there's a world out there!" See that baby seat? Elissa can make the colored buttons flash by moving her legs. Now, when I put her in it, she bats her legs like crazy. She can't get enough of those lights and sounds. Notice the way she looks at your face—like she wants to get into your soul. She really loves this blue smiley-face cushion I bought for 25 cents at a yard sale. Every time she sees it she starts to gurgle, reach, and laugh.

Elissa doesn't cry much—nothing like other babies during the first three months. Actually, I was worried. In the hospital, I asked the doctor whether there was something wrong. Crying is vital to communicating what you need! The same is true of sleeping. I'm almost embarrassed to tell you that I have the only baby in history who has been regularly giving her mom a good night's sleep since she was 2 months old.

Breast-feeding is indescribable. It's like I am literally making her grow. Plus she's getting my total, undivided attention. I'm so glad I could take off work for the first five months. I don't see how anyone could have the luxury of this experience otherwise.

Pick her up. Feel what it's like to hold her—how she melts into you. But lately she's starting to squirm more. See those push-ups, like a rocking machine? It's almost as if she's saying, "Mom, I can't wait to turn over—can't wait to get moving into the world." I plan to be there with my video camera to document every step now that she's really traveling into life.

Elissa is poised at a milestone. Past the first three months of life, she is fully waking up to the world. In this chapter we chart the transformation from lying helplessly to moving into life and the other amazing physical and cognitive changes that occur during infancy. We begin by exploring the basic infant states: eating, crying, and sleeping. Then we scan vision and the emerging motor skills that Kim and her husband are so anxious to observe. Finally, we examine cognition and babies' pathway to mastering language, the capacity that makes our species unique.

What does this young baby see and understand about the tremendous loving object he is facing? That is the mystery we will be exploring in this chapter.

cerebral cortex The outer folded mantle of the brain, responsible for thinking, reasoning, perceiving, and all conscious responses.

axon A long nerve fiber that usually conducts impulses away from the cell body of a neuron.

dendrite A branching fiber that receives information and conducts impulses toward the cell body of a neuron.

synapse The gap between the dendrites of one neuron and the axon of another, over which impulses flow.

synaptogenesis Forming of connections between neurons at the synapses. This process, responsible for all perceptions, actions, and thoughts, is most intense during infancy and childhood but continues throughout life.

myelination Formation of a fatty layer encasing the axons of neurons. This process, which speeds the transmission of neural impulses, continues from birth to early adulthood.

FIGURE 3.1: **The neuron and synapses:** Here is an illustration of the remarkable structure that programs every developing skill, perception, and thought. Notice the dendrites receiving information at the synapses and how impulses flow down the long axon to connect up with the dendrites of the adjoining cells.

Setting the Context: Brain Blossoming and Sculpting

What causes the remarkable changes—from seeing to walking to speaking—that unfold week by week during the first two years of life? To get an answer, let's step back and scan the transformations that are taking place in our master programmer—the human brain—as we travel from birth to our adult years.

The Expanding Brain

The **cerebral cortex,** the outer, furrowed mantle of the brain, is the site of every conscious perception, action, and thought. With a surface area 10 times larger than the monkey's and 100 times larger than the rat's, our cortex is what makes human beings stand apart from any other species on earth.

Because of our immense cortex, humans are also unique in the amount of brain growth that occurs outside of the womb. After birth, our brain volume quadruples. It takes two decades for this expansion to be complete. The fastest growth occurs during infancy. In fact, the cortex only comes "on-line," or starts fully taking over our behavior, a few months *after* birth.

During the first two years of life, as the cortex expands, the brain grows from 25 percent to 75 percent of its final weight (Huttenlocher, 1994; Johnson, 1998, 2001). This expansion builds on the framework that was put in place before birth.

Recall from Chapter 2 that during the middle months of the fetal period the cells destined to compose the brain have migrated to the top of the neural tube. During the final months of pregnancy, and especially the first year of life, they differentiate into their mature form. The cells form long **axons.** They sprout **dendrites**—treelike, branching ends. As the dendrites proliferate at junctions, or **synapses,** the axons and dendrites interconnect (see Figure 3.1).

Synaptogenesis, the process of making these myriad connections, programs every human skill—from Elissa's vigorous push-ups to composing symphonies or solving problems in math. Another change that is critical for our abilities to emerge is called **myelination.** The axons form a fatty encasing layer around their core. Just as a stream of water prevents us from painfully bumping down the slide at a water park, the myelin sheath serves as the lubricant that permits the neural impulses to speedily flow.

Synaptogenesis and myelination occur at different rates in specific regions of the brain. In the visual cortex, the part of the brain responsible for interpreting visual stimuli, the axons are fully myelinated by about age 1. In the frontal lobes, the region of the brain involved in higher reasoning, the myelin sheath is still forming into our early twenties or beyond (Huttenlocher, 2002).

This makes sense. Seeing is a skill we need soon after birth. Visual abilities, as you will learn in this chapter, develop rapidly during our first year of life. But we won't really need the skills to compose symphonies, do higher math, or competently make our way in the complex world until we become full adults. So there are clear parallels between our unfolding real-world abilities and the pattern of physiological maturation manifested by our brain.

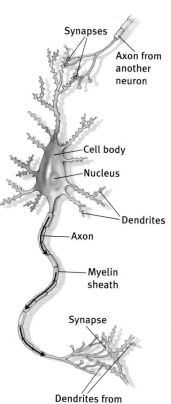

Synapses

Axon from another neuron

Cell body

Nucleus

Dendrites

Axon

Myelin sheath

Synapse

Dendrites from neighboring neurons

Neural Pruning and Brain Plasticity

So far you might imagine that the basic neural principle underlying development is that more extensive connections equal superior skills. That is incorrect. Neural loss is critical to development, too. Following an initial phase of lavishly producing synapses, each region of the cortex undergoes a period of synaptic pruning and neural death (Huttenlocher, 1994, 2002; Johnson, 1998, 2001). This shedding timetable also reflects our expanding abilities. It begins around age 1 in the visual cortex. It starts during late childhood in the frontal lobes (Huttenlocher, 2002; Johnson, 1998). In the same way that careful weeding is critical to sculpting a beautiful garden, getting rid of the unnecessary neurons and connections is essential for those we really require to flower.

Why does the brain undergo this frantic phase of overproduction, followed by gradual cutting back? Neuroscientists believe that having this early oversupply is useful, as it allows us to "recruit" surplus neurons and redirect them to perform other functions, should we have a major sensory deficit or experience a serious brain insult early in life (Amedi and others, 2003; Huttenlocher, 2002; Johnson, 1998, 2001). Actually, our cortex is surprisingly malleable, or **plastic** (able to be changed), particularly during infancy and the childhood years.

Using new brain technologies such as fMRI, which measures the brain's energy consumption, researchers find that among people blind from birth—but not those who lose their sight at older ages—metabolism in the visual cortex is intense while reading Braille (Amedi and others, 2003; Lambert and others, 2004; Melzer and others, 2001). This raises the interesting possibility that, without early stimulation from the eye, the neurons genetically programmed for vision are literally captured, or taken over, to strengthen abilities in touch.

A similar process occurs with language, which is normally represented in distinctive sites in the left hemisphere of the brain. If an infant or young child has a left-hemisphere stroke, the right hemisphere takes over, and only subtle losses in language abilities result. Compare this to the outcome during adulthood once pruning has occurred and language is located firmly in its appropriate places. When adults have a stroke in the left hemisphere, the result can be devastating—a permanent loss in comprehending language or being able to form words (Huttenlocher, 2002).

The bottom-line message is that our understanding of brain plasticity epitomizes the basic nature-combines-with-nurture principle that governs all of human life. Yes, the blueprint for the uniquely human cortex is laid out at conception in our genes. But environmental stimulation is vital in strengthening specific neurons and determining which connections will be pruned. Before the pruning phase, our brain is particularly malleable—permitting us to grow a somewhat different garden should disaster strike. Still, as synaptogenesis occurs until the very end of life, we continue to grow, to learn, to develop intellectually from age 1 to age 101.

[FAQ: How does the brain go through pruning?]

plastic Malleable, or capable of being changed (used to refer to neural or cognitive development).

This resilient baby has survived three major surgeries in which large sections of his brain had to be removed. Remarkably—because the cortex is so *plastic* at this age—he is expected to be left with few, if any, impairments.

Sandy Lora

Sandy Lora

Keeping in mind the basic brain principles—(1) development unfolds "in its own specific neurological time" (you can't teach a baby to do something before the relevant part of the brain comes on-line); (2) stimulation sculpts neurons (our wider-world experiences actually physically change our brain); and (3) mental growth is lifelong (we continue to form new synapses until well into old age)—now it's time to explore how the expanding cortex works magic during the first two years of life.

 TYING IT ALL TOGETHER

1. Christopher and Ashley are arguing about what makes the human brain unique. Christopher says it's the immense size of our cortex. Ashley says it's the fact that we "grow" most of our brain after birth and that the human cortex continues to mature for at least two decades. Who is right—Christopher, Ashley, or both students?

2. Kayla said she wouldn't bother reading this section on the developing brain because she learned that stuff in high school. She knows that the myelin sheath speeds neural impulses. She realizes that the more synaptic connections the neurons form, the higher the level of development. Is Kayla prepared for the test, and if not, where is she wrong?

3. When children with epilepsy have recurring life-threatening seizures, surgeons may remove the portion of the brain in which the seizures are taking place. Remarkably, these children go on to live relatively normal lives. The process that is responsible for this phenomenon is _____.

    a. neural pruning
    b. brain plasticity
    c. myelination

4. Draw a neuron, labeling the axon, dendrites, myelin sheath, and synapses.

Answers to the Tying It All Together questions can be found in the answers section of the book.

Basic Newborn States

Visit a newborn and you will see a set of simple activities: She eats, she cries, she sleeps. In this section we spotlight each basic state.

Eating: The Basis of Living

Eating, the basic foundation for living, undergoes amazing developmental transformations during infancy. Let's briefly scan these transformations and then discuss two environmental, or wider-world, nutritional topics that loom large in the first years of life.

Developmental Changes: From Newborn Reflexes to Two-Year-Olds' Food Cautions

Newborns seem to be eating even when they are sleeping—a fact vividly brought home to me by the loud smacking noises that rhythmically erupted from my son's bassinet. The reason is that babies are born with a powerful **sucking reflex**—they suck virtually all the time. Newborns also are born with a **rooting reflex.** If *anything* touches their cheek, they turn their head in that direction and begin to suck.

Reflexes are automatic activities. Because they are not programmed by the cortex, they are not under conscious control. It is easy to see why the sucking and rooting reflexes are vital to promoting survival the minute we leave the womb. If newborns had to learn to suck, they might die of starvation. Without the rooting reflex, babies might have considerable trouble finding the breast.

Sucking and rooting have clear functions. What about the other infant reflexes shown in Figure 3.2? Do you think the grasping reflex may have helped newborns survive during hunter-gatherer times? Can you think of why newborns, when stood on a

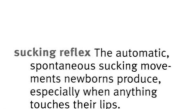

sucking reflex The automatic, spontaneous sucking movements newborns produce, especially when anything touches their lips.

rooting reflex Newborns' automatic response to a touch on the cheek, involving turning toward that location and beginning to suck.

reflex A response or action that is automatic and programmed by noncortical brain centers.

Cathy Melloan / Photo Edit, Inc.

Rooting: Whenever something touches their cheek, newborns turn their head in that direction and make sucking movements.

Simon Fraser / Photo Researchers, Inc.

Sucking: Newborns are programmed to suck, especially when something enters their mouth.

PicturePress / Getty Images

Grasping: Newborns automatically vigorously grasp anything that touches the palm of their hand.

FIGURE 3.2: **Some newborn reflexes:** If the baby's brain is developing normally, each of these reflexes is present at birth and gradually disappears after the first few months of life. In addition to the three illustrated here, other newborn reflexes include the Babinski reflex (stroke a baby's foot and her toes turn outward), the stepping reflex (place a baby's feet on a hard surface and she takes small steps), and the swimming reflex (if placed under water, newborns can hold their breath and make swimming motions).

table, take little steps (the stepping reflex)? Whatever their value, these reflexes, and other characteristic ones, must be present at birth. They must disappear as the cortex grows.

As the cortex matures, the reflexes destined to disappear are often replaced by voluntary processes. Now that she is almost 4 months old, Elissa no longer sucks continually. Her sucking is governed mainly by *operant conditioning*. She sucks in response to reinforcement, when her mother's breast draws near. Still, Sigmund Freud named infancy the oral stage for good reason: During the first year or two of life, the basic theme is "Everything goes immediately into the mouth."

This impulse to taste everything leads to some scary moments as children begin to crawl and walk. There is nothing like the sickening sensation of seeing a baby put a forgotten pin in his mouth, sample the cleanser, or taste a possibly poisonous plant. My personal heart-stopping experience occurred when my son was almost 2. I'll never forget the frantic race to the emergency room after Thomas toddled in to joyously share a new treasure, an open box of pills!

Luckily, there is a mechanism that may help to protect toddlers from sampling every potentially lethal substance they encounter during their first travels into the world. Between age 1½ and 2 children often become picky eaters. They may subsist for months on a few familiar foods, such as peanut butter sandwiches and apple juice. Evolutionary psychologists believe that, like morning sickness, this behavior has an adaptive function. By sticking to foods they know, children reduce the risk of poisoning themselves during the most mobile toddler months (Bjorklund & Pelligrini, 2002; Roberts & Heyman, 2000). Although it is temporary and does not affect development, this 2-year-old food caution gives caregivers headaches as they agonize: "Why is my child refusing to eat the balanced diet he needs?"

What *is* the best diet during the early months of life? When is inadequate food during childhood a truly alarming concern? These questions bring us to two important nutrition-oriented topics: breast-feeding and malnutrition around the world.

Breast Milk: The Best First Food

During the late nineteenth century, even if they survived the hazards of birth, U.S. babies faced enormous perils during their early months of life. Paramount among these threats was a disease called summer diarrhea, which caused a spike in infant mortality in sweltering city tenements during the summer months. The children of immigrant Eastern European Jews, however, were virtually immune to summer diarrhea. They also were less likely to die of other infectious diseases. The reason, argued historians, was that Jewish custom dictated exclusive breast-feeding for a prolonged time (Preston, 1991).

A century ago, because it protected babies against the hazards of impure milk, the decision to breast-feed one's child was a life-saving act. That choice still has an impact today. Breast-fed babies are more alert during their first weeks after birth (Hart and others, 2003). Breast milk provides immunities to middle ear infections and gastrointestinal problems (Bhandari and others, 2003). It makes toddlers more resistant to coming down with colds and the flu (Dubois & Girard, 2005).

[FAQ: Is breast-feeding really better than formula?]

World Health Organization

Providing your baby with the best first food is also a delightful bonding experience—making perfect sense of why this mom in Sumatra seems oblivious to those hordes of children peering in.

Breast milk may have cognitive benefits. Breast-fed babies are more advanced on developmental tests as toddlers (Gomez-Sanchiz and others, 2003; Morley and others, 2004). Compared to formula-fed babies, they even tend to score better on intelligence tests during elementary school (Karns, 2001) and as adults (Mortensen and others, 2002).

Still, we have to be cautious. These findings typically are derived from correlational studies. In North America, women—like Kim—who breast-feed for months tend to be better educated and upper middle class, and so probably provide their children with optimum care in many other ways (Hla and others, 2003; Ramirez, Bravo, & Katsikas, 2005). Depressed mothers—the very people least likely to stimulate their babies—often quickly abandon breast-feeding or may not even begin (Feldman & Eidelman, 2003a; Field, Hernandez-Reif, & Feijo, 2002). Is it really breast milk that makes for superior health, or everything else that goes along with getting this ideal food?

Finally, this optimum first diet may *not* be so ideal when a mother's health is impaired. If a woman is HIV-positive, she should not breast-feed; however, if no high-quality formula is available, she should balance the risk of transmitting this disease against the life-threatening consequences of her baby not getting adequate food (Shapiro and others, 2003). In one study conducted in rural Ethiopia, because the mothers tended to be malnourished, their infants' growth was actually compromised when these babies were given only breast milk (Umeta and others, 2003).

Despite these cautions, the professional community has taken a strong stand. From the American Academy of Pediatrics to the World Health Organization, every major public health organization advocates that infants be exclusively breast-fed for the first six months of life (American Academy of Pediatrics [AAP], 2005; World Health Organization [WHO], 2003a).

How many women around the globe follow the six-month recommendation? The answer, from Ireland to Korea to Peru, is that most mothers probably do not (Earle, 2002; Hla and others, 2003; Stewart-Knox, Gardiner, & Wright, 2003). According to one national U.S poll, only 10 percent of American babies were exclusively breast-fed up to month 6, although 22 percent were still getting some breast milk at that age (Li and others, 2002, 2003). As you saw earlier, extended breast-feeding is more typical among well-educated upper-middle-class women. Given that formula is expensive and breast milk is free, why don't more moderate- and low-income mothers make this choice?

A major reason has to do with the need to work. Although U.S. worksites are mandated by law to permit new mothers to pump their milk, imagine the problems you would face following the six-month requirement as a restaurant server or supermarket clerk who—unlike Kim—had to return soon after delivery to a physically demanding job (Lazarov & Evans, 2000). The fact that working tends to terminate breast-feeding also applies to upper-middle-class U.S. women (Anderson and others, 2002). It is not specific to our part of the world. In a Hong Kong survey, by one month after giving birth half the mothers had abandoned breast-feeding, saying they simply had to return to their jobs or risk getting laid off (Dodgson and others, 2003).

Interestingly, a developing-world nation—Colombia, South America—offers a model of how community support can work wonders at raising breast-feeding rates. Because in this collectivist culture mothers are strongly encouraged to breast-feed and bring their young infants to work, roughly 8 out of 10 Colombian women breast-feed their babies for the first year of life (Ramirez, Bravo, & Katsikas, 2005). Imagine a national movement that made it typical for us to see new mothers carrying their babies to their jobs and openly breast-feeding. Would we be living in a kinder, gentler, more family-friendly nation today?

For the millions of women who find breast-feeding physically or economically impossible or those who, like me, are adoptive parents and cannot participate in the emotional experience Kim describes, there is this final study: In tracking 570 mother–infant pairs, researchers found little difference in feelings of attachment between mothers who bottle-fed their infants and those who used the breast (Else-Quest, Hyde, & Clark, 2003).

Malnutrition: A Serious Developing-World Concern

Breast milk is an equal-opportunity food. It potentially gives *every* child a chance to thrive during the first months of life. However, there comes a time—at around 6 months of age—when a baby must be given some solid food. This is when the stark inequalities in global nutrition hit.

How many children in the developing world suffer from a condition called **undernutrition,** having a serious lack of adequate food? For answers, epidemiologists often look at the prevalence of a state called **stunting,** the percentage of children under age 5 in a given region who rank below the fifth percentile in height, according to the norms for their age (UNICEF, 2002; Wagstaff & Watanabe, 2000). This very short stature, which is a symptom of *chronic* inadequate nutrition, takes a long-term toll on cognition, on learning, on every activity of life (Berkman and others, 2002).

The good news is that during the last decades of the twentieth century, we made tremendous progress in reducing stunting. In 1980, roughly half of all children under 5 in developing countries were stunted. By 2000, the figure had dropped to less than a third (UNICEF, 2002). The bad news is that at this very minute, stunting affects roughly 200 million children around the globe (UNICEF, 2002; see Figure 3.3).

Child undernutrition—as with life expectancy and infant and maternal mortality—is a barometer of a nation's status. Are conditions improving or deteriorating in a particular area of the world? As countries become more affluent, as has recently happened in China, stunting rates decrease. Still, some nations, such as South Africa, have a higher fraction of undernourished children than we would predict by looking at their overall economy (Haddad and others, 2003). The reason is that income inequalities and limited social services are a poisonous recipe for pockets of

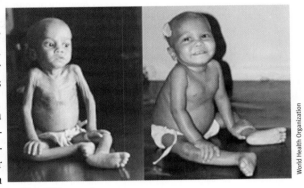

The stunted baby on the left placed next to a normally developing child his age brings home the dramatic physical toll that chronic, severe undernutrition produces even during the first year of life.

undernutrition A chronic lack of adequate food.

stunting Excessively short stature in a child, caused by chronic lack of adequate nutrition.

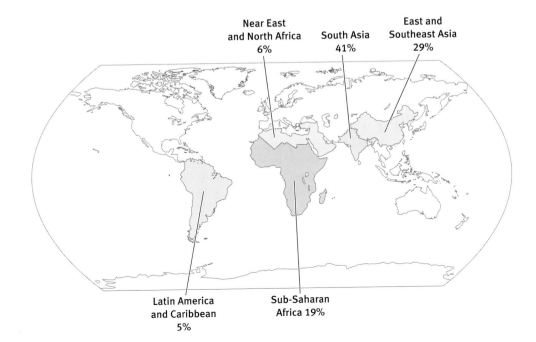

Near East and North Africa 6%
South Asia 41%
East and Southeast Asia 29%
Latin America and Caribbean 5%
Sub-Saharan Africa 19%

FIGURE 3.3: **Fraction of stunted children in different regions:** Stunting still affects an unacceptable number of children throughout the developing world. While the most alarming rates are clearly in South Asia, the place where the prevalence of stunting has actually been increasing is sub-Saharan Africa.
Source: Food and Agriculture Organization of the United Nations, 1999.

TABLE 3.1: Major U.S. Federal Nutrition Programs Serving Young Children

- **Food Stamp Program:** This mainstay federal nutrition program, which served 10 million U.S. households in 2004, provides electronic cards that participants can spend like money to buy food. To qualify for food stamps a family must have an income less than 130 percent of the federal poverty line (set at $1,698 per month for a family of three, as of September 2005) and have no more than $2,000 in resources. Although families with young children make up the majority of food stamp recipients, others—single working adults, the homeless, and legal working immigrants who entered the United States before 1996—also qualify for this aid.

- **Special Supplemental Nutrition Program for Women, Infants, and Children (WIC):** This federally funded grant program is specifically for low-income pregnant women and mothers with children under age 5. To be eligible, a family must be judged nutritionally at risk by a health-care professional and earn below 185 percent of the poverty line. WIC offers a monthly package of supplements tailored to the family's unique nutritional needs (such as infant formula and baby cereals) plus nutrition education and breast-feeding support. As of 2005, 47 percent of all infants in the United States were served by this program.

- **Child and Adult Care Food Program (CACFP):** This program reimburses child-care facilities, day-care providers, after-school programs, and providers of various adult services for the cost of serving high-quality meals. Surveys show that children (roughly 3 million in 2003) in participating programs have higher intakes of key nutrients and eat fewer servings of fats and sweets than do children who attend child-care facilities that do not participate.

Source: U.S. Department of Agriculture (USDA), www.fns.usda.gov/fsp/faqs.htm, accessed November 7, 2005; USDA, www.fns.usda.gov/wic/faqs.htm, accessed November 7, 2005; Food Research and Action Center, www.frac.org/html/federal_food_programs, accessed November 11, 2005.

child undernutrition, even when a nation has ample food to go around. Given that the United States—unfortunately—has wider disparities between the rich and poor than many other developed nations, how many young children are stunted or chronically hungry in the United States?

According to yearly polls sponsored by the U.S. Department of Agriculture, at the turn of this century roughly 10 percent of U.S. households (or 12 million children) were classified as "food insecure" (Tanner & Finn-Stevenson, 2002). Their parents—typically single mothers—reported sometimes being forced to skip meals or to serve their families unbalanced diets. Some 3.7 million families suffered from food insecurity so severe that they were ranked as "hungry"—genuinely deprived of enough food (Parker, 2000). However, the United States does provide young children with a social safety net in the form of the nutrition-related entitlement programs described in Table 3.1. So, in our nation as well as in other developed countries, while poor children may have vitamin deficiencies (Tanner & Finn-Stevenson, 2002), they don't experience the intense, *ongoing* hunger which erodes the life chances of such a high fraction of children around the globe.

Crying: The First Communication Signal

At 2 months, when Jason started crying, I was clueless. I picked him up, rocked him, and kept a pacifier glued to his mouth; called my mother, the doctor, even my local pharmacist, for advice. Since it immediately put Jason to sleep, my husband and I took car rides at three in the morning—the only people on the road were teenagers and other new parents like us. Now that my little love is 10 months old, I know exactly why he is crying, and those lonely countryside tours are long gone.

Crying, that vital way we communicate our feelings at any age, reaches its lifetime peak at around six to eight weeks after birth. Moreover, from Alaska to the Amazon rain forest, babies get fussier during the late afternoon hours (Barr, 2000). Interestingly, a distinctive change in crying occurs at about month 4. As the cortex comes on-line, crying rates dramatically decline, and babies begin to selectively use this basic mode of communication as a tool to express their needs (Barr, 2000).

Anyone who has endured a long plane ride next to a wailing infant has a vivid sense of the grating emotions that can be evoked by the crying sound. Researchers find that we tend to perceive higher-pitched cries as more arousing, signaling that an infant is in more distress (Zeskind & Marshall, 1988). Loud, raspy cries evoke particularly intense discomfort to our ears (Zeskind & Barr, 1997).

Parents, as it turns out, are especially reactive to infant cries. When recording activity in the limbic system (the region of the cortex that processes our emotions), researchers found an interesting difference between parents and nonparents when listening to a tape of a crying infant. Hands-on experience serves as an important sensitizer. The limbic system response of mothers and fathers to infant wailing was more intense (Seifritz and others, 2003).

It's tempting to think of crying as simply a negative state. However, because this basic communication mode is as vital to survival as sucking, when babies cry too little, as Kim worried, this can be a sign of a neurological problem (Zeskind & Lester, 2001). When babies cry, we pick them up, rock them, give them loving care. So, up to a certain point, crying helps cement the infant–parent bond. Crying a good deal is especially useful in certain situations. Because crying can signal a child is relatively healthy, in times of famine "excessive criers" are more likely to survive (Barr, 2000; Soltis, 2004).

Still, there is a limit. When a baby cries continually and cannot be soothed, she may have that bane of early infancy—colic. Watch a baby with colic, arching her back and screaming with pain, and you will immediately understand that this condition is linked to feeding problems (Miller-Loncar and others, 2004). Although colic is primarily due to a glitch in the immature, still-forming digestive system, women who smoke or are especially anxious during pregnancy have babies with higher colic rates (Canivet and others, 2005; Reijneveld and others, 2005). Still, despite what grandmas may (unhelpfully) tell new mothers, anxious parents don't cause colicky babies (Barr, 2000; Meier and others, 2003). We should beware of blaming severely stressed-out parents for this basically biological problem of early infant life (St. James-Roberts & Conroy, 2005).

colic A baby's frantic, continual crying during the first three months of life; caused by an immature digestive system.

The good news is that colic is short-lived. Most parents find, to their relief, that around month 4, suddenly their baby becomes a new, pleasant person overnight (Barr, 2000; Barr & Gunnar, 2000). For this reason, developmentalists become concerned only when excessive crying does not decline after month 5 (Barr, 2000).

Imagine having a baby with colic. You feel completely helpless. You cannot do anything to quiet the baby down. There are few things more damaging to parental self-efficacy than an infant's out-of-control crying.

INTERVENTIONS: What Quiets a Young Baby?

What normally soothes a crying baby? One strategy is to provide a pacifier, a breast, a bottle, or anything that satisfies the need to suck. Another is picking the child up, clasping the baby to your body, rocking, and **swaddling** (wrapping) him. With the caution that every baby is different, what works best?

swaddling Wrapping a baby tightly in a blanket or garment. This technique is calming during early infancy.

Dean Conger / Corbis

Not only are these Mongolian babies getting protection from the intense winter cold, but by being lavishly swaddled, they may feel like they have re-entered their mother's cozy womb.

To answer this question, one researcher (Campos, 1989) explored the effectiveness of swaddling versus providing a pacifier in reducing crying in response to a painful medical event, testing each strategy among 2-week-old infants undergoing heel sticks to draw blood and babies given their first immunizations at 2 months of age. Pacifiers were superior to swaddling at calming the babies. However, for 2-month-olds, swaddling worked almost as well.

Swaddling is not the same as genuine skin-to-skin human contact—wrapping the baby in your arms, carrying her close; massaging and cuddling a child. And the practices of the !Kung San hunter-gatherers of Botswana offer Westerners a lesson here. In this collectivist culture, where mothers strap infants to their bodies as they work and provide continuous feeding on demand, excessively long crying, or colic, is virtually unknown (Barr, 2000; Konner, 1976).

Would interventions to offer more skin-to-skin contact work to reduce crying in our culture, too? To explore this question, researchers randomly assigned new mothers to three groups. One was taught massage therapy, trained to rub the infant's body; another carried their babies around in an infant sling; the third used both techniques. Mothers who massaged their babies and carried them in the sling reported lower crying rates (Elliot and others, 2002). So intensive strategies to increase physical contact really do have a calming effect.

Infant massage is routinely practiced in collectivist cultures (Fikree and others, 2005). As developmentalist Tiffany Field has demonstrated, this age-old technique can work wonders for babies (and everyone else) in our society, too. A pre-bed massage can help ward off infant sleep problems (Field, 2000; Field & Hernandez-Reif, 2001). Training fathers in baby massage gets men more emotionally involved in infant care (Cullen and others, 2000). Moderate-pressure massage helps babies gain weight during the first month of life (Field and others, 2004). Massage is especially effective in helping premature infants thrive (Dieter and others, 2003; Field, 2001). Massage can even decrease the symptoms of cerebral palsy in young children (Hernandez-Reif and others, 2005).

kangaroo care Carrying a young baby in a sling close to the caregiver's body. This technique is useful for soothing an infant.

Kangaroo care, or carrying a baby in a sling like the !Kung San hunter-gatherers, can also help premature infants grow (WHO, 2003b). In one experiment demonstrating this point, developmentalists had one group of mothers with babies in the intensive care unit carry their infants in baby slings for one hour each day. They then compared these children's development to that of a comparison preemie group given standard care. At 6 months, the kangaroo-care preemies scored higher on developmental tests. Their parents were rated as providing a more nurturing home environment, too (Feldman & Eidelman, 2003b).

Imagine having your baby whisked away at birth to spend weeks in the care of strangers. Now think of being able to caress his tiny body, the sense of self-efficacy that would flow from feeling personally responsible for helping him thrive. So it makes sense that any cuddling intervention can have a long-term impact on both the baby and the parent–child bond.

Holding and stroking are lifelong soothers. There is nothing like a cuddle with a loved one or luxuriating in a relaxing massage to erase our troubles. However, soothing and crying also undergo fascinating developmental changes. The same swaddling or long car ride that worked wonders at quieting a 2-month-old evokes agony in a toddler who cannot stand to be confined. First it's swaddling, then watching a mobile, then seeing Mom enter the room that has the magical power to soothe. In preschool, it's monsters that cause wailing; during elementary school, it's failing or being rejected by our social group. As teenagers and emerging adults, we weep for lost love. Finally, among mature adults and old folks (as we reach generativity), we stop crying for ourselves and cry when our loved ones are in pain. Our crying shows just where we are developmentally throughout our lives!

For very premature babies, kangaroo care can make a critical difference in survival. Now imagine how this mother feels being able to touch her ICU baby and take action to help him live.

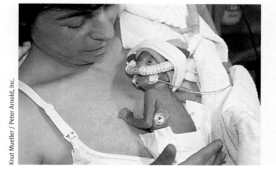

Knut Mueller / Peter Arnold, Inc.

Sleeping: The Main Newborn State

If crying is a crucial baby (and adult) communication signal, sleep is the quintessential newborn state. Visit a relative or friend who has recently given birth. Will her baby be crying or feeding? No, she is almost certain to be asleep. Full-term newborns typically sleep for 18 hours out of a 24-hour day. As Figure 3.4 shows, although they cycle through different stages of arousal, newborns are in the sleeping/drowsy phase about 90 percent of the time (Thoman & Whitney, 1990). And there is a reason for the saying, "She sleeps like a baby." Perhaps because it mirrors the whooshing sound in the womb, noise helps newborns zone out (Anders, Goodlin-Jones, & Zelenko, 1998). The problem for parents, of course, is that babies wake up and start wailing, like clockwork, every three to four hours.

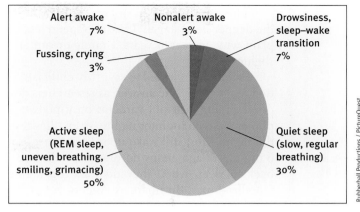

FIGURE 3.4: Newborns sleep most of the time: During each 24-hour period, newborns cycle through various states of arousal. Notice, however, that babies spend the vast majority of their time either sleeping or in the getting-to-sleep phase.
Source: Adapted from Thoman & Whitney (1990).

Developmental Changes: From Signaling, to Self-Soothing, to Shifts in REM Sleep

During the first year of life, infant sleep patterns gradually adapt to the human world (Scher, Epstein, & Tirosh, 2004). Nighttime awakenings become less frequent. Then, by six months, there is a milestone. The typical baby sleeps for six hours a night. At age 1, the typical pattern is roughly 12 hours of sleep a night, with an additional morning and afternoon nap. During year two, the caretaker's morning respite to do housework or rest is regretfully lost, as children give up the morning nap. Finally, by late preschool, sleep often (although not always) occurs only at night (Anders, Goodlin-Jones, & Zelenko, 1998).

In addition to its incredible length and on-again-off-again pattern, infant sleep differs physiologically from our adult pattern. When we fall asleep, we descend through four stages, involving progressively slower brain-wave frequencies, and then cycle back to reach **REM sleep**—a phase of rapid eye movement, when dreaming is intense and our brain-wave frequencies look virtually identical to when we are in the lightest sleep stage (see Figure 3.5). When infants fall asleep, they immediately go into the REM phase and spend most of their time in this state. It is not until adolescence that we have the genuinely adult sleep cycle shown in chart A, with four distinct stages (Anders, Goodlin-Jones, & Zelenko, 1998).

REM sleep The phase of sleep involving rapid eye movements, when the EEG looks almost like it does during waking. REM sleep decreases as infants mature.

FIGURE 3.5: Sleep brain waves and lifespan changes in sleep and wakefulness: In chart A, you can see the EEG patterns associated with the four stages of sleep that first appear during adolescence. After we fall asleep, our brain waves get progressively slower (these are the four stages of non-REM sleep) and then we enter the REM phase during which dreaming is intense. Now notice in chart B the time young babies spend in REM. Could all that REM time be helping to promote brain blossoming, the incredible explosion of synapses—that takes place during the first year of life?
Sources: Adapted from Roffwarg, Muzio, & Dement (1966).

The sleep story does not end at maturity. Older people spend much less time in the deeper sleep stages. They also spend less time in the REM phase—which may explain why, in recent years, I rarely dream and wake up more easily at night, at the slightest sound!

Parents are thrilled to say, "My child is sleeping though the night." Is this perception really true? The answer, as researchers discovered, will come as a surprise. When developmentalists put cameras on tripods next to babies' cribs and used time-lapse photography to monitor nightly sleep, they discovered that babies *never* sleep through the night. Most still wake up several times a night, even at age 2. However, by about 6 months of age, many develop the skills to become **self-soothing,** or put themselves back to sleep when they do wake up (Anders, Goodlin-Jones, & Zelenko, 1998; Goodlin-Jones, Burnham, & Anders, 2000). There is an interesting gender difference here: When it comes to self-soothing, baby girls are superior to baby boys (Goodlin-Jones and others, 2001).

Imagine that you are a new parent. Your first challenge, during early infancy, is to get the baby to develop the skill of nighttime self-soothing. Around age 1, because your child is now put into the crib while still awake, there are issues with getting your baby to *go* to sleep. During preschool and elementary school, the sleep issue shifts again. Now it's problems with getting the child *into* bed: "Mommy, can't I stay up later? Do I *have* to turn off the lights?" (See Anders, Goodlin-Jones, & Sadeh, 2000; Scher, Zukerman, & Epstein, 2005.)

During infancy, as you might imagine, getting the baby to sleep through the night is a consuming parental concern. Although it may make them cranky, parents expect to be sleep-deprived with a very young baby; but once a child has passed the 6-month milestone, they get agitated if the infant has never permitted them a full night's sleep (Minde, 1998). Parents expect periodic sleep problems when their child is ill or under stress; but not the zombie-like irritability that comes from being chronically sleep-deprived for one or two years. There is a poisonous bidirectional effect here: Children with chronic sleep problems produce irritable, overstressed parents (Eckerberg, 2004; Thome & Skuladottir, 2005). Irritable, overstressed parents tend to give children problems with sleep (Benoit and others, 1992; Seifer and others, 1996).

INTERVENTIONS: What Helps a Baby Self-Soothe?

What should parents do when their baby signals (cries out) from her crib? At one end of the continuum stand the traditional behaviorists: "Don't reinforce crying—and be consistent. Never go in and comfort the baby lest you let a variable reinforcement schedule unfold, and the child will cry longer." At the other, we have John Bowlby, with his emphasis on the attachment bond, or Erik Erikson, with his concept of *basic trust*. During the first year of life, you may recall, that both Bowlby and Erikson clearly imply, caregivers should sensitively respond whenever an infant cries. These different academic perspectives are hotly debated by parents, too:

I feel the basic lesson parents need to teach children is how to be independent, not to let your child rule your life, give him time to figure things out on his own, and not be attended to with every whimper.

I am going with my instincts and trying to be a good, caring mommy. Putting a baby in his crib to "cry it out" seems cruel. There is no such thing as spoiling an infant!

Where do you stand on this "Teach 'em" versus "Give unconditional love" controversy? One thing we know, based on our understanding of cortical development, is that babies cannot learn to self-soothe, or regulate their behavior, during the first, reflex-dominated months. But later in the first year of life, there may be advantages to partly heeding the behavioral advice.

Researchers visited the homes of a group of middle-class parents with 1-year-olds to observe baby sleep patterns and parent reactions. They found that, while overall infant fussiness was the main predictor of continual signaling, parents who immediately

self-soothing Children's ability, usually beginning at about 6 months of age, to put themselves back to sleep when they wake up during the night.

picked their babies up did have children who rarely self-soothed (Goodlin-Jones and others, 2001). However, everyone in this study put their children on a variable reinforcement schedule. When crying becomes frantic, and there is a possibility of serious trouble, a caregiver must respond!

To Co-sleep or Not to Co-sleep: A Cultural and Personal Choice

The "Go in and soothe 'em" versus "Let 'em cry it out" controversy has a cultural dimension. The issue of going *in* to get the baby would never arise in most parts of the world. In collectivist cultures, **co-sleeping**, or having the baby in *your* bed, is routine (Latz, Wolf, & Lozoff, 1999; Yang & Hahn, 2002). In Japan, for instance, mothers and fathers often separate to give each child a sleeping partner. The Japanese, and parents in other collectivist societies, believe that co-sleeping is crucial to raising a loving, bonded-to-family adult (Kitahara, 1989).

Ryuichi Sato / Taxi / Getty Images

Does this photo make you slightly nervous? Although this co-sleeping baby probably won't fall off the bed, she may be more vulnerable to having problems if she sleeps face down.

co-sleeping The standard custom, in collectivist cultures, of having a child and parent share a bed.

Realizing that the Western idea of "teaching self-reliance" by having babies sleep alone is looked on with horror by most of the world has allowed co-sleeping—traditionally frowned on by experts in our society (see, for example, Ferber, 1985, 2006)—to "come out of the closet." One British poll showed that, although often initially resistant, many parents came around to the concept of co-sleeping because it helped *them* get a good night's sleep (Ball and others, 2000). How do you feel about this practice? Because cultural feelings against co-sleeping can still run strong, Table 3.2 provides three typical anti-bed-sharing stereotypes and offers some relevant research facts.

Now we turn to more thoroughly explore the issues raised by the third stereotype in the table. What is the risk of a baby smothering while sleeping, or succumbing to that terrifying event called sudden infant death syndrome?

TABLE 3.2: Classic Co-sleeping Stereotypes and Some Relevant Research

1. **Stereotype: Co-sleeping makes a child less independent and mature.**

   Relevant research: Among California parents of preschoolers, researchers looked at three groups: people who actively chose to co-sleep with their child; "reactive co-sleepers," who reluctantly brought a child into their bed because of sleep troubles; and solitary sleepers—those who slept apart from their babies (Keller & Goldberg, 2004). The preschoolers whose parents had actively chosen to co-sleep were rated as more self-reliant (for example, able to dress themselves) and socially independent (for example, more able to make friends by themselves) compared to the other two groups. Although a variety of forces could explain this correlation, according to this finding co-sleeping promotes greater maturity and independence, not less!

2. **Stereotype: Co-sleeping disrupts parents' and children's sleep.**

   Relevant research: Several studies show that co-sleeping infants do awaken more often at night than solitary sleepers. However, co-sleeping babies get *back to sleep* in a shorter time (Latz, Wolf, & Lozoff, 1999; Mao and others, 2004). With regard to adults, one EEG sleep study found that parents who shared a bed with their infant spent a bit less time in the deepest sleep stages. However, because they did not have to go into the child's room, these parents did not spend fewer hours sleeping than the non-bed-sharing moms and dads (Mosko, Richard, & McKenna, 1997). Bottom line: Co-sleeping is *not* detrimental to sleep.

3. **Stereotype: Co-sleeping is dangerous because it can cause a baby to be smothered.**

   Relevant research: Here there *are* a few concerns. Bed-sharing infants spend a good fraction of their sleep time face down or facing their parent (Mao and others, 2004). These particular sleep positions, as you can see in the Focus on a Topic feature on page 86, do not offer the best protection against the ultimate smothering tragedy, SIDS.

WHEN SLEEP IS LETHAL

sudden infant death syndrome (SIDS) The unexplained death of an apparently healthy infant, often while sleeping, during the first year of life.

Sudden infant death syndrome (SIDS) refers to the unexplained death of an apparently healthy infant, often while sleeping. Although it strikes only about 1 in 1,000 babies, SIDS is a top-ranking cause of infant mortality in the United States and the rest of the developed world (Karns, 2001).

SIDS is more common among premature and low-birth-weight babies than full-term infants (Lipsitt, 2003). For some reason, this condition strikes Native American and African American babies and baby boys more frequently (Blackwell and others, 2004; Corr, 1996). Two clearly environmental, or nurture, forces raise the risk of SIDS: living in houses where adults smoke and, especially, being put to bed face down (Blackwell and others, 2004; Carpenter and others, 2004).

What causes SIDS? New research suggests that a genetic variation affecting the development of the autonomic nervous system—which regulates the breathing cycle—might predispose vulnerable infants to this tragic event (Hunt, 2005; Weese-Mayer and others, 2004). As most SIDS deaths take place between months 2 and 5, one researcher suggests that SIDS might be caused by a problem with the transfer from subcortical to cortical functions, when the reflex of shaking one's head in response to breathing problems is waning and the cortex has not yet fully come on-line. When children with initially weak reflexes (or those who are biologically vulnerable) are placed in stressful situations, such as sleeping face down, their breathing mechanism can be overwhelmed (Lipsitt, 2003).

Because a main risk factor for SIDS is putting the baby's face in bedding (that's when infants are most likely to suffocate), in the early 1990s the American Academy of Pediatrics launched a campaign alerting parents to put infants to sleep on their backs. The *Back to Sleep program* was effective. From 1992 to 1997 there was a 43 percent reduction in deaths due to SIDS in the United States (Gore & DuBois, 1998).

Table 3.3 offers a summary in the form of practical tips our research tour offers for caregivers and other people dealing with infants' eating, crying, and sleeping. Now we move on to sensory development and moving into the world.

***TABLE 3.3:* Infants' Basic States: Summary Tips For Caregivers (and Others)**

Eating

- Don't worry about continual newborn sucking and rooting. These are normal reflexes, and they disappear after the first months of life.

- As the baby becomes mobile, be alert to the child's tendency to put everything into the mouth, and baby-proof the home (see the next section's discussion).

- Try to breast-feed exclusively for the first six months—and then continue to breast-feed after introducing solid food. Breast milk is especially valuable in promoting growth when a child has health problems or is born prematurely.

- Family members and friends should encourage and support breast-feeding, especially among "at-risk" new mothers, such as women who are depressed. Employers should make efforts to encourage and support breast-feeding in the workplace.

- After the child is weaned, provide a balanced diet. But don't get frantic if a toddler limits her intake to a few "favorite foods" at around age $1\frac{1}{2}$; this pickiness is normal and temporary.

Crying

- Appreciate that crying is crucial—it's the way babies communicate their needs—and realize that this behavior is at its peak during the first months of life. The frequency of crying sharply declines and the reasons why the child is crying become far clearer after early infancy.

- If a baby has colic, hang in there. This condition typically ends at month four. Moreover, understand that colic has nothing to do with insensitive mothering.

- During the day, carry the infant around in a "baby sling" as much as possible. In addition, employ regular infant massage to soothe the baby.

Sleeping

- Expect to be sleep-deprived for six months, until the typical infant learns to self-soothe; meanwhile, try to take regular naps. After that, expect periodic sleep problems, and understand that children will give up their daytime nap around age 2.

- To promote self-soothing, don't go to an older infant at the first whimper. However, when crying gets frantic and may signal genuine problems, do check on the baby.

- Co-sleeping—having a child sleep in your bed—is a personal decision. Although most of the stereotypes about co-sleeping are wrong, this practice may not be completely safe with young infants, as bed sharing may slightly increase the risk of SIDS.

 ## TYING IT ALL TOGETHER

1. You're a nurse in the obstetrics ward, and new parents often ask you why their babies continually make sucking noises and turn their heads toward anything that touches their cheek and then suck. What should you say?
   a. The sucking noises are called the sucking reflex; the head-turning response is the rooting reflex.
   b. These behaviors are programmed by the lower brain centers to automatically occur at birth, because if infants had to learn to eat, they would die.
   c. These behaviors will start to disappear after about three months as the cortex matures.
   d. You should make all of these comments.

2. As a neonatal nurse, you want to design a questionnaire to predict which of your patients are most likely to abandon breast-feeding or persist. What questions might your informal survey include?

3. Your sister and her husband are under an enormous amount of stress because of their colicky 1-month-old's continual crying. Based on this section, give your sister and her husband two bits of advice for soothing their child. What encouraging information can you give your relatives about colic?

4. Jorge tells you that he's thrilled because last night his 6-month-old finally slept through the night. Is Jorge's child ahead of schedule, behind schedule, or right on time for this milestone? Is Jorge right in saying, "My child is sleeping *through* the night"?

5. Take a poll of your classmates, asking them if they believe in co-sleeping and whether they would immediately go in to quiet a crying infant. Do you find any differences in their answers by ethnicity, by gender, or by age?

Answers to the Tying It All Together questions can be found in the answers section of the book.

Sensory and Motor Development

Eating, sleeping, and crying are easy for us to observe, but what is it like to *be* a newborn? Suppose you could enter into Elissa's consciousness or, better yet, time-travel back to your first days of life. What would you experience through your senses?

One sense is definitely operational before we leave the womb. Using ultrasound, researchers see startle reactions in response to noise in fetuses 6 or 7 months old, showing that rudimentary hearing capacities exist before birth (Fernald and others, 1998). And yes, babies can learn to prefer Mozart in utero, although this passion may not persist beyond the earliest days of life.

Developmentalists had a group of women read the Dr. Seuss story *The Cat in the Hat* aloud several times a day during their last six weeks of pregnancy (DeCasper & Spence, 1987). When the children were born, the researchers used an operant conditioning procedure to see if the newborns had heard the words in the womb. If the babies sucked more (or less) on a pacifier, they were reinforced by hearing the story. The newborns did suck more when given this "reward," showing both that they had heard the words in utero and preferred to hear them again. (Keep in mind for later that this study also demonstrates that newborns can remember events dating from when they were in the womb.)

TABLE 3.4: Some Interesting Facts About Other Newborn Senses

Hearing: Fetuses can discriminate different tones in the womb (Lecanuet and others, 2000). Newborns prefer women's voices, as they are selectively sensitive to higher-pitched tones. At less than 1 week of age, babies recognize their mother's voice (DeCasper & Fifer, 1980). By 1 month of age, they tune in to infant-directed speech (described on page 102), communications tailored to them.

Smell: Newborns can discriminate among a variety of odors and develop preferences for certain smells within the first week of life. They prefer the odor of breast milk to that of amniotic fluid (Marlier, Schaal, & Soussignan, 1998). They also know the distinctive smell of their mother's breast milk and will preferentially turn toward a pad soaked with that fluid (Macfarlane, 1975). Smelling mom's milk helps soothe babies. In one study, infants cried less frantically after a heel stick when presented with that familiar smell (Rattaz, Goubet, & Bullinger, 2005).

Taste: Newborns are sensitive to basic tastes. When they taste a bitter, sour, or salty substance, they stop sucking and wrinkle their faces. They will suck more avidly on a sweet solution, although they will stop if the substance grows too sweet. Having babies suck a sweet solution before a painful experience, such as a heel stick, reduces their agitation and so can be used as a pain-management technique (Fernandez and others, 2003; Gibbins & Stevens, 2001; Rosenstein & Oster, 1988).

Table 3.4 lists some other interesting facts about newborn senses. Now we focus specifically on vision, because the research in this area is so extensive, the findings are so astonishing, and the studies devised to get into babies' heads are so brilliantly planned.

What Do Newborns See?

Imagine you are a researcher who wants to figure out what a newborn can see. What would you do? As you can see in the accompanying photo series, you put the baby into an apparatus, present images, and watch her eyes. Specifically, researchers use the **preferential-looking paradigm**—the principle that human beings are attracted to novelty and look selectively at new things. They also, as the photos show, draw on a process called **habituation**—the fact that we naturally lose interest in a new object after some time.

preferential-looking paradigm A research technique to explore early infant sensory capacities and cognition, drawing on the principle that we are attracted to novelty and prefer to look at new things.

habituation The predictable loss of interest that develops once a stimulus becomes familiar; used to explore infant sensory capacities.

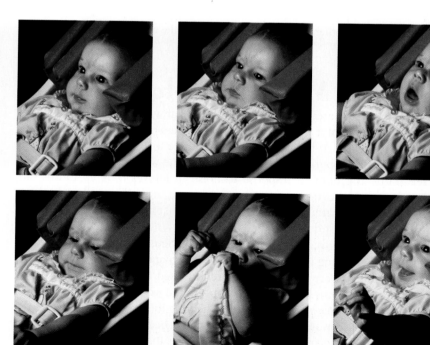

In this preferential-looking study, as an image pops up on the screen, this little girl is at first enthralled. She then *habituates* and gets interested in a new activity (picking at her dress). Finally (hooray!), another enticing new image appears on the screen.

Charles E. Maurer

You can see preferential looking and habituation in operation right now in your life. Notice that if you see or hear something new, you look up with interest. After a minute, you habituate and go back to focus on reading this book.

By showing newborns small- and large-striped patterns and measuring preferential looking, researchers have found that at birth our ability to see clearly at distances is very poor. With a visual acuity score of roughly 20/400 (versus our ideal adult 20/20), a newborn would qualify as legally blind in many states (Kellman & Banks, 1998). Because the visual cortex matures quickly, vision improves rapidly, and by about age 1, infants see just like adults.

What visual capacities *do* we have at birth? At the dawn of the twentieth century the first American psychologist, William James, described the inner life of the newborn as "one buzzing, blooming confusion." In reading these studies exploring size constancy and face perception, you can now judge whether James was correct.

[FAQ: How do researchers measure the sensory and perceptual development of infants?]

[FAQ: What do scientists believe infants really see?]

Seeing a Constant World

Size constancy refers to the fact that we see a given object as being the same size regardless of its distance from us. Right now, as I gaze out my office window at a building several blocks away, the image of this structure on my retina is small. However, I automatically correct for distance and assume that this building is not a miniature toy, but its actual size. To make these kinds of corrections, you might think, we would need considerable real-world experience—for instance, practice in watching buildings get larger as we approach them. You would be wrong.

Consider this ingenious experiment that demonstrated that size constancy is biologically "wired in" at birth (Slater, 2001; Slater, Mattock, & Brown, 1990): Researchers had newborns habituate to a specific cube at different distances, by moving the cube far away and then closer in. Then they presented this now-familiar cube, and an identical cube of a different size, at a distance so that both cast the same-size image on the babies' retinas. The babies preferentially looked at the new cube, the one they had not previously seen—demonstrating that they had size constancy, or really saw the difference in size between the two cubes.

size constancy The principle that we see an object as being the same size regardless of its distance from us.

Focusing on Faces

Without doubt, the most remarkable findings relate to **face-perception studies,** in which researchers explore preferential looking at human faces. When newborns are presented with the paired stimuli in Figure 3.6, they spend more time looking at the face pattern. They will track or follow that facelike stimulus even longer when it is moved from side to side (Farroni, Massaccesi, & Simion, 2002).

The story gets more interesting. Newborns can make amazing distinctions. They prefer to look at a photo of their mother compared to one of a stranger during the first days of life. They can pick out their mother's face from another face with similar features, although not if their mother's hair is covered by a scarf (Bushnell, 1998; Pascalis and others, 1995).

Most interesting, newborns prefer attractive-looking people! Researchers selected photos of attractive and unattractive women, then took infants from the maternity ward and measured preferential looking. The attractive faces got looked at significantly longer—61 percent of the time (Slater and others, 1998). By 3 to 6 months, this preference for good-looking people is entrenched. Babies preferentially look at good-looking infants, at handsome men and pretty women, at good-looking European Americans and African Americans (Slater, 2001). Unhappily, our tendency to gravitate toward people for their looks seems somewhat biologically built-in. (In case you are interested, more symmetrical faces tend to be rated as better-looking.)

There is an interactive component to these perceptions. Newborns look longer at faces that are looking at them (Farroni, Massaccesi, & Simion, 2002). Astonishingly, they imitate facial expressions

face-perception studies Research using preferential looking and habituation to explore what very young babies know about faces.

FIGURE 3.6: **Babies prefer faces:** When shown these three illustrations, newborns looked most at the face like drawing. Might the fact that infants are biologically programmed to selectively look at faces be built into evolution to help ensure that adults give babies loving care?

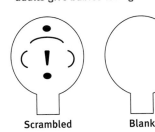

Face   Scrambled   Blank

that an adult makes, such as sticking out the tongue (Maratos, 1998; Meltzoff & Moore, 1977). So if you have wondered why you start stammering when conversing with a very shy person, or have agonized at your humiliating tendency to mimic everyone else's gestures and facial tics, this research offers answers. It's not a personal problem. It's built into our human biology, beginning from day one!

In conclusion, William James was wrong. There is no blooming and buzzing confusion to newborn life. We arrive in the world with a remarkably well developed sensory apparatus. We have a built-in antenna to tune into the human world.

Seeing Depth and Fearing Heights

Psychologists urge caution, however. Just because a beginning capacity is present at birth, let's not fall into the trap of overstating what infants can do (Bornstein, 1998; Bremner, 1998). Visual skills improve with experience. When my 2-year-old son yelled out, *"Toys!!"* while riveted to the window on his first airplane ride, I realized that children have not fully mastered size constancy *years* after birth. Here is an illustration of how a sensory ability takes time to evolve to its mature form. It involves **depth perception,** our ability to see and then eventually to be frightened of heights.

In a classic study called the **visual cliff,** infants were placed on one side of a table with a checkerboard pattern while their mothers were at the other end (see Figure 3.7). The table had a thick, transparent top, but at its midpoint the pattern dropped to the floor level, so it appeared to the babies that if they crawled beyond that point, they would fall. Even when parents smiled and encouraged their babies to crawl to them, 8-month-old infants refused to venture beyond what looked like the drop-off—showing that by this age depth perception exists. Do younger babies have this perception and fear?

To answer this question, developmentalists dangled 2-month-old infants above the drop-off side of the table. The babies' heart rates declined (a sign of interest), showing that by this age they "saw" the difference in depth but were not afraid (Campos, Langer, & Krowitz, 1970). Babies start to *fear* heights about month six or seven, around the time they are getting ready to crawl. At this age their heart rates *accelerate* (showing anxiety) when they are held near the drop-off side (Schwartz, Campos, & Baisel, 1973). Still, there is a nurture (or wider-world experience) component to the age when this biologically programmed fear appears. Early crawlers develop an intense fear of heights at a younger age (Bertenthal, Campos, & Kermoian, 1994).

In sum, while our ability to *see* differences in depth does appear soon after birth, the sick feeling we have when leaning over a balcony—"Wow, I'd better avoid falling into that space below"—only emerges later, when babies are getting mobile and really need that fear to protect them from getting hurt. Now let's look at how the mobility side of life unfolds.

depth perception The ability to see (and fear) heights.

visual cliff A table that appears to "end" in a drop-off at its midpoint; used to test for infant depth perception.

FIGURE 3.7: **The visual cliff:** Even though his mother is on the other side, this 8-month-old child gets anxious about venturing beyond what looks like the drop-off point in the table—demonstrating that by this age babies have depth perception. By using the strategies discussed in the text, researchers then use the same creative visual cliff apparatus to see if babies too young to crawl also see and fear heights.

Mark Richards / Photo Edit, Inc.

Expanding Body Size

Our brain may expand dramatically after birth. Still, it has nothing on the envelope in which we live. Our bodies expand to 21 times their newborn size by the time we reach adulthood (Slater, 2001). This growth rate is most pronounced during infancy, then drastically slows down during childhood, to dramatically increase in velocity again during the preadolescent years. Still, looking at overall height and weight statistics is not revealing. This body sculpting occurs in a definite way.

Imagine taking time-lapse photographs of a baby's head from birth to adulthood and comparing your photos to snapshots of the body. You would not see much change in the overall size and shape of the head. The body, in contrast, would dramatically elongate and thin out. Newborns start out with tiny "frog" legs timed to slowly straighten out by about month 6. Then comes the stocky, bowlegged toddler, followed by the slimmer child of kindergarten and elementary school. So, during childhood growth follows the same principle as it did inside the womb: Development proceeds according to the *cephalocaudal sequence*—from the head to the feet.

Now think of Mickey Mouse, Big Bird, or Oscar the Grouch. They, too, have relatively large heads and small bodies. Might our favorite cartoon characters be enticing because they mimic the proportions of a baby? Did the delicious rounded infant shape evolve to seduce adults into giving babies special care and love?

The tiny frog legs of very early infancy straighten out by month 6 and then become longer and fully functional for carrying us around (as toddlers)—demonstrating the cephalocaudal principle of development.

Mastering Motor Milestones

Actually, all three growth principles spelled out in the previous chapter—*cephalocaudal*, *proximodistal*, and *mass-to-specific*—apply to infant *motor milestones*, the exciting progression of physical abilities during the first year of life. First, babies lift their head, then pivot their upper body, then sit up without support, and finally stand (the cephalocaudal sequence). Infants move their shoulders before they have control of their arms and can make their fingers obey their commands (proximodistal sequence, from interior to outer parts).

But the most important principle programming motor abilities throughout childhood is the mass-to-specific sequence (large before small and detailed). From the wobbly first step at age 1 to the prizewinning pirouette or home run out of the ballpark during the teenage years, big, uncoordinated movements are honed, perfected, and refined as we travel from infancy to adult life.

Babies first joyously lift their heads and upper torsos, then sit up (at about month 5 or 6), and finally, at around age 1, take their first unforgettable steps—demonstrating that the cephalcaudal principle also applies to motor milestones.

Duke University Photography

By giving this infant a Velcro mitten that allows her to pick up the interesting objects she sees, developmentalists find they can accelerate this little girl's grasping-an-object skills.

To appreciate the range of abilities required to make each milestone possible, let's look in more detail at the act of reaching, that landmark event when babies first try to make contact with the world. To make a first swipe at an object, infants must have control of their head and torso. Their neck and arm muscles must be operational (Thelen and others, 1993). Sitting, which happens at around month 6 or 7, allows the baby's reach to become steady and smooth. Sensory abilities are also crucial—having good visual acuity, having the size-perception skills to know what objects are in grasping range, being able to coordinate your vision with the movements of your body and hands. So every motor milestone—from reaching, to sitting, to walking—depends on the minute-to-minute integration of multiple sensory and motor processes, all beautifully coordinated by the brain (Anderson, Campos, & Barbu-Roth, 2004).

Can that first real grasp at the bottle be accelerated by nurture forces or experience? To answer this question, developmentalists came up with an ingenious strategy. They placed Velcro mittens on 3-month-olds, enabling the babies to pick up objects by simply extending their hands. After a week or so of "sticky mitten" practice, the 3-month-olds' grasping skills were equivalent to those of a typical 5-month-old (Needham, Barrett, & Peterman, 2002).

Issues (and Joys) Related to Infant Mobility

Charting all of these milestones does not speak to the joy of witnessing them unfold—that Kodak moment when Kim's baby, Elissa, finally masters turning over, after those vigorous practice push-ups, or when she first connects with the bottle, grasps it, and awkwardly moves it to her mouth. I'll never forget when my own son, after what seemed like years of cruising around holding onto the furniture, ventured (so gingerly) out into thin air, flung up his hands, and, *yes, yes*, took his ecstatic first step!

Nor do the charts mention the hilarious glitches that happen when a skill is first being developed—the first days of creeping, when a baby can only move backward and you find him huddled in the corner in pursuit of objects that get steadily farther way. Or when a child first pulls to a standing position in the crib, and her triumphant expression changes to bewilderment: "Whoops, now tell me, Mom, *how do I get down?*"

But suppose a child is almost 14 months old and has yet to take his first solo step, or is sliding toward 4 years of age and is in danger of being expelled from nursery school because she still is incapable of regularly making it to the toilet in time. And what about the fantasies that set in when an infant is ahead of schedule? "Only 10 months old and already walking. Perhaps my baby is special, a genius."

What typically happens is that within weeks the worries become a memory, and the fantasies about the future are shown to be completely wrong. Except in the case of children who have developmental disorders, the rate at which babies master motor milestones has no relation to their later intelligence. Different regions of the cortex, as we now know, develop at different times. Why should our timetable for walking or grasping an object predict development in a complex function such as grasping the point of this book?

An interesting exception to the rule that early infant individual differences don't predict later cognition involves an ability that doesn't appear on the milestones chart. It concerns *habituation*, discussed in the previous section describing vision. In exploring a variety of infant abilities longitudinally, one researcher was astonished to discover that babies who quickly habituated to stimuli and then later preferentially looked at a new stimulus when it was paired with that same "old" one (showing they remembered what they had seen before) had superior scores on childhood intelligence tests (Fagan, 1988, 2000). The reason is that grasping a stimulus quickly and remembering it is a general capacity that underlies a variety of intellectual skills, from recalling facts better to mastering concepts more quickly to more effortlessly absorbing the messages of this text.

Still, even if a baby's early locomotion (physically getting around) does not mean he will end up an Einstein, moving into the world does usher in many cognitive advances.

Getting a bottle and feeding yourself is a crucial milestone—the first time babies can take independent action to get what they want.

Michael Newman / Photo Edit, Inc.

The Mind-Expanding Effects of Travel

Developmentalists have explored the mind-expanding changes linked to crawling, the one motor milestone that many normal babies actually skip. Crawling provokes more interest in objects at distances. So early crawlers have superior size constancy for far-away objects (Anderson, Campos, & Barbu-Roth, 2004). Early crawlers—compared to other babies—are "mature" in the relationship area, too. They are more attuned to a caregiver's facial expressions. They get upset when a primary caregiver leaves the room at a younger age (Campos and others, 2000). After all, now they need a loving adult on the scene and must carefully monitor her cues ("*Stop,* those are stairs!") to pace their journey into life.

In interviewing mothers of newly crawling babies, developmentalists discovered that crawling is linked to fascinating changes in the parent–child bond (Campos and others, 2000). When their infants started crawling, women reported that they saw their children as more independent, more separate individuals with a mind of their own. Many said this was the first time they began to get angry with and discipline their child. So as babies get mobile, the basic parenting agenda emerges: A child's mission is to explore the world. Parents' job, for the next two decades, lies in setting limits to that exploration, as well as giving love.

INTERVENTIONS: Baby-Proofing, the First Person–Environment Fit

Mobility presents perils. Now safety issues become a major concern. How can care-takers encourage these emerging motor skills and still protect children from getting hurt? The answer is to strive for the right person–environment fit—that is, to **baby-proof** the house.

baby-proofing Making the home safe for a newly mobile infant.

Get on the floor and look at life from the perspective of the child. Cover electrical outlets and put dangerous cleaning substances on the top shelf. Unplug countertop appliances. Take small objects off tables. Perhaps pad the furniture corners, too. The challenge is to anticipate current dangers and to stay one step ahead. There will come a day when that child can pry out those outlet covers or ascend to the top of the cleanser-laden cabinet. As Kim from the chapter-opening vignette is about to learn, those exciting motor milestones have a definite downside, too!

 ## TYING IT ALL TOGETHER

1. You're watching through a one-way mirror as a researcher explores how well newborns can hear. The infant is wearing headphones, and the psychologist presents a tone and watches the baby's face to see if the child looks up with interest. The strategy the researcher is using is called the _____ paradigm.

2. Alicia's daughter has been regularly participating in a visual cliff study. When the baby is placed on the cliff side at 2 months of age, she should _____. At 7 months, she should _____. (Choose from a, b, and c to fill in the blanks.)

   a. show no fear, but give signs that she "sees" the difference by looking interested.
   b. be terribly frightened.
   c. not notice the drop-off at all.

3. Felicity says that babies can see the world remarkably accurately soon after they emerge from the womb. Jason says that visual capacities grow gradually over the first year of life. First make Felicity's case and then make Jason's, citing the research discussed in this section.

4. Charlie crawled and walked at a very young age and grew bored before other babies in a habituation test at the local university. His excited parents are sure that Charlie is gifted and are saving up to send him to Harvard. Which, if any, of Charlie's behaviors might support his parents' dreams?

5. List some steps that you would take to baby-proof the room you are sitting in right now.

Answers to the Tying It All Together questions can be found in the answers section of the book.

TABLE 3.5: Piaget's Stages: Focus on Infancy

Age	Name of Stage	Description
0–2	**Sensorimotor**	The baby manipulates objects to pin down the basics of physical reality. This stage ends with the development of language.
2–7	**Preoperations**	Children's perceptions are captured by their immediate appearances. "What they see is what is real." They believe, among other things, that inanimate objects are really alive and that if the appearance of a quantity of liquid changes (for example, if it is poured from a short, wide glass into a tall, thin one), the amount actually becomes different.
8–12	**Concrete operations**	Children have a realistic understanding of the world. Their thinking is really on the same wavelength as adults. While they can reason conceptually about concrete objects, however, they cannot think abstractly in a scientific way.
12+	**Formal operations**	Reasoning is at its pinnacle: hypothetical, scientific, flexible, fully adult. Our full cognitive human potential has been reached.

sensorimotor stage Piaget's first stage of cognitive development, lasting from birth to age 2, when babies' agenda is to pin down the basics of physical reality.

circular reactions In Piaget's framework, repetitive action-oriented schemas (or habits) characteristic of babies during the sensorimotor stage.

primary circular reactions In Piaget's framework, the first infant habits during the sensorimotor stage, centered on the body.

secondary circular reactions In Piaget's framework, habits of the sensorimotor stage lasting from about 4 months of age to the baby's first birthday, centered on exploring the external world.

Cognition

Why exactly *do* infants have an incredible hunger to explore, to touch, to get into every cleanser-laden cabinet and remove all those outlet plugs? For the same reason that, if you landed on a different planet, you would need to get the basics of reality down.

Imagine stepping out on Mars. You would roam the new environment, exploring the rocks and the sand. While exercising your walking schema, or habitual way of physically navigating, you would need to make drastic changes. On Mars, with its minimal gravity, when you took your normal earthling stride, you would probably bounce up 20 feet. Just like a newly crawling infant, you would have to accommodate, and in the process reach a higher mental equilibrium, or a better understanding of life. Moreover, as a good scientist, you would not be satisfied to perform each movement only once. The only way to pin down the physics of this planet would be to repeat each action over and over again. Now you have the basic principles of Jean Piaget's **sensorimotor stage** (see Table 3.5).

Piaget's Sensorimotor Stage

Specifically, Piaget believed that during our first two years on this planet, our mission is to make sense of physical reality by exploring the world through our senses. Just as in the above Mars example, as they *assimilate*, or fit the outer world to what they are already capable of doing, infants *accommodate* and so gradually mentally advance. (Remember my example in Chapter 1 of how, in the process of assimilating this information to your current knowledge schemas or mental slots, you are accommodating and so expanding what you know.)

Let's take the "everything into the mouth" schema that figures so prominently during the first year of life. As babies mouth each new object—or, in Piagetian terminology, assimilate everything to their mouthing schema—they realize that objects come in different sizes. Some are soft or prickly. Others taste terrible or great. Through continual assimilation and accommodation, during infancy we make a dramatic mental leap—from relying on our small set of reflexes, to reasoning and using symbolic thought.

Circular Reactions: Habits That Pin Down Reality

By meticulously observing his own three children, Piaget discovered that the basic set of actions driving all these advances during infancy were **circular reactions**—habits, or action-oriented schemas, which the child repeats again and again.

From the first birth reflexes, during months 1 to 4, the **primary circular reactions** develop. These are repetitive actions begun by accident, centered about the child's body. A thumb randomly makes contact with his mouth and a 2-month-old removes that interesting object, observes it, and moves it back in and out. Batting her legs was a captivating activity that engaged Kim's baby, Elissa, for hours.

At around 4 months of age, the **secondary circular reactions** appear. These are action-oriented schemas centered on sights and sounds in the *outside* environment. As Kim noticed with Elissa, at about this age the child seems to literally wake up to the wider world. Now her mission is to make sense of this planet where she will spend the next 80 or so years of life. Let's see how Piaget, the master observer, described his daughter Lucienne's first secondary circular reactions:

Lucienne at 0:4 [4 months] is lying in her bassinet. I hang a doll over her feet which . . . sets in motion the schema of shakes. Her feet reach the doll . . . and give it a violent movement which Lucienne surveys with delight. . . . After the first shakes, Lucienne makes slow foot movements as though to grasp and explore. . . . When she tries to kick the doll, and misses . . . she begins again very slowly until she succeeds [without looking at her feet]. (Flavell, 1963, p. 103; original source, Piaget, 1950, p. 159)

During the next few months, secondary circular reactions become more numerous and well coordinated. By about 8 months of age, for instance, babies can simultaneously employ two circular reactions, using both grasping and kicking in concert to explore the world.

Then, around a baby's first birthday, the **tertiary circular reactions** appear. Now the child is no longer constrained by stereotyped schemas. He can operate just like a real scientist, flexibly changing his behavior to make sense of the world. A toddler gets captivated by toilet paper, unrolling sheets and throwing different-sized wads into the bowl. At dinner, he gleefully spits his food at varying velocities and hurls his bottle off the high chair in different directions just to see where it lands.

How important are circular reactions in infancy? Spend time with a young baby, as she bats at her mobile or joyously pinwheels her legs. Try to prevent a 1-year-old from ejecting plates off a high chair, flushing objects down the toilet, or methodically inserting bits of cookie into the computer disk drive. Then you will understand: Infancy is all about the insatiable drive to repeat interesting acts. (See Table 3.6 for a recap of the circular reactions.)

tertiary circular reactions In Piaget's framework, "little-scientist" activities of the sensorimotor stage, beginning around age 1, involving flexibly exploring the properties of objects.

TABLE 3.6: The Circular Reactions: A Summary Table

Primary Circular Reactions: 1–4 months

Description: Repetitive habits center around the child's own body.

Examples: Sucking toes; sucking thumb

Rommel / Masterfile

Secondary Circular Reactions: 4 months–1 year

Description: Child "wakes up to wider world." Habits center on environmental objects

Examples: Grabbing for toys; batting mobiles; pushing one's body to activate the lights and sounds on a swing

Christina Kennedy / Photo Edit, Inc.

Tertiary Circular Reactions: 1–2 years

Description: Child flexibly explores the properties of objects, like a "little scientist."

Examples: Exploring the various dimensions of a toy; throwing a bottle off the high chair in different directions; flushing different objects down the toilet; putting different kinds of food in the VCR or computer

David Young-Wolff / Photo Edit, Inc.

little-scientist phase The time around age 1 when babies use tertiary circular reactions to actively explore the properties of objects, experimenting with them like "scientists."

Piaget's concept of circular reactions offers a new perspective on those obsessions that drive adults crazy during what researchers call the **little-scientist phase** (and parents call the "getting into everything" phase). This is the time, around age 1, when the child begins experimenting with objects in a way that uncannily mimics how a scientist behaves: "Let me try this, then that, and see what happens." The reason it is impossible to derail a 1-year-old from putting oatmeal in the disk drive, or clogging the toilet with toys (making a plumber a parent's new best friend), is that circular reactions allow infants to pin down the basic properties of the world.

Why do *specific* circular reactions, such as flushing objects down the toilet or filling the computer with food, become irresistible during the little-scientist phase? This question brings us to Piaget's ideas about how babies progress from reflexes to the ability to reason and think.

Tracking Early Thinking

How do we know when infants begin to actually think? According to Piaget, one hallmark of thinking is deferred imitation. When Piaget saw Lucienne, at 16 months of age, mimic a tantrum she had seen another child have days earlier, he realized she had the mental skills to keep that image in her mind, mull it over, and translate it into action on her own. Another sign of reasoning abilities is the beginning of make-believe play. To pretend you are cleaning the house or talking on the phone like Mommy, you must realize that something *signifies*, or stands for, something else.

means–end behavior In Piaget's framework, performing a different action to get to a goal—an ability that emerges in the sensorimotor stage as babies approach age 1.

But perhaps the most important sign of emerging reasoning is **means–end behavior**—when the child is able to perform a completely different activity to get to a goal. Turning a doorknob to get outside; manipulating a switch to turn on the light; screwing open a bottle to extract the juice—all of these are examples of "doing something different" to reach a particular end. Let's look at this intellectual feat in action with Lucienne, as Piaget presented his little-scientist 16-month-old with the puzzle of getting a chain out of a matchbox:

> I put the chain inside an empty matchbox, then close the box leaving an opening of 10 mm [about half an inch]. Lucienne . . . tries to grasp the chain through the opening. Not succeeding, she . . . puts her index finger into the slit . . . and then pulls it out. . . . Here begins the experiment. . . . I put the chain back into the box and reduce the opening to 3 mm [about one-tenth of an inch]. . . . She puts her finger inside and gropes to reach the chain, but fails. . . . A pause follows this, during which Lucienne . . . looks at the slit with great attention and then, several times in succession, she opens and shuts her mouth, at first slightly then wider and wider! . . . Soon after . . . , Lucienne . . . puts her finger in the slit and . . . pulls . . . to enlarge the opening.
>
> (adapted from Flavell, 1963, p. 120; original source, Piaget, 1950, pp. 337–338)

In this example we can actually witness Lucienne mentally devising her strategy, as she arrives at a creative *new* means (or method) of getting to that alluring chain. If you have access to a 1-year-old, you might now construct your own means–end task.

First, show the child something she really wants, such as a cookie or a toy. Then put the object in a place where the baby must perform a different type of action to get the treat. For instance, you might put the cookie in a clear container and cover the top with Saran Wrap or a piece of fabric. Will the baby simply ineffectively bang the side of the container, or will she figure out the *different* step (removing the cover) essential to retrieving what she wants? If you conduct your test by putting the cookie in an opaque container, the baby must have another basic understanding: She must realize that—although she may not immediately see it—the cookie is still there.

Object Permanence: Believing in a Stable World

object permanence In Piaget's framework, the understanding that objects continue to exist even when we can no longer see them, which gradually emerges during the sensorimotor stage.

Object permanence refers to the idea that objects exist when we don't see them—a perception that is, obviously, fundamental to our sense of living in a stable world. Suppose you felt that this book disappeared when you averted your eyes or that your house rematerialized out of nothing when you entered your driveway. Piaget believed that this perception is not inborn. Object permanence develops gradually throughout the sensorimotor stage.

Piaget's observations suggested that during babies' first few months, life is a series of disappearing pictures. If an enticing image, such as her mother, passed her line of sight, his child would stare at the place from which the image had vanished as if it would reappear out of thin air. Then, at around month 5, when the *secondary circular reactions* are first flowering, there is a milestone. An object dropped out of sight and his daughter leaned over to look for it, suggesting that she knew it existed independently of her gaze. Still, this sense of a stable object was fragile. The baby quickly abandoned her search after Piaget covered that object with his hand.

Hunting for hidden objects becomes a well-established activity as children approach the first year of life. Actually, uncovering objects that adults hide underneath covers becomes a totally absorbing game. Still, at this age, children make a surprising mistake called the **A-not-B error** (see Figure 3.8). If you put an object in full view of a baby into one out-of-sight location, have the baby get it, and then move it to another place while the child is watching, she will look for it in the initial place!

See if you can perform this classic test if you have access to a 10-month-old: Place an object under a piece of paper (A). Then have the baby find it in that place a few times. Next, remove that object, show it to the infant, and then put it under a different piece of paper (B). What happens? Even though the child was watching you put it in the new location, he will probably look in A again, as if the object had migrated unseen to its original place!

By about their first birthday, children seem to master the basic principle. Move an object to a new location, and they will look in the correct place. However, as Piaget found when he used the same strategy but *covered* the object with his hand, a true sense of stable objects does not emerge until children are almost 2 years old.

Emerging object permanence explains many puzzles about development. Why does peek-a-boo become an all-time favorite activity at around 8 months? The reason is that a child now thinks there is *probably* still someone behind those hands, but doesn't absolutely know for sure.

Emerging object permanence offers a wonderful perspective on why babies are so laid back and then get increasingly possessive as they travel into their second year of life. Those toddler tantrums about objects do not signal a new, awful personality trait called "the terrible twos." They simply show that children have become much smarter. They now have the cognitive skills to know that objects still exist when you take them away.

A-not-B error In Piaget's framework, a classic mistake made by infants in the sensorimotor stage, whereby babies approaching age 1 go back to the original hiding place to look for an object even though they have seen it get hidden in a second place.

All photos: Adele Diamond

FIGURE 3.8: **The A-not-B error:** Before filming these images, researchers had this baby find a covered object in the hole on the right several times. Then, as you can see in the top images, they placed an object in the hole on the left, made sure the infant was watching, and covered each hole with a cloth. Interestingly, notice that even while focusing her attention on the correct hiding place, this baby automatically repeated her previous action and picked up the cloth on the right. (Stay tuned for insights into exactly why this classic A-not-B mistake occurs, later in this section.)

This child is thrilled with his Jack-in-the-box toy because he is just getting the concept of object permanence.

Andy Sacks / Getty Images

Finally, the emerging concept of object permanence, or fascination with disappearing objects, plus means–end behavior, makes perfect sense of that irresistible attraction to the toilet or the compulsion to stick objects in the disk drive or DVD slot. What could be more tantalizing during the little-scientist phase than taking a new action to get to a goal plus causing things to disappear and possibly reappear? It also explains why you can't go wrong if you buy your toddler nephew a pop-up toy.

But during the first year of life there is no need to arrive with any toy. Buy a toy for an infant and he will push it aside to play with the box. Your nephew probably much prefers fiddling with the light switch or buttons on the TV to any fancy mechanical gadget from Toys R Us. Toys only become interesting once we realize that they are different from real life. So, a desire for dolls or action figures—or for anything else that requires make-believe play—shows that a child is emerging from the sensorimotor period and making the transition to symbolic thought. With the concepts of circular reactions, emerging object permanence, and means–end behavior, Piaget masterfully made sense of the puzzling passions of infant life!

Critiquing Piaget

Despite its brilliance, however, Piaget's theory has serious holes. Piaget clearly implies that children only have "a memory" of something when they begin to have the glimmers of object permanence, or to look for hidden objects, at about month 5. But remember that newborns could recall the sounds of *The Cat in the Hat* when that story had been read to them in the womb. Clearly, infants can have memories of events at a far, far younger age.

Piaget's disadvantage was that he had to rely on babies acting (for instance, taking covers off hidden objects) to figure out what they mentally understood. He did not have those creative strategies like preferential looking and charting heart rates to decode what babies know before they can physically respond. Using these techniques, developmentalists realized that infants *generally* understand far more than Piaget gave them credit for.

Now let's look at two specific criticisms researchers have made about Piaget's conceptions about infant life:

[FAQ: How do researchers test infant cognition?]

[FAQ: Do babies think?]

- **Infants grasp the basics of physical reality at a younger age than Piaget believed.** To illustrate this point, developmentalist Renée Baillargeon (1993) presented babies under age 1 with the physically impossible events shown in Figure 3.9. She rotated a screen so that it appeared to pass through a solid object. She showed a tall rabbit—clearly moving behind a screen—that mysteriously materialized on the other side of the gap it had to pass through to reach the place where it arrived. Even young infants looked astonished when they saw these physically impossible events. You could almost hear them thinking, "I know that's not the way objects should behave."

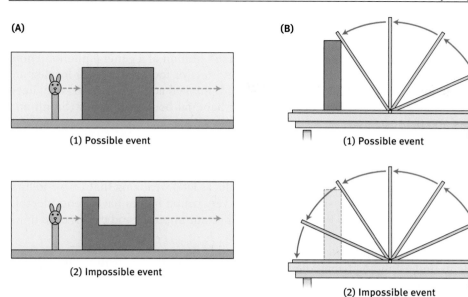

(A)

(1) Possible event

(2) Impossible event

(B)

(1) Possible event

(2) Impossible event

FIGURE 3.9: Baillargeon's impossible events: When babies were shown the rabbit who didn't appear in the opening it had to pass through (A-2) and the screen that passed through a solid object (B-2), even by 4 months of age they looked surprised. The bottom line: Infants understand basic principles about the physical world far earlier than Piaget believed.

Source: Baillargeon & Graber (1987); Baillargeon & DeVos (1991); Baillargeon (1987).

- **Infants' understanding of physical reality emerges gradually.** Moreover, Baillargeon found that babies' understanding of the properties of objects did not arrive in qualitatively different holistic chunks. While babies as young as 3-1/2 months old were surprised when the screen passed through the solid object, the impossible traveling rabbit provoked astonishment only at around month 4 or 5. It took infants until about 9 months of age to understand other basic object permanence phenomena, such as the fact that you can't retrieve an object, such as a bear, from under a blanket that looks as if it's lying flat. The bottom-line message is that our understanding about the real-world properties of objects grows *slowly* during the first year of life. Therefore, developmentalists began to wonder: Is Piaget's model of unitary, qualitatively different stages the best framework for understanding intellectual growth?

Developmentalists who subscribe to an **information-processing theory** approach to understanding cognition believe that the metaphor of a computer with separate processing components offers a better model for understanding babies' maturing minds. For instance, a developmentalist using an information-processing approach would not view means–end behavior as a completely new cognitive capacity that suddenly appeared at a specific age. He would focus on decoding the mental-processing skills involved in this feat (attention, memory, the ability to inhibit an immediate perception, and so on) and explore how each separate skill gradually evolved.

Now turn back to Piaget's description of Lucienne's first secondary circular reactions on page 95. Perhaps you can notice that her careful kicks clearly involve embryonic thinking. An information-processing theorist would trace how the mental skills Lucienne was demonstrating at this age might grow month by month, to culminate in the 16-month means–end feat of getting that chain.

Using this "processing steps" framework not only provides a more linear portrait of cognitive growth, but also means that we can use the same principles to decode thinking at age 1 and age 91. So stay tuned as we return to this influential contemporary model of cognition to explore how memory and thinking develop during *both* childhood and old age.

Before leaving this section, let's return to the A-not-B error—that classic mistake infants make as they approach age 1. It is tempting to see the A-not-B problem as an isolated example illustrating what babies don't know at a given age and then come to fully comprehend. We might be wrong. When developmentalists put the A and B hiding places in the center of a large sandbox, increased the number of "trials" in which

information-processing theory A perspective on understanding cognition in which mental processes are seen as analogous to the way a computer analyzes data, with steps including sensory input, storage, and output.

a child first got the toy in A, and had a parent distract a toddler before she could go to B, they produced the A-not-B error in 2-year-olds! The researchers argue that, rather than being unique, the A-not-B error is one manifestation of a general phenomenon. Our memories for where objects—such as our keys or toothbrush—are located are "body-centered," or solidified through repeated physical actions. All of us may need considerable conscious effort to override our habitual bodily responses (Smith and others, 1999).

Hey, wait a second! Now I realize that I regularly make the A-not-B error myself! Every Thursday I have an appointment that requires me to turn left as I leave my university, rather than right, toward my home. And *every week* I make the same mistake of automatically going right and then, a few blocks later, realizing that I have to turn around! The A-not-B error simply shows that very young babies have a considerable way to go before the part of the brain that inhibits our impulses and causes us to think through different options really comes on-line.

If Piaget were alive today, he would probably be amazed at the strides we have made in understanding babies' developing minds. Still, there is nothing like Piaget's concepts to clue us in to why *real-world* infants behave in all those puzzling ways!

TYING IT ALL TOGETHER

1. You are working at a child-care center, and you notice Darien repeatedly opening and closing a cabinet door. Then Jai comes over and pulls open the door. You decide to latch it. Jai—undeterred—pulls on the door and, when it doesn't open, begins jiggling the latch. And then he looks up, very pleased, as he manages to figure out how to open the latch. Finally, you give up and decide to play a game with Sam. You hide a stuffed bear in a toy box while Sam watches. Then Sam throws open the lid of the box and scoops out the bear. Link the appropriate Piagetian term to each child's behavior: circular reaction; object permanence; means–end behavior.

2. Joe wants to argue, based on this section, that Piaget's theory falls short. Identify which statement is *not* a classic critique of Piaget's theory.

   a. Cognitive development takes place in qualitatively different stages, but not the ones Piaget described.
   b. Infants grasp the facts about physical reality at an earlier age than Piaget assumed.
   c. Children's understanding of the physical world emerges gradually.

Answers to the Tying It All Together questions can be found in the answers section of the book.

Language: The Endpoint of Infancy

Piaget believed the onset of language signals the end of the sensorimotor period, because its emergence shows that children can now think on a abstract, symbolic plane. True, in order to master language, you must grasp the idea that the abstract word-symbol *textbook* refers to what you are reading now. But the real miracle of human language is that we can string together words in novel, immediately understandable ways. What causes us to master this amazing feat, and how does beginning language evolve?

Nature, Nurture, and the Passion to Learn Language

The essential property of human language is its infinite elasticity. How can I come up with this totally new sentence, and why can you understand its meaning, although you have never seen it before? Why does every language have a **grammar**, with nouns, verbs, and rules for putting words into sentences? Why do even deaf children, left to their own devices, construct a genuine language, with its own signing-combination

grammar The rules and word-arranging systems that every human language employs to communicate meaning.

rules? (See Senghas & Coppola, 2001.) According to linguist Noam Chomsky, the reason is that our species is biologically programmed to make "language." We alone possess a language-generating capacity in our genetic code, which Chomsky named the **language acquisition device (LAD)**.

Chomsky developed his nature-oriented concept of a uniquely human LAD in reaction to the behaviorist B. F. Skinner's nurture-oriented proposition that we learn to speak through being reinforced for producing specific words (for instance, Skinner argued that we learn to say "I want cookie" by being rewarded for producing those particular sounds by getting a snack). This pronouncement was another example of the traditional behaviorist principle that "all actions are driven by reinforcement" run amok (see Chapter 1). It defies common sense that we learn to generate billions of new sentences by having other people reinforce us for every word!

Still, Skinner's nurture-oriented perspective on language learning is correct in one basic respect. I speak English instead of Mandarin Chinese because I grew up in New York City, not Beijing. So the way our genetic program for making language gets expressed depends totally on our environmental milieu. Once again, nature plus nurture work in tandem to explain every activity of life!

Developmentalists who adopt a **social-interactionist view** on this core human skill focus on the basic human motivations that propel language (Gleason, 2000; Bruner, 1984; Camaioni, 2001; Hoff-Ginsberg, 1997; Lock, 2001; Snow, 1999). Babies are passionate to communicate with the world. Adults are just as passionate to help babies learn to talk. How does the infant passion to communicate evolve?

Tracking Emerging Speech

The pathway to actually producing language occurs in defined stages. Out of the reflexive crying of the newborn period comes *cooing* (*oooh* sounds) at about month 4. At around month 6, delightful vocal circular reactions called **babbling** emerge. Babbles are alternating consonant and vowel sounds, such as "da da da," that infants playfully repeat with variations of intonation and pitch. Even at this stage the environment is shaping language. In one fascinating study conducted in France, adults who listened to tapes of 8-month-olds were able to pick out from babble sounds whether the baby babbler was French or Chinese (de Boysson-Bardies, Sagart, & Durand, 1984).

The first word emerges out of the babble at around 11 months, although that exact landmark is difficult to define. There is little more reinforcing to paternal pride than when your 8-month-old genius continually repeats your name. But when does "da da da" really refer to Dad? In the first, **holophrase** stage of true speech, one word, liberally accompanied by gestures, literally says it all. When your son says "ja" and points to the kitchen, you know he wants juice . . . or was it a jelly sandwich, or was he referring to his big sister Jane?

Children accumulate their first 50 or so words, centering on the important items in their world (people, toys, and food) slowly (Nelson, 1974). Then, typically between ages 1 1/2 and 2, there is a vocabulary explosion as the child begins to combine words. Because children pare communication down to its essentials, just like an old-style telegram ("Me juice"; "Mommy, no"), this first word-combining stage is called **telegraphic speech**. In Table 3.7, you can see a summary of these basic language landmarks, some examples, and the approximate time during infancy when each milestone occurs.

In the same way as we saw with infant cognition, there is a difference between knowing and acting. Children understand sentences far more complex than the ones they can produce. In one study, babies demonstrated that they knew the difference between the sentences "Where is Big Bird washing Cookie Monster?" and "Where is Cookie Monster washing Big Bird?" when they were only in the holophrase stage (Hirsh-Pasek & Golinkoff, 1991).

language acquisition device (LAD) Chomsky's term for a hypothetical brain structure that enables our species to learn and produce language.

social-interactionist view An approach to language development that emphasizes its social function, specifically that babies and adults have a mutual passion to communicate.

babbling The alternating vowel and consonant sounds that babies repeat with variations of intonation and pitch and that precede the first words.

holophrase First clear evidence of language, when babies use a single word to communicate a sentence or complete thought.

telegraphic speech First stage of combining words in infancy, in which a baby pares down a sentence to its essential words.

TABLE 3.7: Language Milestones from Birth to Age 2*

Age	Language Characteristic
2–4 months	**Cooing:** First sounds growing out of reflexes. *Example:* "oooo"
5–11 months	**Babbling:** Alternate vowel–consonant sounds. *Examples:* "ba-ba-ba," "da-da-da"
12 months	**Holophrases:** First one-word sentences. *Example:* "ja" ("I want juice.")
18 months–2 years	**Telegraphic speech:** Two-word combinations, often accompanied by an explosion in vocabulary. *Example:* "Me juice"

* Babies vary a good deal in the ages at which they begin to combine words.

infant-directed speech (IDS) The simplified, exaggerated, high-pitched tones that adults and children universally use to speak to infants as a way of teaching them language.

Just as they selectively tune in to faces, babies are selectively attuned to speech sounds that are directed toward them. Caregivers, just as interested in connecting to babies, speak to infants in characteristic ways (Hoff-Ginsberg, 1997).

Infant-directed speech (IDS) (what you and I call *baby talk*) has distinctive attributes. It uses simple words, exaggerated tones, elongated vowels, and occurs at a higher pitch than we would use in speaking to adults (Hoff-Ginsberg, 1997). Although it can sound ridiculous to adult ears ("Maaammy taaaaking baaaaby ooooout!" "Maaammy looooves baaaaby!"), it makes a difference in getting the baby's attention (Cooper & Aslin, 1990). So adults naturally use this communication mode with infants, just as we are compelled to pick up and rock a child when she cries.

Interestingly, this style of talking to babies may also be universal and built into our genetic code. In languages from Japanese (Matychuk, 2004) to Norwegian (Englund & Behne, 2005), adults adopt the identical intonations when they talk to infants. Older preschoolers also naturally adopt infant-directed speech when they talk to their toddler and baby siblings (Weppelman and others, 2003).

Do adults use infant-directed speech as a genuine teaching tool? To answer this question, researchers had an insight: "Let's compare the way mothers talk to their infants and to their pets." Mother-to-pet talk did show the same high pitch and exaggerated intonations of infant-directed speech. But it did not have the exaggerated vowels. So those *ooo* sounds that seem so silly are an attempt to train babies in language after all (Burnham, Kitamura, & Vollmer-Conna, 2002).

Does this attempt to teach language work? The answer, as one study showed, seems to be yes. Developmentalists presented babies with nonsense words (Thiessen, Hill, & Saffran, 2005). The infants heard the made-up words either in adult intonations or in infant-directed speech. When reinforced for showing that they heard the breaks between the nonsense words, the babies who heard the utterances spoken in

There is nothing like being able to have a real father-to-daughter discussion for the first time when your toddler begins to combine words. But what might infant-directed speech sound like delivered in Japanese?

Kayte M. Deioma / Photo Edit, Inc.

IDS performed better. Listen carefully to someone speaking to an infant in "baby talk." Doesn't this mode of communication seem tailor-made to emphasize exactly where one word ends and another begins?

TYING IT ALL TOGETHER

1. "We learn to speak by getting reinforced for saying what we want." "We are biologically programmed to learn language." "Babies are passionate to communicate." Identify the theoretical perspective reflected in each of these statements: Skinner's operant conditioning perspective; Chomsky's language acquisition device; a social-interactionist perspective on language.

2. Baby Ginny is 4 months old; Baby Harry is about 7 months old; Baby Sam is 1 year old; Baby David is 2 years old. Identify each child's probable language stage by choosing from the following items: babbling; cooing; telegraphic speech; holophrases.

3. A friend makes fun of adults who use baby talk when speaking to infants. Given the information in this section, is she right?

Answers to the Tying It All Together questions can be found in the answers section of the book.

❧ Final Thoughts: Babies "Connect" with the Human World

Have the studies in this chapter stimulated your interest in designing your own "out of the box" research to get into infants' heads? As developmentalists continue to use their brain power to design creative studies and our knowledge of neural function expands, what more will we know about babies' brains in the next 10 or 20 years?

Just as we come equipped with a passion to master life, one basic message of this chapter is that—from face perception to early language—we arrive on this planet with a strong impulse to connect with the human world. The next chapter focuses on this number-one infant (and adult) agenda by intensively exploring attachment relationships during our first two years of life. ▉

▌ SUMMARY

Setting the Context: Brain Blossoming and Sculpting

Because our uniquely large **cerebral cortex** develops mainly after birth, during the first two years of life the brain mushrooms. **Axons** elongate and develop a fatty cover called myelin. **Dendrites** sprout branches and at **synapses** link up with other cells. **Synaptogenesis** and **myelination** program every infant ability and human skill. Although cortical development continues for two decades, the brain does not simply "develop more synapses." Each brain center undergoes a period of rapid synaptogenesis, followed by gradual pruning (or cutting back). Before pruning occurs, the brain is particularly **plastic,** allowing us to compensate for early brain insults—but synaptogenesis and learning occur throughout life.

Basic Newborn States

Eating undergoes dramatic changes during infancy. We emerge from the womb with **sucking** and **rooting reflexes,** which jumpstart eating, as well as a set of other special birth **reflexes,** which disappear after the early months of life. Although the "everything into the mouth" phase of infancy can make life scary for caregivers, a 2-year-old's food caution can partially protect toddlers from poisoning themselves.

Because of its many health benefits, every public health organization advocates exclusive breast-feeding for the first six months of life—unless the mother has a serious disease. However, only a minority of women worldwide follow the recommendation. Upper-middle-class women in North America are more likely to breast-feed for longer. Low-income mothers (or any mothers) who must immediately return to work find it difficult to breast-feed. A South American country—Colombia—shows that, when cultures strongly support this practice, extended breast-feeding can become the norm.

After weaning, **undernutrition** is a serious concern in the developing world. Although global rates of **stunting** (height retardation due to chronic lack of adequate food) are declining, they still are alarmingly high. Because our country provides food-related entitlement programs—although very poor children may occasionally go hungry, or their parents may have to scrimp on food—in the United States undernutrition and stunting are virtually unknown.

Crying is at its height during early infancy and declines around month 4 as the cortex comes on-line. **Colic,** excessive crying that disappears after early infancy, is basically a digestive-system biological problem. Strategies for quieting crying babies include rocking, holding, **swaddling,** and providing an outlet for the urge to suck. Providing intense skin-to-skin contact through infant massage and **kangaroo care** not only helps quiet babies; these practices also help infants—especially at-risk premature babies—physically grow.

Sleep is the basic newborn state, and from the 18-hour, waking-every-few hours newborn pattern, babies gradually adjust to falling asleep at night. **REM sleep** lessens and shifts to the end of the cycle. Babies, however, really do not ever sleep through the night. At about 6 months, many learn **self-soothing,** putting themselves back to sleep when they wake up. Although there is controversy about whether to "let a baby cry it out" or respond to an infant, during late infancy self-soothing can be fostered by holding off immediately going into an infant's room. **Co-sleeping** (or bed sharing)—the norm in collectivist cultures—although still controversial, is more accepted in the West today.

Sudden infant death syndrome (SIDS)—when a young baby stops breathing, often at night, and dies—is a main cause of developed-world infant mortality. SIDS has environmental correlates, being more common in homes where adults smoke and when babies lie face down. It also may have biological causes. Rates of SIDS deaths have been reduced due to a public health effort urging parents to put babies to sleep on their backs (not stomachs).

Sensory and Motor Development

The **preferential-looking paradigm** (exploring what objects babies look at) and **habituation** (the fact that we get less interested in looking at objects that are no longer "new") are used to determine what very young babies can see. Although at birth visual acuity is poor, newborns possess rudimentary **size constancy. Face-perception studies** show that newborns look at facelike stimuli, recognize their mothers, and even prefer good-looking people from the first weeks of life. **Depth perception** studies using the **visual cliff** show that although they notice differences in depth at a very young age, babies only get frightened of heights around the time they begin to crawl.

Infants' bodies lengthen and thin out as they grow. The cephalocaudal, proximodistal, and mass-to-specific principles apply to how the body changes and emerging infant motor milestones. Although there is no relationship between early motor development and later cognitive abilities, habituation speed (signaling better memory for a stimulus) does correlate with later intelligence. Crawling is linked to widespread maturational changes, plus the need to **baby-proof** the home.

Cognition

During Piaget's **sensorimotor stage,** babies master the basics of physical reality through their senses and begin to symbolize and think. **Circular reactions** (habits the baby repeats) help babies pin down the basics of the physical world. **Primary circular reactions**—body-centered habits, such as sucking one's toes—emerge first. **Secondary circular reactions,** habits centered on making interesting external stimuli last (for example, batting mobiles), begin around month 4. **Tertiary circular reactions, "little-scientist"** activities—like spitting food at different velocities just to see where the oatmeal lands—are the hallmark of the toddler years. A major advance in reasoning that occurs around age 1 is **means–end behavior**—being able to do something new and different to get to a goal.

Piaget's most compelling concept is **object permanence**—knowing that objects still exist when you no longer see them. According to Piaget, this understanding develops gradually during the first years of life. When this knowledge is in the process of developing, infants make the **A-not-B error,** looking for an object in the place where they first found it, even if it has been hidden in another location before their eyes.

Using preferential looking, and watching babies' expressions of surprise at physically impossible events, researchers discovered that babies know more about physical reality at a younger age than Piaget believed. As Piaget's model of distinct qualitative stages also does not fit the continuous way knowledge unfolds, many developmentalists today adopt the **information-processing theory** approach of breaking cognition into steps and tracing how each cognitive ability gradually progresses.

Language: The Endpoint of Infancy

Language, specifically our use of **grammar** and our ability to form infinitely different sentences, sets us apart from any other animal on earth. Although B. F. Skinner believed that we learn to speak through being reinforced, the more logical explanation is Chomsky's idea that we have a biologically built-in **language acquisition device (LAD). Social-interactionists** focus on the mutual passion of babies and adults to communicate.

First, babies coo, then **babble,** then use one-word **holophrases,** and finally, at $1\frac{1}{2}$ or 2, progress to two-word combinations called **telegraphic speech.** Caregivers naturally use **infant-directed speech** (exaggerated intonations and simpler phrases) when they talk to babies. IDS helps teach infants to master this core human skill.

▌ KEY TERMS

cerebral cortex, p. 74

axon, p. 74

dendrite, p. 74

synapse, p. 74

synaptogenesis, p. 74

myelination, p. 74

plastic, p. 75

sucking reflex, p. 76

rooting reflex, p. 76

reflex, p. 76

undernutrition, p. 79

stunting, p. 79

colic, p. 81

swaddling, p. 81

kangaroo care, p. 82

REM sleep, p. 83

self-soothing, p. 84

co-sleeping, p. 85

sudden infant death syndrome (SIDS), p. 86

preferential-looking paradigm, p. 88

habituation, p. 88

size constancy, p. 89

face-perception studies, p. 89

depth perception, p. 90

visual cliff, p. 90

baby-proofing, p. 93

sensorimotor stage, p. 94

circular reactions, p. 94

primary circular reactions, p. 94

secondary circular reactions, p. 94

tertiary circular reactions, p. 95

little-scientist phase, p. 96

means–end behavior, p. 96

object permanence, p. 96

A-not-B error, p. 97

information-processing theory, p. 99

grammar, p. 100

language acquisition device (LAD), p. 101

social-interactionist view, p. 101

babbling, p. 101

holophrase, p. 101

telegraphic speech, p. 101

infant-directed speech (IDS), p. 102

▌ RECOMMENDED RESOURCES

GENERAL READING AND A HISTORICAL ACCOUNT

Bremner, G., and Fogel, A., eds. (2001). *Blackwell handbook of infant development.* Malden, MA: Blackwell Publishers.

This comprehensive overview of infant development is particularly useful for understanding vision, other senses, and motor development.

Fogel, A. (2001). *Infancy: Infant, family, and society.* Belmont, CA: Wadsworth.

This is a basic undergraduate text covering infancy month by month.

Preston, Samuel (1991). *Fatal years: Child mortality in late nineteenth-century America.* Princeton, NJ: Princeton University Press.

This book offers a fascinating glimpse into the U.S. past, citing statistics relating to child illnesses and infant mortality during the late nineteenth and early twentieth centuries.

BASIC STATES

Sameroff, A., Lewis, M., and Miller, S., eds. (2000). *Handbook of developmental psychopathology.* New York: Kluwer.

Chapters in this edited handbook offer comprehensive overviews of crying, sleep, and sleep disorders.

SENSORY AND MOTOR DEVELOPMENT

Simion, F., and Butterworth, G. (Eds.) (1998). *The development of sensory, motor, and cognitive capacities during early infancy: From perception to cognition.* Hove, England: Psychology Press/Erlbaum (UK), Taylor & Francis.

This edited academic book offers excellent coverage of face-perception research.

COGNITION

Baillargeon, R. (1993). The object concept revisited: New directions in the investigation of infants' physical knowledge. In Granrud (ed.), *Visual perception and cognition in infancy* (pp. 265–315). Mahwah, NJ: Erlbaum.

This researcher summarizes her decades of research on "impossible events," showing that babies know more than Piaget gave them credit for.

Flavell, J. (1963). *The developmental psychology of Jean Piaget.* New York: Van Nostrand.

This is the basic resource for summarizing Piaget's theory.

CHAPTER 4

Infancy: Socioemotional Development

Now that we've talked to Kim during pregnancy and paid her a visit when Elissa was a young baby, let's catch up with mother and daughter, almost a year later, now that Elissa is 15 months old.

Elissa had her first birthday in December. She's such a happy baby, but now if you take something away, it's like, "Why did you do that?" Pick her up. For a second everything is fine, and then her face changes and she squirms and her arms go out toward me. She's really busy walking, busy exploring, but she's got an eye on me all the time. The minute I make a motion to leave, she stops what she is doing and races near. I think Elissa has a stronger connection to her dad, because now that I'm working, Jeff has arranged his schedule to watch the baby late in the afternoon . . . but when she's tired or sick, it's still Mom.

At first, it was very difficult to go back to my job. I felt I was neglecting Elissa. Even though I've known the neighbor who keeps her for years, I was terrified. Will this person be taking good care of my little girl? I called about 10 times a day. It was tough on Elissa, too. For the first week she screamed when I left her off. But it's obvious that she's so happy now. Often when Jeff goes to get her, she doesn't want to leave.

It's bittersweet to see my baby separating from me, running into the world, becoming her own little person—with some very strong likes and dislikes. The clashes are becoming more frequent now that I'm turning up the discipline, expecting more in terms of behavior from my "big girl." But the main thing is that it's hard to be apart. I think about Elissa 50 million times during the day. I speed home to see her. I can't wait to see her glowing face in the window, how she jumps up and down, and we run to kiss and cuddle again.

Imagine being Kim, with your child the center of your life. Imagine being Elissa, wanting to be independent but vitally needing your mother close. In this chapter, we focus on **attachment,** the powerful bond of love between caregiver and child.

Our discussion of attachment—which takes up much of this chapter—starts a conversation that we will continue throughout this book. Attachment is the emotional basis both of infancy and of all of human life. After exploring this core one-to-one relationship, we turn outward to the wider world. We examine how that basic marker, socioeconomic status, affects young children's development; then spotlight day care, the setting where so many developed-world babies spend their days. The last section of this chapter focuses directly on **toddlerhood,** the famous time lasting roughly from age 1 to 2 1/2 years.

attachment The powerful bond of love between a caregiver and child (or between any two individuals).

toddlerhood The important transitional stage after babyhood, from roughly 1 year to 2 1/2 years of age; defined by an intense attachment to caregivers and by an urgent need to become independent.

Attachment: The Basic Life Bond

Perhaps you remember being intensely in love. You may be fortunate to be in that wonderful state right now. You cannot stop fantasizing about your beloved. Your moves blend with your partner's. You connect in a unique way. Knowing that this person is there gives you confidence. You can conquer the world. You feel uncomfortable and anxious when you are separated. Your world depends on having your lover close. Now you have some sense of how Elissa feels about her mother and the powerful reciprocal emotions from parent to child.

Setting the Context: How Developmentalists (Slowly) Got Attached to Attachment

During much of the twentieth century, most mainstream U.S. developmentalists seemed oddly indifferent to these intense feelings. In an era when psychology was dominated by behaviorist ideology, studying love, the province of poets, seemed way too unscientific. Behaviorists minimized our human need for attachment, suggesting that the reason babies wanted to be close to their mothers was because this "maternal reinforcing stimulus" provided food. Worse yet, you may remember from Chapter 1 that the early behaviorist John Watson seemed actively *hostile* to attachment when he crusaded against the dangers of "too much" mother love:

> When I hear a mother say "bless its little heart" when it falls down, I . . . have to walk a block or two to let off steam. . . . Can't she train herself to substitute a kindly word . . . for . . . the pick up . . . the coddling? . . . Can't she learn to keep away from the child a large part of the day? [And then he made this memorable statement:] . . . I sometimes wish that we could live in a community of homes [where] . . . we could have the babies fed and bathed each week by a different nurse.
>
> (Watson, 1928/1972, pp. 82–83)

European psychoanalysts, such as John Bowlby, had a different point of view. They were discovering that attachment was far from dangerous. It was the opposite of irrelevant to infant life.

Consider, for instance, a heart-rending 1948 film that showed the fate of babies living in the orphanages that dotted the mid-twentieth-century landscape (Blum, 2002; Karen, 1998). In these efficient, impeccably maintained institutions, Watson and the behaviorists would have predicted that infants should thrive. Why, then, did babies lie listless on cots—dejected, unable to eat, literally withering away?

Now consider the fact that ethologists—the forerunners of today's evolutionary psychologists—were observing that *every* species had a biologically preprogrammed attachment response (or drive to be physically close to their mothers) that came out at a specific point soon after birth. When the famous ethologist Konrad Lorenz (1935) arranged to become this attachment-eliciting stimulus for a set of goslings, the outcome was the classic photograph below. Lorenz became the adored Pied Piper the baby geese were willing to follow to the ends of the earth.

The adoring expressions on the faces of parents and babies as they gaze at each other make it obvious why the attachment relationship in infancy is our basic model for romantic love in adulthood.

Ethologist Konrad Lorenz arranged to become the first living thing that newly hatched geese saw at their species-specific critical time for attachment. He then became the goslings' "mother," the object whom they felt compelled never to let out of their sight.

Still, it took a maverick psychologist named Harry Harlow, who studied monkeys, to convince U.S. psychologists that the behavioral meal-dispenser model of mother love was false. In his classic research Harlow (1958) separated baby monkeys from their mothers at birth and raised them in a cage with a wire-mesh "mother" (which offered food from a milk bottle attached to its chest) and a cloth "mother" (which was soft and provided contact comfort). The babies stayed glued to the cloth mother, making occasional trips to eat from the wire mom. In stressful situations, they scurried to the cloth mother for comfort. Love had won hands down over getting fed!

In Harlow's landmark study, baby monkeys clung to the cloth-covered "mother" (which provided contact comfort) as they leaned over to feed from the wire-mesh "mother"—vividly refuting the behaviorist idea that infants become "attached" to the reinforcing stimulus that feeds them.

Harlow Primate Laboratory, University of Wisconsin

Moreover, as Harlow's research team powerfully documented, there were serious psychological consequences when monkeys were raised without their mothers. The animals rocked in their cages. They couldn't have sex. They were frightened of their peers. Furthermore, there was an intergenerational effect. After being artificially inseminated and giving birth, the "motherless mothers" were uncaring, abusive parents. One mauled her baby so badly that it later died (Harlow and others, 1966; Harlow, C. M., 1986).

Then, in the late 1960s, John Bowlby put all of the evidence together—the orphanage findings, Lorenz's ethological studies, Harlow's research, his own clinical work with children who had been hospitalized or separated from their mothers (Fonagy, 2001; Hinde, 2005). In a pathbreaking series of books, Bowlby (1969, 1973, 1980) argued that there is no such thing as "excessive mother love." Having a loving **primary attachment figure** is crucial to normal development. It is crucial to living fully at any age. By the final decades of the twentieth century, attachment moved to the front burner in developmental science. It remains front and center today.

primary attachment figure The closest person in a child's or adult's life.

Exploring the Attachment Response

Bowlby (1969, 1973) made his case for the crucial importance of attachment on evolutionary grounds. He believed that, like every other species, human beings have a critical period when the attachment response "comes out." As in other species, he argued, attachment is biologically built into our genetic code to allow us to survive. Although the attachment response is programmed to emerge full force during our first years of life, **proximity-seeking behavior**—our need to make contact with an attachment figure—is activated whenever our survival is threatened at *any age*.

Threats to survival, according to Bowlby, come in two categories. They may be activated by disruptions in our internal state. When Elissa clings only to her mother, Kim knows her baby must be ill or tired. When you go to the hospital, you make sure that your family is by your side. You want to know that your "significant other" is easily reachable by cell phone when you have a fever or the flu.

Threats to survival may also be evoked by dangers in the external world. As children, it's a huge dog at the park or a nightmare that propels an anxious trip to our mother's or father's arms. As adults, it's a professor's nasty comment or a humiliating experience at work that may provoke a frantic call to our primary attachment figure, be it our spouse, our parents, or our best friend. (I got insights into the lifelong power of mothers to comfort us in times of trouble when I worked as a clinical psychologist in a nursing home. Rather than calling for their husbands, the elderly women wailed "Mama, Mama" when they were anxious or in pain.)

proximity-seeking behavior Acting to maintain physical contact or to be close to an attachment figure.

A baby's first social smile, which appears at the sight of any face at about 2 to 3 months of age, is biologically programmed to delight adults and charm them into providing love and care.

preattachment phase The first phase of John Bowlby's developmental attachment sequence, during the first three months of life, when infants show no visible signs of attachment.

social smile The first real smile, occurring at about 2 months of age.

attachment in the making The second phase of John Bowlby's developmental attachment sequence, lasting from about 4 to 7 months of age, when infants show a slight preference for their primary caregiver.

clear-cut attachment The critical period for human attachment, lasting from roughly 7 months of age through toddlerhood, characterized by separation anxiety, the need to have a caregiver physically close, and stranger anxiety.

separation anxiety The main signal of clear-cut attachment at about 7 months of age, when a baby gets visibly upset by a primary caregiver's departure.

Although we all need to touch base with our significant others when we feel threatened, adults and older children can be separated from their attachment figures for some length of time. During our first years of life, simply being physically apart from a caregiver elicits distress. Now, let's trace step-by-step how human attachment unfolds.

Attachment Milestones

According to Bowlby, during their first three months of life babies are in what he called the **preattachment phase.** Remember that during this reflex-dominated time infants have yet to really wake up to the world. However, around 2 months of age there is an important milestone called the **social smile.** Bowlby believed that this first real smile does not show true attachment to *a* person. Because it automatically pops up in response to any human face, it is just one example of a variety of reflexive behaviors, such as looking at faces, that biologically program babies to obtain love and care from adults.

Still, a baby's eagerly awaited first smile can be a transforming experience if you are a parent. Suddenly, your relationship with your child is on a different plane. At this point, I have a confession to make: During my first two months as a new mother, I was worried, as I did not feel anything for this beautiful child I had waited so long to adopt. I date Thomas's first endearing smile as the defining event in my lifelong attachment romance.

At roughly 4 months of age infants enter a transitional period, which Bowlby called **attachment in the making.** By now, the environment-focused secondary circular reactions are emerging. The cortex is coming fully on-line. Babies may show a slight preference for their primary caregiver. But still, an outgoing 4- or 5-month-old can be the ultimate party person, happy to be cuddled by anyone—Grandma, a next-door neighbor, or a stranger at the mall.

At around 7 or 8 months of age, all this changes. By this time, infants are hunting for hidden objects—showing that they have the cognitive skills to really miss their caregivers. They also have the motor skills to physically move away. Now that they can crawl, or walk holding on to furniture, children can really get hurt. The stage is set for the crucial event called **clear-cut** (or *focused*) **attachment**—the onset of the full-blown attachment response. This phase of intense attachment will last throughout the toddler years.

Separation anxiety signals this milestone. When Elissa was about 7 or 8 months old, Kim probably noticed one day that her baby got upset when she left the room. Soon afterward, children develop **stranger anxiety.** As you saw in the chapter-opening vignette, infants get agitated when any other person picks them up. So, as children travel toward their first birthday, the universal friendliness of early infancy is a thing of the past. While they may still joyously gurgle at the world from their caregiver's arms, babies forbid any "stranger"—the next-door neighbor or even Grandma when she flies in from out of town—to closely invade their space.

A few months ago, this child would probably not have objected to being held by his family's next-door neighbor; but everything changes at 7 or 8 months of age, during the phase of clear-cut attachment, when stranger anxiety emerges.

Between ages 1 and 2, the distress reaches a peak. Leaving a toddler with a babysitter can be torture. Particularly in unfamiliar situations, the child may cling and cry when a parent makes a motion to leave. It's almost as if an invisible string connects the caregiver and the child. In a park in England, one classic study showed, 1-year-olds tended to play within a certain distance of their mothers. Interestingly, this zone of optimum comfort (about 200 feet) was identical for both the parent and the child (Anderson, 1972).

To see these changes in action, pick up a young baby (such as a 4-month-old) and an older infant (perhaps a baby about 10 months of age) and compare their reactions. Then observe 1-year-olds at a local park. Can you measure this attachment zone of comfort? Do you notice the busily exploring toddlers periodically checking back to make sure a caregiver is still there?

Social referencing is the term developmentalists use to describe this checking-back behavior. As you saw in our discussion of newly crawling babies in Chapter 3, social referencing helps alert the baby to which situations are dangerous and which ones are safe ("Should I climb up this slide, Mommy?" "Does Daddy think this object is OK to explore?"). Therefore, it should come as no surprise that babies reference their caregivers most frequently when they aren't sure whether a given situation is harmful and that, when this person seems distracted, toddlers reference another watching adult. When they notice their parent absorbed in a conversation, 1-year-olds explore less freely (Stenberg, 2003).

This makes good real-world sense. Notice at the mall that when you see a toddler gleefully running away from a caregiver, that adult is often watching closely and in hot pursuit on the baby's heels.

Social referencing demands some complicated interpersonal skills. Babies must be able to pick up on whether the expression on an adult's face or the sound of her voice means encouragement or alarm. They must figure out whether the cues they are getting from the person they are referencing are directed specifically to them.

When do babies have the mental ability to decode whether the messages other people are conveying refer to them? To answer this question—central to making sense of the signals we get from the human world—developmentalists devised a creative experiment (Moses and others, 2001). They had an adult make a negative exclamation, such as "Oh, no!" while the child was walking over to explore a toy. In one condition, the person was clearly watching the baby. In others, the adult was behind a screen or was in the room but examining another object.

By 18 months of age, babies stopped approaching the toy only when the adult was looking at them. This suggests that we begin to develop the ability to "get into another person's head," or decode other people's intentions, sometime between ages 1 and 1½. (We'll be tracing this unfolding capacity to make sense of others' minds in the next chapter.)

Returning to attachment, at what age does this need to be physically close to a caregiver lessen in strength or go away? Although the marker is hazy, children typically leave the phase of clear-cut attachment at about age 3. They still care just as much about their primary attachment figure. But now, according to Bowlby, they have the cognitive skills to carry a **working model**, or internal representation, of this number-one person in their minds (Bretherton, 2005).

The bottom-line message is that the human critical period for attachment is timed to unfold during our most vulnerable time of life. It occurs when children are first really moving into the world and are most in danger of getting hurt. What compensates

Toddlers love to run away from their parents—as long as they can be sure that Mom and Dad are right behind them.

stranger anxiety A signal of the onset of clear-cut attachment at about 7 months of age, when a baby becomes wary of unfamiliar people and refuses to be held by anyone other than a primary caregiver.

social referencing A baby's practice of checking back and monitoring a caregiver's expressions for cues as to how to behave in potentially dangerous exploration situations; linked to the onset of crawling and clear-cut attachment.

working model According to Bowlby's theory, the mental representation of a caregiver that allows children beyond age 3 to be physically apart from a primary caregiver and predicts their behavior in relationships.

This 4-year-old boy has entered the working-model phase of attachment, so he is able to say good-bye to his mother with only slight feelings of anxiety at the door of his preschool.

A toddler's messiness is easy for a grandfather to tolerate when she looks up at him with love—showing why the attachment response overshadows everything else during Piaget's "little scientist" stage.

Mike Brinson / Getty Images

parents for the frustrations of having a Piagetian "little scientist" are enormous gratifications. At the same age when a toddler is continually messing up the house and saying "No!", parents know their child's world revolves totally around them.

Do children differ in the way they express this priceless sense of connection? And if so, what might these differences mean about the quality of the infant–parent bond?

Attachment Styles

These were the questions Mary Ainsworth set out to answer when she developed a classic test of attachment—the **Strange Situation** (Ainsworth, 1967; Ainsworth and others, 1978).

The Strange Situation procedure begins when a caregiver—typically the mother—and a 1-year-old enter a room full of toys. After the child is given time to explore, an unfamiliar adult enters the room. After a brief conversation, the mother leaves, and the baby is alone with the stranger. A few minutes later, the mother returns to comfort the child. Then, the mother leaves the baby totally alone for a minute; the stranger enters; and then the parent returns (see Figure 4.1). By observing the child's reactions to these increasingly stressful separations and reunions through a one-way mirror, developmentalists categorize infants as either *securely* or *insecurely attached.*

Securely attached children use their mother as a secure base, or anchor, to confidently venture out to explore the toys. When she leaves, they may or may not become highly distressed. Most important, however, when she returns, their eyes light up with joy. As with Elissa when Kim comes home, their close relationship is apparent in the way they run and melt into their mother's arms. **Insecurely attached** children react in the following three ways (see Figure 4.2):

- Infants classified as **avoidant** seem excessively detached. They rarely show signs of separation anxiety. Most important, they show little feeling—positive or negative—when their primary attachment figure returns. They seem wooden, unreactive, without much sense of attachment at all.

- Babies with an **anxious-ambivalent attachment** are at the opposite end of the spectrum—clingy, overly nervous, too frightened to freely explore the toys. Terribly distressed by their mother's departure, these infants may show contradictory emotions when she returns—clinging and striking out in anger. Often they are inconsolable, unable to be effectively comforted when their attachment figure comes back.

- Children showing a **disorganized attachment** behave in a bizarre manner. In this worst-case scenario, the child freezes, runs around erratically, or may look frightened and try to flee when the caregiver returns. As you might imagine, babies who

Strange Situation A procedure developed by Mary Ainsworth to measure variations in attachment security at age 1, involving a series of planned separations and reunions with a primary caregiver.

secure attachment The ideal attachment response, when a 1-year-old child responds with joy at being reunited with the primary caregiver in the Strange Situation.

insecure attachment A deviation from the normally joyful response to being reunited with the primary caregiver in the Strange Situation, signaling a problem in the caregiver–child relationship.

avoidant attachment An insecure attachment style characterized by a child's indifference to the primary caregiver when they are reunited in the Strange Situation.

anxious-ambivalent attachment An insecure attachment style characterized by a child's intense distress at separation and by anger and great difficulty being soothed when reunited with the primary caregiver in the Strange Situation.

disorganized attachment An insecure attachment style characterized by responses such as freezing or fear when a child is reunited with the primary caregiver in the Strange Situation.

FIGURE 4.1: **The Strange Situation:** These scenes are from the original Strange Situation study. At left, the baby cries frantically after the mother and the stranger have left the room. At right, the baby is reunited with the mother as the stranger looks on.

Separation

Reunion
Both photos: Mary D. Ainsworth

Secure Attachment
The child is thrilled to see the mother.

Avoidant Attachment
The child is unresponsive to the mother.

Anxious-Ambivalent Attachment
The child cannot be calmed by the mother.

Disorganized Attachment
The child looks frightened by the mother or behaves bizarrely.

have been abused are more likely to show this most "at-risk" type of attachment (Finzi and others, 2000; George & Main, 1979; Lyons-Ruth & Jacobvitz, 1999). Infants in foster care—when they do display insecure attachments—show a disproportionate number of disorganized responses (Cole, 2005).

Developmentalists are careful to point out that insecure attachments (shown in Figure 4.2) do not signal a weakness in the *underlying* sense of connection. Avoidant infants are just as bonded to their caregivers as babies ranked secure. Anxious-ambivalent infants are not more closely attached, even though they show such intense separation distress. To take an analogy from adult life, when a person who cares deeply about you pretends to be indifferent, is this individual less in love than someone who freely expresses her feelings? Is a lover who can't let his partner out of sight more attached than a person who allows his significant other to have an independent life? Although its outward expression differs, *every* infant is closely attached.

The Attachment Dance

Look at a baby and a caregiver together and it is almost as if you are seeing a dance. The partners tune in to each other's signals. They know when to come on stronger and when to back off. They are absorbed and captivated, oblivious to the world. This blissful **synchrony** (Bornstein & Tamis-LeMonda, 2001), which starts to unfold when babies begin to respond emotionally to their caregivers at about 2 or 3 months of age (Lavelli & Fogel, 2005), is what makes the infant–mother relationship our ultimate model for romantic love. Ainsworth and Bowlby believed that the parent's "dancing potential," or sensitivity to a baby's signals, produces secure attachments (Ainsworth and others, 1978). Were they correct?

THE CAREGIVER Decades of studies suggest that the answer is a qualified yes. Sensitive caregivers tend to have babies who are securely attached. Parents who are overly intrusive or misread their baby's signals and, especially, mothers who are depressed, are prone to have infants ranked insecure (Bakermans-Kranenburg, van IJzendoorn, &

synchrony The reciprocal aspect of the attachment relationship, with a caregiver and infant responding emotionally to each other in a sensitive, exquisitely attuned way.

The blissful rapture, the sense of being totally engrossed and in tune with each other, is the reason why developmentalists use the word *synchrony* to describe parent–infant attachment.

[FAQ: What causes different attachment styles to develop?]

Kroonenberg, 2004; Karen, 1998; Main, Hesse, & Kaplan, 2005; Sroufe, 2000; Weinfield and others, 1999). As the prime characteristic of being a sensitive dancer is reaching out to your baby's needs, it makes perfect sense that depression is particularly hazardous to emotional development and the parent–child dance (Dix and others, 2004; Raikes & Thompson, 2006).

Still, there clearly are other forces involved in attachment, as the correlations between caregiver sensitivity and child security are only moderate to weak (Moss and others, 2005; Thompson, 1999; van IJzendoorn & Sagi, 1999; Weinfield and others, 1999). Some highly sensitive mothers have children who rank as insecurely attached. Some intrusive, poorly dancing parents have securely attached daughters and sons. The main reason, as you may have guessed, is that there are *two* partners in the dance.

temperament A person's characteristic, inborn style of dealing with the world.

THE CHILD Listen to any mother comparing her babies ("Sara was fussy; Matthew is much easier to soothe") and you will realize that not all infants are born with the same dancing talent. Specifically, babies differ in their **temperament**—meaning their characteristic, inborn behavioral styles of approaching the world.

[FAQ: What is temperament?]

In a pioneering study, developmentalists classified a group of middle-class babies into three temperamental styles: *Easy* babies—the majority of the children—had rhythmic eating and sleep patterns, were generally positive, and were easily soothed. More wary babies were labeled *slow to warm up*. The researchers classified 1 in 10 babies as *difficult*—hypersensitive, unusually agitated, extremely reactive to every sight and sound (Thomas & Chess, 1977; Thomas, Chess, & Birch, 1968): Here is an example:

> *My 5-month-old wakes up screaming from every nap. Everything seems to bother her—bright sunlight, a rough blanket, any sudden noise. I thought colic was supposed to go away by month 3. I'm getting discouraged and depressed.*

[FAQ: Does temperament influence attachment styles?]

Now look back at the stressful experiences a baby must go through during the Strange Situation. Do you see why some developmentalists have argued that it is biologically based differences in temperamental "reactivity"—not the quality of a mother's caregiving—that determine attachment status at age 1? (See, for example, Kagan, 1984.)

Does a baby's biology (nature) or poor caregiving (nurture) produce insecure attachments? As you might imagine—given the nature-plus-nurture message of this book—the answer is, a little of both (Kochanska, 1998; Rothbart & Bates, 1998). To explore this interaction, researchers engineered a highly stressful event to younger infants. They had the mothers of a group of 4-month-old babies suddenly develop a distant, frozen expression on their faces as they were interacting with their children (see Figure 4.3). Then they rated each baby's distress from minimally to maximally agitated and coded how sensitive each particular mother was at soothing the baby. Finally, they evaluated attachment security months later, at age 1.

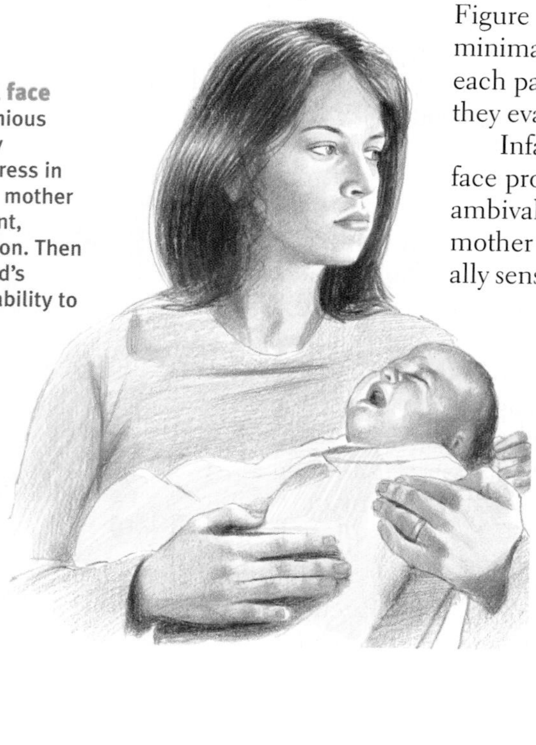

FIGURE 4.3: **The still face procedure:** In this ingenious technique, developed by researchers to elicit distress in 4-month-old babies, the mother suddenly adopts a distant, immobile facial expression. Then researchers rate the child's upset and the mother's ability to soothe her baby.

Infants who cried most frantically during this "still face procedure" were more prone to be labeled anxious-ambivalent in the Strange Situation. However, if a mother with an irritable 4-month-old was rated as unusually sensitive, her nervous baby was more likely to be later categorized as secure (Braungart-Rieker and others, 2001). So an exceptionally sensitive mother can shift her temperamentally at-risk baby from being insecure to secure.

But with the most biologically vulnerable infants, there is a limit to how much parenting can achieve (Kochanska & Coy, 2002). Suppose a child was extremely premature or had some serious disease. Would it be fair to label the baby's attachment issues as the mother's fault?

Moreover, because "it takes two to tango" (that is, the dance is bidirectional), a child's temperament affects the caregiver's sensitivity, too. To use an analogy from real-life dancing, imagine waltzing with a partner who couldn't keep time with the music; or think of a time when you tried to soothe a person who was too agitated to connect. Even a prize-winning dancer or someone with world-class relationship skills would feel incompetent and inept.

THE CAREGIVER'S OTHER ATTACHMENTS

And, to continue the analogy, it takes more than two to tango. Just as a woman's attitudes about being pregnant depend on feeling supported by the wider world (recall Chapter 2), it is difficult to be a sensitive caregiver if your other attachment relationships are not working out. When mothers are unhappily married, for instance, their babies are more likely to be rated as insecurely attached (Crnic, Greenberg, & Slough, 1986; Durrett, Otaki, & Richards, 1984; Moss and others, 2005.)

FIGURE 4.4: Three pathways to insecure attachment

Above left: The mother is too depressed to connect.

Above right: The child has temperamental vulnerabilities.

Left: The caregiver's other attachment relationships make it difficult to "dance" with her baby.

Figure 4.4, spelling out how the caregiver, the baby, and the parent's other relationships interact to shape attachment, illustrates the importance of adopting a developmental systems approach (Belsky, 2005). The quality of the dance of attachment is shaped by many different forces. By assuming that problems were due simply to the parent's personality, Bowlby and Ainsworth were taking an excessively limited view. What about the general theory? Is attachment to a primary caregiver universal? Do infants in different countries fall into the same categories of secure and insecure?

Cultural Variations in Attachment

From Chicago to Capetown, from Naples to New York, Bowlby's and Ainsworth's ideas about attachment get high marks (van IJzendoorn & Sagi, 1999). Babies around the world do get attached to a primary caregiver at roughly the same age. Interestingly, as you can see in Figure 4.5, the percentages of infants ranked secure in different countries are remarkably similar—clustering at roughly 60 to 70 percent (Sroufe, 2000; Tomlinson, Cooper, & Murray, 2005; van IJzendoorn & Sagi, 1999; Weinfeld and others, 1998).

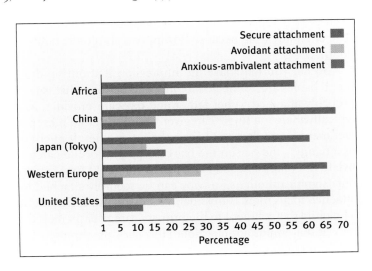

FIGURE 4.5: Snapshots of attachment security (and insecurity) around the world: Around the world, roughly 60 to 70 percent of 1-year-olds are classified as securely attached—although there are interesting differences in the percentages of babies falling into the different insecure categories.

Source: van IJzendoorn & Sagi (1999), p. 729.

This new member of the Efé people of central Africa will be lovingly cared for by the whole community, males as well as females, from his first minutes of life. Because he sleeps with his mother, however, at the "right" age he will develop his primary attachment to her.

Courtesy of Gilda Morelli

The most amazing validation of the universal quality of attachment comes from the Efé, a close-knit, communal hunter-gatherer people living in Africa. Efé newborns freely nurse from any available lactating woman even when their own parent is around. They are dressed, bathed, and cared for by the whole community. But Efé babies still develop a primary attachment to their mothers at the typical age! (See van IJzendoorn & Sagi, 1999.)

Efé infants are the opposite of institutionally reared infants. They live awash in continual attention and unconditional love. Moreover, they sleep cuddled next to their mothers at night. This nighttime sleeping difference, some developmentalists believe, is what may set these babies apart from another, even more unusual community-reared population: infants growing up on a traditional kibbutz (Sagi-Schwartz & Aviezer, 2005; van IJzendoorn & Sagi, 1999).

The kibbutz system was established by Jewish refugees emigrating to Israel in the early and mid-twentieth century. Traumatized by the persecution they had experienced in Europe, and dreaming of a utopian society where human beings would learn to cooperate from the cradle, they decided to found a community where the first lesson children learned from infancy would be to connect with the group.

In the traditional kibbutz, a few months after birth babies entered a "child house," where, under the care of a housemother, they spent the day, ate, and often slept. (The children, however, spent time alone with their parents during a few evening hours.) Interestingly, kibbutz infants did develop a connection to a primary attachment figure, either a parent or the housemother, at the appropriate age—but half of those attachments were ranked insecure (Sagi-Schwartz & Aviezer, 2005; Van IJzendoorn & Sagi, 1999).

However, there were some kibbutz 1-year-olds who lived in the child house during the day but slept in their parents' house. Would their attachment relationships be different?

The fascinating answer, as it turned out, was yes. Developmentalists found that 80 percent of the home-sleeping kibbutz babies were ranked securely attached (Sagi and others, 1994). All of this suggests that being able to sleep near a parent and be comforted during the nighttime hours may be a crucial force in cementing the attachment bond (Sagi-Schwartz & Aviezer, 2005). This makes good sense. What could be more security-promoting than having your attachment figure on the scene when you feel at your most vulnerable, if you wake up with a nightmare or terrified of the dark?

As a final footnote, you might be interested to know that the communal child-sleeping arrangement of the traditional kibbutz has not survived. Children vitally need their parents. Parents vitally need their children close. People abandoned this style of childrearing because Bowlby was absolutely right (Aviezer, Sagi, & van IJzendoorn, 2002).

So far, you may have the impression that during the phase of clear-cut attachment, babies are connected to only one person. That isn't necessarily true. Elissa was probably attached to her father and day-care provider, as well as to Kim. However, typically there is a single caregiver whom the child most prefers. This number-one attachment figure does *not* have to be the mother. It might be Grandma, or the father, or a nanny—the person the baby sleeps with or the caregiver who seems most attentive to the infant's needs. And, just as you and I may connect differently with each of our "significant others," a baby can be securely attached to his father and insecurely attached to his mom (Grossmann, Grossmann, & Zimmermann, 1999; Howes, 1999). The child's attachment to the primary caregiver predicts development best. Now let's look at that important question: How *does* attachment relate to the way children develop and behave?

Does Infant Attachment Predict Success in the Wider World?

Bowlby's core argument, when he developed his concept of the working model, is that our attachment relationships in infancy serve as an inner template that determines how we relate in the wider world (Bretherton, 2005). A baby who acts avoidant with his parents will be aloof and uncaring with friends. He may be cool and dismissing with a teacher's demands. An anxious-ambivalent infant will behave in a needy way in her other love relationships. A secure baby is set up to succeed socially.

In general, Bowlby's argument is supported by the research. From having superior peer relationships (Schmidt, DeMulder, & Denham, 2002; NICHD Early Child Care Research Network, 2006: Thompson, 1999) to showing early signs of conscience (Kochanska & Murray, 2000; Kochanska and others, 2004; Laible & Thompson, 2000, 2002), in every culture (Stams, Juffer, & van IJzendoorn, 2002; van IJzendoorn & Sagi, 1999), babies rated as securely attached do well in a variety of emotional and social areas of life.

Still, we cannot get away from the fact that these studies are all correlational. And simply observing a relationship between two variables does not prove that one *causes* the other one. Given that these forces also predict attachment security, wouldn't it be possible that having an easy, mellow temperament, or growing up with happily married parents, is what causes children to become socially skilled?

And there is another caution. The link between infant attachment security and how a child behaves in other areas of life is strongest when we study behavior over a short timeframe (DeMulder and others, 2000). As we get further away from the testing date, predictions are less reliable (Sroufe and others, 2005; Youngblade & Belsky, 1992). So, yes, you can get insights into how your 1-year-old nephew will probably act in preschool or day care from seeing how he relates to his mom and dad. However, you are on shakier ground if you want to extend that crystal ball much further into his future life.

One obvious reason is that our working model may be subject to revision over time as our dance with our parents changes. When families are under stress, for instance, during a divorce (Moss and others, 2005), or even when a child's beautiful attachment relationship is disrupted by the birth of a baby brother or sister (Teti and others, 1996), attachment security tends to change for the worse. How much does attachment really change as children travel from infancy to adult life?

Does Infant Attachment Predict Adult Relationships?

Imagine your challenge as a researcher who wanted to study attachment security from infancy to adulthood—the time and expense involved in testing babies individually in the Strange Situation and then following families for decades as well as the need to develop new age-appropriate measures of attachment as the children grow up. Luckily, we do have a few of these ambitious longitudinal, infant-to-adult studies (Grossmann, Grossmann, & Kindler, 2005; Hamilton, 2000; Sagi-Schwartz & Aviezer, 2005; Waters and others, 2000). Let's look now at the longest-running, most comprehensive investigation, still being carried out with a "high-risk" group of children, and explore the lessons it offers us about love and life.

In the early 1970s, a University of Minnesota research team recruited a large group of low-income women during their pregnancies (Sroufe, 2002; Sroufe and others, 2002, 2005; Weinfield and others, 1999). Then they regularly tracked the lives of these impoverished, often single, mothers and their babies for almost 30 years. By age 19, 90 percent of the children had experienced at least one very disruptive attachment-related event—from parental drug or alcohol problems to neglect, abuse, or serious maternal depression—at some point during their childhood years.

In Harlow's experiments, female monkeys that had been raised in isolation did not know what to do with their babies, ignoring or even attacking them. However, if an infant kept clinging to its mother and nuzzling her, there was a reasonable chance that it could teach its mother how to respond with love.

Harlow Primate Laboratory, University of Wisconsin

[FAQ: How much does early attachment influence adult relationships?]

Although the majority of the 1-year-olds were initially rated as securely attached, these stresses took their toll. By age 19 the fraction of children labeled secure slid down to 1 in 3. Moreover, as you might imagine, children who had undergone the most intense family stress were most likely to have become insecure (Weinfield, Sroufe, & Egeland, 2000).

As an example, let's look at the life of a child named Tony, whom the researchers ranked as securely attached during infancy. In preschool and early elementary school, Tony, like many other securely attached children in the study, was relating well at school and to his peers. Then, as Tony was approaching adolescence, his parents had a difficult divorce, and his mother began to rely on her son as the man of the house.

When Tony was 14, tragedy struck again: Tony's mother was killed in a car accident. To compound his loss, Tony's father moved to another state, taking the other two children and leaving Tony with an aunt. It should come as no surprise that Tony, robbed of every attachment figure, got into serious trouble in school and at home as a teenager. Angry and depressed, throughout this time Tony was rated as insecurely attached. But when Tony was recently retested at age 26, he seemed to be recouping. He met a loving woman and got married. He was a loving father and a happy man. Tony's attachment status is still classified as avoidant/insecure, but he's on the path to becoming more secure (Sroufe and others, 2005).

So the most blissful infancy cannot inoculate us against unhappy experiences—and attachment insecurity—later on. The good news is that, provided their deprivation is not too long-lasting (O'Connor and others, 2000), children can also move in the opposite direction, becoming secure after facing terrible traumas during their first years of life (Sagi-Schwartz, 2003; Sroufe and others, 2005). Perhaps you have a friend whose family fled the fighting in Rwanda or Kosovo, or know someone who spent her first years of life in an orphanage in Romania, who is succeeding socially as a young adult.

For an ultimate good-news story, let's return to Harlow's monkeys, who faced the most severe attachment deprivation—growing up with no mother at all. In an effort to bring these animals back into the social world, Harlow's research team put young monkeys into a cage with the traumatized animals. (Older animals routinely rejected their socially clueless age-mates). After spending a few months being nuzzled and played with by their young "therapists," the motherless monkeys stopped huddling in corners. They were playing just like their peers. The motherless monkeys could even be taught mother love. When a baby hung in there and clung to an uncaring mother, the infant often brought the parent emotionally back to life! (See C. M. Harlow, 1986.)

Wrapping Up Attachment

The bottom-line message is that early life is more of a sensitive period (or zone of special sensitivity) for attachments than a make-or-break time when inadequate mothering leaves permanent scars. And, while it does provide us with a beautiful beginning, being securely attached in infancy is no guarantee of staying secure throughout life. Finally, when we see insecure attachments we should beware of automatically blaming the mother. The quality of the attachment dance depends on a variety of forces, from the baby's temperament to the mother's other life dances. Now we directly explore two other crucial influences that can potentially affect the quality of a baby's attachment relationships and everything else: poverty and day care.

TYING IT ALL TOGETHER

1. List an example or two of "proximity seeking in distress" in your own life within the past few months.

2. Baby Muriel is 1 month old, Baby Janine is 5 months old, and Baby Ted is 1 year old. List each infant's phase of attachment.

3. Match each of these terms to the correct definition: (1) social referencing; (2) working model; (3) synchrony; (4) Strange Situation.

   a. A researcher measures a child's attachment at age 1 in a series of separations and reunions with the mother.
   b. A toddler keeps looking back at the parent while exploring at a playground.
   c. An elementary school child keeps an image of her parent in mind to calm herself when she gets on the school bus in the morning.
   d. A mother and baby relate to each other as if they are totally in tune.

4. Your cousin is the primary caregiver of her 1-year-old son. On a recent visit to her house, you notice that the baby shows no emotion when his mother leaves the room, and—more important—seems totally indifferent when she returns. How might you classify this child's attachment?

   a. The baby has an avoidant attachment.
   b. The baby has an anxious-ambivalent attachment.
   c. The baby has a secure attachment.

5. Manuel is arguing for the validity of attachment theory as spelled out by Bowlby and Ainsworth. Which argument should Manuel *not* make (that is, which alternative is false)?

   a. Infants around the world get attached to a primary caregiver at roughly the same age.
   b. An infant's attachment security predicts the quality of that child's relationships in preschool.
   c. A child's attachment status as of age 1 never changes.

Answers to the Tying It All Together questions can be found in the answers section of the book.

Contexts of Infant Development

What happens to children in the United States, such as those in the University of Minnesota study, who spend their first years of life in poverty? And what about that crucial wider-world setting of early childhood—day care?

The Impact of Poverty

In Chapter 3, we examined the physical effects of extreme poverty—the alarming rates of stunting in many regions of the developing world. In the United States, you may remember, the kind of wrenching poverty that causes undernutrition is virtually unknown. Still, being poor during early childhood can seriously compromise a person's developing life. What fraction of American infants and toddlers live in poverty? How do child poverty rates in the United States compare with those in other developed countries?

The Prevalence of Poverty

The federal government defines the poverty line as an income level that allows a household to pay for shelter, clothing, and food, with a small bit of money left for extras. In 2005, for instance, a U.S. family of four with an annual income of $19,350 or less qualified as living under the poverty line. (If you estimate how much it *really* costs for a family to satisfy their basic needs in your community, you may understand why many social policy experts argue that these cutoff figures are gross underestimates—minimizing the amount of money it really takes to live.)

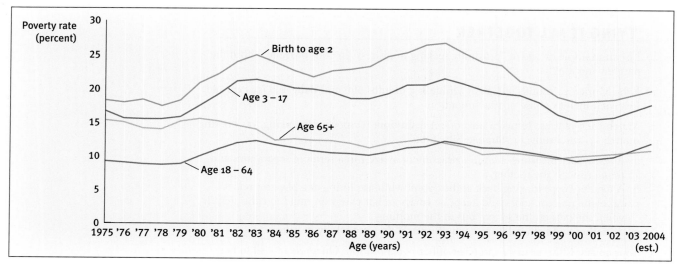

FIGURE 4.6: **Poverty rates by age, 1975 to 2004:** Very young children are more likely to be poor than almost any other age group in the United States. (The rates for women over age 75, although not shown on the chart, are higher.)

Source: National Center for Children and Poverty, (2002); www.nccp.org.

[FAQ: How does socioeconomic status (SES) affect development?]

FIGURE 4.7: **Poverty among children under age 6 in selected countries, 1990s:** The United States has the highest child poverty rates in the developed world.

Source: Shonkoff & Phillips (2000a), p. 277.

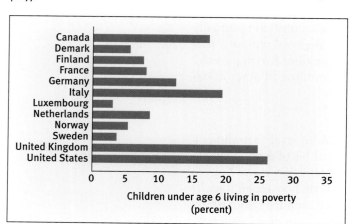

As of 2003, roughly one out of every five U.S. children under age 3 was living in poverty (National Center for Children in Poverty [NCCP], 2005). Moreover, as Figure 4.6 shows, infants and toddlers consistently have higher poverty rates than all other age groups in the United States (except women over age 75) (NCCP, 2002).

A primary reason has to do with the huge number of single mothers. It can be virtually impossible for a woman who is raising children alone to pay for child care, work, and have sufficient money, especially at the beginning of her working years. However, you might be surprised to know that 1 out of every 10 poor children lives in a two-parent family in which the spouses work. Immigrant families, especially Latinos, are at highest risk of having the kinds of low-wage jobs that make their family qualify as "low income" even when a husband and wife both work full time (Koball & Douglas-Hall, 2005).

Equally disheartening, as you can see in Figure 4.7, the United States leads every Western European nation in the fraction of children living far enough below the median income to qualify as "in poverty." Ironically, Scandinavia has a higher fraction of single mothers than the United States. However, in Western European nations the government provides many social supports for mothers and children. Therefore, you might notice that Sweden, Norway, and Denmark can boast of having some of the *lowest* child poverty rates in the world.

Poverty and Cognitive Development

Early-childhood poverty has dramatic, but selective, consequences for later development. Although low-income children have somewhat higher rates of insecure attachment, the impact of poverty tends to be most devastating in the cognitive realm (Duncan & Brooks-Gunn, 2000; Mistry and others, 2004). Even when researchers control for forces such as the mother's education and her marital status, U.S. infants and toddlers who live under the poverty line score considerably lower than their age-mates on early-childhood intelligence tests (Duncan, & Brooks-Gunn 2000).

Early-childhood poverty also makes a difference in high school graduation rates. One developmentalist has estimated that if a poverty-level family with a young child had a few thousand dollars more in income each year, their son or daughter would be almost three times as likely to finish high school (Duncan, & Brooks-Gunn 2000)!

Why does being poor during a child's first years of life have such damaging long-term effects? One possibility is that early-childhood poverty sets up a negative trajectory that is hard to reverse. It is difficult to make up for what you have lost if you enter school already "left behind," not knowing your letters or how to count, without the basic building blocks required to advance (Duncan & Brooks-Gunn, 2000; Mistry and others, 2004). Children living in poverty are far less likely than upper-middle-class children to go to high-quality preschools (Kozol, 2005). As one social critic powerfully puts it, who is more likely to do well on elementary school reading and math tests—children who "spent the years from two to four in lovely Montessori schools . . . in which . . . attentive grown-ups read to them from story books and introduced them . . . to the world of numbers, . . . or the ones who spent those years at home sitting in front of a TV . . . ?" (Kozol, 2005, p. 53).

Early-childhood poverty may also be associated with having other health-compromising conditions that affect cognition. Low-income women are more likely to give birth to less healthy, low-birth-weight infants. Especially when a baby is very premature, that child is vulnerable to having learning problems that persist into late elementary school and the adolescent years (Anderson and others, 2003; Luciana, 2003; see Chapter 2).

Actually, as developmental systems theory might predict, being born into poverty may work to amplify *every* other negative risk factor in a child's life. Using data from a mammoth U.S. study, researchers found that while having a depressed mother was associated with a child's lagging behind on tests of infant and toddler development, this finding mainly applied to lower-income children. If a child had a depressed mother but lived in an affluent family, his development was not compromised, perhaps because the parents had the economic resources to hire caring help (Petterson & Albers, 2001). So although money cannot buy us good mothers, it can help buffer us from an inadequate mother's damaging effects.

Moreover, as anyone who has had serious economic troubles knows well, being poor *makes* people depressed. You are constantly worried over making ends meet. You are living precariously, perhaps moving from apartment to apartment, camping out with various friends. You cannot buy the items your children need to succeed.

Children living in poverty have less access to computers and developmental toys (Yeung and others, 2002). They show higher baseline levels of the stress hormone cortisol (Evans & English, 2002). Living in crowded, substandard housing also interferes with a person's ability to learn (Evans, 2006; Matheny & Phillips, 2001). When a child shares a small room with several brothers and sisters and is subject to constant comings and goings, it's a bit like a brain impeded by excessive neural connections before pruning has occurred: Too much stimulation prevents information from getting in. And if the child lives in an urban area, she cannot escape the household chaos by going outside. Her neighborhood is likely to be a dangerous place.

As parents understand when they struggle to buy a house in a section of town they can't quite afford, where you live makes a difference in your child's life chances. In one national survey in Canada, even controlling for various family characteristics, preschoolers' verbal test scores were related to the affluence of the neighborhood in which they lived (Kohen and others, 2002). Once again, notice the basic developmental systems message here. To understand cognitive development, *even in early childhood*, we need to consider more than a child's genetic capabilities and what's happening at home. We need to look at the wider world.

Despite their problems, however, poor families are not left without support from the U.S. government. There are federal programs designed to improve low-income children's life chances.

[FAQ: Who is responsible for children's growth, parents or society?]

Head Start A federal program offering high-quality day care at a center and other services to help preschoolers aged 3 to 5 from low-income families prepare for school.

INTERVENTIONS: Giving Disadvantaged Children a Cognitive Boost

The most well-known government program is **Head Start.** Initiated in 1965 as part of President Lyndon B. Johnson's Great Society, Head Start is for children aged 3 to 5. Its primary purpose is to offer the kind of high-quality preschool experience that will make disadvantaged children as ready for kindergarten as their middle-class peers. In addition to offering preschool for children, Head Start offers health screenings and social services for families, as well as providing parenting classes.

Early Head Start A federal program that provides counseling and other services to low-income parents and children under age 3.

Early Head Start extends these benefits to children under age 3. The primary emphasis of this program is to help low-income parents be more effective caregivers. One special focus of Early Head Start is getting fathers involved with their babies. Early Head Start also reaches out to support low-income pregnant women with home visits and other services.

Do these programs work? The answer, in the short run, is yes. Parents who participate in Early Head Start are rated as more emotionally supportive. At ages 2 and 3, their children show lower levels of aggression and gains in language development (Love and others, 2003). However, although they score higher than poverty-level children who do not participate, their language abilities still do not approach national norms (U.S. Department of Health and Human Services [USDHHS], 2002).

In a national study, compared to children who did not attend the program or entered other day-care arrangements, Head Start enrollees showed advantages in literacy measures such as pre-reading and vocabulary (but not math abilities) after the program year (USDHHS, 2005). High-quality preschool experiences of *any* kind, researchers emphasize, are vital to reducing the achievement gaps that poverty-level children often show as they enter their school careers (Loeb and others, 2004).

The real issue is whether these programs make a *long-term* difference. Can we really expect a one-shot experience before kindergarten to work miracles at eroding the impact of going to seriously inadequate schools? As you will vividly learn in Chapter 7, low-income children attend the poorest-quality kindergartens. Their elementary and high school educational experiences—without adequate books, with mold-encrusted classrooms and teachers who often quit just a few months into the school year—can be a national shame (Kozol, 1988, 2005).

Actually, however, in predicting how well low-income children will perform intellectually in kindergarten or first grade, what happens at home matters most (NICHD Early Child Care Research Network, 2005; Yeung and others, 2002). To illustrate this fact, let's look at the lives of two children whose mothers enrolled in a teenage poverty program. Sue, at age 4 1/2, scored at the bottom on a vocabulary test; Emily scored near the top.

> *Jane [Sue's mother] . . . herself made it no further than ninth grade. [She and her husband Rich] were evicted from one place after another for failing to make rent payments. . . . Jane . . . keeps her children confined in car seats, playpens, and gated areas. The television is on constantly. . . . Jane's attitude is that if her children are fed and the house is clean, she is a good mom.*

(Luster and others, 2000, pp. 141–142)

These boys attending a Head Start program in Washington State are getting some learning experiences that they probably would not have received at home. The real-life test of Head Start's success is how well children do years later in school.

For this poverty-level family, low socioeconomic status places the three children at a potentially serious long-lasting educational disadvantage.

Six months after Emily was born, Joyce married Emily's father, Bill. . . . They set up the home environment so that it was safe for the child to explore, and they made sure that Emily had interesting and age-appropriate playthings. The relationship between Joyce and Bill had its ups and downs. . . . Whatever problems they had as a couple did not seem to undermine the way either parent dealt with the . . . child.

(Adapted from Luster and others, 2000, p. 142)

Emily's life situation is a good reminder that having two strikes against them does not put poverty-level children out of the academic running. Despite their economic hardships, many low-income parents struggle, with great success, to give their children high-quality experiences. As a student of mine, a single mother with a child in our local gifted program, summed it up: "I live below the poverty line, but I see myself as living a very middle-class life."

The Impact of Child Care

It's easy to insulate ourselves from stories of poverty if we are comfortably well off. Child care affects everyone, from millionaires in mansions to middle-class urban parents to the rural poor. One national study showed that roughly 60 percent of U.S. mothers return to work during their child's first year of life (NICHD Early Child Care Research Network, 2002).

When their children are infants and toddlers, many parents struggle to keep day-care arrangements within the family. Fathers may take off work to become the primary caregiver. Husbands and wives may reduce their work hours or juggle full-time schedules (Shonkoff & Phillips, 2000a, b). If Grandma lives nearby, she may step in to help, perhaps giving up her own job to watch the baby (Guzman, 1999).

Parents who rely on caregivers outside of the family have several options. Well-off families often hire a nanny or baby-sitter. Less affluent parents, or those who want a less expensive option, may turn to **family day care**, where a neighbor or relative cares for a small group of children in her home. The advantage of this flourishing cottage industry—where Kim sent Elissa—is that, as you saw in the chapter-opening vignette, parents often know the caregiver. The downside is lack of government regulation. Only after a day-care provider takes in a certain number of infants and toddlers is that person required to be licensed and inspected by the state.

The big change on the U.S. landscape is the dramatic increase in licensed **day-care centers**. In recent years, more than 1 in 2 U.S. preschoolers attended these center-based programs (Shonkoff & Phillips, 2000b). The comparable figure for infants and toddlers was more than 1 in 5 (see Figure 4.8).

family day care A day-care arrangement in which a neighbor or relative cares for a small number of children in her home for a fee.

day-care center A day-care arrangement in which a large number of children are cared for at a licensed facility by paid providers.

FIGURE 4.8: Day-care arrangements for infants and toddlers with employed mothers, late 1990s: Notice that, while most infants and toddlers with working mothers are cared for by other family members, 1 in 5 attend licensed day-care centers.
Source: Shonkoff & Phillips (2000b), p. 304.

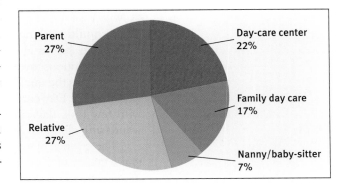

- Parent 27%
- Day-care center 22%
- Family day care 17%
- Nanny/baby-sitter 7%
- Relative 27%

Child Care, Attachment, and Development

Imagine that, like Kim, you are the mother of an infant and must return to work. If you have read about attachment, you are probably wondering, "Will my child be securely attached if I see her only a few hours a day?" You would also worry about finding a reliable child-care provider and about the quality of care your child would be getting: "Is Grandma really stimulating her intellectually?" "Can my baby get the attention she needs at the local day-care center, with all those extra children competing for the caretaker's time?" "What is the *real* impact of having other people give my baby care?"

To answer these questions, in 1989 researchers founded the National Institute of Child Health and Human Development (NICHD) Study of Early Child Care. They selected more than 1,000 newborns in different areas of the country and tracked the progress of these children through a variety of child-care arrangements. In addition to measuring everything from temperament to attachment and from vocabulary to mental health, the researchers evaluated mothers' caregiving skills and the quality of the specific child-care settings in which the children were placed (NICHD Early Child Care Research Network, 2002, 2003, 2005, 2006).

[FAQ: What are the effects of day care on attachment?]

The good news is that putting a baby in day care does not weaken the attachment bond. Infants in day care are still securely attached to their mothers. This is true for children experiencing both a little and a lot of nonparental care. The most important force promoting attachment is the *quality* of the dance—whether a woman is a sensitive caregiver, not whether she works. And remember the lesson from the hunter-gatherer Efé: Those babies developed secure attachments to their mothers despite being cared for by an average of 14 people during their first 18 weeks of life!

[FAQ: Is day care harmful?]

But there is bad news—especially for parents who rely heavily on day care. Quantity can matter, too. The NICHD researchers discovered that babies who spent long hours in day care during their first four years of life were more likely to be rated as "difficult to control" by caregivers and kindergarten teachers (NICHD, Early Child Care Research Network, 2003, 2004, 2006).

These findings would not give much comfort to the millions of working families who need to put their infants and toddlers in day care. The good news is that these correlations are fairly weak. Given that they *are* correlations, the results might be partly due to what developmentalists call "selection effects." Frazzled mothers and fathers may decide to increase a particular child's hours in day care because that infant or toddler is already difficult to handle at home. Still, these findings suggest that parents should be hesitant about relying *extremely* heavily on day care during a child's earliest years of life.

Does this mean that mothers (and fathers) who can afford it should try to stay at home just for the sake of the baby? This advice is far too rigid to capture the nuances. Remember that a caregiver's depression negatively affects a baby's attachment security. So if a mother is unhappy staying at home, is it really better for her child if she doesn't work? Moreover, making blanket pronouncements like "All mothers should stay at home" (or, as in the preceding chapter, breast-feed) is hurtful, because these prescriptions are impossible to fulfill. The United States does not provide for paid parental leave. Many mothers must return to work.

INTERVENTIONS: Deciding Which Child-Care Choice Works Best

What should working parents do? The answer, of course, is to search out the best possible place. Just as Head Start works for low-income preschoolers and the Efé babies given continuous love were securely attached, the main force determining the impact of day care is the quality of the setting itself (NICHD Early Child Care Research Network, 2006). Day-care quality in the United States varies dramatically—from places with few toys, flagrant safety violations, unsupervised infants, and ignored toddlers wandering about, to settings where each child is stimulated, nurtured, and loved.

The essence of good day care, during infancy and at any age, once again boils down to the quality of the dance—that is, the relationship between caretakers and the children in their care. The most lavish physical environment, such as a beautiful center full of toys,

With so few caregivers, these babies in a day-care center (on the left) cannot be getting the one-to-one attention they need at this age to thrive. In contrast, the day-care facility in Sydney, Australia (on the right), shows why child-care programs in this city are the envy of the world.

falls flat without dedicated, attentive staff—people who are warm and caring and provide ample stimulation. At minimum, a low caregiver-to-child ratio is critical to providing the one-to-one loving attention every young child needs (Shonkoff & Phillips, 2000).

Another important dimension is consistency of care. Unfortunately, such consistency is not easy to find. Day-care workers are astonishingly poorly paid, making close to the minimum wage (Whitebook, Howes, & Phillips, 1998). Turnover rates in this field—more than 30 percent per year—are higher than in practically every other industry.

The abysmal salaries translate into low standards. Few states require a high school degree or training in child development for people who care for infants and toddlers. Minimum state-mandated caregiver-to-infant ratios vary widely. They can be as high as one caregiver per 12 children, even during the first year of life! So it is no wonder that in national surveys about one out of every five U.S. day-care settings is labeled "unacceptable" (Shonkoff & Phillips, 2000a). The dismal news is that the typical U.S. infant or toddler spends his time in a setting that, while *marginally* acceptable, is far from being something to write home about.

Our national model of what is possible is the U.S. military, where child-care workers are paid decent salaries and given training, and standards of center-based care are uniformly high. Plus, because the military subsidizes child care, families in the armed services pay considerably less than the typical U.S. parent for this exceptional care (Shonkoff & Phillips, 2000a).

Another model comes from Sydney, Australia. Because this city has rigorous standards for licensed day-care centers, such as a minimum caregiver-to-child ratio of 1 to 5, children entering kindergarten from Sydney child-care centers have superior cognitive and social skills (Love and others, 2003).

But our worldwide model for what is possible in terms of family-friendly policies is Western Europe and, once again, particularly Scandinavia. In Sweden, for example, parents (either mothers or fathers) can take a year off work to care for their babies and get 80 percent of their pay. The United States is the only Western country that does *not* offer new parents any paid leave after a child's birth. Moreover, because European Union countries such as Sweden and France more carefully regulate day-care centers, parents who do go back to work can feel comfortable that when they send their children to child-care centers, they are getting good-quality care.

Still, there is one affluent country that does considerably worse than the United States in terms of center-based care: Israel. In one study conducted in Haifa, the third-largest Israeli city, researchers found that babies attending day-care centers were literally warehoused, with, on average, 17 infants to a room! Given this abysmal caregiver-to-child ratio, it was no wonder that insecure attachments were common among Haifa babies sent to center care (Koren-Karie, Sagi-Schwartz, & Egoz-Mizrachi, 2005; Sagi and others, 2002).

[FAQ: Do children benefit from day care?]

Although the number-one consideration is finding the best possible setting, a baby's temperament also figures into the equation. Just as they have more problems in the Strange Situation, highly anxious infants (and extremely active toddlers) are especially vulnerable to less-than-optimal day care (Crockenberg, 2003; Crockenberg & Leerkes, 2005). Parents might consider their baby's gender, too. In the Haifa study, the negative effect of being sent to center care was most dramatic for boys (Sagi and others, 2002).

Although no more temperamentally difficult than girls, boys have more trouble regulating their emotions during infancy (Calkins and others, 2002). You may recall that this interesting gender difference was also apparent in Chapter 3's discussion of self-soothing. Baby boys have more difficulty calming themselves and going back to sleep after waking up at night (Anders and others, 2000). Male infants are more vulnerable to the negative effects of physical crowding, too (Matheny & Phillips, 2001). So the gender stereotype is true. With the strong caution that variations *between* children outweigh any differences based on sex, males don't seem as biologically able to manage their emotions as females, and this difference shows up as early as the first year of life!

What helps toddlers adjust to day care? As one longitudinal study showed, the main insulating influence is having a secure attachment. Levels of cortisol do rise dramatically during the first week after parents leave their children at day care. (Think of a stressed-out screaming 1-year-old here.) However, securely attached babies have lower cortisol levels and less intense stress responses. This study had another message: Parents who spend more time helping their children get acclimated are likely to have toddlers whose attachments stay secure (Ahnert and others, 2004).

Table 4.1 pulls together all of these messages, as well as providing more detailed guidelines about what to look for in choosing a particular day-care provider. And if you are a working parent who relies heavily on day care, keep these thoughts in mind. Every study shows that *your* responsiveness as a caregiver is what matters most. Moreover, as we saw in the kibbutz studies, by being on the scene at night to give your child comfort, you are positioned to be your baby's primary attachment figure. *You* are the number-one force in making your son or daughter secure.

Now that we have thoroughly examined attachment, poverty, and day care, we turn directly to the topic we have been implicitly talking about all along—being a toddler.

TABLE 4.1: Choosing Day Care: A Section Summary

Overall Considerations

- Consider the caregiver(s). Are they nurturing? Do they love babies? Are they interested in providing a good deal of verbal stimulation to children?
- Look for a low caregiver-to-baby ratio. The ideal is one caregiver for each child.
- Look at the setting. Is it safe and clean? Does it provide appropriate stimulation? (Consider everything from what the bedding is like to whether babies are physically confined and whether there are age-appropriate play materials.)

Additional Suggestions

- For infants and toddlers in full-time care, limit exposure by having a child take occasional vacations or by building in special time with the child every day.
- Consider a child's temperament. Highly anxious babies—or very active toddlers—have special trouble coping with less-than-optimal care.
- Consider a child's gender. Boys are more vulnerable to the negative effects of low-quality day care.
- Consider your whole situation. What is best for the family? Would staying at home make you very depressed? If staying at home would seriously compromise your own well-being, day care may be the best option for your child.
- Make sure to develop a secure attachment with your child, and spend plenty of time helping your baby get acclimated to day care.

Background sources: Whitebook, Howes, & Phillips, 1998; and the authors cited in this section.

TYING IT ALL TOGETHER

1. Hubert is discussing poverty during early childhood in the United States with Heloise. Which of the following statements should he *not* be making?

   a. Being poor during early childhood greatly affects cognitive development and even predicts lower high school graduation rates.
   b. Young children are the poorest segment of the U.S. population (with the exception of women over age 75).
   c. Poverty rates during early childhood are lower in the United States than in other Western nations.

2. Discuss (or list) a few forces *not mentioned in the text* that might negatively impair intellectual development in poor children.

3. Nancy has just put her 6-month-old in day care, and she is terribly anxious about the impact that decision may have on her child. Give one "good news" statement that can ease Nancy's mind, and then be honest and give one "not such good news" statement based on the research.

4. You are making a presentation to a Senate special committee investigating early child care. What should you tell the senators about day-care settings in the United States?

   a. They are uniformly poor.
   b. They are typically good to excellent.
   c. Although they vary in quality, in general, U.S. day care needs a good deal of improvement.

Answers to the Tying It All Together questions can be found in the answers section of the book.

Toddlerhood: Age of Autonomy and Shame and Doubt

Imagine time-traveling back to when you were a toddler. Everything is entrancing—a bubble bath, the dishwasher soap box, the dirt and bugs in your backyard. You are just cracking the language barrier and finally (yes!) traveling into the world on your own two feet. Passionate to set sail into the world, you are also intensely connected to that number-one adult in your life. So, during our second year on this planet, the two agendas that make us human first emerge: We need to be closely connected, and we want to be free, autonomous selves. This is why Erik Erikson (1950) used the descriptive word **autonomy** to describe children's challenge as they emerge from the cocoon of babyhood (see Table 4.2).

Erikson used the words *shame and doubt* to refer to the situation when a toddler's drive for autonomy is not fulfilled. But feeling shameful and doubtful is also

autonomy Erikson's second psychosocial task, when toddlers confront the challenge of understanding that they are separate individuals.

TABLE 4.2: Erikson's Psychosocial Stages

Life Stage	Primary Task
Infancy (birth to 1 year)	Basic trust versus mistrust
Toddlerhood (1 to 2 years)	**Autonomy versus shame and doubt**
Early childhood (3 to 6 years)	Initiative versus guilt
Late childhood (6 years to puberty)	Industry versus inferiority
Adolescence (teens into twenties)	Identity versus role confusion
Young adulthood (twenties to early forties)	Intimacy versus isolation
Middle adulthood (forties to sixties)	Generativity versus stagnation
Late adulthood (late sixties and beyond)	Integrity versus despair

In Erikson's framework, when toddlers develop their first sense of being "a person," their challenge is to have a sense of autonomy—thrill to being independent, without feeling excessively shameful or doubtful.

This toddler has reached a human milestone: She can feel shame, which means that she is beginning to be aware that she has a separate self.

SW Productions / Getty Images

vital to shedding babyhood and entering the human world. During their first year of life, infants show joy, fear, and anger. As babies approach age 2, more complicated, uniquely human emotions emerge—pride, shame, and guilt. The appearance of these **self-conscious emotions** is a milestone. They show that a child is becoming aware of having an actual self. The gift (and sometimes curse) of being human is that we are capable of self-reflection, able to get outside of our heads and observe our actions from an outsider's point of view. Children first show signs of this uniquely human quality when they begin to get ashamed and also clearly feel proud of their behavior at about age 1½ or 2 (Kagan, 1984; Lewis, 1992; Lewis and others, 1989).

self-conscious emotions Feelings of pride, shame, or guilt, which first emerge in toddlerhood and show the capacity to reflect on the self.

socialization The process by which children are taught to obey the norms of society and to behave in socially appropriate ways.

Socialization: The Challenge for 2-Year-Olds

Shame and guilt are vital in another respect. They are essential to **socialization**—the process of being taught to live in the human community.

When do parents begin to seriously socialize their children—or turn the rules and discipline up? For answers, developmentalists surveyed middle-class parents about their rules for their 14-month-olds and returned with the same questionnaire when the children had just turned 2 (Smetana, Kochanska, & Chuang, 2001). Rules for 14-month-olds centered on safety issues: "Don't go into the street," "Stay away from the stove." At age 2, the number of rules had vastly increased, and they were spilling over into the social domain. Parents were expecting their older toddlers to "Share," "Sit at the table," "Brush your teeth," and "Don't disobey, bite, or hit."

Interestingly, other cultural groups, such as the Mayans of Mexico, give much more leeway to children this age. They don't believe that 2-year-olds can control themselves (Mosier & Rogoff, 2003). However, in our society—and many others—the pressure to begin to act "like adults" comes on strong as children reach their second birthdays. No wonder 2-year-olds are infamous for those tantrums called the terrible twos!

When do children have the self-regulating abilities to inhibit their impulses and willingly follow unpleasant rules? To explore this issue, Grayzna Kochanska (1997) and her colleagues devised an interesting procedure. Accompanied by their mothers, young children enter a laboratory full of toys. After playing for a while, the parent gives an unwelcome instruction. She tells the child either to clean up the toy area or not to touch another, easily reachable set of enticing toys.

Not unexpectedly, the research team has discovered that what they call committed compliance—the ability to inhibit one's immediate impulses and *willingly* follow adult requests—improves as children travel from age 1½ to 4. There is an interesting difference, however, depending on the task. It is often easier to comply with an unwanted rule, such as when a parent asks a child to *stop* doing something (not touch the toys), rather than to follow through on an aversive act (making the effort to clean up the toys) (Kochanska, Coy, & Murray, 2001).

This makes good adult sense. Think how much easier it may be for you to hold off when someone tells you not to touch a piece of cake than to perform the heroic task of writing a dreaded term paper or cleaning up the house.

When do children have the beginnings of conscience, the internal sense that they should refrain from doing something they are not supposed to when *not* being watched? To answer this fascinating question, Kochanska and her colleagues used the strategy described earlier, but asked mothers to *leave the room* after delivering their requests. Through a one-way mirror, the researchers then observed how children acted (Kochanska, Coy, & Murray, 2001).

Once again, children find it easier to obey in the "Don't touch that" situation than when asked to do something unpleasant (such as cleaning up the toys). The ability to control oneself and follow unpleasant orders when no one is watching improves with age. Still, the really interesting question is: Which children are best at telling themselves "You've got to listen to what Mom says" when their mothers aren't around?

As we might expect, given their more advanced self-regulation abilities, preschool girls are often (but not always) superior compliers. Temperament, however, is most crucial. Fearful toddlers are more compliant at age 2. They are far less likely to cheat on a game at age 4 than more emotionally intense, uninhibited girls and boys (Aksan & Kochanska, 2004; Kochanska, 2002; Kochanska, Coy, & Murray, 2001; see the How Do We Know box). The bottom line is that exuberant, joyful, fearless, intrepid toddler explorers (no surprise) are more difficult to socialize! (See Kochanska & Knaack, 2003.)

✎ HOW DO WE KNOW . . .

that shy and exuberant children differ dramatically in self-control?

How does Kochanska's research team measure differences in toddler temperament? How do they measure later self-control? Their first step is to design real-world situations tailored to elicit the three primary emotions—fear, anger, and joy—and then observe how toddlers act.

In the situation specially designed to measure differences in fear, a child enters a room filled with frightening toy objects, such as the dinosaur with huge teeth shown below or a black box covered with spider webs. The experimenter asks that boy or girl to perform a mildly risky act, such as putting a hand into the box. To measure variations in anger, the researchers restrain a child in a car seat for a minute or two and then rate how frustrated the toddler gets. To tap into differences in exuberance, the researchers entertain a child with a set of funny puppets. Will the toddler respond with hysterical gales of laughter or be more reserved?

Several years later, the researchers set up a situation tailor-made to provoke noncompliance by asking the child, now age 4, to perform an impossible task (throw Velcro balls at a target from a long distance without looking) to get a prize. Then they leave the room and watch through a one-way mirror to see if the boy or girl will cheat.

As it turns out, toddlers at the high end of the fearless, joyous, and angry continuum show less "morality" at age 4. Without the strong inhibition of fear, their exuberant "get closer" impulses are difficult to dampen down. So they succumb to temptation, sneak closer, and look directly at the target as they hurl the balls (Kochanska & Knaack, 2003).

Courtesy of Grazmya Kochanska

Adam [was a vigorous, happy baby who] began walking at 9 months. From then on, it seemed as though he could never stop.

(10 months) Adam . . . refuses to be carried anywhere. . . . He trips over objects, falls down, bumps himself.

(12 months) The word osside appears. . . . Adam stands by the door, banging at it and repeating this magic word again and again.

(16 months) Adam and his mother take a five-hour plane ride to visit his grandparents. . . . He is miserable unless he is going up and down the aisles.

(19 months) Adam begins attending a toddler group. . . . The first day of the group, Adam climbs to the highest rung of the climbing structure and falls down. . . . The second day, Adam upturns a heavy wooden bench and uses it as a climbing structure. The fourth day, the teacher [devastates Adam's mother] when she says, "I think Adam is not ready for this."

* * *

(13 months) (Erin begins to talk in sentences the same week as she takes her first steps.) . . . Rather suddenly, Erin becomes quite shy. . . . She cries when her mother leaves the room, and insists on following her everywhere.

(15 months) Erin and her parents go to the birthday party of a little friend. . . . For the first half-hour, Erin stays very close to her mother, intermittently hiding her face on her mother's skirt.

(16 months) Father and Erin go to a small grocery store where the friendly owner . . . praises her beautiful eyes and hair. . . . Erin bursts into tears.

(18 months) Erin's mother takes her to a toddlers' gym. Erin watches the children intently with a "tight little face." . . . Her mother berates herself for raising such a timid child.

(Lieberman, 1993, pp. 83–87, 104–105)

Observe any group of 1-year-olds and you will immediately pick out the Erins and the Adams. Some children are wary, careful, and shy. Others are whirlwinds of activity, constantly in motion, literally bouncing off the walls. I remember my own first toddler group at the local Y, when—just like Adam's mother—I first realized how different my exuberant son was from the other children his age. After enduring the horrified expressions of the other mothers as Thomas whirled gleefully around the room while everyone else sat obediently for a snack, I came home and cried. How was I to know that the very qualities that made my outgoing, joyous, vital baby so charismatic during his first year of life might go along with his being so difficult to tame?

The definitive longitudinal studies tracing children with shy temperaments have been carried out by Jerome Kagan (1994) and his students over the past 25 years. Kagan classifies about 1 in 5 middle-class European American toddlers as inhibited. Although they may be perfectly comfortable in familiar situations, these 1-year-olds, like Erin, get nervous when confronted with anything new. In Kagan's lab, inhibited 13-month-olds shy away from approaching a toy robot, a clown, or an unfamiliar person. These are children who take time to venture out in the Strange Situation, get agitated when the stranger enters, and cry bitterly when their parent leaves the room.

My exuberant son—shown enjoying a sink bath at 9 months of age—began to have problems at 18 months, when his strong, joyous temperament collided with the need to "please sit still and listen, Thomas!"

Babies who are destined to be inhibited toddlers show precursors of their later shyness. At 4 months of age, they react with vigorous motor activity, fretting and crying, when confronted with a new object such as a mobile. There is considerable temperamental continuity, too. Inhibited toddlers are more likely to isolate themselves in kindergarten and more prone to be rated shy and fearful in elementary school. At age 13, they tend to be more withdrawn and uncommunicative during an interview with an unfamiliar adult. Their basic biological tendency to be shy even shows up years later, in adulthood. Using MRI brain-scan technology, Kagan's research team finds that, as young adults, his inhibited toddlers show more activity in the limbic system (especially the part of the brain coding negative emotions) when shown a stranger's face on a screen (Schwartz and others, 2003). So for all of you formerly very shy people (your author included) who think you have shed that intense childhood wariness, you still carry your physiology inside.

Still, if you think you have come a long way in conquering your *incredible* childhood shyness, you are probably correct. Most children get less inhibited with age. In a longitudinal study of unusually inhibited and uninhibited 2-year-olds, many (but not all) children drifted toward the middle ranges—being only somewhat shy or active—by the time they entered elementary school (Pfeifer and others, 2002). So both extreme toddler temperamental types do often tend to get mellower as they travel through the childhood years.

INTERVENTIONS: Providing the Right Temperament–Socialization Fit

Faced with a temperamentally timid toddler such as Erin or an exuberant explorer like Adam or Thomas, what specifically can parents do to help?

Socializing a Shy Baby

To see what works best for excessively shy babies, one researcher considered two different parenting strategies (Arcus, 2001). Did the mother quickly pick up her sensitive 4-month-old the minute he got agitated, or let him cry a bit? At months 9 and 13, did she vigorously set limits for her baby, or avoid ever saying no to her inhibited child?

Interestingly, parents who emotionally insulated their infants ended up with the most inhibited toddlers. Parents of fearful children need to be sensitive, loving, and empathic, not discounting their child's distress and—most important—striving for a secure attachment (Shamir-Essakow and others, 2004). However, they should temper their natural tendency to overprotect their highly nervous daughter or son. Gently exposing a fearful baby to some frustrations and new situations teaches that child to cope.

Raising a Rambunctious Toddler

With fearless explorers, the strong temptation is for adults to adopt a socialization strategy called **power assertion**—yelling, screaming, lashing out in frustration at a child who is bouncing off the walls. Parents should resist this tendency. Power assertion is strongly linked to lower levels of conscience development (Kochanska, 2002; Kochanska & Knaack, 2003; Kochanska and others, 2002). As you will see in Chapter 6, using this kind of harsh discipline strongly predicts behavior problems down the road. With fearless toddlers, Kochanska (1995, 1997) has discovered, the best child-rearing strategy lies in promoting an exceptionally strong, loving attachment bond. As my husband insightfully commented, "Punishment doesn't matter much to Thomas. What he does, he does for your love."

Perhaps the most amazing evidence for the taming power of mother love occurred when Kochanska's research team looked specifically at babies rated highly anger prone at 7 months of age—the ones who got most enraged when restrained in a car seat (Kochanska, Aksan, & Carlson, 2005; see the How Do We Know box). As you might imagine, these children—both fearless *and* highly anger prone—were

power assertion An ineffective socialization strategy that involves yelling, screaming, or hitting out in frustration at a child.

most likely to be uncooperative at age 1½. Interestingly, however, if a mother was exceptionally sensitive and loving and—most important—if her easily frustrated child had a secure attachment, she had a toddler who did comply with her requests. With children most at risk for "acting-out" behavior problems, the basic message is clear: Parents should bend over backward to offer love!

Table 4.3 offers a capsule summary of our discussion, showing these different toddler temperaments, their infant precursors, their pluses and potential later dangers, and the lessons for socializing each kind of child. Now let's look at some general temperament-sensitive lessons for raising every child.

An Overall Strategy for Temperamentally Friendly Childrearing

The implication of our discussion is that the main key to socializing children is to foster a secure, loving attachment (Kochanska and others, 2004). However, another key is to understand each child's *specific* temperament and work with that baby's unique behavioral style. This principle was demonstrated decades ago, in the classic study mentioned earlier in this chapter, in which developmentalists classified babies into the categories of "easy," "slow-to-warm-up," and "difficult."

In following the difficult babies as they traveled into elementary school, the researchers found that these highly intense infants were much more likely to have problems with their teachers and peers (Thomas & Chess, 1977; Thomas, Chess, & Birch, 1968). However, some did learn to compensate for their biology and to shine. The key, the researchers discovered, lay in a parenting strategy labeled **goodness of fit**. Parents who took special steps to arrange their children's lives to minimize their vulnerabilities and accentuate their strengths had infants who later did well.

Understanding that their child was easily overwhelmed by stimuli, these parents kept the environment as predictable as possible. They did not compound the problem and get hysterical when faced with their child's distress. They may have offered a quiet environment for studying or encouraged their child to do activities that took advantage of his or her gifts but kept outside distractions to a minimum. They specifically worked to fit the environment to their son's or daughter's temperamental style.

This strategy applies to more than raising children. A basic message of this book is the need to select the environments that fit us temperamentally so that we can really flower.

goodness of fit An ideal parenting strategy that involves arranging children's environments to suit their temperaments, minimizing their vulnerabilities and accentuating their strengths.

TABLE 4.3: **Exuberant and Inhibited Toddler Temperaments: A Summary**

Inhibited, Shy Toddler

- **Developmental precursor:** Responds with intense motor arousal to external stimulation in infancy.

- **Plus:** Easily socialized; shows early signs of conscience; not a discipline problem.

- **Minus:** Shy, fearful temperament can persist into adulthood, making social encounters painful.

- **Child-rearing advice:** Don't overprotect the child. Expose the baby to unfamiliar people.

Matt Carr / Getty Images

Exuberant Toddler

- **Developmental precursor:** Emotionally intense but unafraid of new stimuli.

- **Plus:** Joyous, fearless, outgoing, adventurous.

- **Minus:** Less easily socialized; potential problems with conscience development; at higher risk for later "acting-out" behavior problems.

- **Child-rearing advice:** Avoid power assertion and harsh punishment. Foster a secure attachment and provide lots of love.

Andersen Ross / Getty Images

Final Thoughts

How can we best foster goodness of fit, or person–environment fit, as we travel through life? How much do our inborn temperament (nature) and the external world (nurture) shape the people we become? What happens to babies who are shy or exuberant, difficult or easy, as they travel into elementary school, adolescence, and adult life? How do Ainsworth's categories of attachment play out in adult romantic relationships, and what conditions evoke the clear-cut attachment response at other life stages? Stay tuned as we revisit and explore these tantalizing questions as we move through this book. ▌

TYING IT ALL TOGETHER

1. If Amanda has just turned 2, what prediction are you *not* justified in making?

    a. Amanda wants to be independent, yet closely attached.
    b. Amanda is beginning to show signs of self-awareness and can feel shame.
    c. Amanda's parents haven't begun to discipline her yet.

2. To a colleague at work who confides that she is worried about her timid toddler, what words of comfort can you offer?

3. Think back to your own childhood: Did you fit into either the shy or exuberant temperament type? How did your parents cope with your personality style?

Answers to the Tying It All Together questions can be found in the answers section of the book.

▌SUMMARY

Attachment: The Basic Life Bond

For much of the twentieth century, many psychologists in the United States—because they were behaviorists—minimized the mother–child bond. European psychoanalysts such as John Bowlby were finding, however, that **attachment** was a basic human need. Harlow's studies with monkeys convinced U.S. developmentalists of the importance of attachment, and Bowlby transformed developmental science by arguing that having a loving **primary attachment figure** is biologically built in and crucial to development. Although threats to survival at any age evoke **proximity-seeking behavior**—especially during **toddlerhood**—being physically apart from an attachment figure elicits distress.

According to Bowlby, life begins with a three-month-long **preattachment phase,** which is characterized by the first **social smile.** After an intermediate phase called **attachment in the making,** at about 7 months of age the landmark phase of **clear-cut attachment** begins, signaled by **separation anxiety** and **stranger anxiety.** During this period spanning toddlerhood, children need their caregiver to be physically close, and they rely on **social referencing** to monitor their behavior and ensure that their attachment figure is there. After age 3, children can tolerate separations, as they develop an internal **working model** of their caregiver—which they carry into life.

To explore individual differences in attachment, Mary Ainsworth devised the **Strange Situation.** Using this test, involving a planned series of separations, and especially reunions, developmentalists label 1-year-olds as **securely** or **insecurely attached.** Securely attached 1-year-olds use their primary attachment figure as a secure base for exploration and are delighted when she returns. **Avoidant** infants seem indifferent. **Anxious-ambivalent** children are inconsolable and sometimes

angry when their caregiver arrives. Children with a **disorganized attachment** react in an erratic way and often show fear when their parent reenters the room.

Caregiver–child interactions are characterized by a beautiful **synchrony,** or attachment dance. Although the caregiver's responsiveness to the baby is a major determinant of attachment security at age 1, infant attachment is also affected by the **temperament** of the child and depends on the quality of a caregiver's other relationships, too.

Cross-cultural studies support the idea that attachment to a primary caregiver is universal, with similar percentages of babies in various countries classified as securely attached. Even in an African tribe where infants are cared for by many different adults, children still get attached to their mothers. Studies in the traditional Israeli kibbutz system suggest that the key to fostering a secure attachment lies in having the primary caregiver there to comfort the baby at night. Although babies have one preferred attachment figure, infants can become attached to other caregivers, too.

As Bowlby predicted in his working-model concept, securely attached babies have superior social and emotional skills. Long-term predictions are hazardous, however, because secure attachments during infancy do not insulate us from life traumas (or from becoming insecure). Conversely, some babies with terrible early attachment experiences can construct loving, secure lives.

Contexts of Infant Development

Poverty during the first years of life can have a serious impact on later cognitive development. The United States—because of its high rates of early-childhood poverty—does worse than other developed nations at protecting children from the many negative influences related to being poor. Two federal programs targeted to low-income children and families, **Head Start** and **Early Head Start**, have made progress at improving school readiness among disadvantaged children. However, their impact may be erased by years of inadequate education. Although high-quality preschool experiences are important, the child's home life matters most.

Child care is now a fixture of life. During the first two years of life, many children are cared for by family members—mothers, fathers, and grandmothers. But millions are cared for by non-relatives—by nannies (for affluent parents), in **family day care,** and in the growing number of **day-care centers.**

The NICHD Study of Early Child Care showed that the best predictor of being securely attached at age 1 is the quality of a child's parenting, not number of hours spent in day care. Unfortunately, however, this definitive U.S. child-care study found that children who spend many hours in day care are more likely to be labeled as "difficult" in kindergarten. Although other forces may be responsible for this finding (more temperamentally difficult children may get sent to day care for more hours each day), this research suggests that parents of infants and toddlers should be cautious about relying extremely heavily on full-time nonfamily care.

High-quality day care makes a huge difference—and although settings vary, child care in the United States leaves much to be desired. Caregiver-to-child ratios are often too high. Because day-care workers are so poorly paid, staff turnover is a serious problem. The U.S. military (and Sydney, Australia) offer models for what might be possible in the United States. Western European nations, with their generous paid family-leave policies and well-regulated centers, put the United States to shame.

As quality matters greatly, parents should search for day-care settings with a low caregiver-to-child ratio and loving care providers. Infants who are more temperamentally difficult and male babies seem most vulnerable to poor-quality care. It helps for parents to spend time getting children acclimated to day care, too.

Toddlerhood: Age of Autonomy and Shame and Doubt

Erikson's term **autonomy** captures the essence of toddlerhood, the landmark time of life when we shed babyhood, become able to observe the self, and so really enter the human world. **Self-conscious emotions** such as pride, shame, and guilt emerge and are crucial to **socialization,** which begins in earnest at around age 2. Girls and temperamentally fearful children are superior at inhibiting their behavior, and they show earlier signs of "conscience," obeying adult rules when not being watched. Exuberant, active toddlers are especially hard to socialize.

As young babies, shy toddlers react with intense motor activity to new stimuli. They also are more inhibited in elementary school and adolescence, and show neurological signs of wariness to strangers as adults. Still, over time (and with temperamentally sensitive parenting), many extremely shy toddlers and fearless explorers lose these extreme qualities as they move into their elementary school years.

To help an inhibited baby, be empathic, but don't overprotect the child. Socialize a fearless explorer by avoiding **power assertion**—yelling and screaming—and developing a close, loving attachment bond. While loving, secure attachments are what really make for good socialization (for anger-prone "resistant" children, the more love the better), in raising any child the key is to strive for **goodness of fit**—to tailor one's parenting to a child's unique temperamental needs.

▌ KEY TERMS

attachment, p. 107

toddlerhood, p. 107

primary attachment figure, p. 109

proximity-seeking behavior, p. 109

preattachment phase, p. 110

social smile, p. 110

attachment in the making, p. 110

clear-cut attachment, p. 110

separation anxiety, p. 110

stranger anxiety, p. 110

social referencing, p. 111

working model, p. 111

Strange Situation, p. 112

secure attachment, p. 112

insecure attachment, p. 112

avoidant attachment, p. 112

anxious-ambivalent attachment, p. 112

disorganized attachment, p. 112

synchrony, p. 113

temperament, p. 114

Head Start, p. 121

Early Head Start, p. 122

family day care, p. 123

day-care center, p. 123

autonomy, p. 127

self-conscious emotions, p. 128

socialization, p. 128

power assertion, p. 131

goodness of fit, p. 132

▮ RECOMMENDED RESOURCES

HIGHLY RECOMMENDED POPULAR BOOKS

Blum, D. (2002). *Love at Goon Park: Harry Harlow and the science of affection*. Cambridge, MA: Perseus Publishing.

This beautifully written biography of Harry Harlow covers his primate studies and offers compelling insights into the problems that Harlow confronted from a variety of sources (the feminist movement; the behaviorists) in putting forth his ideas.

Karen, R. (1998). *Becoming attached: First relationships and how they shape our capacity to love*. New York: Oxford University Press.

Written for a popular audience, this book thoroughly catalog the "attachment movement." It's comprehensive, definitive, and a wonderful read.

Lieberman, A. F. (1993). *The emotional life of the toddler*. New York: Free Press.

This sensitively written book gives insights into the inner world of toddlers and discusses different toddler temperaments and child-rearing strategies.

POVERTY AND CHILD CARE WEB SITES

National Center for Children in Poverty, Mailman School of Public Health, Columbia University. www.nccp.org.

This national organization serves as a clearinghouse for information on U.S. child poverty.

National Head Start Association. www.nhsa.org.

This is the official Web site for information about Head Start and Early Head Start.

SCHOLARLY SOURCES FOR ATTACHMENT

Cassidy, J., & Shaver, P. (Eds.) (1999). *Handbook of attachment: Theory, research, and clinical applications*. New York: Guilford Press.

Grossmann, K., Grossmann, K., & Waters, E. (Eds.) (2005). *Attachment from infancy to adulthood*. New York: Guilford Press.

The first book is the definitive academic volume on attachment, with 36 edited chapters covering theory, biological perspectives, attachment throughout the lifespan, clinical applications, and special topics. The second book summarizes the major long-term attachment studies.

TEMPERAMENT

Kagan, J. (1994). *Galen's prophecy*. New York: Basic Books.

Kagan offers an exhaustive look at his own research program on inhibited children and provides an overview of conceptions of temperament from antiquity to the modern age.

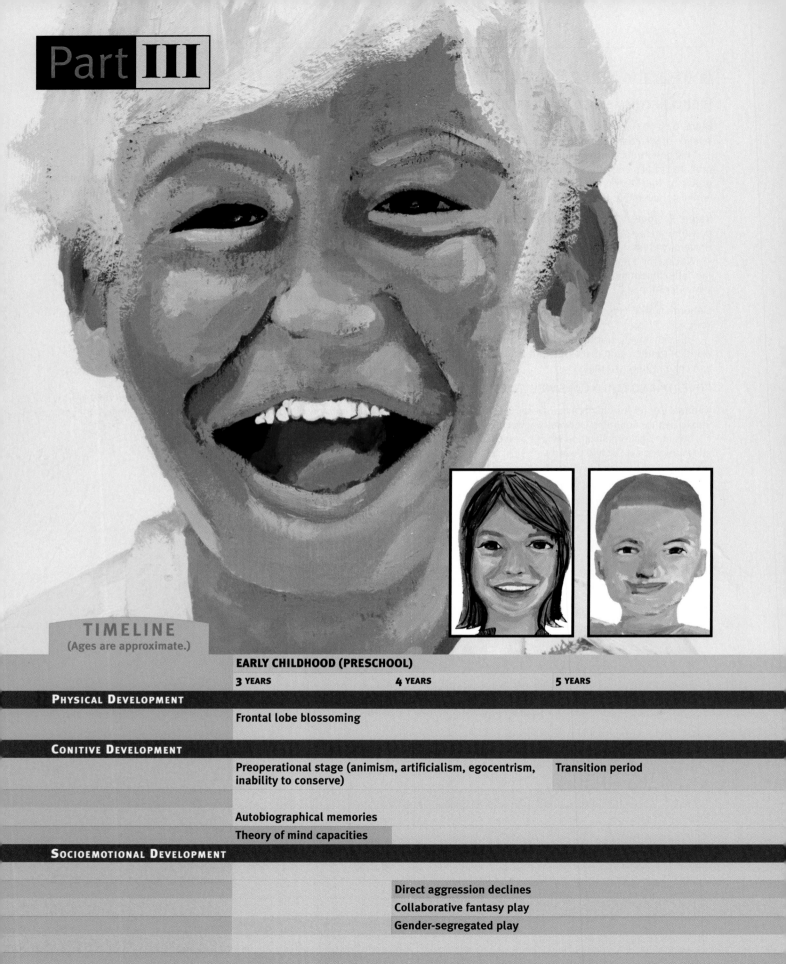

Part III

TIMELINE
(Ages are approximate.)

EARLY CHILDHOOD (PRESCHOOL)

	3 YEARS	4 YEARS	5 YEARS
PHYSICAL DEVELOPMENT			
	Frontal lobe blossoming		
CONITIVE DEVELOPMENT			
	Preoperational stage (animism, artificialism, egocentrism, inability to conserve)		Transition period
	Autobiographical memories		
	Theory of mind capacities		
SOCIOEMOTIONAL DEVELOPMENT			
		Direct aggression declines	
		Collaborative fantasy play	
		Gender-segregated play	

Childhood

In this segment covering childhood, our first two chapters trace children's unfolding abilities. The final chapter looks at those basic settings within which children develop: home and school.

In Chapter 5, "Physical and Cognitive Development," we will examine expanding motor skills and health issues such as obesity. Then comes the heart of this chapter: how children's minds work. If you have ever wondered about the strange ways preschoolers think, need a basic framework for teaching, or want to understand how memory and reasoning develops, this section is for you. Finally, we explore language and two crucial types of knowledge that children master during the preschool years.

In Chapter 6, "Socioemotional Development," our emphasis shifts to school-age children. Here we look at growing self-awareness, aggression, caring acts, play, friendships, and popularity. A special focus of our discussion is on boys and girls who are having difficulties relating to their peers and adults.

In Chapter 7, "Settings for Development: Home and School," we first tackle children's family lives. Is there an ideal way of parenting? Why do some children thrive in spite of devastatingly dysfunctional early lives? What is the impact of spanking, child abuse, and divorce? In the section on school, you will learn all about intelligence tests, what makes schools successful, and how teachers can make every child eager to learn.

The timeline below offers some milestones we will be exploring in the chapters to come.

MIDDLE CHILDHOOD (ELEMENTARY SCHOOL)

6 YEARS	7 YEARS	8 YEARS	9 YEARS	10 YEARS
			Frontal lobe pruning	Frontal lobes continue to mature

Concrete operational stage (identity constancy, seriation, categorization, ability to conserve)

Expansion of executive functions (e.g., memory, selective attention, inhibition)

Self-esteem issues

Relational aggression increases

Games, organized sports

Popularity, bullying are major concerns

CHAPTER 5

These 3-year-olds have amazing skills. They can cut paper with scissors, climb monkey bars, follow directions to move fast and slowly. They are able to tell jokes, communicate about their lives, and occasionally—when they are reminded—remember the teacher's rules. But they clearly have miles to go before they think like adults. What were the children thinking during the pretend feedings at the kitchen corner, and why was Kanesha sure I *had* to know her name? Why did Moriah assume Manuel had more paper when he cut his sheet into pieces, and why did *everyone* have so much trouble remembering the center's rules? This chapter offers answers to these

Physical and Cognitive Development

As the 3-year-olds drift in to Learning Preschool, Ms. Angela fills me in:

"We do free play, then structured games. Then we go outside. At 11 we have snack. We focus on the skills the kids need for school and life: Sit still; follow directions; listen; share. During free play, they need to remember three rules: Four kids to an activity center. Clean up before you leave. Don't take the toys from one center when you go to another place."

In the kitchen corner, Kanesha is busy pretending to scrub pots. "What is your name?" "You know!" says Kanesha, looking at me as if I'm totally dumb. "This is a picnic," Kanesha continues, giving me a plate: "Let's have psghetti and Neruda makeacake." We are having a wonderful time talking as she loads me up with plastic food. The problem is I'm feeling that we aren't communicating. Who is Neruda, that great cook? Then some girls run in with Barbies from the dress-up corner: "Our babies need some food!" We're happily feeding our toys when Ms. Angela pipes up: "No moving stuff from the play centers! Don't you remember our four kids to a center rule?" . . .

I move to the crafts table, where Moriah, a dreamy frail girl, and Manuel are surrounded by paper: "Hey!" Moriah yells, after Manuel cuts his paper into pieces, "Manuel has more than me!" Manuel tenderly gives Moriah his bunny, and gives me a heart-melting, welcoming smile: "I'm [holds up three fingers]." (Moriah and Manuel are obviously interested in what I'm doing.) "I'm taking notes for a book." "Taking nose," both children giggle and hold their noses. Moriah is making beautiful circles with paste. Manuel tries to copy her but can only make random lines. These children are so different in their physical abilities, even though they are the same age. But, oh, no, here come the kids from the kitchen corner with plastic vegetables, forgetting the "don't move the toys" and "four children to a center" rules! Luckily, it's time for structured games.

Ms. Angela shows the class cards picturing a sun, an umbrella with raindrops, and clouds, and asks: "What is the weather today?" Manuel proudly picks the umbrella. "How many people think Manuel is right?" Everyone raises their hands. "Who feels it's sunny?" Everyone yells: "Me!" "Who thinks it's cloudy?" Everyone agrees. Then Ms. Angela puts on a tape: "Dance fast, fast . . . sl o wer sl o w e r . . . Now speed up!" The kids frantically dance around, and it's time to go outside. Soon the wind starts gusting (it really is about to rain), and everyone gets excited: "Let's catch the wind. . . . Oh, he ran away again!" And now (whew!) it's 11:00 and time for snack.

questions—and many others—as we trace physical and cognitive development during **early childhood** (age 3 through kindergarten) and **middle childhood** (elementary school), paying special attention to the early childhood years.

We begin this chapter by looking at physical development, then turn to explore cognition. How do young children's thinking processes grow? Next we chart emerging language. We conclude our discussion by focusing on two kinds of knowledge these preschoolers are developing: understanding that they have a personal past, and understanding that other people have different points of view. The second ability is critical. It may explain why that long decade of life we call childhood exists.

early childhood The first phase of childhood, lasting from age 3 through kindergarten, or about age 5.

middle childhood The second phase of childhood, covering the elementary school years, from about age 6 to 11.

SETTING THE CONTEXT: **Why Childhood?**

Human beings spend a larger fraction of their lifespan before they can physically reproduce than any other species. Macaque monkeys become sexually mature at age 4; our closest cousins, the chimpanzees, at 8 (Poirier & Smith, 1974).

Postponing adulthood is hazardous, because the longer we live in an immature state, the greater our risk of dying without passing on our genes. Why did childhood evolve?

Two Major Learning Challenges

The reason, according to evolutionary theorists, is that we face two kinds of learning challenges that make us different from any other animal on earth (Bjorklund & Pellegrini, 2002).

Special Social Learning Tasks

One uniquely human challenge lies in our need to learn the rules of living in *different* cultures (Bjorklund & Harnishfeger, 1995; Byrne & Whiten, 1988; Geary & Flinn, 2001). Three-year-olds growing up in any society on earth have to be socialized to relate smoothly to their fellow human beings. But, if you have spent time in a different country, you were probably struck with the differences in the basic socialization relationship rules. Do you smile or avoid making eye contact when you are walking down the street? Should you speak openly about your feelings or be more reserved? Learning the detailed rules of living in *specific* societies requires a long period of time.

A second skill that separates us from other animals lies in our ability to build on the knowledge that has been passed down before. Three-year-olds born in biblical times had the same biology as the preschoolers in the vignette; but these twenty-first-century children will grow up to use cell phones and surf the Internet. They might even take vacations on the moon or Mars. It is our capacity to build on the insights of *each* previous generation that allowed our species to progress from living in caves to traveling to outer space.

Can we pinpoint the *specific* talent that allowed human beings to mentally take off? Evolutionary psychologists believe that what makes us special is our finely honed ability to grasp intentions (Tomasello, 2001). We are the only species that regularly places ourselves in other people's shoes and understands their goals. In Chapter 4 you saw this automatic "mind reading" ability ("He must be late, because he's driving fast";

This child is mastering a vital skill in his society, but clearly one that would be irrelevant in the industrialized world. The remarkable human ability to learn the life rules of a diversity of cultures is what makes our species unique.

"She's opening the refrigerator door because she's hungry") get going during the second year of life, when toddlers social-reference a caregiver and understand that that person's expressions and words are intended for them.

Although we take it for granted, this skill represents an enormous evolutionary advance. It means that when the first caveman used a sharp object to crack open a nut, his fellow cave dwellers could immediately appreciate his creative invention and build on this breakthrough to make better tools. But pity the poor chimp Einstein, who developed a new, more efficient method for getting food. Even though his fellow monkeys could "ape" his actions, they might not fully understand *why* he was taking that action—leaving each next monkey genius to literally "reinvent the wheel."

Slow-Growing Frontal Lobes

All this extra learning explains why our huge *cerebral cortex* takes two decades to mature (Bjorklund & Pellegrini, 2002; Geary & Flinn, 2001; Huttenlocher, 2002; recall Chapter 3). The *myelin sheath*—the fatty neural cover—continues to grow into our twenties. *Synaptogenesis* (the process of making billions of connections between neurons) is on a more extended blossoming and pruning timetable, too. This is especially true in the region of the brain responsible for reasoning and thinking through our actions—the **frontal lobes** (Huttenlocher, 2002).

Figure 5.1, which compares the size of our cortex to that of several other species, shows the huge frontal lobes positioned front and center at the top of the brain. During early childhood, the neurons in the visual and motor cortexes are well into their pruning phase, which explains why vision develops so rapidly during early infancy (recall Chapter 3) and why we master basic physical milestones, such as walking, at a relatively young age. However, the frontal lobes are only in their early phase of intense synaptogenesis at the time we start toddling around. Pruning in this part of the brain will not start until about age 9.

Their slow frontal-lobe timetable is the reason why the 3-year-olds in the vignette had so much trouble controlling their behavior. It explains why our ability to plan, think through, and inhibit our actions steadily improves throughout childhood and adolescence (Leon-Carrion, Garcia-Orza, & Perez-Santamaria, 2004; Luna, Garver, Urban, Lazar, & Sweeney, 2004). It even accounts for the high expectations we have of children when the frontal lobes begin their pruning phase in late elementary school. We expect fourth and fifth graders to be able to understand long division and to take responsibility for completing their homework. After all, they can sometimes beat us at baseball and outscore us at the bowling alley, too.

In addition to allowing us to have the inner control to decide to do our homework (rather than watching TV) and the cognitive abilities to grasp long division, the frontal lobes are crucial to mastering every physical ability, from following the rules of baseball, to positioning a bowling ball, to being able to inhibit our impulses and saying "I have to get to the toilet" at about age 2 or 3. Keeping in mind that the slow-growing frontal lobes are the master programmer of *every* skill in this chapter, let's now begin by looking at physical development in the flesh.

frontal lobes The area at the uppermost front of the brain, responsible for reasoning and planning our actions.

FIGURE 5.1: **The human cortex and that of some other species:** Notice the size of our cortex in comparison to other species. Also notice the dramatic increase in the size of our frontal lobes. It is our mammoth cortex and especially our huge frontal lobes that are responsible for everything that makes our species unique.

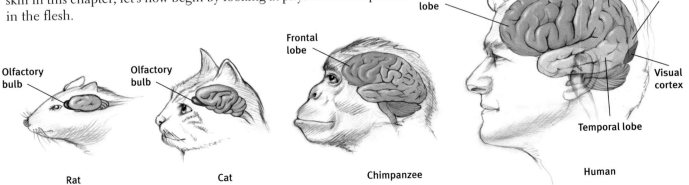

Olfactory bulb

Olfactory bulb

Frontal lobe

Motor cortex

Frontal lobe

Parietal lobe

Occipital lobe

Visual cortex

Temporal lobe

Rat

Cat

Chimpanzee

Human

TYING IT ALL TOGETHER

1. In discussing the qualities that distinguish us from other species, Brandy can list all of the following uniquely human characteristics *except*:

   a. We have a finely tuned ability to understand other people's intentions.
   b. We are able to build on the insights of other people.
   c. We have extremely varied cultures.
   d. We have the ability to keep learning new things.

2. When Steven played hide-and-seek with his 4-year-old nephew, he realized that while Ethan could run very well, he was having a lot of trouble not betraying his hiding place and understanding the rules of the game. The reason is that Ethan's _____ cortex is on an earlier developmental timetable than his _____ lobes.

3. If you just learned that a colleague was in an accident and may have frontal-lobe damage, what should you be thinking?

Answers to the Tying It All Together questions can be found in the answers section of the book.

What tips us off immediately about the ages of the children in these two photographs relates to the *cephalocaudal principle* of development. We know that the children in the top photo are preschoolers because they have squat shapes and relatively large heads, while the longer bodies in the bottom photo are typical of the middle childhood years.

Physical Development

Look at children of different ages at a mall and you will immediately see the *cephalocaudal principle* of physical growth discussed in Chapters 2 and 3. Three-year-olds have relatively large heads and squat, rounded bodies. As children get older, their limbs get longer and their bodies thin out. Although from age 2 to 12 children double their height and weight, after infancy the rate of growth slows down considerably (National Health and Nutrition Examination Survey, 2004). Because they grow at comparable rates, boys and girls are roughly the same size until they reach the preadolescent years.

Now visit a playground or take out samples of your childhood artwork to see the *mass-to-specific* principle—the steady progression from clumsy to sure, swift movements year by year. Three-year-olds have trouble making circles; third graders can draw detailed bodies and faces. At age 4, children catch a ball with both hands; by fourth grade they may be able to hit home runs. You can see the dramatic changes from mass to specific in a few skills displayed in Table 5.1.

TABLE 5.1: Selected Motor Skill Milestones: Progression from Age 2 to Age 6

At age 2	At age 4
Picks up small objects with thumb and forefinger; feeds self with spoon	Cuts paper, approximates circle
Walks unassisted, usually by 12 months	Walks down stairs, alternating feet
Rolls a ball or flings it awkwardly	Catches and controls a large bounced ball across the body

At age 5	At age 6
Prints name	Copies two short words
Walks without holding on to railing	Hops on each foot for 1 meter but still holds railing
Tosses ball overhand with bent elbows	Catches and controls a 10-inch ball in both hands with arms in front of body

Two Types of Motor Talents

Developmentalists divide physical skills into two categories. **Gross motor skills** refer to large muscle movements, such as running, jumping, climbing, and hopping. **Fine motor skills** involve small, coordinated movements, such as drawing circles and writing one's name.

The stereotype that boys are better at gross motor abilities and girls at fine motor tasks is true—although in most areas the differences are small. The largest sex difference in sports-related abilities occurs in throwing speed. During preschool and throughout middle childhood, boys can typically hurl a ball much faster and farther than girls (Geary, 1998; Thomas & French, 1985). Does this mean that girls can't compete with boys on a Little League team? Not necessarily. The boys will have a gross motor advantage: They may be better at running the bases, and they probably will be faster pitchers and more powerful hitters. But the female talent at connecting with the ball, which involves fine motor coordination, may even things out.

Apart from their gender, what accounts for the dramatic differences we can observe between individual preschoolers in their motor skills? To a large degree, nature forces are responsible. Just as children are genetically programmed to be early or late walkers, developmental timetables vary for reaching motor milestones, from catching a ball to forming the letters of one's name. Can nurture forces, or training, help improve young children's skills?

To answer this question, researchers asked kindergarten teachers to coach their classes on fine motor tasks, such as picking up objects using tweezers or tongs (Rule & Stewart, 2002). After six months, they compared this group to an untrained class on a different task—how quickly they could fit pennies into a slot. The children given training were superior, showing that practice can accelerate fine motor development. Because writing is so important in elementary school, this research suggests that perhaps we might pay more attention to teaching fine motor skills to promote school readiness, in addition to simply getting children to understand their letters and the days of the week.

Still, we need to be wary about going too far. Efforts to teach preschoolers to write "just like adults," or to start sports like baseball, are destined to be counterproductive—producing frustration for parents and children alike. As young children don't have the coordination abilities (and, as we'll see later, cognitive capacities) to write well or play organized games, the focus during preschool should be on providing activities—such as cutting or pasting paper, or scaling the monkey bars—appropriate to young children's genetically paced, unfolding motor skills (Zaichkowsky & Larson, 1995). In early childhood, we need to walk a fine line: Provide plenty of chances for preschoolers to exercise their physical capacities, but take care not to push; and be sure to provide the right person–environment fit.

Now that we know what kinds of environments encourage ideal physical development, it's time to look at what can go wrong.

gross motor skills Physical abilities that involve large muscle movements, such as running and jumping.

fine motor skills Physical abilities that involve small, coordinated movements, such as drawing and writing one's name.

[FAQ: How much of the gender differences in developmental milestones is genetic, and how much is environmental?]

[FAQ: Can parents affect the age at which children reach certain milestones?]

Bob Daemmrich / Photo Edit, Inc.

Sean Sprague / The Image Works

While the boys in the photograph at left may have an advantage in the gross motor skills needed to win a potato sack race, the girl in the photo at right might surpass many of the boys in the fine motor talents involved in forming handwritten words.

This starving 3-year-old Afghan boy and his 13-year-old sister are likely to fall far behind in motor skills development because chronic under-nutrition causes weakness and apathy.

Paula Bronstein / Getty Images

[FAQ: What are the results of inadequate nutrition for children between birth and age 8?**]**

[FAQ: What is BMI?**]**

body mass index (BMI) The ratio of weight to height; the main indicator of overweight or underweight.

childhood obesity A body mass index at or above the 95th percentile compared to the U.S. norms established for children in the 1970s.

Environmental Threats to Growth and Motor Skills

One interesting wider-world threat to physical development is extreme life stress. In one case, children living in an orphanage with a sadistic director stopped growing even though they were given adequate food. Other case studies show that when children are removed from abusive homes and placed in caring foster homes, they catch up in terms of growth (Tanner, 1978). Lest you think of stress as only slowing physical development, in Chapter 8 we will explore how family stress may stimulate the hormones programming sexual development, making girls reach puberty at an earlier-than-normal age (Belsky, Steinberg, & Draper, 1991).

The main environmental force impairing growth and motor skills, however, is the problem discussed in Chapter 3: lack of adequate food. In addition to causing stunting, undernutrition impairs gross and fine motor skills because it compromises the development of the bones, muscles, and brain. Even more important, when children are chronically hungry, they are too tired to move much and so don't get the experience crucial to developing their physical skills.

During the 1980s, researchers observed how undernourished children in rural Nepal helped maximize their growth rate by cutting down on play (Anderson & Mitchell, 1984). One expert has suggested that this apathy and inactivity may be more detrimental to malnourished children's physical abilities than the effect of not getting enough nutrients to the body and brain (Tanner, 1978). Notice how, after skipping just one meal, you become lethargic: unwilling to walk, incapable of thinking clearly or moving fast.

Keeping in mind that undernutrition *remains* the top-ranking twenty-first-century global public health threat to physical development, let's now turn to the problem that is currently ringing alarm bells, especially in the developed world: childhood obesity.

Childhood Obesity

Have you ever wondered about the source of the numbers in the charts showing the ideal weights for people of different heights? These statistics come from a regular U.S. national poll called the National Health and Nutrition Examination Study (NHANES). Since the 1960s, the federal government has been literally measuring the size of Americans by charting average caloric intakes, heights, and weights. The statistic researchers use to monitor overweight is called **body mass index (BMI)**—the ratio of a person's weight to height. If a child's BMI is at or above the 95th percentile compared to the norms in the first poll, that boy or girl qualifies as obese.

Childhood obesity started to balloon about 25 years ago. During the late 1980s the NHANES researchers were astonished to find that the fraction of elementary school children qualifying as "seriously overweight" had roughly doubled over a decade (American Obesity Association, 2002; Ogden and others, 2002; see Figure 5.2). Today, 15 percent of U.S. elementary school children are defined as obese—triple the number in the original poll. To bring this difference home, if you entered a second- or third-grade classroom in the early 1970s, one or possibly two children might stand out as seriously overweight. Three or four boys and girls would fit that category today.

This rise in the fraction of children at the top of weight charts is not confined to the United States (Glanz and others, 2005). Rates of childhood obesity are now twice as high in Great Britain as in 1990. They have risen almost fourfold in Egypt over the past 18 years (Ebbeling, Pawlak, & Ludwig, 2002). Obesity is becoming an issue in rapidly developing countries such as South Korea and China, too.

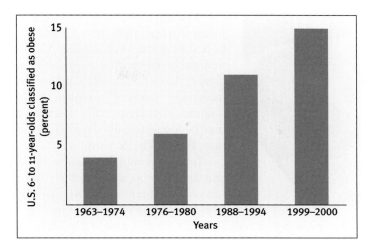

FIGURE 5.2: **Percentage of U.S. children aged 6–11 who are classified as obese:** This chart shows that the prevalence of child obesity almost doubled during the 1980s and is continuing to rise.

Source: Adapted from Centers for Disease Control (2004).

Although the epidemic is global, there is an interesting difference between the developed and developing worlds. In affluent nations, low-income children are more prone to be seriously overweight (Lamerz and others, 2005; Sturm, 2004). In poor regions of the world, childhood obesity is a disease of the well-off (Berkowitz & Stunkard, 2002; Ebbeling, Pawlak, & Ludwig, 2002).

In the United States, there is an ethnic as well as a socioeconomic dimension to the epidemic. Obesity rates are highest among Latino and African American boys and girls (USDHHS, 2004; Zametkin and others, 2003).

Obviously, our genetics have not changed. The real problem, in fact, lies in our being born with the same biology as well before biblical times. Anthropologists believe that our ancestors were in continual motion: tracking game, gathering plant foods, chopping down trees for shelter. They thought nothing of walking ten miles to visit other villages and, to top it off, found time to dance—a major activity in hunter-gatherer times (Berg, 2004). Still, thousands-of-years-old comparisons say nothing about why childhood obesity rates took off around 25 years ago.

To explain the recent surge in overweight, we can point to many "obesogenic" environmental forces, from expanding restaurant portion sizes to the fact that high-fat foods cost families considerably less; from the easy availability of prepackaged caloric snacks to the decline in walking or biking to school. Children are eating out more often, as working parents don't have the time to prepare nutritious sit-down meals. Meals consumed outside of the home tend to be more calorie-dense (think of those "loaded" baked potatoes and huge hamburger platters) (Sturm, 2004). With the Internet and TV, playing outside—that typical childhood vehicle for burning up calories—has sharply declined. In fact, many parents prefer their sons and daughters to stay in the house because roaming the neighborhood can be unsafe. Making matters worse, with funding cutbacks and the pressure to focus on academics, most U.S. public schools no longer offer daily gym (Berg, 2004; Berkowitz & Stunkard, 2002; Sturm, 2004).

You might be interested to know that researchers have not been able to document that children today are consuming significantly more calories than in the past (Berg, 2004). What we do know is that elementary schoolers' intake of high-carbohydrate snack foods, such as chips and pretzels, tripled from the mid-1970s to the mid-1990s. Consumption of sugary soft drinks doubled during that time (Sturm, 2004).

A primary culprit, everyone agrees, is physical inactivity. In one ambitious study, researchers followed a large group of Massachusetts children from preschool to early adolescence, using electronic sensors to monitor activity levels over the years. Children in the upper third in terms of activity had lower BMIs as they traveled into adolescence (Moore and others, 2003). Time spent sitting and watching television, the researchers found, was also an independent predictor of subsequent body fat (Proctor and others, 2003).

[FAQ: How should we prevent or correct obesity?]

This overweight boy in Beijing provides evidence that the obesity epidemic is now global. However, in countries such as China, seriously overweight children are more likely to be wealthy than poor; the opposite is true in the United States.

Reuters / Corbis

Donna Day / Getty Images

This photograph shows exactly why watching a lot of TV is an important risk factor for obesity: total inactivity, plus a tendency to gorge on high-fat snacks.

There is probably a poisonous "nature evokes nurture" influence in operation here. Children who are genetically prone to be heavy may watch more TV because when they do participate in sports they may be teased: "He is too slow and clumsy. Let's not choose Fatty for the team." Less activity and more TV watching, in turn, make children put on more pounds. Then, especially when a child is severely obese, he may be too physically depleted to even move much (Schwimmer, Burwinkle, & Varni, 2003).

Intense parental pressures to diet can backfire. Mothers and fathers who make it their life mission to monitor their son's or daughter's intake may be causing the very eating practices that put on weight. In one observational laboratory study, overweight 8-year-olds (but not normal-weight children) quickly wolfed down food and so consumed more calories, but only when their mothers were around (Laessle, Uhl, & Lindel, 2001). And, of course, continually being criticized for being "fat" does very little for a child's self-esteem.

The good news is that, contrary to popular opinion, overweight children in the United States do not have more serious emotional problems than their normal-sized peers (Zemetkin and others, 2004). Reinforcing the message above, a child's feelings of self-worth are best predicted by looking at his *parents' anxiety* about his weight, not at his actual body mass (Davison & Birch, 2002; Stradmeijer and others, 2000).

The bad news is that Type 2 diabetes—typically a disease of aging, related to being heavy—is showing up at abnormally young ages (Ebbeling, Pawlak, & Ludwig, 2002). High blood pressure among children, a risk factor for heart disease, is also rising (Muntner and others, 2004). So the real worry with serious childhood overweight is long-term: Could this cohort of American children be the first to show a decline in life expectancy and more chronic disease at younger ages?

Table 5.2 summarizes the main messages of our discussion for parents and adults. However, as the problem lies in the twenty-first-century "nutritional environment," perhaps you can think of some ways to provide a better person–environment fit by redesigning your community to make physical activity a *natural* part of daily life.

TABLE 5.2: Physical Development: A Few Practical Messages

General Principles

1. Provide activities appropriate to children's unfolding capacities; for example, preschoolers don't have the physical capacities to play organized sports like T-ball. They need to run around on the playground, to climb, to jump, to exercise their bodies in a way that fits their developing skills.

2. Expect normal individual differences from child to child in physical capacities—and don't be concerned. Children vary in fine and gross motor abilities at every age.

3. If a child is lagging far behind in fine motor abilities, you might play games that would give the child practice at coordination, such as picking up small objects, that could generalize to tasks that come later, such as writing one's name. But, again, make these activities fun and avoid pushing the child.

Overweight

1. Find ways to make the child more physically active. Cut down on TV watching and access to the Internet. Drawing on the child's interests, focus on building some regular physical activity into the daily routine. If possible, provide enticing objects outdoors, such as swings and a slide—and give plenty of time to run around. If going outside is difficult, as young children love helping to clean up, perhaps get the child to sweep the floor or fold laundry, or give the child a regular "helper" task involving exercise around the house.

2. If your family lives within a mile or so of school, have the child walk or bike, rather than being driven, to class.

3. Try to eat family meals at home, and cut down on fast-food meals.

4. Don't keep high-fat, high-carbohydrate (starchy and sugary) foods—especially candy and other snack items—around the house.

5. Avoid monitoring a child's food consumption. This practice is likely to backfire, as the child may eat more quickly and so consume more calories. (Forcing children to limit their intake, leaving them hungry, also ensures that they will try to sneak food later.)

6. Don't make weight a big issue. Appreciate what is really important—your child's inner qualities.

Sources: Blum (2004); Sturm (2004).

TYING IT ALL TOGETHER

1. You are astonished at the physical changes in your 7-year-old niece, Brittany, since you last saw her several years ago. Which example refers to the cephalocaudal principle and which to the mass-to-specific principle? (a) Brittany could barely draw a circle; now she can draw a detailed face; (b) Brittany's body has become much longer and skinnier.

2. Jessica has terrific gross motor skills but trouble with fine motor skills. Select the two sports Jessica would be most likely to excel at from this list: long-distance running; tennis; water ballet; the high jump; bowling.

3. You are giving advice to an international panel on motor skill development. On the basis of this chapter, you should make all of the following statements *except*:

   a. Don't coach children in motor skills; it won't help.
   b. Provide activities appropriate to children's developmental timetables.
   c. Be aware that undernutrition can seriously compromise motor development by making children too tired to move much.

4. Your friend is concerned because her daughter, Tara, has been gaining weight. What is the best advice to give?

   a. Keep reminding Tara that she needs to lose weight.
   b. Encourage Tara to be more physically active.
   c. Carefully monitor exactly what Tara eats.

Answers to the Tying It All Together questions can be found in the answers section of the book.

Cognitive Development

In this section, we turn to the heart of this chapter: cognition. How do children develop intellectually as they travel from age 3 into elementary school? In our search for answers we explore three very different perspectives on mental growth. Let's begin with the ideas of the master theorist Jean Piaget.

Piaget's Preoperational and Concrete Operational Stages

Recall from Chapter 1 that Piaget believed that through assimilation (fitting new information into their existing cognitive structures) and accommodation (changing those cognitive slots to fit input from the world), children undergo qualitatively different stages of cognitive growth. In Chapter 3 we discussed Piaget's sensorimotor stage. Now it is time to tackle the next two stages, illuminated in Table 5.3: the preoperational and concrete operational stages.

As their names imply, we need to discuss these two stages together. **Preoperational thinking** is defined by what children are missing—namely, the ability to step back from their immediate perceptions. **Concrete operational thinking** is defined by what they possess: the ability to reason about the world in a more logical, adultlike way.

preoperational thinking In Piaget's theory, the type of cognition characteristic of children aged 2 to 7, marked by an inability to step back from one's immediate perceptions and think conceptually.

concrete operational thinking In Piaget's framework, the type of cognition characteristic of children aged 8 to 11, marked by the ability to reason about the world in a more logical, adult way.

TABLE 5.3: Piaget's Stages: Focus on Childhood

Age	Name of Stage	Description
0–2	Sensorimotor	The baby manipulates objects to pin down the basics of physical reality. This stage ends with the development of language.
2–7	Preoperations	Children's perceptions are captured by their immediate appearances. "What they see is what is real." They believe, among other things, that inanimate objects are really alive and that if the appearance of a quantity of liquid changes (for example, if it is poured from a short, wide glass into a tall, thin one), the amount becomes different.
8–12	Concrete operations	Children have a realistic understanding of the world. Their thinking is really on the same wavelength as adults'. While they can reason conceptually about concrete objects, however, they cannot think abstractly in a scientific way.
12+	Formal operations	Reasoning is at its pinnacle: hypothetical, scientific, flexible, fully adult. Our full cognitive human potential has been reached.

When children leave infancy and enter the stage of preoperational thought, they have made tremendous mental strides. Still, they often seem on a different planet from adults in terms of the way they reason about the world. The problem is that preoperational children take things at face value. They are unable to look beyond the way objects immediately appear. By about age 7 or 8, children can mentally transcend what first hits their eye. They have entered the concrete operational stage.

The Preoperational Stage: Taking the World at Face Value

We saw some vivid examples of these "from another planet" ways of thinking in the preschoolers' conversations and actions in our chapter-opening vignette. Now let's enter the minds of young children and explore the ways they reason about physical substances and the social world.

STRANGE IDEAS ABOUT SUBSTANCES   The fact that preoperational children are locked into immediate appearances is illustrated by Piaget's (1965) famous **conservation tasks**. In Piaget's terminology, *conservation* refers to our knowledge that the amount of a given substance remains identical despite changes in its shape or form.

In the conservation of mass task, for instance, an adult gives a child a round ball of clay and asks that boy or girl to make another ball "just as big and heavy." Then she reshapes the ball so it looks like a pancake and asks: "Is there still the same amount now?" In the conservation of liquid task, the procedure is similar: Present a child with two identical glasses with equal amounts of liquid. Make sure he tells you, "Yes, they have the same amount of water or juice"; then pour the liquid into a tall, thin glass while the child watches and ask, "Is there more or less juice now, or is there the same amount?"

Typically, when children under age 7 are asked this final question, they give a peculiar answer: "Now there is more clay" or "The tall glass has more juice." "Why?" "Because now the pancake is bigger" or "The juice is taller." Then, when the clay is remolded into a ball or the liquid poured into the original glass, they report: "Now it's the same again." The logical conflict in their statements doesn't bother them at all. In Figure 5.3, you can see these two procedures illustrated step by step as well as some examples of additional Piagetian conservation tasks you might want to perform with children you know.

Why can't young children conserve? For two reasons, Piaget believes. First, children don't grasp a concept called **reversibility**. This is the idea that an operation (or procedure) can be repeated in the opposite direction. Adults automatically accept as

[FAQ: How do young children think about the world?]

conservation tasks Piagetian tasks that involve changing the shape of a substance to see whether children can go beyond the way that substance visually appears to understand that the amount is still the same.

reversibility In Piaget's conservation tasks, the concrete operational child's knowledge that a specific change in the way a given substance looks can be reversed.

[FAQ: How does Piaget's theory tell us what children can and cannot do?]

Type of conservation	Initial step and question	Transformation and next question	Preoperational child's answer
Number	Two equal rows of pennies.  "Are these two rows the same?" (Yes.)	Increase spacing of pennies in one line. "Now is the amount of money the same?"	"No, the longer row has more."
Mass	Two equal balls of clay. 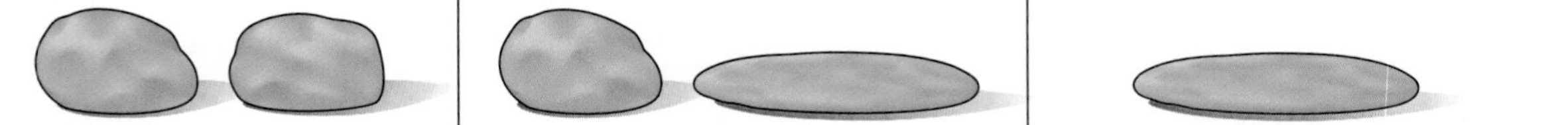 "Do these two balls have the same amount of clay?" (Yes.)	Squeeze one ball into a long pancake shape. "Now is the amount of clay the same?"	"No, the long, thin one has more clay."
Volume of liquid	Two glasses of the same size with liquid.  "Do these glasses have the same amount of juice?" (Yes.)	Pour one into a taller, narrower glass. "Now do these glasses have the same amount of juice?"	"No, the taller glass has more juice."
Matter*	Two identical cubes of sugar.  "Do these cubes have the same amount of sugar?" (Yes.)	Dissolve one cube in a glass of water. "Now is there the same amount of sugar?"	"No, because you made one piece of sugar disappear."

*That is, the idea that a substance such as sugar is "still there" even though it seems to have disappeared (by dissolving).

FIGURE 5.3: Four Piagetian conservation tasks: Can you perform these tasks with a child you know?

given the fact that we can change various substances, such as our nail polish, hairstyle, or the color of our room, and simply reverse them to their original state. Young children lack this fundamental *schema*, or cognitive structure, for interpreting the world.

A second issue lies in an overall perceptual style that Piaget calls **centering**. Young children, Piaget believes, get fixated on the most striking feature of what they immediately see. They interpret things according to what first hits their eye, rather than taking in the entire visual array. In the conservation of liquid task, they get captivated by the height of the liquid. They don't notice that the width of the original container makes up for the height of the current one. When children reach concrete operations, they are able to **decenter**. They can step back from the immediate appearance of a substance and scan the whole picture—understanding that an increase in one dimension makes up for a loss in the other one.

Centering—the tendency to fix on what is visually most striking—causes children to make mistakes on a variety of real-world tasks. It affects **class inclusion**. This is the knowledge that a general category can encompass subordinate elements. Spread 20 Skittles and a few Gummi Bears on a plate and ask a 3-year-old, "Would you rather have the Skittles or the candy?" and she is almost certain to say, "The Skittles," even when you have determined beforehand that both types of candy have equal appeal. She gets mesmerized by the number of Skittles and does not notice that "candy" is the label for both.

Centering interferes with **seriation**—the child's capacity to put objects in order according to some principle, such as size. Place sticks of different lengths in various positions on a table and tell a 5-year-old to arrange them from the smallest to the biggest,

centering In Piaget's conservation tasks, the preoperational child's tendency to fix on the most visually striking feature of a substance and not take other dimensions into account.

decentering In Piaget's conservation tasks, the concrete operational child's ability to look at several dimensions of an object or substance.

class inclusion The understanding that a general category can encompass several subordinate elements.

seriation The ability to put objects in order according to some principle, such as size.

and she is likely to pick the sticks that protrude farthest first. Because, as you can see in Figure 5.4, she looks at (centers on) what first hits her eye, she doesn't consider the actual length of each stick.

These failures are a symptom of a more basic cognitive difficulty. According to Piaget, young children don't have the abstraction skills to understand the concept of a category within which we can classify objects. They don't grasp the idea that it is possible to rank objects in a series at all.

This tendency to focus on immediate appearances explains why, in the opening vignette, Moriah believed that Manuel had more paper when he cut his sheet into sections. Her attention was captured by the spread-out pieces, and she believed that now there must be more paper than before.

The idea that "bigger" automatically equals "more" extends to every aspect of preoperational thought. Ask a 3-year-old if he wants a nickel or a dime, and he will choose the first option. (This is a great source of pleasure to older siblings asked to equally share their funds.) Perhaps because greater height means "older" in their own lives, children even believe that a taller person has been on earth for a longer time:

I was substitute teaching with a group of kindergarten children—at the time I was about 22—and when I met a student's mother at the end of the week, she was shocked. "When I asked Ben about you," she said, "he told me you were much *older than his regular teacher." This teacher was in her mid- to late fifties and looked it. However, then we figured out the difference. This woman was barely 5 feet tall, whereas I am 6 feet two!*

PECULIAR PERCEPTIONS ABOUT PEOPLE Young children's tendency to believe that "what hits my eye right now is real" extends to people. It explains why a 3-year-old thinks her mommy is transformed into a princess when she dresses up for Halloween, or cries bitterly after her first visit to the beauty salon, believing that her short haircut has transformed her into a boy. It makes sense of why a favorite strategy of older sisters and brothers to torture younger siblings is to put on a mask and see the child run in horror from the room. As these examples show, young children lack a concept called **identity constancy**. They don't realize that people are still their essential selves despite changes in the way they visually appear.

I got insights into this identity constancy deficit at my son's fifth birthday party, when I hired a "gorilla" to entertain the guests (some developmental psychologist!). As the hairy six-foot figure rang the doorbell, mass hysteria ensued—requiring the gorilla to take off his head. After the children calmed down, and the gorilla put on his head again to enact his skit, guess what? Pure hysteria again! Why did that huge animal cause such pandemonium? The reason is that the children believed that the gorilla, even though a costume figure, was really alive.

FIGURE 5.4: **A problem with seriation:** When asked to "put these sticks in order, from biggest to smallest," this kindergartener may center on the uppermost part of the table and identify the sticks numbered 2 and 5 as the biggest.

[**FAQ:** What are some examples that illustrate the terminology of Piaget's theory?]

identity constancy In Piaget's theory, the preoperational child's inability to grasp that a person's core "self" stays the same despite changes in external appearance.

When her dad puts on a mask, he suddenly becomes a scary monster to this 4-year-old girl because she has not yet grasped the principle of identity constancy.

Peter Hvizda / The Image Works

Animism refers to the difficulty young children have in sorting out what is really alive. Specifically, preschoolers see inanimate objects—such as dolls or costume figures—as having consciousness, too. Look back at the vignette and you will notice several examples of animistic thinking—for example, the Barbies that were hungry and the wind that ran away. Now think back to when you were age 5 or 6. Do you remember being afraid

His animistic thinking causes this 4-year-old to believe that the bear is really going to enjoy the ride he is about to provide.

the escalator might decide to suck you in? Or perhaps you recall believing, as in the Experiencing the Lifespan box, that your dolls came alive at night.

Listen to young children talking about nature, and you will hear delightful examples of animism: "The sun gets sleepy when I sleep." "The moon likes to follow me in the car." The practice of assigning human motivations to natural phenomena is not something we automatically grow out of as adults. Think of the Greek thunder god Zeus, or the ancient Druids who worshiped the spirits that lived within trees. Throughout history, humans have regularly used animism to make sense of a frightening world.

A related concept is called **artificialism.** Young children believe that everything in nature was made by human beings. Here is an example of this "daddy power" in action from Piaget's 3-year-old daughter, Laurent:

> L was in bed in the evening and it was still light: "Put the light out please" . . . (I switched the electric light off.) "It isn't dark"—"But I can't put the light out outside" . . . "Yes you can, you can make it dark." . . . "How?" . . . "You must turn it out very hard. It'll be dark and there will be little lights everywhere (stars)."
>
> (Piaget, 1951/1962, p. 248)

animism In Piaget's theory, the preoperational child's belief that inanimate objects are alive.

artificialism In Piaget's theory, the preoperational child's belief that human beings make everything in nature.

EXPERIENCING THE LIFESPAN: CHILDHOOD FEARS, ANIMISM, AND THE POWER OF STEPHEN KING

There was one shadow that would constantly cast itself on my bedroom wall. It looked just like a giant creeping towards me with a big knife in his hand.

Our basement was a big hangout. But take away the kids and it was horrifying. I used to believe that Satan lived in my basement. The light switch was at the bottom of the steps, and whenever I switched off the light it was a mad dash to the top. I was so scared that Satan was going to stab my feet with knives.

Boy, do I remember my mom's doll that sat on the top of my dresser. I called it "Chatty Kathy." This doll came to life every night. She would stare at me, no matter where I went.

My mother used to take me when she went to clean house for Mrs. Handler, a rich lady. Mrs. Handler had this huge, shiny black grand piano, and I thought it came alive when I was not looking at it. It was so enormous, dark, and quiet. I remember pressing one of the bass keys, which sounded really deep and loud and it terrified me.

I remember being scared that there was something alive under my bed. I must tell you I sometimes still *get scared*

that someone is under my bed and that they are going to grab me by my ankles. I don't think I will ever grow out of this, as I am 26.

Can you relate to any of these childhood memories collected from my students? Perhaps your enemy was that evil creature lurking in your basement, under your bed, or in the shadows in your room; the frightening stuffed animal on your wall; a huge object (with teeth) such as that piano; or your local garbage truck.

Now you know where that master storyteller Stephen King gets his ideas. King's genius is that he taps into the preoperational kinds of thoughts that we have papered over, though not very well, as adults. When we read King's story about a toy animal that clapped cymbals to signal someone's imminent death, or about Christine, the car with a mind of its own, or about the laundry-pressing machine that loved human blood—these stories fall on familiar childhood ground. Don't you still get a bit anxious when you enter a dark basement? Even today, on a very dark night, do you have an uneasy feeling that some strange monster might be lurking beneath your bed?

Animism and artificialism are perfect illustrations of Piaget's concept of assimilation. The child knows that she is alive and so applies her "alive" schema to every object. Having seen adults perform heroic physical feats, such as turning off lights and building houses, a 3-year-old generalizes the same "big people control things" schema to the universe at large. Imagine that you are a young child taking a family tour around the American West. After you visited that gleaming construction called Las Vegas, wouldn't it make perfect sense to you that people had carved out the Grand Canyon and the Rocky Mountains, too?

The sun and moon examples illustrate another basic aspect of preoperational thought. According to Piaget, young children believe that they are the literal center of the universe, the pivot around which everything else revolves. Their worldview is characterized by **egocentrism**—the inability to understand that other people have different points of view from their own.

By *egocentrism*, Piaget does not mean that young children are vain or uncaring, although they will tell you they are the smartest people on earth and the activities of the heavenly bodies are at their beck and call. Many of their most loving acts show egocentrism. There is nothing more touching than a 3-year-old's offer of a favorite "blankee" if he sees you upset. The child is egocentric, however, because he naturally assumes that what comforts *him* will automatically comfort you.

You can easily pick out examples of egocentrism when having a conversation with a young child. In the opening vignette, for instance, remember that Kanesha got disgusted that I didn't automatically know her name. She didn't feel she had to give me background information about Neruda, this person who cooked so beautifully, because she felt I must know everything that was in her head.

Piaget views egocentrism as a perfect example of centering in the human world. Young children are unable to decenter from their own mental processes. They don't realize that what is in their mind is not in everyone else's awareness, too.

egocentrism In Piaget's theory, the preoperational child's inability to understand that other people have different points of view from their own.

The Concrete Operational Stage: Getting on the Adult Wavelength

Piaget discovered that the transition from preoperations to concrete operations happens gradually. First, children are preoperational in every area. Then, between ages 5 and 7, their thinking gets less static, or "thaws out" (Flavell, 1963). A 6-year-old, when given the conservation of liquid task, might first say the taller glass had more liquid, but then, after it is poured back into a very wide glass, become unsure: "Is it really bigger or not?" She has reached the tipping point when she cannot assimilate her experiences to her existing preoperational schemas and is poised to reason on a higher cognitive plane.

By age 8, the child has reached this higher-level, concrete operational state: "Even though the second glass is taller, the first is wider" (showing decentering); "You can pour the liquid right back into the short glass and it would look the same (illustrating reversibility). Now, she doesn't realize that she ever had a different idea: "Are you silly? Of course it's the same!"

Piaget also found that specific conservations come in at different times. First, at about age 5, children learn number and then later master conservation of mass and liquid. They may not figure out the most difficult conservations until age 11 or 12. Imagine the challenge of understanding the last task in Figure 5.3—realizing that when a packet of sugar is dissolved in water, it still exists, but in its basic molecular form (see page 149).

Still, according to Piaget, age 8 is a landmark for looking beyond immediate appearances, for understanding seriation and categories, for decentering in the physical and social worlds, for abandoning the tooth fairy and the idea that our stuffed animals are alive, for entering the planet of adults.

Table 5.4 shows examples of different kinds of preoperational ideas. Now test yourself by seeing if you can classify each statement in Piagetian terms.

TABLE 5.4: Can You Identify the Type of Preoperational Thought from These Real-World Examples?

Here are your possible choices: (*a*) no identity constancy, (*b*) animism, (*c*) artificialism, (*d*) egocentrism, (*e*) no conservation, and (*f*) inability to use classification.

_____ 1. Heidi was watching her father fix lunch. After he cut her sandwich into quarters, Heidi said, "Oh, Daddy, I only wanted you to cut it in *two* pieces. I'm not hungry enough to eat four!" (Bjorklund & Bjorklund, 1992, p. 168)

_____ 2. My 2-year-old son and I were taking our yearly trip to visit Grandma in Florida. As the plane took off and gained altitude, Thomas looked out the window and said with a delighted grin, "Mommy, TOYS!"

_____ 3. Melanie watched as her father, a professional clown, put on his clown outfit and then began applying his makeup. Before he could finish, Melanie suddenly ran screaming from the room, terrified of the strange clown.

_____ 4. Your child can't understand that he could live in his town and in his state at the same time. He tells you angrily, "I live in Newark, not New Jersey."

_____ 5. As you cross the George Washington Bridge over the Hudson River to New Jersey, your child asks, "Did the same people who built the bridge also make the river?"

Answers: 1 (*e*), 2 (*d*), 3 (*a*), 4 (*f*), 5 (*c*)

INTERVENTIONS: Using Piaget's Ideas at Home and at Work

Piaget's concepts provide wonderful insights into the mysterious workings of young children's minds. For teachers, the theory explains why you need the same-sized cups at a kindergarten lunch table or an argument will erupt, even if the children poured each drink from identical cans. Nurses now understand that rationally explaining the purpose of a painful medical procedure to a 4-year-old may not be as effective as providing a magic doll to help the child cope.

The theory makes sense of why forming a Little League team with a group of 4- or 5-year-olds is an impossible idea. Grasping the rules of a game requires abstract conceptualization—a skill that preoperational children do not yet possess. It tells us why young children are terrified of their dreams, the dark, and scary clowns at the amusement park. So for parents who feel uneasy about playing into their child's fantasies when they provide "anti-monster spray" to calm those bedtime fears, one justification is that, according to Piaget, when your child is ready, she will naturally grow out of her ideas.

Piaget's concepts also give us wonderful insights into children's specific passions at different ages. They explain the power of pretending in early childhood (more about this in Chapter 6) and the irresistible lure of that favorite childhood holiday, Halloween. When a 4-year-old child dresses up as Batman, he may be grappling with the challenge of understanding that you can look different yet still remain your essential self. The theory accounts for why third or fourth graders become captivated with games, such as checkers and soccer, and can be avid collectors of items such as baseball cards. Now that they can understand the concept of rules and categories, concrete operational children are determined to exercise their new conceptual and classification skills.

On a larger level, the theory explains why "real school," the academic part, begins at about age 7 around the world. Children younger than this age—those still in the preoperational stage—don't have the intellectual tools to understand reversibility, a concept critical to understanding mathematics (if 2 plus 4 is 6, then 6 minus 4 must equal 2). Even having the capacity to fully empathize with the teacher's agenda or grasp the purpose of school is a concrete operational skill.

[FAQ: How can Piaget's theories be put to use in the home or work place?]

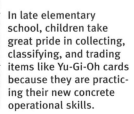

Suzanne Kreiter / The Boston Globe / The New York Times

In late elementary school, children take great pride in collecting, classifying, and trading items like Yu-Gi-Oh cards because they are practicing their new concrete operational skills.

You thought it was just a fun movie, but the *real* reason you loved *Home Alone* was that it was all about giving up your pre-operational worldview to enter the real (concrete operational) world.

The fact that age 8 is an important coming-of-age marker is symbolized by the popular movie *Home Alone*. The plot of this film would have been unthinkable if its hero were 5 or even 6. If the star were 11, the movie would be not be so interesting, because by this age a child could competently take care of himself. Eight is that fragile point when we begin to make the transition to really being able to make it "home alone." It is the age when we shift from worrying about monsters—things that are not real—to grappling with the kinds of dangers that we really face as adults.

Evaluating Piaget

Piaget has clearly transformed the way we think about young children. His ideas are also supported by the new neuroscience findings showing that frontal-lobe pruning sets in when children move fully into concrete operations, by age 9. Still, in important areas, Piaget was incorrect.

We described one problem with Piaget's ideas in Chapter 3: In the same way as he minimized what babies know, Piaget underestimated preoperational children's cognitive capacities. In particular, Piaget overstated young children's egocentrism. If, as we mentioned early in this chapter, toddlers can understand intentions, the first awareness that we all live in "different heads" must dawn on children at a far younger age than 8 (more about this topic later on).

We might also take issue with Piaget's idea that we automatically grow out of animism by age 8 or 9. Maybe he was giving us too *much* credit here. Do you have a good luck charm that keeps the plane from crashing, or a favorite place you go for comfort where you can literally hear the trees whispering to you?

[FAQ: Have Piaget's cognitive tasks been repeated with different populations and in different settings?]

Children around the globe eventually do grasp the basic principles of conservation, supporting Piaget's idea that he was describing a universally unfolding developmental process (Dasen, 1977, 1984). But because nature interacts with nurture, the ages at which children master specific conservation tasks vary from place to place. An interesting example comes from a village in Mexico where weaving is the main adult occupation. Young children in this collectivist culture grasp conservation tasks involving spatial concepts when they are younger than age 7 or 8, because they have so much hands-on training in activities relating to this kind of skill (Maynard & Greenfield, 2003). This brings up a crucial dimension that Piaget's theory leaves out: the impact of teaching in promoting cognitive growth.

Because this girl growing up in Mexico gets so much practice at weaving, we might expect her to grasp concrete operational conservation tasks related to spatial concepts at a relatively early age.

Vygotsky's Zone of Proximal Development

Piaget gives the impression of a child working alone to construct a more adult view of the world. We can't convince young children that their dolls are not alive or that the width of the glass makes up for the height. They have to grow out of those ideas on their own developmental timetable. The Russian psychologist Lev Vygotsky (1962, 1978, 1986) had a different perspective. Vygotsky believed that people propel mental growth.

Vygotsky was born in the same year as Piaget. He showed as much creativity and brilliance at an exceptionally young age, although he died of tuberculosis in his late thirties. Still, Vygotsky's writings have given him towering status in developmental science today. One reason is that Vygotsky was an educator as much as a theorist. He offered a framework for understanding how what *we* do helps children to advance cognitively.

According to Vygotsky, learning takes place within the **zone of proximal development,** which he defined as the difference between what the child can do by himself and his level of "potential development as determined through problem solving under adult guidance or in collaboration with more capable peers" (Vygotsky, 1978, p. 86). Teachers must tailor their instruction to a child's proximal zone. Then, as that child becomes more competent, the instructor should slowly back off and allow the student more responsibility for directing a particular learning activity. This process of sensitive pacing has a special name. It is called **scaffolding** (Wood, Bruner, & Ross, 1976).

You saw scaffolding in operation in Chapter 3, in our discussion of infant-directed speech, the simplified language adults use when talking to babies. Recall that baby talk has a very adult function. It permits caregivers to penetrate a young child's proximal zone for language and so helps scaffold emerging speech. Now let's explore scaffolding firsthand, as we listen in on a mother teaching her 5-year-old daughter how to play her first board game, Chutes and Ladders:

> *Tiffany threw the dice, then looked up at her mother. Her mother said, "How many is that?" Tiffany shrugged her shoulders. Her mother said, "Count them," but Tiffany just sat and stared. Her mother counted the dots aloud, and then said to her daughter, "Now you count them," which Tiffany did. This was repeated for the next five turns. Tiffany waited for her mother to count the dots, then modeled her mother's actions and moved her piece. On her sixth move, however, Tiffany counted the dots on the dice on her own after her mother's request. . . . During the next few moves, her mother still had to ask Tiffany to count how many dots she had. But eventually, Tiffany threw the dice and counted the dots herself and continued to do so, practicing counting and moving the pieces on both her own and her mother's turns.*
>
> (Bjorklund & Rosenblum, 2001)

Notice that this mother was a superb scaffolder. By pacing her interventions to Tiffany's emerging capacities, she paved the way for her child to master the game. But this process did not just flow from parent to child. Tiffany was also teaching her mother how to best respond. Just as your professor is getting new insights into lifespan development from the process of teaching every single class—or at this very minute, as I struggle to write this page, I'm learning how to better connect with Vygotsky's ideas—education is a *bidirectional,* mind-expanding duet (Scrimsher & Tudge, 2003; see also Rogoff, 1990).

In our culture, we have definite ideas about what makes a good scaffolder: Enter a child's proximal zone. Actively instruct, but also be sensitive to a child's input and responses. However, in collectivist societies, such as among the Mayans living in Mexico's Yucatán Peninsula, children learn mainly by observation. They listen in on adult conversations. They watch. They are not explicitly taught the skills they will need for adult life (Rogoff and others, 2003). So the very qualities Westerners see as vital to socializing children are not necessarily part of the ideology of good parenting in other regions of the globe.

zone of proximal development In Vygotsky's theory, the gap between a child's ability to solve a problem totally on his own and his potential knowledge if taught by a more accomplished person.

scaffolding The process of teaching new skills by entering a child's zone of proximal development and tailoring one's efforts to that person's competence level.

[**FAQ:** How can adults contribute to children's cognitive development?]

Daryl Benson / Masterfile

This girl in Thailand is learning to weave just by observing her mother—a strategy that we might find strange in our teaching-oriented culture.

INTERVENTIONS: Becoming an Effective Scaffolder

In our teaching-oriented culture, what exactly do superior scaffolders do? Let's list a few techniques:

- They take care to foster a secure attachment, as they realize that nurturing, responsive interactions are a basic foundation for learning (Laible, 2004).

- They break a larger cognitive challenge, such as learning Chutes and Ladders, into smaller, more manageable steps (Berk & Winsler, 1999).

- They give nonthreatening (but clear) feedback about failure—for instance, hesitating and looking at the correct alternative when the child makes a mistake (Gallimore & Tharp, 1992; Rogoff, 1990).

- They continue helping until they know the child has fully mastered the concept before moving on, as Tiffany's mother did earlier.

- They set an overall framework for the learning task and build in motivation. So, in teaching reading, a first-grade teacher might say: "This is a book about lions. It's about how the author makes friends with a cub. Ooh, this looks like a really interesting book. I can't wait to see what the author says!" (Clay & Cazden, 1992).

In Chapter 7, we'll be looking at these qualities as they relate to elementary school teaching. For now, think of a master scaffolder, or teacher, who stood out in your life. List that person's qualities. Keep your list handy to see if your items fit the teaching talents you'll read about two chapters from now.

Table 5.5 contrasts Vygotsky's and Piaget's perspectives and offers capsule summaries of the backgrounds that helped shape these world-class geniuses' ideas. Although typically described in opposing terms (Rogoff, 1990; Shayer, 2003), these two landmark

TABLE 5.5: **Piagetian and Vygotskian Perspectives on Life and Learning**

Lev Vygotsky (1896–1934)	Jean Piaget (1896–1980)

Biography	
Russian, Jewish, communist (reached teenage years during the Russian Revolution)	Swiss, middle-class family
Basic Interests	
Education, literature, literary criticism. Wanted to know how to stimulate thinking.	Biology, mollusks. Wanted to trace the evolution of thought in stages.
Overall Orientation	
Look at interpersonal processes and the role of society in cognition	Look for universal developmental processes
Basic Ideas	
1. We develop intellectually through social interactions.	1. We develop intellectually through physically acting on the world.
2. Development is a collaborative endeavor.	2. Development takes place on our own inner timetable.
3. People cause cognitive growth.	3. When we are internally ready, we reach a higher level o cognitive development.
Implications for Education	
Instruction is critical to development. Teachers should sensitively intervene within each child's zone of proximal development.	

www.davidsonfilms.com

Bill Anderson / Photo Researchers, Inc.

theories form an ideal complementary pair. Piaget gave us unparalleled insights into the developing structure of childhood cognition. Vygotsky offered us an engine to transform children's lives.

The Information-Processing Perspective

Vygotsky filled in the missing social pieces of Piaget's theory and provided us with a framework for stimulating mental growth. But he did not address the gaps in the theory itself. Exactly *why* are children able to decenter? What specific skills allow children to understand that the width of the glass makes up for the height?

Piaget never mentions how crucial abilities such as memory, concentration, and planning develop. Ms. Angela, the preschool teacher in the opening vignette, might wonder (with good reason) if she was asking too much of her 3-year-olds to remember those free-play rules. Elementary school teachers might want tips for teaching spelling to a third-grade class. Parents might be looking for guidelines as to what to expect from a child at a particular age: "When can my daughter take responsibility for caring for a puppy?" "When will my son have the organizational skills to get ready for school on his own?" Clinical psychologists and caregivers would want to understand why a particular child has so much trouble focusing and obeying at school and at home. To get this information, everyone would gravitate toward the *information-processing approach*.

Recall from Chapter 3 that information-processing theorists view mental growth as continuous rather than progressing in qualitatively distinct stages. They break cognitive processes into components and divide thinking into specific steps. Let's illustrate this approach by examining the information-processing perspective on memory, the basis of all thought.

Making Sense of Memory

Information-processing theorists believe that on the way to becoming "a memory," information passes through different stores, or stages. First, we hold stimuli arriving from the outside world very briefly in a sensory store. Then features that we notice enter the most important store, called working memory.

Working memory is where the "cognitive action" takes place. Here we keep information in awareness and act to either process it or discard it. Working memory is made up of limited-capacity holding bins. It also consists of an "executive processor," which allows us to focus on what we need to remember as well as manipulating the material in working memory to prepare it for permanent storage (Baddeley, 1992). Once we have processed what we need to learn through working memory, it enters a more long-lasting store, and we can recall that information at a later time.

You can get a real-life example of the fleeting quality of the information in working memory when you get a phone number from information and immediately make the call. You know that you can dial the seven-digit number without having to write it down, and your memory will not fail *if you get to finish*. If you are interrupted by a beep from another caller and lose your focus, the number mysteriously evaporates. In fact, for adults the typical bin size of working memory is about the size of a regular phone number: seven chunks of information.

Interestingly, by examining age changes in working memory, information-processing researchers have offered a tantalizing explanation for why young children can't conserve. Memory-bin capacity, as it turns out, expands dramatically between ages 2 and 7—from about two to five bits of information (Dempster, 1981). At about age 6, the executive processor, which allows us to competently massage material through our bins, expands to its adult-like form (Gathercole and others, 2004). These changes, developmentalists speculate, may explain why children reach concrete operations at roughly age 7 or 8 (Case, 1999; Pascual-Leone, 1970). By this age, we finally have the memory capacities to step back from our immediate impressions of a substance and remember that what we saw previously (such as a wider glass) compensates for what we are seeing right now.

Steve Lyne / Getty Images

Does a girl this age have the memory capacity and self-regulation skills necessary to take proper care of a dog? This is the kind of question that an information-processing perspective on cognition can answer.

[**FAQ:** How does the information-processing framework conceptualize memory?]

working memory In information-processing theory, the limited-capacity gateway system, containing all the material that we can keep in awareness at a single time. The material in this system is either processed for more permanent storage or lost.

Exploring Executive Functions

executive functions Any frontal-lobe ability that allows us to inhibit our responses and to plan and direct our thinking.

Executive functions refer to any skill related to managing our memory, controlling our cognitions, planning our behavior, and inhibiting our responses. Executive functions are programmed by the brain's master planner—the frontal lobes. Now let's look at three types of executive functions that make children in concrete operations radically different thinkers than they were at age 4 or 5.

OLDER CHILDREN REHEARSE INFORMATION A major way we learn new information is through **rehearsal.** We repeat material again and again to embed it in memory. In a classic study, developmentalists had kindergarteners, second graders, and fifth graders memorize objects (such as a cat or a desk) pictured on cards (Flavell, Beach, & Chinsky, 1966). During the interval prior to the testing, the research team watched the children's lips to see if they were using the strategy of repeating the names of the objects to themselves. Eighty-five percent of the fifth graders used rehearsal; only 10 percent of the kindergarteners did. So one reason why older children are more capable of learning material is that they understand that they need to rehearse.

rehearsal A learning strategy in which people repeat information to embed it in memory.

And, furthermore, as children get older, their rehearsal strategy becomes better thought out. Researchers asked third, fifth, and eighth graders to memorize a series of words (Ornstein, Naus, & Liberty, 1975). They presented each word individually and gave the children time in between each presentation to rehearse aloud. Third graders just repeated the previous word, for example, saying, *yard, yard, yard, yard.* Older children allotted their rehearsal time more strategically, saying *yard, yard, man, desk,* to make sure they kept in mind all the words they needed to recall.

To bring home the message of this research, if your final exam in this class is cumulative, you know you need to spend most of your time memorizing the last section of this book but still need to go back and review what you learned for the other tests. In third grade you *never* would have grasped this fundamental studying fact.

OLDER CHILDREN UNDERSTAND HOW TO SELECTIVELY ATTEND The ability to manage our awareness so we focus on what we need to know and filter out extraneous information is called **selective attention.** In another classic study illustrating young children's problems in this area, researchers presented boys and girls of different ages with cards. On one half of each card was an animal photo; on the other half was a picture of some household item (see Figure 5.5). The children were instructed to remember only the animals.

selective attention A learning strategy in which people manage their awareness so as to attend only to what is relevant and to filter out unneeded information.

As you might expect, older children were far better at recalling the animal names. But now comes the interesting part: When the children were asked how many household items they could recall, the performance differences between the age groups evaporated—suggesting that the young children wasted effort looking at the objects

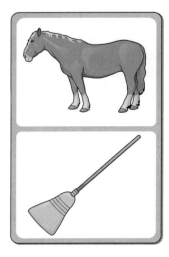

FIGURE 5.5: **A selective attention study:** In this study measuring *selective attention,* children were asked *only* to memorize the animals on the top half of the cards. Then researchers looked for age differences in their memory for the irrelevant household items.

they did not need to know (Bjorklund, 2005). This suggests that, in addition to having smaller memory bins, young children tend to clog their existing bin space with irrelevant information. They can't focus their attention as well on what is relevant and filter out extraneous stimuli.

OLDER CHILDREN ARE SUPERIOR AT INHIBITION In the opening vignette you saw the enormous problems young children have inhibiting their impulses when the 3-year-olds ran into the different activity centers without stepping back and thinking, "That's not what I'm supposed to do." The most fascinating example of inhibition problems occurred during the weather report. Because the temptation to say yes was so strong, the children could not restrain themselves from putting up their hands and agreeing when the teacher asked *any* question about the weather that day.

Given that the exciting news is on this child's mind and the frontal lobes are still under construction, there is no such thing as a secret!

To measure differences in inhibition directly, researchers have developed an ingenious strategy: They ask people to perform some action that contradicts their immediate tendencies. For instance, a person might be told to say the word *black* when he sees the word *white*, or to say the word *night* when he sees a photo of the sun and *day* when shown a picture of the moon (Diamond, Kirkham, & Amso, 2002; Diamond & Taylor, 1996).

Young children and adults with frontal-lobe damage perform very poorly on these kinds of tasks. In fact, notice that many activities in the chapter-opening preschool vignette—such as the "move faster and slower" dance, the center rules, even sitting and listening to the teacher—were designed specifically to train children in the vital skills of following adults' directions and controlling their immediate responses.

The bottom line is that if you think self-control is difficult for you, imagine being a young child. And never, never tell a 4- or 5-year-old to keep a "big secret." Her response is automatically going to be to immediately blurt it out!

[**FAQ:** How can adults help children succeed in school?]

INTERVENTIONS: Using Information-Processing Theory at Home and at Work

So, to bring us back to the questions at the beginning of this section, teachers *cannot* assume that their third graders will automatically understand how to memorize spelling words. Scaffolding study skills, such as the need to rehearse, or teaching strategies to promote selective attention, such as putting large stars next to the relevant words for a test, should be an integral part of education, beginning in elementary school.

Parents will probably need to regularly remind a child to feed the dog even at age 5 or 6. Expect activities requiring many different information-processing tasks, such as getting dressed and remembering to take homework and pencils to class, to be a challenge *throughout* elementary school (and beyond). Actively scaffold organizational strategies, such as helping a second grader get everything ready for school before bedtime and teaching that child to put important items such as a bookbag in specific places. For everyone else, the information-processing research suggests that executive functions, such as using learning strategies, selectively attending, and inhibiting our behavior, are processes that improve gradually over *many years.*

Table 5.6 summarizes these practical messages and provides some additional information-processing tips. Now let's look at the insights the information-processing perspective offers caregivers and clinical psychologists who are interested in understanding children with problems focusing and obeying—boys and girls with attention deficit/hyperactivity disorder, or ADHD.

TABLE 5.6: Information-Processing Tips for Adults to Use with Young and Older Children

Early Childhood

1. Don't expect a child to remember, without considerable prompting, regular chores such as feeding a pet, the details of a movie or show, or the name of the person who telephoned this afternoon.

2. Expect the child to have a good deal of trouble with any situation that involves inhibiting a strong "prepotent impulse"—such as not touching toys, following unpleasant rules, or keeping a secret.

Middle Childhood

1. Don't assume that the child knows how to best master school-related memorization tasks. Actively teach the need to rehearse information, selective attention strategies (such as underlining important points), and other studying skills.

2. Scaffold organizational strategies for school and life. For example, get the child to use a notebook for each class assignment and to keep important objects, such as eyeglasses, in a specific place.

3. Expect situations that involve many different tasks, such as getting ready for school, to present problems. Also expect activities that involve *ongoing* inhibition to give children trouble, such as refraining from watching TV or using the Internet before finishing their homework. Try to build in a regular structure for mastering these difficult executive-functioning tasks: "The rule is that at 8 or 9 P.M., it's time to get everything ready for school"; "Homework must be completed by dinnertime, or the first thing after you get home from school."

4. To promote selective attention (and inhibition), have a child do homework, or any task that involves concentration, in a room away from tempting distractions such as the TV or Internet.

FOCUS ON A TOPIC: ATTENTION DEFICIT/HYPERACTIVITY DISORDER

attention deficit/hyperactivity disorder (ADHD) The most common childhood learning disorder in the United States, disproportionately affecting boys, characterized by excessive restlessness and distractibility at home and at school.

[FAQ: Is ADHD a biological disorder?]

Attention deficit/hyperactivity disorder (ADHD), defined by excessive restlessness and distractibility, is now the top-ranking health disorder among U.S. children. From the mid-1980s to 2001, the number of boys and girls given this diagnosis quadrupled, to roughly 4 million children (MMWR, 2005). Although preschoolers also have this label, ADHD is typically diagnosed in elementary school. During middle childhood, problems sitting still and focusing become clearly apparent and cause special trouble in school and at home.

ADHD is predominantly a male problem, affecting three times as many boys as girls (Biederman, 2005). Almost 10 percent of 10-year-old boys are taking medications for this problem today in the United States! (See Nissen, 2006.)

As twin studies reveal that ADHD has a strong genetic component (Doyle and others, 2005), researchers are feverishly trying to pin down the neurological problem that might be involved (Volkmar, 2005). One hypothesis is that people with ADHD have a lower output of neurotransmitters such as dopamine (Williams & Dayan, 2005). Scientists also use brain scans to look for specific abnormalities when children with ADHD perform learning tasks (Liotti and others, 2005; Mulas and others, 2006; Schulz and others, 2005; Volkmar, 2005). Still, there is no definitive biological test or marker that is diagnostic of ADHD (Furman & Berman, 2004).

What we do know is that a core difficulty with this diagnosis lies in problems with inhibition (Barkley, 1998, 2003; Barkley & Murphy, 2006). When told, for instance, "Don't touch the toys," boys and girls diagnosed with ADHD have unusual trouble not touching.

Watching TV, talking on the phone, and doing homework, all at the same time, would be difficult for anyone, but impossible for a child diagnosed with ADHD.

These children have special problems with selective attention, too (Stins and others, 2005). Researchers asked elementary school children to watch a story on TV (Siklos & Kerns, 2004). In one condition, toys were in the room. In another, there were none. When asked to explain the point of the story, the children diagnosed with ADHD performed just as well as the control group when the toys were not present but did more poorly when these distracting objects were around. So even when they are just as intellectually capable, competing stimuli make children with ADHD get derailed.

As you might imagine, performing several different activities under time pressure, such as getting dressed and ready for school by 7:00 A.M., presents immense problems for children with ADHD. To demonstrate this fact, researchers gave 7- to 13-year-olds with this diagnosis, and a comparison group, six different activities, such as putting puzzles together and completing mazes (Pugzles, Lorch, & others, 2004). They told the children to try as many tasks as possible within 10 minutes and gave them a timer prominently displayed on a computer screen. Then they looked for differences in performance between the two groups. The children diagnosed with ADHD attempted fewer tasks and scanned the clock less frequently—showing special difficulties with time management, or the ability to allocate their time among several tasks.

These problems explain why even the most intellectually gifted child with ADHD can have considerable trouble in school. Classrooms are highly distracting environments. Taking tests well requires allocating one's efforts wisely within a limited period of time.

The same issues with inhibition, selective attention, and time management lead to failures at home. In dealing with their child's difficulties, parents may resort to *power-assertion* disciplinary techniques. They lash out at a 9-year-old who seems incapable of getting his things in order. They scream at a child who seems unwilling to "just sit still." So children with ADHD are *least* likely to get the sensitive, loving parenting that their temperament most demands (Burt and others, 2003). Their failures at school and at home put these children at risk of being labeled "defiant" and highly aggressive (Barkely and others, 2004; Root & Resnick, 2003). The family atmosphere may be poisoned, as mothers in particular become overwhelmed and depressed (Kendall and others, 2005). Given these dangers, what should a caring adult do?

[FAQ: What can we do about my little brother's ADHD?]

INTERVENTIONS: Helping Children with ADHD

The standard treatment for ADHD is to provide psycho-stimulant medications, such as Ritalin. Drugs are useful particularly at reducing the impulsivity, or inhibition problems, basic to ADHD (Barkley & Murphy, 2006; Sutcliff, Bishop, & Houghton, 2006). Medications are most effective when combined with psychosocial interventions, such as using reinforcement for appropriate behavior (Olfson and others, 2003).

Another important strategy is to foster the best possible person–environment fit (Murphy, 2005): Don't put unreasonable demands on a child to do difficult processing tasks. Provide a nondistracting environment during activities that require selective attention, such as completing homework and taking tests.

Even offering regular exercise can help. Researchers gave an elementary school class periodic recess and then compared their classroom behavior on recess and non-recess days. On recess days, the children with ADHD showed lower rates of "inappropriate behavior." In fact, regular recess helped *every* child stay on task and focus better on their schoolwork (Ridgway and others, 2003).

Formal schooling is a fairly recent development on the human landscape. Our ancestors never needed to sit in a classroom for hours. To what degree might this contemporary problem be partly a product of poor childhood–society fit? (See, for instance, Panksepp, 1998; Timimi, 2004.)

Making the environment as free of distractions as possible is the best strategy for helping this boy diagnosed with ADHD stop daydreaming and do his schoolwork.

Royalty-Free / Corbis

[FAQ: Is ADHD overdiag-
nosed, underdiagnosed, or
misdiagnosed?]

This brings up the controversy surrounding the diagnosis of ADHD. Are we over-medicating children for a condition that may sometimes not be "real"? The fact that an astonishing 1 in 10 U.S. fifth-grade boys has had this diagnosis (and the far lower preva-lence of ADHD in Europe) suggests that in the United States this contemporary label may be migrating too widely (Nissen, 2006). Especially troubling is the male tilt to ADHD. As you will see in the next chapter, boys are biologically programmed to run around. Without denying that ADHD can cause considerable heartache to children and adults in today's world, what role might cultural forces play in the frequency of this diagnosis at this particular moment in historical time?

Wrapping Up Cognition

Now that we have reached the end of our survey of cognition, it is clear why our species needs a decade (or two) beyond infancy to master the intellectual challenges of the adult world. And imagine the insights we would be missing if we left out any theory. What if you wanted to make sense of the strange ideas preschoolers have, or needed a general framework for stimulating intellectual growth? What if you wanted some guidance as to what to expect from children in terms of listening, following di-rections, and sitting still? You would have to turn to Piaget, Vygotsky, and the infor-mation-processing perspective. Has a particular theory been especially valuable in helping you understand the children you know?

 ## TYING IT ALL TOGETHER

1. While spending the day with your 3-year-old nephew Mark, you observe many exam-ples of preoperational thought. Give the Piagetian label—egocentrism, animism, no conservation, artificialism, identity constancy—for each of the following:

   a. Mark tells you that the big tree in the garden is watching him. _____
   b. When you stub your toe, Mark gives you his favorite stuffed animal. _____
   c. Mark tells you that his daddy made the sun. _____
   d. Mark says "There's more juice now" when you pour juice from a half-pint carton into a tall, skinny glass. _____
   e. Mark tells you that his sister turned into a princess yesterday when she put on a cos-tume.

2. In a sentence, explain the basic mental difference between an 8-year-old in the con-crete operational stage and a preoperational 4-year-old.

3. Christopher, a preschooler, can recognize every letter of the alphabet and is beginning to sound out words in books. Drawing on Vygotsky's theory, decide which of the fol-lowing Chris's parents should do:

   a. Buy alphabet books, because their son will be able to recognize all the letters.
   b. Buy some "easy-to-read" books just above their son's skill level.
   c. Challenge Chris by getting him books with more complicated stories.

4. Which of the following is *not* an example of an executive function?

   a. A fourth grader rehearses the items he has to learn for a spelling test.
   b. An eighth grader decides "I have to do my homework" right after he gets home from school, rather than watching TV.
   c. You blurt out that you are giving your husband a trip for his birthday.

5. Laura's son has been diagnosed with ADHD. On the basis of what you have read in this chapter, suggest some environmental strategies she might use to help her child.

Answers to the Tying It All Together questions can be found in the answers section of the book.

Language

So far we have been looking at the cognitive and physical milestones in this chapter as if they occurred in a vacuum. But that uniquely human ability, language, is vital to every childhood advance. Vygotsky (1978) actually put *using* language—or speaking—front and center in everything we learn.

[FAQ: What is private
speech, and does it mean
my child is weird?]

Inner Speech

According to Vygotsky, learning takes place when the words a child hears from parents and other scaffolders migrate inward to become talk directed at the self. For instance, using the example of Chutes and Ladders described earlier, after listening to her mother say "Count them" a number of times, Tiffany learned the game by repeating "Count them" to herself. Thinking, according to Vygotsky, is really **inner speech.**

Support for this interesting idea comes from listening to young children monitoring their actions. A 3-year-old might say, "Don't touch!" as she moves near the stove; or she might remind herself to be "a good girl" at preschool that day. Interestingly, in one study researchers observed that when the cognitive demands of a task increased, 5- and 6-year-old children started to talk to themselves much more ("Should I do . . . , this or maybe that . . .") (Fernyhough & Fradley, 2005). This research perfectly explains a behavior we may have observed from time to time in ourselves. If something is *really important*—and if no one is listening—we also may give ourselves advice out loud!

> **inner speech** In Vygotsky's theory, the way by which human beings learn to regulate their behavior and master cognitive challenges, through silently repeating information or talking to themselves.

Developing Speech

How exactly does the ability to use language unfold? Actually, during early childhood language does more than simply unfold. It explodes.

By our second birthday, we are just beginning to put together words (see Chapter 3). By the time we reach kindergarten, we basically have adult language nailed down. When we look at the challenges involved in mastering language, this achievement becomes more remarkable. To speak like adults, children must be able to articulate word sounds. They must be able to string units of meaning together in sentences. They must produce sentences that are grammatically correct. They must be able to understand the meanings of words.

The individual word sounds of language are called **phonemes.** When children begin to speak in late infancy, they can only form single phonemes—for instance, they call their bottle *ba.* They repeat sounds that seem vaguely similar, such as calling their bottle *baba,* when they cannot form the next syllable of the word. By age 3, while children have made tremendous strides in producing phonemes, they still—as you saw in the vignette—have trouble pronouncing multisyllable words (like *psghetti*). Then, early in elementary school, these articulation problems tend to disappear—but not completely. Have you ever had a problem pronouncing a difficult word that you were perfectly able to read on a page?

The basic meaning units of language are called **morphemes** (for example, the word *boys* has two units of meaning: *boy* and the plural suffix *s*). As children get older, their average number of morphemes per sentence—called their **mean length of utterance (MLU)**—expands. A 2-year-old's sentence "Me juice" (2 MLUs) quickly becomes "Me want juice" (3 MLUs) and then, at age 4, "Please give me the juice" (5 MLUS). Also around age 3 or 4, children begin to be fascinated by producing extremely long, jumbled-together sentences strung together by *and* ("Give me juice and crackers and milk and cookies and . . .").

This brings up the steps to mastering grammar, or what is called **syntax.** Here, what's interesting are the classic mistakes that young children make. As parents are well aware, one of the first words that children utter seems to be *No.* First, children typically add this word to the beginning of a sentence ("No eat cheese" or "No go inside"). Next, they move the negative term inside the sentence, next to the main verb ("I no sing" or "He no do it"). A question starts out as a declarative sentence with a rising intonation: "I have a drink, Daddy?" Then it, too, is replaced by the correct word order: "Can I have a drink, Daddy?" Children typically produce grammatically correct sentences by the time they enter school.

Without doubt, however, the most amazing changes occur in **semantics**—understanding word meanings. Here the progression is unbelievable. Children go from three- or four-word vocabularies at age 1 to knowing about 10,000 words by age

> **[FAQ: How do we develop language abilities?]**

> **[FAQ: How do phonemes and morphemes work?]**

> **phoneme** The sound units that convey meaning in a given language—for example, in English, the *c* sound of *cat* and the *b* sound of *bat.*

> **morpheme** The smallest unit of meaning in a particular language—for example, *boys* contains two morphemes: *boy* and the plural suffix *s.*

> **mean length of utterance (MLU)** The average number of morphemes per sentence.

> **syntax** The system of grammatical rules in a particular language.

> **semantics** The meaning system of a language—that is, what the words stand for.

TABLE 5.7: Challenges on the Language Pathway: A Summary Table

Type of Challenge	Description	Example
Phonemes	Has trouble forming sounds	*Baba, psghetti*
Morphemes	Uses few meaning units per sentence	*Me go home*
Syntax (grammar)	Makes mistakes in applying rules for forming sentences	*Me go home*
Semantics	Has problems understanding word meanings	*Calls the family dog a horsey*
Overregularization	Puts irregular pasts and plurals into regular forms	*Foots; runned*
Over/underextension	Applies verbal labels too broadly/narrowly	*Calls every old man grandpa; tells another child he can't have a grandpa because* grandpa *is the name for his grandfather alone.*

overregularization An error in early language development, in which young children apply the rules for plurals and past tenses even to exceptions, so irregular forms sound like regular forms.

overextension An error in early language development in which young children apply verbal labels too broadly.

underextension An error in early language development in which young children apply verbal labels too narrowly.

6! (See Slobin, 1971; Smith, 1926.) Interestingly, around the world, children learn nouns—perhaps because they refer to specific objects and so are more salient— more rapidly than verbs (Bornstein and others, 2004; Imai, Haryu, & Okada, 2005). While we have the other core abilities involved in speaking like adults basically under our belts by the end of early childhood, our vocabularies continue to grow from age 2 to 102.

One interesting mistake young children make while learning language is called **overregularization.** Around age 3 or 4, they often misapply general rules for plurals or past tenses even when exceptions occur. A preschooler, for instance, will say *runned, goed, teached, sawed, mouses, feets,* and *cup of sugars* rather than using the correct irregular form (Berko, 1958).

Another interesting error lies in the semantic mistakes children produce. Also around age 3, children often use what are called **overextensions**—meaning they extend a verbal label too broadly. In Piaget's terminology, they may assimilate the word *horsey* not just to horses but to all four-legged creatures, such as dogs, cats, and lions in the zoo. Or they may use **underextensions**—making name categories too narrow. A 3-year-old may tell you that only her own pet is a dog and insist that all the other neighborhood dogs must be called something else. As children get older, through continual assimilation and accommodation, they sort these glitches out.

Table 5.7 summarizes these language challenges. As an exercise, you might want to have a conversation with a 3- or 4-year-old child. Can you pick out examples of overregularization, overextensions or underextensions, problems with syntax (grammar), or difficulties pronouncing phonemes (word sounds)? Can you figure out the child's MLU?

❧ TYING IT ALL TOGETHER

1. A 5-year-old is talking out loud, making comments such as "Put the big piece here," while constructing a puzzle. What would Vygotsky say about this behavior?

2. You are listening to a 3-year-old named Joshua. Pick out the example of overregularization and the overextension from the following comments.

   a. When offered a piece of cheese, Joshua said, "I no eat cheese."
   b. Seeing a dog run away, Joshua said, "The doggie runned away."
   c. Taken to a petting zoo, Joshua pointed excitedly at a goat and said, "Horsey!"

Answers to the Tying It All Together questions can be found in the answers section of the book.

Specific Cognitive Skills

Language makes us capable of some uniquely human understandings. We are the only species that can see ourselves traveling through time, that is capable of continually reflecting on our evolving life. We are the only species, as mentioned earlier, that regularly transports ourselves into other people's heads, continually imagining what people are thinking and feeling from their own point of view. How do children learn they have an ongoing life history? When do we fully grasp that "other minds" are different from our own?

Constructing Our Personal Past

Autobiographical memories refer to remembering the contents of our personal life histories: from our earliest memories at age 4, to our high school graduation, to that incredible experience we had at work last week (Nelson, 2000; Nelson & Fivush, 2004). Children's understanding that they have a unique autobiography, developmentalists believe, is scaffolded through specific kinds of discussions. Caregivers reminisce with young children: "Remember going on a train to visit Grandma?" "What did we do at the beach last week?" These *past-talk conversations* are teaching a basic lesson: "You have a life story, an ongoing, enduring self" (Nelson, 1999, 2000; Nelson & Fivush, 2004).

Past-talk conversations follow a standard progression. They typically begin with parents doing all the "remembering" in late infancy, when children are just beginning to speak (Harley & Reese, 1999). Then, as preschoolers' language skills improve, adults directly question their children about events they shared: "What did we do on the train when we went to Grandma's?" "Whom did we see at the beach?" Gradually, children become full partners in these mutual stories, and finally, at age 4 or 5, initiate past-talk conversations on their own (Nelson & Fivush, 2004). Let's look at the dramatic changes that take place in children's autobiographies from age 4 to 6:

INTERVIEWER TO 4-YEAR-OLD: Tell me about the Easter egg hunt.

CHILD: I find the golden basket.

INTERVIEWER: You won the golden egg? So tell me more about finding the golden egg.

CHILD: In the tree.

INTERVIEWER TO 6-YEAR-OLD: Can you tell me about the ballet recital?

CHILD: It was driving me crazy.

INTERVIEWER: Really?

CHILD: Yes, I was so scared because I didn't know any of the people and I couldn't see mom and dad. They were way on top of the audience. . . . Ummm, we were on a slippery surface and we all did "Where the Wild Things Are" and we . . . Mine had horns sticking out of it . . . And I had baggy pants.

(adapted from Nelson & Fivush, 2004)

What can adults do to stimulate the kinds of elaborate descriptions this 6-year-old produced? The key is to actively question young children about experiences you shared (Boland, Haden, & Ornstein, 2003; Nelson & Fivush, 2004). Parents differ dramatically in this tendency. Some mothers and fathers rarely talk to a child about what they have done together or ask simple questions such as "What happened at the beach?" Others actively scaffold memories of the past by providing extensive hints. For instance, if a father asks, "What happened when we went to the beach?" and his son doesn't respond, he helps the child by adding details: "Do you remember that we took a walk . . . and what did we pick up?" Needless to say, highly stimulating parent scaffolders have children with richer, more differentiated autobiographical memories (Reese, Haden, & Fivush, 1993).

autobiographical memories Recollections of events and experiences that make up one's life history.

When they get home, this mother can help her daughter construct her "personal autobiography" by starting a dialogue about their wonderful day at the beach and—most important—encouraging the child to talk about her memories.

Paul Avis / Getty Images

In our individualistic society, we put a premium on exploring our inner psychological states. From talk show hosts, to teachers, to mothers and fathers, the first question everyone is primed to ask when we listen to a child recounting an exciting event is, "How did it make you feel?" Might children's autobiographical memories be different in collectivist cultures that put less emphasis on the individual and more on the social group?

An interesting cross-cultural study answered yes. One researcher asked children living in China and in the United States to describe their last birthday or to talk about something that happened recently that was interesting and fun (Wang, 2004). The American children, he discovered, bubbled with past-talk accounts focusing on their feelings. The Chinese children gave more limited descriptions. Their accounts were less likely to feature themselves as the stars of their plots. So even our memories of the past are shaped by the culture in which we live.

When children—in any society—begin to use past-talk conversations, at around age 4 or 5, they use their experiences to connect with other people. Whether we are reminiscing about high school or discussing that amazing event at work, sharing our personal autobiographies is the glue that bonds us to other people at any age. But to really share their personal experiences, children must understand that other people have different experiences from their own. Now we turn to when that special awareness locks in.

Making Sense of Other Minds

Listen to 2- and 3-year-olds having a conversation, and you will get the feeling they are talking "at" each other. It's almost as if you are hearing two disconnected monologues, or mental ships passing in the night. Around age 4 or 5, children really start relating in *give-and-take* ways. They now have reached a human landmark called **theory of mind,** the understanding that we all live in different heads (Lillard, 2000; Wellman, 1990). Developmentalists have devised a special procedure to demonstrate this milestone—*the false-belief task.*

theory of mind Children's first cognitive understanding, which appears at about age 4, that other people have different beliefs and perspectives from their own.

With a friend and a young child, see if you can perform the test for the presence of theory of mind shown in Figure 5.6 (Wimmer & Perner, 1983). Hide a toy in a particular place (location A) while the child and your friend watch. Then have your friend leave the room, and move the toy to another hiding place (location B). Next ask the child where *your friend* will look for the toy when she returns. If the child is under age 4, he will typically answer the second hiding place (location B), even though your friend could not possibly know the toy has been moved. It's as if the child doesn't grasp the fact that what *he* observed can't be in your friend's head, too.

Having a theory of mind is not only vital to having a real give-and-take conversation, it is crucial to grasping a painful fact: Other people may not have your best interests at heart. One developmentalist had children play a game with "Mean Monkey," a puppet the experimenter controlled (Peskin, 1992). Beforehand, the researcher had asked children which sticker they really wanted. Then she had Mean Monkey pick each child's favorite choice. Most 4-year-olds quickly figured out how to play the game and told Mean Monkey the opposite of what they wanted. Three-year-olds never seemed to catch on. They consistently pointed to their favorite sticker and always got the "yucky" one instead.

A remark from one of my students brings home the real-world message of this research. She commented that her 4-year-old nephew had reached the stage where he was beginning to tell lies. Under age 4, children don't fully have the mental abilities to understand that their parents don't know the thoughts in their head. So lying is indeed an important cognitive advance!

The false-belief studies convinced developmentalists that Piaget's ideas about preoperational egocentrism had serious flaws. While perspective-taking abilities continue to develop throughout life—and change in major ways around age 8—children

(1) Another adult and a young child watch while you hide a toy in a place like a desk drawer.

FIGURE 5.6: **The false-belief task:** In this classic test for *theory of mind*, when children under age 4 are asked, "Where will Ms. X look for the toy?" they are likely to say, "Under the bed," even though Ms. X could not possibly know the toy was moved to this new location.

Source: Based on Wimmer & Perner (1983).

(2) The other adult [Ms. X] leaves the room.

(3) You hide the toy under the bed and then ask the child, "Where will Ms. X look for the toy?"

grasp the principle that there are other minds out there years sooner than Piaget would have predicted. Even the age-4 marker may not be accurate. Children show signs of theory of mind well before they can articulate their understanding in words.

Consider this ingenious study: Researchers had toddlers watch two kinds of false-belief sequences (Onishi & Baillargeon, 2005). In one, the person who left and then returned looked for the hidden object in the place where she logically should have—

hiding place A. In the other, the person returned to look for the object in the second hiding place (location B). By 18 months of age, infants appeared surprised when the adult looked in the second hiding place. It was as if they were thinking: "Hey, she wasn't there, so how could she possibly know the object was moved?"

Actually, this finding should come as no surprise. If, as suggested early in this chapter, we start to grasp intentions at about age 1½, we would expect the first glimmers of theory of mind to appear at this very age!

Studies from India, Samoa, and Canada show that the vast majority of children have mastered theory-of-mind tasks by the time they turn 5 (Callaghan and others, 2005). However, there is wide individual variation. Children with superior language abilities often pass verbal false-belief tasks at younger ages (Slade & Ruffman, 2005). But more than language skills are involved. Babies who are securely attached—those with responsive caregivers—tend to develop theory-of-mind abilities earlier (McElwain & Volling, 2004). Conversely, children who have been abused are delayed at mastering false-belief tasks (Pears & Fisher, 2005). So sensitively responding to a baby's feelings helps to scaffold the basic life understanding that other people have different points of view.

Hands-on experience in negotiating with other minds also helps (Avis & Harris, 1991; Tardif & Wellman, 2000). Perhaps because they need to continually jockey for objects—for instance, by saying, "Hey, I want that toy." "Do you?" (Jenkins and others, 2003; Ruffman and others, 1998; Smith, 1998)—having older brothers and sisters helps stimulate theory of mind (Perner, Ruffman, & Leekam, 1994; Ruffman and others, 1998). Moreover, when you are the youngest child in the family, you may be more motivated to develop your "mind-reading" abilities to help you survive (Cummins & Allen, 1998). To illustrate, using an example from our Piaget section, after repeatedly being fooled, a 3-year-old might finally comprehend, "My big brother has a different agenda. When he tells me to take that big piece of money [the nickel], I'd better do the opposite of what he says!"

Interestingly, children and adults with autism, a severe developmental disorder involving difficulties with language and the inability to form relationships, have particular trouble with theory-of-mind tasks even when they perform well on general intelligence tests (Baron-Cohen, 1999; Baron-Cohen, Leslie, & Frith, 1985; Perner and others, 1989; Steele, Joseph, & Tager-Flusberg, 2003). So autism is a particularly devastating condition, because it hinders the ability to genuinely relate to other minds. In fact, returning to the beginning of this chapter, we now know theory of mind is at the heart of being human. It is *really* what makes our species different from any other animal on earth.

Although this big sister probably doesn't intend it, her teasing may be stimulating her 3-year-old sibling's emerging theory of mind.

A. Inden / Zefa / Corbis

TYING IT ALL TOGETHER

1. Andrew said to Madison, his 3-year-old son, "Remember when we went to Grandma and Grandpa's last year? . . . It was your birthday, and what did Grandma make for you? . . . " This _____ conversation will help scaffold Madison's _____.

2. Pick out the statement that would *not* signify that a child has developed a full-fledged theory of mind:

    a. He's having a real give-and-take conversation with you.
    b. He realizes that if you weren't there, you can't know what's gone on—and tries to explain to you what happened while you were absent.
    c. When he has done something he shouldn't do, he is likely to lie.
    d. He's learning to read.

3. Discuss some strategies for stimulating theory of mind.

Answers to the Tying It All Together questions can be found in the answers section of the book.

Final Thoughts

In summary, during early childhood we lay down the basic foundations of self-awareness and the tools for relating to others. In the next chapter we look *directly* at these expanding emotional and social skills—especially (but not exclusively) as children travel into middle childhood. How can we use Piaget's distinctions between the preoperational and concrete operational stages to understand elementary school children's basic concerns? Can the principles of information-processing theory allow us to pinpoint why some children have trouble relating to their peers? What insights does Vygotsky's concept of the zone of proximal development offer for children who are having self-esteem problems, and what insights did this master theorist have about childhood play? Now we look at these questions and many others as we turn to the socioemotional side of life. ▮

▌ SUMMARY

Two Major Learning Challenges

Childhood comprises two phases—**early** and **middle childhood**—and this decade-long period before we are physically able to reproduce lasts longer in our species than in any other animal. We need this time to master the rules of living in particular societies, to absorb the lessons passed down by previous generations, and to take advantage of our finely tuned ability to decode intentions—the talent that has allowed us to advance. The **frontal lobes,** in particular, take two decades to become "adult." As this region of the brain—involved in higher reasoning and planning—gradually develops, every childhood ability improves.

Physical Development

Physical growth slows down after infancy. Girls and boys are roughly the same height during preschool and much of elementary school. Boys are a bit more competent at **gross motor skills.** Girls are slightly superior in **fine motor skills.** Although motor skills can be accelerated by providing training, we need to be careful not to push young children too hard. Stress, and especially undernutrition, impairs physical development by making children too tired to engage in the exercise crucial to promoting physical skills.

The prevalence of **childhood obesity**—defined as a **body mass index (BMI),** or height-to-weight ratio, at the 95th percentile—has dramatically increased during the past 25 years. A variety of forces are implicated in this increasingly global problem. The decline in physical activity is particularly important. Monitoring a child's food intake is not the answer, as it may lead to low self-esteem and make that boy or girl actually eat more. Childhood obesity threatens life expectancy by producing the risk factors for diabetes and cardiovascular disease at abnormally young ages.

Cognitive Development

Piaget's preoperational stage lasts from age 3 to 7. The concrete operational stage lasts from age 8 to 11. **Preoperational thinkers** focus on the way objects and substances (and people) immediately appear. **Concrete operational thinkers** can step back from their visual perceptions and reason on a more conceptual plane. In Piaget's **conservation tasks,** children in preoperations believe that when the shape of a substance has changed, the amount of it has changed. One reason is that young children lack the concept of **reversibility,** the understanding that an operation can be repeated in the opposite way. Another is that children **center** on what first captures their eye and cannot **decenter,** or focus on several dimensions at one time. Centering also affects **class inclusion** (understanding overarching categories) and **seriation** (putting objects in a series from small to big). Preoperational children believe that if something *looks* bigger visually, it always equals "more."

Preoperational children lack **identity constancy;** they don't understand that people are "the same" in spite of changes in external appearance. Their thinking is characterized by **animism** (the idea that inanimate objects are alive) and by **artificialism** (the belief that everything in nature was made by humans). They are **egocentric,** unable to understand that other people have different perspectives from their own. Although Piaget's ideas offer a wealth of insights into children's thinking, he may have underestimated what young children know. Children in every culture do progress from preoperational to concrete operational thinking—but the learning demands of the particular society make a difference in the age at which specific conservations are attained.

Lev Vygotsky, with his concept of the **zone of proximal development,** suggests that learning occurs when adults tailor instruction to a child's capacities and then use **scaffolding** to gradually promote independent performance. Education, according to Vygotsky, is a collaborative, bidirectional learning experience.

Information-processing theory provides another perspective on cognitive growth. In this framework on memory, material must be processed through a limited-capacity system, called **working memory,** in order to be recalled at a subsequent time. As children get older, their memory-bin capacity expands, and the executive processor fully comes on-line. These advances may explain why children reach the stage of concrete operations at age 7 or 8.

Executive functions—the ability to think through our actions and manage our cognitions—dramatically improve over time. Children adopt learning strategies such as **rehearsal.** They get better at **selective attention.** They are better able to inhibit their immediate responses. The research on rehearsal, selective attention, and inhibition provides a wealth of insights that can be applied in real life.

Attention deficit/hyperactivity disorder (ADHD), the most frequently diagnosed childhood disorder in the United States, is far more prevalent among boys than girls. ADHD is largely genetic, but there is no specific brain test for it. Children with ADHD have trouble with executive functions such as inhibition, selective attention, and time management. Medication can be effective in controlling the impulsivity. One key to helping children with ADHD is to strive for a better person–environment fit. ADHD is a controversial diagnosis, with some critics saying that the current rise in prevalence of this condition in the United States may be due to a poor person–environment fit and cultural forces.

Language

Language makes every other childhood skill possible. Vygotsky believed that we learn everything through using **inner speech.** During early childhood, language abilities expand dramatically. **Phonemic** (sound articulation) abilities improve. As the number of **morphemes** in children's sentences increases, their **mean length of utterance (MLU)** expands. **Syntax,** or knowledge of grammatical rules, improves. **Semantic** understanding (vocabulary) shoots up. Common language mistakes young children make include **overregularization** (using regular forms for irregular verbs and nouns), **overextension** (applying word categories too broadly), and **underextension** (applying word categories too narrowly).

Specific Cognitive Skills

Autobiographical memories, the child's understanding of having a personal past, are socialized by caregivers through past-talk conversations during the first years of life. Questioning children about shared life events is key to putting them "in touch" with their personal past.

Theory of mind, a child's knowledge that other people have a different perspective from their own, is measured by the false-belief task. Children typically pass this milestone at about age 4 or 5, although glimmers of this uniquely human quality may appear at age 1½. Language skills, responsive caregiving, and having older siblings to compete with are related to the early development of theory-of-mind capacities. Children with autism have special trouble mastering theory-of-mind tasks.

▌ KEY TERMS

early childhood, p. 139

middle childhood, p. 139

frontal lobes, p. 141

gross motor skills, p. 143

fine motor skills, p. 143

body mass index (BMI), p. 144

childhood obesity, p. 144

preoperational thinking, p. 147

concrete operational thinking, p. 147

conservation tasks, p. 148

reversibility, p. 148

centering, p. 149

decentering, p. 149

class inclusion, p. 149

seriation, p. 149

identity constancy, p. 150

animism, p. 151

artificialism, p. 151

egocentrism, p. 152

zone of proximal development, p. 155

scaffolding, p. 155

working memory, p. 157

executive functions, p. 158

rehearsal, p. 158

selective attention, p. 158

attention deficit/hyperactivity disorder (ADHD), p. 160

inner speech, p. 163

phoneme, p. 163

morpheme, p. 163

mean length of utterance (MLU), p. 163

syntax, p. 163

semantics, p. 163

overregularization, p. 164

overextension, p. 164

underextension, p. 164

autobiographical memories, p. 165

theory of mind, p. 166

▌ RECOMMENDED RESOURCES

Piaget, J. (1951/1962). *Play, dreams, and imitation.* New York: Norton.

Piaget's path-breaking book offers wonderful real-life examples of animism and artificialism, as well providing a look at Piaget's theorizing in the social realm.

Vygotsky, L. S. (1978). *Mind in society: The development of higher mental processes* (edited by Michael Cole, Vera John Steiner, Silvia Scribner, and Ellen Souberman). Cambridge, MA: Harvard University Press.

This is the classic book describing Vygotsky's ideas.

CHAPTER 6

CHAPTER OUTLINE

SETTING THE CHALLENGE: EMOTION REGULATION

PERSONALITY

Observing the Self

INTERVENTIONS: Promoting Realistic Self-Esteem

Doing Good: Prosocial Behavior

INTERVENTIONS: Socializing Prosocial Children

Doing Harm: Aggression

RELATIONSHIPS

Play

INTERVENTIONS: Helping Children Through Play

Girls' and Boys' Play Worlds

Friendships

Popularity

FOCUS ON A TOPIC: Bullying

INTERVENTIONS: Attacking Bullying and Helping Rejected Children

EXPERIENCING THE LIFESPAN: Middle-Aged Reflections on My Middle-Childhood Victimization

FINAL THOUGHTS

Have you ever wondered what makes some children, such as Manuel, stand up to a bully and reach out in caring ways, while others, like Matt, seem insensitive, aggressive, and rude? Perhaps you are curious about what makes people popular, or want to help children like Jimmy and Matt who are having

Socioemotional Development

It is recess at Black Fox Elementary School. Eight-year-old Manuel and his best friend Josh, the class leaders, burst into the yard, starting a game of tag with a ball. Soon six or seven other boys join in, chasing around, having a great time, wrestling and jostling. But then things get serious, changing fast and furiously. In comes Moriah, who had been hanging out with a small group of girls.

"Can I play?"

"No girls allowed!" say the boys.

Then Matt barges in, disrupting the game, shoving and hitting, taking over the ball. A few minutes later, Jimmy, an anxious child who generally plays alone, timidly tries to enter the group.

"Get out!" erupts Matt, "You wuss. You girl!"

Matt pushes Jimmy down roughly and (as usual) a few boys start to laugh. Jimmy starts to cry and slinks away. But suddenly Manuel slows down.

"Hey, cool it, guys," he says. "Hey, man, are you all right? Come join us."

Manuel comforts Jimmy, manages to tell the other boys to lay off, and does his best, as usual, to keep Matt from messing up the game without getting him too angry—as he knows from experience how that will turn out.

problems with their peers. Have you puzzled over the fact that boys love to wrestle or wondered why elementary school children love to hate the other sex—particularly when they get together in groups? Maybe you simply want to understand your own and other people's behavior in a deeper way. If so, this chapter, covering children's emo-tional and social development, is for you.

In the first half of this chapter, we explore topics relating to person-ality; then, we look outward at chil-dren's relationships. Our goal is to offer insights into the social and emotional challenges that children face, particularly during elemen-tary school. But this chapter also has another purpose: to enable us to understand and help boys and girls, such as Matt and Jimmy, who are having problems relating to their peers. With this goal in mind, let's begin by describing a challenge we *all* struggle with, and look at how developmentalists would label Matt's and Jimmy's difficulties in that area of life.

Setting the Challenge: Emotion Regulation

In Chapter 5, we traced how the ability to inhibit our immediate reactions, programmed by the expanding frontal lobes, explains every developing cognitive and physical skill. We need the same self-regulation abilities to succeed socially and emotionally, too (Banfield and others, 2004; Ochsner & Gross, 2004). When we get angry, we must cool down our feelings, rather than lash out. We have to overcome our anxieties and take that frightening science midterm, and conquer our shyness and go to a party because we might meet that special person who will be the love of our life. **Emotion regulation** is the term developmentalists use for the skills involved in managing our feelings so that they don't get in the way of having a productive life (Bridges, Denham, & Ganiban, 2004; Calkins, 2004).

Children with **externalizing tendencies** have special trouble with this challenge. Like Matt, they act on their immediate emotions and often behave disruptively and aggressively. Perhaps you know a child who bursts into every social scene, fighting, bossing people around, wreaking havoc with his classmates and adults.

Children with **internalizing tendencies** have the opposite kind of problem—managing their intense anxiety. Like Jimmy, they hang back in social situations. They seem timid and self-conscious; they often look frightened and depressed.

The beauty of being human is that we all vary in our temperamental tendencies—to be shy or active, boisterous or reserved. Because cultural values differ so much, you might think that if Jimmy grew up in a society that puts a premium on being self-effacing, his shyness would not be a problem. If Matt was raised in a war-like culture, his tendency to aggressively barge in would help him socially succeed. You would be wrong. Socially anxious children are unpopular in collectivist countries such as China and Indonesia as well as in Canada and Illinois. Highly aggressive children—if they are impulsive and unable to regulate their feelings—are rejected around the globe. Serious externalizing and internalizing tendencies *universally* present problems during childhood and throughout life (Ani & Grantham-McGregor, 1998; Coie & Dodge, 1998; Cheah & Rubin, 2004).

In Chapter 4, we examined the temperaments that put toddlers at risk for having internalizing and externalizing problems—being highly exuberant and inhibited. Now let's look at what happens when these tendencies evolve to the point where they cause genuine suffering, as children travel into elementary school.

emotion regulation The capacity to manage one's emotional state.

externalizing tendencies A personality style that involves acting on one's immediate impulses and behaving disruptively and aggressively.

internalizing tendencies A personality style that involves intense fear, social inhibition, and often depression.

 **TYING IT ALL TOGETHER**

1. Krista, a school psychologist, is concerned about two students: Paul, who bursts out in rage and is constantly getting into trouble for fighting and misbehaving; and Jeremy, who is timid and anxious and seems sad most of the time. Krista describes Paul as having _____ tendencies and Jeremy as having _____ tendencies, and she says that issues with emotion regulation are a problem for _____.

   a. externalizing; internalizing; Paul
   b. externalizing; internalizing; both boys
   c. internalizing; externalizing; both boys
   d. internalizing; externalizing; Jeremy

Answers to the Tying It All Together questions can be found in the answers section of the book.

Personality

How do children's perceptions about themselves change as they get older, and how do these changes affect self-esteem? What makes children (and adults) act in caring or hurtful ways?

Observing the Self

Developmentalist Susan Harter (1999) has been exploring the first set of questions in research examining how children view themselves. To make sense of her findings, Harter draws on Piaget's distinction between preoperational and concrete operational thinking—a difference we will be highlighting throughout this chapter. So let's take another brief look at the mental leap that Piaget believes takes place when children reach age 7 or 8. Children in the concrete operational stage:

- Look beyond immediate appearances and think abstractly about inner states.

- Give up their egocentrism and realize they are not the center of the universe, but just one person among many others in this vast world.

To examine how these changes affect **self-awareness**—the way children think about themselves as people—Harter asks boys and girls of different ages to describe themselves. Here are two examples illustrating the responses she finds:

> *I am 3 years old and I live in a big house. . . . I have blue eyes and a kitty that is orange. . . . I love my dog Skipper. . . . I am not scared. I'm never scared! I'm always happy. I have brown hair. . . . I'm really strong.*

> *I'm in fourth grade this year, and I'm pretty popular. . . .That's because I'm nice to people and can keep secrets, although if I get into a bad mood I sometimes say something that can be a little mean. At school I'm feeling pretty smart in certain subjects like . . . Language Arts and Social Studies. . . . But I'm feeling pretty dumb in Math and Science. . . . Even though I'm not doing well in those subjects I still like myself as a person.*

(adapted from Harter, 1999, pp. 37, 48)

Notice that the 3-year-old talks about herself mainly in terms of external facts. In contrast, the fourth grader's self-descriptions are internal and psychological. They are anchored in her feelings, abilities, and inner traits. The 3-year-old describes herself in global, inflated ways as "always happy." The fourth grader lists her deficiencies and strengths in many areas of life. Moreover, while the younger child talks about herself as if she were living in a bubble, the older child focuses on how she measures up compared to her peers. So Harter believes that during concrete operations, children start to realistically evaluate their abilities and decide whether they like or dislike the person they see. **Self-esteem**—the tendency to feel good or bad about ourselves—first becomes a major issue during the middle childhood years.

Actually, around the world, studies show that self-esteem begins to decline during elementary school (Frey & Ruble, 1985, 1990; Harter & Pike, 1984; Lee, J., Super, & Harkness, 2003; Super & Harkness, 2003). A mother may sadly notice this change when her 8-year-old daughter begins to make negative comments such as, "I am not very pretty" or "I can't do math." Caring teachers struggle to cope with the same comparisons, the fact that their fourth graders are exquisitely sensitive to who is popular, which classmates are getting A's, and who needs special academic help.

This all makes perfect sense when we look at Erik Erikson's psychosocial stages. Erikson, as you can see in Table 6.1, labeled the developmental task during middle childhood (from age 6 to 12) as **industry versus inferiority.** During elementary school, we first wake up to the realities of life. We understand that we are not just completely wonderful. We need to learn to work for what we want to achieve. We are vulnerable to feeling inferior, to having the painful sense that we don't measure up.

self-awareness The ability to observe our abilities and actions from an outside frame of reference and to reflect on our inner state.

self-esteem Evaluating oneself as either "good" or "bad" as a result of comparing the self to other people.

industry versus inferiority Erik Erikson's term for the psychosocial task of middle childhood, involving the capacity to work for one's goals.

Maria Sweeney / Getty Images

When they reach concrete operations, children delight in ranking one another on everything from who is the smartest to who is the most popular. As a result, these elementary school children are now in danger of developing self-esteem "issues" for the first time.

In Erikson's framework, during elementary school, our challenge is to learn to work for what we want, and the danger is feeling inferior, that we don't measure up to other people.

TABLE 6.1: Erikson's Psychosocial Stages

Life Stage	Primary Task
Infancy (birth to 1 year)	Basic trust versus mistrust
Toddlerhood (1 to 2 years)	Autonomy versus shame and doubt
Early childhood (3 to 6 years)	Initiative versus guilt
Middle childhood (6 years to puberty)	**Industry versus inferiority**
Adolescence (teens into twenties)	Identity versus role confusion
Young adulthood (twenties to early forties)	Intimacy versus isolation
Middle adulthood (forties to sixties)	Generativity versus stagnation
Late adulthood (late sixties and beyond)	Integrity versus despair

FIGURE 6.1: **How do children view themselves?** Harter has devised this questionnaire format to measure children's feelings of competence in her five different areas of life. The item in the top panel is derived from Harter's scale designed for young children; the questions in the bottom panel are from a similar scale for elementary school children.
Source: Harter (1999), pp. 121–122.

Having this sense of inferiority is essential. It produces industry, or the passion to work to improve ourselves. However, it is a double-edged sword. Not everyone is beautiful or brilliant. Human beings do differ dramatically in the qualities the world prizes. While children vary in self-esteem, some feelings of inferiority are inevitable during elementary school and throughout life.

Still, all is not lost, because entering concrete operations produces another important change. Notice that the fourth grader quoted above compares her abilities in different areas such as personality and school (Marsh, 1993; Marsh, Craven, & Debus, 1999). So as they get older, children's self-esteem doesn't just hinge on one quality. Even if they are not doing well in one particular area, they can take comfort in the places where they really do shine.

Harter's studies suggest that in Western countries, children draw on five basic competence areas to determine their overall self-esteem: *scholastic competence* (their academic talents); *behavioral conduct* (whether they are obedient or "good"); *athletic skills* (their performance at sports); *peer likeability* (their popularity with other children); and *physical appearance* (their looks). To diagnose how a given child feels in each domain, Harter devised the kinds of questions you can see in Figure 6.1.

As we might expect, children who view themselves as "not so good" in several of these areas often report low self-esteem. However, to really understand a given child's self-esteem, it is important to know that person's unique priorities—the value that boy or girl attaches to doing well in a particular area of life.

An examiner points to a girl to a preschooler's right and says, "This girl isn't good at doing puzzles." She then points to a girl to the child's left and says, "This girl is good at doing puzzles." Then she asks the child to point to the appropriate circle under each girl. If "this really fits me," the child points to the large circle. If "this fits me a little bit," the child points to the small circle.

Really True for Me	Sort of True for Me				Sort of True for Me	Really True for Me
☐	☐	Some kids are often *unhappy* with themselves.	BUT	Other kids are pretty *pleased* with themselves.	☐	☐
☐	☐	Some kids feel like they are *just as smart* as other kids their age.	BUT	Other kids aren't so sure and *wonder* if they are as smart.	☐	☐

Here the elementary school child reads the items and checks the box that applies to her.

To understand this point, you might take a minute to rate yourself along Harter's five dimensions: your overall people skills, your politeness or good manners, your intellectual abilities, your looks, and your physical abilities. If you label yourself "not good" in an area you don't really care about (for me, it would be my physical skills), it won't make a dent in your self-esteem. If you care deeply about some particular area and don't feel you are succeeding in it, you would probably get pretty depressed.

This discounting process ("It doesn't matter if I'm not a scholar; I have great relationship skills") is vitally important. It lets us derive our self-esteem from the areas in which we do shine. The problem is that some children take this discounting to an extreme. They minimize their problems in *essential* areas of life.

According to Susan Harter, even when they are failing in other areas of life, children can sometimes derive their self-esteem from the skills in which they shine. Do you think this girl can use this science prize to feel good about herself even if she understands that she is not very popular with the other kids?

Two Kinds of Self-Esteem Distortions

Children with externalizing problems often report high self-esteem even when they are having serious difficulties with their teachers and peers (Hoza and others, 2000; Webster-Stratton & Lindsay, 1999). Perhaps you know an adult whose difficulty managing his anger gets him into continual trouble at home and at work, but who copes by taking the position, "I'm wonderful, and there's nothing wrong." Because this person seems impervious to realistic feedback and has so much difficulty regulating his emotions, he cannot take the needed steps to change his behavior and so ensures that he continues to fail.

Children with internalizing tendencies have the opposite problem. They tend to be highly self-critical. They read failure into neutral situations (Prinstein, Cheah, & Guyer, 2005). They are at risk of developing **learned helplessness** (Abramson, Seligman, & Teasdale, 1978), the feeling that they are powerless to affect their fate, and so should not even attempt to succeed. They give up at the starting gate, assuming, "I know I'm going to fail, so why should I even try?"

So children and adults with externalizing and internalizing tendencies face a similar danger—but for different reasons. When people minimize their real-world difficulties or assume they are totally incompetent, they cut off the chance of working to improve their behavior and so ensure that they *will* fail.

Table 6.2 summarizes these self-esteem problems and their real-world consequences. Then Table 6.3 offers a checklist, based on Harter's five dimensions, for evaluating yourself. Are there areas where you gloss over your deficiencies and say, "I don't have a problem"? Do you have pockets of learned helplessness that are preventing you from living a full life?

learned helplessness A state that develops when a person feels incapable of affecting the outcome of events, and so gives up without trying.

TABLE 6.2: Externalizing and Internalizing Problems, Self-Esteem Distortions, and Consequences—A Summary Table

Description	Self-Esteem Distortion	Consequence
Children with externalizing problems		
Act out "emotions," are impulsive and often aggressive.	May ignore real problems and have unrealistically high self-esteem.	Continue to fail because they don't see the need to improve.
Children with internalizing problems		
Are intensely fearful.	Can read failure into everything and have overly low self-esteem.	Continue to fail because they decide that they cannot succeed and stop working.

TABLE 6.3: Identifying Your Self-Esteem Distortions: A Checklist Using Harter's Five Domains

You have *externalizing issues* if you regularly have thoughts like these:

1. **Academics:** "When I get poor grades, it's because my teachers don't give good tests or teach well." "I have very little to learn from other people." "I'm much smarter than practically everyone else I know."

2. **Physical skills:** "When I play baseball, soccer, etc., and my team doesn't win, it's my teammates' fault, not mine." "I believe it's OK to take physical risks, such as not wearing a seatbelt or running miles in the hot sun, because I know I won't get hurt." "It's all statistics, so I shouldn't be concerned about smoking four packs a day or about drinking a six-pack of beer every night."

3. **Relationships:** "When I have trouble at work or with my family, it's typically my co-workers' or family's fault." "My son (or mate, friend, mother) is the one causing all the conflict between us."

4. **Physical appearance:** "I don't think I have to work to improve my appearance because I'm basically gorgeous."

5. **Conduct:** "I should be able to come to work late (or turn in papers after the end of the semester, talk in class, etc)." "Other people are too uptight. I have a right to behave any way I want to."

Diagnosis: You are purchasing high self-esteem at the price of denying reality. Try to look at the impact of your actions more realistically and take steps to change.

You have *internalizing issues* if you regularly have thoughts like these:

1. **Academics:** "I'm basically stupid." "I can't do well on tests." "My memory is poor." "I'm bound to fail at science." "I'm too dumb to get through college." "I'll never be smart enough to get ahead in my career."

2. **Physical skills:** "I can't play basketball (or some other sport) because I'm uncoordinated or too slow." "I'll never have the willpower to exercise regularly (or stick to a diet, stop smoking, stop drinking, or stop taking drugs)."

3. **Relationships:** "I don't have any people skills." "I'm doomed to fail in my love life." "I can't be a good mother (or spouse or friend)."

4. **Physical appearance:** "I'm basically unattractive." "People are born either good-looking or not, and I fall into the *not* category." "There is nothing I can do to improve my looks."

5. **Conduct:** "I'm incapable of being on time (or getting jobs done or stopping talking in class)." "I can't change my tendency to rub people the wrong way."

Diagnosis: Your excessively low self-esteem is inhibiting your ability to succeed. Work on reducing your helpless and hopeless attitudes and *try for change.*

Giving this child "good boy" stars just to boost his self-esteem is likely to backfire—making him think "I'm the greatest" no matter how he behaves!

INTERVENTIONS: Promoting Realistic Self-Esteem

Our discussion shows why many developmentalists argue that school programs focused on raising self-esteem—those devoted to simply instilling the message, "You are a terrific kid"—may be missing the boat (Damon & Hart, 1992; Seligman and others, 1995). Self-esteem must be anchored in reality. It must come from children's genuine achievements in the world. Telling boys and girls who are not being wonderful that they are wonderful can be dangerous if it encourages a child with externalizing tendencies—who really is having serious troubles—to adopt the worldview "I'm great no matter what I do" (Baumeister, Smart, & Boden, 1999). For any child who is having difficulty in important areas, we need to: (1) enhance *self-efficacy*, or the feeling "I can be competent" and (2) promote *realistic* perceptions about the self. As a caring adult, how might you carry out this two-pronged approach?

ENHANCING SELF-EFFICACY Using Lev Vygotsky's terminology, one key to fostering self-efficacy is to enter the child's proximal zone and put success within striking distance of the developing self. So if a second grader has problems reading, you would first determine the child's actual skill level, then tailor your teaching gradually upward from that point, regularly reinforcing that boy or girl for each small success.

At the same time, you would try to provide a better person–environment fit. You might suggest, for instance, that a very socially anxious child, like Jimmy in the chapter-opening vignette, move to a smaller classroom where making friends is not such an overwhelming task.

ENCOURAGING ACCURATE PERCEPTIONS Next you might try to change the global helpless and hopeless feelings that develop when children are having difficulty in an important area of life (Peterson, Maier, & Seligman, 1987). For a child with internalizing tendencies such as Jimmy, you might give realistic feedback to change his overly critical self-image: "Do you really think the kids hate you? Manuel wanted you to join the game." And, for children who discount their failures and have unrealistically high self-esteem, you would lavishly reinforce the child when she does well but gently give accurate feedback, too (Jenson and others, 2004).

There is a way of softening this painful "I'm not doing so well" message that is the price of entering the real world. Harter (1999) finds that feeling loved by their attachment figures provides a cushion when children realize they are having trouble in an important area of life. Once again, a secure attachment is a buffer that provides us with insulation from life's blows.

Adopting this efficacy-oriented, "I *can* do it" attitude is important, because when children reach concrete operations they tend to see their performance as fixed and due to basic abilities ("I'm just dumb") rather than as changeable and due to hard work ("I can succeed if I try") (Droege & Stipek, 1993; see Chapter 7). This tendency to see "my failed self" as stable is the downside of becoming fully self-aware. We take our failures as well as our successes with us as we travel through time.

Self-Esteem, Asian Style

So far we have been highlighting the need to stimulate realistically high self-esteem. This seems reasonable in Western societies that put a premium on developing the best possible individual self. Does this same emphasis apply around the world?

Studies comparing Japanese and U.S. self-perceptions suggest the answer may be no (Markus & Kitayama, 1991, 1994, 1998). American mothers stress their competence as parents, while Japanese women typically downplay their parenting skills (Holloway & Behrens, 2002). Japanese college students describe themselves in more modest, less self-promoting ways than their U.S. counterparts do. In fact, descriptions that from a Western perspective might indicate excessively low self-esteem are typical in Japan (Kitayama and others, 1997). The reason is that rather than emphasizing personal success, collectivist societies discourage and play down individual differences. They stress relating in a harmonious way to the group (Heine and others, 1999; Markus & Kitayama, 1991, 1994, 1998).

Once again, culture really matters. Even our basic perceptions about ourselves might be very different if we grew up in another part of the world!

Now that we've explored children's overall self-perceptions, it's time to focus on two specific qualities that make us human: the tendencies to act in caring and then hurtful ways.

If this boy has parents who adore him, he is more likely to feel "I'm still OK" even though he worries, "Why am I so dumb in math?"

[FAQ: How does culture affect the development of self-esteem?]

Ask the top-ranking student in this Chinese school "How are you doing?" and he will probably say, "About the same as the other kids." This modesty is typical because in traditional Asian cultures, it's not acceptable to stand out from your group.

What qualities made hundreds of New York City firefighters run into the burning Twin Towers on September 11, knowing that they might be facing death? This is the kind of question that developmentalists who study prosocial behavior want to answer.

prosocial behavior Sharing, helping, and caring actions.

Will this caring 3-year-old become an especially prosocial adult? According to the research described in the text, her chances are good.

Doing Good: Prosocial Behavior

Throughout the morning of September 11, 2001, the nation was riveted by the heroism of the firefighters who ran into the flaming buildings of the World Trade Center, risking almost certain death. We marveled at the "ordinary people" working high in the Twin Towers whose response to this emergency was to help others get out first.

Prosocial behavior is the term developmentalists use to describe such amazing acts of self-sacrifice as well as the minor acts of helping and caring that people perform during daily life. Prosocial behaviors are fully in swing by preschool (Eisenberg, 2003; Eisenberg & Fabes, 1998). Children help the teacher clean up the blocks. They share their toys and give their cookie to a friend.

Prosocial activities become more frequent and varied during elementary school (Fabes and others, 1996). Older children are more likely to act prosocially because they have better skills. They can get a bandage when their playmate cuts his finger or call that injured child's parent on the cell phone. Moreover, when children enter Piaget's concrete operational stage, they have the perspective-taking skills to effectively tailor their help to another person's needs. So while a 3-year-old might give a hurt friend her *own* teddy bear, a 9-year-old might search for the other child's favorite stuffed animal. The older child would understand that her hurt friend's father was the best person to offer comfort—not her own dad.

Individual and Cultural Variations

Amidst these developmental changes lie tantalizing individual differences. In one longitudinal study, developmentalists observed how much young children engaged in sharing and helping activities in preschool classrooms. Then they followed these boys and girls till they were adults. Amazingly, the amount of spontaneous sharing that children showed at ages 3 and 4 was related to reports of prosocial behavior in elementary school, during adolescence, and also in young adulthood (Eisenberg and others, 1999). So, if your 4-year-old niece seems unusually kind and caring, you can predict that she may indeed grow up to be an especially kind and caring adult.

If people differ in their prosocial tendencies, what about cultures? Are children and adults in less competition-oriented societies more prosocial than in the West? Making culture-by-culture comparisons is risky, because in some societies people may be socialized to be highly prosocial within their own group and callous to people defined as "outsiders" (Eisenberg & Fabes, 1998). What we can say is that in collectivist cultures, specific *kinds* of prosocial behaviors, such as sacrificing one's own desires to help family members, is more of a norm (Fuligni, Tseng, & Lam, 1999; Fuligni & Zhang, 2004; Suzuki & Greenfield, 2002). In some cultures there also may be a norm against *reporting* one's prosocial acts (Fu and others, 2001).

Researchers read to Canadian and Chinese boys and girls stories that described a child who did something either prosocial or destructive and then either lied to a teacher or told the truth about that act. While children in both countries said it was important to confess when you did something wrong, there was an interesting difference when it came to admitting to a good deed. Canadian children opted for saying, "Yes, I did that nice thing." Chinese boys and girls said it was important to be modest and lie, saying, "No, it must have been someone else" (Lee, K., and others, 1997).

Decoding Altruism

The fact that admitting to prosocial actions is seen as self-serving in societies that emphasize modesty, such as China or Japan, brings up an interesting point. We *all* act prosocially for a variety of non-prosocial reasons: to get praise ("I'll lend Sara money because everyone will think I am a generous person"); out of fear of punishment ("I'd better help Sara, because otherwise she'll be furious at me"); or for the well-known motive for adult "charitable donations," to show how successful we are ("If I give a Belsky Building to the college, everyone will know I'm very rich"). Genuinely prosocial behaviors involve **altruism.** They are motivated by the desire to help *apart* from getting concrete rewards. Acting altruistically, in turn, depends on experiencing a specific emotional state (Eisenberg, 1992, 2003; Saarni, 1999).

Empathy is the term developmentalists use for directly feeling another person's emotion. You get incredibly anxious when you hear your boss berating a co-worker. You were overcome by horror as you watched the Twin Towers burn.

Sympathy is the more muted feeling that we experience *for* another human being. You feel terrible *for* your co-worker, but don't feel her intense distress. Your heart went out to the people who perished in the Twin Towers that day. Researchers feel that in contrast to empathy, sympathy is actually related to behaving in an altruistic way (Eisenberg, 1992, 2003; Eisenberg & Fabes, 1998; Saarni, 1999).

The reason is that simply experiencing another person's upsetting feelings can provoke a variety of reactions, from becoming immobilized with fear to behaving in a far from caring way (Eisenberg & Fabes, 1998). We can vividly see this when, out of empathic embarrassment, we burst out laughing after a waiter spills a restaurant tray, or when we become paralyzed by terror as we see a highway crash. So to act altruistically, children need to use their emotion-regulating capacities to mute their empathic feelings into a less intense sympathetic response (Eisenberg, 1992; Saarni, 1999).

Behaving altruistically also involves having the information-processing skills to consider different alternatives and select a prosocial act. It requires feeling confident of having the talents to help. Just as I would not be likely to run into a flaming building unless I was a firefighter, the reason children in elementary school typically give for not acting prosocially is that they do not have the skills (Denham, 1998; Eisenberg & Fabes, 1998). Interestingly, therefore, researchers find that children who lack self-confidence (those prone to internalizing disorders), as well as those who are relatively nonempathic (children with externalizing problems), are less prosocial than their peers (Saarni, 1999).

Finally, the fact that studies show people tend to act prosocially when they are happy explains why, when we are immersed in our own problems, we are unlikely to reach out to a friend. It gives us another reason why children with serious internalizing or externalizing problems are unlikely to behave in prosocial ways (Eisenberg, 1992; Eisenberg & Fabes, 1998).

Now, if we return to the chapter-opening vignette, we can decode the qualities that made up Manuel's caring stand. He muted his empathic anxiety into sympathy. He used his information-processing capacities to select a prosocial act. He had the self-confidence and happiness to want to act prosocially. But we still haven't answered that critical question: Exactly what *causes* children like Manuel to act in altruistic ways?

altruism Prosocial behaviors that we carry out for selfless, non-egocentric reasons.

empathy Feeling the exact emotion that another person is experiencing.

sympathy A state necessary for acting prosocially, involving feeling upset *for* a person who needs help.

To respond altruistically to his injured playmate, this boy had to transform his empathy into sympathy, and also had to feel confident that he could take action to help.

As with every other human quality, both nature and nurture are involved. Twin studies suggest there is a genetic component to the tendency to act prosocially (Saudino, Ronald, & Plomin, 2005). Children who are securely attached are more likely to behave in prosocial ways (see Chapter 4). Understanding that providing a loving, secure attachment is the best overall strategy, let's now look at specific techniques that anyone can use to help promote children's prosocial acts.

INTERVENTIONS: Socializing Prosocial Children

[FAQ: How can I have a caring child?]

Giving concrete reinforcements, such as stars or a big prize, for being kind and helpful, as it turns out, is relatively ineffective at fostering prosocial behavior. (In order to teach a child to be altruistic, it doesn't make sense to provide a self-centered motive to be kind!) What works best is to pay attention to prosocial acts and attribute those actions to the child's basic personality—for instance, saying, "You really are a caring person for doing that," instead of "That was a nice thing you did" (Eisenberg, 1992, 2003; Eisenberg & Fabes, 1998). So if you regularly notice the kind things your niece does *and* praise her lavishly for being a kind person, you may be helping to socialize her into becoming a caring adult.

Most studies exploring prosocial behavior center on a style of discipline called **induction** (Hoffman, 1994, 2001). Caregivers who use induction actively scaffold altruism. When a child has done something hurtful, they carefully point out the ethical issue and try to promote the development of an other-centered, sympathetic response. Now imagine that classic situation when your 8-year-old daughter has invited everyone in class but Sara to her birthday party. Instead of punishing your child—or giving that other classic response "Kids will be kids"—here's what you should say: "It's hurtful to leave someone out when everyone else is getting an invitation. Think of how terrible Sara must feel!"

induction The ideal discipline style for socializing prosocial behavior, involving getting a child who has behaved hurtfully to empathize with the pain he has caused the other person.

Induction is effective for several reasons: It offers children feedback about exactly what they did wrong. It moves them off of focusing on their own punishment ("Oh, now I'm really going to get it!") to the *other* child's distress ("Oh gosh, she must feel hurt"). Most important, induction allows for reparations, the chance to make amends. The bottom line is that induction works because it stimulates the important emotion called guilt.

Shame Versus Guilt and Prosocial Acts

[FAQ: What's the best way to discipline my child?]

Think back to an event during childhood when you felt terrible about yourself. Perhaps, for instance, it was the day you were caught cheating and sent to the principal. What you may remember was feeling so ashamed. Developmentalists, however, make a clear distinction between feeling ashamed and experiencing guilt (Mills, 2005; Tangney, 1995, 1998, 2003). **Shame** is the feeling we have when we are *personally* humiliated. **Guilt** is the emotion we experience when we have violated a personal moral standard or hurt another human being.

shame A feeling of being personally humiliated.

guilt Feeling upset about having caused harm to a person or about having violated one's internal standard of behavior.

When parents, like the father in the photograph at left, use shame to discipline, a child's impulse is to get furious and yell back. But by pointing out how disappointed she is in her "good girl," the mother in the photograph at right can produce *guilt*—and so ultimately have a more prosocial child.

Michael Newman / Photo Edit,Inc.

China Tourism Press / Getty Images

Although they appear superficially similar, shame and guilt have very different effects. Shame causes us to withdraw from people. When we feel ashamed, we want to retreat, slink away, and crawl into a hole. We also feel furious at being humiliated and want to strike back. In contrast, guilt connects us to people. We feel terrible about what we have done. We try to apologize and make amends. Shame diminishes us as people. Guilt can cause us to emotionally enlarge (Tangney, 1995, 1998, 2003).

This suggests that socialization techniques involving shame are especially poisonous. If, when you arrived at the principal's office, he shamed you ("In the next school assembly, I'll tell everyone what a terrible person you are!"), you might quickly learn to change your behavior, but at a high emotional price. You would feel humiliated and depressed. You might decide you hated school. But if the principal induced guilt ("I felt so disappointed, because you're such a good kid"), you could take action to enhance self-efficacy ("Oh, Dr. Jones, what can I do to make it up?"). You might end up feeling better about yourself and more connected to school. Has feeling guilty and then apologizing ever made you feel closer to someone you love?

Table 6.4 summarizes these section messages for promoting prosocial behavior and offers an additional tip. And for readers who are thinking, "I'm prosocial, even though I didn't grow up in that kind of home," there is the reality that people can draw on their shaming childhood experiences to construct enormously prosocial adult lives. Perhaps you know someone who grew up in an abusive family whose mission is to work with abused children; or you may have seen a young person learn altruism from stepping in to take care of her siblings when her parents were emotionally impaired. While providing a loving environment is the best way to teach love, people do become altruistic out of adversity, too (McAdams, 2001). You will learn more in Chapter 12 about how some adults transform their childhood tragedies into blessings and construct exemplary prosocial lives.

Before leaving this section, I must stress that there is a difference between being a good, "obedient child" and behaving in a caring, prosocial way. In one study, preschoolers who were most likely to follow adult instructions to not touch forbidden toys (recall the compliance research in Chapter 4) were not necessarily the same children who responded with intense sympathy in simulated distress situations, when an adult dropped a box of toys on her foot and pretended to be hurt (Aksan & Kochanska, 2005).

Might the same temperamentally fearless, exuberant toddlers that adults tend to label as "bad" or "noncompliant" have the potential to be real prosocial heroes? Let's keep this possibility in mind while we look at what *can* happen to these children as they get older, in exploring another basic human trait, aggression.

TABLE 6.4: How to Produce Prosocial Children: A Summary Table

- Pay attention to kind behaviors. Then when a child has done something kind and considerate, tell him that he is "really a caring person."

- Avoid giving children treats or special privileges to reward prosocial acts. Instead, praise the child effusively and point out the positive impact of her behavior.

- When the child has hurt another person, use induction: Clearly point out the moral issue, and alert him to how the other person must feel.

- Avoid teasing and shaming. When the child has done something wrong, tell her you are disappointed and give her a chance to make amends.

- Don't think that you have fulfilled your responsibility to teach altruism by having a child participate in school or church drives to help the unfortunate. Morality isn't magically learned on Sunday. It must be taught in an ongoing way during *day-to-day* life.

When you decide to go after your classmate's purse *(instrumental aggression)*, **you may feel really powerful and good; however, she is going to get furious** *(reactive aggression)* **and want to bop you over the head!**

aggression Any hostile or destructive act.

instrumental aggression A hostile or destructive act initiated to achieve a goal.

reactive aggression A hostile or destructive act carried out in response to being frustrated or hurt.

relational aggression A hostile or destructive act designed to cause harm to a person's relationships.

Doing Harm: Aggression

Aggression refers to any act designed to cause harm, from shaming to shoving, from gossiping to starting unprovoked wars. It should come as no surprise to parents that aggression escalates to a peak at around age 2 or 3. During this critical age for socialization, children are being vigorously disciplined but don't often have the capacity to inhibit their responses. Put yourself in the place of a toddler who is continually being ordered by giants to do impossible things, such as sharing and sitting still. Because being frustrated provokes aggression, it makes perfect sense that biting, hitting, and throwing tantrums are normal during "the terrible twos" (Coie & Dodge, 1998).

As preschoolers become more skilled at regulating their emotions and can make better sense of adults' rules, rates of open aggression (yelling or hitting) dramatically decline. As children get older, the reasons for aggression change. Preschoolers' fights center on objects, such as toys. During elementary school, when children have developed a full-fledged sense of self-esteem, aggression becomes more personal. Children strike out when they have been wounded as human beings (Coie & Dodge, 1998). How exactly do researchers categorize aggressive acts?

Types of Aggression

One way developmentalists classify aggression is by its motive. **Instrumental aggression** is the name for hurtful behavior that is actively initiated to achieve a goal. Johnny kicks Manuel to gain possession of the block pile, or Sally spreads a rumor about Moriah to replace her as Sara's best friend. **Reactive aggression** occurs in response to being hurt, threatened, or deprived. Manuel, infuriated at Johnny, kicks him back.

Its self-determined nature gives instrumental aggression a more calculated, "cooler" emotional tone. When we behave aggressively to get something, we plan our behavior more carefully. We may feel a sense of self-efficacy as we carry out the act. Reactive aggression, in contrast, involves white-hot, disorganized rage. When you hear that your best friend has betrayed you, or even when you have a minor frustrating experience such as being caught in a traffic jam, you get furious and want to blindly lash out.

This feeling is perfectly normal. According to a classic theory called *the frustration–aggression hypothesis,* any time human beings are thwarted, we are biologically programmed to retaliate or strike back.

In addition to its motive—instrumental or reactive—developmentalists also distinguish between different forms of aggression. Hitting and yelling are direct forms of aggression. A more devious type of aggression is called **relational aggression,** any act designed to hurt the person's social relationships (Crick, Bigbee, & Howes, 1996; Crick, Casas, & Nelson, 2002; Crick & Grotpeter, 1995; Henington and others, 1998; Merrell, Buchanan, & Tran, 2006). Not inviting Sara to a birthday party, spreading rumors, or tattling on a disliked classmate are relationally aggressive acts.

Because it targets self-esteem and often involves more sophisticated social skills, relational aggression follows a different developmental path than openly aggressive acts. Just as rates of open aggression are dramatically declining, during middle childhood relational aggression rises. In fact, the overabundance of relational aggression during late elementary school and early adolescence (another intensely frustrating time) may explain why we tend to remember those ages as the "meanest" times of life. And furthermore, although both boys and girls engage in relational aggression, it's girls (no surprise) who adopt this indirect aggression mode most often (Crick, Grotpeter, & Bigbee, 2002; Crick & Rose, 2000; Cullerton-Sen & Crick, 2005; French, Jansen, & Pidada, 2002; Ostrov & Keating, 2004; Russell and others, 2003).

Excluding someone from your group is a classic sign of *relational aggression*—**which really gets going in middle childhood. Can you remember being the target of the behavior shown here when you were in fourth or fifth grade?**

TABLE 6.5: Aggression: A Summary of the Types

What motivated the behavior?

Instrumental aggression: Acts that are actively instigated to achieve a goal.

Examples: "I'll hit Tommy so I can get his toys." "I'll cut off that car so I can get ahead of him." "I want my boss's job, so I'll spread a rumor that he is having an affair."

Characteristics: Emotionally cool and more carefully planned.

Reactive aggression: Acts that occur in response to being frustrated or hurt.

Examples: "Jimmy took my toy, so I'm going to hit him." "That guy shoved me to take my place in line, so I'm going punch him out." "Joe took my girlfriend, so I'm gonna get a gun and shoot him."

Characteristics: Furious, disorganized, impulsive response.

What was its form?

Direct aggression: Everyone can see it.

Examples: Telling your boyfriend you hate his guts. Beating up someone. Screaming at your mother. Having a tantrum. Bopping a playmate over the head with a toy.

Characteristics: At its peak at about age 2 or 3; declines as children get older. More common in boys than in girls, especially physical aggression.

Relational aggression: Carried out indirectly, through damaging or destroying the victim's relationships.

Examples: "Sara got a better grade than me, so I'm going to tell the teacher that she cheated." "Let's tell everyone not to let Sara play in our group." "I want Sara's job, so I'll spread a rumor that she is stealing money from the company." "I'm going to tell my best friend that her husband is cheating on her because I want to break up their marriage."

Characteristics: Occurs mainly during elementary school and may be at its peak during adolescence. More common in girls than in boys.

Table 6.5 summarizes the different types of aggression and gives examples from childhood and adult life. While scanning the table, notice that we all behave in *every* aggressive way. The problem is not that people show instrumental and reactive aggression or are openly or relationally aggressive, but that some children (and adults) are aggressive *too* much of the time.

Understanding Highly Aggressive Children

We have just seen that, as they get older, children typically get much less openly aggressive. However, a small percentage of children remain unusually aggressive into elementary school (Broidy and others, 2003; Dodge & Pettit, 2003). These boys and girls are labeled with externalizing disorders defined by high rates of aggression. They are classified as defiant, antisocial kids.

THE PATHWAY TO PRODUCING PROBLEMATIC AGGRESSION A variety of longitudinal studies suggest that there is a poisonous two-step nature-plus-nurture pathway to being labeled as a highly aggressive child:

Step 1: The toddler's exuberant temperament evokes harsh discipline. When toddlers are highly active and temperamentally fearless, as we saw in Chapter 4, caregivers are tempted to adopt punitive, *power-assertion*, disciplinary techniques (Patterson, 1986, 1992). They shame, threaten, and scream at their "impossible" child: "Sit down. Shut up. You are always giving me trouble." As being shamed and threatened produces frustration, this kind of harsh discipline produces aggression in itself (Rubin and others, 2003; Shaw and others, 2003). Ironically, parents are least likely to use induction with the very toddlers whose temperaments require caring parenting the most (Bates & Bayles, 1988; McFadyen-Ketchum and others, 1996).

Step 2: The child is rejected by teachers and peers in school. Typically, the transition to being labeled "an antisocial child" occurs during early elementary school. As impulsive, by now clearly aggressive, children travel outside the family, they get defined as troublemakers and rejected by their classmates and teachers. By kindergarten, children can clearly identify which classmates are "bad" and need to be avoided (Kupersmidt,

[FAQ: How do you deal with stubborn and willful behavior?]

Regularly using power assertion to discipline an exuberant toddler (which makes him angry and defiant), and then having him be shunned by the other children for his disruptive behavior in elementary school—that's the two-step recipe for producing a highly aggressive child.

Coie, & Dodge, 1990). Regularly being rejected by other children is a powerful stress that amplifies the child's tendency to behave in hostile, aggressive ways (Dodge and others, 2003). So evocative nature-causes-nurture forces make children who are temperamentally prone to high levels of activity and physically acting out their emotions likely to go down an increasingly aggressive path.

A HOSTILE WORLDVIEW Highly aggressive children also tend to think differently in social situations. Numerous studies show that they have a **hostile attributional bias** (Crick & Dodge, 1996; MacBrayer, Milich, & Hundley, 2003; Schultz & Shaw, 2003). They see threat in benign social cues. When a child gets accidentally bumped at the lunch table, he sees a deliberate provocation. Another aggressive child decides that you are her enemy when you look at her the wrong way.

hostile attributional bias The tendency of highly aggressive children to see motives and actions as threatening when they are actually benign.

Aggressive children also feel better about acting aggressively (McConville & Cornell, 2003). Rather than working out their differences, they cope with conflict by lashing out in hostile ways (Hubbard and others, 2001; Leary & Katz, 2005). So the child's behavior actually provokes a more hostile world.

To summarize, let's enter the mind of a highly aggressive child, like Matt in the chapter-opening vignette. As a toddler, your fearless temperament continually got you into trouble with your parents. You have been harshly disciplined for years. In school, you are shunned by your classmates. So you never have a chance to really interact with other children and improve your social skills. In fact, your hostile attributional bias makes perfect sense. You are living in a "sea of negativity" (Jenson and others, 2004). And yes, you are correct: the world *is* out to do you in!

From another perspective, in predicting problems such as Matt's, researchers adopt the developmental systems approach. A *variety* of negative forces, from witnessing family violence (Farver and others, 2005; Jaffee and others, 2003), to living in a crime-ridden city neighborhood (Farever and others, 2005), to coping with divorce (Ram & Hou, 2005), to having a mother who is depressed (Hipwell and others, 2005; Kim-Cohen and others, 2005), raise the risk of antisocial behavior.

Another risk factor for having problems is simply being male. Because they tend to act out their feelings, boys are several times more likely than girls to show the kind of physically aggressive behavior that gets them labeled with an externalizing problem in elementary school (Broidy and others, 2003).

This sex difference in physical aggression is not confined to the United States. In one cross-cultural study, researchers charted the frequency of aggressive acts among boys and girls in villages in Belize, Samoa, Kenya, and Nepal. In every society, boys were more physically aggressive than girls. Moreover, in every culture, acts of aggression were particularly common when boys were playing together in groups (Munroe and others, 2000). How exactly do boys and girls relate when they play in groups? Now it's time to turn to this question and others as we move to part two of this chapter: relationships during the childhood years.

TYING IT ALL TOGETHER

1. You interviewed a 4-year-old and a fourth grader for your class project in lifespan development, but mixed up your interview notes. Which interview statement was made by the 4-year-old?

   a. "My friend Megan is better at math than me."
   b. "Sometimes I get mad at my friends, but maybe it's because I'm too stubborn."
   c. "I have a cat named Kit, and I'm the smartest girl in the world."

2. Pick out which children below have internalizing and externalizing problems and then, for one of these children, design an intervention program using the principles spelled out in this section.

   a. Ryan sees himself as totally wonderful, but he is having serious trouble getting along with his teachers and the other kids.
   b. Sydney doesn't feel she's very good in school but knows she's talented at soccer, her top priority.
   c. Jared is a great student, but every time he gets a B instead of an A, he decides that he's "dumb" and gets too depressed to work.

3. When the teacher yells at Zack and he starts crying, Austin and Gabriel both cringe and feel like crying. In addition, Gabriel feels really sorry for Zack. Although both children feel _____ for Zack, Gabriel feels _____. Is Austin or Gabriel more likely to reach out to comfort Zack?

4. A teacher wants to intervene with a student who has been teasing a classmate. Identify which statement is guilt-producing, which is shame-producing, and which involves the use of induction. Then name which response(s) would help promote prosocial behavior.

   a. "Think of how bad Johnny must feel."
   b. "If that's how you act, you can sit by yourself. You're not nice enough to be with the other kids."
   c. "I'm disappointed in you. You are usually such a good kid."

5. In predicting whether a third grader named David is likely to behave in a prosocial way, you might look for each of the following *except*:

   a. David is self-confident, happy, and well adjusted.
   b. David has a secure attachment, and his parents use induction in disciplining him.
   c. David is very compliant and obedient.
   d. David's identical twin brother, Don, is exceptionally prosocial.

6. Alyssa wants to replace Brianna as Chloe's best friend, so she spreads horrible rumors about Brianna. Brianna overhears Alyssa dissing her and starts yelling and slapping Alyssa. Of the four types of aggression discussed in this section—*direct, instrumental, reactive, relational*—which two describe Alyssa's behavior, and which two fit Brianna's actions?

7. Mark, a fourth grader, feels that everyone is out to get him and has been labeled as a highly aggressive child. Outline the two-step developmental pathway that may have produced this problem, and give the name for Mark's negative worldview.

Answers to the Tying It All Together questions can be found in the answers section of the book.

Relationships

Think back to the times you spent pretending to be a superhero or supermodel, getting together with the girls or boys to play, the hours you spent with your best friends, and whether you were popular during elementary school. Now, beginning with childhood play, moving on to the play worlds of girls and boys, then friendships and popularity, and finally tackling bullying—that issue in the chapter-opening vignette—we look at each topic relating to childhood relationships one by one.

Rough-and-tumble play is not only tremendously exciting, but it seems to be genetically built into being "male."

Photodisc / Getty Images

Play

Developmentalists classify children's "free play" (the non-sports-oriented kind) into different categories. *Exercise play* describes the exciting running and chasing behavior in the chapter-opening vignette. **Rough-and-tumble play** is the name for the shoving, wrestling, and fighting that were also apparent with boys on the playground. Rough-and-tumble play is actually classically boy behavior. As we will see later, it seems biologically built into being male (Bjorklund & Pellegrini, 2002; DiPietro, 1981; Pellegrini & Smith, 1998; Whiting & Whiting, 1975).

Exploring Fantasy Play

Fantasy play, or *pretending,* is different. Here the child takes a stance apart from reality and makes up a scene, often with a toy or other prop (Lillard and others, 2000). While fantasy play can also be very physical, this "as if" quality makes it unique. Children must pretend to be pirates or superheroes as they wrestle and run. Because fantasy play is at the heart of childhood, let's now delve into pretending in depth.

THE DEVELOPMENT AND DECLINE OF PRETENDING Fantasy play begins to emerge in late infancy, as children realize that a symbol can stand for something else. Mothers, research shows, help scaffold emerging fantasy play (Bornstein and others, 1999; Vandermaas-Peeler and others, 2002). In a classic study, developmentalists watched 1-year-olds with their mothers at home. Although toddlers often initiated a fantasy episode, they needed a parent to expand on the scene (Dunn, Wooding, & Hermann, 1977). So a child would pretend to make a phone call, and his mother would amplify the scenario by picking up the real phone and saying, "Hello, this is Mommy speaking. Should I come home now?"

At about age 3, children transfer the skill of pretending with moms to peers. **Collaborative pretend play,** or fantasizing *together* with another child, really gets going at about age 4 (Smolucha & Smolucha, 1998). Because they need to work together to develop the scene, the ability to collaboratively pretend shows that preschoolers have a *theory of mind*—the knowledge that the other person has a different perspective from yours. (You need to understand that your fellow Steven Spielberg may have a different script in his head.) Collaboratively pretending, in turn, teaches young children the vital skill of getting along with different minds (Astington & Jenkins, 1995; Jenkins & Astington, 2000; Youngblade & Dunn, 1995).

Anyone with regular access to a young child can see these changes firsthand. When a 2-year-old has his "best friend" over, they play in parallel orbits—if things go well. More likely, a titanic battle erupts, full of instrumental and reactive aggression, as each child attempts to gain sole possession of the toys. By age 4, children can really play *together.* By age 5 or 6, they can pretend together for hours—with only a few major fights that are usually quickly resolved!

rough-and-tumble play Play that involves shoving, wrestling, and hitting, but in which no actual harm is intended; especially characteristic of boys.

fantasy play Play that involves making up and acting out a scenario; also called *pretend play.*

collaborative pretend play Fantasy play in which children work together to develop and act out the scenes.

Laura Dwight / Photo Edit, Inc.

For these 4-year-old girls (a.k.a. princesses who have dressed up to feed their baby dolls), their *collaborative pretend play* is teaching them vital lessons about how to compromise and get along.

Although fantasy play can continue into early adolescence, when children reach concrete operations, their interest shifts to structured games (Bjorklund & Pellegrini, 2002). At age 3, a child pretends to bake in the kitchen corner; at 9 he wants to actually bake a cake. At age 5, you ran around playing pirates; at 9, you were interested in hitting the ball like the Pittsburgh Pirates do.

THE PURPOSES OF PRETENDING Interestingly, around the world, when children pretend, their fantasy play has some universal plots. Let's listen in at a U.S. preschool:

> **Boy 2:** I don't want to be a Kitty anymore.
>
> **Girl:** You are a husband?
>
> **Boy 2:** Yeah.
>
> **Boys 1 and 2:** Husbands, husbands! (Yell and run around the play house)
>
> **Girl:** Hold it, Bill, I can't have two husbands.
>
> **Boys 1 and 2:** Two husbands. Two husbands!!!
>
> **Girl to the two boys:** We gonna marry ourselves, right?
>
> (adapted from Corsaro, 1985, pp. 102–104)

Why do young children always play "family," and why do they have to assume the "correct" roles when they play mommy and daddy? For answers, we turn to Lev Vygotsky's insights about this central activity of early childhood.

Play allows children to practice adult roles. Vygotsky (1978) believed that pretending allows children to rehearse being adults. The reason girls love pretending to be mommy and baby is that women are the main child-care providers in every society on earth (Bjorklund & Pellegrini, 2002; Geary, 1998; Pellegrini & Smith, 1998; Whiting & Edwards, 1988). Boys play soldiers because this activity offers built-in training for the wars they may face as adults (Hawley, 1999; Pellegrini & Smith, 2005).

Play allows children a sense of control. As the following tea-party conversation suggests, pretending may have a deeper psychological function, too:

> **Girl 1:** (Drinking milk from teacup) Yeah, and let's pretend when Mommy's out until later.
>
> **Girl 2:** Ooooh. Well. I'm not the boss around here, though. 'Cause Mommies play the bosses around here.
>
> **Girl 1:** And us children aren't. (Shakes head sadly)
>
> **Girl 2:** So . . . when you grow up and I grow up we'll be the bosses. . . .
>
> **Girl 1:** (Doubtfully) But maybe we won't know how to punish.
>
> **Girl 2:** I will. I'll put my hand up and spank 'em. That's what my mom does.
>
> **Girl 1:** My mom does too sometimes.
>
> (adapted from Corsaro, 1985, p. 96)

While reading the previous two chapters, you may have been thinking that the so-called carefree years of early childhood are far from free of stress. We expect children to regulate their emotions when their frontal lobes aren't fully functional. We continually discipline toddlers and preschoolers when they may not yet be fully capable of making sense of the rules of the mysterious adult world. Vygotsky (1978) believed that, in response to their feelings of powerlessness, young children enter "an illusory role" in which their desires can be realized. In play, you can be the spanking mommy or the queen of the castle even when you are small and sometimes feel like a slave.

To penetrate the inner world of preschool fantasy play, sociologist William Corsaro (1985, 1997) decided to go undercover. He spent months in a nursery school as a member of the class. (No problem. The children welcomed their new playmate, whom they called Big Bill, as simply a clumsy, greatly enlarged version of themselves.) As Vygotsky would predict, Corsaro found that the plots in preschool play often centered on mastering upsetting events. There were the separation/reunion scenarios ("Help, Help! I'm lost in the forest." "I'll find you.") and the danger/rescue plots ("Get in the house. It's gonna be a rainstorm!"). Sometimes, play scenarios centered on that ultimate frightening event, death:

> **Child 1:** We are dead, we are dead! Help, we are dead! (Puts animals on their sides) . . .

Imagine that, like the supersized preschooler shown here (Professor William Corsaro), you could spend years going down slides, playing family, and bonding with 3- and 4-year-olds—and then get professional recognition for your academic work. What an incredible career!

CHILD 2: You can't talk if you are dead. . . .

CHILD 1: Oh, well, Leah's talked when she was dead, so mine have to talk when they are dead . . . Help, help, we are dead!

(adapted from Corsaro, p. 204)

Notice that these themes are basic to Disney movies and fairy tales. From *Finding Nemo*, *Bambi*, and *The Lion King* to—my personal favorite—*Dumbo*, there is nothing more heart-wrenching than being separated from your parent. From the greedy old witch in *Hansel and Gretel* to the jealous queen in *Sleeping Beauty*, no scenario is as sweet as triumphing over evil and possible death.

Play furthers children's understanding of social norms. Corsaro (1985) found that death was a touchy play topic. When children proposed these plots, their partners might try to change the script. This relates to Vygotsky's third insight about play: Although children's play looks unstructured, it has clear boundaries and rules. Plots involving two husbands or dead animals waking up make children uncomfortable, because they violate the rules of adult life. Preschoolers get even more uneasy when a play partner proposes scenarios with gory themes, such as cutting off people's heads. Wouldn't you get anxious if someone showed an intense interest in decapitation while having a conversation with you?

To explore socially "out of bounds" fantasy play, researchers compared the play of 24 "hard to handle" preschoolers with a control group by observing each child playing with a friend (Dunn & Hughes, 2001). The difficult preschoolers engaged in fantasy play with more violent themes. Moreover, the presence of violent preschool play predicted more externalizing behavior in first grade.

Now that we know play offers children a sense of control and provides a window into preschoolers' inner lives, let's look at how health-care professionals and teachers might use these insights in their work.

INTERVENTIONS: Helping Children Through Play

Nurses on a pediatric ward might be alert to a child's pretend play to get clues into a patient's specific fears about an operation. Then, they might enact their own pretend sequence to speak directly to the child's anxieties (for example, "Little Joe Bear went to sleep for awhile, but when he woke up he began to feel better, and now he's all well, and you will be, too").

Preschool teachers could see the problems looming on the horizon if one of the 4-year-olds in class was obsessed with playing "I'll kill you and cut off your head." They might try to help that child tone down his violent fantasies and encourage him to play in more appropriate ways (Bartolini & Lunn, 2002).

Still, we have to be cautious about heavily intervening in play. By managing (or micromanaging) make-believe, we may be keeping children from learning important lessons on their own. If we decide how children *must* play, we might be going against nature, too. Many teachers get anxious about rough-and-tumble play. Misinterpreting this basic play mode as real aggressive acts, they tend to vigorously punish the very activity that boys most love to engage in when they get together to play (Ardley & Ericson, 2002; Smith, Smees, and others, 2002). But why do female teachers instinctively recoil from rough-and-tumble play? The reason will be apparent as we turn to that other basic characteristic of childhood play: Boys and girls live in separate play worlds.

Girls' and Boys' Play Worlds

[Some] girls, all about five and a half years old, are looking through department store catalogues, . . . concentrating on what they call "girls' stuff" and referring to some of the other items as "yucky boys' stuff." . . . Shirley points to a picture of a couch . . . "All we want is the pretty stuff," says Ruth. Peggy now announces, "If you come to my birthday, every girl in the school is invited. I'm going to put a sign up that says, 'No boys allowed!'" "Oh good, good, good," says Vickie. "I hate boys."

(adapted from Corsaro, 1997, p. 155)

Does this conversation bring back any childhood memories of being 5 or 6? How does **gender-segregated play** develop? What are the characteristics of boy versus girl play, and what causes the sexes to separate into these different, often warring camps?

Exploring the Separate Societies

Visit a neighborhood playground and observe children of different ages. You might notice that toddlers show no sign of gender-segregated play. Starting at about age 3, children begin to gravitate to playing with their own sex (Maccoby & Jacklin, 1987). By kindergarten and early elementary school, gender-segregated play is firmly entrenched. On the playground, boys and girls still do play in mixed groups about one-fourth of the time (Fabes, Martin, & Hanish, 2003). Still, by elementary school, children rarely join a play group unless another member of their own sex is present (Martin & Fabes, 2001). With friendships there is a real split: boys are almost always best friends with boys and girls with girls (Maccoby, 1998).

A visit to any elementary school lunchroom vividly brings home the fact that middle childhood is all about gender-segregated play.

Actually, children are intensely interested in the other society. They thrill at teasing, at chasing, at making raids on the "enemy" camp (Thorne, 1993). Some girls regularly cross the divide and play with the boys. Still, during elementary school, attempts to unite the sexes can be met with resistance. One 11-year-old girl described the teachers in her school who tried to get the boys and girls to play together as "geeky ughs" (Maccoby, 1998).

Now go back to the playground and look at the *way* boys and girls relate. Do you notice that boy versus girl play differs in these following ways?

gender-segregated play Play in which boys and girls associate only with members of their own sex—typical of childhood.

Boys excitedly run around; girls calmly talk. Boys' play is more rambunctious. Even during physical games such as tag, girls play together in calmer and more subdued ways (Maccoby, 1990, 1998). The difference in activity levels is striking if you have the pleasure of witnessing one gender playing with the opposite sex's toys. In one memorable episode, after my son and a friend invaded a girl's stash of dolls, they gleefully ran around the house bashing Barbie into Barbie and using their booty as swords.

Boys compete in groups; girls play collaboratively, one-to-one. Their exuberant, rough-and-tumble play explains why boys tend to burst on the scene, running and yelling, dominating every room. Another difference lies in play group *size*. Boys get together in packs, while girls prefer playing in smaller, more intimate groups (Maccoby, 1990, 1998; Martin & Fabes, 2001).

Boys and girls also differ in the *way* they relate. Boys try to establish dominance and compete to be the best (Maccoby & Jacklin, 1987). This competitive versus cooperative style spills over into children's talk. Girl-to-girl collaborative play really sounds collaborative ("I'll be the doctor, OK?"), whereas boys give each other bossy commands (Maccoby, 1998). Girl-to-girl fantasy play involves nurturing themes. Boys prefer the warrior, superhero mode.

The intensely stereotypic quality of girls' fantasy play came as a shock to me when I spent three days playing with my visiting 7-year-old niece. We devoted day one to setting up a beauty shop, complete with nail polishes and shampoos. We used my sink for hair washing. We had a table for massages and a makeover section featuring all the cosmetics I owned. Then we opened for business for the visiting relatives and, of course—by charging for our services—made money for toys. We spent the last day playing with a "pool party" Barbie combo my niece had carefully selected at Wal-Mart that afternoon.

Boys' and girls' different play interests show why the kindergarteners in the vignette at the beginning of this section came to hate those "yucky" boys. Another reason why girls turn off to the opposite sex is the unpleasant reception they often get from the opposing camp. More than simply establishing dominance, boys seem on a campaign to run "outsiders" off!

Boys live in a more exclusionary, separate world. My niece did choose to buy the Barbies, but she also plays with trucks. She loves soccer and baseball, not just doing her nails. Even though they may say they hate the opposite sex, girls cross the divide. Boys are more likely to avoid that chasm (Boyle, Marshall, & Robeson, 2003; Fabes, Martin, & Hanish, 2003). They won't even go down the Barbie aisle or consider buying a toy labeled "girl." So boys live in a more roped-off gender world.

Now you might be interested in what happened during my final day of pretending with the pool party toys. After my niece said, "Aunt Janet, let's pretend we are the popular girls," our Barbies tried on fancy dresses ("Oh, what shall I wear, Jane?") in preparation for a "popular girls" pool party, where the dolls met up ("Hello, Sara! I'm *so* glad to see you") to discuss—*guess what*—where they shopped and who did their hair!

[FAQ: Are gender differences biological or socialized?]

What Causes Gender-Stereotyped Play?

Why do children, such as my niece, play in these incredibly gender-stereotyped ways? Answers come from exploring three interacting forces: biology (nature), socialization (nurture), and cognitions, or thoughts.

A BIOLOGICAL UNDERPINNING   Ample evidence suggests that gender-segregated play is biologically built in. Children around the world live in separate play societies (Maccoby, 1998). Troops of juvenile rhesus monkeys behave *exactly* like human children. The males segregate into their own groups and engage in rough-and-tumble play (Meaney, Stewart, & Beatty, 1985; Smith, 1982; Pellegrini & Smith, 2005). Grooming activities similar to my niece's beauty-shop behaviors are a prominent activity among young female monkeys, too (Bjorklund & Pellegrini, 2002; Maccoby, 1990, 1998; Suomi, 2004).

Moreover, when pregnant rhesus monkeys are injected with the male sex hormone testosterone, their female offspring also engage in rough-and-tumble play (Udry, 2000). Could a similar effect apply to females in our species, too?

To address this fascinating question, one developmentalist measured the naturally occurring testosterone levels of women pregnant with female fetuses (Udry, 2000). He took maternal blood samples during the second trimester—the time, you may recall from Chapter 2, when the neurons are being formed. Then, years later, when the daughters were about age 17, he asked them to fill out sex-role questionnaires.

Girls who had been exposed to comparatively high levels of prenatal testosterone were more interested in traditionally male occupations, such as engineering, than the lower-hormone-level prenatal group. They were less likely to wear makeup. Even in their twenties, they showed more stereotypically male interests (such as race car driving). So, depending on the dose, prenatal exposure to testosterone seems to help program us to have more "feminized" or "masculinized" brains.

This boy is learning to be more "boylike" as he aggressively pounds a peg into this traditionally male toy, given to him by his parents.

Mel Curtis / Getty Images

THE AMPLIFYING EFFECT OF SOCIALIZATION   The wider world helps biology along. Parents use more induction with girls and more power assertion with boys (Maccoby, 1990, 1998). They buy dolls for their daughters and trucks for their sons. They tend to play with their male and female children in gender-stereotyped ways.

Peers play a particularly powerful role in this programming. For one thing, when they play in mixed-gender groups, children act in less stereotypically masculine or feminine ways (Fabes, Martin, & Hanish, 2003). So if, in the chapter-opening vignette, Manuel and his friends had let Moriah and her friends join their game of tag, they would have toned down their rough-and-tumble play. If a few boys had arrived on the scene at the beginning of this section, the girls might have stopped looking at the catalogs and started running around. Therefore, the very process of splitting into separate play societies seems to train children to behave in ways typical of their own sex (Martin & Fabes, 2001).

This image of 5-year-old girls getting together to enjoy their dolls and reinforce one another for activities such as braiding Barbie's hair shows us exactly why gender-segregated play powerfully reinforces traditional gender role behavior.

Same-sex playmates reinforce one another for selecting the most gender-stereotyped activities ("Let's play with dolls." "Great!"). They mutually model one another as they play together in "gentle" or "rough" ways. The pressure to toe the gender line is also promoted by powerful social sanctions. Popular children tend to closely fit the gender stereotypes. Girls labeled as tomboys are less well liked than "typical" girls. Sensitive, anxious boys rank low on the male popularity totem pole (Coplan and others, 2001; Egan & Perry, 2001; Morison & Masten, 1991). In fact, as early as preschool, teachers view children who don't cross the gender divide—those who play only with their own sex—as more socially competent and mature (Colwell & Lindsey, 2005).

THE IMPACT OF COGNITIONS A cognitive process reinforces these external messages. According to **gender schema theory** (Bem, 1981; Martin & Dinella, 2002), once children understand which basic category (girl or boy) they belong in, they selectively attend to the activities of their own sex.

When do children first grasp their gender label and start this lifelong practice of observing and modeling their group? By the time they begin really talking, at about age 2½, children typically have their gender identity nailed down (Maccoby, 1998). Although they may not learn the real difference until much later (here it helps to have an opposite-sex sibling to see naked), 3-year-olds can tell you that girls have long hair and cry a lot and boys fight and play with trucks. At about age 5 or 6, when they are mastering the similar concept of identity constancy (the knowledge that your essential self doesn't change when you dress up in a gorilla costume), children grasp the idea that once you start out as a boy or girl, you stay that way for life (Kohlberg, 1966). However, mistakes are still common. I once heard my 5-year-old nephew ask my husband, "Was that jewelry from when you were a girl?"

In sum, my niece's beauty-shop activities had a clear biological basis, although a steady stream of nurture influences from adults and playmates helped this process along. Her behavior was also promoted by identifying herself as "a girl" and then spending hours selectively attending to and modeling the women in her life.

But is the sex-segregated childhood play world changing? My students describe having more close friends of the opposite gender during elementary school than I recall from when I was growing up. Reports from the contemporary kindergarten front suggest that the Barbie corner can now—occasionally—be shared by both girls and boys. Do you think our less gender-defined adult culture could be making for less gender-stereotyped play? Were your best friends during elementary school the same sex as you?

[FAQ: How does gender identity develop?]

gender schema theory An explanation for gender-stereotyped behavior that emphasizes the role of cognitions; specifically, the idea that once children know their own gender label (girl or boy), they selectively watch and model their own sex.

Children spend hours modeling their own sex, demonstrating why *gender schema theory* (the idea "I am a boy" or "I am a girl") also encourages behaving in gender-stereotyped ways.

Top: Preschool best friends connect through their shared passion for physical activities such as going down slides. *Bottom:* In late elementary school best friends bond by sharing secrets and plans.

Friendships

This last question brings us to that important topic: friends. *Why* do children choose specific friends, and what benefits do childhood friends provide?

The Core Qualities: Similarity, Trust, and Emotional Support

The essence of friendship is having common interests. We gravitate toward people who share our worldview. The same is true in preschool. An active 4-year-old will tend to make friends with a classmate who also likes to run around. A preschooler who loves the slide or dress-up corner will most likely become best buddies with a child who shares this passion, too (Rose & Asher, 2000; Hartup, 1998; Hartup & Stevens, 1997; Newcomb & Bagwell, 1996).

Mirroring the way they describe themselves, however, young children describe their friendships in terms of external qualities: "She's my best friend because we go down the slide together." As children get older, they shift to talking about inner qualities in describing their friends: "Josh and I are best buddies because he is funny and such a great guy." Around this age children also develop the concept of loyalty ("I can trust Josh to stand up for me") and the sense that friends share their inner lives (Hartup & Stevens, 1997; Newcomb & Bagwell, 1995). Listen to these fourth and fifth graders describing their best friend:

He is my very best friend because he tells me things and I tell him things.

Me and Tiff share our deepest, darkest secrets and we talk about boys, when we grow up, and shopping.

Jessica has problems at home and with her religion and when something happens she always comes to me and talks about it. We've been through a lot together.

(quoted in Rose & Asher, 2000, p. 49)

These quotations would resonate with the ideas of personality theorist Harry Stack Sullivan. Sullivan (1953) believed that a chum (or best friend) fulfills the developmental need for self-validation and intimacy that emerges at around age 9. Sullivan also believed that this special relationship serves as a stepping-stone to a truly adult romance.

The Protecting and Teaching Functions of Friends

In addition to offering emotional support and validating one's feelings, friends stimulate children's personal development in two important ways:

Friends protect and enhance the developing self. Perhaps you noticed this protective function in the quotation above in which the fourth grader spoke about how she helped her best friend when she had problems at home. Friends become crucially important "safe zones" of comfort as children become teenagers and begin separating emotionally from their parents and moving into the wider world (Rubin, Bukowski, & Parker, 1998). You may have noticed that the reasons for shedding a friendship often center on feelings of not being protected: The person we thought was a friend let us down in our hour of need.

Friends teach us to manage our emotions and handle conflicts. Your parents will love you no matter what you do, but the love of a friend is contingent. So to relate to a friend, children must be able to modulate their emotions and attune themselves to the other person's needs (Bukowski, 2001; Denham and others, 2003; Hartup & Stevens, 1997).

This is not to say that friends don't have arguments. In Western cultures, disagreements among friends are often intense. Friendships differ, however, during the conflict resolution phase. Friends in elementary school are more likely than random classmates to deal with conflicts using negotiation (Bukowski, 2001; Hartup, 1998; Hartup & Stevens, 1997). They are committed to preserving their attachment bond.

Furthermore, highly aggressive children, because they respond in a more hostile way when provoked (Leary & Katz, 2005), are less likely to have friends.

Researchers gave fourth and fifth graders a series of vignettes describing conflict situations, such as: "What would you do if your friend wanted to play a different game than you?" Children who most often selected revenge as a motive were least likely to actually have a good friend (Rose & Asher, 1999).

This is not to say that friends are always positive influences. They can bring out a child's worst self, too, by encouraging relational aggression ("We are best friends so you can't play with us") and daring one another to engage in dangerous behavior ("Let's sneak out of the house at 2 A.M."). We will be exploring this dark side of friendship when we look at the pathways to committing delinquent acts during the adolescent years. However, in general, Sullivan seems to be right: Friends do help teach us how to relate as adults.

Scanning the Global Friendship Scene

Although having friends is basic to childhood, there are interesting cultural differences. Israeli researchers looked at conceptions of friendship among Jewish children, who are socialized in an individualistic way, and Bedouin children, who are raised in a collectivist culture. The Jewish children said that disagreeing with a friend is absolutely fine. The Bedouin children stressed the need for harmony, feeling that best friends need to be alike in their thoughts (Elbedour, Shulman, & Kedem, 1997).

There may be interesting differences between individualistic and more collectivist cultures in the intensity of friendships, too. Researchers had Arab and Jewish fourth and fifth graders rate their friendship intimacy through questionnaire items such as "How important is it for you to share your inner feelings with a best friend?" The Jewish children answered yes far more often to these questions, suggesting that their friendships were more emotionally intense (Schraf & Hertz-Lazarowitz, 2003). So childhood friendships may be more important in societies that socialize young people to construct a life apart from their families than in cultures that emphasize staying closely bonded with one's parents and siblings.

Popularity

Friendship is a one-to-one relationship. It involves relating well to a single human being. Being popular, on the other hand, is a group concern. It requires having the talent to rise to the top of the social totem pole. As the following study suggested, having a friend and being popular may involve quite different talents (Walden, Lemerise, & Smith, 1999):

To measure popularity, researchers asked preschoolers to sort photos of their classmates into piles indicating "Don't like," "Like OK," and "Like very much." To measure friendships, they asked the children, "Who do you like to play with the most?" Then they had teachers and parents rate each child on personality tests.

Popular children, those whose photos frequently appeared in the "Like very much" pile, ranked high on overall mental health. Teachers judged these boys and girls as prosocial and outgoing, well adjusted, and interpersonally skilled. The only quality linked to having friends was emotion regulation—having the ability to modify one's feelings and compromise with another human being.

This study beautifully illustrates the core difference between the status-oriented concept of popularity and friendships at any age. We can overlook a good deal in the way of social blunders, immature behaviors, and problems getting along in life and still call someone a close friend—if that person relates well to us. However, to be popular, people cannot blunder socially. We have to "have it all together" to advance to the social ladder's uppermost rungs.

What makes some children popular? What qualities cause children to be rejected by their peers? These are the questions we explore in this section of the chapter.

Creasource / Corbis

Although children differ in social status beginning in preschool, you may remember from your own childhood that the "Who is popular?" question becomes an absorbing issue during later elementary school. As we saw early in this chapter, entering concrete operations makes children especially sensitive to making social comparisons. The urge to rank classmates according to social status is heightened by the confining conditions of childhood itself. In adulthood, popularity fades into the background because we are free to select our own social circles. Children are required to succeed on a daily basis in a small classroom full of random peers.

Who Is Popular and Who Is Unpopular?

How do children vary in popularity during the socially stressful late elementary school years? Here are the categories researchers find when they ask third, fourth, or fifth graders to list the two or three classmates they like most and really dislike:

- *Popular children* are frequently named in the most-liked category and never appear in the disliked group. They stand out as being really liked by everyone.

- *Average children* receive a few most-liked and perhaps one or two disliked nominations. They rank around the middle range of status in the class.

- *Rejected children* land in the disliked category often and never appear in the preferred list. They stand out among their classmates in a negative way.

In addition to these distinctions, some children may be classified as neglected, because they receive no nominations, positive or negative, and so don't appear on the classroom radar screen. Others may be labeled controversial. Their names turn up frequently in both the most-liked and most-disliked lists. The class clown or an aggressive child who is also socially skilled fit this interesting "love 'em or hate 'em" type (Corsaro, 1997). However, these categories are small and highly unstable. What is highly relevant is the popularity–unpopularity distinction. What qualities make children popular? Most important, what traits make children disliked by their peers?

As we just saw, being popular involves having exceptional social skills. In elementary school, popular children tend to be prosocial and kind (Saarni, 1999; Warden & Mackinnon, 2003). One sign of their social talents is revealed in the difficult situation of entering an ongoing group at play. Popular children gradually insinuate themselves into the flow of action. They pace themselves to the group. Rejected children either run away or, like Matt in the opening vignette, insensitively barge right in (Coie & Dodge, 1998). So children who are rejected don't know how to socially behave. Who is rejected during the middle-childhood years?

Rejected children have externalizing (and sometimes internalizing) disorders. Children with externalizing tendencies—especially those who are highly physically aggressive—quickly fall into the rejected category (Dodge and others, 2003; Kupersmidt, Coie, & Dodge, 1990). Highly anxious children—those prone to internalizing disorders—may or may not be rejected. However, a socially anxious child is likely to be avoided as early as first grade (Coplan and others, 2001; Gazelle & Ladd, 2003).

Moreover, a nature-evokes-nurture interaction can set in when a child enters school extremely shy. As children pick up on the fact that people are avoiding them, their shyness gets more intense. So they become less socially competent—and increasingly likely to be rejected—as they advance from grade to grade (Brendgen and others, 2001).

An unfortunate bidirectional process is also occurring. The child's anxiety makes other children nervous. They get uncomfortable and want to retreat when they see this person approach. In response to your own awkward encounters, have you ever been tempted to walk in the opposite direction when you see a very shy person walking down the hall?

His shyness may set this boy up for social rejection in first grade, because his anxiety will make the other children uneasy and he may not have the courage to reach out to his classmates.

Michael Newman / Photo Edit, Inc.

Rejected children don't fit in with the group. Children who stand out as different are also at risk of being rejected. Girls who don't like to play with Barbies; boys who are very quiet (like Jimmy in the vignette) (Coplan and others, 2001; Egan & Perry, 2001; Gleason and others, 2005; Morison & Masten, 1991; Schwartz and others, 1998); low-income children in middle-class schools; sometimes even children who simply like playing alone (Coplan and others, 2001)—all may be set up for rejection during elementary school.

Middle School Meanness

In elementary school, popular children are well liked by both the teachers and their classmates. In middle school, the group norms take a different tilt. Now being rebellious is more of an "in thing," and some aggressive children may be in the popular group (Rodkin and others, 2000; Zeller and others, 2003). Now the talents that help children rise to the top of the social ladder are not necessarily prosocial skills.

When researchers followed several hundred children from fifth to ninth grade (Cillessen & Mayeux, 2004), they found that, for girls in particular, high levels of relational aggression became more linked to being in the popular group year by year. Furthermore, as you can see in Figure 6.2, by ninth grade, being defined as popular became less closely linked to measures of being liked. This explains that familiar paradox: Especially in middle school and early high school, children in the "in-group" or popular crowd may be *personally* disliked by much of the class (Kosir & Pecjak, 2005; Prinstein, 2003; Prinstein & Cillessen, 2003).

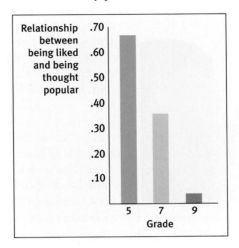

Relationship between being liked and being thought popular

Grade: 5, 7, 9

FIGURE 6.2: How being popular relates to being personally liked for girls in middle school: In this study, children in different grades were asked which classmates were popular and which classmates they liked the most. Notice that by ninth grade, there was little relationship between being viewed as in the "popular" group and being seen as well liked. Did you *really* like the kids in the "in-crowd" at your school?

Source: Cillessen & Mayeux (2004), p. 153.

The Fate of the Rejected

What about children in the out-group? Is being rejected a risk factor for having problems later on? The answer is "sometimes." Aggressive-impulsive children do have serious difficulties during adolescence and their early adult years (Caspi, 2000; Coie & Dodge, 1998). But some traits that get children ranked low-status during childhood do not translate into an unhappy adult life. Consider an awkward little girl named Eleanor Roosevelt, who was socially rejected at age 8, or a boy named Thomas Edison, whose preference for playing alone got him defined as a "problem" child. Because they were so different, these famous adults were dismal failures during elementary school. To get insights into the fleeting quality of childhood peer status, you might organize a reunion of your fifth- or sixth-grade class. You might be surprised at how many "average," "neglected," or "rejected" classmates flowered during their high school or college years.

Will this socially isolated elementary school boy get it together and shine in high school and college? Provided that he is not very aggressive, the answer may be yes.

Alistair Berg / Getty Images

BULLYING

bullying A situation in which one or more children (or adults) harass or target a specific child for systematic abuse.

Children who are shy can excel in the proving ground of life. This is not the case on the proving ground of the playground. While aggressive boys and girls who are also disorganized and impulsive may be a target of harassment, children who are unassertive and anxious are especially vulnerable to **bullying**—being regularly teased, made fun of, and verbally or physically abused by their peers (Gamleil and others, 2003; Orpinas and Horne, 2006).

Having a friend does not prevent a person from being bullied. What matters is a child's overall status in the group. Children who are low in the social hierarchy are typical targets (Eslea and others, 2004; Sandstrom & Cillessen, 2003; Schwartz and others, 1998; Woods & Wolke, 2004). They turn into victims, as you can see in my true confession in the Experiencing the Lifespan box on the next page, when they can't (or won't) strike back (Gamliel and others, 2003). Being targeted breeds more anxiety and further victimization. School becomes such an aversive experience that bullied children often turn off to what happens in class, even when they are highly competent in academics (Buhs & Ladd, 2001; Hodges & Perry, 1999).

The child on the left looks slightly nervous and may not fight back, and unfortunately that means he's an ideal target for the bully on the right.

In studies around the world researchers find that children who are regularly bullied have identical qualities: They are typically anxious, lack confidence, and have few friends (Gini, 2004; Griffin & Gross, 2004; Kallestad & Olweus, 2003; Smith and others, 1999). However, prevalence rates of bullying vary greatly from nation to nation (Griffin & Gross, 2004). One reason is that the definitions of the kinds of behaviors that constitute bullying differ from place to place (Griffin & Gross, 2004; Smith, Cowie, and others, 2002). The same kinds of definitional issues can occur in the United States (Lee, 2006). In one interview study, many preadolescent boys, when questioned about behaviors adults defined as bullying—such as teasing a disliked classmate—described these actions as "just kidding around" (Gamliel and others, 2003).

What we do know is that bullying often takes a different form depending on the child's gender. Girls tend to be bullied through relational aggression. Boys are more often subjected to physical harassment (Cullerton-Sen & Crick, 2005). Most important, we also know that bullying often requires an audience. As you saw in the chapter-opening vignette, typically one child (or a few children) will start the harassment while another group gives the perpetrator positive reinforcement by looking on and laughing. So bullying is a serious problem not because there are so many bullies, but because so many people passively approve. This suggests that interventions to stop bullying are best targeted at the larger group (Batsche & Porter, 2006).

INTERVENTIONS: Attacking Bullying and Helping Rejected Children

Developed by Dan Olweus, the *Olweus Bully Prevention Program* is designed to combat bullying through directly involving the whole school. Early in the year, school administrators hand out questionnaires to assess students' experiences with bullying. Then they plan a schoolwide conference to discuss this problem and form a bullying-prevention committee composed of children from each grade. Throughout the year, teachers and students are on the alert for bullying in their classes. The goal is to develop a schoolwide norm of not tolerating peer abuse (Olweus, Limber, & Mihalic, 1999).

To generally encourage a prosocial atmosphere, some elementary schools provide students with regular coaching in emotion regulation and interpersonal skills. Teachers may offer sessions devoted to getting children to identify their feelings and helping them learn to compromise. Programs may be schoolwide or just for children who are at risk of having problems with teachers and peers (see Table 6.6 for two examples).

TABLE 6.6: Two Sample Programs for Teaching Social Skills and Prosocial Behavior in Elementary School

Promoting Alternative Thinking Strategies (PATHS)

Target group: Kindergarten to fifth grade

Description: Teachers offer "emotional literacy" sessions to their classes three times a week. Children get practice labeling and managing their feelings, picking up on social cues, and using verbal and nonverbal communication skills. Teachers get training in the techniques and also have biweekly sessions with a curriculum consultant.

Outcome data: Compared to control schools, participants show improved self-control and problem-solving skills. Special-needs students have lower rates of problem behavior and depressive symptoms.

Source: Center for the Study and Prevention of Violence. www. Colorado.edu/cspv/blueprints/model/overview.html

Seattle Social Development Project

Target group: Either the elementary school population as a whole or high-risk children

Description: Aimed at training parents and teachers as well as children. Teachers are taught proactive classroom management strategies. Children are taught conflict management. Parents can undergo seven optional sessions of family management training.

Outcome data: Boys at high risk for antisocial behavior showed lower levels of externalizing behaviors in first and second grade, compared to a comparable group. In grade 5, they had less delinquent behaviors, were more attached to their families, and were more committed to school. As high school juniors (five years after the program), they were less involved in violent delinquency and had fewer incidents of drinking and driving.

Sources: Hawkins and others (1992); Hawkins, Von Cleve, & Catalano (1991).

EXPERIENCING THE LIFESPAN: MIDDLE-AGED REFLECTIONS ON MY MIDDLE-CHILDHOOD VICTIMIZATION

It was a hot August afternoon when the birthday present arrived. As usual, I was playing alone that day, maybe reading or engaging in a favorite pastime, fantasizing that I was a princess while sitting in a backyard tree. The gift, addressed to Janet Kaplan, was beautifully wrapped—huge but surprisingly light. This is amazing! I must be special! Someone had gone to such trouble for me! When I opened the first box, I saw another carefully wrapped box, and then another, smaller box, and yet another, smaller one inside. Finally, surrounded by ribbons and wrapping paper, I eagerly got to the last box, and saw a tiny matchbox—which contained a small burnt match.

Around that time, the doorbell rang, and Cathy, then Ruth, then Carol, bounded up. "Your mother called to tell us she was giving you a surprise birthday party. We had to come over right away and be sure to wear our best dresses!" But their excitement turned to disgust when they learned that no party had been arranged. My ninth birthday was really in mid-September—more than a month away. It turned out that Nancy and Marion—the two most popular girls in class—had masterminded this relational aggression plot directed at me.

Why was I selected as the victim among the other third-grade girls? I had never hurt Nancy or Marion. In fact, in confessing their role, they admitted to some puzzlement: "We really don't dislike Janet at all." Researching this chapter has offered me insights into the reasons for this 50-year-old wound.

Although I did have friends, I was fairly low in the classroom hierarchy. Not only was I shy, but I was that unusual girl—a child who genuinely preferred to play alone. But most important, I was the perfect victim. I dislike competitive, status situations. When taunted or teased, I don't fight back.

As an older woman, I still dislike status hierarchies and social snobberies. I'm not a group (or party) person. I far prefer talking one-to-one. I am happy to spend hours alone. Today I consider these attributes a plus (after all, having no problem sitting by myself for many thousands of hours was a prime skill that allowed me to write this text!), but they caused me anguish in middle childhood. In fact, today, when I find myself in status-oriented peer situations, I can still catch glimmers of my long-ago, nervous, third-grade self!

How can you help this tempera-mentally shy preschooler avoid being socially rejected in elementary school? Try to connect him with a good friend or two!

Marcus Mok / Getty Images

social skills training A strategy for teaching emotion regulation and social skills to rejected children, especially boys with externalizing problems.

Social skills training is an intervention developed specifically for children who are already having difficulties getting along with their peers. After watching them in social situations, psychologists or teachers offer rejected boys and girls feedback about what they are doing wrong. The children are taught to stop and think things through before erupting in anger and trained in lecting more appropriate responses. Social skills training is typically used to help children with ex-nalizing problems. Studies show that it can be most effective in helping highly impulsive, aggressive boys (Losel & Beelmann, 2003). What can do to help shy children, such as Jimmy in the opening vignette, who are suffering socially—even though their behavior is not causing problems in the outside world?

One key is to take action as early as possible. In tracking a group of shy kindergarteners as they traveled through elementary school, researchers found that if a child did develop friends in kindergarten or first grade, that boy or girl became less socially anxious over time (Gazelle & Ladd, 2003). So parents need to immediately connect their shy child—preferably in preschool—with a playmate who might become a close friend.

Actually, in helping children at risk for *both* internalizing and externalizing disorders, elementary school is not the best time to intervene. By age 5 or 6, these children have already started to fail socially. The bottom line—especially with children at risk for externalizing disorders—is that parents need to take steps *very early* at home to prevent the pathway to social rejection from emerging. To turn an intrepid explorer into a prosocial hero, provide an excess of love!

Final Thoughts

An underlying message of this chapter has been that parents play a vital role in shaping children's emotional and social skills. But another strong message is that peers are vital in socialization, too. How critical a role do parents versus peers play in determining our behavior and the kind of adult we become? What overall strategies make for good parenting, and what can schools do to help children thrive both socially and academically? Stay tuned for answers in the next chapter, as we shift from looking at the process of development to examining the basic wider-world contexts in which children develop: home and school. ▪

TYING IT ALL TOGETHER

1. When Melanie and Miranda play, they love to make up pretend scenes together. Are these two girls likely to be about age 2, age 5, or age 9?

2. In watching boys and girls at recess in an elementary school, which two of the following observations are you likely to make?

   a. The boys are playing in larger groups.
   b. Both girls and boys love rough-and-tumble play.
   c. Boys are more likely to join the girls' play than the girls are to join the boys'.
   d. The girls are quieter and they are doing more negotiating.

3. Erik and Sophia are arguing about the cause of gender-stereotyped behavior. Erik says the reason why boys like to run around and play with trucks is biological. Sophia argues that gender-stereotyped play is socialized by adults and other chil-

dren. First argue Erik's position and then make Sophia's case by referring to specific data in this section.

4. You are fondly remembering your best friend in later elementary school. Which of the following statements is *not* likely to fit this relationship?

   a. You and your best buddy rarely fought or argued.
   b. You and your best buddy were very similar in interests.
   c. You and your best buddy supported and protected each other.

5. If Emily is the most popular child in her fourth-grade class and Madison is in the popular kids crowd in ninth grade, what can you predict?

   a. Both Madison and Emily are probably very well liked by their classmates.
   b. While the children really like Emily, Madison may not be well liked by many of the kids.

6. Which of the following children is at risk of being rejected in elementary school?

   a. Miguel, a very shy child
   b. Lauren, a tomboy who hates "girls' stuff"
   c. Nicholas, a highly aggressive child
   d. All of these children

7. (a) If a child is being bullied, name the quality that may be making her an easy target. (b) Then, to a parent of a shy preschooler, offer advice to help reduce the chance of that boy or girl being rejected in elementary school. (c) Finally, give a piece of parenting advice to a mother or father of a highly exuberant toddler. (Give a brief answer to each question.)

Answers to the Tying It All Together questions can be found in the answers section of the book.

■ SUMMARY

Setting the Context: Emotion Regulation

Emotion regulation, the ability to manage and control our feelings, is crucial to having a successful life. Children with **externalizing tendencies** often "act out their emotions" and behave aggressively. Children with **internalizing tendencies** have problems managing intense fear. Both of these temperamental tendencies, at their extreme, cause problems during childhood.

Personality

Self-awareness changes dramatically as children move into middle childhood. Concrete operational children think about themselves in psychological terms, realistically scan their abilities, and evaluate themselves in comparison with peers. These more realistic self-perceptions explain why **self-esteem** normally declines during elementary school. Erikson's terms **industry** and **inferiority** also capture the self-esteem challenges children face during middle childhood. Relationships, academics, behavior, sports, and looks are the five areas from which elementary school children derive their self-esteem.

Children with externalizing tendencies minimize their difficulties with other people and may have unrealistically high self-esteem. Children with internalizing tendencies tend to be excessively self-critical, prone to low self-esteem, and may develop **learned helplessness,** the feeling that they are incompetent and incapable of doing well. Because both attitudes keep children from working to improve their behavior, the key to

helping *every* child is to focus on enhancing self-efficacy and to promote realistic views of the self and the world. Stimulating high self-esteem, however, is a Western concern. It is not an issue in Asia, where the cultural ideal is to be self-effacing and modest.

Prosocial behaviors—caring, helpful acts—become more varied and mature as children develop. There also is consistency, with prosocial preschoolers tending to be prosocial later on. In cultures that put a premium on modesty, such as China, there is a norm against telling people about one's caring acts.

Altruism—prosocial activities that are genuinely non-egocentric—involves transforming one's **empathy** (directly experiencing another's feelings) into **sympathy** (feeling for another person); being self-confident (not overly anxious); and being happy. The best way to socialize altruism is to use **induction** (getting a child who has behaved hurtfully to understand the other person's feelings) and to induce **guilt.** Child-rearing techniques involving **shame** (personal humiliation) backfire, making children angry and less likely to act in prosocial ways. Acting altruistically is not the same thing as being compliant or "good."

Aggression, or hurtful behavior, is also basic to being human. Rates of open aggression (hitting, yelling) dramatically decline as children move into the school years. **Instrumental aggression** is hurtful behavior we initiate. **Reactive aggression** occurs in response to being frustrated or hurt. **Relational aggression** refers to acts of aggression designed to damage social relationships.

Relational aggression increases during elementary school and is particularly common among girls.

A two-step pathway produces a highly aggressive child. When toddlers are very active (exuberant), caregivers may respond harshly and punitively—causing anger and aggression. Then, during school, the child's "bad" behavior causes peer rejection that leads to more aggression. Highly aggressive children may develop a **hostile attributional bias.** This "the world is out to get me" outlook is perfectly understandable, since aggressive children may have been living in a hostile, rejecting environment since their earliest years. While a variety of stressful environmental conditions raise the risk of any child's becoming highly aggressive, because boys tend to act out their feelings they are far more likely to be diagnosed as having "problematic aggression" than girls.

Relationships

Play is at the heart of childhood. **Rough-and-tumble play,** play fighting and wrestling, is typical of boys. **Fantasy play** or pretending—typical of all children—begins in later infancy and becomes genuinely mutual at about age 4, with the beginning of **collaborative pretend play.** Fantasy play declines during concrete operations, as children become interested in organized activities.

According to Vygotsky, fantasy play helps children practice adult roles; it offers a sense of mastery; and it teaches the need to adhere to norms and rules. Through examining their fantasy play themes, adults can get insights into children's inner concerns. Although teachers encourage fantasy play, they (perhaps inappropriately) tend to frown on rough-and-tumble play—that activity boys most love.

Gender-segregated play gradually unfolds during preschool, and in elementary school girls and boys typically play only with other members of their own sex. Boy-to-boy play is rambunctious, while girls play together in quiet, collaborative ways. Boys tend to compete in groups; girls play one to one. Boys' play is separate and walled-off from adults' and girls' activities. Gender-stereotyped play seems to have a strong biological basis, but this behavior is also socialized by parents and, especially, by peers as children play together in same-sex groups. According to **gender schema theory,** once children understand that they are a boy or a girl, they attend to and model behaviors of their own sex.

In childhood (and adulthood) we select friends who are similar to ourselves, and when children get older, inner qualities such as personality, loyalty, and sharing feelings become important. Friends provide children with vital emotional support and teach them to modulate their emotions and get along with others. In more collectivist cultures that stress family closeness, childhood friendships may not be as intense.

The one-to-one, symmetrical relationship called friendship involves the ability to regulate our emotions. Popularity involves having the social skills to rise to the top of the social totem pole. Popular children are "the class favorites." Average children are somewhere in the middle range. Rejected children are actively disliked by their peers. Rejected children tend to be socially unskilled. They either have serious externalizing tendencies or are socially anxious or both; or they don't conform to the elementary school group norms. In elementary school popular children are prosocial and well liked by their classmates, but during middle school and high school, children—especially girls—who are at the top of the social hierarchy may be relatively disliked by their peers. Although rejected children with externalizing problems are at risk for having troubles as they travel into adolescence and adult life, shy children and those who don't fit the childhood social mode may flower as they get older.

Children who are unpopular, who are anxious, and, especially, who don't fight back are vulnerable to **bullying.** Because bullies often get reinforced by their classmates, bullying prevention programs help to change the school atmosphere, shifting the social norms toward prosocial behavior. **Social skills training** can teach aggressive boys to modify their anger. Still, with children at risk for being rejected, elementary school is not the best time to intervene. Shy children need to get connected with a friend in preschool. Active explorers need lots of love at home.

▌ KEY TERMS

emotion regulation, p. 174

externalizing tendencies, p. 174

internalizing tendencies, p. 174

self-awareness, p. 175

self-esteem, p. 175

industry versus inferiority, p. 175

learned helplessness, p. 177

prosocial behavior, p. 180

altruism, p. 181

empathy, p. 181

sympathy, p. 181

induction, p. 182

shame, p. 182

guilt, p. 182

aggression, p. 184

instrumental aggression, p. 184

reactive aggression, p. 184

relational aggression, p. 184

hostile attributional bias, p. 186

rough-and-tumble play, p. 188

fantasy play, p. 188

collaborative pretend play, p. 188

gender-segregated play, p. 191

gender schema theory, p. 193

bullying, p. 198

social skills training, p. 200

▌ RECOMMENDED RESOURCES

BOOK FOR A POPULAR AUDIENCE

Thompson, M., and O'Neill, Grace (2001). *Best friends/worst enemies: Understanding the social lives of children*. New York: Ballantine.

This interesting book provides an overview of the core characteristics of childhood friendships and provides advice for parents to help their children in this important area of life. The author's thesis is that friendships—not popularity—are what are really important during childhood.

MORE SCHOLARLY BOOKS

Corsaro, W. A. (1997). *The sociology of childhood*. Thousand Oaks, CA: Pine Forge Press/Sage Publications.

In this lovely book Corsaro describes his firsthand investigations into the play world of nursery school.

Harter, S. (1999). *The construction of the self*. New York: Guilford.

In this academic book Harter summarizes her decades of research on the self.

WEB SITE

www.samhsa.gov.

This Web site, from the U.S. Department of Health and Human Services, outlines the Olweus Bully Prevention Program.

CHAPTER 7

This chapter is dedicated to Cindy Jones and her fourth-grade class

Settings for Development: Home and School

Manuel's parents migrated from Mexico to Las Vegas when he was a baby. Leaving their close extended family was painful, but they knew their son would not have much of a future in their small rural town.

At first, life was going very well. The Las Vegas economy was booming. José joined the Culinary Workers' Union. Maria got a housekeeping job at Caesar's Palace. They sent money to relatives regularly and made a down payment on a condo—carefully chosen to be in the best school district in town. Most important, their baby was turning into an exceptional boy. At age 5 Manuel could repair household appliances. He put together puzzles that would stump a 10-year-old child. He was picking up English beautifully, even though his parents, who only spoke Spanish, could not help him much with reading English and preparing for school.

Then, when Manuel was age 7, everything changed. José was laid off. He started to drink heavily. He came home late to regularly yell at his wife. Maria fell into a depression. This totally involved mother, who had been so strict but very loving—managing her son's activities, teaching him values—was barely able to pay any attention to her child. Although Manuel's first-grade teacher recommended he be tested for the gifted program, when the district psychologist got around to performing the evaluation a year later, Manuel didn't make the cutoff. His performance IQ was off the charts. But growing up in a Spanish-speaking family was a real handicap. His verbal IQ was only 95. And this was the worst time for Manuel to be tested: Maria had recently taken her belongings, moved out, sent for her mother, and filed for divorce.

It's two years later and life is getting back to normal. Maria's becoming the caring mother she used to be. After a rocky third-grade year, Manuel is returning to his old terrific self. The fourth-grade teacher is wonderful. She's creative, gives the children responsibility, understands Manuel's talents, and—most important—appreciates diverse kids. The thorn in Maria's side is Grandma—or, to be exact, Manuel's attitude toward Grandma. Having her mother in the house has been a godsend. Manuel doesn't have to stay home alone at night when Maria works double shifts to keep the family above the poverty line. But Manuel is beginning to be ashamed to bring friends home to see that "old world" lady. He wants to be a regular American boy. The downside of seeing your baby blossom beautifully in this country is watching your heritage get lost.

Is it typical for children, like Manuel, to have a difficult year or two after their parents get divorced? Given that we vitally need to succeed in the wider world, how important are the lessons we learn from our parents as opposed to our peers? What was that test Manuel took, and what strategies can teachers use to make *every* child eager to learn? Now we tackle these questions, and others, as we focus on the main settings within which children develop: home and school.

While our discussion applies to all children, in every home and school, in this chapter we pay special attention to children, such as Manuel, whose families differ from the traditional two-parent, middle-class, European American norm. So let's begin our exploration of home- and school-related topics by scanning the tapestry of families in the twenty-first-century United States.

FIGURE 7.1: **Living arrangements of children in U.S. families:** The first chart (a) shows that the two-parent family is still the most common one—although this family form includes a wide variety of "traditional" and more nontraditional families. The second chart (b) shows the dramatic income differences between two-parent and single-parent families.

Source: Fields (2003); Fields & Casper (2001).

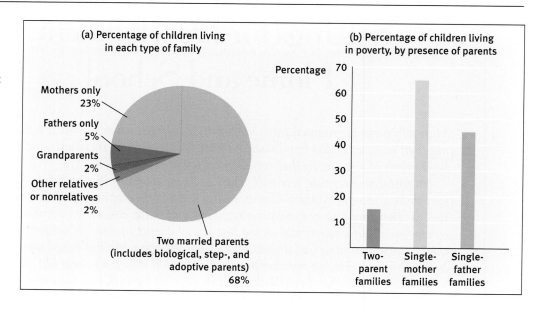

(a) Percentage of children living in each type of family

Mothers only 23%
Fathers only 5%
Grandparents 2%
Other relatives or nonrelatives 2%
Two married parents (includes biological, step-, and adoptive parents) 68%

(b) Percentage of children living in poverty, by presence of parents

Percentage

Two-parent families
Single-mother families
Single-father families

Parenting grandmothers, such as this woman helping her grandson with his homework, show that strong, loving families in the United States come in many forms. What *exactly* is this grandma doing right? This is the question we will explore in this section.

Setting the Context: A Tapestry of Families

At the turn of the century, roughly 7 out of 10 U.S. families with children were categorized as "two-parent." That umbrella category, however, covers a range of family types. There is the *traditional two-parent family*—never remarried with biological children. There are *blended families.* These are families where parents have remarried and in which children grow up with stepparents and often stepsiblings. There are adoptive parents, gay parents, foster parents, and grandparent-headed families.

Finally, there are the legions of *one-parent families.* With regard to these families, as you can see in Figure 7.1, we can make two important generalizations. The majority of single-parent families are headed by women (typically mothers). As two out of three mother-headed families are classified as low-income, for children who grow up in a one-parent family, economic hardship is often a fact of life.

Can children thrive in every type of family? The answer is yes. The key lies in the quality of what parents do. Now let's focus directly on what parents do.

Home

We already know *generally* what parents need to do: It is vital to promote a secure attachment and be sensitive to a given child's unique temperamental needs. Can we outline an overall discipline style that works best? In the early 1970s, developmentalist Diana Baumrind decided that we could.

Parenting Styles

parenting style In Diana Baumrind's framework, how parents align on two dimensions of childrearing: nurturance (or child-centeredness) and discipline (or structure and rules).

Think of a parent you really admire. What is that mother or father doing right? Now think of parents who you feel are not fulfilling this job. Where are they falling short? Most likely your list will center on two functions. Are these people loving and nurturing? Do they provide consistent discipline or rules? By classifying parents on these two dimensions—being responsive or child-centered, and providing "structure" or rules—Baumrind (1971) spelled out the following **parenting styles:**

- **Authoritative parents** rank high on both the nurturing and limit-setting dimensions. They give their children reasonable freedom and lots of love but also have clear expectations and consistent rules. In these families, parents set high standards for their children's behavior. There are consistent bedtimes, rules for completing homework, and specific household chores. However, if a daughter wants to watch a favorite TV program, these parents might relax the rule that homework must be finished before dinner. They could let a son extend his regular 9:00 P.M. bedtime for a party or special event. Although authoritative parents believe firmly in structure, they understand that rules don't take precedence over human needs.

- **Authoritarian parents** are more inflexible. Their child-rearing motto is, "Obey the rules and do what I say." In these families, bedtimes and homework rules are not negotiable. While authoritarian parents typically love their children deeply, their upbringing style can appear to be inflexible, rigid, and sometimes cold.

- **Permissive parents** are at the opposite end of the spectrum from authoritarian parents. Their parenting mantra is, "Give children total freedom and unconditional love." These parents have no set bedtimes for their sons and daughters, and no childhood chores. The child-rearing principle in this household is that children's needs rule.

- **Rejecting-neglecting parents** are the worst of both worlds—low on structure and low on love. Their child-rearing motto is, "Minimize involvement with my child." In this house children are neglected, ignored, and emotionally abandoned. They are left to literally raise themselves (see Figure 7.2 for a visual recap).

As researchers conducted numerous studies using Baumrind's framework, they found that authoritative parenting was correlated with a host of measures of childhood success, predicting everything from academic achievement in adolescence to superior preschool social skills (Maccoby & Martin, 1983). Even the younger generation agrees about the value of using this style. When college students feel good about their lives, they often say their parents raised them in an "authoritative" way (Jackson and others, 2005).

authoritative parents In Diana Baumrind's parenting-styles framework, the best possible child-rearing style, in which parents rank high on both nurturance and discipline, providing both love and clear family rules.

authoritarian parents In Diana Baumrind's parenting-styles framework, a type of childrearing in which parents provide plenty of rules but rank low on child-centeredness, stressing unquestioning obedience.

permissive parents In Diana Baumrind's parenting-styles framework, a type of child-rearing in which parents provide few rules but rank high on child-centeredness, being extremely loving but providing little discipline.

rejecting-neglecting parents In Diana Baumrind's parenting-styles framework, the worst child-rearing approach, in which parents provide little discipline and little nurturing or love.

[**FAQ:** How do parenting styles and family experiences affect a child's sense of self ?]

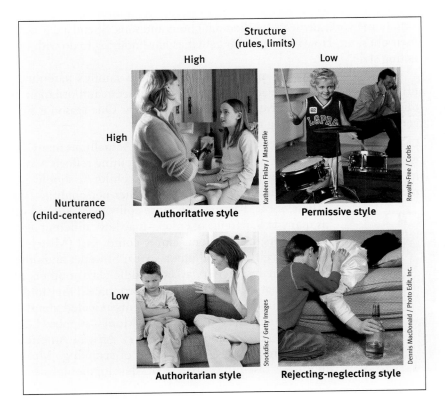

FIGURE 7.2: Parenting styles: A visual summary table.
Source: Adapted from Baumrind (1987).

Questioning and Criticizing the Styles Framework

At first glance, Baumrind's authoritative category offers a wonderful blueprint for the right way to bring up children: Provide plenty of structure and lots of love. However, if you take a minute to classify your own family along these dimensions, you may find a problem. Your mother might have been more permissive and your father more authoritarian, or vice versa.

How often do mothers and fathers *really* differ in their discipline styles? To answer this interesting question, researchers asked married couples to rate their own parenting style and then—using the same questionnaire—to describe their partner's approach. When people rated themselves as authoritarian or permissive, they were more likely to rate their spouse in the same way, saying, "We are both very strict" or "My husband and I are pretty lax." This suggests that with the more extreme discipline styles there is more of a unified family front. But most women in this study labeled themselves as authoritative and ranked their husbands differently—saying either, "He's the permissive one" or, more frequently, "My husband is stricter." Interestingly, going along with the traditional idea of father as more of a disciplinarian, dads also often classified themselves as more "authoritarian" than their wives.

[FAQ: What happens if parents use different parenting styles?]

Does it matter for a child's development that only one parent is authoritative, and should that person be the mother? Suppose one parent is permissive and the other is authoritarian: Can the different approaches balance each other out? We do not know. What we do know is that *fighting* about discipline poisons family life. If one parent is strict and the other is more permissive, the key is to value what the other person brings to the family or, at a minimum, to agree to disagree.

These questions show that we cannot assume that children are exposed to a single child-rearing style. When we look deeper, Baumrind's categories do not reflect the complexity of real-life parenting in *several* important ways:

CHILDREARING INVOLVES A WIDE VARIETY OF BEHAVIORS. For one thing, being a good parent involves far more than simply providing love and discipline (Dodge, 2002; Grusec, Goodnow, & Kuczynski, 2000). As you saw in the chapter-opening vignette, parents arrange the environment. They may move to a different part of town or even to a different country for the sake of their children. They teach values, help with homework, advocate for their daughters and sons. Spend a day with a couple and their children. How many of their activities have nothing to do with *any* defined parenting style?

During that day you may also notice that this family's parenting is difficult to firmly categorize. In some areas of life, they might seem authoritarian. In others, they might appear too permissive from your point of view. One reason is that parents have very different child-rearing priorities and goals.

CHILDREARING REFLECTS CULTURAL AGENDAS. Actually, as many developmentalists have argued, the styles perspective on good parenting reflects a middle-class, European American set of priorities—the idea that children should be raised to be independent and taught to freely express their inner personalities (Greenfield and others, 2003). Parents with more collectivist cultural values—as well as many U.S. parents of color—may have different agendas: Respect your elders; be obedient; family comes first (Mistry, Chaudhuri, & Diez, 2003; Roosa and others, 2002; Shweder and others, 1998).

When researchers asked middle-class mothers and fathers in China what answers would be appropriate if they told their children to "pick up the toys," these parents rejected standard U.S child-negotiating tactics such as, "OK, Mom—suppose I do half and you do half?" (Bowes and others, 2004). African American parents believe more strongly in the value of spanking (Mosby and others, 1999)—a discipline style that developmentalists often rank as

If you asked this loving dad from Africa (who has just become a new American) about the right way to discipline his baby girl, you would almost certainly hear a more positive idea about using physical punishment than if you questioned a developmental scientist. This difference shows that cultures *legitimately* differ about how to bring up children in a caring, nurturing way.

Jeff Greenberg / Photo Edit, Inc.

authoritarian. However, while middle-class European American families who heavily rely on physical punishment are more likely to have children with social and academic difficulties, this is not the case for African American families (Baumrind, Larzelere, & Cowen, 2002; Deater-Deckard and others, 1996; Larzelere, 1994, 1996; Whaley, 2000).

Imagine the very different messages that "Obey what I say" or being spanked might convey if you were a child growing up in a traditional Chinese family or in the African American community. The same discipline style that in one cultural context might be defined as overly authoritarian could be a signal that your parents really loved you very much.

CHILDREARING CHANGES, DEPENDING ON THE ENVIRONMENT. The fact that the activities involved in "good parenting" are relative to the culture we live in is vividly apparent when we look throughout history. You may recall from Chapter 1 that during the eighteenth and nineteenth centuries, affluent parents in cities such as Paris sent their newborns away to be nursed by women in the countryside. Today we would consider these practices abusive. In that era they were vital to ensuring that babies would survive.

Difficult life conditions affect parenting decisions today. From a middle-class perspective, developmentalists tend to rank working-class parents as "overly authoritarian" because they place more emphasis on obedience (Bradley and others, 2001b). However, these parents may feel they need to be stricter to help their children survive in a harsher world (Garcia Coll, Meyer, & Brillon, 1995; Hoff-Ginsberg & Tardif, 1995).

Actually, for children growing up in very dangerous neighborhoods, such as inner-city African Americans, authoritarian parenting is related to *high* achievement (Dearing, 2004; Scarr & Deater-Deckard, 1997). If your mission is to shield your child from the drug dealer on the corner or keep him from getting shot, you don't have the luxury of allowing much negotiation over rules (Burton, 2001; Kelley, Power, & Wimbush, 1992). Think of how your parenting style would change if you moved to a war-torn country or a crime-ridden area of your town. Safety would be your *first* priority, before anything else.

In sum, let's accept the idea that parents should provide clear standards and plenty of love. However, let's understand that parenting styles are affected by people's unique priorities and cultural agendas. Moreover, the best parents vary their child-rearing strategies to provide the best discipline–environment fit.

INTERVENTIONS: Lessons for Thinking About Parents

How can you use this section's insights to relate to parents in a more empathic way in your career and daily life?

- Be culture-friendly. Don't impose your own parenting priorities on other people. Understand that there are a variety of valid child-rearing goals.

- Be aware that dangerous environments demand a more vigilant, rule-oriented kind of parenting—one that may look rigid and less child-centered from a middle-class European American view.

- Before you blame a mother or father for being too strict (or too lax), try to understand the pressures this family is facing. Rather than being judgmental, it is best to be caring and work to provide parents with support.

How Much Do Parents Matter?

Our discussion, however, assumes that parents are in the driver's seat—that what happens at home is the crucial force in determining how children turn out. Why then do some wonderful parents have children with terrible problems? Why do some children with terrible early lives succeed brilliantly as adults?

His aristocratic parents spent their time gallivanting around Europe; they never appeared at the nursery doors. At age 7, he was wrenched from the only person who loved him—his nanny—and shipped off to boarding school. Insolent, angry, refusing to obey orders or sit still, he was regularly beaten by the headmaster and teased by the other boys. Although gifted at writing, he was incapable of rote memorization; he couldn't pass a test. When he graduated at the bottom of his boarding school class, his father informed him that he would never amount to anything. His name was Winston Churchill. He was the man who stood up to Hitler and carried England to victory in the Second World War.

Churchill's upbringing was a recipe for disaster. He had neglectful parents, serious behavior problems, and was a total failure at school. But this dismal childhood produced the leader who saved the modern world.

resilient children Children who rebound from serious early life traumas to construct successful adult lives.

Resilient children, like Churchill, confront terrible conditions such as parental neglect, poverty, and the horrors of war and go on to construct successful, loving lives. What qualities allow these children to thrive? Developmentalists who study these unusual boys and girls find that resilient children typically have outgoing personalities (Kim-Cohen and others, 2004; Rende & Plomin, 1992; Werner & Smith, 1992) and superior emotion-regulation skills (Flores, Cicchetti, & Rogosch, 2005). They may have a special talent, such as Churchill's gift for writing (Masten, 2001; Masten & Coatsworth, 1998). The quality of their attachments is crucial, too. Children who succeed against daunting odds typically have at least one close, caring relationship, if not with a parent, then with a teacher or another adult (such as Churchill's nanny) (Flores, Cicchetti, & Rogosch, 2005; Kim-Cohen and others, 2004; Masten, 2001; Masten & Coatsworth, 1998).

The fact that caring attachments are important shows that to triumph over the odds requires the right nurture. Children cannot thrive without having at least one loving adult in their lives. But these children clearly had to have the right "nature." They had the genetically based temperamental qualities that allowed them to bounce back from severe stress and search out these loving connections, too. Could they have possessed a specific resilience-promoting gene?

Interestingly, rats with two long forms of a gene regulating the transmission of the neurotransmitter serotonin cope amazingly well when subjected to stresses such as loud noises. These fascinating findings enticed developmentalists in the ongoing Dunedin Study to see if there might be a similar genetic protective effect in human beings (Caspi and others, 2003). You may remember from Chapter 1 that in the Dunedin Study, researchers have been tracking the personalities of children born in this New Zealand city from birth into adulthood. At their age-26 evaluation, the research team questioned study participants about the number of stressful events they had experienced over the previous five years. Then, using cutting-edge medical technology, they genotyped each person, looking for the presence of long or short forms of the serotonin-regulating gene.

The researchers discovered that if a person's life had been relatively free of stress, having the long gene did not make a difference in terms of mental health. The findings were very different if these young people experienced four or more major life stresses. Forty-three percent of these severely stressed study participants with two short forms of the gene developed a major depression. The comparable rate for their counterparts with two long forms of the gene was less than half that high. Moreover, having at least one long gene insulated the children who had been abused from becoming depressed during their emerging-adult years. So some people seem blessed by their biology to be resilient human beings!

Does Our Adult Fate Depend Mainly on Our Genes?

In numerous twin and adoption studies, behavioral geneticists have taken aim at Baumrind's nurture-oriented principle that parents are crucially important. They argue that correlations between authoritative parenting and competent, successful children are really caused by shared genetic tendencies. Parents who handle the job of childrearing competently pass down the same biological predispositions to be competent that permit their children to socially succeed (Rowe, 1981, 1983, 2003).

Moreover, behavioral geneticists argue, when we see correlations between parenting styles and children's behavior, we may be confusing the chicken and the egg. Rather than parents determining how children act, the reality is the reverse. Temperamentally easy children evoke warm, authoritative parenting. It is really *children's* personalities that determine parents' child-rearing styles (Bell, 1968; Deater-Deckard, 1996; Deater-Deckard and others, 1996; Plomin & Bergeman, 1991).

Do children's temperaments affect how parents behave? If you think back to the fact that human relationships are inherently bidirectional (and the twin study "nature evokes nurture" research presented in the Experiencing the Lifespan box in Chapter 1), the answer has to be yes. Based on the premise that we actively shape our environments to go along with our inborn temperamental tendencies and skills, developmentalist Sandra Scarr (Scarr & Ricciuti, 1991; Scarr, 1997) came to a controversial conclusion: Given an adequate home life, children grow up to fulfill their unique biological gifts. All parents need to do is provide a reasonably decent upbringing, nothing more.

Is It All in the Peer Group?

Another developmentalist has taken an equally controversial stance. According to Judith Harris (1995, 1998, 2002), our peer group, not our parents, is the main force that shapes our behavior and the adult we become.

Harris begins her argument by disputing the main principle underlying attachment theory—that the lessons we learn from our parents transfer to our other relationships. Learning, Harris believes, is context-specific. We cannot use the same *working model* with our mother and with the classroom bully, or we would never survive. Furthermore, because we live our lives in the wider world, she argues, the messages we absorb from the culture of our contemporaries must take precedence over the lessons we are taught at home.

Any parent can relate to Harris's ideas about the power of peer groups when witnessing a preschooler automatically pick up every bad habit from the other children the first week after entering nursery school. You saw a vivid example of Harris's ideas in operation in our discussion of gender roles in Chapter 6. Remember that as they begin to play in same-sex groups, children socialize one another to behave in gender-stereotyped ways.

The most compelling evidence for Harris's theory may come from looking at what happens to children such as Manuel. Immigrant children quickly shed the cultural customs they learned at home in order to make it as "real" Americans.

These arguments that peers and genetics are very important alert us to the fact that, when we see children "acting out" at a restaurant or at school, we cannot simply leap to the assumption that "it's all the parents fault." As developmental systems theory would predict, a variety of influences—from inborn temperament, to peer groups, to everything else—affect how children behave. But you may be thinking that the idea that parents are *not* important goes way too far. Scarr's statement that all that matters is a "reasonably decent home life" seems particularly offensive. It strikes at the heart of our mission as parents to provide the best upbringing we can!

Look at these exuberant boys, passionate to fit in with their friends. Then ask yourself whether these children are acting the same way they were taught to behave at home. Suddenly, doesn't Judith Harris's theory that "peer groups shape our development" make a good deal of sense?

Skjold Photographs / The Image Works

[FAQ: What role does parenting play in personality development?]

Many developmentalists agree. For children to fully realize their genetic potential, parents should always strive to provide the *best possible* environment (Ceci and others, 1997; Kagan, 1998; Maccoby, 2002). In fact, when children are "at risk" or temperamentally vulnerable, as we know from previous chapters, superior parenting is absolutely required.

Making the Case for Superior Parenting

Imagine, for instance, that your toddler is very active and has trouble regulating his emotions. You know from reading this book that your child's temperament puts him at risk of having externalizing problems as he travels into school. You are determined not to let that pattern unfold. So you inhibit your use of *power assertion*. You take care to provide lots of love. You carefully work to arrange the environment to minimize your child's vulnerabilities and highlight his strengths.

In any at-risk situation—be it growing up in poverty or having a more challenging temperament—developmentalists find that unusually sensitive parenting can indeed make a critical difference (Kim-Cohen and others, 2004; Werner & Smith, 1982). Consider children who are born extremely premature. These very-low-birth-weight babies have two strikes against them. As you saw in Chapter 2, they are biologically vulnerable to having learning and behavior problems. Because they live for months apart from their parents in the neonatal ICU, they may be set up for more parental rejection, too.

Researchers tracked the progress of more than 2,000 extremely-low-birth-weight twins (Tully and others, 2004). They videotaped mothers describing their infants during their first weeks of life. Then they followed the children until they entered kindergarten. If a mother talked about her fragile infant in especially tender, loving terms, that particular child was far less likely to be diagnosed with symptoms of ADHD at age 5.

This finding makes good biological sense. We know that stimulation sculpts neurons. Why wouldn't exceptionally loving mothering be able to mend the biochemistry of the brain (Suomi, 2004)?

[FAQ: How can I use this material to be an effective parent?]

▌INTERVENTIONS: Lessons for Readers Who Are Parents

Now let's summarize our whole discussion, by shifting gears and talking directly to the parent readers of this book:

There are no firm guidelines about how to be an effective parent—except to be loving, set high standards, and provide consistent rules. But it also is critical to be flexible. Adapt your discipline to your life situation and especially to your unique child. You will face special challenges if you live in a dangerous environment (where you may have to exert more control) or have children who are "harder to raise" (where you may have to work harder to stay closely attached). Your ultimate power is limited at best.

However, try to see this message as liberating. Children cannot be massaged into having an idealized adult life. Your child's future does not totally depend on you. Focus on the quality of your relationship and simply enjoy these wonderful years. And if your son or daughter is having problems, draw heart from Winston Churchill's history. Predictions from childhood to adult life can be hazy. Your unsuccessful child may grow up to save the world!

Table 7.1 offers a checklist for every reader to evaluate your personal child-rearing priorities and think more deeply about the qualities you believe are most important to instill in a child.

Now that we've covered the general territory, we turn to specifics. First, we look at that controversial practice, spanking. Then we focus on the worst type of parenting, child abuse. And finally, we explore the life transition in the chapter-opening vignette, divorce.

What do your rankings reveal about the qualities you most admire in human beings?

TABLE 7.1: Checklist for Identifying Your Parenting Priorities

Rank the following goals in order of their importance to you, from 1 (for highest priority) to 8 (for lowest priority). It's OK to use the same number twice if two goals are equally important to you.

_____ Producing an obedient, well-behaved child

_____ Producing a caring, prosocial child

_____ Producing an independent, self-sufficient child

_____ Producing a child who is extremely close to you

_____ Producing an intelligent, creative thinker

_____ Producing a well-rounded child

_____ Producing a happy, emotionally secure child

_____ Producing a spiritual (religious) child

Spanking

Poll your friends and family members about their opinions relating to **corporal punishment**—any discipline technique using physical measures such as spanking—and you are likely to get some strong reactions. Some people firmly believe in the biblical principle, "Spare the rod and spoil the child." They may blame the decline in spanking for every social problem. Others blame corporal punishment for *creating* those same social problems. They believe that parents who rely on "hitting" are implicitly teaching children the message that it is OK to respond in a violent way.

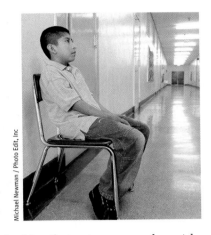

Today when children misbehave in school, we put them in "time-out," rather than paddling them, as we would have done in the past, because we now believe that corporal punishment may teach children that it's fine to hit.

corporal punishment The use of physical force to discipline a child.

Because many Europeans tend to agree with the idea that using corporal punishment offers a model of violence, in most EU countries using physical discipline in school and at home is now against the law (Benjet & Kazdin, 2003). Where do U.S. parents stand on the issue of corporal punishment, and what do developmentalists say?

To begin to answer the first question, researchers polled more than 900 American parents, asking about milder forms of corporal punishment ("Do you spank your child on the bottom with your hand?") as well as more severe practices ("Do you hit your child with a belt?") (Straus & Stewart, 1999).

As you can see in Figure 7.3, although most people don't use physical punishment with an infant, almost everyone (94 percent of Americans) reported using this type of discipline with preschoolers. Moreover, although most parents in this survey said they used only mild forms of corporal punishment, such as spanking, more than one in four reported that they hit their child with a hard object such as a brush or a belt.

The belief that it is perfectly acceptable to use corporal punishment—under certain conditions—is echoed by people who are not yet parents. Researchers gave U.S. college students vignettes describing children who committed various infractions and asked when it might be appropriate to spank a child. Most students felt that a spanking was warranted if a child talked back, took someone's belongings, or (interestingly) hit a playmate, although it was not acceptable to use physical discipline for minor acts of disobedience such as not cleaning a room (Flynn, 1998).

[FAQ: Is spanking bad or good for children?]

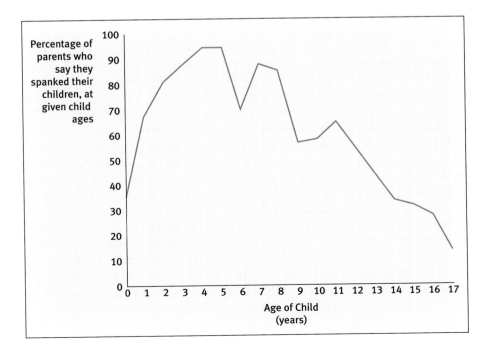

FIGURE 7.3: Prevalence of corporal punishment in the United States, by age of child: Notice from this telephone survey that corporal punishment reaches its peak during the preschool years—although a very high proportion of parents also report hitting their elementary schoolers.

Source: Adapted from Straus & Stewart (1999), p. 59.

[FAQ: Should you spank a child?]

What do developmentalists advise about corporal punishment? Interestingly, within the professional community, there is considerable debate. Some psychologists argue that using physical punishment is *never* appropriate (Gershoff, 2002; Straus & Donnelly, 1994; Straus & Stewart, 1999). As suggested earlier, they feel that hitting a child models violence. It conveys the message that it is acceptable for big people to give small people pain. Spanking, they point out, is also a shame-inducing technique. While it may produce immediate compliance, it is tailor-made to impair prosocial behavior and conscience development (Andero & Stewart, 2002; Benjet & Kazdin, 2003).

Others disagree, believing that mild spanking is not necessarily detrimental (Baumrind, 1996, 1997; Baumrind, Larzelere, & Cowan, 2002; Larzelere, 1994, 1996, 2000; Larzelere & Johnson, 1999; Larzelere & Kuhn, 2005). They suggest that if we totally rule out corporal punishment, we run the risk that caregivers will resort to more emotionally damaging kinds of verbal abuse, such as saying, "I hate you. You will never amount to anything." Still, these developmentalists have the following guidelines about when physical punishment can—and should not—be used:

Parents should never hit an infant. Babies don't know what they are doing wrong. Moreover, infants who are hit regularly have higher baseline rates of the stress hormone cortisol, so spanking a baby may set that child up to be chronically anxious and depressed (Bugenthal, Martorell, & Barraza, 2003). For a preschooler, a few swats on the bottom can be an effective disciplinary technique, especially when a child is engaging in activities that are very dangerous, such as running into the street, and needs to be immediately stopped (Larzelere & Kuhn, 2005). Still, when parents use physical punishment, they should accompany this action by a verbal explanation ("What you did was wrong because . . ."). Ideally, they should reserve a spanking as a backup technique when other strategies, such as time-outs, fail.

[FAQ: How should I discipline my child?]

Every developmentalist, however, is strongly against *heavy* reliance on corporal punishment. The reason is that the "Spare the rod, spoil the child" philosophy comes uncomfortably close to child abuse.

Child Abuse

child maltreatment Any act that seriously endangers a child's physical or emotional well-being.

Child maltreatment—the term for any act that endangers children's physical or emotional well-being—actually goes beyond severe physical punishment to make up four distinct categories. *Physical abuse* refers to bodily injury that leaves bruises. It encompasses everything from overzealous spanking to battering that may lead to a child's death. *Neglect* refers to caregivers' failure to provide adequate supervision and care. It might mean abandoning the child, not providing sufficient food, or even failing to enroll a son or daughter in school. *Emotional abuse* describes acts that cause serious emotional damage, such as terrorizing or exploiting a child. *Sexual abuse* covers the spectrum from rape and incest to fondling and exhibitionistic acts.

[FAQ: How can you tell if a child is being abused?]

Everyone can identify serious forms of maltreatment, but there is a gray zone as to exactly what activities cross the line (Whitaker, Lutzker, & Shelley, 2005). Does *every* spanking that leaves bruises really qualify as physical abuse? If a single mother is forced to leave her toddler in an 8-year-old sibling's care when she goes to work, should we classify her as neglectful? Are parents who walk around naked in the house guilty of exhibitionism or sexual abuse? Emotional abuse is very difficult to prove and prosecute, even though this type of maltreatment may leave the most enduring inner scars.

Even if we had the clearest definitions, it would be impossible to pin down the actual incidence of child abuse. Rates of maltreatment in the United States declined from 1990 to 2002, but at almost 900,000 documented cases in 2002, they still are unacceptably high (National Clearinghouse on Child Abuse and Neglect Information, 2005; Whitaker and others, 2005). Worse yet, many cases are not reported to the authorities. They may be found "accidentally" when a child is discovered with welts, or possibly even severely stunted and near death (Whitaker and others, 2005). What might provoke this kind of violence, and what might we do to help?

Exploring the Risk Factors

As developmental systems theory would predict, several categories of influence may combine to provoke caregivers to act in a physically or emotionally abusive way:

Parents' personality problems are important. People who abuse their children often have psychological disorders, such as depression and, especially, substance abuse (Palusci, Smith, & Paneth, 2005; Rinehart and others, 2005). They tend to be hypersensitive to infant distress (Reijneveld and others, 2004). They may have unrealistic developmental expectations; for example, they may believe that children should be able to sit still or be totally toilet trained at a very young age (Bissada & Briere, 2001; Cicchetti & Toth, 1998; Goodman, Emery, & Haugaard, 1998; Herman-Giddens and others, 1999).

Serious life stress is part of the picture. Parents who maltreat their children are often coping with an overload of problems, from domestic violence to severe poverty. They tend to be isolated from caring family or friends (Bissada & Briere, 2001; Cicchetti & Toth, 1998; Goodman, Emery, & Haugaard, 1998; Herman-Giddens and others, 1999).

Children's vulnerabilities are often influential. Then there is the contribution of the child. Children with difficult temperaments and babies who cry excessively (Reijneveld and others, 2004) are more at risk of being abused (Bissada & Briere, 2001; Cicchetti & Toth, 1998; Goodman, Emery, & Haugaard, 1998). The fact that abusive parents may target just one child was brought home to me when I was working as a clinical psychologist at a city hospital in New York. A mother was referred for treatment by the court for abusing what she called her "spiteful" 10-year-old although she never harmed his "sweet" 3-year-old brother. So disturbances in the attachment relationship are often a core ingredient in the poisonous recipe for producing a battered child.

As you learned in Chapter 4, abused children tend to have insecure attachments. They often have academic and social difficulties (Shonk & Cicchetti, 2001) and, especially, problems regulating their emotions (Ford, 2005). These same deficits, in turn, place these children at higher risk of engaging in domestic violence and maltreating their own children as adults. But it is crucial to point out that *most* abused children go on to be caring, loving parents. People who have been maltreated are not fated to repeat those behaviors or to have problems in their relationships as adults (Trickett, Kurtz, & Pizzigati, 2004).

Interestingly, the Dunedin research team discovered a genetic marker that may protect abused boys from acting out in violent ways (Caspi and others, 2002). The researchers examined various antisocial activities among the 8 percent of 21- to 26-year-old males in the study who had been abused as children. Then they measured the activity of a gene that produces an enzyme regulating aggressive behaviors in mice. If the output of this enzyme was high, a maltreated boy was far less likely to be arrested or to engage in domestic violence during his emerging-adult years. So once again, this exciting research shows there may be specific genes that operate to make us more (or less) resilient to life stress.

INTERVENTIONS: Taking Action Against Child Abuse

What should you do if you suspect child abuse? Teachers, social workers, and health-care professionals are required by law to report the case to child protective services. Children deemed to be in imminent danger are removed from the home, and the cases are referred to juvenile court. Judges do not have the power to punish abusive parents, but they can place their children in foster care and possibly limit or even terminate their parental rights.

Imagine you are a judge who must make the heart-wrenching decision to take a child away from his parents. If you leave the child in an abusive home, that boy or girl may be re-injured or neglected (Palusci, Smith, & Paneth, 2005). But you also

[FAQ: How do you identify a child abuser or a potential abuser?]

[FAQ: Do childhood traumas result in lifelong problems?]

[FAQ: What should you do if you suspect child abuse?]

know that being separated from a primary attachment figure can leave emotional scars. This is why the best strategy is to try, if possible, to keep the child in the family and provide intensive support to help parents be more effective caregivers (National Clearinghouse on Child Abuse and Neglect Information, 2005). The same principle—support the parents so that they can be effective caregivers—applies to the family situation we turn to now: divorce.

Divorce

Child abuse affects a small fraction of children. Millions upon millions of children each year see their parents' marriage break up. How does divorce affect children, and what forces affect how children ultimately adjust?

Let's start with the bad news. Studies around the globe comparing children of divorce with their counterparts in intact married families show that children of divorce are at a statistical disadvantage—academically, socially, and in terms of physical and mental health (Amato, 2000, 2001; Amato & Keith, 1991; Lowenstein, 2005; Troxel & Matthews, 2004). However, these general comparisons are misleading because they paint an overly grim picture. Three out of four children whose parents divorce don't have major mental health problems (Hetherington, Bridges, & Insabella, 1998; Kelly, 2003). When children growing up in divorced families perform more poorly academically or have higher rates of mental health problems, their difficulties might mainly reflect the economic stresses of living in a single-parent family, not the trauma of seeing their parents' marriage break up (Kelly, 2003; McLanahan & Sandefur, 1994).

[FAQ: Is it better to stay in a bad marriage for the sake of the children, or do parents do more harm than good if they stay in a lousy marriage?]

Moreover, the psychological difficulties children tend to manifest after divorce often begin before the couple splits up (Kelly, 2003). Imagine your parents are continually fighting. The family atmosphere is tense. Like Manuel's mother in the chapter-opening vignette, your mother (or father) is depressed and angry. She cannot give you the attention you need. Around the time of the separation, researchers find, childrearing tends to become less competent, and more disorganized, as couples struggle with their feelings and try to rearrange their lives (Hetherington, 1999). Because of their own inner turmoil, many parents have trouble talking openly about their situation—leaving their children confused, angry, and sad. Fortunately, however, most parents do regroup and regain their equilibrium after a year or two (Kelly, 2003).

What forces determine how well children rebound from this trauma? The main key lies in the quality of care the parent who gets custody provides. Can the custodial mother or father be an effective parent? (See Wolchik and others, 2005.) It is also important to look at the relationship between the parents themselves. When husbands and wives battle over visitation rights, continually bad-mouth each other, or try to turn the children against a former partner, children suffer most (Baker, 2005; Kelly, 2003; Siegler, 2005).

Would it be better for couples, such as Maria and José, to stay together for the sake of the children? The answer is probably no. Children in two-parent families with spouses embroiled in chronic conflict are worse off than those whose parents divorce (Doucet & Aseltine, 2003; Weigel, Bennett, & Ballard-Reisch, 2003). In one behavioral-genetic investigation, developmentalists found that living with an antisocial father was particularly harmful to children's development. These children experienced a double whammy: They were genetically at risk for externalizing behaviors *and* they were being trained in being violent at home (Jaffee and others, 2003). Therefore, staying together "for the sake of the children" only makes sense if parents can really "get it together"—at least fairly well—and get along.

Should this unhappy couple stay together "for the sake of their daughter"? The answer, as you can see in the text, depends on whether they can stop continually getting into these terrible arguments.

Timeline (1–2 years)		
Family arguments → Separation, chaotic parenting → Divorce → Reorganizing life		
Interventions		
Couple counseling	Offer support to children at school or via counseling.	Foster authoritative custodial parenting.
	Encourage open discussion by parents with children of what is happening.	Discourage parents from using their children as pawns to express their anger.
	Support parents as they adjust to their new lives.	Discourage parents from fighting over custody.

FIGURE 7.4: Timeline of divorce, with interventions to minimize problems for children

Sources: Pedro-Carroll (2005); Pruett, Insabella, & Gustafson (2005); Wolchik and others (2005).

Figure 7.4 illustrates the problems associated with divorce on a timeline and suggests some interventions that counselors might make. In Chapter 11, we will look at divorce from the adult point of view. Now we turn to that other major setting within which children develop: school.

TYING IT ALL TOGETHER

1. Montana's parents make firm rules but value their children's input about family decisions. Jason's parents have rules for everything and tolerate no *ifs, ands,* or *buts.* Sara's parents don't really have rules. At their house it's always playtime and time to indulge the children. Which parenting style is being used by Montana's parents? by Jason's parents? by Sara's parents?

2. Chloe grew up in a happy middle-class family, but Amber and Sierra both had difficult childhoods. Sierra is struggling in college and often feels very unhappy, but both Amber and Chloe are doing well at school. To which student does the term *resilient* best apply?

3. Melissa's son Jared, now in elementary school, was extremely premature and has a variety of behavior and learning problems. Select the advice that Judith Harris might give, Sandra Scarr might give, and what this chapter would recommend:

   a. "Be the best mother you possibly can; in your son's case, superior parenting is vital."
   b. "There's nothing much you can do except to make sure Jared gets into a good peer group."
   c. "Jared will grow up to fulfill his genetic potential; just do your best to provide a decent home."

4. Your sister is concerned about a friend who uses corporal punishment with her children, who are 12 months and 4 years old. She asks you what the experts say. Which of the following are *two* positions developmentalists might take?

   a. Never spank children of any age.
   b. Mild spanking is OK for the infant.
   c. Mild spanking is OK for the 4-year-old.
   d. Depending on the child, heavy corporal punishment might be OK.

5. As an elementary school teacher, you are concerned about a student who has been coming to school without a coat or jacket this winter. You've also seen what you're pretty sure are burn marks on the child's arms. What kinds of abuse seem to be involved? What should you do? What should the ideal goal be?

6. Your friend Crystal recently had the courage to leave her abusive husband after years of constant fighting. Crystal is feeling good about the separation, but she is worried that maybe she should have stayed with her spouse for the sake of their daughter. Given the research, did Crystal make the right decision for her daughter? What bits of parenting advice can you give Crystal about helping her child?

Answers to the Tying It All Together questions can be found in the answers section of the book.

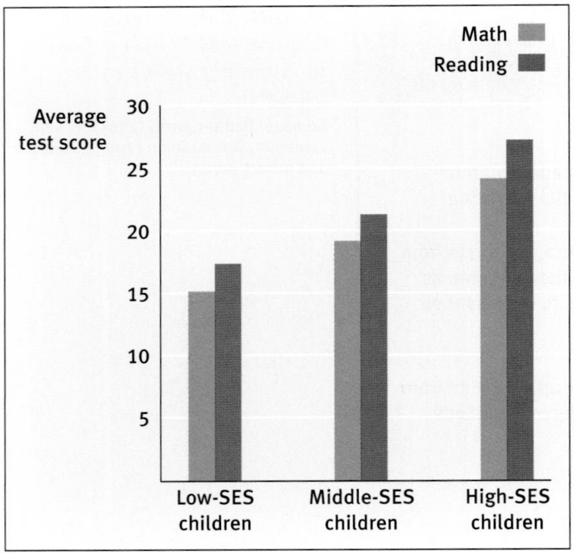

FIGURE 7.5: Socioeconomic status and kindergartners' scores on tests of readiness for reading and math: As children's socioeconomic status rises, so do average scores on tests of math and reading readiness. Notice the dramatic differences between low-income and affluent children.

Source: Lee & Burkham (2002), p.18.

School

What was that test Manuel took, and what does intelligence really mean? What makes for good teaching and superior schools? Before looking carefully at these school-related topics, let's begin by setting the framework—stepping back and, once again, exploring the impact of that basic marker, poverty, on young children's cognitive skills.

Setting the Context: Unequal at the Starting Gate

In Chapter 4 you learned that living in poverty for the first years of life has its most damaging effects on cognition. Figure 7.5 reveals that devastation by offering some sobering statistics with regard to the entering U.S. kindergarten class of 1998 (Lee & Burkam, 2002). Notice that children from low-income families, on average, do markedly worse than their upper-middle-class counterparts on tests of reading readiness and math. When we compare poverty level Latino and African American children to the wealthiest European Americans, the gap in scores widens to a chasm. The most disadvantaged children enter school academically several years behind their most affluent counterparts.

The reasons for these inequalities become apparent when developmentalists visit young children's homes to rate various aspects of family life. As one national survey showed, children growing up in poverty-level U.S. families had few books. Their parents infrequently read to them. They rarely had home computers. They practically never went to museums (Bradley and others, 2001a).

I must emphasize that low-income parents care as much about their sons' and daughters' education as corporate CEOs. But when you are working long hours to provide the bare necessities, children's basic needs—and safety—take priority over anything else. Here is how one parent at an inner-city school described the situation:

I mean some of us are scraping to put food on the table, clothes on their backs . . ., keeping the kids off of the street corner. That's our job, you know, taking care of business and making sure that they have the opportunity to go to school each day. 'Cause with no clothes, or if they wind up in trouble with the system, then school ain't a possibility for them.

(quoted in Lawson, 2003, pp. 91–92)

This dispiriting scene is common in many public schools attended by low-income children in the United States. If your classroom had broken windows and shades, inadequate heating and air-conditioning, and few books—how well would you be able to learn?

For first-generation immigrant families, language barriers can add to the difficulties. If parents only speak Spanish or Swahili, they cannot help their children with classroom work. The downside of having a United Nations in our educational system is that many young children need to grapple with the challenge of learning a new language at school. In 1998, for instance, 30 percent of Latino kindergarteners had parents who only spoke Spanish at home (Lee & Burkam, 2002).

We would think that when children start a race miles behind, they should be given every chance to catch up. The reality is the reverse. Using the same 1998 Department of Education data, researchers found that—from class size, to the quality of teacher training, to the attractiveness of the physical building—kindergartens serving poor children ranked at the bottom of the educational heap. Here is the dismal—but not unexpected—conclusion that the researchers reached:

The consistency of these findings across aspects of school quality that are themselves very different from one another is both striking and troubling. The least advantaged of America's children, who also begin their formal schooling at a substantial cognitive disadvantage, are systematically mapped into our nation's worst schools.

(Lee & Burkam, 2002, p. 77)

Now let's keep these inequalities in mind as we explore the controversial topic of intelligence tests.

Intelligence and IQ Tests

What does it mean to be intelligent? Ask your classmates the question, and they will probably mention a wide range of qualities from doing well at academics to being able to perform well in the wider world (Sternberg, Grigorenko, & Kidd, 2005). Traditional intelligence tests are designed to measure purely academic skills. Intelligence tests, however, differ from **achievement tests,** the yearly evaluations children take to measure their knowledge in various subjects. What exactly *do* these tests measure? To frame this surprisingly cloudy issue, let's look briefly at how the first IQ test was devised and what scores on that test soon came to signify.

[FAQ: What makes a person intelligent?]

achievement tests Measures that evaluate a child's knowledge in specific school-related areas.

A Bit of History

In 1905 the French government commissioned psychologist Alfred Binet to devise a test to predict which children would have trouble with standard classroom learning. To address this challenge, Binet got a large sample of children of different ages and then measured their performance on different tasks, such as memory or vocabulary. By determining how the average child performed at each given age, he then could classify a given boy or girl as either ahead or behind compared to the "typical child." If a 6-year-old finished the tests an average 8-year-old could master, she was labeled as having a mental age of 8. If that same child only mastered tasks an average 4-year-old might complete, her mental age was defined as 4.

Binet never believed that he was measuring a global entity called intelligence. He simply wanted to determine which children might be eligible for alternative schools. But when his test was transported across the Atlantic in the early twentieth century by eager Americans, the measure took on a life of its own (Bergin & Cizek, 2001; Fancher, 1985; Schlinger, 2003; White, 2000).

At that time, the nation was coping with a flood of immigrants. Many people felt that these new arrivals—often from Eastern Europe—were of "lower quality" (that is, biologically inferior). It would help if scientists had an "objective" way to classify how people differed from each other in innate intellectual gifts (Gould, 1981). So Binet's test was adapted to be given to everyone, of any age, as a kind of X-ray into the basic quality of people's minds (Fancher, 1985; Gould, 1981; Kamin, 1974).

Today, luckily, we have retreated from that early racist use of the IQ test. We use intelligence tests very selectively during childhood to predict school performance, and we are far more careful about generalizing to people's real-world abilities based on their test results. However, the basic issue is still hotly debated: Do tests such as Binet's scale really measure an abstract quality called "intelligence"? Does an IQ test predict anything beyond school-related skills? Let's approach these hot-button issues by examining the intelligence test that children typically take today: the WISC.

Examining the WISC

The **WISC (Wechsler Intelligence Scale for Children),** now in its third revision, was devised by David Wechsler and has supplanted Binet's measure as the standard childhood test. Like Binet's test, the WISC samples a child's performance in a variety of areas. However, as Table 7.2 shows, the WISC is divided into two sections. One involves answering questions (the Verbal Scale), and the other involves manipulating materials (the Performance Scale). This allows testers to give a child a separate IQ score for each part.

WISC (Wechsler Intelligence Scale for Children) The standard intelligence test used in childhood, consisting of a Verbal Scale (questions for the child to answer), a Performance Scale (materials for the child to manipulate), and a variety of subtests.

TABLE 7.2: The WISC-III Subtests and Sample Kinds of Items

Verbal Scale

Subtest	Sample (simulated) item
Information (tests factual knowledge)	Who is George Bush?
Similarities (analogies)	Cat is to kitten as dog is to _____.
Vocabulary (defining words)	What is a table?
Comprehension (social judgment)	What do you do if you are lost in Manhattan?
Arithmetic	Mary has five apples and gives two away. How many does she have left?
Digit span (memory)	Repeat these seven digits forward. . . . backward. . . .

Performance Scale

(involves manipulating, arranging, or identifying materials within a time limit)

Picture completion	What is missing in this picture?
Block design	Arrange these blocks to look like the photograph on the card.
Picture arrangement	Arrange these pictures in the correct sequence to tell a story.
Object assembly	Put these puzzle pieces together.
Coding	Using the key above, put each symbol in the correct space below.

Source: WISC-III, Psychological Corporation (Wechsler, 1991).

Achievement tests are taken in groups. The WISC is administered individually by a trained psychologist, a process that includes several hours of testing and concludes with a written report. If the child scores at the 50th percentile for his age group, his IQ is defined as 100. If that child's IQ is 130, he ranks at roughly the 98th percentile, or in the top 2 percent of children his age. If a child's score is 70, he is at the opposite end of the distribution, performing in the lowest 2 percent of children that age. Put on a graph, this score distribution, as you can see in Figure 7.6, looks like a bell-shaped curve.

When do children take this time-intensive test? The answer, most often, is during elementary school when there is some major question about classroom work. School personnel then use the IQ score as one component of a multifaceted assessment, which includes achievement test scores, teachers' ratings, and parents' input, to determine whether a boy or girl needs special help (Sattler, 2001). If a child's low score (under 70) and other behaviors warrant this designation, she may be classified as **mentally retarded.** If a child's IQ is far higher than would be expected compared to her performance on achievement tests, she is classified as having a **specific learning disability**—an umbrella term for any impairment in language or difficulties related to listening (such as ADHD), thinking, speaking, or processing information in reading, spelling, or math.

mentally retarded The label for significantly impaired intellectual functioning, defined as when a child (or adult) has an IQ of 70 or below accompanied by evidence of deficits in learning abilities.

specific learning disability The label for any impairment in language or any deficit related to listening, thinking, speaking, reading, writing, spelling, or understanding mathematics; diagnosed when a score on an intelligence test is much higher than a child's performance on achievement tests.

FIGURE 7.6: **The bell-shaped curve:** The WISC scores are arranged to align in a normal distribution. Notice from the chart that about 68 percent of the population has scores between 85 and 115 and about 95 percent of the scores are between 70 and 130.

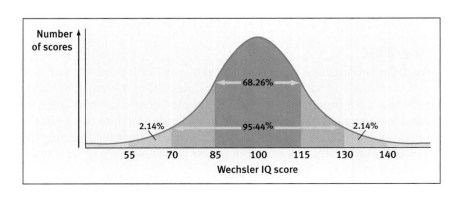

Although children with learning disabilities often score in the average range on IQ tests, they have considerable trouble with schoolwork. Many times they have a debilitating brain-based language impairment called **dyslexia** that undercuts every academic skill. Dyslexia involves a host of reading-related difficulties, such as having trouble fluently recognizing written words or accurately processing sentences. Children with this most common learning disability have extremely poor spelling, too (Bender, 1998; Keogh & MacMillan, 1996).

My son, for instance, has dyslexia, and our experience shows just how valuable testing can be. Because Thomas was falling behind the third grade, my husband and I arranged to have our son tested. Thomas was defined as having a learning disability because his IQ score was above average but his achievement scores were well below the norm for his grade. Although we were aware of our son's reading problems, the testing was vital in easing our anxieties. Thomas—just as we thought—was capable intellectually. Now we just had to get our son through school with his sense of self-efficacy and self-esteem intact!

Often teachers and parents urge testing for a happier reason: They want to confirm their impression that a child is intellectually advanced. If the child's IQ exceeds a certain number, typically 130, in the top 2 percent (see Figure 7.6), she is labeled **gifted** and eligible for special programs. In U.S. public schools, intelligence testing is mandated by law before children can be assigned to a gifted program or remedial class (Canter, 1997; Sattler, 2001).

Table 7.3 offers a fact sheet about dyslexia. The Experiencing the Lifespan on page 222 provides a firsthand view of what it is like to deal with—and triumph over—this condition. Now that we have explored the measure and when it is used, we turn to that vital issue—what the scores really mean.

It's hard to imagine Tom Cruise having "self-esteem issues" today, but things may have been very different as he struggled to cope with dyslexia during his childhood years.

This second grader, taking a subtest of the WISC performance scale, will be tested for at least an hour and a half. Then the examiner will write a report and compare his scores with those of other children his age. If this boy's IQ is at least 130—ranking him at roughly the top 2 percent of his age group—he will be eligible for his school's gifted program.

TABLE 7.3: Some Interesting Facts About Dyslexia (and Specific Learning Disabilities)

- In 2002, 8 percent of U.S elementary school children were classified with a specific learning disability other than ADHD. Dyslexia is by far the most common reason for this catchall diagnosis. In fact, 80 percent of children with a specific learning disability other than ADHD are dyslexic.

- Specific learning disabilities are a mainly male diagnosis. Dyslexia, for instance, affects roughly three times as many boys as girls around the world.

- Researchers have targeted genes on chromosomes 6, 12, and 15 that seem to be involved in dyslexia. While there is strong evidence that dyslexia is biologically based (23 to 65 percent of children with dyslexia have a parent who has the condition), problems with learning to read may have a variety of genetic and environmental causes.

- Late-appearing language (entering the word-combining phase of speech at an older-than-typical age, such as close to age 2½ [see Chapter 3]) and phonemic deficits (the inability to differentiate different sounds [see Chapter 5]) are early predictors of dyslexia.

- New research suggests that children prone to dyslexia may even be identified during their first weeks after birth—by looking at the pattern of their brain waves evoked by different sounds. These newborns have a slightly slower shift from positivity to negativity on "event related potentials" when exposed to noises of different frequencies (Guttorm and others, 2005).

- Although many children with dyslexia eventually learn to read, this condition persists to some extent. Children who had serious trouble mastering reading in school still read more haltingly as adults.

- Children with dyslexia are at higher risk for developing other mental health problems—such as depressive and anxiety disorders. They are at *much* higher risk of being diagnosed with ADHD (Arnold and others, 2005).

dyslexia A brain-based learning disability that is characterized by reading difficulties, lack of fluency, poor word recognition, and problems in spelling.

gifted The label for superior intellectual functioning characterized by an IQ score of 130 or above, showing that a child ranks in the top 2 percent of his age group.

Sources: Kavale & Forness (2003); Sattler (2001); Shaywitz & Shaywitz (2001); Turner & Rack, (2004).

Aimee Holt, a colleague of mine who teaches our school psychology students, is beautiful and intelligent, the kind of golden girl you might imagine would have been a great childhood success. When I sat down to chat with Amy about her struggles with dyslexia and other learning disabilities, I found first impressions can be very misleading:

When I was in first grade, the teachers at school told my parents I was mentally retarded. I didn't notice the sounds that went along with the letters of words. I walked into walls and fell down a lot. My parents refused to consider putting me in a special school and finally got me accepted at a private school, contingent on getting a good deal of help. I spent my elementary school years being tutored for an hour before school, an hour afterwards, and all summer.

Socially, elementary school was a nightmare . . . I have memories of kids laughing at me, calling me stupid. There was a small group of people that I was friendly with, but we were all misfits. One of my closest friends had an inoperable brain tumor. Because of my problems coordinating my vision with my motor skills, I couldn't really participate in normal activities, such as sports or dance. By seventh grade, after years of working every day with my wonderful reading teacher, I was reading at almost grade level.

Then when we moved to Tennessee in my freshman year of high school, I felt like a completely new person had emerged. Nobody knew that I had learning difficulties. We moved to a rural community, so I got to be a top student, because I'd had the same classes in my Dallas private school the year before. In the tenth and eleventh grades, I was making A's and B's. I got a scholarship to college, where I was a straight-A student (with a GPA of 3.9).

My mom is the reason I've done so well. She always believed in me, always felt I could make it; she never gave up. Plus, as I mentioned, I had an exceptional reading teacher who ended up working as a leader in the field. My goal was always to be an elementary school teacher, but, after teaching for years and realizing that a lot of the kids in my classes were not being accurately diagnosed, I decided to go back to graduate school to get my Ph.D.

Today, in addition to teaching, I do private tutoring with children like me. First, I get kids to identify word sounds (phonemes) because children with dyslexia have a problem decoding the specific sounds of words. I'll have the children identify how many sounds they hear in a word . . . "Which sounds rhyme, which don't?" . . . "If I change the word from cat to hat, what sound changes?" Most children naturally pick up on these reading cues. Kids with dyslexia need to have these skills directly taught.

Many children I tutor are in fourth or even sixth grade and have had years of feeling like a total failure. They develop an attitude of "Why try? I'm going to be a failure anyway." I can tell them that I've been there and that they can succeed. So I work on academic self-efficacy—teaching them to put forth effort. Most of these kids are really intelligent, but as they progress through school, their verbal IQ drops because they are not being exposed to written material at their grade level. I try to get them to stay in the regular classroom, with modifications such as books on tape and oral testing, to prevent that false drop in their knowledge base. I was so fortunate—with a wonderful mother, an exceptional reading teacher, getting the help I needed at exactly the right time— that I feel my mission is to give something back.

Decoding the Meaning of the IQ Test

reliability In measurement terminology, a basic criterion of a test's accuracy that scores must be fairly similar when a person takes the test more than once.

The first question we need to grapple with in looking at the meaning of the test relates to a basic measurement criterion called **reliability**. When people take a test thought to measure a basic trait, such as IQ, more than one time, their results should not really vary. Imagine that IQ scores randomly gyrated from gifted to average year by year. Clearly, such a test would be worthless. It would not tell us anything about a stable entity called intelligence.

The good news is that, in general, IQ test performance does typically remain fairly stable. In one impressive study, people's IQ scores remained fairly similar when they first took the test in childhood and then many decades later in old age! (See Deary and others, 2000.) Still, when we look at individual children, the IQ can sometimes change markedly. Interestingly, scores are most likely to change a good deal when children have undergone major life stresses.

This research tells us exactly why Manuel in the chapter-opening vignette was being tested at the wrong time: We should never evaluate a child during a family crisis such as a divorce. But being reliable is only the first requirement. The test must be **valid**. This means it must predict what it is supposed to be measuring. Is the WISC a valid test?

validity In measurement terminology, a basic criterion for a test's accuracy involving whether that measure reflects the real-world quality it is supposed to measure.

If our predictor is academic performance, the answer is yes. A child who gets an IQ score of 130 will most likely perform well in the gifted class. A child's whose

IQ is 80 will probably need remedial help. But now we turn to the really controversial question: whether the test measures genetic learning potential or biological
smarts.

ARE THE TESTS A GOOD MEASURE OF GENETIC GIFTS? When we are evaluating
children living in poverty (or boys and girls growing up in immigrant families who
may not be familiar with our cultural norms), logic tells us that the answer should be
no. The test score cannot offer a good portrait of a child's innate abilities. Look back
at the items on the WISC Verbal Scale (Table 7.2 on p. 220), in particular, and you
will immediately see that if parents stimulate a child's vocabulary, she will be at a clear
advantage. If a family cannot afford to take their children to museums or to buy them
books and learning toys, they will be handicapped on the test.

Our logical impression that the test can't reflect the genetic capacities of disadvantaged children is scientifically correct. For low-income children, the IQ score mainly
reflects environmental forces. For upper-middle-class children, the test score is more
reflective of genetically based abilities and gifts (Turkheimer and others, 2003).

Now imagine that you are an upper-middle-class child. You were raised by attentive parents, regularly read to, and taken to museums. Your IQ score is only 95 or 100.
Is your potential limited for life?

DO IQ SCORES PREDICT REAL-WORLD PERFORMANCE? When, as often happens, a
student comes up after this class lecture and proudly admits that his IQ is 130 or 140,
he is not thinking of school learning. He is assuming that his score measures a basic
"smartness" that carries over to every life activity. In measurement terminology, this
student would agree with the ideas of theorist Charles Spearman. Spearman believed
that a score on an IQ test reflects a general underlying, all-encompassing intelligence
factor called "g."

Psychologists hotly debate the existence of "g" (Schlinger, 2003). Many do believe
that the IQ test *generally* predicts intellectual capacities. They argue that we can use
the IQ score as a summary measure of a person's inherent cognitive potential for any
life task (Gottfredson, 1998, 2005; Herrnstein & Murray, 1994; Jensen, 1992, 1998;
Rushton & Jensen, 2005). Others believe that people have unique intellectual weaknesses and strengths. There is no one-dimensional quality called intelligence (Canter, 1997; Eisner, 2004; Howe, 1988a, b; McGrew and others, 1997; Schlinger, 2003).
These critics argue that it is inappropriate to rank people on a single continuum from
highly intelligent to not very smart (Gould, 1981; Sternberg, 1997; Sternberg and others, 2005).

Tantalizing evidence of the existence of "g" lies in the fact that people differ in
the overall speed with which they process information (Jensen, 1998; Rushton &
Jensen, 2005). You may remember from Chapter 3 that infants who easily grasp the
essence of a stimulus and habituate more quickly later perform at high levels on intelligence tests. Intelligence test scores also correlate with various indicators of life
success, such as occupational status (Rushton & Jensen, 2005). However, the gateway to high-status professions, such as law and medicine, is school performance,
which is what the tests predict (Sternberg, 1997; Sternberg, Grigorenko, & Bundy,
2001; Wagner, 1997).

One problem with believing that IQ tests offer an X-ray into basic intellectual capacities is that people may carry around their test-score ranking as an inner wound
(Williams, 1998). A psychologist supervisor once confessed to me that he was really
not that intelligent because his IQ was only 105. He devalued the criterion the scores
were supposed to predict—his many years of real-life success—by accepting what, in
his case, was an invalid score!

A high test score can produce its own real-world problems. Suppose the student
who told me his IQ was 140 decided he was so intelligent, he didn't have to open a
book in my class. He might be in for a nasty surprise both in college and in life when
he found out that what *really* matters is your ability to work.

"g" Charles Spearman's term
for a general intelligence
factor that he claimed
underlies all cognitive
activities.

Even the firmest advocate of "g" would admit that people have different talents. Some of us are marvelous mechanically and miserable at math, wonderful at writing but impossible at reading maps. If a child such as Manuel in our chapter-opening vignette is so gifted mechanically, shouldn't we nurture that talent even though he does not qualify as exceptional in every area of life? (See Canter, 1997; Kaufman, 2000; McGrew and others, 1997; Sternberg & Grigorenko, 2000.)

Toward a Broader View of Intelligence

But if intelligence involves different abilities, such as mechanical talents, perhaps we should go beyond the IQ test to sample those skills in a broader way. Psychologists Robert Sternberg and Howard Gardner have devoted distinguished careers to providing this broader view of what it means to be smart.

STERNBERG'S SUCCESSFUL INTELLIGENCE Robert Sternberg (1984, 1996, 1997) is a man on a mission. In hundreds of publications, this contemporary psychologist has transformed the way we think about intelligence. Sternberg's passion comes from the heart. He began his school career with a problem:

> *As an elementary school student, I failed miserably on the IQ tests. . . . Just the sight of the school psychologist coming into the classroom to give a group IQ test sent me into a wild panic attack. . . . You don't need to be a genius to figure out what happens next. My teachers in the elementary school grades certainly didn't expect much from me. . . . So I gave them what they expected. . . . Were the teachers disappointed? Not on your life. They were happy that I was giving them what they expected.*
>
> (1997, pp. 17–18)

Sternberg believes that traditional intelligence tests can do damage in the school environment. As you might imagine, the relationship between IQ scores and schooling is somewhat bidirectional. Children who attend inferior schools, or who miss months of classroom work due to illness, perform more poorly on intelligence tests (Brody, 1997; Perkins & Grotzer, 1997; Sternberg, 1997). Worse yet, Sternberg argues, when school personnel decide to assign children to lower-track, less demanding classes on the basis of their low test scores, their IQs gradually erode, year by year.

Most important, Sternberg (1984) believes that conventional intelligence tests are too limited. Although they do measure one type of intelligence, they do not cover the total terrain.

IQ tests, according to Sternberg, measure only **analytic intelligence.** They test how well people can solve academic-type problems having a single solution. They do not measure **creative intelligence,** the ability to "think outside the box," to come up with innovations, or to formulate problems in new ways. Nor do they measure a third type of intelligence called **practical intelligence,** common sense, or "street smarts."

Brazilian street children who make their living selling candy or flowers and who don't have any real formal education show impressive levels of practical intelligence.

analytic intelligence In Robert Sternberg's framework on successful intelligence, the facet of intelligence involving performing well on academic-type problems.

creative intelligence In Robert Sternberg's framework on successful intelligence, the facet of intelligence involved in producing novel ideas or innovative work.

practical intelligence In Robert Sternberg's framework on successful intelligence, the facet of intelligence involved in knowing how to act competently in real-world situations.

Being an inspired writer *(creative intelligence)* or knowing how to put up a tent and camp alone in the woods *(practical intelligence)* doesn't necessarily go along with being a "genius" at school. That's why Robert Sternberg believes that the standard IQ test (which measures *analytic intelligence*) does not tap into many of the skills we need to be successful in life.

They understand how to handle money in the real world. However, they do poorly on standard mathematics tests and measures of traditional IQ (Sternberg, 1984, 1997; Wagner & Sternberg, 1984). Others, such as Winston Churchill, can be terrible scholars who flower after they leave their academic careers. Then there are the people who excel at IQ test taking and traditional schooling but fail abysmally once they enter the real world. Sternberg argues that to be **successfully intelligent** in life requires a balance of all three skills.

GARDNER'S MULTIPLE INTELLIGENCES Howard Gardner (1998) did not have Sternberg's problem with intelligence tests:

> As a child I was a good student and a good test taker . . . but . . . music in particular and the arts were important parts of my life. Therefore when I asked myself what optimal human development is, I became more convinced that [we] had to . . . broaden the definition of intelligence to include these activities, too.
>
> (1998, p. 3)

Gardner, unlike Sternberg, is not passionately opposed to standard intelligence tests. Still, he believes that using the single IQ score is far less informative than trying to measure children's unique talents and gifts. (Gardner's motto is: "Ask not *how intelligent* you are, but *how are* you intelligent.") According to Gardner's **multiple intelligences theory** (2004), human abilities come in eight, and possibly nine, distinctive forms.

In addition to the verbal and mathematical skills measured by traditional psychometric tests, people may be gifted in interpersonal intelligence, or skillful at understanding other people. Their talents may lie in intrapersonal intelligence, the skill of understanding oneself, or in spatial intelligence, the ability to grasp where objects are arranged in space. (You might rely on a friend who is gifted in spatial intelligence to intuitively understand just how to arrange the furniture in your house or remember where any item is by simply scanning a room.) Some people have high levels of musical intelligence, kinesthetic intelligence (the ability to use the body well), or naturalist intelligence (the gift for dealing with animals or plants and trees). There may even be a spiritual intelligence, too.

EVALUATING THE THEORIES These different perspectives on intelligence are very exciting. Some of you may be thinking, "I believe that I'm gifted in practical or musical intelligence. I always knew there was more to intelligence than being successful at school!" But let's use our practical intelligence to offer some criticisms of these approaches. What is Gardner's rationale for selecting these particular eight (or nine) intelligences, rather than others? Parents and teachers may marvel at a 6-year-old's creative or kinesthetic intelligence, but unfortunately it is analytic intelligence that will get this child into the gifted program at school, not his artistic productions or how well his body moves (Eisner, 2004).

We can also criticize Sternberg's ideas. Is there really such a thing as creative or practical intelligence apart from a particular field? For instance, adopting the idea that there is a single "creative" intelligence might lead to the conclusion that Michelangelo would also be a talented musician or that Mozart could beautifully paint the Sistine Chapel.

The bottom line is that neither Gardner nor Sternberg has developed good replacements for our current all-purpose IQ test. But this does not matter. Their mission is larger than simply changing the way we test children. They want to transform the way school systems teach.

INTERVENTIONS: Lessons for Schools

Gardner's theory has been enthusiastically embraced by some innovative schools determined to build in equal time during the school day for *each* form of intelligence, rather than simply focusing on traditional academic skills (Hoerr, 2004; Kornhaber & Gardner, 2006; Kornhaber, Fierros, & Veenema, 2004; Kornhaber & Krechevsky,

successful intelligence In Robert Sternberg's framework, the optimal form of cognition, involving having a good balance of analytic, creative, and practical intelligence.

multiple intelligences In Howard Gardner's perspective on intelligence, the principle that there are eight separate kinds of intelligence—verbal, mathematical, interpersonal, intrapersonal, spatial, musical, kinesthetic, naturalist—plus a possible ninth form, called spiritual intelligence.

Being a terrific guitarist *(musical intelligence)* or a world-class gymnast *(kinesthetic intelligence)* doesn't necessarily mean that you will also shine in reading or math. That's why Howard Gardner believes that schools need to broaden their focus to teach to the *different* kinds of intelligences that we all possess.

1995). However, to fully implement his ideas requires revolutionizing the way we structure education. Therefore, the most widespread use of multiple intelligences theory has been in helping "nontraditional learners" succeed in traditional, analytic-intelligence schools (Schirduan & Case, 2004). Here is how Mark, a dyslexic teenager who had been failing in class, describes how he uses his spatial intelligence to cope with the maze of facts in history:

> I'll picture things; for example, if we are studying the French revolution . . . Louis the 16th . . ., I'll have a picture of him in my mind [and I'll visualize] the castle and peasants to help me learn.
>
> (quoted in Schirduan & Case, 2004, p. 93)

Sternberg's research team has conducted an experiment demonstrating that teaching with every type of intelligence in mind produces better classroom performance. The researchers divided third-grade classes at a public school into two groups. One was taught social studies by standard methods. The other was given instruction carefully balanced among the three types of intelligence. The children taught according to Sternberg's theory performed at a higher level even on standard multiple-choice tests (Sternberg, Torff, & Grigorenko, 1998). (In Table 7.4, I have used my creative intelligence to illustrate how a teacher might draw on Sternberg's different intelligences to test you on the material you are learning right now.)

So the real potential of these innovative ideas about intelligence is to enrich the way standard classrooms operate. How exactly do classrooms operate?

TABLE 7.4: Test Items a Professor Might Use to Evaluate Students on This Section Based on Using Sternberg's Three Components of Intelligence

Questions Measuring Analytic Intelligence

- Compare and contrast Gardner's and Sternberg's theories of intelligence.
- List Gardner's eight intelligences and offer a criticism of his theory. Then list Sternberg's three intelligences and offer a critique of his theory.

Questions Measuring Creative Intelligence

- Devise some items to measure one of Gardner's intelligences. Then do the same for one of Sternberg's intelligences.
- Construct a test of practical intelligence at being an undergraduate at your college. First make up a set of questionnaire items. Then explain how you would validate your test of "practical intelligence at X University"—that is, what real-world criteria might you use to show that performance on your test predicts practical intelligence at your school?
- List other possible intelligences that may be missing from Gardner's theory.
- Make up your own theory of intelligence and make the case for your ideas.

Questions Measuring Practical Intelligence

- Identify your strongest intelligences using Gardner's and Sternberg's theories and explain how you might apply them to studying for tests in this course.

Based on your unique intellectual strengths (analytic, creative, or practical), what questions would you most prefer an instructor to give in class?

Classroom Learning

The diversity of intelligences, cultures, and educational experiences at home is matched by the incredible diversity of American schools. There are small rural schools and large urban schools, public schools and private schools, highly traditional schools where students wear uniforms and schools that teach to Gardner's intelligences. There are single-sex schools, religious schools, magnet schools that cater to gifted students, and alternative schools for children with behavior problems or learning disabilities.

Can students thrive in every kind of school? The answer is yes, *provided* schools have an intense commitment to student learning and teachers can excite students to learn. The rest of this chapter focuses on these challenges.

Examining Successful Schools

What qualities make a school successful? We can get insights from surveying elementary schools that are beating the odds. These schools, while located in low-income areas and serving large numbers of children whose parents do not speak English, have students who are thriving.

In the Vista School, located on a Native American reservation in Washington State, virtually all the children are eligible for a free lunch. More than half come from families where English is not the primary language spoken at home. However, Vista consistently boasts dramatic improvements on statewide reading and math tests (Borko and others, 2003). According to Ms. Thompson, the principal, "Our job is not to make excuses for students, but just to give them every possible opportunity. At Vista, teachers refuse to dumb down the curriculum. We offer tons of high-level conceptual work" (quoted in Borko and others, 2003, p. 177).

At Beacon Elementary School, also in Washington State, two out of every three students exceed state-mandated writing standards despite coming from impoverished backgrounds. Here Susie Murphy, the principal, comments: "You can look around at other schools . . . and people would say, these kids are poor. You just need to love them. Or you can come to a school like this where the philosophy is that the best way to love them is to give them an education so they can make choices in their life" (quoted in Borko and others, 2003, p. 186). Beacon teachers, she continues, "are here in this building by choice. They are committed to proving that kids who live in poverty can learn every bit as well as other kids" (p. 192). At Beacon, teachers are also committed to providing high-level challenging work, such as intensive experience in writing in a variety of genres. The school regularly builds in opportunities for the teachers to share ideas: "We have mini-workshops in geometry, or problem solving. Our whole staff talks about the general focus and where math is going" (p. 194).

Lest you think that a passion for excellence and mutual collaboration is only important in the United States, now let's travel to Japan, a country renowned for its exceptional student achievement scores on international tests in the sciences and math. An integral facet of the Japanese educational system is the "lesson plan." Teachers in each school get together at the beginning of the year to decide on an objective, such as improving how to teach fractions. Then they meet regularly to problem-solve, practice new approaches in their classrooms, and discuss what did or didn't work. At the end of the year, they publish their insights in manuals that are often eagerly devoured countrywide (Fernandez & Yoshida, 2004; Stigler & Hiebert, 1999).

A school's physical appearance can also make a real difference in whether children "beat the odds." This boy attends a model public school, designed and built by a well-known architect and located in an impoverished section of New York City. Who do you think would be more likely to love reading: this child or someone who attended the rundown school in the photograph on page 218?

Tony Cenicola / The New York Times / Redux

The teacher in this Japanese science class will regularly consult with his colleagues about the best way to teach his students how to build robots. Outstanding teaching is a national priority in Japan, and—most important—exceptional teaching is viewed as a *teachable* skill.

[FAQ: What is involved in learning?]

intrinsic motivation The drive to act based on the pleasure of taking that action in itself, not for an external reinforcer or reward.

extrinsic motivation The drive to take an action because that activity offers external reinforcers such as praise, money, or a good grade.

The bottom line is that successful schools set high standards and believe that every child can succeed. Teachers offer an excess of nurture—both to their students and to one another. In terms of Baumrind's parenting-styles framework, these schools would be classified as authoritative in their approach.

Now that we have the general outlines for what is effective, it's time to tackle the challenge *every* teacher faces: getting students to be eager to learn.

Producing Eager Learners

But to go to school on a summer morn,
O! it drives all joy away;
Under a cruel eye outworn,
The little ones spend the day
In sighing and dismay.

—William Blake, "The Schoolboy" (1794)

Jean Piaget believed that the hunger to learn is more important than food or drink. Why then do children over the centuries lament, "I hate school"? The reason is that learning loses its joy when it becomes a requirement instead of an activity we choose to engage in for ourselves.

THE PROBLEM: AN EROSION OF INTRINSIC MOTIVATION. Developmentalists divide motivation into two distinct categories. **Intrinsic motivation** refers to self-generated activities—actions we take purely from our inner desires. When Piaget described our hunger to learn, he was referring to intrinsic motivations. **Extrinsic motivation** refers to activities that we undertake in order to get external reinforcers, such as praise or pay, or a good grade.

Unfortunately, the learning activity you are currently engaged in falls into the extrinsic category. You know you will be tested on what you are reading. Worse yet, if you decided to pick up this book for an intrinsic reason—because you wanted to learn about human development—the very fact that you might be graded would make your basic interest fall off.

Numerous studies show that when adults give external reinforcers for activities that are intrinsically motivating, children are less likely to want to perform those activities for themselves (Lepper and others, 1997; Morgan, 1984; Stipek, 1996, 1997). In one classic example, researchers selected preschoolers who were intrinsically interested in art. When they gave a "good player" award (an outside reinforcer) for the art projects, the children later showed a dramatic decline in their interest in doing art for fun (Lepper, Greene, & Nisbett, 1973). This research makes sense of the question you may have wondered about: "Why, after taking that literature class, am I so much less interested in reading on my own?"

Young children enter kindergarten brimming with intrinsic motivation. When does this love affair with school turn sour? Think back to your childhood, and you will realize that the enchantment typically ends during the early years of elementary school, when teachers begin to provide those external reinforcers—grades (Stipek, 1997). To make matters worse, during first or second grade classroom learning becomes more abstract and removed from life. Boring, rote activities, like filling in worksheets and memorizing multiplication tables, have replaced the creative hands-on projects of kindergarten. Ironically, then, school has been transformed into the very setting where Piaget's little-scientist activities are *least* likely to occur.

Then, as children fully enter Piaget's stage of concrete operations—around age 8 or 9—they begin really comparing their performance to that of their peers. This competitive orientation erodes intrinsic motivation (Ames, 1986; Ames & Archer, 1988; Dweck, 1986; Self-Brown & Mathews, 2003; Stipek, 1997.) The focus shifts from "I want to improve for myself" to "I want to do better than my friends."

In sum, several forces explain why children naturally come to dislike school: School involves extrinsic reinforcers (grades). School learning, because it often involves rote

Compare the activities of the kindergarten class of "little scientists" at left with those of the second graders in the photograph at right and you will immediately understand why by about age 8 many children begin to say, "I hate school."

memorization, is not intrinsically interesting. In school, children are not free to set their own internal learning goals. Their performance is judged by a fixed outside standard: how they measure up to the rest of the class.

It is no wonder, therefore, that developmentalists find an alarming decline in intrinsic motivation as children travel through school (Lepper, Corpus, & Iyengar, 2005). Susan Harter (1981) asked children to choose between the following two statements: "Some kids work really hard to get good grades" (referring to extrinsic motivation) or "Some kids work really hard because they like to learn new things" (measuring intrinsic motives). When she gave her measure to hundreds of California public school children, intrinsic motivation scores fell off from third to ninth grade.

Still, external reinforcers can be vitally important. They are sometimes the hook that gets us intrinsically involved. Have you ever reluctantly read a book for a class assignment and found yourself captivated by the subject matter? Perhaps you enrolled in this course because it was a requirement for graduation, but are becoming so interested in the material that you want to make some aspect of developmental science your future career. Given that extrinsically motivating activities are basic to school and life, how can we make them work best?

THE SOLUTION: MAKING EXTRINSIC LEARNING PART OF US. To answer this question, Edward Deci and Richard Ryan (1985, 2000) make the point that extrinsic learning tasks vary on a continuum. We engage in some types of extrinsic learning totally unwillingly: "I have to take that terrible anatomy course because it is a requirement for graduation." We enthusiastically embrace other extrinsic tasks, which may not be inherently interesting, because we identify with their larger goal: "I want to memorize every bone of the body, because that information is vital to my plan to become a nurse." In the first situation, the learning activity seems completely irrelevant. In the second, the task has become intrinsic because it is connected to our inner self. Therefore the key to transforming school learning from a chore into a pleasure is to make extrinsic learning relate to children's internal goals and desires.

The most boring tasks take on an intrinsic aura when they speak directly to children's passions. Imagine, for instance, how a first grader's motivation to sound out words might change if a teacher, knowing that a particular student was captivated by dinosaurs, gave that child the job of sounding out dinosaur names. Deci and Ryan (2000) believe that learning becomes intrinsic when it satisfies our basic need for relatedness (attachment). Think back, for instance, to the discussion of schools that beat the odds. Now imagine how motivated those children were to learn to read and write when they understood that their success would make their beloved school proud. Finally, extrinsic tasks take on an intrinsic feeling when they foster our need for autonomy, or offer us choices of *how* to do our work (Ryan and others, 2006).

Studies around the globe suggest that when teachers and parents take away children's autonomy—by controlling, criticizing, or micromanaging learning tasks—their actions erode self-efficacy and intrinsic motivation (Chirkov & Ryan, 2001; Grolnick

[FAQ: How can I conduct my class to get my students to love learning?]

Masterfile

Using computers in the classroom can draw on children's basic interest in video games to make academics intrinsically more interesting. But in order to make this learning *truly* intrinsic, this teacher cannot micromanage or hover over her students, or be overly critical. These boys need to feel that they can control their learning and master the concepts at their own pace.

and others, 2002; Zuckerman and others, 1978; Swann & Pittman, 1977; Wong, Wiest, & Cusick, 2002). We can see this principle in our own lives. By continually denigrating our work, or hovering over every move, a controlling supervisor has the uncanny ability to turn us off to the most intrinsically interesting job.

Our basic need for autonomy offers clues as to why high-level conceptual learning tasks might be effective with *every child*. One researcher asked third-grade teachers to abandon their typical strategy of teaching writing skills by having children fill in sentences or copy words. He urged them to do activities such as writing creative essays and not to worry about what learning objectives they did or did not cover in class. This change produced a dramatic shift from extrinsic motivations (children saying "I'm doing this for a good grade") to intrinsic motivations (students saying "I really love this stuff"). Moreover, to the teachers' surprise, their classes performed just as well on the standard end-of-year achievement test as if they had specifically taught to the test.

Even more exciting, the low-ability students did not find the higher-level tasks overwhelming. Their scores on the end-of-year tests rose the *most*. So giving high-level conceptual work may be the most intelligent strategy for students across the board (Miller, 2003)!

Table 7.5 summarizes these three messages for teachers: Focus on relevance, enhance relatedness, and provide autonomy. The table also pulls together other teaching tips based on our discussion of Gardner's and Sternberg's perspectives on intelligence and our look at what makes schools successful. Now let's conclude our discussion by paying a visit to a class that embodies all of these teaching lessons.

TABLE 7.5: Lessons for Teachers: A Recap of This Chapter's Insights

1. **Foster relevance.** For instance, in teaching reading, tailor the books you are assigning so that they fit children's passions. And entice students to learn to read in other ways, such as getting first and second graders energized by telling them that now they will now be able to break a code that the world uses just like a detective!

2. **Foster relatedness.** Develop a secure, loving attachment with every student. Continually tell each child how proud you are when that person tries hard or succeeds.

3. **Foster autonomy.** As much as possible, give your students freedom to plan their own work. Don't give time limits, such as "It's 9:30 and this has to be done by 10:00." Don't hover, take over tasks, or make negative comments. Stand by to provide informational comments and careful scaffolding (see Chapter 5) when students ask. Build in assignments that allow high-level thinking, such as using essays in preference to rote work such as copying sentences or filling out worksheets.

Teaching Tips Based on Gardner's and Sternberg's Theories

1. Offer balanced assignments that capitalize on students' different kinds of intelligence—creative work such as essays; practical-intelligence activities such as calculating numbers to make change at a store; single-answer analytic tasks (using Sternberg's framework); and classroom time devoted to music, dance, the arts, and caring for plants (capitalizing on Gardner's ideas).

2. Explicitly teach students to use their different intelligences in mastering classroom work.

Additional Teaching Tips

1. Don't rely on IQ test scores, especially in assessing the abilities of low-income and ethnic-minority students.

2. Avoid overpraising children for being "brilliant." Compliment them for hard work.

3. Go beyond academics to teach children interpersonal skills.

4. Strive for excellence. Expect all students to succeed.

5. Foster collaborative working relationships with your colleagues.

6. Minimize grade-oriented comparisons (such as who got As, Bs, Cs, etc.). Emphasize the importance of *personal improvement* to students. Experiment with giving grades for individual progress.

TEACHING AT ITS FINEST

When you enter Cindy Jones's fourth-grade classroom in Murfreesboro, Tennessee, you immediately realize that this teacher is special. You see a corner cluttered with evidence of enduring attachments—letters and gifts from former students now living around the world, and provocative sayings that dot the walls: "Teachers are united mind workers." "Fair means everyone gets what they need. Not everyone gets the same." Your eye is captured by colorful posters of interesting women and men from every culture who made a difference in history. You see beautiful birds, creative projects the children have completed, and canned goods neatly stacked to be delivered to families in need. Offering caring, making learning intrinsically motivating, and teaching to students' different intelligences are clearly what this class is all about.

To help foster Gardner's interpersonal and intrapersonal intelligences, Cindy has divided the class into teams: the Red Hot Patriots, the Shooting Stars, and the Lightning Bolts. In making up the teams, Cindy strives for a balance. She puts students with learning problems together with children who are reading at the twelfth-grade level; she puts children from different cultures, and outgoing and shy students, on each team. Children get points for tackling tasks that are personally hard, for taking responsibility, and for doing something positive for another child. Cindy tells me:

> Don't let them know, but I arrange the points so that every team wins each third week. I also tone down the competition by giving points for rooting for and helping the other teams. When children say they want to switch to be with a friend, I never say yes. Life involves relating to all kinds of people. That's an important lesson I want to instill. When conflicts come up, they take the responsibility to have a group pow-wow to work things out.

The teams are the subtext that keeps the year humming along. But each day unfolds according to a specific plan:

8:30–9:30 (CURRENT EVENTS) The morning begins with a high-intensity curtain-raiser that combines relevance and autonomy: Cindy has the children bring in some interesting fact they learned from reading the newspaper or watching the news. She tells me her goal here is "to seize the teachable moment," or to relate this material to the academic content in class. For instance, when a girl reports that she heard that a woman just died at age 107, Cindy says, "Let's calculate her birth date. How do you find out in what year she was born? What kinds of events were happening when she was a little girl? Imagine the way the world will have changed when you get that old."

9:30–10:30 (CENTERS) During this hour the students circulate in small groups among areas designated for reading, studying, computer activities, and using worksheets to practice for the upcoming statewide exams. Now, I wonder, how will Cindy handle this completely extrinsic task? The answer, I discover, is to connect this activity to children's feelings of autonomy and relatedness: "Slow and steady." "Fill everything in." "You can do it." "Get mad at the test-makers. You need an attitude for these terrible tests." "Josh, I'm going to put a tattoo on your hand so when you invite me to your wedding, it will say 'Josh, slow up.'" For a girl with serious reading problems: "Brittany, would you be the class role model for a child in kindergarten this year?"

10:30–11:30 (GRAMMAR) Now comes a hilarious exercise in understanding the purpose of punctuation, showing how the most rote learning can be fun: "I bought PAPER . . . BAGS . . . FISH . . . GLUE . . . paper bags . . . fish . . . glue . . . Suppose I bought two things? . . . three things? . . . Or, suppose I decided to buy fish glue?" "Who got that one right, and who had trouble?" "David, I'm so glad you are explaining that to Jason, just like he gave you help on spelling last week."

Then there is some downtime before lunch listening to classical music, followed by an afternoon seminar discussing how the children feel about the piece: "Was the composer successful in conveying his ideas?" The children learn to disagree without arguing. The shy children are encouraged to give their thoughts. The day ends with the test on a social studies chapter, during which Cindy and I *leave the room.* Cindy explains, "I make it clear to the children that I trust them . . . but they also work to earn my trust."

Because this class—like any other—has its share of students who are hard to manage, at the end of the day Cindy has a few children fill out a sheet listing goals for improvement to take home. The difference is that in Cindy's class the children assume responsibility for monitoring their *own* behavior and reporting honestly on the day: Cindy asks questions like "Think carefully: Do you give yourself a smiley-face sticker for focusing today or not talking back?" Then, in the evening, she calls parents to brainstorm about solutions to problems and about the child's progress: "I try to call or e-mail when there is good news to report, or just to say hi, not just when something goes wrong." In fact, the intimate dance of attachment between parents and this teacher makes this class stand out. There is a seamless web of socialization between what happens at school and what goes on at home.

Perhaps the most defining moment of my day spent observing this captivating class occurred when Cindy reminded these fourth graders that there would be a holiday the next Monday and the students all groaned and said, "Oh no!" Yes, outstanding teachers can make school such an exciting experience that children hate vacation time!

Final Thoughts

Throughout this chapter's discussion, you may have noticed a few fundamental themes. Outstanding teachers like Cindy, as well as outstanding parents, have clear priorities. They provide structure or high standards for their children. They understand each child's gifts and weaknesses. They flexibly tailor their behavior to the needs of a given child.

I also hope that this chapter has encouraged you to think more deeply about the many forces involved in development, what it means to be intelligent, and what schools can do to make learning a positive experience for every child. And I hope you have been sensitized to the crucial role that the cultural and social context plays in every aspect of development, too. Other cultural groups have a good deal to teach us about the child-rearing values our society holds dear. Children who grow up in poverty have trouble performing well on intelligence tests or in school. We need to provide the kind of environment that allows parents to effectively parent and school systems to teach in a way that permits *every* child to succeed. ▮

⊗ TYING IT ALL TOGETHER

1. Devin, from an upper-middle-class family, and Adam, from a low-income family, will be starting kindergarten this fall. With regard to academic performance now and in the future, which of the following statements is most likely to be accurate?

    a. Devin and Adam will perform equally well on school readiness tests, but Adam will fall behind because he is likely to go to a poor-quality kindergarten.
    b. Devin will outperform Adam on school readiness tests, and the gap will probably widen because Adam will go to a poorer-quality kindergarten.

2. Malik hasn't been doing well in school, and his achievement test scores have consistently been well below average for his grade. On the WISC, Malik gets an IQ score of 115. What is your conclusion?

    a. Malik is gifted but performing below his potential.
    b. Malik has a learning disability.

    c. Malik may be mildly mentally retarded.

    d. Malik is goofing off at school and needs to be disciplined.

3. You are telling a friend about the deficiencies of relying on a child's IQ score. Pick out the *two* arguments you might make.

    a. The tests are not reliable; children's scores *typically* change a lot during the elementary school years.

    b. The tests are not valid predictors of school performance.

    c. As people have different abilities, a single IQ score may not tell us very much about a child's unique gifts.

    d. As poor children are at a disadvantage in taking the test, you should not use the test as an index of "genetic school-related talents" for low-income children.

4. Josh doesn't do well in reading or math, but he excels in music and dance, and he really gets along with all kinds of children. In terms of Sternberg's theory of successful intelligence, Josh is not good in _____, but he is skilled in _____ and _____. In terms of Gardner's theory of _____ _____, Josh is strong in which intelligences?

5. A friend of yours who is the principal of a school in a low-income district of your city asks you how her school can beat the odds. You could give all of the following pieces of advice *except*:

    a. Have the teachers regularly meet to work together and share ideas.

    b. Be sure the teachers make the material very simple so that all students experience success.

    c. Make sure that all the teachers share a commitment to having every child learn.

    d. Encourage the teachers to give the children lots of creative, conceptually interesting work.

6. (a) Define intrinsic and extrinsic motivation. (b) Give an example of a task in your life right now that is driven by each kind of motivation. (c) From reading the chapter, can you come up with some ways to make the extrinsic tasks you do feel more intrinsic?

Answers to the Tying It All Together questions can be found in the answers section of the book.

▌ SUMMARY

Home

The composition of two-parent families varies dramatically, from the never-divorced two-parent family to different types of blended families. Most single-parent families are headed by women, and boys and girls growing up in these families are at risk of being poor. Children however, can thrive in any kind of family, depending on the care parents provide.

According to Diana Baumrind's **parenting styles** framework, based on the dimensions of providing rules and nurturing, child-rearing can be classified as **authoritative, authoritarian, permissive, and rejecting-neglecting.** Although many studies show that authoritative parents who provide clear rules and are also highly child-centered tend to raise the most well-adjusted, competent children, there are questions about this framework. Mothers and fathers often have different parenting styles. Good parents do more than just provide discipline. Parenting reflects cultural agendas. Difficult environments demand a stricter, more authoritarian approach to childrearing.

Resilient children, those who do well in spite of difficult early experiences, tend to have a good temperament, other talents, and, typically, one close, secure attachment. Researchers find there may be a specific gene that promotes resilience, insulating some people from falling apart in the face of overwhelming life stress.

Taking the behavioral-genetic position that children's biologically based temperaments drive parenting and our genetic talents shape our adult fate, developmentalist Sandra Scarr has suggested all parents need to do is provide an "acceptable upbringing." Judith Harris also disputes the importance of parenting, arguing that peer groups are the main socializing force in children's lives. While many forces drive development, many developmentalists disagree with these extreme positions, pointing out that the quality of childrearing does matter and that children who are at risk—either environmentally or biologically—require the best possible parenting to succeed. Parents need to be flexible, tailoring their childrearing to their environment and to their children's needs. They should also relax and enjoy these fleeting years.

Corporal punishment, particularly mild spanking, is widespread in the United States, particularly during the preschool years. Experts differ as to whether spanking is detrimental, but no developmentalist believes that it is appropriate to hit a baby or subscribes to the idea that children need to be severely physically punished in order grow up to be competent adults. Severe corporal punishment qualifies as child abuse.

The behaviors that constitute the four forms of **child maltreatment**—physical abuse, neglect, emotional abuse, and sexual abuse—can *sometimes* be hard to classify. The true incidence of abuse can be unclear. However, we do know that parents' personality problems, intense environmental stress, and lack of attachment to a given child are the main risk factors that lead to children being abused. Abused children often have serious emotional problems and are at risk for antisocial acts later in life, although many victims of abuse do construct successful adult lives. There may be a genetic marker that predicts whether abused boys respond to maltreatment by acting in antisocial ways as adults. If possible, when children are being maltreated, it is desirable not to break up the family but to give parents the help they need to parent more effectively.

Children of divorce are at risk for a host of negative life outcomes. However, most boys and girls survive this common childhood change without serious emotional scars. The key to making divorce less traumatic lies in enhancing the quality of the custodial parenting and in keeping the parents from fighting over the children. Living in a chronically conflict-ridden home or with an antisocial father is often worse for children than having their parents divorce.

School

Many children from low-income families enter kindergarten well behind their affluent counterparts in terms of basic academic skills. These inequalities at the starting gate are magnified by the fact that poor children are likely to attend the poorest-quality kindergartens.

Achievement tests measure a child's body of knowledge. Although they also test cognitive abilities, IQ tests measure something more basic—but there is controversy over what that basic quality is. The original intelligence test, devised at the turn of the twentieth century, was intended to predict which children would be able to master schoolwork. In the United States, however, the test was soon adapted to be used for everyone as an index of basic intellectual gifts. Today, IQ tests are used only when there are questions about children's school performance, but controversy surrounding the true meaning of IQ scores remains intense.

The **Wechsler Intelligence Scale for Children (WISC),** with its verbal and performance scales, is the childhood intelligence test in widest use today. This time-intensive test, involving a variety of subtests, is given individually to a child. If the child's IQ score is below 70—and if other indicators warrant this designation—that boy or girl may be labeled **mentally retarded.** If the child's score is much higher than his performance on achievement tests, he is classified as having a **specific learning disability,** such as **dyslexia.** If a child's IQ score is at or above 130, she is considered **gifted** and is eligible to be placed in an accelerated class.

IQ scores satisfy the measurement criterion called **reliability,** meaning that people tend to get roughly the same score if the test is taken more than once. However, stressful life experiences can artificially lower a child's score. The test must also be **valid,** meaning that it predicts what it was devised to measure: performance in school. While some psychologists claim that performance on the test reflects a single, overall quality called **"g"** that relates to cognitive performance in every area of life, others feel that intelligence involves multiple independent abilities. These critics argue that it is inappropriate to rank people as intelligent or not based on their IQ scores. For poor children in particular, the IQ score cannot be viewed as an index of genetic gifts.

Robert Sternberg and Howard Gardner argue that we need to expand our measures of intelligence beyond traditional tests. Sternberg believes that there are three types of intelligence: **analytic intelligence** (academic abilities), **creative intelligence,** and **practical intelligence** (real-world abilities, or "street smarts"). **Successful intelligence** requires having a balance among all three of these skills. Gardner, in his **multiple intelligences theory,** describes eight (or possibly nine) distinct types of intelligences. Although neither of these psychologists has developed alternatives to conventional IQ tests, their ideas have generated a good deal of excitement and have been used to transform how some schools teach.

Schools that serve poor but high-achieving children share a mission to have every child succeed. They assume that poor children can do well at high-level conceptual work. Teachers support and mentor one another. They provide a nurturing environment for everyone.

Why do many children come to dislike school? The reason is that classroom learning is based on **extrinsic motivation** (external reinforcers such as grades), which impairs **intrinsic motivation** (the desire to learn for the sake of learning). School learning is inherently less interesting, because it often involves rote learning removed from life. Being evaluated in comparison to the class also erodes a child's interest in learning for its own sake. Studies show a disturbing decline in intrinsic motivation as children progress through elementary school.

Teachers (and parents) can make extrinsic learning tasks more intrinsic. The keys are to make material relevant to children's interests, to foster relatedness (or a close attachment), and to provide autonomy, or give students choices about how to do their work. Because it offers more autonomy, conceptual work is preferable to rote learning tasks for students at all levels of ability. With exceptional teaching, students can love school!

▌ KEY TERMS

▌ RECOMMENDED RESOURCES

HOME

Harris, J. (1998). *The nurture assumption*. New York: Free Press.

In this lively, well-written critique of the belief that parenting is all-important, Judith Harris puts forth her controversial argument that peer groups, not parents, are our main socializers.

Kotlowitz, A. (1992). *There are no children here*. New York: Anchor Books.

This book offers a riveting firsthand account of parenting under the worst environmental conditions. Kotlowitz, a journalist, describes the year he spent observing a family in the Henry Horner housing projects in Chicago.

Manchester, W. (1983). *The last lion: Winston Spencer Churchill, visions of glory, 1874–1932*. New York: Little, Brown.

This biography of Churchill's early years offers a glimpse into what parenting and schooling (and life) were like among the British aristocracy 100 years ago. The way they brought up children—never seeing them—would be seen as abusive today.

TOP-PICK PARENTING MOVIES

Life Is Beautiful (1998, Miramax Films; directed by Roberto Benigni).

In this uplifting Italian movie, a Jewish father and comedian makes his 5-year-old son believe the two of them are undergoing a wonderful comic experience (that's not really real) when they are captured by the Nazis and sent to a concentration camp during World War II. This film is an incredible metaphor for the power of parental love to insulate children from the worst horrors of the world and make "life beautiful."

Dumbo (1941, Walt Disney Pictures; directed by Ben Sharpsteen).

This classic movie is also a masterpiece about parent love—and it resonates with many *other* messages of this chapter, too. *Highly recommended to show in class, as it is only an hour long.*

INTELLIGENCE

Gardner, H. (2004). *Frames of mind*. New York: Basic Books.

In this classic book, Gardner describes his theory of multiple intelligences.

Gould, S.J. (1996; 1981). *The mismeasure of man*. New York: Norton.

In this devastating critique of attempts to test for "intelligence" and so label specific groups as "biologically inferior," Gould offers a hair-raising tour of the ups and downs of IQ testing.

Sternberg, R. (1996). *Successful intelligence*. New York: Putnam.

This popular book is a joy to read as well as being informative, laying out Sternberg's ideas about successful intelligence and studies in an understandable form.

SCHOOL

Kidder, T. (1990). *Among schoolchildren*. New York: Avon.

This marvelous book chronicles a year in the life of Chris Zajak, a passionately committed fifth-grade teacher.

Kozol, J. (1991). *Savage inequalities*. New York: Crown Publishers.

This social critic offers a firsthand journalistic account of the dramatic inequalities in U.S. schools in Chicago, New York, and other cities—as he visits public schools serving poor (often minority) and upper-middle-class children and simply documents the differences in supplies, the buildings, class sizes, and everything else.

Lee, L.E., and Burkam, D.T. (2002). *Inequality at the starting gate: Social background differences in achievement as children begin school*. Washington, DC: Economic Policy Institute.

This academic book provides statistics documenting ethnic and socioeconomic differences in achievement and learning situations as children start school. It also surveys the poor-quality kindergartens that low-income and ethnic-minority children typically attend.

Stigler, J., and Hiebert, J. (1999). *The teaching gap*. New York: Free Press.

This slim book offers a look at Japanese education and the lessons it offers for U.S. schools.

TOP-PICK IDEAL TEACHER MOVIE

Mr. Holland's Opus (1995, Buena Vista Pictures; directed by Stephen Herek).

This wonderful movie is all about the power of a teacher—in this case, a high school music teacher—to permanently change lives. (It also relates to ideal parenting.)

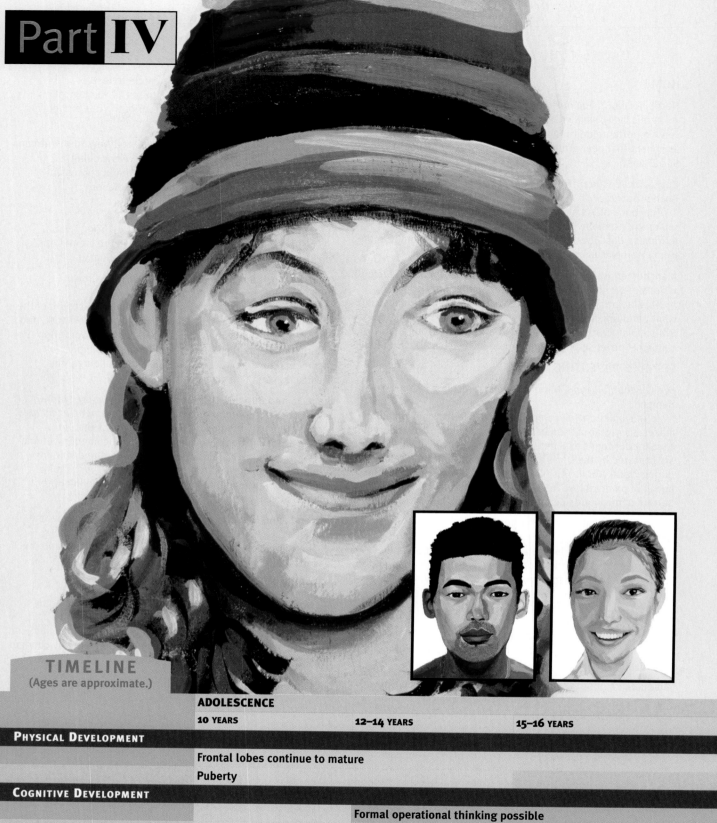

Part IV

TIMELINE
(Ages are approximate.)

	ADOLESCENCE		
	10 YEARS	12–14 YEARS	15–16 YEARS
PHYSICAL DEVELOPMENT			
	Frontal lobes continue to mature		
	Puberty		
COGNITIVE DEVELOPMENT			
		Formal operational thinking possible	
			Morality advances to conventional level
SOCIOEMOTIONAL DEVELOPMENT			
		Adolescent egocentrism	
	Emotional storms/risk taking		
		Parent–child conflict at its height	
	Same-sex cliques	Crowds	Mixed-sex cliques

Adolescence and Emerging Adulthood

This section deals with the process of "coming of age," but it covers more than just the teenage years. That's because today puberty can take place as early as age 9 or 10, and many of us take well into our twenties to fully construct an adult life.

Chapter 8, "Physical Development," focuses mainly on the early years of adolescence. Although much of our discussion here is devoted to an in-depth exploration of the emotional and physical impact of puberty, in this chapter we also look at body image concerns (and eating disorders), and teenage sexuality.

In Chapter 9, "Cognitive and Socioemotional Development," we focus on the dramatic advances in reasoning and morality that take place during adolescence and explore teenagers' emotional states. We also look at how teenagers relate to their parents and their peers.

Chapter 10, "Constructing an Adult Life," tackles the challenges of making the transition to adulthood in the 21st -century developed world. In this chapter you will get insights into how to approach college, choose a career, and find a mate. If you are a traditional college student or a 20-something young adult, this chapter is all about your life.

The timeline below traces some of the major milestones during this long two-decade phase of life.

EMERGING ADULTHOOD

18–19 YEARS	MID-20S		LATE 20S

Constructing an adult life—work or college

Identity and intimacy issues are paramount   Identity achievement in all areas of life

Career/college issue/adult romantic relationships

CHAPTER 8

puberty The hormonal and physical changes by which children become sexually mature human beings.

How do children *really* feel during **puberty,** the name for all of the internal and external changes related to physically becoming adult? In this chapter we look at this question and others as we focus on physical development mainly during the early adolescent years. In most of this chapter we chart

Physical
Development

Samantha and her twin brother, Sam, were so much alike—in their physical features, their personalities, their academic talents. Except for the sex difference, they almost seemed like identical twins. Then, when Samantha was 10, she started to tower over Sam and the rest of the fifth-grade class.

Yes, there was a downside to being first to develop—needing to hide behind a locker when you dressed for gym; not having anyone to talk to when you got your period at age 10. But, oh, what fun! From being a neglected, pudgy elementary school child by sixth grade, Samantha leaped into the ranks of most popular, especially with the older boys. At age 12, Samantha was smoking and drinking. By 14, she regularly defied her helpless parents and often left the house at 2 A.M.

Samantha's parents were frantic, but their daughter couldn't care less. Everything else was irrelevant compared to exploring being an adult. It took a life-changing tenth-grade trip to Costa Rica with Caroline, and a pregnancy scare, to get Samantha on track. Samantha had abandoned Caroline, her best friend during elementary school, for her new "mature" friends. But when the girls got close again that memorable summer, Caroline's calming influence woke Samantha up. Samantha credits comments like "Why are you putting yourself in danger by having unprotected sex?" with saving her life. Plus, her lifelong competition with her brother didn't hurt. Although Sam was also an early developer, when he shot up to 6 feet in the spring of seventh grade, he became a sports star and was also great at school.

Now that Samantha is 30, married, and expecting her first child, it's interesting for the three of them to get together and really talk (for the first time) about the early adolescent years. Sam remembers the thrill of getting so much stronger and his first incredible feelings of being in love. Samantha recalls being excited about her changing body, but she also remembers the constant dieting and her terrible anxiety about being too fat. Then there is Caroline, who says she sailed through middle school because she didn't begin to menstruate until age 16. Everyone goes through puberty, but why does everyone react in such different ways?

puberty—exploring what sets off this watershed in human life; examining how the changes unfold; making sense of why people such as Samantha, Sam, and Caroline undergo this transformation at such different ages. Why did Samantha—but not Sam—have so much trouble coping with being an "early-maturing" child, and

what can we do to make puberty a less stressful experience for *every* boy and girl?

Then we examine body image issues, such as Samantha's dieting frenzy; and finally, we look at sexuality. When do our first sexual feelings appear, and what influences predict when teenagers begin

having intercourse? Are there really differences between girls and boys in their attitudes about sex? As you read this chapter, you might think back to what it was like to be 10 or 12 or 14. How did you feel about your body during puberty? When did you begin dating and fantasizing about having sex?

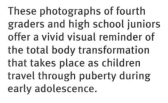

These photographs of fourth graders and high school juniors offer a vivid visual reminder of the total body transformation that takes place as children travel through puberty during early adolescence.

Puberty

Compare photos of yourself from late elementary school and high school, and you will get a vivid sense of the incredible changes that occur during berty. From the size of our thighs to the shape of our nose, we we become a totally different-looking per- during the early teenage years. Although children's timetables vary, today puberty—which lasts about years from start to finish—typically is a pre-teen and early adolescent change (Archibald, Graber, & Brooks-Gunn, 2003). Moreover, today, as you saw with Samantha, who started menstruating at age 10 has just gotten pregnant at age 30, the gap between being physically able to have children and actually *having* children can be twice as long as infancy and childhood combined.

This lack of person–environment fit, when our body is telling us to have sex and society is telling us to "just say no" to intercourse, explains why teenage sexuality is such an important worry today. Our concerns are actually surprisingly recent. They are mainly a product of living in the twenty-first-century developed world.

Setting the Context: Culture, History, and Puberty

> *As my sisters and I went about doing our daily chores, we choked on the dust stirred up by the herd of cattle and goats that had just arrived in our compound.... These animals were my bride wealth, negotiated by my parents and the family of the man who had been cho- sen as my husband.... I am considered to be a woman, so I am ready to marry, have chil- dren, and assume adult privileges and responsibilities. My name is Telelia ole Mariani. I am 14 years old.*
>
> (quoted in Wilson, Ngige, & Trollinger, 2003, p. 95)

puberty rite A "coming of age" ritual, usually beginning at some event such as first menstruation, held in tradi- tional cultures to celebrate children's transition to adulthood.

As this quotation from a girl in rural Nigeria illustrates, throughout most of human his- tory and even today in a few agrarian societies, people never worried much about teenage pregnancy. Girls got married right after they became sexually mature (Schlegel, 1995; Schlegel & Barry, 1991). The fact that a young person's changing body used to be the signal to enter a new stage of life produced a different cultural attitude toward the physical changes. In industrialized societies, we need to minimize puberty because we don't want teenagers to act on their sexuality for years. In many traditional cultures, the whole community would get together to celebrate the changes in a com- ing-of-age ceremony called the **puberty rite**.

For this rural Vietnamese boy, reaching puberty means it's time to assume his adult responsibili- ties as a fisherman. This is the reason why having *puberty rites* to mark the end of childhood makes excellent sense in less industrialized cultures, but not in our own.

Celebrating Puberty

Puberty rites were more than just parties. They were thrilling events, carefully scripted to highlight the child's passage into adult life. Typically, a boy or girl was removed from the family and, under the guidance of same-sex adult role models, asked to perform challenging tasks. There was intense anxiety ("Can I really do this thing?") and feelings of awe and self-efficacy as the young person returned, to be joyfully reunited with the community in a different, adult way (Weisfeld, 1997).

So, at his fourteenth or fifteenth birthday, a boy might be spirited away at night by the males in the village to a secret campsite, to hunt, raid an enemy camp, and perhaps be initiated into the mysteries of sex (Weisfeld, 1997). A girl's first menstruation was the signal for a community-wide festival to celebrate her arrival into womanhood.

Consider, for instance, the Navajo four-day Kinaalda ceremony (Markstrom & Iborra, 2003). At the beginning of her first or second menstrual cycle, guided by a female mentor who had been carefully selected by the family, the girl performed the long-distance running ritual, sprinting for miles. (Imagine the motivation to train for this event, when you understood that the length of your run symbolized how long you would live.) The female role model massaged the girl's body and painted her face as she supervised the strenuous task of grinding corn (a symbol of fertility) for a cake. On the final day, the girl served the cake during a joyous, all-night community sing. The Navajo believe that when females begin menstruating they possess unique spiritual powers, so everyone would gather around for the girl's blessings as they gave her a new adult name.

Today, however, children may reach puberty at age 10 or even 9. At that age—in *any* society—could a person really be ready for adult life? The answer is no. In the past we reached puberty at a much older age.

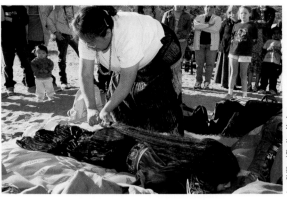

As the female mentor symbolically welcomes her into adulthood, this newly menstruating Navajo girl is undergoing a traditional cultural ritual that will be an unforgettable highlight of her life. Plus, the female tourists watching this ceremony are getting insights into a very different, positive way of looking at menarche!

[FAQ: Is the age of puberty declining?]

The Declining Age of Puberty

You can see this dramatic age decline, called the **secular trend in puberty,** illustrated in Figure 8.1. In 1830 the average age of **menarche,** or first menstruation, in Northern Europe was over 17 (Tanner, 1978). Today, in the developed world, it has dropped to well under 13 (Parent and others, 2003). A century ago, girls could not get pregnant until their late teens. Today, girls can have babies *before* they enter their teenage years.

secular trend in puberty A century-long decline in the average age at which children reach puberty in the developed world.

menarche A girl's first menstruation.

Finland ———
Sweden ———
Norway ———
Italy (north) ———
U.K. (south) ———
U.S.A. (middle class) ———

Average age at menarche (years)

16
15
14
13
12

1860 1880 1900 1920 1940 1960

Year

FIGURE 8.1: **The secular trend in puberty:** Notice that the average age of puberty has dramatically declined in developed countries since the 1890s. What impact do you think this change alone has made on teenage pregnancy rates?

Source: Tanner (1978), p. 103.

If they had grown up a century ago, these seventh graders at a summer computer camp would really have looked like girls. Due to the *secular trend in puberty,* they look like women today.

Peter Hvizdak / The Images Works

Researchers use menarche as their marker for exploring the secular trend in puberty because it is an obvious sign of possibly being able to have a child. The male signal of fertility, **spermarche,** or first ejaculation of live sperm, is a hidden event. But, just as with girls, the age of puberty has been steadily declining for boys.

In addition, because it reflects improving nutrition, just as you saw with stunting rates in Chapter 3, epidemiologists use the secular trend in puberty as an index of a nation's economic development. In impoverished countries, such as Senegal, girls on average reach menarche when they are over 16. In rapidly developing nations with huge income inequalities, such as India, affluent urban girls begin to menstruate at the same average age as girls in the United States (about 12½). The comparable figure for poor rural girls is well over 15 (Parent and others, 2003).

Given that nutrition levels are somehow involved, what *exactly* sets puberty off? For answers, we now focus on the hormone systems that program the physical changes of puberty.

The Hormonal Programmers

Puberty is programmed by two independent command centers. One system, located in the adrenal glands at the top of the kidneys, begins to release its hormones at about age 6 to 8, several years before children show any observable signs of puberty. The **adrenal androgens,** whose output increases to reach a peak in the early twenties, eventually produce (among other events) pubic hair development, skin changes, body odor, and, as you will see later in this chapter, our first feelings of sexual desire (McClintock & Herdt, 1996).

About two years later the most important command center kicks in. Called the **HPG axis,** because it involves the hypothalamus (in the brain), the pituitary (a gland at the base of the brain), and the **gonads** (the *ovaries* and the *testes*), this system sets in motion the major body changes.

As Figure 8.2 shows, puberty is set off by a three-phase chain reaction. At about age 9 or 10, after a suppression that has lasted since infancy, pulsating bursts of the initial hypothalamic hormone stimulate the pituitary gland to step up production of its hormones. This causes the ovaries and testes to secrete several closely related compounds called *estrogens* and the hormone called **testosterone** (Cameron, 1990; Ebling, 2005; Sisk & Foster, 2004).

As the blood concentrations of estrogens and testosterone float upward, these hormones unleash a physical transformation. Estrogens produce the changing female shape by causing the hips to widen and the uterus and breasts to enlarge. They also set in motion the cycle of reproduction, stimulating the ovaries to produce eggs. Testosterone causes the penis to lengthen, promotes the growth of facial and body hair, and is responsible for a dramatic increase in muscle mass and other internal masculine changes.

Boys and girls both produce estrogens and testosterone. Testosterone and the adrenal androgens are the desire hormones. They are responsible for sexual arousal in females and males. However, women produce mainly estrogens. The concentration of testosterone is roughly eight times higher in boys after puberty than it is in girls; in fact, this classic "male" hormone is responsible for all physical changes in boys.

Now, to return to our earlier question, what primes the triggering hypothalamic hormone? As you might imagine, the signal is set off when the body reaches a certain level of maturation (Sisk & Foster, 2004). Throughout childhood, our bones elongate

spermarche A boy's first ejaculation of live sperm.

adrenal androgens Hormones produced by the adrenal glands that program various aspects of puberty, such as growth of body hair, skin changes, and sexual desire.

HPG axis The main hormonal system programming puberty; it involves a triggering hypothalamic hormone that causes the pituitary to secrete its hormones, which in turn cause the ovaries and testes to develop and secrete the hormones that produce the major body changes.

gonads The sex organs—the ovaries in girls and the testes in boys.

testosterone The hormone responsible for the maturation of the organs of reproduction and other signs of puberty in men, and for hair and skin changes during puberty and for sexual desire in both sexes.

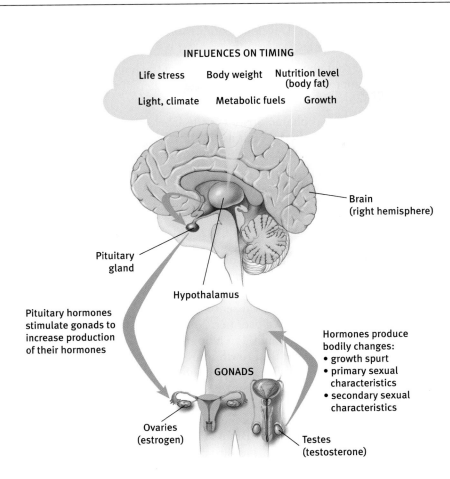

INFLUENCES ON TIMING

Life stress   Body weight   Nutrition level (body fat)

Light, climate   Metabolic fuels   Growth

Brain (right hemisphere)

Pituitary gland

Hypothalamus

Pituitary hormones stimulate gonads to increase production of their hormones

GONADS

Hormones produce bodily changes:
• growth spurt
• primary sexual characteristics
• secondary sexual characteristics

Ovaries (estrogen)

Testes (testosterone)

FIGURE 8.2: **The HPG axis: The three-phase hormonal sequence that triggers puberty:** As you can see here, in response to various genetic and environmental influences, the hypothalamus releases a hormone that stimulates the pituitary gland to produce its own hormones, which cause the ovaries in girls and the testes in boys to grow and secrete estrogens and testosterone, producing the physical changes of puberty.

and in the process gradually ossify (harden). Puberty occurs once the skeleton reaches a certain level of ossification, which explains why children who are stunted due to poor nutrition reach puberty at older ages (Tanner, 1955, 1978).

A critical chemical tied to the onset of puberty is a hormone called *leptin,* which is sensitive to the amount of body fat (Ebling, 2005). Scientists find that underfeeding laboratory rats inhibits the concentration of leptin, keeping the animals in a prolonged infantile state (Parent and others, 2003). You might be interested to know that severe dieting and reaching a low level of body fat can cause women to stop menstruating and ovulating too.

But in making sense of the puzzle of puberty, we need to take into account more than simply the amount of body fat. Boys and girls who migrate from impoverished to affluent countries during middle childhood reach puberty at an unusually early age (Parent and others, 2003). This suggests that a dramatic *change* in nutrition may activate the production of leptin, which primes the hypothalamic puberty pump.

Actually, as Figure 8.2 illustrates, the hypothalamic trigger is sensitive to a variety of signals—from leptin levels to the amount of exposure to heat and light (given comparable nutrition, children who live in warmer climates tend to reach puberty comparatively early) to environmental stress (more about this fascinating force later) (Ebling, 2005; Parent and others, 2003; Sanders & Reinisch, 1990). This complexity is mirrored by the diversity of the physical changes.

The Physical Changes

Puberty causes a total *psychological* as well as physical transformation. As the hormones flood the brain, they affect the neurotransmitters, making teenagers more emotional and more interested in taking risks (Nelson and others, 2005; see Chapter 9 for

primary sexual characteristics Physical changes of puberty that directly involve the organs of reproduction, such as the growth of the penis and the onset of menstruation.

secondary sexual characteristics Physical changes of puberty that are not directly involved in reproduction.

growth spurt A dramatic increase in height and weight that occurs during puberty.

more about this topic). Developmentalists divide the physical changes into the following three categories:

- **Primary sexual characteristics** refer to all of the body changes directly involved in the reproductive process. The growth of the penis and the onset of menstruation are examples of primary sexual characteristics.

- **Secondary sexual characteristics** is the label for the hundreds of other changes that accompany puberty, such as the development of the breasts, the growth of pubic hair, voice changes, and alterations in the texture of the skin.

- The **growth spurt** is another change that merits its own category. Puberty produces a dramatic increase in height and weight.

Now let's offer a motion picture of these changes, first in girls and then in boys.

For Girls

As you saw with Samantha in the chapter-opening vignette, the first sign of puberty in girls is the growth spurt. During late childhood, girls' growth picks up speed, accelerates, and then a few years later begins to decrease (Abbassi, 1998). On a visit to my 11-year-old niece I got a vivid sense of this "peak velocity" phase of growth. Six months earlier, I had towered over her. Now she insisted on standing back-to-back to demonstrate: "Look, Aunt Janet, I'm taller than you!"

About six months after the growth spurt begins, girls begin to develop breasts and pubic hair. On average, girls' breasts take about five years to grow to their adult form (Archibald, Graber, & Brooks-Gunn, 2003; Tanner, 1955, 1978).

Interestingly, menarche tends to occur relatively late in this process, in the middle to final stages of breast and pubic hair development, when girls' growth is winding down (Archibald, Graber, & Brooks-Gunn, 2003). So you can tell your 12-year-old niece, who has just begun to menstruate, that while her breasts are still works in progress, she is probably about as tall today as she will be as an adult.

When they reach menarche, can girls get pregnant? Yes, but there is often a window of infertility until the system fully gears up. Does the sequence of changes occur in the same way for every girl? The answer is no. Because the hormonal signals are so complex for both girls and boys, the pattern of puberty varies from child to child. In some girls, pubic hair development (programmed by the adrenal androgens) is well under way before the breasts start to enlarge. Occasionally, a girl grows significantly taller after she begins to menstruate (Dorn and others, 1999).

The difference in the *rate of change* can be remarkable. In comparing breast development among rural and urban girls in Zambia, Africa, researchers found that while the better-nourished urban girls began developing breasts roughly two years sooner, the rural girls sped through each phase of breast development to reach the adult stage at the same age as their city counterparts (Gillett-Netting, Meloy, & Campbell, 2004). Scientists also observe this catch-up growth—or accelerated maturation—in children whose growth has been retarded due to famine. Given adequate nutrition, the hormones that program development go into overdrive. It's almost as if the body is saying, "It's time to get going very fast" (Parent and others, 2003).

In tracking puberty in females, researchers focus on charting pubic hair and breast development, because these classic external secondary sexual changes can be measured in stages. The internal changes are equally dramatic. During puberty the uterus grows, the vagina lengthens, and the hips develop a cushion of fat. The vocal cords get longer. The heart gets bigger, and the red blood cells carry more oxygen. So, in addition to looking very different after puberty, girls become much stronger (Archibald, Graber, & Brooks-Gunn, 2003). The increases in strength and stamina and in height and weight, as we see now, are much more pronounced in boys.

For Boys

In boys, researchers also chart how the penis, the testicles, and pubic hair develop in distinctive stages. However, because these organs of reproduction begin developing first, boys still look like children to the outside world for at least a year or two after their bodies start changing. Voice changes, the growth of body hair, and that other clearly visible sign of being a man—needing to shave—all take place after the growth of the testes and penis are well underway (Tanner, 1978). Now let's pause to look at perhaps the most obvious signals that a boy is becoming a man— the tremendous transformations in size, shape, and physical strength (Huddleston & Ge, 2003).

You may remember from our discussion in Chapter 5 that during elementary school, boys and girls are roughly the same size. Then, during their growth spurt, boys get about 8 *inches taller*, compared to 4 inches for girls (Tanner, 1978). During puberty boys also become much stronger than the opposite sex.

One reason lies in the tremendous increase in muscle mass that is produced by the flood of testosterone. Another lies in the dramatic cardiovascular changes. At puberty, boys' hearts increase in weight by more than one-third. In particular, notice in Figure 8.3 that compared to females, after puberty males have many more red blood cells and a much greater capacity for carrying oxygen in their blood (Tanner, 1978).

Because that landmark change, shaving, occurs fairly late in the sequence of puberty, we can be sure that this 14-year-old boy has been looking like a man for some time in the ways that you and I can't see.

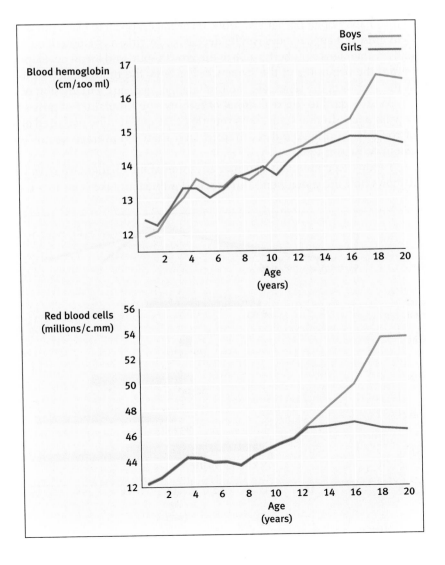

FIGURE 8.3: **Changes in blood hemoglobin and red blood cells during puberty in males and females:** At puberty, increases in the amount of hemoglobin in the blood and in the number of red blood cells cause children of both sexes to get far stronger. But notice that these changes are more pronounced in boys than in girls. *Source:* Tanner (1955), p. 103.

By comparing this photograph of Haley Joel Osment taken in 2002 *(left)* with the one taken two years later in 2004 *(right)*, can you pick out the ways puberty subtly transforms the face of a boy into that of a man?

[FAQ: How much later do boys reach puberty than girls?]

The visible signs of these changes are a big chest, wide shoulders, and a muscular frame. The real-world consequence is that after puberty teenage boys have a built-in advantage in gross motor skills that makes them far superior at sports, from football to baseball to bowling, over the opposite sex.

Do you have access to a group of seventh- or eighth-grade boys? If so, you might notice that growth during puberty takes place in the opposite pattern to the one that occurs earlier in life. Rather than following the *cephalocaudal* and *proximodistal* sequences, from the head downward and from the middle of the body outward, at puberty the hands, feet, and legs grow first. While this happens for both sexes, because their growth is so dramatic, these changes are especially obvious in boys.

Their unusually long legs and large feet explain why, in their early teens, boys look so gawky. Adding to the problem is the crackly voice produced by the growing larynx, the wispy look of beginning facial hair, and the fact that during puberty a boy's nose and ears grow before the rest of his face catches up. To make matters worse, the increased activity of the sweat glands and enlarged pores gives us that recipe for the teenage condition that causes such emotional pain: acne. Although girls also suffer from acne, boys are somewhat more vulnerable to this condition because testosterone, which males produce in abundance, produces changes in the hair and skin.

Are Boys on a Later Timetable? A Bit

Now visit a sixth-grade class and you will be struck by the gender difference mentioned in the chapter-opening vignette. Boys, on average, appear to reach puberty two years later than girls. But appearances can be deceiving. In girls, as we described earlier, the externally visible signs of puberty, such as the growth spurt and breast development, take place toward the beginning of the sequence. For boys, the more hidden developments, such as the growth of the testes, are the first changes to occur (Huddleston & Ge, 2003).

With regard to the real signal of fertility, the timetables of girls and boys are not very far apart. In one study, boys reported that spermarche occurred at an average age of roughly 13, only about six months later than the average age of menarche today (Stein & Reiser, 1994).

Figure 8.4 graphically summarizes some of the changes we have been discussing. It shows how the testes, penis, breasts, and pubic hair take years to grow. It reveals that

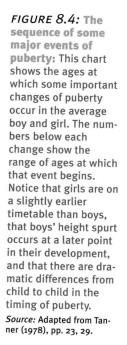

FIGURE 8.4: The sequence of some major events of puberty: This chart shows the ages at which some important changes of puberty occur in the average boy and girl. The numbers below each change show the range of ages at which that event begins. Notice that girls are on a slightly earlier timetable than boys, that boys' height spurt occurs at a later point in their development, and that there are dramatic differences from child to child in the timing of puberty.

Source: Adapted from Tanner (1978), pp. 23, 29.

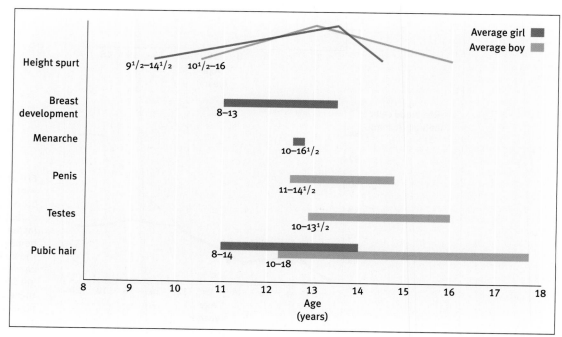

menstruation occurs fairly late in the process for females, and illustrates that the height spurt occurs at a slightly later point in boys' development than girls'. Now let's turn to explore the numbers inside the chart. Why do children undergo puberty at such different ages?

Individual Differences in Puberty Timetables

I'm seventeen already. But I still look like a kid. I get teased a lot, especially by the other guys. . . . Girls aren't interested in me, either, because most of them are taller than I am. When will I grow up?

(adapted from an on-line chat room)

The gender difference in puberty timetables can cause anxiety. As an early-maturing girl, I vividly remember slumping to avoid the humiliation of having my partner's head encounter my chest in sixth-grade dancing class! But nature's cruelest blow may relate to the individual differences in timing. What accounts for the five-year difference in puberty timetables between children who live in the same environment (Parent and others, 2003)?

Not unexpectedly, genetic forces are very important. Identical twins reach puberty at more similar ages than fraternal twins (Mustanski and others, 2004). There are also genetically programmed timetable ethnic differences. Asian American children tend to be slightly behind other U.S. children. African American boys and girls, on average, are ahead of other North American groups (Freedman and others, 2002; Sun and others, 2002). In one recent survey, the average African American girl reached menarche at about her twelfth birthday, a full six months earlier than the typical European American girl (Wu, Mendola, & Back, 2002).

A longitudinal study conducted in Mississippi has suggested that this ethnic gap is widening. From the 1970s to the late 1990s, the median age at menarche for African American girls in this state decreased by nine months, versus two months for European American girls (Freedman and others, 2002).

An interesting nature-plus-nurture interaction related to diet seems to be responsible. Researchers measured the food intake of a group of African American girls and compared these findings to what elderly black women in their seventies and eighties remembered eating during childhood (Talpade & Talpade, 2001). The older women reported consuming a meager two meals a day. This study suggests that during the last half-century, the African American diet in particular has become far more caloric. Unfortunately, this dietary change has not had totally positive effects. As you may remember from Chapter 5, obesity rates have recently been skyrocketing among African American elementary school girls and boys.

Overweight and Early Puberty

This brings up interesting questions. Do children who are overweight tend to reach puberty earlier? And, given that many more elementary school children *are* seriously overweight today, is the secular trend in puberty continuing? The answer to both questions seems to be yes. Although this finding is most striking for girls, children with a high BMI (body mass index) tend to reach puberty at a younger age. Moreover, for everyone, the age of puberty *still* seems be declining (Anderson, Dallal, & Must, 2003). And all signs point to the obesity-promoting environment, specifically the recent rise in childhood body fat.

So far it seems as if we have identified the main lifestyle influence involved in the secular trend in puberty: It's the obesity epidemic. But remember that the hypothalamic timer is influenced by many environmental forces. Now let's look at the most interesting nurture force that affects when we physically mature: the nurturing that we get during early life.

Bananastock / Jupiter Images

Look at female middle school friends—such as these girls getting ready for a dance—and you will be struck with the differences in puberty timetables. In this section, you will find out why children mature earlier or later than their peers.

[FAQ: Why do some children reach puberty early and others late?]

Stress, Absent Fathers, and Early Puberty

Drawing on an *evolutionary psychology* perspective, about a decade ago psychologists devised a compelling hypothesis. When family stress is intense, they argued, it would make sense to build in a mechanism to accelerate sexual maturity and free a child from the inhospitable nest (Belsky, Steinberg, & Draper, 1991; Ellis, 2004). According to this theory, an unhappy early life increases the level of stress hormones, which prompts the body to put the hypothalamic signal forward, causing a child to reach puberty at a younger age.

You may be amazed to know that this prediction has considerable research support. Early-maturing girls tend to report more stressful childhoods (Moffitt and others, 1992). They show more symptoms of distress, such as sleep disorders, in their childhood years (Tremblay & Frigon, 2005). Late-maturing girls report having had a happier, closer, more harmonious family life (Ellis, 2004; Ellis and others, 1999).

Another fascinating family risk factor—for both girls and boys—relates to growing up in the absence of a biological father. The presence of a stepfather doesn't really alter the age of puberty much. What seems to be particularly influential is being raised by a single mother, particularly during a child's first years of life (Bogaert, 2004; Ellis, 2004; Quinlan, 2003).

So with puberty we can vividly see the developmental-systems principle that a variety of forces combine to influence every aspect of who we are and that all systems interrelate. This biological process is sensitive to our emotional state. What happens to us hormonally years later may be affected by our relationships during our earliest years. And since we know that many forces set off the hypothalamic timer, the fact that mental distress affects puberty makes excellent biological sense.

Finally, notice that socioeconomic status—the basic marker that shapes so many aspects of life—affects even our puberty timetable. However, as we saw with childhood obesity in Chapter 5, living in poverty has a different impact on children in the developed and developing worlds. In impoverished countries, because it produces stunting, low socioeconomic status predicts reaching puberty later. In affluent countries, because they are more likely to grow up with single mothers, to have more stressful childhoods, and to be overweight, children at the lower end of the economic totem pole are more likely to mature at an earlier age.

Table 8.1 summarizes our discussion by spelling out questions that would predict a child's chance of reaching puberty at a younger-than-average age. If you were an early maturer, how many—if any—of these forces applied to you?

Now that we've described the physical process, it's time to shift to an insider's perspective. In this next section we explore how children feel about three classic signs of puberty—breast development, menstruation, and first ejaculation—and then look at whether it *really* matters if a boy or girl reaches puberty relatively early or late.

[FAQ: How do kids feel during puberty?]

If you were an early maturer, how well does this profile fit your experience?

TABLE 8.1: **Questions to Ask to Predict an Elementary School Child's Chances of Reaching Puberty Early**

1. When did this child's parents reach puberty? Ask about first menstruation for mother; voice change for father; 12 or under = early for mother; under 14 = early for father.

2. Is this child African American?

3. Is this child overweight?

4. Is this child under considerable stress?

5. Did this child grow up in a single-parent, mother-headed family?

An Insider's View of Puberty

If you think back to how you felt about your changing body during puberty, you probably remember a mixture of emotions: fear, pride, uncertainty, embarrassment, excitement. Now imagine how you would react if a researcher asked you to describe your inner state. Would you want to talk about how you *really* felt? (See Brooks-Gunn & Reiter, 1990.) The intense reluctance of pre-teens to discuss what is happening ("Yuck! Just don't go there!") explains why, when researchers study reactions to puberty, they often ask adults to remember this time of life. When developmentalists do decide to explore young teenagers' feelings, they may use indirect measures, such as having children tell stories about pictures, to reveal their inner concerns.

The Breasts

Researchers used this indirect strategy to explore how girls feel in relation to their parents while undergoing that most visible sign of becoming a woman—breast development (Brooks-Gunn and others, 1994). They asked girls to tell a story about the characters in a drawing that showed an adult female (the mother) taking a bra out of a shopping bag while an adolescent girl and an adult male (the father) watched (see Figure 8.5). While girls often talked about the mother in the picture as being excited and happy, they typically described the teenager as humiliated by her father's presence in the room. Moreover, girls in the middle of puberty told the most negative stories about the fathers, suggesting that body embarrassment is at its height when children are actually undergoing the physical changes.

Because our society strongly values this symbol of being a woman (and today bigger is definitely better!), other research suggests that U.S. girls feel proud of their developing breasts (Brooks-Gunn & Warren, 1988). However, among girls in ballet schools, where there are strong social pressures to look lean and prepubescent, one study showed that breast development evoked distress (Brooks-Gunn & Warren, 1985). The same principle—that children's reactions to puberty depend on the messages they get from the wider world—holds true for menstruation, too.

FIGURE 8.5: Getting your first bra: To measure how girls undergoing puberty feel around their parents—without asking them directly—researchers used this specially constructed card and asked children of different ages to describe what is happening and "How do the mother, the father and the girl feel?"
Source: Brooks-Gunn and others (1994), p. 549.

Chris Hondros / Getty Images

Imagine how these girls auditioning at a premier ballet academy in New York City will feel when they develop breasts and perhaps find that their womanly body shape interrupts their career dreams, and you will understand why children's reactions to puberty depend totally on their unique environment.

Menstruation

Think of being a Navajo girl and believing that when you begin to menstruate, you enter a special spiritual state. Compare this with the less-than-glowing portrait most societies paint about "that time of the month" (Brooks-Gunn & Ruble, 1982; Costos, Ackerman, & Paradis, 2002; Simes & Berg, 2001). From the advertisements for pills strong enough to handle *even* menstrual pain to the "just grin and bear it" attitudes of many mothers, it's no wonder that girls in many regions of the world approach this change with mixed emotions (Marván, Vacio, & Espinosa-Hernández, 2003). When they do begin to menstruate, girls tend to be pleasantly surprised, thinking, "It isn't as bad as I thought it would be" (Brooks-Gunn & Ruble, 1982).

In the West we tend to discuss menstruation in general terms, so girls are somewhat prepared for what will happen. This is not the situation in Islamic countries such as Pakistan. As one Pakistani woman in an interview study recalled: "When my menses started, I did not know what had happened to me. I cried so much. . . . When [my mother] came back, I told her I was going to die" (quoted in Hennink, Rana, & Iqbal, 2005, p. 322). Another woman, however, had happier memories: "When it started with me, . . . my mother . . . briefed me all about it. I felt very strange, but I also felt good. She was so caring" (p. 322). These studies highlight the fact that with regard to explaining puberty, mothers around the world serve as confidantes for their daughters (Brooks-Gunn & Reiter, 1990).Who talks to boys about first ejaculation, and how do male adolescents feel about their signal of becoming men?

First Ejaculation

Mothers must discuss menstruation with their daughters because this change demands specific coping techniques. Spermarche, as we mentioned earlier, is a hidden experience — one that doesn't require instructions from the outside world. Still, when researchers questioned a group of 18-year-old boys, most had vivid memories of this event (Stein & Reiser, 1994):

I woke up the next morning and my sheets were pasty. . . . After you wake up your mind is kind of happy and then you realize: "Oh my God, this is my wet dream!"

(quoted in Stein & Reiser, 1994, p. 380)

My mom, she knew I had them. It was all over my sheets and bedspread and stuff, but she didn't say anything, didn't tease me and stuff, and I was kind of glad. She never asked if I wanted to talk about it—I'm glad. I never could have said anything to my mom.

(quoted in Stein & Reiser, 1994, p. 377)

Most of these boys reported that they felt they needed to be secretive. They didn't want to let *anyone* know. And notice from the second quotation—as you saw earlier with fathers and pre-teen girls—that boys also see the changes of puberty as especially embarrassing around the parent of the opposite sex.

Is this tendency for children to want to hide their changing bodies around the parent of the other gender programmed into evolution to help teenagers begin to emotionally separate from their families? We can only speculate about this interesting question. Where we do have a good deal of scientific data—from decades of studies—is on the emotional impact that being early or late has on children.

Being Early: It Can Be a Problem for Girls

Imagine being an early-maturing girl. How would you feel if you looked like an adult while everyone else in your class still looked like a child? Now imagine being a late maturer and thinking, "What's wrong with my body? Will I *ever* grow up?"

Actually the timing of development does matter, but mainly for girls. The research for boys is ambiguous. Some studies show that being early is difficult for males, while others reveal that, as with Sam in the opening vignette, boys who mature early—being so much taller and stronger—are at an advantage socially over their peers. Sometimes researchers find that being late and looking like a child when everyone else looks adult can provoke boys to prove themselves as men by getting into trouble as teens (Duncan and others, 1985; Graber and others, 1997; Simmons & Blyth, 1987; Williams & Dunlop, 1999). However, every study throughout the developed world agrees: *Early-maturing girls are vulnerable to having a host of difficulties during their adolescent years.*

As you saw with Samantha in the chapter-opening vignette, early-maturing girls often are more popular (Michael & Eccles, 2003). The bad news is that the problems attached to this popularity can outweigh the pluses.

Early-maturing girls are at special risk of developing acting-out, externalizing problems. Because we select friends who are "like us," early-maturing girls tend to gravitate toward becoming friends with older girls and boys. So they may get involved in risky activities, such as smoking and drinking, at a younger age (Silbereisen and others, 1989).

Because they are so busy exploring adulthood, the result can be a disconnect from school (Archibald, Graber, & Brooks-Gunn, 2003). Early-maturing girls tend to get worse grades than their classmates in the sixth and seventh grades (Simmons & Blyth, 1987). Once set in motion, this poor performance can be difficult to reverse. In one longitudinal study in Sweden, by their twenties early-maturing girls were several times less likely to have graduated from high school than their later-developing peers (Stattin & Magnusson, 1990).

This 13-year-old cheerleader is getting a lot of attention from the 18-year-old football star. Unfortunately, she may be too young to assert herself and say no if they start to date and he pressures her to have sex.

Then there is the main concern with having a mature body early on: having unprotected sex. Because they may not have the cognitive abilities to resist this social pressure and often have older boyfriends, early-maturing girls are more likely to have intercourse at a younger age (Silbereisen & Kracke, 1997). They are less likely to use contraception, making them much more vulnerable to becoming pregnant as teens (Ellis, 2004). How would you feel if you were a sixth- or seventh-grade girl being pursued by high school boys? Would you have the presence of mind to "just say no"?

Early-maturing girls are at special risk of getting anxious and depressed. As if this were not enough, early-maturing girls are also more prone to feel bad about themselves (Kaltiala-Heino, Kosunen, & Rimpela, 2003). In particular, they are vulnerable to feeling dissatisfied about their weight (Ge and others, 2001). The reason is that early-maturing girls tend not only to be heavier when they approach puberty but also to end up being shorter because their height spurt occurs at an earlier point in their development than that of other girls (Duncan and others, 1985; Must and others, 2005; Tanner, 1978). Late-maturing girls feel better about their bodies because they are more likely to fit the ultra-slim model shape. Maturing early sets girls up for a poor body image and low self-esteem.

So far I've been painting a dismal portrait of early-maturing girls. But, as with any aspect of development, it's important to look at the whole context of a person's life. Early maturation, interestingly, does not produce body image issues for African American girls. One reason, as we will see in the next section, is that African American women have a healthier, more inclusive idea about beauty and body size (Michael & Eccles, 2003).

Moreover, these negative effects happen only when girls enter the high-risk setting of dating and having older friends (Stattin & Magnusson, 1990). If a girl attends a single-sex school, has strong family or religious values, or, unlike Samantha in the vignette, stays close to her elementary school friends, her puberty timetable will not matter.

Another fascinating, wider influence that affects children's chances of getting into trouble relates to the educational structure of their town. In a classic study exploring puberty, developmentalists traced the lives of two groups of pre-teens in Milwaukee: boys and girls in school districts with separate junior high schools (what we now call middle school) and those who attended a K–8 (kindergarten through eighth grade) school (Simmons & Blyth, 1987; Simmons, Carlton-Ford, & Blyth, 1987). We might think that the early-maturing girls in K–8 schools would have more problems because they look so different from everyone else. We would be wrong. Girls who transferred to a junior high school had more troubles. In fact, for *every child* who moved to the larger, more anonymous junior high, academic performance tended to decline and self-confidence typically became shakier. Therefore, many of the problems that seem to be basic to reaching puberty, such as getting more anxious or becoming less interested in academics, may be in part a function of changing schools.

Wrapping Up Puberty

Now let's summarize the messages of our discussion:

- **Children's reactions to puberty depend on the environment in which they physically mature.** Negative feelings are more likely to occur when a society looks down on a given sign of development (as with menstruation) or when the physical changes are not valued in a person's particular group (as with breast development in ballerinas). Changing schools during puberty magnifies the stress of the body changes (Eccles & Midgley, 1989; Eccles & Roeser, 2003).

- **With early-maturing girls, we need to take special care to arrange the right body–environment fit.** While having an adult body at a young age can be dangerous for girls, wider-world influences, such as staying in the same school from kindergarten through eighth grade, can reduce the tendency for early-maturing girls to get into trouble as teens.

- **Communication about puberty can be vastly improved.** Although this is true for every child, mothers do tend to discuss puberty with their daughters; so experts suggest that boys, in particular, often enter puberty without any guidance about what to expect (Gaddis & Brooks-Gunn, 1985; Omar, McElderry, & Zakharia, 2003; Paikoff & Brooks-Gunn, 1991).

INTERVENTIONS: Minimizing Puberty Distress

Given these findings, what are the lessons for parents? What changes should society make?

LESSONS FOR PARENTS It's tempting for parents to avoid discussing puberty because children are so sensitive about their changing bodies. This reluctance is a mistake. Developmentalists urge parents to discuss what is happening with a same-sex child. They also advise beginning these discussions when the child is at an age when talking is emotionally easier, before the actual changes take place. Fathers, in particular, need to make special efforts to talk about puberty with their sons (Graber, Petersen, & Brooks-Gunn, 1996; Paikoff & Brooks-Gunn, 1991).

Parents should not heighten the embarrassment by teasing children about their changing bodies. Mothers need to avoid complaining too much about menstruation (Rembeck & Gunnarsson, 2004). Finally, parents with an early-maturing daughter should make special efforts to get their child involved in positive activities, especially with friends her own age, and possibly to switch their daughter to a more nurturing K–8 school.

LESSONS FOR SOCIETY This brings up the influence of the wider environment. Should we move *any* child to a large middle school during a time of intense bodily change? (See Eccles & Roeser, 2003.) If we cannot switch to K–8 school systems, at a minimum we should try to make middle schools more intimate, perhaps by having schools within a school, in which groups of students attend all their classes together in separate, cozier units.

It is extremely difficult for children who are in the midst of puberty to adjust to a huge middle school like this one—having to make new friends, being a small fish in a sea of unfamiliar faces. This is why most developmentalists believe that during the prime puberty years, children should ideally attend smaller K–8 schools.

David Frazier / Photo Edit, Inc.

We also need to provide adequate education about puberty. However, if you think back to what you personally wanted to know about your changing body ("My breasts don't look right"; "My penis has a strange shape"), you will realize that simply laying out biological facts is not enough (Diorio & Munro, 2003). In one U.S. survey, adolescents reported that they got their first formal education about puberty at around age 13 or even 15 (Omar, McElderry, & Zakharia, 2003)—*after* the changes had taken place. (That's like locking the barn door after the horses have been stolen!) Sex education classes in the United States and the United Kingdom focus heavily on what not to do, telling teenagers, "Don't have intercourse" and emphasizing the hazards of teen pregnancy (Kidger, 2005; Welles, 2005). Suppose we decided to really *celebrate* puberty, as the Navajo do? Perhaps this might start us on a revolution, where we celebrated every body size.

 ## TYING IT ALL TOGETHER

1. Reading about traditional puberty rites, Luis thinks that they sound like an awesome idea but that they wouldn't make much sense in the twenty-first century. What is the *main* reason why we would find it difficult to celebrate puberty today?

   a. Today puberty occurs a decade or two before we actually *can* enter adult life.
   b. Today we reach puberty at such different ages.

2. You notice that your 11-year-old cousin is going from looking like a child to looking like a young woman. (a) Outline the three-phase hormonal sequence that is setting off the physical changes, and (b) name the three classes of hormones involved in puberty. (c) Which change is happening first?

3. Kendra and Anthony are both 12 years old. Kendra recently shot up in height and is just beginning to develop breasts. Anthony still looks physically like a child. Statistically speaking, you can predict that Kendra [is already menstruating/is not yet menstruating] and that Anthony [has not yet reached puberty/may or may not have reached puberty].

4. All of the following facts about Brianna suggest that she may be on an early puberty timetable *except*:

   a. She is African American.
   b. She grew up in a single-parent household.
   c. Her mother was an early maturer.
   d. She is a dancer and is very thin.

5. Which girl is at highest risk for getting into trouble (e.g., with drugs, academics, or having unprotected sex) as a teen?

   a. Kimberly, who matured early and goes to the local middle school
   b. Jennifer, who matured early and goes to an all-girls school
   c. Melanie, who matured late and goes to a K–8 school

6. You are on a national advisory committee charged with developing programs to help children deal better with the changes of puberty. On the basis of what you've read in this chapter, what recommendations might you make?

Answers to the Tying It All Together questions can be found in the answers section of the book.

Body Image Issues

What do you daydream about?

Being skinny.

—Amanda (quoted in Martin, 1996, p. 36)

Puberty is a time of intense physical preoccupations, and there is hardly a teenager who isn't concerned about some body part. How important is it for young people to be *generally* satisfied with how they look?

FIGURE 8.6: Satisfaction with physical appearance among boys and girls in the third through the eleventh grade: Girls feel increasingly dissatisfied with their physical appearance as they get older. Boys feel just about as self-assured in high school as they were in third grade.

Source: Harter (1999), p. 163.

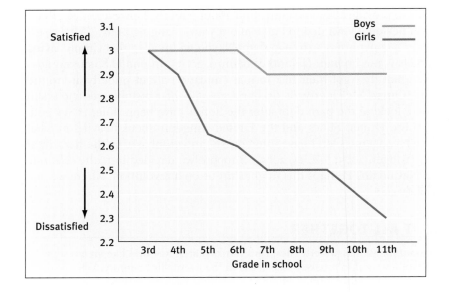

Exactly when did our culture develop the idea that women should be unrealistically thin? Historians trace this change to the 1960s and 1970s, when extremely slim actresses like Audrey Hepburn became our cultural ideal.

Norman Parkinson Limited / Corbis

Consider this finding: Susan Harter (1999) explored how feeling competent in each of five dimensions—scholastic abilities, conduct, athletic skills, peer likeability, and appearance (see Chapter 6)—related to teenagers' overall self-esteem. She found that being happy about one's looks far outweighed *anything else* in determining whether adolescents generally felt good about themselves. This finding is not just true of teenagers in the United States. It appears in surveys that Harter and her colleagues have conducted in a variety of Western countries among people at various stages of life. If we are happy with the way we look, we are almost certain to be happy with who we are as human beings.

Feeling physically appealing is centrally important to everyone. But given the premium society puts on female beauty, girls (no surprise) are more likely than boys to feel unhappy with their looks. As Figure 8.6 shows, this gender gap in satisfaction widens grade by grade as children travel through adolescence. Also notice that the gender split begins well before puberty, during elementary school, when children reach the concrete operational stage and begin to compare themselves to their peers.

Still, while this tendency for women to be more critical of their appearance may be ageless, one reason that females today are at especially high risk for low self-esteem (Feingold & Mazzella, 1998) is that, especially in Western cultures, we expect women to be abnormally thin. For this reason, in this next section we turn specifically to look at worries about weight (and body shape) in girls and boys.

Exploring the Concerns

With surveys showing that roughly one out of every two U.S. teenage girls is currently trying to lose weight, puberty sets off a dieting epidemic among females in the Western world (Cauffman & Steinberg, 1996; Ricciardelli & McCabe, 2004). Although boys also worry about being too heavy, males may have another concern: They want to build their muscles up—spending hours at the gym, perhaps using protein powders and anabolic steroids to increase their body mass (Field and others, 2005; Harvey & Robinson, 2003; McCabe & Ricciardelli, 2005; McCreary & Sasse, 2000; Nishizawa and others, 2003; Ricciardelli & McCabe, 2004).

During puberty, children of both sexes get attuned to every facial flaw. But unlike girls, this teenage boy may decide "I'm too thin" and try to spend time building up his muscles.

Estelle Rancurel / Getty Images

These preoccupations may be promoted in part by biological forces. As you will see in the next chapter, the hormones of puberty make children intensely self-conscious. But a variety of environmental influences are also involved. Teenagers tend to become more interested in dieting and building up their muscles when they start dating. Another force that sets off the pressure to diet is being teased by one's family and friends: "You're getting a little chunky; isn't it time to lose weight?" (Barker & Galambos, 2003; Compian, Gowen, & Hayward, 2004; McCabe & Ricciardelli, 2003).

Especially influential culprits are the media (Field and others, 2005; Wiseman, Sunday, & Becker, 2005). In one typical experiment, researchers asked a group of teenage girls to watch TV ads featuring fashion models. Compared to a control group who watched commercials that were not appearance-oriented, the girls exposed to ultra-thin models were suddenly dissatisfied with their bodies (Hargreaves & Tiggemann, 2003). In a comparable study in which male college students viewed clothing worn by male models, they experienced similar emotions. So *both* genders are vulnerable to feeling bad about themselves when they are exposed to the unrealistic, idealized media images of how people should look (Baird & Grieve, 2006).

A graphic example of the power of the media to change a whole culture's attitudes about weight occurred in a remote corner of the world—the island of Fiji, in Polynesia. In this society, where people always appreciated ample-sized women, eating disorders had been virtually unknown. Then, during the 1990s, a few years after television was introduced in a province on that island, teenage girls began to complain about being too fat and developed the same dieting concerns we have in the West (Becker and others, 2002).

Still, some U.S. children are more immune to the media messages. In Albert Bandura's social learning framework, these girls don't model the images on TV because they don't see those media models as "similar to myself." When one researcher asked African American and European American high school students to describe the models in women's magazines, both groups agreed that the media portrayed the female form in an unrealistic way (Milkie, 1999). However, African American girls rejected what they saw as "white culture," while European American girls admitted that they used the images as their standard for how to look, because, in their words, "this is what everybody cares about." As suggested earlier, African American girls have an emotional advantage entering puberty because they don't buy into the thin ideal. Black women are beautiful at many sizes!

There is a clear difference, however, between deciding "I need to lose some pounds" and being obsessed with losing weight. Many teenagers diet. Relatively few (about 1 in 10 teenage girls, depending on the survey) cross the line and develop an **eating disorder**, making being thin the sole focus of their lives. What transforms the decision to diet into a single-minded obsession that can actually end in death? For answers, let's look at the symptoms and causes of the two main eating disorders: anorexia and bulimia.

David Hancock

Although she might be horrified to know it, this British TV personality—on a visit to Fiji—may have unknowingly helped to infect her young female admirers with the Western dieting mania.

eating disorder A pathological obsession with getting and staying thin. The two best-known eating disorders are *anorexia nervosa* and *bulimia nervosa*.

[**FAQ:** How do eating disorders develop?]

George Simhoni / Masterfile

Because most African Americans don't buy into the idea that the key to beauty lies in being slim, they can be joyous and comfortable with bodies that come in many sizes.

Eating Disorders

anorexia nervosa A potentially life-threatening eating disorder characterized by pathological dieting (resulting in severe weight loss and extreme thinness) and by a distorted body image.

Anorexia nervosa, the most serious eating disorder, affects roughly 1 in 1,000 teenagers, the vast majority of whom are girls. To qualify, a person must have starved to the point of being 85 percent of ideal body weight or less. (This means that if your ideal weight for your height is 110 pounds, you now weigh *under* 95 pounds [American Academy of Pediatrics, Committee on Adolescence, 2003].) A basic feature of this disorder—among both girls and boys—is a distorted body image (Gila and others, 2005; Skrzypek, Wehmeier, & Remschmidt, 2001). Even when people look skeletal, they feel fat and are driven to cut their food intake down to virtually nothing. A child or adult with anorexia may consume a single pea for lunch, misuse laxatives, and continuously exercise.

Anorexia becomes life-threatening when the person's food intake can no longer support vital functions (Herzog and others, 1999). When she reaches two-thirds of her ideal weight or less, that's a signal the child needs to be hospitalized and fed—by force, if necessary—to stave off death (Rome and others, 2003; American Academy of Pediatrics, Committee on Adolescence, 2003). A student of mine last semester, who now runs a self-help group for people with eating disorders at our university, provided a vivid reminder of the enduring physical toll anorexia can cause. Alicia informed the class that she had permanently damaged her heart muscle during her teenage bout with this devastating disease.

bulimia nervosa An eating disorder characterized by cycles of bingeing and purging (by inducing vomiting or taking laxatives) in an obsessive attempt to lose weight.

Bulimia nervosa is a less life-threatening problem because the child's weight often stays within a normal range. However, because this disorder involves bingeing (periodic eating sprees in which thousands of calories may be consumed in a matter of hours) and purging (getting rid of the food by inducing vomiting), bulimia can also seriously compromise health. In addition to producing deficiencies of basic nutrients, the purging episodes can cause mouth sores, ulcers in the esophagus, and the loss of enamel in the teeth as a result of the child's throat and mouth being continuously exposed to stomach acid (Rome and others, 2003; American Academy of Pediatrics, Committee on Adolescence, 2003).

These two diseases seem to have different cultural dynamics. Although anorexia rates have stayed relatively stable, in recent decades the prevalence of bulimia has dramatically increased. Therefore, bulimia qualifies as a mental disorder unique to the contemporary developed world. While in different cultures and historical times vulnerable teenagers may have developed other emotional problems, in our weight-obsessed society they "choose" bulimia today (Keel & Klump, 2003).

Because in the past it was almost always upper-middle-class girls who developed eating disorders, psychologists traditionally viewed the person's search for perfection and anger at authority figures as the causes. Bombarded by pressures to be perfect, they reasoned, the girl unconsciously gets back at her rejecting, controlling parents by choosing to be "perfect" at controlling her weight (Muuss, 1986). However, anorexia and now bulimia have migrated well beyond middle-class female teenagers, appearing in more boys and in every socioeconomic group. They are leaking out to affect elementary school children, too (Rome and others, 2003).

Actually, behavioral-genetics studies show that there is a hereditary component to the drive to be thin, especially in girls (Keski-Rahkonen and others, 2005). This does not rule out a nature-plus-nurture combination, however. Girls who develop eating disorders are more likely to report having tense family interactions (Swarr & Richards, 1996). Not infrequently, their parents also have their own "issues" about weight. What may happen is that girls who are biologically susceptible to developing eating disorders tend to have parents, particularly mothers, who have their own troubled attitudes about thinness and who nag their daughters about weight: "What are you eating? You don't need that dessert!" (Pike & Rodin, 1991). This environmental pressure tends to push temperamentally vulnerable children over the line.

At bottom, however, eating disorders reflect far more than simply problems with eating. They are a symptom of a general tendency to be anxious and depressed (Johnson & Wardle, 2005). Studies show that elementary school girls who go on to

This young woman, who was rushed to the hospital weighing 62 pounds, needs to get on the scale backwards because, if she gains even a pound, her distorted body image may cause her to feel "fat" and refuse to eat anything.

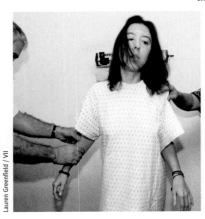

Lauren Greenfield / VII

Now that we know the diagnostic categories and risk factors for eating disorders, it's time to get an insider's perspective. Here is what Mary, a counselor at my university's women's center, told me when we sat down to chat about her clients with eating disorders:

With eating disorders, denial is big. A lot of times, people won't bring their problem in as the issue that troubles them but, after talking for a while, they finally feel comfortable enough to say that they abuse laxatives or exercise incessantly. Sometimes a person talks seemingly innocently and I'm thinking:"Hmm, sounds like you have an eating disorder."

You won't find it in the standard diagnostic criteria, but to me the key is, "Is this person's self-worth defined by how much she weighs?" Also, with eating disorders the whole day focuses around what the person is going to eat. Because secrecy is involved, a fair amount of planning goes into a binge. A person might go to the drive-through at six fast food restaurants to hide the fact that she is buying six meals that she will eat right now.

So there's the obsession about obtaining the food, the obsession about what the food is going to be, and the obsession about weight. Gaining half a pound becomes a crisis. Losing half a pound makes the person's day. People often have a magic number where everything in life is going to fall into place. Sometimes

I get a call from a client who says, "I always thought if I weighed such-and-such everything would be OK." Then they do a reality check and say, "I think I need help."

It's a progressive disease. You start out bingeing and purging once every few weeks. Somebody who is pretty well into the illness will be doing it several days a week. A good day is when you fight the urge. A bad day is when you skip class or put your kid at the babysitter so you can binge and purge all day. Every case is individual, but I feel at the core of all eating disorders is the sense that "I'm not good enough." I frequently find people have controlling parents who don't let them make decisions, telling them exactly what to wear, exactly what to eat: "You have to make 'our family' look good, get the highest grades, be in such-and-such activity." You are not allowed to have problems. "Everything's OK in this family." These are people who are used to being controlled by everyone—parents, boyfriends. They don't have the concept of directing their life. They come in saying, "I hate to take up your time but my boyfriend wants me to be here."

My goal is to have them take control of their life. We work on self-esteem issues, a sense of having value. Most people are more than willing to talk about how worthless a person they are. So that's my opening. It's a slow process. The most gratifying experience is seeing people grow, become assertive, take responsibility for their lives.

develop eating disorders as teenagers are prone to making negative comparisons: "I'm less popular, less good-looking than so-and-so" (Leon and others, 1999; Ricciardelli & McCabe, 2004; Stice & Whitenton, 2002). At the core of an eating disorder lies low *self-efficacy*—a sense of being helpless and out of control of one's life. (See my interview with the women's center counselor in the Experiencing the Lifespan box.)

Unfortunately, even when a teenager recovers from her problem, this general sense of insecurity can persist. In one longitudinal study, even though they had been described as "cured" of their problem, women who had had an eating disorder as teens suffered from unusually low self-esteem well into their emerging-adult years (Striegel-Moore, Seeley, & Lewinsohn, 2003).

Table 8.2 offers a summary of these various influences in a checklist for determining if a person has serious body dissatisfaction. If these forces ring true for you or someone you love, a few strategies that might help are given on the next page.

At this clinic in Florida, teenagers and women with eating disorders participate in group therapy to learn how to cope with their anxiety and reduce the feelings of low self-efficacy that are at the root of their debilitating symptoms.

TABLE 8.2: Is a Teenager at Risk for Serious Body Dissatisfaction? A Checklist

(Background influences: Has this child reached puberty? Is this child female, European American, and dating?)

1. Is this child temperamentally prone to anxiety and depression?
2. Does this child suffer from low self-esteem?
3. Is being pencil-thin this child's ideal?
4. Have friends and family members repeatedly teased this child about her weight?
5. Is this child under intense pressure from her mother to be thin?
6. Does this child rely heavily on the images on TV or fashion models for her standard of how to look ?
7. Is this child becoming obsessed with dieting?

INTERVENTIONS: Improving Teenagers' Body Image

Our discussion shows that some dissatisfaction with one's body is normal. We cannot expect girls (and now boys) to be immune from a society that asks human beings to try to reshape their bodies to fit an unattainable goal (Brownell, 1991).

Our first impulse might be to teach children that their appearance doesn't matter. What really counts are inner qualities such as being kind and smart. But this may be impossible when the wider world is saying otherwise, and, as we saw from Harter's research, feeling satisfied with our looks looms critically important in determining our self-esteem. What we can say is that society's "standards" are less objective than they appear. Furthermore, how we feel about ourselves is crucial in shaping our physical appeal.

In one study in which researchers tried to examine whether physically attractive people are happier, they had a surprising amount of trouble getting raters to agree on who was good-looking and who was not (Diener, Wolsic, & Fujita, 1995). These difficulties in getting consistent ratings were most apparent when the method the study authors used was not still photographs but videos—that is, when the raters evaluated people as they "came alive," or behaved in real life. The message seems to be that beauty is more in the eye of the beholder than we might think. Moreover, our personality as it shines forth in action may take over, making reliable ratings based on so-called objective visual cues particularly difficult. After meeting someone and having a conversation, haven't you ever had the insight, "She's far from good-looking, but she's one of the *most* attractive people I've ever met"?

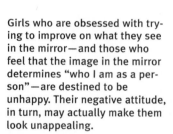

Lauren Greenfield / VII Photo

Girls who are obsessed with trying to improve on what they see in the mirror—and those who feel that the image in the mirror determines "who I am as a person"—are destined to be unhappy. Their negative attitude, in turn, may actually make them look unappealing.

[FAQ: What interventions have shown positive results in helping teens at risk for eating disorders?]

How can we convince teenagers (or anyone else) that who they are as people is very important in determining their physical appeal? The good news is that many boys and girls intuitively grasp this idea. When Harter (1999) surveyed a group of teenagers about how they viewed the connection between looks and self-esteem, about 60 percent said they believed that the external image shaped their feelings: "When I look in the mirror and don't like what I see, I feel bad about myself." The other 40 percent said: "When I am feeling upset and look in the mirror, I don't like the way I look." Teenagers who adopted the idea that there is an "objective image" out there were much more likely to feel vulnerable, out of control, and dissatisfied with their appearance. Those who understood that their feelings about themselves determined what they (and others) saw were more upbeat about both their looks and their lives.

This finding may explain why programs designed to prevent adolescent eating disorders that use hands-on exercises to teach children the message that "I am in control of my own beauty" have been remarkably effective. It's particularly important to inoculate girls against the media images that equate beauty with being pencil thin and to give them a sense of self-efficacy about their own ability to determine how they look (Stice & Shaw, 2003). This need to empower children of *both* sexes to resist outside pressures also looms large as we turn now to explore the final topic in this chapter, sexuality.

✿ TYING IT ALL TOGETHER

1. Kimberly, an eleventh grader, tells you, "I am ugly," but knows she is terrific in sports and academics. According to Harter's studies, Kimberly

    a. probably has high self-esteem.

    b. probably has low self-esteem.

    c. may or may not have low self-esteem.

2. Daniel works out at the gym, trying to build up his muscle mass. Amy is regularly on a diet, trying for that Barbie doll figure. Jasmine, who is far below her ideal body weight, is always exercising and has cut her food intake down to virtually nothing. Sophia, whose weight is normal, goes on periodic eating sprees followed by purges. Identify which *two* of these teenagers have a genuine eating disorder, and name each person's specific problem.

3. Your teenage daughter says, "Mom, I look in the mirror and think I'm fat and ugly." According to this chapter, what should your response be?

   a. "Looks don't matter—you've got brains and you're a good person, and those are the things that really count."
   b. "It's all in your power. If you feel really good about yourself as a human being, you'll feel like you look good, and other people will see you as attractive."
   c. "It's all in your power. Just lose all that extra weight and you'll look great!"

4. You are an adolescent specialist interested in setting up a prevention program for teens at risk of developing eating disorders. Devise a checklist to identify people who would be most likely to benefit from your program.

Answers to the Tying It All Together questions can be found in the answers section of the book.

Sexuality

548: Immculate ros: Sex sex sex that all you think about?

559: Snowbunny: people who have sex at 16 r sick:

560: Twonky: I agree

564: ooooCaFfEinNe; no sex until ur happily married—Thtz muh rule

566: Twonky: I ag4ree with that too.

567: Snowbunny: me too caffine!

(quoted in Subrahmanyam, Greenfield, & Tynes, 2004, p. 658)

Sex is the elephant in the room of teenage life. Everyone knows it's a top-ranking issue, but the adult world shies away from even mentioning it. Celebrated in the media, ignored (or condemned) by society, the minefield issue of when and whether to have sex is left for teenagers to decide on their own as they filter through the intense conflicting messages and—as you can see above—vigorously stake out their positions in on-line chats.

It is a minefield issue that contemporary young people negotiate in different ways. Take a poll of your classmates. Some people, as with the teenagers quoted above, may advocate abstinence, believing that everyone should remain a virgin until marriage. Others are likely to believe that having sex within a loving relationship is fine. Some students, if they are being honest, will admit, "I want to try out the sexual possibilities, but I promise to use contraception!"

This increasing acceptability (within limits) of carving out our own personal sexual path was highlighted in a 50-year longitudinal survey of a U.S. high school senior class, shown in Figure 8.7 (on page 260). Notice that the major changes in the acceptability of having intercourse as a teenager occurred after the sexual revolution of the 1960s (see the changes in seniors' ideas from 1950 to 1975). However, as you can see in the 2000 survey, our attitudes are still evolving in some interesting ways (Caron & Moskey, 2002). By the turn of this century, more young people—and, more important, many more *parents*—believed that it was acceptable for teenagers to have intercourse. But more teenagers than ever feel that they can decide to *not* have sex and still be popular and grown-up. Teenagers are confident of being able to resist the pressure from their romantic partners and wait to have sex until they are married. They now say that when they do have intercourse, they

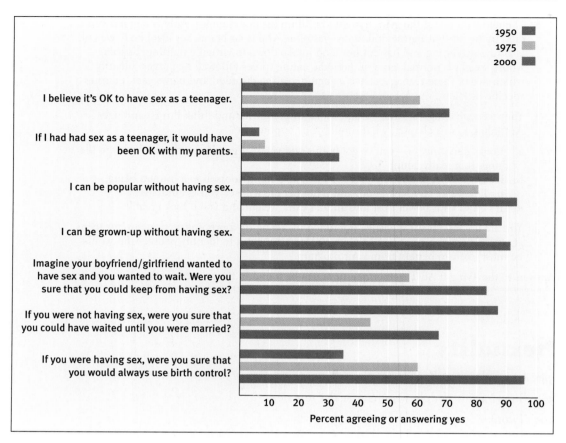

FIGURE 8.7:
Percentage of high school seniors agreeing with various ideas about sex in 1950, 1975, and 2000: Notice from this chart that in 2000, teenagers felt more confident about being able to chart their own sexual path than their counterparts in 1975 did. How would you have answered these questions as a senior in high school?

Source: Adapted from Caron & Moskey (2002), p. 520.

[FAQ: When do we first feel sexual desire?]

will always use birth control. How are these encouraging attitudes being translated into action? Let's begin our exploration of teenage sexual practices in the United States at the starting gate—with desire.

Exploring Sexual Desire

> David, age 14: *Since a year or so ago, I just think about sex and masturbation ALL THE TIME! I mean I just think about having sex no matter where I am and I'm aroused all the time. Is that normal?*
>
> Expert's reply: *Welcome to the raging hormones of adolescence!*
>
> (adapted from a teenage sexuality on-line advice forum)

At what age does sexual desire begin? Although scientists had long assumed that the answer was probably in the middle of puberty, when testosterone is pumping through the body, research with homosexual adults caused them to rethink this idea. When gay women and men were asked to recall a watershed event in their lives—the age when they first realized that they were physically attracted to a person of the same sex—their responses centered around age 10. At that age the output of the adrenal androgens is rising but testosterone production has not yet fully geared up (McClintock & Herdt, 1996). So our first sexual feelings seem to be programmed by the adrenal androgens and appear well before we undergo the visible changes of puberty, by about fourth grade!

How do sex hormone levels relate to the intensity of teenagers' sexual interests? According to researchers, we need a threshold androgen level to prime our initial feelings of sexual desire (Udry, 1990; Udry & Campbell, 1994; Halpern and others, 1993). Then signals from the environment feed back to heighten the interest in sex. As children see their bodies changing, they begin to think of themselves in a new, sexual way.

Having a boy look at you at the community pool or noticing men watching you as you walk down the street—these experiences help stimulate androgen production and cause intense feelings of sexual desire.

Reaching puberty evokes a different set of signals from the outside world. A ninth-grade boy finds love notes in his locker. A seventh-grade girl notices men looking at her differently as she walks down the street. It is the physical changes of puberty and how outsiders react to those changes that usher us fully into our lives as sexual human beings. Now let's look directly at which young people begin to act on those desires by having intercourse as teens.

[FAQ: How many teens are having sex?]

Who Is Having Intercourse?

Today, the average age of first intercourse in the United States is the late teens. But about one out of four teenagers has begun to have sex by age 15 (Klein and Committee on Adolescence, 2005).

As developmental systems theory suggests, a variety of forces predict what researchers call the *transition to intercourse*. One influence, for both boys and girls, is biological—being on an earlier puberty timetable (Lam and others, 2002). There's also a social class and ethnic difference, with low-SES children and African American girls and boys, on average, becoming sexually active at younger ages (Brewster, 1994; Browning, Leventhal, & Brooks-Gunn, 2005; Rowe & Rogers, 1994).

In predicting who is having sex as a teenager, we might also look to a person's television viewing practices for clues. Developmentalists asked more than 1,000 sexually inexperienced teenagers about the kinds of TV programs they watched. A year later, they returned to question the same group of teens about their sexual activities. The researchers found that *even when they controlled for every other factor*, they could predict which boys and girls were more likely to have become sexually active just from their prior TV-watching practices. Teens who reported watching a heavy diet of programs rated high in sexually oriented talk were twice as likely to have had intercourse in the intervening year as the children who did not (Collins and others, 2004).

Should we blame TV programs oversaturated with sexual innuendos for *causing* teenagers to start having sex? A bidirectional influence is probably in operation here. If a teenager is *already* very interested in sex, that boy or girl will gravitate toward watching programs that fit this passion. For me, the tip-off was raiding my parents' library to read the steamy scenes in that forbidden book, D.H. Lawrence's *Lady Chatterley's Lover*. Today, parents know that their daughter has entered a different mental space when she abandons the Discovery Channel in favor of *Sex and the City* DVDs. (For boys, it's when your passion shifts from playing video games to watching video porn.) Swimming in this sea of media sex would then naturally further inflame a teenager's desires.

Television, however, is doing more than simply stoking teenagers' passions. It seems to be changing their perceptions, making them inflate the amount of sex that is happening in real life. Children who watch sexually oriented TV programs are more likely to think that their friends are having intercourse, even when they really aren't (Brown, Halpern, & L'Engle, 2005; Eggermont, 2005; Rich, 2005).

Although his mother may be well aware of what her teenage son is thinking when he reads *Playboy*, she may not realize that her child's obsession with reading this magazine may actually predict his making the transition to having sexual intercourse.

To learn whether their daughters are sexually active, European American parents might try to find out about the sexual activities of these best friends. For Latino parents, knowing that your daughter has a boyfriend alerts them to the fact that she may be in the danger zone.

This brings up the crucial influence of peers. As suggested earlier in our discussion of early-maturing girls, we can predict a teenager's—particularly a female teenager's—chance of having intercourse by looking at the company she chooses. Having an older boyfriend (or girlfriend) dramatically raises the chance of becoming sexually active during the early teens (Marin & others, 2006). In one study, developmentalists discovered that if a virgin girl's two best friends were nonvirgins, they could predict that the girl would have made the transition to intercourse within the next year (Billy & Udry, 1985). However, there is an interesting ethnic difference. This "look to her best friends" principle may apply only to European American girls, not to African American or Latina teens. One researcher found that for Latina girls, the only tip-off as to whether a child was engaging in sexual activity is: "Is my daughter beginning to date?" (Cavanagh, 2004).

Studies show that there tends to be a progression over time from breast fondling to genital contact to intercourse (O'Sullivan & Brooks-Gunn, 2005). Latino parents tend to be stricter with their daughters than with their sons—often forbidding dating until age 16. But when these girls do start dating, they seem to plunge rapidly into deep romantic relationships and having intercourse (Raffaelli, 2005). So for Latina teens the very act of having a boyfriend—and possibly being pressured by that romantic partner—is the main force propelling becoming sexually involved.

This image of boyfriends seducing their girlfriends leads us to that major category of adolescent you may have been thinking of when you imagined who is more likely to be having sex as a teen. It's got to be boys!

FOCUS ON A TOPIC: ## THE SEXUAL DOUBLE STANDARD

> *It's different for boys, it's like . . . if they have sex with somebody and then they are rewarded . . . and all the guys are just like "That's great!" You have sex, and you're a girl and its like "Slut." That's how it is . . .*

(quoted in Martin, 1996, p. 86)

sexual double standard A cultural code that gives men greater sexual freedom than women. Specifically, society expects males to want to have intercourse and expects females to remain virgins until they marry and to be more interested in relationships than in having sex.

These complaints from a 16-year-old girl named Erin refer to the well-known **sexual double standard.** Boys are expected to want sex; girls are supposed to resist. Teenage boys get considerable reinforcement for "getting to home base." Intercourse is fraught with ambivalence and danger for girls: "Should I do it? Will he love me if I do it? Will he love me if I don't? Will I get pregnant? What will my friends and my parents think?" (Martin, 1996; Schwartz & Rutter, 1998; Tolman, 1999).

Is it really true, then, that teenage boys are more likely to be having sex than teenage girls? If we look at the statistics relating to African American and Latino adolescents, the answer is yes. But in a recent national survey of high school seniors, more European American girls (45 percent) reported having had sex than European American boys (41 percent) (Child Trends, 2005c). The fact that a majority of European American boys in the United States are still virgins by at least age 17 suggests that there is something wrong with seeing teenage boys as simply passionate to have sex.

Basic to the stereotype of the double standard is the idea that girls are looking for committed relationships and that boys mainly want sex. A rare study in which researchers actually interviewed an ethnically mixed group of boys undergoing puberty about their attitudes came to a very different conclusion (Tolman and others, 2004). Many of these eighth graders said that they wanted a girlfriend, but for the emotional connection. They seemed to be yearning for the kind of intimate relationship they could not get with their male friends. Read what one 13-year-old named Skater had to say:

> [I want] Someone with the same interests as me. . . . Not just like [a] makeout body, you know . . . , like you don't just hang around them to make out, you just hang around them like regular friends. . . . [And then he added that this relationship would be different] 'cause it would feel more open . . . we'd feel closer.
>
> (quoted in Tolman and others, 2004, p. 240)

Here is how another 13-year-old boy named Boo talked about his girlfriend of about a year:

> She's, like, one of the few people that actually like cares about me . . . I'm more able to tell her things. . . . Like, other people, like my other friends, they would just be, like, whatever, go away or I'll see you next week. [And then he added I'd be] lost [if we broke up].
>
> (quoted in Tolman and others, 2004, p. 240)

The boys in this study stressed the importance of needing to act macho when they were around their male friends. (Several mentioned that it was important to show that they wanted to "get some" in order to prove that they were not gay.) But they also expressed considerable ambivalence about just having sex.

And it's not just girls who feel bad when external pressures lead them to compromise their inner selves. One 13-year-old described his first French kiss (in a game of kiss or dare at a party) as "terrible, disgusting and nasty, 'cause like I didn't really want to. . . . It was like a big rip-off. . . . Like, 'cause it didn't mean anything, it was just, like, really dumb. [He pauses.] In a way, that's just, like, rude to myself" (quoted in Tolman and others, 2004, p. 246).

Yes, in surveys teenage boys report having sex as a higher priority in their relationships than do girls. But both teenage boys and girls put their highest priority on intimacy (Ott and others, 2006). It's really all about attachment and love—not just about raging hormones—for *both* sexes during the adolescent years.

Are male teenagers intensely interested in caring and closeness? The adoring expressions on the faces of this couple tell us that adolescent boys' love relationships involve far more than just physical desire.

Wrapping Up Sexuality: Contemporary Trends

In summary, teenagers today feel more comfortable about charting their own sexual path. Many feel free *not* to become sexually active. Boys are reporting that they are primarily interested in a relationship, not "just having sex." These changes are reflected in the encouraging statistics you can see in Figure 8.8: fewer U.S. teenagers having intercourse; lower rates of teenage pregnancy; more adolescents reporting using condoms when they last did have sex.

Still, with 4 out of every 10 girls getting pregnant before age 20, the United States remains the teenage pregnancy capital of the Western world (Klein and the Committee on Adolescence, 2005). Moreover, the decline in rates of intercourse has been accompanied by a rise in the prevalence of oral sex. In 2002, one out of every four teenagers who reported never having had intercourse said that they had engaged in oral sex (Child Trends Data Bank, 2005b).

Young people report many advantages to making this choice. As only a minority of teenagers define oral sex as "real" sex, teenagers who engage in oral sex can still say

FIGURE 8.8: **Some new trends in teenage sexuality from national U.S. surveys:** The news about teenage sex is good! Fewer young people are having intercourse, the teenage pregnancy rate is at an historic low, and more sexually active adolescents report using condoms.

Source: Centers for Disease Control and Prevention (2006).

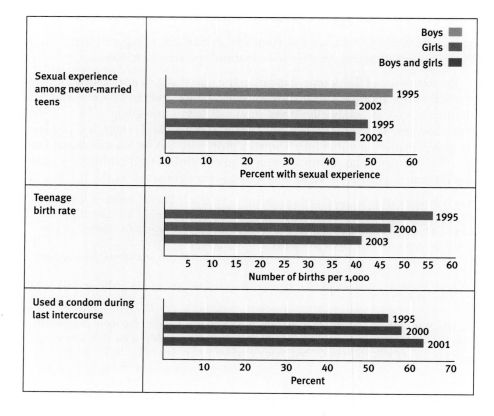

How likely is this couple to progress from making out to having intercourse? If they are affluent and live in the United States, they may put their limit at oral sex, so they can say that they are still virgins.

that they are virgins (Pitts & Rahman, 2001). Obviously, oral sex eliminates at least one major risk: You can't get pregnant. Young people also see oral sex as less emotionally dangerous: There's less potential for getting hurt, less chance of getting a bad reputation and feeling guilty or bad about oneself (Halpern-Felsler and others, 2005). Interestingly, the teenagers most likely to report only oral sex experience are the very young people who might feel that having intercourse would be a special threat. Oral sex is most popular among affluent, upper-middle-class teens (Child Trends Data Bank, 2005a).

How do you feel about this new trend toward oral sex? Do you see it as an example of a dangerous practice and a new route to low female self-esteem, as it's typically boys who get the benefits of this activity? Or do you see it as an intelligent way of dealing with a body that wants to "just say yes" when society is saying no?

INTERVENTIONS: Toward Teenager-Friendly Sex Education

All of this leads us back to the issue alluded to in our discussion of puberty: the best way to educate teenagers about sex. Given that many adolescents today see oral sex as a guilt-free alternative to intercourse, we need to stress that this activity does carry the risk of getting a sexually transmitted disease (STD). At a minimum, any sex education program adults develop should be sensitive to the complex attitudes, feelings, and perceptions that contemporary teenagers bring to their exciting, emerging new sexual selves.

Unfortunately, however, many sex education courses in the United States focus on urging teens to "just say no." Today, in 21 states, public school sex education programs are required by law to heavily stress abstinence (Guttmacher Institute, 2006). Programs often begin in high school—too late for many early-maturing girls—and often focus on issues such as preventing AIDS or STDs. Teenagers want more from these courses than mere moralizing or memorizing a frightening list of sexually transmitted diseases. Consider, for instance, this comment from a girl named Kristin when she was asked what a sex education class should teach:

> *Umm what are the right circumstances and wrong circumstances to have sexual inter-course. . . . But umm, I think they should learn about what emotional steps they should go through to see if they are prepared to have sexual intercourse.*
>
> (quoted in Martin, 1996, p. 124)

Another 16-year-old, named Tracy, added that in her sex education course,

> *They just taught, like, VD and stuff like. . . . Maybe they could have stressed more, talked about relationships or something. 'Cause when I [started] high school, . . . I had no clue of what boys were like, you know.*
>
> (quoted in Martin, 1996, p. 125)

So, with sex education, what teenagers are really hungering for is information about *relationships*, not just information about sex.

Table 8.3 pulls together this section's insights by spelling out some considerations in devising a teenage sexuality program. Although contemporary young people in the United States are doing far better at negotiating the minefield of sexual choices than teenagers were a few decades ago, clearly the adult world can do more to help.

TABLE 8.3: Designing a Teenager-Friendly Sex Education Program: A Section Summary Table

---

1. Explore the sexual attitudes and beliefs of your group of teens, and tailor your interventions to those varying attitudes.

2. Provide realistic information about who is having sex to counter the unrealistic TV and movie images.

3. Design your interventions to fit the ethnic realities of your group. While fostering a culture of responsible sexuality is important for everyone, for European American girls direct your interventions to the role of influences from other girls; for Latinas, stress that having "a boyfriend" doesn't mean you should have sex.

4. As every girl could benefit from interventions focused on increasing self-efficacy, build in the message that "you have control of your body," and offer role-playing practice in how to assert oneself to say no in sexual situations.

5. Don't neglect boys. Pay special attention to teaching boys to resist the peer pressure to be "players."

6. Design your program to fit the group norms. Is having oral sex standard practice in this population? If so, explicitly discuss this issue rather than focusing solely on intercourse.

7. Go beyond providing information just about sex. Teach teens about handling *relationships*.

Final Thoughts

Any program to help teenagers cope with their changing bodies and emerging sexual feelings has to take into account what teenagers are really like "as people." Are adolescents really emotionally vulnerable, more prone to take risks and to get into trouble, as the stereotypes of teenagerhood suggest? What new reasoning capacities emerge as children leave childhood behind? In the next chapter, we turn to these topics as we explore cognition and personality during the teenage years. ■

TYING IT ALL TOGETHER

1. As a parent, you are determined to talk to your children about sex when they are experiencing their *first* sexual feelings. What should your target age be?

   a. Around age 10, when the output of the adrenal androgens is rising
   b. Around age 12, when testosterone levels are rising
   c. Around age 10, when the output of testosterone is rising

2. Your friend, a European American mother, thinks her teenage daughter may be having sex and asks for your opinion. All the following questions are relevant for you to ask this friend *except*

   a. Is your daughter's best friend having sex?
   b. Is your daughter's school teaching abstinence?
   c. Is your daughter obsessed with watching sexually oriented TV shows?
   d. Does your daughter have an older boyfriend?

3. Tom is discussing recent trends in teenage sex. He should mention all of the following *except*

   a. Today, more teenage boys than girls—in every ethnic group—have sex during high school.
   b. Teenagers today feel freer to say no to sex.
   c. Today, rates of teenage intercourse are down.
   d. Today, oral sex may be a substitute for intercourse, especially among affluent kids.

4. Based on what you have learned in this chapter, in a sentence spell out how you would change the current focus of U.S. sex education classes to make these programs genuinely responsive to teenagers' needs.

Answers to the Tying It All Together questions can be found in the answers section of the book.

■ SUMMARY

Puberty

Today, the physical changes of **puberty** occur during early adolescence, and there can be decades between the time children physically mature and the time they fully enter adult life. Because in agrarian societies a person's changing body used to be the signal to get married, many cultures devised **puberty rites** to welcome the physical changes. The **secular trend in puberty** has magnified the separation between puberty and full adulthood, the fact that **menarche** (and **spermarche**) have been occurring at much younger ages.

Two hormonal command centers program puberty. The adrenal glands produce **adrenal androgens** starting in middle childhood. The **HPG axis,** the main system that sets the bodily changes in motion, involves the hypothalamus, the pituitary, and the **gonads** (ovaries and testes), which produce estrogens and **testosterone** (found in both males and females). Leptin levels and a variety of environmental influences trigger the initial hypothalamic hormone.

The physical changes of puberty are divided into **primary sexual characteristics, secondary sexual characteristics,** and **the growth spurt.** Although in females puberty begins with the growth spurt and menarche occurs late in the process, the rate and sequence of this total-body transformation varies from child to child. Because for males the externally visible changes of puberty occur later and the organs of reproduction are the first to start developing, the puberty timetables of the sexes are not as far apart as they appear to be.

The striking individual differences in the timing of puberty are mainly genetically programmed. African American children tend to reach puberty at a younger age. Being overweight is tied to reaching puberty earlier. Puberty may be accelerated by childhood stress. Growing up in a single-mother family has also been linked to developing at an earlier than average age.

How children feel about their changing bodies varies, depending on the social environment. Breast development often evokes positive emotions. Menstruation produces ambivalence; first ejaculation is rarely talked about. Mothers tend to discuss puberty with their daughters, but sons are left more in the dark about the changes. Children tend to be embarrassed about their changing bodies when they are around the parent of the opposite sex.

Girls who mature early are at greater risk of getting into trouble as teens (for example, taking drugs, getting pregnant, or doing poorly in school) because they get involved with older friends. Because they often end up heavier and shorter, these girls tend to have a poor body image and are more prone to be anxious and depressed. Research shows that it is better for *all* children to attend a school that offers K–8 education during this time of dramatic body change.

Parents need to talk about puberty with their children, especially their sons. We need to be alert to the potential for problems with early-maturing girls, and schools should be structured to provide the best person–environment fit for adolescents undergoing puberty. We need better, more sensitive education about puberty in schools.

Body Image Issues

How children feel about their looks is closely tied to their overall self-esteem. Girls tend to feel worse about their looks than boys do, partly because society expects women to be unrealistically thin. At puberty many girls start to diet. Boys sometimes diet and also tend to focus on building up their muscle mass. Media images play an important role in causing teenage body dissatisfactions.

The **eating disorders** called **anorexia nervosa** (severe underweight resulting from obsessive dieting) and **bulimia nervosa** (chronic bingeing and, often, purging) are most likely to strike middle-class teenage girls. Genetic tendencies, parental pressures to be thin, and, especially, a general feeling of low self-efficacy are at the core of these problems. We need to convince children that beauty is less "objective" than it appears and that how people feel about themselves is important in determining their physical appeal. We also need to inoculate teenagers against the destructive media images that promote unrealistic ideals of slimness.

Sexuality

Studies suggest that teenagers today feel freer to make their own sexual decisions, including whether or not to begin to have intercourse. While sexual desire is triggered by the adrenal androgens and first switches on around age 10, sexual signals from the outside world feed back to cause children to really become interested in sex.

Forces that predict making the transition to intercourse include being on an earlier puberty timetable; watching sexy TV programs; having a best friend who has become sexually active (for European American girls); having an older boyfriend (for all girls); or simply having a boyfriend (for Latina girls). Although the **sexual double standard** suggests that boys just want sex and girls are interested in relationships, teenage boys are as interested in close relationships and love as girls are.

The good news about teenage sexuality in the United States is that rates of sexual activity and teenage pregnancy are dropping and fewer children are having intercourse during their high school years. However, more upper-middle-class U.S. teens than ever are engaging in oral sex. Sex education programs in high schools need to focus more on helping teenagers deal with relationships, rather than simply stressing abstinence or the risk of getting sexually transmitted diseases.

▮ KEY TERMS

puberty, p. 238

puberty rite, p. 240

secular trend in puberty, p. 241

menarche, p. 241

spermarche, p. 242

adrenal androgens, p. 242

HPG axis, p. 242

gonads, p. 242

testosterone, p. 242

primary sexual characteristics, p. 244

secondary sexual characteristics, p. 244

growth spurt, p. 244

eating disorder, p. 255

anorexia nervosa, p. 256

bulimia nervosa, p. 256

sexual double standard, p. 262

▮ RECOMMENDED RESOURCES

PUBERTY

Archibald, A.B., Graber, J.A., & Brooks-Gunn, J. (2003). Pubertal processes and physiological growth in adolescence. In G.R. Adams & M.D. Berzonsky (Eds.), *The Blackwell handbook of adolescence* (pp. 24–47). Ames, IA: Blackwell Publishing.

This excellent scholarly review article covers the physiology and psychology of puberty.

BODY IMAGE ISSUES

Brumberg, J. (1988). *Fasting girls*. Cambridge, MA: Harvard University Press.

This is a compelling social history of anorexia and the twentieth-century obsession with weight control.

Martin, K.A. (1996). *Puberty, sexuality and the self: Boys and girls at adolescence*. New York: Routledge.

This interesting, brief book is filled with quotes from the author's interviews with 55 adolescents who describe their feelings about puberty, their bodies, and sexuality.

Simmons, R., and Blyth, D. (1987). *Moving into adolescence*. Hawthorne, NY: Aldine.

This book describes the classic Milwaukee research on "moving through puberty" discussed in the text.

SEXUALITY

Tolman, D.L., Spencer, R., Harmon, T., Rosen-Reynoso, M., and Striepe, M. (2004). Getting close, staying cool: Early adolescent boys' experiences with romantic relationships. In N. Way & J.Y. Chu (Eds.), *Adolescent boys: Exploring diverse cultures of boyhood* (pp. 235–255). New York: New York University Press.

In this unique interview study, eighth-grade boys discuss their desire for intimacy and the social pressure to be "players," or macho men.

WEB SITE

The Guttmacher Institute: www. guttmacher.org

This organization's Web site is a wonderful source of information on research on adolescent sexuality and sex education programs in the United States.

CHAPTER 9

Cognitive and Socioemotional Development

Samantha's father began to worry when his daughter was in sixth grade. Suddenly, his sweet little princess was becoming so selfish, so moody, and so rude. She began to question everything, from her 10 o'clock curfew to why poverty exists. At the same time, she had to have clothes with exactly the right designer label and immediately buy the latest CD. She wanted to be a total individual, but her friends shaped every decision. She got hysterical if anyone looked at her the wrong way. Worse yet, Samantha was beginning to get in with a bad crowd—staying out all night; not doing her homework; cutting class.

Her twin brother, Sam, couldn't have been more different. Sam was obedient, an honor student, captain of the basketball team. He seemed to mellowly sail into his teenage years. Actually, Sam defied the categories. He was smart, a jock; he really had heart. Sam volunteered with disabled children. He effortlessly moved from the brains to the popular kids to the artsy "Goths" groups at school. Still, this model child could also give his parents palpitations. The most heart-stopping example happened when the police picked up Sam and a carload of buddies for drag racing on the freeway. Sam's puzzled explanation: "Something just took over and I stopped thinking, Dad."

If you looked beneath the surface, however, both of his children were really great. They were thoughtful, caring, and capable of having the deepest discussions about life. They simply seemed to get caught up in the moment and lose their minds—especially when they were with their friends. What really is going on in the teenage mind?

Think of our contradictory stereotypes about the teenage mind. Teenagers are supposed to be idealistic, thoughtful, and introspective; concerned with larger issues; pondering life in deeper ways; but also impulsive, moody, and out of control. We expect them to be the ultimate radicals, rejecting everything adults say, and the consummate conformists, dominated by the crowd, driven by the latest craze, totally influenced by their peers (Buchanan and others, 1990; Montemayor, 1983). In this chapter, we will make sense of these contradictory ideas.

Setting the Context: How High School Defined Adolescence into a Life Stage

Youth are heated by nature as drunken men by wine.

Aristotle (n.d.)

I would that there were no age between ten and twenty-three . . . , for there's nothing in between but getting wenches with child, wronging the ancientry, stealing, fighting. . . .

William Shakespeare, *The Winter's Tale*, Act III

As these quotations illustrate, throughout history, wise observers of human nature have described young people as being emotional, hotheaded, and out of control. When, in 1904, G. Stanley Hall first identified a new life stage characterized by **"storm and stress,"** which he called "adolescence," he was only echoing these timeless ideas. Moreover, as the mission of the young is to look at society in fresh, new ways, it makes sense that most cultures would view each new generation in ambivalent terms. They would praise young people for their energy and passion; they also would fear them as a menace and threat.

However, until fairly recently young people never had years to explore life or rebel against society, because they had to take on adult responsibilities at an early age. As you may remember from Chapter 1, adolescence only became a distinct stage of life in the United States during the 1930s, when—for most children—going to high school became routine (Goldscheider & Goldscheider, 1999; Mintz, 2004; Modell, 1989; Palladino, 1996).

Look into your family history, and you may find a great-grandparent who finished high school or went to college. However, a century ago, children in the United States often left school after sixth or seventh grade to find work (Mintz, 2004). But during the Great Depression of the 1930s, there was little work to actually find. Idle and at loose ends, many young people took to roaming the countryside, angry, demoralized, and depressed. Alarmed by the situation (and aware that in Germany similar disaffected youth were fueling Adolf Hitler's rise to power), the federal government took action. At the same time it instituted the Social Security system to provide for the elderly (to be discussed in Chapter 13), the Roosevelt administration implemented an ambitious national youth program to lure young people to school. The program worked. By 1939, 75 percent of all U.S. teenagers were attending high school.

Roosevelt's massive social experiment boosted the intellectual skills of a whole generation of Americans. But it produced a generation gap between these young people and their parents, many of whom had been first-generation immigrants, and led to our familiar adolescent culture, with its special hairstyles, music, and dress (Mintz, 2004; Modell, 1989). When teenagers spend their days with people their own age, they band together as a group with their own concerns. They see themselves as more of a "generation" (or, in developmental science terminology, a cohort), separate from the adult world.

This sense of a young generation reacting *against* society reached its height during the late 1960s and early 1970s. With "Never trust anyone over 30" as its slogan, the huge teenage baby-boom cohort rejected the conventional rules relating to marriage and gender roles and transformed the way we live our adult lives today.

"storm and stress" G. Stanley Hall's phrase for the intense moodiness, emotional sensitivity, and risk-taking tendencies that characterize the life stage he labeled *adolescence.*

As this famous 1930s photograph of a migrant family traveling across the arid Southwest to search for California jobs illustrates, during the Great Depression there was no chance to go to high school and no real adolescence because children had to work to support their families at a very young age.

LOC / SSPL / The Image Works

TABLE 9.1: **Stereotypes About Adolescence: True or False?**

T/F	1. Adolescents think about life in deeper, more thoughtful ways than children do.
T/F	2. Adolescence is when we begin to develop our personal moral code for living.
T/F	3. Adolescents are highly sensitive to what other people think.
T/F	4. Adolescents are unusually susceptible to peer influences.
T/F	5. Adolescents are highly emotional, compared to other age groups.
T/F	6. Adolescents are often emotionally disturbed.
T/F	7. Adolescents take more risks than do people in other age groups.
T/F	8. Parents find that adolescence is the "worst" life stage.
T/F	9. Adolescents reject their parents' basic ideas and worldviews.
T/F	10. Getting in with a bad crowd makes it more likely for teenagers to "go down the wrong path."

In the following pages, we explore the experience of being an adolescent in the contemporary developed world—a time in history when we expect to go to high school and can count on spending a decade or more insulated from adult life. For most of this chapter we look at the mysterious teenage mind, exploring why adolescents, like Samantha and Sam, seem both remarkably mature and immature. Then we turn to relationships, charting how teenagers separate from their parents and relate to one another in groups. At the end of this chapter we highlight a few problems facing the millions of young people growing up in areas of the world where teenagers still can't count on having a life stage called adolescence at all.

Before delving into our discussion, you might want to take the "Stereotypes About Adolescence: True or False?" quiz in Table 9.1. While you read this chapter, you can check out the truth of each of your ideas. You will also find answers to these questions at the end of the chapter, on page 299.

The Mysterious Teenage Mind

Thoughtful and introspective, but impulsive, moody, and out of control; peer-centered conformists and rebellious risk takers: Can teenagers *really* be all these things? In our search to explain these contradictions, let's first look at three classic theories of teenage thinking. Then we'll turn to the exciting research relating to teenage storm and stress.

Three Classic Theories of Teenage Thinking

Have a thoughtful conversation with a 16-year-old and a 10-year-old, and you are likely to be struck by the remarkable mental growth that occurs during adolescence. It's not so much that teenagers know much more than they did in fourth or fifth grade, but that adolescents *think* in a different way. With an elementary school child in the concrete operational stage you can have a rational talk about daily life. With a teenager you can have a rational talk about *ideas*. This ability to reason abstractly about concepts is the defining quality of Jean Piaget's formal operational stage (see Table 9.2 on the next page).

Formal Operational Thinking: Abstract Reasoning at Its Peak

Children in concrete operations are able to look beyond the way objects immediately appear. They realize that when Mommy puts on a mask, she's still Mommy "inside." They understand that when you pour a glass of juice or milk into a different-shaped glass, the amount of liquid remains the same. Piaget believed that when children

TABLE 9.2: Piaget's Stages: Focus on Adolescence

Age	Name of Stage	Description
0–2	Sensorimotor	The baby manipulates objects to pin down the basics of physical reality.
2–7	Preoperations	Children's perceptions are captured by their immediate appearances. "What they see is what is real." They believe, among other things, that inanimate objects are really alive and that if the appearance of a quantity of liquid changes (for example, if it is poured from a short, wide glass into a tall, thin one), the amount actually becomes different.
8–12	Concrete operations	Children have a realistic understanding of the world. Their thinking is really on the same wavelength as adults'. While they can reason conceptually about concrete objects, however, they cannot think abstractly in a scientific way.
12+	Formal operations	Reasoning is at its pinnacle: hypothetical, scientific, flexible, fully adult. Our full cognitive human potential has been reached.

formal operational stage Jean Piaget's fourth and final stage of cognitive development, reached at around age 12 and characterized by teenagers' ability to reason at an abstract, scientific level.

reach the **formal operational stage,** at around age 12, this ability to think abstractly takes a qualitative leap. Teenagers are able to reason logically in the realm of pure thought. Specifically, according to Piaget:

Adolescents can think logically about concepts and hypothetical possibilities. Ask a fourth- or fifth-grader to put objects such as sticks in order from small to large, and he will have no problem performing this *seriation* task. But present a child with a similar task verbally: "Bob is taller than Sam and Sam is taller than Bill. Who is the tallest?" and that boy or girl will be lost. The reason is that it's during adolescence when we first become capable of logically manipulating concepts in our minds (Elkind, 1968; Flavell, 1963).

Moreover, if you give a child in the concrete operational stage a reasoning task that begins, "Suppose snow is blue," she will probably refuse to go further, saying, "That's not true!" Adolescents in formal operations have no problem tackling that challenge, because once our thinking is liberated from concrete objects, we are comfortable reasoning about concepts that may *not* be real.

Adolescents can think like real scientists. When our thinking processes occur on an abstract plane, we have the capacity to approach problems in a genuinely scientific way. We can devise a strategy to rule out alternative interpretations and scientifically prove that something is true.

Piaget designed the following exercise to reveal the presence of this new scientific thought: He presented children with the pendulum apparatus you can see in Figure 9.1 and the set of four strings and different weights. Notice that two of the strings are shorter than the other two and that the bigger weights also differ in their heaviness. Their challenge, as described in the figure, was to find out which factor determined how quickly the pendulum swung from side to side. Was it the length of the string, the heaviness of the weight, or the height from which the string was released?

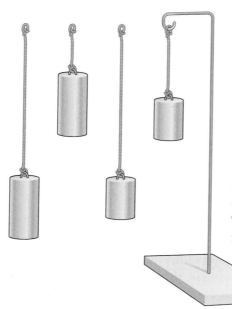

FIGURE 9.1: Piaget's pendulum apparatus: A task to assess whether children can reason scientifically: Piaget presents the child with the different weights and string lengths illustrated here and shows the boy or girl how to attach them to the pendulum (and to one another). Then he says, "Your task is to discover what makes the pendulum swing more or less rapidly from side to side—is it the length of the string, the heaviness of the weight, or the height (and force) from which you release the pendulum?" and watches to see what happens.

Step back and consider how to approach this problem and you will realize that the key lies in being systematic—in keeping everything constant but the factor whose influence you want to assess (recall our explanation of an experiment in Chapter 1). To test whether it's the heaviness of the weight, you must keep the string length and the height from which you drop it constant, varying only the weight. Then you need to isolate another variable, keeping everything else the same. And when you vary the length of the string keeping everything else the same, you will realize that the string length alone determines how quickly the pendulum moves.

The advances in scientific thinking that allow teenagers to solve the pendulum problem are the core qualities that make it possible for this University of Maryland undergraduate to be a real research collaborator in his professor's chemistry lab.

Elementary school children, Piaget discovered, approach such problems haphazardly. Only adolescents are capable of using this systematic strategy to find the solution to this task (Flavell, 1963; Ginsburg & Opper, 1969).

HOW DOES THIS CHANGE IN THINKING APPLY TO REAL LIFE? This new ability to think hypothetically and scientifically explains why it's not until we're in high school that we can thrill to a poetic metaphor or comprehend chemistry experiments (Kroger, 2000). It's only during high school that we have the capacity to join the debate team and argue the case for and against capital punishment, no matter what we *personally* believe. In fact, reaching the formal operational stage explains why teenagers are famous for debating *everything* in their lives. A 10-year-old who wants to stay up till 2 A.M. to watch a new video will just keep saying, "I don't want to go to bed." A teenager will lay out his case logically, point by point: "Mom, I got enough sleep last night. Besides, I only need six hours. I'll just be lying in bed with my eyes open. I can sleep after school tomorrow."

[FAQ: Do adolescents benefit in any way from their styles of thinking?]

Do *all* adolescents, however, really reach formal operations, in the sense of being able to reason using the scientific method? The answer is definitely no. When one developmentalist explored how people go about solving problems such as the pendulum task, she found that the metaphor of "real scientists" did not fit most *adults*. Worse yet, when asked to debate a controversial issue, such as capital punishment, many adults in this study simply restated the premise in different words. They did not even grasp the idea that they needed concrete data to back up their points (Kuhn, 1989).

Still, even if most people don't reason like real scientists or master debaters, at any age, we can vividly see the qualities involved in formal operational thinking when we look at how adolescents—especially older teenagers—reason about their *own lives*.

If you are a traditional emerging-adult student, you might think back to the complex organizational skills it took to get into college. You may have learned about your options from an adviser; researched each possibility on the Internet; visited campuses and talked to current students; and constructed different applications to showcase your talents. Then, when you got accepted, you needed to reflect on your future self again: "This school works in terms of finances, but is it too large for me? How will I feel about moving far from home?" Would you have been able to mentally weigh these different possibilities, and rationally project yourself into the future in this way, at age 10, 12, or even 14?

The bottom line is that reaching concrete operations allows us to be on the same wavelength as the adult world. Reaching formal operations allows us to *act* in the world like adults.

Discussing your plans with an adviser, filling out college applications, and realistically assessing your interests and talents involve the kind of future-oriented adult thinking that only becomes possible in late adolescence. So, even if they don't reason at the formal operational level on Piaget's laboratory tasks, these Portland, Maine, high school seniors are probably firmly formal operational in terms of thinking about their own lives.

Kohlberg's Stages of Moral Judgment: Developing Internalized Moral Values

This new ability to reflect on ourselves as people allows us to reflect on our personal values. Therefore, drawing on Piaget's theory, developmentalist Lawrence Kohlberg (1981, 1984) has argued that it is only during adolescence that we become capable of developing a moral code that guides our lives. To measure the presence of this moral code, Kohlberg constructed ethical dilemmas. He then had people reason about these scenarios and asked raters to chart the responses according to the three levels of moral thought that are outlined in Table 9.3. Before looking at the table, you might take a minute to respond to the "Heinz dilemma," the most famous problem on Kohlberg's test of moral judgment:

> *A woman was near death from cancer. One drug might save her. The druggist was charging . . . ten times what the drug cost him to make. The . . . husband, Heinz, went to everyone he knew to borrow the money but he could only get together about half of what it cost. [He] asked the . . . druggist to sell it cheaper or let him pay later. But the druggist said NO! Heinz broke into the man's store to steal the drug. . . . Should he have done that? Why?*

If you thought in terms of whether Heinz would be personally punished or rewarded for his actions, you would be classified as operating at the lowest level of morality, the **preconventional level.** Responses such as "Heinz should not take the drug because he will go to jail," or "Heinz should take the drug because if he does this good thing, then his wife will treat him well," suggest that—because your focus is solely on the external consequences for Heinz—you are not demonstrating *any* internalized moral sense.

If you made comments such as "Heinz should [or shouldn't] steal the drug because it's a person's duty to obey the law [or to stick up for his wife]" or "Yes, human life is sacred, but the rules must be obeyed," your response would be classified at the

preconventional level of morality In Lawrence Kohlberg's theory, the lowest level of moral reasoning, in which people approach ethical issues by considering the personal punishments or rewards of taking a particular action.

TABLE 9.3: **Kohlberg's Three Levels of Moral Reasoning, with Sample Responses***

Preconventional level:

Description: person operates according to a punishment-and-reward mentality

Reasons given for acting in a certain way : (1) to avoid being punished by the authorities; (2) to serve one's own interests, although the person also shows signs of recognizing that other people may have different interests

Examples: (1) Heinz shouldn't steal the drug because he will go to jail. (2) Heinz should steal the drug because his wife will love him more.

Conventional level:

Description: person's morality centers on the need to obey society's rules

Reasons given for acting in a certain way: (1) to be a "good person" in one's own and other people's eyes; (2) the need to keep the social system going and avoid a breakdown in society

Examples: (1) Heinz should steal the drug because that's what "a good husband" does; or, Heinz should not steal the drug because good citizens don't steal. (2) Heinz can't steal the drug—even though it might be best—because if one person decides to steal, so will another and then another and then the laws would all break down.

Postconventional level:

Description: person has a personal moral code that transcends society's rules

Reasons given for acting in a certain way: (1) talks about abstract concepts, such as taking care of the welfare of all people; (2) belief in universally valid moral principles that transcend anything society says

Examples: (1) Although it's wrong for Heinz to steal the drug, there are times when rules must be disobeyed to provide for people's welfare. (2) Heinz *must* steal the drug, because the obligation to save a human life transcends every other consideration.

---

*Within each general moral level, the reasons and examples numbered (1) reflect a slightly lower sub-stage of moral reasoning than those numbered (2).

Source: Adapted from Reimer, Paolitto, & Hersh, 1983.

conventional level—right where adults typically are. This shows your morality revolves around the need to uphold society's rules.

People who reason about this dilemma using their own moral guidelines *apart* from the rules of society are operating at Kohlberg's highest **postconventional level.** As the table shows, a response showing postconventional reasoning might be, "No matter what society says is wrong or right, Heinz had to steal the drug, because nothing outweighs the universal principle of saving a life."

When he conducted studies with children of different ages, Kohlberg discovered that at age 13, preconventional answers were universal in every culture. By the time they were 15 or 16, most children around the world were reasoning at the conventional level. Still, most of us stop right there. Although some adults advanced to thinking postconventionally, no one consistently reasoned at the highest stage on Kohlberg's different vignettes (Reimer, Paolitto, & Hersh, 1983; Snarey, 1985).

HOW DOES KOHLBERG'S THEORY APPLY TO REAL LIFE? Kohlberg's categories get us to think more deeply about our values. Do you have a moral code that guides your actions? Would you intervene, no matter what the costs, to save a person's life? They give us interesting insights into other people. While reading about Kohlberg's preconventional level, you might have thought: "I know someone just like this. This person has no sense of ethics. He only cares about whether or not he gets caught!"

Still, Kohlberg's research has been severely criticized. For one thing, as we just saw, if so few adults reason at Kohlberg's highest level, does a distinct stage of postconventional thought really exist? (See Modgil & Modgil, 1986; Reimer, Paolitto, & Hersh, 1983.) Critics have questioned the connection between talk and actions. Does how people reason in response to artificial scenarios really relate to the qualities, such as sympathy and self-efficacy, that predict acting prosocially in real life? (Recall our discussion in Chapter 6.) In fact, when a group of outstandingly prosocial teenagers—community leaders who set up programs for the homeless—took Kohlberg's test, researchers rated their answers at the very same conventional level as non-prosocial teens! (See Reimer, 2003.)

Concerns about the *validity of* Kohlberg's scale (does it actually predict real-world morality?) are heightened when we look around. All of us know people who can spout the highest ethical principles, but in reality behave pretty despicably: the minister who lectures his congregation about the sanctity of marriage while cheating on his wife; the chairman of the ethics committee in the state legislature who has been taking bribes for years.

Still, when he describes the advances in moral thinking that take place during adolescence, Kohlberg has an important point. Teenagers are famous for questioning society's rules, for seeing the injustice of the world, and for getting involved in idealistic causes (as you can see in the Experiencing the Lifespan box on the next page). Unfortunately, this ability to step back and see the world as it should be, but rarely is, may produce the emotional storm and stress of teenage life.

conventional level of morality In Lawrence Kohlberg's theory, the intermediate level of moral reasoning, in which people respond to ethical issues by considering the need to uphold social norms.

postconventional level of morality In Lawrence Kohlberg's theory, the highest level of moral reasoning, in which people respond to ethical issues by applying their own moral guidelines apart from society's rules.

[**FAQ:** Do people move between levels of moral development?]

Demonstrating solidarity with their people by staging a walkout from their classes to join this 2006 national immigrant rights rally is a crucial life experience for these Latino high school students. It's also a teenage developmental landmark, as advances in moral reasoning make adolescents highly attuned to social injustices.

Monica Almeida / The New York Times

In my niece Olivia's room there are no photos of teen idols, no cosmetics, no closet overflowing with clothes. The peace symbols and posters with titles such as "U.S. out of my uterus" show that this 16-year-old has a clear moral vision. Here's how Olivia explains the passions that dominate her life:

I volunteer at a soup kitchen on weekends. I am active in the Young People's Socialist League—that's a grassroots organization centering on social justice. I went to a couple of their protests against local greengrocers. They pay illegal immigrants, like, $2 an hour and take advantage of the fact that they can't complain to the police.

I began to really get into social activism in eighth grade. I had a really cool teacher, and one time we were talking about how we were appalled at the fact that in the last presidential election only 36 percent of the people went out to vote, and he lent me a book called *Marx for Beginners*. So, after reading that, I began to think about how we could have a radical restructuring of society where the people are empowered. I became really enraged at the fact that for so many thousands of years the common man has been screwed over, and still is being screwed over, and continues to be screwed over all over the world. The capital is there, the money is there, and so the fact that poverty exists is really remarkable. We have such vast inequalities in wealth. So basically my anger at that prompted me to get involved in the Young People's Socialist League.

My friends are wonderful, but a lot of the other kids at school are really superficial. In our town, you have a lot of racial and class divisions. Everyone talks about what a diverse community it is, but the white kids live on the north end and the poor minority kids live on the south end. At school, there's a lot of separatism in the races. You might be friendly on the surface, but there's no real diffusion or mixing. There's also this mad scramble to get into college. Parents are putting a lot of pressure on the kids. If they don't get a 95, there is going to be hell to pay. Some kids in the AP chemistry class were cheating . . . white kids from the north end. And they had already been inducted into the National Honor Society. So when these kids were caught, the department pretended like the whole thing never happened. If you are white and it looks like your parents have a lot of money, or if you are the kind of kid who looks like they are going to an Ivy League school, they are not interested in whether you cheat or not. It's a very Machiavellian system.

I try to do the best job I can, but I'm not interested in the "get the grade, get the grade" mentality. I told my parents if they pressured me about grades, I wasn't going to college. My plan is to apply to the United World College for my senior year. That's this real cool, rigorous academic program. They take high school students to places where you can make a difference, like in India and Africa. In Westchester we are the third richest county in the nation, so you don't get a chance to see real poverty. I'm trying to learn more about the income inequality gap between nations. It's really of mammoth proportions. I want to spend these years taking time to read as much as I can.

Elkind's Adolescent Egocentrism: Explaining Teenage Storms

Developmentalist David Elkind (1978) has also drawn on Piaget's theory, but his goal is to make sense of teenagers' emotional states. Elkind believes that when children start to make the transition to formal operational thought at about age 12, they suddenly see beneath the surface of adult pronouncements and rules. They realize that a 10 o'clock bedtime, rather than being carved in stone, is an arbitrary number capable of being contested and changed. Most important, as you vividly saw in the Experiencing the Lifespan box with Olivia, the social activist, they become aware of the difference between what adults *say* they do and how they really act. The same people who tell you to appreciate diversity or to treat everyone equally, as Olivia realized, let the rich kids cheat. The same parents and teachers who punish you for missing your curfew or being late to class can't get to the dinner table or a meeting on time.

This realization that the emperor has no clothes ("Those godlike adults are no better than me"), according to Elkind, leads to anger, anxiety, and the impulse to rebel. From arguing with a ninth-grade English teacher over a grade to testing the limits by drinking or driving very fast, teenagers are well known for doing *everything* just because it is against the rules.

Most important, Elkind draws on formal operational thinking to make sense of the classic symptom you saw with Samantha in the chapter-opening vignette—namely, the fact that young teenagers are unusually sensitive to what other people think. According to Elkind, when children first become attuned to seeing the flaws in other people's behavior, this feeling turns inward, to become an obsession with what others think about their *own* personal flaws. This leads to a psychological phenomenon named **adolescent egocentrism**—the distorted feeling that one's *own* actions are at the absolute center of everyone else's consciousness.

So 13-year-old Melody drives her parents crazy by objecting to everything from the way they dress to how they chew their food. When her mother comes to pick her up from school, she will not let this humiliating person emerge from the car: "Oh, Mom, I don't know you!" She does not spare herself: A minuscule pimple is a monumental misery; stumbling and spilling her food on the cafeteria lunch line is a source of shame for months ("Everyone is laughing at me! My life is over!"). According to Elkind, this intense self-consciousness is caused by a key component of adolescent egocentrism called the **imaginary audience.** By that term he meant that teenagers—especially young adolescents—literally feel that they are on stage, with everyone watching everything they do.

A second component of adolescent egocentrism is the **personal fable.** Teenagers feel that their own lives are totally special and unique. So Melody believes that no one has *ever* had so disgusting a blemish. She has the *most* embarrassing mother in the world.

These mental distortions explain the comically exaggerated emotional storms we laugh about in young teens. Unfortunately, the personal fable can also lead to potentially tragic acts. Boys, as you saw in the chapter-opening vignette, may put their lives at risk by deciding to drag race on the freeway, because they imagine that they are invincible and can never die. A girl does not bother to use contraception when she has sex because, she reasons, "Yes, *other* girls can get pregnant, but that will never happen to me. Plus, even if I do get pregnant, I will be the center of attention, a real heroine."

Look at the worried expressions on the faces of these freshman cheerleaders and you can almost hear them thinking, "If I make a mistake during the game, everyone will laugh at me for my whole life!" According to David Elkind, the *imaginary audience* can make daily life intensely humiliating for young teens.

adolescent egocentrism David Elkind's term for the tendency of young teenagers to feel that their actions are at the center of everyone else's consciousness.

imaginary audience David Elkind's term for the tendency of young teenagers to feel that everyone is watching their every action; a component of adolescent egocentrism.

personal fable David Elkind's term for the tendency of young teenagers to believe that their lives are special and heroic; a component of adolescent egocentrism.

Studying Three Aspects of Storm and Stress

Are teenagers really unusually sensitive to other people's reactions? Are they intensely emotional, as the concept of adolescent egocentrism implies? Is Elkind (like other wise observers from Aristotle to Shakespeare to G. Stanley Hall) on target in saying that risk taking is intrinsic to being a "hotheaded youth"? Now we turn to the developmental-science research relating to these three aspects of teenage storm and stress.

Are Adolescents More Socially Sensitive?

In the previous chapter you learned that when they reach puberty, children become highly attuned to their body size and often start to diet. You saw that we can predict whether a particular teenager has become sexually active by looking at that person's social group.

When researchers tried to pinpoint what concerned teenagers in these areas of life and others, they discovered, as Elkind would believe, that everything comes down to: "What will other people think?" From being overweight, to deciding whether to have intercourse (or oral sex); from having a fight with your parents, to getting pregnant as an unmarried teen, the issue is: "Will I be laughed at or rejected? How will my friends respond?" (Bell & Bromnick, 2003).

Neuroscientists speculate that the hormones of puberty may sensitize the regions of the cortex involved in processing our emotions, and so set teenagers up physiologically to be unusually alert to social cues (Nelson and others, 2005). In one tantalizing study, researchers took brain wave recordings from the amygdala (the brain's emotional center) of people of different ages while they watched photographs of fearful faces. Adolescents, they discovered, showed more intense amygdala activation than adults to this emotional social cue. Then they recorded from the frontal lobes while asking the participants to shift from focusing on their feelings (for example, "Tell me how frightened this face makes you feel") to making a more purely intellectual judgment (such as "Estimate the

[FAQ: Is adolescence really stressful?]

[FAQ: What does current brain imaging research reveal about adolescent functioning?]

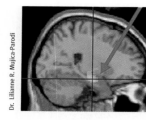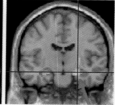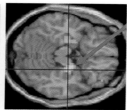

Dr. Lilianne R. Mujica-Parodi

These brain scans taken when people looked at fear-inducing stimuli show lit-up areas in the amygdala. During adolescence, as you can see in the text, this "emotional center" of the brain may be especially active.

[FAQ: Why are teenagers so susceptible to peer influences?]

width of this person's nose"). When asked to make the nonemotional assessment, teenagers showed *less activity* in their frontal lobes than older people (Monk and others, 2003). (Recall that the frontal lobes are the region of the cortex responsible for being able to step back from our feelings and rationally think through our responses.)

This physiological finding reinforces the message of the research described in the How Do We Know box. While adolescents *can* think rationally in nonemotional situations, their attention gets captivated by arousing interpersonal stimuli. That may explain why the most levelheaded teenagers, like Sam in the chapter-opening vignette, sometimes do such crazy things when with their friends (Steinberg, 2004, 2005).

ᛥ How do we know . . .

that adolescents make riskier decisions when they are with their peers?

Their heightened sensitivity to social stimuli gives us strong indirect evidence that teenagers might tend to do more dangerous things in arousing situations with their friends. An ingenious laboratory study vividly demonstrated the truth of this statement (Gardner & Steinberg, 2005). Researchers asked younger teenagers (aged 13 to 16), emerging adults (aged 18 to 22), and adults (aged 24-plus) to play a computer game in which they had the chance to earn more points by taking risks, such as continuing to drive a car after a traffic light had turned yellow. They assigned the members of each age group to two conditions: they either played the game alone or they played it while two friends were watching and giving advice.

The chart below shows the intriguingly different findings for young teenagers and for people over age 24. Notice that while being with other people had no significant impact on risky decision making in the adults, it had an enormous effect on young teens, who were much more likely to risk crashing the car by driving farther after the yellow light appeared when they were playing the game in the presence of their friends. The bottom line: Watch for risky behavior when groups of teenagers are together—a fact to consider the next time you see a car full of adolescents in the next lane, barreling down the road with music playing full blast!

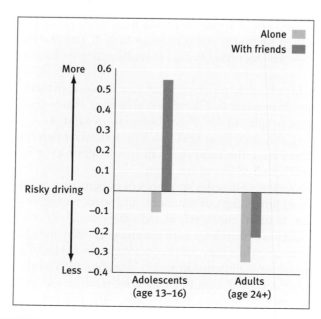

Even their strides in the ability to reason abstractly may accentuate teenagers' sensitivity to social cues. Developmentalists gave adolescents a variety of tests of cognition and personality. They found that superior performance on scales measuring abstract reasoning was correlated with heightened social anxiety (Rosso and others, 2004). So here, too, Elkind seems to be right. Especially when teenagers can *really* think postformally, they do become self-conscious, overly attuned to thinking how they appear from an outsider's view.

If we enter the mind of an especially thoughtful, intelligent child reaching puberty, this all makes perfect sense. You start to rethink everything you were taught to believe. You are physiologically set up to be especially sensitive to the smallest facial cue. You then start second guessing your own behavior: "Am I acting right?" "Is there something wrong with me?"

Imagine being the boy driving this car—listening to deafening music, captivated by your friends, perhaps thinking, "To prove myself to that gorgeous girl in the back seat, I need to go very fast." Now we understand from the developmental science research on the adolescent brain that our fears of carloads of teenagers have a real basis!

Are Adolescents More Emotional, More Emotionally Disturbed, or Both?

Given this heightened sensitivity to other people's emotions, it should come as no surprise that our second major stereotype about teenage storm and stress is also correct. Adolescents *are* more emotionally intense than adults. Developmentalists could not arrive at this conclusion by using surveys in which they asked young people to reflect on how they *generally* felt. They needed a method to chart the minute-to-minute ups and downs of teenagers' emotional lives.

Imagine that you could get inside the head of a 16- or 17-year-old as that person went about daily life. Several decades ago, Mihaly Csikszentmihalyi and Reed Larson (1984) accomplished this feat through an innovative procedure called the **experience-sampling technique.** The researchers asked students at a suburban Chicago high school to carry pagers programmed to emit a signal at random intervals during each day for a week. When the beeper went off, each teenager filled out a chart like the one you can see illustrated in Figure 9.2 on the next page. Notice if you scan Greg's record that the experience-sampling procedure gives us insights into what experiences make teenagers (and people of any other age) feel joyous or distressed. Let's now look at what the charts revealed about the intensity of adolescents' moods.

experience-sampling technique A research procedure designed to capture moment-to-moment experiences by having people carry pagers and take notes describing their activities and emotions whenever the signal sounds.

The records showed that adolescents *do* live life on a more intense emotional plane than adults do. Teenagers—both boys and girls—reported experiencing euphoria and deep depression far more often than a comparison sample of adults. Teenagers also had more roller-coaster shifts in their moods. While a 16-year-old was more likely to be back to normal 45 minutes after feeling terrific, an adult was likely to still feel happier than average hours after reporting an emotional high.

Does this mean that adolescents' moods are irrational? The researchers concluded that the answer was no. As Greg's experience-sampling chart shows, teenagers don't get excited or down in the dumps for no reason. It's "rapping" with their friends that makes them elated. It's a boring class or boring job that makes them very, very bored.

Does this mean that most adolescents are emotionally disturbed? Now the answer is *definitely* no. Although the distinction can escape parents when their child wails, "I got a D on my chemistry test; I'll kill myself," there is a difference between being highly *emotional* and being emotionally disturbed. The researchers found that adolescents whose moods varied most dramatically were just as well adjusted as their friends who lived life on a steadier plane.

[FAQ: Are teenagers more likely to have emotional problems?]

Actually, when developmentalists ask teenagers to step back and evaluate their lives, they get an upbeat picture of how young people generally feel. Surveys around the world show that most adolescents are confident, zestful, and hopeful about the future. Only a minority of teens (roughly one in four) feel extremely

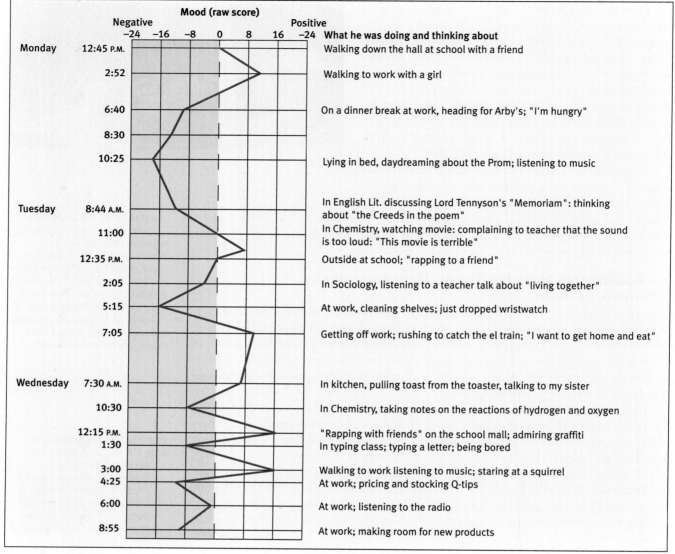

Mood (raw score)

| | | Negative | | | | Positive | | | What he was doing and thinking about |

FIGURE 9.2: Three days in the life of Gregory Stone: an experience-sampling record: This chart is based on three days of self-reports by a teenager named Greg Stone as he was randomly beeped and asked to rate his moods and what he was doing at that moment. By looking at the ups and downs of Greg's mood, can you identify the kinds of activities that he really enjoys or dislikes? Now as an exercise, you might want to monitor your own moods for a few days and see how they change in response to your own life experiences. What insights does your internal mental checklist reveal about which activities are most enjoyable for you?
Source: Adapted from Csikszentmihalyi & Larson (1984), p. 111.

upset or unhappy with their lives (Arnett, 1999; Bacchini and Magliulo, 2003; Offer and others, 1988). Furthermore, telling your parents "I hate you" doesn't mean you don't love them (Steinberg, 2001). Most teenagers report feeling close to their families. Their attachments remain resilient even when they vehemently disagree with their mothers' and fathers' ideas.

So the stereotypic impression that most teenagers are unhappy or emotionally distressed is definitely not true. Still, the picture is not completely rosy. The hormonal changes of puberty do heighten adolescents' reactivity to stress (Arnett, 1999; Arnsten & Shansky, 2004; Cameron, 2004). As children go through puberty, they produce more of the stress hormone cortisol in response to negative life events (Walker, Sabuwalla, & Huot, 2004). (Interestingly, cortisol is excreted by the adrenal glands, which, you may recall from Chapter 8, are intimately involved in programming puberty itself.)

Moreover, as children travel into late adolescence, they become susceptible to the kinds of mental disorders they may have to battle during adult life. *Every* serious psychological disorder, from schizophrenia to substance abuse, has a typical age of onset either in the late teens or early twenties (Compas, Connor, & Hinden, 1998).

You can see a good example of this pattern illustrated in Figure 9.3. Notice how, beginning at around age 15, rates of depression rise dramatically, particularly in girls (Keenan & Hipwell, 2005; Lucht and others, 2003). By the end of adolescence the

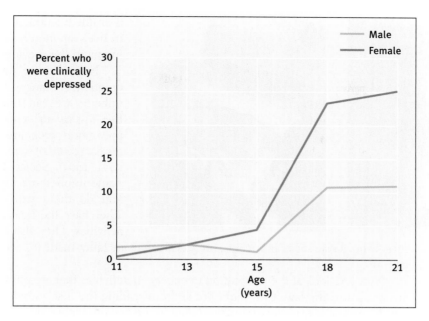

FIGURE 9.3: **Rates of clinical depression in adolescents, by age and gender (the Dunedin study):** As you can see here, at age 15 depression rates are not much higher for females than for males. By age 18, however, the adult pattern appears, with women twice as likely to be clinically depressed as males. This finding—that our adult patterns of mental illness tend to emerge by late adolescence or in our early twenties—is classic for a variety of mental disorders.
Source: Hankin and others (1998), p. 613.

adult gender difference is well established. Women are twice as susceptible to developing depression as men as they travel through life (Nolen-Hoeksema & Girgus, 1994; Wade, Cairney, & Pevalin, 2002). So not only do the hormones of puberty intensify our emotions and social sensitivities, they also activate our predispositions to developing specific emotional problems as adults (Dahl & Hariri, 2005; Walker, Sabuwalla, & Huot, 2004).

I saw this distressing process happen with a close colleague and his wife, both of whom have suffered from serious mood disorders. Their children were all successful, well adjusted, and happy throughout elementary school. But when they became older teenagers, their family history of depression kicked in. *Each* child began to develop symptoms of this devastating disease.

[**FAQ:** Are teenagers depressed?]

Are Adolescents Risk Takers?

Doing something and getting away with it. . . . You are driving at 80 miles an hour and stop at a stop sign and a cop will turn around the corner and you start giggling. Or you are out drinking or maybe you smoked a joint, and you say "hi" to a police officer and he walks by. . . .
(quoted in Lightfoot, 1997, p. 100)

Last Friday we dropped acid. . . . At school you have to be straight and set your mind on something, but when you are free to be with your closest friends you can get wild and un-inhibited. It's a different way to relate—a different way of being close.
(quoted in Lightfoot, 1997, p. 99)

These quotations, taken from an interview study of teens, show that (no surprise) the third storm-and-stress stereotype is *definitely* true. From experimenting with the latest drug to having the thrill of driving very fast, pushing the envelope—in sometimes dangerous ways—is a basic feature of teenage life (Dahl, 2004; Lightfoot, 1997; Steinberg, 2004, 2005).

Consider data from an annual national poll of U.S. teens relating to the use of social drugs (Eaton and others, 2006). This survey showed that in 2005 the vast majority of all U.S. high school seniors report having consumed alcohol at least once. One in four teens reported binge drinking (defined as having five or more drinks at a time for males and four or more drinks in a row for females) in the previous month. (For some other interesting facts about adolescents and alcohol, see Table 9.4.) Despite years of government-sponsored anti-smoking campaigns, most teenagers have tried cigarettes. Around one in four adolescents smokes regularly. While the use of other illegal drugs such as heroin and methamphetamine is uncommon, in this recent survey

The image of an isolated teen injecting drugs is extremely rare. The other scene is much more typical—experimenting with alcohol and, often, being initiated into your adult smoking career when you are with your friends.

a sizable fraction of teenagers (one in five) reported having used marijuana in the previous 30 days.

Now that we understand the emotional changes that occur at puberty, we can understand why the "just say no" school-based drug-prevention programs have had a dismal record of success (Steinberg, 2004, 2005). Social drugs, as their name implies, *are* intensely social. You do them with your friends. They have the lure of being adult activities. They also are against the rules. The classic social lubricants, such as alcohol, are tailor-made to reduce social anxiety, too.

Now let's look at the temptation to engage in activities that are physically dangerous or against the law. You might notice from reading the first quotation in this section that there is truth to Elkind's concept of the personal fable. For many teenagers, doing things that can get you into trouble (and not being caught) is part of the thrill of being alive (Lightfoot, 1997). This tendency to tempt fate and engage in risky activities is the glue that binds teenagers to their friends. It makes for lifelong memorable experiences, too. When the adolescents quoted above meet up again at age 30 or 40, they can reminisce about the time they did acid together, or drove too fast and barely missed getting pulled over by that cop. Do you remember the joy of doing something that was against the law—with your friends—when you were 14 or 15? If so, you have plenty of company. In one national poll, two out of three U.S. teenagers reported having committed an illegal act (Krueger and others, 1994).

Younger children also rebel, disobey and test the limits. But if you have ever seen a group of teenage boys hanging from the top of a speeding car, you know that the kinds of risks adolescents take can be threatening to life. At the very age they are most physically robust, teenagers—particularly male teenagers—are most likely to die of preventable causes such as accidents (Dahl, 2004). So, yes, parents can legitimately worry about their children—particularly their sons—when they haven't made it home from a party yet and it's already 2 A.M.!

TABLE 9.4: Some Interesting Facts About Alcohol and Teens

1. The earlier a teenager is exposed to alcohol, the more likely that person is to abuse alcohol later in life. Specifically, beginning to drink heavily under age 16 is a risk factor for persistent problem drinking (Pitkanen, Lyyra, & Pulkkinen, 2005).

2. There are ethnic group differences in teenage drinking, with European American teens being most prone to drink heavily, followed by Mexican Americans and then African Americans (Stewart & Power, 2003).

3. Being involved in high school sports is linked to excessive teenage drinking for European Americans but is negatively correlated with alcohol use for other groups (Eitle & Eitle, 2003).

4. Teenagers who drink heavily show signs of compromised brain function. In one study, teenagers who abused alcohol had smaller hippocampuses (the brain region involved in short-term memory). Various studies show that teens who regularly drink excessively have lower reaction times, lower verbal and performance IQs, and poorer reading scores compared to their peers (Zeigler and others, 2005).

5. The frequency of binge drinking (see text) and what is called harmful drinking (regularly consuming more than 4 drinks in a row for males and more than 2 drinks in a row for females) is highest during adolescence and emerging adulthood, and then tends to decline as people get older. However, if a male teenager engages in harmful drinking, that behavior is likely to persist well into early adulthood (McCarty and others, 2004).

Different Teenage Pathways

In high school I really got it together. I connected with my lifelong friends, and my love of music.

All I remember was my church group—getting involved in mission work. It was actually the best time of my life.

As a teenager, I really began to love school for the first time—I had some terrific teachers. I'll never forget the incredible feeling when I won that special prize in history my senior year.

Are you having trouble identifying with this teenage risk-taking portrait? Perhaps you remember becoming totally absorbed in academics during high school. Maybe your passion was singing in the chorus, participating in church activities, or, as with Olivia in the Experiencing the Lifespan box, agitating to change the world. Moreover, there is a tremendous difference between taking occasional risks, such as staying out after curfew or speeding, and getting into serious trouble with drugs or the law. Many teenagers engage in minor risk taking. Only a minority of adolescents gets involved in genuinely delinquent behavior or emotionally falls apart (Arnett, 1999).

Which Teens Tend to Have Serious Problems?

Who is most at risk of getting emotionally derailed? With children who are genetically vulnerable, as we saw earlier, developing a serious mental disorder is a tragedy that we may not be able to predict. However, when we look at delinquent behaviors, such as substance abuse or committing illegal acts, we can see early warning signs of what is to come.

At-risk teens tend to have emotional problems earlier on. It should come as no surprise that if an elementary school child is having the kinds of externalizing problems discussed in Chapter 6, that boy or girl is especially vulnerable to getting into trouble as a teen (Broidy and others, 2003; Laird and others, 2005). One reason is that children whose aggressive behavior is causing them to fail socially gravitate toward antisocial groups of friends, who then give one another reinforcement for doing dangerous things (we'll discuss this unfolding process in detail later).

Actually, any situation that disconnects children from conventional reinforcements is a warning sign—be it failing in school due to learning disabilities (Lynam, Moffitt, & Stouthamer-Loeber, 1993) or simply failing to connect with any passion in life (Hunter & Csikszentmihalyi, 2003). Young people who say that their only goal in life is "just having fun" are more likely to engage in delinquent acts (Dubois and others, 1999; Dubois & Tevendale, 1999).

At-risk teens tend to have poor family relationships. Feeling disconnected from one's parents is an especially potent indicator of later troubles (Brendgen and others, 2005; Pardini, Loeber, & Stouthamer-Loeber, 2005). In one longitudinal study, researchers found that children who reported high levels of family conflict during seventh grade tended to get involved with undesirable peer groups by late in the eighth grade. This in turn led to their getting into more serious trouble during high school (Goldstein, Davis-Kean, & Eccles, 2005).

Teenagers who say they don't get along with their parents complain about both too little and too much involvement. They may report: "My mother and father are clueless about my life." Or they may complain that their parents are too intrusive: "They want to micromanage every act" (Goldstein, Davis-Kean, & Eccles, 2005). In essence, these young people are describing an insecure attachment. Teenagers want to know they can disagree with their parents and be listened to and respected. They need to be able to openly discuss their feelings and still understand they are unconditionally loved (Allen and others, 2003). To use the attachment metaphor spelled out in Chapter 4, parents of teens must be exceptionally skillful dancers. They must provide limits and respect their child's need for independence. They should understand when to back off and when to stay close (Allen and others, 2003).

[FAQ: How can relationships with parents counteract harmful peer influences?]

If you interviewed this 17-year-old who has been picked up for stealing and dealing drugs, you might find a history of externalizing behaviors during elementary school, poor family relationships, and deviant behaviors that began to escalate in the young teenage years (or, because every person is different, you might not find any of these classic risk factors!). The good news is that even severe *adolescence limited turmoil* only infrequently leads to *life-course difficulties.*

adolescence-limited turmoil Antisocial behavior that, for most teens, is specific to adolescence and does not persist into adult life.

life-course difficulties Antisocial behavior that, for a fraction of adolescents, persists into adult life.

Still, when we see these correlations between teenagers' reporting poor family relationships and later getting into trouble, we have to be careful about just blaming mothers and fathers. Suppose a child is doing dangerous things, such as having unprotected sex or taking drugs. Would that person tell her parents about her activities? And if she did, would she expect her family to "just understand"? Yes, experts do believe that being authoritative and keeping open the lines of communication are vital in parenting adolescents (Steinberg, 2001). But let's also understand that human relationships are bidirectional. Negative teenage behavior naturally evokes negative parental reactions (Neiderhiser and others, 2004). When children begin to engage in antisocial activities, they tend to hide what they are doing from their families (Kerr & Stattin, 2000; Stattin & Kerr, 2000). So it's very difficult for parents to act authoritatively in their child's life.

At-risk teens begin getting into trouble at younger ages. Another warning sign occurs when a child starts to engage in problem behaviors, such as drinking, taking drugs, or cutting classes, during middle school. As you saw with early-maturing girls in Chapter 8, when teenagers get involved in deviant activities at a young age, their problems tend to escalate during subsequent years (Moffitt, 1993).

Moreover, once a young person starts drinking heavily or taking drugs, that child is more likely to get into fights or start failing at school. If a child is getting into fights or failing at school, that boy or girl is prone to become depressed and to abuse alcohol more (Wiesner, Kim, & Capaldi, 2005). As developmental systems theory would predict, when one major area of life tends to unravel, everything else tends to come unglued, too (Capaldi & Stoolmiller, 1999).

However, it is important to make a distinction between what adolescent specialists call **adolescence-limited turmoil** (antisocial behavior during the teenage years) and **life-course difficulties** (antisocial behaviors that continue into adult life) (Moffitt, 1993). From the teenage rebel Benjamin Franklin, who ran away to Philadelphia at age 17 (see Chapter 1), to that angry school failure Winston Churchill (discussed in Chapter 7), some of the most difficult teenagers can become exceptional adults. Perhaps you have a friend who used to stay out all night partying, drinking, or taking drugs, but has become an extremely responsible parent. Or you may know someone who was in continual trouble in high school, but is succeeding brilliantly after finding the right person–environment fit at work. If so, you understand a main message of the next chapter: We change the *most* during our emerging-adult years.

Which Teens Thrive?

Finally, we need to understand that for every teenager who gets into trouble, there are many other young people, such as the children quoted at the beginning of this section, who feel better than ever during adolescence (Prinstein & La Greca, 2002). What forces promote thriving or really coming into one's own as a teen?

For answers, we can provide a mirror image of the very qualities just described: Teenagers thrive when they have close family relationships and prosocial friends; when they are succeeding academically and connected to strong schools; when they

The determined expression on 15-year-old Michelle Wie's face as she tees off during the men's U.S. Open in Hawaii says it all: Having a life passion and special skill the world prizes allows teenagers to really thrive.

have a special passion, such as the arts or sports; or some quality, such as attractiveness, that society prizes (Masten, 2004). Having a strong religious faith is especially helpful (Dowling and others, 2004). Religion offers teenagers personal insulation from getting into trouble. It tends to embed teens in a caring, prosocial community, too.

Actually, the impact of the wider community may be especially crucial during adolescence, because during this pivotal life stage children are separating from their parents and moving into the world. To paraphrase the old saying: "It may take a village to raise a child, but it *really* takes a nurturing village to help a teenager thrive." (Table 9.5 offers a checklist based on these considerations to help you evaluate whether a child you love is at risk of getting into trouble or is set up to thrive as a teenager.)

TABLE 9.5: Predicting Whether a Child Is Likely to Have Problems or to Thrive as a Teenager: A Section Summary Checklist

T/F	1. Does this child have close family relationships?
T/F	2. Does this child have nurturing relationships with other competent and caring adults?
T/F	3. Does this child live in a community with good schools and good after-school programs for teenagers?
T/F	4. Does this child have close friends who are prosocial?
T/F	5. Is this child religious?
T/F	6. Does this child have a life passion or a special talent?

Source: Adapted from Masten (2004), p. 315.

If the answer to most or all of these questions is "false," a boy or girl is at high risk of getting into trouble in adolescence. The more "true" responses, the greater the probability that the child will thrive as a teen.

How many teenagers are thriving, or at least functioning very well? We can get hints by looking at a study that dispels a powerful storm-and-stress stereotype—that parents *hate* this life stage. Researchers interviewed several hundred mothers and fathers of teenagers, asking how their relationships with their children had changed. The majority of these parents said that they felt closer to their sons and daughters than ever before! (See Shearer, Crouter, & McHale, 2005.) We tend to focus on the teenagers who are getting into trouble and to forget that adolescence is a time of tremendous mental growth.

Wrapping Things Up: The Blossoming Teenage Brain

Now let's put it all together: the incredible mental growth; the heightened morality; the intense emotionality; and sensitivity to what others think. Give teenagers an intellectual problem and they can reason in mature, adult ways. But they tend to get overwhelmed in emotionally arousing situations, especially when they are with their friends.

According to adolescence specialists, these qualities make perfect sense when we look at the developing brain (Dahl, 2004). The frontal lobes, as you may recall, continue to mature into the mid-twenties (Giedd, 2004). At the same time, the hormones of puberty target the emotional centers of the brain (Kelley, Schochet, & Landry, 2004). As developmentalist Laurence Steinberg (2004, 2005) has beautifully described it, it's like starting the engine of adulthood with an unskilled driver. This heightened emotional sensitivity when the brain's master planner is not yet fully formed makes adolescence a potentially risky time.

But from an evolutionary standpoint, it is developmentally logical to start with an emotional engine in high gear. Their risk-taking tendencies propel teenagers to venture forth and experience what life has to offer. Their intense awareness of social cues helps adolescents confront the challenge of forming loving relationships as adults. Although it can make for a more dangerous few years, the unique qualities of the teenage mind are beautifully tailored to help young people separate from their families and begin to construct a successful adult life (Dahl, 2004).

INTERVENTIONS: Making the World Fit the Teenage Mind

Table 9.6 summarizes some of these messages in a chart for parents. Now let's explore the ramifications of our discussion for society as a whole.

Don't punish adolescents as if they were mentally just like adults. Given that the adolescent brain is a work in progress, it doesn't make sense to have the same legal sanctions for adolescents who commit crimes that we do for adults. The worst-case example is the death penalty. The United States is one of only a handful of countries, including Iran, Saudi Arabia, and Nigeria, that permit the execution of people under age 18.

Are fathers and their adolescent sons emotionally distant? In contrast to our stereotypes, if you asked this Australian man—like many parents—he might say he feels closer than ever today to his baby boy.

[FAQ: How does one deal with bad adolescent behavior?]

TABLE 9.6: **Tips for Parents of Teens**

1. Understand that strong emotions may not have the same meaning for your child that they do for you. So try not to take random comments like "I hate myself" or "I'm the dumbest person in the world" very seriously. Also let negative comments such as "I hate you" roll off your back. Just because your child gets furious at you, don't think she doesn't love you!

2. Do worry if you see a general pattern developing, with your child becoming more withdrawn, angry, or depressed over weeks or months. Getting involved with peers who are clearly in trouble or starting down a problem path at a younger age is a warning sign that your child may need special help.

3. Keep the lines of communication open, and provide rules. But know when to get involved and when to back off.

4. Try to get your child connected with some passion or activity she really loves.

In a Fort Lauderdale court, 13-year-old Lionel Tate, shown here with his mother, was tried for first-degree murder (carrying a mandatory life sentence of 25 years with no possibility of parole) for causing the death of his 6-year-old playmate Tiffany. Lionel, who said he was practicing wrestling moves and had no clue that the child would die, was ultimately put on probation and given special help, although his 2001 trial symbolized the fact that over the last decade of the twentieth century we have begun to accept the idea that it's OK to apply adult sanctions to teenagers who commit crimes.

youth development program Any after-school program, or structured activity outside of the school day, that is devoted to promoting thriving in teenagers.

In recent decades there has been a tendency to punish younger and younger teenagers like adults. Rather than simply locking adolescents up, it seems logical that at this young age we focus on rehabilitation. In fact, because teenagers' frontal lobes are undergoing so much growth, adolescence may offer a special neurological window of opportunity to turn people's lives around (Cauffman, 2004). As Laurence Steinberg and virtually every other adolescence expert has suggested with regard to the legal system, "less guilty by reason of adolescence" is the way to go (Steinberg & Scott, 2003).

Limit adolescents' access to potentially dangerous adult activities. Moreover, given adolescents' susceptibility to immediate, heat-of-the-moment influences, Steinberg (2004) makes the point that simply trying to teach teenagers to think through their decisions more carefully may not be effective. We need to provide external barriers to risky behavior, too. Raising the age of getting a driver's license to 17 or 18; increasing the cost of cigarettes to help deter children from smoking (Turner, Mermelstein, & Flay, 2004); vigilantly enforcing laws against underage drinking—all these measures offer teenagers some insulation from getting into trouble until their brains finish growing up.

Capitalize on adolescents' strengths. At the same time, we need to harness in a positive way the energy that can come out in taking dangerous risks (Cauffman, 2004; Dahl, 2004). Teenagers take tremendous pleasure in feeling self-efficacy. Their greatest joy lies in experiences of communion—in feeling close and connected to others (Masten, 2004). As you can see in Figure 9.4, teenagers are most likely to get into serious trouble when they are hanging around with their friends in the afternoon (Goldstein and others, 2005; Osgood, Anderson, & Shaffer, 2005). Why not take this unstructured time and fill it with activities that promote caring connections and enrich the self?

Youth development programs fulfill this mission. They provide efficacy-promoting, nurturing activities for teenagers to do after school (Dworkin, Larson, & Hansen, 2003; Mahoney and others, 2005; Roth & Brooks-Gunn, 2003). From 4H clubs, to teenage church groups, to after-school basketball teams, these programs ideally foster a set of qualities that developmentalist Richard Lerner has named the five Cs: competence, confidence, character, caring, and connections. They provide the kind of environment that allows young people to thrive (Lerner, Dowling, & Anderson, 2003; Lerner and others, 2005).

Unfortunately, however, communities differ in the richness of their after-school resources (Pittman, Tolman, & Yohalem, 2005). Upper-middle-class towns and neighborhoods, not unexpectedly, tend to have more sports facilities and community centers. They offer the most varied opportunities to get involved in the arts. Moreover, as youth development programs involve voluntary participation, the boys and girls who

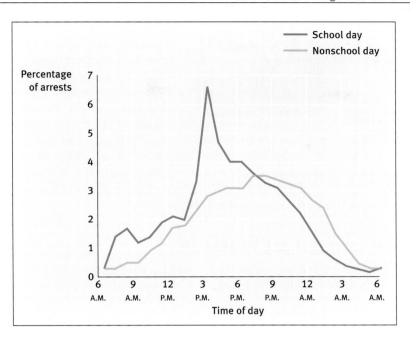

FIGURE 9.4: Juvenile arrests for aggravated assault, by time of day: Notice that teenagers are most likely to get arrested after school, as researchers find that the risk of teenagers engaging in *many* deviant activities spikes during the late afternoon hours, when adolescents have "time on their hands" and are most likely to be hanging out with their friends. This explains why *youth development programs* can be so helpful at preventing delinquency.

Source: Osgood, Anderson, & Shaffer (2005), p. 46.

seek out these activities tend to be teenagers who are *already* thriving (Reis, Colbert, & Hebert, 2005). Therefore, it may be especially useful to rethink the one setting where *every* young person spends the day: high school.

Change high schools to provide a better adolescent–environment fit. How can we make high schools genuinely captivating places? Once again, the experience-sampling method has offered clues. In charting the emotions of students during various high school periods, Csikszentmihalyi and his colleagues found that passive activities, such as listening to lectures and watching videos, almost always produced boredom. Teenagers were happiest when they were directing their own learning, either while working on group projects or by themselves (Shernoff and others, 2003). Given that the main mode of instruction in high school (and college) involves lectures, it makes perfect sense for many young people to zone out in their classes and find school an unpleasant place.

In surveys, teenagers say that they are yearning for the same kinds of academic experiences that characterize high-quality elementary schools (described in Chapter 7). They want more autonomy-supporting activities, specifically work that encourages them to think independently (Greene and others, 2004; Nolen, 2003). They need caring connections with teachers. They would love more courses that are directly relevant to their own lives (Wagner, 2000).

Service learning classes, involving hands-on volunteer activities, in particular, can make a lasting difference in later development (McIntosh, Metz, & Youniss, 2005; Reinders & Youniss, 2006). Here is what one African American young man had to say about his junior-year course in which he volunteered at a soup kitchen : "I was on the brink of becoming one of those hoodlums the world so fears. This class was one of the major factors in my choosing the right path" (quoted in Yates & Youniss, 1998, p. 509).

Finally, experts urge, we might rethink the school day to take account of teenagers' unique sleep requirements. As you may recall from your own adolescence, the hormones of puberty push the sleep cycle to begin at a later hour (Carskadon, Acebo, & Jenni, 2004; Dahl, 2004). The typical teenager goes to bed well after 11 P.M., and often must get up by 6 or 7 A.M. to get to school on time. Because adolescents actually need roughly 10 hours of sleep to function at their best, during the school week the typical teen accumulates a net sleep deficit of roughly two hours per night (Hansen

These high school girls are taking enormous pleasure in, and deriving a tremendous feeling of self-efficacy from, spending their Thanksgiving serving dinners to the homeless and impoverished elderly in their south Texas town. Was some teenage service learning experience life-changing for you?

Could this have been you in high school, particularly toward the end of the week? Did you decide not to take early-morning classes this semester because you realized the same thing would happen to you today? Do you think that we are making a mistake by resisting teenagers' biological clocks and insisting that their school day start at 8 A.M.?

and others, 2005; Yang and others, 2005). Spending one's school days in a zombie-like state is destined to make the most intrinsically motivating class torture. It is tailor-made to make any person irritable and depressed. Therefore, simply starting the school day a couple of hours later might go a long way toward reducing adolescent storm and stress!

Take a minute to think back to your high school—what you found problematic; what helped you cope; what may have allowed you to thrive. Do you have other ideas about how we might change schools, or any other aspect of the environment, to help teenagers make the most of these special years?

 ## TYING IT ALL TOGETHER

1. Robin, a teacher, is about to transfer from fourth grade to the local high school, and she is excited by all the things that her older students will be able to do. Based on what you have learned about Piaget's formal operational stage and Kohlberg's theory of moral reasoning, pick out which two *new* capacities Robin is likely to find among her high school students.

   a. The high schoolers will be able to memorize poems.
   b. The high schoolers will be able to summarize the plots of stories.
   c. The high schoolers will be able to debate different ideas even if they don't personally agree with them.
   d. The high schoolers will be able to develop their own set of moral principles.

2. The basketball team that Eric coaches is having its year-end conference tournament. The star forward has the flu and won't be able to play. Terry, who made all-state last year, offers to fill in, without telling the conference organizers. Eric agonizes about the ethical issue. It doesn't seem right to deprive his guys, who have worked so hard, of their shot at the championship; but he knows that putting Terry in is against team policy. For each of the following possible decisions, fill in the moral reasoning level (preconventional, conventional, or postconventional) that Eric is using:

   a. Yes. We need to put Terry in, because that's our best shot at winning.
   b. No. Going against the basic rules of the tournament is wrong.
   c. No. If someone finds out, the team will be in huge trouble.
   d. Yes. If I put Terry in, the team will feel that I went all out for them and maybe vote me coach of the year.
   e. No. If it were a question of saving someone's life, I would feel justified in going against the rules and putting Terry in. But my guys have to understand that any victory would be meaningless if it violated the basic principle that honesty comes first.

3. A 14-year-old worries that everyone is watching every mistake she makes; at the same time, she is fearless when her friends dare her to take life-threatening risks like bungee jumping off a cliff. According to Elkind, this feeling that everyone is watching her illustrates _____; the risk taking is a sign of _____; and both are evidence of the overall process called _____ _____.

4. Your teenage nephew, David, is spending the summer with you. He's a typical teenager, so you can expect all of the following *except*:

   a. intense mood swings.
   b. depression, as most adolescents have psychological problems.
   c. a high degree of sensitivity to what his peers think.
   d. a tendency to engage in risky behavior when this normally levelheaded kid is with his friends.

5. There has been an alarming rise in teenage crimes in your town, and you are at a community meeting to explore possible solutions. Given what you know about the teenage mind, which of the following interventions should you *definitely* support?

   a. Push the state legislature to punish teenage offenders as adults. Let them pay for their crimes!

b. Consider instituting a teenage curfew and heavily taxing the sale of liquor.

c. Set up a variety of exciting after-school activities so adolescents don't spend their time just hanging around with friends.

d. Consider postponing the beginning of the school day to 10 A.M.

e. Present more lectures in the high school devoted to teaching teenagers how to avoid getting into trouble.

Answers to the Tying It All Together questions can be found in the answers section of the book.

Teenage Relationships

Now that we have explored the teenage mind, it's time to look outward to examine those two adolescent relationship agendas: the push to separate from one's parents and the pull to congregate in groups with one's peers.

Separating from Parents

When I'm with my dad fishing, or when my family is eating dinner, and we get going on some story, or just when Mom and I share a laugh—it's times like these when I feel completely content, loved, the best about life, the world and myself.

In their original experience-sampling study, Csikszentmihalyi and Larson (1984) discovered that teenagers' most uplifting experiences occurred when they were with their families—sharing a joke around the dinner table or having a close moment with Mom or Dad. Unfortunately, however, taken as a whole, those moments were few. In fact, the charts revealed a finding that might not surprise us. Teenagers *generally* felt more upbeat with their friends than with their parents. When adolescents were with their families, unhappy emotions outweighed positive ones ten to one.

The Issue: Pushing for Autonomy

Why does family life produce a few peak moments and so many dramatic lows? (See Holmbeck, 1996.) As developmentalists point out, if our home life is basically good, our family provides our cocoon. Home is the place where we can relax, be totally ourselves, and feel completely loved. However, in addition to providing our safe haven, our parents must be a source of pain. The reason is that parents' job is both to love us and to limit us. When this parental limiting function gets into high gear, teenage distress becomes acute. Consider this quotation from a child in the original experience-sampling study:

Finally, I get a Sunday off; I don't have to work, so I can sleep a little later. But now I have to go to church. . . . They always wake you up, and they act like they are always cheerful . . . but they are really hostile if you don't want to go . . . [then on the way things get worse]. . .I asked them to change the channel—they were listening to some opera stuff. They just ignored me. . . . Jesus Christ, at least they could answer me!

(quoted in Csikszentmihalyi and Larson, 1984, p. 141)

What specifically do teenagers and their parents argue about? Studies dating from the Depression era to the 1960s to today agree: Conflicts do not typically occur over large concerns such as politics, the state of the world, or even the merits of being religious, but rather the minutiae of daily life—going to church, doing your homework, or cleaning your room (Laursen & Collins, 1994; Montemayer, 1983; Smetana, Daddis, & Chuang, 2003). Conflicts relating to independence loom large. Even here the disagreement is often not about the basic outlines, or what should happen, but at *what age*.

Researchers asked Dutch teenagers and their parents to estimate the ideal age for achieving a range of independence-related tasks, from leaving home, to staying out late, to dating, to first having sex (Dekovic, Noom, & Meeus, 1997). They found remarkable consensus about the sequence in which these events should occur. However, teenagers believed that they should be achieving each milestone at an earlier age than their parents did. The difference of opinion was most intense among parents and younger teens.

Passing a driving test and *finally* getting the keys to the car is a joyous late-teenage transition into adult liberation. It's almost the developed-world equivalent of a puberty rite!

The Process: Separating to Become Close in a New Way

Parent–adolescent conflict tends to reach its high point while children are in the middle of puberty (Arnett, 1999; Holmbeck, 1996; Montemayor, 1983; Paikoff & Brooks-Gunn, 1991; Steinberg, 2005). When Laurence Steinberg and a colleague videotaped sons and mothers having a conversation, they found that if a boy was undergoing puberty, he was most likely to challenge, to contradict, and to argue with his parent's point of view (Steinberg & Hill, 1978). From an evolutionary perspective, the hormonal surges of puberty may propel this struggle for power, setting in motion the dance of separation that is intrinsic to becoming an independent adult.

As suggested in Chapter 8, the physical changes of puberty themselves may also promote the impulse to separate. Parents are probably less interested in cuddling their suddenly-shaving six-foot-tall son, or having their 120-pound daughter sit on their lap. Remember that when they reach puberty, children also try to put a halt to much of the physical contact, as they struggle to hide their newly developing bodies from their families' sight.

As teenagers push for freedom, assert their rights, and gradually win more autonomy, they establish a new relationship with their parents as adults. Although studies show that conflict can be intense through mid-adolescence, it often (but not always) subsides during the later teenage years (Holmbeck, 1996; Larson and others, 1996; Smetana, Daddis, & Chuang, 2003).

By late adolescence, the frontal lobes are rapidly reaching maturity. Rebelling for the sake of rebelling becomes less interesting. It's time to get going on preparing for college or thinking about a career. The person's main agenda shifts to constructing an adult life (Steinberg, 2005). Even the major social markers of independence around age 16 or 17 eliminate important sources of family strain. Think about how getting your first real job, or getting your license and perhaps first car, removed an important area of family conflict by reducing the need to ask your parents for money or to depend on them when you needed to get around.

These eagerly awaited adult milestones put distance between our families and ourselves in the most basic physical way. The experience-sampling charts showed that ninth-graders spent 25 percent of their time with family members. Among high school seniors, the figure dropped to 14 percent (Csikszentmihalyi and Larson, 1984).

Being able to have a real woman-to-woman talk with your grown-up daughter can make the older teenage years a delight.

So the actual process of separating from our families makes it possible to have a more harmonious family life. The delicate task for parents, as suggested earlier, is to keep an eye on their sons and daughters but increasingly to allow them space to shape their own lives (Fuligni & Eccles, 1993; Steinberg, 2001). One mother of a teenager explained what ideally should happen when she said: "I don't treat her like a young child anymore, but we're still very, very close. Sort of like a friendship, but not really, because I'm still in charge. She's my buddy" (quoted in Shearer, Crouter, & McHale, 2005, p. 674).

Cultural Variations on a Theme

In individualistic societies many parents encourage children to construct an independent life. As you just saw in the quotation above, they ultimately want an adult-to-adult relationship that is less hierarchical, more like a friendship. What about teenagers who grow up in immigrant families with more collectivist norms? Do they have the same kinds of clashes with their parents? Do they need to feel independent from their families, too?

To explore this question, researchers asked three sets of immigrant teenagers—Korean Americans, Armenian Americans, and Mexican Americans—to respond to different scenarios relating to parent–child differences of opinion: "A popular band is giving a concert. You and your friends want to go, but your parents say no. What would you do and why?" "Your parents want you to attend a family dinner, but you want to go out with your friends instead. How would you act?" They compared the answers of these first-generation ethnic-minority children with those of European Americans of the same age. To see if their findings differed by stage of adolescence, the researchers gave the questionnaires to people in their mid-teens, late teens, and early twenties (Phinney and others, 2005).

As it turned out, the immigrant children were less likely to report that they would negotiate, more likely to say that they would automatically obey what their parents said. (Recall our Chapter 7 discussion of cultural differences in authoritative versus authoritarian child-rearing styles.) But there was an interesting age pattern. The Mexican Americans and Armenian Americans in their early twenties did speak about the need to follow their own desires. Therefore, with some (but not all) immigrant children, the push to be autonomous still does happen, but not until the twenties rather than at age 15!

Immigrant and ethnic-minority teenagers may have an interesting push/pull issue. On the one hand, as the photo below shows, they may feel closer to their parents as they connect with their ethnic roots and encounter discrimination in the wider world (Grotevant & Cooper, 1998). On the other hand, coming from a first-generation immigrant family has the potential to make for more distance. You want to become a "real" American. You think: "My parents have such old-fashioned attitudes. They have nothing to do with my life." As Judith Harris' theory of peer group socialization might predict (recall Chapter 7), anytime children must create a radically different adult lifestyle, parent–child disagreements may go beyond bickering about family rules. They may involve a basic separation in attitudes and worldviews (Arnett, 1999).

This line of reasoning suggests that there may be intriguing cohort differences with regard to parent–child closeness. When I poll my students, many of them say that they are best friends with their parents. I'm not sure I would have gotten the same information had I been asking this question in the late 1960s, when the baby-boom cohort was in college and rebellion against the older generation was in vogue. Do you think that mid-life baby boomers and their children are closer because they are more likely to share basic values? Or perhaps the baby boomers are the first cohort who even made an effort to be "best friends" with their daughters and sons! Whatever the answer, as we saw earlier, the *quality* of children's relationships with their parents makes a difference. It helps to determine which peer group a teenager chooses to join.

Spencer Grant / Photo Edit, Inc.

Ask the teenage sons posing for this photograph with their Latino father and Native American mom if they agree with the individualistic idea that it's important for them to separate from their parents and they might say no. For ethnic-minority teens, adolescence can be a time to connect with your heritage and, in the case of the emerging-adult son on the right, embed your European American girlfriend into your warm, caring family.

Why do teenagers get together in groups and gravitate to specific kinds of friends? How much do groups shape how adolescents behave? In this section, we look at answers to these interesting questions and others.

Peter Griffith / Masterfile

clique A small peer group composed of roughly six teenagers who have similar attitudes and who share activities.

crowd A relatively large teenage peer group.

Connecting in Groups

Go to your local pizza place or mall on a weekend or after school and you will see teenagers in groups, "hanging out," getting together with "their" crowd. Why do *groups* of friends become important during adolescence? What function does this typical teenage arrangement serve?

Defining Groups by Size: Cliques and Crowds

Developmentalists classify teenage peer groups into categories. **Cliques** are intimate groups having a membership size of about six. Your group of closest friends would constitute a clique. **Crowds** are larger groupings. Your crowd comprises both your best buddies and a more loose-knit set of people you get together with less regularly.

In a pioneering observational study in Sydney, Australia, conducted more than 40 years ago, one researcher found that these different-sized groups serve a fascinating purpose: They are the vehicles that convey teenagers to relationships with the opposite sex (Dunphy, 1963).

As you can see in the photos in Figure 9.5, children enter their pre-teen years belonging to unisex cliques, the close associations of same-gender best friends that we described in Chapter 6. Relationships start to change when cliques of boys and girls enter a public space and "accidentally" meet. You may see this fascinating stage of development by observing at your local mall. Notice the bands of sixth- or seventh-grade girls who have supposedly arrived to check out the stores, but who really have another agenda: They know that Sam or José and his buddies will be there. A major mode of interaction when these groups meet is loud teasing. When several cliques get together to walk around the store or go to a movie, they have melded into that larger, first genuinely mixed-sex group called a crowd (Cotterell, 1996).

The crowd is an ideal medium to bridge the gap between the sexes, because there is safety in numbers. Children can still be with their own gender while they are crossing into that "foreign" land. Gradually, out of these large-group experiences, small heterosexual cliques form. You may recall this stage during high school, when your dating activities occurred in a small group of girls *and* boys. Finally, at the end of adolescence the structure collapses. It seems babyish to get together as a group. You want to be with your romantic partner alone.

How accurate is this very old study? Today, the phase of hanging out together in groups seems to have a more extended timetable. With less than one in three seniors reporting in a recent national U.S. poll that they date regularly, traditional dating—at least in the United States—is at an all-time low (Child Trends Data Bank, 2005a). But the basic progression outlined in this research still rings true (Smetana, Campione-Barr, & Metzger, 2006): First teenagers get together in large mixed-sex crowds; then they date together in smaller groups; then they go out in pairs, or form one-to-one relationships.

FIGURE 9.5: **The steps from unisex elementary cliques to adult romantic relationships: A visual summary:** Unisex cliques meld into large heterosexual crowds, then re-form as heterosexual cliques, and then break up into one-to-one dating relationships. Does this sequence match your own experience?

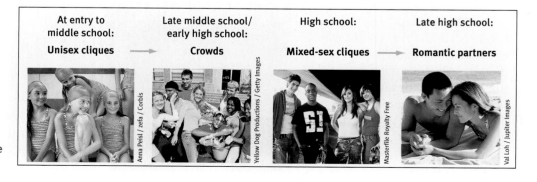

At entry to middle school:	Late middle school/ early high school:	High school:	Late high school:
Unisex cliques →	**Crowds**	**Mixed-sex cliques** →	**Romantic partners**

Anna Peisl / zefa / Corbis

Yellow Dog Productions / Getty Images

Masterfile Royalty Free

Val Loh / Jupiter Images

What Is the Purpose of Crowds?

Crowds have other functions. They allow teenagers to connect with other people who share their values and ideas. Just as we select friends who fit our personalities, we gravitate to the crowd that fits our interests. We disengage from a crowd when its values diverge from ours. As one academically focused teenager lamented: "I see some of my friends chang-

It might be a mutual love of music and nature that caused these teenagers to form this clique of best friends. Moreover, sharing this experience on the beach would further solidify their intense emotional bond.

ing. . . .They are getting into parties and alcohol. . . . We used to be good friends . . . and now, I can't really relate to them anymore. . . . That's kind of sad" (quoted in Phelan, Davidson, & Yu, 1998, p. 60). Adventuresome teenagers, such as Sam in the chapter-opening vignette, may move from crowd to crowd to explore different lifestyles (Cotterell, 1996; Stone & Brown, 1998).

Crowds also offer a roadmap for finding "our kind of people" in an overwhelming social world (Smetana, Campione-Burr, & Metzger, 2006). Interestingly, distinctive crowds are most prominent in large high schools. If you went to a small school you can probably recall having a circle of friends, but your class was less likely to be split into clear crowds, such as "the Goths" or "the brains," who shared activities, attitudes, and a special type of dress. Therefore, one developmentalist has suggested that the impersonal, large public high school plays a vital role in the development of the teenage crowd (Cotterell, 1996). When each class is filled with unfamiliar faces, it is helpful to develop an easy mechanism for finding a smaller set of people just like you. Teenagers adopt a specific look—like having blue hair and wearing grungy jeans—to signal: "I'm your type of person. It's OK to be friends with me."

What Are the Kinds of Crowds?

Throughout the developed world, researchers find a good deal of consistency in crowd categories. The brains (or, sometimes, the nerds), the popular kids (hotshots or preppies), the troublemakers (burnouts, dirts, freaks, or druggies), and perhaps the Goths (artsy types, alternatives) appear in large high schools in many affluent nations (Cotterell, 1996). Interestingly, however, perhaps because sports are not as central to the teenage experience in other countries, "the jocks" are a uniquely North American type of crowd.

How much mixing occurs between different crowds? To answer this question, researchers went into a large public high school and asked the students to map the

crowds at school according to their status and their relative social closeness (that is, how similar they were in values and ideas) (Stone & Brown, 1998). They found that when children straddled different crowds, they tended to be friends with adjacent groups. So a boy in the jock crowd would, most likely, associate with the popular kids. He would not have anything to do with the groups that were ranked socially very different, such as the rebels (or the bad kids).

As you pass this group of "punks" on the street, you may think, "Why do they dress in this crazy way?" But for this group, their outlandish hair and clothes are a message that "I'm very different, and I don't agree with what society says," and most important, they are a signal to attract other fellow minds: "I'm like you. I'm safe. I have the same ideas about the world."

FIGURE 9.6: Feelings of depression in late elementary school and high school for children who ended up in three different high school crowds: In this "follow-back" study researchers tested children in grades four and six and then looked at their depression levels in high school and explored their particular high school crowds. Notice that the boys and girls in the high-status "populars" and "jocks" crowds became happier during high school. The children destined to be in the "brains" crowd felt happiest during elementary school. The teens who became "burnouts" were more depressed than any other group both in late elementary school and in high school. If you remember being in one of these high school crowds, how do these findings relate to your feelings in elementary school versus high school?

Source: Prinstein & La Greca (2002), p. 340.

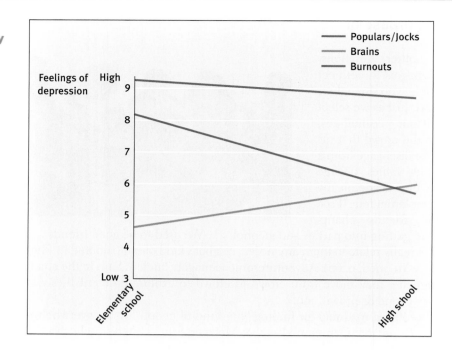

Moreover, the jocks and the popular kids were highest-status crowds. The brains were not very popular at all. Although *parents* may be happy when their child associates with the intellectuals, being academically minded does not gain teenagers many positive points in the peer world (at least in the standard public high school).

In another longitudinal study, tracking children as they moved from elementary school to high school, researchers found that the children who were in specific high school crowds tended to travel certain emotional pathways (Prinstein & La Greca, 2002). Notice in Figure 9.6 above that the boys and girls who ended up in the high-status popular kids and jocks crowds became more self-confident during their teenage years. (These are the people who would tell you, "I wasn't very happy in elementary school, but high school was my best time of life.") The brains group followed the opposite path—happiest during elementary school, but less self-confident as teens. (Once again, being academically oriented is associated with feeling great in elementary school, but it doesn't give teenagers much mileage in terms of self-esteem.)

Finally, as the figure shows, the teenagers in the burnout, troublemakers group were the most unhappy before adolescence and *stayed* at the low end of the happiness continuum in high school. We already know that failing socially in middle childhood predicts gravitating toward groups of "bad" peers. Now let's explore in detail why joining that crowd makes a teenager even more likely to fail.

"Bad Crowds"

The classic defense that parents give for a teenager's delinquent behavior is, "My child got in with a bad crowd." Without ignoring the principle of selection (birds of a feather flock together), there are powerful reasons why bad crowds *do* cause kids to do bad things.

For one thing, as we know, teenagers are heavily influenced by their peers. Each group also has a leader, the person who most embodies the group's goals. So if children join the brains group, their school performance is likely to improve because everyone will be jockeying for prestige and leadership status by competing for grades. (That's why parents are delighted when their children associate with the brainy kids.) In delinquent groups, the leader or person the group models tends to be the most antisocial member. Therefore, the activities of this most acting-out role model set the standard for how the others want to behave.

As a group euphoria sets in and people start surging for the stage, these teenagers at a rock festival in England might trample one another—and then later be horrified that they could ever have acted this way.

So, in the same way you felt compelled to jump into the icy water at camp when the bravest of your bunkmates took the plunge, if one group member begins robbing stores or selling drugs, the rest must follow the leader or risk being called "chicken." Moreover, when children compete for status by getting into trouble, this creates ever-wilder antisocial modeling and propels the group toward taking increasingly risky actions.

This tendency is compounded by the very fact of being in a group. When teenagers get together with their friends, as we saw earlier in this chapter, a kind of euphoria occurs (Larson & Kleiber, 1993). Talk gets looser and more outrageous. People feed off one another's energy. A group "high" emerges. This intensely pleasurable feeling explains why "chilling out" with friends is a favorite teenage activity. It also shows why in groups we act in ways that would be unthinkable when we are alone. From rioting at rock concerts or driving 100 miles an hour on the freeway in a car with our buddies, groups *do* cause normally sensible people to act in irrational, sometimes dangerous ways (Cotterell, 1996).

By videotaping groups of boys, developmentalists have documented the **deviancy training,** or socialization into delinquency, that occurs as a function of simply talking with friends in a group (Dishion, McCord, & Poulin, 1999). The researchers find that "at-risk" pre-teens forge friendships through specific kinds of conversations: They laugh; they egg one another on; they reinforce one another as they discuss committing antisocial acts. So peer interactions in early adolescence are a medium by which problem behavior gets established, solidified, and entrenched.

The pressure to engage in this kind of talk is intensified because, as suggested earlier, friendship "choice" among "at-risk" children is not free. Put yourself in the place of a child whose aggressive activities are causing him to live in a hostile world (see Chapter 6). You aren't getting along with your family or your teachers, and you can't fit in socially with the regular kids. You vitally need to connect with other children like yourself because you have failed at gaining entry anywhere else (Dishion, Andrews, & Crosby, 1995; Hartup & Stevens, 1999; Laird and others, 2005). Once in the group, your *hostile attributional bias* is reinforced by your buddies. Your friends tell you that it's fine to go against the system. For the first time, you may find acceptance in an unfriendly world.

In middle-class settings, it is typically children with emotional problems who naturally gravitate toward delinquent groups. In the most economically deprived neighborhoods, however, there may be few jocks or brains to hang out with. Thriving is difficult because the whole community is a toxic place. The only major crowd may be the antisocial group called a gang.

deviancy training Socialization of a young teenager into delinquency through conversations centered on performing antisocial acts.

To combat the sense of brotherhood, status, and power discussed in the text, in this innovative program designed to defuse Cambodian street gangs in Lowell, Massachusetts, a Buddhist monk offers "at-risk" teenagers the same sense of being brothers by teaching them to pray, meditate, and feel in control of themselves in a peaceful way.

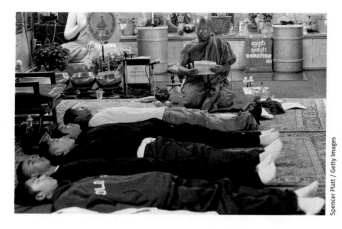

gang A close-knit, delinquent peer group. Gangs form mainly under conditions of economic deprivation; they offer their members protection from harm and engage in a variety of criminal activities.

The **gang,** a close-knit, delinquent peer group, embodies society's worst nightmares. Gang members share a collective identity, which they often express by adopting specific symbols and claiming control over a certain territory or turf (Shelden, Tracy, & Brown, 1997). This predominantly male group is found in many different cultures and historical times. However, with gangs the socioeconomic context looms large. Adverse economic conditions foster gangs.

Gangs provide teenagers with status. They offer a child physical protection in a dangerous neighborhood (Shelden, Tracy, & Brown, 1997). There may be economic motives to join. Anytime teenagers don't see a way of succeeding financially as adults, the gang offers an alternative pathway to making a living (for example, by selling drugs or stealing). Under these conditions, what began as time-limited adolescent turmoil is more likely to turn into a life-course criminal career.

Moreover, in societies where young people can't count on an adult future, the protected phase of life called adolescence may also disappear. Unfortunately, adolescence has been eliminated for the approximately 1 million children who enter the sex trade every year (United Nations Children's Fund, 2002a). Some of these boys and girls are street children. They live together in gangs in cities in Latin America or Southeast Asia. Sometimes, as in Thailand or Nepal, impoverished parents may feel forced to sell their daughters into the sex industry or to ship them to other countries as domestics, in order for the family to survive (Santa Maria, 2002).

Adolescence has also been eliminated for the hundreds of thousands of child soldiers in the developing world. The main combatants in the conflicts in the poor regions of the globe are boys in their teens. Many are abducted and coerced into fighting as young as age 10 (United Nations Children's Fund, 2002a).

Yes, many teenagers in the affluent areas of the globe are thriving. But unacceptably large numbers of children in the least-developed regions of the world can't count on having an adolescence insulated from adulthood, because they have little chance of constructing a reasonable adult life.

This 14-year-old soldier in Sierra Leone and this teenage prostitute on a Rio de Janeiro street offer a stark testament that, in many areas of the world, young people still do not really have an adolescence.

Final Thoughts

In Chapter 10, we explore the process of constructing an adult life among young people fortunate enough to live in the affluent West. What happens after we leave high school and grapple with the challenge of finding our place in the world of work? How can you be successful in college? How do romantic relationships evolve, and what predicts being "successful" in love? As we focus on the life stage called emerging adulthood, we will be tackling these immensely relevant issues that many of you may be grappling with right now in your own lives. ▪

TYING IT ALL TOGETHER

1. Chris and her parents are arguing again. If they're like most traditional European American families, you can be pretty sure that their arguments concern which of the following topics?

   a. How their community treats the homeless
   b. How late Chris's curfew should be
   c. Issues such as Chris's cleaning her room and doing chores

2. Based on this chapter, at what age might arguments between Chris and her parents be most intense: age 14, 18, or 21?

3. Your pre-teen niece, Heather, hangs around with a small group of girlfriends. You see them at the mall giggling at a group of boys. According to the standard pattern, what is the next step?

   a. Heather and her friends will begin going on dates with the boys.
   b. Heather and her clique will meld into a large heterosexual crowd.
   c. Heather and her clique will form another small clique composed of both girls and boys.

4. Mom #1 says, "Getting involved with the 'bad kids' makes teens get into trouble." Mom #2 disagrees: "It's the kid's personality that causes him to get into trouble." Mom #3 says, "You both are correct—but also partly wrong. The kid's personality causes him to gravitate toward the 'bad kids' and then that peer group encourages antisocial acts." Which mother is right?

5. You want to set up a program to help prevent "at-risk" pre-teens from becoming delinquents. First make up a short checklist to assess who might be appropriate for your program. Then, applying the principles in this chapter, set up a program to turn your potentially "troublemaking teens" around.

Answers to the Tying It All Together questions can be found in the answers section of the book.

▌ SUMMARY

The Mysterious Teenage Mind

Wise observers have described the "hotheaded" qualities of youth for millennia. However, adolescence, the life stage first identified by G. Stanley Hall in the early 1900s and characterized by **"storm and stress,"** became a reality in the United States only in the late 1930s, when high school became universal under President Franklin Roosevelt.

According to Jean Piaget, when teenagers reach the **formal operational stage,** they can think abstractly about hypothetical possibilities and reason scientifically. Although even adults don't typically think like scientists, older teenagers use the kinds of skills involved in formal operations to plan their lives in an adult way.

According to Lawrence Kohlberg, reaching formal operations makes it possible for people to develop a set of values that guides their lives. By examining how they reason about ethical dilemmas, Kohlberg has classified people at the **preconventional level** (a level of moral judgment in which only punishment and reward are important); the **conventional level** (moral judgment that is based on obeying social norms); and the highest, **postconventional level** (moral reasoning that is based on one's own moral ideals, apart from society's rules). By the middle of adolescence, most teenagers reach the conventional level, but very few adults advance to Kohlberg's postconventional stage. Despite this issue and other problems with Kohlberg's scale, adolescence is when we first become attuned to society's contradictions and flaws.

According to David Elkind, this new ability to evaluate the flaws of the adult world produces **adolescent egocentrism.** The **imaginary audience** (the feeling that everyone is watching everything one does) and the **personal fable** (the feeling that one's life is utterly unique) are two components of this intense early-teenage sensitivity to what others think.

Studies suggest that many storm-and-stress stereotypes about teenagers are true. Adolescents are extremely sensitive to social cues (and are also more susceptible to being influenced by their peers in arousing situations). Research using the **experience-sampling technique** shows that teens are more emotionally intense than adults. However, most adolescents are upbeat, happy, and not emotionally disturbed, although in later adolescence people begin to develop the characteristic emotional problems that they may battle as adults. Finally, teenagers are definitely risk takers. The lure of testing the limits—especially when teens are with their friends—makes the adolescent years a more dangerous time, especially for males.

The small minority of teenagers who get into *serious* trouble with drugs or the law tend to have prior emotional problems (especially with aggression) and poor peer relationships, and to feel distant from their families. Antisocial activities that start early are a risk factor for serious trouble down the road. However, **adolescence-limited turmoil** only infrequently becomes **life-course difficulties.** Many problem teens go on to construct fulfilling lives as adults. Children who thrive as teens have personal strengths and interpersonal resources and tend to live in nurturing communities. Parents, not infrequently, feel closer to their children than ever during the adolescent years.

The unique characteristics of the developing teenage brain are what make adolescence a relatively dangerous life stage. The frontal lobes are still far from mature. Puberty heightens teenagers' social sensitivities and emotional states. The lessons for society are: Don't punish teenagers who break the law in the same ways that adult offenders are punished; provide ex-

ternal barriers that limit teenagers' chances of getting into trouble; channel teenage passions in a positive way through **youth development programs;** set up high school courses so that they capture teenagers' interests; adjust the school day to fit adolescent sleep needs.

Teenage Relationships

Teenagers' conflicts with their parents tend to center on mundane issues (cleaning up their room, curfew, etc.), and struggles are most intense during puberty. In late adolescence, children ideally develop a more adult, friend-like relationship with their parents. Cultural differences and historical forces affect the separation process, the extent of conflict, and the degree to which parents and their children become "friends."

Teenage peer groups comprise **cliques** and **crowds.** These different-sized groups function to convey adolescents, in stages, toward romantic involvement. Crowds (such as the jocks or the brains) give teenagers an easy way of finding people like themselves in large high schools. The popular kids and the jocks (in contrast to the lower-status brains) feel better about themselves in high school than during elementary school. Children who enter delinquent groups tend to be unhappy before high school and remain the unhappiest during their teenage years.

Entering a "bad crowd" smoothes the way to more antisocial behavior. The reason is that the group members model the most antisocial leader and compete for leadership by trying to perform the most delinquent acts. **Deviancy training,** in which preteens egg one another on by talking about doing dangerous things, leads directly to antisocial behavior as "at-risk" children travel into high school. **Gangs,** mainly male teenage peer groups that engage in criminal acts, are most common in communities where economic conditions make it difficult for people to construct a fulfilling adult life. In impoverished regions of the world, where constructing an adult life is difficult, young people may not have an adolescence at all.

▌KEY TERMS

storm and stress, p. 270

formal operational stage, p. 272

preconventional level of morality, p. 274

conventional level of morality, p. 275

postconventional level of morality, p. 275

adolescent egocentrism, p. 277

imaginary audience, p. 277

personal fable, p. 277

experience-sampling technique, p. 279

adolescence-limited turmoil, p. 284

life-course difficulties, p. 284

youth development program, p. 286

clique, p. 292

crowd, p. 292

deviancy training, p. 295

gang, p. 296

▮ RECOMMENDED RESOURCES

THE MYSTERIOUS TEENAGE MIND

Brown, B., Larson, R. W., & Saraswathi, T. S. (Eds.). (2002). *The world's youth: Adolescence in eight regions of the globe.* Cambridge, U.K.: Cambridge University Press.

This terrific edited book offers chapters describing the issues facing teenagers in every major region of the world, from the Middle East to Europe, India, and China. It's very highly recommended.

Csikszentmihalyi, M., and Larson, R. (1984). *Being adolescent: Conflict and growth in the teenage years.* New York: Basic Books.

This is the classic experience-sampling study described in the chapter. It's also very interesting reading.

Dahl, R., & Spear, L. (Eds.) (2004). *Adolescent brain development: Vulnerabilities and opportunities.* New York: New York Academy of Sciences.

This neuroscience-focused book is highly academic but required reading for anyone interested in the latest research on the adolescent brain. Chapters cover everything from hormonal changes to frontal lobe development to teenage sleep changes.

TEENAGE RELATIONSHIPS

Mahoney, J. L., Larson, R., & Eccles, J. (Eds.). (2005). *Organized activities as contexts of development.* Mahwah, NJ: Erlbaum.

The articles gathered in this book cover a range of topics relevant to activities promoting youth development.

(Answers to the quiz in Table 9.1:
1. T, 2. T, 3. T, 4. T, 5. T, 6. F, 7. T, 8. F, 9. F, 10. T)

CHAPTER 10

Can you relate to Sam's experience—his need to take time off from college and to travel, his worries about falling behind in his timetable for constructing an adult life? If so, you might agree with the young people in Figure 10.1. You are no longer children, but you have not yet

Constructing an Adult Life

After graduating from high school with honors, Sam looked forward to pursuing his teenage dream of becoming a doctor. But his freshman year of college was more like a nightmare. His courses felt irrelevant. He zoned out during lectures. Especially after a night of clubbing, he found it impossible to get to class. Sam knew he was too immature to make it through sophomore year, much less graduate. The only solution seemed to be to drop out for a while and extend his part-time job at Banana Republic to 40 hours a week.

Sam was getting by financially—and having much more fun—although he still needed to rely on his parents for help with the car payments and rent. Then national headquarters eliminated his branch store, and Sam was suddenly fired. What followed was a series of temporary jobs that never paid more than $200 a week. Finally, Sam's parents intervened and helped their wayward son to enroll in bartending school.

After getting his certificate, Sam spent some time with a buddy in Florida, then moved to California and got a job tending bar at a Hilton hotel. Next came a year at the Amsterdam Marriott, followed by some exciting months traveling through the Far East. Then, at age 23, completely broke, Sam moved back home with his parents for six months.

Sam played with the idea of returning to college, but the timing never felt right. Now he knows it is time to finish his degree. He recently met a wonderful woman, and they have just started living together. If things work out, they plan to get engaged. Sam is getting anxious about his complete lack of progress toward his medical school dream. After all, his life plan was to be married, in a private practice, and have a child by age 35. Life should be an eternal adventure, but at age 28 it's time for a person to consider growing up!

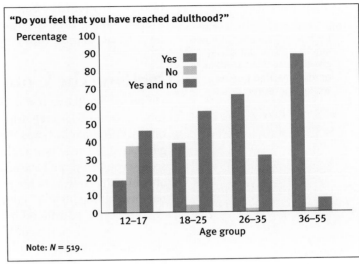

"Do you feel that you have reached adulthood?"

Note: N = 519.

FIGURE 10.1: Have you reached adulthood? When asked, "Do you feel that you have reached adulthood?" people of different ages responded differently. Notice that people aged 18 to 25 are unsure about the answer to this question. They are often on the fence, saying "yes and no." If you are in this age group, how would you answer this question?
Source: Arnett (2004).

entered the real-world activities that society views as marking full adulthood: financial independence, marriage, parenthood, beginning a lifelong career. Because this life stage does not fit neatly into the category "adult" or "adolescent," developmentalists have overlooked this in-between period when we are focused on constructing an adult life. The problem, says Jeffrey Arnett (2000, 2004), is that we need a new category. We need to label *emerging adulthood* as a distinct life stage.

This chapter is devoted to this new life phase. First, we'll explore the features of emerging adulthood and focus on topics relating to this extended "coming of age." Then we'll examine *identity*, our major psychological challenge during these years. The last half of this chapter centers on the most important concerns of emerging adults: work, college, and finding love.

Emerging into Adulthood

emerging adulthood The phase of life that begins after high school, tapers off toward the late twenties, and is devoted to constructing an adult life.

role The characteristic behavior that is expected of a person in a particular social position, such as student, parent, married person, worker, or retiree.

As you learned in Chapter 1, **emerging adulthood** starts after high school and tapers off by the late twenties. Its function is exploration, trying out options before committing to adult **roles**. Emerging adults are not quite ready to settle down. They feel too young to get married or to have children. They are not financially or emotionally secure. Like Sam, they may be exploring many trial pathways—changing majors, taking time off from college, traveling the world, moving from job to job, testing out relationships before they commit (Arnett, 2000, 2004).

Setting the Context: Culture and History

Emerging adulthood is a product of living in the developed world at this moment in history. This more leisurely trip to adulthood—taking time to decide on a career, putting off starting a family—was made possible by our dramatic twentieth-century longevity gains. Imagine reaching adulthood a half-century ago. With a life expectancy in the mid-sixties, you could not have afforded the luxury of spending almost a decade constructing an adult life. Now, with life expectancy floating up to the late seventies in industrialized nations, putting off adult commitments until an older age makes excellent sense.

Emerging adulthood has been promoted by social changes. A half-century ago, high school graduates could easily climb to the top rungs of a career. Today, most emerging adults attend college. It typically takes almost six years to get an undergraduate degree, especially since most young people work to help pay for their college years (Astin, 1999; National Center for Education Statistics, 2004b).

Finally, our attitude toward adulthood itself is shifting. Emerging adulthood took hold in an individualistic late-twentieth-century Western culture that stresses self-expression and "doing your own thing," in which people make dramatic life changes *throughout* their adult years.

Longevity, higher education, and personal freedom have made this new life stage possible. Still, the forces that drive emerging adulthood vary from place to place. For snapshots of this variability, let's travel to Italy and Sweden.

Italy: Living with Family, Searching Hard for a Job

cohabitation Sharing a household in an unmarried romantic relationship.

In Italy, strong labor unions and a preference for hiring men with families make it difficult for young people to find jobs that pay well enough to support an independent life. The Italian culture has strong norms against **cohabitation,** or living together, and having babies before marriage. Students often attend universities close to home and, on average, take seven years to complete their degree. So Italian emerging adults typically spend their twenties in their parents' home (Rossi, 1997). In Italy, financial problems loom large in driving emerging adulthood. The markers of being adult—*mestiere, matrimonio, e macchina* (a steady job, marriage, and a car)—are difficult to reach until people are in their thirties and can find a well-paying job (Cook & Furstenberg, 2002).

Many Italian men in their late twenties are still living with their parents because they cannot afford to leave the nest. If you were in this situation, how would you react?

Sweden: Living Independently, with Government Help

At the opposite extreme is Sweden, a country with a strong national norm stressing independence. The Swedish government subsidizes university attendance. Employers make an effort to hire young workers. The nation is committed to helping young people get on their feet financially. So Swedish emerging adults can survive economically, and **nest-leaving**—moving out of our parents' home to live independently—routinely occurs at age 18.

Moreover, because being married is not seen as important for having children, in Sweden the timing of these adult landmarks is reversed. Cohabiting couples and their children get the same partner benefits as married couples (Duvander, 1999). Swedish women have their first baby at an average age of 28. The typical age of settling down to marriage is 30 for women and 32 for men. In this nation, the twenties really do qualify as a stress-free interlude—a time for exploring, for traveling the world, and for enjoying life (Cook & Furstenberg, 2002).

The United States: Alternating Between Independence and Dependence

Emerging adulthood in the United States has features of both the Swedish and Italian scenes. Unmarried couples often live together during their emerging-adult years. And—although not as common as in Sweden—many American women have babies before they get married. As in Sweden, the U.S. individualistic culture encourages independence and moving out of our parents' home at 18. But, like Italy, the United States has no state-sponsored avenues for getting a job. This makes for a bumpier, less predictable pathway to constructing an adult life (Cook & Furstenberg, 2002).

This erratic path was evident when researchers tracked people as they entered and moved through the emerging-adult years (Cohen and others, 2003). Developmentalists followed several hundred upstate New York men and women from age 17 to 27. They monitored traditional markers of adulthood, such as becoming financially independent, living alone, getting married, and having children. They found an overall shift to more mature adult status as people moved deeper into their twenties. But notice from Figure 10.2 that when we look at individuals, we see considerable variability and dramatic movement backward and forward. So, in his early twenties, a man might be well on the way to marriage, in a steady committed relationship, cohabiting with the idea of getting married. At 25, he might break up with his fiancée and begin dating again. A woman could be financially independent at 21, with a job that paid her bills, then slide backward, depending on her parents' help after losing her job or deciding to return to school.

If you are in your twenties, take a minute to construct your own timeline toward independence. Does your pathway show that our progress to adulthood occurs in fits and starts? Now think of several friends and relatives in their late twenties. Consider their pathways in terms of marriage, parenthood, career, financial independence, and leaving home. Wait a second! Some people on your list may *never* have qualified as emerging adults! Each person's path to adulthood is influenced by many forces.

nest-leaving Moving out of a childhood home and living independently.

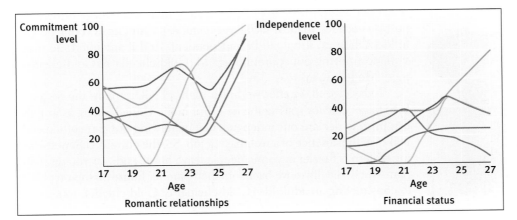

FIGURE 10.2: **The ups and downs of the emerging-adult years:** In a 10-year study tracing how young people develop from age 17 to 27, researchers discovered that many emerging adults move backward and forward on their way to constructing an adult life. These graphs illustrate the adult pathways of five different people in the areas of financial independence and romantic relationships.
Source: Cohen and others (2003).

Do you think this emerging-adult mother living in Los Angeles would agree that she is not an adult?

A. Ramey / Photo Edit, Inc.

- **Emerging adulthood varies from person to person.** We all go through adolescence and childhood. We do not all become emerging adults. People who get married, become self-supporting, or have children at age 18 or 21 might actually be offended by being called emerging adults. They are fully grappling with adult life. Others whose lives remain works in progress in the relationship area may have been financially self-supporting since age 16 or 17. So emerging adulthood is defined by its variability both from person to person and also within different aspects of ourselves (Arnett, 2000, 2004).

- **Emerging adulthood varies by culture and socioeconomic status.** If you recently immigrated from Asia, Africa, or Latin America, you might find the idea of emerging slowly into adulthood bizarre. In a poll conducted at Beijing University, students believed that "adulthood" definitely begins at about age 21 (Nelson, Badger, & Wu, 2004). So our cultural background shapes our emerging-adult years. Economic resources influence emerging adulthood, too. If your parents are fairly well off, as for Sam in the chapter-opening vignette, they can support you as you explore the world. However, this life stage feels different if age 18 is your marker for being financially free. If you are one of the many college students working long hours to finance school, constructing an adult life may still take well into your twenties (Astin, 1999; Engle, n.d.). But these years may often feel more like pure struggle than carefree fun.

So this unpredictable, structure-free time of life varies from person to person. It is limited by our culture and by our socioeconomic status. Now, we turn to the boundaries of this new life stage.

Beginning and End Points

In contemporary North America, we often view the entry point of emerging adulthood as the time when young people first move out of their parents' house. Its exit point is that hazy age when we expect people to settle down to adult life.

Leaving Home: Past and Present

[FAQ: When does adulthood start?]

This 22-year-old is working as a server in a restaurant and living at home while looking for a journalism job. Do you think this return to the nest feels to her like a return to childhood?

Over the past century, this entry point has undergone fascinating changes. Before World War II, young people traditionally moved out of their parents' house only when they fully entered adult roles. Women left home when they got married. Men moved out when they were financially established or, if work was not available in their area, to search out a job (Goldscheider & Goldscheider, 1999; Modell, 1989; Modell, Furstenberg, & Hershberg, 1976).

During the Great Depression of the 1930s, this meant that the average age of nest-leaving was the mid-twenties for both women and men—a statistic we might consider amazingly old today. A decade later, with the massive military call-up for World War II, the age marker for males leaving home slid down to the late teens. The draft, plus the mushrooming number of people deciding to attend college during the postwar decades, made it socially acceptable for American young people to leave the nest simply to be independent. And it anchored the milestone for moving out at around age 18 (Goldscheider & Goldscheider, 1999; Modell, 1989).

Today, age 18, or after we finish high school, remains the frequent U.S. target date for leaving the nest. But in the United States, as in Italy, this push to declare our independence by moving out can collide with reality in the absence of a well-paying job. So, the current U.S. nest-leaving pattern is fuzzier as young people leave home and—as you saw with Sam—periodically move back into their parents' house on their pathway to constructing an adult life (Goldscheider & Goldscheider, 1999).

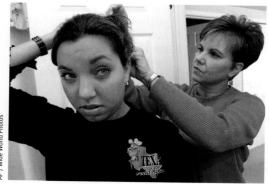

AP / Wide World Photos

The good news from the older generation's side is that many parents accept these re-entries (Goldscheider & Goldscheider, 1999; Riche, 1990; Schnaiberg & Goldenberg, 1989). They understand that their emerging-adult children may need to move back home for refueling and rest. The bad news from the young people's side is that moving back may make them feel that they are sliding into a life state they thought they had left behind (Schnaiberg & Goldenberg, 1989). For insights into how living under the parents' roof can interfere with a person's normal developmental need to become an adult, take a look at these complaints from a study exploring the nest-residing experiences of young Australians (White, 2002, pp. 221–222, 225):

> We are encouraged to have our own opinion. But because [my parents] own the house their opinion is the only one that actually gets implemented.
>
> (female student, age 23, employed part time)

> I think I'd feel a lot more mature if I was out of home. . . . My parents often say, "I wouldn't do that because this could happen." . . . That doesn't give me time to learn or grow as an individual.
>
> (female student, age 19, employed part time)

Researchers find an interesting ethnic difference in moving out. Because more collectivist cultures encourage family closeness, Hispanic Americans and Asian Americans are more likely to stay in the nest until they marry. They don't have the same drive to leave home or to feel physically free as young European Americans do (Goldscheider & Goldscheider, 1993, 1999).

There is an interesting gender difference in nest-leaving, too. Men tend to live with their parents longer than women do. They are more likely to return home after moving out (Cohen and others, 2003; Goldscheider & Goldscheider, 1999). Do you think that mothers and fathers give live-in sons more space to be adult—greater freedom to come and go—than they give their daughters? Is the nest more male-friendly because sons tend to get the perks of living at home, such as meals and laundry, without being pressured to help with household chores? What role might the older U.S. male marriage timetable (roughly age 27, versus age 25 for females) play in these interesting statistical gender differences in moving out?

Whatever the answer, one thing is clear: Even the most relaxed parent is likely to become uncomfortable with a child who is still living at home at a certain age—particularly if that person is making little progress toward constructing an adult life. When do we expect people to finalize their passage to adulthood? The answer brings up a classic concept in adult development.

The Ticking of the Social Clock

Our feelings about how late is too late reflect our culture's **social clock,** the idea that we chart our adult progress by referring to shared **age norms** (Neugarten, 1972, 1979). These norms act as guideposts that tell us which behaviors are appropriate at particular ages. If our passage matches up with the normal timetable in our culture, we are defined as **on time;** if not, we are **off time**—either too early or too late, depending on where we are expected to be at a given age.

So, in the developed world today, exploring our options is considered on time during our twenties, but quickly becomes off time if it extends well into the next decade of life. A parent whose 35-year-old son is "just dating," shows no signs of deciding on a career, or moves back home for the third or fourth time may become impatient: "Will my child ever grow up?" A woman traveling through her thirties may grow uneasy: "I'd better hurry up if I want a family," or "Do I still have time to go to medical school?"

Social clock markers are specific to the time and place in which we live. In my 80-year-old mother's cohort, women expected to be married in their early twenties (Elder, 1981; Modell, 1989; Modell, Furstenberg, & Hershberg, 1976). By their mid-twenties they were in danger of being labeled "old maids." Today, this marriage marker seems excessively rigid and far too young.

social clock The concept that we regulate our passage through adulthood by an inner timetable that tells us which life activities are appropriate at certain ages.

age norms Cultural ideas about the appropriate ages for engaging in particular activities or life tasks.

on time Being on target in a culture's timetable for achieving adult life tasks.

off time Being too late or too early in a culture's timetable for achieving adult life tasks.

Take a minute to plot your personal social clock timetable for marriage (if you are not married), for having children and grandchildren, for retirement. Do your specific life plans agree with these age norms?

TABLE 10.1 Australian Students' Settings for the Social Clock, Mid-1990s

Best Age for . . .	Average Ages as Given . . .	
	. . . By Males	. . . By Females
. . . a man to marry	25.1	25.96
. . . a woman to marry	23.04	24.48
. . . a woman to have a baby	26.41	26.65
. . . most people to become grandparents	52.89	54.05
. . . most people to be ready to retire	60.03	62.66

Source: Adapted from Peterson (1996).

The social revolution of the late 1960s, as you learned in Chapter 1, has produced a more *age-irrelevant society*. Today, the social clock norms are far looser. A woman can get married at 40 or 50, or decide to never marry at all. We celebrate people who go back to school at 60 and begin new careers at 85. Still, the social clock guidelines linger. Notice from Table 10.1 that during the 1990s, Australian college students had no trouble deciding on the "right" ages for marriage, parenthood, and retirement—suggesting that even in our choice-oriented Western culture, people still have clear ideas about which behaviors are appropriate at given ages.

Imagine that you are off time. How might having the uneasy sense that your personal social clock is "too fast" or "too slow" affect your emotional state? To answer this question, researchers surveyed more than 8,000 American adults, relating reports of feeling off time to overall self-esteem (Rook, Catalano, & Dooley, 1989). Although being too early was no problem, feeling too late was linked to distress.

This makes sense. With the exception of teenage pregnancies, it doesn't much matter if we start a family or enter our career early, at 20 or 21. But if we reach a certain age not having accomplished our goals, we get anxious: "Will I ever fulfill my dreams?"

The social clock pressures to get our adult life in order may partly explain why emerging adulthood is both an exhilarating *and* an emotionally difficult time. In a comprehensive survey of U.S. mental illness rates, University of Michigan researchers (Kessler and others, 1994) interviewed more than 8,000 Americans, ranging in age from 18 to 52. They discovered that rates of mental disorders reached a peak during emerging adulthood—ages 18 to 24. Huge yearly polls of U.S. freshman college classes reinforce this impression of considerable stress (Engle, n.d.; Sax and others, 1999). In 2002, one in every four freshmen agreed with the statement, "I feel overwhelmed by everything I do." More than 40 percent said they were inclined to seek counseling for a personal concern.

For some emerging adults, the problem may be dealing with an unhappy love affair, or partying, missing class, and flunking out of school. For others there may be serious economic troubles, the demands of single motherhood, or the painful realization that you don't have the skills to get a college degree—wrenching issues that threaten your ability to survive in the adult world. Or a person might appear to be doing very well but still feel anxious, disoriented, and depressed. The reason for this inner turmoil is that during emerging adulthood we undergo a fundamental mental makeover. We decide *who* to be as adults.

 TYING IT ALL TOGETHER

1. You are giving a toast at your friend Sarah's twenty-first birthday party, and you want to offer some predictions on what the next years might hold for her. Given your new understanding of emerging adulthood, which of the following would *not* be a safe prediction?

    a. Sarah may not reach all the standard markers of adulthood until her late twenties.

b. Sarah's pathway to adulthood will flow smoothly, with steady, predictable steps forward toward adult life.

c. Sarah may spend roughly six years completing college.

d. Sarah might need to move back in with her parents at some point before her thirtieth birthday.

2. If Maria moves back home after graduation so that she can pay off her college loans more quickly, what is the main risk she may face? (a) Her parents will resent their daughter's invading their space or (b) Maria will feel she is sliding back into the role of a child.

3. Which person is most likely to be worrying about a social clock issue?

a. Adam, who graduated from college three years early at age 18.

b. Martha, age 50, who lost her job as a project manager and wants to apply to nursing school.

c. Lee, 28, who has just become a father.

d. They are all equally likely to worry about social clock issues.

Answers to the Tying It All Together questions can be found in the answers section of the book.

Constructing an Identity

Erik Erikson was the theorist who highlighted the challenge of transforming our childhood self into the person we will be as adults. As you may recall, he called this process the search for **identity** (see Table 10.2).

Time spent wandering through Europe to find himself sensitized Erikson to the difficulties young people face in constructing an adult self. Erikson's lifelong fascination with identity as a major developmental task crystallized when he worked as a psychotherapist in a Massachusetts psychiatric hospital for troubled teens. Erikson discovered that many of his young patients suffered from a problem he labeled **identity confusion**. They literally found it impossible to move ahead:

> [The person feels as] if he were moving in molasses. It is hard for him to go to bed and face the transition into . . . sleep; and it is equally hard for him to get up. . . . Such complaints as . . . "I don't know" . . . "I give up" . . . "I quit" . . . are often expressions of . . . despair.
>
> (Erikson, 1968, p. 169)

Some young people felt a frightening sense of falseness about themselves: "If I smoke a cigarette, if I tell a girl I like her, if I make a gesture, if I try to read a book, this third voice is at me all the time—'You're doing this for effect; you're a phony'" (quoted in Erikson, 1968, p. 173). Others could not cope with having any future at all and planned to end their lives on their eighteenth birthday or some other symbolic date.

identity In Erikson's theory, the life task of deciding who to be as a person in making the transition to adulthood.

identity confusion Erikson's term for a failure in identity formation, marked by the lack of sense of a future adult path.

TABLE 10.2 Erikson's Psychosocial Stages

Life Stage	Primary Task
Infancy (birth to 1 year)	Basic trust versus mistrust
Toddlerhood (1 to 2 years)	Autonomy versus shame and doubt
Early childhood (3 to 6 years)	Initiative versus guilt
Late childhood (6 years to puberty)	Industry versus inferiority
Adolescence (teens into twenties)	**Identity versus role confusion**
Young adulthood (twenties to early forties)	Intimacy versus isolation
Middle adulthood (forties to sixties)	Generativity versus stagnation
Late adulthood (late sixties and beyond)	Integrity versus despair

In Erikson's framework, emerging adults are grappling with the challenge of identity, transforming themselves from their childhood selves into the people they will be as adults. Problems with identity formation can lead to role confusion, a feeling of being disconnected from any possible adult self. As you will see later in this chapter, at this age, young people also begin their search for intimacy.

This total derailment, which Erikson called confusion—an aimless drifting, or a literal shutting down—differs from the active search process he labeled *moratorium* (1980). Taking time out to explore various possibilities for an adult life, Erikson argued, is crucial to forming a solid adult identity. Having witnessed Hitler's Holocaust, Erikson believed vehemently that young people must discover their *own* identities. He had seen a destructive process of identity formation firsthand. To cope with that nation's serious economic problems following its defeat in World War I, many German teenagers leaped into pathological identities by entering totalitarian organizations such as the Hitler Youth.

Can we spell out the different ways people tackle the challenge of constructing an adult self? James Marcia answered yes.

Marcia's Identity Statuses

Marcia (1966, 1987) devised four **identity statuses** to elaborate on and measure Erikson's powerful ideas:

- **Identity diffusion** best fits Erikson's description of the most troubled teens—young people drifting aimlessly toward adulthood without any goals: "I don't know where I am going." "Nothing in life has any appeal."

- **Identity foreclosure** describes an individual who adopts an identity without any self-exploration or thought. At its violent extreme, foreclosure might apply to a Hitler Youth member or a young person who becomes a suicide bomber in his teens. In general, however, researchers define young people as being in foreclosure

identity statuses Marcia's four categories of identity formation: identity diffusion, identity foreclosure, moratorium, and identity achievement.

identity diffusion An identity status in which the person is aimless or feels totally blocked, without any adult life path.

identity foreclosure An identity status in which the person decides on an adult life path (often one spelled out by an authority figure) without any thought or active search.

This young person may fit Marcia's category of *identity diffusion*. She seems listless and depressed.

The young man in the background plans to take over this barber shop when his father retires. People who follow their parents' career choices without exploring other possibilities are in *identity foreclosure*.

This college student, volunteering as a tutor in a local public school to see if she wants a career as a teacher, is in *identity moratorium*.

South African singer Buddy Masondo *(left)*, following his life's passion, is in *identity achievement*.

when they uncritically adopt a life path handed down by some authority: "My parents want me to take over the family business, so that's what I will do."

- The person in **moratorium** is engaged in the healthy search for an adult self. While this internal process may provoke anxiety because it involves wrestling with different philosophies and ideas, it is critical to arriving at the final stage.

- **Identity achievement** is this end point: "I've thought through my life. I want to be a musician and songwriter, no matter what my family says."

Criticisms of Marcia's Categories

Marcia's identity statuses offer a marvelous framework for pinpointing what may be going wrong (or right) in a young person's life. Perhaps while reading through these categories you were thinking, "I have a friend or coworker in diffusion. Now I understand exactly what this person's problem is!" Still, despite their clarity and usefulness, Marcia's categories have been criticized.

Marcia originally believed that as we move through the teenage years into adulthood, we progress from diffusion to moratorium to achievement. Who thinks much about their adult life in ninth or tenth grade? At that age, your agenda is to cope with puberty (see Chapter 8). You test the limits. You sometimes act in ways that seem tailor-made to undermine your adult life. A true moratorium search should begin only during emerging adulthood, when we see real adulthood looming in full view. By our late twenties, we should have finalized the search for an adult identity.

However, many people stay stuck in one category; others move backward and forward over time (Waterman, 1999). Because of this variability, some developmentalists argue that rather than seeing people as moving from stage to stage, we should view each status as a unique state on its own (Berzonsky, 2003; Berzonsky & Adams, 1999; Kunnen & Bosma, 2003; Van Hoof, 1999a, b).

Critics have also questioned the logic of Marcia's view that we can definitely categorize people as being in diffusion or moratorium (Kroger, 2000; Kroger & Haslett, 1991). Does lumping a person into a *single* status really make sense? You may know a young person who is clearly in identity achievement in terms of religion or relationships but in moratorium or diffusion in some other area of life (Goossens, 2001).

If you are an older student, you will probably relate to a third criticism of Marcia's work, the idea that it is possible to reach our final identity as emerging adults. Many developmentalists believe that identity formation does not end in our twenties—that our identity is evolving as we travel through life (Bauer & McAdams, 2004; Hooker & McAdams, 2003; McAdams, 1998, 2003). This push to make plans and have goals is what makes us human. It is essential at any age. Moreover, revising our identity is vital to living fully, because our lives are always prone to being disrupted—as we change careers, retire, become widowed, or adapt to our children's leaving the nest (McAdams, 2001b). So, yes, identity issues are front and center during emerging adulthood, but let's not forget that we are works in progress throughout our entire lives.

A final troubling aspect of Marcia's framework is the value judgment implicit in viewing foreclosure as "bad" (Van Hoof, 1999a, b). Few of us would be happy to see a young person adopt the identity of a suicide bomber, but what's wrong with agreeing with your parents' ideas about how to live? Is it pathological to decide as a young teenager to become a carpenter or a teacher, a committed Jew or Baptist, and then stick to that identity as you travel through life? Actually, foreclosure has traditionally been the standard pattern throughout the world.

Culture and Identity Formation

Identity is a modern Western concept. For most of history, we never had to search out an adult path. That path was clearly marked out from a young age. Now the traditional guideposts are eroding around the globe (Arnett, 2002).

moratorium An identity status in which the person actively searches out various possibilities to find a truly solid adult life path. A mature style of constructing an identity.

identity achievement An identity status in which the person decides on a definite adult life path after searching out various options.

[FAQ: Can a person's identity status change over time?]

[FAQ: How do cultural issues affect development?]

These young Tibetans at an ATM, while firmly committed to their own culture, are still participating in our modern global society.

Mark Richards / Photo Edit, Inc.

bicultural identity A dual identity based on identification with both one's traditional culture and the norms of the global society.

Although some emerging adults still live relatively isolated lives, other young people in the developing world travel. They listen to rap music. They surf the Internet. They are fully exposed to Western ideas. Many of these young people adopt **bicultural identities.** They identify with both their unique culture and the world at large (Farver, Narang, & Bhadha, 2002).

The passion to participate in Western culture and stay connected to one's roots is not specific to young people living in India, Africa, or the Middle East. It is played out on every developed-world street (Yeh, Carter, & Pieterse, 2004): "How can I meld my cultural identity as Honduran or West Indian with being American or British? How can I take advantage of the freedoms of this new culture without feeling guilty about abandoning my people?"

One solution, a group of Indian-heritage college students realized, would be to provide settings that merge the best of both worlds: Give emerging adults from South Asia a nightclub where they can embrace Western ways and simultaneously feel they are making a statement of solidarity with their culture. At "Desi" (meaning someone from the homeland) nightclubs in Philadelphia, young people drink, dance, listen to live rap music, and simultaneously feel they are standing up for their cultural roots. However, we can see the burdens of some classic identity issues crashing down on José, one of the party promoters. José, a college junior who has earned thousands of dollars renting out the facilities and arranging for bands, has to keep his life a secret from his parents: "They know I am a leader, to help Indian people grow together. They just don't know which way." Although his family wants him to be an accountant, José has different dreams: His role model is Beanie Siegel, a South Philadelphia gangsta rapper. He dreams of getting into the music business and owning a string of clubs one day (Bahadur, 2002).

As we struggle to define an identity, whether in opposition to our parents or not, we face two tasks. One is to choose a career. The other is to find love. The rest of this chapter tackles these agendas.

✿ TYING IT ALL TOGETHER

1. You overheard your psychology professor saying that his daughter Emma has all the symptoms of Erikson's identity confusion. Emma must be ——————, which in Marcia's identity status framework is a sign of ——————.

   a. drifting aimlessly and seeing no adult future; diffusion.
   b. drifting aimlessly and seeing no adult future; moratorium.
   c. exploring different possible life paths; foreclosure.
   d. exploring different possible life paths; diffusion.

2. Joe said, "Because we Malloys have worked for generations on the family farm, I know that this must be my career." Kayla replied, "I don't know what my career will be. I'm searching out different possibilities." Joe's identity status is ——————; Kayla's is ——————. (Choose from: moratorium, foreclosure, diffusion, achievement.)

3. Discuss some of the difficulties inherent in developing a bicultural identity.

Answers to the Tying It All Together questions can be found in the answers section of the book.

Finding a Career

Choosing a fulfilling career ranks as a number-one issue in constructing an adult identity. In a famous statement, Sigmund Freud, when asked to sum up the definition of ideal mental health, answered with the simple words "the ability to love and work." Let's look now at finding ourselves in the world of work.

Teens' Career Dreams

When did you begin seriously thinking about your career? What influences are drawing you to psychology, journalism, nursing, education, or business—a compelling class, a caring mentor, or just the conviction that this field would fit your talents best? How do young people feel about their careers, their futures, the act of working?

To answer such questions, Mihaly Csikszentmihalyi and Barbara Schneider (2000) began a pioneering study of teenagers' career dreams. They selected 33 schools to reflect the demographic diversity of the United States, and tested and interviewed students from sixth grade to their senior year. To chart how the young people felt—when relaxing at home with family, when hanging out with friends, when working at school—they used the *experience-sampling method* (discussed in Chapter 9). Let's turn to their insights.

The Up Side: High Goals

Almost every young person expects to go to college. As you can see in Table 10.3, almost everyone plans to have a professional career. The tendency to aim high appears regardless of gender or social class: Whether male or female, rich or poor, teenagers of every ethnicity have lofty career goals.

The Down Side: Unrealistic Ideas

When Csikszentmihalyi and Schneider asked young people about their interests and matched these answers to the teenagers' chosen occupations, they typically found a reasonable fit. Young people who ranked being wealthy as their top priority were more likely to select occupations such as businessperson. Those who wanted to be doctors said they were fine with the idea of working very hard. Few people wanted to be ballerinas or astronauts or sports figures—at least after junior high.

Where teenagers are understandably vague is in appreciating the steps and barriers to implementing these dreams (Vondracek & Skorikov, 1997). Can 10 percent of the teenage population (see Table 10.3) really make it through medical school? Is a psychology Ph.D. a good bet if a person hates reading or is in the bottom half of his high school class? Career disappointment seems to lurk right around the corner for many young people as they emerge from the cocoon of high school.

Can we predict who is set up for a rough or relatively smooth passage into adult life? Without minimizing the important role of external barriers, such as dealing with poverty, racism, or other life stresses, clues may come from looking at an internal quality: whether or not young people like to work.

TABLE 10.3 Expected Occupations of Teens in Csikszentmihalyi and Schneider's Study

Rank	Career Goal	Percentage of Teens ($n = 3{,}891$)
1.	Doctor	10
2.	Businessperson	7
3.	Lawyer	7
4.	Teacher	7
5.	Athlete	6
6.	Engineer	5
7.	Nurse	4
8.	Accountant	3
9.	Psychologist	3
10.	Architect	3

Source: Adapted from Csikszentmihalyi & Schneider (2000).

A Core Ability: Enjoying Work

Using the experience-sampling records and interviews, Csikszentmihalyi and Schneider (2000) classified the teenagers in their study into two categories: workers and players. *Workers* enjoy being productive and having a sense of accomplishing tasks. *Players* hate the idea of working and find gratification only in their leisure lives. Players see their futures as hazy. They speak in terms of what they want to avoid, rather than what they want to do. So being at the upper end of the player spectrum puts a teenager at risk of being in career diffusion during the emerging-adult years. Here is what two players had to say during their senior year in high school (quoted in Csikszentmihalyi & Schneider, 2000, p. 86):

> *My main goal . . . is not to have a 9-to-5 job where I sit in an office . . . and type or whatever. It's like, I get ill almost thinking about that.*

> *None of my friends really know what they want to do. I mean, you know they want to go to college . . . but no one is really sure exactly where they are going to be. . . . They just talk about how they want to, you know, be friends and have barbecues.*

These worker/player differences may partly reflect the nature-based temperamental tendencies we have been exploring throughout this book. Because having the ability to regulate our emotions is important to persisting at work, being highly exuberant, in particular, may set children up for player-like problems with identity diffusion as they make the transition into adult life.

Still, all is not lost. For many young people, emerging adulthood is a watershed life stage in terms of personal growth.

A Core Trait: Personality Changes

Several studies offer strong hints that the twenties are the time when our personalities change the most. In one of psychology's most remarkable longitudinal studies, researchers traced the lives of children born during the early twentieth century throughout their entire lifespan (Clausen, 1991; Eichorn and others, 1981). Because several generations of researchers followed this California sample, developmentalists were able to collect data about personality stability and change over an amazing 60 years. Notice from Figure 10.3 that childhood was the time of greatest personality stability. Emerging adulthood, from late adolescence to the mid-thirties, was the life stage when people typically changed the most (Haan, Millsap, & Hartka, 1986).

Recent research reinforces this message. Developmentalists followed children from late elementary school through their early twenties (Shiner, Masten, & Tellegen, 2002). In measuring "positive emotionality" in the early twenties, the researchers were astonished to discover that having this upbeat attitude toward life was unrelated to *any* measure of how a child had been functioning at age 8 or 10.

Perhaps the most convincing evidence that emerging adulthood is the time we may change the most comes from a thoroughly researched set of traits. Developmentalists, as you will see later in this book, often measure personality by ranking people along five underlying dimensions: basic mental health, extraversion (outgoingness), willingness to try new things, agreeableness (or ability to compromise and get along), and conscientiousness (McCrae & Costa, 1986). Although studies around the world show that these core aspects of who we are remain relatively stable after age 30, they do shift a good deal during our twenties. Most interestingly, conscientiousness shifts upward dramatically during the emerging-adult years (Costa & McCrae, 2002; McCrae and others, 2000).

[FAQ: How does childhood temperament become adult personality?]

[FAQ: Is personality set at a very young age? Does personality change much throughout the lifespan?]

FIGURE 10.3: Change in personality over different phases of the lifespan: In this classic study in lifespan development, researchers explored changes in personality over different segments of the lifespan. Notice that there is less change during childhood and adolescence than during adulthood. Notice also that emerging adulthood is the time when personality changes the most.

Source: Adapted from Haan, Millsap, & Hartka (1986).

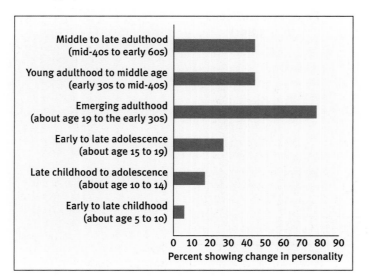

Some young people may lock into their conscientious-worker identity in college. Others become workers and find happiness only when they leave the classroom and enter the world of work. An absorbing inner state can help a teenage player lock passionately into a career.

A Core Goal: Finding Flow

Think back over the past week to the times you felt really energized and alive. You might be surprised to discover that many events you looked forward to—relaxing at home after work or watching a favorite TV program—do not come to mind. Many of life's most uplifting experiences occur when we connect deeply with people. Others take place when we are immersed in some compelling task. Csikszentmihalyi names this intense task absorption **flow.**

Flow happens during any activity that stretches our capacities, be it climbing a mountain or mastering the material in this book. People also differ in the kinds of activities that cause flow. For some of us, it's hiking in the Himalayas that produces this feeling. For me, it has been writing this book. When we are in flow, we enter an altered state of consciousness in which we forget the outside world. Problems disappear. We lose a sense of time. The activity feels infinitely worth doing for its own sake. Flow makes us feel completely alive.

Csikszentmihalyi (1990), who has spent his career studying flow, finds that some people rarely experience this feeling. Others feel flow several times a day. If you feel flow only during a rare mountain-climbing experience or, worse, when robbing a bank, Csikszentmihalyi argues that it will be difficult to construct a satisfying life. The challenge is to find flow in ways related to your career.

Flow depends on being *intrinsically motivated.* We must be mesmerized by what we are doing right now for its own sake, not for an extrinsic reward. There is also a future-oriented dimension to feeling flow. Flow, according to Csikszentmihalyi, happens when we are working toward a goal.

For example, the idea that this book would be published in about six years was the goal that propelled my mammoth project over time. But what really riveted me to my chair for hours at a time was the actual process of writing. Getting into a flow state is often elusive. On the days when I couldn't construct a paragraph, I'd get anxious. But if I could not regularly find flow in my writing, I would never have written this book.

Figure 10.4 tells us exactly why finding flow can be difficult. Reaching that state depends on a delicate person–environment fit. When a task seems beyond our capacities, we become anxious. When an activity is too simple, we grow bored. Ideally, the activities in which we feel flow can alert us to the careers in which we want to spend our lives. Think about some situation in which you recently felt flow. If you are in moratorium or worry you may be sliding into career diffusion, can you use this feeling to clue you in to a particular field?

Drawing on the compelling concept of flow, plus our discussion of identity, let's now explore two different paths that emerging adults follow.

[FAQ: Can early effects be changed later in development? How does the past affect my future?]

flow Csikszentmihalyi's term for a feeling of total absorption in a challenging, goal-oriented activity.

[FAQ: Is career fulfillment within my control? If so, how?]

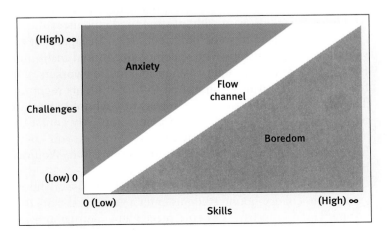

FIGURE 10.4: **The zone of flow:** Notice that the flow zone (white area) depends on a delicate matching of our abilities and the challenge involved in a particular real-world task. If the task is too difficult or beyond our capacities, we land in the upper, red area of the chart and become anxious. If the task is too easy, we land in the lower, gray area of the chart and become bored. Moreover, as our skills increase, the difficulty of the task must also increase to provide us with the sense of being in flow.

Which theorist's ideas about teaching and what stimulates mental growth does this model remind you of? (Turn page upside down for answer.)
Source: Adapted from Csikszentmihalyi (1990).

Answer: Vygotsky

Emerging Directly into the Workforce

Photodisc

This 21-year-old is working in a secondary labor market job in New York City. Do you think he is dreaming of a primary labor market career as a chef?

secondary labor market A category of low-wage jobs providing few benefits and little security.

primary labor market A category of jobs offering good salaries and benefits such as health care and retirement plans.

Two of every three U.S teenagers enroll in college after high school (Engle, n.d.). Then the ranks start to thin. Like Sam in the chapter-opening vignette, fully one in four college students drops out by the end of freshman year (Rosenbaum, 2001). Twice that number will exit before the end of their senior year. According to 2001 U.S. data, by their late twenties, only about one in four U.S. emerging adults has completed a four-year college degree (National Center for Education Statistics, 2004b). What is the fate of these legions of emerging adults who do not complete college?

People who do not go to college, or who never finish their degree, can have very fulfilling careers. Some rank high on Robert Sternberg's practical or creative intelligence but do not do well at academics. When they find their person–environment fit in the work world, they blossom. Consider the career of college failure Woody Allen, or even that of Bill Gates, who found his college courses too confining and left Harvard to pioneer a new field.

Unfortunately, however, as Sam learned, people who enter the labor force in their late teens often spend their first working years in the **secondary labor market,** a group of jobs offering low pay and little security (Rosenbaum, 2001; Smith & Rojewski, 1993). The stereotype of "unreliable teenager" can linger into the early twenties. It is not until the mid-twenties that some employers view young people as good promotion material at work (Arnett, 2000; Hamilton, 1986).

Moreover, noncollege emerging adults are at a double disadvantage when they search for jobs. Many **primary labor market** jobs—those that offer good salaries and benefits such as health care—require an associate's degree, technical certification, or a B.A. (Rosenbaum, 2001).

In interviewing a group of noncollege emerging adults, researchers found that a satisfying experience was possible if a person's job offered a chance for advancement, friendly co-workers, and an opportunity to enhance work skills (Blustein and others, 1997). One key to happiness was a quality that psychologists call *career maturity*—the person's ability to undertake an active, moratorium-like exploration with regard to possible careers. People did best when they reached out for help, both to friends and to other adults, and had an open-minded, flexible approach to searching out work. Another key to satisfaction, as you may have guessed, was being in flow.

During my first weeks as a server, I was terrified that I wouldn't be able to keep up. Now, I am in the flow of things. I served 20 customers on Saturday. Time passed so quickly. When closing rolled around, I thought it was like 7 o'clock.

When I paint houses I enter a kind of altered state—I will be working for 14 hours and I get amazed when I notice it's dark.

In theory, the United States has many avenues for finding flow-inducing careers: job fairs, newspaper ads, Internet sites, employment agencies, and word of mouth. However, with a few notable exceptions, we leave people emerging right into the workforce to sink or swim without structured guidance after they leave high school.

This is not true in some other countries. In Japan, for instance, employers develop close relationships with specific educational institutions (Rosenbaum, 2001; Rosenbaum & Kariya, 1989). When looking for workers, companies turn to these feeder schools and feel committed to hire students recommended by the faculty. This practice not only makes for a stress-free **school-to-work transition,** it also helps with a classic teenage high school complaint: "My courses are totally irrelevant; I am just marking time to get my degree." Suppose you knew your performance in high school was critical to your future employment. Wouldn't you be more highly invested in your classes?

school-to-work transition The change from the schooling phase of life to the work world.

Germany offers another model for the school-to-work transition. In fourth or sixth grade, non–college-bound students enter a vocational track that leads directly to a job in a particular industry. The centerpiece of the German program is an apprenticeship system. Employers partner with schools to offer on-the-job training. Graduates emerge with a guaranteed job in a particular firm (Cook & Furstenberg, 2002; Hamilton, 1990; Rosenbaum, 2001).

Many of us would instinctively reject the German approach because it labels people as "noncollege material" at an early age. The great benefit of the U.S. system, in contrast to the Japanese and especially the German system, is that it gives people continual second chances. Theoretically, we can reinvent ourselves in the work world no matter how poorly we performed in school. Moreover, many high school guidance counselors now encourage every high school senior to enroll in college, no matter how dismal their grades (Kerckhoff, 2002; Rosenbaum, 2001).

One observer, however, suggests that this uncritical positive stance has costs: It contributes to a kind of preoperational thinking, a magical fantasy that "college will turn me around." In truth, the best predictor of succeeding in college is succeeding in high school. Six years after entering, only one of five public high school graduates with an average of C or below receives a four-year college degree (Engle, n.d.). By comparison, more than three of four A-average high school students go on to get their degree.

INTERVENTIONS: Helping Young People Find Careers Outside the College Path

Because finishing college is a long shot for a young person in the lower half of a public school class, experience in the work world may be a more productive route to advancing in a career (Rosenbaum, 2001). Employers look for qualities such as reliability, initiative, and the ability to get along with co-workers—skills that can best be demonstrated by a track record at work.

Joining the work world directly from high school does not mean never returning to college, as many readers are well aware. In Sweden the social clock for college is actually *programmed* to start ticking a few years after high school (Cook & Furstenberg, 2002). The reasoning is that time in the "real world" helps young people home in on what they want to study during their college years.

As conscientiousness shifts upward during the twenties, putting off college for a few years may improve academic performance. I cannot tell you how many times students have told me, "I was too young to be in college at 18. Now I have the motivation to succeed." Their grades show it, too!

Still, we should not let society off the hook. The carefully planned school-to-work transitions in Germany and Japan suggest that the United States can do far more to strengthen the link between school and work, for both non–college-bound young people and people bound for Ph.D.'s (Kerckhoff, 2003; Youniss & Ruth, 2002). Why not establish government-sponsored initiatives to develop links among high schools, colleges, and relevant employers in each community? If you knew that your high school teachers or college professors had the power to get you your first postgraduation job, wouldn't you be more committed to each class and feel more secure about emerging into the world of work?

Table 10.4 pulls together some career-search tips based on our discussion of emerging adulthood, identity, and finding a career. Let's turn next to the setting you are in right now.

These two young German apprentices can look forward to guaranteed jobs in their field when they finish their training.

[FAQ: What do school administrators need to know about adult development?]

TABLE 10.4 Some Career-Search Tips

1. Don't be overly concerned that you have not decided on a particular career during college. Many people take considerable time to explore various possibilities before settling on a satisfying career.

2. Conduct an active moratorium career search by reaching out to other people for advice and exploring a number of potential fields.

3. Use the activities that give you flow as guidelines for choosing a satisfying career. If you feel in diffusion right now, remember that your work orientation can change dramatically if you find a job that gives you a sense of flow.

4. Don't feel you must go directly to college—especially if academics are not your "thing." Build up a track record at work. If you do decide to take the college path later, you may be a better student.

Emerging Directly into College

College offers a marvelous opportunity for exploring your identity. You can venture far from your hometown or stick close by, be a big fish in a little pond (attending a community college or small private school) or be a little fish in a big pond (enrolling in a large public or private university). Whether you want to explore deaf culture or agriculture, some school will fit your needs. What do the studies exploring college satisfaction suggest about being successful during these special years?

As you can see by looking at the flow chart in Figure 10.5, a variety of forces combine to predict college happiness and success (Tinto, 1987). The bottom-line message is that the key to college fulfillment lies in becoming emotionally connected to school.

This sense of being embedded in a caring community explains why students at small residential colleges are often highly satisfied with their undergraduate experience (Astin, 1999; Engle, n.d.). It tells us why living far from campus and working long hours increase the risk of dropping out (Astin, 1993; Bachman & Schulenberg, 1993; Horowitz, 1992; Worrell, 1997). One of the best predictors of happiness relates to the faculty (Astin, 1993; Umbach & Porter, 2002). Do students feel connected to their professors, or do they have the sense of being a number passing through? Now let's pull this research together to offer some tips for making the most of your undergraduate years.

FIGURE 10.5: **Predicting college success—a flow chart:** What we bring to college, in terms of family background, skills, and school experiences, affects our motivation to succeed as undergraduates. Once in college, our academic talents and relationships with the faculty, as well as our school activities and relationships with friends, help foster the sense of engagement that is vital to succeeding happily. Competing commitments (yellow box), however, tend to interfere with forming an emotional connection to college life. *Source:* Adapted from Tinto (1987).

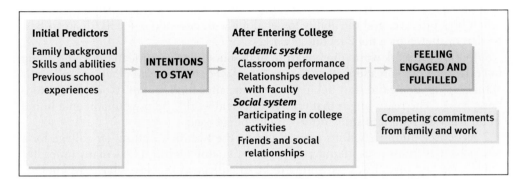

▮INTERVENTIONS▮ Making College a Flow Zone

Immerse yourself in the college milieu. Following this advice is easy at a small residential college: You live on campus. The college experience is at your doorstep, ready to be embraced. At a large university, especially a part-time commuter school, you may need to make active efforts to get involved in campus life. Choose, if possible, to live in a college dormitory or move close to school. If you are taking a full load of classes, try to avoid working full time. Join a college organization, or two or three. Working for the college newspaper or becoming active in the drama club not only will provide you with a rich source of friends, but can help promote your career identity, too.

Connect your classes to potential careers. Because the link between college courses and specific careers is often ill-defined, take steps to institute your personal school-to-work program. Set up independent studies involving volunteer work. If you are interested in science, work in a professor's lab. If your passion is politics, do an internship with a local legislator. In one study, college seniors mentioned that the highlight of their undergraduate experience occurred during a mentored project in the real world (Light, 2001).

Make connections with your professors. College takes on a different flavor when students feel close ties with professors. Take several courses with a favorite nurturing professor. Visit your adviser every semester, and—if this person doesn't seem all that responsive—ask your favorite instructor to be your adviser. (She will be flattered.)

College is an ideal time to connect with people from different backgrounds. So go for it!

As this senior describes, feeling cared about by a professor can be a peak experience in your personal life:

He began by asking me which single book had the biggest impact on me. He was the first professor who was interested in what matters to me. . . . You can't imagine how excited I was.
(quoted in Light, 2001, pp. 82–83)

Capitalize on the diverse human connections college provides. As you saw during adolescence, the crowds and cliques we select as undergraduates propel the direction of our future self (Astin, 1993). At college, it is tempting to find a single clique and then not reach out to other crowds. Resist this impulse. Students—particularly European Americans—report that one of the major growth experiences college offers is the chance to get to know people of different backgrounds, religions, and races (Hu & Kuh, 2003). Let's see what another undergraduate had to say:

I have re-evaluated my beliefs. . . . At college, there are people of all different religions around me. . . . Living . . . with these people marks an important difference. . . . [It] has made me reconsider and ultimately reaffirm my faith.
(quoted in Light, 2001, p. 163)

How can you break out of your social circle and promote your own Eriksonian moratorium search? One strategy, again, is to spend your first years living in a diverse college residence hall. Another is to participate in the *inclusive* activities on campus that give you flow. Writing for the newspaper, becoming active in student government, or even taking a college-sponsored weekend trip (rather than going with a friend) will not only help you establish your identity, but will also smooth your way to that other central goal of constructing an adult life—finding love.

[FAQ: How can I change?]

✿ TYING IT ALL TOGETHER

1. Mai Lee, who just graduated from high school, seems to be happy only when hanging out with friends or watching TV. According to Csikszentmihalyi's framework, which category does Mai Lee fit into?

2. Hannah was recently chosen as a member of a national women's soccer team. She loves the challenge and the feeling that she is exercising all of her skills. Time flies by while she's in practice. She says she'd find a way to play soccer even if she couldn't be paid for it. For Hannah, soccer is a (an) ———————— experience.

   a. career diffusion
   b. off-time
   c. secondary labor
   d. flow

3. As a member of the President's Commission to Improve the School-to-Work Transition in the United States, you've been asked to offer three suggestions, based on your knowledge of what the Japanese and Germans do. Which of the following suggestions does *not* reflect either the Japanese or German approach?

a. Let's have every elementary school child enter either a college or noncollege path.
b. Let's develop an apprenticeship program, attached to certain employers, so people get on-the-job training and then have a postgraduation job at a particular firm.
c. Let's get employers in each community connected to a given "feeder" high school and have them commit to hiring the school's graduates whom their teachers recommend.
d. Let's encourage every student to enter college immediately after graduating from high school.

4. You are a college adviser and a student named David comes to you for help with a decision. David's boss has offered him a full-time job and promised to give him a work schedule that won't conflict with his classes. David is tempted, but he is worried about the impact that taking this job will have on his plans to get connected to college and ultimately have the grades to go to medical school. What should you advise David to do, and why?

Answers to the Tying It All Together questions can be found in the answers section of the book.

Finding Love

intimacy Erikson's first adult task, involving connecting with a partner in a mutual loving relationship.

[FAQ: How can I find the right mate?**]**

How do twenty-first-century emerging adults negotiate Erikson's first task of adult life (see Table 10.5)—**intimacy,** the search for a soul mate or enduring love? How do romantic relationships develop, and why do they sometimes fall apart? What insights does the social science research on relationships offer for finding an ideal mate? We now explore these questions one by one.

TABLE 10.5 Erikson's Life Stages and Their Psychological Tasks

Life Stage	Primary Task
Infancy (birth to 1 year)	Basic trust versus mistrust
Toddlerhood (1 to 2 years)	Autonomy versus shame and doubt
Early childhood (3 to 6 years)	Initiative versus guilt
Late childhood (6 years to puberty)	Industry versus inferiority
Adolescence (teens into twenties)	Identity versus role confusion
Young adulthood (twenties to early forties)	**Intimacy versus isolation**
Middle adulthood (forties to sixties)	Generativity versus stagnation
Late adulthood (late sixties and beyond)	Integrity versus despair

In addition to finding their identity, emerging adults begin to struggle with the first adult task, intimacy, forming a close one-to-one relationship with a partner. Problems with intimacy can lead to isolation, feeling adrift from the human world.

Setting the Context: New Forms of Finding Love

Daolin Yang, 77, a grandfather, is retired and lives in Hebie Province, China. . . . At age 15, he married his wife Yufen, then 13, in a village. . . . A matchmaker proposed the marriage on behalf of the Yang family. They have been married for 62 years and reared three children. . . . He says that they married first and dated later. It is "cold at the start and hot in the end." The relationship gets better and better over the years.

(Xia & Zhou, 2003, p. 231)

This long-lasting love story reminds us that finding a mate on our own, like identity, is a uniquely Western phenomenon. Still, even in our individualistic society, the landscape of love is evolving. It has changed in three major ways within the past 30 years.

How did this couple meet— through the Internet, at church, at work? You might be surprised to know that finding mates on our own is a very recent practice in human history.

Virtual Dating

The most striking new transformation is **virtual dating**—finding an ideal mate on the Internet. What is online romance *really* like? As one British researcher discovered, dating online has many of the same features as real-life dating (Hardey, 2002). At first there is some flirting. You try not to come on too strong in your e-mail encounters or to appear too aloof. In stages, you get more personal and reveal more of yourself. You typically tell your cyberspace partner the truth. (After all, your goal is to eventually meet!) If you don't get an e-mail within a certain time, you know the relationship is off. Here is how one English woman in the study describes the pleasure she takes in online romance:

> I would say it is like a striptease! . . . I start with a full-clothed version of me, that I put up as an advertisement—makeup and posh frock to get men interested! Then as I write e-mails and get to know someone I reveal more of the real me and if we both seem to like what we see . . . we . . . arrange a meeting. If I decide I'm no longer interested I can easily say so and that's the end of it.

> (quoted in Hardey, 2002, p. 578)

Virtual dating can lead to disappointments. That sensitive and funny artist who looked so handsome in the photo may be very different in the flesh. When you meet, the chemistry may just not be there. Even so, the enthusiastic testimonials this researcher gathered suggest that finding love in cyberspace may continue to be a very popular way to select a mate. How many couples do you know who met on the Internet and got married? So far, I have counted three!

virtual dating Internet dating and love relationships.

Nontraditional Partners

A second shift in the love landscape is the rise in interracial dating. In a turn-of-the-century nationwide U.S. poll, one in three European Americans reported dating someone of a different ethnic or racial group. More than half of all the African Americans, Hispanic Americans, and Asian Americans in this survey had dated someone of a different ethnicity or race (Yancey & Yancey, 2002). In a study specifically exploring the dating practices of emerging adults, one of four students at East Carolina State University reported having dated interracially (Knox and others, 2000). This finding shows that among young people in the South, that once-taboo practice—dating across the color line—is breaking down.

Cross-gender walls are cracking, too. This is not to say that **homophobia**, or intense fear and dislike of gays and lesbians, is absent. People still hold stereotypes such as those described in Table 10.6 on the next page. But in today's cohort of emerging adults, same-sex relationships are far more acceptable than they were even a decade ago (Savin-Williams, 2001). On a few U.S. campuses, politically correct students— particularly women—see using the labels "gay" or "straight" to describe their sexuality as old-fashioned and passé (Diamond & Savin-Williams, 2003).

homophobia Intense fear and dislike of gays and lesbians.

TABLE 10.6 Homosexual Stereotypes and Scientific Facts

Stereotype: Overinvolved mothers and distant fathers "cause" boys to be homosexual.

Scientific Fact: There is no evidence that this or any other parenting problem causes homosexuality. The causes of homosexuality (which occurs in many mammals and so may play an adaptive function in evolution) are unknown (Pillard, 1997).

Stereotype: Through counseling, homosexuals can change their sexual orientation from gay to straight.

Scientific Fact: Outcome studies exploring "reparation therapy"—strongly discouraged by every major U.S. mental health organization but practiced by a few Christian ministries—are nonexistent. One researcher did conduct a telephone poll of people who said they had successfully undergone this therapy (Spitzer, 2003). Although complete change was rare, these people did report that they had changed their orientation from predominantly homosexual to heterosexual. The strong caution here is that this study comes from a very self-selected sample—men and women anxious to report success.

Stereotype: Homosexuals have an unhappy life.

Scientific Fact: In one survey of the Dutch population, gay men did report lower self-esteem and lower feelings of mastery—two indications of less happiness—than reported by heterosexual males. However, the researchers found no signs of lower quality of life among lesbians. Moreover, the elevated distress among gay men may logically reflect the toll of experiencing discrimination in the wider world and may have nothing to do with emotional problems basic to being gay and male (Sandfort, de Graaf, & Bijl, 2003).

Stereotype: Homosexual parents have pathological family interactions and disturbed children.

Scientific Fact: British researchers compared groups of lesbian-mother, two-parent heterosexual, and single-mother families (Golombok and others, 2003). They rated the parents and their elementary-school-aged children on various measures of child rearing and mental health. Boys and girls raised in lesbian families had no problems with their gender identity and had no signs of impaired mental health. In fact, the lesbian mothers showed some signs of superior parenting—hitting their children less frequently and engaging in more fantasy play.

Stereotype: People decide to be gay at various points in life.

Scientific Fact: As you saw in Chapter 8, children's first awareness of having homosexual feelings typically takes place at a remarkably uniform age—roughly age 9 or 10, when the body starts producing androgens. In one U.S. study exploring other developmental milestones, participants reported having their first same-sex encounter at an average age of 16, and initially disclosing their sexual identity to a heterosexual best friend and then to a family member at roughly ages 17 and 19 (Maguen and others, 2002). (See the discussion of coming out to family on page 324.) Each of these milestones, however, occurs at older ages in China, which has strong taboos against homosexuality, about shaming the family, and about openly discussing sex (Wong & Tang, 2004).

Cohabitation

A third "new" love feature—*cohabitation*, or sharing a household in an unmarried romantic relationship—doesn't really qualify as all that new. It began to blossom during the flower-child years of the late 1960s. Notice from Figure 10.6 how cohabitation rates first leaped up during the 1970s and then continued to make inroads in American life during the final decades of the twentieth century.

Couples who live together range in age from 17 to 97, but rates of cohabitation are highest between the ages of 18 and 24 (Fields & Casper, 2001). Therefore social scientists suggest that cohabitation is now fulfilling many of the intimacy needs that marriage once did, especially during the emerging-adult years (Goldscheider & Waite, 1991; Popenoe, 1993; Qian & Preston, 1993).

Still, cohabitation is qualitatively different from the married state. Couples who live together are more interested in independence than are those who ultimately wed (Cunningham & Antill, 1994). They tend to differ more in religion and ethnicity (Fields & Casper, 2001; Schoen & Weinick, 1993). They are far less likely to share finances or to own their own home (Axinn & Barber, 1997). For many people, like Sam in the chapter-opening vignette, cohabitation operates as a midway state: "I'm not ready for a more permanent commitment, but I still want to be with the person I love."

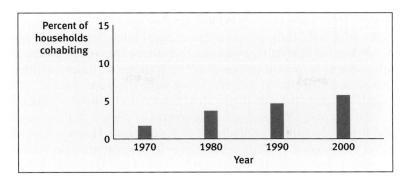

FIGURE 10.6: The fraction of "households cohabiting," 1970–2000: Rates of cohabitation (shown here as a percentage of U.S. households with two or more unrelated adults) rose dramatically during the 1970s, then continued to increase, but more slowly, during the final two decades of the twentieth century.
Source: Fields & Casper (2001).

Living together is often viewed as a midway state in another respect. Many people see it as an essential step on the pathway to getting married (Smock & Gupta, 2002). Let's spell out the typical path: As your relationship becomes more serious, you move in together. Your reasoning is logical: "Before we get married, we need to live together. Then we will find out if we can have a marriage that can last."

Statistically speaking, however, this conclusion is wrong. Polls in a variety of European countries as well as Canada and the United States show that married couples who report previous cohabitation, especially several of these experiences, are more likely to report having gotten divorced (Kiernan, 2002; Schoen, 1992; Thomson & Colella, 1992).

One key to understanding this correlation lies in *selection forces*—the fact that a nonrandom sample is choosing the "living together before marriage" state (Hoelter & Stauffer, 2002; Smock & Gupta, 2002). As you will see later in this chapter, people tend to be relatively consistent in their approach to love relationships. It makes sense that a person with a history of exiting close relationships before marriage would be more likely to exit from marriage, too.

More general attitudes may also be involved. Highly religious emerging adults are less likely to cohabit before marriage (Kiernan, 2002; Turcotte & Belanger, 1997). These same people tend to have stronger-than-average moral strictures against divorce. In this case, the correlation between cohabitation and later divorce is due to a third variable, religious commitment, rather than to any issue basic to living together.

To prove that living together is bad for marriage, we would have to do an impossible experiment: randomly assign couples to cohabit or not, see them get married, then track which marriages last. Without this study, we cannot blame a friend's divorce on the fact that she and her husband lived together before the ceremony took place.

The cohabitation statistics offer an excellent example of the problems of generalizing from a global correlation to diverse groups. Some couples who cohabit would never consider marriage. Others move in together to see if they might be compatible. Still others cohabit when they definitely plan to get engaged. The main issue—if you are living with someone you love—is to explore your motivations. For different emerging adults, cohabitation means very different things.

This tour of the changing social context of finding a mate tells us nothing about how people really connect. Do opposites attract, or do we choose our mirror selves? How do relationships develop and progress?

[FAQ: Is cohabitation good or bad for marriage?]

Traditional Looks at Love: Similarity and Structured Relationship Stages

Bernard Murstein's now-classic **stimulus-value-role theory** (1970) views mate selection as a three-phase process. During the **stimulus phase,** we see a potential partner and make our first decision: "Could this be a good choice for me?" "Would this person want me?" Since we know nothing about the person, our judgment is based on superficial signs, such as looks or the way the individual dresses. In this assessment, we compare our own reinforcement value to the other person's along a number of dimensions (Murstein,

stimulus-value-role theory Murstein's mate-selection theory that similar people pair up and that the path to commitment goes through three phases (called the stimulus, value-comparison, and role phases).

stimulus phase In Murstein's theory, the initial mate-selection stage, in which judgments about a potential partner are based on external characteristics such as appearance.

value-comparison phase In Murstein's theory, the second mate-selection stage, in which judgments about a partner are made on the basis of similar values and interests.

role phase In Murstein's theory, the final mate-selection stage, in which committed partners work out their future life together.

[FAQ: How do we choose our mates?]

homogamy The principle that we select a mate who is similar to us.

1999): "True, I am not as good-looking, but she may find me desirable because I am better educated." If the person seems of equal value, we decide to go on a date.

When we start dating, we enter the **value-comparison phase.** Here, our goal is to select the right person by matching up in terms of inner qualities and traits: "Does this person share my interests? Do we have the same values?" If this person seems "right," we enter the **role phase,** in which we decide how to work out our shared lives.

So at a party, Michael scans the room and decides that Samantha with the tattoos and frumpy-looking Abigail are out of the question. He can do much better than that! Erika, surrounded by all those men, may be *too* beautiful. He gravitates to Ashley, who seems very appealing. Her dress and her way of speaking suggest that she might be athletic or intellectual, and maybe—like him—a bit shy. As Michael and Ashley begin dating, he discovers to his delight that they really are on the same wavelength. They enjoy the same movies; they both love the mountains; they have the same worldview. The romance could still end. On their third or tenth date, there may be a revelation that "this person is way too different." But if things go smoothly, Michael and Ashley will begin planning their future. Should they move to California when they graduate? Will their wedding be small and intimate or big and expensive?

The "equal-reinforcement-value partner" part of Murstein's theory explains why we intuitively expect couples to fit in terms of their social status. We're not surprised if the best-looking girl in high school dates the captain of the football team. When we find what appear to be serious partner value mismatches, we search for reasons to explain these discrepancies (Murstein, Reif, & Syracuse-Siewert, 2002): "That handsome young lawyer must have low self-esteem or 'a mother complex' to have settled for that unattractive older woman." "Perhaps he chose that woman because she has millions in the bank."

Most important, Murstein's theory suggests that opposites definitely do *not* attract. In love relationships, as in childhood and adolescent friendships, the driving force is **homogamy** (similarity). Our goal is to find a soul mate, a person who matches us not just in external status but in basic interests, needs, and attitudes about life.

Homogamy is propelled by our personal choices. We actively put ourselves in situations that give us a sense of flow. If your passion is politics, you may join the college Democrats and meet your soul mate. If you are devoted to your religion, you might find the love of your life at the local Bible study group.

Homogamy is promoted by a passive process, the fact that human beings naturally swim in similar social ponds. A Jewish young man is apt to date and marry within his religion simply by virtue of growing up in a mainly Jewish environment and having mainly Jewish friends. The valedictorian of your high school class who attends an Ivy League school naturally finds herself in the ideal place to meet her intellectual mate. Because birds of a feather cluster together, we meet, date, and marry our own kind (Laumann and others, 1994).

The process of passive selection even applies to neighborhoods, as a large-scale sociological study of mate-selection practices in Chicago demonstrated (Laumann and others, 2004). Researchers fanned out to interview residents about their dating and mating activities in this major U.S. city that, while segmented into definite neighborhoods, is a model of the diversity of American life. They discovered to their surprise that African Americans living on Chicago's South Side were unlikely to date African Americans from the west side of the city. The serious dating scene in Chicago was circumscribed by neighborhood because people connect through their local social networks. They may meet at their neighborhood church or fitness center or through their high school friends.

These young people sharing their passion for fitness may be in Murstein's *value-comparison* phase. Will they make it to the *role phase*?

Finally, we tend to date and marry similar others because of our *personal* need to have our partner mesh with our family and friends. It is an illusion that people simply choose a mate entirely on their own. Because we enter the landscape of adult love embedded in a network of other close love relationships, the input of close attachment figures weighs heavily in our romantic choices (Baxter & Widenmann, 1993). In one survey conducted at a California state university, although undergraduates said they would have no problem dating interracially, many still said that—all other things being equal—they would prefer marrying within their ethnic group (Fiebert and others, 2004). Have you had second thoughts about a romantic partner or decided to break off a relationship because your friends didn't like that person or because your family disapproved?

Ed Kashi / Corbis

Pleasing your family is still a primary consideration in mate selection in many countries. This bride may have married the person whom her parents picked out— judging by the look on her face!

The idea that family approval outweighs all other concerns is fundamental to the practice of arranged marriages. As you saw with the love story from China at the beginning of this section, throughout most of human history parents selected their child's marital partner, and the partners only later learned to love. It explains the power of Shakespeare's *Romeo and Juliet*: "If you fall in love with someone your family disapproves of, you will suffer a terrible fate." Even in our individualistic society, parents sometimes still take firm control of dating and selecting a mate. The Experiencing the Lifespan box below offers a vivid example of the steps a traditional culture takes to monitor dating and to ensure that young people marry someone of their own kind.

On the next page, we focus on a situation that in the not-so-distant past could have caused horror and banishment from your family and community. Let's say that you are gay and decide to reveal your sexual orientation to your parents, the people you have always loved the most.

EXPERIENCING THE LIFESPAN: ANOTHER PERSPECTIVE ON U.S. DATING AND MATING

To keep in mind that selecting love relationships on our own is far from universal even in our choice-oriented society, listen to Alara, an immigrant from India:

Dating is not allowed in my religion. That is a very strict rule. If I were to date someone and he was not Hindu, I couldn't marry him. If I met a Hindu I might be allowed to see him, but it wouldn't be dating in the traditional sense. You can't date for the experience. It's always for the purpose of marriage.

We have loosened up a bit. My parents had an arranged marriage. My mother's and father's parents were best friends—and my two grandpas decided that my parents would marry each other when they were little children. Mom says if she had had a choice she would not have married Dad. They used to argue all the time. Now that we are grown up, Mom moved back to Pittsburgh and teaches school there, and my dad still lives in Springfield. They still say they are married, but they really don't talk much.

When I was in kindergarten, we moved from India to Pittsburgh, where there is a large Indian community. Eight years ago, my dad got a better job offer, and we moved to western Massachusetts. In Pittsburgh, all my friends were Indian, either Hindu or Muslim; after we went to Springfield I didn't have one Indian friend. They were all Americans. They were real cool, but I always felt their values were different.

My brother is 29 and about to get married. He met Shukla, his fiancée, at a friend's wedding. She lives in California. Every time he visits, her mom chaperones them. They are not allowed to be alone together. My sister is also engaged, but, once again, when they see each other, my mom always has to be there.

I did have a problem with our practices, but I've accepted them. When I lived at home, I didn't date. Then, when I went to college I went crazy for about a year. I fell in love with a Baptist guy, but after a while I realized I had to end the relationship. My mom, it would have broken her heart. I care too much about my family. People would look down on my parents if I married outside our religion. And, suppose I married my Baptist boyfriend, I mean, what religion would my children be? I want to give my children a firm sense of identity. So I'm comfortable waiting until I meet the right Hindu man.

COMING OUT TO MOM AND DAD

Rachel Epstein / The Image Works

This young San Francisco couple got married in February 2004. Some gay young people have trouble proudly admitting their sexual identity.

Imagine you are a parent, and your child has just informed you that he or she is gay. You may have suspected the truth for years, but the revelation can hit like a bomb-shell. Believing that this lifestyle is just fine in the abstract is different from feeling that this lifestyle is just fine for *your child.* If this is your only child, you may feel a sense of mourning as you realize that your fantasies of grandparenthood will be less easily fulfilled. You may worry about telling other family members or even be anxious about what "the neighbors" may think. Most important, you have fears for the future: Will your baby be exposed to prejudice and have trouble finding fulfilling love? In a series of interviews with U.S. teenagers and emerging adults, Rich Savin-Williams (2001; Savin-Williams & Ream, 2003) explored how young people deliver this news and how it is received.

The media are rife with hair-raising stories of parents banishing gay offspring from the house. Savin-Williams found this portrait to be seriously off-kilter. Only 4 percent of the young people in his study described outright parental rejection or verbal abuse. Many parents did wrestle with intense feelings. However, after a short period of adjustment, the majority rallied around their child. Few sons or daughters felt that their relationship with their parents deteriorated after coming out. Most reported that they felt either closer or just as close as before.

Coming out is a gradual process. People first must be clear about their feelings. Then they typically confide in a good friend. Finally, they decide if and when to tell their family the news. Most of the people in Savin-Williams's study made the an-nouncement at about age 19. There was considerable variability, however—from the young people who came out as young as age 13 to those who said they would never tell.

Imagine you are a gay emerging adult who has yet to come out to your parents. How can you predict how they will respond? Savin-Williams suggests the key lies in know-ing your family. Once again, the best predictor of future behavior is past behavior. If your parents are homophobic or intolerant, it's a good bet they will react poorly to your news. If you feel that coming out may put you in genuine jeopardy, you should trust your gut instincts and not tell. But if you and your family have a close, caring relation-ship, revealing your sexual orientation will not make a dent in that enduring bond.

The strong caution is that these upbeat data have been filtered only from the child's side of the equation and only from the young people who felt comfortable enough to tell their families, not from those who were reluctant to tell the truth. Still, Savin-Williams's research makes an important point: Gay young people are like all young people. We cannot assume that they are alienated or distant from their parents. We cannot assume that they relate in *any* stereotyped way. Diversity is a hallmark of fam-ily relationships among young people with same-sex orientations, just as it is with other teenagers and emerging adults.

New Looks at Love: Irrationality, Unpredictability, and Attachment Styles

So far, we have looked at love as a realistic process of matching up. We look for similarity in our partner. We expect our mate to mesh well with our family and friends. We get in-volved in predictable stages. But there is far less predictability to romance in the real world.

Irrationality and Unpredictability

[FAQ: Why do people fall in or out of love?]

Researchers find that, rather than seeing a realistic image, people in highly satisfying relationships tend to view their mates through rose-colored glasses (Murray & Holmes, 1997). They inflate their partner's virtues. They describe the person in more glowing terms than either friends or the person would describe their own personality (Murray and others, 2000). They overestimate the extent to which they and their partner are alike. They see more similarities than really exist when asked to describe the other person's values and day-to-day feelings (Murray and others, 2002). They interpret neutral or negative actions through a more positive lens (Gable, Reis, & Downey, 2003; more about this in Chapter 11). So science confirms George Bernard Shaw's classic observation: "Love is a gross exaggeration of the difference between one person and everyone else."

Moreover, the inner experience of commitment does not translate neatly into structured phases such as stimulus, value-comparison, and role periods. We have doubts and ups and downs; our feelings about the relationship and our partner fluctuate.

To get firsthand insights into this emotional ebb and flow, researchers asked couples who were seriously dating to graph their chances (from 0 to 100 percent) of marrying their partner (Surra & Hughes, 1997; Surra, Hughes, & Jacquet, 1999). They then had the young people return each month to chart changes in their commitment level and asked them to describe the reasons for any dramatic relationship turning points, for better or worse.

You can see interesting examples of these turning points in Table 10.7. Notice that relationships do often hinge on homogamy issues ("This person is really right for me") and the input of family and friends. Still, other causes may be turning points—from social comparisons ("Our relationship seems better than theirs") to the simple insight, "I'm really too young to get involved."

Sometimes people know exactly when their relationship has reached a critical turning point. As one woman reported, "He told me to sit down and . . . he had something to tell me . . . , and then he just looked at me and he said, 'I love you'" (quoted in Surra, Hughes, & Jacquet, 1999, p. 139). At other times, everything seems to be going according to schedule, when an event that has nothing to do with you or your partner intrudes: "I talked to my dad . . . who felt he got married too young so he was a little bit more encouraging against getting married" (quoted in Surra, Hughes, & Jacquet, 1999, p. 138).

One of the most interesting findings in this study and others is that we can often predict the outcome of a relationship by looking at its overall features. Some relationships accelerate gradually to a higher level of commitment, with couples getting closer and closer over time. Others are **event-driven**, punctuated by intense highs and lows. People start out passionately involved, then repeatedly fight and break up, to become passionately involved again. Event-driven relationships are more fragile. Dramatic ups and downs are a sign that a romance is less likely to endure (Arriaga, 2001; Surra, Hughes, & Jacquet, 1999).

So, yes, relationships may progress in stages, and we can definitely spell out the principle that homogamy matters in love. But we should not ignore the messy reality of real-world romance: It helps to exaggerate your partner's good qualities and his soul-mate-like similarity to you. (That's what love is all about!) Relationships have unpredictable twists and turns. If a romance involves *many* dramatic twists and turns, however, that relationship is at risk of being derailed.

Now let's take a different perspective, as we shift from exploring the qualities of relationships to examining the personalities of the partners in the romance.

***TABLE 10.7* Some Major Positive (+) and Negative (−) Turning Points in a Relationship**

Personal Compatibility/Homogamy

We spent a lot of time together. +

We had a big fight. −

We had similar interests. +

He was acting like a jerk. −

She said she was still upset about me going out without her. −

Compatibility with Family and Friends

My friends kept saying that Sue was bad for me. −

She met my whole family. +

I fit right in with his family. +

Her dad just hated me. −

We had a better relationship than my friends did. +

Other Random Forces

I just turned 21, so I don't want to be tied down to anyone. −

The guy I used to date started calling me. −

We always got along better in hot weather. +

Source: Adapted from Surra, Hughes, & Jacquet (1999).

If you are in a relationship, have you experienced any of these turning points?

event-driven relationship An erratic love relationship characterized by dramatic shifts in feelings and sense of commitment, with the couple repeatedly breaking up, then getting back together again.

[FAQ: How do I enhance or evaluate my primary relationship?]

adult attachment styles
The various ways in which adults relate to romantic partners, based on Mary Ainsworth's infant attachment styles. Classified as secure and preoccupied/ambivalent insecure or avoidant/dismissive insecure.

preoccupied/ambivalent insecure attachment
An excessively clingy, needy style of relating to loved ones.

avoidant/dismissive insecure attachment A standoffish, excessively disengaged style of relating to loved ones.

Adult Attachment Styles

Think back to Chapter 4's discussion of the different infant attachment styles (page 112). Remember that Mary Ainsworth (1973) found that *securely attached* babies run with hugs and kisses when Mom appears in the room. *Avoidant* infants act cold, aloof, and indifferent in the Strange Situation when the caregiver returns. *Anxious/ambivalent* babies are overly clingy, afraid to explore the toys, and angry and inconsolable when their caregiver arrives. Now think of your own romantic relationships, or the relationships of family members or friends. Wouldn't these same attachment categories apply to adult romantic love? Cindy Hazan and Phillip Shaver (1987) had the same insight: Let's draw on Ainsworth's dimensions to classify people into specific **adult attachment styles.**

People with the **preoccupied/ambivalent** type of insecure attachment fall quickly and deeply in love (see the box below). But, because they are engulfing and needy in their relationships, they often end up being rejected or feeling chronically unfulfilled. Adults with an **avoidant/dismissive** form of insecure attachment are at the opposite end of the spectrum—withholding and aloof, reluctant to engage. You

---

❧ HOW DO WE KNOW . . .

that a person is securely or insecurely attached?

How do developmentalists classify adults as either securely or insecurely attached? In the *current relationship interview,* they ask people questions about their goals and feelings about their romantic relationships; for example, "What happens when either of you is in trouble? Can you rely on each other to be there emotionally?" Trained evaluators then code the responses.

People are labeled securely attached if they coherently describe the pluses and minuses of their own behavior and of the relationship; if they talk freely about their desire for intimacy; and if they adopt an other-centered perspective, seeing nurturing the other person's development as a primary goal. Those who describe their relationship in formal, stilted ways, emphasize "autonomy issues," or talk about the advantages of being together in nonintimate terms ("We are buying a house"; "We go places"), are classified as avoidant/dismissive. Those who express total dependence ("I can't function unless she is nearby"), anger about not being treated correctly, or fears of being left are classified as preoccupied/ambivalent.

This in-depth interview technique is extremely time-intensive. But many attachment researchers argue that it reveals a person's attachment style better than questionnaires in which people simply check "yes" or "no" to indicate whether items on a scale apply to them.

Avoidant/dismissive insecure attachment
- **Definition:** Unable to get close in relationships.
- **Signs:** Uncaring, aloof, emotionally distant. Unresponsive to loving feelings. Abruptly disengages at signs of involvement. Unlikely to be in a long-term relationship.

Secure attachment
- **Definition:** Capable of genuine intimacy in relationships.
- **Signs:** Empathic, sensitive, able to reach out emotionally. Balances own needs with those of partner. Has affectionate, caring interactions. Probably in a loving, long-term relationship.

Preoccupied/ambivalent insecure attachment
- **Definition:** Needy and engulfing in relationships.
- **Signs:** Excessively jealous, suffocating. Needs continual reassurance of being totally loved. Unlikely to be in a loving, long-term relationship.

Source: Crowell, Fraley, & Shaver (2002).

may have dated this kind of person, someone whose main mottos seem to be "stay independent," "don't share," and "avoid getting emotionally close" (Feeney, 1999).

Securely attached people are emotionally fully open to love. They give their partner space to differentiate, yet are firmly committed. Like Ainsworth's secure infants, their faces light up when they talk about their partner. Their joy in their love shines through.

Decades of studies exploring these different attachment styles through interviews and questionnaires show that insecurely attached adults have trouble with relationships. Securely attached adults are successful in the world of love (Crowell, Fraley, & Shaver, 1999; Feeney, 1999; Mikulincer and others, 2002; Morgan & Shaver, 1999).

Securely attached adults have happier marriages. They report more satisfying romances (Crowell, Fraley, & Shaver, 1999; Feeney, 1999; Mikulincer and others, 2002; Morgan & Shaver, 1999). They are more likely to *be* romantically involved (Bookwala, 2003). Securely attached adults are more sensitive to their partner's signals. They give support when needed. They hold off when their loved one does not need their help (Simpson and others, 2002). Using the metaphor of mother–infant attachment described in Chapter 4, adults with secure attachments know how to dance, or to really be emotionally responsive and in tune.

Recall that John Bowlby and Ainsworth believe that the dance of attachment between caregiver and baby is the basis for feeling securely attached in infancy and for dancing well in every other relationship in life. If you listen to friends bemoaning their relationship missteps, you will hear similar ideas: "The reason I act so clingy and jealous is that during my childhood I felt unloved." "It's hard for me to warm up and show my love because my mom was so rejecting and cold." How enduring are adult attachment styles, and how much can they change?

To answer this question, researchers measured the attachment styles of several hundred women at intervals over two years (Cozzarelli and others, 2003). They found that almost one half of the women had changed categories over that time. So the good news is that we can change our status from insecure to secure. And—as will come as no surprise to many readers—we can also move in the opposite direction, temporarily feeling insecurely attached after a terrible experience with love. The best way to conceptualize attachment styles, then, is as somewhat enduring and consistent, arising in part from our ongoing experiences in love and the world (Feeney, 1999).

One reason attachment styles have a tendency to stay stable is that they operate as a self-fulfilling prophecy. A preoccupied, clingy person does tend to be rejected repeatedly. An avoidant individual remains locked in isolation simply because piercing that armored shell takes such a heroic effort. A secure, loving person lives awash in warm, caring responses.

Are there normal developmental changes in our sense of attachment security as we travel through adult life? Stay tuned for Chapter 12, where we examine research relevant to this question as we chart how personality changes from emerging adulthood to the older years.

By now you are probably impressed with the power of Ainsworth's attachment-styles framework in offering guidelines for how to sensibly select a mate. Bowlby's (1969) analyses of the forces that universally drive attachment responses are equally powerful at offering insights into love relationships that make little logical sense. Remember that Bowlby believes that our biologically programmed attachment response is automatically activated in situations in which we feel vulnerable. So it is natural to fall in love with surgeons, psychotherapists, or other powerful people when we are in pain.

The principle that stress provokes proximity-seeking behavior also explains why exciting, unreliable partners (who are bad for us) and passionate, event-driven relationships have such uncanny appeal. It even normalizes the trouble that victims of abuse sometimes have shedding their addiction to a battering mate. We may not need years of therapy to understand these so-called pathological love choices. We can treat them as examples of distortions of the normal human impulse to seek security when we are in distress (Morgan & Shaver, 1999). Attachment theory allows us to look at *every* love relationship through a new and revealing lens.

secure attachment The genuine intimacy that is ideal in love relationships.

[FAQ: How does early attachment shape later love relationships?**]**

[FAQ: How can I evaluate my primary relationship?]

INTERVENTIONS: **Evaluating Your Own Relationship**

How can you use this information to help ensure smoother-sailing love? Try to select someone who is similar to you in values and interests. Be attentive to how well your choice meshes with the people you care about the most. Focus on the outstanding "special qualities" of your partner. Be wary of stormy, event-driven relationships. Look for a partner who is securely attached. Take care, however, to note the message of the research on relationship turning points: If things don't work out, it easily may have *nothing* to do with you, your partner, or any problem basic to how well you get along! If you want to evaluate your own relationship now, you might take the questionnaire based on these chapter points in Table 10.8.

TABLE 10.8 Evaluating Your Own Relationship: A Section Summary Checklist

	Yes	No
1. Are you and your partner similar in interests and values?	❑	❑
You don't have to be clones of each other, but the research shows that the more similar you are in attitudes and basic worldviews, the greater your chances of a happy relationship.		
2. Do your other "attachment figures," such as close friends and family, like your partner?	❑	❑
Not everyone needs to adore your partner, but if your most central attachment figures really dislike your partner, problems may arise.		
3. Do you each believe that your partner is unique and wonderful, the absolute best?	❑	❑
Deciding that this person has no human flaws is not necessary—but seeing your partner as "unique and special" predicts staying together as well as being happy.		
4. Is your relationship progressing toward greater commitment at a fairly steady rate?	❑	❑
If you have minor arguments, that's fine; but if you and your partner repeatedly have huge fights, break up, and get back together, that's not a good sign.		
5. Is your partner able to fully reach out in love, neither intensely jealous nor aloof?	❑	❑
Some jealousy or hesitation about commitment can be normal, but in general your partner should be securely attached and able to love.		

If you checked "yes" for all five of these questions, your relationship is in excellent shape. If you checked "no" for every question, your "relationship" does not exist! One or two no's mixed in with yesses suggest areas that need additional work.

 TYING IT ALL TOGETHER

1. You are getting serious with your significant other and are considering cohabiting, but are worried about the impact if you decide to get married. According to the text:

   a. You should definitely decide to cohabit. Living together before marriage reduces the chance of divorce.
   b. You should definitely *not* cohabit. Living together before marriage causes marriages to break up.
   c. You should ask your parents and friends. They will know what is right.
   d. There are no firm research guidelines. For different people, cohabitation means very different things.

2. Natasha and Akbar met at a friend's New Year's Eve party and just started dating. They are about to find out whether they share similar interests, backgrounds, and worldviews. This couple is in Murstein's (choose one) *stimulus/value-comparison/role* phase of romantic relationships.

3. Jared and Brittany are arguing about how people choose a partner. Jared says that opposites attract because they balance each other's weaknesses. Brittany says that we

look for someone just like us, someone who shares our values, interests, and attitudes. Who is right?

4. Kinasha is clingy and always feels rejected. Rena runs away from intimate relationships. Sam is affectionate and loving. Which of the following alternatives gives the correct combination of attachment statuses for these three people?

    a. Kinasha's attachment category is preoccupied/ambivalent insecure; Rena's is avoidant/dismissive insecure; Sam's is secure.

    b. Kinasha's attachment category is avoidant/dismissive insecure; Rena's is preoccupied/ambivalent insecure; Sam's is controlled insecure.

    c. Kinasha's category is ambivalent secure; Rena's is aloof secure; Sam's is controlled secure.

    d. Kinasha's attachment status is needy; Rena's is ambivalently insecure; Sam's is controlled insecure.

Answers to the Tying It All Together questions can be found in the answers section of the book.

❧ Final Thoughts

In this chapter, we have only begun our exploration into two major adult agendas, finding love and finding satisfying work. In Chapter 11, we continue this discussion as we look more deeply at relationships and work during the first half of adult life. What happens when people get married, and how do marriages change over time? How can we categorize love relationships, and are there specific couple communication strategies that can alert us to whether relationships are destined to founder or work out? Do careers go through specific phases, and what strategies—other than finding flow—can you use to have a satisfying career? How has the landscape of career and marriage changed in the Western world over the past 30 years? In the next chapter, we explore these topics and others, as well as provide an in-depth look at parenting—the third major adult role.

▐ SUMMARY

Emerging Adulthood

Psychologists have identified a new life phase called **emerging adulthood.** This in-between, not-quite-fully-adult time of life, beginning after high school and tapering off by the late twenties, involves testing out adult **roles.** Emerging adulthood is specific to living in the developed world today, although this life stage differs from country to country. In Italy, young people typically live at home and have trouble becoming financially independent adults. In Sweden, **cohabitation** and having babies before marriage are widespread. Government help, plus the emphasis placed on hiring young people, makes **nest-leaving** at age 18 the norm in Sweden.

In the United States, people often move backward and forward as they progress to becoming "full adults." However, the real U.S. pattern is tremendous variability. Emerging adulthood differs dramatically from person to person and is affected by cultural and socioeconomic forces.

Today, U.S. adults often leave the nest and become independent at around age 18, but they may periodically move back in with their parents. The danger of moving back is the potential for sliding into a less adult state. Sons tend to stay in the nest longer than daughters and are also more likely to move back home.

Social clock pressures, or **age norms,** set the boundaries of the emerging-adult stage of life. Exploring is **on time,** or appropriate, in the twenties, but is **off time** if it extends well into the thirties. Social clock issues, as well as other concerns, make emerging adulthood a time of special stress.

Constructing an Identity

Deciding on one's **identity,** Erikson's first task in becoming an adult, is the major challenge facing emerging adults. Erikson believed that exploring various possibilities and taking time to ponder this vital question is critical to developing a solid adult self. At the opposite pole lies **identity confusion**—drifting and seeing no adult future.

Marcia identified four **identity statuses: identity diffusion** (drifting aimlessly), **identity foreclosure** (leaping into an identity without any thought), **moratorium** (exploring different pathways), and **identity achievement** (settling on an identity). Marcia's statuses clearly spell out Erikson's ideas. But the statuses are less developmental than Marcia imagined. They often vary in different areas of a person's life, and for all of us identity development is lifelong. Moreover, foreclosure is not necessarily pathological. Traditionally, it has been the only accepted life path. Today, some young people in the developing world and emerging adults who relocate to developed countries form **bicultural identities**—identifying with both their own cultural traditions and those of our modern global society.

Finding a Career

In a pioneering study of career aspirations, researchers found that teenagers have high career goals. The downside is that many adolescents have unrealistic career dreams. Teenagers who are workers seem better able to lock into a career identity. Players (or highly work-averse teenagers) may be more likely to end up in career diffusion. Players, however, may turn into workers, as emerging adulthood is the time of life when personality changes most.

Flow is a feeling of total absorption in a challenging task. The hours seem to pass like minutes, intrinsic motivation is high, and our skills are in balance with the demands of a given task. Flow states can alert us to our ideal careers.

Although most people do enter college, only a minority complete their degree. Young people who emerge directly into the workforce tend to end up in the **secondary labor market,** rather than in more desirable **primary labor market** jobs. Career maturity and finding a sense of flow in a job are the keys to feeling satisfied when emerging directly into the work world.

Japan and Germany are models for a well-organized **school-to-work transition,** and they suggest that the United States could do more to strengthen the connection between high school and careers. Although the U.S. unstructured pathway has the benefit of giving everyone a second chance, it can produce anxiety as young people flounder in their search for jobs. Another problem is the contemporary emphasis on college for all. Because the odds of making it through college are far lower for students in the bottom half of their high school class, experts suggest first developing a track record at work.

For young people who emerge into college, the key to undergraduate satisfaction lies in feeling engaged at school. Tips for achieving this goal include living on or near campus, avoiding full-time work, using these years to explore career-relevant work, making connections with professors, and getting to know other students of different ethnic backgrounds.

Finding Love

The second emerging-adult task, **intimacy**—finding committed love—has changed dramatically over the past 30 years. We now find love on the Internet through **virtual dating.** Interracial dating and gay relationships are far more acceptable, although **homophobia,** an intense fear and dislike of gays, still exists.

Cohabitation, living together before marriage, is a common feature of Western life.

Cohabitation may be substituting for marriage during the emerging-adult years, but living together outside of marriage is statistically associated with a higher risk of divorce after being wed. The correlation between cohabitation and divorce does not mean that living together causes divorce. Cohabitation has different meanings for different emerging adults.

Stimulus-value-role theory spells out a three-stage process leading to marriage. First, we select a potential partner who looks appropriate (the **stimulus phase**); then, during the **value-comparison** phase, we find out whether that person shares our interests and worldview. Finally, during the **role phase,** we plan our lives together. **Homogamy,** people's tendency to choose similar partners and partners of equivalent status to themselves, is the main principle underlying this theory.

The chances of finding a homogamous partner are enhanced by the fact that people select activities where they find similar others and tend to meet people in their own social group. The need to have a partner mesh with our other attachment figures also promotes homogamy.

When gay young people come out to their parents, the parent–child bond is not typically threatened. People who have close, loving relationships with their parents are not in danger of losing that enduring love.

A good deal of irrationality is involved in romance. We tend to idealize a partner and exaggerate our similarities. Relationships have turning points rather than progressing in a smooth, patterned way. Stormy, **event-driven relationships** are less likely to endure.

Researchers have spelled out three **adult attachment styles.** Adults ranked as insecurely attached—either **preoccupied/ambivalent** (overly clingy and engulfing) or **avoidant/dismissive** (overly aloof and detached)—have poorer-quality love relationships. **Securely attached** adults tend to be successful in love and marriage. Adult attachment styles can change. Just as Ainsworth's ideas have enriched our understanding of individual differences in adult relationships, Bowlby's ideas make sense of why people make inappropriate love choices.

▌ KEY TERMS

▮ RECOMMENDED RESOURCES

Arnett, J. J. (2004). *Emerging adulthood: The winding road from the late teens through the twenties*. New York: Oxford University Press.

This is the definitive book on emerging adulthood.

Csikszentmihalyi, M. (1990) *Flow: The psychology of optimal experience*. New York: Harper.

In this compelling book written for a popular audience, Csikszentmihalyi spells out the facets and wide-ranging aspects of flow.

Csikszentmihalyi, M., & Schneider, B. (2000). *Becoming adult: How teenagers prepare for the world of work*. New York: Basic Books.

This book exploring teenage career dreams will be especially good reading for budding researchers interested in seeing how a huge research project is planned and conducted.

Goldscheider, F., & Goldscheider, C. (1999). *The changing transition to adulthood*. Thousand Oaks, CA: Sage.

This is a definitive historical study of U.S. nest-leaving.

Light, R. (2001). *Making the most of college: Students speak their minds*. Cambridge, MA: Harvard University Press.

This readable book is full of tips for maximizing the college experience.

Savin-Williams, R. C. (2001). *Mom, Dad, I'm gay: How families negotiate coming out*. Washington, DC: American Psychological Association.

Compelling interviews make this scientific study of coming out to parents fascinating reading.

Part V

TIMELINE
(Ages are approximate.)

	EARLY ADULTHOOD	
	20S	30S
PHYSICAL DEVELOPMENT		
COGNITIVE DEVELOPMENT	Fluid IQ declines; crystallized IQ rises	
SOCIOEMOTIONAL DEVELOPMENT		
PERSONALITY	Mental health lower	
LIFE ROLES AND RELATIONSHIPS	Marriage (fourth-year divorce danger zone)	
	Parenthood	
	Establishment phase of career	

Early and Middle Adulthood

This unit on early and middle adulthood covers the time when we are immersed in adult life (roughly our late twenties), but have not yet reached the age when society defines us as senior citizens (our mid-sixties).

Chapter 11, "Relationships and Roles," examines marriage, parenthood, and work. In the marriage section, you will learn about how different societies view this core relationship and how marriages change over time; you will also learn about couple communications and divorce. A special focus of our discussion is exploration of the insights the research offers about having a happy relationship that lasts. In the parenthood section, we trace how becoming parents changes a marriage, and we examine the challenges of motherhood and fatherhood. How have our work lives and work priorities been changing? What qualities make for happiness in a career? These are the kinds of questions we will be looking at in the last section of this chapter: work.

In much of Chapter 12, "Midlife," we focus on the question: "How do people change over the adult years?" Once again, as we survey the research on adult personality and intellectual change, you will get fascinating information about how to have a fulfilling adult life. The last sections of this chapter explore topics specific to mid-life: grandparenthood, caring for elderly parents, and age-related changes in sexuality.

The timeline on these pages spells out some of the milestones that we will discuss during our survey of this 40-year period—the longest in human life.

MIDDLE ADULTHOOD				
40S	50S		LATE 50S	EARLY 60S
Concerns about declining sexuality	Menopause			
Mental health higher				
Generative strivings at peak				
Empty nest (long-term marriages get happier)				
	Grandparenthood			
	Maintenance phase of career		Retirement	
Career peak				
Creativity peak				

CHAPTER 11

Do you know someone like Kevin who is struggling to be a caring husband and an involved father and to support his family? Perhaps you have a friend who, after one divorce, is determined to make a second marriage work. Or you may know a person who is working at a job that is boring or not particularly flow-inducing, and is dreaming of a more rewarding career. If so, you know a twenty-first-century adult.

This section of the book is devoted to being an adult. It covers that long period from the end of emerging adulthood until the senior citizen years. This chapter explores our primary adult relationships: marriage, parenthood, and work. In Chapter 12, we focus on changes in our inner self

Relationships
and Roles

Home at 5 A.M. from the night shift at the Nissan plant and hopefully to bed at 6. Then Mary wakes up and gets the kids ready for school to make it to her accountant job at 8.

Kevin's first marriage, right out of high school, ended in a disastrous divorce. He feels blessed to have this second chance for happiness at age 35. Mary and Kevin met six years ago at a community-wide faith celebration. They share the same values. They understand what marriage is all about—it's about compromise, family, and love. The racial difference hasn't mattered. They are together in their passion for the Lord.

This time, Kevin is trying to be the best possible husband. One divorce in a lifetime was one more than enough! He cooks dinner and helps the kids with their homework. He puts the twins to bed on the evenings when Mary comes home stressed out from work at 8 or 9 P.M.

Kevin's job on the assembly line is incredibly dull. He would love a more fulfilling career. But working nights lets him pick up the kids from school, take them to soccer practice, and get in good family time before leaving for work at 10 P.M. The health benefits at Nissan are great, and there's plenty of overtime. By working double shifts last spring, Kevin was able to finance a family trip to Disney World. Knowing you have the money to give your children this experience is the best feeling a man can have. It's a 24/7 struggle, but this marriage must work for life!

TABLE 11.1: Stereotypes About Family and Work: A Quiz

Write "True" or "False" next to each of the following statements. To see how accurate your beliefs about family and work are, look at the correct answers, printed upside down below the table. As you read through the chapter, you'll find out exactly *why* each statement is true or false.

_____ 1. Americans today are not as interested in getting married as they were in the past.

_____ 2. Poor people often don't get married, because they are basically less interested in having a permanent commitment.

_____ 3. People are happiest in the honeymoon phase of a marriage.

_____ 4. Having children brings married couples closer.

_____ 5. People who don't have children are self-absorbed and narcissistic.

_____ 6. Mothers used to spend more time with their children than they do today.

_____ 7. Men work longer hours today than they did in the 1950s.

_____ 8. The average workweek in the United States is 40 hours.

_____ 9. Young people today are more obsessed with getting ahead than in the past.

_____ 10. You will be a better worker if you care more about your work life than your family life.

Answers: 1. F, 2. F, 3. T, 4. F, 5. F, 6. F, 7. F, 8. F, 9. F, 10. F

as we move into middle age, and we look at topics such as grandparenthood and menopause. Before beginning your reading, you might want to take the quiz about family and work in Table 11.1. In the following pages you will learn *why* each stereotype is right or wrong.

Although we will discuss them separately, the main theme in this chapter is that we cannot look at marriage, parenthood, and career as isolated parts of life. Our work situation determines when we decide to get married. Our feelings about our job spill over into our married life. Having children dramatically changes a marriage and—as you saw with Kevin—determines our career choices. Marriage, parenthood, and career are *tri-directional*, interlocking roles. Moreover, as developmental systems theory would predict, how we approach these core adult roles depends on the time in history and the society in which we live.

Marriage

Imagine being a time traveler from 40 years ago. How strange Kevin's marriage would seem! As recently as 1970, 9 out of every 10 U.S. husbands were the primary breadwinners (Raley, Mattingly, & Bianchi, 2006). So you might be shocked to hear that Kevin had a lower-status job than his spouse. The idea that a man—even with a working wife—would be cooking dinners or regularly helping the children with their homework would also strike you as bizarre (Council on Families in America, 1995; Furstenberg & Cherlin, 1991).

Forty years ago, Kevin would not have been worried about getting *another* divorce. With 9 out of every 10 married couples staying together for life, he would probably have stayed married—no matter how unhappily—to his first wife. Today, with husbands and wives facing a fifty-fifty chance of experiencing this familiar transition, Kevin has good reason to be concerned about having a relationship that can last. How did we get to where we are today with regard to our ideas about married life?

Setting the Context: The Changing Landscape of Marriage

Throughout much of human history, as you saw in Chapter 10, people often got married based on practical concerns. With many marriages being arranged by the brides' and grooms' parents, and with daily life being so difficult, most couples did not have the luxury of marrying simply for love. In addition, before the twentieth century, life expectancy was so low that the typical marriage only lasted about 20 years before one partner died.

Then, during the early decades of the previous century, as medical advances allowed people to routinely live into later life, Western societies developed the idea that people should get married in their early twenties and be lovers and best friends for a half century or more. The traditional marriage of the 1950s, with defined gender roles, reflected this idealized vision of enduring love (Cherlin, 2004; Coontz, 1992).

In the last third of the twentieth century, our ideas about marriage in the West took a dramatic turn. The women's movement told us that women should have careers and that husbands and wives should share the child care. As a result of the 1960s lifestyle revolution, which stressed personal fulfillment, we rejected the idea that people should stay in an unhappy marriage for life (Cherlin, 2004; Furstenberg & Cherlin, 1991). People could get divorced, decide to have babies without being married, and even choose not to get married at all.

The outcome has been a late-twentieth-century change that social scientists call the **deinstitutionalization of marriage.** What they mean is that marriage has been transformed from a standard life "institution" into a more optional choice.

deinstitutionalization of marriage The decline in marriage and the emergence of alternate family forms that occurred during the last third of the twentieth century.

From the 1950s stay-at-home mom to the two-career marriage with fully engaged dads—over the last third of the twentieth century, a revolution occurred in our ideas about "traditional" married life. How do you feel about these lifestyle changes?

TABLE 11.2: Some Signs of the Deinstitutionalization of Marriage in the United States During the Late Twentieth Century*

Sign	1960–1970 (percent)	Late 1990s (percent)
Childbirths outside of marriage	5	30+
Probability of marriage ending in divorce	about 14	about 50
Married-couple households	71	53
Children living with one parent	9	40
People living alone	17	26

*Rough data from 1960 and 1970 and from 1990 and 2000.

Sources: Furstenberg & Cherlin (1991); Fields & Casper (2001).

Table 11.2 shows statistics related to this change in the United States: a tremendous rise in divorce rates, an increase in having children without being married, the large percentage of adults living alone or in a variety of family forms other than marriage. Although the specific statistics vary from country to country, researchers find similar shifts away from conventional marriage in other developed nations over the past 40 years. But around the world, ideas about marriage vary tremendously, perhaps more than at any previous time in history. To get insights into this diversity, let's travel to Egypt and Scandinavia.

Egypt (and Much of the Middle East): Male-Dominated Marriage

As in other traditional Islamic nations, the 1960s social revolutions have not taken place in Egypt, where getting married is still the only acceptable life path. Many Egyptian women do have jobs and they are attending universities in increasing numbers. However, according to Islamic law, when a woman gets married, she is expected to stay at home. In Egypt, as in many other Middle Eastern countries, there is no thought that women and men should have equal status (Moghadam, 2004). Husbands can forbid their wives to work if they feel that their job will interfere with family life. While getting a divorce is extremely difficult for women—involving lengthy court battles—until recently, if a man wanted to end his marriage, he could simply tell his wife, "I no longer want you around" (Yount & Agree, 2004). Moreover, when an Egyptian couple does get divorced, the husband automatically gets custody of any son over age 10 and any daughter over age 12.

Given these conditions, it is no wonder that a young unmarried Egyptian woman in an interview study gave this unromantic answer when a researcher asked what she hoped for from married life: "I don't believe in love. The only kind of love [I know] is for my mother and sister . . . I want to marry a man who is rich, successful and able to take responsibility" (Amin & Al-Bassusi, 2004, p. 1295).

Scandinavia: Marriage Doesn't Matter

In comparison, Scandinavian ideas about marriage seem to be from a different planet. With one in two babies being born to single mothers in Norway, Sweden, and Denmark (versus roughly one in three in England, Canada, and the United States), in Scandinavia, having children has become almost irrelevant to getting married (Cherlin, 2004). With rates of cohabitation reaching almost 50 percent in Sweden, the deinstitutionalization of marriage is virtually complete (see

If you talked to this couple living in Cairo and then visited this Scandinavian family enjoying a picnic by a lake, the difference in scenery would be symbolic of a totally different approach to men's and women's roles and married life. In fact, there would be a fifty-fifty chance that the Swedish parents would not be married at all!

FIGURE 11.1: **Married and cohabiting couples aged 30–39, selected EU countries:** Rates of marriage versus cohabitation among people in their prime marriage years vary a good deal in different European nations. Notice that in Sweden, among couples in their thirties, living together is just as common as being married.

Source: Adapted from Kiernan (2004), p. 982.

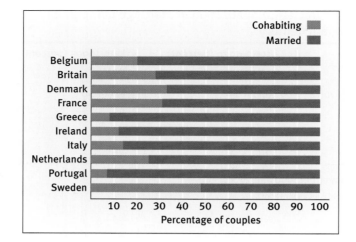

[FAQ: Is our interest in marriage similar to that of our parents?]

Figure 11.1). It's not that Scandinavian adults are anti-marriage. They simply see getting married as one among a number of *equally acceptable* alternatives for living a fulfilling life (Kiernan, 2002, 2004).

The United States: Dreaming of Marriage for Life

Where do we stand in the United States? Given the dismal divorce statistics, you might think our interest in getting married would have declined. You would be mistaken. Polls show roughly 8 out of 10 U.S. teenagers and emerging adults still want to be married (Waite & Gallagher, 2000; Goldscheider & Waite, 1991; Martin and others, 2003; Thornton & Young-DeMarco, 2001). Although we understand that it is perfectly possible to live rich, fulfilling lives and stay single, in the United States we still firmly believe that being married is the ideal way to construct an adult life (Cherlin, 2004; Waite & Gallagher, 2000). However, Americans are realists. Before deciding to have that wedding ceremony, we want to have certain foundations in place.

Take a minute to think about your requirements for getting married if you are single—or, if you are married, think of your personal goals before you were wed. In addition to finding the right person, if you are like most people you probably believe that entering an enduring commitment demands reaching a certain place in your development. It's important to have a solid sense of identity, to know who you are as a human being. It's also a good idea to feel settled on a career and to be fairly financially secure (Edin, Kefalas, & Reed, 2004). In the United States—as around the world—men are reluctant to get married until they can support a family (Palkovitz, 2002; Smock, Manning, & Porter, 2005). Therefore, as you saw in Chapter 10, because we select partners according to *homogamy*, the marriage market for low-income adults—especially poverty-level single mothers—is very poor (Edin and others, 2004; Lichter, Batson, & Brown, 2004; Schoen & Cheng, 2006). Even when couples are firmly committed to each other, they can find it difficult to move from living together to getting engaged (Smock, Manning, & Porter, 2004).

Read what Candace, a 25-year-old on workers' compensation, had to say about her marriage plans:

> *Um, we have certain things that we want to do before we get married. We both want very good jobs, and we both want a house, and we want reliable transportation. . . . He's been looking out for jobs everywhere and we— . . . we're trying. We just want to have—we gotta have everything before we say, "Let's get married."*

(quoted in Smock, Manning, & Porter, 2005, p. 690)

And 30-year old Donald put it more bluntly:

> *[I would marry her] if I was to hit the lottery and could take her somewhere and we wouldn't have to worry about no problems for the rest of our life.*

(quoted in Smock and others, 2005, p. 691)

As these comments imply, social scientists believe that in recent decades we have elevated marriage into a badge of achievement (Cherlin, 2004; Edin and others, 2004; Smock and others, 2004). For very low-income young people, the status symbol is *getting married.* Having a wedding means that a couple has the financial resources to commit to each other in a genuinely permanent way (Cherlin, 2004; Edin and others, 2004; Lichter, Batson, & Brown, 2004; Sweeney, 2002).

Another major achievement—for everyone—lies in managing to stay married for life. I got insights into the awe young people feel about this milestone when a college-student server came up to my husband and me at a local restaurant and shyly asked for our secret when we said we had been married for 27 years.

Is our dream of finding a soul mate for life too idealistic? Should churches and synagogues be encouraging cohabiting couples to "just get married," given that their decision *not to get married* may be a rational choice? How can we fulfill our dream of staying together happily for decades when there are so many alternatives to getting married and it is so easy to get divorced? In this section, we explore this last crucially important question, as we look at the tantalizing insights the social science research offers about how to have enduring, happy relationships. Let's begin, however, by examining what *typically* happens over time, as we trace how marital happiness normally changes through the years.

Why do the joyous expectations of the wedding day fade? Can we predict whether this couple will stay happily married for life? These are the kinds of questions we will tackle later in the chapter.

The Main Marital Pathway: Downhill and Then Up

Many of us enter marriage (or any love relationship) with blissful expectations. Soon disenchantment sets in. Hundreds of studies conducted over the past 40 years in Western countries show that marital satisfaction is at its peak during the honeymoon and then begins to decrease (Blood & Wolfe, 1960; Glenn, 1990; Rollins & Feldman, 1970; Tucker & Aron, 1993). As the decline is steepest during the first few years and tends to slow or level off, some researchers believe that if couples can make it beyond the first four years of married life, they have passed the main danger zone for getting divorced (Bradbury & Karney, 2004; Hetherington & Kelly, 2002).

Notice the interesting similarity to John Bowlby's ideas about the different attachment phases discussed in Chapter 4. In the first year or two of their relationship, people are in the phase of clear-cut attachment when they are madly in love and see their significant other as the absolute center of their lives. As they move into the *working model* phase of their relationship—developing more separate lives, getting involved in the wider world—they face the risk of disconnecting emotionally from their spouse.

For couples who pass the four-year danger zone and survive the stresses of raising children and the challenges of parenting adolescents, the good news is that there is a positive change to look forward to later on. According to the **U-shaped curve of marital satisfaction,** marriages get happier when the children leave the house and husbands and wives have the luxury of focusing on each other again (White & Edwards, 1990; Glenn, 1990). Look around and you can see these wonderful empty-nest couples—traveling, enjoying being with each other, entering a "second honeymoon" after the children have left.

Still, to paraphrase Leo Tolstoy's memorable introduction to *Anna Karenina,* marriages—at any life stage—are very different. The close, contented empty-nest couples have little in common with married people who stay together miserably—the ones who only argue or barely talk. And luckily, the dismal decline statistics do not fit everyone. Roughly 1 in 10 couples bucks the trend to less happiness, feeling *more in love* over time (Karney & Bradbury, 1997). To understand

U-shaped curve of marital satisfaction The most common pathway of marital happiness in the West, in which satisfaction is highest at the honeymoon, declines during the child-rearing years, then rises after the children grow up.

The so-called "difficulties" of the empty nest are highly overrated. In fact, many couples find that, when the children leave, they can joyously rekindle marital love!

what makes these marriages special, and to get deeper insights into what changes for the worse, let's step back and survey the characteristics of *every* type of relationship as we turn to a contemporary psychologist's conceptualizations about love.

The Triangular Theory Perspective on Happiness

triangular theory of love
Robert Sternberg's categorization of love relationships into three facets: passion, intimacy, and commitment. When arranged at the points of a triangle, their combinations describe all the different kinds of adult love relationships.

According to Robert Sternberg's (1986, 1988, 2004) **triangular theory of love,** we can break adult love relationships into three components: passion (sexual arousal), intimacy (feelings of closeness), and commitment (typically marriage, but also exclusive, lifelong cohabiting relationships). When we arrange them on a triangle, as you can see in Figure 11.2, we get a portrait of the different kinds of relationships in life.

With passion alone, we have a crush. This is the wonderful fantasy obsession for the girl down the street or a handsome professor we don't really know. With intimacy alone, we have the warm feelings of caring that we have for a best friend. *Romantic love* combines these two qualities. Walk around your campus, and you can immediately see this type of relationship. Couples are passionate and clearly know each other well, but have probably not made a final commitment to get married or to form a lifelong, exclusive bond.

On the marriage side of the triangle, commitment alone results in what some observers call "empty marriages." In these emotionally barren, loveless marriages (luckily fairly infrequent today), people stay together physically but live totally separate lives. Intimacy plus commitment produces *companionate marriages,* the best-friend relationships that long-married couples may have after passion is gone. Finally, notice from the bottom of the diagram that a few married couples stay together because they share sexual passion and nothing else. The ideal in our culture is the relationship you can see at the center of the triangle—one that combines passion, intimacy, and commitment. Sternberg calls this ideal state **consummate love.**

consummate love In Robert Sternberg's triangular theory of love, the ideal form of love, in which a couple's relationship involves all three of the major facets of love: passion, intimacy, and commitment.

Why is consummate love so fragile? One reason, according to Sternberg, is that as familiarity increases, passion naturally falls off. It's hard to keep lusting after your mate when you wake up together day after day for years (Klusmann, 2002). As couples enter into the working-model phase of their marriage, and genuinely move out into the world, intimacy can also decline. You and your partner don't talk the way you used to. Work or the children are more absorbing. There is a danger of becoming "ships passing in the night."

According to Sternberg, therefore, the key to living happily for a lifetime is to understand the natural course of relationships and to realize that marriage takes work.

FIGURE 11.2: **Sternberg's triangle: The different types of love:** The three facets of love form the points of this triangle. The relationships along the triangle's sides reflect combinations of the facets. At the center is the ideal relationship: consummate love.

Source: Adapted from Sternberg (1988).

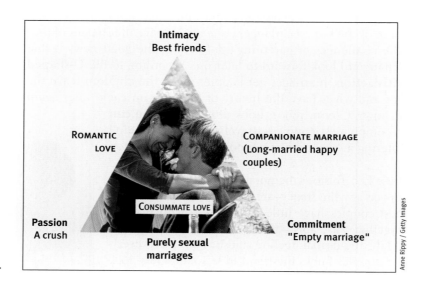

As couples get involved in "the real world," they may disengage from each other and feel bored and distant.

But *exactly* what kind of work is involved? For clues, one group of psychologists decided to turn to the romance side of the triangle and explore the inner experience of falling in love.

When we fall in love, they discovered, our self-concept expands enormously. Feelings of self-efficacy are intense. We feel powerful, competent, special; capable of doing wonderful things (Aron and others, 2002). Given that romantic love causes a joyous feeling of self-expansion, could married couples recapture passion and intimacy by sharing exciting activities that expand the self?

To test this interesting proposition, the psychologists asked married volunteers to list their most exciting activities—the passions that gave them a sense of flow (see Chapter 10). Then they instructed one group of husbands and wives to engage in the stimulating activities *both* partners had picked out (for example, going to concerts, hiking, or skiing) very frequently over 10 weeks. As they predicted, marital happiness rose dramatically among these couples compared to control groups who were told to engage in pleasant but not especially interesting activities (such as going out to dinner) or just to follow their normal routine (Reissman, Aron, & Bergen, 1993).

This tantalizing study suggests that to revitalize marriages, it's not necessary to take a romantic trip to Tahiti. It may not even be all that important to go out regularly for candlelit dinners. People should simply *continue* to engage in the exciting, flow-inducing activities that brought them together in the first place. Using Chapter 10's example, if you met the love of your life at a meeting of the college Democrats, keep working together on campaigns. Since Kevin and Mary connected through their spirituality, they might do mission work together as the years pass. The problem is that during the later, working-model phase of a relationship, the activities that give people a sense of flow tend to migrate outside of married life. When work does become more compelling (or flow-inducing, or self-enhancing), people may find their partner dull. Worse yet, they may fall in love with someone who is on the scene to witness their most efficacious self emerge: "My co-worker (or secretary) understands who I really am!" Keeping passions *within a* marriage may help keep marital passion alive.

But simply sharing exciting activities is not enough. People need to get along in normal day-to-day life.

[FAQ: Why do people fall in (or out of) love?]

This couple is doing more than sharing a wonderful experience—they are actually "working" on their relationship. Engaging in mutually exciting activities helps keep passion and intimacy alive in a marriage.

Couple Communications and Happiness

Have you ever gone to an engagement party and come away with the disturbing impression: "That marriage will never make it beyond the first few years"? Imagine you had a crystal ball that could predict which marriages (or intimate relationships) would last. By conducting longitudinal studies tracking the lives of engaged couples, researchers find they can tell with uncanny accuracy *before* the wedding which relationships are likely to fall apart.

Consider the Denver Family Development Project (Clements, Stanley, & Markman, 2004). More than 100 engaged couples filled out a variety of questionnaires. Psychologists observed how the partners communicated by watching them discuss problem issues in their relationships. The qualities that characterized the relationships of couples who later divorced were probably the same ones you were intuitively picking up when you got the uneasy feeling, "This isn't going to last." When people begin their married lives by treating each other in more wary, less loving ways, they are more likely to get divorced (Fincham & Bradbury, 1993; Huston and others, 2001; Kurdek, 2002). In fact, we can tell a good deal about whether a relationship is destined for divorce by simply watching people talk. Now let's look at four communication styles that spell trouble in married life (Driver and others, 2003; Gottman, 1994, 1999; Noller & Feeney, 2002; Rogge & Bradbury, 2002):

[FAQ: What kinds of communication styles should I avoid with my significant other?]

- *Unhappy couples engage in a low ratio of positive to negative interactions.* People can fight a good deal and still have a happy marriage. The key is to make sure that the number of caring, loving comments strongly outweighs the critical ones. In videotaping couples talking about problems in his "love lab," relationship researcher John Gottman (1994) has discovered that anytime the ratio of positive to negative interactions dips below 5 to 1, the risk of getting divorced is exceptionally high.

- *Unhappy couples get personally hurtful when they argue.* When happily married couples fight, they confine themselves to the problem: "I don't like it when I come home and the house is messy. What can we do?" Unhappy couples personalize their conflicts. They use put-downs and sarcasm. They look disgusted. They roll their eyes. Expressions of contempt for the other person as a human being are poisonous to married life.

- *Unhappy couples engage in demand–withdrawal conversations.* Another classic way of relating that signals a marriage is in trouble occurs when one partner regularly pushes for more emotional involvement and the other tries to back off (Eldridge & Christensen, 2002; Noller and others, 2005). As this **demand–withdrawal communication pattern** escalates, it takes a bitter, personal turn:

demand–withdrawal communication A pathological type of interaction in which one partner, most often the woman, presses for more intimacy and the other person, most often the man, tends to back off.

WIFE (WORRIED VOICE): Is there something wrong, honey?

HUSBAND (DISTANT VOICE): Nope. Not a thing.

WIFE: I can tell that you are annoyed at me—I can see it in your face. What's wrong?

HUSBAND (SOUNDING ANNOYED): I already told you, there's nothing wrong. Will you lay off of me? I just need some time to myself.

WIFE (DISGUSTEDLY): Oh, you are impossible. You never talk to me.

HUSBAND (CONTEMPTUOUSLY): You are such a terrible nag!

(adapted from Gottman, 1994, p. 138)

You would not be surprised to learn that—as in the example above—women typically demand more involvement. Wives tend to want to talk about feelings, but husbands withdraw and attempt to shut the discussion off (Eldridge & Christensen, 2002). Among men prone to batter their wives, however, this gender pattern is reversed. The man peppers his wife with suspicious questions: "Who did you see?

Where did you go?" She tries to get away. The problem is that abusive husbands have a *hostile attributional bias* (Schweinle & Ickes, 2002). Just as we saw with highly aggressive elementary school children in Chapter 6, they tend to read personal rejection into benign events.

- *Unhappy couples see their partner through an unrealistically suspicious lens.* Happy couples minimize their partners' angry comments, attributing them to random situational forces: "John is is being grumpy because he doesn't feel well today." Distressed couples see even caring actions in a negative light: "She cooked me that great dinner; so she must be having an affair!" (Bradbury & Fincham, 1990; Honeycutt, 1993).

This woman's body language during a fight with her partner tells us a good deal about her attachment style. The problem with the pathological communication styles described in the text is that they can turn a secure, loving attachment into a suspicious and ultimately adversarial relationship.

The bottom-line message is that, in unhappy relationships, the other person has been transformed from a loving, reliable ally into a potential enemy. Couples who are not getting along have developed insecure attachment styles (Feeney & Noller, 2002; Murray and others, 2003).

Communal Versus Exchange Mentalities and Happiness

Most people subscribe to a securely attached **communal model of love,** believing that we should give to our partner without expecting to get anything in return (Clark, Graham, & Grote, 2002). When securely attached couples have disagreements (and sometimes make hurtful statements), they are frantic to get back into synchrony. They reach out; they tell their partner how much they care. They become closer after having an argument than before (Murray and others, 2003). In contrast, if couples *consistently* adopt an **exchange model of love,** which involves keeping score to make sure that "if I do this for you, you must do this for me," their marriages have fallen off track.

To some extent, these insecure, exchange patterns of relating reflect enduring personality problems. In one amazing 40-year longitudinal study tracing the lives of people about to be married, if a friend reported that "this person has mental health problems" at the engagement, this judgment outweighed any other influence in predicting marital problems over the years (Kelly & Conley, 1987).

communal model of love An ideal approach to love relationships in which the partners give everything without expecting to get anything in return.

exchange model of love An unsatisfying approach to love relationships in which the partners attempt to "keep score" and give to the other person only when the partner gives to them.

Faced with the many chores of married life, it's important to work as a team and negotiate about who does what. But if this husband and wife adopt an *exchange mentality*—saying, "You didn't do the shopping last week, so I won't do the cleaning today"—their marriage is destined for problems.

FIGURE 11.3: **A husband's and wife's ratings of their marriage:** This chart shows concretely how work pressures can negatively affect a marriage. This couple participating in a marital-happiness study rated the quality of their relationship periodically during the first four years. When the wife's ratings unexpectedly declined dramatically (starting after day 1,100), researchers discovered that she was experiencing severe stress at work.

Source: Bradbury & Karney (2004), p. 873.

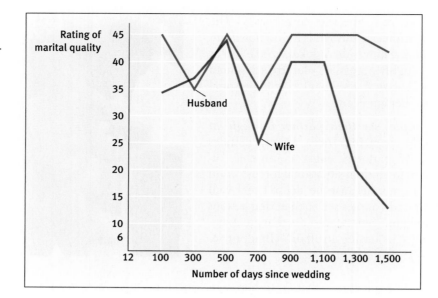

[FAQ: What factors influence marital success?]

To some extent, however, people adopt an exchange mentality in response to external pressures: A couple is having financial problems, or is overburdened at home and work. So they revert to continual "scorekeeping": "I'll only take the kids to the baseball game on Friday if you take them on Monday. You aren't doing your fair share around the house!" (Clark, Graham, & Grote, 2002).

So to stay happily together for life, we need to understand that marriages normally change over time *and* that the quality of relationships ebbs and flows, depending on the other stresses in a couple's lives (Bradbury & Karney, 2004; see Figure 11.3). We also should realize that in order to be genuinely happy, *both* partners should try to give 100 percent!

INTERVENTIONS: **Staying Together Happily for Life**

How can you draw on *all* of these research insights to have an enduring happy relationship? Understand the natural time course of love. Take steps to preserve intimacy and passion by sharing exciting activities you both enjoy. Be very, very positive after you get negative. Avoid getting personal when you fight. Beware of falling into the demand–withdrawal pattern. Watch out for irrational suspicions of your mate. Don't get into a continual "score-keeping" mentality in your relationship. Monitor the natural tendency to bring problems from your outside life home. When you see that your partner is under stress, take special care to reach out in a loving way. Table 11.3 offers

TABLE 11.3: **Evaluating Your Close Relationship: A Checklist**

Answer these questions as honestly as you can. The more "yes" boxes you check, the stronger your relationship is likely to be.

	Yes	No
1. Do you have realistic expectations about your relationship—realizing that passion and intimacy don't magically last forever?	❑	❑
2. Do you engage in activities that your partner feels as passionate about as you do?	❑	❑
3. Do you try to solve differences of opinion in a constructive way?	❑	❑
4. Do you try to adhere to the "we" mentality of unconditional love and avoid scorekeeping?	❑	❑
5. Do you try not to let outside stresses affect your relationship?	❑	❑
6. Do you make special efforts to be considerate when your partner is having problems?	❑	❑

a checklist based on these points to evaluate your current relationship or to keep on hand for the love relationships you will have as you travel through life.

As a final caution, however, it is important to be aware that the concept of "working at a marriage" or even trying to communicate well with a spouse is a primary goal only in modern individualistic societies. In traditional collectivist cultures, relationships among members of the extended family take clear priority over the emotional bond that exists between a husband and wife. Moreover, even today in some areas of the world, like the Philippines, divorce is illegal (Jones, 2005). In the West, this is obviously not the case. As we know, today divorce has become a predictable transition of twenty-first-century life.

Divorce

Researchers stress that, just as we saw in Chapter 7 when we described its impact on children, in looking at divorce we need to think of this major life change as having specific phases (Hetherington & Kelly, 2002).

When people first consider divorce, there is a period of unhappiness and ambivalence as they weigh the costs of leaving against the benefits (Hopper, 1993; Kelly, 2000). You and your spouse are not getting along, but perhaps you should just hang on and hope things will get better. For women, financial considerations may loom large: "Can I afford the loss in income after a divorce?"

Sometimes, what tips the balance in favor of divorce is an extramarital affair. In tracking thousands of U.S. married couples, researchers discovered that the stereotype that having an affair breaks up an otherwise happy marriage is false. When people decide to have an affair, it is a symptom that they are already unhappy in their married lives. Still, there is a bidirectional process in operation here. The affair itself widens the emotional chasm that already exists between a husband and wife (Previti & Amato, 2004).

Once a couple definitely decides to separate, they experience an overload of other changes. One partner needs to move, or a spouse may need to find a different, better-paying job. There are the legal hassles and anxieties about telling other loved ones: "Will my friends still be friends? How will my family feel?" If the couple has children, there is the anguish of dealing with their intense distress. The stress does gradually lessen as people adjust to their new situation and the actual parting gets farther away in time (Barnet, 1990; Mitchell-Flynn & Hutchinson, 1993). But imagine regularly battling with your spouse over the children and having to cope with all the parenting, and you can see why psychologists have labeled divorce "a chronic stressor" in women's lives (Bursik, 1991).

Still, coping with divorce and its aftermath can have a silver lining. It can show people that they are more capable than they thought. Divorce can produce emotional growth and enhanced efficacy feelings, as well as anguish and regrets (Hetherington & Kelly, 2002; Hopper, 1993; Stewart and others, 1997).

Jon Feingersh / Getty Images

Norbert Schaefer / Corbis

Being a single mother is intensely stressful, but it can also be a relief compared to the ambivalence and fighting prior to getting a divorce. Divorce can also enhance efficacy feelings and give women a chance to realize "I can make it on my own."

A 30-year-long study tracing women's lives suggests that the perception of divorce as a growth experience may vary in interesting ways, depending on a person's life stage. Women who got divorced in their twenties highlighted issues relating to their personal development. They said that their divorce caused them to rethink their basic life goals. Those who divorced in their thirties, many of whom had young children, focused on their husbands' emotional problems. They often reported that they needed to leave for the children's sake. For women who got divorced in their forties, once again, the main issue propelling their decision had to do with personal growth. As one woman reported: "Time is running out. . . . [I had] the sense I was treading water, . . . When could I live just for me?" (quoted in Young, Stewart, & Miner-Rubino, 2001, p. 218).

[FAQ: How are men affected by divorce?]

Divorce has its own unique impact on men. Because women still typically get primary custody of the children, after a divorce there is a tendency for many men to disengage from their families—not paying child support or perhaps not seeing the children at all (Furstenberg & Cherlin, 1991; Graham & Beller, 2002; Lamb, 2002). While the temptation is to blame men for "opting out," the Experiencing the Lifespan box poignantly shows how difficult it can be to be a full-fledged father when you have the standard twice-a-week visitation schedule, and picking up the children can be fraught with anxieties: "Will my daughter or son be there this time?"

What often happens is that after a divorce, as with Kevin in the chapter-opening vignette, men remarry, have other children, or become stepfathers. They try to construct new relationships to make up for those they may have lost. However, for stepfathers it can be challenging to fully establish these new connections (Hetherington & Kelly, 2002). Stepfathers have to deal with the delicate issue of whether they qualify as "real fathers" even when they desperately want to take a fully involved parenting role. As one man in an interview study commented about his relationship with his stepdaughter, "Sometimes I feel like I'm on the outside looking in because— sometimes I wish she was mine. . . . In my heart I feel like I'm her father" (quoted in Marsiglio, 2004, p. 31).

But other stepdads decide to just jump right in. Another man in this study informed the interviewer: "I don't introduce her as my stepdaughter, because I didn't step on her. I introduce her 'This is my daughter.' . . . She's a part of me. I'd go crazy if something happened to her" (quoted in Marsiglio, 2004, p. 32). And another person described how before he remarried he laid down the law to his fiancée: "I'm either going to be . . . all father or nothing at all. . . . I can't have like half a relationship. . . . I'm going to be there all the way" (quoted in Marsiglio, 2004, p. 29).

In this next section, we turn to the emotions these fathers were feeling as we look directly at parenthood, that second important adult role.

Noncustodial fathers can have trouble staying involved because they have to struggle to be on the scene during important times during their children's lives. Imagine how hard it may have been for this divorced dad to get the chance to attend his daughter's Thanksgiving school play since that event took place on his "ex-wife's day."

David H. Wells / The Image Works

EXPERIENCING THE LIFESPAN: VISITOR FATHER

Fatherhood is the critical experience of Henry's life. When Joanna was a preschooler, their destination was the zoo or the playground. As she grew older, Henry took Joanna for music lessons and taught her sports. His presence was hard won and, he feels, too rare. Henry had been demoted from father to person with visitation rights.

Henry and his wife separated when Joanna was almost 2. According to their divorce agreement, the child was supposed to be available every two weeks; but often Henry's ex-wife took off with the baby or gave him some excuse when he came to pick his daughter up. Henry never knew for sure if Joanna would be waiting there when he arrived.

Henry felt his only option was to sue for joint custody, the right to have Joanna on weekends and every other day. When they met in court, however, to Henry's astonishment the judge ordered a psychiatric evaluation to determine if *he* was emotionally fit. One judge asked point blank: "Why would a man want to take care of a

2-year-old?" Eventually, Henry won the right to have Joanna one afternoon per week, every other weekend, alternate holidays, and the month of July.

Over the next 10 years Henry went to court periodically to try to force a greater role in his daughter's life. Once he sued for full custody. While no one denied that Henry was a good father, a psychologist testified that a child needed a mother during the early years.

For years, Henry felt terrible about not being able to see his daughter every day. His work suffered. He was often upset. Now that Joanna is 12, he has adjusted. His daughter has her own room in his apartment. He feels secure that she knows this is her second home. Henry feels he reached an emotional landmark when, during "his time" this past summer, he was able to let go and allow Joanna to attend sleep-away camp. Still, the heartache of not being on the scene to watch his child grow up never really goes away.

TYING IT ALL TOGETHER

1. Jared is making the case that during the late twentieth century there was an historic "deinstitutionalization of marriage." Which *two* of the following phenomena should Jared should use to support this argument?

    a. Today, one of every two marriages ends in divorce.
    b. Today, many more women have babies without being married.
    c. Today, marital satisfaction declines over the first few years of marriage.

2. Four couples are celebrating their silver anniversaries. Which relationship has followed the "classic" marital pathway?

    a. After being extremely happy with each other during the first three years, Ted and Elaine now find that their marriage has gone steadily downhill.
    b. Steve and Betty's marriage has had many unpredictable ups and downs over the years.
    c. Dave and Erika's marital satisfaction declined, especially during the first four years, but has improved now that their children have left home.
    d. Lee and Marta's marriage has become stronger over the years.

3. Describe the triangular theory to a friend, and give an example of (a) romantic love, (b) consummate love, and (c) a companionate marriage. Can you think of couples who fit each category? At what stage of life are couples most likely to have companionate marriages?

4. At dinner, a married couple you know are berating each other for not "pulling their weight in the marriage." The main problem here is that this couple:

    a. is embroiled in demand–withdrawal interactions.
    b. is personalizing their conflicts.
    c. has adopted an exchange model of relationships.

5. You are a marriage counselor. Drawing on the three perspectives in this section (triangular theory; couple communications; and communal vs. exchange mentalities), formulate one concrete suggestion for "homework" that you might give couples who come to your office for help.

6. Your best friend is getting a divorce. If this person is male and has children, the main problem is likely to be _____. If this person is female, the main problem is likely to be _____.

Answers to the Tying It All Together questions can be found in the answers section of the book.

Parenthood

I have never felt the joy that my daughter brings me when I wake up and see her . . . when you are laying there and . . . and feel this little hand tapping on your hand . . . that has been the most joyful thing I ever have experienced. . . . I've never been able to get that type of joy anywhere else.

(quoted in Palkovitz, 2002, p. 96)

Setting the Context: More Parenting Possibilities, Fewer Children

Take an informal poll of the parents you know and you will hear similar comments: "The love and joy you have with children are impossible to describe." The great benefit of the 1960s lifestyle revolution is that we have expanded the number of people who can fully participate in this life-changing experience, from stepparents, to gay couples, to never-married adults. Our twenty-first-century tapestry of nontraditional families, described in Chapter 7, offers many chances to fulfill this core identity of adult life.

At the same time, people have more freedom *not* to be parents—and increasing numbers of adults are making that choice. One sign of the times is the decline in **fertility rates** in many affluent regions of the world. (This term refers to the average number of children women in a given nation can expect to have during their lives.) And whatever happened to those huge Spanish or Italian families? As you can see in Figure 11.4, adults in these southern European countries now have some of the lowest childbearing rates in the world.

One reason why fertility has dropped well below the replacement level (2.1 children per couple) in every European nation may lie in the slower progress people are making toward adulthood. Remember from Chapter 10 that in Italy, for instance, many people are well into their thirties before they have the financial resources to leave home and marry. Moreover, at least in the developed world, when a nation has a poor economy—as you can see in the dismal Russian fertility statistics in the figure—young people are particularly unwilling to bring babies into the world.

Alarmed by their shrinking populations, newspapers in some European countries such as Great Britain are quick to paint this cohort of young people as selfish,

---

In the past, gay couples such as these women could never have hoped to be parents. In fact, they would have had to hide their relationship from the outside world. Today, they have the benefits of living in a society where this crucial life dream can be fulfilled.

fertility rate The average number of children a woman in a given country has during her lifetime.

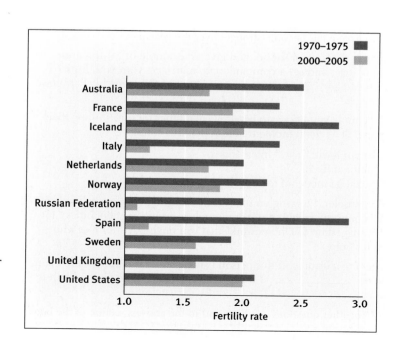

FIGURE 11.4: **Fertility rates in selected developed countries, 1970–1975 and 2000–2005:** This chart reveals just why declining fertility is a crucial concern in Western Europe, where fertility rates are now well below the replacement level (2.1 children) in every country. Notice in particular the extremely low fertility rates in Russia and southern Europe.

Source: United Nations Development Programme (2003).

irresponsible, or even unpatriotic. They bombard their readers with dire warnings about having an unhappy old age (Brown & Ferree, 2004). They are incorrect. Researchers find that people who choose not to have children are not more narcissistic (Gerson, Posner, & Morris, 1991). Provided that they have freely made this decision, childless adults are just as happy later in life as people who do become parents (Connidis & McMullin, 1993). Moreover, the stereotype that having children makes a marriage stronger (or that having a child saves an unhappy marriage) is equally false. How does having a baby *really* change married life?

The Transition to Parenthood

To get a full portrait of how becoming parents affects a marriage, researchers have conducted several in-depth longitudinal studies, selecting U.S. couples when the wife was pregnant and tracking those families for a few years after the baby's birth (Belsky, Lang, & Rovine, 1985; Belsky & Rovine, 1990; Belsky, Spanier, & Rovine, 1983; Cowan & Cowan, 1988, 1992; Feeney and others, 2001). Understanding that parenthood arrives via many routes, they have explored how having a child affects the bond between lesbian partners, too (Goldberg & Sayer, 2006). Here are the main conclusions of these studies tracing the transition to parenthood:

- *Parenthood makes couples less intimate and romantic.* Look back to the infancy chapters—especially the discussion of infant sleep in Chapter 3—and you will immediately see why a baby's birth is destined to change marital passion and intimacy for the worse. In fact, look at any couple struggling with an infant at your local restaurant and you will understand why researchers find that feelings about one's spouse shift from lover to "fellow worker" after the baby arrives (Belsky, Lang, & Rovine, 1985; Belsky & Rovine, 1990). One father aptly summarized what happens when he commented: "Instead of channeling our love towards just each other . . . we have channeled our love together towards them" (adapted from Palkovitz, 2002, p. 176).

- *Parenthood produces more traditional (and potentially conflict-ridden) marital roles.* If the couple is heterosexual, having children tends to make gender roles more distinct. Even when spouses have been sharing the household tasks equally, women often take over most of the housework and child care after the baby is born. Typically this occurs because the wife decides to leave her job or reduce her hours at work (Singley & Hynes, 2005). However, even when both spouses work full time, mothers still typically do more of the diaper changing and the laundry and household chores than fathers. This change can provoke conflicts centering on issues related to **marital equity.** Wives may feel angry at their husbands for not doing their "fair share" around the house (Feeney and others, 2001).

marital equity Fairness in the "work" of a couple's life together. If a relationship lacks equity, with one partner doing significantly more than the other, the outcome is typically marital dissatisfaction.

Parenthood also can bring up conflicts relating to different discipline styles if one parent is more permissive while the other adopts an authoritarian child-rearing approach (recall Chapter 7). One unhappy wife described this kind of clash when she informed her husband: "What's really getting to me . . . is that we hardly ever agree on how to handle [the baby]. I think you are too rough, and you think I'm spoiling her, and none of us wants to change" (quoted in Cowan & Cowan, 1992, p. 112).

These examples show how that outside stress—the baby's birth—can poison the atmosphere between husbands and wives. However, most people adapt to this change in their relationship, although, on average, the research shows their marital satisfaction does tend to decline (Belsky & Rovine, 1990; Cowan & Cowan, 1992; Feeney and others, 2001). About one in three couples reports that having a child has *increased* their feelings of love for their spouse (Belsky & Rovine, 1990).

To predict which marriages greatly deteriorate, decline slightly, or improve, the studies show we can get our best clues from the pre-baby relationship. Was the couple securely attached before the birth? (See Alexander and others, 2001; Feeney and others, 2003; Paley and others, 2005.) Did they discuss issues in their relationship

Will this young couple's relationship seriously deteriorate after the baby? Will it improve? To answer these questions, we need to look at what their marriage was like *before* having a child.

constructively before the child arrived? Agreeing on the division of labor is extremely important (Feeney & Noller, 2002). It doesn't matter whether the wife (or husband) is actually doing more. What really matters is whether a couple has similar views about how to arrange the household chores (Barnett & Baruch, 1988; Saginak & Saginak, 2005). In the words of one research team, "The transition to parenthood seems to act as an amplifier, tuning couples into their strengths and turning up the volume on existing difficulties in managing their . . .[love]" (Cowan & Cowan, 1992, p. 206).

Now that we've looked at its impact on a marriage, let's turn to the experience of parenthood from mothers' and fathers' points of view.

Exploring Motherhood

We've already talked about the incredible love that mothers feel for their children, especially in the infancy section of this book. But motherhood has its downside. National surveys show that mothers of young children report the *lowest* levels of day-to-day happiness, compared to women who are not parents or who are in the empty-nest stage of life (McLanahan & Adams, 1989; Umberson & Gove, 1989). Here are some reasons why.

The Motherhood Experience

Motherhood, as an in-depth survey revealed, is tailor-made to destroy basic conceptions women have about themselves (Genevie & Margolies, 1987). In this revealing poll of American mothers, one in two women admitted that they did not control their tempers well. Among the situations that made them most irate, challenges to their authority ranked first. Disobedience, disrespect, and even typical behaviors such as a child's whining might provoke reactions bordering on rage. When confronted with real-life children, these mothers found that their ideal of being calm, empathic, and always in control came tumbling down (Genevie & Margolies, 1987).

Given the bidirectional quality of the parent–child bond, it should come as no surprise that a main force in this survey that affected how closely a woman fit her motherhood ideal lay in the quality of her relationship with a given child. Children who were temperamentally difficult provoked more irritation and lowered a mother's self-esteem. An easy child (recall Chapter 4) had the opposite effect, evoking loving feelings and making that mother feel competent about herself. As one woman wrote:

> Lee Ann has been my godsend. My other two have given me so many problems and are rude and disrespectful. Not Lee Ann. . . . I disciplined her in the same way . . . , except that she seemed to require less of it. Usually she just seemed to do the right thing. She is . . . my chance for supreme success after two devastating failures.
>
> (quoted in Genevie & Margolies, 1987, pp. 220–221)

These emotions destroy another ideal that we have about motherhood: Mothers are supposed to love all their children equally. Although they said they tried not to let their preferences show, many women in this study did admit they had favorites. Typically a favorite child was "easy" and successful in the wider world. However, what was most important, again, was the quality of the attachment relationship, the feeling of being totally loved by a particular child. As one mother reported:

> There will always be a special closeness with Darrell. He likes to test my word. . . . There are times he makes me feel like pulling my hair out. . . . But when he comes to "talk" to mom that's an important feeling to me.
>
> (quoted in Genevie & Margolies, 1987, p. 248)

Not only does the experience of motherhood vary dramatically from child to child, it shifts from minute to minute and day to day:

> Good days are getting hugs and kisses and hearing "I love you." The bad days are hearing "you are not my friend." Good days are not knowing the color of the refrigerator because of the paintings and drawings all over it. Bad days are seeing a new drawing on a just painted wall.
>
> (quoted in Genevie & Margolies, 1987, p. 412)

In sum, motherhood is incredibly wonderful—*and* absolutely terrible. It evokes the most uplifting emotions *and* offers intensely painful insights into the self. Now, drawing on this study, let's explore how outside influences—the media, friends, family members, and some experts—can amplify mothers' distress.

Expectations and Motherhood Stress

The world provides women with an airbrushed view of motherhood—from the movie stars who wax enthusiastic about the joys of having babies (much better than that terrible old career) to the family members who gush at bleary-eyed new mothers who haven't slept for weeks: "How wonderful you must feel!" By portraying motherhood as total bliss, are we doing women a disservice when they realize that their own experience does not live up to this glorified image? (See Douglas & Michaels, 2004.)

What compounds the problem are unrealistic performance pressures. Good children, as you saw in the above quotation, make a mother feel competent. "Difficult" children can make a woman feel like a failure. Despite all we know about the crucial role of genetics, peers, and the wider society in affecting development (see Chapter 7), mothers still bear the weight of responsibility for the way their children turn out (Coontz, 1992; Crittenden, 2001; Douglas & Michaels, 2004; Garey & Arendell, 2001).

Then there is the weight of the child-rearing demands we put on women today: the need to cram in the right amount of reading, to give a child lessons, to produce a perfect child. The media expect mothers to be infinitely patient and caring. Social critics talk in anguished terms about how today's working mothers are not giving children the attention they received in "the good old days."

But these statements about an epidemic of uninvolved mothers can be subjected to scientific scrutiny. And we have a fascinating study that *proves* the mother-bashing critics are wrong. When developmentalists compared diary reports of mothers' involvement over the past 40 years, they discovered that in the late 1990s mothers spent *more* time with their children than their counterparts did a generation ago (Sayer, Bianchi, & Robinson, 2004). In particular, notice from Figure 11.5 the dramatic increase in the amount of time spent teaching and playing. This cohort of young-adult

The blissful image of a mother and baby is nothing like contending with the reality of continual sleep deprivation and a screaming newborn—explaining why the idealized motherhood messages can make the first months of new motherhood come as a total shock.

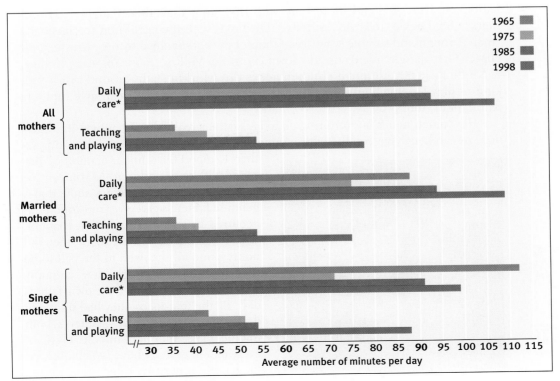

FIGURE 11.5: Minutes per day devoted to hands-on child care by U.S. mothers: Notice in particular that, in contrast to our myths, in recent years mothers are spending much more time teaching and playing with their children than in previous decades.

Source: Adapted from Sayer, Bianchi, & Robinson (2004).

*Refers to routine kinds of care, such as helping the child get dressed.

This photograph shows the reality of motherhood today. Young working mothers are spending much *more* time teaching their children than their own, stay-at-home mothers did in the past!

mothers is spending almost *twice as much time* engaging in child cognition-stimulating activities as their own mothers spent with them!

Given that national surveys show the average U.S. working mother (including part-time workers) clocks in about 39 hours a week at a job, today's mothers are behaving heroically. Although they work longer days (42 hours a week, on average), single mothers spend *just as much time* with their children as married women do (retrieved May 15, 2005, from www.familiesandwork.org).

We also need to give a round of applause to twenty-first-century fathers. As with Kevin in the chapter-opening vignette, fathers today are struggling to become very involved in family life.

Exploring Fatherhood

As women entered the workforce in large numbers in the 1970s, it became a badge of honor for fathers, in addition to fulfilling the traditional male *breadwinner* role, to change the diapers. What social scientists called the *new nurturer father* became our upper-middle-class masculine ideal. In addition, according to psychologists, we expect fathers to be good sex-role models, giving children a road map for how men should ideally behave. And sometimes we even want them to be ultimate authority figures, the people responsible for laying down the family rules (as in the old saying: "Wait until your father gets home!").

These different requirements can leave today's fathers facing a confusing set of contradictory demands (Lamb, 1986, 1997). Like Kevin in the chapter-opening vignette, surveys show that many fathers want to be breadwinners and to be fully involved with the family (Galinsky & others, 2005; Milkie & others, 2004; Palkovitz, 2002). The vision of the male as authority figure can conflict with being a loving nurturer—which may partly explain why some women, as you saw earlier, get angry at their husbands for being too insensitive and rough with the children. Given that there are many "right" ways to be a father, how do contemporary men carry out their role?

[FAQ: How do fathers behave?]

How Fathers Act

As we would expect from the principle that they should be good sex-role models, fathers on average spend more time with their sons than their daughters (Bronstein, 1988; Dickie, 1987; Jones, 1985). They play with their children in classically "male," rough-and-tumble ways (see Chapter 6). Fathers love to run, wrestle, and chase. They dangle infants upside down (Belsky & Volling, 1987; Yogman, Cooley, & Kindlon, 1988). Although children adore this whirl-the-baby-around-by-the-feet kind of play (in our house we called it "going to Six Flags"), it can give mothers palpitations, too.

[FAQ: How are fathers' roles changing?]

How much hands-on nurturing do today's fathers really do? To answer this question, researchers have conducted the same diary studies described earlier, asking fathers to report the number of minutes they spend with their children. As you can see in Figure 11.6, their findings show that a genuine father-as-caregiver revolution has occurred in recent years (Sayer, Bianchi, & Robinson, 2004). In the 1970s, men did not respond all that well to the call to be new nurturers (although they certainly were doing more than their own fathers did). By the mid-1980s, they had started to do far more. Today many fathers—both middle class and non–middle class, of every ethnic group—have *fully* embraced the hands-on nurturer role.

As you look at this photograph, think back to the thrilled expressions on the faces of the boys engaging in rough-and-tumble play in Chapter 6 and you can understand why this "hang 'em upside down" daddy play style is a compelling bonding experience for *both* fathers and their sons.

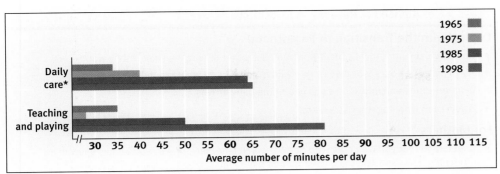

1965 ■
1975 ■
1985 ■
1998 ■

Daily care*

Teaching and playing

30 35 40 45 50 55 60 65 70 75 80 85 90 95 100 105 110 115
Average number of minutes per day

*Refers to routine kinds of care, such as helping the child get dressed.

FIGURE 11.6: **Minutes per day devoted to hands-on child care by married U.S. fathers:** This chart shows that more married fathers today are genuinely embracing the nurturing role, spending far more time teaching and playing with their children than their predecessors did.
Source: Adapted from Sayer, Bianchi, & Robinson (2004).

Still, if you look back to Figure 11.5 on page 351 and compare the average number of minutes per day mothers and fathers spend, you will notice that men still lag well behind women in the amount of care they typically provide. Furthermore, the statistics don't tell us which parent is taking bottom-line responsibility for managing the children—making that dentist appointment, arranging for babysitting, planning the meals, and being on call when a child is sick. Having bottom-line responsibility may not translate into many hours spent physically with a daughter or son, but the weight and worry make this aspect of parenting a 24-hour job.

On the basis of our earlier discussion of society's expectations, it seems likely that mothers still typically take bottom-line responsibility for their children's care. When we look at where the parenting buck stops, the enduring gender dimension of being a parent is fully revealed (Lamb, 1997).

Variations in Fathers' Involvement

If you look at the fathers you know, however, you will be struck by the amazing diversity. There are divorced men who never see their children and traditional "I never touch a diaper" dads. There also are fathers who take on *all* of the care (for instance, 5 percent of all American households are headed by single dads). What statistical forces predict how involved a given father is likely to be?

In two-parent families one strong clue, researchers find, comes from looking at the man's gender-role conceptions. A father with a traditional view of women's roles is far less likely to be willing to pitch in around the house (Bulanda, 2004; Pasley, Futris, & Skinner, 2002). As one uninvolved father explained the situation, "Well, she's the housewife and she's the emotional one. I go to work . . . and I'm the disciplinarian guy" (quoted in Matta & Knudson-Martin, 2006, p. 27). Another influence lies in the other demands placed on the couple's lives. For example, as women increase their time at work, men often respond by doing more child care and household chores (Evertsson & Nermo, 2004). And as we might expect, a third force depends on the attitudes of the partner in the parenthood duet: the woman. When a wife makes fun of her husband's diaper-changing ability, or gets angry with him for being too rough with their child, or shows signs of being jealous of her husband's relationship with the children, the message gets across. Women can be crucial gatekeepers. They are able to either encourage or put up barriers to their husband's entry into the nurturing role (Cowan & Bronstein, 1988; Grossman, 1987; Tamis-LeMonda & Cabrera, 2002).

In sum, to understand how men approach being fathers, we need to take a developmental systems theory perspective. We should look at how a man views the father's role and whether he can sensitively respond to his wife's need for help (Matta & Knudson-Martin, 2006). We also need to understand his wife's expectations and how she *actually* acts when her husband does the hands-on child care. We may want to find out if the man has daughters or sons. We would definitely need to know about the demands of a couple's working lives.

Contemporary fathers differ dramatically in how willing they are to change diapers. To explain this young man's behavior, we would predict that he has "father as nurturer" gender-role ideas and—very important—a wife who has been praising him, rather than making fun of his diaper-changing skills.

BURGER / Photo Researchers, Inc.

TABLE 11.4: Advice for Parents: A Checklist

Coping with the Transition to Parenthood

- Don't expect your romantic feelings about each other to stay the same—they won't.
- Try to agree on your respective roles—who is going to do what around the house.
- Work on your communication skills before the baby arrives.
- Enjoy—and work together as a team!

For Mothers

- Understand that *you won't and can't be the perfect mother*—in fact, sometimes you will be utterly terrible—and accept yourself for being human!
- Don't buy into the fantasy of producing a perfect child. Children cannot be micromanaged into being perfect. Focus on enjoying and loving your child as he or she is (see also Chapter 7).
- Don't listen to people who say that working outside the home automatically means that you can't be an involved mother. Remember the findings discussed in this section.

For Fathers

- Understand that your role is full of contradictions—and that there is no "perfect" way to be a dad.
- Do what makes you feel comfortable, but also be flexible and responsive to the needs of your partner and the conditions of your life.
- Know your priorities. If fulfilling the breadwinner role is most important to you, don't beat yourself up for spending long hours at a job; but also take care to fully communicate and explain your feelings to your spouse and children.

This last consideration brings up the greatest barrier that may keep today's fathers from being completely involved. As you saw in the chapter-opening vignette, many men still view being the breadwinner as central to their fatherhood role (Tamis-LeMonda & Cabrera, 2002). So having a demanding work schedule, one that involves traveling or spending time at the office on weekends, can force the most passionately interested parent—male or female—to be less involved with the children (Willott & Griffin, 2004). How much do career pressures *really* impinge on family life? We sum up the messages of our parenthood section in Table 11.4, and then we explore this question and others as we turn to the third vital adult role: work.

 ## TYING IT ALL TOGETHER

1. Jenna and Charlie are expecting their first child, and Jenna plans to keep working full time. According to the research on the transition to parenthood, after the baby is born, this couple is prone to:

   a. become more affectionate.
   b. share the household chores and child care equally.
   c. have conflicts relating to marital equity, as Jenna will most likely be doing most of the child care.

2. Ashley, a new mother, is feeling unexpectedly stressed and unhappy. Ashley and other mothers might cope better if they experienced which *two* of the following?

   a. got a less rosy, more accurate picture about motherhood from the media
   b. had more experts giving them parenting advice
   c. had less pressure placed on them to "be perfect" from the outside world

3. Your grandmother is lamenting that children today don't get the attention from their parents that they got in the good old days. How should you respond, based on this chapter? Be specific with regard to both mothers and fathers.

4. Brandon, husband and father of three, puts in a 50-hour week at work, and he somehow finds lots of time to play with and take care of his children. Brandon is fulfilling both the _____ and _____ roles.

5. Construct a questionnaire to predict how heavily involved in child care a particular man is likely to be and give it to some fathers you know.

Answers to the Tying It All Together questions can be found in the answers section of the book.

Work

How has the world of work been changing in the United States, and how do careers differ for men and women? Are there normal developmental changes in how people feel about their careers, and what forces make for happiness at a job? How can you construct a fulfilling work life?

Setting the Context: The Changing Landscape of Work

We begin our discussion by looking at the shifting conditions of the work world and examining the career paths of men and women.

General Trends: More Variability, Greater Work Fragility, and Longer Hours

You can see one major change in careers during the late twentieth century in the Experiencing the Lifespan box below. Forty years ago, Mike would almost certainly never have found his ideal job in his fifties. Right after high school or college, men typically settled into their permanent life's work. Once in a job, they often stayed in the same organization until they retired (Super, 1957). Today this pattern, called the **traditional stable career**, is no longer the typical path. The average U.S. worker shifts jobs every four years (Bird, 1994). Like Mike, many people totally change direction, starting new careers as they travel through life. In the twenty-first-century West, workers tend to have **boundaryless careers** (DeFillippi & Arthur, 1994; Stahl, Miller, & Tung, 2002).

As with Mike, this less structured career path has clear advantages. People are not locked into a single occupation. They have more freedom to flexibly tailor their work life to find a sense of flow in their jobs (Mirvis & Hall, 1994). In tracking the careers of rural Iowa high school seniors over 25 years, researchers found that people who had traditional stable careers (about 30 percent of the sample) experienced lower career satisfaction in midlife (Jepsen & Choudhuri, 2001). Still, the boundaryless career has become common for a more negative reason: greater job insecurity.

traditional stable career A career path in which people settle into their permanent life's work in their twenties and often stay with the same organization until they retire.

boundaryless career Today's most common career path for Western workers, in which people change jobs or professions periodically during their working lives.

EXPERIENCING THE LIFESPAN: FINDING AN IDEAL CAREER AT 50

To get vivid insights into the boundaryless career, read this interview with my student Mike:

I've put in a lot of mileage in my 30 years at work. In 1970, I dropped out of high school to work as a manager at Pizza Hut. Then, six years later, I was robbed and realized: "I've got to look for a calmer job!" I went into the steel pipe industry, loading trucks. I sold clothes for J.C. Penney. Then I got my GED and finally got a job at Honeywell, selling heating and air-conditioning systems. It was like I was in heaven. I had a secretary, profit sharing, a great medical plan. The work was so easy. I could cold call and within a few months I was being invited for dinner. Then management decided on cost-cutting measures. We'd just had a sales contest and out of 169 reps I'd come in second. That Tuesday, I went into the office expecting my boss to commend me. I was devastated when he said, "Mike, there's no easy way to tell you this. I have to lay you off."

My next job was selling medical equipment. Then I worked for another heating and air-conditioning firm. Manufacturing

went on strike and they laid off the sales force. I was desperate. A friend at the police department helped me get this job.

I've been a police officer for the past three years. I hope to make commander before I turn 55. Police officers are always on display. You're emotionally on the job 24 hours a day. I'm basically a trusting person. Training teaches you not to trust people. Being a deputy sheriff in a rural county, I go out on patrol without a partner. Last week, I pulled over a car that was driving all over the road. When I asked for the driver's license, the man gets out of the car and starts coming at me. I got lucky. When I pulled my gun, he backed down. I'm basically a nonviolent person. I hope until the day I die that I never have to take a life.

Much of what we do involves helping people. Sometimes a child will call: "I've seen Daddy beat Mommy." I hurt for those people. I've had several women call and say, "Thank you, officer, for saving my life." It's those times when I know the disappointments had a purpose. Finally, at age 50, I've found the perfect field.

Take-out Chinese dinner at your desk faced with mountains of paperwork at 6 or 7 P.M.— welcome to the so-called 40-hour workweek today!

Forty or fifty years ago, the United States had what the writer Tom Wolfe called "a magic economy." Because large corporations, such as General Motors, employed huge numbers of Americans, workers entered their careers feeling secure about having a well-paying lifetime job. Now, with downsizing and the demise of many of those mid-twentieth-century titans of U.S. industry, job insecurity has become a fact of life.

Job insecurity may partly explain why U.S. workers are working harder than ever. It is not true that when men were the main breadwinners, they worked longer hours than they do today. Men (and, of course, women) today are putting in more hours at their jobs than their parents or grandparents did.

Consider, for instance, findings from the National Survey of the Changing Workforce (NSCW), a U.S. poll that has regularly been monitoring the hours that workers put in at their jobs. This survey documents what many of us intuitively already know: The 40-hour workweek is now largely a thing of the past. The typical male worker spends an average of 49 hours a week on his so-called 40-hour-a-week job (Galinsky, Kim, & Bond, 2001; Galinsky and others, 2005).

Why has work been expanding well beyond 9 to 5? One reason may be that competitive pressures and reinforcements favor working longer hours. Your co-worker starts regularly staying at the office until 7 P.M. In order to be promoted, you feel compelled to stay at your desk an extra hour or two. Soon, anyone who leaves the office at 5 is defined as slacking off (Schor, 1991). Furthermore, as companies continue to downsize, each individual worker has more to do. Since your company got rid of so many employees, everyone *must* work well into dinnertime to take up the slack.

The technology revolution has played its own part, with people able to stay in touch with their work 24/7 via BlackBerries, pagers, and cell phones. In the most recent NSCW survey, one in three U.S. workers reported being contacted after hours at least once a week via one of these "labor-saving devices" (Galinsky and others, 2005). Has your boss ever called to "request" that you come in to work on a weekend? Do you repeatedly get intrusive calls from your employer at home? Do you feel completely comfortable about telling your supervisor if (or when) this happens: "I'm sorry. This is my time to relax"?

Finally, even our standard working hours have expanded well out of the traditional weekday slots. Who are the one in five U.S. workers who work weekends, evenings, or night shifts? As one national poll showed, they make up the millions of typically low-wage service employees who keep our economy afloat (Presser, 2003). Although they complained about feeling sleep deprived, many night-shift workers in this survey who were parents reported that they preferred this schedule. Put yourself in the place of a person who, like Kevin, can support the family by working nights and spend afternoons and evenings with the children. Provided your partner could work a more typical schedule, wouldn't you make the same choice?

Women's Work

Women face the same twenty-first-century work conditions and pressures as men. However, their career paths differ from men's in the following ways:

- **Women have less continuous careers than men.** Because, as you saw earlier, they are still often the primary nurturers, women are more likely to move in and out of the workforce or to work part time for significant periods during their lives. So a woman decides to give up teaching for a few years, or to cut down her hours at the law firm, when she has her baby. Most often it is after her second child that she simply feels that she *must* give up her job. Making this choice, however, can have enduring economic consequences. It often leads to lower lifetime earnings, fewer chances of advancement, and a greater chance of sliding into poverty in old age (Belsky, 2001; O'Rand, 1988).

- **Women have different occupations and get lower wages.** Compounding their more erratic work lives are the facts that jobs are still segmented by gender and that stereotypically female jobs pay comparatively low wages. About 98 percent of secretaries, clerks, and child-care workers are female (Charles, 1992; Cohen, 2004; Reskin, 1993). Even in nations such as Sweden, where the government provides incentives for companies to hire women in traditionally male fields, there are very few female chemists or engineers (Anker, Malkas, & Korten, 2003).

Have you ever been astonished to see a woman climb into the cockpit of your plane? If so, you have had a vivid reminder that *occupational segregation* is still prevalent in many jobs today.

occupational segregation The separation of men and women into different kinds of jobs and career paths.

To what degree is this **occupational segregation** due to nature (biologically driven preferences) or nurture (socialization pressures in the wider world)? Whatever the answer, in addition to having lower-paying occupations (Kanazawa, 2005), women are far less likely to be promoted to management positions within a given field (Anker, Malkas, & Korten, 2003). These forces all take their toll in terms of pay. In March 2006, for instance, the average weekly salary of women who worked full time in the United States was about $530—roughly $150 less than the weekly wages of the average man who worked full time! (See U.S. Bureau of Labor Statistics, 2006.)

So far we have highlighted the variability that exists in the work world as we examined the boundaryless career and explored the different career paths men and women take. Now let's turn to a theory that spells out some predictable stages to our lives at work.

Looking at Careers from a Lifespan Perspective

In his **lifespan theory of careers**, Donald Super (1957) identifies four phases to careers. During adolescence and emerging adulthood we are in a period of *moratorium*, actively searching for the right career. Once we have found our work identity, we enter the *establishment* phase. During this time, typically lasting from our twenties into our early forties, we are working very hard to advance in our career. In our late forties and fifties we reach the *maintenance* phase, as we enjoy being at our career peak, become less interested in personal success and more interested in nurturing the younger generation, and care more about ethical concerns at work (Pogson and others, 2003). Finally, we enter the *decline* phase, during which we retire, and so disengage from the world of work.

lifespan theory of careers Donald Super's identification of four career phases: *moratorium* in adolescence and emerging adulthood; *establishment* in young adulthood; *maintenance* in midlife; and *decline* in late life.

Although Super developed his ideas in the 1950s, they resonate today. In the most recent NSCW poll, workers in their twenties and thirties said they were more interested in working hard to get ahead in their careers than did the baby boomers in their forties and fifties or people about to retire (Galinsky and others, 2005).

Super's theory fits our *social clock norms*—general ideas about what activities are appropriate at different adult stages (see Chapter 10). Even in our less age-stratified society, we expect people to be at specific places in their careers at certain times of life.

Working as a salesperson at Target is "on target" for a 20-year-old. It is less appropriate if a worker is 45—especially if that person is a male. My midlife students who have returned to school to get training for a new career must cope with their anxiety about being seriously *off time* (see Chapter 10) in their career social clock: "Am I too old to get hired in my new field?" So, despite all the variability, there *are* predictable changes related to age in our attitudes about work.

But even though it still remains true that during their earlier work lives people are most likely to want to advance at a job, the most recent NSCW poll revealed some interesting changes in young men's feelings about climbing the status rungs. In the early 1990s, two out of three male U.S. workers in their twenties and thirties wanted to move into higher-status jobs. In the most recent poll, conducted in 2002, only one in two made that claim (Galinsky and others, 2005).

Because today's young men are more interested in being hands-on fathers, they may care less about working the kinds of backbreaking schedules it takes to get promoted at work. Experts, in fact, tie this interesting change in aspirations directly to the fact that U.S. workers—with or without children—believe they *already* are working too many hours at their jobs. People want to reduce their working hours to, yes, the number of hours they are *supposed to be working*—35 or 40 hours per week (Galinsky and others, 2005)! If you already feel overextended at work, why would you want to be promoted and, most likely, find yourself with even more to do?

Finding Career Happiness

Although many U.S. workers do want to work fewer hours, however, people still care vitally about finding fulfilling, flow-inducing careers. So let's turn to look at two strategies for achieving that goal.

Strategy 1: Find a Career That Fits Your Personality

According to John Holland's (1985) classic theory, the key to finding career fulfillment is to match our job to our personality. People who are sociable should not work in solitary cubicles. Someone strong in Howard Gardner's naturalistic intelligence (recall Chapter 7) should search for a profession that involves working with nature, perhaps choosing landscaping or working with animals, over a job 50 stories up in a corporate tower. The closer we get to our ideal personality–career fit, Holland argues, the more satisfied and successful we will be at our jobs.

To promote this fit, Holland classifies six personality types, described in Table 11.5, and fits them to occupations. Based on their answers to items on a career inventory, people get a three-letter code, showing the three main categories into which they fit, in descending order of importance. If a person's ranking is SAE (social, artistic, and entrepreneurial), that individual might find fulfillment directing an art gallery or setting up and managing a beautiful restaurant. If your code is SIE (social, investigative, and entrepreneurial), you might be better off developing and marketing a medicine for heart disease, or spending your work life as a practicing veterinarian.

Still, even when people have found their optimum personality–work fit, there is no guarantee that they will be happy at a job. What if your job as a gallery manager or vet involved mountains of paperwork and very little time exercising your creative or social skills? In predicting career happiness, it is vital to consider the demands of the actual workplace, too.

TABLE 11.5: **Holland's Six Personality Types**

Realistic type: These people enjoy manipulating machinery or working with tools. They like physical activity and being outdoors. If you fit this profile, your ideal career might be in construction, appliance repair, or car repair.

Investigative type: These people like to find things out through doing research, analyzing information, and collecting data. If you fit this pattern, you might get special satisfaction in some scientific career.

Artistic type: These people are creative and nonconforming, and they love to freely express themselves in the arts. If this is your type, a career as a decorator, dancer, musician, or writer might be ideal.

Social type: These people enjoy helping others and come alive when they are interacting with other human beings. If this description fits you, a career as a bartender, practicing physician, or social worker might be right.

Entrepreneurial type: These people like to lead others, and they enjoy working on organizational goals. As this kind of person, you might find special joy as a company manager or in sales.

Conventional type: These people have a passion for manipulating data and getting things organized. If you fit this type, you would probably be very happy as an accountant, administrative assistant, or clerk.

Take a minute to think about your three-letter code. Can you use this framework to come up with your ideal career?

Strategy 2: Find a Workplace That Fits Your Needs

What specific qualities constitute an ideal work environment? On this point the NSCW poll respondents are very clear. People want to work in jobs that let them expand their skills. They want autonomy to exercise their creativity. They want to have input into decision making at work. They want supportive colleagues and employers who are sensitive to their needs. Remember from Chapter 7 that these are the very qualities—autonomy, nurturing, and relatedness—that define ideal school environments. Workers in the United States are looking for **intrinsic career rewards**.

Bill Varie / Corbis

Having too many tasks piled on you—exceeding any possible person–work task fit—explains why *role overload* is destined to cause burnout and intense career distress.

Extrinsic career rewards, such as salary, can also be crucially important, depending on a person's life situation. As you saw with Kevin in the chapter-opening vignette, people will accept work that is not intrinsically rewarding when their job allows them to fulfill the breadwinner role. There is also an interesting global difference in work priorities. In developing nations, especially those with wide income inequalities and few social services, studies show that only extrinsic benefits, such as pay or job security, matter to workers' happiness (Huang & Van de Vliert, 2003). People have the luxury of viewing work as an intrinsically gratifying, flow-inducing experience only if they are so fortunate as to live in a society where their basic economic needs are likely to be fulfilled.

Remember from Chapter 10 that flow states require the demands of a given task to perfectly match our skills. Therefore, no job can be intrinsically satisfying or flow-inducing under conditions of **role overload**—meaning when people have way too much to do. Work also becomes unsatisfying when people feel **role conflict**—when they are continually torn between competing life demands (such as family and work).

The good news, as Figure 11.7 shows, is that U.S. workers give their jobs high marks for being intrinsically motivating even though they often want to work fewer hours. The reason may be that the actual time we spend at work matters less than the quality of our working conditions. If people are continually interrupted, forced to waste time on meaningless activities, or asked to do too many tasks at once, any job feels impossibly burdensome and difficult to carry out (Galinsky and others, 2005).

How common is work–family conflict? Very. Because they are working more hours, men report feeling particularly deprived of family time (Milkie and others, 2004). People are less likely to complain about their family interfering with their job responsibilities. Instead, they want their work to give them enough time for their family lives.

How do you feel about the importance of your work compared to your family life? A **work-centric worker** puts top priority on his or her career. A **dual-centric worker** gives family and career equal weight. A **family-centric worker** puts family life before the job. If you are like the vast majority of younger workers, you probably rank yourself as either family-centric or dual-centric. The surprise is that the NSCW study

intrinsic career rewards Work that provides inner fulfillment and allows people to satisfy their needs for creativity, autonomy, and relatedness.

extrinsic career rewards Work that is performed for external reinforcers, such as prestige or a high salary.

role overload A job situation that places so many requirements or demands on workers that it becomes impossible to do a good job.

role conflict A situation in which a person is torn between two or more major sets of responsibilities—for instance, parent and worker—and cannot do either job adequately.

work-centric worker A worker who puts his or her job above family life.

dual-centric worker A worker who puts equal importance on family and career.

family-centric worker A worker who puts family life above a job.

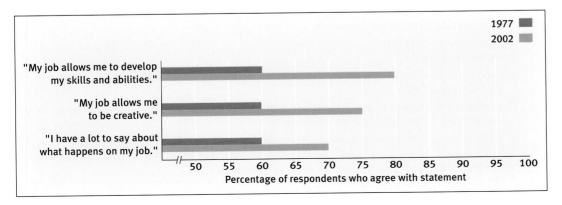

FIGURE 11.7: U.S. workers' ratings of their jobs as intrinsically motivating, 1977 and 2002: Notice that U.S. workers are more likely today to give their jobs high marks for providing intrinsic satisfaction—even though they are working longer hours.

Source: Bond, Galinsky, & Hill (2004): www.familiesandwork.org.

Rolf Bruderer / Corbis

His boss may be surprised to learn that this dual-centric worker, who puts equal priority on his career and family life, will actually make the best kind of employee.

shows that having these attitudes would actually make you happier and more productive on the job (Galinsky and others, 2005). In contrast to our stereotypes, the researchers find that workaholics are not better employees. People do better at their work when they care as much (or more) about their families as their working lives!

INTERVENTIONS: Making Work More People-Friendly

Table 11.6 shows the overwork scale used in the NSCW survey so that you can rate your work stress level compared to that of the average U.S. employee. For any reader who scores in the moderate range (needs help) and certainly for anyone in the highly stressed overloaded zone, here are some strategies that might help.

LESSONS IF YOU ARE A WORKER

- Try to minimize interruptions while you are working on tasks (close your door and post a do-not-disturb sign or don't answer your phone).

- Make it a policy to finish one task before you start another.

- On days when you feel completely overloaded, employ stress management techniques. Close the door; relax; build in regular mental health breaks—perhaps walk around the office or get out for a 15-minute jog. Not only will you be better able to focus on work but you might live longer, too.

- Build in a wall between your work life and your outside life. Resist the temptation to bring a briefcase full of papers home or to check e-mails at home during the evening or on the weekend. Mentally shut off your "work brain" and try to enjoy your family outside of working hours.

TABLE 11.6: How Overworked Are You?

Circle the number that corresponds to your answer to each question: 1 = never; 2 = rarely; 3 = sometimes; 4 = often; 5 = very often.

		Score			
1. Within the last month, how often have you felt overwhelmed by how much work you had to do?	1	2	3	4	5
2. How often within the last month have you felt that you didn't have time to step back and process or reflect on the work you are doing?	1	2	3	4	5
3. Within the last month, how often have you felt overworked?	1	2	3	4	5
4. During a typical workweek, how often do you have to work on too many tasks at the same time?	1	2	3	4	5
5. During a typical workweek, how often do interruptions make it difficult to get your work done?	1	2	3	4	5
6. How often do co-workers, supervisors, managers, or clients contact you—or you, them—about work-related matters outside normal working hours?	1	2	3	4	5
7. While you are on vacation, how often do you do any work related to your job (working on projects, calling in to work or being called from work, checking e-mail, etc.)?	1	2	3	4	5

Total score _____

Interpreting Your Total Score:

If your score is 10 or below, you rank at the bottom 10 percent of the workforce, meaning that you are not overworked.

If your score is below 14, you are at the bottom third of the workforce, meaning that you are generally not overworked.

If your score is between 15 and 20, you rank in the middle third of the workforce. There is room for improvement and you are moderately overworked.

If your score is 21 or above, you rank in the top third of workers and are highly overworked.

If your score is 26 or more, you are dangerously overworked (top 10 percent of the workforce). This high level of overwork may have serious negative consequences for your health and job performance.

Source: Galinsky & others (2005).

LESSONS IF YOU ARE AN EMPLOYER

- Evaluate what work is busywork and what jobs really need to be done—and cut out the busywork.

- Provide your workers with a work-focused, distraction-free environment.

- Resist the impulse to micromanage, let your staff be creative, and don't foster destructive competition. You will have a more productive, happier workforce if you provide a nurturing, collegial environment that lets people exercise their autonomy and flow.

- Understand that being sensitive to your workers' family lives may improve their productivity. Allow workers freedom to take time off for family needs. But simply having a policy that permits "family time" is not enough. Create an environment that makes people feel secure that they won't be penalized when they do take time off (Clark, 2001; Thompson, Beauvais, & Lyness, 1999).

- Finally, try not to overwork your workers. A 40-hour-a-week job should mean 40 hours!

Final Thoughts

In the United States, the federal government basically takes a hands-off position with regard to regulating work hours, allowing employers free rein to "ask" their employees to pile on extra hours at their so-called 9-to-5 jobs. Another stance common in the United States is the practice of marginalizing part-time work. Part-time positions typically pay less per hour than full-time work, and very few of those jobs offer health insurance. This leaves many workers with the choice of either continuing full time or quitting their jobs when they have children, even though they would prefer part-time work. Finally, the typical U.S. employee gets about two weeks of vacation a year.

The situation in Europe is almost from a different planet. The European Union (EU) sets the typical workweek by law at 35 hours. Governments actively encourage employers to provide high-quality part-time work, especially for people during their child-rearing years. In Sweden, for instance, parents have the legal right to work six hours a day at their jobs (at prorated pay) until their children reach the age of 8. Moreover, since their governments all provide citizens with universal health care, European workers don't have to worry about losing their health benefits when they work part time. Another telling difference relates to vacation time. In contrast to our paltry average two weeks, in the EU a month of vacation is the norm! Can we learn some lessons from Europe about how to help make work more family-friendly in the United States? ▨

TYING IT ALL TOGETHER

1. Michael is unhappy about his job. His grandfather is trying to make him feel better by contrasting the career situation today with "the good old days." What can this grandfather legitimately say (i.e., pick the true answer)?

    a. "Your problem isn't so bad! In my day, people had to stick with their careers, even if they didn't really like them."
    b. "Your problem isn't so bad! In my day, most people worked much longer hours than today."
    c. "Your problem isn't so bad! In my day, we had much less job security."

2. Which of the men described below does *not* fit into any of Super's phases in his lifespan theory of careers but instead is following a work pattern common in today's world?

    a. Ethan, a 30-year-old, is working very hard to advance in his career.
    b. Brad, a 40-year-old, is looking for a whole new career.
    c. Tom, a 50-year-old, has risen through the ranks of the company and is now enjoying being at the peak of his career.
    d. John, a 60-year-old, is thinking about retirement.

3. In the previous question, which person clearly has a traditional stable career and which person has a boundaryless career?

4. Vanessa, a bubbly, outgoing 30-year-old, has what her friends see as a perfect job: She's a researcher in a one-person office with flexible hours; a large, quiet workspace; a boss who is often away; job security; and great pay. Yet Vanessa is unhappy with the job. According to Holland's theory, what is the problem?

5. Which of the following people would be most likely to experience role conflict?
   a. a work-centric worker who needs to spend weekends in the office
   b. a dual-centric worker whose job requires frequent long trips overseas
   c. a family-centric worker who was recently passed over for a promotion

6. Imagine you are in charge of formulating federal employment policy for the current administration. Come up with some incentives that would put pressure on U.S. employers to avoid overworking their workers.

Answers to the Tying It All Together questions can be found in the answers section of the book

∎ SUMMARY

Marriage

Marriages used to be practical unions often arranged by families. In the early twentieth century, as life expectancy increased dramatically, we developed the modern idea that couples should be best friends and lovers for 50 years. During the late twentieth century, with the women's movement and the increasing acceptability of divorce, marriage became **deinstitutionalized**—less of a standard path in the Western world. In contrast to Egypt, where male-dominated marriage is universal, and Scandinavia, where not getting married is perfectly fine, in the United States we still care deeply about getting married—but are reluctant to enter that state unless we feel fairly financially secure. Couples can expect a decline in marital happiness, especially during the first four years of married life; but for those who stay together, there is often a **U-shaped curve of marital satisfaction,** with happiness rising at the empty-nest stage.

According to Sternberg's **triangular theory of love,** married couples start out with **consummate love,** but passion and intimacy can decline as partners live separate lives. To preserve passion and intimacy, one strategy may be to share mutual passions with one's mate. Research shows that unhappy couples communicate in various destructive ways: being less positive, getting personally hurtful, engaging in **demand–withdrawal communications,** and seeing their partners through an overly suspicious lens. Adopting an **exchange model of love** (versus a securely attached **communal model of love**) also can be poisonous to married life.

Divorce, that common adult event, has several phases. There is a pre-divorce phase of marital unhappiness, then the upheaval of the separation, and possibly long-term stresses relating to conflicts around the children. Although women tend to suffer financially after a divorce, coping with this event can result in emotional growth. Because mothers usually get custody of the children after a divorce, fathers often face the problem of losing their children and perhaps the need to establish new families. Men cope in different ways with challenges of stepparenthood.

Parenthood

Although many more people *can* become parents in our twenty-first-century society, more people are choosing not to have children. A major concern in Europe is declining **fertility rates.**

Despite our negative stereotypes, adults who choose not to have children are not more self-centered or prone to be more unhappy in old age.

The transition to parenthood tends to lessen romance and intimacy. Gender roles become more traditional. Conflicts centering around **marital equity** can arise. Still, there is tremendous variability, with some couples growing closer after the baby is born. The quality of a couple's relationship before becoming parents predicts how a marriage will fare after the baby arrives.

Motherhood has extreme lows as well as highs—and this experience is tailor-made to destroy women's idealized images of themselves. Society conveys a sanitized view of what motherhood is like. We tend to blame mothers for their children's "deficiencies," and we sometimes berate working women for not spending enough time with their children. In contrast to our images of an epidemic of "uninvolved" mothers, twenty-first-century women spend much more time (especially teaching time) with their children than in the past. Contemporary mothers (and fathers) are giving their children unparalleled attention and love—even while they hold down jobs.

Fathers are expected to be breadwinners and nurturers as well as good sex-role models and sometimes the disciplinarians. During the past 15 years, men have stepped in as genuine caregiving partners, although women may still tend to have bottom-line responsibility for directing children's lives. Fathers play with their children in traditionally male, active ways, and they vary in their involvement, depending on their sex-role attitudes, the attitudes of their spouse toward their getting involved, and the couple's work schedules. Feeling committed to the male role of breadwinner, and needing to work long hours, can interfere with men's (and women's) "child-care time."

Work

We used to have **traditional stable careers.** Today, partly due to job insecurity, we are more likely to have **boundaryless careers.** The average U.S. worker spends much more than 40 hours at a normal full-time job. Another emerging work trend, the practice of working nonstandard shifts, helps full-time workers be full-time parents. Women have less continuous careers than men; in addition, **occupational segregation** and lower pay for women are still prevalent in the world of work.

Super's **lifespan theory of careers,** with moratorium, establishment, maintenance, and decline phases of work, is still relevant today. But the current cohort of young men care less about climbing the ladder of success, because they feel they are already working too many hours.

One key to job happiness is to choose a career that fits our personality. Another is having a work environment that permits creativity and autonomy. U.S. workers are mainly looking for **intrinsic career rewards,** but **extrinsic career rewards,** such as pay, become paramount when considerations such as supporting a family or having enough money to survive loom large.

U.S. workers give their jobs high marks for being intrinsically satisfying. People feel in **role overload** when their work is not flow-inducing—not when they are working long hours. **Role conflict** is very common today, especially for men. **Family-centric** and **dual-centric workers** feel more productive and are happier at their jobs than **work-centric workers.** All workers should try to avoid distractions, take regular mental health breaks, and build a wall between work and family time. Employers should make work conditions more flow-inducing and build in chances for their employees to take time off for family. European nations, with their family-friendly work policies, offer lessons for the United States.

▌ KEY TERMS

deinstitutionalization of
    marriage, p. 336
U-shaped curve of marital
    satisfaction, p. 339
triangular theory of love, p. 340
consummate love, p. 340
demand–withdrawal
    communication, p. 342

communal model of love,
    p. 343
exchange model of love,
    p. 343
fertility rate, p. 348
marital equity, p. 349
traditional stable career,
    p. 355

boundaryless career, p. 355
occupational segregation,
    p. 357
lifespan theory of careers,
    p. 357
intrinsic career rewards,
    p. 359

extrinsic career rewards,
    p. 359
role overload, p. 359
role conflict, p. 359
work-centric worker, p. 359
dual-centric worker, p. 359
family-centric worker, p. 359

▌ RECOMMENDED RESOURCES

MARRIAGE

Gottman, J. (1994). *Why marriages succeed and fail—and how you can make yours last.* New York: Simon & Schuster.

The author, a psychologist, sums up his decades of research exploring which communication styles make marriages effective and offers advice for having happy, healthy relationships.

Hetherington, M., and Kelly, J. (2002). *For better or for worse: Divorce reconsidered.* New York: Norton.

Enriched by personal life stories, this book summarizes the findings of a landmark 25-year study of divorce and traces its impact on men, women, and children.

Sternberg, R. J. (1988). Triangulating love. In R. J. Sternberg and M. L. Barnes (eds.), *The psychology of love* (pp. 119–138). New Haven, CT: Yale University Press.

In this article, Sternberg spells out his triangular theory of love.

Waite, L., & Gallagher, M. (2000). *The case for marriage.* New York: Random House.

As they summarize the social science findings relating to marriage, the authors make the case that marriage is a health-enhancing state.

PARENTHOOD

Cowan, C., and Cowan, P. (1992). *When partners become parents.* New York: Basic Books.

This book offers a readable account of one classic study exploring the transition to parenthood.

Douglas, S., and Michaels, M. W. (2004). *The mommy myth: The idealization of motherhood and how it has undermined women.* New York: Free Press.

The authors explore the pernicious effects of the "perfect mom" myth on contemporary women.

Genevie, L., and Margolies, E. (1987*). The motherhood report.* New York: Macmillan.

This national survey, described in the chapter, offers a compelling, honest portrait of the motherhood experience.

Palkovitz, R. (2002). *Involved fathering and men's psychological development.* Mahwah, NJ: Erlbaum.

In this intensive study of fathers, men talk about the pleasures and problems of fatherhood.

CAREERS

Gornick, J. C., and Meyers, M. K. (2003). *Families that work: Policies for reconciling parenthood and employment.* New York: Russell Sage Foundation.

This book provides a devastating critique of the family-unfriendly work policies of the United States compared to European countries. It's a bit academic but well worth reading.

Families and Work Institute, www.familiesandwork.org

This organization—the source for the chapter's information about work and careers—sponsors the National Surveys of the Changing Workforce. Check out its Web site for readable summaries of the study's findings and for tips about how to make your work situation more satisfying.

CHAPTER 12

Midlife

Today, at age 52, I am calm, in control, confident about my ideas. There is some regret about the wrinkles and the added pounds—but you might be surprised at how minor these concerns are. Getting through menopause was a problem, but now that it's over I feel wonderful. Sex with Kevin is better than before. My fear relates to my mind. After years spent crunching numbers as an accountant, I plan to go back to school to get a social work degree. I've always volunteered on weekends at church. I want to devote myself full time during these next precious decades to helping "at risk" young people succeed. Having grown up during the civil rights movement here in Nashville, I learned social activism at a young age. But can I make it in the classroom at my age? Then there are the anxieties about time. Cotonia and Joshua recently moved in after the divorce. Kevin wants to reduce his hours at Nissan to watch our precious grandbaby while my daughter is at work—but I can't put that responsibility totally on my husband. Child care is a grandma's job!

Still, my life experience will help me cope with these challenges, and I can rely on my life love, Kevin, to cheer me on. I'm basically the same person that I was at 20, just as caring, energetic, and outgoing, with the added depth only age can bring. And it's now or never. I feel the clock ticking when I look around. My good friend Susan just died of cancer. My baby brother Jay retired after having his stroke last year. I get my inspiration from Mom, at age 75 still running the beauty shop six days a week. Mom—well, she's supposed to be old, but she's really middle-aged.

When you think of middle age, what images come to your mind? As is true of Mary, you may imagine people at the peak of their powers: wise, mature, competently mastering adult life. You also might think of sexual decline, menopause, and fears about mental loss (Lachman, 2004). You might imagine vigorous, healthy grandparents or people struggling to care for their disabled parents in old age. In this chapter, devoted to the long life stage that psychologist Carl Jung (1933) poetically labeled "the afternoon of life," we explore these challenges and changes.

Let's start by setting some boundaries. When do people move into their middle years? When does life's afternoon shade into the evening of life?

Although they are both in their mid-fifties, this German industrialist enjoying his vacation villa in Acapulco looks middle-aged, while we might label this disabled Cuban man elderly. This illustrates just why chronological age is an imperfect marker of our "real" place on the life cycle during the middle years.

Setting the Context: Pinning Down Middle Age

If you are like most adults in our culture, you probably believe we enter middle age at about age 40 and leave this stage at age 60 or 65 (Etaugh & Bridges, 2006; Lachman, 2004; Lachman & Bertrand, 2001). Not everyone would agree. In various U.S. surveys, roughly *half* of all people in their late sixties and seventies call themselves middle-aged (Lachman, 2004). They may be right. When a woman, such as Mary's mother, is healthy and working in her seventies, should we call that person middle-aged or old? When someone is just starting a family at age 45 or 50, is that individual middle-aged or a young adult?

At the other extreme, you may know a middle-aged person who really qualifies as "old": a colleague in his fifties coping with serious heart disease; a relative, such as Mary's brother, who was forced by poor health to retire at a too young, *off-time* age.

These definitional problems are compounded by the fact that middle age begins and ends earlier in regions of the globe where life expectancy is comparatively low. In one cross-cultural poll, students in Bahrain, Brazil, and Indonesia believed that we enter middle age at 30 and begin old age at roughly age 45! (See Eyetsemitan and others, 2003.)

So, just as we saw with emerging adulthood in Chapter 10, middle age is a hazy, ill-defined life stage. People who fit into this chronological category are a tremendously diverse group. Diversity is actually the basic feature of the middle years—this time of losses and gains; of looking forward to the future and realizing that much of life now lies behind. Diversity—of change patterns, and from person to person—*plus* consistency is the basic message of the chapter you are about to read.

The Evolving Self

Do we get more mature as we age, or are we the same people at age 50 as at 25? Is Mary right to be worried about going back to school at her age, and how do our intellectual abilities really change as we travel through adult life? These questions have been hotly debated for decades. The reasons for the controversies will become clear as we explore the developmental science research relating to those compelling human questions: "How do personality and intelligence change during adulthood?" and "How can we have a fulfilling adult life?"

[FAQ: Do our personalities change as we grow older?]

Exploring Personality

We actually have three *contradictory* views about how our personalities tend to change over the years. One is that people basically stay the same: "If Calista is bossy and self-centered in college, she will be bossy and self-centered in the nursing home." Another is that entering new life stages or having life-changing experiences produces radical transformations in our basic self: "Since giving birth to my child, I'm a completely different person." "Coming close to death in my car accident last summer transformed how I think about the world." Then, there is the change that we all hope for, the one that Mary describes and many middle-aged and older women also report (Stewart, Ostrove, & Helson, 2001; Zucker, Ostrove, & Stewart, 2002). As we get older, we should grow more competent, confident, better at coping with stress. Which point of view is true? The answer, as developmentalists have discovered, is *each* idea, depending on which aspect of personality we chart!

How We Don't Change (Much): Examining the "Big Five"

Today, psychologists often measure personality by ranking people according to five core psychological predispositions, or traits (Costa & McCrae, 1988; McCrae, Costa, & Piedmont, 1993). As you read the following list, take a minute to think of where you stand on these categories, which researchers label the **Big Five traits:**

Big Five traits Five core psychological predispositions—neuroticism, extraversion, openness to experience, conscientiousness, and agreeableness—that underlie personality.

- *Neuroticism* refers to our general tendency toward mental health versus psychological disturbance. Are you basically resilient, stable, and well-adjusted, someone who bounces back after setbacks and copes well with stress? Or are you hostile, highstrung, and incredibly obsessive, a person whom people might label as psychologically disturbed? (Children with serious externalizing and internalizing tendencies, for instance, would rank high on neuroticism.)

- *Extraversion* describes outgoing attitudes, such as warmth, gregariousness, activity, and assertion. Are you sociable, friendly, a real "people person," someone who thrives on going to parties? Or are you most comfortable curling up alone with a good book? Do you get antsy when you are by yourself, thinking "I've got to get out and be with people," or would you find happiness living a reflective, solitary life?

- *Openness to experience* refers to our tendency to be risk-takers and seek out new experiences. Do you love traveling the world, sampling different cuisines, taking chances, having people shake up your preconceived ideas? Do you think life should be a continual adventure and relish getting out of your comfort zone? Or are you basically cautious, risk averse, comfortable mainly with what you already know?

- *Conscientiousness* describes having the kind of industrious worker personality described in Chapter 10. Are you hardworking, self-disciplined, and reliable, someone others count on to take on demanding jobs and get things done? Or are you erratic and irresponsible, prone to renege on obligations and forget appointments, a person your friends and co-workers really can't trust?

- *Agreeableness* has to do with kindness, empathy, and the ability to compromise. Are you pleasant, loving, and easy to get along with? Or are you stubborn, hot-tempered, someone who continually gets offended and regularly gets into fights? (Agreeable people, for instance, have secure attachment styles.)

Big Five scores vary a bit in different cultures. Residents of more individualistic nations, such as the United States, tend to rank higher on extraversion and openness to experience. Citizens growing up in collectivist regions of the globe, such as Asia and Africa, score higher on agreeableness than people in the West (Allik & McCrae, 2004). Still, around the world, research shows we can boil personality down to these five basic dimensions. Moreover, these core personality styles—on average—do not change much after age 30. The bottom-line answer, based on decades of studies with the Big Five and related personality tests, to the question "How will I change?" is "Not very much" (Costa & McCrae, 2002; McCrae & Costa, 1990; McCrae and others, 2000; Schaie, Willis, & Caskie, 2004).

[FAQ: Is personality stable, or do our predispositions change as we age?]

The idea that our basic personality doesn't change much may fit in with your personal experience. Contact an old college acquaintance decades later and you will probably be amazed at how much of the same person reemerges: "She's just as much a party person at 60 as she was at 20!" "He's got the same problems with wife number three as he had with wife number one!"

Let's now follow the same approach as throughout this book, exploring how "nature evokes nurture" forces might work to solidify our basic personality tendencies and make us *more* like ourselves as we age.

Take Sara, who ranked high on conscientiousness in her early twenties. Her *worker* personality ensured that she did well in college and got an excellent first job. As she travels through the work world, she is regularly praised for her industriousness and eventually is promoted to an executive position at a firm. Sara is a committed, loyal friend who works hard on her marriage, and—because we match up by *homogamy*—has an equally conscientious mate. At age 55, Sara's life is a testament to the power of hard work in building a fulfilling life. She is the treasured rock on which her family and employees depend.

Now, imagine José, a friend of yours, who ranked low on agreeableness at age 30. Because José is so hostile, he has continually lost jobs and has had several failed marriages. At age 60, when you bump into José after not seeing him for decades, he seems even more bitter, demoralized, and disgusted than before.

[FAQ: Why do some people's temperaments change as they age?]

Still, these are *average* tendencies. When developmentalists conduct longitudinal studies, they find that some people change a good deal. What specifically causes these core dimensions of personality to shift? In following men from late middle age into their sixties, researchers found that changes in these basic traits most often occur in response to *other* major changes (Mroczek & Spiro, 2003). A lifelong extrovert might withdraw into a shell after developing serious memory problems. A disagreeable 60-year-old might become much more mellow after finding a loving new mate (Costa & McCrae, 2002; McCrae and others, 2000; Small and others, 2003). So, yes, in general, you can predict that a 30-year-old extrovert will still love to socialize at 50 or 65. But you could be very wrong.

Knowing that someone is extroverted, conscientious, or disagreeable gives us the basic outlines of personality. But it tells us little about the specifics of a given individual's life. Think of several friends you would rank high on conscientiousness. One person might be a committed, full-time mother; another might be a company manager; yet another might have found the outlet for her conscientiousness in teaching or being a nurse. In order to really understand what makes human beings tick, we have to move closer and ask them about their lives. This is the strategy that developmentalist Dan McAdams and his colleagues have been using to explore personality during the adult years (McAdams, 2006; McAdams & Logan, 2004). Let's eavesdrop on one of McAdams's interviews:

> I was living in a rural North Dakota town and was the mother of a 4-year-old son. One summer afternoon . . . Jeff left without me and was hit by a car. When I got there, he was lying in the street unconscious . . . . I felt sure he was dying, and I didn't know of anything I could do to preserve his life. My friend did, though, and today [Jeff] is 18 years old and very healthy. That feeling of being helpless and hopeless while I was sure I was watching my son die was a turning point. I decided I would never feel it again and I became an E.M.T.
> (quoted in McAdams, de St. Aubin, & Logan, 1993, p. 228)

When they listen to life stories such as these, McAdams and his colleagues get a drastically different portrait of how much our personality changes. Although this woman might have always ranked relatively high in conscientiousness, the *specific path* her life took was responsive to this life-changing event. In McAdams's opinion, once we fill in the rich details of human experience, we do see lives being transformed.

How We Do Change: Examining Generativity

In addition to exploring the twists and turns of our human journey through autobiographies, McAdams's research team has focused on rigorously testing the ideas of the pioneering theorist who *does* believe that we change dramatically at different life stages: Erik Erikson. Does **generativity,** or nurturing the next generation, become our priority during the middle years? Is Erikson (1969) correct that fulfilling our generativity is the key to feeling fulfilled as midlife adults? When people in their forties or fifties lack a feeling of generativity, are they stagnant, at loose ends, demoralized, and depressed? (See Table 12.1.)

To fully capture Erikson's complex concept, the developmentalists devised three different types of measures: They constructed a questionnaire designed to measure overall generative attitudes. (You can see the first ten items on this scale in Table 12.2.) They asked people to write about their primary goals or priorities (for example, "What are the main agendas in your life now?"). They questioned adults about specific generative activities, asking them, for instance, "Have you volunteered to help the homeless or taught someone else a skill within the past two months?" (See McAdams, 2001; McAdams, de St. Aubin, & Logan, 1993; McAdams and others, 1997.)

When the researchers gave their measures to young, middle-aged, and elderly people, they found few age differences in generative attitudes or activities. People were just as likely to care about making a difference in the world and do good works at age 20 or 50 or 85. They did discover striking age differences in generative *priorities*—with emerging adults ranking very low on this particular scale (McAdams, Hart, & Maruna, 1998). Young people's goals centered on identity issues. A 20-year-old might say, "I want to make my job more interesting" or "My plan is to figure out what I want to do with my life." Mid life and older people were more likely to report: "I want to be a positive role model," "I want to help my teenage son," or "I want to work for justice and peace in the world."

TABLE 12.1: Erikson's Psychosocial Stages

Life Stage	Primary Task
Infancy (birth to 1 year)	Basic trust versus mistrust
Toddlerhood (1 to 2 years)	Autonomy versus shame and doubt
Early childhood (3 to 6 years)	Initiative versus guilt
Late childhood (6 years to puberty)	Industry versus inferiority
Adolescence (teens into twenties)	Identity versus role confusion
Young adulthood (twenties to early forties)	Intimacy versus isolation
Middle adulthood (forties to sixties)	**Generativity versus stagnation**
Late adulthood (late sixties and beyond)	Integrity versus despair

According to Erikson, in midlife our mission shifts to giving to others (generativity). Adults who don't feel generative stagnate, feeling no real purpose to their lives.

generativity In Erikson's theory, the seventh psychosocial task, in which people in midlife find meaning from nurturing the next generation, caring for others, or enriching the life of others through their work. According to Erikson, when midlife adults have not achieved generativity, they feel stagnant, without a sense of purpose in life.

TABLE 12.2: McAdams's Generative Concern Scale

True	False	
❏	❏	1. I try to pass along the knowledge I have gained through my experiences.
❏	❏	2. I do not feel that other people need me.
❏	❏	3. I think I would like the work of a teacher.
❏	❏	4. I feel as though I have made a difference to many people.
❏	❏	5. I do not volunteer to work for a charity.
❏	❏	6. I have made and created things that have had an impact on other people.
❏	❏	7. I try to be creative in most things that I do.
❏	❏	8. I think that I will be remembered for a long time after I die.
❏	❏	9. I believe that society cannot be responsible for providing food and shelter to all homeless people.
❏	❏	10. Others would say that I have made unique contributions to society

Answers: 1. T, 2. F, 3. T, 4. T, 5. F, 6. T, 7. T, 8. T, 9. F, 10. T

Source: McAdams & St. Aubin (1992), pp. 1003–1015.

How do you score on this test measuring overall generative motivations?

Adults of every age get great pleasure from engaging in generative activities. But for this college student, her work volunteering at a nursing home may rank a distant second to "getting my career and life together," while for this elderly Hispanic man, cultivating a Los Angeles community garden that provides poor people with free vegetables may rank as his first priority in life.

This makes sense. Remember from Chapter 6 that prosocial behaviors are in full swing by early childhood. There is no reason to think that our basic human drive to be nurturing changes at *any* life stage. But, just as Erikson would predict, we need to resolve issues relating to our personal development before our *primary* concern shifts to giving to others in the wider world.

Erikson, however, was wrong in one respect. Although generative strivings do become our main focus in midlife, priorities centered on nurturing the next generation can be just as intense at age 90 as at 45 (McAdams, 2001a, 2006; Zucker and others, 2002). To bring home this point, you might poll the older adults in your family. Ask them: "What are your top-ranking goals?" I'll bet you will often hear generativity-oriented comments, such as "I want to be a role model for my grandchildren" or "I need to make sure my wife is well provided for if I die."

Is Erikson correct when he says that fulfilling our generativity is the key to happiness during adult life? Highly generative people do often score above average on measures of life satisfaction (McAdams, Hart, & Maruna, 1998). Still, when we think of outstandingly generative role models such as Martin Luther King, Jr., or Mother Teresa, phrases such as "happy" and "satisfied with life" do not come to mind. What does come to mind is having a deep sense of purpose and living an immensely meaningful life. And yes, exceptionally generative people do report having tremendously meaningful, fulfilling adult lives (Grossbaum & Bates, 2002; Peterson, 1998; Stewart & Vandewater, 1998; Zucker and others, 2002).

Moreover, when people are not fulfilling their generativity, their lives lack meaning. In Erikson's words, they feel *stagnant*—purposeless and at loose ends. Read what one developmentalist had to say about a woman named Deborah, who scored very low on generativity in a longitudinal study of women's lives:

In response to a question about career wishes, Deborah, who at the time was in her late forties, wrote, "I have yet to think this one out fully . . . . Luck has always played a major role in my life." In reference to the birth of her first child, Deborah wrote, "All actions automatic. No emotional involvement . . . ; totally self-preserving but very unpleasant." After many years of marriage, Deborah underwent a difficult divorce. She began to work in a "blur of meaningless jobs."

(adapted from Peterson, 1998, p. 12)

As this case history suggests, generativity is not automatically evoked by simply having children. It does not naturally unfold at a certain age. People vary in the degree to which they reach this developmental milestone at age 40 or 50, just as they differ in identity status at age 20 or 25.

Do the life stories of exceptionally generative people differ from those of less generative adults? To answer this question, McAdams's research team selected people with unusually high scores on the generative concern scale illustrated in Table 12.2 on page 369—adults such as Mary in the chapter-opening vignette, whose priorities centered on doing good works—and asked them to tell their life stories. Would these autobiographies differ from those of people such as Deborah in the previous example, who ranked low on fulfilling Erikson's midlife task?

The answer was yes. The life stories of unusually generative adults had a cluster of themes demonstrating what the researchers called a **commitment script.** Specifically, they often described early memories of feeling especially fortunate: "I was my grandmother's favorite"; "I was a miracle child who should not have survived." They frequently reported feeling unusually sensitive to the suffering of others from a young age. They also talked about having an identity revolving around generative values that never wavered from their teenage years. A 50-year-old minister in one of McAdams's studies was a teenage prostitute, then a con artist, and spent two years in a federal prison, but throughout her life, she reported, "I was always doing ministry."

Generative adults were far from free of internal conflicts. Because taking vigorous action to make a difference involves being very assertive (recall that this quality is also involved in acting prosocially during childhood), highly generative people struggled with tensions relating to those basic poles of human experience: They needed to be powerful and dominant, and also to be gentle and caring. Often they were discouraged about the state of the world. However, they were at heart optimistic, believing that people were basically good and that everything turns out for the best (McAdams, 2006).

Perhaps the most striking characteristic of generative adults' autobiographies was that they were defined by **redemption sequences**—examples of devastating events that turned out in a positive way (McAdams, 2001a; McAdams & Bowman, 2001; McAdams, Hart, & Maruna, 1998). For instance, in the example just mentioned, the woman minister would view the humiliation of being sent to prison as the best thing that ever happened, the pivotal experience in turning her life around. Earlier in our discussion, recall how the North Dakota mother talked about her son's frightening accident as the tragic event that allowed her to connect with the perfect flow-inducing, generative career.

In contrast, highly nongenerative adults often described **contamination sequences**—blissful life experiences that went wrong: "My wedding was beautiful, but then my husband and I started to fight"; "I was thrilled to learn I was pregnant, but felt nothing after my child was born." In sum, early memories of feeling personally blessed, an enduring sensitivity to others' misfortunes, and having the ability to turn tragedies into growth experiences seem to be the basic ingredients for constructing an extremely generative adult life.

Although the impulse to be generative is probably universal, built into our humanity and programmed to fully blossom during adulthood, it may differ depending on our gender. Women are more likely to fulfill their generativity by doing hands-on child care. As you saw in Chapter 11, men feel incredibly generative while carrying out the breadwinner role.

The society we live in shapes our outlets for generativity, too. In traditional collectivist cultures generativity was programmed into the structure of living. As they aged, people automatically became teachers or elders who passed down wisdom to the young (de St. Aubin, McAdams, & Kim, 2004). In our individualistic society—from nurturing our co-workers to being the best possible parent to volunteering at the local nursing home—we have the freedom to carve out the unique generative path that gives us flow.

Finally, as they searched out their generative exemplars, McAdams and his colleagues discovered a tantalizing ethnic difference. African American men and women, they discovered, were overrepresented in the group of exceptionally generative adults (Hart and others, 2001; McAdams, 2006). Is this because the church, with its emphasis on good works, plays such an important role in the black community? Does a history of coping with discrimination make people more sensitive to suffering and help steer them to living a generative life? In support of this second possibility, themes highlighting steady progress toward overcoming adversity were central in highly generative African Americans' autobiographies (McAdams & Bowman, 2001).

commitment script In Dan McAdams's research, a type of autobiography produced by highly generative adults that involves childhood memories of feeling special, being unusually sensitive to others' misfortunes, and having a strong, enduring generative mission from adolescence, and that often includes redemption sequences.

redemption sequence In Dan McAdams's research, a characteristic theme of highly generative adults' autobiographies, in which they describe tragic events that turned out for the best.

contamination sequence In Dan McAdams's research, a characteristic theme of nongenerative adults' autobiographies, in which they describe joyous events that turned out badly.

This group project to restore the oldest black Baptist church in South Carolina is typical in the African American experience, where a mission to be of service—especially in a caring community that revolves around the church—is standard.

Karen Kasmauski/Corbis

Do you believe that dealing with adversity makes us more giving, generative people? Did some painful experience in your own life change your priorities, transforming you into a more loving human being? If so, you might agree with the adults in one study who highlighted a crucial *negative* experience as the defining event that caused them to become wise (Bluck & Glück, 2004).

The idea that coping with life's setbacks produces emotional growth may underlie our third idea about personality. We do not expect 20-year-olds to have enough real-world experience to be fully mature. As we get older and live life, we expect to become more self-confident, competent, and better able to handle stress. Do people really become more mature as they move into midlife?

Do We Get More Mature with Age?

Compelling evidence that getting older *does* bring maturity comes from one of psychology's earliest longitudinal studies. During the 1930s, psychologists selected the "best and brightest" members of a class of Harvard undergraduates to interview and then talked to the men at several points as they moved into their middle years (Valliant, 1977). As each person returned to discuss his life, raters coded the interviews for **defense mechanisms,** basic unconscious strategies that, Freudian psychoanalysts believe, are used for coping with upsetting events. Although, according to Freud and his followers, we all adopt defense mechanisms in handling life, the researchers ranked these styles of coping on a hierarchy from extremely maladaptive to fully mature (see Table 12.3).

Let's take the case of a man who is laid off from his job. At the most pathological extreme, this person might adopt psychotic defenses, retreating into a fantasy world. At a slightly higher level, he would engage in self-destructive acts, such as drinking, taking drugs, or acting out against the world. At the next level up on the maturity hierarchy, he might develop a phobia ("I can't leave the house"), get depressed, or deny his upsetting emotions ("I'm not worried at all"). At the most mature level, this man would cope with adversity in productive ways: focusing on what he still had; using humor; making redemption sequences his basic mode of operation, transforming this misfortune into a chance to enrich his life.

[FAQ: How consistent is personality across the life-span?]

defense mechanisms In Freudian psychoanalytic theory, unconscious strategies that people use for coping with upsetting events.

TABLE 12.3: **A Hierarchy of Defense Mechanisms, Ranked from Most Pathological to Fully Mature, and Examples Illustrating Each Style of Thinking in Response to a Life Stress**

Stressful event: How does Mr. Jones handle getting fired?

Psychotic mechanisms

"My boss didn't fire me. I'll show up for work tomorrow." "Sorry, I'm the boss of this company. I can't fire anyone." "I control the world."

Immature mechanisms

"I hate myself. I'm going to turn to drugs or drinking." "I'll make them pay. I'll make life miserable for them, too."

Neurotic mechanisms

"It really wasn't bad. I'm not upset at all." "I'm getting anxiety attacks and becoming phobic." "I'm so depressed that I'm having trouble functioning."

Mature mechanisms

"It's terribly distressing, but I need to count my blessings. I'm healthy. The kids are wonderful. We'll survive this and come out stronger."

"Well, there goes life again!" *(humor)*

"This is a chance for me to become a full-time dad—to really get to know the kids. It's a blessing in disguise!" "I'll use my time while I send out résumés to volunteer at the local homeless shelter." *(redemption sequence)*

As undergraduates, the Harvard men used mainly immature defenses, but over the years the balance shifted. After age 35, the men were much more likely to use mature defenses in handling the stresses of life.

Although their criteria for measuring maturity were different, in another classic longitudinal study—tracking 1959 graduates from Mills College (an exclusive female college in California)—other researchers found similar changes (Helson, Jones, & Kwan, 2002). By their forties, the Mills women became more self-confident and decisive. Amazingly, by midlife all of the women who had been rated as excessively clingy in their love relationships during their twenties were now ranked as securely attached! Moreover, in contrast to the old stereotype of menopausal women as depressed and demoralized, notice from Figure 12.1 that the Mills women felt better about their lives in their early fifties than at *any* other age (Mitchell & Helson, 1990).

Although these studies trace the lives of highly educated people, we can see the same transformations in men and women in every segment of society. There is the reformed criminal who spends his time lecturing at high schools: "It's too late for me, but maybe I can help keep other teenagers from taking my path" (Maruna, 2001; Maruna, LeBel, & Lanier, 2004). There is the youthful drug abuser, who after painfully going through rehab, decides to return to school to become an addictions counselor at age 40 or 45.

We even have recent cross-sectional research exploring the feelings of randomly selected adults that supports the findings of the Mills and Harvard studies. As you may recall from Chapter 10, rates of mental disorders are at their peak in our twenties and decline as we get older (Kessler and others, 1994). When researchers examined the emotions of several hundred U.S. adults of various ages, they discovered that the frequency of upsetting emotions lessened and feelings of happiness rose from the twenties to the seventies (Mroczek, 2001). You may recall that in the amazing 300,000-person on-line poll discussed in Chapter 1, self-esteem scores rose from the twenties to a high point in the sixties—although they did decline in advanced old age (Robins and others, 2002). The findings of that study are a bit suspect. Do you think that people who surf the Internet or who choose to spend time taking on-line personality polls constitute a *representative sample*, or do they differ in some systematic way from the typical adult? Still—at least in our society—the evidence clearly shows that, *on average*, we can expect to get more self-confident and happier as we age!

But averages don't apply to everyone. Perhaps you know someone, such as Deborah in our earlier example of low generativity, who has remained mired in identity diffusion.

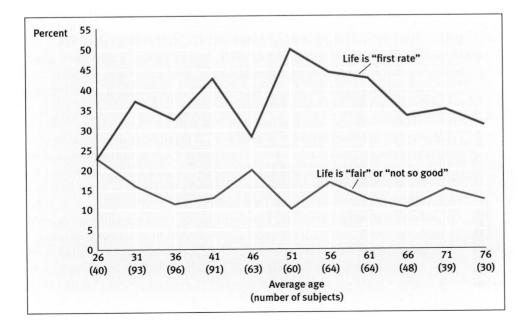

FIGURE *12.1*: Satisfaction with life peaks among women in their early fifties*: Notice from this chart that, in their early fifties, women were most likely to describe life as "first rate."

Source: Mitchell & Helson (1990). Copyright 1990, reprinted with permission of Cambridge University Press.

*The graphs for each curve do not add up to 100 percent because they do not include responses that fell into an intermediate category.

Like many people in their fifties, this woman is clearly at the peak of her powers. If you met her at age 25, could you see the seeds of the amazingly self-assured, competent older woman in this photograph? Given that young people who are already mature tend to grow the most with age, the answer is probably yes.

The teenage football hero and the beauty queen who descend into depression and drug abuse as they get older are classic life stories, too. Can we predict who is likely to grow happier and more mature? When the psychologists conducting the Mills College study gave the women a test that measured maturity, they found that the people who ranked high on that scale during their emerging-adult years were most likely to grow emotionally as they aged (Helson & Roberts, 1994).

The bottom-line message is that, once again, we can see consistency even when we are exploring change. Highly generative midlife adults report always having generative identities. People who grow most over the years tend to think about life in a mature way as young adults.

Wrapping Up Personality

Now let's summarize *all* of these messages. Having read this chapter, here is what you might tell an emerging-adult friend who wants insights into the person she will be at 40 or 55:

- Your core personality will probably not change much, unless you undergo a major change in your life.

- Your priorities will probably shift toward more generative concerns.

- You are likely to cope better with stress and to feel more self-confident and happier, especially if you are relatively mature right now.

- Still, take these predictions with a grain of salt. People vary in generativity and in the extent to which they change and grow. Life-changing experiences at every time of life can set you on a different life path.

Individual consistency, diversity from person to person, different pathways of change depending on the way we conceptualize personality—we can see the same themes when we explore how people develop intellectually during adult life.

Exploring Intelligence

Remember from Chapter 7 that when psychologists measure intelligence during childhood, they look mainly at how elementary schoolers perform on standard intelligence tests. Sometimes they explore alternate ideas about what it means to be smart, such as Gardner's multiple intelligences or Sternberg's successful intelligence. Developmentalists use standard IQ tests and nontraditional strategies to trace adult intelligence, too.

Taking the Traditional Approach: Looking at Standard IQ Tests

Think of your intellectual role model. Most likely your mind will immediately gravitate to someone who is 50 or 80—not a person who is 20 or 25. In fact, if you are like most adults, you probably assume that in general people get more intelligent over the years (Sternberg & Berg, 1992).

How will this young woman's cognitive abilities change as she ages? By comparing how adults of different ages performed on intelligence tests, early researchers came to the dismal conclusion that this twenty-something adult might be at her mental peak today.

Mid-twentieth-century psychologists had a different idea: They believed that people reach their intellectual peak in their twenties, and then intelligence steadily declines (Botwinick, 1967). They based these disturbing conclusions on studies using the newly developed Wechsler Adult Intelligence Scale.

The **Wechsler Adult Intelligence Scale (WAIS)** has the same format as the WISC, the standard IQ test for children described in Chapter 7. It has verbal and performance scales. The verbal scale measures different types of knowledge, such as vocabulary and adults' ability to solve math problems. The performance scale asks test-takers to perform relatively unfamiliar activities, such as putting together puzzles or arranging blocks. On this part of the test, speed is essential. People must complete the items within a limited time.

When psychologists tested adults to get their standards for how people should normally perform on the WAIS at different ages, they discovered that, starting in the twenties, in each older age group average scores declined. They also found the interesting pattern you can see in Figure 12.2. While verbal scores stayed stable or declined to a lesser degree, average scores on the performance scale steadily slid down, starting in the twenties (Botwinick, 1967).

These findings would not give Mary or any other midlife student confidence about venturing into a college classroom full of 20-year-olds. Luckily, however, the researchers were making a serious logical error. They were not taking into account the huge educational differences between different cohorts during that particular time in U.S. history. While virtually all of the young people taking the test had gone to high school (high school enrollment was mandatory after 1940), many middle-aged or elderly people taking the original WAIS had probably left school in the seventh or eighth grade. The psychologists were comparing apples to oranges—adults with far less education to those with much more.

How does our performance on standard intelligence tests *really* change as we travel through adult life? To answer this question, in the early 1960s researchers began the **Seattle Longitudinal Study**—the definitive study of intelligence and age (Schaie, 1988, 1996; Schaie, Willis, & Caskie, 2004; Schaie & Zanjani, 2006).

Imagine being a developmentalist interested in charting how people change intellectually during adulthood. If you were to carry out a cross-sectional study—comparing different age groups at the same time—your findings would certainly be biased in a negative way. Older cohorts would be at a disadvantage, not having had as much experience taking tests, typically having gone to school for far fewer years. But if you carried out a longitudinal study, you would be faced with the incredibly difficult task of following adults for a half century or more. Even then, you would end up with a far-too-positive portrait of how the *average* person changes over time. The volunteers who enrolled in your study would probably be highly educated men and women who cared about making a contribution to science. Over the years, as people dropped out of your research, you would be left with an increasingly self-selected group, the tiny fraction of older people who were especially proud of proving their intellectual capacities and—as they reached their seventies—those healthy enough to take your tests (Baltes & Smith, 1997).

Faced with these contrasting biases (longitudinal research will be too positive; cross-sectional research is going to be biased in a negative way), the researchers devised a brilliant solution: They decided to combine the two kinds of studies, then factor out the biases of each research method, and so isolate the "true" impact of age on IQ.

Wechsler Adult Intelligence Scale (WAIS) The standard test to measure adult IQ, involving verbal and performance scales, each of which is made up of various subtests.

Seattle Longitudinal Study The definitive study of the effect of aging on intelligence, carried out by K. Warner Schaie, involving simultaneously conducting and comparing the results of cross-sectional and longitudinal studies carried out with a group of Seattle volunteers.

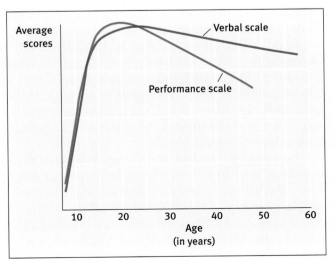

FIGURE 12.2: Age-related changes in mean scores on the performance and verbal scales of the WAIS: This chart shows the pattern of decline from a study using the early form of the WAIS. Notice how average scores on the performance scale regularly slid down starting in the twenties, while scores on the verbal scale remained more stable with age. *Source:* Botwinick (1967).

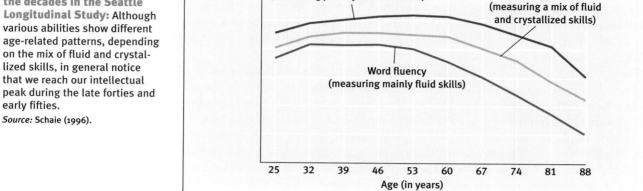

FIGURE 12.3: Changes in a few intellectual abilities over the decades in the Seattle Longitudinal Study: Although various abilities show different age-related patterns, depending on the mix of fluid and crystallized skills, in general notice that we reach our intellectual peak during the late forties and early fifties.

Source: Schaie (1996).

First, the research team selected groups of people enrolled in a Seattle health organization who were 7 years apart in age, tested them, and compared their scores. Then they followed each group longitudinally, testing them at 7-year intervals. At each evaluation, they selected another cross-sectional sample, some of whom they also followed over time.

Using an IQ test that, unlike the WAIS, measured five basic cognitive abilities, they got a much more encouraging portrait of how we change intellectually—one that fits our intuitive sense of how people should perform. Notice in looking at Figure 12.3 that on this measure—involving capacities such as vocabulary and our ability to mentally rotate designs in space—overall we can expect to reach our intellectual peak during our late forties and early fifties. Still, the Seattle study showed the same pattern as on the WAIS. On a test involving quick verbal responses, people performed at their best in their thirties, and then scores rapidly declined. On a vocabulary test, scores rose well into the fifties and only began to fall off—but very slowly—during later life (Schaie, 1996; Schaie, Willis, & Caskie, 2004). Now let's look at a theory that makes sense of all these findings and tells us a good deal about our intellectual abilities in the real world.

Two Types of Intelligence: Crystallized and Fluid Skills

Psychologists today often divide intelligence into two basic categories. **Crystallized intelligence** refers to our knowledge base, the storehouse of information that we have accumulated over the years. The verbal scale of the WAIS, with its tests of vocabulary and math, mainly measures crystallized skills. **Fluid intelligence** involves our ability to reason quickly when facing totally new intellectual challenges. The WAIS performance scale, with its emphasis on putting together blocks or puzzles within a time limit, tends to measure fluid skills.

Fluid intelligence—because it depends on our nervous system being at its biological peak—is at its high point in our early twenties and then declines. Because it measures the knowledge that we have amassed over years, crystallized intelligence follows a different path. This type of intelligence tends to increase as we age—until late middle age, when crystallized skills begin to slowly fall off (Kaufman, 2001). The reason is that at this time in life, our rate of forgetting outpaces the amount of new knowledge that we can absorb.

Interestingly, if we look over the whole lifespan, fluid and crystallized skills develop in different ways. In early childhood, both types of intelligence increase at the same rate. Then, after we enter school and our knowledge base grows by leaps and bounds, our fluid abilities grow more slowly than our crystallized skills do. As you just saw, the gap widens during early and middle adulthood, when our fluid abilities are declining and our crystallized capacities continue to expand. Finally, when people reach advanced old age (or, as you will see, when they are close to death), *both* crystallized and fluid abilities rapidly fall off (Li and others, 2004; McArdle and others, 2002; Singer and others, 2003).

crystallized intelligence A basic facet of intelligence, consisting of a person's knowledge base, or storehouse of accumulated information.

fluid intelligence A basic facet of intelligence, consisting of the ability to quickly master new intellectual activities.

[FAQ: How does age affect learning?]

During elementary school, as children learn new academic skills such as writing, their crystallized intelligence grows by leaps and bounds. However, especially if the man in the photograph at left hasn't drawn a picture for some time, his grandchild's wall drawings will certainly surpass his own productions, due to his rapidly declining fluid skills.

The losses on tests of fluid intelligence are a symptom of a more general process. As we get older, we get slower. We cannot process information as quickly as before. This means that when situations require very quick responses and multitasking, people are likely to notice their abilities getting worse at a relatively young age. For example, by your late thirties, it seems harder to dribble a basketball when you have to keep your attention on the opposing team. You realize that while doing the cooking you are having more trouble juggling conversations with guests at your dinner party than before. These fluid losses, as you will see in Chapter 14, gradually progress to the point where they interfere with many aspects of living when we reach old age.

So the beauty of the distinction between fluid and crystallized intelligence is that it makes sense not only of IQ test performances but of *all* of our performances in daily life. It accounts for why people in fast-paced jobs, such as assembly-line workers and air-traffic controllers, worry about being over the hill in their forties. It makes sense of why factory bosses and airline CEOs can expect to reach their professional peak in late middle age. Anytime an activity heavily depends on quickness and new learning, age presents problems. Whenever an intellectual challenge involves stored knowledge or experience, people can continue to improve well into their fifties and beyond.

Suppose your job heavily depends on speed—perhaps you are a food server or an assembly-line worker. Can your crystallized intelligence, or knowledge of how to do your work, make up for these biologically based fluid losses? Developmentalist Paul Baltes says yes. Baltes (1993) believes that our experience can indeed compensate somewhat for declining fluid skills. In one study proving this point, researchers developed a test of food-server intelligence. They watched older and younger servers at their jobs. Older, more experienced servers not only outscored the young workers on the specially devised test, but they also served more customers during both busy and quiet times at work (Perlmutter, Kaplan, & Nyquist, 1990). Even in jobs depending on speedy information processing, our knowledge of *how* to do our work—up to a point—outweighs the automatic losses in fluid abilities that occur with age!

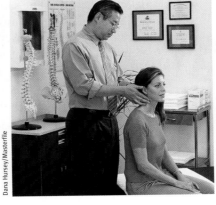

As their job demands speedy mental processing, thinking on their feet, and responding quickly, these professional hockey players may feel "aged" in their thirties. But at age 50, this doctor will probably feel his diagnostic skills are continuing to get better because his life work depends almost exclusively on crystallized skills.

FIGURE 12.4: **Age-related changes in the career paths of geniuses and of less eminent creators:** These charts show that people reach their peak period of creativity at different points in midlife, depending on when they start their creative careers. However, the most gifted geniuses stand head and shoulders above their contemporaries at every age.

Source: Simonton (1997).

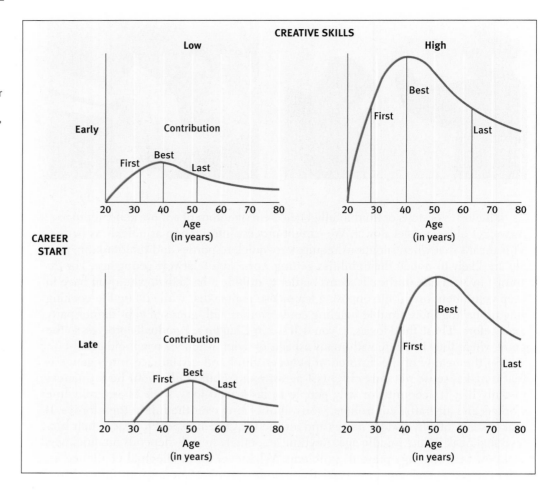

Is the middle-aged fashion designer on the left at his creative peak? According to the research, the answer is yes. How proficient will this young man watching ultimately be at designing suits? For answers, we would want to look at this person's creative talents right now.

Suppose you are an artist or a writer. When can you expect to do your finest work? Researchers find that the age for optimum creativity differs, depending on the specific art form. When a type of creative activity is heavily dependent on physical skills or being totally original, such as dancing or writing poetry, people tend to perform best in their thirties. If the form of creativity depends just on crystallized experience, such as writing nonfiction or history or, in my case, producing college textbooks (!), people perform at their best in their early sixties (Simonton, 1997, 2002). But, in tracing the lives of people famous for their creative work, one researcher discovered that who we are *as people*, or our enduring abilities, outweighs the changes that occur with age. As you can see in Figure 12.4, true geniuses outshine everyone else at *any* age (Simonton, 1997).

So the basic message with regard to creativity or any type of intellectually challenging work is the same as with personality. Expect to reach your creative peak in middle age (in most fields). Still, expect to be the same person—to a large degree—that you were when you were younger. If you are exceptionally competent and creative at 30, you can stay exceptionally competent and creative at 70 or even 95. To illustrate this point, here are two quotations taken from an interview study of creative people over age 60 (Csikszentmihalyi, 1996).

A 70-year-old poet named Anthony Hecht commented:

I'm not as rigid as I was. And I can feel this in the quality and texture of the poems themselves. They are freer metrically, they are freer in general design. The earliest poems that I wrote were almost rigid in their eagerness not to make any errors. I'm less worried than that now.

(p. 215)

Grandma Moses, who gained artistic fame in old age and died at age 101, and Frank Lloyd Wright, shown here lecturing at the young age of 91, are testaments to the fact that people can be exceptionally creative until the very limit of human life.

And the historian C. Vann Woodward, in his mid-80s, said:

Well, [today] I have . . . changed my mind and the reasons and conclusions about what I have written. For example, that book on Jim Crow. I have done four editions of it and I am thinking of doing a fifth, and each time it changes. And they come largely from criticisms that I have received. I think the worst mistake you could make as a historian is to be indifferent or contemptuous of what is new. You learn that there is nothing permanent in history. It's always changing.

(p. 216)

From Sigmund Freud, who kept putting forth masterpieces in psychology well into his eighties, to Frank Lloyd Wright, who was still actively designing world-class buildings into his ninth decade of life, history is full of examples showing that creativity can burn bright until well into old age.

Staying IQ Smart

Returning to normally creative people, such as you and me, what specific qualities might help *any* person stay cognitively sharp well into later life? What forces might cause our IQ scores and our real-life intellectual capacities to decline at a younger-than-normal age?

HEALTH MATTERS The Seattle researchers discovered that one key to staying intelligent with age lies in keeping healthy—specifically, avoiding heart disease. Men and women diagnosed with heart problems during their fifties lost points earlier on every one of the Seattle tests than the other volunteers (Schaie, 1996).

The most interesting evidence that illness affects IQ relates to an eerie phenomenon called **terminal drop.** While conducting the earliest longitudinal studies of intelligence, developmentalists were astonished to discover that they could predict

terminal drop A research phenomenon in which a dramatic decline in an older person's scores on vocabulary tests and other measures of crystallized intelligence predicts having a terminal disease.

We might think that spending hours each day for your whole adult life fashioning a rock garden into waves would be incredibly boring. But his heart-healthy diet and the physical exercise this elderly Japanese monk is getting while he carries out this Zen-like task may be doing wonders at keeping him mentally sharp.

which older people were more likely to die or to become seriously ill within the next few years by "larger than expected" losses in their verbal IQ (Cooney, Schaie, & Willis, 1988; Riegel & Riegel, 1972). If a person's scores on tests of vocabulary and other crystallized measures dramatically decline, they found, these changes may be an ominous early warning signal of a soon-to-be diagnosed life-threatening disease.

This research haunted me the summer when I noticed that my father had suddenly aged mentally. My dad, who was always an intellectual whiz, had lost interest in the world. He was disoriented and unable to remember basic facts, such as where I lived. A few months later, my worst fears were confirmed: My father was diagnosed with liver cancer, the illness that was to quickly end his life.

MENTAL EXERCISE MAY MATTER Because, as you may recall from Chapter 3, environmental stimulation promotes synaptogenesis, the second key to keeping our IQ fine-tuned should be simple: Exercise your mind! The most interesting research supporting this idea relates to a topic discussed in the previous chapter: work environments. Our impulse to search for intrinsically motivating jobs, as it turns out, may have long-term cognitive benefits. People who work in complex jobs become more intellectually flexible as the years pass. Routine work, such as flipping hamburgers, is associated with earlier-than-normal cognitive decline (Schooler, 1990, 1999, 2001; Schooler, Mulatu, & Oates, 2004). The developmentalists who have conducted these studies around the globe have extended their findings to homemakers, too. Engaging in mentally enriching activities—from reading to attending lectures—helps *everyone* become more mentally flexible with age.

Still, we need to be cautious. People who search out complex professions, love lectures, or join book clubs are probably *already* intellectually interested (and upper-middle class) to begin with. Given that who we are as people endures—and, as we know, socioeconomic status matters a great deal—we would need to conduct an impossible experiment to *prove* that mental stimulation causes IQ to rise (or prevents decline). We would have to randomly assign one group of young adults to "exercise their minds" for decades and compare their IQs to those of a control group in later middle age. Without this defining "clinical trial," therefore, one group of gerontologists specializing in cognitive aging has pronounced the "use your brain or lose it" principle completely unproved (Salthouse, Berish, & Miles, 2002).

But wait a second! We do have concrete evidence proving that providing enriched environments promotes synaptogenesis in the brains of laboratory rats. Neuroscientists put rats in a large cage with a variety of wheels and swings and compared their cortexes with those of control groups after varying lengths of time. Although the effect works better with young animals, even adult rats who are exposed to this "treatment" have thicker, heavier brains! (See Diamond, 1988, 1993.) Let's tentatively accept the idea, then, that just as physical exercise strengthens our muscles, mental exercise *may* make for a more resilient brain.

Having the fast-paced, difficult challenge of designing the Chinese edition of Vogue (like figuring out where to put these photographs to highlight the main points in this chapter!) is the kind of intellectually complex work that is tailor-made to help these Shanghai women stay mentally flexible as they age.

In sum, people in their forties and fifties are at the peak of their mental powers. But they will have much more trouble mastering totally new cognitive challenges (those involving fluid skills) when they are under time pressure. To preserve their cognitive capacities, they should take care of their health and make sure to regularly challenge their minds. And you can tell any worried older friend who—like Mary in the chapter-opening vignette—is considering going back to school that she should *definitely* go for it!

INTERVENTIONS: Keeping a Fine-Tuned Mind

Now let's look at the lessons the research offers for any person, whether middle-aged or young, who wants advice about how to stay mentally sharp as the years pass.

- Develop a hobby or passion that challenges your mind—preferably when you are young. Keep practicing your passion as you age.

- Throughout life, put yourself in intellectually challenging situations. If your job is not mentally stimulating, search out a more intrinsically rewarding career. If you are unable to find flow-inducing work, exercise your mental capacities outside your job, through volunteer work or hobbies that stretch your mind.

- As you age, watch your physical health. In particular, guard against developing heart disease.

- Understand that as you get older, new activities involving complex information processing will be more difficult. To cope with the losses you experience, you might adopt the following three-part strategy advocated by Paul Baltes called **selective optimization with compensation.**

As we move into the older years and notice we cannot function as well as we used to, Baltes believes that we need to (1) *selectively* focus on our most important activities, shedding less important priorities; (2) *optimize*, or work harder, to perform at our best in these most important areas of life; and (3) *compensate*, or rely on external aids when we cannot cope on our own (Baltes, 2003; Baltes & Carstensen, 2003; Krampe & Baltes, 2003).

Let's take the example of a woman whose passion is gourmet cooking. As she reaches her fifties, she might need to give up some less important passion such as gardening, conserving her strength for the hours she spends at the stove *(selection)*. She would need to work harder to prepare complex dishes demanding split-second timing, such as her prize-winning soufflés *(optimization)*. She might put a chair in the kitchen rather than stand for hours preparing meals, or give up preparing elaborate dinner party feasts all by herself and rely on her guests to bring an appetizer or dessert *(compensation)*.

selective optimization with compensation Paul Baltes's three principles for successful aging (and living): (1) selectively focusing on what is most important, (2) working harder to perform well in those top-ranking areas, and (3) relying on external aids to cope effectively.

What can this white-haired female college student do to ensure that she can keep up with her twenty-something classmates in this computer course? She can try to take just this one class, rather than four or five, this term (selection); spend more time studying (optimization), and perhaps ask the instructor if she can tape the lectures, so she doesn't have to just rely on her notes (compensation).

TABLE 12.4: Using Selective Optimization with Compensation to Construct a Fulfilling Life

Selection: List your top-ranking priorities. Estimate how much time you spend on these agendas.

1. _____ hrs _____

2. _____ hrs _____

3. _____ hrs _____

Can you increase the time you spend on these most critical agendas and decrease the time you spend on less important concerns?

Optimization: List several strategies that you could use to perform better in your top-priority areas.

1. _____

2. _____

3. _____

Compensation: List some external aids that might help you be more successful in managing your time or succeeding.

1. _____

2. _____

3. _____

List the people to whom you can turn to help you when you feel overloaded. Think of friends and family who can take over some of your less important jobs.

1. _____

2. _____

3. _____

Although Baltes originally spelled out these guidelines to apply to successful aging, people who use these strategies report being more successful at work and more satisfied with their overall lives (Freund & Baltes, 2002; Wiese, Freund, & Baltes, 2003). Baltes believes that his theory offers insights for living wisely and successfully at any age (Baltes & Freund, 2003). So Table 12.4 offers a selective-optimization-with-compensation checklist to fill out to enhance your own life.

Taking a Nontraditional Approach: Examining Postformal Thought

So far we have been talking about the insights relating to intelligence that we can get from traditional IQ tests. But look back at the quotations from the elderly poet Anthony Hecht and the elderly historian C. Vann Woodward on pages 378–379. The qualities these master creators were describing have nothing to do with putting together puzzles or blocks. What stands out about these people is their passion for learning, their receptiveness to new ideas, and their sensitivity to their inner lives. Given that standard IQ tests were devised to predict performance in school, perhaps it would make sense to devise a test to capture the qualities that are central to being intelligent during adult life.

Jean Piaget, as we know, devoted his life to describing qualitative changes in cognition that occur as children get older. So developmentalists decided to draw inspiration from this master theorist to construct an adult-relevant measure of IQ (Labouvie-Vief, 1992; Rybash, Hoyer, & Roodin, 1986; Sinnott, 1989, 1991, 1998, 2003).

Piaget, you may recall, believed that we develop cognitively through hands-on experience with the world. Although Piaget believed that the pinnacle of mental development occurs when we reach formal operations as teenagers, wouldn't years of hands-on experience as adults lead to a higher form of reasoning called **postformal thought**? Let's look at the qualities that differentiate this uniquely adult intelligence from formal operational thought.

postformal thought A uniquely adult form of intelligence that involves being sensitive to different perspectives, making decisions based on one's inner feelings, and being interested in exploring new questions.

Postformal thought is relativistic. As you saw in Chapter 9, adolescents in formal operations argue rationally with their parents about absolute rights and wrongs. As we grow older and acquire more life experience, we realize that most real-world problems do not have clear-cut answers. Postformal thinkers accept the validity of different perspectives. They embrace the ambiguities of life.

This awareness that the truth is relative does not mean that postformal thinkers avoid making decisions or having strong beliefs. As you saw with C. Vann Woodward, people who reason postformally make better decisions precisely *because* they are open to changing their ideas when faced with the complexity of life.

Postformal thought is feeling-oriented. Teenagers in formal operations feel that by using logic, they can make sense of the world. Postformal thinkers go beyond rationality to reason in a different way. Because there is often no objectively "right" answer to many of life's dilemmas, thinking postformally means relying more on one's gut feelings as the basis for making decisions. As with Anthony Hecht, people who reason postformally are less rigid, more open to new experiences, free to be fully in touch with their inner lives.

Postformal thought is question-driven. Adolescents want to get the correct answers and to finish or solve tasks. Postformal thinkers are less focused on solutions. As you saw with both Woodward and Hecht, people who think postformally thrive on the process of developing new questions, and of reconsidering their opinions. They relish coming up with new and interesting ways of looking at the world.

Clearly, we cannot measure this kind of intelligence by giving people tests in which each question has a single correct answer. We need to adopt the strategy that Lawrence Kohlberg used with his moral dilemmas: Present people with everyday situations and examine the *way* they reason about life. How would you respond to this sample situation the researchers devised?

> *John is known to be a heavy drinker, especially when he goes to parties. Mary, John's wife, warns him that if he gets drunk one more time, she will leave him and take the children. John goes to an office party and comes home drunk. Does Mary leave him? How sure are you of your answer?*

The researchers originally predicted that if you are in your twenties, you will answer this question in a rigid way: "Mary said she would leave, so of course she should. Yes, I am sure I am right." Middle-aged or elderly people, in contrast, would think through the consequences of leaving for Mary, for John, and for the children. They would realize that any answer they gave would be a judgment call.

Unfortunately, however, the researchers' prediction that postformal thinking would increase in middle age and later life was wrong. This type of thinking is indeed at a low ebb during the teens. (Adolescents, you may recall, are famous for rigidly sticking to what their peers think!) However, emerging adults are just as likely to reason postformally as people of any other age (Labouvie-Vief, Hakim-Larson, & Hobart, 1987; Sinnott, 1989). Have you noticed yourself using this relativistic, person-centered kind of thinking when facing some complex real-world issue? Do you agree with the psychologists who believe that reasoning postformally is important to constructing a fulfilling adult life?

This brings us back to the compelling question we posed early in this chapter: How can you have a fulfilling adult life? Table 12.5, on the following page, summarizes *all* of the lessons we have learned from our discussion of cognition and personality in a chart offering tips for flourishing during adult life.

So far we have been talking about issues that are relevant to everyone—people in their twenties, their forties and fifties, and people aged 95. In the next section of this chapter, we will turn to explore transitions that are unique to the middle years.

TABLE 12.5: How to Flourish During Adulthood: A Summary Table

1. Develop a generative mission. If you feel that you're at loose ends or that your life lacks purpose, try volunteering or helping others—it's addictive!

2. Try to view your failures and upsetting life experiences as learning lessons. Understand that life's tragedies and disappointments offer us our best opportunities to grow.

3. Draw on mature defenses such as humor, and focus on what you still have, when you fail or experience an upsetting event.

4. Develop a life passion and stay interested in that passion as you age.

5. To keep your mind fine-tuned as you age, take care of your physical health. In particular, avoid heart disease.

6. In general, be interested in learning and developing as a person.

7. When you feel in role overload (or any time), establish priorities, work hard in your most important areas, and rely on external aids to help you perform at your best.

8. Think postformally: Be open to different perspectives; question your established ideas and ways of thinking; be aware of your inner feelings and use them as a guide to make wise life choices.

 TYING IT ALL TOGETHER

1. Tim is going to the twentieth reunion of his college graduating class, and he can't wait to find out how his classmates have changed. Statistically speaking, which *two* changes is Tim likely to find in the people he meets?

    a. They will be less introverted and more outgoing.
    b. They will have different life priorities, caring more about nurturing the next generation.
    c. They will be more self-assured and confident.
    d. They will be more depressed and burned out.

2. You are interviewing your role model, your mother, about her life. She's your role model because she has always been the most caring, nurturing person you know. In describing her life, is your mom most likely to describe (a) negative life events that turned out for the best, (b) a life full of happy events, or (c) a life full of depressing events?

3. Adam is an air traffic controller and Mick is a historian. Explain which man is likely to reach his career peak earlier and tell the reasons why.

4. Your author is writing another textbook on lifespan development. She is also learning a new video game. Identify each type of intellectual skill involved and describe how my abilities in each of these areas are likely to change as I move into my sixties.

5. Rick says, "I've got way too much on my plate. I can't seem to do anything well." Sara says, "I don't feel my life has much meaning." Which theories of ideal development, discussed in this chapter, would be most helpful to address each of these problems, and what might each theory advise?

6. Kayla is considering whether to break up with her boyfriend, Mark, because, she says, "He doesn't give me the attention I need." Name the advice a postformal thinker would certainly *not* give to Kayla.

    a. "Leave the bum!"
    b. "Think of what is going on from Mark's perspective—for instance, is he overworked?"
    c. "Whatever choice you make, be sure to look at all the angles."
    d. "There may be no 'right decision.' Go with your gut."

Answers to the Tying It All Together questions can be found in the answers section of the book.

Midlife Roles and Issues

Two ways in which middle-aged adults can fulfill their generativity are through being grandparents and caring for their own aged parents. A major concern we expect in midlife is coping with sexual decline. Now we look at each of these "aging phase of life" topics.

Grandparenthood

The grandparents always took . . . at least the first grandchild to raise because that's always the way the Lakota did it. They think that . . . they're more mature and have had more experience and they could teach the children a lot more than the young parents . . . . I'm still trying to carry on that tradition because my grandmother raised me most of the time up until I was nine years old. . . .

(quoted in Weibel-Orlando, 1999, p. 187)

This comment from Mrs. Big Buffalo, a Native American grandmother living in South Dakota, reminds us that every adult role, from spouse to parent to worker to grandparent, is shaped by our culture. In our society, if we saw grandparents raising their grandchildren, we would probably automatically assume that there was a serious problem with the parents' ability to provide care.

Still, even in the contemporary United States, our sense of the appropriate roles for grandparents differs by ethnic group. African American grandparents see their mission as providing considerable grandchild care—often at great personal cost (Winston, 2006). European Americans take a more hands-off stance. In addition, for everyone, the "traditional jobs" of grandparents are continuing to evolve. Today, with so many single parents and working mothers, middle-class grandparents have stepped in to do more hands-on child care than they typically did even a few decades ago.

Grandparenting Functions

What are the *basic* functions of grandparents? In subsistence societies, grandparents may literally help the youngest generation physically survive. In one study in rural Ethiopia, the presence of a grandmother in a family reduced the odds of a grandchild dying during the early years of life (Gibson & Mace, 2005). In our affluent, individualistic culture grandparents often serve as **family watchdogs,** stepping in during a crisis to stabilize the family. At these times their value is illuminated, their hidden importance revealed. Grandparents are the family's safety net (Troll, 1983).

family watchdogs A basic role of grandparents, which involves monitoring the younger family's well-being and intervening to provide help in a crisis.

This view of grandparents as family watchdogs is supported by tracing what happens when adult children get divorced. After a divorce, grandparents often make an effort to see the grandchildren more frequently (Ehrenberg & Smith, 2003). As Mary and Kevin in the chapter-opening vignette did, they may have their newly single child and the grandchildren move in with them for a time (Wilks & Melville, 1990).

Even when their children are not undergoing stressful life transitions, the role of family stabilizer is important. Grandparents can serve as mediators, helping the younger generations resolve their differences (Hagestad, 1985; Kennedy, 1990). In one poignant international example, researchers in Bulgaria found that the presence of a loving grandparent acted as an emotional buffer, reducing the tendency for adolescent girls and boys living in economically struggling families to become seriously depressed (Botcheva & Feldman, 2004).

Grandparents are the cement that keeps the extended family close. They are the command center for family news: "Hey, Mom. How are my little sister Amy and the children *really* doing since her divorce? Is there anything I can do to help?" From Christmas holiday get-togethers to Thanksgiving dinners, "Grandma's house" is often the central meeting point—the place where siblings gather to regularly reconnect with one another as they move out into life. As one developmentalist beautifully put it:

Grandparents serve as symbols of connectedness within and between lives; as people who can listen and have the time to do so; as reserves of time, help, and attention; as links to the unknown past; as people who are sufficiently varied, flexible, and complex to defy easy categories and clear-cut roles.

(Hagestad, 1985, p. 48)

You may notice this complexity and flexibility in action in your own family. One of your grandparents might be a shadowy figure, while another qualifies as a second mother or best friend. Some grandparents love to jump on trampolines with the

From jumping on trampolines to taking the grandchildren to the local lake, grandparents fulfill this joyous life role in their own distinctive, personal ways.

grandchildren; others show their love in traditional, "baking cookies" ways. You may have an "intellectual grandma" who takes you to lectures and a "fishing grandpa" who takes you out on the lake.

Which Grandparents Are More or Less Involved?

In terms of being involved in their grandchildren's lives, what forces determine how active a particular grandparent is likely to be? Gender matters. Just as they do with their own children, women tend to take a more hands-on approach with their grandchildren than do men (Cherlin & Furstenberg, 1985; Reitzes & Mutran, 2004). Physical proximity makes a difference (Cherlin & Furstenberg, 1985). If you live in rural Iowa, your grandparents are more likely to be a major presence in your life, because—living in a less mobile community—they are more likely to live nearby (King and others, 2003). Another predictor of involvement is age. Middle-aged grandparents are more likely to be "very active." Grandparents who are elderly tend to be more peripherally involved (Cherlin & Furstenberg, 1985).

Generative feelings are probably important—whether a particular man or woman is really fulfilling Erikson's midlife task (Belsky, 1999). In fact, because grandparenthood *is* a prime way of expressing generativity, people who feel fulfilled in this core "older" family role tend to feel more content with their overall lives (Reitzes & Mutran, 2004). As one woman reported, "I cannot tell you how wonderful it is to take care of the grandchildren every Friday afternoon. My whole world lights up when they walk in the room. And the fact that I don't have to be there every day to discipline Karen and Matt makes being a grandma pure joy."

Grandparent Problems

Grandparents relish their freedom to "spoil" the grandchildren and send them back to Mom and Dad. But, because their access to the children depends on the generation in between, grandparents are not really very free at all. Grandparents cannot criticize how the grandchildren are being raised or they may risk being cut off from visits. Sometimes, they are forced to be less involved simply because of their position in family life.

Maternal grandparents tend to be more involved with their grandchildren than paternal grandparents (Hodgson, 1992; Kennedy, 1990). The main reason is that women control the family's social relationships. Because daughters tend to be closer to their own mothers, mothers of sons are at risk of being grandmas of second rank (Hagestad, 1985).

Being second rank to the other grandmother produced heartache for a close friend of mine. Her daughter-in-law decided to move across the country to be close to her own mother in Seattle, rather than stay in New York City, and my friend was put in the position of being the distant grandma she never wanted to be.

[FAQ: Why are some grandparents so "cool" and young and others so "old"?]

This allegiance to one's family of origin can have devastating effects after a divorce. When the wife gets custody, she may prevent her ex-husband's parents from *ever* seeing the grandchildren again. In this situation, paternal grandparents have to petition for visitation privileges, rights that are granted only when the court deems it in the best interest of the children (Henderson, 2005). Therefore, any paternal grandmother who wants to be closely involved must do what may not always come naturally: go *out of her way* to be a supportive, nurturing mother-in-law! (See Fingerman, 2004.)

Mothers of daughters may have the opposite problem. They may end up being *too* involved. Let's spell out a typical scenario: Your daughter wants you to watch the baby full time while she is at work. She feels more comfortable having you provide the care. She believes that relying on a day-care center would be a needless expense. You don't want to disappoint your child. Still, you want to have your own life. The role conflict and feelings of ambivalence are especially intense when grandparents must assume a more demanding job. They need to become full-time parents again.

Caregiving grandparents take full responsibility for raising their grandchildren. In recent decades the ranks of these totally involved grandparents have swelled. More than 6 percent of U.S. children live in grandparent-headed households today (Goyer, 2005). In the most extreme cases, a caregiving grandparent may petition the court for custody, taking action to formally adopt a granddaughter or grandson.

caregiving grandparents Grandparents who have taken on full responsibility for raising their grandchildren.

How does it feel to take full legal responsibility for raising a grandchild? As we might expect, these parents the second time around are typically deeply distressed, mourning the fact that their own son or daughter, often because of drug or alcohol problems, is incapable of performing this job (Baird, 2003; Kelley & Whitley, 2003). They may feel angry at being forced into this "off-time" role. But they often feel a passionate, generative, "watchdog" mission to protect their flesh and blood (Hayslip & Patrick, 2003). Here is what one woman had to say to the police after her drug-abusing daughter absconded with the grandchild and stole her car:

> [The police in a different state] said to me, "Ma'am, if you don't get here in 72 hours, then your grandson will be put in the [state protective services system] and you will have to fight to get him." I said, "I will fight from the moment I get there if my grandson is not there for me."
>
> (quoted in Climo, Terry, & Lay, 2002, p. 25)

And another woman summed up the general feeling of the custodial grandmothers in this interview study when she blurted out: "Nobody is going to take [my grandson] away from me. I have done everything except give birth to him" (quoted in Climo, Terry, & Lay, 2002, p. 25).

These custodial grandmothers, who were mainly in their late fifties, complained about feeling physically drained: "Some days I feel really old, like I just can't keep up with him" (quoted in Climo, Terry, & Lay, 2002, p 23). They had mixed emotions about their situation: "Some days I feel real blessed by it, other days I want to sit and cry" (p. 25). They sometimes described redemption sequences, too: "God has given me this wonderful little boy to raise and I'm thinking, 'How many people get the opportunity to do it a second time?'" (p. 26).

Parent Care

Ask friends and family members and they will tell you that becoming a grandparent is one of the main joys of being middle-aged. Words such as *joy* and *fulfillment* do not come to mind with regard to the other classic midlife role: caring for elderly parents. Developmentalists who study **parent care** use terms such as *burden*, *strain*, *hassles*, and *distress* (Hunt, 2003; Pearlin and others, 1990; Zarit, Reever, & Bach-Peterson, 1980).

parent care Adult children's care for their disabled elderly parents.

Even though the message that they must care for their elderly family members has been carefully socialized in their culture, the emotions are no different in China (Holroyd, 2003) or among Asian immigrants to the United States (Spitzer and others, 2003). In fact, in one international comparison, South Korean caregivers felt more depressed than their counterparts in the United States, perhaps because in that collectivist culture children are expected to do *all* of the care (Kim & Lee, 2003).

Caring for parents violates the basic idea in our culture that parents give to their children, not the reverse (Belsky, 1999). It can produce role conflict when a woman is working and must reduce her hours or give up her job. If, as is increasingly true, a caregiving daughter is in her sixties or seventies, parent care may interfere with a person's retirement plans or the need to care for her frail, disabled spouse. More rarely, a woman is pulled between two intergenerational commitments, simultaneously caring for elderly parents and watching the grandchildren full time (Kinsella & Velkoff, 2001).

There is a reason why we are describing women here. Men do take over the caregiving if there are no sisters and the father needs care (Daire, 2002; Kramer & Thompson, 2002; Matthews, 2002). However, around the globe, parent care is typically a daughter's or daughter-in-law's job (Harris & Long, 1999; Spitzer and others, 2003; Kinsella & Velkoff, 2001).

What forces make this job easier? One factor, as you might imagine, is having an enduring, loving attachment to that parent. In a longitudinal study, researchers found that when a daughter was close to her parents as a teenager, she felt better about providing parent care decades later, when she was middle-aged (Daire, 2002; Silverstein and others, 2002). Caregiving daughters and their mothers feel better when they are sensitive and support one another's need for autonomy (McGraw & Walker, 2004). Finally, the severity of the older person's problems affects the level of caregiver stress (Pinquart & Sörenson, 2004). Caring for an aged parent, as we will see in Chapter 14, is especially difficult when the parent has Alzheimer's disease. Still, some children find that caring for a disabled parent offers its own redemption sequence. It is a chance to repay a beloved mother or father for years of love (Kramer & Thompson, 2002).

How can midlife adults balance their strong sense of **intergenerational solidarity**, or loving obligation, to their parents and children with the need to have their own lives? This is the question that women such as Mary struggle with as they strive to be generative with both the grandchildren and their parents and to live autonomous lives.

Will this middle-aged child find parent care a labor of love or an impossible stress? The key lies in how burdensome the demands are, the sensitivity of her mom, and whether this daughter feels a generative mission to repay her mother for her own years of loving care.

Dennis MacDonald/Photo Edit, Inc.

Body Image, Sex, and Menopause

Physical disabilities lie far in the future for most midlife adults. Still, as you can see in the Experiencing the Lifespan box, fiftyish adults take great pleasure in cataloguing each sign of bodily decay. Take it from me—these external signs of aging are unimportant. Remember from the discussion of teenage body image in Chapter 8 that *we* determine our own beauty. Perhaps because young women's reference standards are so unattainable (movie stars and fashion models), when researchers compared a group of college students and older women, they found that the *young women* actually felt worse about their bodies than the middle-aged adults! (See Greenleaf, 2005.) However, when we are 20 or 30, the thought of experiencing gray

intergenerational solidarity Middle-aged adults' feeling of loving obligation to both the older and the younger generations.

EXPERIENCING THE LIFESPAN: CONFRONTING AN AGING FACE

Letty Pogrebin, a feminist and founding editor of Ms. *magazine, has written a humorous book exposing the female body on "the far side of 50." Here is her frank account of her 55-year-old image as witnessed in the mirror—and some comments on what set her straight:*

Remember the opening scene from Mommie Dearest, when the aging Joan Crawford wakes up, takes off her lubricated sleep mask, . . . and plunges her face into a bowl of steaming hot water and then into a sinkful of ice cubes? Well, I have what she was trying to prevent.

Under my eyes are puffy fat pads surrounded by dark circles, each unfortunate feature trying its best to call attention to the other. My wrinkles materialized almost overnight when I was 49. Now the lines in my face remind me of my palms. When I raise my eyebrows, my forehead pleats, and when my eyebrows come down the pleats stay. . . . The cheerful parentheses at the corners of my smile have started looking downtrodden, and my top lip is beginning to produce those spidery . . . creases that soak up lipstick. . . .

Just this year, my jaw, the Maginot Line of facial structure, surrendered to the force of gravity. On each side of my chin the muscles have pulled loose from the bone. Once I had a

right-angle profile; now there's a hypotenuse between my chin and neck . . . . Which brings me, regrettably, to my neck, with its double choker of lines; and my chest, creased like crepe paper; and my shoulders and arms, which are holding their own for now except for the elbows, which are rough enough to shred a carrot. I don't yet have loose skin on the underside of my upper arm—you know, the part that keeps waving after you've stopped—but I can see it coming.

. . .

These days I'm into the truth and the truth is I'm not crazy about my looks but I can live with them. . . . What jolted me out of my low-grade Body Image Blues was the death of friends felled by cancer in the prime of their lives. After the third funeral. . ., I saw my body, not as face, skin, hair, figure, but as the vehicle through which I could experience everything my friend would never know again. . . . Ordinary pleasures seemed so precious that I vowed to set my priorities straight before some fatal illness did it for me. Since then I have been trying to focus on the things that really matter. And I can assure you that being able to wear a bikini isn't one of them.

Source: Pogrebin (1996), pp. 128–129, 153.

---

hair, wrinkles, or sagging skin can be alarming, because these changes seem to signal the end of the sexual self. What *really* happens sexually to both men and women as they age?

The physiological findings for middle-aged men are somewhat depressing. According to the classic studies conducted by William Masters and Virginia Johnson, males need more time to develop an erection. They are more likely to lose an erection before ejaculation occurs. Their ejaculations become less intense. By their fifties, most men are not able to have another erection for 12 to 24 hours after having had sex (Masters & Johnson, 1966). These changes explain the billion-dollar market for erection-stimulating aids. Desire remains intact, but by late middle age, many men feel they need some extra help to fully implement their plans.

In contrast, females get more sexual, reaching their peak of desire in their early thirties (Schmitt and others, 2002). But by late middle age, most women do report having less interest in sex than men (Michael, 1994; Verwoerdt, Pfeiffer, & Wang, 1969). One reason is not so hard to guess: fewer sexual signals coming in from the outside world.

As they move into their fifties, more women are likely to be without a partner (due to widowhood or divorce). Or they may be in a long-term *companionate* relationship with an older spouse. (Recall from the last chapter that over time, sexual desire naturally tends to decline in any relationship.) Moreover, just as signals from the outside world accentuate our first feelings of sexual desire during puberty, when the outer world stops viewing older women as sexual human beings, desire turns off (Kenrick and others, 1993). Menopause takes a toll on sexuality, too.

Menopause typically occurs at about age 50, when estrogen production falls off dramatically and women stop ovulating. Specifically, the defining marker of having reached menopause is not having menstruated for a year. As estrogen production declines and a woman approaches this marker, the menstrual cycle becomes more irregular. During this winding-down period, which is called *perimenopause*, some

menopause The age-related process, occurring at about age 50, in which ovulation and menstruation stop due to the loss of estrogen.

Yes, the secret is that many couples do stay passionate well into middle age and beyond—provided they make staying sexy and interested in sex a life priority!

Andy Ryan/Getty Images

women experience minor mood changes and other physical symptoms, such as night sweats and hot flashes (sudden sensations of heat) (see Table 12.6).

Although some women can sail through menopause without *any* symptoms, this estrogen loss produces definite changes in the reproductive tract. Normally, the walls of the vagina have thick folds that expand easily to admit a penis and to accommodate childbirth. After menopause, the vaginal walls thin out and become smooth and more fragile. The vagina shortens, and its opening narrows. The size of the clitoris and labia decreases. Masters and Johnson (1966) found it takes longer after arousal for lubrication to begin. Women don't produce as much fluid as before. These changes can make having intercourse so painful that some women stop having sex.

If women lose interest in sex after menopause, is this due to pain during intercourse, some subtle hormonal shift, or the fact that society doesn't react to older women as sexual human beings? Whatever the answer, once again, diversity is the main message with sexuality. As you saw in the chapter-opening vignette, some women find sex more exciting after menopause (Hvas, 2001). Some couples are very sexually active well into their seventies and beyond (Brecher and *Consumer Reports* editors, 1985; Wiley & Bortz, 1996). Table 12.7 summarizes the male/female changes described in this section and offers some advice for staying passionate about sex.

[FAQ: What is the relationship between menopause and sexual activity?]

[FAQ: Is there such a thing as "male menopause"?]

TABLE 12.6: Stereotypes and Facts About Menopause

1. **The stereotype:** Women have terrible physical symptoms while going through menopause.

   The facts: In longitudinal studies, researchers find that an upsurge of minor physical complaints does occur during the few years preceding menopause: lack of energy, backaches, and joint stiffness. Anywhere from 30 to 70 percent of U.S. women experience hot flashes and some sleeplessness. Still, there is tremendous variability. Women are most likely to report considerable physical and psychological distress, particularly when they are undergoing other life stresses (Avis and others, 2003).

2. **The stereotype:** Women are very moody while going through menopause.

   The facts: Statistically speaking, women do show an increase in minor symptoms of anxiety and depression as they approach menopause, when estrogen levels are waning (Avis and others, 2004). Still, these changes do not affect all women, and, after reaching menopause, many women report feeling better than they ever have. Remember that the Mills College study (described in the text) showed that a larger fraction of women feel that their lives are more satisfying during their early fifties than at any other age.

3. **The stereotype:** Women feel empty, "dried up," old, and asexual after menopause.

   The facts: Many women greet menopause with a sense of relief; for instance, one-third of the women in Taiwan and almost half of all Australian women in a cross-cultural study said that they were happy not to have to deal with menstruation every month (Fu, Anderson, & Courtney, 2003). In a Danish study, women reported other positive emotions, such as feeling that they were entering a new, freer stage of life. Some said that their sex life was much better now that they had no worries about getting pregnant (Hvas, 2001).

TABLE 12.7: Staying Passionate About Sex with Age

For Men

Problem	Solutions
Trouble maintaining or achieving an erection.	1. Understand that some physiological slowing down is normal, and do not be alarmed by occasional problems performing. Sexual relations need to occur more slowly; manual stimulation may be necessary to fully achieve erection and orgasm. 2. Stay healthy. Avoid sexually impairing conditions such as heart disease. If possible, avoid medications that have clear sexual side effects (such as antidepressants and blood pressure pills). 3. If troubled by chronic problems performing, explore the medicines that are now available for treating these problems (e.g., Viagra).

For Women

Problem	Solutions
No sexual signals coming from the outside world.	1. Stay sexy, be conscious of your physical appearance. 2. Try to find a partner who really appreciates you as a sexual human being.
Decline in estrogen levels makes having sexual intercourse painful.	1. Consider using lubricants, such as K-Y Jelly, when having sex. 2. Consider hormone replacement therapy (but discuss this with your doctor).

Final Thoughts

The bottom-line message of this chapter is that—from intelligence to personality to developing new, generative roles—the middle years are a high point of life. Readers in their twenties should look forward to their forties and fifties with joy! What about being age 65 or 80? Stay tuned, as we move now into the older years.

In the next chapter, we start where we are now leaving off by first describing personality and cognition. Then we turn to two major late-life transitions, widowhood and retirement. In Chapter 14 you will learn all about physical aging and how that process can progress to the kinds of impairments that require parent care. ▪

 ## TYING IT ALL TOGETHER

1. Emma has two grandmothers, Karen and Louise. Grandma Karen is much more involved with Emma than is Grandma Louise. List several characteristics that might explain why Karen is the more active, hands-on grandmother.

2. Poll your class. Do most people report being closest to their maternal grandmother (or grandfather)? For the students who were closer to a paternal grandparent, explore why that might be.

3. Kim is caring for her elderly mother, who just had a stroke. Each of the following factors should make Kim's job feel easier *except*

    a. Kim and her mother were very close when Kim was growing up.
    b. Kim and her mother respect each other's "space" and are sensitive to each other.
    c. Kim grew up in a culture that stresses the importance of caring for older family members.

4. For the following statements regarding age change in sexuality, select the right gender: *Males/Females* decline the most physiologically at a younger age, but *male/female* age changes in sexuality are most affected by social issues (such as not having a partner). As they reach their fifties, *males/females* report having less interest in sex. *Males/Females* have the most untapped sexual potential in later life.

5. If Judy is going through menopause, she will *definitely*

    a. experience hot flashes.
    b. have mood swings.
    c. lose interest in sex.
    d. undergo reproductive tract changes, such as a thinning of her vaginal walls.

Answers to the Tying It All Together questions can be found in the answers section of the book.

■ SUMMARY

The Evolving Self

Although the boundaries of middle age span from about age 40 to the early sixties, many older adults describe themselves as middle-aged. Diversity—among people and change processes—plus consistency are the defining characteristics of the middle years.

Research on the **Big Five traits** shows that personality doesn't change much after age 30 unless people experience other major life changes. Interviews paint a different picture, suggesting that we change a good deal as we travel through life. Dan McAdams's research exploring Erikson's **generativity** shows that our priorities shift to "other-centered concerns" during midlife. Generativity remains crucially important in later life, and fulfilling Erikson's midlife task is intimately tied to having a fulfilling adult life.

In their autobiographies, highly generative adults produce a **commitment script** and describe **redemption sequences**—negative events that turned out for the best. Nongenerative adults describe **contamination sequences**—good events that turned out badly. Perhaps because they need to struggle with adversity, many African Americans are exceptionally generative.

Two classic longitudinal studies showed that people become more mature in middle age. College men adopt more mature **defense mechanisms** as they move into midlife. Women become more self-confident in their forties and are especially happy in their early fifties. Although the main theme of the developmental science research is that we grow emotionally after youth, tremendous individual differences are also the norm. Being relatively mature as a young adult predicts a flowering in midlife. Diversity of changes and individual consistency characterize personality as people travel through adult life.

Early studies using the **Wechsler Adult Intelligence Scale (WAIS)** found that people reach their intellectual peak in their twenties—although scores on the timed performance scale tests declined more rapidly than did scores on the verbal scale. The **Seattle Longitudinal Study**—which controlled for the biases of this research—showed the same change pattern, but it also indicated that we reach our intellectual peak in midlife.

Fluid intelligence, the capacity to master unfamiliar cognitive challenges quickly, is at its height early in adulthood, and then it declines. **Crystallized intelligence,** our knowledge base, rises or stays stable until well into middle age. In work situations demanding speed, crystallized knowledge can sometimes make up for losses in fluid intelligence. Creativity reaches its peak in midlife, although our basic talents are the best predictors of our creative accomplishments at any age.

Staying healthy and stimulating the mind are two keys to preventing age-related cognitive decline. **Terminal drop,** a significant loss on verbal (crystallized) tests, can indicate that a person has a fatal disease. Using **selective optimization with compensation** helps people to successfully cope with age-related losses and to live more successfully at any life stage.

Postformal thinkers are sensitive to diverse perspectives, interested in exploring questions, and attuned to their inner feelings in making life decisions. While there are no systematic age differences in this type of thinking after emerging adulthood, the ability to think postformally may be very helpful in constructing a fulfilling adult life.

Midlife Roles and Issues

Grandparents often act as the **family watchdogs,** stepping in when their children and grandchildren need help. Gender, proximity to the grandchildren, and personality shape how people carry out this often joyous but unstructured role. Because women tend to be closer to their own mothers, paternal grandmothers are at risk of being less involved with the grandchildren than they want to be. The problem for maternal grandparents lies in being pressured to do too much. The extreme case of taking "too much care" occurs when people become **caregiving grandparents** or must take full custody and raise the child.

Parent care is another family role that middle-aged daughters may have to assume. While often stressful, a variety of forces affect how people feel when caring for a disabled parent. Midlife adults feel a strong sense of **intergenerational solidarity** with their parents, their grandchildren, and their children.

Another midlife concern involves declining sexuality. For males, erectile capacity steadily declines. Although women tend to feel most passionate in their thirties, **menopause** has the side effect of making intercourse more painful. Because of this pain, as well as the fact that they may not have interested partners, many older women may lose interest in sex. Still, women (and men) can stay very sexually active well into later life.

▌ KEY TERMS

Big Five traits, p. 367

generativity, p. 369

commitment script, p. 371

redemption sequence, p. 371

contamination sequence,
   p. 371

defense mechanisms, p. 372

Wechsler Adult Intelligence
   Scale (WAIS), p. 374

Seattle Longitudinal Study,
   p. 375

crystallized intelligence, p. 376

fluid intelligence, p. 376

terminal drop, p. 379

selective optimization with
   compensation, p. 381

postformal thought, p. 382

family watchdogs, p. 385

caregiving grandparents,
   p. 387

parent care, p. 387

intergenerational solidarity,
   p. 388

menopause, p. 389

▌ RECOMMENDED RESOURCES

BOOKS

Brecher and associates (1985). *Sex after fifty.* Boston: Little Brown.

   This survey of elderly sex offers an upbeat view of sexuality in the later years.

McAdams, D.P. (2006). *The redemptive self: Stories Americans live by.* New York: Oxford University Press.

   This fascinating book summarizes McAdams's decades of research exploring generativity, looks carefully at redemption and contamination sequences, and explores themes of redemption throughout history and in our contemporary culture. It even has a chapter that focuses on the downside of redemption sequences and autobiographies. McAdams makes the point that the redemption sequence (using life's tragedies to promote growth and development) is also a particularly American cultural theme.

McAdams, D.P., & de St. Aubin, E. (Eds.). (1998). *Generativity and adult development: How and why we care for the next generation.* Washington, D.C.: American Psychological Association.

   This academic book contains a collection of articles relating to generativity—both careful empirical research and biographical articles.

WEB SITE

www.aarp.org (American Association of Retired Persons).

   This Web site offers a wealth of data on caregiving grandparents as well as resources for people who must assume this role.

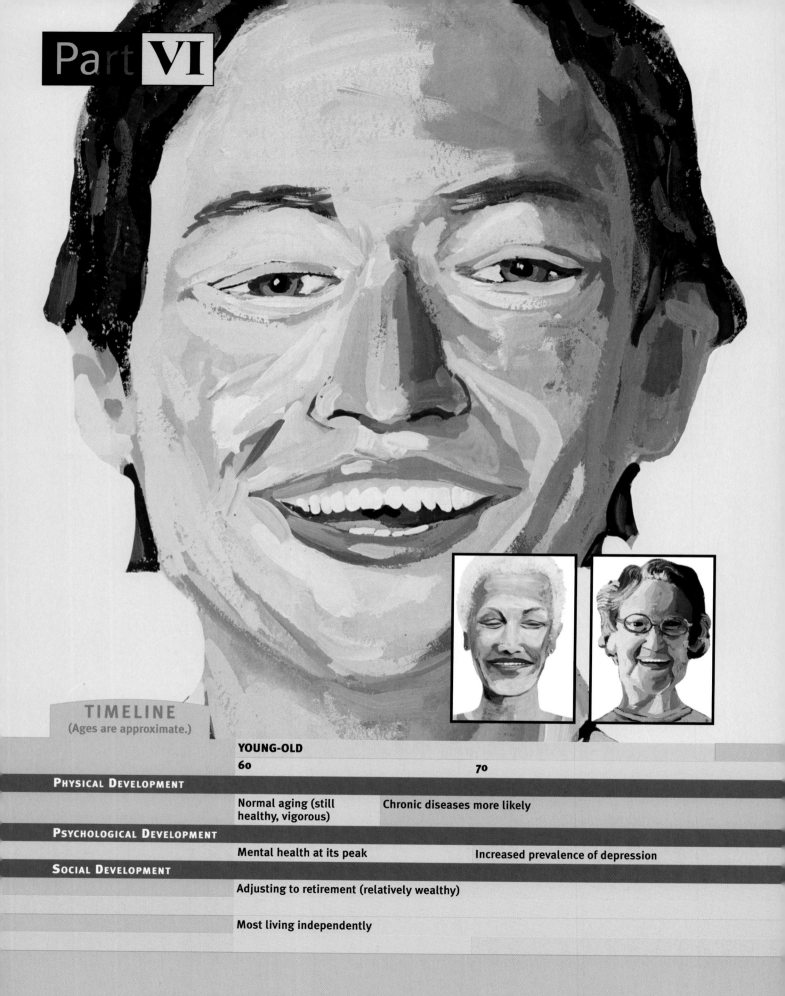

Part VI

TIMELINE
(Ages are approximate.)

YOUNG-OLD

	60	70
PHYSICAL DEVELOPMENT		
	Normal aging (still healthy, vigorous)	Chronic diseases more likely
PSYCHOLOGICAL DEVELOPMENT		
	Mental health at its peak	Increased prevalence of depression
SOCIAL DEVELOPMENT		
	Adjusting to retirement (relatively wealthy)	
	Most living independently	

Later Life

The chapters devoted to this last stage of life take a developmental approach to senior citizenhood (our sixties and beyond). In Chapter 13 we cover issues relevant to both the young-old and old-old years. In Chapter 14 we emphasize concerns that tend to become pressing priorities in advanced old age.

Chapter 13, "Later Life: Cognitive and Socioemotional Development," offers an in-depth look at memory in later life. As you read this section, you will learn a good deal about how memory changes with age and also how to have a better memory at any age. Then we spell out a provocative theory of later-life personality and look at older people's emotional states. Finally, we turn to the major later-life transitions: retirement and widowhood.

Chapter 14, "The Physical Challenges of Old Age," begins by describing the aging process and how it progresses into disease and disability. Next we explore sensory and motor changes and dementia, and finally look at the living arrangements and health-care options people have when old-age frailties strike. This chapter will open your eyes to the challenges of physical aging and hopefully get you to look at the physical environment in a new, age-friendly way.

The timeline on these pages summarizes some major landmarks we will be discussing on our journey through later life.

OLD-OLD

80	90	100

ADL problems, increasing frailty (multiple chronic diseases, sensory and motor impairments)

Increased risk of dementia

Poverty a serious risk

Most women widowed

Increasing numbers of people in assisted-living residences or nursing homes

CHAPTER 13

Later Life: Cognitive and Socioemotional Development

When Sadie was 59 and Saul was 61, they both retired. They were healthy, active, and—with Saul's investments and their pensions—moderately well off. It was time to enjoy these final decades, to focus on the moment, to revel in their life. Saul had risen through the ranks to become president of the local bank. Although he loved his job, he wanted to take early retirement to pursue his second love— traveling. If truth be told, his company pressed him for early retirement by offering a pension package that he could not refuse. Sadie and Saul never had children, but they had their nieces and nephews and many friends. They were looking forward to following their passions in this exciting new phase of life.

For about 10 years, things went wonderfully. They enrolled in Elderhostel, took trips around the world, met exciting new friends of different ages. Saul even got elected president of the synagogue one year. They were happier than ever before. Then, at age 75, Saul's heart disease worsened and he died.

It has been hard for Sadie to function. How can you go on without your high school sweetheart, your best friend for almost 60 years? Sadie takes comfort from her widowed friends, particularly her next-door neighbor and "older sister in spirit," Lillian. Sadie and Saul were there for Lillian when she lost her husband, Jack, in 1985. Now it is Lillian's turn—spry and vigorous at age 83—to serve as a caring sounding board for Sadie to talk (or not to talk) about Saul.

Sadie feels Saul's comforting presence in the house. She even finds herself mentally consulting her husband for advice. But for the most part (knock wood), she's been amazed at her inner strength. After being hit with Saul's medical bills, Sadie found that her income was alarmingly low. She scoured the county for jobs, thinking, "Who would want to hire an old lady of 74?" She was wrong and will start her job as a children's books consultant at Barnes & Noble next week. Tonight she plans to celebrate by opening a bottle of champagne with Saul!

Sadie's life changed dramatically from the time she entered retirement until after Saul got ill and died. This two-chapter sequence captures the developmental shifts as people travel through the *young-old* (sixties and seventies) and *old-old* (over age 80) years. In the current chapter we focus on cognition and the socioemotional side of later life. In Chapter 14, we follow Sadie as she moves into her eighties and confronts the physical frailties of advanced old age.

Sadie and Saul's lives differ dramatically from those of many of their counterparts around the globe—in religion, in lifestyle, in having the freedom to travel the world. Still, in one respect they are the same as every person their age: Their cohort is the fastest-growing life stage.

Setting the Context: Scanning the New Older World

Sadie and Saul are members of an expanding army. At the turn of this century in North America, about one of every nine people was over age 65. In Europe, the fraction was an astonishing one in six (Kinsella & Velkoff, 2001). Although it still lags well behind, much of the developing world is poised to catch up (see Figure 13.1). Within 25 years, in countries as varied as Singapore, Malaysia, and Colombia, the percentage of older adults in the population will be more than triple what it is now (U.S. Census Bureau, 2001).

What accounts for this unparalleled increase in older adults? One force, as you learned in Chapter 1, lies in our historic strides in life expectancy, first during the earlier twentieth century in the industrialized West (see, for instance, Figure 13.2) and—more recently—in the rapidly modernizing areas of the developing world. A second influence, particularly in North America and Europe, is the baby boom cohort, now flooding into later life. As of this writing, the leading edge of the baby boomers is turning 60. By 2030, this massive cohort will all be well into their older years.

Finally, the late-twentieth-century decrease in fertility discussed in Chapter 11 is also making for an older world. When birth rates decline, the **median age** of a nation—meaning the cutoff age at which half of the population is older and half is younger—tends to rise. Recall that with fertility dipping below replacement levels in many industrialized nations, as Figure 13.2 shows, the median age of the population in some affluent countries is now well into middle age.

Life expectancy, the baby boomers, and low fertility rates set the stage for our new older world. Now let's offer some predictions about what will happen roughly two decades from now. In 2030 in Japan, where average life expectancy is now 81 and fertility rates are among the lowest in the world, the median age of the population will be roughly 50. In Italy, one out of *every two* people will be at least 52. And in that same year, one in every five Americans and one in four Europeans will be over age 65 (Kinsella & Velkoff, 2001).

What will it be like to live in a nation where so many of your neighbors are senior citizens? To answer this question, we need to return to the second crucial fact about later life. Just as an emerging adult has little in common with an eighth grader, being 90—statistically speaking—is very different from being age 60 or 65.

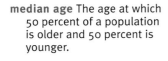

median age The age at which 50 percent of a population is older and 50 percent is younger.

Rising life expectancy, declining fertility, the baby boomers reaching old age—all of these forces explain why the median age of the population is increasing and why, in the decades to come, more people will look closer in age to this elderly woman than her 22-year-old granddaughter.

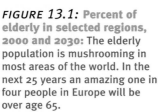

FIGURE 13.1: Percent of elderly in selected regions, 2000 and 2030: The elderly population is mushrooming in most areas of the world. In the next 25 years an amazing one in four people in Europe will be over age 65.

Source: Adapted from Kinsella & Velkoff (2001), Table 2-1, p. 9.

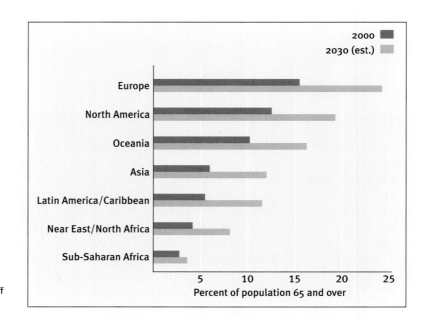

Jens Lucking / Getty Images

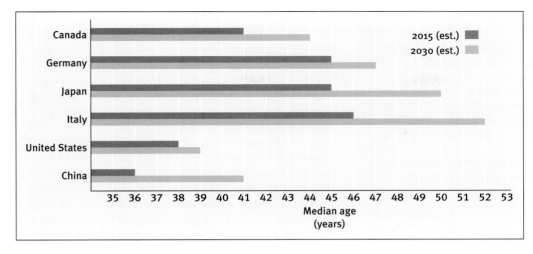

FIGURE 13.2: Predicted median age of the population, selected countries, in 2015 and 2030: A few years from now, the median age of the population—the point at which half the people are younger and half are older—will be middle-aged in Canada and Western Europe. Also, notice how high the median ages will be in Italy, Germany, and Japan in a few decades. How do you think living in these "most-aged nations" will affect residents' daily lives?

Source: Kinsella & Velkoff (2001).

We celebrate our amazing twentieth-century progress in raising life expectancy at birth. An equally interesting, less well-known statistic concerns the late-twentieth-century increase in **late-life life expectancy** (see Figure 13.3). This phrase refers to the number of years we can expect to live once we have turned 65. When they reach their sixty-fifth birthdays, contemporary U.S. adults, such as Sadie and Saul, have a fifty-fifty chance of surviving for almost 20 more years (Clark & Quinn, 2002; Hardy, 2002; Kinsella & Velkoff, 2001). These decades of travel through later life can produce dramatic changes. This is why developmentalists divide the elderly into two groups: The **young-old,** people in their sixties and seventies, are typically healthy and often relatively well off financially. The **old-old,** people over age 80, are far more likely to suffer from old-age disabilities and to be poor.

The health and wealth differences between the young-old and the old-old may explain our strangely contradictory stereotypes about later life. There is the image of the wealthy senior citizen traveling the world, and the portrait of the frail older person in a nursing home; the vision of the upbeat, vigorous older adult, and the depressed person with a dementing disease. Take a minute to classify your older family members and friends. While you may know an inspiring person who is still working or walking miles in advanced old age, do you agree that being 60 is very different from being 90 or 95?

late-life life expectancy The number of additional years a person in a given country can expect to live once reaching age 65.

young-old People in their sixties and seventies.

old-old People age 80 and older.

The faces of this 65-year-old golfer and this 90-year-old Chinese woman say it all. In terms of lifestyle, personality, memory, health, and everything else, we cannot stereotype "the elderly," and there is a world of difference between being young-old and old-old.

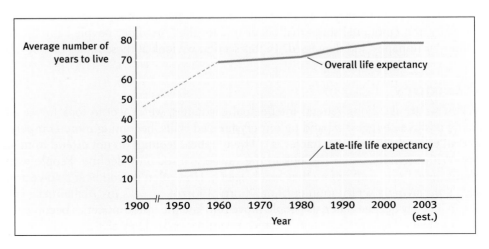

FIGURE 13.3: Life expectancy and late-life life expectancy in the United States, selected years: There has been an incredible increase in overall life expectancy at birth in the United States, particularly during the twentieth century's first half. Late-life life expectancy has also been slowly rising in the past 50 years.

Source: Kinsella & Velkoff (2001).

The hair is gray. . . . The brows are gone, the eyes are blear. . . . The nose is hooked and far from fair. . . . The ears are rough and pendulous. . . . The face is sallow, dead and drear. . . . The chin is purs'd . . . the lips hang loose. . . . Aye such is human beauty's lot! . . . Thus we mourn for the good old days . . . , wretched crones, huddled together by the blaze. . . . With many a man ' tis just the same.

(excerpted from an Old English poem called "Lament of the Fair Heaulmiere" [or Helmet-maker's girl], quoted in Minois, 1989, p. 230)

Many of us assume that people had better values and attitudes toward old age in "the good old days." Poems such as the one above show that we need to give that stereotype a much closer look.

In ancient times, old age was seen as a miracle of nature because it was so rare. Where there was no written language, older people were greatly valued for their knowledge. However, this elevated status applied only to a few people—typically men—who were upper class. For slaves, servants, and women, old age was often a cruel time. Moreover, just as we do today, many cultures made a clear distinction between active, healthy older people and those who were disabled and ill.

In many traditional cultures, for instance, the same person who had been revered several years earlier was subjected to barbaric treatment once he outlived his usefulness—that is, became decrepit or senile. Samoans killed their elderly in elaborate ceremonies in which the victim was required to participate. Other societies left their older people to die of neglect. Michelangelo and Sophocles, who were revered as old men, stand as symbols of the age-friendly attitudes of the cultures in which they lived. However, the images portrayed in their creative works celebrated youth and beauty. Even in Classical Greece and Renaissance Italy—societies known for being extremely enlightened—people believed old age was the worst time of life.

As historian Georges Minois (1989) concluded in a survey of how Western cultures treated their elders, "It is the tendency of every society to live and go on living: it extols the strength and fecundity that are so closely linked to youth and it dreads the . . . decrepitude of old age. Since the dawn of history . . . young people have regretted the onset of old age. The fountain of youth has always constituted Western man's most irrational hope" (p. 303).

(The information in this box is taken from Minois, 1989, and Fischer, 1977.)

As a final comment, we assume that our twenty-first-century society marginalizes the elderly—robbing them of dignity and opportunities they had in some wonderful past. This stereotype is also untrue. Notice in reading the Experiencing the Lifespan box above that throughout history people also made a distinction between vigorous older people and those who were mentally and physically impaired. Ironically, because we are not killing off our frail elderly, our age may actually be the most age-friendly age of all!

Now, keeping in mind that the sixties—statistically speaking—are very different from being 90 or 95, let's begin where we left off in the previous chapter by exploring the evolving self.

The Evolving Self

What happens to memory as we grow old? Are there specific changes in our emotional priorities and emotional states that occur in later life? Are older people calm and together, or unhappy and depressed? In this section we look at these topics one by one.

Memory

When we think of our general intellectual capacities, we expect to look forward to many positive changes: expanding our crystallized skills, becoming more competent and in control of life (see Chapter 12). These upbeat feelings do not extend to memory. With memory, when we look to the future, we see only decline. People worry about these losses well before they reach age 65. How often do you hear a 50-year-old say, "I'm having a senior moment," or, "Sorry, I forgot. . . . It's my Alzheimer's kicking in"? A few decades later, as people move into late life, these anxieties become top-ranking fears (Dark-Freudeman, West, & Viverito, 2006). They also begin to migrate to the wider world.

In a classic study, psychologists filmed actors aged 20, 50, and 70 reading an identical speech. During the speech each person made a few references to memory problems, such as "I forgot my keys." Adults then watched only the young, middle-aged, or older actor and wrote about what the person was like. Many of the people who saw the 70-year-old described him as forgetful. No one who heard the identical words read by the younger adults even mentioned memory (Rodin & Langer, 1980).

If this man said, "I forgot my keys," while telling you his story, would you be thinking, "Maybe his memory is going"? If a 16-year-old made the same comment, wouldn't you think, "That's a typical disorganized teen"? Can you remember a time when your old-age stereotypes caused you to read ominous implications into an elderly relative's random memory lapses?

This is one of many studies suggesting that people are selectively attuned to memory problems in later life. Once someone is over 75 or 80, we see memory lapses in a more ominous light. When a young person forgets something, we pass off the problem as due to external forces: "He was distracted" or "She had too much else going on." When that person is old, we leap to more serious assumptions: "Perhaps this is the beginning of Alzheimer's disease" (Erber & Prager, 1999; Erber & Rothberg, 1991). When you last were with an elderly family member and she forgot a name or appointment, did the idea that "My grandma is declining mentally" cross your mind?

[FAQ: How does memory change in old age?]

Scanning the Facts

Does memory really begin to decline by middle age? Are older people's memory capacities really much worse than those of younger adults? Unfortunately, the answer to both questions is yes. In hundreds of laboratory studies testing everything from the ability to recall unfamiliar faces to the names of new places, from remembering the content of paragraphs to recalling where objects are located in space, the elderly perform more poorly than the young (Park, 2000; Salthouse, 2000; Zacks, Hasher, & Li, 2000).

As the memory task gets more difficult, the performance gap between the young and old dramatically expands. When psychologists ask people to identify a photograph they have previously seen, older age groups often do as well as the typical 20-year-old (Craik & McDowd, 1987). The elderly score far more poorly when they need to come up with the names of the people pictured in the photos completely on their own. (The distinction here is analogous to taking an easy multiple-choice exam rather than a difficult short-answer test.)

Situations involving time pressure present special problems—being given a few minutes to study what you need to remember, versus an hour; being tested right after learning the information or after some time has elapsed. So do **divided-attention tasks**—situations that demand memorizing material while simultaneously monitoring something else. These kinds of multitasking challenges give us trouble at any age, as you know when you are studying at the library and are distracted by conversations or must keep your eye on the clock so as not to miss a 3:30 class.

divided-attention task A difficult memory challenge involving memorizing material while simultaneously monitoring something else.

Moreover, as the demands on memory become increasingly difficult, losses show up at younger ages (Crook & Larrabee, 1992; Zelinski & Burnight, 1997). Actually, as you can see in Figure 13.4 on page 402, on a range of challenging speed-oriented memory tests, losses appear as early as the thirties (Salthouse, 2003). Returning to the previous chapter, it makes sense that when people are asked to remember totally unfamiliar, random bits of information under time pressure,

Shifting her attention from scanning a computer, remembering what is on the screen, and taking notes on what she just read is easy for this young woman. But this kind of memory task, researchers find, gets far more difficult when we reach later life.

FIGURE 13.4: Age-related changes in performance on eight memory tests: This chart shows the average scores when different age groups took the Wechsler Memory Scale III. This test measures, among other abilities, people's immediate and delayed memory for stories, arbitrary pairs of words, faces, and lists of unrelated words. As you can see, age-related declines in performance on many of the memory scale tasks began to show up as young as the thirties.

Source: Salthouse (2003), Figure 1, p. 162.

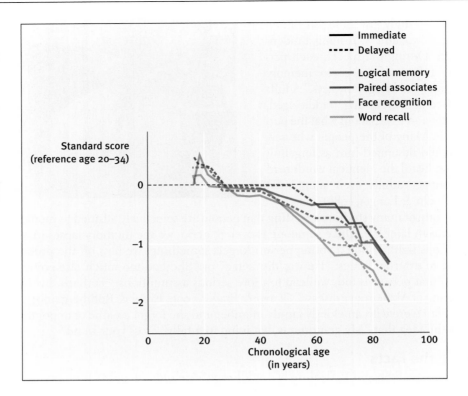

we would start to see age declines at a remarkably young age. These are prime examples of *fluid intelligence tasks.*

What exactly is going wrong? We can get insights from examining two different ways of conceptualizing memory: the information-processing and memory-systems approaches.

An Information-Processing Perspective on Memory Change

Remember from Chapter 5 that developmentalists who adopt an *information-processing theory* perspective on cognition see having a "memory" as progressing through defined stages. The gateway system, in which we take action to transform information into more permanent storage, is called *working memory.*

Working memory, you may recall, contains a limited memory-bin space, the amount of information we can keep in our awareness. It includes an executive processor that controls attention and works to transform the ephemeral contents of this temporary storage facility into material we can recall at a later time. Remember that during childhood, as the frontal lobes mature, bin capacity of working memory increases. Unfortunately, in the older years, the same phenomenon happens in reverse: Working memory-bin space declines (Park, 2000; Salthouse, 1994, 2000).

Researchers have offered different explanations for this loss. One possibility is that because older people process information more slowly, they simply cannot fit as many items into their memory bins and transfer them into storage as fast (Luszcz, Bryan, & Kent, 1997; Salthouse, 1991, 1992, 1996, 2000; Salthouse & Ferrer-Caja, 2003; Zimprich & Martin, 2002). Another explanation targets the problem as lying in selective attention. According to this perspective, when older people need to memorize information, irrelevant thoughts intrude and their existing bin space gets filled with extraneous "noise" (Hasher & Zacks, 1988; Zacks & Hasher, 1997).

According to *the frontal-lobe hypothesis of cognitive aging,* however, the underlying biological cause for both of these problems is the same: age-related neural deterioration in our master planner, the frontal lobes (see Figure 13.5; Friedman, 2003; Prull, Gabrieli, & Bunge, 2000; Reuter-Lorenz, 2000; Tisserand &

FIGURE 13.5: "Frontal lobe" losses: A good candidate for age losses in memory.

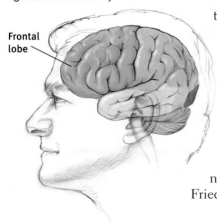

Frontal lobe

Jolles, 2003; Andrés, Parmentier, & Escera, 2006). Do we have concrete physiological evidence that older frontal cortexes operate differently when confronted with memory tasks? The answer is yes.

Brain scans provide a window into the intensity of neural activity when adults are given cognitive challenges. When young people must memorize simple information (such as recalling one or two letters or words), limited regions of the left frontal cortex get activated. As the memory demands become difficult (for instance, in tasks involving divided attention), activation spreads to the right hemisphere of the brain. But when older adults are given *any* memory task, easy or hard, *both* the right and left hemispheres light up. This finding has suggested to many neuropsychologists that to compensate for frontal-lobe deterioration, older people are forced to use a wider area of the cortex when they are engaged in unfamiliar activities that challenge their minds (Friedman, 2003; Grady & Craik, 2000; Prull, Gabrieli, & Bunge, 2000; Reuter-Lorenz and others, 2001).

This finding seems very depressing. Does our brain have to work on overdrive to remember *everything* in later life? Luckily, the answer is no. It is only in *specific* memory situations that older people need to engage in this intense mental work.

A Memory-Systems Perspective on Change

Think of the amazing resilience of some memories and the incredible vulnerability of others. Why do you automatically remember how to hold a tennis racquet even though you have not been on a court for years? Why is "George Washington," the name of our first president, locked in your mind while you are incapable of remembering what you had for dinner three days ago? These kinds of memories seem to differ in a way that goes beyond how much effort went into embedding them into our minds. They appear to be qualitatively different in a fundamental way.

According to the **memory-systems perspective** (Craik, 2000; Tulving, 1985), there are three basic types of memory:

- **Procedural memory** refers to information that we automatically remember, without conscious reflection or thought. An important real-life example involves physical skills. Once we have learned a complex motor activity, such as how to hit a tennis ball, we automatically remember how to perform that skill once we are in that situation again.

- **Semantic memory** is our fund of basic factual knowledge. Remembering that George Washington was our first president and knowing what a tennis racquet is are examples of the kinds of information in this well-learned, crystallized database.

- **Episodic memory** refers to the ongoing events of daily life. When you remember getting on the tennis court last Thursday or what you had for dinner last night, or when a psychologist asks you to recall a random series of names in a memory experiment, you are drawing on material in episodic memory.

As you can see in these examples and those described in Table 13.1 on page 404, episodic memory is by far the most fragile system. A month or year from now you will still remember who George Washington was (semantic memory). You will recall how to hold the tennis racquet and hit the ball (procedural memory). However, even a week later you are likely to forget what you had for dinner on a particular night. Remembering any isolated event—from what day we last played tennis, to what we ate last Tuesday, to the paragraph you are reading right now—is especially vulnerable to the passage of time.

As the findings of the memory study displayed in Figure 13.6 on page 404 show, on tests of semantic memory older people typically do almost as well as the young (Craik & Jennings, 1992; Salthouse, 1991; Zacks, Hasher, & Li, 2000). Procedural memory is amazingly long-lasting, as we know when we get on the tennis court after not having played for years, and effortlessly hit the ball. The real age loss occurs in episodic memory—our ability to remember the ongoing details of daily life (Nilsson, 2003).

memory-systems perspective A framework that divides memory into three types: procedural, semantic, and episodic memory.

procedural memory In the memory-systems perspective, the most resilient (longest-lasting) type of memory; refers to material, such as well-learned physical skills, that we automatically recall without conscious awareness.

semantic memory In the memory-systems perspective, a moderately resilient (long-lasting) type of memory; refers to our ability to recall basic facts.

episodic memory In the memory-systems perspective, the most fragile type of memory, involving the recall of the ongoing events of daily life.

TABLE 13.1: Examples of the Differences Among Procedural, Semantic, and Episodic Memory

Procedural Memory	Semantic Memory	Episodic Memory
You get into your blue Toyota and automatically know how to drive.	You know that you have a blue Toyota.	You memorize where you left your blue Toyota in the parking lot of the amusement park.
You automatically find yourself singing the words to "Jingle Bells" when the melody comes on the radio.	You remember that "Jingle Bells" is a song.	You remember the last time you heard "Jingle Bells."
You begin to get excited as you approach your college campus for the fall semester of your senior year.	You know that you are a student at *X* University and that you are a psychology major.	You memorize the locations of classrooms and your professors' names during the first week of the new semester.
I unconsciously find the letters I am typing now on my computer.	I know that I am writing a book called *Experiencing the Lifespan*.	I remember that today I must go to the library and photocopy an article on memory that I will need in preparing this chapter.

This decline in episodic memory is what people notice in their forties when they realize they are having more trouble remembering the name of a person at a party or where they parked the car. Our databank of semantic memories, or crystallized information, stays intact until well into later life unless we have a fatal disease (recall the discussion of *terminal drop* in Chapter 12). People with Alzheimer's disease can retain procedural memories after the other memory systems are largely gone. They can walk, dress themselves, and even remember (to the horror of caregivers) how to turn on the ignition and drive a car after losing their ability to recall basic facts such as where they live.

Why is this particular memory system the last to go? The reason, according to neuropsychologists, is that procedural memory resides in a different region of the brain. When we first learn a complex motor skill, such as driving a car or playing tennis, our frontal lobes are heavily involved. Then, after we have thoroughly

FIGURE 13.6: Age differences in episodic and semantic memory: These charts show how the age gap between the old and young shrinks when we test semantic memory versus episodic memory. To test episodic memory, researchers asked young adults and older people to memorize names linked to unfamiliar faces (this would be like memorizing the names of people you were just introduced to). To study semantic memory, the researchers asked participants to name famous people and well-known objects (such as brooms or lamps) pictured in photographs. Notice that the older people did as well as the young when they were asked to recall the names of famous people and of well-known objects (chart B), but their performance was markedly worse when asked to memorize new names (chart A).

Source: Rendell, Castel, & Craik (2005), pp. 58, 64.

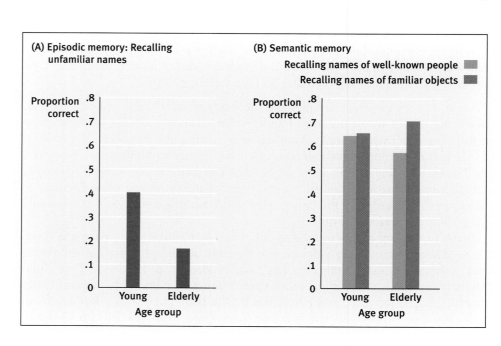

learned that activity, this knowledge becomes automatic and migrates to a lower brain center, which frees up our frontal cortex for mastering other higher-level thinking tasks (Friedman, 2003). Actually, this is all to the good. If I had to focus on simultaneously remembering how to type these words on my computer, would I ever be able to do the enormously complicated mental work of figuring out how to clearly describe the concepts I am explaining right now?

In sum, the message with regard to age and memory is both a bit worse and also far better than we might have thought: As we get older, we do not have to worry much about being able to remember familiar material. Our storehouse of crystallized knowledge is "really there." We will, however, have more trouble memorizing isolated bits of new information, and these losses in episodic memory will show up at a surprisingly early age.

Interventions: Keeping Memory Fine-Tuned

What should people do when they notice that their ability to remember life's ongoing details is getting worse? Let's now look at three approaches:

USE SELECTIVE OPTIMIZATION WITH COMPENSATION The first strategy is to use Baltes's three-step process, spelled out in Chapter 12: (1) Selectively focus on what you want to remember—that is, don't let your working memory-bin space get clogged with irrelevant thoughts. (2) Optimize, or work hard to manipulate material in this system into permanent memory. (3) Use compensation, or external memory aids, when you do not feel confident about remembering some piece of information without help.

For example, to remember where you parked your car at the airport: (1) Take care to actively focus on *where* you are parking when you drive into the airport; don't daydream or get distracted by the need to catch the plane. (2) Work hard to encode that specific location in your brain. (3) Write down "G6, bus stop 4" on a card and stick that information in your wallet so you won't have to remember that spot all on your own.

The compensation, or "write information down," principle is easy to follow, although you still have to remember where you put the card! Now let's look at what older people—or any person—can do to slide information more effortlessly through their memory bins:

USE MNEMONIC TECHNIQUES Have you ever noticed that some episodic events are locked in memory (such as your wedding day or the time you and your significant other had that terrible fight), while others quickly fade? Emotional events embed themselves solidly into memory because they activate wider regions of the brain (Dolcos & Cabeza, 2002). Therefore, the key to memorizing any isolated bit of information is to make that material stand out emotionally.

Mnemonic techniques are strategies to make information emotionally vivid. When you use the jingle "Thirty days hath September . . ." to remember the number of days in a particular month or, when introduced to a person, you realize, "I won't forget this person's name, because my sister is also named Alice," you are using a mnemonic technique.

One way of making material stand out is to conjure up a striking visual image. To remember where you parked at the airport, take a visual snapshot of the location: "Here's the marker G6 right over my head." To remember G6, imagine your 6-year-old niece, Gina, driving your Toyota. (I've actually been drawing on this fundamental "images help us remember" principle in my strategy of using photos to directly illustrate many of the concepts and terms in this text.)

[FAQ: What can be done to minimize cognitive deficits in old age?

mnemonic technique A strategy for aiding memory, often by using imagery or enhancing the emotional meaning of what needs to be learned.

Although his main goal is to greet this woman in a warm, personal way, in order to remember his new friend's name, this elderly man might want to step back and use the mnemonic strategy of forming a mental image, thinking, "I'll remember it's Mrs. Silver because of her hair."

Ronnie Kaufman / Getty Images

The fact that we learn emotionally vivid information without much effort may explain why our memory for facts varies in such puzzling ways in real life. A history buff soaks up every detail about the Civil War but remains clueless about where he left his socks. Because your passion is developmental science, you do well with very little studying in this course, but it takes you hours to memorize a single page in your biology text. Interestingly, when they are asked to remember emotionally vivid material, older people tend to perform almost as well as the young! (See Kensinger, Krendl, & Corkin, 2006.)

ENHANCE MEMORY SELF-EFFICACY Because being motivated looms so large in making our memory processes better or worse, this brings up the thought that perhaps laboratory memory tests may not be fair to older adults. If you were 70 or 80, imagine how you would feel if you entered a traditional memory study: Wouldn't you be frightened, thinking, "Perhaps this test might show I have Alzheimer's disease"?

How much do these kinds of internal stereotypes handicap older people on standard memory tests? For answers, psychologists devised an interesting experiment. Prior to administering a memory test to elderly volunteers, the researchers assigned their study participants to read different newspaper reports (Hess and others, 2003). One group read an article that had the message, "It's a biological fact that as people get older, memory seriously declines." The other group's article had a more upbeat behavioral message: "The problem is not biological. Older people are just out of practice. The elderly are no less capable than the young." As they had predicted, on the subsequent test the older adults who read the positive "You can do it" article far outperformed the people exposed to the negative ("It's hopeless and biological") information.

Therefore, a critical third strategy for improving memory in old age, or at any age, is to promote *memory self-efficacy* (Cavanaugh, 1996, 2000; Cavanaugh & Green, 1990). Take the biological data referring to neural loss very lightly. Understand that with extra effort, *anyone's* memory can be really good (Cavanaugh, 1996, 2000; Grandmaison & Simard, 2003; Hess and others, 2003). Just as believing that intelligence is a fixed genetic entity hurts children, when older people believe they have a basic brain deficit—and so withdraw from challenging learning situations—they *ensure* that their memory will be poor!

In fact, we all intuitively understand that—in the real world—with regard to memory our motivation does matter a great deal. Despite firmly believing that memory is "deficient" in old age, whom would you trust more to remember to feed your cat when you are on vacation—the teenager next door or your elderly neighbor down the street?

Shifting Emotional Priorities

Everyone believes that memory declines with age. But think of our contradictory stereotypes about late-life personality. Are older people unhappy, demoralized, and depressed? Or are the elderly peaceful, calm, and together? To make sense of these contradictions, let's first look at a provocative theory that makes the upbeat case, and then conclude by turning to research that directly examines older people's emotional states.

Focusing on Time Left to Live: Socioemotional Selectivity Theory

Imagine that, like Sadie and Saul, you are elderly and well aware that you may have only a few years left to live. How might your priorities about what is important in life change? The idea that our place on the lifespan alters our agendas and goals is the basic premise of Laura Carstensen's **socioemotional selectivity theory.**

According to Carstensen (1995; Carstensen, Fung, & Charles, 2003), during the first half of adult life our basic push is to look to the future. We are eager to make it in the wider world. We want to reach a better place at some later date. As we grow older and realize that our future is limited, we refocus our priorities. We want to make the most of our present life.

socioemotional selectivity theory A theory of aging (and the lifespan) put forth by Laura Carstensen, describing how the time we have left to live affects our priorities and social relationships. Specifically, Carstensen believes that as people reach later life, they focus on enhancing the quality of the present and place priority on spending time with their closest attachment figures.

Socioemotional selectivity theory, with its principle that older people focus only on the activities they really love, makes perfect sense of why we see young people looking bored because they feel they "must" go to a party (when they would rather stay home), while the elderly couple on the right are passionately getting into the swing of things.

Carstensen believes that this focus on making the most of every moment means that old age has the potential to be the *happiest* time of life. When our agenda lies in the future, we often forgo our immediate desires in the service of a later goal. Instead of telling off the professor or boss who insults us, we hold our tongue because this authority figure holds the key to getting ahead. We are nice to that nasty person or go to that dinner party we would rather pass up in order to advance socially or in our career. We accept the anxiety-ridden months we face when we first move to an unfamiliar city or begin a new job because we expect to feel better than ever in a year or two.

In later life we are less interested in where we *will* be going. So we refuse to let insulting remarks pass, to waste time with unpleasant people, or to enter anxiety-provoking situations because they may have a payoff at some later point. Almost unconsciously, we decide, "I don't have that long to live. I have to spend my time doing what makes me feel good emotionally *right now*."

Furthermore, when our passion lies in making the most of the present, Carstensen argues, our social priorities change. During childhood, adolescence, and emerging adulthood our basic thrust is to leave our attachment figures. We want to expand our social horizons, form new close relationships, and connect with exciting new people who can teach us new things. Once we have achieved our life goals, we are less interested in developing new close attachments. We already have our family and network of caring friends. So we center our lives on our spouse, our best friends, our children—the people we love the most.

Socioemotional selectivity theory, with its principle that in old age we choose to spend as much time as possible with our closest attachment figures, explains why simply spending time with each other and their grandchild is this elderly Chinese couple's passion in life.

To test whether this age-related shift really does occur, Carstensen's research team asked elderly and young people, "Who would you rather spend time with—a close family member, a recent acquaintance, or the author of a recent book?" Young people's choices were spread among the three possible partners. Older people chose overwhelmingly to be with the family member, their closest attachment figure in life (Fung, Lai, & Ng, 2001).

When Do We Prioritize the Present Regardless of Our Life Stage?

Is this shift in priorities *simply* a function of being old? The answer, the researchers found, is no. People with AIDS also voted to spend an evening with a familiar close person. So did people who were asked to imagine that they were about to move across the country alone. According to Carstensen, whenever we see our future as limited, we selectively pare down our social contacts, spending as much time as possible with the people we care about the most.

Socioemotional selectivity theory explains why—although normally we are content to live a continent away—when we are in danger of losing a loved one, we want to be physically close. You fly in from California to spend time with your beloved grandma in New York when she is seriously ill. You insist on spending the weekend with your high school friend who is leaving for a tour of duty in Iraq.

The theory accounts for the choices my cousin Clinton made when he was diagnosed with lymphoma in his early twenties. An exceptionally gifted architect, Clinton gave up his promising career and retired to rural New Hampshire to build houses, hike, and ski for what turned out to be another quarter-century of life. Clinton's funeral, when he died at age 50, was an unforgettable celebration—a testament to a person who, although his life was shorter than most, was able to live fully for longer than many people who survive to twice this age. Have you ever seen the principles of socioemotional selectivity theory in operation in your own life?

Later-Life Emotional States

This passion to make the most of every moment and to spend time with our loved ones when we see the future as limited makes good psychological sense. But is Carstensen correct when she says that people are actually *happier* in later life?

The Upside: Calmer and More in Control

One classic late-twentieth-century study of mental disorders implies that the answer may be yes. In this landmark epidemiologic study of mental illness, the researchers found that people over age 65 had strikingly lower rates of emotional problems than adults of any other age (Weissman and others, 1985).

Older people, Carstensen's research team finds, are better at regulating their emotions (Carstensen and others, 2000; Charles, Reynolds, & Gatz, 2001). They seem to actively shut out upsetting stimuli in the interest of preserving a positive emotional state.

In asking different age groups to reminisce about their lives, Carstensen and her colleagues discovered that older people—in contrast to younger adults—dwelled more on happy memories than on sad events (Kennedy, Mather, & Carstensen, 2004). When the psychologists gave elderly and young people photos of joyous and distressing scenes, the older adults, but not the young people, looked more often at the happy images than the upsetting ones (Mather & Carstensen, 2003). Then, in a follow-up study, when the researchers recorded the activity of the amygdala—recall that this is the region of the brain that processes our emotions—the elderly volunteers showed more intense brain activation to the positive photos, too (Mather and others, 2004). So, yes, in later life people may be happier—in the sense of being superior at maintaining a calm, pleasant emotional state.

The Downside: A Less Exciting Emotional Life and Perhaps the Potential to Become Depressed

However, this emphasis on emotional control can come at a price. When your priority is minimizing upsetting emotions, you may eliminate the highs as well as the lows. In synthesizing the findings of many studies exploring age differences in positive and nega-

This homeless Russian woman is holding a plate of food she just got from an emergency distribution center as the temperature in Moscow went down to a bone-chilling 20° below zero one January day. If a society does not provide adequate services for its elderly citizens and when people are poor and isolated, old age can be a dismal life stage.

Alexander Natruskin / Reuters / Corbis

tive emotions around the globe, one researcher discovered that while older people were less prone to feel furious or extremely upset, they also reported fewer intensely positive emotions, such as exuberant joy (Pinquart, 2001). And, unfortunately, only in certain countries—such as Great Britain and the United States—did age bring more positive emotions. In Eastern European countries (which have few social services for the elderly), older people were far less happy than the young.

The bottom line is that, just as at any life stage, the wider context of our lives has everything to do with having a fulfilling old age. If your nation provides its citizens with ample retirement income, you are more likely to be happy than if you are left to languish in poverty during your "golden years." Our older years are (no surprise) more likely to be golden when we live surrounded by loving attachment figures, versus feeling marginalized, abandoned, and alone (Rothermund & Brandstadter, 2003; Sugisawa and others, 2002). Moreover, there is a difference when researchers specifically focus on the young-old versus the old-old. Yes, depression rates are indeed low among people in their sixties; but the prevalence of this problem climbs dramatically after age 75 (Rothermund & Brandstadter, 2003).

In sum, people are most likely to be happy focusing on the present when they can fully *enjoy* their present lives. Happiness is indeed common among young-old people living in affluent regions of the world. When the disabilities of advanced old age strike, while people may say "I feel peaceful," the word *happy* does not really apply. As one woman in an assisted-living facility put it, "I don't like the word *happy*. I'm grateful for my family. I'm grateful that I can get out of bed each day. I can stand up. I can go to dinner. I wouldn't call that happiness—I'm just grateful" (quoted in Johnson & Barer, 1997, p. 172).

Still, let's not stereotype every old-old person as living in a demoralized holding pattern, waiting for death. Some very old adults take enormous pleasure from simply surviving to see another day. Listen to this immigrant woman who lived alone in a dangerous urban neighborhood:

> When I get up I wiggle my toes. Good, they still obey. I open my eyes. Good, I can see. I walk down to the ocean. Good, it's still there . . . (shining and beautiful). About tomorrow I never know. After all, I'm 89. I can't live forever.
>
> (adapted from a quote in Myerhoff, 1978, p. 1)

And as this obituary of a 92-year-old doctor makes clear, let's not forget that people can live active, passionate, generative lives well into advanced old age:

> Salvator Altchek, the $5 doctor to the melting pot of Brooklyn, especially the poorest residents, died on Tuesday. He was 92. He continued to work until two months ago. He generally attended to the health needs of anyone who showed up in his basement office—charging 5 or 10 dollars if he charged at all. For more than a half-century, he began his work day at 8 A.M. and often made house calls until late at night. He knew everyone and everyone knew him. Once when he was held up at gunpoint, the robber, recognizing him, reached into his own pocket and gave him 10 dollars. His last spoken thought was to remember that he owed a patient a medical report.
>
> (adapted from Martin, 2002, p. 40)

Do you have an old-age generative role model, such as Dr. Altchek? At age 89, could you, too, extract joy from simply seeing the ocean or knowing that you are still alive to wiggle your toes? What steps can you personally take to prepare for living fully in advanced old age? For hints, you might want to turn back to consult Table 12.5 on page 384. Now let's look at the lessons our current discussion offers for readers who work with—and care about—older adults.

[FAQ: How can one live well in old age?]

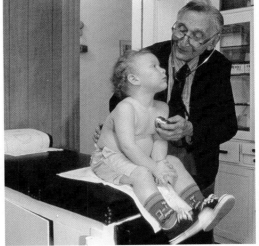

Dr. Altchek practices his generative passion in his final decades.

Alessandra Sanguinetti

INTERVENTIONS **Using the Memory and Emotions Research at Home and Work**

How can we help older people improve their memory skills? How should you think about the relationship priorities of older loved ones, and when should you worry about their emotional states? Here are some suggestions:

- As late-life memory difficulties are most likely to show up in situations where there is "lots going on" and older people must remember new information very fast, give elderly people extra time to learn new material and provide a noise-free, non-distracting environment (more about this environmental engineering in Chapter 14).

- Don't stereotype older adults as having a "bad memory." Be aware of the crucial role of low self-efficacy in making people's memory capacities worse. Work to enhance efficacy feelings by suggesting this chapter's memory tips.

- Give older adults chances to exercise their *personal* passions. Remember that when we are emotionally engaged, material slides more effortlessly through our working memory bins.

- Using the insights that socioemotional selectivity theory offers, don't expect older people to automatically want to socialize or make new friends. When an elderly loved one says, "I don't want to go to the senior citizen center. All I care about is my family," she may be making an age-appropriate response!

- Don't stereotype older people as unhappy—in fact, assume the reverse is true, especially in the young-old years. However, be alert to depression in someone who is old-old, physically frail, and socially isolated. The key to preventing depression in old age is the same as at any age: being interested in the world, having loving relationships, and living a generative life.

 ## TYING IT ALL TOGETHER

1. You are advising a national task force that is drawing up guidelines for programs to help the elderly. On the basis of this section, what might you suggest?

   a. Let's focus mainly on combating negative late-life stereotypes because, while nonexistent in the past, discrimination against the elderly is now an alarming problem.
   b. Let's provide many different kinds of programs, as older people are incredibly varied in their health, lifestyles, preferences, and needs.
   c. Let's target people in their sixties for the most help, as physical disabilities become prevalent at that age.

2. Christopher is planning on teaching lifespan development at the senior center. He's excited, but until now he's taught only younger people. He is concerned about older people and memory and wonders what he might do differently. Based on your understanding of which memory situations give older people the most trouble, suggest some changes Christopher might make in his teaching.

3. Classify each of the following memory challenges as involving episodic memory, semantic memory, or procedural memory:

   a. Someone asks you your street address.
   b. Someone asks you what you just read in this chapter.
   c. You to go bike riding.

4. Which of the abilities above will an older loved one retain the longest if she gets Alzheimer's disease, and why?

5. When Mandy asked her grandfather if he had chicken last night, he thought for a moment and then said, "You know, it's incredible. I remember the name of every state capital, but I don't remember what I had for dinner last night!" Mandy's grandfather's comment illustrates that _____ memory is much more fragile than _____ memory.

6. You are eavesdropping on four elderly friends at a local café as they discuss their feelings about life. According to socioemotional selectivity theory, which *two* of the following comments might you expect to hear?

   a. Frances says, "Now that I've gotten older, I want to start meeting as many new people as possible."
   b. Allen reports, "I've been enjoying life in the past few years more than ever. I'm taking time to savor every moment—and what a pleasure it is to do just what I want!"
   c. Milly mentions, "I've been trying to spend as much time as possible with my family. These are the people who matter to me the most."

7. In what life situations might you worry about an older person being at high risk for depression?

Answers to the Tying It All Together questions can be found in the answers section of the book.

Later-Life Transitions

Now let's look at how people fulfill their generativity, pursue their passions, and implement their basic human need to be closely attached as they confront the major life transitions of retirement and widowhood.

Retirement

When they retired at age 59 and 61, Sadie and Saul were right on target for the current social clock norms. Over the last half of the twentieth century, at the same time that late-life life expectancy was floating upward, the average retirement age was sliding down. In 1950, three out of every four U.S. workers stayed at their jobs until at least age 65. Today the average retirement age is closer to 60, and only one in ten U.S. adults is still in the labor force at or after the "traditional" retirement age (Kinsella & Velkoff, 2001). Moreover, in 1950, the typical American worker could expect to spend only six years in the retired state before he died. Today, a new retiree can expect to live for almost two extra decades of life! (See Hardy, 2002.)

What caused retirement to expand from a short pause before death to a stage of life that lasts as long as childhood and adolescence? What does retirement look like around the world? Why do people decide to retire, and what happens when they take that step?

Setting the Context: Scanning the Global Scene

Retirement is a socially constructed life stage. It became possible when governments began to provide a financial cushion for their older citizens to live without working. As government income-support programs proliferated during the last half of the twentieth century, retirement became a full stage of life in much of the developed world (see Figure 13.7).

This cushion, however, does not exist in many developing countries, where people must continue to work until they are disabled or die. In Bangladesh, Jamaica, and Mexico, more than half of all elderly people are in the labor force. In Rwanda, a third of all women and half of all men over age 75 are still working. Compare this to France or Luxembourg, where life expectancy is far longer and only 2 *percent* of the population stay at their jobs after age 65 (Kinsella & Velkoff, 2001).

Even in relatively affluent countries, however, government-funded retirement programs vary from extremely generous to nil. For insights into these differences, let's first visit Germany, stop off in Hong Kong, and conclude by focusing on the United States.

Christopher P. Baker / Lonely Planet Images

If he lived in another, more affluent country, this 65-year-old Jamaican man would probably already have retired. But because his nation does not provide its citizens with retirement income, he may need to work until he is well into his seventies or even older.

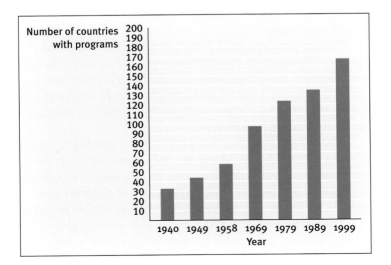

FIGURE 13.7: Number of countries with government-funded old-age retirement programs, 1940–1999: Notice that by the end of the twentieth century, many countries provided their citizens with income-support programs for the elderly (and other needy groups). Notice also that the number of governments that established these programs began to rapidly take off in the 1960s.

Source: Kinsella & Velkoff (2001), Figure 11-2, p. 117.

GERMANY: MORE COMFORTABLE AFTER RETIREMENT THAN BEFORE Germany stands out as a model of what the government can provide to retirees. In fact, in the late nineteenth century Germany instituted the first public government-funded retirement program in the world. Retirement in Germany is mainly financed by employee and employer payroll taxes, in a system similar to the one we have in the United States. In Germany, unlike in the United States, however, the guiding philosophy is to keep people financially *comfortable* during their older years. When the typical German worker retires, the government replaces roughly three-fourths of that person's working income for life. In Germany, retirees have no worries about falling into poverty in old age. Because the government stipend rises depending on increases in the cost of living, older people in this nation actually have *more* spending power as they travel further into their retirement years (Hungerford, 2003).

HONG KONG: RELYING ON PERSONAL SAVINGS AND FEELING INSECURE At the opposite extreme is Hong Kong, which provides its older citizens with no government-funded retirement help. This cohort of middle-aged and young-old people in Hong Kong is in a difficult position. Until recently, in this collectivist culture children automatically were expected to support their parents in old age. But, as in the rest of the Far East, Hong Kong is making the transition to an individualistic society in which the younger generation no longer feels compelled to "honor thy parents' financial needs."

Late-middle-aged adults in Hong Kong, caught in these cultural crosswinds, express considerable anxiety about their old-age fate. They have not been encouraged to save for retirement. They know they must depend on their children's goodwill. Many are looking forward with trepidation to what will happen to them when they get old (Lee & Law, 2004).

THE UNITED STATES: DIVERSE ECONOMIC SITUATIONS AND DETERIORATING FINANCES The United States lies about midway between these extremes. Our federal government does offer the famous old-age insurance program called Social Security. But the income Social Security provides does not allow for a comfortable retirement. Our nation does encourage workers to save for retirement through private pension plans, but this source of income varies dramatically in adequacy. The most vulnerable American adults typically enter retirement with no pensions at all.

Social Security, the landmark government program instituted by President Franklin D. Roosevelt at the height of the Great Depression of the 1930s, operates as a safety net. It is designed to stave off late-life poverty rather than to ensure a comfortable old age. Employees and employers pay into this universal program during their working years to finance the current crop of retirees; then, when it is their turn to retire, these elderly adults get a stipend financed by the current working population for as long as they live. The problem, however, is that the Social Security system offers one of the lowest old-age stipends in the Western world (Hardy, 2002). On average, Social Security replaces slightly more than half of the typical person's income at work (Kinsella & Velkoff, 2001).

Private pensions (and personal savings) are supposed to take up the slack. Workers put aside a portion of each paycheck, and these funds, often matched by employer contributions, go into a tax-free account that accumulates equity. Then, when people retire, they typically get a lump-sum payment or regular stipend on which to live. Furthermore, some employers (but a rapidly declining number) offer health-care coverage to their retired employees.

The central role of private pensions in financing retirement reflects the premium that the United States places on individual initiative. As with health care, or our hands-off approach to regulating working hours (recall Chapter 11), we are leery about the expense and welfare-state implications of a federal government plan. We prefer to provide tax incentives, to encourage workers to plan for retirement on their own.

The problem is that, just as many U.S. workers do not have health-care coverage (to be discussed in Chapter 14), people who work in low-wage jobs, such as servers or

---

[FAQ: What financial resources are available for seniors?**]**

Social Security The U.S. government's national retirement support program.

private pensions The major source of nongovernmental income support for retirees, in which the individual worker and the employer put a portion of each paycheck into an account to help finance retirement.

the cashiers at your local convenience store (who are often female and minority), are not likely to have pensions, either (Stanford & Usita, 2002). To be eligible for this source of income, people typically need to work for a company in a "regular" full-time job. Pension plans vary in their generosity and are subject to being drastically cut or eliminated when a company goes bankrupt. This means that, unlike Social Security, this source of income is actually *insecure*.

As people move further into retirement and their pension income and savings erode, they depend on Social Security for a larger chunk of their income. This spells financial trouble. Unlike in Germany, studies show that the average American retiree experiences declining living standards as he travels into his old-old years (Hungerford, 2003).

The bottom-line message is that the U.S. income inequalities highlighted throughout this book persist in later life. Low-income workers—because they rely primarily on Social Security—start out their retirement years as low-income elderly. Women, like Sadie in the chapter-opening vignette, who have entered retirement firmly middle class are vulnerable to sliding into old-age poverty after their medical bills mount during their husband's final illness and death (Stanford & Usita, 2002).

Now that we have sketched out the economic picture, it's time to offer a motion picture of retirement over time.

Making the Retirement Choice

Why do people decide to retire? Being able to live without working is the top-ranking reason: "I have enough money to enjoy my life." However, a second reason is poor health: "I was too ill to continue at work" (Szinovacz, 2003; Taylor & Doverspike, 2003). Disability can strike anyone, rich or poor, but—as should come as no surprise—health concerns loom large in the retirement decision at the lower ends of the socioeconomic scale (McNamara & Williamson, 2004).

At the upper end of the economic spectrum, as with Saul in the chapter-opening vignette, workers may be lured to retire at a younger-than-normal age by pensions. **Age discrimination** at work is illegal. People cannot be laid off for being a certain age. But put yourself in the position of an employer. Your older, long-standing employees have higher salaries. They cost you more in benefits such as health care. So you offer these workers a special carrot, a one-shot pension incentive to retire. However, there can be an implicit threat: Retire now, and get these terrific benefits, or find yourself without a job.

> **age discrimination** Illegally laying off workers or failing to hire or promote them on the basis of age.

Listen to this engineer from Bell Labs:

> *We were all encouraged to retire. . . . We were offered a sweetener with the notion that if we didn't take retirement at that time our chances would be less favorable next year. . . . And after all they could hire young technicians at half the price they were paying us.*
>
> (quoted in Williamson, Rinehart, & Blank, 1992, p. 41)

And here is what a supervisor at Bethlehem Steel had to say:

> *They said if we didn't leave the company voluntarily (taking the early retirement incentive), they would have to reduce the work force at their discretion. Ordinarily we were a two-man office, but when my boss retired a year before, he was not replaced. . . . After vacation you would have twice as much work because it wasn't being done by anyone else.*
>
> (quoted in Williamson, Rinehart, & Blank, 1992, p. 43)

The tactic of encouraging retirement by producing role overload works. In studying Norwegian men, researchers found that a main predictor of taking early retirement was working in a boring, low-autonomy, non-flow-inducing job (Blekesaune & Solem, 2005).

On a positive note, because the United States (unlike Japan) has no widespread mandatory retirement laws, people who want to stay at their jobs are free to continue working well beyond the traditional retirement age. Who are the one in ten U.S. adults who say no to retirement and stay in the labor force beyond age 65?

Richard Mellouli / Sygma / Corbis

While this French actor named Jean Marais might tell you he loved his creative career on the stage, like some older adults, he chose to retire to spend time on a new later-life creative passion—producing pottery.

As you might expect, these people are healthy and often highly educated (McNamara & Williamson, 2004; Rix, 2002). They tend to be workers, such as Dr. Altchek, mentioned earlier, who find tremendous flow in their careers. In fact, you can predict an older family member's retirement decision by asking: "Do you absolutely love what you do? Do you hate the idea of leaving work?"

But your prediction might be wrong. People can adore their jobs but retire to fulfill some nonwork identity. As socioemotional selectivity theory would predict, you know your future is limited, and you have the money and want to pursue your passion for being a pilot or painter. Perhaps, as in the chapter-opening vignette, you want to spend your final decades of life seeing the world or spending quality time with your spouse.

Life as a Retiree

The good news is that, provided people *choose* to retire—and don't feel they were pressured out of the workforce—they typically feel they made the right choice (Warr and others, 2004). Retirees report fewer day-to-day stresses (Bossé and others, 1991). They take better care of their health than they did during their working years (Midanak and others, 1995). Actually, as with Sadie and Saul, retirement has many similarities to emerging adulthood. It is a time to explore new lifestyles, to construct different identities, to travel the world.

Just as we saw during emerging adulthood, however, there may be glitches on the pathway to finding a retirement identity. According to a classic theory, people go through predictable stages in adapting to retirement (Atchley, 1977). First, there is a honeymoon period when everything is rosy. A man luxuriates in his freedom, goes fishing, travels, and packs in activities. A woman makes lunch dates and exercises for hours. Then a letdown sets in. Something may be missing. One person may be doing too much and end up exhausted. Another may feel at loose ends without something productive to do. At this point, the person might reconsider: "How do I want my life to go?" Finally, after a year or two, people connect with their identity as retirees.

Based on what we know about personality consistency during adulthood, these new retirement identities often have much in common with who that person was before (Atchley, 1989). A conscientious person is not going to be happy sitting on the beach. She will need to be productive during her retirement years. Actually, for many U.S. retirees, relaxing on the beach is the opposite of what retiring is all about (Ekerdt, 1986). People use these years to fulfill their generative impulses (Savishinsky, 2004). Often they spend this time being of service in ways that build on their lifelong passions, talents, and skills. A social activist joins the Peace Corps or works for Amnesty International. A business executive volunteers his services at SCORE (Senior Corps of Retired Executives), giving advice to young people who are setting up small businesses. Like Saul in the chapter-opening vignette, he may find a new, unpaid executive career as the president of the local synagogue or church. Sometimes, people construct a late-life identity as a student or scholar of life.

A dazzling array of options are available to older adults who decide to use retirement as a time for expanding their minds, from reduced-cost programs for returning students at universities to special older-adult institutes such as **Elderhostel.**

Read what one joyous participant had to say about his experience at this well-known education-travel program, in which people age 55 and over can choose from thousands of courses taught by the best professors on campus for one exciting summer week.

These older people are enrolled in an English class in a special senior citizens' college in Japan. Because many people use their retirement years to devote themselves to the human passion for learning, special educational programs such as Elderhostel are flourishing in nations around the world.

Tom Wagner / Corbis

After my program at the University of Notre Dame in Indiana I have an overwhelming memory. It was simply wonderful. . . . Dr. James Ellis . . . made mankind come alive, showed us how our species is swiftly and not wisely changing the world. His illustrations were stunning: "We Americans are using 75 percent of the world's calories." (And I didn't want to make him a liar as I passed through the cafeteria line.) . . . Next, Sandy Vanslinger put us through our paces in the aerobics class. . . . With my damaged ticker I was concerned, but . . . I felt great. . . . The quality of the program was so magnificent that I felt I was in heaven. . . . Notre Dame, I won't forget you!

(quoted in Mills, 1993, pp. 108–111)

Perhaps the most compelling example of blossoming during retirement occurs when discrimination or poverty prevents people from pursuing their passions and they lock into their *real* career identities after they retire:

Growing up African American during the 1940s, medical school was a distant dream. Now that I'm retired from the post office, I volunteer at the local hospital. I wear a white coat. People call me Doc. After 50 years—I've finally found my ideal career!

As these examples show, many contemporary retirees see retirement as the opposite of retiring from life. These years are for vigorously connecting to the world (Ekerdt, 1986). However, there is a different cultural model of retirement. In the Hindu perspective, later life is a time to disengage from worldly concerns. Ideally, people become wandering ascetics, renouncing their connections to loved ones and earthly pleasures in preparation for death (Savishinsky, 2004). Although this goal of disengagement is rarely followed in practice (after all, our need to be closely attached is a basic human drive!), let's not assume that our "do not go gently into the sunset," keep-active retirement ideal applies around the world.

Undoing the Retirement Choice

And let's not assume that the retirement decision is permanent, either. In a national survey, one-half of all U.S. workers said they had returned to the workforce for at least some time after formally leaving work (McNamara & Williamson, 2004). Unfortunately, retirees do not typically get lured back to work by the prospect of exciting, well-paying new jobs. The main reason they return, as you saw with Sadie, is that they need the income to live (Rix, 2002).

Consider Joe Janson, an engineer who took early retirement from an $83,000-a-year job. After the company eliminated his health insurance, Joe, with two teenage children and a wife to support, was forced to look for new work. "If I have to," he said, "I will drive a school bus" (Porter & Walsh, 2005, p. 14). Another distraught early retiree, Jon Lemoine, said, "You'd be surprised at who won't hire you because of your age." After being laid off as a manager at AT&T in his early fifties, Jon got a job as a maintenance worker at a Sam's Club. Still unable to make ends meet, he finally took a full-time position as a security guard (Porter & Walsh, 2005, p. A-l). Do you know someone who retired in his fifties or sixties, finding himself reluctantly needing to work to make ends meet?

Elderhostel An education-travel program that offers people age 55 and older special learning experiences at universities and other locations across the United States and around the world.

| FOCUS ON A TOPIC: | SOCIAL POLICY RETIREMENT ISSUES |

Now let's summarize these section messages by focusing on some critical social issues with regard to the retirement years.

- **The old-old and retirees who rely just on Social Security are at high risk of being poor.** For the legions of low-wage workers without pensions, retirement spells financial trouble. Low-income people are faced with a double whammy: They probably need post-retirement jobs the most and also are least likely to *actually* find this work. Then there is the alarming situation many middle-class people, such as Sadie, face as they travel into their old-old years. Imagine spending your adult life comfortably well off but living your final days in dire poverty. How can we prevent "getting poorer" from being the main theme of the old-old years? (See Vartanian & McNamara, 2002.)

- **Older workers are an at-risk group.** Our discussion shows that—from being offered pension incentives to retire early, to not being able to find anything but a low-wage job after you are forced out—implicit age discrimination at work is alive and well (Palmore, 1990a; Rosen & Jerdee, 1995; Rix, 2002). Still, there may be a silver lining. Until now, employers have had their pick of a huge pool of workers. When the massive baby-boom cohort retires, this inexhaustible labor supply will dry up. Many baby boomers say they want to work during retirement (Rix, 2002). Will employers respond by changing their negative attitudes toward older employees?

- **Retirement is an at-risk life stage.** These negative attitudes may need to be revised in response to simple demographic pressures: the burden we *all* face in supporting the massive army that is marching into later life. In 1950, there were about 16 workers for every U.S. retiree. In 2010, when the leading edge of the baby boomers will have reached their sixties, the **old-age dependency ratio,** or the proportion of working adults to retirees, will swell to roughly three to one. Social Security was never intended to finance an entire stage of life. It was instituted when life expectancy was far lower, as a cushion when physical problems made it impossible for people to work. The U.S. government has already raised the age of eligibility for full Social Security benefits to 67. Will retirement return to its original meaning as a support for old-age physical incapacity as the twenty-first century unfolds?

old-age dependency ratio
The fraction of people over age 60 to younger working-age adults (ages 15 to 59). This ratio is expected to rise dramatically as the baby boomers retire.

Widowhood

While many of us may look forward to retirement with joy, that emotion does not apply to widowhood. In a classic study of life stress, researchers ranked the death of a spouse as life's most traumatic change (Holmes & Rahe, 1967). Today many younger adults will have some built-in lifestyle preparation for coping with this trauma because they have lived alone for some time after being divorced. However, as with Sadie and Saul, most people who are currently in their seventies and eighties got married in their early twenties and then stayed married for life.

Imagine losing your life partner after 50 or 60 years. You are unmoored and adrift, cut off from your main attachment figure. Tasks that may have been totally foreign, such as understanding the finances or fixing the faucet, fall on you alone. You must remake an identity whose central focus has been "married person" since your emerging-adult years. British psychiatrist Colin Parkes (1987) beautifully described how the world tilts: "Even when words remain the same, their meaning changes. The family is no longer the same as it was. Neither is home or a marriage" (p. 93).

How do people mourn this life loss and adapt over time to losing a partner? How do widows and widowers cope, and what specific strategies seem to help?

This photo of an Iraqi woman whose husband has just been killed in a car-bomb explosion in Baghdad offers vivid insights into the horrors of the first moments of widowhood. In the next few months, she may replay that terrible day in her mind and keep asking herself, "Why didn't I insist that he stay home that morning?" Or, she might keep thinking, "If only he had passed that point just an hour or two earlier, he might still be alive."

Wathiq Khuzaie / Getty Images

The Experience of Mourning

During the early days and months after a loved one dies, people are often obsessed with the events surrounding the final event (Lindemann, 1944; Parkes, 1972): Especially if the death was relatively sudden, husbands and wives often report repeatedly going over a spouse's final days or hours. They may feel the impulse to search for their beloved, even though they know intellectually that they are being irrational. Notice that these responses have uncanny similarities to those of a toddler who frantically searches for a caregiver when she leaves the room. With widowhood—as some of the poignant comments of the women I gathered in the Experiencing the Lifespan box show—John Bowlby's clear-cut attachment response reemerges at full force.

EXPERIENCING THE LIFESPAN: VISITING A WIDOWED PERSON'S SUPPORT GROUP

What is it like to lose your mate? What are some of the hardest things to endure in the first year after a spouse dies? Here are the responses I got when I visited a local support group for widowed people and asked the women in the room these kinds of questions:

"I've noticed that even when I'm in a crowd, I feel lonely."

"I find the weekends and evenings hard, especially now that it gets dark so early."

"Sundays are my worst. You sit in church by yourself. People avoid you when you are a widow."

"I think the hardest thing is when you had a handyman and then you lose your handyman. You would be amazed at how much fixing there is that you didn't know about. My hardest jobs were George's jobs. For instance, every time I have a car problem I break down and cry."

"I was married to a handyman and a cook. He spoiled me rotten. You don't realize it until they are gone."

"For me, it's the incessant doctors' bills. I got one yesterday. It's that continual painful reminder of the death."

"And you get all this stuff from Medicare, from Social Security. This year will be the last I file with him."

"You just don't know what to do. I didn't know anything, didn't know how much money we had . . . didn't know about the insurance. . . . My friends would help me out but, you know, it's funny—you don't ask."

"You have friends, but you can't really talk to them. You don't bring him up, and neither does anyone else."

"The thing that upsets me is that I'm scared that no one but me will remember that he was alive."

In traditional cultures, widows are supposed to be in mourning for the rest of their lives (Hsu and others, 2004; Klass & Goss, 2003). In individualistic Western societies, we expect widowed people to "recover" in the sense of remaking a satisfying new life (Rando, 1992–1993; Worden, 1982). People still care deeply about their spouse. The working model of a partner remains. However, this mental image is incorporated into the survivor's evolving identity as that person continues to travel through life (Silverman & Klass, 1996).

As they struggle to reconstruct their lives, people often say that they have the sense their spouse is still "really" there (Field and others, 1999; Klass & Walter, 2001). Experts believe that this palpable sense of connection, which they refer to as **continuing bonds,** provides mourners with a sense of self-efficacy and mutes the feelings of grief. One widowed friend described this sense of solace when she wrote: "I am never lonely. . . . I feel that my husband has expanded into the world of total freedom and contracted into my heart and inner self" (see Klass & Walter, 2001).

Does conjuring up the image of the lost loved one *really* help reduce the pain? To shed light on this interesting question, developmentalists decided to use the *experience-sampling technique.* They gave beepers to newly widowed people and to a group whose spouses had died roughly two years earlier. Then they asked their volunteers to describe what they were thinking and feeling each time the signal went off (Field & Friedrichs, 2004). Not unexpectedly, the newly bereaved were thinking about their partners very often. But instead of being a source of comfort, these mental images were likely to provoke intense pain. In contrast, two years after the loss, thoughts of one's husband or wife, when they did occur, were associated with both pleasant and negative moods.

This makes sense. When a wound is very fresh (or when widowed people are in the midst of the clear-cut attachment phase of mourning), they cannot use their memories of their loved one in a positive way. As they move into the working-model phase of mourning (that is, when they are actively remaking their lives), their feelings become less raw and more bittersweet. You still get sad when you think of your life love, but you also feel enormously blessed for the years you had together.

Perhaps, however, the newly bereaved can turn to another place for comfort: religion. Do people really become more religious after a spouse (or loved one) dies, as many of us believe? Does religion help widows and widowers cope? To answer these questions—and trace how people adjust to their loss over time—

continuing bonds A widow's or widower's ongoing sense of the deceased spouse's presence "in spirit."

Now that she is in the working-model phase of widowhood, this woman can take tremendous pleasure in this family reunion party. But while enjoying a dance with her grandson, she might get sad as she thinks, "Wouldn't my husband be thrilled to be here?" Maybe she even believes that her husband is there "in spirit," looking down on everyone on this joyous day.

Chuck Savage / Corbis

developmentalists conducted an ambitious longitudinal study. They evaluated the personalities of more than 1,000 married couples, then followed the small subset who became widowed over the next two years (Brown & others, 2004).

The researchers found that during the first six months after the death, people did attend religious services more frequently and felt more spiritually connected to God. However, this rise in religiosity (or religious signs) was temporary. It declined to the pre-bereavement level at 24 months. Did turning to religion mute the pain? The answer here was also a qualified yes. Widowed people who felt more spiritually connected to God did grieve less intensely, although they were no less depressed than were those who did not turn for comfort to their faith in a higher being.

Now that we understand what normally happens and have explored how people use religion and draw on the sense that their spouse is physically present to help them construct a new life, let's examine who is most at risk for having special trouble moving on.

Having Trouble Moving On

It's been two years and I still can't get Teresa out of my mind. The children live miles away. I never see my old buddies from the plant . . . and after all, being men, we never were that close. How do you go on when everything you had is completely lost?

Intuitively, we might expect women to cope better with the death of a spouse than men. Women are more emotionally embedded in other relationships. They can use their loving attachments with their children and grandchildren—and, as you saw in the chapter-opening vignette, draw comfort from their widowed friends. Just as having a friend at age 5 helps ease the trauma of the first day at school, this nurturing network of friends can reach out at age 75 and smooth the passage into the widowed state.

Although the research is mixed, our intuition seems accurate to a point (Belsky, 1999; Rubinstein, 1986). Men are more likely to become disabled after their spouse dies (van den Brink and others, 2004). They are at higher risk of dying after being widowed, unless they find a new mate (Belsky, 2001). Because their remarriage options are limited, the most vulnerable group is old-old widowed men. Imagine losing your life mate at 80 or 85, and you will understand why, for elderly men living alone, suicide is a major concern (Belsky, 2001).

However, rather than making generalizations based on gender and age in predicting who has problems coping, we need to look at a variety of forces (Bonanno & Kaltman, 1999). How emotionally resilient is the widowed person? Does that individual have other attachments or a life passion to cushion the blow? (See Carr, 2004.) We also need to look at the person's *married* attachment style. People who are securely attached to their partner tend to have other secure attachments in the wider world. Men *and* women who are totally dependent on their spouse have special trouble constructing a new identity when their mate dies (Bonanno and others, 2002; Field, Gal-Oz, & Bonanno, 2003).

Notice the parallel to the different types of attachment discussed in Chapters 4 and 10. When we have an insecure attachment, we cannot use our memories of the other person as a base for exploration. So, we tend to stagnate, mired in eternal grief.

Finally, the experience of widowhood is shaped by the cultural context. Because, as we know, collectivist societies prize the bond to the wider family over the one-to-one relationship with a partner, in these cultures being widowed may not be as wrenching a loss as in the West (Sugisawa and others, 2002). In some African societies where males have total power, widowhood can have nightmarish aspects that go well beyond losing a spouse.

Among the Igbo of West Africa, for instance, new widows must "prove" that they did not kill their spouse by sleeping with their husband's corpse. Because property rights revert to the paternal side of the family, after the man's death his relatives feel perfectly free take the newly bereaved woman's possessions and force her off her land (Cattell, 2003; Sossou, 2002). Given this totally male-dominated tilt to their society, it

[FAQ: Why do older men commit suicide at such high rates?]

This young Iraqi man in Fallujah mourning the death of his wife will have the (unfortunate) benefit of knowing many other people in a similar situation as he struggles to cope with this off-time tragedy. How he ultimately adjusts to losing his spouse, however, will depend on his personality, his support network, and whether he is able to reconnect in love with his family and perhaps find another life mate.

Scott Nelson / Getty Images

is no wonder that an African widow in her sixties made this comment when asked about her single state: "I've had so much of this bossing by men. I have my house, my garden. Why should I have a man take my money and spend it on drink and other women? I am the boss now" (quoted in Cattell, 2003, p. 59).

Widowed People Are Resilient!

So far I have highlighted the trauma of widowhood, except for this last ecstatic quote. However, we may be making a serious error in overemphasizing the pain (Bonanno, 2004). Most people—male or female—who lose a spouse cope very well (Bonanno and others, 2002). Support groups for widowed people, such as the one mentioned in the Experiencing the Lifespan box on page 417, are counterproductive unless a person is having considerable trouble adjusting to the death (Caserta & Lund, 1993).

The most interesting evidence that widowhood has mixed effects comes from the study mentioned earlier, in which researchers evaluated the personalities of married couples and then traced what happened after their spouses died. Wives, they discovered, with the lowest self-esteem during their marriage got *more* self-confident after their husbands died (Carr, 2004). Were these particular husbands infantilizing these wives or putting them down during their married lives? The answer is probably no. Women, such as Sadie, who have lived in a marriage for their whole adult lives may not realize how well they can cope on their own. When you discover that yes, you *can* prepare the tax return or fix the faucet, and that you do not fall apart when finding yourself suddenly single after 50 or 60 years, you have learned an important lesson about who you are. As in the Chinese proverb, within the worst crisis lies an opportunity (or, in Chapter 12's terminology, a potential redemption sequence). Life's traumas, handled successfully, can promote emotional growth.

Furthermore, this study has a lesson for the rest of us. Widows who reported having the most help from friends and family did not feel better. They actually had lower self-worth (Carr, 2004). So perhaps we need to apply Chapter 5's childhood principles of scaffolding to widowhood: Give people the support they need, but don't overprotect them. Don't rob widows or widowers of the chance to learn self-efficacy and connect with their confident new single selves. (Table 13.2 summarizes these section messages by offering guidelines to thriving during retirement and surviving widowhood.)

[FAQ: How can you help someone suffering from grief?]

TABLE 13.2: **Advice for Thriving During Retirement and Surviving Widowhood: A Summary Table**

Retirement

1. Understand that it may take you some time to find your retirement identity. Be aware that after a joyous beginning, you may feel let down as the first-year anniversary approaches.

2. Use this time to further your passions. Draw on your previous interests for clues as to how to engineer a fulfilling retirement life. Look into the interesting new volunteer opportunities and educational programs that are available to retirees.

3. Be prepared for unpleasant economic surprises. You may need to go back to work to make ends meet, and if you are like most people, your economic status will worsen the longer you live. Plan ahead for this contingency by conserving your retirement nest egg.

Widowhood

1. Develop a network of attachments and fulfilling identities outside of your marriage before being widowed, to cushion the loss of your life love.

2. You might want to draw on your faith in God, particularly in the first months, and use the feeling that your spouse is with you as you struggle to remake a competent new life.

3. Graciously accept emotional support from your friends and family—but don't let them take over your life.

4. Try to see this tragedy as a challenge, an opportunity for understanding that you can function on your own. You may find that you are more resilient than you ever thought.

Final Thoughts

As we turn now to explore physical aging, we continue to highlight the same themes: Old-age impairments are not necessarily the tragedy we expect when we look from an outsider's view. People often confront the challenges of physical aging in a proactive, efficacious way. Don't infantilize frail older people. Be wary of doing either too little or too much for them. Most important, understand that the wider world is vitally important in determining how well people function physically in their older years. ■

TYING IT ALL TOGETHER

1. Joe is looking forward to retiring from his job as a public school teacher and living happily ever after without working. Although Joe is likely to be able to draw on _____, the threat looming on the horizon is _____.

   a. both Social Security and a pension; the mushrooming old-age dependency ratio
   b. a huge amount of money from Social Security; a dramatic increase in younger workers
   c. a pension but no Social Security; the mushrooming old-age dependency ratio
   d. mainly his personal savings; age discrimination

2. Given current conditions, at roughly what age will Joe be most likely to retire: his mid-fifties, his early sixties, 65, or his seventies?

3. Which of the following retirement experiences is *not* typical? (Based on this chapter, pick out the most unusual pattern.)

   a. Alice couldn't wait to retire, but now she hates retirement and is desperate to get back to work.
   b. Barry wanted to retire, and he has been enjoying traveling, vacationing, and visiting his children and grandchildren.
   c. Denise took some time to find her retirement niche but finally settled into a satisfying routine.
   d. Joe retired but went back to work part time because he needed the money.

4. Many social policy experts believe that we will soon need to raise the age of eligibility for getting full Social Security benefits to 70. Discuss the pros and cons of this idea.

5. Isabel's husband, Frank, just died, and her friends are especially worried because during her 52-year marriage Isabel was very dependent on Frank for practical things like handling the finances and doing home repairs. Should Isabel's friends (a) immediately step in to take over these jobs or (b) offer Isabel a good deal of emotional support but be careful to let her try to learn these tasks on her own?

6. An elderly relative of yours has just been widowed. List the signals mentioned in the chapter that might set off alarm bells that this person is at risk for having a rocky time.

Answers to the Tying It All Together questions can be found in the answers section of the book.

SUMMARY

Setting the Context: Scanning the New Older World

The **median age** of the population is rising, **late-life life expectancy** is expanding, and the baby boomers are moving into later life; all these forces are converging to make the twenty-first century the "age of the old." The most important fact to know about the elderly population is that there is a dramatic difference between being **young-old** and being **old-old.**

The Evolving Self

Everyone believes that as people get older, memory declines. Elderly people do perform less well than the young on most memory tasks. Memory challenges involving speedy responses and **divided attention tasks** produce the most severe deficits, and many losses in challenging tasks have their onset at a surprisingly young age.

Using the information-processing perspective, researchers find that as people age, working memory-bin capacity declines, either because people cannot fit as much information into this system and move it into permanent memory (because of an overall age-related slowing of their mental processes) or because of problems screening out task-irrelevant thoughts. Using the **memory-systems perspective,** studies reveal few age-related losses in **semantic memory** or **procedural memory** but dramatic declines in **episodic memory.** To improve memory in old age (or at any age), use selective optimization with compensation, employ **mnemonic techniques,** and foster memory self-efficacy.

Socioemotional selectivity theory suggests that in old age (or at any age), when people see their future as limited, they focus on maximizing the quality of their current life, prefer to be with their closest attachment figures, and have the potential to be happier than at any other life stage. The elderly do tend to be calmer than younger people and to focus more on pleasant events. However, when older people don't have government-funded old-age financial support and when they are socially isolated, later life is a depressing life stage. Affluent young-old people are indeed likely to be happy. During advanced old age, when physical limitations make enjoying the present difficult, rates of depression rise.

Later-Life Transitions

Government programs offering older people financial support have made retirement a full stage of life in much of the developed world. Germany provides such generous old-age funding that the average retiree in that nation actually gets more financially comfortable over the years. In Hong Kong, where the government does not offer old-age assistance, people approach retirement full of anxiety. In the United States, **Social Security** only provides a meager income to retirees.

Private pensions, the second source of retirement income, vary in availability and adequacy. Low-income workers, because they often rely totally on Social Security, are likely to be low-income retirees. Middle-class people in their sixties are vulnerable to falling into poverty as they travel into their old-old years and come to depend mainly on Social Security to live.

Most people retire because they can afford to live without working, but at the lower ends of the economic spectrum, workers are more likely to retire for health reasons. Pension enticements often lure upper-income workers to retire at a younger-than-normal age. Although overt **age discrimination** is illegal, employers use pension incentives, plus the threat of being downsized (let go from a job), to induce late-middle-aged employees to retire.

People who work beyond the traditional retirement age are often healthy and well-educated, and hate the idea of leaving work.

Once people do retire, they are generally happy, although they may need some time to develop their retirement identities. People use this time to be generative, to further their education (through programs such as **Elderhostel**), and to keep active—often following similar passions as they did during their younger years. However, many retirees must return to work today, because they need the money to make ends meet. The major social issues with regard to retirement include an alarming descent into poverty, particularly during the old-old years, workforce discrimination against older employees, and changes in the **old-age dependency ratio** that may soon make it impossible to finance retirement as an extended life stage.

Widowhood qualifies as the number-one life stress, especially for the cohort of old-old people who have lived their whole adult lives in the married state. The early symptoms of bereavement have much in common with the separation response of an infant whose caregiver leaves the room. By about the second year after being widowed, people typically begin to recover, in the sense of beginning to construct a satisfying new life. **Continuing bonds,** having a sense of the deceased partner's presence, can ultimately offer people comfort, although thoughts of one's spouse are typically painful during the first months after the death. Religion, however, can help to ease the trauma of bereavement.

Because they have a richer web of close attachments, women often cope better with widowhood than men. The most at-risk group is old-old men. Having had a secure attachment to one's spouse and good options for constructing a new life predict how well people handle this trauma. Cultural forces shape the experience of widowhood, too. Finally, we need to beware of seeing widowhood as an *impossible* trauma. Don't overprotect widowed people. Let them connect with their "efficacious" self.

▮ KEY TERMS

median age, p. 398

late-life life expectancy, p. 399

young-old, p. 399

old-old, p. 399

divided-attention task, p. 401

memory-systems perspective, p. 403

procedural memory, p. 403

semantic memory, p. 403

episodic memory, p. 403

mnemonic technique, p. 405

socioemotional selectivity theory, p. 406

Social Security, p. 412

private pensions, p. 412

age discrimination, p. 413

Elderhostel, p. 414

old-age dependency ratio, p. 416

continuing bonds, p. 417

▮ RECOMMENDED RESOURCES

WEB SITE

AARP (American Association of Retired Persons); www.aarp.org

This premier organization for older Americans provides a clearinghouse for resources relating to coping with retirement and widowhood. The AARP is also a good general source for every aging-related topic, from caregiving grandparents to nursing home care.

BOOKS

Kinsella, K., and Velkoff, V. A. (2001). *An aging world: 2001* (U.S. Census Bureau Series P95/01-1). Washington, D.C.: U.S. Bureau of the Census.

This monograph, which is available on-line (www.census.gov/prod/2001pubs/P95-01-1.pdf), is a treasure trove of information about the elderly worldwide. It includes data on population aging, family life, retirement, pensions, and much more.

Myerhoff, B. (1977). *Number our days.* New York: Simon & Schuster.

This beautiful, uplifting, highly recommended anthropological study explores the lives of old-old, often impoverished immigrant people who attended a Jewish senior citizens center during the 1970s in California. It shows that the human spirit endures (and that elderly human beings remain full human beings, with all their foibles) until the very end of life.

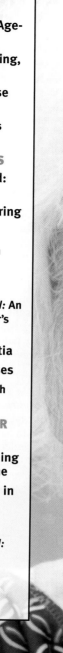

CHAPTER 14

What is the enemy Sadie is battling? How does physical aging turn into disease, disability, and sometimes the need for a nursing home? What is causing Sadie's vision problems, and how frequently does a fall result in admission into long-term care? This chapter offers answers to these questions and many more.

In the following pages we focus on the kinds of impairments that some gerontologists (for example, Rowe & Kahn, 1998) label as signs of "unsuccessful aging," describing what *can* go seriously physically wrong during the old-old years. I believe that equating "successful aging" with walking miles at age 90 is equally misguided and

wrong. Successful aging means drawing on Carstensen's *socioemotional selectivity theory* and Baltes's principles of *selective optimization with compensation* to live fully no matter how our body behaves. Successful aging is epitomized by my 85-year-old colleague with serious kidney failure, who is following his goal of "dying at the blackboard" as

The Physical Challenges of Old Age

At age 76, Sadie was vigorous and fit. She walked a mile each day and worked full time at the bookstore. She was the most beloved employee they had. However, because of her night vision problems, Sadie no longer drove after dusk. Unfortunately, her medical checkups showed ominous signs. Sadie's atherosclerosis was progressing. The bone loss that had first shown up on the scan in her fifties was getting much worse. By age 79, Sadie felt uncomfortable driving down Main Street during rush hour. When she realized it was impossible to see the titles of some paperback books, Sadie knew it was time to quit her job.

Two years later, at age 81, Sadie was having trouble cooking and cleaning. She began to worry: "What will happen when I can't take care of myself?" Lillian, her close friend, now 90 and still as spry and vigorous as a 60-year-old, suggested that Sadie move in with her. Sadie politely said no. She was determined to actively plan for her future, and that future did not involve burdening loved ones with her care. Lillian vowed, "I'd rather be in the cemetery than in an old person's home!" Sadie, knowing those prejudices were from a different generation, disagreed. It was time to prepare for her future and check out the new advances in long-term care. But after going on-line to scan the assisted-living facilities in her area, Sadie almost had a heart attack. The average rates at some facilities ($4,000 a month) were higher than at a four-star hotel! Eventually she located a nursing home at the forefront of geriatric care. The Stein Center was only 50 miles away and, best of all, had a rabbi on staff and served kosher meals. Sadie immediately put her name on the waiting list—and none too soon. Three years later she fell, breaking her hip, and could no longer live at home.

Today, Sadie uses a walker. She needs help getting dressed and using the toilet. However, when I visited her, she was surprisingly upbeat. True, Sadie admits that life at 87 can be difficult—not simply because of a person's physical state. The real problem is losing your life partner after 60 wonderful years. Still, the facility is wonderful. She loves the activities and many of her helpers. Old ladies can hang on to their passions, too. The discussion group, using books on tape, that Sadie formed at the center just won a national prize!

he shuffles by, using his walker, to class. Bob Womack, an award-winning teacher, has been inspiring students and shaking up their prejudices for the past 50 years. This is Bob's finest teaching hour.

Aging successfully depends on having Bob's grit and generative mission. But successful aging also depends on the wider world: that is, whether a society offers older people the support they need for functioning at their best. The real issue in later life is not so much being ill, but living as fully as possible in the face of chronic disease. The way people live and function in late life depends on nature (our biological capacities and enduring personality) combined with nurture—having the right person–environment fit.

How can you take action to engineer the right person–environment fit for older loved ones? How well is our nation doing at providing the best possible body–environment fit to older adults? Let's begin our search for answers by offering an overview of physical aging itself.

This 70-year-old Japanese mountaineer showing off a certificate for being the oldest man to climb Mount Everest seems to have little in common with a bent-over woman of the same age who can barely get down the street. However, their aging process is identical. Although aging progresses at different rates, normal aging changes are predictable, are biologically programmed into being human, and advance in tandem with the advancing years.

[FAQ: What are the normal signs of aging?]

normal aging changes The universal, often progressive signs of physical deterioration intrinsic to the aging process.

chronic disease Any long-term illness that requires ongoing management. Most chronic diseases are age-related and are the endpoint of normal aging changes.

Tracing Physical Aging

Sadie has atherosclerosis, or fatty deposits on her artery walls. She has trouble seeing at night and has been losing density in her bones. These are just a few of the many body signs called **normal aging changes.**

Normal aging changes vary in their time of onset. Some, such as Sadie's bone density loss and night vision troubles, begin in midlife. Others, such as atherosclerosis and the losses in mental processing speed that we described in Chapters 12 and 13, begin in our early thirties or even before. Normal aging changes, however, all have similar features: They are universal and genetically programmed into our DNA. They occur in every member of our species to some degree. They are progressive, growing more pronounced as the years pass.

Three Basic Principles of Age-Related Disease

Over time, as the following principles reveal, normal aging changes shade into disease, then disability, and finally—by a specific barrier age—universal death.

Chronic disease is often normal aging "at the extreme." Many physical losses, when they occur to a moderate degree, are called normal. When these changes become more extreme, they have a different label: **chronic disease** (Elias, Elias, & Elias, 1990). Sadie's bone density loss and atherosclerosis are a perfect case in point. These changes, as they progress, produce those familiar old-age illnesses—osteoporosis and heart disease.

The National Health Interview Survey (NHIS), an annual government poll of health conditions among the U.S. population, tells us other interesting illness facts. Notice from scanning Figure 14.1 that arthritis is the top-ranking chronic illness in later life (Centers for Disease Control [CDC], 2005). As we travel up the age ladder,

FIGURE 14.1: Prevalence of selected chronic health conditions among U.S. adults in middle and later life: As people travel through later life, the rates of many age-related chronic diseases rise dramatically. Although every chronic illness can impair the ability to fully enjoy life, many common chronic diseases don't actually result in death.

Source: National Center for Health Statistics (2005).

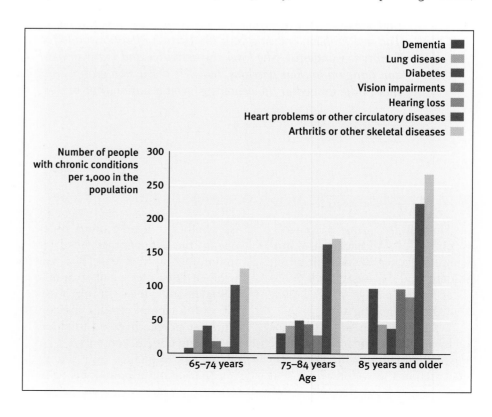

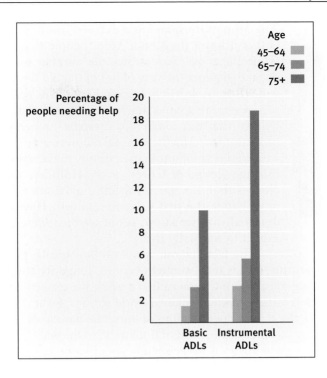

FIGURE 14.2: Percentages of people needing assistance with instrumental ADLs and basic ADLs in middle and later life: Although in middle age and even in the young-old years the fraction of people with ADLs is relatively small, the risk of having these kinds of problems increases dramatically over age 75.
Source: National Center for Health Statistics (2005).

our chance of having a variety of illnesses increases. Like arthritis, many age-related diseases are not fatal. They interfere with the ability to function in the world. So the outcome of chronic illness is not just death, but what gerontologists call **ADL (activities of daily living) problems**—difficulties handling life.

ADL impairments are a serious risk during the old-old years. ADL limitations come in two categories. **Instrumental ADL problems** refer to difficulties in performing tasks required for living independently, such as the troubles with cooking and cleaning that Sadie had before her fall. **Basic ADL problems** mean being incapable of performing fundamental self-care activities. When people have these severe kinds of losses—in the ability to stand, to get to the bathroom, or to feed themselves—they need full-time caregiving help.

Notice from Figure 14.2 that the risk of developing instrumental ADL impairments rises dramatically by the late seventies. It's fifty-fifty over age 85. Even more ominous, in the age group over 85, roughly one in four people living in their own homes has a basic ADL problem or elemental life difficulty, such as walking to the toilet or rising from a chair (Crimmins, Saito, & Reynolds, 1997). The fraction of very old people with these severe problems is actually higher, because, as you saw with Sadie, these are the kinds of difficulties that cause people to enter a nursing home.

The good news is that, like Lillian in the chapter-opening vignette, people *do* live into advanced old age virtually disability-free. The bad news is that during the old-old years, serious problems with physically coping become a definite risk.

ADL (activities of daily living) problems Difficulty in performing everyday tasks that are required for living independently. ADLs are classified as either basic or instrumental.

instrumental ADL problems Difficulties in performing everyday household tasks, such as cooking and cleaning.

basic ADL problems Difficulty in performing essential self-care activities, such as rising from a chair, eating, and getting to the toilet.

Stockbytea / Getty Images

Here you can see the real enemy in old age: It's ADL impairments, not specific illnesses. Moreover, if this 85-year-old man's difficulties walking independently to the toilet are permanent, he may be forced to enter a nursing home.

Jamal Saidi / Reuters / Corbis

Although our species-specific human maximum lifespan is about 105 years, there are always a handful of people who make it beyond that age barrier. Here is a 2004 photograph of a Lebanese woman who is still working and—at an amazing 126 years old—may be the oldest person on Earth.

[FAQ: What can I do now to prolong good health and promote successful aging?]

socioeconomic/health gap
The disparity, found in nations around the world, between the health of the rich and poor. At every step up on the socioeconomic ladder, people survive longer and enjoy better health.

The human lifespan has a defined limit. A final fact about the aging process is that it has a fixed end. More people than ever are surviving past age 100 (Kinsella, 2005). Since 1950, the number of centenarians has doubled every decade, making the very oldest of the old the fastest-growing age group worldwide (Robine & Michel, 2004; Kinsella & Velkoff, 2001). But no human being survives more than a few years beyond that ultimate age. Some biologists believe that our *maximum lifespan*—about age 105—is totally genetically programmed (Hayflick, 2004). Others argue that an accelerating pattern of wear and tear on our tissues simply makes death inevitable for everyone after this age (Judge & Corey, 2000; Holliday, 2004; Kirkwood, 1999). What is clear is that our species-specific maximum lifespan has not really changed much since the first humans evolved (Hayflick, 1987). What has increased drastically, as we know, is our *average life expectancy*, the time that we can expect to normally live.

The fact that our species is biologically programmed to die after roughly a century makes our twentieth-century longevity strides even more remarkable. You may recall from Chapter 1 that average life expectancies have zoomed into the upper seventies in many developed-world nations. So at this moment in history, babies born in the most affluent regions of the globe have a very good chance of surviving to striking distance of the limit of human life. Our odds of approaching this biological limit are even higher if we *personally* are affluent and if we are female. Just as they affect every aspect of development, socioeconomic status and gender dramatically shape our physical aging path.

Socioeconomic Status, Aging, and Disease

Throughout this book we have highlighted the impact socioeconomic status has on many aspects of life. Now it's time to explore the influence this basic marker has on the rate at which we age and die.

Specifically, within each nation, researchers have documented a **socioeconomic/health gap.** As we move up the social-status ladder rung by rung, we tend to live healthier and to survive for a longer time.

The fact that *each* step up in social status translates into a longer lifespan was first discovered in Great Britain more than 25 years ago. Researchers were surprised to find that they could predict a male British government worker's risk of dying of heart disease by looking at his ranking on the civil service hierarchy (Batty and oth-

Comparing this elegant, well-dressed, 100-year-old San Francisco man to this impoverished 60-year-old woman shuffling down a New York City street vividly brings home the basic message of this section: Statistically speaking, socioeconomic status is closely related to the rate at which we age and die.

Kevin Horan / Getty Images

Thomas Hoepker / Magnum Photos

ers, 2003; Hemingway and others, 2000; Reid and others, 1974). Since this classic study was published, social scientists have documented a similar socioeconomic/health gap in many countries (Adler & Ostrove, 1999). Whether researchers measure heart disease mortality, overall life expectancy, self-rated health, or ADL difficulties, from affluent Finland (Mackenbach & Bakker, 2003) to poverty-stricken Bangladesh (Kabir & others, 2003), people who are more affluent live longer and enjoy better health.

The relationship between income and illness becomes stronger during midlife, when normal aging changes are progressing to chronic diseases. You can get hints of what is happening by just looking around. Notice how by their late thirties and forties people start to show clear differences in their aging rates. Although there are many exceptions, notice also that people who appear to be poor often look physically older than their chronological age.

We can trace the origins of this accelerated aging process back to the childhood years. Recall from Chapter 5 that childhood obesity—a major risk factor for premature heart attacks and strokes—is more common at the lower end of the socioeconomic spectrum. When epidemiologists measured high blood pressure and cholesterol in one midwestern public high school, they found that these ominous predictors of cardiovascular disease showed up most often among students whose mothers did not have a high school degree (Goodman and others, 2005).

Still, the size of the socioeconomic/health gap varies from country to country. In nations with large income inequalities and those without universal government-funded medical care, low-income people tend to die at a *much younger* age (Adler & Ostrove, 1999; Wilkinson, 1996). This may partly explain why even though the United States spends more money on health care per person than any other nation, our country (with its millions of uninsured adults and large income gaps between the rich and the poor) has a lower average life expectancy (age 77.2) than much of the rest of the developed world (Kinsella & Velkoff, 2001).

Actually, if you are an adult living below the poverty line in the United States, your aging pathway has uncomfortable statistical similarities to that of a person living in an impoverished nation such as Bangladesh (Kabir and others, 2003). Expect an average life expectancy in the mid-sixties, about a decade younger than the national norm. Expect to develop ADL difficulties at a far younger than normal age. In fact, among U.S. adults living under the poverty line, "old-age" disabilities may really qualify as problems of midlife (Johnson & Crystal, 1997).

These alarming statistics, however, are correlations. They don't tell us about causes. Imagine developing heart disease or cancer in your forties. You could lose your job. You would have tremendous medical bills. You would probably find yourself sliding down the socioeconomic scale. In addition to poverty producing chronic illness, wouldn't being ill *cause* people to become poor? Keeping in mind that the poverty–illness relationship is complex and bidirectional (Adda, Chandola, & Marmot, 2003), let's now scan the forces linked to low socioeconomic status that might accelerate physical aging and smooth the path to chronic disease.

Low-income people are more likely to engage in high-risk behaviors such as smoking (Marmot, 1999; Pampel & Rogers, 2004; Pickering, 1999). Actually, the real social-class difference lies in *giving up* smoking. Among college graduates in their late fifties and early sixties, as a turn-of-the-century Health Interview Survey revealed, roughly 2 out of 5 people reported they used to smoke; only 1 in 9 still did. In contrast, far fewer non–high school graduates said they were former smokers. One in three were still smoking now, in late middle age.

Low-income adults are less likely to engage in health-promoting activities. They are less prone to regularly exercise (Grzywacz & Marks, 2001); they eat fewer fruits and vegetables than their upper-middle-class counterparts do. The next time you are at the supermarket, check out the prices of packaged foods such as chips or cookies compared to fresh carrots, strawberries, or plums. What food choices would you make if you had to worry about saving every dime?

Being able to afford these high-quality fresh fruits and vegetables is just one advantage that will help this 70-year-old upper middle class man live a longer, disease-free life than a low-income person of the same age. Another important force is having this loving wife to worry about and watch over his health.

Vicky Kasala / Getty Images

This brings up the devastating impact of life stress (Baum, Garofalo, & Yali, 1999; Taylor & Seeman, 1999). Low-income adults often work in non-flow-inducing, low-autonomy jobs. They are less likely to be embedded in supportive, nurturing relationships or to be married (Waite & Gallagher, 2000). Living in more dangerous, "toxic" neighborhoods also takes a toll (Altschuler, Somkin, & Adler, 2004). In the most crime-ridden U.S. neighborhoods, life expectancy is an alarming 15 years under the national norm (Olden, 1998).

Now combine this cascade of risk factors with problems related to getting medical care. If you are an immigrant or an impoverished adult, you may not feel comfortable visiting a health-care provider: "How can I talk to that upper-middle-class doctor who has no understanding of my life?" You may not be fully aware that a symptom such as your pain in the chest or lump in the breast needs to be looked at *right away*.

Then there are the economic hurdles relating to *getting* care. Although the *Medicaid* program covers health care for the lowest-income U.S. adults, because of its low reimbursement rates, few doctors accept Medicaid patients. Suppose the only health-care provider who accepts your insurance is many miles away or, worse yet, you are one of roughly 45 million Americans without *any* health insurance (Robert Wood Johnson Foundation, 2005). Would you risk getting fired from work to have a pain in your chest or lump in your breast checked out, especially if there was little you could do if you did learn the worst?

These life-shortening influences—from poor health habits to lack of knowledge about the symptoms of serious illnesses to inadequate access to medical care—are not specific to the United States. Consider this report from Russia:

> When the chest pains first gripped him that February day in 1998, Anatoly Iverianov was driving a tractor. . . . "I had a glass of vodka," he said. "I thought it would help." . . . It didn't. Mr. Iverianov was having a heart attack. Within six months he suffered another. Two years later he is impoverished, embittered, and sick. . . . His disability pension is a pittance, he is bored and useless at home. . . . Russia's elaborate system of state-run health care . . . is desperately under-financed. Hospitals are critically short of money. . . . Paying for care, on or under the table, is now the norm. Mr. Iverianov, the 45-year-old heart patient . . . is a caricature of what ails the country. He treats chest pain with vodka. He smokes. . . . His diet is "bread, potatoes and the occasional chicken." Mr. Iverianov's story does not have a happy ending . . . Just before 3 P.M. on November 21 he was brought once more to Central Clinic Hospital by ambulance. . . . Doctors suspected a heart attack. Three hours later, he died. Mr. Iverianov would have turned 46 this month.
>
> (Wines, 2000, p. A1)

Our immediate impulse is to blame people who don't take care of their health and then die of heart attacks at a young age. Why agonize over the fate of men such as Mr. Iverianov, who are digging their own graves by drinking and smoking so much? This example reminds us that the issue with regard to poor health habits and illness is more subtle and complex. Suppose you couldn't fulfill your provider role and felt out of control of your life? How hard would it be for you to resist those classic stress reducers, alcohol and cigarettes? Yes, we need to empower people to follow good health habits. But the common practice of blaming the victim—for heart disease, for cancer, or even for obesity (see Chapter 5)—when the reinforcers *all* converge to promote unhealthy living also seems shortsighted and unfair.

Interestingly, around the globe, researchers find that health relates more strongly to social-class standing for males than for females (Mustard & Etches, 2003). Are men especially vulnerable to acting out their frustrations at being low on the socioeconomic totem pole by engaging in the kinds of destructive health practices described above? Are women better insulated from the health effects of being poor because they are more embedded in caring relationships at every life stage? What *exactly* are the health and aging differences between women and men?

If these Spanish laborers get heart attacks at age 50 or 55, we might be tempted to blame their "poor health habits" for their disease. But if there were few jobs in your town, you were unable to support a family, and you had little to do during the day, wouldn't you spend your time smoking and drinking with your friends?

Bruno Barbey / Magnum Photos

Gender, Aging, and Disease

Women, as you learned in Chapter 2, are the more biologically resilient sex. Their second X chromosome gives them a survival advantage from the time they are in the womb. During the aging phase of life, the main reason for this superior survival rate can be summed up in one phrase: fewer early heart attacks. Illnesses of the cardiovascular system (the arteries and their pump, the heart) are the top-ranking killers for both women and men. Heart disease alone accounts for roughly 30 percent of deaths during adult life (American Heart Association, 2001). However, because estrogen helps to slow the natural process by which fat deposits clog the arteries, men are roughly twice as likely as women to die of a heart attack in midlife (American Heart Association, 2001).

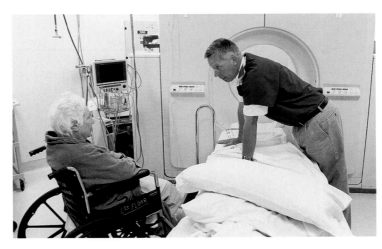

Years of experience with the medical system, being sensitive to her body's signals, understanding that "When I don't feel well, I need to go for tests such as this MRI"—all of these forces explain why this woman may be likely to have her cancer diagnosed at an early stage and so outlive the average man her age.

Their markedly increased biological susceptibility to early heart attacks means men tend to "die quicker and sooner." For women, the aging pattern is "surviving longer but being more frail" (Kinsella, 2000; Kinsella & Velkoff, 2001).

It makes sense that more disability is the price of traveling to the lifespan train's final stops. However, you might be interested to know that the phrase "living sicker" applies to women *throughout* adult life. Women visit doctors more frequently; they are more often confined to bed by disease. On a variety of health indicators, they rank as more ill (Gijsbers van Wijk, and others, 1992; Gold and others, 2002; McCullough & Laurenceau, 2004; Verbrugge, 1990).

To explain this interesting paradox—higher life expectancy in the face of poorer health—we can look to nature forces. During the first half of adulthood, only women experience the physical ailments related to pregnancy and menstruation. In their older years, females are more susceptible to arthritis as well as the famous bone condition osteoporosis—illnesses that produce ADL problems but do not directly result in death.

We need to look to nurture forces, too. In their role as the family health protectors, women are more sensitive to signs of disease in their loved ones and themselves. They visit physicians more readily and are more attuned to the need to take care of their health (Verbrugge, 1990; von Bothmer & Fridlund, 2005; Wilcox & Stefanick, 1999). To demonstrate this gender difference in sensitivity to illness, you might want to take the poll in Table 14.1 and compare your ratings with those of class members of the opposite sex. Does the fact that men are more resistant to staying in bed or seeing a doctor (another symptom of the asking-for-directions issue) partly explain why women outlive men by at least five years throughout the developed world? (See Kinsella & Velkoff, 2001.)

Whatever its causes, the female survival advantage that begins before birth endures to the very end of life. When faced with old-age health problems that doctors judge equally severe, women are almost twice as likely to outlive the opposite sex! (See Leveille and others, 2000.)

TABLE 14.1: Rate Your "Health Orientation"

	Never/ Unimportant				Always/ Very Important
Health Practices					
1. Interest in exercising	1	2	3	4	5
2. Interest in healthful eating	1	2	3	4	5
Sensitivity Toward Illness					
3. Interest in seeing a doctor regularly	1	2	3	4	5
4. Tendency to stay in bed when sick	1	2	3	4	5
5. Use of over-the-counter medications	1	2	3	4	5
Overall Interest in Health Issues					
6. Read magazine articles related to health	1	2	3	4	5
7. Watch TV programs and visit Web sites related to health	1	2	3	4	5
8. Think about my health	1	2	3	4	5

What do your answers tell you about your overall interest in health?

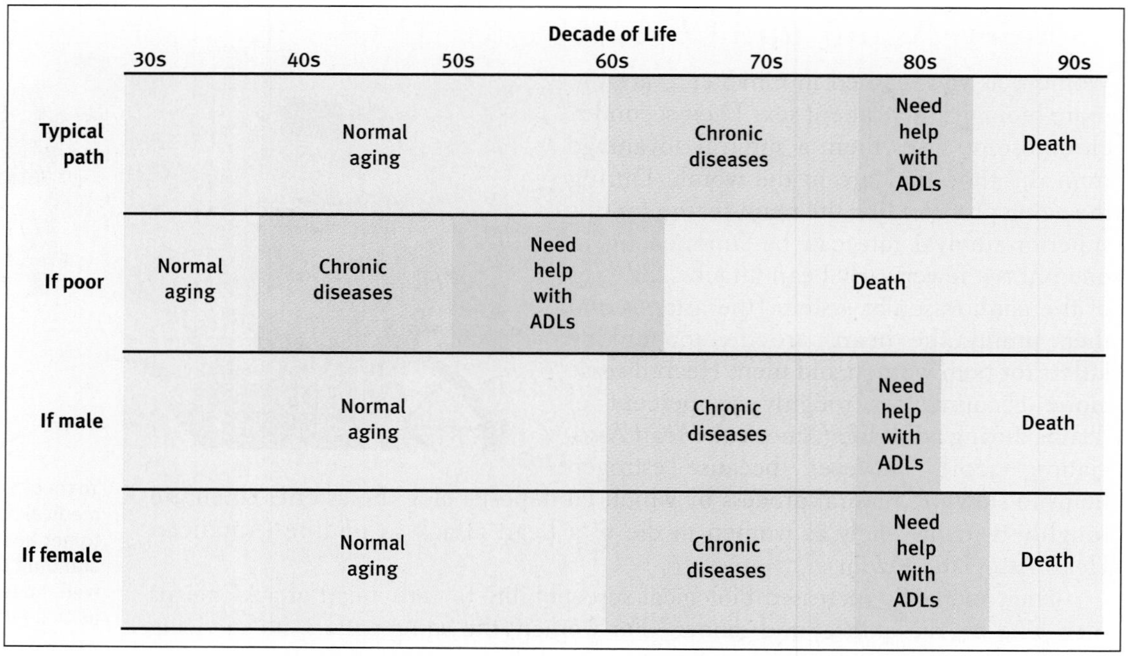

FIGURE 14.3:
The pathway from normal aging changes to death, and how that path varies by socio-economic status and gender

		Decade of Life					
	30s	40s	50s	60s	70s	80s	90s
Typical path		Normal aging			Chronic diseases	Need help with ADLs	Death
If poor	Normal aging	Chronic diseases		Need help with ADLs	Death		
If male		Normal aging			Chronic diseases	Need help with ADLs	Death
If female		Normal aging			Chronic diseases	Need help with ADLs	Death

INTERVENTIONS: Taking a Broader View of What Causes Disease

Our discussion clearly implies that to slow the progression from normal aging to illness to ADL problems, we should intervene at the first stage. Efforts such as high school smoking cessation programs will have health and longevity payoffs decades down the road. But encouraging young people to not try cigarettes or to get more exercise "for their future health" can fall flat when the future seems limitless and a person cannot imagine being "old."

The good news is that it's almost never too late. Even when people give up smoking and start exercising in their sixties, they improve their odds of living longer, disability-free (Kaplan, 1992; Stessman and others, 2002). But is putting out the message to follow good health practices really enough? What good is telling someone to exercise or watch her diet when she is working two jobs to make ends meet and cannot afford to go to the gym or buy healthful, high-cost foods? Why post public service advertisements telling people to "Visit the doctor to have your blood pressure checked" if many adults don't have health insurance and cannot afford medical care? Now that we have documented the socioeconomic/health gap, what can we do to reduce the *real* root cause of early chronic disease and premature death: inequalities in social class? (See Isaacs & Schroeder, 2004.)

Figure 14.3 provides a timeline illustrating the pathway from normal aging to disease to ADL problems to death, and shows how that pattern can statistically vary by our gender and social class. Now that we understand the overall process, let's spotlight two major causes of ADL impairments: sensory-motor declines and dementia.

 TYING IT ALL TOGETHER

1. In her late fifties, Edna's doctor found considerable bone erosion and atherosclerosis during a checkup. At 70, Edna's been diagnosed with osteoporosis and heart disease. What is going on?

    a. Edna suddenly developed these chronic diseases.
    b. Over the decades, Edna's normal aging changes progressed to chronic disease.

2. Marjorie has problems cooking and cleaning the house. Sara cannot dress herself or get out of bed without having help. Marjorie has _____ impairments and Sara has _____ impairments.

3. You are an epidemiologist studying health and longevity rates in three neighborhoods: a low-income area, a middle-class section of town, and Millionaires' Row. Based on the text, what should you find?

  a. People in Millionaires' Row live longest. Next come residents of the middle-class neighborhood. People living in the low-income section of town die at the youngest ages.
  b. People in the low-income section of town die at much younger ages, but there are no differences in health and longevity between the middle-class residents and those on Millionaires' Row.
  c. You won't find significant differences in life expectancy in these neighborhoods.

4. Nico and Hiromi are arguing about men's versus women's health. Nico says that women are healthier during adult life; Hiromi thinks that men are. Who is right?

  a. Nico is right: Women live longer and are healthier during adult life.
  b. Hiromi is right: Men live longer and are healthier during adult life.
  c. Nico and Hiromi are each partly right: Women tend to live longer, but men tend to be healthier during adult life.

Answers to the Tying It All Together questions can be found in the answers section of the book.

Sensory-Motor Changes

What happens to vision, hearing, and motor abilities as we grow old, and how can people take action to minimize sensory-motor declines?

Our Windows on the World: Vision

One way aging affects our sight becomes evident during midlife. By their late forties and fifties, people have trouble seeing close objects. The year I turned 50, this change struck like clockwork when I had to buy glasses to read.

Presbyopia, the term for age-related difficulties with seeing close objects, is one of those classic signs, like gray hair, showing that people are no longer young. When I squint to make out sentences, the fact of my age crosses my consciousness. I imagine my students have this same thought ("Dr. Belsky is middle-aged") when they see me struggle with this challenge in class.

Other age-related changes in vision progress more gradually. Older people have special trouble seeing in dim light. They are more bothered by *glare*, a direct beam of light hitting the eye. They cannot distinguish certain colors as clearly or see visual stimuli as distinctly as before.

What is it like to be in the early stages of this progression? It can be annoying to ask the server what the impossibly faint restaurant bill comes to or to fumble your way into a neighbor's seat at a darkened movie theater. For me, the most hair-raising experiences relate to driving at night. Once, a curve of the highway exit ramp loomed out of the dark and I was inches from death. But apart from some hesitation about night driving, especially on unfamiliar roads, these problems have virtually no effect on my life or the lives of most middle-aged adults.

Unfortunately, this may not be true a few decades from now. As Figure 14.4 illustrates, seeing in glare-filled environments such as a lighted medicine cabinet, or even making out the print on a white page, can be a real challenge during the old-old years.

presbyopia Age-related midlife difficulty with near vision, caused by the inability of the lens to bend.

FIGURE 14.4: How an 85-year-old might see the world: Age-related visual losses, such as sensitivity to glare, make the world look fuzzier at age 80 or 85. So, as these images show, everything from finding a bottle of pills in the medicine cabinet to reading the print in books such as this text can be a difficult task.

Nicole Villamora

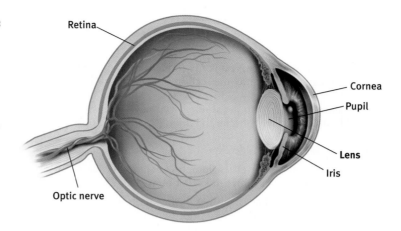

FIGURE 14.5: The human eye: Deterioration in many structures of the eye contributes to making older adults' vision poor. However, as discussed in the text, it is changes in the lens, shown here, that are responsible for presbyopia and also contribute greatly to impaired dark vision and sensitivity to glare—the classic signs of "aging vision."

lens A transparent, disk-shaped structure in the eye, which bends to allow us to see close objects.

[FAQ: How can I help my grandparent deal with poor vision?]

Because she is lucky enough to have one of the few chronic conditions that can easily be cured, a day or so after her cataract surgery, this woman may say, "It's a miracle. I can see far better than I have for years."

All of these signs of normal aging—presbyopia, problems seeing in the dark, and increased sensitivity to glare—are mainly caused by changes in a structure toward the front of the eye called the lens (see Figure 14.5). The disk-shaped **lens** allows us to see close objects by bending or curving outward. As people reach midlife, the transparent lens thickens and develops impurities, and so can no longer bend. This clouding and thickening not only produce presbyopia but also limit vision in dimly lit places where people need as much light as possible to see.

These changes also make older adults far more sensitive to glare. Notice how when sunlight hits a dirty window, the rays scatter and it becomes impossible for you to see out. Because they are looking at the world through a cloudier lens, older people see far less well when a beam of light shines in their eye. When this normal age-related lens clouding becomes so pronounced that the person's vision is seriously impaired, the outcome is that familiar late-life chronic condition—a *cataract.*

The good news is that cataracts are curable. The physician simply removes the defective lens and inserts a contact lens. The bad news is that the other three top-ranking old-age vision conditions—macular degeneration (deterioration of the receptors promoting central vision), glaucoma (a buildup of pressure that can damage the visual receptors), and diabetic retinopathy (a leakage from the blood vessels of the retina into the body of the eye)—do tend to permanently impair sight.

INTERVENTIONS: Clarifying Sight

To lessen the impact of the normal vision losses basic to getting old, the key is to modify the wider world. Older people should make sure their homes are well lit but avoid overhead light fixtures, especially fluorescent bulbs shining down directly on a bare floor, as these produce glare. Appliances should be designed with nonreflective materials and adjustable lighting. Putting enlarged letters and numbers on appliances will make items such as the stove and computer keyboard easier to use (Pirkl, 1995).

If the person's problems have progressed to the chronic disease stage, it's important to explore the medical interventions that are continually being developed. Then, when the impairments are really permanent and seriously limit sight, the best strategy is to adopt Paul Baltes's *compensation* mode, relying on external aids to preserve one's passions. Avid readers such as Sadie, gerontologists find, don't reduce their reading when they become visually impaired (Ryan and others, 2003). They experiment with low-vision aids or books on tape. Or, as the principles of *socioemotional selectivity theory* suggest, they decide to center their priorities on what is really important in life (Brennan & Cardinali, 2000). Sometimes, as the following comments show, people make lemonade when life hands them lemons, or, in developmental science terms, find *redemption sequences* in their losses:

> *I bought large-print books, then used magnifiers. To me, trying books on tape meant giving up and admitting my vision was terribly poor; but since my local librarian convinced me to take home a tape, I've become addicted. It's like a gifted parent is reading to you . . .*

and now I can tune in to the world of literature, even while doing the housework or relaxing in the tub.

My vision problems have an unexpected bonus. They bring out the best in strangers (I always get seats on the bus). I'm being pampered by my family like never before.

Interestingly, researchers find that people tend to cope better when vision impairments strike in old age rather than during midlife, at more of an "off-time" age (Boerner, 2004). From getting a heart attack in the forties to developing cancer at a younger-than-average age, any late-life illness that occurs before our *social clock* would predict causes special pain.

Our Bridge to Others: Hearing

Although we tend to worry most about losing our sight in old age, our fears may be a bit misplaced. Hearing impairments actually can present more barriers to living fully in later life. The reason is that while poor vision limits our contact with the physical world, hearing losses prevent us from understanding language, our bridge to other minds. So when we lose the ability to hear, we are deprived of fully entering the human world.

Unfortunately, hearing problems are very common in later life. They may affect roughly one in three people over age 70. The statistics are particularly alarming for men. Around the world, males are several times more likely than women to develop hearing losses in midlife (Belsky, 1999).

The main reason is that hearing impairments have a clear environmental cause: exposure to noise. Men are more likely to be construction workers; they operate heavy machinery, ride motorcycles, and go to NASCAR races. These high-noise environments set people up to have hearing handicaps at an unusually young age. Government regulations mandate hearing protection devices for workers in noisy occupations—as you may have noticed when you last glanced at the ground crew before your plane took off. But people must take responsibility for protecting their hearing on their own. Ominously, rates of age-associated hearing problems have doubled since the 1970s (Strawbridge and others, 2000). From being surrounded by the jangle of horns when we are stalled in traffic to the continual chatter of cell phones, the reason is that today we have noisier daily lives.

Presbycusis—the characteristic age-related hearing loss—is caused by the atrophy or loss of the hearing receptors, located in the inner ear (see Figure 14.6 on the next page). So this condition is permanent. The receptors encoding our perception of high-pitched tones are most vulnerable. This means older people have special difficulties hearing tones that are of higher pitch. (For instance, if musicians are playing a guitar and a drum *equally* loudly, to an older person the guitarist's melody will sound more faint.)

Put yourself in the place of someone with presbycusis. Because of your problem hearing higher-pitched sounds, listening to conversations feels a bit like hearing a radio that is filled with static. Because your impairment has been progressing gradually, you may not be sure you *have* a problem, thinking, "Other people are talking too softly." If you are like most older adults, unless family members pressure you, you probably don't think of getting a professional checkup, and you certainly don't want to buy a hearing aid (Duijvestijn and others, 2003; Hietanen and others, 2004; Karlsson & Rosenhall, 1998; Meister & von Wedel, 2003). Hearing aids are hard to manage and they do not work all that well—or so you have been told (Stephens, Vetter, & Lewis, 2003). Besides, these devices are for "old people." And, after all, you can hear fairly well in quiet situations. It's only when it gets noisy that you can't hear at all.

Being in a wheelchair seriously compromises anyone's quality of life. But this woman's hearing impairment, which makes having a conversation with her husband practically impossible, may be even more important in cutting her off from the outside world.

presbycusis Age-related difficulty in hearing, particularly high-pitched tones, caused by the atrophy of hearing receptors located in the inner ear.

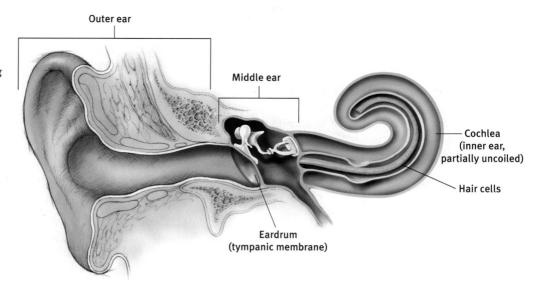

Outer ear

Middle ear

Cochlea (inner ear, partially uncoiled)

Hair cells

Eardrum (tympanic membrane)

FIGURE 14.6: The human ear: Presbycusis is caused by the selective loss of the hearing receptors in the inner ear—called hair cells—that allow us to hear high-pitched tones—so these changes are permanent.

elderspeak A style of communication used with an older person who seems to be physically impaired, involving speaking loudly and with slow, exaggerated pronunciation, as if talking to a baby.

Even though this aged woman may have spent her life as a Shakespeare scholar or a well-known scientist, her emerging-adult granddaughter will be tempted to talk to her frail, tiny grandma in elderspeak. How often have you automatically used this patronizing type of speech with a cognitively sharp person in her eighties or nineties just because she looked as if she *might* be impaired?

Ole Graf / zeta / Corbis

Think of the pitch of the background noises surrounding you right now: the hum of a computer, the slamming of a door, the sound of a car motor starting up. These sounds are all lower in pitch than speech. This explains why hearing-impaired people are prone to complain about "all that noise." Background sounds overpower the higher-pitched conversations they are trying to understand.

Imagine having a conversation with a hearing-impaired relative—having to repeat things continually, needing to always shout to make yourself understood. Although you still may love your grandpa dearly, you now find yourself withdrawing when he enters the room. Now imagine that you are a hearing-impaired person and faced with the choice of saying "Please repeat that" or guessing at what the speaker has said, and you will understand why this problem can take such a human toll (Stark & Hickson, 2004; Strawbridge and others, 2000; Wallhagan, Strawbridge, & Kaplan, 1996). Hearing losses impair the quality of every relationship in life.

▌INTERVENTIONS:▌ Amplifying Hearing

Because the level of background noise is important in determining how well older people hear, the solution is to choose one's social settings with special care. Don't go to a noisy restaurant. Try to avoid places with low ceilings or bare floors, as they magnify sound. Install wall-to-wall carpeting in the house, because it will help absorb background noise. Get rid of noisy appliances, such as a rattling air conditioner or fan.

When having a conversation with an older adult with a hearing problem, speak clearly. Enunciate words distinctly (Souza & Hoyer, 1996). But try to avoid *elderspeak*, the tendency to talk more slowly and in exaggerated tones ("HOW *ARE* YOU, *DAR-LING*? WHAT IS FOR *DINNER* TODAY?").

Elderspeak—a mode of communication we tend to naturally fall into when an older person looks physically (and so mentally) impaired—has unfortunate similarities to infant-directed speech. We use simpler phrases and grammar, and employ infantile "loving" words, such as *darling*, that we would never adopt when formally addressing a "real" adult (Kemper & Mitzner, 2001). The elderly have mixed feelings about this type of talk. From family members, elderspeak can indicate that the person cares. But from strangers elderspeak can come off as incredibly patronizing (O'Connor & St. Pierre, 2004). I'll never forget going out to dinner with a friend in his late eighties who needed to use a walker and cringing at how the 18-year-old server treated this intellectual man like a 2-year-old!

For your own future hearing, the message rings out loud and clear. Avoid high-noise environments, and cover your ears when you pass by noisy places. Why do we hear so much about the need to exercise, and yet there is a deafening silence about the need to protect our hearing? How many of you readers religiously work out to prevent age-related diseases like heart attacks, but then attend rock concerts without a thought? Think of the noise level at your fitness center. Could the very place you are going to improve your health be one force that is insidiously producing this very common late-life chronic disease?

Motor Performances

Late-life hearing loss can present problems when we talk to individual older adults. What everyone finds distressing when we think of the general category "old person" lies in the motor realm. The elderly are so slow!

Slowness tends to put older people out of sync with the physical world. It can make driving or getting across the street a challenging feat. It causes missteps in the world of relationships, too. If you find yourself behind an elderly person at the supermarket checkout counter or an older driver going 40 in a 65-mile-per-hour zone, notice that your immediate reaction is to get intensely annoyed. So the slowing that age brings may help explain why our fast-paced, time-oriented society has such negative prejudices against the elderly.

The slowness that is such a symbol of old age is mainly caused by the loss in information-processing speed that starts decades earlier, in young adulthood, described in Chapters 12 and 13. This slowed **reaction time**—or decline in the ability to respond quickly to sensory input—affects every action, from accelerating when the traffic light turns green to counting change at the checkout counter to performing well on a fluid IQ test.

Age changes in the skeletal structures propelling action compound the slowness: With *osteoarthritis*, the joint cartilage wears away, making everything from opening a jar to running for the bus an endurance test. With **osteoporosis,** the bones become porous, brittle, and fragile, and tend to break easily. Although men can also develop osteoporosis, women, as is well known, are more susceptible to this disease. The main reason is that females have frailer, smaller bones. Small-boned, slender women (therefore most often females of Asian and European American descent) are at highest risk of developing osteoporosis. With this illness, the fragile bones break at the slightest pressure and cannot knit themselves back together. Hip fractures are a special danger. As you saw with Sadie in the chapter-opening vignette, falling and breaking a hip is one of the primary causes for needing to enter a nursing home (Jette and others, 1998).

INTERVENTIONS: Managing Motor Problems

Once again, when these difficulties strike in later life, the strategy is to achieve a delicate person–environment fit: Keep as physically active as possible and exercise moderately, as keeping active can help prevent ADL problems from developing or getting worse (Jette and others, 1999; Miller and others, 2000). But make sure not to overdo it, and, especially in the old-old years, take care to guard against falls.

This fall-prevention strategy may also best be achieved by taking steps to remodel one's home: Provide the best possible lighting and install low-pile wall-to-wall carpeting to prevent tripping. Put grab bars in places such as the bathtub, where falls are likely to occur. To make instrumental ADLs such as cooking easier, install cabinet doors that open to the touch and put shelves within easy reach. A popular strategy in Europe—although it hasn't caught on in the United States—is to wear hip pads that cushion falls and so reduce the danger of landing in a nursing home.

You are at the bank. You need to get to work, and at the head of this long line is a slow elderly person. Experiences such as these are what cause us to dislike old people and automatically link "old age" with an image of being annoyingly slow.

reaction time The speed at which a person can respond to a stimulus. A progressive increase in reaction time is universal to aging.

osteoporosis An age-related chronic disease in which the bones become porous, fragile, and more likely to break. Osteoporosis is most common in thin women and so most common in females of European and Asian descent.

The simple act of going down steps—which we take for granted—can be an ordeal when people have ADL impairments. Imagine being this woman and knowing that, because of your osteoporosis, any misstep might land you in a wheelchair and perhaps even require you to enter a nursing home.

TABLE 14.2: Age-Related Sensory-Motor Changes and Interventions: A Summary

Changes	Interventions
Vision	
Problems with seeing in dimly lit places, sensitivity to glare	• Use strong, indirect light, and avoid using fluorescent bulbs.
	• Look for home appliances with large letters, nonreflective surfaces, and adjustable lighting.
	• Consider giving up driving at night or in the rain.
	• If your eyesight becomes severely impaired, use low-vision aids.
Hearing	
Loss of hearing for high-pitched tones	• Reduce background noise.
	• Speak distinctly, facing the person, but avoid elderspeak.
	• Install wall-to-wall carpeting and double-paned windows in a home.
Motor abilities	
Slower reaction time	• Be careful in speed-oriented situations.
Osteoporosis and osteoarthritis	• Exercise moderately, but don't overdo it.
	• Modify your home to prevent falls.
	• Install low-pile carpeting to prevent tripping.
	• Install grab bars and other assistive devices.
	(The lighting interventions suggested above will also help prevent falls.)

Table 14.2 summarizes the main points of this sensory-motor section, with special emphasis on highlighting what older adults and their loved ones can do to produce the right person–environment fit at home. Another problem, however, lies right outside the person's doors. Unless people live in a city with good mass transit, they *must* drive.

FOCUS ON A TOPIC: DRIVING IN OLD AGE

Imagine that you are an older adult, such as Sadie. You know your vision problems are making driving dangerous. So you stop driving during rush hour. For years you have been uncomfortable about driving at night and in the rain (Charness & Bosman, 1995). But you cannot imagine giving up your car completely. Abandoning driving means confronting the crucial loss of independent selfhood that you first gained when you got your license as a teen (Liddle & McKenna, 2003). In our car-focused society, it might mean that you have to leave your home and enter a nursing home.

Actually, driving is a special concern for older adults because it involves many sensory and motor skills. In addition to demanding adequate vision, driving is affected by hearing losses, because you might notice that we become alert to the location of other cars partly by their sound. To drive well, people must have the muscle strength to push down the pedals and the joint flexibility to turn the wheel. And, as anyone behind an older driver when the light turns green immediately realizes, driving is especially sensitive to increases in reaction time.

Because people like Sadie naturally limit how much they drive, when researchers look just at age-group differences in crashes, older adults have far lower accident rates than do drivers aged 18 to 25. But if we consider the number of accidents per miles driven, as you can see in Figure 14.7, among people over age 75 driving is a perilous practice indeed (Jette & Branch, 1992; Stamatiadis, 1996).

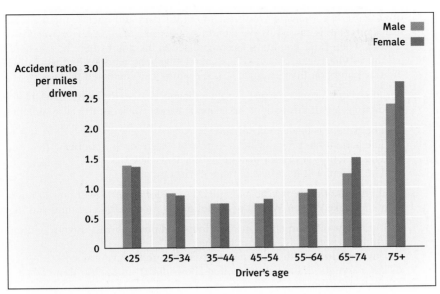

FIGURE *14.7:* **Accident rates in U.S. urban areas, by age and gender:** Driving is especially dangerous for drivers age 75 and over. Notice from the chart that if we look at per-person miles driven, by this age accident rates are higher than they are for even that other high-risk population—teenagers and emerging adults.

Source: Stamatiadis (1996).

What steps should society take to reduce these hazards? Some experts advocate yearly license renewals accompanied by vision tests for people once they are over a certain age (Stamatiadis, Agent, & Ridgeway, 2003). Still, a simple eye screening might not pick up the core vision deficits. Older people have trouble clearly discriminating visual images. They have difficulty quickly processing the changing array of visual stimuli we encounter while on the road (Ball & Rebok, 1994; Roenker and others, 2003; Sims and others, 2000). As many wrecks are caused by cognitive impairments, to really weed out dangerous drivers might require giving older adults who are at risk a battery of neuropsychological tests (Bieliauskas, 2005). Should we rely on family members or ask physicians to report impaired older drivers, as is now specified by law in Oregon? (See Snyder & Bloom, 2004.) Would you have the courage to rob an older loved one of his adult status by taking away his keys?

None of these interventions speaks to the larger issue: "If I can't drive, I may have to leave my home." We need to redesign the driving environment by putting adequate lighting on road signs, streets, highways, and, especially, exit ramps. We might extend the yellow light signal time and provide more traffic lights, reducing the need for those left turns into traffic that are an accident waiting to happen for people of any age.

Most important, we need to change how we build communities—to have stores located within walking distance of homes and, especially, to invest in more cost-efficient transportation systems that don't involve cars. This mandate is mandatory in view of that huge group fast accelerating down the highway into later life: the baby boomers.

On your way home today, try to identify the most hazardous places for older drivers. Think of how you could redesign lights, signals, and intersections to make them more user-friendly for older adults. The same need to take action to provide the right person–environment fit, as we will see in the next section, is crucial when dealing with the devastating cognitive problems of later life: dementing diseases.

Divided-attention tasks, such as the need to look away from the road while consulting a map, are particularly hazardous when combined with the other age-related changes that make driving basically more difficult in late life. Today, due to advances in technology, this couple might buy a GPS device to make their retirement trips safer. In addition to changing the wider environment, can you also list some ways to redesign this new red convertible to make it more age-friendly for this man and his wife?

Patti McConville / Getty Images

✿ TYING IT ALL TOGETHER

1. Roy, who is 55, is having trouble seeing in the dark and in glare-filled environments. Roy's problem is caused by the clouding of his _____ (cornea/iris/lens). At age 75, when Roy's condition has progressed to the point where he can't see much at all, he will have _____ (a cataract/diabetic retinopathy/macular degeneration), a condition that _____ (cannot/can) be cured by surgery.

2. Dr. Jones has just given a 45-year-old a diagnosis of presbycusis. All of the following predictions about this patient are accurate *except* (pick out the false statement):

   a. The patient is likely to be a male.
   b. The patient has probably been exposed to high levels of noise.
   c. The patient is at risk for becoming socially isolated.
   d. The patient will hear best in noisy environments.

3. Your grandmother is 75 years old and asks you for advice about how to remodel her home to make it safer. Which of the following modifications should you suggest?

   a. Install low-pile carpeting on your floors and put grab bars in your bathroom.
   b. Put fluorescent lights in your ceilings.
   c. Buy appliances with larger numerals and nonreflective surfaces.
   d. Put a skylight in the bathroom that allows direct sunlight to shine down on your medicine cabinet.
   e. Get rid of your noisy air conditioners and fans.

4. Your state legislature is considering a law to require annual eye exams for drivers over the age of 65. Your representative asks you to testify about this issue. Using the points in this section, explain to the legislature why such a law may not be very effective and offer some alternate strategies that might minimize the dangers of needing to drive in old age.

Answers to the Tying It All Together questions can be found in the answers section of the book.

Dementia

dementia The general term for any illness that produces serious, progressive, usually irreversible cognitive decline.

[FAQ: How can I tell if a family member is suffering from dementia?]

Dementia is the general label for any illness that produces serious, progressive, often irreversible cognitive decline. Dementia involves the total erosion of our personhood, the complete unraveling of the inner self. Younger people can also develop a dementing disease if they experience a brain injury or an illness such as AIDS. However, because—as we will describe later in our discussion—dementias are typically produced by two illnesses basic to the aging process, these conditions almost always strike people in later life.

What are the general symptoms of *any* later-life dementia? As the first-person account in the Experiencing the Lifespan box poignantly reveals, in the earlier stages of these diseases, people show memory impairments that go far beyond normal age-related episodic forgetting. They forget basic *semantic information*, core facts about their lives such as the name of their town or how to get home.

As the symptoms progress, every aspect of thinking is impaired. Abstract reasoning becomes difficult. Older adults can no longer think through options when making decisions. Their language abilities are compromised. People may be unable to name common objects, such as a shoe or a bed. Judgment is gone. Older adults often act inappropriately—undressing in public, running out in traffic, yelling in the street. They wander aimlessly and behave recklessly, unaware that they are endangering their lives (McCarty and others, 2000).

As these diseases reach their later stages, there is the loss of all functions. People may be unable to speak or move. Ultimately, they are bedridden, unable to remember how to eat or even swallow well. At this point, complications such as infections or pneumonia often occur and lead to death.

AN INSIDER'S PORTRAIT OF ALZHEIMER'S DISEASE

Hal is handsome, distinguished, a young-looking 69. He warmly welcomes me into his immaculate apartment at the assisted-living facility. Copies of National Geographic *and* Scientific American *are neatly laid out in stacks on the coffee table. Labeled photos of family members adorn the walls. Index cards organized in piles on the desk list his daughters' names and phone numbers, and provide reminders about the city and the state where he lives.*

Hal taught university chemistry for years. After his wife died, he kept active with volunteer work and church activities. About two years ago his mind began to unravel. In addition to the forgetfulness, his children worried about the rambling conversations, the disorganized letters, the long-distance calls at all hours of the night. Concerned about Hal's ability to keep living on his own, his daughters planned to move him to Tennessee this coming fall. Their plans were cut short when Hal set out to drive across the country to Nashville but could not remember where he was going or who he was going to see. Luckily, Hal had the presence of mind to check himself into a local hospital, where he learned that he had the illness whose symptoms he graciously consents to describe:

I first noticed that I had a problem giving short speeches. All of a sudden you have a blank and like . . . what do I put in there . . . and I couldn't do it. I can speak. You are listening to me and you don't hear any pauses, but if you get me into something. . . . I just had one of these little pauses. I knew what I wanted to say and I couldn't get into it, so I think a little bit and wait and try to get around to it. It's there . . . I know it's there . . . but where do I use it? . . . Then, you have to sit down and think and sort. I went to the hospital because I knew there was something wrong. When I got there, they wanted to know about my life. I said: "If you provide me with some information about what you think will happen to me and if I find that it's a good argument, then I'll tell you about myself." When I was told I had Alzheimer's, I thought, "Oh, brother, this is a terrible place to be." The psychiatrist, Dr. West—Oh, I got that right!—helped me a lot. Now, I tell everyone what I have. They are kind of shocked, but it doesn't bother me.

I'm not ashamed of my Alzheimer's and I'm not ashamed of anyone else's Alzheimer's.

It's ups and downs; and then one day you are in a deep valley. You can't get tied up in the hills and valleys because they just lead you around and it makes you more frustrated than ever. . . . If I can't get things, I just give up and then try to calm down and come back to it. You have to work very hard to get back to where you were. Like, when I read, I get confused; but then I just stop and try again a month later. Or the people here: I know them by face, by sight, by what they wear, but I cannot get that focus down to memorize any names. I remember things from when I was five. It's what's happening now that doesn't make a lot of sense. Now, I think it's time for us to stop and let me show you the pictures on my wall and tell you who these people are. . . .

As we walk to my car after this interview, Hal's daughter fills me in:

My father seems a lot happier now that he is here. The big problem is the frustration, when he tries to explain things and I can't understand and neither of us connect. Then he gets angry and I get angry. My father has always been a very organized, very intellectual person, so feeling dependent and out of control is overwhelming for him. We had to get a power of attorney [a legal order declaring guardianship]. I think he understood it conceptually, but he hasn't come to grips emotionally with it. The fact that he can't write checks is devastating. He has days where he gets paranoid, decides that there is a conspiracy out for him. It's tiny things. A letter came to the wrong place and he went down and exploded at the people at the desk.

The good news is that we put him on medication that seems to help. Also, they can handle this here. If we get home health services to come in, they will keep him until he gets very bad. For me the worst thing is remembering how my father was. You expect a certain response from him and you get this strange response. It's like there's a different person inside.

The Dimensions of Dementia

How long does this devastating decline process take? There is a fuzzy period between having moderate memory problems and having full-blown symptoms (Bäckman and others, 2004; Petersen & O'Brien, 2006; Rivas-Vazquez and others, 2004). So labeling the point when people have crossed the line from what is called mild cognitive impairment into full-fledged dementia can be difficult (Morris, 2006). The deterioration progresses at different rates from person to person and also varies depending on the specific dementing disease (Tulving & Craik, 2000). But, in general, dementia amply deserves the label *chronic* disease. On average, the time from diagnosis until death is approximately four to eight years (Rivas-Vazquez and others, 2004; Larson and others, 2004).

This 100-year-old Chinese man showing off his calligraphy skills is a testament to the fact that people can remain extremely intellectually sharp in their areas of special expertise well into advanced old age.

The good news is that dementias are not illnesses of the young-old years. They typically strike in advanced old age (Blennow, de Leon, & Zetterberg, 2006). Is dementia the inevitable price of living a very long time? Luckily, the answer is no. When Danish researchers evaluated the cognitive capacities of every person in that nation who had their hundredth birthday during 1996, they discovered that one in three centenarians showed *no* signs of memory impairment (Andersen-Ranberg, Vasegaard, & Jeune, 2001). In another study, when psychologists gave people over age 100 various cognitive tests, some of these oldest adults outperformed the typical 20-year-old on measures of crystallized IQ (Hagberg and others, 2001). In an even more heartening survey, when researchers tested every person over age 90 living outside of a nursing home in the Italian city of Bologna, only *one in three* older adults showed the kind of significant memory loss that might qualify as even the beginning of a dementing disease (Pioggiosi and others, 2006). So yes, people can live sound in mind (as well as in body) until the very limit of human life.

Dementia's Two Main Causes

What specific illnesses produce the terrible symptoms we have been charting? Although there are some rare dementing diseases, typically the person will be diagnosed with *Alzheimer's disease* or *vascular dementia* or—most likely in the old-old years—some combination of those two illnesses (Anderson & Craik, 2000; Langa, Foster, & Larson, 2004).

Alzheimer's disease directly attacks the core structure of human consciousness, our neurons. With this illness the neurons literally decay or wither away. They are replaced by strange wavy structures called *neurofibrillary tangles* and thick, bullet-shaped bodies of protein called *senile plaques* (Terry, 2006).

Vascular dementia refers to impairments in the vascular (blood) system, or network of arteries feeding the brain. Here the person's cognitive problems are caused by multiple small strokes.

In real life, it is often difficult to make distinctions between these two diseases (Whitehouse, 2003). Strokes, because they limit the blood supply to the brain, cause neurons to die (Hachinski, 2000). When a person develops the symptoms of dementia, particularly in advanced old age, strokes or seriously impaired circulation, as well as Alzheimer's changes, are typically working together to produce the devastating neural decay (Langa, Foster, & Larson, 2004; Romàn, 2003).

Understanding that several pathways produce the impairments, scientists are vigorously attacking dementia on various fronts. Given that Alzheimer's disease often has a vascular component, they are hoping that drugs that reduce the risk factors for cardiovascular problems, such as blood pressure medications, might help stave off the neural loss (Sano, 2003). The most intense research effort, however, centers on decoding what is causing the plaques and tangles to take over the brain. Do the plaques cause the tangles to develop, or are the tangles at

Alzheimer's disease A type of age-related dementia characterized by neural atrophy and abnormal by-products of that atrophy, such as senile plaques and neurofibrillary tangles.

vascular dementia A type of age-related dementia caused by multiple small strokes.

[FAQ: What causes Alzheimer's disease?]

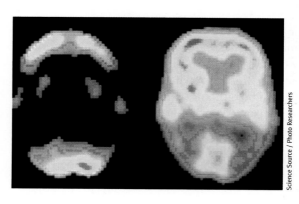

This photo shows PET-scan images of the metabolic activity of a normal brain (right) and one with Alzheimer's (left). Notice how the neural devastation described in the text is literally shutting down a person's brain.

the core of the disease? (See Adlard & Cummings, 2004; and Hardy, 2004.) Much research centers specifically on amyloid, a fatty substance that constitutes the plaques. If scientists can prevent the accumulation of this material, or inhibit the protein precursor to its development, perhaps they can inhibit the process by which the neurons start to be eaten away (Adlard & Cummings, 2004; Hardy, 2004; Schenk, 2006).

The discovery of a genetic marker for Alzheimer's disease may aid this effort. Roughly 15 percent of the U.S. population possesses the APOE-4 marker. People in the unlucky fraction of the population with at least one copy of this gene tend to develop Alzheimer's symptoms approximately a decade earlier than the average person (Blennow, de Leon, & Zetterberg, 2006) and are also prone to experience accelerated age-related memory decline (Blacker & Lovestone, 2006).

This breakthrough in the genetics of Alzheimer's, however, poses difficult choices. Children who have witnessed a parent develop this devastating illness are (no surprise) terrified of getting the disease (Anderson, Towsley, & Gaugler, 2004; Gerritsen, Kuin, & Steverink, 2004). Knowing they don't have the genetic marker would ease their minds. But having the marker does not mean that a given individual will definitely get Alzheimer's. It only shows that person is at higher risk. Would you decide to be tested? The answer, if you are like many people, hinges on whether there are strategies to ward off the blow (Cutler & Hodgson, 2003). Where are we today in terms of preventing and treating Alzheimer's and other dementing diseases?

[FAQ: What is the best way to deal with Alzheimer's disease and other forms of dementia?]

INTERVENTIONS: Dealing with Dementing Diseases

Memory-stimulating medicines can slow the transition from experiencing moderate memory problems to getting the symptoms of full-blown dementia, at least for some time (Farlow & Inglis, 2002; Giacobini, 2003; Peskind and others, 2006; Wallin and others, 2004). (When my mother was prescribed one of these pills, she said, "It was like a fog lifted from my mind within an hour.") Researchers are currently testing medicines that may slow the progression of the illness when it is more advanced (Karaman and others, 2004).

Perhaps the most interesting findings on the prevention side relate to exercise (not mental but physical exercise). Longitudinal studies suggest that—perhaps because exercise promotes vascular function—people who run, or walk, or work out regularly have a lower risk of developing the symptoms of late-life dementia (Abbott and others, 2004; Lindsay and others, 2004; Richards, Hardy, & Wadsworth, 2003). Still, as this evidence is correlational, researchers urge caution (Lautenschlager & Almeida, 2006). It has not been proven that getting on a treadmill every day for decades will prevent Alzheimer's or any other dementing disease. Moreover, there is no way of halting the disease process once it has begun. Therefore, with dementia the main interventions are environmental. Once again, they involve providing the best disease–environment fit for the person and helping dementia's second casualty—caregivers.

FOR THE PERSON WITH DEMENTIA: USING EXTERNAL AIDS AND MAKING LIFE PREDICTABLE AND SAFE Creative external aids such as Hal's strategy of using note cards can be used to jog memory, particularly when people are in the beginning stages of the illness (Kasl-Godley & Gatz, 2000; Noyes, Daley, & French, 2000). A prime concern is safety. To prevent people from wandering off (or driving off!), caregivers need to double-lock or put buzzers on doors. They must deactivate dangerous appliances, such as the stove, and put toxic substances, such as household cleaners, out of reach. Many nursing facilities have innovative specialized Alzheimer's units, where the living environment is designed to promote cognitive capacities and the staff is skilled in dealing with dementing diseases. At every stage of the illness, the goals are to (1) protect people and keep them functioning as well as possible for as long as possible and (2) be caring and offer loving support.

So far, I have mainly discussed what others can do for dementia—as if the disease process had magically evaporated a human being. This assumption is wrong. The real profiles in courage are the people in the early stages of these illnesses who are getting together to problem-solve and offer each other support (Kasl-Godley & Gatz, 2000; Noyes, Daley, & French, 2000). What does it feel like to be losing your basic anchor, your inner self? We already got insights from Hal in the Experiencing the Lifespan box on page 439. Now let's read what other people with dementia have to say:

> We were all going along quite productively in our lives until we were confronted by memory loss, confusion, nervousness. . . . It's as if you are reading a book and someone has torn the pages out.
>
> (quoted in Snyder, 1999, p. 1)

> I'm almost 71 and I'm not amazed that people die. So it isn't the death. It's the loss of oneself while you're still alive.
>
> (quoted in Snyder, 1999, p. 57)

Outsiders can compound this sense of inner disorientation when they develop their own kind of memory problem—centering only on the label and forgetting about the real human being inside. A woman named Bea vividly described this situation when she was first told her diagnosis:

> The last person who interviewed me was the neurologist. He was very indifferent and said it was just going to get worse. . . . He had no feelings for me whatsoever. . . . Health care professionals need to be compassionate. . . . There but for the grace of God go I.
>
> (quoted in Snyder, 1999, pp. 17–18)

Later, she continued:

> We've never tried to hide that I have Alzheimer's. But everyone acts like they don't want to get near because they might catch it. They don't know how to deal with it. I was always so social before but now I don't like to be around people.
>
> (quoted in Snyder, 1999, p. 22)

Can people with Alzheimer's be generative? Listen to Bea describing her current life plan: "I'd like to be a good example for someone coming along" (quoted in Snyder, 1999, p. 26). Can they keep their sense of humor and self-efficacy intact? Jean, another woman in this interview study, shows that she can:

> My advice to people with Alzheimer's is: Don't have it! But if you do . . . , learn what you can do. . . . Just have as clear a picture as you can about all of the possibilities. . . . To family members I say, "Don't baby me and don't pretend it isn't there."
>
> (quoted in Snyder, 1999, pp. 71–72)

Can people with dementia teach us what it means to be wise and fully mature? Judge for yourself, as you read what a loving dad named Booker has to say about the cycle of life:

> I'm blessed to have a wonderful daughter. I sent her to . . . school and college and now she takes care of all of my business. I depend on her. I'm in her hands. I'm in my baby phase now, so to speak. So sometimes I call her "my mumma." . . . Yes, she's my mumma now. [Booker smiled appreciatively.] . . . She's my backbone. She's such a blessing to me.
>
> (quoted in Snyder, 1999, p. 103)

FOR THE CAREGIVER: COPING WITH LIFE TURNED UPSIDE DOWN Imagine caring for a loved one with dementia. You know that the illness is permanent. You must helplessly witness your beloved father or brother or husband deteriorate. As the disease progresses and enters its middle phase, you must deal with a loved human being who has turned alien, where the tools used in normal encounters no longer apply. Your relative may be physically and verbally abusive. She may be agitated and wake and wander in the night. As your family member becomes incontinent and needs total care, you typically suffer the guilt of putting your loved one in a nursing home. Or you decide to put your life on hold for years as you care for this person every minute of the day.

[FAQ: How do family caregivers cope with taking care of loved ones affected by Alzheimer's disease?]

TABLE 14.3: Tips for Helping People with Dementia

1. Provide clear cues to alert the person to the surroundings, such as using note cards with important names and addresses and labeling rooms and objects around the home (for example, use a picture of the toilet and tub at the door to the bathroom); use strong, contrasting colors to highlight the difference between different rooms in the house.

2. As a protection from getting injured, double-lock the doors, turn off the stove, and take away the person's car keys.

3. Offer a highly predictable, structured daily routine.

4. Don't take insulting comments personally. Try to understand that "it's the disease talking."

5. Try to see the silver lining; this is a time to understand what's really important in life and show your love.

6. Join a caregiver support group.

7. *Remember that there is a real person in there.* Especially in the early stages of the disease, don't take over every aspect of life. Respect the individual's personhood.

Alzheimer's caregiver support groups and Internet chat rooms sponsored by the Alzheimer's Association offer travelers negotiating this frightening terrain a forum to share their anguish and offer advice: "I notice that she seems to get worse during the night." "What works for you?" "My husband hit me the other day, and I was devastated." "Keep telling yourself it's the illness. People with dementia can't help how they act." Often, the key lies less in managing the person than in changing one's feelings, attitudes, and responses:

> *Accept the fact that the patient won't be able to live up to even minimum standards of behavior. . . . Let it go. . . . I realized I never knew what would happen but I . . . decided that wasn't a reason not to do things. He was happier and I was happier if the ordinary standards of life just didn't apply.*
>
> *My approach to the world is more confident. . . . I used to find my mother terribly embarrassing—you overcome that. . . . Understand that the behavior is not voluntary, that they have no control.*
>
> (quoted in Aneshensel and others, 1995, p. 170)

As these quotations show, dementia offers its own redemption sequence. Dealing with dementia teaches us what is really important in life.

Table 14.3 offers some tips for coping with dementing diseases. Until we solve the biological puzzle, we need to make life as easy as possible for the millions of older adults and caregiving families coping "36 hours a day" with these devastating conditions of later life.

So far we have explored how older people and their loved ones can *personally* take action to promote the best person–environment fit when old-age frailties strike. In the next section of the chapter, we explore what society is doing to help.

 TYING IT ALL TOGETHER

1. Your grandmother has just been diagnosed with dementia. Describe the two disease processes that typically cause this condition.

2. Mary, age 50, is terrified of getting a dementing disease. Which of the following statements can you make that are both accurate and comforting?

   a. Dementia is typically an illness of the "old-old" years.
   b. Even by their nineties, many people don't have dementia.
   c. Dementia is extremely rare at any age.
   d. If you have the APOE-4 marker, your chance of getting Alzheimer's is virtually nil.

3. Mrs. Jones has just been diagnosed with early Alzheimer's disease. Her relatives might help by:

    a. taking steps to keep her safe in her home.
    b. encouraging her to attend an Alzheimer's patient support group.
    c. treating her like a human being.
    d. doing all of the above.

Answers to the Tying It All Together questions can be found in the answers section of the book.

Options and Services for the Frail Elderly

Suppose that, like Sadie, you are developing ADL problems. Cooking and cleaning are becoming difficult. You are among the roughly three in four U.S. women in their eighties who are widowed; and, as with the majority of older widows in the developed world, you live alone (Federal Interagency Forum on Aging Related Statistics, 2000; Kinsella & Velkoff, 2001). You start out by mainly using selection and optimization. You focus on your most essential activities. You spend more time on each important life task. You are determined to live independently for as long as possible. But you know that the time is coming when you will enter Baltes's full-fledged compensation mode. You will need to depend on other people for your daily needs. Where can you turn?

Setting the Context: Scanning the Global Elder-Care Scene

For most of human history and in many regions of the developing world today, older people would never confront this challenge. Families always lived in multigenerational households (Johnson & Climo, 2000; Kinsella & Velkoff, 2001). When the oldest generation needed help, loving caregivers were right on the scene.

In African villages, caring for the frail elderly was a duty assumed by any relative or shared by the whole community. In Asia, traditionally a first-born son would take his parents in, and the daughter-in-law was expected to provide care (Johnson & Climo, 2000).

Today, however, this support network is fraying. In an era of wrenching poverty, when wide swaths of Africa have been decimated by war and the ravages of AIDS, it's natural for middle-aged and younger adults to put top priority on their children's needs (Aboderin, 2004; Cliggett, 2001; Shaibu & Wallhagen, 2002; van der Geest, 2002). In rapidly Westernizing Asia, where many women are now in the labor force, the traditional collectivist norms are being replaced by more individualistic ideas: "People don't have to sacrifice everything for their parents"; "Think of your husband and children first" (Zhan, 2004). So today, residents of affluent, rapidly developing nations such as South Korea and China are turning to more Western society-wide models of providing elder care (Levande, Herrick, & Sung, 2000; Chow and others, 2004).

The Scandinavian countries, in particular, offer excellent models for the kinds of comprehensive services an enlightened society can provide. In Sweden, Norway, and Denmark, government-funded home health services swing into operation to help impaired older people "age in place"—meaning stay in their own homes. Residents can get cash grants to remodel their homes in the ways discussed earlier in this chapter. Innovative elderly housing alternatives dot the countryside—from multigenerational villages with a central community center providing health care to small nursing facilities with attractive private rooms (Johri, Beland, & Bergman, 2003).

Medicare The U.S. government's program of health insurance for elderly people.

alternatives to institutionalization Services and settings designed to keep older people who are experiencing age-related disabilities that don't merit intense 24-hour care from having to enter nursing homes.

continuing care retirement community A housing option characterized by a series of levels of care for elderly residents, ranging from independent apartments to assisted living to nursing home care. People enter the community in relatively good health and move to sections where they can get more care when they become disabled.

assisted-living facility A housing option providing care for elderly people who have instrumental ADL impairments and can no longer live independently but may not need a nursing home.

day-care program A service for impaired older adults who live with relatives, in which the older person spends the day at a center offering various activities.

In Scandinavia—as in every nation around the globe—families still take on the main responsibility of caring for the older generation. But because their governments fully fund services designed to help their disabled older citizens, older people living in these nations (and others such as Germany) do not have to worry about what will happen to them should they get physically impaired (Pinquart, Sörenson, & Davey, 2003).

Alternatives to Institutions in the United States

In the United States we do have these worries. The reason is that **Medicare,** our health insurance system for the elderly, pays only for services defined as cure-oriented. It does not cover help with activities of daily living—the very ongoing services with cooking or cleaning or bathing that might keep people out of a nursing home when they are having some trouble functioning in life.

What choices do disabled older people in the United States (and people who love them) have, *other* than going to a nursing home? Here are the main **alternatives to institutionalization** that exist today:

- A **continuing care retirement community** is a residential complex that provides different levels of services from independent apartments to nursing home care. Continuing care is designed to provide people with the ultimate person–environment fit. Residents arrive in relatively good health and then get the appropriate type of care as their physical needs change. With this type of housing, older adults are purchasing peace of mind. They don't have to worry about burdening their children if they develop ADL problems. They know exactly where they will be going if and when they need nursing home care.

- An **assisted-living facility** is specifically for people who are currently experiencing ADL limitations but do not have the kinds of problems with dressing or feeding themselves that require full-time, 24-hour care. Assisted living—which has mushroomed in popularity in the United States over the past decade—offers care in a less medicalized, homey setting. Residents often have private rooms with their own furniture. The staff is attuned to older adults' need for independence (Ball and others, 2004). These settings do not have the overtones of an anonymous, institutional "old-age home" (Phillips & Hawes, 2005).

- **Day-care programs** are specifically for older people who live with their families. Much like its namesake for children, adult day care provides activities and a place for an impaired older person to go when family members are at work and feel uncomfortable about leaving that person alone. One great advantage of day care is that it allows relatives to care for frail older loved ones in their own home, without having to give up their other responsibilities in life (Schacke & Zank, 2006).

[FAQ: What options do elderly people have when it becomes difficult to live in their own homes, and how is the decision to leave one's home made?]

[FAQ: How should caregivers evaluate an elderly person's need for assisted-living facilities?]

Assisted living has become an enticing option for relatively wealthy people with ADL impairments. At the facility shown on the left, a man and his wife with Alzheimer's disease can be taken care of and still live together in their own homey room. The breathtaking atrium on the right shows that top-of-the-line housing of this type looks like a luxurious hotel.

G. Paul Burnett / The Image Works

Jim Wilson / The New York Times / Redux

home health services Nursing-oriented and house-keeping help provided in the home of an impaired older adult (or any other impaired person).

- **Home health services** help people age "in place" (at home). Paid caregivers come to the house to cook, clean, and help the older adult with personal care activities such as bathing.

The problem is that these alternatives are typically costly and not covered by Medicare. So they are mainly available to affluent older adults (Branch, 2001). To offer an insight into the going rates at assisted-living facilities, a colleague is currently paying roughly $5,000 a month to house his father with vascular dementia at one of these places. Can you devise some innovative, lower-cost options for helping frail older adults? We are in especially dire need of housing that bridges the gap from living independently to needing the setting specially tailored for people who *are* severely physically impaired—the nursing home.

Nursing Home Care

nursing home/long-term-care facility A residential institution that provides shelter and intensive caregiving, primarily to older people who need help with basic ADLs.

Nursing homes, or **long-term-care facilities,** provide shelter and services to people with basic ADL problems—individuals who really *do* require 24-hour intensive caregiving help. Although adults of every age live in nursing homes, it should come as no surprise that the main risk factor for entering these institutions is being very old. The average nursing home resident is in his—or, I should say, her—late eighties and nineties. Because, as we know, females live sicker well into advanced old age, women make up roughly three out of every four residents in long-term-care facilities (J. K. Belsky, 2001; Freedman, 1996).

What causes people to enter nursing homes? Often, as you saw in the chapter-opening vignette, an older adult arrives after some physically incapacitating event, such as falling and breaking a hip. Given that dementia requires such daunting 24/7 care, roughly half of the nursing home population has been diagnosed with some dementing disease.

In predicting who ends up in a nursing home, both nature and nurture forces are involved. Yes, the person's biology (or physical state) does matter a good deal. But so does the environment, specifically whether or not family members are available to provide care. A spouse is the first line of defense against a nursing home. Children, particularly caregiving daughters, as you saw in Chapter 12, come second. People such as Sadie, who have no close living relatives, are at very high risk of ending their lives in long-term care (Belsky, 2001).

Just as the routes by which people arrive differ, residents take different paths once they enter nursing homes. Sometimes a nursing home is a short stop before returning home. Or it may be a short interlude before death. Some residents live for years in long-term care.

Visit any home for the aged and you will be struck by the fact that the men are missing in action, because females live much longer with ADL-impairments than males!

Syracuse Newspapers / The Image Works

You might be surprised to learn who is paying for these residents' care. Because people start out paying the huge costs out of their own pockets and "spend down" until they are impoverished, it is Medicaid, the U.S. health-care system for the poor, that finances our nation's nursing homes.

Evaluating Nursing Homes

Nursing homes are often viewed as dumping grounds where residents are abused or left to languish unattended until they die. How accurate are these stereotypes? Many times the generalizations are unfair. A few twenty-first-century nursing homes are rich in services, with state-of-the-art features such as private rooms and a full complement of activities specifically tailored to residents' needs. However, about one in four U.S. nursing homes provides seriously substandard care. They are deemed dangerous, placing residents at genuine physical risk (Wiener, 2003). Even the best nursing home has psychological liabilities, the identity-eroding losses basic to institutional life. Imagine being a nursing home resident and having to share a small room with a stranger. You are required to eat the foods the facility serves, at predetermined hours (Kane, 1995–1996; Kane, Kane, & Ladd, 1998). Then, of course, you have to cope with the loss of self-efficacy that results from needing to depend on other people for help with your most intimate physical needs.

This brings up the front-line caregiver in the nursing home, the **certified nurse assistant or aide.** Just as you saw during life's early years, caregiving at the upper end of the lifespan is low-status work. Nursing home workers, like their counterparts in day-care centers, make poverty-level wages. In 2001, the average salary of a nursing home aide was a meager $8 an hour. Staff turnover rates at nursing homes are high. Many facilities are also chronically understaffed (Quadagno & Stahl, 2003; Wiener, 2003). So even when an aide loves what she does, the conditions of the job can make it difficult to provide adequate care. Having worked in long-term care, I can testify that residents are indeed sometimes left lying in urine for hours. They wait inordinately long for help getting to the bathroom or being fed. One reason is that it can take 45 minutes to get the person to the toilet and back and hours to feed the eight or so people in your care when dinner arrives!

Still, when we actually talk to people who work in nursing homes, we get a different portrait of what this job is all about. Here's what Jayson, a mellow, six-foot-tall, 200-pound giant says about his work as an activities director at a Philadelphia nursing home:

> At first I was put off by the smells. . . . As time went by, I started seeing that these people [residents] need love. . . . Then I got moved to the Alzheimer's unit . . . and I found this to be like my most—how would I say this—the best task I ever had. . . . If you just come in here and say, "Okay, I got a job to do and I'm just doing my job," . . . then you're in the wrong field. . . . When somebody here dies, we all talk, we say how much we miss the person. . . . Some of them cry. . . . Some of them go to their funerals. . . . I actually spoke at some of the funerals. . . . I say how much this person meant to me.
>
> (quoted in Black & Rubinstein, 2005, pp. S-4–6)

certified nurse assistant or aide The main hands-on care provider in a nursing home, who helps elderly residents with basic ADL problems.

This photograph of a nursing home in Japan shows the scene that would greet you in any long-term-care facility around the world: People with basic ADL impairments (and often dementia) are languishing in wheelchairs. Even when the staff has the best intentions, they simply cannot give adequate attention to the impaired residents' needs.

A few years ago, I attended an unforgettable memorial service at a Florida nursing home. Person after person rose to eulogize this woman, a gifted poet and playwright, a passionate advocate who had worked with immense self-efficacy to make a difference in her fellow residents' lives. Then Mrs. Alonzo's son told his story. He said that he had never really known his mother. When he was young, she became schizophrenic and was shunted from institution to institution. Found at age 68 dehydrated and curled up in a ball in a tiny apartment, Mrs. Alonzo had been delivered to the nursing home to await death. It was only in this place, where life is supposed to end, that she fully blossomed as a human being.

If you think that this story is unique, that personal growth is virtually impossible in a nursing home, listen to this friend of mine, a psychologist who, like Jayson, finds her generativity in nursing home work:

My most amazing success entered treatment two years ago. This severely depressed resident had had an abusive childhood and marriage and suffered from enduring feelings of powerlessness and low self-esteem, and yet was very, very bright. I think that being sent to our institution allowed this woman to make the internal changes that she had been incapable of before. She began to look at her past and see how her experiences had shaped her poor sense of self and then to see her inner strengths. She and I formed a very close, very strong relationship.

So then she decided to work on becoming closer to her children. She had been aloof as a mother, and she told me that once her younger child had asked her to say that she loved her and she couldn't get the words out. Now, at age 89, she called this daughter, told her that she did love her and that she was sorry she couldn't say it for all of these years. Her daughters said that I had presented them with a miracle, the loving mother they always wanted. The nurses marveled at how my patient had been transformed. She made friends on the floor and became active in the residents' council. In the year and a half we saw one another she used to tell me, "I never believed I could change at this age."

As she finished her story, my friend's eyes filled with tears: "My patient died a few months ago, and I still miss her so much."

For Jayson, who, after being shot and lingering near death, reported seeing an angel visit him in the form of a little old man, his career is a calling from God. At age 36, he is flourishing in this consummately generative job. What about nursing home residents? Can people flourish within this most unlikely setting of life? For some uplifting answers, you might want to read the Experiencing the Lifespan box above.

Final Thoughts

Dealing with the physical challenges of old age is a major social challenge we must confront in the developed world in a few decades as the baby boomers move into their old-old years. Unfortunately, we cannot rely on medical miracles to magically erase the impairments that are the downside of our progress in getting so many people close to the biological maximum of life. We need to make preparations for the looming old-old army right now.

Our personal challenge as we live into our older years is to reach Erikson's stage of **integrity**, "the acceptance of one's one and only life cycle" (see Table 14.4). We need to feel that we have lived a fulfilling life in order to accept the fact that we are soon to die. And here is where making our own preparations is vital. At the beginning of this chapter you learned how my colleague Bob Womack is achieving integrity by determining to fulfill his generativity and core identity as an educator until the last possible day of life. In Erikson's wise words, finding our identity and fulfilling our generativity—in our own personal way—is the key to accepting death at any age.

The Experiencing the Lifespan box above suggests that—although Erikson doesn't specifically mention it—the quality of our attachment relationships is also crucial to reaching integrity. If we feel connected in love to the people we care about most in life, death loses some of its pain. Plus, the story of this woman who got it together in the nursing home enriches Erikson's masterful ideas that have guided our lifespan

integrity In Erikson's framework, the successful old-age task in which people believe that they have fulfilled their "human purpose in living." This feeling is necessary for a person to accept impending death.

TABLE 14.4: Erikson's Psychosocial Stages and Tasks

Life Stage	Primary Task
Infancy (birth to 1 year)	Basic trust versus mistrust
Toddlerhood (1 to 2 years)	Autonomy versus shame and doubt
Early childhood (3 to 6 years)	Initiative versus guilt
Middle childhood (6 years to puberty)	Industry versus inferiority
Adolescence (teens into twenties)	Identity versus role confusion
Young adulthood (twenties to early forties)	Intimacy versus isolation
Middle adulthood (forties to sixties)	Generativity versus stagnation
Late adulthood (late sixties and beyond)	**Integrity versus despair**

In old age, Erikson believes, our task is to reach integrity, the feeling that we have lived meaningful lives and accomplished what we needed to do as human beings. Without this inner sense, older people feel despair because they cannot change the past and are terribly afraid of dying.

tour in another way: It reminds us that it's never too late to accomplish developmental tasks that we may have missed. People can find their real identity (or authentic self), fulfill their generativity, connect with loved ones, and so reach integrity in their final months of life!

In the next chapter, we continue this theme of inner development and also highlight the crucial importance of making connections with loved ones as we focus directly on life's endpoint—death. ▮

 TYING IT ALL TOGETHER

1. An 85-year-old woman and her family come to a geriatric counselor for advice about the best arrangement for her future care. Match the letter of each item below with the number of the suggestion that would be most appropriate if this elderly client:

   _____ a. is affluent, is worried about living alone, and has no ADL problems.
   _____ b. has ADL impairments (but can still get around) and is living with the family—who want to continue to care for her at home.
   _____ c. has instrumental ADL impairments (but can still perform basic self-care activities), can no longer live alone, and has a good amount of money saved up.
   _____ d. has basic ADL impairments.
   _____ e. is beginning to have ADL impairments, lives alone, and has very little money (but does not qualify for Medicaid).

   (1) a continuing-care retirement facility
   (2) an assisted-living facility
   (3) a day-care program
   (4) a nursing home
   (5) There are no good alternatives you can suggest; people in this situation must struggle to cope at home.

2. Joey and Jane have tried every alternative, but they now realize that their mother needs a nursing home. Which of the following statements about this mother's situation—and nursing homes in general—is *not* true?

   a. Their mom is probably old-old and widowed.
   b. Medicare will completely cover their mom's expenses.
   c. The quality of the facilities their mom will possibly go to can vary greatly.

3. What steps can you take to ensure that you reach integrity before you die?

   a. have a fulfilling identity
   b. fulfill your generativity
   c. have loving, intimate attachments
   d. all of the above

Answers to the Tying It All Together questions can be found in the answers section of the book.

▮ SUMMARY

Tracing Physical Aging

Normal aging changes shade into **chronic disease** and finally, during the old-old years, may result in impairments in **activities of daily living (ADLs),** either less incapacitating **instrumental ADL problems** or **basic ADL problems**—troubles with basic self-care. Although no human being lives beyond the maximum lifespan (about age 105), the statistical odds of getting fairly close to this limit are good when people live in an affluent country, rank high on that nation's socioeconomic status ladder, and are female.

The **socioeconomic/health gap** refers to the fact that as social status rises—within each nation—people live healthier for a longer time. A variety of forces, from health-compromising lifestyles to lack of knowledge about illnesses to inadequate access to medical care, make low income a major risk factor for early disability and death. Another risk factor for dying earlier is being male. Men tend to die quicker primarily because they have heart attacks at younger ages. Women live longer but report more health problems at every stage of adult life. The female "health orientation," or sensitivity to illness, may help promote longevity, too.

Sensory-Motor Changes

The classic age-related vision problems—**presbyopia** (impairments in near vision), difficulties seeing in dim light, and problems with glare—are caused by a rigid, cloudier **lens.** Modifying lighting can help compensate for these losses. Cataracts, the endpoint of a cloudy lens, can be easily treated, although the other major age-related vision impairments can often result in a more permanent loss of sight. Elderly people cope fairly well with age-related vision losses.

The old-age hearing impairment **presbycusis** can present special problems because it limits a person's contact with the human world. Because chronic exposure to noise causes this selective loss for high-pitched tones, men are at higher risk of having hearing handicaps, especially at younger ages. To help a hearing-impaired person, limit low-pitched background noise and speak distinctly—but avoid **elderspeak,** the impulse to talk to the older person like a baby. For your own future hearing, protect yourself against excessive noise.

"Slowness" in later life is due to the age-related slowing in **reaction time** and skeletal conditions such as arthritis and **osteoporosis** (thin, fragile bones). Osteoporosis is a special concern because falling and breaking a hip is a major reason for entering a nursing home. With age-related mobility problems, the key is to keep as active as possible and take care to modify one's home to reduce the risk of falls and injury.

Although older people drive less often, accident rates per miles driven rise sharply among drivers over age 75. Solutions to the problem, such as mandatory vision testing over a certain age, may not work so well, as driving involves many sensory, motor, and cognitive skills. Modifying the driving environment and developing creative alternatives to cars is critical, because when older people can no longer drive, they may have to leave their homes and enter nursing homes.

Dementia

Dementia, the most feared old-age condition, is typically caused by **Alzheimer's disease** (neural atrophy accompanied by senile plaques and neurofibrillary tangles) and/or **vascular dementia** (small strokes). Dementia progresses gradually over years, and the risk of developing this devastating disease accelerates in advanced old age—although even at age 100 a significant percentage of people are still mentally sharp. Scientists are trying to understand why the plaques and tangles develop. A genetic test can tell if people are at high risk of developing Alzheimer's disease. Although medications may slow the downslide into Alzheimer's disease, this devastating illness cannot be cured or prevented. The key is to make environmental modifications to keep the person safe—and understand that older adults with dementia are still people. Caregiver support groups offer family members vital help in coping with this illness in a loved one.

Options and Services for the Frail Elderly

Elderly people in developed countries live apart from their families. In many developing nations, they traditionally lived in multigenerational households, with a built-in family support network when they became frail. However, in the rapidly modernizing developing world and in many African nations, this support is fraying. Scandinavia, with its rich array of services, offers a model for government-supported elder care. In the United States the major **alternatives to institutionalization—continuing care retirement communities, assisted-living facilities, day-care programs,** and **home health services**—are typically costly. These options are not covered by **Medicare.** We need creative services to keep frail older people from prematurely entering that setting designed for the most impaired older adults—the nursing home.

Being female and very old, and not having available family members, are the main risk factors for entering **nursing homes,** or **long-term-care facilities.** Nursing homes vary dramatically in quality. The **certified nursing assistant or aide,** the main caregiver, while very poorly paid, can find a generative mission in nursing home work. Society needs to prepare for the onslaught of baby boomers as they enter their old-old years. Although the best personal preparation for reaching **integrity** is having fulfilled each adult life task "on time," people can reach every Eriksonian milestone during their final years—or even months—of life.

▮ KEY TERMS

normal aging changes,
    p. 424

chronic disease, p. 424

ADL (activities of daily living)
    problems, p. 425

instrumental ADL problems,
    p. 425

basic ADL problems, p. 425

socioeconomic/health gap,
    p. 426

presbyopia, p. 431

lens, p. 432

presbycusis, p. 433

elderspeak, p. 434

reaction time, p. 435

osteoporosis , p. 435

dementia, p. 438

Alzheimer's disease,
    p. 440

vascular dementia,
    p. 440

Medicare, p. 445

alternatives to institutionali-
    zation, p. 445

continuing care retirement
    community, p. 445

assisted-living facility,
    p. 445

day-care program, p. 445

home health services,
    p. 446

nursing home/long-term-care
    facility, p. 446

certified nurse assistant or
    aide, p. 447

integrity, p. 448

▮ RECOMMENDED RESOURCES

GENERAL SOURCE

National Center for Health Statistics (www.cdc.gov/nchs)
    This treasure trove of health data offers up-to-date statistics on everything from life expectancy to nursing homes to state-by-state breakdowns of chronic disease.

SOCIOECONOMIC/HEALTH GAP

Adler, N., Marmot, M., McEven, B.S., and Stewart, J., Eds. (1999). *Socio-economic status and health in industrial nations: Social, psychological, and biological pathways.* New York: New York Academy of Sciences.
    This scholarly book focuses on socioeconomic health disparities throughout the lifespan. Chapters cover specific causes (such as stress and smoking), basic physiological mechanisms, interventions, country-by-country comparisons, and other topics.

DEMENTIA

Alzheimer's Association (www.alz.org)
    This organization provides information about everything from the latest biomedical investigations to interviews with researchers to basic statistics. On-line chats are also available on the Web site.

Mace, N., and Rabins, P. (1999). *The thirty-six-hour day: A family guide to Alzheimer's.* Baltimore: Johns Hopkins Press.
    This is the classic self-help book on caring for people with dementing diseases.

Snyder, S. (1999). *Speaking our minds: Personal reflections from individuals with Alzheimer's.* New York: Freeman.
    This fascinating book provides in-depth interviews with seven people in the early stages of Alzheimer's disease.

Tanzi, R., and Parson, A. (2000). *Decoding darkness: The search for the genetic causes of Alzheimer's disease.* Cambridge, MA: Perseus.
    In this book, a science writer and a biomedical researcher team up to offer an account of the race to understand the hereditary aspects of Alzheimer's disease.

CHAPTER 15

My father died in the "normal" late-twentieth-century way. Although we knew nothing about the actual process by which people die, we had plenty of time to plan for the event. Dad's death came at the "right" time, at the end of a long life. The kind of death Stewart's mother faced on September 11 was horrifying, unexpected—totally outside the norm.

Today, as Figure 15.1 on page 454 illustrates, our pathways to death take three basic forms (Enck, 2003; Institute of Medicine, 1997). As happened most dramatically in the World Trade Center tragedy, roughly one out of every six or seven people in developed-world nations

Death and Dying

I was getting in the car to drive to work when Amy screamed, "Stewart! Come listen to the news!" We figured out pretty quickly that it came in right about the floor where she worked, the 96th. By the time the tower came down, we knew for sure that she died. With a normal death, you prepare for the grieving process. With a shocking death, it hits you by surprise. My wife was about to give birth to our first child, and my mother had plane tickets to come down on Friday. You get into the part of it where you mentally play back the events. Mom (typical, for her) had gone in to work early so she could leave for a dentist appointment. If she'd been a less responsible person, she would not have been there at 8:46. The other weird part of it is, like, the whole country feels they own pieces of this tragedy and need to constantly remind you about it. So it doesn't go away.

My mom didn't have young children, but she was looking forward to retirement, to being a grandmother, and so she was cheated of all those things. Not only did she die in this horrible way—she died at an unacceptably early age.

* * * *

In his seventies my father seemed immortal. While he often joked about being an "old man," he had no major infirmities. At age 81, mortality hit. For a few months Dad had been listless—not his old self, suddenly looking old. Then came the unforgettable call: "The doctor says it's cancer of the liver. Jan, I'm going to die."

Because medicine never admits defeat, the plan was three rounds of chemotherapy, punctuated by "recovery" at home. The doctor said, "Maybe we can lick this thing," but the treatments were agonizing. Worse yet, recovery never happened. My father got weaker. After a few months he could barely walk. Then, before going into the hospital for the third round, my mother called: "Last night we cried together and decided not to continue. We're calling in hospice. I think it's time for you to come down." My father had two more weeks to live.

A day or two before you die, you slip into a coma. It's the preceding week or two that lasts for years. Everyone has been summoned to bustle around a train that cannot be derailed. Yes, you can talk, but what do you say? My father was never a verbal man. Then, as if on cue, the disease picks up speed. From the wheelchair to becoming bedridden, the voice that mutates into a whisper, followed by waiting . . . for what? You force yourself to be at the bedside when the breathing gets slow and rattled, but you are terrified. You have never seen a dying person. You don't know how things will go. Above all, you hope that things go quickly. You can't stand to see your father suffer anymore.

dies without any warning—as a result either of an accident or, more often, of a sudden fatal, age-related event, such as a heart attack or stroke (Enck, 2003; see the red line in Figure 15.1). My father's death fit the pattern when illnesses such as cancer are discovered at an advanced stage. Here, as you can see in the blue line, a person is diag-nosed with a fatal disease and then steadily declines.

The prolonged, erratic pattern shown in yellow, however, is probably the most common dying pathway in our contemporary age of extended chronic disease. After developing cancer, kidney problems, or heart disease, people battle that condition, helped by medical technology, until death eventually occurs (Enck, 2003; Walter, 2003).

So today deaths in affluent countries typically occur slowly. They are dominated by medical procedures. They have a protracted, uncertain course (Walter, 2003). For most of human history, people died in a very different way.

FIGURE 15.1: Three pathways to death: Although some people die suddenly, the pattern in blue and especially that in yellow are the most common pathways by which people die today.

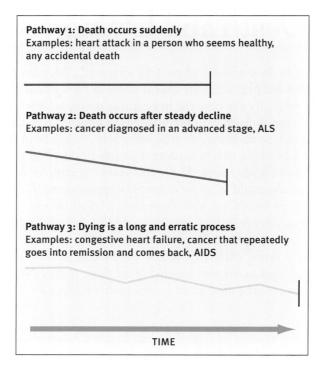

Pathway 1: Death occurs suddenly
Examples: heart attack in a person who seems healthy, any accidental death

Pathway 2: Death occurs after steady decline
Examples: cancer diagnosed in an advanced stage, ALS

Pathway 3: Dying is a long and erratic process
Examples: congestive heart failure, cancer that repeatedly goes into remission and comes back, AIDS

TIME

Setting the Context: A Short History of Death

She contracted a summer cholera. After four days she asked to see the village priest, who came and waited to give her the last rites. "Not yet, M. le Curé, I'll let you know when the time comes." Two days later: "Go and tell M. le Curé to bring me Extreme Unction."

(reported in Walter, 2003, p. 213)

As you can see in this nineteenth-century description of the death of a French peasant woman, before modern medicine, death typically arrived quickly. People let nature take its course. There was nothing they could do. Dying was familiar, predictable, and normal. It was firmly embedded in daily life (Wood & Williamson, 2003).

According to the historian Philippe Ariès (1974, 1981), while life in the Middle Ages was unimaginably horrid and "wild," death was often "tame." Famine, childbirth, and infectious disease ensured that death was an expected presence throughout the lifespan. People died, as they lived, in full view of the community and then were buried in the churchyard in the center of town.

During the eighteenth and nineteenth centuries, death began to move off center stage when—because of fears about disease and overcrowding—villagers decided to relocate burial sites to cemeteries outside of town (Kastenbaum, 2004). Then a more dramatic change took place about a century ago, when doctors began to vigorously wage war against disease. The early-twentieth-century conquest of many infectious illnesses moved dying toward the end of the lifespan, relocating it to old age. Today, with three out of four deaths in the United States taking place among people over age 65 (and many happening in the late eighties and nineties), the actors in the death drama are often a marginal, atypical group—nothing like you or me.

Moreover, as medicine took over, the scene of death shifted to hospitals and nursing homes, so the actual physical process of dying was removed from view. Now, when a person dies, often in the inner recesses of the intensive care

For most of human history, death was ever present—"up close and personal"—and occurred in the midst of normal life. Here is an eighteenth-century painting entitled "The Last Request," in which a dying young woman is offering her final words to her spouse.

These men in Afghanistan are honoring their 8-year-old nephew, who has just died of pneumonia, by following the traditional Muslim ritual of personally wrapping the body in a shroud. Compare this image with our sanitized U.S. funeral, with the body encased in its coffin, the well-dressed mourners, the church filled with flowers, and all preparations taken care of by the funeral home.

unit, we cover the body and erase all signs of its presence as it's stealthily shipped to the funeral home (Kastenbaum, 2004; Nuland, 1994). According to one social critic, by the middle of the twentieth century death had become the new "pornography"—disgusting, abnormal, never to be seen or talked about (Gorer, 1965).

To appreciate how appropriate the word *pornographic* is with regard to our feelings about the organic reality of death, let's pause for a moment to look at a few standard deathbed practices in different cultures. Imagine, for instance, performing the traditional Islamic end-of-life ritual. As a death becomes imminent, loved ones prop the person up to sit facing Mecca and pronounce the confession of faith. After death, they cleanse the body with water and soap, arrange the corpse in a sleeping position (sometimes inserting perfume-soaked cotton balls in the armpits and between the legs to offer a pleasant smell), shroud the body, and carry it to the burial site.

Or consider the deathbed duties of a family member living in Japan about a century ago: When the end approaches, the child seated closest to the ill person performs a symbolic resuscitation, dipping a bamboo chopstick into water to wet the lips. At the moment of death the eyes are closed, the person's hands are folded into a position of prayer, and the body is lovingly dressed in its carefully chosen death robe. A son designated to inherit the household shaves his father's head, cuts his nails, and performs the bathing ritual, designed to wash away his sins (Suzuki, 2003). Would you be able to participate in these activities? Could you give your relative the personal, hands-on care that people throughout history automatically provided to their dying loved ones in societies around the world?

Still, although we may be just as likely as ever to recoil from the physical act of dying, beginning with the 1960s lifestyle revolutions, Western attitudes toward *talking* about death totally changed (Kastenbaum, 2004, 2005). Particularly in North America, university courses on death and dying became the rage (Doka, 2003; Wass, 2004). The social norms drastically shifted from the standard 1950s practice of concealing a devastating diagnosis (never mentioning, for instance, the "C word") in favor of honestly telling people, "Yes, you have cancer, and there's not much we can do." No longer do people in our society see planning the way we die as ghoulish. Today, we urge everyone to document in writing their personal preferences for "a good, dignified death."

In this chapter we will focus on this modern Western **death awareness movement** as we explore what dying is like in our age of death-defying technology and extended, uncertain chronic disease. What feelings do people have as they approach death? Is there a way of improving the way doctors deal with the terminally ill? What issues and choices do people and their families face as they struggle to plan for this "final act"? In our search for answers, we will be moving back and forth between the perspectives of the two major players in the drama of dying: the person and the health-care system.

[FAQ: Why do we study death and dying today?]

death awareness movement The late-twentieth-century trend in Western societies toward openly talking about death and improving the psychological conditions under which people die.

TYING IT ALL TOGETHER

1. Imagine that you were born in the seventeenth or eighteenth century. Which of the following statements about your pathway of dying would *not* be true ?

   a. You would probably have died relatively quickly of an infectious disease.
   b. You would have died in a hospital.
   c. You would have seen death all around you from a young age.
   d. You would probably have died at a relatively young age.

2. If you follow the typical twenty-first-century pattern, as you approach death you can expect to decline (quickly/slowly and erratically) due to (an accident/an age-related chronic disease).

3. Margaret says that today we live in a death-denying society. Ella says, "No, that's not true. Today we are more accepting of death than ever." First make Ella's case and then Margaret's, referring to the information in this section.

Answers to the Tying It All Together questions can be found in the answers section of the book.

The Dying Person

How do people react when they are diagnosed with a fatal illness? What are their emotions as they struggle with this devastating news? The first person to study these topics in a systematic, scientific way was a young psychiatrist named Elisabeth Kübler-Ross.

Kübler-Ross's Stages of Dying: Description and Critique

While working as a consultant at a Chicago hospital during the 1960s, Kübler-Ross became convinced that the health-care system was neglecting the emotional needs of the terminally ill. As part of a seminar for medical students, she got permission to interview dying patients about their feelings. Many people, she found, were relieved to talk openly about their diagnosis. Many, she discovered, knew that their condition was probably terminal, even though the medical staff and family members had made valiant efforts to conceal that fact. Kübler-Ross published her discovery that open communication was important to dying people in *On Death and Dying*, a slim bestseller that ushered in a revolution in the way we treat the terminally ill.

Kübler-Ross (1969), in her **stage theory of dying**, originally proposed that people progress through five distinctive emotions in coming to terms with death: *denial, anger, bargaining, depression,* and *acceptance*. Let's briefly look at each of these stages.

When a person first gets some terrible diagnosis, such as "You have advanced lung cancer," her immediate reaction is denial. She thinks, "There must be a mistake." She may take trips to doctor after doctor, searching for a new, more favorable set of tests. When these efforts fail, denial gives way to anger.

In the anger stage, the person lashes out, bemoaning her fate, railing at other people. One individual may get enraged at a physician: "He should have picked up my illness earlier on!" Others may direct their fury at a friend or family member: "Why did I get this disease, while my brother, who has smoked a pack of cigarettes a day since he was 20, remains in perfect health?"

Eventually, this emotion yields to a more calculating one: bargaining. Now the person pleads for more time, promising to be good if she can put off death a bit. Kübler-Ross (1969) gives this example of a woman who begged God to let her live long enough to attend the marriage of her oldest son:

The day preceding the wedding she left the hospital as an elegant lady. Nobody would have believed her real condition. She . . . looked radiant. I wondered what her reaction would

---

Kübler-Ross's stage theory of dying The landmark theory, developed by psychiatrist Elisabeth Kübler-Ross, that people who are terminally ill progress through five stages in confronting their death: denial, anger, bargaining, depression, and acceptance.

be when the time was up for which she had bargained. . . . I will never forget the moment she returned to the hospital. She looked tired and somewhat exhausted and before I could say hello, said, "Now don't forget I have another son."

(1969, p. 83)

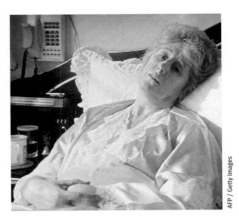

Then, once reality fully sinks in, the person gets depressed and, ultimately, reaches the stage of acceptance. By this time the individual is quite weak and no longer feels upset, angry, or depressed. She may even look forward to the end.

Kübler-Ross deserves enormous credit for alerting us to the fact that there is a living, breathing person inside of the diagnosis "terminal cancer" or "end-stage heart disease." The problem is that her original ideas were embraced in an overly rigid, simplistic way. Here are three reasons why we *cannot* take this famous theory as the final word about death:

Terminally ill people do *not* always want to discuss their situation. Although she never intended this message, many people read into Kübler-Ross's theory the idea that patients universally want to talk about their fate. This is emphatically not true. When one researcher questioned dying patients about their feelings about "death talk," she found that people broach this subject selectively—and often reluctantly (McGrath, 2004). In the words of one respondent: "They're scary subjects and . . . we don't want to touch on it too much. . . . It's very personal" (p. 836). Patients avoid these discussions, this interview study showed, to protect loved ones: "Because you don't want them to . . . get really upset so you . . . hold everything back. . . . My sister is good but I couldn't load off onto her, she would just break" (p. 837). Sometimes, they shy away from this topic to emotionally protect themselves: "I think I've got as much as I can cope with. So I can't get her upset . . . and then have to try to calm her down" (p. 839).

The bottom line is that people who are dying behave just as they do when they are fully living (which they are!). They are leery about bringing up painful subjects. People don't shed their sensitivity to others and feelings about what topics are socially appropriate to discuss when they have a terminal disease. As life is drawing to a close, preserving the quality of our attachment relationships is actually a *paramount* agenda—and this, as you will see, is a main message we will highlight later in our discussion (Kastenbaum, 2004).

Not all cultures see "openness" as an ideal way to behave. Even the concept that it's preferable to tell the truth to terminally ill patients is not universally shared. This idea reflects the premium that our Western individualistic culture puts on honest communication. In collectivist societies that stress social harmony, many people feel that revealing these kinds of painful facts is hurtful. So doctors in China and Japan do not typically follow the Western practice of telling patients when they have a fatal disease (Fetters, 1998; Chan, 2004; Long, 2004). Once again, notice that behaviors our culture defines as "caring and sensitive" may be viewed as insensitive and rude in other parts of the globe.

People do *not* pass through distinctive stages in adjusting to death. Most important, people facing death do not react in anything like a universal, cookie-cutter way! In fact, uncritically accepting Kübler-Ross's stages can be dangerous if it encourages us to distance ourselves from dying loved ones (Kastenbaum, 2004). Instead of understanding that becoming depressed is a perfectly reasonable reaction when a person is facing a life-threatening illness, if friends and family see this feeling as "a phase," they might view it as somehow not real.

According to Kubler-Ross's famous *stage theory of dying*, we would label this terminally ill woman as being in the "depression phase" and then expect her to reach acceptance. But do people really die in this patterned way? As you will see on the next page, the answer is no.

Having members of a congregation praying by one's bedside can offer solace and a sense of connection during a person's final days. But to be really sensitive, this minister and church members would also need to respect this man's privacy, taking their cues from him as to whether he *really* wanted to discuss his impending death.

It's perfectly understandable for an ill person to get angry when others respond insensitively or don't call or visit; but if we see this response through the lens of stage theory, we might dismiss these natural feelings of hurt as "predictable" signs of the anger stage.

Therefore, experts today view Kübler-Ross's contributions with mixed emotions. Yes, she pioneered an important topic. But her theory inadvertently encouraged its own kind of insensitivity to the terminally ill (Kastenbaum, 2004).

The More Realistic View: Many Different Emotions

People who are dying *do* get angry, bargain, deny their illness, and become depressed (Corr, 1991, 1992; Sandstrom, 2003). However, as one psychiatrist argues, it's more appropriate to view these feelings as "a complicated clustering of intellectual and affective states, some fleeting, lasting for a moment, or a day" (Schneidman, 1976, p. 6). When—as is often true today—an ill person may be diagnosed with an incurable, fatal disease, and then live on for years or decades, thoughts of dying may arise only during a medical crisis (Willems and others, 2004). Even when people theoretically "know" that their illness is terminal, the awareness that "I am dying" may not fully penetrate in a definitive way (Chochinov & others, 2000; Groopman, 2004; McGrath, 2004). This emotional state, called **middle knowledge,** is beautifully described in the following quotation:

> *Patients seem to know and want to know, yet they often talk as if they did not know and did not want to be reminded of what they have been told. Many patients rebuke their doctors for not having warned them about complications in treatment or the course of an illness even though the doctors may have been scrupulous about keeping them informed. These instances of seeming denial are usually examples of middle knowledge.*
>
> (Weisman, 1984, p. 459)

And, as anyone who has witnessed a loved one facing approaching death is well aware, an emotion that often burns strong until almost the final days of life is hope (Groopman, 2005; Little & Sayers, 2004). If the person is religious, he may believe in divine intervention: "God will provide a miraculous cure." Someone else may pin her hopes on meditation, alternative therapies, or exercise. Another source of hope—as Kübler-Ross suggested—is the idea that the medical predictions can be wrong: "True, I have that diagnosis, but I know of cases where a doctor told a person with my illness she had six months left and she has been living for 10 years."

Finally, in an era when our illness-to-death path can last for decades, being diagnosed with a life-threatening illness can produce interesting new feelings. It can energize people, promote further development, and stimulate the search for new, more satisfying identities and life goals. Let's read what three young men with AIDS had to say (quoted in Sandstrom, 2003):

> *I feel like AIDS has sort of been a blessing, because, well, it's helped me grow a lot as a person. I've come out of my shell emotionally. . . . I mean it's ironic . . . but because of AIDS I've learned how to enjoy life and enjoy people. . . . It's been a very positive experience.*
>
> (p. 470)

> *It's helped me to set priorities, you know. . . . I'm better able to sort out what's really important and what isn't. . . . I think I've changed in that respect.*
>
> (p. 470)

> *One of my concerns is that I haven't made a dent in the world. And so I've decided to do some advocacy things . . . and that's . . . helped take the focus off the fact that I might be dying. . . . It's made me feel like I'm finally making a contribution to the world.*
>
> (p. 471)

In sum, people react to the challenge of dying in the same ways as they react to the challenges of living. They get anxious and depressed, angry and "in denial." They are calm, accepting, and often hopeful. Sometimes, they feel fully alive for the first time in life.

middle knowledge The idea that terminally ill people can know that they are dying yet at the same time not completely grasp or come to terms emotionally with that fact.

Diagnosed in his early twenties with testicular cancer that had spread to his brain, Lance Armstrong went on to triumph over his often fatal disease and win the Tour de France many times. In the process, he became a symbol to patients with advanced cancer around the world that "Yes, you may be able to beat this thing."

Eric Gaillard / Reuters / Corbis

AIDS, that extended chronic disease, is typical of of the common twenty-first-century pathway to death discussed at the beginning of this chapter. Patients are in limbo, unsure if they are really dying. They have good days and bad days. They can live for a very long time in the shadow of death. But AIDS is unusual because it often strikes at an age that is clearly *off time* in terms of our social clock—often during the young adult years.

Drawing on Erik Erikson's theory, we might predict that facing death in our twenties or thirties is uniquely difficult and painful. How can you reach inintegrity, or the sense that you have accomplished your life goals, if your life may end just when you are finding your identity, mastering intimacy, or discovering your generative path? (See Rando, 1984.) The elderly—although they may be just as afraid of the pain of dying as younger people are—almost always say that they are not afraid of death (J.K. Belsky, 1999). (As an 80-year-old colleague of mine with an inoperable brain tumor calmly explained the situation to his daughter, who couldn't understand why he rejected the chemotherapy that could buy him extra months of life: "Life is a play, with a beginning, middle, and end.")

But it's not always possible to generalize about people's coping styles on the basis of their age. Even children can face death in brave, accepting ways. One oncologist told the story of a 9-year-old patient with cancer, who, when his illness reached its final phase, calmly planned his funeral, picked out his burial clothes, and gave away his favorite toys to his brother and friends (Wolfe, 2004). What we do know is that deaths that occur at an off-schedule time in the life life cycle haunt *parents* for the rest of their lives.

AP Photo / Todd Warshaw

Magic Johnson, shown here carrying the Olympic flame, is a testament to how being diagnosed HIV-positive can be the signal for a person to construct a new, more gratifying, generative life. Since he learned about his illness 25 years ago, Johnson has had several successful business ventures, written a book, appeared as a regular commentator on TNT, and—most important—devoted his life to philanthropic work. His Magic Johnson Foundation has donated millions of dollars to help inner-city children and adults succeed.

Dave Einsel / Getty Images

Being robbed of the chance to be a loving husband and father at the threshold of adult life is impossibly unfair. Imagine being at this funeral of a private who, right after getting married to his 18-year-old sweetheart (shown here), left for Iraq and was killed by a roadside bomb at the terribly off-time age of 23.

FOCUS ON A TOPIC: *THE DEATH OF A CHILD*

My first son passed away at age 24 from bone cancer. It's been over 40 years since he died, but not a day goes by when I don't miss him. My younger boy just died from heart disease, last month, at age 62. I don't understand it. I'm 90. Why didn't the Lord take me instead?

When I worked in a nursing home, I realized that the death of a child outweighs any other loss. It doesn't matter whether their "baby" dies at age 6 or in his sixties; parents never fully come to terms with that unnatural event (Hayslip & Hansson, 2003). People do *eventually* go on to construct a fulfilling life. However, when a child dies, it's hard to move on to the working-model, "recovery" stage of mourning (see the discussion of widowhood in Chapter 13). Parents are typically immobilized by intense grieving for several years (Bernstein, 1997; Hayslip & Hansson, 2003; Singg, 2003).

As you just saw in the quotation above, a child's death may evoke powerful feelings of survivor guilt: "Why am I still alive?" If the death occurred suddenly due to an accident, there is disbelief and possibly guilt at having failed in one's fundamental mission as a parent: "I couldn't protect my baby!" (Cole & Singg, 1998). If the child died of an incurable genetic disorder such as cystic fibrosis, or after a long illness such as cancer, parents seem better able to cope (Singg, 2003). But even when they are confident

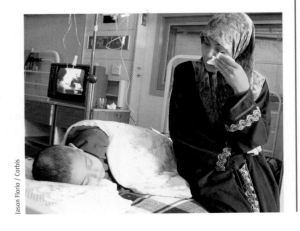

Jason Florio / Corbis

This photograph from Iraq of a terminally ill cancer patient and his grieving mother has its own universal theme. No event is harder to cope with than the death of a child.

[FAQ: Should you tell terminally ill children they are dying?]

[FAQ: How can you help someone suffering from grief?]

that medically everything possible has been done, mothers and fathers may still have nagging concerns: "Maybe I *could* have done something else emotionally for my daughter or son."

When a child has inoperable cancer *and seems to understand that he is dying,* should parents explicitly talk about death? To thoroughly explore this question, Swedish researchers interviewed *every* family who had lost a child to cancer in that country over a period of several years (Kreicbergs and others, 2004). No parent who reported having a conversation about death with an ill daughter or son had any regrets. In contrast, more than half of the mothers and fathers who believed that their child understood what was happening but never discussed this topic felt guilty later on. So discussing death helps *parents* feel that they did everything they could do emotionally to help.

What can health-care providers do to ease a family's pain? Attend the funeral. Write condolence letters to honor the struggle of the parents and the courage of the child (Wolfe, 2004). Listen to people share their stories (Rallison & Moules, 2004). And prior to death, when the child's illness reaches its advanced stage, sensitively broach the possibility of dying, while not destroying feelings of hope (Rallison & Moules, 2004). Moreover, experts urge, when death becomes imminent, it helps to invite parents to share the hands-on care. After watching a man pace the room helplessly, his hands clenched together as his son was dying of AIDS, a nurse described how she gave this father one last chance to be a parent in the final moments of his son's life:

> I adjusted the damp cloth on the young man's head and the father asked if he could do that. I handed him the cloth, and as he stroked his son's face with it, he told me about the times he had bathed his son when he was a little boy and prepared him for bed. I asked if he would like to do this now. . . . He then proceeded to bathe his son, who died later that evening. At the wake, the father came up to me, smiled and said proudly that his son had died in clean pajamas. . . . [Along with his pain] he will always have [that] memory.
>
> (quoted in Brabant, 2003, pp. 480–481)

Because it is clearly off time, most of us would never see the death of a child as appropriate or right. What overall qualities are involved in having what psychologists call "a good death"?

In Search of a Good Death

We can get interesting insights into the core dimensions of "a good death" by turning to religious sources, such as Old Testament writings (Spronk, 2004). According to the Bible, death is appropriate after a long life, showing why deaths that occur prematurely cause us special pain. The Bible specifies that death should be peaceful, explaining why surveys reveal that people—no matter what their religion—dislike the idea of dying after being "tortured" by machines (Willems and others, 2004) and don't want to die after years of suffering from extended chronic illnesses, such as Alzheimer's disease (Long, 2004; Walter, 2003; Wood & Williamson, 2003). Death is "best" when it occurs in the "homeland" (not far away), accounting for why—around the globe—people say they want to die at home surrounded by their attachment figures and why we universally reject the sanitized, impersonal dying that takes place in the recesses of intensive care units (Long, 2004).

My personal example of a good death came to my grandmother, Lillian Sheerr, one beautiful summer day. Grandma, at age 98, was just beginning to get slightly frail. One afternoon, before preparing dinner for her visiting grandchildren and great-grandchildren (which she insisted on doing), she got in her car to drive to the hairdresser and—on leaving the driveway—was hit by an oncoming car. Of the eight people involved in the accident no one was hurt but Grandma, who was killed

The principle that good deaths must occur "near the homeland" is embedded in many religious traditions—not just Judeo-Christian ones. This nineteenth-century depiction shows a Hindu funeral ceremony, with the deceased making his final passage surrounded by loving community members while being carried ceremoniously to the grave.

instantly. They said she never felt any pain. My grandma got the death she deserved—because she was a saint in her life.

Given that our chances of being killed instantly in an accident at our doorstep, without any frailties at the limit of human life, are virtually nil, how can we expand on the criteria mentioned above to spell out more specific dimensions of a good death? One psychologist offers the following guidelines (Corr, 1991, 1992):

1. We want to minimize our physical distress, to be as free as possible from debilitating pain.

2. We want to maximize our psychological security, reduce fear and anxiety, and feel in control of how we die.

3. We want to enhance our relationships and be as close as possible emotionally to the people we care about most.

4. We want to foster our spirituality and have the sense that there was integrity and purpose to our lives.

Minimize pain and fear; be close to loved ones; enhance spirituality; feel that our life has meaning—these are all messages of the few studies that have explored "good deaths" among people in their final weeks of life (Breitbart and others, 2004; Nakashima & Canda, 2005; Tang, Aaronson, & Forbes, 2004). Some of this research suggests that people classified as having optimum deaths do tend to have a strong religious faith (Kacela, 2004; Nakashima & Canda, 2005). But it's not necessary to believe in an afterlife or any specific religion. Actually, in one study conducted with terminally ill people, the main dimension that related to feeling comfortable about dying was having had a sense of purpose in life (Ardelt & Koenig, 2006).

So Erikson may have been right in saying that the key to accepting death is fulfilling our life tasks and, especially, our generative missions. And in Erikson's (1963) poetic words, appreciating that one's "individual life is the accidental coincidence of . . . one lifecycle within . . . history" (p. 268) can be important in embracing death, too:

> Barbara turned on the lamp beside her bed. Her eyes were sunken and her skin was pale. It would not be long, I thought. . . . "Are you afraid?" I asked. "You know, not really, not as much as I thought. . . . I have strange comforting thoughts. . . . When fear starts to creep up on me, I conjure up the idea that millions and millions of people have passed away before me, and millions more will pass away after I do . . . I guess if they all did it, so can I."
> (Groopman, 2004, pp. 137–138)

What are your priorities for a good death? Table 15.1 on page 462 offers an expanded checklist based on the principles in this section, to help you evaluate your top-ranking death goals. In the next section, we turn to how well the health-care system is doing at helping people fulfill their plans for a dignified death.

Did this relatively young cancer patient (who later died) have a "good" death? According to the research, much depended on whether he believed he had fulfilled his generative life-mission, and so reached Erikson's integrity, accepting the fact that his personal death was a natural part of the cycle of life.

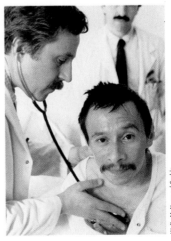

TABLE 15.1: Evaluating Your Priorities for a Good Death: A Checklist

When you think about dying, rank how important each of these criteria might be to you as: (1) of utmost importance; (2) important, but not primary; or (3) relatively unimportant.

_____ 1. Not being a burden to my family.

_____ 2. Being at peace with death—that is, not being anxious about dying.

_____ 3. Not being in physical pain.

_____ 4. Having control over *where* I die—that is, being able to choose whether to die at home or in the hospital.

_____ 5. Having control over *how* I die—that is, being able to choose whether to be kept alive through medical interventions or to die naturally. Being able to end my life if I am terminally ill and in great pain.

_____ 6. Feeling close to my loved ones.

_____ 7. Feeling close to God.

_____ 8. Feeling that I have fulfilled my mission on earth or made a difference in the world.

Do your top-ranking priorities for dying tell you anything about your priorities for living?

 TYING IT ALL TOGETHER

1. Sara is arguing that Kübler-Ross's conceptions about dying are "fatally flawed." Pick out the argument she should *not* use to make her case (that is, identify the false alternative):
   a. People who are dying do not necessarily want to talk about death.
   b. In more collectivist cultures, openly discussing terminal diagnoses with patients is often seen as insensitive.
   c. People do not go through "stages" in adjusting to impending death.
   d. People who are dying simply accept that fact.

2. If your uncle has recently been diagnosed with advanced lung cancer, he should feel (many different emotions/only depressed/only angry), but in general he should have (hope/a feeling of acceptance/a lot of anger).

3. You are a psychologist who works with the terminally ill and their families. All other things being equal, which client is likely to find it easiest to cope with impending death: a 16-year-old girl, a 30-year-old man, an 80-year-old woman, a parent of a dying 8-year-old child?

4. As a hospital administrator, outline some steps you might take to help patients have a good death by reducing their fear and increasing their feelings of having control over how they die.

Answers to the Tying It All Together questions can be found in the answers section of the book.

The Health-Care System

How does the traditional health-care system deal with dying patients? In this section we first take a critical look at standard hospital terminal care and then explore some new health-care options designed to tame twenty-first-century death.

What's Wrong with Traditional Hospital Care for the Dying?

Although most of us can expect to die in a hospital, social scientists have known for decades that the traditional hospital approach to the dying has glaring flaws. Consider the findings of this pathbreaking 1960s study in which sociologists entered hospitals and unobtrusively observed how the medical staff organized "the work" of terminal care (Glaser and Straus, 1968).

The researchers found that when a person was admitted to the hospital, nurses and doctors set up predictions about what pattern that individual's dying was likely to follow. This implicit **dying trajectory** then governed how the staff acted.

There actually were several distinctive dying trajectories. In "the expected swift death," for instance, a patient would arrive (usually in the emergency room) whose death was imminent, perhaps from an accident or heart attack, and who had no chance of surviving. "Expected lingering while dying" was another pathway. In this case a man or woman would enter the hospital with advanced cancer or end-stage heart disease, and slowly decline. Or the patient might follow the "entry–reentry" path that is typical of contemporary chronic diseases: admitted and stabilized medically, then discharged, perhaps to return periodically until the final crisis before death.

The problem, however, was that dying schedules cannot be easily predicted. When someone mistakenly categorized as "expected to linger" was moved to a unit in the hospital where she was not carefully monitored, this mislabeling tended, not infrequently, to hasten death. A particularly interesting situation happened when "expected swift death" changed to "lingering." Doctors would call loved ones to the bedside to say goodbye, only to find that the person began to improve. This "final goodbye" scenario could play out time and time again. The paradox, as you can see in the following example, was that if it was "off schedule," *living* might be transformed into a negative event!

> One patient who was expected to die within four hours had no money, but needed a special machine in order to last longer. A private hospital at which he had been a frequent paying patient for 30 years agreed to receive him as a charity patient. He did not die immediately but started to linger indefinitely, even to the point where there was some hope he might live. The money problem, however, created much concern among both family members and the hospital administrators. . . .The doctor continually had to reassure both parties that the patient (who lived for six weeks) would soon die; that is, to try to change their expectations back to "certain to die on time."
>
> (Glaser & Straus, 1968, pp. 11–12)

The bottom-line message here is that deaths don't occur according to a pre-programmed timetable. Hospitals are structured according to the assumption that they do. This incompatibility makes for an inherently messy dance of terminal care.

Unfortunately, in the decades since this research was conducted, conditions have not changed. Critics still target bumpy, disorganized dying scenarios as a major problem in modern hospital deaths (Brabant, 2003; Good and others, 2004; Yabroff, Mandelblatt, & Ingham, 2004). Hospital personnel still set up projections for when they think patients will die. When dying proceeds according to schedule, health-care providers classify the death as "good." As one resident in a study exploring physicians' perceptions reported: "I felt good that he died in a comfortable way. . . . I guess I just knew it would happen in 24 hours so it doesn't come as a shock" (quoted in Good and others, 2004, p. 944). When trajectories are mislabeled, the death is defined as "bad": "She came in for a bone marrow transplant to cure her [cancer] . . . and got pulmonary toxicity and died" (p. 945). Good deaths happen when there is smooth communication between the medical team and patients' families. Bad deaths are rife with disagreements, anger, and hurt. In fact, because of the potential for miscommunication, traditional hospital dying may be more turbulent in the twenty-first century than ever before.

One reason is that today, unlike in the past, patients do not typically spend weeks or months in a hospital. They often enter this setting when they are within days of death. Therefore the health-care professionals on the death scene are usually not emotionally involved with the person (Good and others, 2004). They have little understanding of patients' and families' needs. Compounding this situation are issues related to living in our multicultural society. Suppose the attending doctor on the floor where your relative is dying is a recent immigrant from Beijing or Bangladesh, or your parents only speak Spanish or Swahili. How would it be possible for everyone to really communicate at this intensely emotional time?

dying trajectory The fact that hospital personnel make projections about the particular pathway to death that a seriously ill patient will take and organize their care according to that assumption.

It takes tremendous sensitivity to communicate well with the anguished family members of a dying patient. This attending physician may have an exceptionally difficult job because she has probably just met these parents at the door of the intensive-care unit and may be wondering whether they do or do not want the staff to use heroic measures to keep their son artificially alive.

Royalty-Free / Corbis

Most important, today, the quantum leap in our death-defying technologies lets us extend the act of dying well beyond the time that nature would intend. Physicians can offer nutrition to people through a tube into the stomach, effectively bypassing the body's normal signal to stop eating in preparation for death. They can put critically ill patients on ventilators, machines that breathe for the person, well beyond the time the lungs would normally have given out. Caring physicians often agonize about using these heroic measures, but as the following comment shows, their mission to cure makes it difficult to resist the lure of the machines:

> We were realizing that we were going to hurt him [a 40-year-old lung cancer patient who had had multiple surgeries and several strokes] if we, for example, . . . kept trying to keep a body alive that was not wanting to be alive. And everyone figured "what the heck, give it a shot."
>
> (quoted in Good and others, 2004, p. 945)

Today, health-care workers are faced with agonizing ethical choices: How long do you vigorously wage war against death, and when should you say "enough is enough"? Shifting from the cure-at-all-costs mode can be very difficult. To paraphrase one observer, it's like "deciding to play baseball while the football game is in full swing" (Chapple, 1999). With the understanding that we can never take the mess out of dying, just as we can never take the mess out of living, let's now explore how the traditional health-care system is taking action to tame death today.

palliative care Any intervention designed not to cure illness but to promote dignified dying.

end-of-life care instruction Courses in medical and nursing schools devoted to teaching health-care workers how to provide the best palliative care to the dying.

INTERVENTIONS: Providing Superior Palliative Care

Palliative care refers to any strategy designed not to cure people but to promote dignified dying. Palliative care includes educating health-care personnel about how to deal with dying patients; modifying the hospital structure; or providing that well-known alternative to dying in a hospital, hospice care. Let's now scan and critique each of these three interventions one by one.

Educating Health-Care Providers

In recent decades, **end-of-life care instruction** has become an integral component of medical and nursing training (Wass, 2004). Courses cover everything from the best drugs to control pain without "knocking the person out" to the ethics of withdrawing treatment, from tips on talking about death with patients to ways of providing sensitive end-of-life care to people from different cultural groups.

Imagine being this doctor and knowing the terminally ill patient whose chart you are reading is about to ask, "What is my prognosis?" Wouldn't it be helpful to have some *end-of-life care instruction* during your training to guide you about how best to respond?

Unfortunately, much of this training consists of lectures that are removed from the realities of hands-on clinical work. Instruction can be spotty. The irony is that paramedics, the very health-care workers who encounter death on a daily basis, get almost no training in end-of-life care (Wass, 2004). In one medical school survey, 8 out of 10 deans described death education as very important. Most said that they believed this topic was given insufficient emphasis at their school. However, they blamed the problem on "time constraints" and not having faculty members with that specific expertise (Sullivan and others, 2004).

Rob Melnychuk / Jupiter Images

Training in being sensitive to the needs of seriously ill patients and families is critically important. From the physicians who (perhaps out of their own fear) decide to take Kübler-Ross's concept of "honesty" literally, saying, "Your illness is terminal and there's nothing we can do," to the story of the woman in Chapter 14 whose neurologist coldly stated, "You have Alzheimer's disease," many of us have horror stories about health-care providers who—when delivering a devastating diagnosis—totally left their humanity behind.

Still, even the most humane physician will have trouble bucking an institutional structure where the push to provide a cure at all costs impedes good end-of-life care. Therefore, some modern medical centers have developed a new in-hospital alternative designed to promote the best possible death.

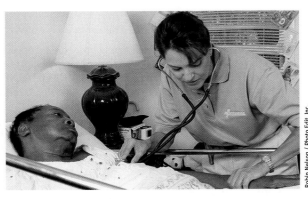

Robin Nelson / Photo Edit, Inc.

Changing Hospitals: Palliative Care Units

A **palliative care service** is a special unit or service within a traditional hospital that is devoted to end-of-life care. Upon entering an institution that offers these state-of-the-art programs, certain groups of patients—for instance, old-old people with multiple chronic illnesses and people with advanced cancer— have their care managed by a team of providers specifically trained in when to shift from "football to baseball mode" (recall the analogy mentioned earlier; Chapple, 1999; Ellershaw, 2001). Patients enrolled in the palliative care service are not denied cure-oriented interventions. However, as their illness progresses and becomes terminal, the vigor of life-prolonging treatments gradually shifts to providing the best possible palliative care (Paice, Muir, & Shott, 2004).

But perhaps it's unfair to ask health-care professionals to embrace the enemy. Physicians in particular may shy away from dying patients because it means they failed in their mission to cure—and of course they are human like the rest of us (Kastenbaum, 2004; Wass, 2004). Therefore, the best way to ensure dignified dying might be to remove that process completely from the hospital, with its death-defying machines.

Palliative care services, with their focus on pain control and letting patients spend their final days in a more natural setting, provide an alternative to dying in the medicalized recesses of intensive care. In this palliative care unit, a nurse is taking the blood pressure of a patient who has had a stroke and is suffering from end-stage heart disease.

palliative care service A service or unit in a hospital that is devoted to end-of-life care.

hospice movement A movement, which became widespread in recent decades, focused on providing palliative care to dying patients outside of hospitals and especially on giving families the support they need to care for the terminally ill at home.

Unhooking Death from Hospitals: Hospice Care

This is the philosophy that underlies the **hospice movement,** which gained momentum in the 1970s, along with the natural childbirth movement. Like birth, hospice activists argued, death is a natural process. We need to let this natural process occur in the most natural way (Brabant, 2003; Leming, 2003).

Hospice workers are skilled in techniques to minimize patients' physical discomfort. They are trained in providing a supportive psychological environment, one that assures patients and family members that they will not be abandoned in the face of approaching death.

Initially, hospice care was delivered only in an inpatient setting called a hospice, much like the palliative care hospital services described above. Although there are still inpatient hospice facilities in many cities, the current emphasis of the hospice movement—at least in the United States—is on providing backup care that allows people to die with dignity at home. As you can see in my interview in the Experiencing the Lifespan box on page 466, multidisciplinary hospice teams go into the person's home, offering care on a part-time, scheduled, or daily basis. They provide 24-hour help in a crisis, giving family caregivers the support they need to allow their relative to spend his final days at home. Their commitment does not end after the person dies: An important component of hospice care is bereavement counseling.

Hospice care has struck a tremendous chord. As I mentioned earlier in this chapter, surveys around the globe show that most people want to spend their final days of life at home (Long, 2004). Since the first American hospice was established in Connecticut in 1974, the U.S. hospice movement has mushroomed, especially in recent years (see Figure 15.2 on page 466).

Hospice care is specifically for the terminally ill. For a patient to enroll, a physician must certify that the person is within six months of death. However, today people have the option of entering hospice programs without abandoning all curative care. They can end their lives helped by hospice personnel in traditional medical settings such as hospitals and nursing homes. Moreover, as Medicare fully covers hospice care, this option is available to elderly people on every economic rung (Brabant, 2003; Leming, 2003).

EXPERIENCING THE LIFESPAN: *HOSPICE TEAM*

What is hospice care really like? How do people who work in hospice feel about what they do? For answers, here are some excerpts from an interview I conducted with the team (nurse, social worker, and volunteer coordinator) who manages our local hospice.

Usually, we get referrals from physicians. People may have a wide support system in the community or be new to the area. Even when there are many people involved, there is almost always one primary caregiver, typically a spouse or adult child.

We see our role as empowering families, giving them the support to care for their loved ones at home. We go into the home as a team to make our initial assessment: What services does the family need? We provide families training in pain control, in making beds, in bathing. A critical component of our program is respite services. Volunteers come in for part of each day. They may take the children out for pizza, or give the primary caregiver time off, or bathe the person, or just stay there to listen.

Families will say initially, "I don't think I can stand to do this." They are anxious because it's a new experience they have never been through. At the beginning they call a lot. Then you watch them really gain confidence in them-

selves. We see them at the funeral and they thank us for helping them give their loved one this experience. Sometimes, the primary caregiver can't bear to keep the person at home to the end. We respect that, too.

The whole thing about hospice is choice. Some people want to talk about dying. Others just want you to visit, ask about their garden, talk about current affairs. We take people to see the autumn leaves, to see Santa Claus. Our main focus is: What are your priorities? We try to pick up on that. We had a farmer whose goal was to go to his farm one last time and say goodbye to his tractor. We got together egg crates, a big tank of oxygen, and carried him down to his farm. We have one volunteer who takes a client to the mall.

We keep in close touch with the families for a year after, providing them counseling or referring them to bereavement groups in the community. Some families keep in contact with notes for years. We run a camp each summer for children who have lost a parent.

We have an unusually good support system among the staff. In addition to being with the families at 3 a.m., we call one another at all times of the night. Most of us have been working here for years. We feel we have the most meaningful job in the world.

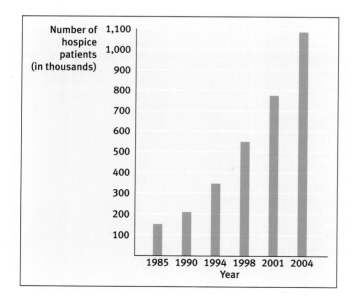

FIGURE 15.2: **Increase in number of hospice patients in the United States (selected years since 1985):** The number of people enrolling in hospice has grown exponentially in recent years.

Source: **National Hospice and Palliative Care Organization (n.d.).**

Still, fewer than one in four deaths in the United States occur among patients enrolled in hospice care (Brabant, 2003). Ethnic and racial minorities, in particular, are less likely than European Americans to use this service (National Hospice and Palliative Care Organization, n.d.). Hospice care has not caught on, in particular, with the Latino community. According to 2003 data, this major ethnic group made up only 4.5 percent of hospice enrollees. Why might people avoid this option even when they say they want to die in a natural way?

Barriers to Hospice Care

One reason, as we saw earlier, is that people are reluctant to give up hope. Making the decision to enter hospice means admitting "I am going to die" (National Hospice and Palliative Care Organization, n.d.). People of color or low-income patients—those who have not gotten the best curative care from the medical system—may have the perception that "I'll be abandoning my best shot at treatment if I enter hospice care" (Ardelt, 2003; Dresser, 2004). Because it means openly labeling a person's condition as terminal, family members may naturally be reluctant to broach the idea of hospice to loved ones—a feeling that is likely to be especially strong among immigrants from collectivist societies in which openly talking about a person's condition is taboo. This cultural difference may explain why the hospice movement has not taken hold in countries such as China, Korea, and Japan (Chan, 2004; Long, 2004).

Moreover, to enter hospice a patient must have a good family support system. As you saw in the Experiencing the Lifespan box above, since the person will typically be dying

at home, there must be a spouse or network of caring relatives committed to the physically and emotionally draining tasks of day-to-day caregiving.

Another barrier may lie in the hospice gatekeeper—
the physician (Feeg & Elebiary, 2005). Even when they
are very open to hospice (Kaplowitz and others, 1999),
doctors often want to put a positive spin on diagnoses.
They believe, with good reason, that it's cruel to take
away hope. As one physician put it, "A tumor has not always read the textbook and a treatment can have an unexpectedly dramatic effect" (quoted in Groopman,
2004, p. 210). The good news is that—because dying trajectories *are* unpredictable—providing hope is perfectly
compatible with telling the truth!

For these reasons, as you saw with my father in the chapter-opening vignette, people typically enter hospice when their death is fairly imminent. In 2003, one in three
hospice patients died within a week of enrollment. In that year the median time spent
in hospice before death occurred was 21 days (National Hospice and Palliative Care
Organization, n.d.).

As the Experiencing the Lifespan box suggested, hospice care can offer tremendous solace to the dying person and loved ones, allowing families to offer one last
demonstration of love as they care for the patient at home. Without minimizing these
benefits, so beautifully described by the hospice team, let's point out some cautions
about actually dying at home.

Although this wife probably would say she wouldn't have it any other way, caring for a beloved husband at home puts a tremendous burden on the caregiver and—as you will see later in this section—can be difficult from the perspective of the dying person as well.

[FAQ: What are the choices on where people can spend their final days?]

The Case Against Dying at Home

Deciding to care for a loved one at home demands a daunting commitment. True,
hospice volunteers do come to relieve the family periodically, but if you are a spouse
or caregiving child, you are basically on call 24/7. You may need to take time off from
work, perhaps for months. You may be under severe financial strain (Tilden and others, 2004). Even with the backup provided by the hospice team, it may be too
anxiety-provoking to manage the crises associated with impending death, so you may
need to transfer your loved one to an inpatient setting in his final days (Arras &
Dubler, 1994).

There are problems from the patient's perspective, too. Imagine spending your
final weeks of life being totally taken care of by your family. You don't have any privacy. Loved ones must bathe you and dress you; they must care for your every need.
You may be embarrassed about being seen naked and incontinent; you may want time
alone to cry out, to vent your anguish and pain. In a hospital, care is impersonal. At
home, there is the humiliation of having to depend on the people you love most for
each intimate bodily act.

Most important, care by strangers equals care that is free from guilt. As you saw
in the "death talk" study discussed earlier in this chapter, when people are approaching death, they often want to protect their loved ones—to shield them from pain. Witnessing the toll that your disease is taking on your family may multiply the pain of
dying itself.

For these reasons, when researchers actually *ask* seriously ill people about their
preferences, they find less than overwhelming enthusiasm about dying at home
(Thomas, Morris, & Clark, 2004). In one interview study, when women with advanced breast cancer were questioned, many suggested they were ambivalent about
taking that route (Hays and others, 1999). One patient said, "I guess it would depend
on if you are not in great pain." Another was confident about pain control ("There's
too many pharmaceutical companies out there") but less comfortable about the idea
of blood ("Hemorrhaging concerns me. That would be so frightening [to my chil-
dren])" (p. 9). A widow mentioned that she definitely wanted to die in the hospital

FIGURE 15.3: **Family reports of major worries of 63 dying patients:** As people are dying, worries about attachment-related issues outweigh everything else. (Losing control over bodily functions is in itself a "relationship issue," as patients want to spare their loved ones the need to care for them should they become incontinent.)

Source: Hickman, Tilden, & Tolle, (2004).

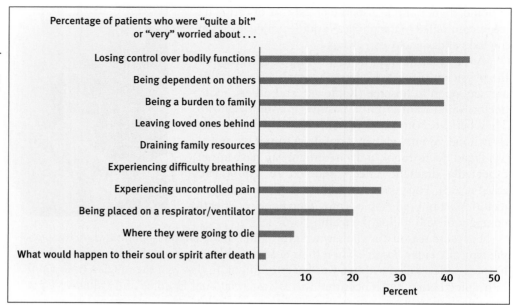

because "I would not want my son to come into the bedroom one day and find me dead. That would be too traumatic for a 16-year-old" (p. 10).

When researchers polled family members about what bothered their terminally ill loved one most, we see similar themes. Notice in Figure 15.3 that as death looms on the horizon, concerns relating to *where* people meet their death fade into the background. People worry mainly about attachment-related issues—being a burden, draining family resources, feeling dependent—even more, you may be surprised to learn, than about being in pain (Hawkins and others, 2005; Hickman, Tilden, & Tolle, 2004; Kastenbaum, 2004). (Now you might want to see how this research compares with your responses to the death anxieties checklist you completed in Table 15.1 on page 462.) If preserving our connections to loved ones is crucially important at the end of life, the best choice may *not* necessarily be to die at home.

Table 15.2 summarizes these points by comparing the pros and cons of home and hospital deaths. Now that we have surveyed the health-care possibilities, it's time to continue our search for a "good" twenty-first-century death by returning to the dying person.

TABLE 15.2: Hospital Death Versus Home Death: Pros and Cons

The case for dying in a hospital

1. Potential for better management of the physical aspects of dying.
2. No fear of burdening your family with your care.
3. Privacy to vent your feelings, without family members around.
4. Avoiding the embarrassment of depending on loved ones for help with your intimate body functions.

The case for dying at home

1. Avoiding having life-prolonging machines used on you.
2. Spending your final days surrounded by the people you care about most.
3. Spending your final days in the physical setting you love best.
4. Having full freedom to follow your own cultural and religious preferences relating to dying.

Given these considerations, where would you prefer to meet death—in a hospital or at home?

TYING IT ALL TOGETHER

1. In a sentence, describe to a friend the basic message of the classic research describing the various dying trajectories discussed on page 463.

2. Based on this section, which statement most accurately reflects doctors' reactions to the terminally ill?
   a. Doctors are always insensitive to dying patients' needs.
   b. Doctors are faced with agonizing choices about using modern technologies to "prolong death."
   c. Because they see their mission as curing illness, doctors *always* strongly believe in the value of using death-defying technologies.

3. Sara is arguing that we are making tremendous strides in improving end-of-life care in traditional medical settings. Martha says no—we have a very long way to go. First make Sara's case and then make Martha's, citing the evidence discussed in this section.

4. Which patient are you most likely to find enrolled in a hospice program?
   a. an old-old man with end-stage heart disease who lives alone and has no living family members
   b. a man with end-stage lung cancer who lives with his wife and daughters
   c. a Hispanic man who has just had a stroke

5. Melanie is arguing that there's no way she will die in a hospital. She wants to end her life at home, surrounded by her husband and children. Using the information in this section, try to convince Melanie that there might be a downside to spending her final days at home.

6. Your grandmother is dying. According to the text, her main priority is likely to be:
   a. feeling close to her attachment figures—you and your parents.
   b. dying at home.
   c. having her pain controlled.

Answers to the Tying It All Together questions can be found in the answers section of the book.

The Dying Person: Taking Control of How We Die

In this section we explore two strategies people can take to control their final passage and so promote a "good death." The first is an option that our society strongly encourages: People should make their wishes known in writing about their treatment preferences, in case they become permanently mentally incapacitated. The second approach is much more controversial: People might be allowed to get help if they want to end their lives.

[FAQ: Can people control the timing of their own death?]

Giving Instructions: Advance Directives

An **advance directive** is the name for any written document spelling out instructions with regard to life-prolonging treatment when people are irretrievably ill and cannot communicate their wishes. There are four basic types of advance directives: two that the individual drafts and two that are filled out by other people, called surrogates, when the ill person is already seriously mentally impaired.

- In the **living will,** mentally competent individuals leave instructions about their treatment wishes for life-prolonging strategies should they become comatose or permanently incapacitated. Although people typically fill out living wills in order to refuse aggressive medical interventions, it is important to point out that this document can also specify that every possible heroic measure be carried out.

advance directive Any written document spelling out instructions with regard to life-prolonging treatment if individuals become irretrievably ill and cannot communicate their wishes.

living will A type of advance directive in which people spell out their wishes for life-sustaining treatment in case they become permanently incapacitated and unable to communicate.

durable power of attorney for health care A type of advance directive in which people designate a specific surrogate to make health-care decisions if they become incapacitated and are unable to make their wishes known.

Do Not Resuscitate (DNR) order A type of advance directive filled out by surrogates (usually a doctor in consultation with family members) for impaired individuals, specifying that if they go into cardiac arrest, efforts should not be made to revive them.

Do Not Hospitalize (DNH) order A type of advance directive put into the charts of impaired nursing home residents, specifying that in a medical crisis they should not be transferred to a hospital for emergency care.

- In a **durable power of attorney for health care,** individuals designate a specific surrogate, such as a spouse or a child, to make end-of-life decisions "in their spirit" when they are incapable of making those choices known.

- A **Do Not Resuscitate (DNR) order** is filled out when the sick person is already mentally impaired, usually by the doctor in consultation with family members. This document, most often placed in a nursing home or hospital chart, stipulates that if a cardiac arrest takes place, health-care professionals should not try to revive the patient.

- A **Do Not Hospitalize (DNH) order** is specific to nursing homes. This document specifies that in case of a medical crisis, a mentally impaired resident is not to be transferred to a hospital for emergency care.

Advance directives have an admirable goal. Ideally, they provide a clear road map so that family members and doctors are not forced to guess what care the permanently incapacitated person *might* want. However, there are serious issues, especially with regard to the most well-known advance directive—the living will.

One difficulty is that people are reluctant to plan for their death in writing. Do you or your parents have a living will? Estimates suggest that only about 5 to 25 percent of the U.S. population does (Pevey, 2003). Doctors don't do much better. In one survey of thousands of Finnish physicians, only 13 percent had filled out a living will (Hildén, Louhiala, & Palo, 2004).

The concept of putting one's personal plans in writing flies in the face of strong cultural norms. In collectivist societies it might be seen as insulting. It would mean that you don't trust loved ones to make decisions about your care (Chan, 2004). When people have been deprived of good access to health care, as alluded to earlier in the section on hospice care, they naturally are reluctant to sign documents stipulating that treatment be withheld (Wetle, 1994). So people who fill out living wills tend to be well-educated and affluent—those most at risk of getting "too much care" (Laakkonen and others, 2004; Pevey, 2003; Sachs, 1994). Moreover, these documents were developed in response to a health-care system with strong incentives to overtreat people. With the growth of cost-containing efforts in medicine, the climate is shifting away from using expensive technologies to preserve life. When patients perceive that the danger may be receiving *too little* care, they may be less interested in signing a document focused on spelling out what interventions doctors should not provide.

The main problem, however, is that these documents don't work that well! Somehow Grandma's living will gets lost in the transition to the hospital, or family members override the document and say, "Grandma really wanted (or didn't want) that particular intervention" (Pevey, 2003). The information in the typical living will is very vague (Reisfield & Wilson, 2004). Does "no aggressive treatments" mean not putting in the feeding tube that has allowed my aunt to survive for a year after brain surgery? What exactly does "no heroic measures" mean?

The solution has been to press for more specificity ("I don't want to be on a ventilator, but I do want a feeding tube"), but would that really be feasible? Would you want to try to micromanage every detail of your future medical treatment in advance? Yes, before you get Alzheimer's disease you might think, "Let me die if I become like that," but you've never been there. Perhaps if you were in this state, you would want modern medicine to pull out all the stops to keep you alive. For this reason, surveys show that many older people don't want to be tightly bound by the instructions they give in their living wills (Reisfield & Wilson, 2004; Seymour and others, 2004). They prefer to leave their doctors and surrogates considerable leeway as to the specifics of their care (Danis and others, 1991; Hawkins and others, 2005; Sehgal and others, 1992).

These considerations suggest that the most useful advance directive is the durable power of attorney (Hawkins and others, 2005). Granted, deciding on a specific family member to carry out one's wishes can lead to jealousy ("Why did Mom give power of attorney to my brother and not me?"). It might not work in cultures where decision making is expected to be a shared family enterprise, such as among the Chinese or Japanese (Chan, 2004). Still, having a designated surrogate can reduce the potential for the kinds of conflicts that may crop up, especially when a parent is elderly and widowed and there are several siblings. Suppose you believe that Mom's suffering should not be prolonged, while your brother insists that treatment continue at all costs. Issues such as these can poison family relationships for years (or life).

By now, some readers may be getting uneasy, not so much about keeping people alive too long but about the opposite problem—letting them die too soon. Let's ratchet up the anxiety a few notches as we move to the next step in the search for death with dignity: actively helping people take their own lives.

Deciding When to Die: Active Euthanasia and Physician-Assisted Suicide

A physician was called to the room of a 20-year-old dying of ovarian cancer. The alcohol drip attached to the I.V. was causing her to vomit profusely, and she said, "Let's get this over with." The doctor wrote, "I could not give her health, but I could give her rest," instructed the nurse to prepare a syringe of morphine, which he then injected into the I.V. Four minutes later, the patient stopped breathing.

(as reported in Walker, 2003)

How do you feel about this doctor's decision, reported in an anonymous article in the *Journal of the American Medical Association* in 1988? Let's first make some distinctions. **Passive euthanasia**, withdrawing potentially life-saving interventions, such as a feeding tube, is legal in the United States and other countries. (That's what advance directives specify.) **Active euthanasia**—taking *action* to help a person die—is currently against the law in every nation except Belgium and the Netherlands (see Table 15.3 on page 472). However, a variation on active euthanasia called **physician-assisted suicide** has been legalized in Oregon. Under very strict conditions, at a terminally ill patient's request, physicians in that state can prescribe a medication the individual can personally take to bring on death.

The distinction between the two types of euthanasia, although a bit murky, lies in intentions. When we withdraw some heroic measure, we don't specifically wish for death. When doctors, as in the quotation above, give a patient a lethal dose of morphine or, as in physician-assisted suicide, prescribe a lethal substance for a terminally ill person, they *want* that individual to die.

Although active euthanasia is almost universally against the law, studies suggest that these kinds of practices that hasten death do regularly occur around the world (Bilsen and others, 2004). Polls suggest that people do accept some form of "restricted" active euthanasia—for instance, if an individual is terminally ill and in great pain (Walker, 2003). But there is considerable resistance to actually making these practices legal. Why?

One reason is that killing violates the religious principle that only God can give or take a life. This is why people in the right-to-life movement passionately oppose both physician-assisted suicide and active euthanasia (Ardelt, 2003; Walker, 2003). Apart from religious considerations, there are other reasons many of us might be leery about taking this step.

By agreeing to legalize these practices, critics fear, we may be opening the gates to involuntary euthanasia, allowing doctors and families to "pull the plug" on people who are impaired but don't want to die (Ardelt, 2003; Walker, 2003). Even when someone requests help to end his life, we don't know whether the patient is being pressured into that decision by unscrupulous relatives who are anxious to get their inheritance or want to be spared the expense of waiting for the person to die.

Another issue relates to trusting the patient's *own* current feelings and thoughts. People who request physician-assisted suicide are

passive euthanasia Withholding potentially life-saving interventions that might keep a terminally ill or permanently comatose patient alive.

active euthanasia A deliberate intervention that helps a terminally ill patient die.

physician-assisted suicide A type of active euthanasia in which a physician prescribes a lethal medication to a terminally ill person who wants to die.

[**FAQ:** When will people have the right to choose how and when they will die?]

Here is a standard euthanasia kit, available at pharmacies throughout Belgium, that doctors can purchase to help patients die. Do you think we should make *active euthanasia* legal in the United States and provide these kinds of "toxic cocktails" to physicians in our country?

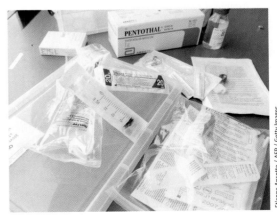

Etienne Ansotte / AFP / Getty Images

TABLE 15.3: Euthanasia and Physician-Assisted Suicide: A Fact Sheet on the Experience in the Netherlands and in Oregon

The Netherlands*

In 2001, both active euthanasia (physicians can administer a lethal injection) and physician-assisted suicide (a doctor can prescribe a lethal medication for the patient to take) were legalized in this country.

Requirements: People do not have to be terminally ill, but a physician must certify that the individual's suffering is "unbearable." The patient must persistently request that his life be terminated in repeated discussions with the primary physician, report that his suffering is unbearable, and state that he wants to die. An independent doctor must also confirm that the patient's suffering is permanent and incurable. Finally, after the death, the primary physician must submit a full report to the coroner, and a pathologist must perform an autopsy and report the findings to a review committee.

Additional facts:

- Slightly more than half of the doctors in the Netherlands have performed this procedure; 12 percent say that they would refuse to do so.

- In 2005, this nation reported 1,933 cases of active euthanasia and physician-assisted suicide.

Oregon†

Oregon's Death with Dignity Act was approved by the state legislature in 1994, but due to legal proceedings, its implementation was put off until 1997. In Oregon, *only* physician-assisted suicide is legal, and doctors can prescribe a lethal medication only when the person is terminally ill.

Requirements: The person must make two requests to the prescribing doctor at least 15 days apart and make one written request witnessed by two people. Two doctors must confirm that the patient is within six months of death, mentally capable, and not depressed. The prescribing doctor must inform the patient of alternative choices and must have given the prescription to the Oregon Health Department.

Additional facts:

- In 2005, 38 people utilized this option.

- Compared to the overall population of deaths, people who used this approach were younger, more apt to be Asian American, divorced, and well educated. People with cancer or amyotrophic lateral sclerosis (ALS) were most likely to decide to end their lives in this way.

- Although a slim majority of Oregon doctors said that they approved of the legislation, only one in three said that they would be willing to prescribe a lethal medication themselves.

*Belgium is the only other country in which active euthanasia is fully legal.
†Physician-assisted suicide is also legal in Switzerland.

Sources: Ardelt (2003); Associated Press (2006); Pietsch (2004); State of Oregon Department of Human Services (n.d.).

During the 1990s, Dr. Jack Kevorkian ignited a nationwide controversy when he reported having helped many terminally ill patients die and made numerous media appearances proudly showing off this "suicide machine." For the reasons spelled out in the text, many people reacted with horror, and now the man dubbed "Dr. Death" is serving a sentence of 10 to 25 years in prison for second-degree murder!

almost always depressed (Arnold, 2004; Parker, 2004). If the depression were treated, they might feel differently about ending their lives. One psychiatrist cited the case of a young man in his thirties diagnosed with leukemia and given a 25 percent chance of survival (Hendin, 1994). Fearing both the side effects of the treatment and being a burden to his family, he begged for assistance in killing himself:

> Once the young man and I could talk about the possibility of his dying—what separation from his family and the destruction of his body meant to him—his desperation subsided. He accepted medical treatment and used the remaining months of his life to become closer to his wife and parents. Two days before he died, he talked about what he would have missed without the opportunity for a loving parting.
>
> (Hendin, 1994, Dec. 16, p. A19)

There are also excellent arguments on the other side. Should patients be forced to unwillingly endure the pain and humiliation of dying when doctors have the tools to mercifully end life? Knowing the agony that terminal disease can cause, is it really being humane to stand by and let nature gradually take its course? Do you believe that legalizing active euthanasia or physician-assisted suicide is a true advance in caring for the dying or its opposite, the beginning of a "slippery slope" that might end in sanctioning the killing of anyone whose quality of life is impaired?

A Looming Social Issue: Age-Based Rationing of Care

There is an age component to the "slippery slope" of withholding care. As I suggested earlier, people with DNR or DNH orders in their charts are typically elderly, near the end of their natural lives. We already use passive euthanasia at the upper end of the lifespan on a case-by-case basis, holding off from giving aggressive treatments to people we deem "too frail." Should we formally adopt the principle "don't use death-defying strategies" for people after they reach a certain age?

Daniel Callahan (1988), a prominent biomedical ethicist, has taken the position that the answer must be yes. There is a time when "the never-to-be-finished fight against death" must stop. According to Callahan, waging total war for everyone might be acceptable if we all had equal access to health care. But in the United States, Medicare pays for expensive life-prolonging strategies, while millions of younger Americans have no health insurance at all. Let's read Callahan's arguments in favor of **age-based rationing of care:**

1. *After a person has lived out a natural lifespan, medical care should no longer be oriented to resisting death.* While stressing that no precise cutoff age can be set, Callahan puts this marker at around the eighties. This does not mean that life at this age has no value, but rather that when people reach their old-old years, death in the near future is inevitable and this process cannot be vigorously defied.

2. *The existence of medical technologies capable of extending the lives of elderly persons who have lived out a natural lifespan creates no presumption that the technologies must be used for that purpose.* Callahan believes that the proper goal of medicine is to stave off premature death. We should not become slaves to our death-defying technology by blindly using each intervention on every person, no matter what that individual's age.

Is Callahan "telling it like it should be" from a logical, rational point of view, or do his proposals give you chills? As you consider this issue, you might be interested to know that we already practice age-based rationing of health care at the opposite end of the lifespan. At a major medical center in my city, babies born before the "cutoff" date of 25 weeks of pregnancy are given no heroic measures. If they survive in the uterus to 26 weeks, however, doctors pull out all the stops. Age-based rationing of care—and when to use aggressive medical measures—is an issue that applies to both the very beginning and the very end of life!

age-based rationing of care The controversial idea that society should not use expensive life-sustaining technologies on people in their old-old years.

Final Thoughts

Age-based rationing of health care is a major social challenge looming on the horizon. Expect these kinds of conversations to continue in the coming decades as the huge baby-boom cohort enters its old-old years.

But the basic message of this chapter takes us back to the heart of our universal human concern. As we approach death, notice that our life comes full circle, and we

care only about what mattered during our first year of life—being connected to the people we most love. OK, during most of the lifespan, self-efficacy is important. But when we come right down to it, attachment trumps everything else! ▨

 ## TYING IT ALL TOGETHER

1. Your mother asks you whether she should fill out an advance directive. Given what you now know from this chapter, what should your answer be?

    a. Go for it! The best thing to do is to fill out a living will so you can be sure your preferences will be fulfilled.
    b. Go for it! But the best alternative might be to discuss your preferences with us and complete a durable power of attorney.
    c. Avoid advance directives like the plague, because your preferences will never be fulfilled.

2. David and Janet are arguing about legalizing physician-assisted suicide. David is furious that this practice is not legal and feels that "people should have the right to die." Janet is terribly worried about formally institutionalizing this practice. First make David's case and then support Janet's argument, using the points in this section.

Answers to the Tying It All Together questions can be found in the answers section of the book.

▌ SUMMARY

The Dying Person

Today, we have three major pathways to death: We may die suddenly, without warning; we may steadily decline; and, most often, we may battle an ultimately fatal, chronic condition for a prolonged time. Before modern medicine, people died quickly and everyone had a good deal of hands-on experience with death. Today, we have "moved" death to old age and keep the act of dying hidden from view. Although the physical process of dying is still "off the horizon," the late-twentieth-century **death awareness movement** has promoted more open discussion of that taboo subject and efforts to promote a dignified death.

Elisabeth Kübler-Ross, in her **stage theory of dying,** proposed that people pass through denial, anger, bargaining, depression, and acceptance when they learn they have a fatal disease. However, we cannot take this landmark theory as the final truth. Not every ill person wants to talk about impending death. Not every culture feels that being honest is the best way to approach the terminally ill. Most important, people feel many different emotions, especially hope, when they confront a possibly fatal illness. They may experience a state called **middle knowledge,** both knowing and not fully comprehending their fate. Sometimes, when people live for years with a life-threatening disease, this knowledge allows them to get their lives together and approach living in a different way.

Parents have an enormously difficult time coping with that off-time event, the death of a child. If a terminally ill child seems to know he or she is dying, it helps parents feel they did everything possible when they openly discuss death with their daughter or son. Health-care workers can help families by attending the funeral, sensitively bringing up the possibility of death when the illness enters its terminal phase, and inviting parents to share in the hands-on care during a child's final hours.

The Old Testament injunction that dying at peace after a long life surrounded by our loved ones is the best possible way for life to end resonates today. Most people want to die at home and reject being kept artificially alive by medical interventions. Specifically, people want to end their lives relatively free of pain and anxiety, feel in control of how they die, and die feeling close to loved ones. Spirituality—believing that we have fulfilled our purpose in living and appreciating that our death is part of the universal human cycle of life—is also important in accepting death.

The Health-Care System

A classic study of **dying trajectories** showed that because dying doesn't proceed according to a predetermined plan but medical personnel assume it does, the way hospitals manage death leaves much to be desired. Communication problems among patients and families and medical personnel, along with the fact that medical technologies can extend life well beyond the time the body "wants" to die, increase the potential for undignified hospital deaths today. Interventions to provide better **palliative care** include: (1) offering **end-of-life care instruction** to health-care personnel; (2) establishing hospital-based **palliative care services;** and (3) removing the scene of dying from hospitals to the hospice.

The **hospice movement** offers backup services that allow families to let their loved ones spend their final months dying naturally, typically at home. Although more people than ever use hospice care, this well-established program has not caught on with ethnic minorities. Enrolling in hospice means labeling the patient as definitely dying. It also demands that family members be committed to providing hands-on care. Interestingly, home deaths get less attractive when people realize that they are most worried about attachment-related issues, such as not burdening their families.

The Dying Person: Taking Control of How We Die

Advance directives—the **living will** and **durable power of attorney for health care,** filled out by the individual in health, and the **Do Not Resuscitate (DNR)** and **Do Not Hospitalize (DNH)** orders, filled out by surrogates when the person is mentally impaired—provide information about whether to use heroic measures when individuals cannot make their treatment wishes known. As there are special problems with the living will, the best advance directive may be the durable power of attorney, which gives a specific surrogate decision-making power to direct one's care.

With **active euthanasia** and **physician-assisted suicide,** physicians move beyond **passive euthanasia** (withdrawing treatments) to actively take steps that promote the death of seriously ill people who want to end their lives. Paramount among the objections to legalizing active euthanasia is the idea that we may be opening the door to killing people who don't really want to die. A related issue is **age-based rationing of care,** whether to hold off on using expensive death-defying technologies with people who are in their old-old years. The bottom-line message of this chapter is that love (or, in developmental science terminology, our attachments) matters more than anything else.

▍ KEY TERMS

death awareness movement, p. 455

Kübler-Ross's stage theory of dying, p. 456

middle knowledge, p. 458

dying trajectory, p. 463

palliative care, p. 464

end-of-life care instruction, p. 464

palliative care service, p. 465

hospice movement, p. 465

advance directive, p. 469

living will, p. 469

durable power of attorney for health care, p. 470

Do Not Resuscitate (DNR) order, p. 470

Do Not Hospitalize (DNH) order, p. 470

passive euthanasia, p. 471

active euthanasia, p. 471

physician-assisted suicide, p. 471

age-based rationing of care, p. 473

▍ RECOMMENDED RESOURCES

GENERAL BOOKS

Kastenbaum, R. (2004). *On our way: The final passage through life and death.* Berkeley: University of California Press.

This highly recommended book, covering everything from the history of burials and cremations to mass deaths such as the plague to a no-holds-barred account of what happens to the body after death, offers a rollicking tour of death throughout the ages. It's a total tour de force and very funny!

THE DYING PERSON

Groopman, J. (2004). *The anatomy of hope.* New York: Random House.

This beautifully written collection of case studies of dying explores "good" and "bad" deaths.

Kübler-Ross, E. (1969). *On death and dying.* New York: Macmillan.

This is Elisabeth Kübler-Ross's classic book on death and dying.

Nuland, S. B. (1994). *How we die: Reflections on life's final chapter.* New York: Random House.

This is an excellent book for learning about a topic not discussed in this chapter: what happens to people physically when they die of common fatal illnesses (AIDS, cancer, or heart disease) or from accidents.

THE HEALTH-CARE SYSTEM

Glaser, B., and Strauss, A. L. (1968). *Time for dying.* Chicago: Aldine.

This academic book describes the classic study of mismanaged dying trajectories, discussed in the text.

The National Hospice and Palliative Care Organization. www.nhpco.org

This is the Web site of a premier national organization devoted to hospice care. It offers a wealth of facts and data about this organization, and spells out the principles of palliative care.

SOCIAL ISSUES

Callahan, D. (1988). *Setting limits: Medical goals in an aging society.* New York: Simon & Schuster.

Check out this controversial book for the arguments in favor of age-based rationing of health care. Although written several decades ago, the same arguments may flare up again in the next few decades as the baby boomers become old-old.

ANSWERS TO TYING IT ALL TOGETHER QUESTIONS

CHAPTER 1 The People and the Field **P. 2**

Setting the Context: Basic Markers That Shape the Lifespan

1. d. The incidence of child poverty has increased in tandem with the rise in single parenthood.

2. Maria is probably in her late forties or early fifties; Sara is probably in her early sixties; Rosa is, most likely, in her eighties.

3. Jim might argue that life is better today because we have a much more open society, with individual freedom—especially for women and people of color. Joe might counter that these lifestyle changes have produced a divorce-prone society, an explosion of single parenthood, and increased female and child poverty rates.

4. Pablo has a collectivist worldview, while Peter's worldview is individualistic.

Lenses for Looking at the Lifespan: Theories

1. (1) c; (2) a; (3) b; (4) d; (5) f; and (6) e.

2. b. This suggestion involves providing an appropriate person–environment fit by taking into account the fact that children need to run around.

3. According to Piaget, the act of mouthing everything refers to assimilation. Changing one's mouthing behavior to fit the characteristics of the object is an example of accommodation.

4. Samantha might argue that behaviorism is an ideal approach to human development because it is simple, easy to implement, results-oriented, and very positive about people's capacity to change. Behaviorism's simple, action-oriented concepts—be consistent, reinforce positive behavior, draw on principles of modeling and stimulate efficacy feelings—can help us improve the quality of life for both children and adults.

    Sally might argue that behaviorism's premise that nurture is all-important neglects the powerful impact of nature or genetic forces in determining who we are. She might cite the value of using multiple perspectives—the insights of attachment theory evolutionary psychology, behavioral geneticists Piaget and Erikson's ideas—to understand development. Behaviorism is too simplistic and offers a far too limited understanding of the forces that shape our behavior as we travel through life.

The Tools of the Trade: Research Methods

1. Craig is conducting a correlational study, and Jessica is conducting a true experiment.

2. a. Jessica; b. Craig; c. Jessica; d. Jessica; e. Craig; f. Craig.

3. Cecila is conducting a cross-sectional study, and Jamel is conducting a longitudinal study.

4. You would first select the participants for your study by choosing a particular age group. Then you would test all participants on your question of interest and subsequently retest your group at regular intervals over an extended period of time. In addition to the huge time and money investment, you would face the problem of keeping track of your study's

participants for many years, getting them to the testing site, and contend with the issue of dropouts. The people who continue in your study will probably be an exceptionally motivated and elite group, and your findings will reflect this bias.

CHAPTER 2 Prenatal Development, Pregnancy, and Birth **P. 34**

The First Step: Fertilization

1. Your sketch should include the cervix, uterus, fallopian tubes, ovaries, and ova.

2. The testes are the parallel structure to the ovaries in the male reproductive system.

3. Tell Tiff that the best time to have intercourse is around the time of ovulation, as fertilization typically occurs when the ovum is in the upper part of the fallopian tube. The chain of events that leads from ovulation to fertilization begins with sexual intercourse, during which millions of sperm are ejaculated. A few find their way to the fallopian tubes and drill into the ovum. When one sperm burrows to the ovum's nucleus, the others are shut out, and the two nuclei merge to form a single 46-chromosome cell.

3. c. Twenty percent more males than females are conceived; and roughly 5 percent more males than females are born. The father's chromosome determines the baby's sex: If a Y-carrying sperm penetrates the ovum, the baby will be a boy (XY); if an X-carrying sperm leads to fertilization, the baby will be a girl (XX).

Prenatal Development

1. a. Organs form rapidly during the embryonic stage; neurons migrate to the top of the brain during the fetal stage; the blastocyst forms during the germinal stage.

2. From the neural tube, a mass of cells differentiates during the late embryonic phase. Then, during the next months of pregnancy, the cells migrate to the top of the neural tube, completing their migration by week 25. In late pregnancy, the neurons begin to elongate and differentiate into their mature form.

3. (a) The head develops before the arms; (b) the arms develop before the hands; (c) the fingers develop before fingernails form.
    Examples during childhood: (a) An infant can move its head before it can turn over or sit; (b) a baby can move its shoulders before it has the ability to reach out and grasp a desirable toy; (c) a child can first grasp a crayon, then make swiggles, then draw a person's face.

Pregnancy

1. During the first trimester, Samantha will probably feel tired and have morning sickness. During the second trimester, she will feel better physically and experience the joy and sense of connection when she feels the baby move. During the third trimester, she is likely to feel uncomfortable and anxiously await her baby's birth.

2. Samantha is likely to feel best—both physically and emotionally—during the second trimester.

3. Two wider-world forces that suggest a woman may need special help coping with pregnancy are being under economic stress and, especially, not having a supportive partner or caring social network.

4. Your answers here will differ, but here are some possibilities: You might make a systematic effort to include dads in your pregnancy and birth educational materials and encourage males to be present for all the prenatal exams; you might specifically alert women about the need to be sensitive to their partner; you could set up a support group specifically for fathers-to-be.

Threats to the Developing Baby

1. Teratogen A, which caused limb malformations, most likely wreaked its damage during *the embryonic stage* of prenatal development and was taken during *the first trimester* of pregnancy. Teratogen B, which caused developmental disorders, probably did its damage during *the fetal stage* and was taken during the *second or third trimesters*.

2. The principle that teratogens exert their damage during the sensitive period for the development of a particular organ.

3. d. Typically, there should be no problem with one glass of wine, as it is below the teratogenic threshold; but—as individual fetuses may be especially vulnerable—the best approach is not to drink at all during pregnancy.

4. Jennifer. Down syndrome—the chromosomal disorder—is typically caused by an unlikely, random event. Having already given birth to a child with cystic fibrosis, the recessive genetic disorder, Jennifer has a one-in-four chance of each subsequent child having that disease.

5. You can say that the CVS test is a more dangerous procedure—with a slightly higher risk of limb malformations and miscarriage—but its advantage is that your child's genetic fate can be determined in the first trimester, and so you won't need to go through the trauma of a full labor. Amniocentesis is a safe procedure, and this test can determine a fuller complement of genetic disorders. But because this test must be performed in the second trimester, you will have to endure a full labor should you decide to end the pregnancy.

6. Your checklist to determine whether in vitro fertilization might be an appropriate strategy might include the following questions: Are your fallopian tubes blocked? Is there a problem with the sperm reaching or penetrating the egg? Do you have ample funds (or exceptional health insurance)? Could you (women especially) spend several days each month undergoing a difficult procedure? Do you live near a major medical center or could you take time off each month to visit one? How much is it worth to you to have your own "biological child"? Could you live with a higher possibility of miscarrying and a slightly higher risk of giving birth to a child with a birth defect?

Birth

1. Melissa is in stage 1, effacement and dilation of the cervix. Margo is in stage 2, birth.

2. c. Holland has a low rate of maternal mortality, and a significant percentage of women give birth at home.

3. Lo Sue: This operation has saved countless lives—and we vitally need it to protect the baby and sometimes the mother's health. If Lo Sue lived in

China, she might say, "Having a c-section will help ensure I give birth to my one healthy baby and allow me to have my child on a lucky day." Sara: Birth is a natural process that should occur in a natural way. C-section rates have increased dramatically over the past few decades, which suggests that many of these procedures are not really necessary. C-sections are more expensive and, although typically very safe, because they are operations, they may lead to a higher risk of complications.

The Newborn

1. Baby David is in excellent health.

2. c. Birth is typically very safe in the developed world, but maternal and infant mortality remain a serious problem in the least developed countries.

3. b. Developmental lags are predictable, and while many babies do outgrow their problems, there is a higher risk of the child having enduring disabilities.

4. Sally: The United States—like other developed world countries—has made tremendous strides in conquering infant mortality. Samantha: We should be ashamed because our country has higher rates of infant mortality than many other developed countries. Low-income women in the United States often do not have equal access to high-quality prenatal care.

5. Some possible answers: Provide better access to prenatal care by increasing the number of nurse practitioners and obstetrician-gynecologists in under-served African American neighborhoods, perhaps by providing special monetary incentives to health-care providers to treat these women; provide better preventative health care by offering free screening for health-compromising conditions, such as diabetes and high blood pressure, that make pregnancies among this ethnic group riskier; launch a vigorous public awareness campaign encouraging women to see a health-care provider right away in the first trimester; make it easier for women to actually *see* a health-care provider by providing incentives to employers to encourage pregnant employees to take time off work to get prenatal care.

CHAPTER 3 Infancy: Physical and Cognitive Development **P. 72**

Setting the Context: Brain Blossoming and Sculpting

1. Both Christopher and Ashley are right. We are unique in our massive cerebral cortex, in growing most of our brain "outside of the womb," and because our brain does not reach its adult form for two decades.

2. Kayla is partly right (with regard to the myelin sheath) and partly wrong because synaptic loss and neural pruning are essential to fostering our emerging abilities.

3. b. Their remarkable brain plasticity may allow young children to "recruit" neurons to compensate for the part of the brain that the surgeons remove.

4. Make your drawing from memory and then see how closely it mirrors Figure 3.1 on page 74.

Basic Newborn States

1. d. All these statements are correct. The sucking reflex (automatic sucking) and rooting reflex (head turning and sucking) are present at birth to help ensure the infant's survival. As the cortex matures, these reflexes disappear.

2. Your questionnaire might include items such as the following: Will you have to go back to work full-time after the baby's birth to make ends meet? How soon do you plan to return to work (if at all)? Will your employer support your breast-feeding? Does your community or culture encourage breast-feeding? What is your annual household income? What is the highest school grade you've completed? (Low SES—recall from the text— predicts prematurely abandoning breast feeding.) Do you suffer from depression? Was your baby born prematurely?

3. Tell your sister and her husband to learn baby massage and get a baby sling and carry the child around (kangaroo care), as these techniques reduce crying. (Also, they might make heavy use of a pacifier!) The encouraging information you should provide is that this is a short-lived problem. Colic typically goes away by the fourth month.

4. Jorge's child is right on schedule, but he's wrong to say his child is sleeping through the night. The baby has simply learned to self-soothe.

5. The answers here will depend on the class.

Sensory and Motor Development

1. The correct answer is the *preferential-looking paradigm*.

2. a and b. At 2 months, Alicia's baby should show interest in the visual cliff, but no fear (a). At 7 months, the baby should be afraid of the cliff (b).

3. Felicity should cite the research on newborn size perception and the evidence from the face-perception studies that babies know remarkable things about faces from the first week of life. Jason should cite the research on depth perception using the visual cliff—while babies can see differences in depth early on, infants only start to fear heights about the time they become able to crawl.

4. Charlie's early motor skills won't predict his arriving at Harvard (or anything else related to early emerging cognitive skills), although his parents are correct that babies, like their son, who habituate quickly do tend to do well on childhood intelligence tests.

5. Steps to baby-proof a room might include: providing electrical outlet covers; relocating sharp, poisonous, and breakable objects out of a baby's reach; putting carpet or rugs on hard floor surfaces; padding furniture corners; installing latches on cabinet doors; and so on.

Cognition

1. circular reaction = Darien; means–end behavior = Jai; object permanence = Sam.

2. a. Developmentalists criticize the whole *concept* that development occurs in qualitatively distinct stages. They haven't suggested different qualitative benchmarks than Piaget did.

Language: The Endpoint of Infancy

1. The idea that we learn language by reinforcement reflects Skinner's operant conditioning perspective; Chomsky hypothesized that we are biologically programmed to acquire language; and the social-interactionist perspective on language development emphasizes the fact that babies and adults have a passion to communicate.

2. Baby Ginny is cooing; Baby Harry is babbling; Baby Sam is speaking in holophrases (one-word stage); and Baby David is using telegraphic speech.

3. NO! The friend is wrong. Baby talk, or in developmental science terms, infant-directed speech (IDS), gets an infant's attention and helps promote early language development.

CHAPTER 4 Infancy: Socioemotional Development P. 106

Attachment: The Basic Life Bond

1. Examples of proximity-seeking will vary, but any example such as "I called Mom when that terrible thing happened at work" should illustrate the basic point: When we are under stress, our immediate impulse is to contact our primary attachment figure.

2. Muriel = preattachment; Janice = attachment in the making; Ted = clear-cut attachment.

3. (1) b; (2) c; (3) d; (4) a.

4. a. The baby has an avoidant attachment.

5. c. A child's attachment status *can* change over time.

Contexts of Infant Development

1. c. The United States has the highest child poverty rate in the Western world.

2. Possible answers might include: not being able to buy nutritious foods; greater chance of being exposed to environmental toxins, such as peeling paint from living in deteriorated housing; less access to adequate health care; and so on.

3. The good news is that the quality of her parenting is the main force in determining her child's attachment. Being on the scene at night also helps cement the attachment response The bad news is that children who spend long hours in day care during their first four years of life have a higher chance of being ranked "difficult" in kindergarten.

4. c. Day-care facilities in the United States vary dramatically, but in general they need a good deal of improvement.

Toddlerhood: Age of Autonomy *and* Shame and Doubt

1. c. In our culture, parents typically start serious discipline around age 2.

2. You might tell her that most children grow out of their shyness, even if they do not completely shed this temperamental tendency. But be sure to tell her the advantages of being shy: Her baby will be easier to socialize, is not likely to have a behavior problem, and may have a stronger conscience, too.

3. Answers here will vary.

CHAPTER 5 Physical and Cognitive Development P. 138

Setting the Context: Why Childhood?

1. d. Animals also can keep learning new things.

2. Ethan's *motor* cortex is on an earlier developmental timetable than his *frontal* lobes.

3. This is a disaster! Your colleague might have trouble with everything from regulating his physical responses to analyzing problems to inhibiting his actions.

Physical Development

1. (a) mass-to-specific; (b) cephalocaudal.

2. Long-distance running and the high jump would be most appropriate for Jessica, as these sports depend mainly on gross motor skills.

3. a. Coaching children can help them improve their motor skills, provided they are developmentally ready.

4. b. Your friend should focus on getting Tara to be active—the other strategies are often counterproductive.

Cognitive Development

1. a. animism; b. egocentrism; c. artificialism; d. can't conserve; e. identity constancy.

2. Children in concrete operations have the ability to step back from their immediate perceptions, while children in the preoperational stage center on immediate appearances and cannot think abstractly.

3. b. These books will be in Chris's proximal zone.

4. c. Blurting out your birthday secret shows a *glitch* in executive functioning.

5. Laura should avoid putting her son in demanding situations involving time management; she should provide her child with a distraction-free learning environment; and she should give her son plenty of physical exercise. Also, she needs to rely heavily on positive reinforcement and definitely avoid power assertion (yelling and screaming).

Language

1. Vygotsky would say it's normal—the way children learn to think through their actions and control their behavior.

2. b = overregularization; c = overextension. The other language mistake has to do with grammar or syntax.

Specific Cognitive Skills

1. This *past talk* conversation will help stimulate Madison's *autobiographical memory.*

2. d. All the others are signs the child has a theory of mind.

3. Promote a secure attachment and talk about feelings a good deal—your own and a child's; work to stimulate language abilities; give your child experience playing with other children, particularly those who are a bit older.

CHAPTER 6 Socioemotional Development P. 172

Setting the Context: Emotion Regulation

1. b. Children with externalizing tendencies behave impulsively and aggressively; children with internalizing tendencies are excessively shy, anxious, and seem depressed. Both boys have difficulties with emotion regulation.

Personality

1. c. Young children tend to see themselves in terms of external facts and as "all great."

2. Every child except Sidney has self-esteem problems. Ryan's problem is unrealistically high self-esteem. To intervene, lavishly reinforce Ryan for appropriate behavior and give him plenty of love, but make sure to point out his realistic deficiencies. Then help stimulate self-efficacy by entering Ryan's proximal zone and teaching some emotion regulation skills (see the end of the chapter). Jared's problem is unrealistically low self-esteem—his mind-set is excessively negative. Continually point out reality ("No one does well all the time. You are a fabulous student.") and get Jared to identify his "hopeless and helpless perceptions" and substitute more accurate kinds of responses.

3. empathy; sympathy. Gabriel is more likely to be able to offer comfort to Zack.

4. a. induction; this is a good strategy; b. shame; this is a bad strategy; c. guilt; this is a good strategy.

5. c. Obedience does not necessarily predict prosocial behavior.

6. Alyssa = instrumental, relational; Brianna = direct, reactive.

7. Step 1: Mark's exuberant temperament as a toddler evoked harsh discipline from his parents—which made Mark aggressive and angry. Step 2: Then Mark was rejected by his peers (and teachers) in school—which made him even angrier and more defiant. Mark has a hostile attributional bias.

Relationships

1. This type of play is typical at about age 4 or 5 (younger children don't really pretend *together*, and older children become more interested in structured games).

2. a and c. Rough-and-tumble play is boy behavior; girls, not boys, are more likely to cross the gender divide.

3. Erik can cite the fact that gender-stereotyped play occurs in primates (and in societies around the world). He can also cite the study showing masculine type behaviors may be programmed by prenatal testosterone. Sophia can say that parents buy their children gender-stereotyped toys and play with their sons and daughters in "feminine" or "masculine" ways. Most important, she should cite the evidence that kids teach other kids to play in stereotypic ways as they begin to segregate into same-sex play groups, and also mention the finding that in mixed-sex groups boys and girls play in much more similar ways.

4. a. In our culture, disagreements among friends are common (what really matters is whether you can work out your differences).

5. b. By middle school and high school, kids who are in the "in-group" may not be personally well liked.

6. d. Children who are aggressive, socially anxious, and who stand out as different are all at higher risk of being rejected in elementary school.

7. (a) She seems anxious and has trouble standing up for herself. (b) Get the child involved with a friend. (c) Provide lots of love.

CHAPTER 7 Settings for Development: Home and School **P. 204**

Home

1. Montana's parents are authoritative. Jason's parents are authoritarian. Sara's parents are permissive.

2. Amber is resilient.

3. a. this chapter's advice; b. Judith Harris's advice; c. Sandra Scarr's advice.

4. a and c. Some experts feel that spanking should never be used. Other developmentalists feel mild spanking is appropriate with preschoolers (never infants).

5. a. Neglect and physical abuse. b. Report the problem to child protective services. c. If the child is removed from the home the ultimate goal should be to reunite him with the family, and help teach the parents better parenting skills.

6. Yes, tell Crystal she made the right decision, as living in an atmosphere poisoned by chronic fighting can often be worse for children's development. As for parenting advice, tell Crystal to talk openly with her daughter about the situation and to let her daughter freely explore her feelings about the divorce. She should expect some problems for the first year or so and possibly—*if it is needed*—get counseling for her daughter. She should try to minimize any other life disruptions (e.g., keep her child in the same school). Crystal should also make sure to not bad-mouth her former spouse. It's best if they can both agree on custody arrangements.

School

1. b. Low-income children often start school well behind their affluent peers and fall further behind as the years pass because they attend the poorest-quality schools.

2. b. When a child scores well below normal on academic progress/school learning measures such as achievement tests but has an above-average IQ score, it means he or she has a learning disability.

3. c and d. The IQ score doesn't tell us about children's unique abilities; and the tests don't reflect genetic potential in disadvantaged children.

4. Analytic intelligence; creative intelligence; practical intelligence; multiple intelligences. Josh's strengths using Gardner's framework are in musical, kinesthetic, and interpersonal intelligences.

5. b. Schools that beat the odds insist on high standards—they don't "dumb down" the work.

6. (a) Intrinsic motivation is self-generated—we work for the sheer joy of working. Extrinsic motivation comes from external reinforcers such as grades. (b) Answers here will vary.(c) You need to make that task relevant to a larger personal goal; you need to increase your sense of autonomy (e.g., choosing when or in what way you do the assignment); you need to feel that if you succeed at that task you will be pleasing someone you really care about.

CHAPTER 8 Physical Development **P. 238**

Puberty

1. a. Today we physically develop a decade or more before we reach adult life. (Puberty rites are designed to celebrate the person's entry into "real" adulthood, and that can't happen today.)

2. (a) The initial hypothalamic hormone triggers the pituitary to produce its hormones, which trigger the growth of the ovaries and testes and cause them to produce hormones, which in turn trigger the physical changes. (b) Estrogens, testosterone, and the adrenal androgens. (c) Your cousin will start to grow much taller.

3. It is probable that Kendra *is not yet menstruating yet*, as that event occurs relatively late in the sequence. Anthony *may or may not have reached puberty*, as "hidden events," such as the growth of reproductive organs, begin while boys still "look like children."

4. d. Dancers, especially if they diet vigorously, are likely to reach puberty late.

5. a. Maturing early and going to middle school are both "risk factors" for having more trouble as teens.

6. You might suggest: changing to K–8 schools (get rid of middle school); instituting more "honest" puberty education at a younger age, possibly in a format (such as on-line) where children could talk anonymously about their concerns; instituting a public awareness program encouraging parents to talk about puberty with a same-sexed child before the changes occur; encouraging parents to be alert to problems if they have an early maturing girl; getting parents to celebrate the changes (without embarrassing their children!).

Body Image Issues

1. b. According to Harter's research, the major correlate of overall self-esteem is feeling good about the way one looks.

2. Jasmine and Sophia would be classified as having eating disorders. Jasmine has the symptoms of anorexia nervosa; Sophia has the symptoms of bulimia nervosa.

3. b. The best strategy is to tell children their personality determines their looks, not that looks don't matter or that they need to drastically change how they look.

4. Your checklist could include the following questions: Is this child female? Is this child temperamentally anxious? Does the child suffer from low self-esteem? Does this child want *above all* to be ultra thin and to use the models in the media as her standard for the right weight? Do this child's parents, particularly her mother, pressure her about weight? Is this child becoming obsessed with dieting?

Sexuality

1. a. The adrenal androgens program our first feelings of sexual desire.

2. b. The other forces are relevant; whether the child's school teaches abstinence is not.

3. a. A lower percentage of European American boys report having had sex by their senior year of high school than their European American female counterparts.

4. Sex education programs should focus on how to deal with relationships and not just warn children against STDs or moralize about teenage pregnancy or the "sexual act."

CHAPTER 9 Cognitive and Socioemotional Development **P. 268**

The Mysterious Teenage Mind

1. c and d. Piaget argues that only after reaching formal operations can we take hypothetical positions and debate different points of view. According to Kohlberg, we first develop an internalized sense of moral values during adolescence.

2. a. preconventional; b. conventional; c. preconventional; d. preconventional; e. post conventional

3. The imaginary audience; the personal fable; adolescent egocentrism

4. b. Most adolescents are upbeat and not depressed. Only a small minority of teenagers has emotional problems.

5. b, c, and d. The other alternatives don't take into account that the teenage brain is still very much a work in progress and that teenagers have unique sleep patterns. Neither do they capitalize directly on teenagers' interests.

Teenage Relationships

1. b and c. Chris and her parents are more likely to argue about Chris's curfew and issues such as cleaning up Chris's room.

2. At age 14. In the late teens, relationships often improve.

3. b. Heather and her clique will meld into a large heterosexual crowd.

4. Mom #3 is correct. Children gravitate to certain peers based on their personality, but joining a deviant peer group encourages kids to get into trouble.

5. Checklist: (1) Is this child aggressive and being rejected by the mainstream kids? (2) Does this child have problems with his parents? (3) Is this child failing at school (does she have learning disabilities)? (4) Does this child have few real interests (other than having fun)?

   A program would involve: getting children involved in caring groups capitalizing on the 5 Cs; perhaps putting them in a more nurturing classroom situation; possibly working with parents to be more authoritative; definitely trying to get children connected with a different set of peers.

CHAPTER 10 Constructing an Adult Life **P. 300**

Emerging Into Adulthood

1. b. Studies suggest that in the United Stated our pathway to adulthood is not smooth and steady, but rather, occurs in fits and starts.

2. b. Maria's parents may be okay with having her move back, but she runs the risk of sliding into a childlike status while living under their roof.

3. b. Social clock issues become salient when people feel behind the normal timetable for their age, so Martha, who is starting a new career at age 50, is likely to be most worried about the ticking of the social clock.

Constructing an Identity

1. a. Emma's aimless drifting and her inability to see an adult future define Marcia's diffusion status.

2. b. Joe is in foreclosure, defined by uncritically accepting an identity handed down by an authority. Moratorium is defined by exploring many different possible identities, as Kayla is doing.

3. a. Feeling pulled between wanting to adhere to your traditions and being a global citizen may cause feelings of anxiety ("Shouldn't I make a choice between my own culture and the wider world?"). There may be issues related to feeling distant from your family—needing to "give up" their values and feeling guilty about hurting the people you most love. There may also be the anxieties related to feeling "different" than other people, or encountering discrimination because your traditions are different than the mainstream culture.

Finding a Career

1. b. Csikszentmihalyi would use the term *players* to describe teenagers such as Mai Lee who dislike working.

2. d. Hannah is experiencing a sense of flow.

3. d. Encouraging all students to enter college immediately after high school is typical of the United States, not the Japanese or German systems.

4. If David can afford it, you should strongly encourage him not to work full time, as this will prevent him from getting fully immersed in his studies and college life.

Finding Love

1. d. Cohabitation means very different things for different people.

2. b. Natasha and Akbar are in Murstein's *value-comparison* phase.

3. Bittany is right. We look for people who are similar to ourselves.

4. a. Kinasha's status is preoccupied. Rena is avoidant/dismissing. Sam is securely attached.

CHAPTER 11 Relationships and Roles **P. 334**

Marriage

1. a and b. The decline in marital satisfaction is a reliable research finding dating from the 1950s. It has nothing to do specifically with the deinstitutionalization of marriage.

2. c. This is the classic pattern.

3. According to the triangular theory, we can classify the types of love relationships according to three dimensions—passion, intimacy, and commitment—and by looking at their combinations, we get the love relationships in life. (a) The couple are firmly together and loving (they have intimacy and passion) but have decided not to get married or enter into a more permanent relationship. (b) The couple have intimacy, passion, and commitment (have it all!). (c) This couple are best friends (intimate) and married (committed) but have no passion. . . . This next one is

for you. Long-married older couples are most likely to have companionate marriages.

4. c. When couples berate one another for not pulling their weight, this is a sign of thinking in terms of an exchange mentality.

5. Triangular theory suggestion would revolve around rekindling passion and intimacy by engaging in exciting activities you both enjoy together. Couple communications suggestions might involve: (1) increasing the ratio of positive comments to negative comments; (2) taking steps to change one's overly negative interpretations of a partner's actions; (3) keeping fights from getting personal or avoiding getting into the demand withdrawal pattern; (4) getting couples to avoid continual scorekeeping (i.e., exchange mentality) in the marriage, possibly by getting them to practice random acts of caring toward their partners without expecting anything in return.

6. For a man, the biggest problem is likely to be losing the ability to see the children frequently, as the former spouse often has custody. For a woman, the economic strain of being the sole breadwinner.

Parenthood

1. c. Conflicts centering on marital equity can arise because women tend to do most of the childcare, even when they work full time.

2. a and c. We may have too many experts giving us advice today—leading people to feel they must be perfect.

3. That's not true! Mothers today are spending as much time with their children as in the past. In particular, they are doing more teaching. Dads are spending *a lot* more time teaching and playing and doing much more routine care, such as feeding and diaper changing.

4. breadwinner; nurturer

5. Ask about his gender role ideas; whether his wife supports and reinforces his competence in the nurturer role; his feelings about being the primary breadwinner (for example, having a higher status or more lucrative job than his wife); whether he has to work long hours.

Work

1. a. In the past, people often had to stay with a job, even if they hated it.

2. b. Super's mid-twentieth-century framework does not fit today's boundary-less careers.

3. Tom has a traditional stable career. Brad has a boundaryless career.

4. According to Holland's theory, Vanessa's job does not fit her sociable personality; that is, she is unhappy because her work situation provides a poor personality-work fit.

5. b. Being equally committed to both family and work, long trips overseas would be very upsetting for a dual centric worker.

6. Offer tax breaks for companies that offer family-friendly policies; pass laws penalizing employers who have their employees work over a certain number of hours; return to the prior practice of having the typical salaried

employee (who has now often been redefined as a manager) paid time-and-a-half for working beyond a 40-hour week.

CHAPTER 12 Midlife P. 366

The Evolving Self

1. b and c. Answer a refers to a Big Five trait. The research shows that life priorities become more generative and that people get more self-assured in midlife.

2. a. Your mom will describe redemption sequences.

3. Adam will reach his career peak earlier because his job is more heavily dependent on fluid skills. History draws almost exclusively on crystallized skills.

4. Textbook writing is a crystallized skill, so I should be just as good in my sixties as I am now (provided I don't get ill). Playing the video game is a fluid skill, so I should be terrible now and get much worse in my sixties.

5. Rick's problem—"too much on his plate"—would benefit from using Baltes's selective optimization with compensation. He should (1) prioritize and shed his less-important jobs, (2) work harder in the top-ranking areas, and (3) use external aids whenever possible to help. Sara's problem seems to be a lack of generativity. She should try to get involved in activities that relate to "giving"—volunteering, etc.—and trying to make a difference in other people's lives.

6. a. Post-formal thought involves looking at life from the other person's per-spective, thinking things through, and going with your feelings. A person who thinks this way would not immediately say, "Leave the bum!"

Mid-life Roles and Issues

1. Karen may be younger, live closer to Emma, and be a more generative person. Most likely, she is the maternal grandma.

2. Answers here will vary.

3. c. Caregivers in collectivist cultures feel just as stressed by parent care.

4. *Males* decline most physiologically; *female* sexuality is most affected by social/ partner issues. Women report *less* sexual interest than men. *Females* have the most untapped sexual potential in later life.

5. d. Not all women experience the other symptoms, but all do show repro-ductive tract changes.

CHAPTER 13 Later Life: Cognitive and Socioemotional Development P. 398

The Evolving Self

1. b. Age discrimination has been a problem throughout the ages; physical disabilities occur during the old-old years. The correct answer is that older people vary tremendously—perhaps more than at any other life stage.

2. Christopher might slow down his presentation of the material and not overload his older students with too many facts. He should explicitly tie the course content into students' existing "knowledge base" or crystallized skills (for example, capitalize on their semantic memory capacities). He

should strive to make the material personally relevant. He needs to make sure he teaches in a distraction-free environment. He also might consider having shorter class sessions.

3. a. semantic memory b. episodic memory c. procedural memory

4. c. Bike riding is a well-learned automatic activity that does not involve conscious thinking and is therefore "procedural," residing in a lower center of the brain.

5. episodic; semantic

6. b and c. According to socioemotional selectivity theory, in later life people focus on enjoying the present moment and try to spend as much time as possible with their closest attachment figures—their families.

7. When an elderly person is isolated—without close relationships—and economically deprived or old-old and in poor health, depression is a serious risk.

Later Life Transitions

1. a. Middle-class workers such as Joe retire with both pensions and Social Security. The threat on the horizon is the fact that when all of the baby boomers reach retirement age, the old-age dependency ratio, or number of workers putting money into Social Security, versus older people "dependent" on that system will decline, leading to this financial mainstay no longer being able to support the huge numbers of people in their retirement years.

2. Joe is most likely to retire in his early sixties.

3. a. Most people are happy after they decide to retire, but they may take some time to find their new "retirement niche." Today however, increasing numbers of retirees reluctantly need to take post-retirement jobs to make ends meet.

4. Pros: This will make the retirement system solvent and keep Social Security designed to do what it always was envisioned to do—give people a financial cushion when they are too old to work. It might encourage older people to be productive for longer and get society more used to the fact that people *can* be highly productive until well into later life. Cons: This strategy will eliminate the decades-long retirement we all have been expecting to enjoy. Having so many older workers might make it harder for younger people to advance at work or even get jobs at the beginning of their working years. Workers who are in poor health would be forced to stay in the labor force longer.

5. (2) Isabel needs emotional support, but by taking over the practical tasks, friends are depriving her of the efficacy feelings that might be derived from learning she can take care of herself all by herself.

6. One risk factor for having problems coping is being male. In particular, old-old men in lifelong marriages are at risk of becoming depressed or committing suicide. Being emotionally fragile and socially isolated, having few interests or attachments outside of the marriage, and having an insecure married attachment style are other risk factors. The bottom-line force that sets a person up for special trouble after being widowed is not having the internal or external resources to develop a satisfying new life.

CHAPTER 14 The Physical Challenges of Old Age P. 422

Tracing Physical Aging

1. b. Normal aging changes, as they become more severe, often shade into chronic illness.

2. Margery has instrumental ADL problems. Sara has basic ADL problems.

3. a. As people ascend the social status rungs, they live longer in better health.

4. c. They are both partly right: Women live longer but experience more health problems than men.

Sensory-Motor Changes

1. lens; a cataract; can be cured by surgery

2. d. The patient's hearing will be most impaired in noisy environments.

3. a, c, and e. All of the others will make grandma's eyesight worse.

4. Tell the lawmakers that eye exams won't work because driving is dependent on multiple sensory and motor skills; and the vision problems older people have that affect driving may not be picked up by a standard eye-chart test. To help older people, you might want the lawmakers to sponsor bills to change the driving environment by putting adequate lighting on exit ramps, more traffic signals at intersections (especially left-turn signals), and extending the yellow-light-signal time. Most importantly, however, we should devote money to fostering initiatives that don't depend on driving—investing in better public transportation, giving tax breaks to developers who build shopping centers in residential neighborhoods, promoting alternatives to using cars.

Dementia

1. The illnesses are Alzheimer's disease, deterioration of the neurons and their replacement with senile plaques and tangles; and vascular dementia, small strokes. (If grandma is old-old, she's likely to have both illnesses.)

2. a and b. Answer c is wrong because a reasonable fraction of people do get dementia at the uppermost ends of life; and having the APOE-4 marker (answer d) increases the likelihood that a person will have the illness.

3. d. Every strategy can help.

Options and Services for the Frail Elderly

1. a. 1; b. 3; c. 2; d. 4; e. 5

2. b. Medicare covers only care defined as cure-oriented, not custodial care.

3. d. Everything is important.

CHAPTER 15 Death and Dying P. 452

Setting the Context: A Short History of Death

1. b. People in the seventeenth and eighteenth century didn't die in hospitals.

2. slowly and erratically; an age-related chronic disease

3. Ella's case: We talk about death to terminally ill patients. We try to get people to document their wishes for a dignified death. We have many death education classes and are making active efforts to think about how

to take good care of the terminally ill. Margaret's case: Today we are totally disconnected from—and frightened about—the physical reality of death. We also use euphemisms for death like "passing away."

The Dying Person

1. d. People go through many different emotions in confronting a terminal diagnosis, but primarily they feel hope.

2. many different emotions; hope

3. an 80-year-old woman

4. Possible answers: provide counselors on call to the person; make sure you offer plenty of medications to calm anxiety; give patients time to express their preferences and make sure that their preferences—with regard to see-ing family, pain control, and everything else—are fulfilled by the staff.

The Health-Care System

1. Although medical personnel set up predictions about how patients are likely to die, death doesn't always go according to schedule, so their pre-dictions can be very wrong!

2. b. Doctors agonize over whether to use heroic measures to simply prolong dying.

3. Sara's case: We now have courses focused on teaching health-care workers how to approach dying people and provide end-of-life care, and some hos-pitals have established special palliative-care units. Martha's case: Health-care personnel still often feel compelled to use aggressive medical measures, even when they are concerned about the ethics of doing so. The whole medical system is cure-oriented, making it very difficult to shift to palliative care.

4. b. People who enroll in hospices tend to have loving family members liv-ing in the home who are committed to providing care.

5. You might not want to burden your family by having them feel compelled to providing you with intense nursing care for months. How would you feel having loved ones see you naked and incontinent—would you want that to be their last memory of you? Maybe you would want privacy to vent your feelings in a setting where you did not always have to worry about how loved ones would feel. Would you want people to need to cope with the fear of seeing you die?

6. a. It's all about attachment!

The Dying Person: Taking Control of How We Die

1. b. Given the problems with living wills, the best alternative may be the durable power of attorney.

2. David's case: People who don't want to live should have their preferences respected. We should not torture people by making them suffer helplessly when they want their lives to end. Janet's case: There is the potential for abuse if relatives pressure the person into making this decision "for the good of the family." People may decide they want to die because they are depressed, and if that condition is treated, they might change their minds. Even worse, legalizing these practices leaves the door open to society deciding to kill people when *we* think the quality of their life is not good.

Glossary

A

accommodation In Piaget's theory, enlarging our mental capacities to fit input from the wider world.

achievement tests Measures that evaluate a child's knowledge in specific school-related areas.

active euthanasia A deliberate intervention that helps a terminally ill patient die.

active forces The nature-interacts-with-nurture principle that our genetic temperamental tendencies and predispositions cause us to actively choose to put ourselves into specific environments.

ADL (activities of daily living) problems Difficulty in performing everyday tasks that are required for living independently. ADLs are classified as either basic or instrumental.

adolescence-limited turmoil Antisocial behavior that, for most teens, is specific to adolescence and does not persist into adult life.

adolescent egocentrism David Elkind's term for the tendency of young teenagers to feel that their actions are at the center of everyone else's consciousness.

adoption study Behavioral genetic research strategy, designed to determine the genetic contribution to a given trait, that involves comparing adopted children with their biological and adoptive parents.

adrenal androgens Hormones produced by the adrenal glands that program various aspects of puberty, such as growth of body hair, skin changes, and sexual desire.

adult attachment styles The various ways in which adults relate to romantic partners, based on Mary Ainsworth's infant attachment styles. Classified as secure and insecure (preoccupied/ambivalent or avoidant/dismissive).

adult development The scientific study of the developing adult.

advance directive Any written document spelling out instructions with regard to life-prolonging treatment if individuals become irretrievably ill and cannot communicate their wishes.

age discrimination Illegally laying off workers or failing to hire or promote them on the basis of age.

age norms Cultural ideas about the appropriate ages for engaging in particular activities or life tasks.

age of viability The earliest point at which a baby can survive outside the womb.

age-based rationing of care The controversial idea that society should not use expensive life-sustaining technologies on people in their old-old years.

aggression Any hostile or destructive act.

alternatives to institutionalization Services and settings designed to keep older people who are experiencing age-related disabilities that don't merit intense 24-hour care from having to enter nursing homes.

altruism Prosocial behaviors that we carry out for selfless, non-egocentric reasons.

Alzheimer's disease A type of age-related dementia characterized by neural atrophy and abnormal by-products of that atrophy, such as senile plaques and neurofibrillary tangles.

amniocentesis A second-trimester procedure that involves inserting a syringe into a woman's uterus to extract a sample of amniotic fluid, which is tested for a variety of genetic and chromosomal conditions.

amniotic sac A bag-shaped, fluid-filled membrane that contains and insulates the fetus.

analytic intelligence In Robert Sternberg's framework on successful intelligence, the facet of intelligence involving performing well on academic-type problems.

animism In Piaget's theory, the preoperational child's belief that inanimate objects are alive.

anorexia nervosa A potentially life-threatening eating disorder characterized by pathological dieting (resulting in severe weight loss and extreme thinness) and by a distorted body image.

A-not-B error In Piaget's framework, a classic mistake made by infants in the sensorimotor stage, whereby babies approaching age 1 go back to the original hiding place to look for an object even though they have seen it get hidden in a second place.

anxious-ambivalent attachment An insecure attachment style characterized by a child's intense distress at separation and by anger and great difficulty being soothed when reunited with the primary caregiver in the Strange Situation.

Apgar scale A quick test used to assess a just-delivered baby's condition by measuring heart rate, muscle tone, respiration, reflex response, and color.

artificialism In Piaget's theory, the preoperational child's belief that human beings make everything in nature.

assimilation In Jean Piaget's theory, the first step promoting mental growth, involving fitting environmental input to our existing mental capacities.

assisted reproductive technology (ART) Any infertility treatment in which the egg is fertilized outside the womb.

assisted-living facility A housing option providing care for elderly people who have instrumental ADL impairments and can no longer live independently but may not need a nursing home.

attachment The powerful bond of love between a caregiver and child (or between any to individuals).

attachment in the making The second phase of John Bowlby's developmental attachment sequence, lasting from about 4 to 7 months of age, when infants show a slight preference for their primary caregiver.

attachment theory Theory, formulated by John Bowlby, centering on the crucial importance to our species' survival of being closely connected with a caregiver during early childhood and being attached to a significant other during all of life.

attention deficit/hyperactivity disorder (ADHD) The most common childhood learning disorder in the United States, disproportionately affecting boys, characterized by excessive restlessness and distractibility at home and at school.

authoritarian parents In Diana Baumrind's parenting-styles framework, a type of childrearing in which parents provide plenty of rules but rank low on child-centeredness, stressing unquestioning obedience.

authoritative parents In Diana Baumrind's parenting-styles framework, the best possible child-rearing style, in which parents rank high on both nurturance and discipline, providing both love and clear family rules.

autobiographical memories Recollections of events and experiences that make up one's life history.

autonomy Erikson's second psychosocial task, when toddlers confront the challenge of understanding that they are separate individuals.

average life expectancy A person's fifty-fifty chance at birth of living to a given age.

avoidant attachment An insecure attachment style characterized by a child's indifference to the primary caregiver when they are reunited in the Strange Situation.

avoidant/dismissive insecure attachment A standoffish, excessively disengaged style of relating to loved ones.

axon A long nerve fiber that usually conducts impulses away from the cell body of a neuron.

B

babbling The alternating vowel and consonant sounds that babies repeat with variations of intonation and pitch and that precede the first words.

baby boom cohort The huge age group born between 1946 and 1964.

baby-proofing Making the home safe for a newly mobile infant.

basic ADL problems Difficulty in performing essential self-care activities, such as rising from a chair, eating, and getting to the toilet.

behavioral genetics Field devoted to scientifically determining the role that hereditary forces play in determining individual differences in behavior.

bicultural identity A dual identity based on identification with both one's traditional culture and the norms of the global society.

bidirectionality The crucial principle that people affect one another, or that interpersonal influences flow in both directions.

Big Five traits Five core psychological predispositions—neuroticism, extraversion, openness to experience, conscientiousness, and agreeableness—that underlie personality.

birth defect A physical or neurological problem that occurs prenatally or at birth.

blastocyst The hollow sphere of cells formed during the germinal stage in preparation for implantation.

body mass index (BMI) The ratio of weight to height; the main indicator of overweight or underweight.

boundaryless career Today's most common career path for Western workers, in which people change jobs or professions periodically during their working lives.

bulimia nervosa An eating disorder characterized by cycles of binging and purging (by inducing vomiting or taking laxatives) in an obsessive attempt to lose weight.

bullying A situation in which one or more children (or adults) harass or target a specific child for systematic abuse.

C

caregiving grandparents Grandparents who have taken on full responsibility for raising their grandchildren.

centering In Piaget's conservation tasks, the preoperational child's tendency to fix on the most visually striking feature of a substance and not take other dimensions into account.

cephalocaudal sequence The developmental principle that growth occurs in a sequence from head to toe.

cerebral cortex The outer folded mantle of the brain, responsible for thinking, reasoning, perceiving, and all conscious responses.

certified nurse assistant or aide The main hands-on care provider in a nursing home, who helps elderly residents with basic ADL problems.

cervix The neck, or narrow lower portion, of the uterus.

cesarean section (c-section) A method of delivering a baby surgically by extracting the baby through incisions in the woman's abdominal wall and in the uterus.

child development The scientific study of development from birth through adolescence.

child maltreatment Any act that seriously endangers a child's physical or emotional well-being.

childhood obesity A body mass index at or above the 95th percentile compared to the U.S. norms established for children in the 1970s.

chorionic villus sampling (CVS) A relatively risky first-trimester pregnancy test for fetal genetic disorders.

chromosome A threadlike strand of DNA located in the nucleus of every cell that carries the genes, which transmit hereditary information.

chronic disease Any long-term illness that requires ongoing management. Most chronic diseases are age-related and are the endpoint of normal aging changes.

circular reactions In Piaget's framework, repetitive action-oriented schemas (or habits) characteristic of babies during the sensorimotor stage.

class inclusion The understanding that a general category can encompass several subordinate elements.

clear-cut attachment The critical period for human attachment, lasting from roughly 7 months of age through toddlerhood, characterized by separation anxiety, the need to have a caregiver physically close, and stranger anxiety.

clique A small peer group composed of roughly six teenagers who have similar attitudes and who share activities.

cognitive behaviorism (social learning theory) A behavioral worldview that emphasizes that people learn by watching others and that our thoughts about the reinforcers determine our behavior. Cognitive behaviorists focus on charting and modifying people's thoughts.

cohabitation Sharing a household in an unmarried romantic relationship.

cohort The age group with whom we travel through life.

colic A baby's frantic, continual crying during the first three months of life; caused by an immature digestive system.

collaborative pretend play Fantasy play in which children work together to develop and act out the scenes.

collectivist cultures Societies that prize social harmony, obedience, and close family connectedness over individual achievement.

commitment script In Dan McAdams's research, a type of autobiography produced by highly generative adults that involves childhood memories of feeling special, being unusually sensitive to others' misfortunes, and having a strong, enduring generative mission from adolescence, and that often includes redemption sequences.

communal model of love An ideal approach to love relationships in which the partners give everything without expecting to get anything in return.

concrete operational thinking In Piaget's framework, the type of cognition characteristic of children aged 8 to 11, marked by the ability to reason about the world in a more logical, adult way.

conservation tasks Piagetian tasks that involve changing the shape of a substance to see whether children can go beyond the way that substance visually appears to understand that the amount is still the same.

consummate love In Robert Sternberg's triangular theory of love, the ideal form of love, in which a couple's relationship involves all three of the major facets of love: passion, intimacy, and commitment.

contamination sequence In Dan McAdams's research, a characteristic theme of nongenerative adults' autobiographies, in which they describe joyous events that turned out badly.

contexts of development Fundamental markers, including cohort, socioeconomic status, culture, and gender, that shape how we develop throughout the lifespan.

continuing bonds An ongoing sense of the deceased spouse's presence "in spirit."

continuing care retirement community A housing option characterized by a series of levels of care for elderly residents, ranging from independent apartments to assisted living to nursing home care. People enter the community in reatively good health and move to sections where they can get more care when they become disabled.

conventional level of morality In Lawrence Kohlberg's theory, the intermediate level of moral reasoning, in which people respond to ethical issues by considering the need to uphold social norms.

corporal punishment The use of physical force to discipline a child.

correlational study A research strategy that involves relating two or more variables.

co-sleeping The standard custom, in collectivist cultures, of having a child and parent share a bed.

creative intelligence In Robert Sternberg's framework on successful intelligence, the facet of intelligence involved in producing novel ideas or innovative work.

cross-sectional study A developmental research strategy that involves testing different age groups at the same time.

crowd A relatively large teenage peer group.

crystallized intelligence Basic facet of intelligence consisting of a person's knowledge base, or storehouse of accumulated information.

D

day-care center A day-care arrangement in which a large number of children are cared for at a licensed facility by paid providers.

day-care program A service for impaired older adults who live with relatives, in which the older person spends the day at a center offering various activities.

death awareness movement The late-twentieth-century trend in Western societies toward openly talking about death and improving the psychological conditions under which people die.

decentering In Piaget's conservation tasks, the concrete operational child's ability to look at several dimensions of an object or substance.

defense mechanisms In Freudian psychoanalytic theory, unconscious strategies that people use for coping with upsetting events.

deinstitutionalization of marriage The decline in marriage and the emergence of alternate family forms that occurred during the last third of the twentieth century.

demand–withdrawal communication A pathological type of interaction in which one partner, most often the woman, presses for more intimacy and the other person, most often the man, tends to back off.

dementia The general term for any illness that produces serious, progressive, usually irreversible cognitive decline.

dendrite A branching fiber that receives information and conducts impulses toward the cell body of a neuron.

depth perception The ability to see (and fear) heights.

developed world The most affluent countries in the world.

developing world The more impoverished countries of the world.

developmental disorders Learning impairments and behavioral problems during infancy and childhood.

developmental systems perspective An all-encompassing outlook on development that stresses the need to embrace a variety of theories, and the idea that all systems and processes interrelate.

developmentalists (developmental scientists) Researchers and practitioners whose professional interest lies in the study of some aspect of human development.

deviancy training Socialization of a young teenager into delinquency through conversations centered on performing antisocial acts.

disorganized attachment An insecure attachment style characterized by responses such as freezing or fear when a child is reunited with the primary caregiver in the Strange Situation.

divided-attention task A difficult memory challenge involving memorizing material while simultaneously monitoring something else.

DNA (deoxyribonucleic acid) The material that makes up genes, which bear our hereditary characteristics.

Do Not Hospitalize (DNH) order A type of advance directive put into the charts of impaired nursing home residents specifying that in a medical crisis they should not be transferred to a hospital for emergency care.

Do Not Resuscitate (DNR) order A type of advance directive filled out by surrogates (usually a doctor in consultation with family members) for impaired individuals specifying that if they go into cardiac arrest, efforts should not be made to revive them.

dominant disorder An illness that a child gets by inheriting one copy of the abnormal gene that causes the disorder.

Down syndrome The most common chromosomal abnormality, causing mental retardation, susceptibility to heart disease, and other health problems; and distinctive physical characteristics, such as slanted eyes and stocky build.

dual-centric worker A worker who puts equal importance on family and career.

durable power of attorney for health care A type of advance directive in which people designate a specific surrogate to make health-care decisions if they become incapacitated and are unable to make their wishes known.

dying trajectory The fact that hospital personnel make projections about the particular pathway to death that a seriously ill patient will take and organize their care according to that assumption.

dyslexia A brain-based learning disability that is characterized by reading difficulties, lack of fluency, poor word recognition, and problems in spelling.

E

early childhood The first phase of childhood, lasting from age 3 through kindergarten, or about age 5.

Early Head Start A federal program that provides counseling and other services to low-income parents and children under age 3.

eating disorder A pathological obsession with getting and staying thin. The two best-known eating disorders are *anorexia nervosa* and *bulimia nervosa*.

egocentrism In Piaget's theory, the preoperational child's inability to understand that other people have different points of view from their own.

Elderhostel An educational/travel program that offers people age 55 and older special learning experiences at universities and other locations across the United States and around the world.

elderspeak A style of communication used with an older person who seems to be physically impaired, involving speaking loudly and with slow, exaggerated pronunciation, as if talking to a baby.

embryonic stage The second stage of prenatal development, lasting from week 3 through week 8.

emerging adulthood The phase of life that begins after high school, tapers off toward the late twenties, and is devoted to constructing an adult life.

emerging adulthood The phase of life that begins after high school, tapers off toward the late twenties, and is devoted to constructing an adult life.

emotion regulation The capacity to manage one's emotional state.

empathy Feeling the exact emotion that another person is experiencing.

end-of-life care instruction Courses in medical and nursing schools devoted to teaching health-care workers how to provide the best palliative care to the dying.

episodic memory In the memory-systems perspective, the most fragile type of memory; involving the recall of the ongoing events of daily life.

Erikson's psychosocial tasks In Erik Erikson's theory, the challenges we face as we travel through the eight stages of the lifespan.

event-driven relationship An erratic love relationship characterized by dramatic shifts in feelings and sense of commitment, with the couple repeatedly breaking up, then getting back together again.

evocative forces The nature-interacts-with-nurture principle that our genetic temperamental tendencies and predispositions evoke, or produce, certain responses from other people.

evolutionary psychology Theory or worldview highlighting the role that inborn, species-specific behaviors play in human development and life.

exchange model of love An unsatisfying approach to love relationships in which the partners attempt to "keep score" and give to the other person only when the partner gives to them.

executive functions Any frontal-lobe ability that allows us to inhibit our responses and to plan and direct our thinking.

experience-sampling technique A research procedure designed to capture moment-to-moment experiences by having people carry pagers and take notes describing their activities and emotions whenever the signal sounds.

externalizing tendencies A personality style that involves acting on one's immediate impulses and behaving disruptively and aggressively.

extrinsic career rewards Work that is performed for external reinforcers, such as prestige or a high salary.

extrinsic motivation The drive to take an action because that activity offers external reinforcers such as praise, money, or a good grade.

F

face-perception studies Research using preferential looking and habituation to explore what very young babies know about faces.

fallopian tube One of a pair of slim, pipelike structures that connect the ovaries with the uterus.

family day care A day-care arrangement in which a neighbor or relative cares for a small number of children in her home for a fee.

family watchdogs Basic role of grandparents that involves monitoring the younger family's well-being and intervening to provide help in a crisis.

family-centric worker A worker who puts family life above a job.

fantasy play Play that involves making up and acting out a scenario; also called *pretend play.*

fertility rate The average number of children a woman in a given country has during her lifetime.

fertilization The union of sperm and egg.

fetal alcohol syndrome (FAS) A cluster of birth defects caused by the mother's alcohol consumption during pregnancy.

fetal stage The final period of prenatal development, lasting seven months, characterized by physical refinements, massive growth, and the development of the brain.

fine motor skills Physical abilities that involve small, coordinated movements, such as drawing and writing one's name.

flow Csikszentmihalyi's term for a feeling of total absorption in a challenging, goal-oriented activity.

fluid intelligence Basic facet of intelligence consisting of the ability to quickly master new intellectual activities.

formal operational stage Jean Piaget's fourth and final stage of cognitive development, reached at around age 12 and characterized by teenagers' ability to reason at an abstract, scientific level.

frontal lobes The area at the uppermost front of the brain, responsible for reasoning and planning our actions.

G

"g" Charles Spearman's term for a general intelligence factor that he claimed underlies all cognitive activities.

gang A close-knit, delinquent peer group. Gangs form mainly under conditions of economic deprivation; they offer their members protection from harm and engage in a variety of criminal activities.

gender schema theory An explanation for gender-stereotyped behavior that emphasizes the role of cognitions; specifically, the idea that once children know their own gender label (girl or boy), they selectively watch and model their own sex.

gender-segregated play Play in which boys and girls associate only with members of their own sex—typical of childhood.

gene A segment of DNA that contains a chemical blueprint for manufacturing a particular protein.

generativity In Erikson's theory, the seventh psychosocial task, in which people in midlife find meaning from nurturing the next generation, "caring for others, or enriching the life of others through their work." According to Erikson, when mid-life adults have not achieved generativity, they feel stagnant, without a sense of purpose in life.

genetic counselor A professional who counsels parents-to-be about their own or their children's risk of developing genetic disorders, as well as about available treatments.

genetic testing A blood test to determine whether a person carries the gene for a given genetic disorder.

germinal stage The first 14 days of prenatal development, from fertilization to full implantation.

gerontology The scientific study of the aging process and older adults.

gestation The period of pregnancy.

gifted The label for superior intellectual functioning characterized by an IQ score of 130 or above, showing that a child ranks in the top 2 percent of his age group.

gonads The sex organs—the ovaries in girls and the testes in boys.

goodness of fit An ideal parenting strategy that involves arranging children's environments to suit their temperaments, minimizing their vulnerabilities and accentuating their strengths.

grammar The rules and word-arranging systems that every human language employs to communicate meaning.

gross motor skills Physical abilities that involve large muscle movements, such as running and jumping.

growth spurt A dramatic increase in height and weight that occurs during puberty.

guilt Feeling upset about having caused harm to a person or about having violated one's internal standard of behavior.

H

habituation The predictable loss of interest that develops once a stimulus becomes familiar; used to explore infant sensory capacities.

Head Start A federal program offering high-quality day care at a center and other services to help preschoolers aged 3 to 5 from low-income families prepare for school.

holophrase First clear evidence of language, when babies use a single word to communicate a sentence or complete thought.

home health services Nursing-oriented and housekeeping help provided in the home of an impaired older adult (or any other impaired person).

homogamy The principle that we select a mate who is similar to us.

homophobia Intense fear and dislike of gays and lesbians.

hormones Chemical substances released in the bloodstream that target and change organs and tissues.

hospice movement A movement, which became widespread in recent decades, focused on providing palliative care to dying patients outside of hospitals and especially on giving families the support they need to care for the terminally ill at home.

hostile attributional bias The tendency of highly aggressive children to see motives and actions as threatening when they are actually benign.

HPG axis Main hormonal system programming puberty that involves a triggering hypothalamic hormone that causes the pituitary to secrete its hormones, which in turn cause the ovaries and testes to develop and secrete the hormones that produce the major body changes.

I

identity achievement An identity status in which the person decides on a definite adult life path after searching out various options.

identity confusion Erikson's term for a failure in identity formation, marked by the lack of sense of a future adult path.

identity constancy In Piaget's theory, the preoperational child's inability to grasp that a person's core "self" stays the same despite changes in external appearance.

identity diffusion An identity status in which the person is aimless or feels totally blocked, without any adult life path.

identity foreclosure An identity status in which the person decides on an adult life path (often one spelled out by an authority figure) without any thought or active search.

identity In Erikson's theory, the life task of deciding who to be as a person in making the transition to adulthood.

identity statuses Marcia's four categories of identity formation: identity diffusion, identity foreclosure, moratorium, and identity achievement.

imaginary audience David Elkind's term for the tendency of young teenagers to feel that everyone is watching their every action; a component of adolescent egocentrism.

implantation The process in which a blastocyst becomes embedded in the uterine wall.

in vitro fertilization An infertility treatment in which conception occurs outside the womb; the developing cell mass is then inserted into the woman's uterus so that pregnancy can occur.

individualistic cultures Societies that prize independence, competition, and personal success.

induction The ideal discipline style for socializing prosocial behavior, involving getting a child who has behaved hurtfully to empathize with the pain he has caused the other person.

industry versus inferiority Erik Erikson's term for the psychosocial task of middle childhood, involving the capacity to work for one's goals.

infant mortality Death during the first year of life.

infant-directed speech (IDS) The simplified, exaggerated, high-pitched tones that adults and children universally use to speak to infants as a way of teaching them language.

infertility The inability to conceive after a year of unprotected sex. (Includes the inability to carry a child to term.)

information-processing theory A perspective on understanding cognition in which mental processes are seen as analogous to the way a computer analyzes data, with steps including sensory input, storage, and output.

inner speech In Vygotsky's theory, the way by which human beings learn to regulate their behavior and master cognitive challenges, through silently repeating information or talking to themselves.

insecure attachment A deviation from the normally joyful response to being reunited with the primary caregiver in the Strange Situation, signaling a problem in the caregiver–child relationship.

instrumental ADL problems Difficulties in performing everyday household tasks, such as cooking and cleaning.

instrumental aggression A hostile or destructive act initiated to achieve a goal.

integrity Erik Erikson's eighth psychosocial stage, in which elderly people approaching their final years decide that their life missions have been fulfilled and so can fully accept impending death.

intergenerational solidarity Middle-aged adults' feeling of loving obligation to both the older and the younger generations.

internalizing tendencies A personality style that involves intense fear, social inhibition, and often depression.

intimacy Erikson's first adult task, involving connecting with a partner in a mutual loving relationship.

intrinsic career rewards Work that provides inner fulfillment and allows people to satisfy their needs for creativity, autonomy, and relatedness.

intrinsic motivation The drive to act based on the pleasure of taking that action in itself, not for an external reinforcer or reward.

kangaroo care Carrying a young baby in a sling close to the caregiver's body. This technique is useful for soothing an infant.

Kübler-Ross's stage theory of dying The landmark theory, developed by psychiatrist Elisabeth Kübler-Ross, that people who are terminally ill progress through five stages in confronting their death: denial, anger, bargaining, depression, and acceptance.

language acquisition device (LAD) Chomsky's term for a hypothetical brain structure that enables our species to learn and produce language.

late-life life expectancy The number of additional years a person in a given country can expect to live once reaching age 65.

learned helplessness A state that develops when a person feels incapable of affecting the outcome of events, and so gives up without trying.

lens A transparent, disk-shaped structure in the eye, which bends to allow us to see close objects.

life-course difficulties Antisocial behavior that, for a fraction of adolescents, persists into adult life.

lifespan development The scientific field covering all of human development.

lifespan theory of careers Donald Super's identification of four career phases: *moratorium* in adolescence and emerging adulthood; *establishment* in young adulthood; *maintenance* in mid-life; and *decline* in late life.

little-scientist phase The time around age 1 when babies use tertiary circular reactions to actively explore the properties of objects, experimenting with them like "scientists."

living will A type of advance directive in which people spell out their wishes for life-sustaining treatment in case they become permanently incapacitated and unable to communicate.

longitudinal study A developmental research strategy that involves testing an age group repeatedly over many years.

low birth weight (LBW) A body weight at birth of less than 5 1/2 pounds.

marital equity Fairness in the "work" of a couple's life together. If a relationship lacks equity, with one partner doing significantly more than the other, the outcome is typically marital dissatisfaction.

mass-to-specific sequence The developmental principle that large structures (and movements) precede increasingly detailed refinements.

maximum lifespan The biological limit of human life (about 105 years).

mean length of utterance (MLU) The average number of morphemes per sentence.

means–end behavior In Piaget's framework, performing a different action to get to a goal—an ability that emerges in the sensorimotor stage as babies approach age 1.

median age The age at which 50 percent of a population is older and 50 percent is younger.

Medicare The U.S. government's program of health insurance for elderly people.

memory-systems perspective A framework that divides memory into three types: procedural, semantic, and episodic memory.

menarche A girl's first menstruation.

menopause The age-related process, occurring at about age 50, in which ovulation and menstruation stop due to the loss of estrogen.

mentally retarded The label for significantly impaired intellectual functioning, defined as when a child (or adult) has an IQ of 70 or below accompanied by evidence of deficits in learning abilities.

middle childhood The second phase of childhood, covering the elementary school years, from about age 6 to age 11.

middle knowledge The idea that terminally ill people can know that they are dying yet at the same time not completely grasp or come to terms emotionally with that fact.

miscarriage The naturally occurring loss of a pregnancy and death of the fetus.

mnemonic technique A strategy for aiding memory, often by using imagery or enhancing the emotional meaning of what needs to be learned.

modeling Learning by watching and imitating others.

moratorium An identity status in which the person actively searches out various possibilities to find a truly solid adult life path. A mature style of constructing an identity.

morpheme The smallest unit of meaning in a particular language—for example, *boys* contains two morphemes: *boy* and the plural suffix *s*.

multiple intelligences In Howard Gardner's perspective on intelligence, the principle that there are eight separate kinds of intelligence—verbal, mathematical, interpersonal, intrapersonal, spatial, musical, kinesthetic, naturalist—plus a possible ninth form, called spiritual intelligence.

myelination Formation of a fatty layer encasing the axons of neurons. This process, which speeds the transmission of neural impulses, continues from birth to early adulthood.

N

natural childbirth A general term for labor and birth without medical interventions.

naturalistic observation A measurement strategy that involves directly watching and coding behaviors.

nature Biological or genetic causes of development.

neonatal intensive care unit (NICU) A special hospital unit that treats at-risk newborns, such as low-birth-weight and very-low-birth-weight babies.

nest-leaving Moving out of a childhood home and living independently.

neural tube A cylindrical structure that forms along the back of the embryo and develops into the brain and spinal cord.

neuron A nerve cell.

non-normative transitions Unpredictable or atypical life changes that occur during development.

normal aging changes The universal, often progressive signs of physical deterioration intrinsic to the aging process.

normative transitions Predictable life changes that occur during development.

nursing home/long-term-care facility A residential institution that provides shelter and intensive caregiving, primarily to older people who need help with basic ADLs.

nurture Environmental causes of development.

O

object permanence In Piaget's framework, the understanding that objects continue to exist even when we can no longer see them, which gradually emerges during the sensorimotor stage.

occupational segregation The separation of men and women into different kinds of jobs and career paths.

off time Being too late or too early in a culture's timetable for achieving adult life tasks.

old-age dependency ratio The fraction of people over age 60 to younger working-age adults (ages 15 to 59). This ratio is expected to rise dramatically as the baby boomers retire.

old-old People age 80 and older.

on time Being on target in a culture's timetable for achieving adult life tasks.

operant conditioning According to the traditional behavioral perspective, the law of learning that determines any voluntary response. Specifically, we act the way we do because we are reinforced for acting in that way.

osteoporosis An age-related chronic disease in which the bones become porous, fragile, and more likely to break. Osteoporosis is most common in thin women and so most common in females of European or Asian descent.

ovary One of a pair of almond-shaped organs that contain a woman's ova, or eggs.

overextension An error in early language development in which young children apply verbal labels too broadly.

overregularization An error in early language development, in which young children apply the rules for plurals and past tenses even to exceptions, so irregular forms sound like regular forms.

ovulation The moment during a woman's monthly cycle when an ovum is expelled from the ovary.

ovum An egg cell containing the genetic material contributed by the mother to the baby.

P

palliative care Any intervention designed not to cure illness but to promote dignified dying.

palliative care service A service or unit in a hospital that is devoted to end-of-life care.

parent care Adult children's care for their disabled elderly parents.

parenting style In Diana Baumrind's framework, how parents align on two dimensions of childrearing: nurturance (or child-centeredness) and discipline (or structure and rules).

passive euthanasia Withholding potentially life-saving interventions that might keep a terminally ill or permanently comatose patient alive.

permissive parents In Diana Baumrind's parenting-styles framework, a type of child-rearing in which parents provide few rules but rank high on child-centeredness, being extremely loving but providing little discipline.

personal fable David Elkind's term for the tendency of young teenagers to believe that their lives are special and heroic; a component of adolescent egocentrism.

person–environment fit The extent to which the environment is tailored to our biological tendencies and talents. In developmental science, fostering this fit between our talents and the wider world is an important goal.

phoneme The sound units that convey meaning in a given language—for example, in English, the c sound of *cat* and the b sound of *bat*.

physician-assisted suicide A type of active euthanasia in which a physician prescribes a lethal medication to a terminally ill person who wants to die.

Piaget's cognitive developmental theory Jean Piaget's principle that from infancy to adolescence, children progress through four qualitatively different stages of intellectual growth.

placenta The structure projecting from the wall of the uterus during pregnancy through which the developing baby absorbs nutrients.

plastic Malleable, or capable of being changed (used to refer to neural or cognitive development).

postconventional level of morality In Lawrence Kohlberg's theory, the highest level of moral reasoning, in which people respond to ethical issues by applying their own moral guidelines apart from society's rules.

postformal thought A uniquely adult form of intelligence that involves being sensitive to different perspectives, making decisions based on one's inner feelings, and being interested in exploring new questions.

power assertion An ineffective socialization strategy that involves yelling, screaming, or hitting out in frustration at a child.

practical intelligence In Robert Sternberg's framework on successful intelligence, the facet of intelligence involved in knowing how to act competently in real-world situations.

preattachment phase The first phase of John Bowlby's developmental attachment sequence, during the first three months of life, when infants show no visible signs of attachment.

preconventional level of morality In Lawrence Kohlberg's theory, the lowest level of moral reasoning, in which people approach ethical issues by considering the personal punishments or rewards of taking a particular action.

preferential-looking paradigm A research technique to explore early infant sensory capacities and cognition, drawing on the principle that we are attracted to novelty and prefer to look at new things.

preoccupied/ambivalent insecure attachment An excessively clingy, insecure style of relating to loved ones.

preoperational thinking In Piaget's theory, the type of cognition characteristic of children aged 2 to 7, marked by an inability to step back from one's immediate perceptions and think conceptually.

presbycusis Age-related difficulty in hearing, particularly high-pitched tones, caused by the atrophy of hearing receptors located in the inner ear.

presbyopia Age-related midlife difficulty with near vision, caused by the inability of the lens to bend.

primary attachment figure The closest person in a child's or adult's life.

primary circular reactions In Piaget's framework, the first infant habits during the sensorimotor stage, centered on the body.

primary labor market A category of jobs offering good salaries and benefits such as health care and retirement plans.

primary sexual characteristics Physical changes of puberty that directly involve the organs of reproduction, such as the growth of the penis and the onset of menstruation.

private pensions The major source of nongovernmental income support for retirees, in which the individual worker and the employer put a portion of each paycheck into an account to help finance retirement.

procedural memory In the memory-systems perspective, the most resilient (longest-lasting) type of memory; refers to material, such as well-learned physical skills, that we automatically recall without conscious awareness.

prosocial behavior Sharing, helping, and caring actions.

proximity-seeking behavior Acting to maintain physical contact or to be close to an attachment figure.

proximodistal sequence The developmental principle that growth occurs from the most interior parts of the body outward.

puberty rite A "coming of age" ritual, usually beginning at some event such as first menstruation, held in traditional cultures to celebrate children's transition to adulthood.

puberty The hormonal and physical changes by which children become sexually mature human beings.

Q

qualitative research Occasional developmental science data-collection strategy that involves interviewing people to obtain information that cannot be quantified on a numerical scale.

quantitative research Standard developmental science data-collection strategy that involves testing groups of people and using numerical scales and statistics.

quickening A pregnant woman's first feeling of the fetus moving inside her body.

R

reaction time The speed at which a person can respond to a stimulus. A progressive decline in reaction time speed is universal to aging.

reactive aggression A hostile or destructive act carried out in response to being frustrated or hurt.

recessive disorder An illness that a child gets by inheriting two copies of the abnormal gene that causes the disorder.

redemption sequence In Dan McAdams's research, a characteristic theme of highly generative adults' autobiographies, in which they describe tragic events that turned out for the best.

reflex A response or action that is automatic and programmed by non-cortical brain centers.

rehearsal A learning strategy in which people repeat information to embed it in memory.

reinforcement Behavioral term for reward.

rejecting-neglecting parents In Diana Baumrind's parenting-styles framework, the worst child-rearing approach, in which parents provide little discipline and little nurturing or love.

relational aggression A hostile or destructive act designed to cause harm to a person's relationships.

reliability In measurement terminology, a basic criterion of a test's accuracy that scores must be fairly similar when a person takes the test more than once.

REM sleep The phase of sleep involving rapid eye movements, when the EEG looks almost like it does during waking. REM sleep decreases as infants mature.

representative sample A group that reflects the characteristics of the overall population.

resilient children Children who rebound from serious early life traumas to construct successful adult lives.

reversibility In Piaget's conservation tasks, the concrete operational child's knowledge that a specific change in the way a given substance looks can be reversed.

role conflict A situation in which a person is torn between two or more major sets of responsibilities—for instance, parent and worker—and cannot do either job adequately.

role overload A job situation that places so many requirements or demands on workers that it becomes impossible to do a good job.

role phase In Murstein's theory, the final mate-selection stage, in which committed partners work out their future life together.

role The characteristic behavior that is expected of a person in a particular social position, such as student, parent, married person, worker, or retiree.

rooting reflex Newborns' automatic response to a touch on the cheek, involving turning toward that location and beginning to suck.

rough-and-tumble play Play that involves shoving, wrestling, and hitting, but in which no actual harm is intended; especially characteristic of boys.

S

scaffolding The process of teaching new skills by entering a child's zone of proximal development and tailoring one's efforts to that person's competence level.

school-to-work transition The change from the schooling phase of life to the work world.

Seattle Longitudinal Study The definitive study of the effect of aging on intelligence, carried out by K. Warner Schaie, involving simultaneously conducting and comparing the results of cross-sectional and longitudinal studies carried out of a group of Seattle volunteers.

secondary circular reactions In Piaget's framework, habits of the sensorimotor stage lasting from about 4 months of age to the baby's first birthday, centered on exploring the external world.

secondary labor market A category of low-wage jobs providing few benefits and little security.

secondary sexual characteristics Physical changes of puberty that are not directly involved in reproduction.

secular trend in puberty A century-long decline in the average age at which children reach puberty in the developed world.

secure attachment The genuine intimacy that is ideal in love relationships.

secure attachment The ideal attachment response, when a 1-year-old child responds with joy at being reunited with the primary caregiver in the Strange Situation.

selective attention A learning strategy in which people manage their awareness so as to attend only to what is relevant and to filter out unneeded information.

selective optimization with compensation Paul Baltes's three principles for successful aging (and living): (1) selectively focusing on what is most important, (2) working harder to perform well in those top-ranking areas, and (3) relying on external aids to cope effectively.

self-awareness The ability to observe our abilities and actions from an outside frame of reference and to reflect on our inner state.

self-conscious emotions Feelings of pride, shame, or guilt, which first emerge in toddlerhood and show the capacity to reflect on the self.

self-efficacy According to cognitive behaviorism, an internal belief in our competence that predicts whether we initiate activities or persist in the face of failures, and predicts the goals we set.

self-esteem Evaluating oneself as either "good" or "bad" as a result of comparing the self to other people.

self-report strategy A measurement strategy that involves having people report on their feelings and activities through questionnaires.

self-soothing Children's ability, usually beginning at about 6 months of age, to put themselves back to sleep when they wake up during the night.

semantic memory In the memory-systems perspective, a moderately resilient (long-lasting) type of memory; refers to our ability to recall basic facts.

semantics The meaning system of a language—that is, what the words stand for.

sensitive period The time when a certain developmental process is occurring or a body structure is most vulnerable to damage by a teratogen.

sensorimotor stage Piaget's first stage of cognitive development, lasting from birth to age 2, when babies' agenda is to pin down the basics of physical reality.

separation anxiety The main signal of clear-cut attachment at about 7 months of age, when a baby gets visibly upset by a primary caregiver's departure.

seriation The ability to put objects in order according to some principle, such as size.

sex-linked single-gene disorder An illness, carried on the mother's X chromosome, that typically leaves the female offspring unaffected but has a fifty-fifty chance of striking each male child.

sexual double standard A cultural code that gives men greater sexual freedom than women. Specifically, society expects males to want to have intercourse and expects females to remain virgins until they marry and to be more interested in relationships than in having sex.

shame A feeling of being personally humiliated.

single-gene disorder An illness caused by a single gene.

size constancy The principle that we see an object as being the same size regardless of its distance from us.

social clock The concept that we regulate our passage through adulthood by an inner timetable that tells us which life activities are appropriate at certain ages.

social referencing A baby's practice of checking back and monitoring a caregiver's expressions for cues as to how to behave in potentially dangerous exploration situations; linked to the onset of crawling and clear-cut attachment.

Social Security The U.S. government's national retirement support program.

social skills training A strategy for teaching emotion regulation and social skills to rejected children, especially boys with externalizing problems.

social smile The first real smile, occurring at about 2 months of age.

social-interactionist view An approach to language development that emphasizes its social function, specifically that babies and adults have a mutual passion to communicate.

socialization The process by which children are taught to obey the norms of society and to behave in socially appropriate ways.

socioeconomic status (SES) A basic marker referring to status on the educational and—especially—income rungs.

socioeconomic/health gap The disparity, found in nations around the world, between the health of the rich and poor. At every step up on the socioeconomic ladder, people survive longer and enjoy better health.

socioemotional selectivity theory A theory of aging (and the lifespan) put forth by Laura Carstensen, describing how the time we have left to live affects our priorities and social relationships. Specifically, Carstensen believes that as people reach later life, they focus on enhancing the quality of the present and place priority on spending time with their closest attachment figures.

specific learning disability The label for any impairment in language or any deficit related to listening, thinking, speaking, reading, writing, spelling, or understanding mathematics; diagnosed when a score on an intelligence test is much higher than a child's performance on achievement tests.

spermarche A boy's first ejaculation of live sperm.

stimulus phase In Murstein's theory, the initial mate-selection stage, in which judgments about a potential partner are based on external characteristics such as appearance.

stimulus-value-role theory Murstein's mate-selection theory that similar people pair up and that the path to commitment goes through three phases (called the stimulus, value-comparison, and role phases).

"storm and stress" G. Stanley Hall's phrase for the intense moodiness, emotional sensitivity, and risk-taking tendencies that characterize the life stage he labeled *adolescence*.

Strange Situation A procedure developed by Mary Ainsworth to measure variations in attachment security at age 1, involving a series of planned separations and reunions with a primary caregiver.

stranger anxiety A signal of the onset of clear-cut attachment at about 7 months of age, when a baby becomes wary of unfamiliar people and refuses to be held by anyone other than a primary caregiver.

stunting Excessively short stature in a child, caused by chronic lack of adequate nutrition.

successful intelligence In Robert Sternberg's framework, the optimal form of cognition, involving having a good balance of analytic, creative, and practical intelligence.

sucking reflex The automatic, spontaneous sucking movements newborns produce, especially when anything touches their lips.

swaddling Wrapping a baby tightly in a blanket or garment. This technique is calming during early infancy.

sympathy A state necessary for acting prosocially, involving feeling upset *for* a person who needs help.

synapse The gap between the dendrites of one neuron and the axon of another, over which impulses flow.

synaptogenesis Forming of connections between neurons at the synapses. This process, responsible for all perceptions, actions, and thoughts, is most intense during infancy and childhood but continues throughout life.

synchrony The reciprocal aspect of the attachment relationship, with a caregiver and infant responding emotionally to each other in a sensitive, exquisitely attuned way.

syntax The system of grammatical rules in a particular language.

T

telegraphic speech First stage of combining words in infancy, in which a baby pares down a sentence to its essential words.

temperament A person's characteristic, inborn style of dealing with the world.

teratogen A substance that crosses the placenta and harms the fetus.

terminal drop A research phenomenon in which a dramatic decline in an older person's scores on vocabulary tests and other measures of crystallized intelligence predicts having a terminal disease.

tertiary circular reactions In Piaget's framework, "little-scientist" activities of the sensorimotor stage, beginning around age 1, involving flexibly exploring the properties of objects.

testes Male organs that manufacture sperm.

testosterone The hormone responsible for the maturation of the organs of reproduction and other signs of puberty in men, and for hair and skin changes during puberty and sexual desire in both sexes.

theory Any perspective explaining why people act the way they do. Theories allow us to predict behavior and also suggest how to intervene to improve behavior.

theory of mind Children's first cognitive understanding, which appears at about age 4, that other people have different beliefs and perspectives from their own.

toddlerhood The important transitional stage after babyhood, from roughly 1 year to 2 ½ years of age; defined by an intense attachment to caregivers and by an urgent need to become independent.

traditional behaviorism A behavioral worldview that focuses on charting and modifying only "objective," externally visible behaviors.

traditional stable career A career path in which people settle into their permanent life's work in their twenties and often stay with the same organization until they retire.

triangular theory of love Robert Sternberg's categorization of love relationships into three facets: passion, intimacy, and commitment. When arranged at the points of a triangle, their combinations describes all of the different kinds of adult love relationships.

trimester One of the 3-month-long segments into which pregnancy is divided.

true experiments The only research strategy that can determine that something causes something else; involves randomly assigning people to different treatments and then looking at the outcome.

twentieth-century life expectancy revolution The dramatic increase in average life expectancy that occurred during the first half of the twentieth century in the developed world.

twin study Behavioral genetic research strategy, designed to determine the genetic contribution of a given trait, that involves comparing identical twins with fraternal twins (or with other people).

twin/adoption studies Behavioral genetic research strategy that involves comparing the similarities of identical twin pairs adopted into different families, to determine the genetic contribution to a given trait.

U

ultrasound In pregnancy, an image of the fetus in the womb that helps to date the pregnancy, assess the fetus's growth, and identify abnormalities.

umbilical cord The structure that attaches the placenta to the fetus, through which nutrients are passed and fetal wastes are removed.

underextension An error in early language development in which young children apply verbal labels too narrowly.

undernutrition A chronic lack of adequate food.

U-shaped curve of marital satisfaction The most common pathway of marital happiness in the West, in which satisfaction is highest at the honeymoon, declines during the child-rearing years, then rises after the children grow up.

uterus The pear-shaped muscular organ in a woman's abdomen that houses the developing baby.

V

validity In measurement terminology, a basic criterion for a test's accuracy involving whether that measure reflects the real-world quality it is supposed to measure.

value-comparison phase In Murstein's theory, the second mate-selection stage, in which judgments about a partner are made on the basis of similar values and interests.

vascular dementia A type of age-related dementia caused by multiple small strokes.

very low birth weight (VLBW) A body weight at birth of less than 3 1/4 pounds.

virtual dating Internet dating and love relationships.

visual cliff A table that appears to "end" in a drop-off at its midpoint; used to test for infant depth perception.

W

Wechsler Adult Intelligence Scale (WAIS) The standard test to measure adult IQ, involving verbal and performance scales, each of which is made up of various subtests.

WISC (Wechsler Intelligence Scale for Children) The standard intelligence test used in childhood, consisting of a Verbal Scale (questions for the child to answer), a Performance Scale (materials for the child to manipulate), and a variety of subtests.

work-centric worker A worker who puts his or her job above family life.

working memory In information-processing theory, the limited-capacity gateway system, containing all the material that we can keep in awareness at a single time. The material in this system is either processed for more permanent storage or lost.

working model According to Bowlby's theory, the mental representation of a caregiver that allows children beyond age 3 to be physically apart from a primary caregiver and predicts their behavior in relationships.

Y

young-old People in their sixties and seventies.

youth development program Any after-school program, or structured activity outside of the school day, that is devoted to promoting thriving in teenagers.

Z

zone of proximal development In Vygotsky's theory, the gap between a child's ability to solve a problem totally on his own and his potential knowledge if taught by a more accomplished person.

zygote A fertilized ovum.

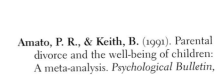

Abbassi, V. (1998). Growth and normal puberty. *Pediatrics, 102,* 507–511.

Abbott, R. D., White, L. R., Ross, G. W., Masaki, K. H., Curb, J. D., & Petrovitch, H. (2004). Walking and dementia in physically capable elderly men. *Journal of the American Medical Association, 292,* 1447–1453.

Aboderin, I. (2004). Decline in material family support for older people in urban Ghana, Africa: Understanding processes and causes of change. *Journals of Gerontology: Series B: Psychological Sciences and Social Sciences, 59B,* S128-S137.

AbouZahr, C., & Wardlaw, T. (2001). Maternal mortality at the end of a decade: Signs of progress? *Bulletin of the World Health Organization, 79,* 561–568.

Abrahamsson, A., Springett, J., Karlsson, L., & Ottosson, T. (2005). Making sense of the challenge of smoking cessation during pregnancy: A phenomenographic approach. *Health Education Research, 20,* 367–378.

Abramson, L. Y., Seligman, M. E., & Teasdale, J. D. (1978). Learned helplessness in humans: Critique and reformulation. *Journal of Abnormal Psychology, 87,* 49–74.

ACOG Practice Bulletin. (2001). Prenatal diagnosis of fetal chromosomal abnormalities. *Obstetrics & Gynecology, 97*(5, Pt 1), Suppl. 1–12.

Adda, J., Chandola, T., & Marmot, M. (2003). Socio-economic status and health: Causality and pathways. *Journal of Econometrics, 112,* 57–63.

Adlard, P. A., & Cummings, B. J. (2004). Alzheimer's disease—A sum greater than its parts? *Neurobiology of Aging, 25,* 725–733.

Adler, N. E., Marmot, M., McEwen, B. S., & Stewart, J. (Eds.). (1999). *Socioeconomic status and health in industrial nations: Social, psychological, and biological pathways* (Vol. 896). New York: New York Academy of Sciences.

Adler, N. E., & Ostrove, J. M. (1999). Socioeconomic status and health: What we know and what we don't. In N. E. Adler, M. Marmot, B. S. McEwen, & J. Stewart (Eds.), *Socioeconomic status and health in industrial nations: Social, psychological, and biological pathways* (pp. 3–15). New York: New York Academy of Sciences.

Ahnert, L., Gunnar, M. R., Lamb, M. E., & Barthel, M. (2004). Transition to child care: Associations with infant-mother attachment, infant negative emotion, and cortisol elevations. *Child Development, 75,* 639–650.

Ainsworth, M. D. S. (1967). *Infancy in Uganda: Infant care and the growth of love.* Baltimore: Johns Hopkins Press.

Ainsworth, M. D. S. (1973). The development of infant-mother attachment. In B. M. Caldwell & H. N. Ricciuti (Eds.), *Review of child development research* (Vol. 3, pp. 1–94). Chicago: University of Chicago Press.

Ainsworth, M. D. S., Blehar, M. C., Waters, E., & Wall, S. (1978). *Patterns of attachment: A psychological study of the strange situation.* Hillsdale, NJ: Erlbaum.

Aksan, N., & Kochanska, G. (2004). Links between systems of inhibition from infancy to preschool years. *Child Development, 75,* 1477–1490.

Aksan, N., & Kochanska, G. (2005). Conscience in childhood: Old questions, new answers. *Developmental Psychology, 41,* 506–516.

Aldred, H. E. (1997). *Pregnancy and birth sourcebook: Basic information about planning for pregnancy, maternal health, fetal growth and development.* Detroit, MI: Omnigraphics.

Alexander, R., Feeney, J., Hohaus, L., & Noller, P. (2001). Attachment style and coping resources as predictors of coping strategies in the transition to parenthood. *Personal Relationships, 8,* 137–152.

Allen, J. P., McElhaney, K. B., Land, D. J., Kuperminc, G. P., Moore, C. W., O'Beirne-Kelly, H., & Kilmer, S. L. (2003). A secure base in adolescence: Markers of attachment security in the mother-adolescent relationship. *Child Development, 74,* 292–307.

Allik, J., & McCrae, R. R. (2004). Toward a geography of personality traits: Patterns of profiles across 36 cultures. *Journal of Cross-Cultural Psychology, 35,* 13–28.

Altschuler, A., Somkin, C. P., & Adler, N. E. (2004). Local services and amenities, neighborhood social capital, and health. *Social Science & Medicine, 59,* 1219–1229.

Alzheimer's Disease Education & Referral Center [ADEAR]. (2004). Estrogen-alone hormone therapy could increase risk of dementia in older women. Retrieved January 13, 2006, from http://www.alzheimers.org/nianews/nianews66.html

Amato, P. R. (2000). The consequences of divorce for adults and children. *Journal of Marriage & the Family, 62,* 1269–1287.

Amato, P. R. (2001). Children of divorce in the 1990s: An update of the Amato and Keith (1991) meta-analysis. *Journal of Family Psychology, 15,* 355–370.

Amato, P. R., & Keith, B. (1991). Parental divorce and the well-being of children: A meta-analysis. *Psychological Bulletin, 110,* 26–46.

Amedi, A., Raz, N., Pianka, P., Malach, R., & Zohary, E. (2003). Early 'visual' cortex activation correlates with superior verbal memory performance in the blind. *Nature Neuroscience, 6,* 758–766.

American Academy of Pediatrics [AAP], Committee on Adolescence. (2003). Identifying and treating eating disorders. *Pediatrics, 111,* 204–211.

American Academy of Pediatrics [AAP], Committee on Drugs. (2000). Use of psychoactive medication during pregnancy and possible effects on the fetus and newborn. *Pediatrics, 105,* 880–887.

American Academy of Pediatrics [AAP], Section on Breastfeeding. (2005). Breastfeeding and the use of human milk. *Pediatrics, 115,* 496–506.

American Heart Association. (2001). 2002 *Heart and Stroke Statistical Update.* Dallas, TX: American Heart Association.

American Obesity Association. (2002). AOA fact sheets: Obesity—A global epidemic. Retrieved October 4, 2006, from http://www.obesity.org/subs/fastfacts/obesity_global_epidemic.shtml

Ames, C. (1986). Effective motivation: The contribution of the learning environment. In R. S. Feldman (Ed.), *The social psychology of education: Current research and theory* (pp. 235–256). New York: Cambridge University Press.

Ames, C., & Archer, J. (1988). Achievement goals in the classroom: Students' learning strategies and motivation processes. *Journal of Educational Psychology, 80,* 260–267.

Amin, S., & Al-Bassusi, N. H. (2004). Education, wage work, and marriage: Perspectives of Egyptian working women. *Journal of Marriage and Family, 66,* 1287–1299.

Andero, A. A., & Stewart, A. (2002). Issue of corporal punishment: Re-examined. *Journal of Instructional Psychology, 29,* 90–96.

Anders, T., Goodlin-Jones, B., & Sadeh, A. (2000). Sleep disorders. In C. H. Zeanah, Jr. (Ed.), *Handbook of infant mental health* (2nd ed., pp. 326–338). New York: Guilford Press.

Anders, T., Goodlin-Jones, B., & Zelenko, M. (1998). Infant regulation and sleep-wake state development. *Zero to Three*, 19(2), 9–14.

Andersen-Ranberg, K., Vasegaard, L., & Jeune, B. (2001). Dementia is not inevitable: A population-based study of Danish centenarians. *Journals of Gerontology: Series B: Psychological Sciences and Social Sciences*, 56B, P152-P159.

Anderson, D. I., Campos, J. J., & Barbu-Roth, M. A. (2004). A developmental perspective on visual proprioception. In G. Bremner & A. Slater (Eds.), *Theories of infant development* (pp. 30–69). Malden, MA: Blackwell.

Anderson, E. S., Jackson, A., Wailoo, M. P., & Petersen, S. A. (2002). Child care decisions: Parental choice or chance? *Child: Care, Health and Development*, 28, 391–401.

Anderson, J. W. (1972). Attachment behaviour out of doors. In N. Blurton Jones (Ed.), *Ethological studies of child behaviour* (pp. 199–215). Oxford, England: Cambridge University Press.

Anderson, K. A., Towsley, G. L., & Gaugler, J. E. (2004). The genetic connections of Alzheimer's disease: An emerging source of caregiver stress. *Journal of Aging Studies*, 18, 429–443.

Anderson, N. D., & Craik, F. I. M. (2000). Memory in the aging brain. In E. Tulving & F. I. M. Craik (Eds.), *The Oxford handbook of memory* (pp. 411–425). New York: Oxford University Press.

Anderson, P., Doyle, L. W., Callanan, C., Carse, E., Casalaz, D., Charlton, M. P., Davis, N., Duff, J., Ford, G., Fraser, S., Hayes, M., Kaimakamis, M., Kelly, E., Opie, G., Watkins, A., Woods, H., & Yu, V. (2003). Neurobehavioral outcomes of school-age children born extremely low birth weight or very preterm in the 1990s. *Journal of the American Medical Association*, 289, 3264–3272.

Anderson, R., & Mitchell, E. M. (1984). Children's health and play in rural Nepal. *Social Science & Medicine*, 19, 735–740.

Anderson, S. E., Dallal, G. E., & Must, A. (2003). Relative weight and race influence average age at menarche: Results from two nationally representative surveys of US girls studied 25 years apart. *Pediatrics*, 111, 844–850.

Andrés, P., Parmentier, F. B. R., & Escera, C. (2006). The effect of age on involuntary capture of attention by irrelevant sounds: A test of the frontal hypothesis of aging. *Neuropsychologia*, 44, 2564–2568.

Aneshensel, C. S., Pearlin, L. I., Mullan, J. T., Zarit, S. H., & Whitlatch, C. J. (1995). *Profiles in caregiving: The unexpected career*. San Diego, CA: Academic Press.

Ani, C. C., & Grantham-McGregor, S. (1998). Family and personal characteristics of aggressive Nigerian boys: Differences from and similarities with Western findings. *Journal of Adolescent Health*, 23, 311–317.

Anker, R., Malkas, H., & Korten, A. (2003). *Gender-based occupational segregation in the 1990's* (Declaration/WP/16/2003). Geneva, Switzerland: International Labour Office.

Archibald, A. B., Graber, J. A., & Brooks-Gunn, J. (2003). Pubertal processes and physiological growth in adolescence. In G. R. Adams & M. D. Berzonsky (Eds.), *Blackwell handbook of adolescence* (pp. 24–47). Malden, MA: Blackwell.

Arcus, D. (2001). Inhibited and uninhibited children: Biology in the social context. In T. D. Wachs & G. A. Kohnstamm (Eds.), *Temperament in context* (pp. 43–60). Mahwah, NJ: Erlbaum.

Ardelt, M. (2003). Physician-assisted death. In C. D. Bryant (Ed.), *Handbook of death & dying* (pp. 424–434). Thousand Oaks, CA: Sage.

Ardelt, M., & Koenig, C. S. (2006). The role of religion for hospice patients and relatively healthy older adults. *Research on Aging*, 28, 184–215.

Ardley, J., & Ericson, L. (2002). "We don't play like that here!": Understanding aggressive expressions of play. In C. R. Brown & K. C. Marchant (Eds.), *Play in practice: Case studies in young children's play* (pp. 35–48). St. Paul, MN: Redleaf.

Ariès, P. (1962). *Centuries of childhood: A social history of family life*. New York: Knopf.

Ariès, P. (1974). *Western attitudes toward death: From the Middle Ages to the present* (P. M. Ranum, Trans.). Baltimore: Johns Hopkins University Press.

Ariès, P. (1981). *The hour of our death* (H. Weaver, Trans.). New York: Knopf.

Arnett, J. J. (1999). Adolescent storm and stress, reconsidered. *American Psychologist*, 54, 317–326.

Arnett, J. J. (2000). Emerging adulthood: A theory of development from the late teens through the twenties. *American Psychologist*, 55, 469–480.

Arnett, J. J. (2002). The psychology of globalization. *American Psychologist*, 57, 774–783.

Arnett, J. J. (2004). *Emerging adulthood: The winding road from the late teens through the twenties*. New York: Oxford University Press.

Arnold, E. M. (2004). Factors that influence consideration of hastening death among people with life-threatening illnesses. *Health & Social Work*, 29, 17–26.

Arnold, E. M., Goldston, D. B., Walsh, A. K., Reboussin, B. A., Daniel, S. S., Hickman, E., & Wood, F. B. (2005). Severity of emotional and behavioral problems among poor and typical readers. *Journal of Abnormal Child Psychology*, 33, 205–217.

Arnsten, A. F. T., & Shansky, R. M. (2004). Adolescence: Vulnerable period for stress-induced prefrontal cortical function? Introduction to part IV. In R. E. Dahl & L. P. Spear (Eds.), *Adolescent brain development: Vulnerabilities and opportunities* (Vol. 1021, pp. 143–147). New York: New York Academy of Sciences.

Aron, A., Norman, C. C., Aron, E. N., & Lewandowski, G. (2002). Shared participation in self-expanding activities: Positive effects on experienced martial quality. In P. Noller & J. A. Feeney (Eds.), *Understanding marriage: Developments in the study of couple interaction* (pp. 177–194). New York: Cambridge University Press.

Arras, J. D., & Dubler, N. N. (1994). Bringing the hospital home: Ethical and social implications of high-tech home care. *Hastings Center Report*, 24(Suppl. 5), S19–28.

Arriaga, X. B. (2001). The ups and downs of dating: Fluctuations in satisfaction in newly formed romantic relationships. *Journal of Personality and Social Psychology*, 80, 754–765.

Associated Press. (2006). Euthanasia on the rise in Netherlands. Retrieved October 18, 2006, from The Christian Post Web site: http://world.christianpost.com/article.htm?aid=8565&dat=20060502

Astin, A. W. (1993). *What matters in college? Four critical years revisited*. San Francisco: Jossey-Bass.

Astin, A. W. (1999). How the liberal arts college affects students. *Daedalus*, 128(1), 77–100.

Astington, J. W., & Jenkins, J. M. (1995). Theory of mind development and social understanding. *Cognition & Emotion, 9,* 151–165.

Atchley, R. C. (1977). *The social forces in later life: An introduction to social gerontology* (2nd ed.). Belmont, CA: Wadsworth.

Atchley, R. C. (1989). A continuity theory of normal aging. *Gerontologist, 29,* 183–190.

AVERT. (2005, November 22, 2005). AIDS and HIV statistics for Sub-Saharan Africa. Retrieved January 24, 2006, from http://www.avert.org/subaadults.htm

Aviezer, O., Sagi, A., & van IJzendoorn, M. H. (2002). Balancing the family and the collective in raising children: Why communal sleeping in kibbutzim was predestined to end. *Family Process, 41,* 435–454.

Avis, J., & Harris, P. L. (1991). Belief-desire reasoning among Baka children: Evidence for a universal conception of mind. *Child Development, 62,* 460–467.

Avis, N. E., Assmann, S. F., Kravitz, H. M., Ganz, P. A., & Ory, M. (2004). Quality of life in diverse groups of midlife women: Assessing the influence of menopause, health status and psychosocial and demographic factors. *Quality of Life Research, 13,* 933–946.

Avis, N. E., Ory, M., Matthews, K. A., Schocken, M., Bromberger, J., & Colvin, A. (2003). Health-related quality of life in a multiethnic sample of middle-aged women: Study of Women's Health Across the Nation (SWAN). *Medical Care, 41,* 1262–1276.

Axinn, W. G., & Barber, J. S. (1997). Living arrangements and family formation attitudes in early adulthood. *Journal of Marriage and the Family, 59,* 595–611.

Bacchini, D., & Magliulo, F. (2003). Self-image and perceived self-efficacy during adolescence. *Journal of Youth and Adolescence, 32,* 337–349.

Bachman, J. G., & Schulenberg, J. (1993). How part-time work intensity relates to drug use, problem behavior, time use, and satisfaction among high school seniors: Are these consequences or merely correlates? *Developmental Psychology, 29,* 220–235.

Bäckman, L., Wahlin, Å., Small, B. J., Herlitz, A., Winblad, B., & Fratiglioni, L. (2004). Cognitive functioning in aging and dementia: The Kungsholmen project. *Aging, Neuropsychology, and Cognition, 11,* 212–244.

Baddeley, A. D. (1992). Working memory: The interface between memory and cognition. *Journal of Cognitive Neuroscience, 4,* 281–288.

Bahadur, G. (2002, June 13). Young South Asians in America meet, greet at "Desi parties". *Philadelphia Inquirer,* p. A-1 (local).

Baillargeon, R. (1987). Young infants' reasoning about the physical and spatial properties of a hidden object. *Cognitive Development, 2,* 179–200.

Baillargeon, R. (1993). The object concept revisited: New direction in the investigation of infants' physical knowledge. In C. Granrud (Ed.), *Visual perception and cognition in infancy* (pp. 265–315). Hillsdale, NJ: Erlbaum.

Baillargeon, R., & DeVos, J. (1991). Object permanence in young infants: Further evidence. *Child Development, 62,* 1227–1246.

Baillargeon, R., & Graber, M. (1987). Where's the rabbit? 5.5-month-old infants' representation of the height of a hidden object. *Cognitive Development, 2,* 375–392.

Baird, A. H. (2003). Through my eyes: Service needs of grandparents who raise their grandchildren, from the perspective of a custodial grandmother. In B. Hayslip, Jr. & J. H. Patrick (Eds.), *Working with custodial grandparents* (pp. 59–65). New York: Springer.

Baird, A. L., & Grieve, F. G. (2006). Exposure to male models in advertisements leads to a decrease in men's body satisfaction. *North American Journal of Psychology, 8,* 115–121.

Baker, A. J. L. (2005). The long-term effects of parental alienation on adult children: A qualitative research study. *American Journal of Family Therapy, 33,* 289–302.

Bakermans-Kranenburg, M. J., van IJzendoorn, M. H., & Kroonenberg, P. M. (2004). Differences in attachment security between African-American and white children: Ethnicity or socio-economic status? *Infant Behavior & Development, 27,* 417–433.

Ball, H. L., Hooker, E., & Kelly, P. J. (2000). Parent-infant co-sleeping: Fathers' roles and perspectives. *Infant and Child Development, 9,* 67–74.

Ball, K., & Rebok, G. W. (1994). Evaluating the driving ability of older adults. *Journal of Applied Gerontology, 13,* 20–38.

Ball, M. M., Perkins, M. M., Whittington, F. J., Hollingsworth, C., King, S. V., & Combs, B. L. (2004). Independence in assisted living. *Journal of Aging Studies, 18,* 445–465.

Baltes, M. M., & Carstensen, L. L. (2003). The process of successful aging: Selection, optimization and compensation. In U. M. Staudinger & U. Lindenberger (Eds.), *Understanding human development: Dialogues with lifespan psychology* (pp. 81–104). Dordrecht, Netherlands: Kluwer Academic.

Baltes, P. B. (1987). Theoretical propositions of life-span developmental psychology: On the dynamics between growth and decline. *Developmental Psychology, 23,* 611–626.

Baltes, P. B. (1993). The aging mind: Potential and limits. *Gerontologist, 33,* 580–594.

Baltes, P. B. (2003). On the incomplete architecture of human ontogeny: Selection, optimization, and compensation as foundation of developmental theory. In U. M. Staudinger & U. Lindenberger (Eds.), *Understanding human development: Dialogues with lifespan psychology* (pp. 17–43). Boston: Kluwer Academic Publishers.

Baltes, P. B., Featherman, D. L., & Lerner, R. M. (Eds.). (1988). *Life-span development and behavior, Vol. 8.* Hillsdale, NJ: Erlbaum.

Baltes, P. B., & Freund, A. M. (2003). The intermarriage of wisdom and selective optimization with compensation: Two meta-heuristics guiding the conduct of life. In C. L. M. Keyes & J. Haidt (Eds.), *Flourishing: Positive psychology and the life well-lived* (pp. 249–273). Washington, DC: American Psychological Association.

Baltes, P. B., Reese, H. W., & Lipsitt, L. P. (1980). Life-span developmental psychology. *Annual Review of Psychology, 31,* 65–110.

Baltes, P. B., & Smith, J. (1997). A systemic-wholistic view of psychological functioning in very old age: Introduction to a collection of articles from the Berlin Aging Study. *Psychology and Aging, 12,* 395–409.

Bandura, A. (1977). *Social learning theory.* Englewood Cliffs, NJ: Prentice Hall.

Bandura, A. (1986). *Social foundations of thought and action: A social cognitive theory.* Englewood Cliffs, NJ: Prentice-Hall.

Bandura, A. (1989). Human agency in social cognitive theory. *American Psychologist, 44,* 1175–1184.

Bandura, A. (1992). Exercise of personal agency through the self-efficacy mechanism. In R. Schwarzer (Ed.), *Self-efficacy: Thought control of action* (pp. 3–38). Washington, DC: Hemisphere.

Bandura, A. (1997). *Self-efficacy: The exercise of control.* New York: Freeman.

Banfield, J. F., Wyland, C. L., Macrae, C. N., Munte, T. F., & Heatherton, T. F. (2004). The cognitive neuroscience of self-regulation. In R. F. Baumeister & K. D. Vohs (Eds.), *Handbook of self-regulation: Research, theory, and applications* (pp. 62–83). New York: Guilford Press.

Barker, E. T., & Galambos, N. L. (2003). Body dissatisfaction of adolescent girls and boys: Risk and resources factors. *Journal of Early Adolescence, 23,* 141–165.

Barkley, R. A. (1998). *Attention-deficit hyperactivity disorder: A handbook for diagnosis and treatment* (2nd ed.). New York: Guilford Press.

Barkley, R. A. (2003). Attention-deficit/hyperactivity disorder. In E. J. Mash & R. A. Barkley (Eds.), *Child psychopathology* (2nd ed., pp. 75–143). New York: Guilford Press.

Barkley, R. A., Fischer, M., Smallish, L., & Fletcher, K. (2004). Young adult follow-up of hyperactive children: Antisocial activities and drug use. *Journal of Child Psychology and Psychiatry, 45,* 195–211.

Barkley, R. A., & Murphy, K. R. (2006). *Attention-deficit hyperactivity disorder: A clinical workbook* (3rd ed.). New York: Guilford Press.

Barnet, H. S. (1990). Divorce stress and adjustment model: Locus of control and demographic predictors. *Journal of Divorce, 13,* 93–109.

Barnett, R. C., & Baruch, G. K. (1988). Correlates of fathers' participation in family work. In P. Bronstein & C. P. Cowan (Eds.), *Fatherhood today: Men's changing role in the family* (pp. 66–78). Oxford, England: Wiley.

Baron-Cohen, S. (1999). The evolution of a theory of mind. In M. C. Corballis & S. E. G. Lea (Eds.), *The descent of mind: Psychological perspectives on hominid evolution* (pp. 261–277). New York: Oxford University Press.

Baron-Cohen, S., Leslie, A. M., & Frith, U. (1985). Does the autistic child have a "theory of mind"? *Cognition, 21,* 37–46.

Barr, R. G. (2000). Excessive crying. In A. J. Sameroff, M. Lewis, & S. M. Miller (Eds.), *Handbook of developmental psychopathology* (2nd ed., pp. 327–350). Dordrecht, Netherlands: Kluwer.

Barr, R. G., & Gunnar, M. (2000). Colic: The "transient responsivity' hypothesis. In R. G. Barr, B. Hopkins, & J. A. Green (Eds.), *Crying as a sign, a symptom, & a signal: Clinical, emotional, and developmental aspects of infant and toddler crying* (pp. 41–66). New York: Cambridge University Press.

Bartolini, V., & Lunn, K. (2002). "Teacher, they won't let me play!": Strategies for improving inappropriate play behavior. In C. R. Brown & K. C. Marchant (Eds.), *Play in practice: Case studies in young children's play* (pp. 13–20). St. Paul, MN: Redleaf.

Bates, J. E., & Bayles, K. (1988). Attachment and the development of behavior problems. In J. Belsky & T. Nezworski (Eds.), *Clinical implications of attachment* (pp. 253–299). Hillsdale, NJ: Erlbaum.

Batsche, G. M., & Porter, L. J. (2006). Bullying. In G. G. Bear & K. M. Minke (Eds.), *Children's needs III: Development, prevention, and intervention* (pp. 135–148). Washington, DC: National Association of School Psychologists.

Batty, G. D., Shipley, M. J., Marmot, M. G., & Smith, G. D. (2003). Leisure time physical activity and disease-specific mortality among men with chronic bronchitis: Evidence from the Whitehall Study. *American Journal of Public Health, 93,* 817–821.

Bauer, J. J., & McAdams, D. P. (2004). Personal growth in adults' stories of life transitions. *Journal of Personality, 72,* 573–602.

Baum, A., Garofalo, J. P., & Yali, A. M. (1999). Socioeconomic status and chronic stress. Does stress account for SES effects on health? In N. E. Adler, M. Marmot, B. S. McEwen, & J. Stewart (Eds.), *Socioeconomic status and health in industrial nations: Social, psychological, and biological pathways* (pp. 131–144). New York: New York Academy of Sciences.

Baumeister, R. F., Smart, L., & Boden, J. M. (1999). Relation of threatened egotism to violence and aggression: The dark side of high self-esteem. In R. F. Baumeister (Ed.), *The self in social psychology* (pp. 240–284). New York: Psychology Press.

Baumrind, D. (1971). Current patterns of parental authority. *Developmental Psychology, 4*(1, Pt. 2), 1–103.

Baumrind, D. (1996). The discipline controversy revisited. *Family Relations: Journal of Applied Family & Child Studies, 45,* 405–414.

Baumrind, D. (1997). Necessary distinctions. *Psychological Inquiry, 8,* 176–182.

Baumrind, D., Larzelere, R. E., & Cowan, P. A. (2002). Ordinary physical punishment: Is it harmful? Comment on Gershoff (2002). *Psychological Bulletin, 128,* 580–589.

Baxter, L. A., & Widenmann, S. (1993). Revealing and not revealing the status of romantic relationships to social networks. *Journal of Social and Personal Relationships, 10,* 321–337.

Beasley, J. (1997). Sickle cell newborn screening: Frequently asked questions (FAQs). Retrieved January 21, 2006, from Sickle Cell Information Center Web site: http://www.scinfo.org/faqNBS.htm

Becker, A. E., Burwell, R. A., Herzog, D. B., Hamburg, P., & Gilman, S. E. (2002). Eating behaviours and attitudes following prolonged exposure to television among ethnic Fijian adolescent girls. *British Journal of Psychiatry, 180,* 509–514.

Beckmann, C. R. B., Ling, F. W., Laube, D. W., Smith, R. P., Barzansky, B. M., & Herbert, W. N. P. (2002). *Obstetrics and gynecology* (4th ed.). Baltimore: Lippincott Williams & Wilkins.

Behague, D. P., Victora, C. G., & Barros, F. C. (2002). Consumer demand for caesarean sections in Brazil: Informed decision making, patient choice, or social inequality? A population based birth cohort study linking ethnographic and epidemiological methods. *BMJ, 324,* 942.

Behrman, R. E., & Butler, A. S. (Eds.). (2006). *Preterm birth: Causes, consequences, and prevention.* Washington, DC: National Academies Press.

Bell, J. H., & Bromnick, R. D. (2003). The social reality of the imaginary audience: A ground theory approach. *Adolescence, 38,* 205–219.

Bell, R. Q. (1968). A reinterpretation of the direction of effects in studies of socialization. *Psychological Review, 75,* 81–95.

Bellenir, K. (Ed.). (2004). *Genetic disorders sourcebook* (3rd ed.). Detroit, MI: Omnigraphics.

Bellinger, D., Leviton, A., Waternaux, C., Needleman, H., & Rabinowitz, M. (1987). Longitudinal analyses of prenatal and postnatal lead exposure and early cognitive development. *New England Journal of Medicine, 316,* 1037–1043.

Belsky, J. (2005). Attachment theory and research in ecological perspective: Insights from the Pennsylvania Infant and Family Development Project and the NICHD Study of Early Child Care. In K. E. Grossmann, K. Grossmann, & E. Waters (Eds.), *Attachment from infancy to adulthood: The major longitudinal studies* (pp. 71–97). New York: Guilford Press.

Belsky, J., Lang, M. E., & Rovine, M. (1985). Stability and change in marriage across the transition to parenthood: A second study. *Journal of Marriage and the Family, 47,* 855–865.

Belsky, J., & Rovine, M. (1990). Patterns of marital change across the transition to parenthood: Pregnancy to three years postpartum. *Journal of Marriage & the Family, 52,* 5–19.

Belsky, J., Spanier, G. B., & Rovine, M. (1983). Stability and change in marriage across the transition to parenthood. *Journal of Marriage & the Family, 45,* 567–577.

Belsky, J., Steinberg, L., & Draper, P. (1991). Childhood experience, interpersonal development, and reproductive strategy: An evolutionary theory of socialization. *Child Development, 62,* 647–670.

Belsky, J., & Volling, B. L. (1987). Mothering, fathering, and marital interaction in the family triad during infancy: Exploring family system's processes. In P. W. Berman & F. A. Pedersen (Eds.), *Men's transitions to parenthood: Longitudinal studies of early family experience* (pp. 37–63). Hillsdale, NJ: Erlbaum.

Belsky, J. K. (1999). *The psychology of aging: Theory, research, and interventions* (3rd ed.). Pacific Grove, CA: Brooks/Cole.

Belsky, J. K. (2001). Aging. In J. Worell (Ed.), *Encyclopedia of women and gender: Sex similarities and differences and the impact of society on gender* (Vol. 1, pp. 95–108). San Diego, CA: Academic Press.

Bem, S. L. (1981). Gender schema theory: A cognitive account of sex typing. *Psychological Review, 88,* 354–364.

Bender, W. N. (1998). *Learning disabilities: Characteristics, identification, and teaching strategies* (3rd ed.). Boston: Allyn and Bacon.

Bengtson, V. L. (1989). The problem of generations: Age group contrasts, continuities and social change. In V. L. Bengtson & K. W. Schaie (Eds.), *The course of later life: Research and reflections* (pp. 25–54). New York: Springer.

Benjet, C., & Kazdin, A. E. (2003). Spanking children: The controversies, findings and new directions. *Clinical Psychology Review, 23,* 197–224.

Benn, P. A., Egan, J. F. X., Fang, M., & Smith-Bindman, R. (2004). Changes in the utilization of prenatal diagnosis. *Obstetrics & Gynecology, 103,* 1255–1260.

Benoit, D., Zeanah, C. H., Boucher, C., & Minde, K. K. (1992). Sleep disorders in early childhood: Association with insecure maternal attachment. *Journal of the American Academy of Child & Adolescent Psychiatry, 31,* 86–93.

Berg, E. Z. (2004). Gender and its effects on psychopathology. *American Journal of Psychiatry, 161,* 179.

Bergin, D. A., & Cizek, G. J. (2003). Alfred Binet. In J. Palmer (Ed.), *Fifty major thinkers on education: From Confucius to Dewey* (pp. 160–164). London: Routledge.

Berk, L. E., & Winsler, A. (1999). NAEYC research into practice series: Vol. 7. *Scaffolding children's learning: Vygotsky and early childhood education.* Washington, DC: National Association for the Education of Young Children.

Berkman, D. S., Lescano, A. G., Gilman, R. H., Lopez, S. L., & Black, M. M. (2002). Effects of stunting, diarrhoeal disease, and parasitic infection during infancy on cognition in late childhood: A follow-up study. *Lancet, 359,* 564–571.

Berko, J. (1958). The child's learning of English morphology. *Word, 14,* 150–177.

Berkowitz, R. I., & Stunkard, A. J. (2002). Development of childhood obesity. In T. A. Wadden & A. J. Stunkard (Eds.), *Handbook of obesity treatment* (pp. 515–531). New York: Guilford Press.

Bernstein, J. R. (1997). *When the bough breaks: Forever after the death of a son or daughter.* Kansas City, MO: Andrews and McMeel.

Bertenthal, B. I., Campos, J. J., & Kermoian, R. (1994). An epigenetic perspective on the development of self-produced locomotion and its consequences. *Current Directions in Psychological Science, 3,* 140–145.

Berzonsky, M. D. (2003). The structure of identity: Commentary on Jane Kroger's view of identity status transition. *Identity, 3,* 231–245.

Berzonsky, M. D., & Adams, G. R. (1999). Reevaluating the identity status paradigm: Still useful after 35 years. *Developmental Review, 19,* 557–590.

Besser, A., Priel, B., & Wiznitzer, A. (2002). Childbearing depressive symptomatology in high-risk pregnancies: The roles of working models and social support. *Personal Relationships, 9,* 395–413.

Bhandari, N., Bahl, R., Mazumdar, S., Martines, J., Black, R. E., & Bhan, M. K. (2003). Effect of community-based promotion of exclusive breastfeeding on diarrhoeal illness and growth: A cluster randomised controlled trial. *Lancet, 361,* 1418–1423.

Biederman, J. (2005). Attention-deficit/hyperactivity disorder: A selective overview. *Biological Psychiatry, 57,* 1215–1220.

Bieliauskas, L. A. (2005). Neuropsychological assessment of geriatric driving competence. *Brain Injury, 19,* 221–226.

Billy, J. O., & Udry, J. R. (1985). The influence of male and female best friends on adolescent sexual behavior. *Adolescence, 20,* 21–32.

Bilsen, J. J. R., Vander Stichele, R. H., Mortier, F., & Deliens, L. (2004). Involvement of nurses in physician-assisted dying. *Journal of Advanced Nursing, 47,* 583–591.

Bird, A. (1994). Careers as repositories of knowledge: A new perspective on boundaryless careers. *Journal of Organizational Behavior, 15,* 325–344.

Birren, J. E., & Birren, B. A. (1990). The concepts, models, and history of the psychology of aging. In J. E. Birren & K. W. Schaie (Eds.), *Handbook of the psychology of aging* (3rd ed., pp. 3–20). San Diego, CA: Academic Press.

Bissada, A., & Briere, J. (2001). Child abuse: Physical and sexual. In J. Worell (Ed.), *Encyclopedia of women and gender: Sex similarities and differences and the impact of society on gender* (pp. 219–232). San Diego, CA: Academic Press.

Bjorklund, D. F. (2005). *Children's thinking: Cognitive development and individual differences* (4th ed.). Belmont, CA: Wadsworth.

Bjorklund, D. F., & Bjorklund, B. R. (1992). *Looking at children: An introduction to child development.* Belmont, CA: Brooks/Cole.

Bjorklund, D. F., & Harnishfeger, K. K. (1995). The evolution of inhibition mechanisms and their role in human cognition and behavior. In F. N. Dempster & C. J. Brainerd (Eds.), *Interference and inhibition in cognition* (pp. 141–173). San Diego, CA: Academic Press.

Bjorklund, D. F., & Pellegrini, A. D. (2002). *The origins of human nature: Evolutionary developmental psychology.* Washington, DC: American Psychological Association.

Bjorklund, D. F., & Rosenblum, K. E. (2001). Children's use of multiple and variable addition strategies in a game context. *Developmental Science, 4,* 184–194.

Black, H. K., & Rubinstein, R. L. (2005). Direct care workers' response to dying and death in the nursing home: A case study. *Journals of Gerontology: Series B: Psychological Sciences and Social Sciences, 60B,* S3–S10.

Blacker, D., & Lovestone, S. (2006). Genetics and dementia nosology. *Journal of Geriatric Psychiatry and Neurology, 19,* 186–191.

Blackwell, C. C., Moscovis, S. M., Gordon, A. E., Al Madani, O. M., Hall, S. T., Gleeson, M., Scott, R. J., Roberts-Thomson, J., Weir, D. M., & Busuttil, A. (2004). Ethnicity, infection and sudden infant death syndrome. *FEMS Immunology and Medical Microbiology, 42,* 53–65.

Blake, W. (1794). The schoolboy. Retrieved October 21, 2006, from University of Dundee Web site: http://www.dundee.ac.uk/english/wics/blake/blake2.htm#e25

Blekesaune, M., & Solem, P. E. (2005). Working conditions and early retirement: A prospective study of retirement behavior. *Research on Aging, 27,* 3–30.

Blennow, K., de Leon, M. J., & Zetterberg, H. (2006). Alzheimer's disease. *Lancet, 368,* 387–403.

Blood, R. O., & Wolfe, D. M. (1960). *Husbands and wives: The dynamics of family living.* Oxford, England: Free Press Glencoe.

Bluck, S., & Glück, J. (2004). Making things better and learning a lesson: Experiencing wisdom across the lifespan. *Journal of Personality, 72,* 543–572.

Blum, D. (2002). *Love at Goon Park: Harry Harlow and the science of affection.* Cambridge, MA: Perseus.

Blum, H. P. (2004). Separation-individuation theory and attachment theory. *Journal of the American Psychoanalytic Association, 52,* 535–553.

Blustein, D. L., Phillips, S. D., Jobin-Davis, K., Finkelberg, S. L., & Roarke, A. E. (1997). A theory-building investigation of the school-to-work transition. *Counseling Psychologist, 25,* 364–402.

Bodenhorn, N., & Lawson, G. (2003). Genetic counseling: Implications for community counselors. *Journal of Counseling & Development, 81,* 497–501.

Boerner, K. (2004). Adaptation to disability among middle-aged and older adults: The role of assimilative and accommodative coping. *Journals of Gerontology: Series B: Psychological Sciences and Social Sciences, 59B,* P35–P42.

Bogaert, A. F. (2005). Age at puberty and father absence in a national probability sample. *Journal of Adolescence, 28,* 541–546.

Bogren, L. Y. (1983). Couvade. *Acta Psychiatrica Scandinavica, 68,* 55–65.

Boland, A. M., Haden, C. A., & Ornstein, P. A. (2003). Boosting children's memory by training mothers in the use of an elaborative conversational style as an event unfolds. *Journal of Cognition and Development, 4,* 39–65.

Bonanno, G. A. (2004). Loss, trauma, and human resilience: Have we underestimated the human capacity to thrive after extremely aversive events? *American Psychologist, 59,* 20–28.

Bonanno, G. A., & Kaltman, S. (1999). Toward an integrative perspective on bereavement. *Psychological Bulletin, 125,* 760–776.

Bonanno, G. A., Wortman, C. B., Lehman, D. R., Tweed, R. G., Haring, M., Sonnega, J., Carr, D., & Nesse, R. M. (2002). Resilience to loss and chronic grief: A prospective study from preloss to 18-months postloss. *Journal of Personality and Social Psychology, 83,* 1150–1164.

Bond, J. T., Galinsky, E., & Hill, E. J. (2004). When work works: Flexibility: A critical ingredient in creating an effective workplace. Retrieved October 22, 2006, from Families and Work Institute Web site: http://familiesandwork.org/3w/research/downloads/3w.pdf

Bondas, T., & Eriksson, K. (2001). Women's lived experiences of pregnancy: A tapestry of joy and suffering. *Qualitative Health Research, 11,* 824–840.

Bookwala, J. (2003). Being "single and unattached": The role of adult attachment styles. *Journal of Applied Social Psychology, 33,* 1564–1570.

Borko, H., Wolf, S. A., Simone, G., & Uchiyama, K. P. (2003). Schools in transition: Reform efforts and school capacity in Washington state. *Educational Evaluation and Policy Analysis, 25,* 171–201.

Bornstein, M. H. (1998). Stability in mental development from early life: Methods, measures, models, meanings, and myths. In F. Simion & G. Butterworth (Eds.), *The development of sensory, motor and cognitive capacities in early infancy: From perception to cognition* (pp. 301–332). Hove, England: Psychology Press.

Bornstein, M. H., Cote, L. R., Maital, S., Painter, K., Park, S.-Y., Pascual, L., Pecheux, M.-G., Ruel, J., Venuti, P., & Vyt, A. (2004). Cross-linguistic analysis of vocabulary in young children: Spanish, Dutch, French, Hebrew, Italian, Korean, and American English. *Child Development, 75,* 1115–1139.

Bornstein, M. H., Haynes, O. M., Pascual, L., Painter, K. M., & Galperin, C. (1999). Play in two societies: Pervasiveness of process, specificity of structure. *Child Development, 70,* 317–331.

Bornstein, M. H., & Tamis-LeMonda, C. S. (2001). Mother-infant interaction. In G. Bremner & A. Fogel (Eds.), *Blackwell handbook of infant development* (pp. 269–295). Malden, MA: Blackwell.

Bossé, R., Aldwin, C. M., Levenson, M. R., & Workman-Daniels, K. (1991). How stressful is retirement? Findings from the Normative Aging Study. *Journals of Gerontology: Series B: Psychological Sciences and Social Sciences, 46,* P9–P14.

Botcheva, L. B., & Feldman, S. S. (2004). Grandparents as family stabilizers during economic hardship in Bulgaria. *International Journal of Psychology, 39,* 157–168.

Botwinick, J. (1967). *Cognitive processes in maturity and old age.* New York: Springer.

Bouchard, T. J. (1994, June 17). Genes, environment, and personality. *Science, 264,* 1700–1701.

Bowes, J. M., Chen, M.-J., San, L. Q., & Yuan, L. (2004). Reasoning and negotiation about child responsibility in urban Chinese families: Reports from mothers, fathers, and children. *International Journal of Behavioral Development, 28,* 48–58.

Bowlby, J. (1969). *Attachment and loss: Vol. 1. Attachment.* New York: Basic Books.

Bowlby, J. (1973). *Attachment and loss: Vol. 2. Separation: Anxiety and anger.* New York: Basic Books.

Bowlby, J. (1980). *Attachment and loss: Vol. 3. Loss: Sadness and depression.* New York: Basic Books.

Boyle, D. E., Marshall, N. L., & Robeson, W. W. (2003). Gender at play: Fourth-grade girls and boys on the playground. *American Behavioral Scientist, 46,* 1326–1345.

Brabant, S. (2003). Death in two settings: The acute care facility and hospice. In C. D. Bryant (Ed.), *Handbook of death & dying* (pp. 475–484). Thousand Oaks, CA: Sage.

Bradbury, T. N., & Fincham, F. D. (1990). Attributions in marriage: Review and critique. *Psychological Bulletin, 107,* 3–33.

Bradbury, T. N., & Karney, B. R. (2004). Understanding and altering the longitudinal course of marriage. *Journal of Marriage and Family, 66,* 862–879.

Bradley, R. H., Corwyn, R. F., Burchinal, M., McAdoo, H. P., & Garcia Coll, C. (2001a). The home environments of children in the United States Part II: Relations with behavioral development through age thirteen. *Child Development, 72,* 1868–1886.

Bradley, R. H., Corwyn, R. F., McAdoo, H. P., & Garcia Coll, C. (2001b). The home environments of children in the United States Part I: Variations by age, ethnicity, and poverty status. *Child Development, 72,* 1844–1867.

Branch, L. G. (2001). Community long-term care services: What works and what doesn't? *Gerontologist, 41,* 305–306.

Braungart-Rieker, J. M., Garwood, M. M., Powers, B. P., & Wang, X. (2001). Parental sensitivity, infant affect, and affect regulation: Predictors of later attachment. *Child Development, 72,* 252–270.

Brecher, E. M., & the editors of Consumer Reports books. (1984). *Love, sex, and aging: A Consumers Union report.* Boston: Little, Brown.

Breitbart, W., Gibson, C., Poppito, S. R., & Berg, A. (2004). Psychotherapeutic interventions at the end of life: A focus on meaning and spirituality. *Canadian Journal of Psychiatry, 49,* 366–372.

Bremner, J. G. (1998). From perception to action: The early development of knowledge. In F. Simion & G. Butterworth (Eds.), *The development of sensory, motor and cognitive capacities in early infancy: From perception to cognition* (pp. 239–255). Hove, England: Psychology Press.

Bremner, J. G., & Fogel, A. (Eds.). (2001). *Blackwell handbook of infant development.* Malden, MA: Blackwell.

Brendgen, M., Vitaro, F., Bukowski, W. M., Doyle, A. B., & Markiewicz, D. (2001). Developmental profiles of peer social preference over the course of elementary school: Associations with trajectories of externalizing and internalizing behavior. *Developmental Psychology, 37,* 308–320.

Brendgen, M., Wanner, B., Morin, A. J. S., & Vitaro, F. (2005). Relations with parents and with peers, temperament, and trajectories of depressed mood during early adolescence. *Journal of Abnormal Child Psychology, 33,* 579–594.

Brennan, M., & Cardinali, G. (2000). The use of preexisting and novel coping strategies in adapting to age-related vision loss. *Gerontologist, 40,* 327–334.

Brennan, P. A., Grekin, E. R., Mortensen, E. L., & Mednick, S. A. (2002). Relationship of maternal smoking during pregnancy with criminal arrest and hospitalization for substance abuse in male and female adult offspring. *American Journal of Psychiatry, 159,* 48–54.

Bretherton, I. (2005). In pursuit of the internal working model construct and its relevance to attachment relationships. In K. E. Grossmann, K. Grossmann, & E. Waters (Eds.), *Attachment from infancy to adulthood: The major longitudinal studies* (pp. 13–47). New York: Guilford Press.

Brewster, K. L. (1994). Race differences in sexual activity among adolescent women: The role of neighborhood characteristics. *American Sociological Review, 59,* 408–424.

Bridges, L. J., Denham, S. A., & Ganiban, J. M. (2004). Definitional issues in emotion regulation research. *Child Development, 75,* 340–345.

Brody, N. (1997). Intelligence, schooling, and society. *American Psychologist, 52,* 1046–1050.

Broidy, L. M., Nagin, D. S., Tremblay, R. E., Bates, J. E., Brame, B., Dodge, K. A., Fergusson, D., Horwood, J. L., Loeber, R., Laird, R., Lynam, D. R., Moffitt, T. E., Pettit, G. S., & Vitaro, F. (2003). Developmental trajectories of childhood disruptive behaviors and adolescent delinquency: A six-site, cross-national study. *Developmental Psychology, 39,* 222–245.

Bronfenbrenner, U. (2005). *Making human beings human: Bioecological perspectives on human development.* Thousand Oaks, CA: Sage.

Bronstein, P. (1988). Father-child interaction: Implications for gender-role socialization. In P. Bronstein & C. P. Cowan (Eds.), *Fatherhood today: Men's changing role in the family* (pp. 107–124). Oxford, England: Wiley.

Brooks-Gunn, J., Newman, D. L., Holderness, C. C., & Warren, M. P. (1994). The experience of breast development and girls' stories about the purchase of a bra. *Journal of Youth and Adolescence, 23,* 539–565.

Brooks-Gunn, J., & Reiter, E. O. (1990). The role of pubertal processes. In S. S. Feldman & G. R. Elliott (Eds.), *At the threshold: The developing adolescent* (pp. 16–53). Cambridge, MA: Harvard University Press.

Brooks-Gunn, J., & Ruble, D. N. (1982). The development of menstrual-related beliefs and behaviors during early adolescence. *Child Development, 53,* 1567–1577.

Brooks-Gunn, J., & Warren, M. P. (1985). The effects of delayed menarche in different contexts: Dance and nondance students. *Journal of Youth and Adolescence, 14,* 285–300.

Brooks-Gunn, J., & Warren, M. P. (1988). The psychological significance of secondary sexual characteristics in nine- to eleven-year-old girls. *Child Development, 59,* 1061–1069.

Brown, B. B., Larson, R. W., & Saraswathi, T. S. (2002). *The world's youth: Adolescence in eight regions of the globe.* New York: Cambridge University Press.

Brown, J. A., & Ferree, M. M. (2005). Close your eyes and think of England: Pronatalism in the British print media. *Gender & Society, 19,* 5–24.

Brown, J. D., Halpern, C. T., & L'Engle, K. L. (2005). Mass media as a sexual super peer for early maturing girls. *Journal of Adolescent Health, 36,* 420–427.

Brown, S. L., Nesse, R. M., House, J. S., & Utz, R. L. (2004). Religion and emotional compensation: Results from a prospective study of widowhood. *Personality and Social Psychology Bulletin, 30,* 1165–1174.

Brownell, K. D. (1991). Dieting and the search for the perfect body: Where physiology and culture collide. *Behavior Therapy, 22,* 1–12.

Browning, C. R., Leventhal, T., & Brooks-Gunn, J. (2005). Sexual initiation in early adolescence: The nexus of parental and community control. *American Sociological Review, 70,* 758–778.

Brumberg, J. J. (1988). *Fasting girls: The emergence of anorexia nervosa as a modern disease.* Cambridge, MA: Harvard University Press.

Bruner, J. (1984). Interaction, communication, and self. *Journal of the American Academy of Child Psychiatry, 23,* 1–7.

Buchanan, C. M., Eccles, J. S., Flanagan, C., Midgley, C., Feldlaufer, H., & Harold, R. D. (1990). Parents' and teachers' beliefs about adolescents: Effects of sex and experience. *Journal of Youth and Adolescence, 19,* 363–394.

Bugental, D. B., Martorell, G. A., & Barraza, V. (2003). The hormonal costs of subtle forms of infant maltreatment. *Hormones and Behavior, 43,* 237–244.

Buhs, E. S., & Ladd, G. W. (2001). Peer rejection as antecedent of young children's school adjustment: An examination of mediating processes. *Developmental Psychology, 37,* 550–560.

Bukowski, W. M. (2001). Friendship and the worlds of childhood. In D. W. Nangle & C. A. Erdley (Eds.), *New directions for child and adolescent development: No. 91. The role of friendship in psychological adjustment* (pp. 93–105). San Francisco: Jossey-Bass.

Bulanda, R. E. (2004). Paternal involvement with children: The influence of gender ideologies. *Journal of Marriage and Family, 66,* 40–45.

Buller, D. J. (2005). *Adapting minds: Evolutionary psychology and the persistent quest for human nature.* Cambridge, MA: MIT Press.

Burnham, D., Kitamura, C., & Vollmer-Conna, U. (2002, May 24). What's new, pussycat? On talking to babies and animals. *Science, 296,* 1435.

Bursik, K. (1991). Correlates of women's adjustment during the separation and divorce process. *Journal of Divorce & Remarriage, 14,* 137–162.

Burt, S. A., Krueger, R. F., McGue, M., & Iacono, W. (2003). Parent-child conflict and the comorbidity among childhood externalizing disorders. *Archives of General Psychiatry, 60,* 505–513.

Burton, L. M. (2001). One step forward and two steps back: Neighborhoods, adolescent development, and unmeasured variables. In A. Booth & A. C. Crouter (Eds.), *Does it take a village? Community effects on children, adolescents, and families* (pp. 149–159). Mahwah, NJ: Erlbaum.

Bushnell, I. W. R. (1998). The origins of face perception. In F. Simion & G. Butterworth (Eds.), *The development of sensory, motor and cognitive capacities in early infancy: From perception to cognition* (pp. 69–86). Hove, England: Psychology Press.

Byrne, R. W., & Whiten, A. (Eds.). (1988). *Machiavellian intelligence: Social expertise and the evolution of intellect in monkeys, apes, and humans.* New York: Clarendon Press/Oxford University Press.

Calkins, S. D. (2004). Early attachment processes and the development of emotional self-regulation. In R. F. Baumeister & K. D. Vohs (Eds.), *Handbook of self-regulation: Research, theory, and applications* (pp. 324–339). New York: Guilford Press.

Calkins, S. D., Dedmon, S. E., Gill, K. L., Lomax, L. E., & Johnson, L. M. (2002). Frustration in infancy: Implications for emotion regulation, physiological processes, and temperament. *Infancy, 3,* 175–197.

Callaghan, T., Rochat, P., Lillard, A., Claux, M. L., Odden, H., Itakura, S., Tapanya, S., & Singh, S. (2005). Synchrony in the onset of mental-state reasoning: Evidence from five cultures. *Psychological Science, 16,* 378–384.

Callahan, D. (1988). *Setting limits: Medical goals in an aging society.* New York: Simon and Schuster.

Camaioni, L. (2001). Early language. In G. Bremner & A. Fogel (Eds.), *Blackwell handbook of infant development* (pp. 404–426). Malden, MA: Blackwell.

Cameron, J. L. (1990). Factors controlling the onset of puberty in primates. In J. Bancroft & J. M. Reinisch (Eds.), *Adolescence and puberty* (pp. 9–28). New York: Oxford University Press.

Cameron, J. L. (2004). Interrelationships between hormones, behavior, and affect during adolescence: Complex relationships exist between reproductive hormones, stress-related hormones, and the activity of neural systems that regulate behavioral affect. Comments on part III. In R. E. Dahl & L. P. Spear (Eds.), *Adolescent brain development: Vulnerabilities and opportunities* (Vol. 1021, pp. 134–142). New York: New York Academy of Sciences.

Campos, J. J., Anderson, D. I., Barbu-Roth, M. A., Hubbard, E. M., Hertenstein, M. J., & Witherington, D. (2000). Travel broadens the mind. *Infancy, 1,* 149–219.

Campos, J. J., Langer, A., & Krowitz, A. (1970, October 9). Cardiac responses on the visual cliff in prelocomotor human infants. *Science, 170,* 196–197.

Campos, R. G. (1989). Soothing pain-elicited distress in infants with swaddling and pacifiers. *Child Development, 60,* 781–792.

Canivet, C. A., Ostergren, P. O., Rosen, A. S., Jakobsson, I. L., & Hagander, B. M. (2005). Infantile colic and the role of trait anxiety during pregnancy in relation to psychosocial and socioeconomic factors. *Scandinavian Journal of Public Health, 33,* 26–34.

Canter, A. S. (1997). The future of intelligence testing in the schools. *School Psychology Review, 26,* 255–261.

Capaldi, D. M., & Stoolmiller, M. (1999). Co-occurrence of conduct problems and depressive symptoms in early adolescent boys: III. Prediction to young-adult adjustment. *Development and Psychopathology, 11,* 59–84.

Caplan, A. L., Blank, R. H., & Merrick, J. C. (Eds.). (1992). *Compelled compassion: Government intervention in the treatment of critically ill newborns.* Totowa, NJ: Humana Press.

Caron, S. L., & Moskey, E. G. (2002). Changes over time in teenage sexual relationships: Comparing the high school class of 1950, 1975, and 2000. *Adolescence, 37,* 515–526.

Carpenter, R. G., Irgens, L. M., Blair, P. S., England, P. D., Fleming, P., Huber, J., Jorch, G., & Schreuder, P. (2004). Sudden unexplained infant death in 20 regions in Europe: Case control study. *Lancet, 363,* 185–191.

Carr, D. (2004). Gender, preloss marital dependence, and older adults' adjustment to widowhood. *Journal of Marriage and Family, 66,* 220–235.

Carskadon, M. A., Acebo, C., & Jenni, O. G. (2004). Regulation of adolescent sleep: Implications for behavior. In R. E. Dahl & L. P. Spear (Eds.), *Adolescent brain development: Vulnerabilities and opportunities* (Vol. 1021, pp. 276–291). New York: New York Academy of Sciences.

Carstensen, L. L. (1995). Evidence for a life-span theory of socioemotional selectivity. *Current Directions in Psychological Science, 4,* 151–156.

Carstensen, L. L., Fung, H. H., & Charles, S. T. (2003). Socioemotional selectivity theory and the regulation of emotion in the second half of life. *Motivation and Emotion, 27,* 103–123.

Carstensen, L. L., Pasupathi, M., Mayr, U., & Nesselroade, J. R. (2000). Emotional experience in everyday life across the adult life span. *Journal of Personality and Social Psychology, 79,* 644–655.

Case, R. (1999). Conceptual development. In M. Bennett (Ed.), *Developmental psychology: Achievements and prospects* (pp. 36–54). New York: Psychology Press.

Caserta, M. S., & Lund, D. A. (1993). Intrapersonal resources and the effectiveness of self-help groups for bereaved older adults. *Gerontologist, 33,* 619–629.

Caspi, A. (2000). The child is father of the man: Personality continuities from childhood to adulthood. *Journal of Personality and Social Psychology, 78,* 158–172.

Caspi, A., Begg, D., Dickson, N., Harrington, H., Langley, J., Moffitt, T. E., & Silva, P. A. (1997). Personality differences predict health-risk behaviors in young adulthood: Evidence from a longitudinal study. *Journal of Personality and Social Psychology, 73,* 1052–1063.

Caspi, A., Henry, B., McGee, R. O., Moffitt, T. E., & Silva, P. A. (1995). Temperamental origins of child and adolescent behavior problems: From age three to age fifteen. *Child Development, 66,* 55–68.

Caspi, A., McClay, J., Moffitt, T., Mill, J., Martin, J., Craig, I. W., Taylor, A., & Poulton, R. (2002, August 2). Role of genotype in the cycle of violence in maltreated children. *Science, 297,* 851–854.

Caspi, A., Moffitt, T. E., Cannon, M., McClay, J., Murray, R., Harrington, H., Taylor, A., Arseneault, L., Williams, B., Braithwaite, A., Poulton, R., & Craig, I. W. (2005). Moderation of the effect of adolescent-onset cannabis use on adult psychosis by a functional polymorphism in the catechol-O-methyltransferase gene: Longitudinal evidence of a gene X environment interaction. *Biological Psychiatry, 57,* 1117–1127.

Caspi, A., & Silva, P. A. (1995). Temperamental qualities at age three predict personality traits in young adulthood: Longitudinal evidence from a birth cohort. *Child Development, 66,* 486–498.

Caspi, A., Sugden, K., Moffitt, T. E., Taylor, A., Craig, I. W., Harrington, H., McClay, J., Mill, J., Martin, J., Braithwaite, A., & Poulton, R. (2003, July 18). Influence of life stress on depression: Moderation by a polymorphism in the 5-HTT gene. *Science, 301,* 386–389.

Cassidy, J., & Shaver, P. R. (Eds.). (1999). *Handbook of attachment: Theory, research, and clinical applications.* New York: Guilford Press.

Cattell, M. G. (2003). African widows: Anthropological and historical perspectives. *Journal of Women & Aging, 15,* 49–66.

Cauffman, E. (2004). The adolescent brain: Excuse versus explanation: Comments on part IV. In R. E. Dahl & L. P. Spear (Eds.), *Adolescent brain development: Vulnerabilities and opportunities* (Vol. 1021, pp. 160–161). New York: New York Academy of Sciences.

Cauffman, E., & Steinberg, L. (1996). Interactive effects of menarcheal status and dating on dieting and disordered eating among adolescent girls. *Developmental Psychology, 32,* 631–635.

Cavanagh, S. E. (2004). The sexual debut of girls in early adolescence: The intersection of race, pubertal timing, and friendship group characteristics. *Journal of Research on Adolescence, 14,* 285–312.

Cavanaugh, J. C. (1996). Memory self-efficacy as a moderator of memory change. In F. Blanchard-Fields & T. M. Hess (Eds.), *Perspectives on cognitive change in adulthood and aging* (pp. 488–507). New York: McGraw-Hill.

Cavanaugh, J. C. (2000). Metamemory from a social-cognitive perspective. In D. C. Park & N. Schwarz (Eds.), *Cognitive aging: A primer* (pp. 115–130). New York: Psychology Press.

Cavanaugh, J. C., & Green, E. E. (1990). I believe, therefore I can: Self-efficacy beliefs in memory aging. In E. A. Lovelace (Ed.), *Aging and cognition: Mental processes, self-awareness, and interventions* (pp. 189–230). Oxford, England: North-Holland.

Ceci, S. J., Rosenblum, T., de Bruyn, E., & Lee, D. Y. (1997). A bio-ecological model of intellectual development: Moving beyond h-sup-2. In R. J. Sternberg & E. L. Grigorenko (Eds.), *Intelligence, heredity, and environment* (pp. 303–322). New York: Cambridge University Press.

Center for the Study and Prevention of Violence. (n.d.). Blueprints Model Programs overview. Retrieved May 8, 2006, from University of Colorado at Boulder Web site: http://www.colorado.edu/cspv/blueprints/model/overview.html

Centers for Disease Control and Prevention. (2005). Monitoring progress in arthritis management—United States and 25 states, 2003. *Morbidity and Mortality Weekly Report, 54,* 484–488.

Centers for Disease Control and Prevention. (2006). National Youth Risk Behavior Survey: 1991–2005. Trends in the prevalence of sexual behaviors. Retrieved October 10, 2006, from http://www.cdc.gov/HealthyYouth/yrbs/pdf/trends/2005_YRBS_Sexual_Behaviors.pdf

Centers for Disease Control and Prevention [CDC]. (2004). *2002 Assisted Reproductive Technology (ART) report.* Atlanta, GA: Centers for Disease Control and Prevention (CDC).

Centers for Disease Control and Prevention, National Center on Birth Defects and Developmental Disabilities. (n.d.). Fetal alcohol information. Retrieved January 20, 2006, from http://www.cdc.gov/ncbddd/fas/fasask.htm

Central Intelligence Agency. (2005). The world factbook 2005. Retrieved September 30, 2006, from https://www.cia.gov/cia/download2005.htm

Chan, H. M. (2004). Sharing death and dying: Advance directives, autonomy and the family. *Bioethics, 18,* 87–103.

Chapple, H. S. (1999). Changing the game in the intensive care unit: Letting nature take its course. *Critical Care Nurse, 19,* 25–34.

Charles, M. (1992). Cross-national variation in occupational sex segregation. *American Sociological Review, 57,* 483–502.

Charles, S. T., Reynolds, C. A., & Gatz, M. (2001). Age-related differences and change in positive and negative affect over 23 years. *Journal of Personality and Social Psychology, 80,* 136–151.

Charness, N., & Bosman, E. A. (1995). Compensation through environmental modification. In R. A. Dixon & L. Bäckman (Eds.), *Compensating for psychological deficits and declines: Managing losses and promoting gains* (pp. 147–168). Hillsdale, NJ: Erlbaum.

Cheah, C. S. L., & Rubin, K. H. (2004). European American and Mainland Chinese mothers' responses to aggression and social withdrawal in preschoolers. *International Journal of Behavioral Development, 28,* 83–94.

Cherlin, A., & Furstenberg, F. F. (1985). Styles and strategies of grandparenting. In V. L. Bengtson & J. F. Robertson (Eds.), *Grandparenthood* (pp. 97–116). Thousand Oaks, CA: Sage.

Cherlin, A. J. (2004). The deinstitutionalization of American marriage. *Journal of Marriage and Family, 66,* 848–861.

Child Trends. (2005a). Child Trends DataBank: Dating. Retrieved October 11, 2006, from http://www.childtrendsdatabank.org/indicators/73Dating.cfm

Child Trends. (2005b). Child Trends DataBank: Oral sex. Retrieved October 11, 2006, from http://www.childtrends-databank.org/indicators/95OralSex.cfm

Child Trends. (2005c). Child Trends DataBank: Sexually experienced teens. Retrieved October 11, 2006, from http://www.childtrendsdatabank.org/indicators/24SexuallyExperienced Teens.cfm

Chirkov, V. I., & Ryan, R. M. (2001). Parent and teacher autonomy-support in Russian and U. S. adolescents: Common effects on well-being and academic motivation. *Journal of Cross-Cultural Psychology, 32*, 618–635.

Chochinov, H. M., Tataryn, D. J., Wilson, K. G., Enns, M., & Lander, S. (2000). Prognostic awareness and the terminally ill. *Psychosomatics: Journal of Consultation Liaison Psychiatry, 41*, 500–504.

Chow, E. S. L., Kong, B. M. H., Wong, M. T. P., Draper, B., Lin, K. L., Ho, S. K. S., & Wong, C. P. (2004). The prevalence of depressive symptoms among elderly Chinese private nursing home residents in Hong Kong. *International Journal of Geriatric Psychiatry, 19*, 734–740.

Cicchetti, D., & Toth, S. L. (1998). Perspectives on research and practice in developmental psychopathology. In W. Damon (Series Ed.) & I. E. Sigel & K. A. Renninger (Vol. Eds.), *Handbook of child psychology: Vol. 4. Child psychology in practice* (5th ed., pp. 479–483). New York: Wiley.

Cillessen, A. H. N., & Mayeux, L. (2004). From censure to reinforcement: Developmental changes in the association between aggression and social status. *Child Development, 75*, 147–163.

Clark, M. S., Graham, S., & Grote, N. (2002). Bases for giving benefits in marriage: What is ideal? What is realistic? What really happens? In P. Noller & J. A. Feeney (Eds.), *Understanding marriage: Developments in the study of couple interaction* (pp. 150–176). New York: Cambridge University Press.

Clark, R. L., & Quinn, J. F. (2002). Patterns of work and retirement for a new century: Emerging trends and policy implications. *Generations, 26*(2), 17–24.

Clark, S. C. (2001). Work cultures and work/family balance. *Journal of Vocational Behavior, 58*, 348–365.

Clausen, J. S. (1991). Adolescent competence and the shaping of the life course. *American Journal of Sociology, 96*, 805–842.

Clay, M. M., & Cazden, C. B. (1992). A Vygotskian interpretation of Reading Recovery. In L. C. Moll (Ed.), *Vygotsky and education: Instructional implications and applications of sociohistorical psychology* (pp. 206–222). New York: Cambridge University Press.

Clements, M. L., Stanley, S. M., & Markman, H. J. (2004). Before they said "I do": Discriminating among marital outcomes over 13 years. *Journal of Marriage and Family, 66*, 613–626.

Cliggett, L. (2001). Survival strategies of the elderly in Gwembe Valley, Zambia: Gender, residence and kin networks. *Journal of Cross-Cultural Gerontology, 16*, 309–322.

Climo, J. J., Terry, P., & Lay, K. (2002). Using the double bind to interpret the experience of custodial grandparents. *Journal of Aging Studies, 16*, 19–35.

Cohen, P., Kasen, S., Chen, H., Hartmark, C., & Gordon, K. (2003). Variations in patterns of developmental transmissions in the emerging adulthood period. *Developmental Psychology, 39*, 657–669.

Cohen, P. N. (2004). The gender division of labor: "Keeping house" and occupational segregation in the United States. *Gender & Society, 18*, 239–252.

Coie, J. D., & Dodge, K. A. (1998). Aggression and antisocial behavior. In W. Damon (Series Ed.) & N. Eisenberg (Vol. Ed.), *Handbook of child psychology: Vol 3. Social, emotional, and personality development* (5th ed., pp. 779–862). Hoboken, NJ: Wiley.

Cole, B., & Singg, S. (1998). *Relationship between parental bereavement reaction factors and selected psychosocial variables.* Paper presented at the Annual Meeting of the American Psychological Society, Washington, DC.

Cole, S. A. (2005). Infants in foster care: Relational and environmental factors affecting attachment. *Journal of Reproductive and Infant Psychology, 23*, 43–61.

Coles, R. (1970). *Erik H. Erikson: The growth of his work.* Boston: Little, Brown.

Collins, R. L., Elliott, M. N., Berry, S. H., Kanouse, D. E., Kunkel, D., Hunter, S. B., & Miu, A. (2004). Watching sex on television predicts adolescent initiation of sexual behavior. *Pediatrics, 114*, e280–289.

Colwell, M. J., & Lindsey, E. W. (2005). Preschool children's pretend and physical play and sex of play partner: Connections to peer competence. *Sex Roles, 52*, 497–509.

Compas, B. E., Connor, J. K., & Hinden, B. R. (1998). New perspectives on depression during adolescence. In R. Jessor (Ed.), *New perspectives on adolescent risk behavior* (pp. 319–362). New York: Cambridge University Press.

Compian, L., Gowen, L. K., & Hayward, C. (2004). Peripubertal girls' romantic and platonic involvement with boys: Associations with body image and depression symptoms. *Journal of Research on Adolescence, 14*, 23–47.

Condon, J. T., Boyce, P., & Corkindale, C. J. (2004). The First-Time Fathers Study: A prospective study of the mental health and wellbeing of men during the transition to parenthood. *Australian and New Zealand Journal of Psychiatry, 38*, 56–64.

Connidis, I. A., & McMullin, J. A. (1993). To have or have not: Parent status and the subjective well-being of older men and women. *Gerontologist, 33*, 630–636.

Cook, T. D., & Furstenberg, F. F. (2002). Explaining aspects of the transition to adulthood in Italy, Sweden, Germany, and the United States: A cross-disciplinary, case synthesis approach. *Annals of the American Academy of Political & Social Science, 580*, 257–287.

Cooney, T. M., Schaie, K. W., & Willis, S. L. (1988). The relationship between prior functioning on cognitive and personality dimensions and subject attrition in longitudinal research. *Journals of Gerontology, 43*, P12–P17.

Coontz, S. (1992). *The way we never were: American families and the nostalgia trap.* New York: Basic Books.

Cooper, R. P., & Aslin, R. N. (1990). Preference for infant-directed speech in the first month after birth. *Child Development, 61*, 1584–1595.

Coplan, R. J., Gavinski-Molina, M. H., Lagace-Seguin, D. G., & Wichmann, C. (2001). When girls versus boys play alone: Nonsocial play and adjustment in kindergarten. *Developmental Psychology, 37*, 464–474.

Corr, C. A. (1991–1992). A task-based approach to coping with dying. *Omega: Journal of Death and Dying, 24*, 81–94.

Corr, C. A. (1996). Children, development, and encounters with death and bereavement. In C. A. Corr & D. M. Corr (Eds.), *Handbook of childhood death and bereavement* (pp. 3–28). New York: Springer.

Corsaro, W. A. (1985). *Friendship and peer culture in the early years.* Norwood, NJ: Ablex.

Corsaro, W. A. (1997). *The sociology of childhood.* Thousand Oaks, CA: Pine Forge Press/Sage.

Costa, P. T., & McCrae, R. R. (1988). From catalog to classification: Murray's needs and the five-factor model. *Journal of Personality and Social Psychology, 55,* 258–265.

Costa, P. T., & McCrae, R. R. (2002). Looking backward: Changes in the mean levels of personality traits from 80 to 12. In D. Cervone & W. Mischel (Eds.), *Advances in personality science* (pp. 219–237). New York: Guilford Press.

Costos, D., Ackerman, R., & Paradis, L. (2002). Recollections of menarche: Communication between mothers and daughters regarding menstruation. *Sex Roles, 46,* 49–59.

Cotterell, J. (1996). *Social networks and social influences in adolescence.* New York: Routledge.

Council on Families in America. (1995). *Marriage in America: A report to the nation.* New York: Institute for American Values.

Cowan, C. P., & Bronstein, P. (1988). Fathers' roles in the family: Implications for research, intervention, and change. In P. Bronstein & C. P. Cowan (Eds.), *Fatherhood today: Men's changing role in the family* (pp. 341–347). Oxford, England: Wiley.

Cowan, C. P., & Cowan, P. A. (1988). Who does what when partners become parents: Implications for men, women, and marriage. *Marriage & Family Review, 12,* 105–131.

Cowan, C. P., & Cowan, P. A. (1992). *When partners become parents: The big life change for couples.* New York: Basic Books.

Cozzarelli, C., Karafa, J. A., Collins, N. L., & Tagler, M. J. (2003). Stability and change in adult attachment styles: Associations with personal vulnerabilities, life events, and global construals of self and others. *Journal of Social & Clinical Psychology, 22,* 315–346.

Crade, M., & Lovett, S. (1988). Fetal response to sound stimulation: Preliminary report exploring use of sound stimulation in routine obstetrical ultrasound examinations. *Journal of Ultrasound in Medicine, 7,* 499–503.

Craik, F. I. M. (2000). Age-related changes in human memory. In D. C. Park & N. Schwarz (Eds.), *Cognitive aging: A primer* (pp. 75–92). New York: Psychology Press.

Craik, F. I. M., & Jennings, J. M. (1992). Human memory. In F. I. M. Craik & T. A. Salthouse (Eds.), *The handbook of aging and cognition* (pp. 51–110). Hillsdale, NJ: Erlbaum.

Craik, F. I. M., & McDowd, J. M. (1987). Age differences in recall and recognition. *Journal of Experimental Psychology: Learning, Memory, and Cognition, 13,* 474–479.

Crick, N. R., Bigbee, M. A., & Howes, C. (1996). Gender differences in children's normative beliefs about aggression: How do I hurt thee? Let me count the ways. *Child Development, 67,* 1003–1014.

Crick, N. R., Casas, J. F., & Nelson, D. A. (2002). Toward a more comprehensive understanding of peer maltreatment: Studies of relational victimization. *Current Directions in Psychological Science, 11,* 98–101.

Crick, N. R., & Dodge, K. A. (1996). Social information-processing mechanisms on reactive and proactive aggression. *Child Development, 67,* 993–1002.

Crick, N. R., & Grotpeter, J. K. (1995). Relational aggression, gender, and social-psychological adjustment. *Child Development, 66,* 710–722.

Crick, N. R., Grotpeter, J. K., & Bigbee, M. A. (2002). Relationally and physically aggressive children's intent attributions and feelings of distress for relational and instrumental peer provocations. *Child Development, 73,* 1134–1142.

Crick, N. R., & Rose, A. J. (2000). Toward a gender-balanced approach to the study of social-emotional development: A look at relational aggression. In P. H. Miller & E. Kofsky Scholnick (Eds.), *Toward a feminist developmental psychology* (pp. 153–168). Florence, KY: Taylor & Frances/Routledge.

Crimmins, E. M., Saito, Y., & Reynolds, S. L. (1997). Further evidence on recent trends in the prevalence and incidence of disability among older Americans from two sources: The LSOA and the NHIS. *Journals of Gerontology: Series B: Psychological Sciences and Social Sciences, 52B,* S59–S71.

Crittenden, A. (2001). *The price of motherhood: Why the most important job in the world is still the least valued.* New York: Metropolitan Books.

Crnic, K. A., Greenberg, M. T., & Slough, N. M. (1986). Early stress and social support influences on mothers' and high-risk infants' functioning in late infancy. *Infant Mental Health Journal, 7,* 19–33.

Crockenberg, S. C. (2003). Rescuing the baby from the bathwater: How gender and temperament (may) influence how child care affects child development. *Child Development, 74,* 1034–1038.

Crockenberg, S. C., & Leerkes, E. M. (2005). Infant temperament moderates associations between childcare type and quantity and externalizing and internalizing behaviors at 2 1/2 years. *Infant Behavior & Development, 28,* 20–35.

Crook, T. H., 3rd, & Larrabee, G. J. (1992). Changes in facial recognition memory across the adult life span. *Journals of Gerontology: Series B: Psychological Sciences and Social Sciences, 47,* P138–141.

Crowell, J. A., Fraley, R. C., & Shaver, P. R. (1999). Measurement of individual differences in adolescent and adult attachment. In J. Cassidy & P. R. Shaver (Eds.), *Handbook of attachment: Theory, research, and clinical applications* (pp. 434–465). New York: Guilford Press.

Csikszentmihalyi, M. (1990). *Flow: The psychology of optimal experience.* New York: Harper & Row.

Csikszentmihalyi, M. (1996). *Creativity: Flow and the psychology of discovery and invention.* New York: HarperCollins.

Csikszentmihalyi, M., & Larson, R. (1984). *Being adolescent: Conflict and growth in the teenage years.* New York: Basic Books.

Csikszentmihalyi, M., & Schneider, B. L. (2000). *Becoming adult: How teenagers prepare for the world of work.* New York: Basic Books.

Cullen, C., Field, T., Escalona, A., & Hartshorn, K. (2000). Father-infant interactions are enhanced by massage therapy. *Early Child Development and Care, 164,* 41–47.

Cullerton-Sen, C., & Crick, N. R. (2005). Understanding the effects of physical and relational victimization: The utility of multiple perspectives in predicting social-emotional adjustment. *School Psychology Review, 34,* 147–160.

Cummins, D. D., & Allen, C. (Eds.). (1998). *The evolution of mind.* New York: Oxford University Press.

Cunningham, J. D., & Antill, J. K. (1994). Cohabitation and marriage: Retrospective and predictive comparisons. *Journal of Social and Personal Relationships, 11,* 77–93.

Cutler, S. J., & Hodgson, L. G. (2003). To test or not to test: Interest in genetic testing for Alzheimer's disease among middle-aged adults. *American Journal of Alzheimer's Disease and Other Dementias, 18,* 9–20.

CysticFibrosis.com. (n.d.). CysticFibrosis.com. Retrieved January 20, 2006, from http://www.cysticfibrosis.com/info/index.html

Dahl, R. E. (2004). Adolescent brain development: A period of vulnerabilities and opportunities. In R. E. Dahl & L. P. Spear (Eds.), *Adolescent brain development: Vulnerabilities and opportunities* (Vol. 1021, pp. 1–22). New York: New York Academy of Sciences.

Dahl, R. E., & Hariri, A. R. (2005). Lessons from G. Stanley Hall: Connecting new research in biological sciences to the study of adolescent development. *Journal of Research on Adolescence, 15,* 367–382.

Dahl, R. E., & Spear, L. P. (Eds.). (2004). *Adolescent brain development: Vulnerabilities and opportunities.* New York: New York Academy of Sciences.

Daire, A. P. (2002). The influence of parental bonding on emotional distress in caregiving sons for a parent with dementia. *Gerontologist, 42,* 766–771.

Damon, W., & Hart, D. (1992). Self-understanding and its role in social and moral development. In M. H. Bornstein & M. E. Lamb (Eds.), *Developmental psychology: An advanced textbook* (3rd ed., pp. 421–464). Hillsdale, NJ: Erlbaum.

Danis, M., Southerland, L. I., Garrett, J. M., Smith, J. L., Hielema, F., Pickard, C. G., Egner, D. M., & Patrick, D. L. (1991). A prospective study of advance directives for life-sustaining care. *New England Journal of Medicine, 324,* 882–888.

Dark-Freudeman, A., West, R. L., & Viverito, K. M. (2006). Future selves and aging: Older adults' memory fears. *Educational Gerontology, 32,* 85–109.

Dasen, P. R. (1977). *Piagetian psychology: Cross-cultural contributions.* New York: Gardner Press.

Dasen, P. R. (1984). The cross-cultural study of intelligence: Piaget and the Baoule. *International Journal of Psychology, 19,* 407–434.

Davison, K. K., & Birch, L. L. (2002). Processes linking weight status and self-concept among girls from ages 5 to 7 years. *Developmental Psychology, 38,* 735–748.

de Boysson-Bardies, B., Sagart, L., & Durand, C. (1984). Discernible differences in the babbling of infants according to target language. *Journal of Child Language, 11,* 1–15.

de St. Aubin, E., McAdams, D. P., & Kim, T.-C. (2004). The generative society: An introduction. In E. de St. Aubin, D. P. McAdams, & T.-C. Kim (Eds.), *The generative society: Caring for future generations* (pp. 3–13). Washington, DC: American Psychological Association.

Dearing, E. (2004). The developmental implications of restrictive and supportive parenting across neighborhoods and ethnicities: Exceptions are the rule. *Journal of Applied Developmental Psychology, 25,* 555–575.

Deary, I. J., Whalley, L. J., Lemmon, H., Crawford, J. R., & Starr, J. M. (2000). The stability of individual differences in mental ability from childhood to old age: Follow-up of the 1932 Scottish Mental Survey. *Intelligence, 28,* 49–55.

Deater-Deckard, K. (1996). Within family variability in parental negativity and control. *Journal of Applied Developmental Psychology, 17,* 407–422.

Deater-Deckard, K., Dodge, K. A., Bates, J. E., & Pettit, G. S. (1996). Physical discipline among African American and European American mothers: Links to children's externalizing behaviors. *Developmental Psychology, 32,* 1065–1072.

Deave, T. (2005). Associations between child development and women's attitudes to pregnancy and motherhood. *Journal of Reproductive and Infant Psychology, 23,* 63–75.

DeCasper, A. J., & Fifer, W. P. (1980, June 6). Of human bonding: Newborns prefer their mothers' voices. *Science, 208,* 1174–1176.

DeCasper, A. J., & Spence, M. J. (1987). Prenatal maternal speech influences newborns' perception of speech sounds. *Annual Progress in Child Psychiatry & Child Development, 20,* 5–25.

Deci, E. L., & Ryan, R. M. (1985). The general causality orientations scale: Self-determination in personality. *Journal of Research in Personality, 19,* 109–134.

Deci, E. L., & Ryan, R. M. (2000). The "what" and "why" of goal pursuits: Human needs and the self-determination of behavior. *Psychological Inquiry, 11,* 227–268.

DeFillippi, R. J., & Arthur, M. B. (1994). The boundaryless career: A competency-based perspective. *Journal of Organizational Behavior, 15,* 307–324.

Dekovic, M., Noom, M. J., & Meeus, W. (1997). Expectations regarding development during adolescence: Parental and adolescent perceptions. *Journal of Youth and Adolescence, 26,* 253–272.

Dempster, F. N. (1981). Memory span: Sources of individual and developmental differences. *Psychological Bulletin, 89,* 63–100.

DeMulder, E. K., Denham, S., Schmidt, M., & Mitchell, J. (2000). Q-sort assessment of attachment security during the preschool years: Links from home to school. *Developmental Psychology, 36,* 274–282.

Denham, S. A. (1998). *Emotional development in young children.* New York: Guilford Press.

Denham, S. A., Blair, K. A., DeMulder, E., Levitas, J., Sawyer, K., Auerbach-Major, S., & Queenan, P. (2003). Preschool emotional competence: Pathway to social competence. *Child Development, 74,* 238–256.

Dezoete, J., MacArthur, B., & Tuck, B. (2003). Prediction of Bayley and Stanford-Binet scores with a group of very low birthweight children. *Child: Care, Health and Development, 29,* 367–372.

Diamond, A., Kirkham, N., & Amso, D. (2002). Conditions under which young children can hold two rules in mind and inhibit a prepotent response. *Developmental Psychology, 38,* 352–362.

Diamond, A., & Taylor, C. (1996). Development of an aspect of executive control: Development of the abilities to remember what I said and to "Do as I say, not as I do." *Developmental Psychobiology, 29,* 315–334.

Diamond, L. M., & Savin-Williams, R. C. (2003). Explaining diversity in the development of same-sex sexuality among young women. In L. D. Garnets & D. C. Kimmel (Eds.), *Psychological perspectives on lesbian, gay, and bisexual experiences* (2nd ed., pp. 130–148). New York: Columbia University Press.

Diamond, M. C. (1988). *Enriching heredity: The impact of the environment on the anatomy of the brain.* New York: Free Press.

Diamond, M. C. (1993). An optimistic view of the aging brain. *Generations, 17*(1), 31–33.

Dickie, J. R. (1987). Interrelationships within the mother-father-infant triad. In P. W. Berman & F. A. Pedersen (Eds.), *Men's transitions to parenthood: Longitudinal studies of early family experience* (pp. 113–143). Hillsdale, NJ: Erlbaum.

Diener, E., Wolsic, B., & Fujita, F. (1995). Physical attractiveness and subjective well-being. *Journal of Personality and Social Psychology, 69,* 120–129.

Dieter, J. N. I., Field, T., Hernandez-Reif, M., Emory, E. K., & Redzepi, M. (2003). Stable preterm infants gain more weight and sleep less after five days of massage therapy. *Journal of Pediatric Psychology, 28,* 403–411.

Dimitrovsky, L., Levy-Shiff, R., & Schattner-Zanany, I. (2002). Dimensions of depression and perfectionism in pregnant and nonpregnant women: Their levels and interrelationships and their relationship to marital satisfaction. *Journal of Psychology: Interdisciplinary and Applied, 136,* 631–646.

Diorio, J. A., & Munro, J. (2003). What does puberty mean to adolescents? Teaching and learning about bodily development. *Sex Education, 3,* 119–131.

DiPietro, J. A. (1981). Rough and tumble play: A function of gender. *Developmental Psychology, 17,* 50–58.

Dishion, T. J., Andrews, D. W., & Crosby, L. (1995). Antisocial boys and their friends in early adolescence: Relationship characteristics, quality, and interactional process. *Child Development, 66,* 139–151.

Dishion, T. J., McCord, J., & Poulin, F. (1999). When interventions harm: Peer groups and problem behavior. *American Psychologist, 54,* 755–764.

Dix, T., Gershoff, E. T., Meunier, L. N., & Miller, P. C. (2004). The affective structure of supportive parenting: Depressive symptoms, immediate emotions, and child-oriented motivation. *Developmental Psychology, 40,* 1212–1227.

Dodge, K. A. (2002). Mediation, moderation, and mechanisms in how parenting affects children's aggressive behavior. In J. G. Borkowski, S. L. Ramey, & M. Bristol-Power (Eds.), *Parenting and the child's world: Influences on academic, intellectual, and social-emotional development* (pp. 215–229). Mahwah, NJ: Erlbaum.

Dodge, K. A., Lansford, J. E., Burks, V. S., Bates, J. E., Pettit, G. S., Fontaine, R., & Price, J. M. (2003). Peer rejection and social information-processing factors in the development of aggressive behavior problems in children. *Child Development, 74,* 374–393.

Dodge, K. A., & Pettit, G. S. (2003). A biopsychosocial model of the development of chronic conduct problems in adolescence. *Developmental Psychology, 39,* 349–371.

Dodgson, J. E., Henly, S. J., Duckett, L., & Tarrant, M. (2003). Theory of planned behavior-based models for breastfeeding duration among Hong Kong mothers. *Nursing Research, 52,* 148–158.

Doka, K. J. (2003). The death awareness movement: Description, history, and analysis. In C. D. Bryant (Ed.), *Handbook of death & dying* (pp. 50–55). Thousand Oaks, CA: Sage.

Dolcos, F., & Cabeza, R. (2002). Event-related potentials of emotional memory: Encoding pleasant, unpleasant, and neutral pictures. *Cognitive, Affective & Behavioral Neuroscience, 2,* 252–263.

Dooley, D., & Prause, J. (2005). Birth weight and mothers' adverse employment change. *Journal of Health and Social Behavior, 46,* 141–155.

Dorn, L. D., Nottelmann, E. D., Susman, E. J., Inoff-Germain, G., Cutler, G. B., & Chrousos, G. P. (1999). Variability in hormone concentrations and self-reported menstrual histories in young adolescents: Menarche as an integral part of a developmental process. *Journal of Youth and Adolescence, 28,* 283–304.

Dorris, M. (1989). *The broken cord.* New York: Harper & Row.

Doucet, J., & Aseltine, R. H. (2003). Childhood family adversity and the quality of marital relationships in young adulthood. *Journal of Social and Personal Relationships, 20,* 818–842.

Douglas, S. J., & Michaels, M. W. (2004). *The mommy myth: The idealization of motherhood and how it has undermined women.* New York: Free Press.

Dowling, E. M., Gestsdottir, S., Anderson, P. M., von Eye, A., Almerigi, J., & Lerner, R. M. (2004). Structural relations among spirituality, religiosity, and thriving in adolescence. *Applied Developmental Science, 8,* 7–16.

Doyle, A. E., Biederman, J., Seidman, L. J., Reske-Nielsen, J. J., & Faraone, S. V. (2005). Neuropsychological functioning in relatives of girls with and without ADHD. *Psychological Medicine, 35,* 1121–1132.

Dresser, R. (2004). Death with dignity: Contested boundaries. *Journal of Palliative Care, 20,* 201–206.

Driver, J., Tabares, A., Shapiro, A., Nahm, E. Y., & Gottman, J. M. (2003). Interactional patterns in marital success and failure: Gottman laboratory studies. In F. Walsh (Ed.), *Normal family processes: Growing diversity and complexity* (3rd ed., pp. 493–513). New York: Guilford Press.

Droege, K. L., & Stipek, D. J. (1993). Children's use of dispositions to predict classmates' behavior. *Developmental Psychology, 29,* 646–654.

DuBois, D. L., Felner, R. D., Brand, S., & George, G. R. (1999). Profiles of self-esteem in early adolescence: Identification and investigation of adaptive correlates. *American Journal of Community Psychology, 27,* 899–932.

Dubois, D. L., & Tevendale, H. D. (1999). Self-esteem in childhood and adolescence: Vaccine or epiphenomenon? *Applied & Preventive Psychology, 8,* 103–117.

Dubois, L., & Girard, M. (2005). Breastfeeding, day-care attendance and the frequency of antibiotic treatments from 1.5 to 5 years: A population-based longitudinal study in Canada. *Social Science & Medicine, 60,* 2035–2044.

Duijvestijn, J. A., Anteunis, L. J. C., Hoek, C. J., van den Brink, R. H. S., Chenault, M. N., & Manni, J. J. (2003). Help-seeking behaviour of hearing-impaired persons aged ≥ 55 years; effect of complaints, significant others and hearing aid image. *Acta Oto-Laryngologica, 123,* 846–850.

Duncan, G. J., & Brooks-Gunn, J. (2000). Family poverty, welfare reform, and child development. *Child Development, 71,* 188–196.

Duncan, P. D., Ritter, P. L., Dornbusch, S. M., Gross, R. T., & Carlsmith, J. M. (1985). The effects of pubertal timing on body image, school behavior, and deviance. *Journal of Youth and Adolescence, 14,* 227–235.

Dunn, J., & Hughes, C. (2001). "I got some swords and you're dead!": Violent fantasy, antisocial behavior, friendship, and moral sensibility in young children. *Child Development, 72,* 491–505.

Dunn, J., Wooding, C., & Hermann, J. (1977). Mothers' speech to young children: Variation in context. *Developmental Medicine & Child Neurology, 19,* 629–638.

Dunphy, D. C. (1963). The social structure of urban adolescent peer groups. *Sociometry, 26,* 230–246.

Durrett, M. E., Otaki, M., & Richards, P. (1984). Attachment and the mother's perception of support from the father. *International Journal of Behavioral Development, 7,* 167–176.

Duvander, A.-Z. E. (1999). The transition from cohabitation to marriage: A longitudinal study of the propensity to marry in Sweden in the early 1990s. *Journal of Family Issues, 20,* 698–717.

Dweck, C. S. (1986). Motivational processes affecting learning. *American Psychologist, 41,* 1040–1048.

Dworkin, J. B., Larson, R., & Hansen, D. (2003). Adolescents' accounts of growth experiences in youth activities. *Journal of Youth and Adolescence, 32*, 17–26.

Earle, S. (2002). Factors affecting the initiation of breastfeeding: Implications for breastfeeding promotion. *Health Promotion International, 17*, 205–214.

Eaton, D. K., Kann, L., Kinchen, S., Ross, J., Hawkins, J., Harris, W. A., Lowry, R., McManus, T., Chyen, D., Shanklin, S., Lim, C., Grunbaum, J. A., & Wechsler, H. (2006, June 9). Youth risk behavior surveillance—United States, 2005. *MMWR Surveillance Summaries, 55*(5), 1–108.

Ebbeling, C. B., Pawlak, D. B., & Ludwig, D. S. (2002). Childhood obesity: Public-health crisis, common sense cure. *Lancet, 360*, 473–482.

Ebling, F. J. P. (2005). The neuroendocrine timing of puberty. *Reproduction, 129*, 675–683.

Eccles, J. S., & Midgley, C. (1989). Stage-environment fit: Developmentally appropriate classrooms for young adolescents. In C. Ames & R. Ames (Eds.), *Research on motivation in education: Vol. 3. Goals and cognitions* (pp. 13–44). New York: Academic Press.

Eccles, J. S., & Roeser, R. W. (2003). Schools as developmental contexts. In G. R. Adams & M. D. Berzonsky (Eds.), *Blackwell handbook of adolescence* (pp. 129–148). Malden, MA: Blackwell.

Eckerberg, B. (2004). Treatment of sleep problems in families with young children: Effects of treatment on family well-being. *Acta Paediatrica, 93*, 126–134.

Edin, K., Kefalas, M. J., & Reed, J. M. (2004). A peek inside the black box: What marriage means for poor unmarried parents. *Journal of Marriage and Family, 66*, 1007–1014.

Egan, S. K., & Perry, D. G. (2001). Gender identity: A multidimensional analysis with implications for psychosocial adjustment. *Developmental Psychology, 37*, 451–463.

Eggermont, S. (2005). Young adolescents' perceptions of peer sexual behaviours: The role of television viewing. *Child: Care, Health and Development, 31*, 459–468.

Ehrenberg, M. F., & Smith, S. T. L. (2003). Grandmother-grandchild contacts before and after an adult daughter's divorce. *Journal of Divorce & Remarriage, 39*, 27–43.

Eichorn, D. H., Clausen, J. A., Haan, J., Honzik, M. P., & Mussen, P. H. (Eds.). (1981). *Present and past in middle life.* New York: Academic Press.

Eisenberg, N. (1992). *The caring child.* Cambridge, MA: Harvard University Press.

Eisenberg, N. (2003). Prosocial behavior, empathy, and sympathy. In M. H. Bornstein, L. Davidson, C. L. M. Keyes, & K. A. Moore (Eds.), *Well-being: Positive development across the life course* (pp. 253–265). Mahwah, NJ: Erlbaum.

Eisenberg, N., & Fabes, R. A. (1998). Prosocial development. In W. Damon (Series Ed.) & N. Eisenberg (Vol. Ed.), *Handbook of child psychology: Vol 3. Social, emotional, and personality development* (5th ed., pp. 701–778). Hoboken, NJ: Wiley.

Eisenberg, N., Guthrie, I. K., Murphy, B. C., Shepard, S. A., Cumberland, A., & Carlo, G. (1999). Consistency and development of prosocial dispositions: A longitudinal study. *Child Development, 70*, 1360–1372.

Eisner, E. W. (2004). Multiple intelligences: Its tensions and possibilities. *Teachers College Record, 106*, 31–39.

Eitle, D., & Eitle, T. M. (2003). Segregation and school violence. *Social Forces, 82*, 589–615.

Ekerdt, D. J. (1986). The busy ethic: Moral continuity between work and retirement. *Gerontologist, 26*, 239–244.

Elbedour, S., Shulman, S., & Kedem, P. (1997). Adolescent intimacy: A cross-cultural study. *Journal of Cross-Cultural Psychology, 28*, 5–22.

Elder, G. H. (1981). Social history and life experience. In D. H. Eichorn, J. A. Clausen, J. Haan, M. P. Honzik, & P. H. Mussen (Eds.), *Present and past in middle life* (pp. 3–31). New York: Academic Press.

Elder, G. H., & Caspi, A. (1988). Economic stress in lives: Developmental perspectives. *Journal of Social Issues, 44*, 25–45.

Eldridge, K. A., & Christensen, A. (2002). Demand-withdraw communication during couple conflict: A review and analysis. In P. Noller & J. A. Feeney (Eds.), *Understanding marriage: Developments in the study of couple interaction* (pp. 289–322). New York: Cambridge University Press.

Elias, M. F., Elias, J. W., & Elias, P. K. (1990). Biological and health influences on behavior. In J. E. Birren & K. W. Schaie (Eds.), *Handbook of the psychology of aging* (3rd ed., pp. 79–102). San Diego, CA: Academic Press.

Elkind, D. (1968). Cognitive development in adolescence. In J. F. Adams (Ed.), *Understanding adolescence* (pp. 128–158). Boston: Allyn and Bacon.

Elkind, D. (1976). *Child development and education: A Piagetian perspective.* Oxford, England: Oxford University Press.

Elkind, D. (1978). Understanding the young adolescent. *Adolescence, 13*, 127–134.

Ellershaw, J. (2002). Clinical pathways for care of the dying: An innovation to disseminate clinical excellence. *Journal of Palliative Medicine, 5*, 617–621.

Elliott, M. R., Reilly, S. M., Drummond, J., & Letourneau, N. (2002). The effect of different soothing interventions on infant crying and on parent-infant interaction. *Infant Mental Health Journal, 23*, 310–328.

Ellis, B. J. (2004). Timing of pubertal maturation in girls: An integrated life history approach. *Psychological Bulletin, 130*, 920–958.

Ellis, B. J., McFadyen-Ketchum, S., Dodge, K. A., Pettit, G. S., & Bates, J. E. (1999). Quality of early family relationships and individual differences in the timing of pubertal maturation in girls: A longitudinal test of an evolutionary model. *Journal of Personality and Social Psychology, 77*, 387–401.

Else-Quest, N. M., Hyde, J. S., & Clark, R. (2003). Breastfeeding, bonding, and the mother-infant relationship. *Merrill-Palmer Quarterly, 49*, 495–517.

Enck, G. E. (2003). The dying process. In C. D. Bryant (Ed.), *Handbook of death & dying* (pp. 457–467). Thousand Oaks, CA: Sage.

Engle, S. (n.d.). Degree attainment rates at colleges and universities: College completion declining, taking longer, UCLA study shows. Retrieved September 6, 2006, from Higher Education Research Institute Web site: http://www.gseis.ucla.edu/heri/darcu_pr.html

Englund, K. T., & Behne, D. M. (2005). Infant directed speech in natural interaction—Norwegian vowel quantity and quality. *Journal of Psycholinguistic Research, 34*, 259–280.

Erber, J. T., & Prager, I. G. (1999). Age and memory: Perceptions of forgetful young and older adults. In T. M. Hess & F. Blanchard-Fields (Eds.), *Social cognition and aging* (pp. 197–217). San Diego, CA: Academic Press.

Erber, J. T., & Rothberg, S. T. (1991). Here's looking at you: The relative effect of age and attractiveness on judgments about memory failure. *Journals of Gerontology: Series B: Biological Sciences and Medical Sciences, 46*, P116–P123.

Erikson, E. H. (1950). *Childhood and society*. Oxford, England: Norton.

Erikson, E. H. (1963). *Childhood and society* (2nd ed.). New York: Norton.

Erikson, E. H. (1968). *Identity: Youth and crisis*. New York: Norton.

Erikson, E. H. (1969). *Gandhi's truth: On the origins of militant nonviolence*. New York: Norton.

Erikson, E. H. (1980). *Identity and the life cycle*. New York: Norton.

Eslea, M., Menesini, E., Morita, Y., O'Moore, M., Mora-Merchan, J. A., Pereira, B., & Smith, P. K. (2004). Friendship and loneliness among bullies and victims: Data from seven countries. *Aggressive Behavior, 30,* 71–83.

Etaugh, C. A., & Bridges, J. S. (2006). Midlife transitions. In J. Worell & C. D. Goodheart (Eds.), *Handbook of girls' and women's psychological health: Gender and well-being across the lifespan* (pp. 359–367). New York: Oxford University Press.

EUROCAT. (2004). *EUROCAT special report: A review of environmental risk factors for congenital anomalies*. Newtownabbey, Northern Ireland: Author.

Evans, G. W. (2006). Child development and the physical environment. *Annual Review of Psychology, 57,* 423–451.

Evans, G. W., & English, K. (2002). The environment of poverty: Multiple stressor exposure, psychophysiological stress, and socioemotional adjustment. *Child Development, 73,* 1238–1248.

Evertsson, M., & Nermo, M. (2004). Dependence within families and the division of labor: Comparing Sweden and the United States. *Journal of Marriage and Family, 66,* 1272–1286.

Eyetsemitan, F., Gire, J. T., Khaleefa, O., & Satiardama, M. P. (2003). Influence of the cross-cultural environment on the perception of aging and adult development in the developing world: A study of Bahrain, Brazil and Indonesia. *Asian Journal of Social Psychology, 6,* 51–60.

Fabes, R. A., Eisenberg, N., Smith, M. C., & Murphy, B. C. (1996). Getting angry at peers: Associations with liking of the provocateur. *Child Development, 67,* 942–956.

Fabes, R. A., Martin, C. L., & Hanish, L. D. (2003). Young children's play qualities in same-, other-, and mixed-sex peer groups. *Child Development, 74,* 921–932.

Fagan, J. F. (1988). Evidence for the relationship between responsiveness to visual novelty during infancy and later intelligence: A summary. *Cahiers de Psychologie Cognitive/Current Psychology of Cognition, 8,* 469–475.

Fagan, J. F. (2000). A theory of intelligence as processing: Implications for society. *Psychology, Public Policy, and Law, 6,* 168–179.

Fancher, R. E. (1985). Spearman's original computation of g: A model for Burt? *British Journal of Psychology, 76,* 341–352.

Farlow, M., & Inglis, F. (2002). Issues in the management of Alzheimer's disease. *Primary Care Psychiatry, 8,* 107–108.

Farroni, T., Massaccesi, S., & Simion, F. (2002). La direzione dello sguardo di un'altra persona puo dirigere l'attenzione del neonato? [Can the direction of the gaze of another person shift the attention of a neonate?]. *Giornale Italiano di Psicologia, 29,* 857–864.

Farver, J. A. M., Narang, S. K., & Bhadha, B. R. (2002). East meets West: Ethnic identity, acculturation, and conflict in Asian Indian families. *Journal of Family Psychology, 16,* 338–350.

Farver, J. A. M., Xu, Y., Eppe, S., Fernandez, A., & Schwartz, D. (2005). Community violence, family conflict, and preschoolers' socioemotional functioning. *Developmental Psychology, 41,* 160–170.

Federal Interagency Forum on Aging-Related Statistics. (2000). *Older Americans 2000: Key indicators of well-being* (017-022-01504-8). Washington, DC: U.S. Government Printing Office.

Feeg, V. D., & Elebiary, H. (2005). Exploratory study on end-of-life issues: Barriers to palliative care and advance directives. *American Journal of Hospice and Palliative Medicine, 22,* 119–124.

Feeney, J. A. (1999). Adult romantic attachment and couple relationships. In J. Cassidy & P. R. Shaver (Eds.), *Handbook of attachment: Theory, research, and clinical applications* (pp. 355–377). New York: Guilford Press.

Feeney, J. A., Alexander, R., Noller, P., & Hohaus, L. (2003). Attachment insecurity, depression, and the transition to parenthood. *Personal Relationships, 10,* 475–493.

Feeney, J. A., Hohaus, L., Noller, P., & Alexander, R. P. (2001). *Becoming parents: Exploring the bonds between mothers, fathers, and their infants*. New York: Cambridge University Press.

Feeney, J. A., & Noller, P. (2002). Allocation and performance of household tasks: A comparison of new parents and childless couples. In P. Noller & J. A. Feeney (Eds.), *Understanding marriage: Developments in the study of couple interaction* (pp. 411–436). New York: Cambridge University Press.

Feingold, A., & Mazzella, R. (1998). Gender differences in body image are increasing. *Psychological Science, 9,* 190–195.

Feldman, R., & Eidelman, A. I. (2003a). Direct and indirect effects of breast milk on neurobehavioral and cognitive development of premature infants. *Developmental Psychobiology, 43,* 109–119.

Feldman, R., & Eidelman, A. I. (2003b). Skin-to-skin contact (kangaroo care) accelerates autonomic and neurobehavioural maturation in preterm infants. *Developmental Medicine & Child Neurology, 45,* 274–281.

Ferber, R. (1985). *Solve your child's sleep problems*. New York: Simon and Schuster.

Ferber, R. (2006). *Solve your child's sleep problems* (New, revised, and expanded ed.). New York: Fireside.

Fernald, A., Pinto, J. P., Swingley, D., Weinberg, A., & McRoberts, G. W. (1998). Rapid gains in speed of verbal processing by infants in the 2nd year. *Psychological Science, 9,* 228–231.

Fernandes, O., Sabharwal, M., Smiley, T., Pastuszak, A., Koren, G., & Einarson, T. (1998). Moderate to heavy caffeine consumption during pregnancy and relationship to spontaneous abortion and abnormal fetal growth: A meta-analysis. *Reproductive Toxicology, 12,* 435–444.

Fernandez, C., & Yoshida, M. (2004). *Lesson study: A Japanese approach to improving mathematics teaching and learning*. Mahwah, NJ: Erlbaum.

Fernandez, M., Blass, E. M., Hernandez-Reif, M., Field, T., Diego, M., & Sanders, C. (2003). Sucrose attenuates a negative electroencephalographic response to an aversive stimulus for newborns. *Journal of Developmental & Behavioral Pediatrics, 24,* 261–266.

Fernyhough, C., & Fradley, E. (2005). Private speech on an executive task: Relations with task difficulty and task performance. *Cognitive Development, 20,* 103–120.

Fetters, M. D. (1998). The family in medical decision making: Japanese perspectives. *Journal of Clinical Ethics, 9,* 132–146.

Fiebert, M. S., Karamol, H., & Kasdan, M. (2000). Interracial dating: Attitudes and experience among American college students in California. *Psychological Reports, 87*(3, Pt 2), 1059–1064.

Field, A. E., Austin, S. B., Camargo, C. A., Jr., Taylor, C. B., Striegel-Moore, R. H., Loud, K. J., & Colditz, G. A. (2005). Exposure to the mass media, body shape concerns, and use of supplements to improve weight and shape among male and female adolescents. *Pediatrics, 116*, e214–220.

Field, N. P., & Friedrichs, M. (2004).- Continuing bonds in coping with the death of a husband. *Death Studies, 28*, 597–620.

Field, N. P., Gal-Oz, E., & Bonanno, G. A. (2003). Continuing bonds and adjustment at 5 years after the death of a spouse. *Journal of Consulting and Clinical Psychology, 71*, 110–117.

Field, N. P., Nichols, C., Holen, A., & Horowitz, M. J. (1999). The relation of continuing attachment to adjustment in conjugal bereavement. *Journal of Consulting and Clinical Psychology, 67*, 212–218.

Field, T. (2000). Infant massage therapy. In C. H. Zeanah, Jr. (Ed.), *Handbook of infant mental health* (2nd ed., pp. 494–500). New York: Guilford Press.

Field, T. (2001). Massage therapy facilitates weight gain in preterm infants. *Current Directions in Psychological Science, 10*, 51–54.

Field, T., & Hernandez-Reif, M. (2001). Sleep problems in infants decrease following massage therapy. *Early Child Development and Care, 168*, 95–104.

Field, T., Hernandez-Reif, M., Diego, M., Feijo, L., Vera, Y., & Gil, K. (2004). Massage therapy by parents improves early growth and development. *Infant Behavior & Development, 27*, 435–442.

Field, T., Hernandez-Reif, M., & Feijo, L. (2002). Breastfeeding in depressed mother-infant dyads. *Early Child Development and Care, 172*, 539–545.

Fields, J. (2003). *Children's living arrangements and characteristics: March 2002* (Current Population Reports P20-547). Washington, DC: U.S. Census Bureau.

Fields, J., & Casper, L. M. (2001). *America's families and living arrangements: March 2000* (Current Population Reports P20-537). Washington, DC: U.S. Census Bureau.

Fikree, F. F., Ali, T. S., Durocher, J. M., & Rahbar, M. H. (2005). Newborn care practices in low socioeconomic settlements of Karachi, Pakistan. *Social Science & Medicine, 60*, 911–921.

Fincham, F. D., & Bradbury, T. N. (1993). Marital satisfaction, depression, and attributions: A longitudinal analysis. *Journal of Personality and Social Psychology, 64*, 442–452.

Fingerman, K. L. (2004). The role of offspring and in-laws in grandparents' ties to their grandchildren. *Journal of Family Issues, 25*, 1026–1049.

Finkel, D., & Pedersen, N. L. (2004). Processing speed and longitudinal trajectories of change for cognitive abilities: The Swedish Adoption/Twin Study of Aging. *Aging, Neuropsychology, and Cognition, 11*, 325–345.

Finzi, R., Cohen, O., Sapir, Y., & Weizman, A. (2000). Attachment styles in maltreated children: A comparative study. *Child Psychiatry & Human Development, 31*, 113–128.

Fischer, D. H. (1977). *Growing old in America.* New York: Oxford University Press.

Flavell, J. H. (1963). *The developmental psychology of Jean Piaget.* New York: Van Nostrand.

Flavell, J. H. (1971). Stage-related properties of cognitive development. *Cognitive Psychology, 2*, 421–453.

Flavell, J. H., Beach, D. R., & Chinsky, J. M. (1966). Spontaneous verbal rehearsal in a memory task as a function of age. *Child Development, 37*, 283–299.

Flores, E., Cicchetti, D., & Rogosch, F. A. (2005). Predictors of resilience in maltreated and nonmaltreated Latino children. *Developmental Psychology, 41*, 338–351.

Flynn, C. P. (1998). To spank or not to spank: The effect of situation and age of child on support for corporal punishment. *Journal of Family Violence, 13*, 21–37.

Fogel, A. (2001). *Infancy: Infant, family, and society* (4th ed.). Belmont, CA: Wadsworth.

Fonagy, P. (2001). *Attachment theory and psychoanalysis.* New York: Other Press.

Food and Agriculture Organization of the United Nations. (1999). Children suffering from undernutrition, by region. Retrieved September 27, 2006, from http://www.fao.org/news/factfile/ff9903-e.htm

Food Research and Action Center. (n.d.). Child and Adult Care Food Program. Retrieved March 24, 2006, from http://www.frac.org/html/federal_food_programs/programs/cacfp.html

Ford, D. H., & Lerner, R. M. (1992). *Developmental systems theory: An integrative approach.* Newbury Park, CA: Sage.

Ford, J. D. (2005). Treatment implications of altered affect regulation and information processing following child maltreatment. *Psychiatric Annals, 35*, 410–419.

Freedman, D. S., Khan, L. K., Serdula, M. K., Dietz, W. H., Srinivasan, S. R., & Berenson, G. S. (2002). Relation of age at menarche to race, time period, and anthropometric dimensions: The Bogalusa Heart Study. *Pediatrics, 110*, e43.

Freedman, V. A. (1996). Family structure and the risk of nursing home admission. *Journals of Gerontology: Series B: Psychological Sciences and Social Sciences, 51*, S61–69.

Freid, V. M., Prager, K., MacKay, A. P., & Xia, H. (2003). *Chartbook on trends in the health of Americans. Health, United States, 2003.* (DHHS Publication No. 2003-1232). Hyattsville, MD: National Center for Health Statistics.

French, D. C., Jansen, E. A., & Pidada, S. (2002). United States and Indonesian children's and adolescents' reports of relational aggression by disliked peers. *Child Development, 73*, 1143–1150.

Freund, A. M., & Baltes, P. B. (2002). Life-management strategies of selection, optimization and compensation: Measurement by self-report and construct validity. *Journal of Personality and Social Psychology, 82*, 642–662.

Frey, K. S., & Ruble, D. N. (1985). What children say when the teacher is not around: Conflicting goals in social comparison and performance assessment in the classroom. *Journal of Personality and Social Psychology, 48*, 550–562.

Frey, K. S., & Ruble, D. N. (1990). Strategies for comparative evaluation: Maintaining a sense of competence across the life span. In R. J. Sternberg & J. Kolligian, Jr. (Eds.), *Competence considered* (pp. 167–189). New Haven, CT: Yale University Press.

Fried, L. P. (1997, November). *Quantitative methods in aging research.* Paper presented at the annual meeting of the Gerontological Society of America, Cincinnati, OH.

Friedman, D. (2003). Cognition and aging: A highly selective overview of event-related potential (ERP) data. *Journal of Clinical and Experimental Neuropsychology, 25,* 702–720.

Fu, G., Lee, K., Cameron, C. A., & Xu, F. (2001). Chinese and Canadian adults' categorization and evaluation of lie- and truth-telling about pro-social and antisocial behaviors. *Journal of Cross-Cultural Psychology, 32,* 720–727.

Fu, S.-Y., Anderson, D., & Courtney, M. (2003). Cross-cultural menopausal experience: Comparison of Australian and Taiwanese women. *Nursing & Health Sciences, 5,* 77–84.

Fuligni, A. J., & Eccles, J. S. (1993). Perceived parent-child relationships and early adolescents' orientation toward peers. *Developmental Psychology, 29,* 622–632.

Fuligni, A. J., Tseng, V., & Lam, M. (1999). Attitudes toward family obligations among American adolescents with Asian, Latin American, and European backgrounds. *Child Development, 70,* 1030–1044.

Fuligni, A. J., & Zhang, W. (2004). Attitudes toward family obligation among adolescents in contemporary urban and rural China. *Child Development, 75,* 180–192.

Fung, H. H., Lai, P., & Ng, R. (2001). Age differences in social preferences among Taiwanese and mainland Chinese: The role of perceived time. *Psychology and Aging, 16,* 351–356.

Furman, L., & Berman, B. W. (2004). Rethinking the AAP Attention Deficit/Hyperactivity Disorder Guidelines. *Clinical Pediatrics, 43,* 601–603.

Furstenberg, F. F., & Cherlin, A. J. (1991). *Divided families: What happens to children when parents part.* Cambridge, MA: Harvard University Press.

Furstenberg, F. F., & Cherlin, A. J. (2002). *Divided families: What happens to children when parents part* (Reissue ed.). Cambridge, MA: Harvard University Press.

Gable, S. L., Reis, H. T., & Downey, G. (2003). He said, she said: A quasi-signal detection analysis of daily interactions between close relationship partners. *Psychological Science, 14,* 100–105.

Gaddis, A., & Brooks-Gunn, J. (1985). The male experience of pubertal change. *Journal of Youth and Adolescence, 14,* 61–69.

Galinsky, E., Bond, J. T., Kim, S., Backon, L., Brownfield, E., & Sakai, K. (2005). *Overwork in America: When the way we work becomes too much.* New York: Families and Work Institute.

Galinsky, E., Kim, S. S., & Bond, J. T. (2001). *Feeling overworked: When work becomes too much.* New York: Families and Work Institute.

Gallimore, R., & Tharp, R. (1992). Teaching mind in society: Teaching, schooling, and literate discourse. In L. C. Moll (Ed.), *Vygotsky and education: Instructional implications and applications of sociohistorical psychology* (pp. 175–205). New York: Cambridge University Press.

Gamliel, T., Hoover, J. H., Daughtry, D. W., & Imbra, C. M. (2003). A qualitative investigation of bullying: The perspectives of fifth, sixth and seventh graders in a USA parochial school. *School Psychology International, 24,* 405–420.

Garcia Coll, C. T., Meyer, E. C., & Brillon, L. (1995). Ethnic and minority parenting. In M. H. Bornstein (Ed.), *Handbook of parenting: Vol. 2. Biology and ecology of parenting* (pp. 189–209). Hillsdale, NJ: Erlbaum.

Gardner, H. (1998). A multiplicity of intelligences. *Scientific American Presents, 9*(4), 18–23.

Gardner, H. (2004). *Frames of mind: The theory of multiple intelligences.* New York: Basic Books.

Gardner, M., & Steinberg, L. (2005). Peer influence on risk taking, risk preference, and risky decision making in adolescence and adulthood: An experimental study. *Developmental Psychology, 41,* 625–635.

Garey, A. I., & Arendell, T. (2001). Children, work, and family: Some thoughts on "mother blame". In R. Hertz & N. L. Marshall (Eds.), *Working families: The transformation of the American home* (pp. 293–303). Berkeley, CA: University of California Press.

Gath, A. (1993). Changes that occur in families as children with intellectual disability grow up. *International Journal of Disability, Development and Education, 40,* 167–174.

Gathercole, S. E., Pickering, S. J., Ambridge, B., & Wearing, H. (2004). The structure of working memory from 4 to 15 years of age. *Developmental Psychology, 40,* 177–190.

Gazelle, H., & Ladd, G. W. (2003). Anxious solitude and peer exclusion: A diathesis-stress model of internalizing trajectories in childhood. *Child Development, 74,* 257–278.

Ge, X., Elder, G. H., Regnerus, M., & Cox, C. (2001). Pubertal transitions, perceptions of being overweight, and adolescents' psychological maladjustment: Gender and ethnic differences. *Social Psychology Quarterly, 64,* 363–375.

Geary, D. C. (1998). *Male, female: The evolution of human sex differences.* Washington, DC: American Psychological Association.

Geary, D. C., & Flinn, M. V. (2001). Evolution of human parental behavior and the human family. *Parenting: Science and Practice, 1,* 5–61.

Genevie, L. E., & Margolies, E. (1987). *The motherhood report: How women feel about being mothers.* New York: Macmillan.

George, C., & Main, M. (1979). Social interactions of young abused children: Approach, avoidance, and aggression. *Child Development, 50,* 306–318.

Gerritsen, D., Kuin, Y., & Steverink, N. (2004). Personal experience of aging in the children of a parent with dementia. *International Journal of Aging & Human Development, 58,* 147–165.

Gershoff, E. T. (2002). Corporal punishment by parents and associated child behaviors and experiences: A meta-analytic and theoretical review. *Psychological Bulletin, 128,* 539–579.

Gerson, M.-J., Posner, J.-A., & Morris, A. M. (1991). The wish for a child in couples eager, disinterested, and conflicted about having children. *American Journal of Family Therapy, 19,* 334–343.

Giacobini, E. (2003). Cholinergic function and Alzheimer's disease. *International Journal of Geriatric Psychiatry, 18*(Suppl. 1), S1-S5.

Gibbins, S., & Stevens, B. (2001). Mechanisms of sucrose and non-nutritive sucking in procedural pain management in infants. *Pain Research & Management, 6,* 21–28.

Gibson, M. A., & Mace, R. (2005). Helpful grandmothers in rural Ethiopia: A study of the effect of kin on child survival and growth. *Evolution and Human Behavior, 26,* 469–482.

Giedd, J. N. (2004). Structural magnetic resonance imaging of the adolescent brain. In R. E. Dahl & L. P. Spear (Eds.), *Adolescent brain development: Vulnerabilities and opportunities* (Vol. 1021, pp. 77–85). New York: New York Academy of Sciences.

Gijsbers van Wijk, C. M., Kolk, A. M., Van den Bosch, W. J., & Van den Hoogen, H. J. (1992). Male and female morbidity in general practice: The nature of sex differences. *Social Science & Medicine*, 35, 665–678.

Gila, A., Castro, J., Cesena, J., & Toro, J. (2005). Anorexia nervosa in male adolescents: Body image, eating attitudes and psychological traits. *Journal of Adolescent Health*, 36, 221–226.

Gilbert, E. S., & Harmon, J. S. (1998). *Manual of high risk pregnancy & delivery* (2nd ed.). St. Louis, MO: Mosby.

Gilbert-Barness, E. (2000). Maternal caffeine and its effect on the fetus. *American Journal of Medical Genetics*, 93, 253.

Gillett-Netting, R., Meloy, M., & Campbell, B. C. (2004). Catch-up reproductive maturation in rural Tonga girls, Zambia? *American Journal of Human Biology*, 16, 658–669.

Ginsburg, H., & Opper, S. (1969). *Piaget's theory of intellectual development: An introduction*. Englewood Cliffs, NJ: Prentice-Hall.

Glanz, K., Sallis, J. F., Saelens, B. E., & Frank, L. D. (2005). Healthy nutrition environments: Concepts and measures. *American Journal of Health Promotion*, 19, 330–333.

Glaser, B. G., & Strauss, A. L. (1968). *Time for dying*. Chicago: Aldine.

Glazier, R., Elgar, F., Goel, V., & Holzapfel, S. (2004). Stress, social support and emotional distress in a community sample of pregnant women. *Journal of Psychosomatic Obstetrics & Gynecology*, 25, 247–255.

Gleason, J. B. (2000). *The development of language* (5th ed.). Needham Heights, MA: Allyn & Bacon.

Gleason, T. R., Gower, A. L., Hohmann, L. M., & Gleason, T. C. (2005). Temperament and friendship in preschool-aged children. *International Journal of Behavioral Development*, 29, 336–344.

Glenn, N. (1990). Quantitative research on marital quality in the 1980s: A critical review. *Journal of Marriage and the Family*, 52, 818–831.

Gokyildiz, S., & Beji, N. K. (2005). The effects of pregnancy on sexual life. *Journal of Sex & Marital Therapy*, 31, 201–215.

Gold, C. H., Malmberg, B., McClearn, G. E., Pedersen, N. L., & Berg, S. (2002). Gender and health: A study of older unlike-sex twins. *Journals of Gerontology: Series B: Psychological Sciences and Social Sciences*, 57B, S168–S176.

Goldberg, A. E., & Sayer, A. (2006). Lesbian couples' relationship quality across the transition to parenthood. *Journal of Marriage and Family*, 68, 87–100.

Goldberg, J., Holtz, D., Hyslop, T., & Tolosa, J. E. (2002). Has the use of routine episiotomy decreased? Examination of episiotomy rates from 1983 to 2000. *Obstetrics & Gynecology*, 99, 395–400.

Goldscheider, F., & Goldscheider, C. (1993). Whose nest? A two-generational view of leaving home during the 1980s. *Journal of Marriage & the Family*, 55, 851–862.

Goldscheider, F. K., & Goldscheider, C. (1999). *The changing transition to adulthood: Leaving and returning home*. Thousand Oaks, CA: Sage.

Goldscheider, F. K., & Waite, L. J. (1991). *New families, no families? The transformation of the American home*. Berkeley, CA: University of California Press.

Goldstein, S. E., Davis-Kean, P. E., & Eccles, J. S. (2005). Parents, peers, and problem behavior: A longitudinal investigation of the impact of relationship perceptions and characteristics on the development of adolescent problem behavior. *Developmental Psychology*, 41, 401–413.

Golombok, S., Perry, B., Burston, A., Murray, C., Mooney-Somers, J., Stevens, M., & Golding, J. (2003). Children with lesbian parents: A community study. *Developmental Psychology*, 39, 20–33.

Gomez-Sanchiz, M., Canete, R., Rodero, I., Baeza, J. E., & Avila, O. (2003). Influence of breast-feeding on mental and psychomotor development. *Clinical Pediatrics*, 42, 35–42.

Good, M.-J. D., Gadmer, N. M., Ruopp, P., Lakoma, M., Sullivan, A. M., Redinbaugh, E., Arnold, R. M., & Block, S. D. (2004). Narrative nuances on good and bad deaths: Internists' tales from high-technology work places. *Social Science & Medicine*, 58, 939–953.

Goodlin-Jones, B. L., Burnham, M. M., & Anders, T. F. (2000). Sleep and sleep disturbances: Regulatory processes in infancy. In A. J. Sameroff, M. Lewis, & S. M. Miller (Eds.), *Handbook of developmental psychopathology* (2nd ed., pp. 309–325). Dordrecht, Netherlands: Kluwer.

Goodlin-Jones, B. L., Burnham, M. M., Gaylor, E. E., & Anders, T. F. (2001). Night waking, sleep-wake organization, and self-soothing in the first year of life. *Journal of Developmental & Behavioral Pediatrics*, 22, 226–233.

Goodman, E., McEwen, B. S., Huang, B., Dolan, L. M., & Adler, N. E. (2005). Social inequalities in biomarkers of cardiovascular risk in adolescence. *Psychosomatic Medicine*, 67, 9–15.

Goodman, G. S., Emery, R. E., & Haugaard, J. J. (1998). Developmental psychology and law: Divorce, child maltreatment, foster care and adoption. In W. Damon (Series Ed.) & I. E. Sigel & K. A. Renninger (Vol. Eds.), *Handbook of child psychology: Vol. 4. Child psychology in practice* (5th ed., pp. 775–874). Hoboken, NJ: Wiley.

Goossens, L. (2001). Global versus domain-specific statuses in identity research: A comparison of two self-report measures. *Journal of Adolescence*, 24, 681–699.

Gore, T., & Dubois, R. (1998). The "Back to Sleep" campaign. *Zero To Three*, 19(2), 22–23.

Gorer, G. (1965). *Death, grief, and mourning in contemporary Britain*. London: Cresset Press.

Gornick, J. C., & Meyers, M. K. (2003). *Families that work: Policies for reconciling parenthood and employment*. New York: Russell Sage Foundation.

Gottfredson, L. S. (1998). Jensen, Jensenism, and the sociology of intelligence. *Intelligence*, 26, 291–299.

Gottfredson, L. S. (2005). What if the hereditarian hypothesis is true? *Psychology, Public Policy, and Law*, 11, 311–319.

Gottman, J. (1994). *Why marriages succeed or fail: And how you can make yours last*. New York: Simon & Schuster.

Gottman, J. M. (1999). *The marriage clinic: A scientifically based marital therapy*. New York: Norton.

Gould, S. J. (1981). *The mismeasure of man*. New York: Norton.

Goyer, A. (2006). Intergenerational relationships: Grandparents raising grandchildren. Retrieved October 23, 2006, from AARP Foundation Grandparent Information Center Web site: http://www.aarp.org/research/international/perspectives/nov_05_grandparents.html

Graber, J. A., Lewinsohn, P. M., Seeley, J. R., & Brooks-Gunn, J. (1997). Is psychopathology associated with the timing of pubertal development? *Journal of the American Academy of Child & Adolescent Psychiatry*, 36, 1768–1776.

Graber, J. A., Petersen, A. C., & Brooks-Gunn, J. (1996). Pubertal processes: Methods, measures, and models. In J. A. Graber, J. Brooks-Gunn, & A. C. Petersen (Eds.), *Transitions through adolescence: Interpersonal domains and context* (pp. 23–53). Hillsdale, NJ: Erlbaum.

Grady, C. L., & Craik, F. I. M. (2000). Changes in memory processing with age. *Current Opinion in Neurobiology, 10,* 224-231.

Graham, J. W., & Beller, A. H. (2002). Nonresident fathers and their children: Child support and visitation from an economic perspective. In C. S. Tamis-LeMonda & N. Cabrera (Eds.), *Handbook of father involvement: Multidisciplinary perspectives* (pp. 431–453). Mahwah, NJ: Erlbaum.

Grandmaison, E., & Simard, M. (2003). A critical review of memory stimulation programs in Alzheimer's disease. *Journal of Neuropsychiatry & Clinical Neurosciences, 15,* 130–144.

Green, E. G., Deschamps, J.-C., & Paez, D. (2005). Variation of individualism and collectivism within and between 20 countries: A typological analysis. *Journal of Cross-Cultural Psychology, 36,* 321–339.

Greene, B. A., Miller, R. B., Crowson, H. M., Duke, B. L., & Akey, K. L. (2004). Predicting high school students' cognitive engagement and achievement: Contributions of classroom perceptions and motivation. *Contemporary Educational Psychology, 29,* 462–482.

Greenfield, P. M., Keller, H., Fuligni, A., & Maynard, A. (2003). Cultural pathways through universal development. *Annual Review of Psychology, 54,* 461–490.

Greenleaf, C. (2005). Self-objectification among physically active women. *Sex Roles, 52,* 51–62.

Gregory, A. M., Caspi, A., Eley, T. C., Moffitt, T. E., O'Connor, T. G., & Poulton, R. (2005). Prospective longitudinal associations between persistent sleep problems in childhood and anxiety and depression disorders in adulthood. *Journal of Abnormal Child Psychology, 33,* 157–163.

Griffin, R. S., & Gross, A. M. (2004). Childhood bullying: Current empirical findings and future directions for research. *Aggression and Violent Behavior, 9,* 379–400.

Grolnick, W. S., Gurland, S. T., DeCourcey, W., & Jacob, K. (2002). Antecedents and consequences of mothers' autonomy support: An experimental investigation. *Developmental Psychology, 38,* 143–155.

Groopman, J. E. (2004). *The anatomy of hope: How patients prevail in the face of illness.* New York: Random House.

Grossbaum, M. F., & Bates, G. W. (2002). Correlates of psychological well-being at midlife: The role of generativity, agency and communion, and narrative themes. *International Journal of Behavioral Development, 26,* 120–127.

Grossman, F. K. (1987). Separate and together: Men's autonomy and affiliation in the transition to parenthood. In P. W. Berman & F. A. Pedersen (Eds.), *Men's transitions to parenthood: Longitudinal studies of early family experience* (pp. 89–112). Hillsdale, NJ: Erlbaum.

Grossmann, K., Grossmann, K. E., & Kindler, H. (2005). Early care and the roots of attachment and partnership representations: the Bielefeld and Regensburg longitudinal studies. In K. E. Grossmann, K. Grossmann, & E. Waters (Eds.), *Attachment from infancy to adulthood: The major longitudinal studies* (pp. 98–136). New York: Guilford Press.

Grossmann, K. E., Grossmann, K., & Waters, E. (Eds.). (2005). *Attachment from infancy to adulthood: The major longitudinal studies.* New York: Guilford Press.

Grossmann, K. E., Grossmann, K., & Zimmermann, P. (1999). A wider view of attachment and exploration: Stability and change during the years of immaturity. In J. Cassidy & P. R. Shaver (Eds.), *Handbook of attachment: Theory, research, and clinical applications* (pp. 760–786). New York: Guilford Press.

Grotevant, H. D., & Cooper, C. R. (1998). Individuality and connectedness in adolescent development: Review and prospects for research on identity, relationships, and context. In E. E. A. Skoe & A. L. von der Lippe (Eds.), *Personality development in adolescence: A cross national and life span perspective* (pp. 3–37). New York: Routledge.

Grusec, J. E., Goodnow, J. J., & Kuczynski, L. (2000). New directions in analyses of parenting contributions to children's acquisition of values. *Child Development, 71,* 205–211.

Grzywacz, J. G., & Marks, N. F. (2001). Social inequalities and exercise during adulthood: Toward an ecological perspective. *Journal of Health and Social Behavior, 42,* 202–220.

Guttmacher Institute. (2006). *State policies in brief: Sex and STD/HIV education.* New York: Author.

Guttorm, T. K., Leppanen, P. H. T., Poikkeus, A.-M., Eklund, K. M., Lyytinen, P., & Lyytinen, H. (2005). Brain event-related potentials (ERPs) measured at birth predict later language development in children with and without familial risk for dyslexia. *Cortex, 41,* 291–303.

Guzman, L. (1999). *The use of grandparents as child care providers* (NSFH No. 84). Madison, WI: A National Survey of Families and Households.

Haan, N., Millsap, R., & Hartka, E. (1986). As time goes by: Change and stability in personality over fifty years. *Psychology and Aging, 1,* 220–232.

Hachinski, V. (2000). Vascular factors in cognitive impairment—Where are we now? In R. N. Kalaria & P. Ince (Eds.), *Vascular factors in Alzheimer's disease* (pp. 1–5). New York: New York Academy of Sciences.

Haddad, L., Alderman, H., Appleton, S., Song, L., & Yohannes, Y. (2003). Reducing child malnutrition: How far does income growth take us? *World Bank Economic Review, 17,* 107–131.

Hagberg, B., Alfredson, B. B., Poon, L. W., & Homma, A. (2001). Cognitive functioning in centenarians: A coordinated analysis of results from three countries. *Journals of Gerontology: Series B: Psychological Sciences and Social Sciences, 56B,* P141–P151.

Hagestad, G. O. (1985). Continuity and connectedness. In V. L. Bengtson & J. F. Robertson (Eds.), *Grandparenthood* (pp. 31–48). Thousand Oaks, CA: Sage.

Hall, G. S. (1969). *Adolescence.* New York: Arno Press. (Original work published 1904)

Halpern, C. T., Udry, J. R., Campbell, B., & Suchindran, C. (1993). Testosterone and pubertal development as predictors of sexual activity: A panel analysis of adolescent males. *Psychosomatic Medicine, 55,* 436–447.

Halpern-Felsher, B. L., Cornell, J. L., Kropp, R. Y., & Tschann, J. M. (2005). Oral versus vaginal sex among adolescents: Perceptions, attitudes, and behavior. *Pediatrics, 115,* 845–851.

Hamilton, C. E. (2000). Continuity and discontinuity of attachment from infancy through adolescence. *Child Development, 71,* 690–694.

Hamilton, S. F. (1986). Excellence and the transition from school to work. *Phi Delta Kappan, 68,* 239–242.

Hamilton, S. F. (1990). *Apprenticeship for adulthood: Preparing youth for the future*. New York: Free Press.

Hankin, B. L., Abramson, L. Y., Moffitt, T. E., Silva, P. A., McGee, R., & Angell, K. E. (1998). Development of depression from preadolescence to young adulthood: Emerging gender differences in a 10-year longitudinal study. *Journal of Abnormal Psychology, 107,* 128–140.

Hansen, M., Janssen, I., Schiff, A., Zee, P. C., & Dubocovich, M. L. (2005). The impact of school daily schedule on adolescent sleep. *Pediatrics, 115,* 1555–1561.

Hansen, M., Kurinczuk, J. J., Bower, C., & Webb, S. (2002). The risk of major birth defects after intracytoplasmic sperm injection and in vitro fertilization. *New England Journal of Medicine, 346,* 725–730.

Hardey, M. (2002). Life beyond the screen: Embodiment and identity through the Internet. *Sociological Review, 50,* 570–585.

Hardy, J. (2004). The uncertain anatomy of Alzheimer's disease. *Neurobiology of Aging, 25,* 719–720.

Hardy, M. A. (2002). The transformation of retirement in twentieth-century America: From discontent to satisfaction. *Generations, 26*(2), 9–16.

Hargreaves, D., & Tiggemann, M. (2003). The effect of "thin ideal" television commercials on body dissatisfaction and schema activation during early adolescence. *Journal of Youth and Adolescence, 32,* 367–373.

Harley, K., & Reese, E. (1999). Origins of autobiographical memory. *Developmental Psychology, 35,* 1338–1348.

Harlow, C. M. (Ed.). (1986). *From learning to love: The selected papers of H. F. Harlow.* New York: Praeger.

Harlow, H. F. (1958). The nature of love. *American Psychologist, 13,* 673–685.

Harlow, H. F., Harlow, M. K., Dodsworth, R. O., & Arling, G. L. (1966). Maternal behavior of rhesus monkeys deprived of mothering and peer associations in infancy. *Proceedings of the American Philosophical Society, 110,* 58–66.

Harris, J. R. (1995). Where is the child's environment? A group socialization theory of development. *Psychological Review, 102,* 458–489.

Harris, J. R. (1998). *The nurture assumption: Why children turn out the way they do.* New York: Free Press.

Harris, J. R. (2002). Beyond the nurture assumption: Testing hypotheses about the child's environment. In J. G. Borkowski, S. L. Ramey, & M. Bristol-Power (Eds.), *Parenting and the child's world: Influences on academic, intellectual, and social-emotional development* (pp. 3–20). Mahwah, NJ: Erlbaum.

Harris, P. B., & Long, S. O. (1999). Husbands and sons in the United States and Japan: Cultural expectations and caregiving experiences. *Journal of Aging Studies, 13,* 241–267.

Hart, H. M., McAdams, D. P., Hirsch, B. J., & Bauer, J. J. (2001). Generativity and social involvement among African Americans and White adults. *Journal of Research in Personality, 35,* 208–230.

Hart, S., Boylan, L. M., Carroll, S., Musick, Y., & Lampe, R. M. (2003). Brief report: Breast-fed one-week-olds demonstrate superior neurobehavioral organization. *Journal of Pediatric Psychology, 28,* 529–534.

Harter, S. (1981). A new self-report scale of intrinsic versus extrinsic orientation in the classroom: Motivational and informational components. *Developmental Psychology, 17,* 300–312.

Harter, S. (1999). *The construction of the self: A developmental perspective.* New York: Guilford Press.

Harter, S., & Pike, R. (1984). The Pictorial Scale of Perceived Competence and Social Acceptance for Young Children. *Child Development, 55,* 1969–1982.

Hartup, W. W. (1998). Cooperation, close relationships, and cognitive development. In W. M. Bukowski, A. F. Newcomb, & W. W. Hartup (Eds.), *The company they keep: Friendship in childhood and adolescence* (pp. 213–237). New York: Cambridge University Press.

Hartup, W. W., & Stevens, N. (1997). Friendships and adaptation in the life course. *Psychological Bulletin, 121,* 355–370.

Hartup, W. W., & Stevens, N. (1999). Friendships and adaptation across the life span. *Current Directions in Psychological Science, 8,* 76–79.

Harvey, J. A., & Robinson, J. D. (2003). Eating disorders in men: Current considerations. *Journal of Clinical Psychology in Medical Settings, 10,* 297–306.

Hasher, L., & Zacks, R. T. (1988). Working memory, comprehension, and aging: A review and a new view. In G. H. Bower (Ed.), *Advances in research and theory: Vol. 22. The psychology of learning and motivation* (pp. 193–225). San Diego, CA: Academic Press.

Haslam, C., & Lawrence, W. (2004). Health-related behavior and beliefs of pregnant smokers. *Health Psychology, 23,* 486–491.

Hawkins, J. D., Catalano, R. F., Morrison, D. M., O'Donnell, J., Abbott, R. D., & Day, L. E. (1992). The Seattle Social Development Project: Effects of the first four years on protective factors and problem behaviors. In J. McCord & R. E. Tremblay (Eds.), *Preventing antisocial behavior: Interventions from birth through adolescence* (pp. 139–161). New York: Guilford Press.

Hawkins, J. D., Von Cleve, E., & Catalano, R. F. (1991). Reducing early childhood aggression: Results of a primary prevention program. *Journal of the American Academy of Child & Adolescent Psychiatry, 30,* 208–217.

Hawkins, N. A., Ditto, P. H., Danks, J. H., & Smucker, W. D. (2005). Micromanaging death: Process preferences, values, and goals in end-of-life medical decision making. *Gerontologist, 45,* 107–117.

Hawley, P. H. (1999). The ontogenesis of social dominance: A strategy-based evolutionary perspective. *Developmental Review, 19,* 97–132.

Hayflick, L. (1987). The human life span. In G. Lesnoff-Caravaglia (Ed.), *Realistic expectations for long life* (pp. 17–34). New York: Human Sciences Press.

Hayflick, L. (2004). "Anti-aging" is an oxymoron. *Journals of Gerontology: Series A: Biological Sciences and Medical Sciences, 59A,* 573–578.

Hays, J. C., Galanos, A. N., Palmer, T. A., McQuoid, D. R., & Flint, E. P. (2001). Preference for place of death in a continuing care retirement community. *Gerontologist, 41,* 123–128.

Hayslip, B., Jr., & Hansson, R. O. (2003). Death awareness and adjustment across the life span. In C. D. Bryant (Ed.), *Handbook of death & dying* (pp. 437–447). Thousand Oaks, CA: Sage.

Hayslip, B., Jr., & Patrick, J. H. (Eds.). (2003). *Working with custodial grandparents.* New York: Springer.

Hazan, C., & Shaver, P. (1987). Romantic love conceptualized as an attachment process. *Journal of Personality and Social Psychology, 52,* 511–524.

HealthLink. (2002). Bad news about hormone replacement therapy. Retrieved September 24, 2006, from Medical College of Wisconsin Web site: http://healthlink.mcw.edu/article/1025191125.html

Heine, S. H., Lehman, D. R., Markus, H. R., & Kitayama, S. (1999). Is there a universal need for positive self-regard? *Psychological Review, 106,* 766–794.

Helson, R., Jones, C., & Kwan, V. S. Y. (2002). Personality change over 40 years of adulthood: Hierarchical linear modeling analyses of two longitudinal samples. *Journal of Personality and Social Psychology, 83,* 752–766.

Helson, R., & Roberts, B. W. (1994). Ego development and personality change in adulthood. *Journal of Personality and Social Psychology, 66,* 911–920.

Hemingway, H., Shipley, M., Macfarlane, P., & Marmot, M. (2000). Impact of socioeconomic status on coronary mortality in people with symptoms, electrocardiographic abnormalities, both or neither: The original Whitehall study 25 year follow up. *Journal of Epidemiology & Community Health, 54,* 510–516.

Henderson, T. L. (2005). Grandparent visitation rights: Successful acquisition of court-ordered visitation. *Journal of Family Issues, 26,* 107–137.

Hendin, H. (1994, December 16). Scared to death of dying [Op-Ed]. *New York Times,* p. A19.

Henington, C., Hughes, J. N., Cavell, T. A., & Thompson, B. (1998). The role of relational aggression in identifying aggressive boys and girls. *Journal of School Psychology, 36,* 457–477.

Hennink, M., Rana, I., & Iqbal, R. (2005). Knowledge of personal and sexual development amongst young people in Pakistan. *Culture, Health & Sexuality, 7,* 319–332.

Herman-Giddens, M. E., Brown, G., Verbiest, S., Carlson, P. J., Hooten, E. G., Howell, E., & Butts, J. D. (1999). Underascertainment of child abuse mortality in the United States. *Journal of the American Medical Association, 282,* 463–467.

Hernandez-Reif, M., Field, T., Largie, S., Diego, M., Manigat, N., Seoanes, J., & Bornstein, J. (2005). Cerebral palsy symptoms in children decreased following massage therapy. *Early Child Development and Care, 175,* 445–456.

Herrnstein, R. J., & Murray, C. A. (1994). *The bell curve: Intelligence and class structure in American life.* New York: Free Press.

Hertzog, C. (1996). Research design in studies of aging and cognition. In J. E. Birren, K. W. Schaie, R. P. Abeles, M. Gatz, & T. A. Salthouse (Eds.), *Handbook of the psychology of aging* (4th ed., pp. 24–37). San Diego, CA: Academic Press.

Herzog, D. B., Dorer, D. J., Keel, P. K., Selwyn, S. E., Ekeblad, E. R., Flores, A. T., Greenwood, D. N., Burwell, R. A., & Keller, M. B. (1999). Recovery and relapse in anorexia and bulimia nervosa: A 7.5-year follow-up study. *Journal of the American Academy of Child & Adolescent Psychiatry, 38,* 829–837.

Hess, T. M., Auman, C., Colcombe, S. J., & Rahhal, T. A. (2003). The impact of stereotype threat on age differences in memory performance. *Journals of Gerontology: Series B: Psychological Sciences and Social Sciences, 58B,* P3–P11.

Hetherington, E. M. (1999). *Coping with divorce, single parenting, and remarriage: A risk and resiliency perspective.* Mahwah, NJ: Erlbaum.

Hetherington, E. M., Bridges, M., & Insabella, G. M. (1998). What matters? What does not? Five perspectives on the association between marital transitions and children's adjustment. *American Psychologist, 53,* 167–184.

Hetherington, E. M., & Kelly, J. (2002). *For better or for worse: Divorce reconsidered.* New York: Norton.

Hickman, S. E., Tilden, V. P., & Tolle, S. W. (2004). Family perceptions of worry, symptoms, and suffering in the dying. *Journal of Palliative Care, 20,* 20–27.

Hietanen, A., Era, P., Sorri, M., & Heikkinen, E. (2004). Changes in hearing in 80-year-old people: A 10-year follow-up study. *International Journal of Audiology, 43,* 126–135.

Hildén, H. M., Louhiala, P., & Palo, J. (2004). End of life decisions: Attitudes of Finnish physicians. *Journal of Medical Ethics, 30,* 362–365.

Hinde, R. A. (2005). Ethology and attachment theory. In K. E. Grossmann, K. Grossmann, & E. Waters (Eds.), *Attachment from infancy to adulthood: The major longitudinal studies* (pp. 1–12). New York: Guilford Press.

Hipwell, A. E., Murray, L., Ducournau, P., & Stein, A. (2005). The effects of maternal depression and parental conflict on children's peer play. *Child: Care, Health and Development, 31,* 11–23.

Hirsh-Pasek, K., & Golinkoff, R. M. (1991). Language comprehension: A new look at some old themes. In N. A. Krasnegor, D. M. Rumbaugh, R. L. Schiefelbusch, & M. Studdert-Kennedy (Eds.), *Biological and behavioral determinants of language development* (pp. 301–320). Hillsdale, NJ: Erlbaum.

Hla, M. M., Novotny, R., Kieffer, E. C., Mor, J., & Thiele, M. (2003). Early weaning among Japanese women in Hawaii. *Journal of Biosocial Science, 35,* 227–241.

Hodges, E. V. E., & Perry, D. G. (1999). Personal and interpersonal antecedents and consequences of victimization by peers. *Journal of Personality and Social Psychology, 76,* 677–685.

Hodgson, L. G. (1992). Adult grandchildren and their grandparents: Their enduring bond. *International Journal of Aging & Human Development, 34,* 209–225.

Hoelter, L. F., & Stauffer, D. E. (2002). What does it mean to be "just living together" in the new millennium? An overview. In A. Booth & A. C. Crouter (Eds.), *Just living together: Implications of cohabitation on families, children, and social policy* (pp. 255–271). Mahwah, NJ: Erlbaum.

Hoerr, T. (2004). How MI informs teaching at New City School. *Teachers College Record, 106,* 40–48.

Hoff-Ginsberg, E. (1997). *Language development.* Belmont, CA: Brooks/Cole.

Hoff-Ginsberg, E., & Tardif, T. (1995). Socioeconomic status and parenting. In M. H. Bornstein (Ed.), *Handbook of parenting: Vol. 2. Biology and ecology of parenting* (pp. 161–188). Hillsdale, NJ: Erlbaum.

Hoffman, M. L. (1994). Discipline and internalization. *Developmental Psychology, 30,* 26–28.

Hoffman, M. L. (2001). Toward a comprehensive empathy-based theory of prosocial moral development. In A. C. Bohart & D. J. Stipek (Eds.), *Constructive & destructive behavior: Implications for family, school, & society* (pp. 61–86). Washington, DC: American Psychological Association.

Hofstede, G. (1981). Cultures and organizations. *International Studies of Management and Organization, 10*(4), 15–41.

Hofstede, G. (2001). *Culture's consequences: Comparing values, behaviors, institutions, and organizations across nations* (2nd ed.). Thousand Oaks, CA: Sage.

Holland, J. L. (1985). *Making vocational choices: A theory of vocational personalities and work environments* (2nd ed.). Englewood Cliffs, NJ: Prentice-Hall.

Holliday, R. (2004). The multiple and irreversible causes of aging. *Journals of Gerontology: Series A: Biological Sciences and Medical Sciences, 59A,* 568–572.

Holloway, S. D., & Behrens, K. Y. (2002). Parenting self-efficacy among Japanese mothers: Qualitative and quantitative perspectives on its association with childhood memories of family relations. In J. Bempechat & J. G. Elliott (Eds.), *Learning in culture and context: Approaching the complexities of achievement motivation in student learning* (pp. 27–43). San Francisco: Jossey-Bass.

Holmbeck, G. N. (1996). A model of family relational transformations during the transition to adolescence: Parent-adolescent conflict and adaptation. In J. A. Graber, J. Brooks-Gunn, & A. C. Petersen (Eds.), *Transitions through adolescence: Interpersonal domains and context* (pp. 167–199). Hillsdale, NJ: Erlbaum.

Holmes, T. H., & Rahe, R. H. (1967). The social readjustment rating scale. *Journal of Psychosomatic Research, 11,* 213–218.

Holroyd, E. E. (2003). Chinese family obligations toward chronically ill elderly members: Comparing caregivers in Beijing and Hong Kong. *Qualitative Health Research, 13,* 302–318.

Honeycutt, J. M. (1993). Marital happiness, divorce status and partner differences in attributions about communication behaviors. *Journal of Divorce & Remarriage, 21,* 177–205.

Hooker, K., & McAdams, D. P. (2003). Personality and Adult Development: Looking Beyond the OCEAN. *Journals of Gerontology: Series B: Psychological Sciences and Social Sciences, 58B,* P311–P312.

Hopper, J. (1993). The rhetoric of motives in divorce. *Journal of Marriage & the Family, 55,* 801–813.

Horowitz, T. R. (1992). Dropout: Mertonian or reproduction scheme? *Adolescence, 27,* 451–459.

Howe, M. J. (1988a). Intelligence as an explanation. *British Journal of Psychology, 79,* 349–360.

Howe, M. J. (1988b). The hazards of using correlational evidence as a means of identifying the causes of individual ability differences: A rejoinder to Sternberg and a reply to Miles. *British Journal of Psychology, 79,* 539–545.

Howes, C. (1999). Attachment relationships in the context of multiple caregivers. In J. Cassidy & P. R. Shaver (Eds.), *Handbook of attachment: Theory, research, and clinical applications* (pp. 671–687). New York: Guilford Press.

Hoza, B., Waschbusch, D. A., Pelham, W. E., Molina, B. S. G., & Milich, R. (2000). Attention-deficit/hyperactivity disordered and control boys' responses to social success and failure. *Child Development, 71,* 432–446.

Hrdy, S. B. (1999). *Mother nature: A history of mothers, infants, and natural selection.* New York: Pantheon Books.

Hsu, M.-T., Kahn, D. L., Yee, D.-H., & Lee, W.-L. (2004). Recovery through reconnection: A cultural design for family bereavement in Taiwan. *Death Studies, 28,* 761–786.

Hu, S., & Kuh, G. D. (2003). Diversity experiences and college student learning and personal development. *Journal of College Student Development, 44,* 320–334.

Huang, X., & Van de Vliert, E. (2003). Where intrinsic job satisfaction fails to work: National moderators of intrinsic motivation. *Journal of Organizational Behavior, 24,* 159–179.

Hubbard, J. A., Dodge, K. A., Cillessen, A. H. N., Coie, J. D., & Schwartz, D. (2001). The dyadic nature of social information processing in boys' reactive and proactive aggression. *Journal of Personality and Social Psychology, 80,* 268–280.

Huddleston, J., & Ge, X. (2003). Boys at puberty: Psychosocial implications. In C. Hayward (Ed.), *Gender differences at puberty* (pp. 113–134). New York: Cambridge University Press.

Huizink, A. C., Mulder, E. J., & Buitelaar, J. K. (2004). Prenatal stress and risk for psychopathology: Specific effects or induction of general susceptibility? *Psychological Bulletin, 130,* 115–142.

Hungerford, T. L. (2003). Is there an American way of aging? Income dynamics of the elderly in the United States and Germany. *Research on Aging, 25,* 435–455.

Hunt, C. E. (2005). Gene-environment interactions: Implications for sudden unexpected deaths in infancy. *Archives of Disease in Childhood, 90,* 48–53.

Hunt, C. K. (2003). Concepts in caregiver research. *Journal of Nursing Scholarship, 35,* 27–32.

Hunter, J. P., & Csikszentmihalyi, M. (2003). The positive psychology of interested adolescents. *Journal of Youth and Adolescence, 32,* 27–35.

Huston, T. L., Caughlin, J. P., Houts, R. M., Smith, S. E., & George, L. J. (2001). The connubial crucible: Newlywed years as predictors of marital delight, distress, and divorce. *Journal of Personality and Social Psychology, 80,* 237–252.

Huth-Bocks, A. C., Levendosky, A. A., Bogat, G., & von Eye, A. (2004). The impact of maternal characteristics and contextual variables on infant-mother attachment. *Child Development, 75,* 480–496.

Huttenlocher, P. R. (1994). Synaptogenesis, synapse elimination, and neural plasticity in human cerebral cortex. In C. A. Nelson (Ed.), *Threats to optimal development: Integrating biological, psychological, and social risk factors* (pp. 35–54). Hillsdale, NJ: Erlbaum.

Huttenlocher, P. R. (2002). *Neural plasticity: The effects of environment on the development of the cerebral cortex.* Cambridge, MA: Harvard University Press.

Hvas, L. (2001). Positive aspects of menopause: A qualitative study. *Maturitas, 39,* 11–17.

Imai, M., Haryu, E., & Okada, H. (2005). Mapping novel nouns and verbs onto dynamic action events: Are verb meanings easier to learn than noun meanings for Japanese children? *Child Development, 76,* 340–355.

Institute of Medicine. (1997). Brandt, E. N., Jr., & Pope, A. M. (Eds.) *Enabling America: Assessing the role of rehabilitation science and engineering.* Washington, DC: National Academy Press.

Isaacs, S. L., & Schroeder, S. A. (2004). Class—The ignored determinant of the nation's health. *New England Journal of Medicine, 351,* 1137–1142.

Islam, M. K., & Gerdtham, U.-G. (2006). *The costs of maternal-newborn illness and mortality.* Geneva, Switzerland: World Health Organization.

Ito, M., & Sharts-Hopko, N. C. (2002). Japanese women's experience of childbirth in the United States. *Health Care For Women International, 23,* 666–677.

Jackson, L. M., Pratt, M. W., Hunsberger, B., & Pancer, S. M. (2005). Optimism as a mediator of the relation between perceived parental authoritativeness and adjustment among adolescents: Finding the sunny side of the street. *Social Development, 14,* 273–304.

Jacobson, J. L., & Jacobson, S. W. (1994). Prenatal alcohol exposure and neurobehavioral development: Where is the threshold? *Alcohol Health & Research World, 18,* 30–36.

Jaffee, S. R., Moffitt, T. E., Caspi, A., & Taylor, A. (2003). Life with (or without) father: The benefits of living with two biological parents depend on the father's antisocial behavior. *Child Development, 74,* 109–126.

Jain, A. E., & Lacy, T. (2005). Psychotropic drugs in pregnancy and lactation. *Journal of Psychiatric Practice, 11,* 177–191.

Jenkins, J. M., & Astington, J. W. (2000). Theory of mind and social behavior: Causal models tested in a longitudinal study. *Merrill-Palmer Quarterly, 46,* 203–220.

Jenkins, J. M., Turrell, S. L., Kogushi, Y., Lollis, S., & Ross, H. S. (2003). A longitudinal investigation of the dynamics of mental state talk in families. *Child Development, 74,* 905–920.

Jensen, A. R. (1992). Spearman's hypothesis: Methodology and evidence. *Multivariate Behavioral Research, 27,* 225–233.

Jensen, A. R. (1998). The suppressed relationship between IQ and the reaction time slope parameter of the Hick function. *Intelligence, 26,* 43–52.

Jenson, W. R., Olympia, D., Farley, M., & Clark, E. (2004). Positive psychology and externalizing students in a sea of negativity. *Psychology in the Schools, 41,* 67–79.

Jepsen, D. A., & Choudhuri, E. (2001). Stability and change in 25-year occupational career patterns. *Career Development Quarterly, 50,* 3–19.

Jette, A. M., Assmann, S. F., Rooks, D., Harris, B. A., & Crawford, S. (1998). Interrelationships among disablement concepts. *Journals of Gerontology: Series A: Biological Sciences and Medical Sciences, 53A,* M395-M404.

Jette, A. M., & Branch, L. G. (1992). A ten-year follow-up of driving patterns among the community-dwelling elderly. *Human Factors, 34,* 25–31.

Jette, A. M., Lachman, M., Giorgetti, M. M., Assmann, S. F., Harris, B. A., Levenson, C., Wernick, M., & Krebs, D. (1999). Exercise—It's never too late: The Strong-for-Life program. *American Journal of Public Health, 89,* 66–72.

Johnson, C. L., & Barer, B. M. (1997). *Life beyond 85 years: The aura of survivorship.* New York: Springer.

Johnson, F., & Wardle, J. (2005). Dietary restraint, body dissatisfaction, and psychological distress: A prospective analysis. *Journal of Abnormal Psychology, 114,* 119–125.

Johnson, M. H. (1998). The neural basis of cognitive development. In W. Damon (Series Ed.) & D. Kuhn & R. S. Siegler (Vol. Eds.), *Handbook of child psychology: Vol. 2. Cognition, perception, and language* (pp. 1–49). New York: Wiley.

Johnson, M. H. (2001). Functional brain development during infancy. In G. Bremner & A. Fogel (Eds.), *Blackwell handbook of infant development* (pp. 169–190). Malden, MA: Blackwell.

Johnson, N. E., & Climo, J. J. (2000). Aging and eldercare in lesser developed countries. *Journal of Family Issues, 21,* 683–691.

Johnson, R. W., & Crystal, S. (1997). Health insurance coverage at midlife: Characteristics, costs, and dynamics. *Health Care Financing Review, 18,* 123–148.

Johri, M., Beland, F., & Bergman, H. (2003). International experiments in integrated care for the elderly: A synthesis of the evidence. *International Journal of Geriatric Psychiatry, 18,* 222–235.

Jones, C. (1985). Father-infant relationships in the first year of life. In S. M. H. Hanson & F. W. Bozett (Eds.), *Dimensions of fatherhood* (pp. 92–114). Beverly Hills, CA: Sage.

Jones, G. W. (2005). The "flight from marriage" in south-east and east Asia. *Journal of Comparative Family Studies, 36,* 93–119.

Judge, D. S., & Carey, J. R. (2000). Postreproductive life predicted by primate patterns. *Journals of Gerontology: Series A: Biological Sciences and Medical Sciences, 55A,* B201-B209.

Jung, C. G. (1933). *Modern man in search of a soul.* Oxford, England: Harcourt.

Kaaja, E., Kaaja, R., & Hiilesmaa, V. (2003). Major malformations in offspring of women with epilepsy. *Neurology, 60,* 575–579.

Kabir, Z. N., Tishelman, C., Agüero-Torres, H., Chowdhury, A. M. R., Winblad, B., & Höjer, B. (2003). Gender and rural-urban differences in reported health status by older people in Bangladesh. *Archives of Gerontology and Geriatrics, 37,* 77–91.

Kacela, X. (2004). Religious maturity in the midst of death and dying. *American Journal of Hospice & Palliative Care, 21,* 203–208.

Kagan, J. (1984). *The nature of the child.* New York: Basic Books.

Kagan, J. (1994). *Galen's prophecy: Temperament in human nature.* New York: Basic Books.

Kagan, J. (1998). *Galen's prophecy: Temperament in human nature.* Boulder, CO: Westview Press.

Kallestad, J. H., & Olweus, D. (2003). Predicting teachers' and schools' implementation of the Olweus bullying prevention program: A multilevel study. *Prevention & Treatment, 6*(1).

Kaltiala-Heino, R., Kosunen, E., & Rimpela, M. (2003). Pubertal timing, sexual behaviour and self-reported depression in middle adolescence. *Journal of Adolescence, 26,* 531–545.

Kamin, L. J. (1974). *The science and politics of I.Q.* Oxford, England: Erlbaum.

Kanazawa, S. (2005). Is "discrimination" necessary to explain the sex gap in earnings? *Journal of Economic Psychology, 26,* 269–287.

Kane, R. A. (1995–1996). Transforming care institutions for the frail elderly: Out of one shall be many. *Generations, 14*(4), 62–68.

Kane, R. A., Kane, R. L., & Ladd, R. C. (1998). *The heart of long term care.* New York: Oxford University Press.

Kaplan, G. A. (1992). Health and aging in the Alameda County Study. In K. W. Schaie, D. G. Blazer, & J. S. House (Eds.), *Aging, health behaviors, and health outcomes* (pp. 69–88). Hillsdale, NJ: Erlbaum.

Kaplowitz, S. A., Osuch, J. R., Safron, D., & Campo, S. (1999). Physician communication with seriously ill cancer patients: Results of a survey of physicians. In B. de Vries (Ed.), *End of life issues: Interdisciplinary and multidimensional perspectives* (pp. 205–228). New York: Springer.

Karaman, Y., Erdogan, F., Köseoglu, E., Turan, T., & Ersoy, A. Ö. (2004). A 12-month study of the efficacy of rivastigmine in patients with advanced moderate Alzheimer's disease. *Dementia and Geriatric Cognitive Disorders, 19,* 51–56.

Karen, R. (1998). *Becoming attached: First relationships and how they shape our capacity to love.* London: Oxford University Press.

Karlsson, A. K., & Rosenhall, U. (1998). Aural rehabilitation in the elderly: Supply of hearing aids related to measured need and self-assessed hearing problems. *Scandinavian Audiology, 27,* 153–160.

Karney, B. R., & Bradbury, T. N. (1997). Neuroticism, marital interaction, and the trajectory of marital satisfaction. *Journal of Personality and Social Psychology, 72,* 1075–1092.

Karns, J. T. (2001). Health, nutrition, and safety. In G. Bremner & A. Fogel (Eds.), *Blackwell handbook of infant development* (pp. 693–725). Malden, MA: Blackwell.

Kasl-Godley, J., & Gatz, M. (2000). Psychosocial intervention for individuals with dementia: An intergration of theory, therapy, and a clinical understanding of dementia. *Clinical Psychology Review, 20,* 755–782.

Kastenbaum, R. (2004). *On our way: The final passage through life and death.* Berkeley, CA: University of California Press.

Kastenbaum, R. (2005). Is death better in utopia? *Illness, Crisis, & Loss, 13,* 31–48.

Kato, K., & Pedersen, N. L. (2005). Personality and coping: A study of twins reared apart and twins reared together. *Behavior Genetics, 35,* 147–158.

Kaufman, A. S. (2000). Seven questions about the WAIS-III regarding differences in abilities across the 16 to 89 year life span. *School Psychology Quarterly, 15,* 3–29.

Kaufman, A. S. (2001). WAIS-III IQs, Horn's theory, and generational changes from young adulthood to old age. *Intelligence, 29,* 131–167.

Kavale, K. A., & Forness, S. R. (2003). Learning disability as a discipline. In H. L. Swanson, K. R. Harris, & S. Graham (Eds.), *Handbook of learning disabilities* (pp. 76–93). New York: Guilford Press.

Keel, P. K., & Klump, K. L. (2003). Are eating disorders culture-bound syndromes? Implications for conceptualizing their etiology. *Psychological Bulletin, 129,* 747–769.

Keenan, K., & Hipwell, A. E. (2005). Preadolescent clues to understanding depression in girls. *Clinical Child and Family Psychology Review, 8,* 89–105.

Keller, M. A., & Goldberg, W. A. (2004). Co-sleeping: Help or hindrance for young children's independence? *Infant and Child Development, 13,* 369–388.

Kelley, A. E., Schochet, T., & Landry, C. F. (2004). Risk taking and novelty seeking in adolescence: Introduction to part I. In R. E. Dahl & L. P. Spear (Eds.), *Adolescent brain development: Vulnerabilities and opportunities* (Vol. 1021, pp. 27–32). New York: New York Academy of Sciences.

Kelley, M. L., Power, T. G., & Wimbush, D. D. (1992). Determinants of disciplinary practices in low-income Black mothers. *Child Development, 63,* 573–582.

Kelley, S. J., & Whitley, D. M. (2003). Psychological distress and physical health problems in grandparents raising grandchildren: Development of an empirically-based intervention model. In B. Hayslip, Jr. & J. H. Patrick (Eds.), *Working with custodial grandparents* (pp. 127–144). New York: Springer.

Kellman, P. J., & Banks, M. S. (1998). Infant visual perception. In W. Damon (Series Ed.) & D. Kuhn & R. S. Siegler (Vol. Eds.), *Handbook of child psychology: Volume 2: Cognition, perception, and language* (pp. 103–146). Hoboken, NJ: Wiley.

Kelly, E. L., & Conley, J. J. (1987). Personality and compatibility: A prospective analysis of marital stability and marital satisfaction. *Journal of Personality and Social Psychology, 52,* 27–40.

Kelly, J. B. (2000). Children's adjustment in conflicted marriage and divorce: A decade review of research. *Journal of the American Academy of Child & Adolescent Psychiatry, 39,* 963–973.

Kelly, J. B. (2003). Changing perspectives on children's adjustment following divorce: A view from the United States. *Childhood: A Global Journal of Child Research, 10,* 237–254.

Keltner, N. L., & Hall, S. (2005). Neonatal serotonin syndrome. *Perspectives in Psychiatric Care, 41,* 88–91.

Kemper, S., & Mitzner, T. L. (2001). Language production and comprehension. In J. E. Birren & K. W. Schaie (Eds.), *Handbook of the psychology of aging* (5th ed., pp. 378–398). San Diego, CA: Academic Press.

Kendall, J., Leo, M. C., Perrin, N., & Hatton, D. (2005). Service needs of families with children with ADHD. *Journal of Family Nursing, 11,* 264–288.

Kennedy, G. E. (1990). College students' expectations of grandparent and grandchild role behaviors. *Gerontologist, 30,* 43–48.

Kennedy, Q., Mather, M., & Carstensen, L. L. (2004). The role of motivation in the age-related positivity effect in autobiographical memory. *Psychological Science, 15,* 208–214.

Kenrick, D. T., Groth, G. E., Trost, M. R., & Sadalla, E. K. (1993). Integrating evolutionary and social exchange perspectives on relationships: Effects of gender, self-appraisal, and involvement level on mate selection criteria. *Journal of Personality and Social Psychology, 64,* 951–969.

Kensinger, E. A., Krendl, A. C., & Corkin, S. (2006). Memories of an emotional and a nonemotional event: Effects of aging and delay interval. *Experimental Aging Research, 32,* 23–45.

Keogh, B. K., & MacMillan, D. L. (1996). Exceptionality. In D. C. Berliner & R. C. Calfee (Eds.), *Handbook of educational psychology* (pp. 311–330). New York: Macmillan Library Reference.

Kerckhoff, A. C. (2002). The transition from school to work. In J. T. Mortimer & R. W. Larson (Eds.), *The changing adolescent experience: Societal trends and the transition to adulthood* (pp. 52–87). New York: Cambridge University Press.

Kerr, M., & Stattin, H. (2000). What parents know, how they know it, and several forms of adolescent adjustment: Further support for a reinterpretation of monitoring. *Developmental Psychology, 36,* 366–380.

Keski-Rahkonen, A., Bulik, C. M., Neale, B. M., Rose, R. J., Rissanen, A., & Kaprio, J. (2005). Body dissatisfaction and drive for thinness in young adult twins. *International Journal of Eating Disorders, 37,* 188–199.

Kessler, R. C., McGonagle, K. A., Zhao, S., Nelson, C. B., Hughes, M., Eshleman, S., Wittchen, H. U., & Kendler, K. S. (1994). Lifetime and 12-month prevalence of DSM-III-R psychiatric disorders in the United States: Results from the National Comorbidity Study. *Archives of General Psychiatry, 51,* 8–19.

Kidger, J. (2005). Stories of redemption? Teenage mothers as the new sex educators. *Sexualities, 8,* 481–496.

Kiernan, K. (2002). Cohabitation in Western Europe: Trends, issues, and implications. In A. Booth & A. C. Crouter (Eds.), *Just living together: Implications of cohabitation on families, children, and social policy* (pp. 3–31). Mahwah, NJ: Erlbaum.

Kiernan, K. (2004). Redrawing the boundaries of marriage. *Journal of Marriage and Family, 66,* 980–987.

Kim, J.-S., & Lee, E.-H. (2003). Cultural and noncultural predictors of health outcomes in Korean daughter and daughter-in-law caregivers. *Public Health Nursing, 20,* 111–119.

Kim-Cohen, J., Moffitt, T. E., Caspi, A., & Taylor, A. (2004). Genetic and environmental processes in young children's resilience and vulnerability to socioeconomic deprivation. *Child Development, 75,* 651–668.

Kim-Cohen, J., Moffitt, T. E., Taylor, A., Pawlby, S. J., & Caspi, A. (2005). Maternal depression and children's antisocial behavior: Nature and nurture effects. *Archives of General Psychiatry, 62,* 173–181.

King, V., Silverstein, M., Elder, G. H., Bengtson, V. L., & Conger, R. D. (2003). Relations with grandparents: Rural midwest versus urban Southern California. *Journal of Family Issues, 24,* 1044–1069.

Kinsella, K. (2000). Demographic dimensions of global aging. *Journal of Family Issues, 21,* 541–558.

Kinsella, K. (2005). Future longevity-demographic concerns and consequences. *Journal of the American Geriatrics Society, 53*(Suppl. l9), S299–S303.

Kinsella, K., & Velkoff, V. A. (2001). *An aging world: 2001* (Series P95/01-1). Washington, DC: U.S. Census Bureau.

Kirkwood, T. B. L. (1999). *Time of our lives: The science of human aging.* New York: Oxford University Press.

Kisilevsky, B. S., Muir, D. W., & Low, J. A. (1992). Maturation of human fetal responses to vibroacoustic stimulation. *Child Development, 63,* 1497–1508.

Kitahara, M. (1989). Childhood in Japanese culture. *Journal of Psychohistory, 17,* 43–72.

Kitayama, S., Markus, H. R., Matsumoto, H., & Norasakkunkit, V. (1997). Individual and collective processes in the construction of the self: Self-enhancement in the United States and self-criticism in Japan. *Journal of Personality and Social Psychology, 72,* 1245–1267.

Kitzinger, S. (2000). *Rediscovering birth.* New York: Pocket Books.

Klass, D., & Goss, R. (2003). The politics of grief and continuing bonds with the dead: The cases of Maoist China and Wahhabi Islam. *Death Studies, 27,* 787–811.

Klass, D., & Walter, T. (2001). Processes of grieving: How bonds are continued. In M. S. Stroebe, R. O. Hansson, W. Stroebe, & H. Schut (Eds.), *Handbook of bereavement research: Consequences, coping, and care* (1st ed., pp. 431–448). Washington, DC: American Psychological Association.

Klein, J. D., & Committee on Adolescence. (2005). Adolescent pregnancy: Current trends and issues. *Pediatrics, 116,* 281–286.

Klusmann, D. (2002). Sexual motivation and the duration of partnership. *Archives of Sexual Behavior, 31,* 275–287.

Knox, D., Zusman, M. E., Buffington, C., & Hemphill, G. (2000). Interracial dating attitudes among college students. *College Student Journal, 34,* 69–71.

Koball, H., & Douglas-Hall, A. (2005). Most low-income parents are employed. Retrieved March 28, 2006, from Columbia University, National Center for Children in Poverty Web site: http://www.nccp.org/pub_pel05.html

Kochanska, G. (1995). Children's temperament, mother's discipline, and security of attachment: Multiple pathways to emerging internalization. *Child Development, 66,* 597–615.

Kochanska, G. (1997). Multiple pathways to conscience for children with different temperaments: From toddlerhood to age 5. *Developmental Psychology, 33,* 228–240.

Kochanska, G. (1998). Mother-child relationship, child fearfulness, and emerging attachment: A short-term longitudinal study. *Developmental Psychology, 34,* 480–490.

Kochanska, G. (2002). Committed compliance, moral self, and internalization: A mediational model. *Developmental Psychology, 38,* 339–351.

Kochanska, G., Aksan, N., & Carlson, J. J. (2005). Temperament, relationships, and young children's receptive cooperation with their parents. *Developmental Psychology, 41,* 648–660.

Kochanska, G., Aksan, N., Knaack, A., & Rhines, H. M. (2004). Maternal parenting and children's conscience: Early security as moderator. *Child Development, 75,* 1229–1242.

Kochanska, G., & Coy, K. C. (2002). Child emotionality and maternal responsiveness as predictors of reunion behaviors in the Strange Situation: Links mediated and unmediated by separation distress. *Child Development, 73,* 228–240.

Kochanska, G., Coy, K. C., & Murray, K. T. (2001). The development of self-regulation in the first four years of life. *Child Development, 72,* 1091–1111.

Kochanska, G., Gross, J. N., Lin, M.-H., & Nichols, K. E. (2002). Guilt in young children: Development, determinants, and relations with a broader system of standards. *Child Development, 73,* 461–482.

Kochanska, G., & Knaack, A. (2003). Effortful control as a personality characteristic of young children: Antecedents, correlates, and consequences. *Journal of Personality, 71,* 1087–1112.

Kochanska, G., & Murray, K. T. (2000). Mother-child mutually responsive orientation and conscience development: From toddler to early school age. *Child Development, 71,* 417–431.

Kohen, D. E., Brooks-Gunn, J., Leventhal, T., & Hertzman, C. (2002). Neighborhood income and physical and social disorder in Canada: Associations with young children's competencies. *Child Development, 73,* 1844–1860.

Kohlberg, L. (1966). Moral education in the schools: A developmental view. *School Review, 74,* 1–30.

Kohlberg, L. (1981). *The meaning and measurement of moral development.* Worcester, MA: Clark University Press.

Kohlberg, L. (1984). *The psychology of moral development: The nature and validity of moral stages.* San Francisco: Harper & Row.

Konner, M. J. (1976). Relations among infants and juveniles in comparative perspective. *Social Science Information, 15,* 371–402.

Koren-Karie, N., Sagi-Schwartz, A., & Egoz-Mizrachi, N. (2005). The emotional quality of childcare centers in Israel: The Haifa study of early childcare. *Infant Mental Health Journal, 26,* 110–126.

Kornhaber, M., Fierros, E. G., & Veenema, S. A. (2004). *Multiple intelligences: Best ideas from research and practice.* Boston: Pearson/A and B.

Kornhaber, M., & Gardner, H. (2006). Multiple intelligences: Developments in implementation and theory. In M. A. Constas & R. J. Sternberg (Eds.), *Translating theory and research into educational practice: Developments in content domains, large-scale reform, and intellectual capacity* (pp. 255–276). Mahwah, NJ: Erlbaum.

Kornhaber, M., & Krechevsky, M. (1995). Expanding definitions of teaching and learning: Notes from the MI underground. In P. W. Cookson & B. L. Schneider (Eds.), *Transforming schools.* New York: Garland.

Kosir, K., & Pecjak, S. (2005). Sociometry as a method for investigating peer relationships: What does it actually measure? *Educational Research, 47,* 127–144.

Kotimaa, A. J., Moilanen, I., Taanila, A., Ebeling, H., Smalley, S. L., McGough, J. J., Hartikainen, A.-L., & Jarvelin, M.-R. (2003). Maternal smoking and hyperactivity in 8-year-old children. *Journal of the American Academy of Child & Adolescent Psychiatry, 42,* 826–833.

Kotlowitz, A. (1992). *There are no children here: The story of two boys growing up in the other America.* New York: Anchor Books.

Kozol, J. (1988). *Rachel and her children: Homeless families in America.* New York: Crown.

Kozol, J. (1991). *Savage inequalities: Children in America's schools.* New York: Crown.

Kozol, J. (2005). *The shame of the nation: The restoration of apartheid schooling in America.* New York: Crown.

Kramer, B. J., & Thompson, E. H. (2002). *Men as caregivers: Theory, research, and service implications.* New York: Springer.

Krampe, R. T., & Baltes, P. B. (2003). Intelligence as adaptive resource development and resource allocation: A new look through the lenses of SOC and expertise. In R. J. Sternberg & E. L. Grigorenko (Eds.), *The psychology of abilities, competencies, and expertise* (pp. 31–68). New York: Cambridge University Press.

Kreicbergs, U., Valdimarsdóttir, U., Onelöv, E., Henter, J.-I., & Steineck, G. (2004). Talking about death with children who have severe malignant disease. *New England Journal of Medicine, 351,* 1175–1186.

Kroger, J. (2000). *Identity development: Adolescence through adulthood.* Thousand Oaks, CA: Sage.

Kroger, J., & Haslett, S. J. (1991). A comparison of ego identity status transition pathways and change rates across five identity domains. *International Journal of Aging & Human Development, 32,* 303–330.

Krueger, R. F., Schmutte, P. S., Caspi, A., Moffitt, T. E., Campbell, K., & Silva, P. A. (1994). Personality traits are linked to crime among men and women: Evidence from a birth cohort. *Journal of Abnormal Psychology, 103,* 328–338.

Krumm, J. (2002). Genetic discrimination: Why Congress must ban genetic testing in the workplace. *Journal of Legal Medicine, 23,* 491–521.

Kübler-Ross, E. (1969). *On death and dying.* New York: Macmillan.

Kuhn, D. (1989). Children and adults as intuitive scientists. *Psychological Review, 96,* 674–689.

Kunnen, E. S., & Bosma, H. A. (2003). Fischer's skill theory applied to identity development: A response to Kroger. *Identity, 3,* 247–270.

Kupersmidt, J. B., Coie, J. D., & Dodge, K. A. (1990). The role of poor peer relationships in the development of disorder. In S. R. Asher & J. D. Coie (Eds.), *Peer rejection in childhood* (pp. 274–305). New York: Cambridge University Press.

Kurdek, L. A. (2002). Predicting the timing of separation and marital satisfaction: An eight-year prospective longitudinal study. *Journal of Marriage and Family, 64,* 163–179.

Laakkonen, M.-L., Pitkala, K. H., Strandberg, T. E., Berglind, S., & Tilvis, R. S. (2004). Living will, resuscitation preferences, and attitudes towards life in an aged population. *Gerontology, 50,* 247–254.

Labouvie-Vief, G. (1992). A neo-Piagetian perspective on adult cognitive development. In R. J. Sternberg & C. A. Berg (Eds.), *Intellectual development* (pp. 197–228). New York: Cambridge University Press.

Labouvie-Vief, G., Hakim-Larson, J., & Hobart, C. J. (1987). Age, ego level, and the life-span development of coping and defense processes. *Psychology and Aging, 2,* 286–293.

Lachman, M. E. (2004). Development in midlife. *Annual Review of Psychology, 55,* 305–331.

Lachman, M. E., & Bertrand, R. M. (2001). Personality and the self in midlife. In M. E. Lachman (Ed.), *Handbook of midlife development* (pp. 279–309). Hoboken, NJ: Wiley.

Laessle, R. G., Uhl, H., & Lindel, B. (2001). Parental influences on eating behavior in obese and nonobese preadolescents. *International Journal of Eating Disorders, 30,* 447–453.

Laible, D. J. (2004). Mother-child discourse surrounding a child's past behavior at 30 months: Links to emotional understanding and early conscience development at 36 months. *Merrill-Palmer Quarterly, 50,* 159–180.

Laible, D. J., & Thompson, R. A. (2000). Mother-child discourse, attachment security, shared positive affect, and early conscience development. *Child Development, 71,* 1424–1440.

Laible, D. J., & Thompson, R. A. (2002). Mother-child conflict in the toddler years: Lessons in emotion, morality, and relationships. *Child Development, 73,* 1187–1203.

Laird, R. D., Pettit, G. S., Dodge, K. A., & Bates, J. E. (2005). Peer relationship antecedents of delinquent behavior in late adolescence: Is there evidence of demographic group differences in developmental processes? *Development and Psychopathology, 17,* 127–144.

Lam, T. H., Shi, H. J., Ho, L. M., Stewart, S. M., & Fan, S. (2002). Timing of pubertal maturation and heterosexual behavior among Hong Kong Chinese adolescents. *Archives of Sexual Behavior, 31,* 359–366.

Lamb, M. E. (1986). The changing role of fathers. In M. E. Lamb (Ed.), *The father's role: Applied perspectives* (pp. 3–27). New York: Wiley.

Lamb, M. E. (1997). *The role of the father in child development* (3rd ed.). Hoboken, NJ: Wiley.

Lamb, M. E. (2002). Infant-father attachments and their impact on child development. In C. S. Tamis-LeMonda & N. Cabrera (Eds.), *Handbook of father involvement: Multidisciplinary perspectives* (pp. 93–117). Mahwah, NJ: Erlbaum.

Lambert, S., Sampaio, E., Mauss, Y., & Scheiber, C. (2004). Blindness and brain plasticity: Contribution of mental imagery? An fMRI study. *Cognitive Brain Research, 20,* 1–11.

Lamerz, A., Kuepper-Nybelen, J., Wehle, C., Bruning, N., Trost-Brinkhues, G., Brenner, H., Hebebrand, J., & Herpertz-Dahlmann, B. (2005). Social class, parental education, and obesity prevalence in a study of six-year-old children in Germany. *International Journal of Obesity, 29,* 373–380.

Langa, K. M., Foster, N. L., & Larson, E. B. (2004). Mixed dementia: Emerging concepts and therapeutic implications. *Journal of the American Medical Association, 292,* 2901–2908.

Larson, E. B., Shadlen, M. F., Wang, L., McCormick, W. C., Bowen, J. D., Teri, L., & Kukull, W. A. (2004). Survival after initial diagnosis of Alzheimer disease. *Annals of Internal Medicine, 140,* 501–509.

Larson, R., & Kleiber, D. (1993). Daily experience of adolescents. In P. H. Tolan & B. J. Cohler (Eds.), *Handbook of clinical research and practice with adolescents* (pp. 125–145). New York: Wiley.

Larson, R. W., Richards, M. H., Moneta, G., Holmbeck, G., & Duckett, E. (1996). Changes in adolescents' daily interactions with their families from ages 10 to 18: Disengagement and transformation. *Developmental Psychology, 32,* 744–754.

Larzelere, R. E. (1994). Should the use of corporal punishment by parents be considered child abuse? No. In M. A. Mason & E. Gambrill (Eds.), *Debating children's lives: Current controversies on children and adolescents* (pp. 204–209, 217–218). Thousand Oaks, CA: Sage.

Larzelere, R. E. (1996). A review of the outcomes of parental use of nonabusive or customary physical punishment. *Pediatrics, 98,* 824–828.

Larzelere, R. E. (2000). Child outcomes of nonabusive and customary physical punishment by parents: An updated literature review. *Clinical Child and Family Psychology Review, 4,* 199–221.

Larzelere, R. E., & Johnson, B. (1999). Evaluations of the effects if Sweden's spanking ban on physical child abuse rates: A literature review. *Psychological Reports, 85,* 381–392.

Larzelere, R. E., & Kuhn, B. R. (2005). Comparing child outcomes of physical punishment and alternative disciplinary tactics: A meta-analysis. *Clinical Child and Family Psychology Review, 8,* 1–37.

Latz, S., Wolf, A. W., & Lozoff, B. (1999). Cosleeping in context: Sleep practices and problems in young children in Japan and the United States. *Archives of Pediatrics & Adolescent Medicine, 153,* 339–346.

Laumann, E. O., Ellingson, S., Mahay, J., Paik, A., & Youm, Y. (Eds.). (2004). *The sexual organization of the city.* Chicago: University of Chicago Press.

Laumann, E. O., Gagnon, J. H., Michael, R. T., & Michaels, S. (1994). *The social organization of sexuality: Sexual practices in the United States.* Chicago: University of Chicago Press.

Laursen, B., & Collins, W. A. (1994). Interpersonal conflict during adolescence. *Psychological Bulletin, 115,* 197–209.

Lautenschlager, N. T., & Almeida, O. P. (2006). Physical activity and cognition in old age. *Current Opinion in Psychiatry, 19,* 190–193.

Lavelli, M., & Fogel, A. (2005). Developmental changes in the relationship between the infant's attention and emotion during early face-to-face communication: The 2-month transition. *Developmental Psychology, 41,* 265–280.

Lawrence, F. R., & Blair, C. (2003). Factorial invariance in preventive intervention: Modeling the development of intelligence in low birth weight, preterm infants. *Prevention Science, 4,* 249–261.

Lawson, M. A. (2003). School-family relations in context: Parent and teacher perceptions of parent involvement. *Urban Education, 38,* 77–133.

Lawton, M. P. (1977). The impact of environment on aging and behavior. In J. E. Birren & K. W. Schaie (Eds.), *Handbook of the psychology of aging* (pp. 276–301). New York: Van Nostrand Reinhold.

Lazarov, M., & Evans, A. (2000). Breast-feeding—Encouraging the best for low-income women. *Zero to Three, 21*(1), 15–23.

Leary, A., & Katz, L. F. (2005). Observations of aggressive children during peer provocation and with a best friend. *Developmental Psychology, 41,* 124–134.

Leavitt, J. W. (1986). *Brought to bed: Childbearing in America, 1750 to 1950.* New York: Oxford University Press.

Lecanuet, J. P., Graniere-Deferre, C., Jacquet, A. Y., & DeCasper, A. J. (2000). Fetal discrimination of low-pitched musical notes. *Developmental Psychobiology, 36,* 29–39.

LeClere, F. B., & Wilson, J. B. (1997). *Advance data from vital and health statistics: No. 288. Smoking behavior of recent mothers, 18–44 years of age, before and after pregnancy: United States, 1990* (PHS 97-1250). Hyattsville, MD: National Center for Health Statistics.

Lee, C. (2006). Exploring teachers' definitions of bullying. *Emotional & Behavioural Difficulties, 11,* 61–75.

Lee, J., Super, C. M., & Harkness, S. (2003). Self-perception of competence in Korean children: Age, sex and home influences. *Asian Journal of Social Psychology, 6,* 133–147.

Lee, K., Cameron, C. A., Xu, F., Fu, G., & Board, J. (1997). Chinese and Canadian children's evaluations of lying and truth telling: Similarities and differences in the context of pro- and antisocial behaviors. *Child Development, 68,* 924–934.

Lee, V. E., & Burkam, D. T. (2002). *Inequality at the starting gate: Social background differences in achievement as children begin school.* Washington, DC: Economic Policy Institute.

Lee, W. K. M., & Law, K. W.-K. (2004). Retirement planning and retirement satisfaction: The need for a national retirement program and policy in Hong Kong. *Journal of Applied Gerontology, 23,* 212–233.

Leitner, Y., Fattal-Valevski, A., Geva, R., Bassan, H., Posner, E., Kutai, M., Many, A., Jaffa, A. J., & Harel, S. (2000). Six-year follow-up of children with intrauterine growth retardation: Long-term, prospective study. *Journal of Child Neurology, 15,* 781–786.

Leming, M. R. (2003). The history of the hospice approach. In C. D. Bryant (Ed.), *Handbook of death & dying* (pp. 485–494). Thousand Oaks, CA: Sage.

Leon, G. R., Fulkerson, J. A., Perry, C. L., Keel, P. K., & Klump, K. L. (1999). Three to four year prospective evaluation of personality and behavioral risk factors for later disordered eating in adolescent girls and boys. *Journal of Youth and Adolescence, 28,* 181–196.

Leon-Carrion, J., Garcia-Orza, J., & Perez-Santamaria, F. J. (2004). Development of the inhibitory component of the executive functions in children and adolescents. *International Journal of Neuroscience, 114,* 1291–1311.

Lepper, M. R., Corpus, J. H., & Iyengar, S. S. (2005). Intrinsic and extrinsic motivational orientations in the classroom: Age differences and academic correlates. *Journal of Educational Psychology, 97,* 184–196.

Lepper, M. R., Greene, D., & Nisbett, R. E. (1973). Undermining children's intrinsic interest with extrinsic reward: A test of the "overjustification" hypothesis. *Journal of Personality and Social Psychology, 28,* 129–137.

Lepper, M. R., Sethi, S., Dialdin, D., & Drake, M. (1997). Intrinsic and extrinsic motivation: A developmental perspective. In S. S. Luthar, J. A. Burack, D. Cicchetti, & J. R. Weisz (Eds.), *Developmental psychopathology: Perspectives on adjustment, risk, and disorder* (pp. 23–50). New York: Cambridge University Press.

Lerner, J. V., & Lerner, R. M. (1994). Explorations of the goodness-of-fit model in early adolescence. In W. B. Carey & S. C. McDevitt (Eds.), *Prevention and early intervention: Individual differences as risk factors for the mental health of children: A festschrift for Stella Chess and Alexander Thomas* (pp. 161–169). Philadelphia: Brunner/Mazel.

Lerner, R. M. (1998). Theories of human development: Contemporary perspectives. In W. Damon (Series Ed.) & R. M. Lerner (Vol. Ed.), *Handbook of child psychology: Vol. 1: Theoretical models of human development* (5th ed., pp. 1–24). Hoboken, NJ: Wiley.

Lerner, R. M. (2003). What are SES effects effects of? A developmental systems perspective. In M. H. Bornstein & R. H. Bradley (Eds.), *Socioeconomic status, parenting, and child development* (pp. 231–255). Mahwah, NJ: Erlbaum.

Lerner, R. M., Dowling, E., & Roth, S. L. (2003). Contributions of lifespan psychology to the future elaboration of developmental systems theory. In U. M. Staudinger & U. Lindenberger (Eds.), *Understanding human development: Dialogues with lifespan psychology* (pp. 413–422). Dordrecht, Netherlands: Kluwer Academic.

Lerner, R. M., Dowling, E. M., & Anderson, P. M. (2003). Positive youth development: Thriving as the basis of personhood and civil society. *Applied Developmental Science, 7,* 172–180.

Lerner, R. M., Lerner, J. V., Almerigi, J. B., Theokas, C., Phelps, E., Gestsdottir, S., Naudeau, S., Jelicic, H., Alberts, A., Ma, L., Smith, L. M., Bobek, D. L., Richman-Raphael, D., Simpson, I., Christiansen, E. D., & von Eye, A. (2005). Positive youth development, participation in community youth development programs, and community contributions of fifth-grade adolescents: Findings from the first wave of the 4-H Study of Positive Youth Development. *Journal of Early Adolescence, 25,* 17–71.

Levande, D. I., Herrick, J. M., & Sung, K.-T. (2000). Eldercare in the United States and South Korea: Balancing family and community support. *Journal of Family Issues, 21,* 632–651.

Leveille, S. G., Penninx, B. W. J. H., Melzer, D., Izmirlian, G., & Guralnik, J. M. (2000). Sex differences in the prevalence of mobility disability in old age: The dynamics of incidence, recovery, and mortality. *Journals of Gerontology: Series B: Psychological Sciences and Social Sciences, 55B,* S41-S50.

Lewis, M. (1992). *Shame: The exposed self.* New York: Free Press.

Lewis, M., Sullivan, M. W., Stanger, C., & Weiss, M. (1989). Self development and self-conscious emotions. *Child Development, 60,* 146–156.

Lewis, M. W. (2003). Maternal-fetal bonding among pregnant women attending prenatal care: An ecological model. *Dissertation Abstracts International 63*(10), 3730A. (UMI No. 3066870)

Li, R., Ogden, C., Ballew, C., Gillespie, C., & Grummer-Strawn, L. (2002). Prevalence of exclusive breastfeeding among US infants: The third National Health and Nutrition Examination Survey (Phase II, 1991–1994). *American Journal of Public Health, 92,* 1107–1110.

Li, R., Zhao, Z., Mokdad, A., Barker, L., & Grummer-Strawn, L. (2003). Prevalence of breastfeeding in the United States: The 2001 National Immunization Survey. *Pediatrics, 111,* 1198–1201.

Li, S.-C., Lindenberger, U., Hommel, B., Aschersleben, G., Prinz, W., & Baltes, P. B. (2004). Transformations in the couplings among intellectual abilities and constituent cognitive processes across the life span. *Psychological Science, 15,* 155–163.

Lichter, D. T., Batson, C. D., & Brown, J. B. (2004). Welfare reform and marriage promotion: The marital expectations and desires of single and cohabiting mothers. *Social Service Review, 78,* 2–25.

Liddle, J., & McKenna, K. (2003). Older drivers and driving cessation. *British Journal of Occupational Therapy, 66,* 125–132.

Lieberman, A. F. (1993). *The emotional life of the toddler.* New York: Free Press.

Light, R. J. (2001). *Making the most of college: Students speak their minds.* Cambridge, MA: Harvard University Press.

Lightfoot, C. (1997). *The culture of adolescent risk-taking.* New York: Guilford Press.

Lillard, A. S. (1998). Playing with a theory of mind. In O. N. Saracho & B. Spodek (Eds.), *Multiple perspectives on play in early childhood education* (pp. 11–33). Albany, NY: State University of New York Press.

Lillard, A. S., Zeljo, A., Curenton, S., & Kaugars, A. S. (2000). Children's understanding of the animacy constraint on pretense. *Merrill-Palmer Quarterly, 46,* 21–44.

Lindemann, E. (1944). Symptomatology and management of acute grief. *American Journal of Psychiatry, 101,* 141–148.

Lindsay, J., Sykes, E., McDowell, I., Verreault, R., & Laurin, D. (2004). More than the epidemiology of Alzheimer's disease: Contributions of the Canadian Study of Health and Aging. *Canadian Journal of Psychiatry, 49,* 83–91.

Liotti, M., Pliszka, S. R., Perez, R., Kothmann, D., & Woldorff, M. G. (2005). Abnormal brain activity related to performance monitoring and error detection in children with ADHD. *Cortex, 41,* 377–388.

Lipsitt, L. P. (2003). Crib death: A biobehavioral phenomenon? *Current Directions in Psychological Science, 12,* 164–170.

Little, M., & Sayers, E.-J. (2004). While there's life . . . hope and the experience of cancer. *Social Science & Medicine, 59,* 1329–1337.

Lock, A. (2001). Preverbal communication. In G. Bremner & A. Fogel (Eds.), *Blackwell handbook of infant development* (pp. 370–403). Malden, MA: Blackwell.

Loeb, S., Fuller, B., Kagan, S. L., & Carrol, B. (2004). Child care in poor communities: Early learning effects of type, quality, and stability. *Child Development, 75,* 47–65.

Logsdon, M., & Davis, D. W. (2003). Professional support for pregnant and parenting women. *MCN: The American Journal of Maternal/Child Nursing, 28,* 371–376.

Long, S. O. (2004). Cultural scripts for a good death in Japan and the United States: Similarities and differences. *Social Science & Medicine, 58,* 913–928.

López Bernal, A. (2001). Timing of parturition. *Lancet, 358*(Suppl. 1), S51.

Lorenz, K. (1935). Der Kumpan in der Umwelt des Vogels. Der Artgenosse als auslosendes Moment sozialer Verhaltungsweisen. [The companion in the bird's world. The fellow-member of the species as releasing factor of social behavior.]. *Journal fur Ornithologie. Beiblatt. (Leipzig), 83,* 137–213.

Losel, F., & Beelmann, A. (2003). Effects of child skills training in preventing antisocial behavior: A systematic review of randomized evaluations. *Annals of the American Academy of Political and Social Science, 587,* 84–109.

Love, J. M., Harrison, L., Sagi-Schwartz, A., Van IJzendoorn, M. H., Ross, C., Ungerer, J. A., Raikes, H., Brady-Smith, C., Boller, K., Brooks-Gunn, J., Constantine, J., Kisker, E. E., Paulsell, D., & Chazan-Cohen, R. (2003). Child care quality matters: How conclusions may vary with context. *Child Development, 74,* 1021–1033.

Lowenstein, L. F. (2005). Causes and associated features of divorce as seen by recent research. *Journal of Divorce & Remarriage, 42,* 153–171.

Lucht, M., Schaub, R. T., Meyer, C., Hapke, U., Rumpf, H. J., Bartels, T., von Houwald, J., Barnow, S., Freyberger, H. J., Dilling, H., & John, U. (2003). Gender differences in unipolar depression: A general population survey of adults between age 18 to 64 of German nationality. *Journal of Affective Disorders, 77,* 203–211.

Luciana, M. (2003). Cognitive development in children born preterm: Implications for theories of brain plasticity following early injury. *Development and Psychopathology, 15,* 1017–1047.

Luna, B., Garver, K. E., Urban, T. A., Lazar, N. A., & Sweeney, J. A. (2004). Maturation of cognitive processes from late childhood to adulthood. *Child Development, 75,* 1357–1372.

Luster, T., Bates, L., Fitzgerald, H., Vandenbelt, M., & Key, J. P. (2000). Factors related to successful outcomes among preschool children born to low-income adolescent mothers. *Journal of Marriage and Family, 62,* 133–146.

Luszcz, M. A., Bryan, J., & Kent, P. (1997). Predicting episodic memory performance of very old men and women: Contributions from age, depression, activity, cognitive ability, and speed. *Psychology and Aging, 12,* 340–351.

Lynam, D., Moffitt, T. E., & Stouthamer-Loeber, M. (1993). Explaining the relation between IQ and delinquency: Class, race, test motivation, school failure, or self-control? *Journal of Abnormal Psychology, 102,* 187–196.

Lyons-Ruth, K., & Jacobvitz, D. (1999). Attachment disorganization: Unresolved loss, relational violence, and lapses in behavioral and attentional strategies. In J. Cassidy & P. R. Shaver (Eds.), *Handbook of attachment: Theory, research, and clinical applications* (pp. 520–554). New York: Guilford Press.

MacBrayer, E. K., Milich, R., & Hundley, M. (2003). Attributional biases in aggressive children and their mothers. *Journal of Abnormal Psychology, 112,* 698–708.

Maccoby, E. E. (1990). Gender and relationships: A developmental account. *American Psychologist, 45,* 513–520.

Maccoby, E. E. (1998). *The two sexes: Growing up apart, coming together.* Cambridge, MA: Belknap Press of Harvard University Press.

Maccoby, E. E. (2002). Gender and group process: A developmental perspective. *Current Directions in Psychological Science, 11,* 54–58.

Maccoby, E. E., & Jacklin, C. N. (1987). Gender segregation in childhood. In H. W. Reese (Ed.), *Advances in child development and behavior* (Vol. 20, pp. 239–287). San Diego, CA: Academic Press.

Maccoby, E. E., & Martin, J. A. (1983). Socialization in the context of the family: Parent-child interaction. In P. H. Mussen (Series Ed.) & E. M. Hethenington (Vol. Ed.), *Handbook of child psychology: Vol. 4. Socialization, personality, and social development* (4th ed., pp. 1–101). New York: Wiley.

Mace, N. L., & Rabins, P. V. (1999). *The 36-hour day: A family guide to caring for persons with Alzheimer disease, related dementing illnesses, and memory loss in later life* (3rd ed.). Baltimore: Johns Hopkins University Press.

Macfarlane, A. (1975). Olfaction in the development of social preferences in the human neonate, *Ciba Foundation Symposium: Vol. 33. Parent-infant interactions* (pp. 103–117). New York: Elsevier.

Mackenbach, J. P., & Bakker, M. J. (2003). Tackling socioeconomic inequalities in health: Analysis of European experiences. *Lancet, 362,* 1409–1414.

Magnusson, D., Stattin, H., & Allen, V. L. (1985). Biological maturation and social development: A longitudinal study of some adjustment processes from mid-adolescence to adulthood. *Journal of Youth and Adolescence, 14,* 267–283.

Maguen, S., Floyd, F. J., Bakeman, R., & Armistead, L. (2002). Developmental milestones and disclosure of sexual orientation among gay, lesbian, and bisexual youths. *Journal of Applied Developmental Psychology, 23,* 219–233.

Mahoney, J. L., Larson, R., & Eccles, J. S. (Eds.). (2005). *Organized activities as contexts of development: Extracurricular activities, after-school, and community programs.* Mahwah, NJ: Erlbaum.

Mahoney, J. L., Larson, R. W., Eccles, J. S., & Lord, H. (2005). Organized activities as development contexts for children and adolescents. In J. L. Mahoney, R. W. Larson, & J. S. Eccles (Eds.), *Organized activities as contexts of development: Extracurricular activities, after-school and community programs* (pp. 3–22). Mahwah, NJ: Erlbaum.

Main, M., Hesse, E., & Kaplan, N. (2005). Predictability of attachment behavior and representational processes at 1, 6, and 19 years of age: The Berkeley Longitudinal Study. In K. E. Grossmann, K. Grossmann, & E. Waters (Eds.), *Attachment from infancy to adulthood: The major longitudinal studies* (pp. 245–304). New York: Guilford Press.

Manchester, W. R. (1983). *The last lion, Winston Spencer Churchill: Vol. 1. Visions of glory, 1874–1932.* Boston: Little, Brown.

Mao, A., Burnham, M. M., Goodlin-Jones, B. L., Gaylor, E. E., & Anders, T. F. (2004). A comparison of the sleep-wake patterns of cosleeping and solitary-sleeping infants. *Child Psychiatry & Human Development, 35,* 95–105.

Maratos, O. (1998). Neonatal, early and later imitation: Same order phenomena? In F. Simion & G. Butterworth (Eds.), *The development of sensory, motor and cognitive capacities in early infancy: From perception to cognition* (pp. 145–160). Hove, England: Psychology Press.

March of Dimes Birth Defects Foundation. (2005). During your pregnancy: Amniocentesis. Retrieved January 21, 2006, from http://www.marchofdimes.com/pnhec/159_520.asp

Marcia, J. E. (1966). Development and validation of ego-identity status. *Journal of Personality & Social Psychology, 3,* 551–558.

Marcia, J. E. (1987). The identity status approach to the study of ego identity development. In T. Honess & K. Yardley (Eds.), *Self and identity: Perspectives across the lifespan* (pp. 161–171). New York: Routledge.

Marieb, E. N. (2004). *Human anatomy & physiology* (6th ed.). New York: Pearson Education.

Marin, B. V., Kirby, D. B., Hudes, E. S., Coyle, K. K., & Gomez, C. A. (2006). Boyfriends, girlfriends and teenagers' risk of sexual involvement. *Perspectives on Sexual and Reproductive Health, 38,* 76–83.

Markstrom, C. A., & Iborra, A. (2003). Adolescent identity formation and rites of passage: The Navajo Kinaaldá ceremony for girls. *Journal of Research on Adolescence, 13,* 399–425.

Markus, H. R., & Kitayama, S. (1991). Culture and the self: Implications for cognition, emotion, and motivation. *Psychological Review, 98,* 224–253.

Markus, H. R., & Kitayama, S. (1994). A collective fear of the collective: Implications for selves and theories of selves. *Personality and Social Psychology Bulletin, 20,* 568–579.

Markus, H. R., & Kitayama, S. (1998). The cultural psychology of personality. *Journal of Cross-Cultural Psychology, 29,* 63–87.

Marlier, L., Schaal, B., & Soussignan, R. (1998). Neonatal responsiveness to the odor of amniotic and lacteal fluids: A test of perinatal chemosensory continuity. *Child Development, 69,* 611–623.

Marmot, M. (1999). Epidemiology of socioeconomic status and health: Are determinants within countries the same as between countries? In N. E. Adler, M. Marmot, B. S. McEwen, & J. Stewart (Eds.), *Socioeconomic status and health in industrial nations: Social, psychological, and biological pathways* (pp. 16–29). New York: New York Academy of Sciences.

Marsh, H. W. (1993). The multidimensional structure of academic self-concept: Invariance over gender and age. *American Educational Research Journal, 30,* 841–860.

Marsh, H. W., Craven, R., & Debus, R. (1999). Separation of competency and affect components of multiple dimensions of academic self-concept: A developmental perspective. *Merrill-Palmer Quarterly, 45,* 567–601.

Marsiglio, W. (2004). When stepfathers claim stepchildren: A conceptual analysis. *Journal of Marriage and Family, 66,* 22–39.

Martin, C. L., & Dinella, L. M. (2002). Children's gender cognitions, the social environment, and sex differences in cognitive domains. In A. McGillicuddy-De Lisi & R. De Lisi (Eds.), *Biology, society, and behavior: The development of sex differences in cognition* (pp. 207–239). Westport, CT: Ablex.

Martin, C. L., & Fabes, R. A. (2001). The stability and consequences of young children's same-sex peer interactions. *Developmental Psychology, 37,* 431–446.

Martin, D. (2002, September 15). Salvator Altchek, 'the $5 doctor' of Brooklyn, dies at 92. *New York Times,* p. 40.

Martin, J. A., Hamilton, B. E., Menacker, F., Sutton, P. D., & Mathews, T. J. (2005, November 15). *Preliminary births for 2004: Infant and maternal health.* Hyattsville, MD: National Center for Health Statistics.

Martin, J. A., Hamilton, B. E., Sutton, P. D., Ventura, S. J., Menacker, F., & Munson, M. L. (2003, December 17). Births: Final data for 2002. *National Vital Statistics Reports, 52*(10).

Martin, K. A. (1996). *Puberty, sexuality, and the self: Boys and girls at adolescence.* New York: Routledge.

Martin, P. D., Specter, G., Martin, D., & Martin, M. (2003). Expressed attitudes of adolescents toward marriage and family life. *Adolescence, 38,* 359–367.

Maruna, S. (2001). *Making good: How ex-convicts reform and rebuild their lives.* Washington, DC: American Psychological Association.

Maruna, S., LeBel, T. P., & Lanier, C. S. (2004). Generativity behind bars: Some "redemptive truth" about prison society. In E. de St. Aubin, D. P. McAdams, & T.-C. Kim (Eds.), *The generative society: Caring for future generations* (pp. 131–151). Washington, DC: American Psychological Association.

Marván, M. L., Vacio, A., & Espinosa-Hernández, G. (2003). Menstrual-related changes expected by premenarcheal girls living in rural and urban areas of Mexico. *Social Science & Medicine, 56,* 863–868.

Massimini, K. (Ed.). (2000). *Health reference series: Genetic disorders sourcebook* (2nd ed.). Detroit, MI: Omnigraphics.

Masten, A. S. (2001). Ordinary magic: Resilience processes in development. *American Psychologist, 56,* 227–238.

Masten, A. S. (2004). Regulatory processes, risk, and resilience in adolescent development. In R. E. Dahl & L. P. Spear (Eds.), *Adolescent brain development: Vulnerabilities and opportunities* (Vol. 1021, pp. 310–319). New York: New York Academy of Sciences.

Masten, A. S., & Coatsworth, J. D. (1998). The development of competence in favorable and unfavorable environments: Lessons from research on successful children. *American Psychologist, 53,* 205–220.

Masters, W. H., & Johnson, V. E. (1966). *Human sexual response.* Boston: Little, Brown.

Matheny, A. P., & Phillips, K. (2001). Temperament and context: Correlates of home environment with temperament continuity and change, newborn to 30 months. In T. D. Wachs & G. A. Kohnstamm (Eds.), *Temperament in context* (pp. 81–101). Mahwah, NJ: Erlbaum.

Mather, M., Canli, T., English, T., Whitfield, S., Wais, P., Ochsner, K., Gabrieli, J. D. E., & Carstensen, L. L. (2004). Amygdala responses to emotionally valenced stimuli in older and younger adults. *Psychological Science, 15,* 259–263.

Mather, M., & Carstensen, L. L. (2003). Aging and attentional biases for emotional faces. *Psychological Science, 14,* 409–415.

Matta, D. S., & Knudson-Martin, C. (2006). Father responsivity: Couple processes and the coconstruction of fatherhood. *Family Process, 45,* 19–37.

Matthews, S. H. (2002). Brothers and parent care: An explanation for sons' underrepresentation. In B. J. Kramer & E. H. Thompson (Eds.), *Men as caregivers: Theory, research, and service implications* (pp. 234–249). New York: Springer.

Matychuk, P. (2004). A case study on the role of child-directed speech (CDS) in child language acquisition. *Dissertation Abstracts International, 64*(8), 2864A. (UMI No. AAI3100465)

Maynard, A. E., & Greenfield, P. M. (2003). Implicit cognitive development in cultural tools and children: Lessons from Maya Mexico. *Cognitive Development, 18,* 489–510.

Mazurkewich, K. (2004, August 26). Facing one-child rule, Chinese top world in caesareans. *Wall Street Journal,* p. B1.

McAdams, D. P. (1998). Ego, trait, identity. In P. M. Westenberg, A. Blasi, & L. D. Cohn (Eds.), *Personality development: Theoretical, empirical, and clinical investigations of Loevinger's conception of ego development* (pp. 27–38). Mahwah, NJ: Erlbaum.

McAdams, D. P. (2001a). Generativity in midlife. In M. E. Lachman (Ed.), *Handbook of midlife development* (pp. 395–443). Hoboken, NJ: Wiley.

McAdams, D. P. (2001b). The psychology of life stories. *Review of General Psychology, 5,* 100–122.

McAdams, D. P. (2003). Identity and the life story. In R. Fivush & C. A. Haden (Eds.), *Autobiographical memory and the construction of a narrative self: Developmental and cultural perspectives* (pp. 187–207). Mahwah, NJ: Erlbaum.

McAdams, D. P. (2006). *The redemptive self: Stories Americans live by.* New York: Oxford University Press.

McAdams, D. P., & Bowman, P. J. (2001). Narrating life's turning points: Redemption and contamination. In D. P. McAdams, R. Josselson, & A. Lieblich (Eds.), *Turns in the road: Narrative studies of lives in transition* (pp. 3–34). Washington, DC: American Psychological Association.

McAdams, D. P., & de St. Aubin, E. (1992). A theory of generativity and its assessment through self-report, behavioral acts, and narrative themes in autobiography. *Journal of Personality and Social Psychology, 62,* 1003–1015.

McAdams, D. P., & de St. Aubin, E. (Eds.). (1998). *Generativity and adult development: How and why we care for the next generation.* Washington, DC: American Psychological Association.

McAdams, D. P., de St. Aubin, E., & Logan, R. L. (1993). Generativity among young, midlife, and older adults. *Psychology and Aging, 8,* 221–230.

McAdams, D. P., Diamond, A., de St. Aubin, E., & Mansfield, E. (1997). Stories of commitment: The psychosocial construction of generative lives. *Journal of Personality and Social Psychology, 72,* 678–694.

McAdams, D. P., Hart, H. M., & Maruna, S. (1998). The anatomy of generativity. In D. P. McAdams & E. de St. Aubin (Eds.), *Generativity and adult development: How and why we care for the next generation* (pp. 7–43). Washington, DC: American Psychological Association.

McAdams, D. P., & Logan, R. L. (2004). What is generativity? In E. de St. Aubin, D. P. McAdams, & T.-C. Kim (Eds.), *The generative society: Caring for future generations* (pp. 15–31). Washington, DC: American Psychological Association.

McArdle, J. J., Ferrer-Caja, E., Hamagami, F., & Woodcock, R. W. (2002). Comparative longitudinal structural analyses of the growth and decline of multiple intellectual abilities over the life span. *Developmental Psychology, 38*, 115–142.

McCabe, M. P., & Ricciardelli, L. A. (2003). Sociocultural influences on body image and body changes among adolescent boys and girls. *Journal of Social Psychology, 143*, 5–26.

McCabe, M. P., & Ricciardelli, L. A. (2005). A longitudinal study of body image and strategies to lose weight and increase muscles among children. *Journal of Applied Developmental Psychology, 26*, 559–577.

McCarty, C. A., Ebel, B. E., Garrison, M. M., DiGiuseppe, D. L., Christakis, D. A., & Rivara, F. P. (2004). Continuity of binge and harmful drinking from late adolescence to early adulthood. *Pediatrics, 114*, 714–719.

McCarty, H. J., Roth, D. L., Goode, K. T., Owen, J. E., Harrell, L., Donovan, K., & Haley, W. E. (2000). Longitudinal course of behavioral problems during Alzheimer's disease: Linear versus curvilinear patterns of decline. *Journals of Gerontology: Series A: Biological Sciences and Medical Sciences, 55A*, M200-M206.

McClearn, G. E. (1993). Genetics, systems, and alcohol. *Behavior Genetics, 23*, 223–230.

McClintock, M. K., & Herdt, G. (1996). Rethinking puberty: The development of sexual attraction. *Current Directions in Psychological Science, 5*, 178–183.

McConville, D. W., & Cornell, D. G. (2003). Aggressive attitudes predict aggressive behavior in middle school students. *Journal of Emotional and Behavioral Disorders, 11*, 179–187.

McCrae, R. R., & Costa, P. T. (1986). Clinical assessment can benefit from recent advances in personality psychology. *American Psychologist, 41*, 1001–1003.

McCrae, R. R., & Costa, P. T. (1990). *Personality in adulthood.* New York: Guilford Press.

McCrae, R. R., Costa, P. T., Ostendorf, F., Angleitner, A., Hrebíčková, M., Avia, M. D., Sanz, J., Sánchez-Bernardos, M. L., Kusdil, M. E., Woodfield, R., Saunders, P. R., & Smith, P. B. (2000). Nature over nurture: Temperament, personality, and life span development. *Journal of Personality and Social Psychology, 78*, 173–186.

McCrae, R. R., Costa, P. T., & Piedmont, R. L. (1993). Folk concepts, natural language, and psychological constructs: The California Psychological Inventory and the five-factor model. *Journal of Personality, 61*, 1–26.

McCreary, D. R., & Sasse, D. K. (2000). An exploration of the drive for muscularity in adolescent boys and girls. *Journal of American College Health, 48*, 297–304.

McCreight, B. S. (2004). A grief ignored: Narratives of pregnancy loss from a male perspective. *Sociology of Health and Illness, 26*, 326–350.

McCullough, M. E., & Laurenceau, J.-P. (2004). Gender and the natural history of self-rated health: A 59-year longitudinal study. *Health Psychology, 23*, 651–655.

McElwain, N. L., & Volling, B. L. (2004). Attachment security and parental sensitivity during infancy: Associations with friendship quality and false-belief understanding at age 4. *Journal of Social and Personal Relationships, 21*, 639–667.

McFadyen-Ketchum, S. A., Bates, J. E., Dodge, K. A., & Pettit, G. S. (1996). Patterns of change in early childhood aggressive-disruptive behavior: Gender differences in predictions from early coercive and affectionate mother-child interactions. *Child Development, 67*, 2417–2433.

McGrath, P. (2004). Affirming the connection: Comparative findings on communication issues from hospice patients and hematology survivors. *Death Studies, 28*, 829–848.

McGraw, L. A., & Walker, A. J. (2004). Negotiating care: Ties between aging mothers and their caregiving daughters. *Journals of Gerontology: Series B: Psychological Sciences and Social Sciences, 59B*, S324-S332.

McGrew, K. S., Flanagan, D. P., Keith, T. Z., & Vanderwood, M. (1997). Beyond g: The impact of Gf-Gc specific cognitive abilities research on the future use and interpretation of intelligence tests in the schools. *School Psychology Review, 26*, 189–210.

McIntosh, H., Metz, E., & Youniss, J. (2005). Community service and identity formation in adolescents. In J. L. Mahoney, R. W. Larson, & J. S. Eccles (Eds.), *Organized activities as contexts of development: Extracurricular activities, after-school and community programs* (pp. 331–351). Mahwah, NJ: Erlbaum.

McLanahan, S. (2004). Diverging destinies: How children are faring under the second demographic transition. *Demography, 41*, 607–627.

McLanahan, S., & Adams, J. (1989). The effects of children on adults' psychological well-being: 1957–1976. *Social Forces, 68*, 124–146.

McLanahan, S., & Sandefur, G. D. (1994). *Growing up with a single parent: What hurts, what helps.* Cambridge, MA: Harvard University Press.

McNamara, T. K., & Williamson, J. B. (2004). Race, gender, and the retirement decisions of people ages 60 to 80: Prospects for age integration in employment. *International Journal of Aging & Human Development, 59*, 255–286.

Meaney, M. J., Stewart, J., & Beatty, W. W. (1985). Sex differences in social play: The socialization of sex roles. In J. S. Rosenblatt, C. Beer, M.-C. Busnel, & P. J. B. Slater (Eds.), *Advances in the study of behavior* (Vol. 15, pp. 1–58). New York: Academic Press.

Meier, P., Wolke, D., Gutbrod, T., & Rust, L. (2003). The influence of infant irritability on maternal sensitivity in a sample of very premature infants. *Infant and Child Development, 12*, 159–166.

Meister, H., & von Wedel, H. (2003). Demands on hearing aid features—Special signal processing for elderly users? *International Journal of Audiology, 42*(Suppl. l2), 2S58–52S62.

Meltzoff, A. N., & Moore, M. K. (1977, October 7). Imitation of facial and manual gestures by human neonates. *Science, 198*, 75–78.

Melzer, P., Morgan, V. L., Pickens, D. R., Price, R. R., Wall, R. S., & Ebner, F. F. (2001). Cortical activation during Braille reading is influenced by early visual experience in subjects with severe visual disability: A correlational fMRI study. *Human Brain Mapping, 14*, 186–195.

Ment, L. R., Vohr, B., Allan, W., Katz, K. H., Schneider, K. C., Westerveld, M., Duncan, C. C., & Makuch, R. W. (2003). Change in cognitive function over time in very low-birth-weight infants. *Journal of the American Medical Association, 289*, 705–711.

Merrell, K. W., Buchanan, R., & Tran, O. K. (2006). Relational aggression in children and adolescents: A review with implications for school settings. *Psychology in the Schools, 43,* 345–360.

Michael, A., & Eccles, J. S. (2003). When coming of age means coming undone: Links between puberty and psychosocial adjustment among European American and African American girls. In C. Hayward (Ed.), *Gender differences at puberty* (pp. 277–303). New York: Cambridge University Press.

Michael, R. T., Gagnon, J. H., Laumann, E. O., & Kolata, G. (1994). *Sex in America: A definitive survey.* Boston: Little, Brown.

Midanik, L. T., Soghikian, K., Ransom, L. J., & Tekawa, I. S. (1995). The effect of retirement on mental health and health behaviors: The Kaiser Permanente Retirement Study. *Journals of Gerontology: Series B: Psychological Sciences and Social Sciences, 50B,* S59–S61.

Mikulincer, M., & Florian, V. (1999). Maternal-fetal bonding, coping strategies, and mental health during pregnancy—The contribution of attachment style. *Journal of Social & Clinical Psychology, 18,* 255–276.

Mikulincer, M., Florian, V., Cowan, P. A., & Cowan, C. P. (2002). Attachment security in couple relationships: A systemic model and its implications for family dynamics. *Family Process, 41,* 405–434.

Milkie, M. A. (1999). Social comparisons, reflected appraisals, and mass media: The impact of pervasive beauty images on black and white girls' self concepts. *Social Psychology Quarterly, 62,* 190–210.

Milkie, M. A., Mattingly, M. J., Nomaguchi, K. M., Bianchi, S. M., & Robinson, J. P. (2004). The time squeeze: Parental statuses and feelings about time with children. *Journal of Marriage and Family, 66,* 739–761.

Miller, M. E., Rejeski, W. J., Reboussin, B. A., Ten Have, T. R., & Ettinger, W. H. (2000). Physical activity, functional limitations, and disability in older adults. *Journal of the American Geriatrics Society, 48,* 1264–1272.

Miller, S. D. (2003). How high and low challenge tasks affect motivation and learning: Implications for struggling learners. *Reading & Writing Quarterly: Overcoming Learning Difficulties, 19,* 39–57.

Miller-Loncar, C., Bigsby, R., High, P., Wallach, M., & Lester, B. (2004). Infant colic and feeding difficulties. *Archives of Disease in Childhood, 89,* 908–912.

Mills, E. S. (1993). *The story of Elderhostel.* Hanover, NH: University Press of New England.

Mills, R. S. L. (2005). Taking stock of the developmental literature on shame. *Developmental Review, 25,* 26–63.

Minde, K. (1998). The use of psychotropic medication in preschoolers: Some recent developments. *Canadian Journal of Psychiatry, 43,* 571–575.

Miniño, A. M., Arias, E., Kochanek, K. D., Murphy, S. L., & Smith, B. L. (2002, September 16). Deaths: Final data for 2000. *National Vital Statistics Reports, 50*(16).

Minois, G. (1989). *History of old age: From antiquity to the Renaissance* (S. H. Tenison, Trans.). Chicago: University of Chicago Press.

Mintz, S. (2004). *Huck's raft: A history of American childhood.* Cambridge, MA: Belknap Press of Harvard University Press.

Mirvis, P. H., & Hall, D. T. (1994). Psychological success and the boundaryless career. *Journal of Organizational Behavior, 15,* 365–380.

Mistry, J., Chaudhuri, J., & Diez, V. (2003). Ethnotheories of parenting: Integrating culture and child development. In R. M. Lerner, F. H. Jacobs, & D. Wertlieb (Eds.), *Handbook of applied developmental science: Promoting positive child, adolescent, and family development through research, policies, and programs* (pp. 233–256). Thousand Oaks, CA: Sage.

Mistry, R. S., Biesanz, J. C., Taylor, L. C., Burchinal, M., & Cox, M. J. (2004). Family income and its relation to preschool children's adjustment for families in the NICHD Study of Early Child Care. *Developmental Psychology, 40,* 727–745.

Mitchell, V., & Helson, R. (1990). Women's prime of life: Is it the 50s? *Psychology of Women Quarterly, 14,* 451–470.

Mitchell-Flynn, C., & Hutchinson, R. L. (1993). A longitudinal study of the problems and concerns of urban divorced men. *Journal of Divorce & Remarriage, 19,* 161–182.

MMWR. (1994, August 26). Down syndrome prevalence at birth—United States, 1983–1990. *Morbidity and Mortality Weekly Report, 43,* 617–622.

MMWR. (2002, May 24). Fetal alcohol syndrome—Alaska, Arizona, Colorado, and New York, 1995–1997. *Morbidity and Mortality Weekly Report, 51,* 433–435.

MMWR. (2005, September 2). Mental health in the United States: Prevalence of diagnosis and medication treatment for attention-deficit/hyperactivity disorder—United States, 2003. *Morbidity and Mortality Weekly Report, 54,* 842–847.

Modell, J. (1989). *Into one's own: From youth to adulthood in the United States, 1920–1975.* Berkeley, CA: University of California Press.

Modell, J., Furstenberg, F., & Hershberg, T. (1976). Social change and transitions to adulthood in historical perspective. *Journal of Family History, 1,* 7–32.

Modgil, S., & Modgil, C. (Eds.). (1986). *Lawrence Kohlberg: Consensus and controversy.* Philadelphia: Falmer Press.

Moffitt, T. E. (1993). Adolescence-limited and life-course-persistent antisocial behavior: A developmental taxonomy. *Psychological Review, 100,* 674–701.

Moffitt, T. E., Caspi, A., Belsky, J., & Silva, P. A. (1992). Childhood experience and the onset of menarche: A test of a sociobiological model. *Child Development, 63,* 47–58.

Moghadam, V. M. (2004). Patriarchy in transition: Women and the changing family in the Middle East. *Journal of Comparative Family Studies, 35,* 137–162.

Monk, C. S., McClure, E. B., Nelson, E. E., Zarahn, E., Bilder, R. M., Leibenluft, E., Charney, D. S., Ernst, M., & Pine, D. S. (2003). Adolescent immaturity in attention-related brain engagement to emotional facial expressions. *Neuroimage, 20,* 420–428.

Montemayor, R. (1983). Parents and adolescents in conflict: All families some of the time and some families most of the time. *Journal of Early Adolescence, 3,* 83–103.

Moore, L. L., Gao, D., Bradlee, M. L., Cupples, L. A., Sundarajan-Ramamurti, A., Proctor, M. H., Hood, M. Y., Singer, M. R., & Ellison, R. C. (2003). Does early physical activity predict body fat change throughout childhood? *Preventive Medicine: An International Journal Devoted to Practice and Theory, 37,* 10–17.

Morgan, D. L. (1998). Facts and figures about the baby boom. *Generations, 22*(1), 10–15.

Morgan, H. J., & Shaver, P. R. (1999). Attachment processes and commitment to romantic relationships. In J. M. Adams & W. H. Jones (Eds.), *Handbook of interpersonal commitment and relationship stability* (pp. 109–124). Dordrecht, Netherlands: Kluwer Academic.

Morgan, M. (1984). Reward-induced decrements and increments in intrinsic motivation. *Review of Educational Research, 54*, 5–30.

Morison, P., & Masten, A. S. (1991). Peer reputation in middle childhood as a predictor of adaptation in adolescence: A seven-year follow-up. *Child Development, 62*, 991–1007.

Morley, R., Fewtrell, M. S., Abbott, R. A., Stephenson, T., MacFadyen, U., & Lucas, A. (2004). Neurodevelopment in children born small for gestational age: A randomized trial of nutrient-enriched versus standard formula and comparison with a reference breastfed group. *Pediatrics, 113*, 515–521.

Morris, J. C. (2006). Mild cognitive impairment is early-stage Alzheimer disease. *Archives of Neurology, 63*, 15–16.

Mortensen, E. L., Michaelsen, K. F., Sanders, S. A., & Reinisch, J. M. (2002). The association between duration of breastfeeding and adult intelligence. *Journal of the American Medical Association, 287*, 2365–2371.

Mosby, L., Rawls, A. W., Meehan, A. J., Mays, E., & Pettinari, C. J. (1999). Troubles in interracial talk about discipline: An examination of African American child rearing narratives. *Journal of Comparative Family Studies, 30*, 489–521.

Moses, L. J., Baldwin, D. A., Rosicky, J. G., & Tidball, G. (2001). Evidence for referential understanding in the emotions domain at twelve and eighteen months. *Child Development, 72*, 718–735.

Moses-Kolko, E. L., Bogen, D., Perel, J., Bregar, A., Uhl, K., Levin, B., & Wisner, K. L. (2005). Neonatal signs after late in utero exposure to serotonin reuptake inhibitors: Literature review and implications for clinical applications. *Journal of the American Medical Association, 293*, 2372–2383.

Mosier, C. E., & Rogoff, B. (2003). Privileged treatment of toddlers: Cultural aspects of individual choice and responsibility. *Developmental Psychology, 39*, 1047–1060.

Mosko, S., Richard, C., & McKenna, J. (1997). Maternal sleep and arousals during bedsharing with infants. *Sleep: Journal of Sleep Research & Sleep Medicine, 20*, 142–150.

Moss, E., Cyr, C., Bureau, J.-F., Tarabulsy, G. M., & Dubois-Comtois, K. (2005). Stability of attachment during the preschool period. *Developmental Psychology, 41*, 773–783.

Mroczek, D. K. (2001). Age and emotion in adulthood. *Current Directions in Psychological Science, 10*, 87–90.

Mroczek, D. K., & Spiro, A. (2003). Modeling intraindividual change in personality traits: Findings from the Normative Aging Study. *Journals of Gerontology: Series B: Psychological Sciences and Social Sciences, 58B*, P153–P165.

Mulas, F., Capilla, A., Fernández, S., Etchepareborda, M. C., Campo, P., Maestú, F., Fernández, A., Castellanos, F. X., & Ortiz, T. (2006). Shifting-related brain magnetic activity in attention-deficit/hyperactivity disorder. *Biological Psychiatry, 59*, 373–379.

Munroe, R. L., Hulefeld, R., Rodgers, J. M., Tomeo, D. L., & Yamazaki, S. K. (2000). Aggression among children in four cultures. *Cross-Cultural Research: The Journal of Comparative Social Science, 34*, 3–25.

Muntner, P., He, J., Cutler, J. A., Wildman, R. P., & Whelton, P. K. (2004). Trends in blood pressure among children and adolescents. *Journal of the American Medical Association, 291*, 2107–2113.

Murphy, K. (2005). Psychosocial treatments for ADHD in teens and adults: A practice-friendly review. *Journal of Clinical Psychology, 61*, 607–619.

Murray, S. L., Bellavia, G. M., Rose, P., & Griffin, D. W. (2003). Once hurt, twice hurtful: How perceived regard regulates daily marital interactions. *Journal of Personality and Social Psychology, 84*, 126–147.

Murray, S. L., & Holmes, J. G. (1997). A leap of faith? Positive illusions in romantic relationships. *Personality and Social Psychology Bulletin, 23*, 586–604.

Murray, S. L., Holmes, J. G., Bellavia, G., Griffin, D. W., & Dolderman, D. (2002). Kindred spirits? The benefits of egocentrism in close relationships. *Journal of Personality and Social Psychology, 82*, 563–581.

Murray, S. L., Holmes, J. G., Dolderman, D., & Griffin, D. W. (2000). What the motivated mind sees: Comparing friends' perspectives to married partners' views of each other. *Journal of Experimental Social Psychology, 36*, 600–620.

Murstein, B. I. (1970). Stimulus-value-role: A theory of marital choice. *Journal of Marriage & the Family, 32*, 465–481.

Murstein, B. I. (1999). The relationship of exchange and commitment. In J. M. Adams & W. H. Jones (Eds.), *Handbook of interpersonal commitment and relationship stability* (pp. 205–219). Dordrecht, Netherlands: Kluwer Academic.

Murstein, B. I., Reif, J. A., & Syracuse-Siewert, G. (2002). Comparison of the function of exchange in couples of similar and differing physical attractiveness. *Psychological Reports, 91*, 299–314.

Musick, K., & Mare, R. D. (2004). Family structure, intergenerational mobility, and the reproduction of poverty: Evidence for increasing polarization? *Demography, 41*, 629–648.

Must, A., Naumova, E. N., Phillips, S. M., Blum, M., Dawson-Hughes, B., & Rand, W. M. (2005). Childhood overweight and maturational timing in the development of adult overweight and fatness: The Newton Girls Study and its follow-up. *Pediatrics, 116*, 620–627.

Mustanski, B. S., Viken, R. J., Kaprio, J., Pulkkinen, L., & Rose, R. J. (2004). Genetic and environmental influences on pubertal development: Longitudinal data from Finnish twins at ages 11 and 14. *Developmental Psychology, 40*, 1188–1198.

Mustard, C. A., & Etches, J. (2003). Gender differences in socioeconomic inequality in mortality. *Journal of Epidemiology & Community Health, 57*, 974–980.

Muuss, R. E. (1986). Adolescent eating disorder: Bulimia. *Adolescence, 21*, 257–267.

Myerhoff, B. G. (1978). *Number our days.* New York: Dutton.

Nakashima, M., & Canda, E. R. (2005). Positive dying and resiliency in later life: A qualitative study. *Journal of Aging Studies, 19*, 109–125.

National Center for Children in Poverty [NCCP]. (2002). Early childhood poverty: A statistical profile. Retrieved March 29, 2006, from Columbia University Web site: http://www.nccp.org/media/ecp02-text.pdf

National Center for Education Statistics. (2004a). *The condition of education 2004* (NCES 2004–077). Washington, DC: U.S. Government Printing Office.

National Center for Education Statistics. (2004b). Student effort and educational progress. Retrieved September 6, 2006, from National Center for Education Statistics Web site: http://www.nces.ed.gov/programs/coe/list/i3.asp

National Center for Health Statistics. (2005). *Health, United States, 2005: With chartbook on trends in the health of Americans.* Hyattsville, MD: National Center for Health Statistics.

National Clearinghouse on Child Abuse and Neglect Information. (2005). Child maltreatment 2003: Summary. Retrieved October 20, 2005, from National Clearinghouse on Child Abuse and Neglect Information Web site: http://www.acf.hhs.gov/programs/cb/pubs/cm03/index.htm

National Health and Nutrition Examination Survey. (2000). Clinical growth charts. Retrieved October 4, 2006, from National Center for Health Statistics (U.S. Department of Health & Human Services [USDHHS]) Web site: http://www.cdc.gov/nchs/about/major/nhanes/growthcharts/clinical_charts.htm

National Hospice and Palliative Care Organization. (n.d.). NHPCO's 2004 facts and figures. Retrieved October 17, 2006, from http://www.nhpco.org/files/public/Facts_Figures_for2004data.pdf

Needham, A., Barrett, T., & Peterman, K. (2002). A pick me up for infants' exploratory skills: Early simulated experiences reaching for objects using 'sticky' mittens enhances young infants' object exploration skills. *Infant Behavior & Development, 25,* 279–295.

Neiderhiser, J. M., Reiss, D., Pedersen, N. L., Lichtenstein, P., Spotts, E. L., Hansson, K., Cederblad, M., & Ellhammer, O. (2004). Genetic and environmental influences on mothering of adolescents: A comparison of two samples. *Developmental Psychology, 40,* 335–351.

Nelson, E. E., Leibenluft, E., McClure, E., & Pine, D. S. (2005). The social reorientation of adolescence: A neuroscience perspective on the process and its relation to psychopathology. *Psychological Medicine, 35,* 163–174.

Nelson, K. (1974). Concept, word, and sentence: Interrelations in acquisition and development. *Psychological Review, 81,* 267–285.

Nelson, K. (1999). The developmental psychology of language and thought. In M. Bennett (Ed.), *Developmental psychology: Achievements and prospects* (pp. 185–204). New York: Psychology Press.

Nelson, K. (2000). Narrative, time and the emergence of the encultured self. *Culture & Psychology, 6,* 183–196.

Nelson, K., & Fivush, R. (2004). The emergence of autobiographical memory: A social cultural developmental theory. *Psychological Review, 111,* 486–511.

Nelson, L. J., Badger, S., & Wu, B. (2004). The influence of culture in emerging adulthood: Perspectives of Chinese college students. *International Journal of Behavioral Development, 28,* 26–36.

Neugarten, B. (1972). Personality and the aging process. *Gerontologist, 12*(1, Pt. 1), 9–15.

Neugarten, B. L. (1979). Time, age, and the life cycle. *American Journal of Psychiatry, 136,* 887–894.

Newcomb, A. F., & Bagwell, C. L. (1995). Children's friendship relations: A meta-analytic review. *Psychological Bulletin, 117,* 306–347.

Newcomb, A. F., & Bagwell, C. L. (1996). The developmental significance of children's friendship relations. In W. M. Bukowski, A. F. Newcomb, & W. W. Hartup (Eds.), *The company they keep: Friendship in childhood and adolescence* (pp. 289–321). New York: Cambridge University Press.

NICHD Early Child Care Research Network. (2002). Parenting and family influences when children are in child care: Results from the NICHD Study of Early Child Care. In J. G. Borkowski, S. L. Ramey, & M. Bristol-Power (Eds.), *Parenting and the child's world: Influences on academic, intellectual, and social-emotional development* (pp. 99–123). Mahwah, NJ: Erlbaum.

NICHD Early Child Care Research Network. (2003). Does amount of time spent in child care predict socioemotional adjustment during the transition to kindergarten? *Child Development, 74,* 976–1005.

NICHD Early Child Care Research Network. (2004). Type of child care and children's development at 54 months. *Early Childhood Research Quarterly, 19,* 203–230.

NICHD Early Child Care Research Network. (2005). *Child care and child development: Results from the NICHD Study of Early Child Care and Youth Development.* New York: Guilford Press.

NICHD Early Child Care Research Network. (2006). Child-care effect sizes for the NICHD Study of Early Child Care and Youth Development. *American Psychologist, 61,* 99–116.

Nilsson, L.-G. (2003). Memory function in normal aging. *Acta Neurologica Scandinavica, 107*(Suppl. 179), 7–13.

Nilsson L. (with Hamberger L.). (1990). *A child is born.* New York: Delacorte Press.

Nishizawa, Y., Kida, K., Nishizawa, K., Hashiba, S., Saito, K., & Mita, R. (2003). Perception of self-physique and eating behavior of high school students in Japan. *Psychiatry and Clinical Neurosciences, 57,* 189–196.

Nissen, S. E. (2006). ADHD drugs and cardiovascular risk. *New England Journal of Medicine, 354,* 1445–1448.

Nolen, S. B. (2003). Learning environment, motivation, and achievement in high school science. *Journal of Research in Science Teaching, 40,* 347–368.

Nolen-Hoeksema, S., & Girgus, J. S. (1994). The emergence of gender differences in depression during adolescence. *Psychological Bulletin, 115,* 424–443.

Noller, P., & Feeney, J. A. (2002). Communication, relationship concerns, and satisfaction in early marriage. In A. L. Vangelisti, H. T. Reis, & M. A. Fitzpatrick (Eds.), *Stability and change in relationships* (pp. 129–155). New York: Cambridge University Press.

Noller, P., Feeney, J. A., Roberts, N., & Christensen, A. (2005). Withdrawal in couple interactions: Exploring the causes and consequences. In R. E. Riggio & R. S. Feldman (Eds.), *Applications of nonverbal communication* (pp. 195–213). Mahwah, NJ: Erlbaum.

Noyes, L. E., Daley, P., & French, K. (2000). Community-based services help people in the early stages of Alzheimer's disease and other cognitive impairments. *American Journal of Alzheimer's Disease, 15,* 309–313.

Nuland, S. B. (1994). *How we die: Reflections on life's final chapter.* New York: Random House.

O'Connor, B. P., & St. Pierre, E. S. (2004). Older persons' perceptions of the frequency and meaning of elderspeak from family, friends, and service workers. *International Journal of Aging & Human Development, 58,* 197–221.

O'Connor, T. G., Rutter, M., Beckett, C., Keaveney, L., Kreppner, J. M., & The English & Romanian Adoptees Study Team. (2000). The effects of global severe privation on cognitive competence: Extension and longitudinal follow-up. *Child Development, 71,* 376–390.

O'Rand, A. M. (1988). Convergence, institutionalization, and bifurcation: Gender and the pension acquisition process. In G. L. Maddox & M. P. Lawton (Eds.), *Annual review of gerontology and geriatrics, Vol. 8: Varieties of aging* (pp. 132–155). New York: Springer.

O'Sullivan, L. F., & Brooks-Gunn, J. (2005). The timing of changes in girls' sexual cognitions and behaviors in early adolescence: A prospective, cohort study. *Journal of Adolescent Health, 37,* 211–219.

Ochsner, K. N., & Gross, J. J. (2004). Thinking makes it so: A social cognitive neuroscience approach to emotion regulation. In R. F. Baumeister & K. D. Vohs (Eds.), *Handbook of self-regulation: Research, theory, and applications* (pp. 229–255). New York: Guilford Press.

Offer, D., Ostrov, E., Howard, K. I., & Atkinson, R. (1988). *The teenage world: Adolescents' self-image in ten countries.* New York: Plenum.

Ogden, C. L., Flegal, K. M., Carroll, M. D., & Johnson, C. L. (2002). Prevalence and trends in overweight among US children and adolescents, 1999–2000. *Journal of the American Medical Association, 288,* 1728–1732.

Oishi, S., Hahn, J., Schimmack, U., Radhakrishan, P., Dzokoto, V., & Ahadi, S. (2005). The measurement of values across cultures: A pairwise comparison approach. *Journal of Research in Personality, 39,* 299–305.

Olden, K. (1998, February 16). The complex interaction of poverty, pollution, health status. *The Scientist, 12,* 7.

Olfson, M., Gameroff, M. J., Marcus, S. C., & Jensen, P. S. (2003). National trends in the treatment of attention deficit hyperactivity disorder. *American Journal of Psychiatry, 160,* 1071–1077.

Olweus, D., Limber, S., & Mihalic, S. F. (1999). *Blueprints for violence prevention: Book 9. Bullying Prevention Program.* Boulder, CO: Center for the Study and Prevention of Violence, Institute of Behavioral Science, University of Colorado at Boulder.

Omar, H., McElderry, D., & Zakharia, R. (2003). Educating adolescents about puberty: What are we missing? *International Journal of Adolescent Medicine and Health, 15,* 79–83.

Onishi, K. H., & Baillargeon, R. (2005, April 8). Do 15-month-old infants understand false beliefs? *Science, 308,* 255–258.

Ornstein, P. A., Naus, M. J., & Liberty, C. (1975). Rehearsal and organizational processes in children's memory. *Child Development, 46,* 818–830.

Orpinas, P., & Horne, A. M. (2006). *Bullying prevention: Creating a positive school climate and developing social competence.* Washington, DC: American Psychological Association.

Osgood, D. W., Anderson, A. L., & Shaffer, J. N. (2005). Unstructured leisure in the after-school hours. In J. L. Mahoney, R. W. Larson, & J. S. Eccles (Eds.), *Organized activities as contexts of development: Extracurricular activities, after-school and community programs* (pp. 45–64). Mahwah, NJ: Erlbaum.

Ostrov, J. M., & Keating, C. F. (2004). Gender differences in preschool aggression during free play and structured interactions: An observational study. *Social Development, 13,* 255–277.

Ott, M. A., Millstein, S. G., Ofner, S., & Halpern-Felsher, B. L. (2006). Greater expectations: Adolescents' positive motivations for sex. *Perspectives on Sexual and Reproductive Health, 38,* 84–89.

Paice, J. A., Muir, J. C., & Shott, S. (2004). Palliative care at the end of life: Comparing quality in diverse settings. *American Journal of Hospice & Palliative Care, 21,* 19–27.

Paikoff, R. L., & Brooks-Gunn, J. (1991). Do parent-child relationships change during puberty? *Psychological Bulletin, 110,* 47–66.

Paley, B., Cox, M. J., Kanoy, K. W., Harter, K. S. M., Burchinal, M., & Margand, N. A. (2005). Adult attachment and marital interaction as predictors of whole family interactions during the transition to parenthood. *Journal of Family Psychology, 19,* 420–429.

Palkovitz, R. J. (2002). *Involved fathering and men's adult development: Provisional balances.* Mahwah, NJ: Erlbaum.

Palladino, G. (1996). *Teenagers: An American history.* New York: Basic Books.

Palmore, E. B. (1990a). *Ageism: Negative and positive.* New York: Springer.

Palmore, E. B. (1990b). Predictors of outcome in nursing homes. *Journal of Applied Gerontology, 9,* 172–184.

Palusci, V. J., Smith, E. G., & Paneth, N. (2005). Predicting and responding to physical abuse in young children using NCANDS. *Children and Youth Services Review, 27,* 667–682.

Pampel, F. C., & Rogers, R. G. (2004). Socioeconomic status, smoking, and health: A test of competing theories of cumulative advantage. *Journal of Health and Social Behavior, 45,* 306–321.

Panksepp, J. (1998). Attention deficit hyperactivity disorders, psychostimulants and intolerance of childhood playfulness: A tragedy in the making? *Current Directions in Psychological Science, 7,* 91–98.

Pardini, D. A., Loeber, R., & Stouthamer-Loeber, M. (2005). Developmental shifts in parent and peer influences on boys' beliefs about delinquent behavior. *Journal of Research on Adolescence, 15,* 299–323.

Parent, A.-S., Teilmann, G., Juul, A., Skakkebaek, N. E., Toppari, J., & Bourguignon, J.-P. (2003). The timing of normal puberty and the age limits of sexual precocity: Variations around the world, secular trends, and changes after migration. *Endocrine Reviews, 24,* 668–693.

Park, D. C. (2000). The basic mechanisms accounting for age-related decline in cognitive function. In D. C. Park & N. Schwarz (Eds.), *Cognitive aging: A primer* (pp. 3–21). New York: Psychology Press.

Parker, L. (2000). The federal nutrition programs: A safety net for very young children. *Zero to Three, 21*(1), 29–36.

Parker, M. (2004). Medicalizing meaning: Demoralization syndrome and the desire to die. *Australian and New Zealand Journal of Psychiatry, 38,* 765–773.

Parkes, C. M. (1972). *Bereavement: Studies of grief in adult life.* New York: International Universities Press.

Parkes, C. M. (1987). *Bereavement: Studies of grief in adult life* (2nd ed.). Madison, CT: International Universities Press.

Pascalis, O., de Schonen, S., Morton, J., Deruelle, C., & Fabre-Grenet, M. (1995). Mother's face recognition by neonates: A replication and an extension. *Infant Behavior & Development, 18,* 79–85.

Pascual-Leone, J. (1970). A mathematical model for the transition rule in Piaget's developmental stages. *Acta Psychologica, Amsterdam, 32,* 301–345.

Pasley, K., Futris, T. G., & Skinner, M. L. (2002). Effects of commitment and psychological centrality on fathering. *Journal of Marriage and Family, 64,* 130–138.

Patterson, G. R. (1986). Performance models for antisocial boys. *American Psychologist, 41,* 432–444.

Patterson, G. R. (1992). Developmental changes in antisocial behavior. In R. D. Peters, R. J. McMahon, & V. L. Quinsey (Eds.), *Aggression and violence throughout the life span* (pp. 52–82). Thousand Oaks, CA: Sage.

Pearlin, L. I., Mullan, J. T., Semple, S. J., & Skaff, M. M. (1990). Caregiving and the stress process: An overview of concepts and their measures. *Gerontologist, 30,* 583–594.

Pears, K. C., & Fisher, P. A. (2005). Emotion understanding and theory of mind among maltreated children in foster care: Evidence of deficits. *Development and Psychopathology, 17,* 47–65.

Pedersen, N. L. (1996). Gerontological behavior genetics. In J. E. Birren, K. W. Schaie, R. P. Abeles, M. Gatz, & T. A. Salthouse (Eds.), *Handbook of the psychology of aging* (4th ed., pp. 59–77). San Diego, CA: Academic Press.

Pedro-Carroll, J. L. (2005). Fostering resilience in the aftermath of divorce: The role of evidence-based programs for children. *Family Court Review, 43*, 52–64.

Pellegrini, A. D., & Smith, P. K. (1998). Physical activity play: Consensus and debate. *Child Development, 69*, 609–610.

Pellegrini, A. D., & Smith, P. K. (2005). Play in great apes and humans. In A. D. Pellegrini & P. K. Smith (Eds.), *The nature of play: Great apes and humans* (pp. 3–12). New York: Guilford Press.

Perkins, D. N., & Grotzer, T. A. (1997). Teaching intelligence. *American Psychologist, 52*, 1125–1133.

Perlmutter, M., Kaplan, M., & Nyquist, L. (1990). Development of adaptive competence in adulthood. *Human Development, 33*, 185–197.

Perner, J., Frith, U., Leslie, A. M., & Leekam, S. R. (1989). Exploration of the autistic child's theory of mind: Knowledge, belief, and communication. *Child Development, 60*, 689–700.

Perner, J., Ruffman, T., & Leekam, S. R. (1994). Theory of mind is contagious: You catch it from your sibs. *Child Development, 65*, 1228–1238.

Peskin, J. (1992). Ruse and representations: On children's ability to conceal information. *Developmental Psychology, 28*, 84–89.

Peskind, E. R., Potkin, S. G., Pomara, N., Ott, B. R., Graham, S. M., Olin, J. T., & McDonald, S. (2006). Memantine treatment in mild to moderate Alzheimer disease: A 24-week randomized, controlled trial. *American Journal of Geriatric Psychiatry, 14*, 704–715.

Petersen, R. C., & O'Brien, J. (2006). Mild cognitive impairment should be considered for DSM-V. *Journal of Geriatric Psychiatry and Neurology, 19*, 147–154.

Peterson, B. E. (1998). Case studies of midlife generativity: Analyzing motivation and realization. In D. P. McAdams & E. de St. Aubin (Eds.), *Generativity and adult development: How and why we care for the next generation* (pp. 101–131). Washington, DC: American Psychological Association.

Peterson, C., Maier, S. F., & Seligman, M. E. P. (1993). *Learned helplessness: A theory for the age of personal control.* New York: Oxford University Press.

Peterson, C. C. (1996). The ticking of the social clock: Adults' beliefs about the timing of transition events. *International Journal of Aging & Human Development, 42*, 189–203.

Petterson, S. M., & Albers, A. B. (2001). Effects of poverty and maternal depression on early child development. *Child Development, 72*, 1794–1813.

Pevey, C. (2003). Living wills and durable power of attorney for health care. In C. D. Bryant (Ed.), *Handbook of death & dying* (pp. 891–898). Thousand Oaks, CA: Sage.

Pfeifer, M., Goldsmith, H. H., Davidson, R. J., & Rickman, M. (2002). Continuity and change in inhibited and uninhibited children. *Child Development, 73*, 1474–1485.

Phelan, P., Davidson, A. L., & Yu, H. C. (1998). *Adolescents' worlds: Negotiating family, peers, and school.* New York: Teachers College Press.

Phillips, C. D., & Hawes, C. (2005). Care provision in housing with supportive services: The importance of care type, individual characteristics, and care site. *Journal of Applied Gerontology, 24*, 55–67.

Phinney, J. S., Kim-Jo, T., Osorio, S., & Vilhjalmsdottir, P. (2005). Autonomy and relatedness in adolescent-parent disagreements: Ethnic and developmental factors. *Journal of Adolescent Research, 20*, 8–39.

Piaget, J. (1950). *The psychology of intelligence.* Oxford, England: Harcourt.

Piaget, J. (1962). *Play, dreams and imitation in childhood.* New York: Norton. (Original work published 1951)

Piaget, J. (1965). *The moral judgment of the child* (Paperback ed.). New York: Free Press.

Piaget, J. (1971). *The psychology of intelligence.* London: Routledge & Kegan Paul. (Original work published 1950)

Pickering, T. (1999). Cardiovascular pathways: Socioeconomic status and stress effects on hypertension and cardiovascular function. In N. E. Adler, M. Marmot, B. S. McEwen, & J. Stewart (Eds.), *Socioeconomic status and health in industrial nations: Social, psychological, and biological pathways* (pp. 262–277). New York: New York Academy of Sciences.

Pietsch, J. H. (2004). Health care decision making and physician-aid-in-dying in Hawaii. *Journal of Legal Medicine, 25*, 303–332.

Pike, K. M., & Rodin, J. (1991). Mothers, daughters, and disordered eating. *Journal of Abnormal Psychology, 100*, 198–204.

Pillard, R. (1997). The search for a genetic influence on sexual orientation. In V. A. Rosario (Ed.), *Science and homosexualities* (pp. 226–241). New York: Routledge.

Pinquart, M. (2001). Age differences in perceived positive affect, negative affect, and affect balance in middle and old age. *Journal of Happiness Studies, 2*, 375–405.

Pinquart, M., & Sörensen, S. (2004). Associations of caregiver stressors and uplifts with subjective well-being and depressive mood: A meta-analytic comparison. *Aging & Mental Health, 8*, 438–449.

Pinquart, M., Sörensen, S., & Davey, A. (2003). National and regional differences in preparation for future care needs: A comparison of the United States and Germany. *Journal of Cross-Cultural Gerontology, 18*, 53–78.

Pioggiosi, P. P., Berardi, D., Ferrari, B., Quartesan, R., & De Ronchi, D. (2006). Occurrence of cognitive impairment after age 90: MCI and other broadly used concepts. *Brain Research Bulletin, 68*, 227–232.

Pirkl, J. J. (1994). *Transgenerational design: Products for an aging population.* New York: Van Nostrand Reinhold.

Pitkanen, T., Lyyra, A. L., & Pulkkinen, L. (2005). Age of onset of drinking and the use of alcohol in adulthood: A follow-up study from age 8–42 for females and males. *Addiction, 100*, 652–661.

Pittman, K., Tolman, J., & Yohalem, N. (2005). Developing a comprehensive agenda for the out-of-school hours: Lessons and challenges across cities. In J. L. Mahoney, R. W. Larson, & J. S. Eccles (Eds.), *Organized activities as contexts of development: Extracurricular activities, after-school and community programs* (pp. 375–397). Mahwah, NJ: Erlbaum.

Pitts, M., & Rahman, Q. (2001). Which behaviors constitute "having sex" among university students in the UK? *Archives of Sexual Behavior, 30*, 169–176.

Plomin, R. (1994). The Emanuel Miller Memorial Lecture 1993. Genetic research and identification of environmental influences. *Journal of Child Psychology and Psychiatry, 35*, 817–834.

Plomin, R. (2003). General cognitive ability. In R. Plomin, J. C. DeFries, I. W. Craig, & P. McGuffin (Eds.), *Behavioral genetics in the postgenomic era* (pp. 183–201). Washington, DC: American Psychological Association.

Plomin, R., & Bergeman, C. S. (1991). The nature of nurture: Genetic influence on "environmental" measures. *Behavioral and Brain Sciences, 14,* 373–427.

Plomin, R., DeFries, J. C., Craig, I. W., & McGuffin, P. (2003a). Behavioral genetics. In R. Plomin, J. C. DeFries, I. W. Craig, & P. McGuffin (Eds.), *Behavioral genetics in the postgenomic era* (pp. 3–15). Washington, DC: American Psychological Association.

Plomin, R., DeFries, J. C., Craig, I. W., & McGuffin, P. (2003b). Behavioral genomics. In R. Plomin, J. C. DeFries, I. W. Craig, & P. McGuffin (Eds.), *Behavioral genetics in the postgenomic era* (pp. 531–540). Washington, DC: American Psychological Association.

Plomin, R., DeFries, J. C., & McClearn, G. E. (1980). *Behavioral genetics: A primer.* San Francisco: Freeman.

Plomin, R., & McClearn, G. E. (Eds.). (1993). *Nature, nurture, & psychology.* Washington, DC: American Psychological Association.

Plomin, R., & Spinath, F. M. (2004). Intelligence: Genetics, genes, and genomics. *Journal of Personality and Social Psychology, 86,* 112–129.

Pogrebin, L. C. (1996). *Getting over getting older: An intimate journey.* Boston: Little, Brown.

Pogson, C. E., Cober, A. B., Doverspike, D., & Rogers, J. R. (2003). Differences in self-reported work ethic across three career stages. *Journal of Vocational Behavior, 62,* 189–201.

Poirier, F. E., & Smith, E. O. (1974). Socializing functions of primate play. *American Zoologist, 14,* 275–287.

Popenoe, D. (1993). American family decline, 1960–1990: A review and appraisal. *Journal of Marriage and the Family, 55,* 527–542.

Porter, E., & Walsh, M. W. (2005, February 9). Retirement turns into a rest stop as benefits dwindle. *New York Times,* p. A1.

Presser, H. B. (2003). *Working in a 24/7 economy: Challenges for American families.* New York: Sage.

Preston, S. H. (1991). *Fatal years: Child mortality in late nineteenth-century America.* Princeton, NJ: Princeton University Press.

Previti, D., & Amato, P. R. (2004). Is infidelity a cause or a consequence of poor marital quality? *Journal of Social and Personal Relationships, 21,* 217–230.

Prinstein, M. J. (2003). Social factors: Peer relationships. In A. Spirito & J. C. Overholser (Eds.), *Evaluating and treating adolescent suicide attempters: From research to practice* (pp. 191–213). San Diego, CA: Academic Press.

Prinstein, M. J., Cheah, C. S. L., & Guyer, A. E. (2005). Peer victimization, cue interpretation, and internalizing symptoms: Preliminary concurrent and longitudinal findings for children and adolescents. *Journal of Clinical Child and Adolescent Psychology, 34,* 11–24.

Prinstein, M. J., & Cillessen, A. H. N. (2003). Forms and functions of adolescent peer aggression associated with high levels of peer status. *Merrill-Palmer Quarterly, 49,* 310–342.

Prinstein, M. J., & La Greca, A. M. (2002). Peer crowd affiliation and internalizing distress in childhood and adolescence: A longitudinal follow-back study. *Journal of Research on Adolescence, 12,* 325–351.

Proctor, B. D., & Dalaker, J. (2003). *Poverty in the United States: 2002* (No. P60-222). Washington, DC: U.S. Government Printing Office.

Proctor, M. H., Moore, L. L., Gao, D., Cupples, L. A., Bradlee, M. L., Hood, M. Y., & Ellison, R. C. (2003). Television viewing and change in body fat from preschool to early adolescence: The Framingham Children's Study. *International Journal of Obesity, 27,* 827–833.

Profet, M. (1997). *Pregnancy sickness: Using your body's natural defenses to protect your baby-to-be.* Reading, MA: Addison-Wesley.

Pruett, M. K., Insabella, G. M., & Gustafson, K. (2005). The collaborative divorce project: A court-based intervention for separating parents with young children. *Family Court Review, 43,* 38–51.

Prull, M. W., Gabrieli, J. D. E., & Bunge, S. A. (2000). Age-related changes in memory: A cognitive neuroscience perspective. In F. I. M. Craik & T. A. Salthouse (Eds.), *The handbook of aging and cognition* (2nd ed., pp. 91–153). Mahwah, NJ: Erlbaum.

Pugzles Lorch, E., Eastham, D., Milich, R., Lemberger, C. C., Polley Sanchez, R., Welsh, R., & van den Broek, P. (2004). Difficulties in comprehending causal relations among children with ADHD: The role of cognitive engagement. *Journal of Abnormal Psychology, 113,* 56–63.

Qian, Z., & Preston, S. H. (1993). Changes in American marriage, 1972 to 1987: Availability and forces of attraction by age and education. *American Sociological Review, 58,* 482–495.

Quadagno, J., & Stahl, S. M. (2003). Challenges in nursing home care: A research agenda. *Gerontologist, 43,* 4–6.

Quinlan, R. J. (2003). Father absence, parental care, and female reproductive development. *Evolution and Human Behavior, 24,* 376–390.

Raffaelli, M. (2005). Adolescent dating experiences described by Latino college students. *Journal of Adolescence, 28,* 559–572.

Rahman, A., Iqbal, Z., & Harrington, R. (2003). Life events, social support and depression in childbirth: Perspectives from a rural community in the developing world. *Psychological Medicine, 33,* 1161–1167.

Raikes, H. A., & Thompson, R. A. (2006). Family emotional climate, attachment security and young children's emotion knowledge in a high risk sample. *British Journal of Developmental Psychology, 24,* 89–104.

Raley, S. B., Mattingly, M. J., & Bianchi, S. M. (2006). How dual are dual-income couples? Documenting change from 1970 to 2001. *Journal of Marriage and Family, 68,* 11–28.

Rallison, L., & Moules, N. J. (2004). The unspeakable nature of pediatric palliative care: Unveiling many cloaks. *Journal of Family Nursing, 10,* 287–301.

Ram, B., & Hou, F. (2005). Sex differences in the effects of family structure on children's aggressive behavior. *Journal of Comparative Family Studies, 36,* 329–341.

Ramirez, A., Bravo, I. M., & Katsikas, S. (2005). Infant feeding decisions and practices in the U.S. and Colombia. *Journal of Prenatal & Perinatal Psychology & Health, 19,* 237–249.

Rando, T. A. (1984). *Grief, dying, and death: Clinical interventions for caregivers.* Champaign, IL: Research Press.

Rando, T. A. (1992–1993). The increasing prevalence of complicated mourning: The onslaught is just beginning. *Omega: Journal of Death and Dying, 26,* 43–59.

Rattaz, C., Goubet, N., & Bullinger, A. (2005). The calming effect of a familiar odor on full-term newborns. *Journal of Developmental & Behavioral Pediatrics, 26,* 86–92.

Reese, E., Haden, C. A., & Fivush, R. (1993). Mother-child conversations about the past: Relationships of style and memory over time. *Cognitive Development, 8,* 403–430.

Reid, D. D., Brett, G. Z., Hamilton, P. J., Jarrett, R. J., Keen, H., & Rose, G. (1974). Cardiorespiratory disease and diabetes among middle-aged male civil servants. A study of screening and intervention. *Lancet, 1,* 469–473.

Reijneveld, S., Lanting, C., Crone, M., & Van Wouwe, J. (2005). Exposure to tobacco smoke and infant crying. *Acta Paediatrica, 94,* 217–221.

Reijneveld, S. A., van der Wal, M. F., Brugman, E., Sing, R. A. H., & Verloove-Vanhorick, S. P. (2004). Infant crying and abuse. *Lancet, 364,* 1340–1342.

Reimer, J., Paolitto, D. P., & Hersh, R. H. (1983). *Promoting moral growth: From Piaget to Kohlberg* (2nd ed.). New York: Longman.

Reimer, K. (2003). Committed to caring: Transformation in adolescent moral identity. *Applied Developmental Science, 7,* 129–137.

Reinders, H., & Youniss, J. (2006). School-based required community service and civic development in adolescents. *Applied Developmental Science, 10,* 2–12.

Reis, S. M., Colbert, R. D., & Hébert, T. P. (2005). Understanding resilience in diverse, talented students in an urban high school. *Roeper Review, 27,* 110–120.

Reisfield, G. M., & Wilson, G. R. (2004). Advance care planning redux: It's time to talk. *American Journal of Hospice & Palliative Care, 21,* 7–9.

Reissman, C., Aron, A., & Bergen, M. R. (1993). Shared activities and marital satisfaction: Causal direction and self-expansion versus boredom. *Journal of Social and Personal Relationships, 10,* 243–254.

Reitzes, D. C., & Mutran, E. J. (2004). Grandparenthood: Factors influencing frequency of grandparent-grandchildren contact and grandparent role satisfaction. *Journals of Gerontology: Series B: Psychological Sciences and Social Sciences, 59B,* S9–S16.

Rembeck, G. I., & Gunnarsson, R. K. (2004). Improving pre-and postmenarcheal 12-year old girls' attitudes toward menstruation. *Health Care for Women International, 25,* 680–698.

Rende, R., & Plomin, R. (1992). Diathesis-stress models of psychopathology: A quantitative genetic perspective. *Applied & Preventive Psychology, 1,* 177–182.

Rendell, P. G., Castel, A. D., & Craik, F. I. M. (2005). Memory for proper names in old age: A disproportionate impairment? *The Quarterly Journal of Experimental Psychology A: Human Experimental Psychology, 58A,* 54–71.

Reskin, B. (1993). Sex segregation in the workplace. *Annual Review of Sociology, 19,* 241–270.

Reuter-Lorenz, P. A. (2000). Cognitive neuropsychology of the aging brain. In D. C. Park & N. Schwarz (Eds.), *Cognitive aging: A primer* (pp. 93–114). New York: Psychology Press.

Reuter-Lorenz, P. A., Marshuetz, C., Jonides, J., Smith, E. E., Hartley, A., & Koeppe, R. (2001). Neurocognitive ageing of storage and executive processes. *European Journal of Cognitive Psychology, 13,* 257–278.

Ricciardelli, L. A., & McCabe, M. P. (2004). A biopsychosocial model of disordered eating and the pursuit of muscularity in adolescent boys. *Psychological Bulletin, 130,* 179–205.

Rich, M. (2005). Sex screen: The dilemma of media exposure and sexual behavior. *Pediatrics, 116,* 329–331.

Richards, M., Hardy, R., & Wadsworth, M. E. J. (2003). Does active leisure protect cognition? Evidence from a national birth cohort. *Social Science & Medicine, 56,* 785–792.

Riche, M. F. (1990). The boomerang age. *American Demographics, 12,* 27–30, 52–53.

Ridgway, A., Northup, J., Pellegrin, A., LaRue, R., & Hightsoe, A. (2003). Effects of recess on the classroom behavior of children with and without Attention-Deficit Hyperactivity Disorder. *School Psychology Quarterly, 18,* 253–268.

Riegel, K. F., & Riegel, R. M. (1972). Development, drop, and death. *Developmental Psychology, 6,* 306–319.

Righetti, P., Dell'Avanzo, M., Grigio, M., & Nicolini, U. (2005). Maternal/paternal antenatal attachment and fourth-dimensional ultrasound technique: A preliminary report. *British Journal of Psychology, 96,* 129–137.

Rinehart, D. J., Becker, M. A., Buckley, P. R., Dailey, K., Reichardt, C. S., Graeber, C., VanDeMark, N. R., & Brown, E. (2005). The relationship between mothers' child abuse potential and current mental health symptoms: Implications for screening and referral. *Journal of Behavioral Health Services & Research, 32,* 155–166.

Rivas-Vazquez, R. A., Mendez, C., Rey, G. J., & Carrazana, E. J. (2004). Mild cognitive impairment: New neuropsychological and pharmacological target. *Archives of Clinical Neuropsychology, 19,* 11–27.

Rix, S. E. (2002). The labor market for older workers. *Generations, 26(2),* 25–30.

Robert Wood Johnson Foundation. (2005). 2005 annual report. Retrieved September 20, 2006, from Robert Wood Johnson Foundation Web site: http://www.rwjf.org/publications/annualreportlist.jsp

Roberts, S. B., & Heyman, M. B. (2000). Micronutrient shortfalls in young children's diets: Common, and owing to inadequate intakes both at home and at child care centers. *Nutrition Reviews, 58,* 27–29.

Robine, J.-M., & Michel, J.-P. (2004). Looking forward to a general theory on population aging. *Journals of Gerontology: Series A: Biological Sciences and Medical Sciences, 59A,* 590–597.

Robins, R. W., Trzesniewski, K. H., Tracy, J. L., Gosling, S. D., & Potter, J. (2002). Global self-esteem across the life span. *Psychology and Aging, 17,* 423–434.

Robinson, D. S. (2005). Psychotropic drugs and pregnancy: Guidance for antidepressants. *Primary Psychiatry, 12,* 22–23.

Rodin, J., & Langer, E. J. (1980). Aging labels: The decline of control and the fall of self-esteem. *Journal of Social Issues, 36,* 12–29.

Rodkin, P. C., Farmer, T. W., Pearl, R., & Van Acker, R. (2000). Heterogeneity of popular boys: Antisocial and prosocial configurations. *Developmental Psychology, 36,* 14–24.

Roenker, D. L., Cissell, G. M., Ball, K. K., Wadley, V. G., & Edwards, J. D. (2003). Speed-of-processing and driving simulator training result in improved driving performance. *Human Factors, 45,* 218–233.

Roffwarg, H. P., Muzio, J. N., & Dement, W. C. (1966, April 29). Ontogenetic development of the human sleep-dream cycle. *Science, 152,* 604–619.

Rogge, R. D., & Bradbury, T. N. (2002). Developing a multifaceted view of change in relationships. In A. L. Vangelisti, H. T. Reis, & M. A. Fitzpatrick (Eds.), *Stability and change in relationships* (pp. 228–253). New York: Cambridge University Press.

Rogoff, B. (1990). *Apprenticeship in thinking: Cognitive development in social context.* New York: Oxford University Press.

Rogoff, B., Paradise, R., Arauz, R. M., Correa-Chavez, M., & Angelillo, C. (2003). Firsthand learning through intent participation. *Annual Review of Psychology, 54,* 175–203.

Rollins, B. C., & Feldman, H. (1970). Marital satisfaction over the family life cycle. *Journal of Marriage & the Family, 32,* 20–28.

Román, G. C. (2003). Stroke, cognitive decline and vascular dementia: The silent epidemic of the 21st century. *Neuroepidemiology, 22,* 161–164.

Rome, E. S., Ammerman, S., Rosen, D. S., Keller, R. J., Lock, J., Mammel, K. A., O'Toole, J., Rees, J. M., Sanders, M. J., Sawyer, S. M., Schneider, M., Sigel, E., & Silber, T. J. (2003). Children and adolescents with eating disorders: The state of the art. *Pediatrics, 111,* e98–108.

Rook, K. S., Catalano, R., & Dooley, D. (1989). The timing of major life events: Effects of departing from the social clock. *American Journal of Community Psychology, 17,* 233–258.

Roosa, M. W., Morgan-Lopez, A. A., Cree, W. K., & Specter, M. M. (2002). Ethnic culture, poverty, and context: Sources of influence on Latino families and children. In J. M. Contreras, K. A. Kerns, & A. M. Neal-Barnett (Eds.), *Latino children and families in the United States: Current research and future directions* (pp. 27–44). Westport, CT: Praeger.

Root, R. W., & Resnick, R. J. (2003). An update on the diagnosis and treatment of attention-deficit/hyperactivity disorder in children. *Professional Psychology: Research and Practice, 34,* 34–41.

Rose, A. J., & Asher, S. R. (1999). Children's goals and strategies in response to conflicts within a friendship. *Developmental Psychology, 35,* 69–79.

Rose, A. J., & Asher, S. R. (2000). Children's friendships. In C. Hendrick & S. S. Hendrick (Eds.), *Close relationships: A sourcebook* (pp. 47–57). Thousand Oaks, CA: Sage.

Rosen, B., & Jerdee, T. H. (1995). *The persistence of age and sex stereotypes in the 1990s.* Washington, DC: American Association of Retired Persons.

Rosenbaum, J. E. (2001). *Beyond college for all: Career paths for the forgotten half.* New York: Russell Sage Foundation.

Rosenbaum, J. E., & Kariya, T. (1989). From high school to work: Market and institutional mechanisms in Japan. *American Journal of Sociology, 94,* 1334–1365.

Rosenstein, D., & Oster, H. (1988). Differential facial responses to four basic tastes in newborns. *Child Development, 59,* 1555–1568.

Rossi, G. (1997). The nestlings: Why young adults stay at home longer: The Italian case. *Journal of Family Issues, 18,* 627–644.

Rosso, I. M., Young, A. D., Femia, L. A., & Yurgelun-Todd, D. A. (2004). Cognitive and emotional components of frontal lobe functioning in childhood and adolescence. In R. E. Dahl & L. P. Spear (Eds.), *Adolescent brain development: Vulnerabilities and opportunities* (Vol. 1021, pp. 355–362). New York: New York Academy of Sciences.

Roth, J. L., & Brooks-Gunn, J. (2003). What exactly is a youth development program? Answers from research and practice. *Applied Developmental Science, 7,* 94–111.

Rothbart, M. K., & Bates, J. E. (1998). Temperament. In W. Damon (Series Ed.) & N. Eisenberg (Vol. Ed.), *Handbook of child psychology: Vol. 3. Social, emotional, and personality development* (5th ed., pp. 105–176). New York: Wiley.

Rothermund, K., & Brandtstädter, J. (2003). Depression in later life: Cross-sequential patterns and possible determinants. *Psychology and Aging, 18,* 80–90.

Rowe, D. C. (1981). Environmental and genetic influences on dimensions of perceived parenting: A twin study. *Developmental Psychology, 17,* 203–208.

Rowe, D. C. (1983). A biometrical analysis of perceptions of family environment: A study of twin and singleton sibling kinships. *Child Development, 54,* 416–423.

Rowe, D. C. (2003). Assessing genotype-environment interactions and correlations in the postgenomic era. In R. Plomin, J. C. DeFries, I. W. Craig, & P. McGuffin (Eds.), *Behavioral genetics in the postgenomic era* (pp. 71–86). Washington, DC: American Psychological Association.

Rowe, D. C., & Rodgers, J. L. (1994). A social contagion model of adolescent sexual behavior: Explaining race differences. *Social Biology, 41,* 1–18.

Rowe, J. W., & Kahn, R. L. (1998). *Successful aging.* New York: Pantheon Books.

Royal College of Obstetricians and Gynaecologists [RCOG]. (1999). Alcohol consumption in pregnancy. Retrieved January 25, 2006, from http://www.rcog.org.uk/index.asp?PageID=509

Rubertsson, C., Waldenström, U., & Wickberg, B. (2003). Depressive mood in early pregnancy: Prevalence and women at risk in a national Swedish sample. *Journal of Reproductive and Infant Psychology, 21,* 113–123.

Rubertsson, C., Waldenström, U., Wickberg, B., Radestad, I., & Hildingsson, I. (2005). Depressive mood in early pregnancy and postpartum: Prevalence and women at risk in a national Swedish sample. *Journal of Reproductive and Infant Psychology, 23,* 155–166.

Rubin, K. H., Bukowski, W., & Parker, J. G. (1998). Peer interactions, relationships, and groups. In W. Damon (Series Ed.) & N. Eisenberg (Vol. Ed.), *Handbook of child psychology: Vol 3. Social, emotional, and personality development* (5th ed., pp. 619–700). Hoboken, NJ: Wiley.

Rubin, K. H., Burgess, K. B., Dwyer, K. M., & Hastings, P. D. (2003). Predicting preschoolers' externalizing behaviors from toddler temperament, conflict, and maternal negativity. *Developmental Psychology, 39,* 164–176.

Rubinstein, R. L. (1986). The construction of a day by elderly widowers. *International Journal of Aging & Human Development, 23,* 161–173.

Ruffman, T., Perner, J., Naito, M., Parkin, L., & Clements, W. A. (1998). Older (but not younger) siblings facilitate false belief understanding. *Developmental Psychology, 34,* 161–174.

Rule, A. C., & Stewart, R. A. (2002). Effects of practical life materials on kindergartners' fine motor skills. *Early Childhood Education Journal, 30,* 9–13.

Rushton, J. P., & Jensen, A. R. (2005). Thirty years of research on race differences in cognitive ability. *Psychology, Public Policy, and Law, 11,* 235–294.

Russell, A., Hart, C. H., Robinson, C. C., & Olsen, S. F. (2003). Children's sociable and aggressive behavior with peers: A comparison of the US and Australian, and contributions of temperament and parenting styles. *International Journal of Behavioral Development, 27,* 74–86.

Ryan, E. B., Anas, A. P., Beamer, M., & Bajorek, S. (2003). Coping with age-related vision loss in everyday reading activities. *Educational Gerontology, 29,* 37–54.

Ryan, R. M., Deci, E. L., Grolnick, W. S., & La Guardia, J. G. (2006). The significance of autonomy and autonomy support in psychological development and psychopathology. In D. Cicchetti & D. J. Cohen (Eds.), *Developmental psychopathology, Vol. 1: Theory and method* (2nd ed., pp. 795–849). Hoboken, NJ: Wiley.

Rybash, J. M., Hoyer, W. J., & Roodin, P. (1986). *Adult cognition and aging: Developmental changes in processing, knowing, and thinking.* New York: Pergamon Press.

Saarni, C. (1999). *The development of emotional competence.* New York: Guilford Press.

Sachs, G. A. (1994). Increasing the prevalence of advance care planning. *Hastings Center Report,* 24(Suppl. 6), S13–16.

Sagi, A., Koren-Karie, N., Gini, M., Ziv, Y., & Joels, T. (2002). Shedding further light on the effects of various types and quality of early child care on infant-mother attachment relationship: The Haifa Study of Early Child Care. *Child Development,* 73, 1166–1186.

Sagi, A., van IJzendoorn, M. H., Aviezer, O., Donnell, F., & Mayseless, O. (1994). Sleeping out of home in a Kibbutz communal arrangement: It makes a difference for infant-mother attachment. *Child Development,* 65, 992–1004.

Sagi-Schwartz, A. (2003). Introduction to the special issue: Extreme life events and catastrophic experiences and the development of attachment across the life span. *Attachment & Human Development,* 5, 327–329.

Sagi-Schwartz, A., & Aviezer, O. (2005). Correlates of attachment to multiple caregivers in kibbutz children from birth to emerging adulthood: The Haifa Longitudinal Study. In K. E. Grossmann, K. Grossmann, & E. Waters (Eds.), *Attachment from infancy to adulthood: The major longitudinal studies* (pp. 165–197). New York: Guilford Press.

Saginak, K. A., & Saginak, M. A. (2005). Balancing work and family: Equity, gender, and marital satisfaction. *Family Journal: Counseling and Therapy for Couples and Families,* 13, 162–166.

Sahyoun, N. R., Lentzner, H., Hoyert, D., & Robinson, K. N. (2001). *Aging trends: Trends in causes of death among the elderly* (No. 1). Hyattsville, MD: Centers for Disease Control and Prevention.

Salisbury, A., Law, K., LaGasse, L., & Lester, B. (2003). Maternal-fetal attachment. *Journal of the American Medical Association,* 289, 1701.

Salthouse, T. A. (1991). *Theoretical perspectives on cognitive aging.* Hillsdale, NJ: Erlbaum.

Salthouse, T. A. (1992). The information-processing perspective on cognitive aging. In R. J. Sternberg & C. A. Berg (Eds.), *Intellectual development* (pp. 261–277). New York: Cambridge University Press.

Salthouse, T. A. (1994). Aging associations: Influence of speed on adult age differences in associative learning. *Journal of Experimental Psychology: Learning, Memory, and Cognition,* 20, 1486–1503.

Salthouse, T. A. (1996). General and specific speed mediation of adult age differences in memory. *Journals of Gerontology: Series B: Psychological Sciences and Social Sciences,* 51B, P30–P42.

Salthouse, T. A. (2000). Pressing issues in cognitive aging. In D. C. Park & N. Schwarz (Eds.), *Cognitive aging: A primer* (pp. 43–54). New York: Psychology Press.

Salthouse, T. A. (2003). Memory aging from 18 to 80. *Alzheimer Disease and Associated Disorders,* 17, 162–167.

Salthouse, T. A., Berish, D. E., & Miles, J. D. (2002). The role of cognitive stimulation on the relations between age and cognitive functioning. *Psychology and Aging,* 17, 548–557.

Salthouse, T. A., & Ferrer-Caja, E. (2003). What needs to be explained to account for age-related effects on multiple cognitive variables? *Psychology and Aging,* 18, 91–110.

Sameroff, A. J., Lewis, M., & Miller, S. M. (Eds.). (2000). *Handbook of developmental psychopathology* (2nd ed.). New York: Kluwer.

Samson, J. F., & de Groot, L. (2001). Study of a group of extremely preterm infants (25–27 weeks): How do they function at 1 year of age? *Journal of Child Neurology,* 16, 832–837.

Sanders, S. A., & Reinisch, J. M. (1990). Biological and social influences on the endocrinology of puberty: Some additional considerations. In J. Bancroft & J. M. Reinisch (Eds.), *Adolescence and puberty* (pp. 50–62). New York: Oxford University Press.

Sandfort, T. G. M., de Graaf, R., & Bijl, R. V. (2003). Same-sex sexuality and quality of life: Findings from the Netherlands Mental Health Survey and Incidence Study. *Archives of Sexual Behavior,* 32, 15–22.

Sandstrom, K. L. (2003). On coming to terms with death and dying: Neglected dimensions of identity work In C. D. Bryant (Ed.), *Handbook of death & dying* (pp. 468–474). Thousand Oaks, CA: Sage.

Sandstrom, M. J., & Cillessen, A. H. N. (2003). Sociometric status and children's peer experiences: Use of the daily diary method. *Merrill-Palmer Quarterly,* 49, 427–452.

Sano, M. (2003). Current concepts in the prevention of Alzheimer's disease. *CNS Spectrums,* 8, 846–853.

Santa Maria, M. (2002). Youth in Southeast Asia: Living within the continuity of tradition and the turbulence of change. In B. B. Brown, R. W. Larson, & T. S. Saraswathi (Eds.), *The world's youth: Adolescence in eight regions of the globe* (pp. 171–206). New York: Cambridge University Press.

Sattler, J. M. (2001). *Assessment of children: Cognitive applications* (4th ed.). La Mesa, CA: Jerome M. Sattler.

Saudino, K. J., Ronald, A., & Plomin, R. (2005). The etiology of behavior problems in 7-year-old twins: Substantial genetic influence and negligible shared environmental influence for parent ratings and ratings by same and different teachers. *Journal of Abnormal Child Psychology,* 33, 113–130.

Savin-Williams, R. C. (2001). *Mom, dad, I'm gay. How families negotiate coming out.* Washington, DC: American Psychological Association.

Savin-Williams, R. C., & Ream, G. L. (2003). Sex variations in the disclosure to parents of same-sex attractions. *Journal of Family Psychology,* 17, 429–438.

Savishinsky, J. (2004). The volunteer and the Sannyasin: Archetypes of retirement in America and India. *International Journal of Aging & Human Development,* 59, 25–41.

Sax, L. J., Astin, A. W., Korn, W. S., & Mahoney, K. M. (1999). *The American freshman: National norms for Fall 1999.* Los Angeles: Higher Education Research Institute.

Sayer, L. C., Bianchi, S. M., & Robinson, J. P. (2004). Are parents investing less in children? Trends in mothers' and fathers' time with children. *American Journal of Sociology,* 110, 1–43.

Scarr, S. (1992). Developmental theories for the 1990s: Development and individual differences. *Child Development,* 63, 1–19.

Scarr, S. (1997). Behavior-genetic and socialization theories of intelligence: Truce and reconciliation. In R. J. Sternberg & E. L. Grigorenko (Eds.), *Intelligence, heredity, and environment* (pp. 3–41). New York: Cambridge University Press.

Scarr, S., & Deater-Deckard, K. (1997). Family effects on individual differences in development. In S. S. Luthar, J. A. Burack, D. Cicchetti, & J. R. Weisz (Eds.), *Developmental psychopathology: Perspectives on adjustment, risk, and disorder* (pp. 115–136). New York: Cambridge University Press.

Scarr, S., & Ricciuti, A. (1991). What effects do parents have on their children? In L. Okagaki & R. J. Sternberg (Eds.), *Directors of development: Influences on the development of children's thinking* (pp. 3–23). Hillsdale, NJ: Erlbaum.

Schacke, C., & Zank, S. R. (2006). Measuring the effectiveness of adult day care as a facility to support family caregivers of dementia patients. *Journal of Applied Gerontology, 25,* 65–81.

Schaie, K. W. (1988). The impact of research methodology on theory building in the developmental sciences. In J. E. Birren & V. L. Bengtson (Eds.), *Emergent theories of aging* (pp. 41–57). New York: Springer.

Schaie, K. W. (1996). Intellectual development in adulthood. In J. E. Birren, K. W. Schaie, R. P. Abeles, M. Gatz, & T. A. Salthouse (Eds.), *Handbook of the psychology of aging* (4th ed., pp. 266–286). San Diego, CA: Academic Press.

Schaie, K. W., Willis, S. L., & Caskie, G. I. L. (2004). The Seattle longitudinal study: Relationship between personality and cognition. *Aging, Neuropsychology, and Cognition, 11,* 304–324.

Schaie, K. W., & Zanjani, F. A. K. (2006). Intellectual development across adulthood. In C. Hoare (Ed.), *Handbook of adult development and learning* (pp. 99–122). New York: Oxford University Press.

Schenk, D. (2006). Treatment of Alzheimer's disease: The beginning of a new era: Dale Schenk, ISOA—October 5th-6th, 2005. *Current Alzheimer Research, 3,* 177.

Scher, A., Epstein, R., & Tirosh, E. (2004). Stability and changes in sleep regulation: A longitudinal study from 3 months to 3 years. *International Journal of Behavioral Development, 28,* 268–274.

Scher, A., Zukerman, S., & Epstein, R. (2005). Persistent night waking and settling difficulties across the first year: Early precursors of later behavioural problems? *Journal of Reproductive and Infant Psychology, 23,* 77–88.

Schirduan, V., & Case, K. (2004). Mindful curriculum leadership for students with attention deficit hyperactivity disorder: Leading in elementary schools by using multiple intelligences theory (SUMIT). *Teachers College Record, 106,* 87–95.

Schlegel, A. (1995). The cultural management of adolescent sexuality. In P. R. Abramson & S. D. Pinkerton (Eds.), *Sexual nature, sexual culture* (pp. 177–194). Chicago: University of Chicago Press.

Schlegel, A., & Barry, H., III. (1991). *Adolescence: An anthropological inquiry.* New York: Free Press.

Schlinger, H. D. (2003). The myth of intelligence. *Psychological Record, 53,* 15–32.

Schmidt, M. E., DeMulder, E. K., & Denham, S. (2002). Kindergarten social-emotional competence: Developmental predictors and psychosocial implications. *Early Child Development and Care, 172,* 451–462.

Schmitt, D. P., Shackelford, T. K., Duntley, J., Tooke, W., Buss, D. M., Fisher, M. L., Lavellée, M., & Vasey, P. (2002). Is there an early-30s peak in female sexual desire? Cross-sectional evidence from the United States and Canada. *Canadian Journal of Human Sexuality, 11,* 1–18.

Schnaiberg, A., & Goldenberg, S. (1989). From empty nest to crowded nest: The dynamics of incompletely-launched young adults. *Social Problems, 36,* 251–269.

Schneidman, E. (Ed.). (1976). *Death: Current perspectives.* Palo Alto, CA: Mayfield.

Schoen, R. (1992). First unions and the stability of first marriages. *Journal of Marriage and the Family, 54,* 281–284.

Schoen, R., & Cheng, Y.-H. A. (2006). Partner choice and the differential retreat from marriage. *Journal of Marriage and Family, 68,* 1–10.

Schoen, R., & Weinick, R. M. (1993). Partner choice in marriages and cohabitations. *Journal of Marriage and the Family, 55,* 408–414.

Schooler, C. (1990). Psychosocial factors and effective cognitive functioning in adulthood. In J. E. Birren & K. W. Schaie (Eds.), *Handbook of the psychology of aging* (3rd ed., pp. 347–358). San Diego, CA: Academic Press.

Schooler, C. (1999). The workplace environment: Measurement, psychological effects, and basic issues. In S. L. Friedman & T. D. Wachs (Eds.), *Measuring environment across the life span: Emerging methods and concepts* (pp. 229–246). Washington, DC: American Psychological Association.

Schooler, C. (2001). The intellectual effects of the demands of the work environment. In R. J. Sternberg & E. L. Grigorenko (Eds.), *Environmental effects on cognitive abilities* (pp. 363–380). Mahwah, NJ: Erlbaum.

Schooler, C., Mulatu, M. S., & Oates, G. (2004). Occupational self-direction, intellectual functioning, and self-directed orientation in older workers: Findings and implications for individuals and societies. *American Journal of Sociology, 110,* 161–197.

Schor, J. (1991). *The overworked American: The unexpected decline of leisure.* New York: Basic Books.

Schraf, M., & Hertz-Lazarowitz, R. (2003). Social networks in the school context: Effects of culture and gender. *Journal of Social and Personal Relationships, 20,* 843–858.

Schultz, D., & Shaw, D. S. (2003). Boys' maladaptive social information processing, family emotional climate, and pathways to early conduct problems. *Social Development, 12,* 440–460.

Schulz, K. P., Tang, C. Y., Fan, J., Marks, D. J., Newcorn, J. H., Cheung, A. M., & Halperin, J. M. (2005). Differential prefrontal cortex activation during inhibitory control in adolescents with and without childhood attention-deficit/hyperactivity disorder. *Neuropsychology, 19,* 390–402.

Schupf, N., Pang, D., Patel, B. N., Silverman, W., Schubert, R., Lai, F., Kline, J. K., Stern, Y., Ferin, M., Tycko, B., & Mayeux, R. (2003). Onset of dementia is associated with age at menopause in women with Down's syndrome. *Annals of Neurology, 54,* 433–438.

Schwartz, A. N., Campos, J. J., & Baisel, E. J. (1973). The visual cliff: Cardiac and behavioral responses on the deep and shallow sides at five and nine months of age. *Journal of Experimental Child Psychology, 15,* 86–99.

Schwartz, C. E., Wright, C. I., Shin, L. M., Kagan, J., & Rauch, S. L. (2003, June 20). Inhibited and uninhibited infants "grown up": Adult amygdalar response to novelty. *Science, 300,* 1952–1953.

Schwartz, D., Dodge, K. A., Coie, J. D., Hubbard, J. A., Cillessen, A. H. N., Lemerise, E. A., & Bateman, H. (1998). Social-cognitive and behavioral correlates of aggression and victimization in boys' play groups. *Journal of Abnormal Child Psychology, 26,* 431–440.

Schwartz, P., & Rutter, V. (1998). *The gender of sexuality.* Thousand Oaks, CA: Pine Forge Press.

Schweinle, W. E., & Ickes, W. (2002). On empathic accuracy and husbands' abusiveness: The "overattribution bias". In P. Noller & J. A. Feeney (Eds.), *Understanding marriage: Developments in the study of couple interaction* (pp. 228–250). New York: Cambridge University Press.

Schwimmer, J. B., Burwinkle, T. M., & Varni, J. W. (2003). Health-related quality of life of severely obese children and adolescents. *Journal of the American Medical Association, 289,* 1813–1819.

Scrimsher, S., & Tudge, J. (2003). The teaching/learning relationship in the first years of school: Some revolutionary implications of Vygotsky's theory. *Early Education and Development, 14,* 293–312.

Sehgal, A., Galbraith, A., Chesney, M., Schoenfeld, P., Charles, G., & Lo, B. (1992). How strictly do dialysis patients want their advance directives followed? *Journal of the American Medical Association, 267,* 59–63.

Seifer, R., Sameroff, A. J., Dickstein, S., Hayden, L. C., & Schiller, M. (1996). Parental psychopathology and sleep variation in children. *Child and Adolescent Psychiatric Clinics of North America, 5,* 715–727.

Seifritz, E., Esposito, F., Neuhoff, J. G., Luthi, A., Mustovic, H., Dammann, G., von Bardeleben, U., Radue, E. W., Cirillo, S., Tedeschi, G., & Di Salle, F. (2003). Differential sex-independent amygdala response to infant crying and laughing in parents versus nonparents. *Biological Psychiatry, 54,* 1367–1375.

Self-Brown, S. R., & Mathews, S. (2003). Effects of classroom structure on student achievement goal orientation. *Journal of Educational Research, 97,* 106–111.

Seligman, M. E. P., Reivich, K., Jaycox, L., & Gillham, J. (1995). *The optimistic child.* Boston: Houghton Mifflin.

Senghas, A., & Coppola, M. (2001). Children creating language: How Nicaraguan sign language acquired a spatial grammar. *Psychological Science, 12,* 323–328.

Seymour, J., Gott, M., Bellamy, G., Ahmedzai, S. H., & Clark, D. (2004). Planning for the end of life: The views of older people about advance care statements. *Social Science & Medicine, 59,* 57–68.

Shaibu, S., & Wallhagen, M. I. (2002). Family caregiving of the elderly in Botswana: Boundaries of culturally acceptable options and resources. *Journal of Cross-Cultural Gerontology, 17,* 139–154.

Shamir-Essakow, G., Ungerer, J. A., Rapee, R. M., & Safier, R. (2004). Caregiving representations of mothers of behaviorally inhibited and uninhibited preschool children. *Developmental Psychology, 40,* 899–910.

Shapiro, R. L., Lockman, S., Thior, I., Stocking, L., Kebaabetswe, P., Wester, C., Peter, T., Marlink, R., Essex, M., & Heymann, S. J. (2003). Low adherence to recommended infant feeding strategies among HIV-infected women: Results from the pilot phase of a randomized trial to prevent mother-to-child transmission in Botswana. *AIDS Education and Prevention, 15,* 221–230.

Shaw, D. S., Gilliom, M., Ingoldsby, E. M., & Nagin, D. S. (2003). Trajectories leading to school-age conduct problems. *Developmental Psychology, 39,* 189–200.

Shayer, M. (2003). Not just Piaget; not just Vygotsky, and certainly not Vygotsky as alternative to Piaget. *Learning and Instruction, 13,* 465–485.

Shaywitz, S. E., & Shaywitz, B. A. (2001). The neurobiology of reading and dyslexia. *Focus on Basics, 5*(A), 11–15.

Shearer, C. L., Crouter, A. C., & McHale, S. M. (2005). Parents' perceptions of changes in mother-child and father-child relationships during adolescence. *Journal of Adolescent Research, 20,* 662–684.

Shelden, R. G., Tracy, S. K., & Brown, W. B. (1997). *Youth gangs in American society.* Belmont, CA: Wadsworth.

Shernoff, D. J., Csikszentmihalyi, M., Shneider, B., & Shernoff, E. S. (2003). Student engagement in high school classrooms from the perspective of flow theory. *School Psychology Quarterly, 18,* 158–176.

Shiner, R. L., Masten, A. S., & Tellegen, A. (2002). A developmental perspective on personality in emerging adulthood: Childhood antecedents and concurrent adaptation. *Journal of Personality and Social Psychology, 83,* 1165–1177.

Shonk, S. M., & Cicchetti, D. (2001). Maltreatment, competency deficits, and risk for academic and behavioral maladjustment. *Developmental Psychology, 37,* 3–17.

Shonkoff, J. P., & Phillips, D. A. (2000a). *From neurons to neighborhoods: The science of early childhood development.* Washington, DC: National Academy Press.

Shonkoff, J. P., & Phillips, D. A. (2000b). Growing up in child care. In J. P. Shonkoff & D. A. Phillips (Eds.), *From neurons to neighborhoods: The science of early childhood development* (pp. 297–327). Washington, DC: National Academy Press.

Shweder, R. A., Goodnow, J., Hatano, G., LeVine, R. A., Markus, H., & Miller, P. (1998). The cultural psychology of development: One mind, many mentalities. In W. Damon (Series Ed.) & R. M. Lerner (Vol. Ed.), *Handbook of child psychology: Vol. 1. Theoretical models of human development* (5th ed., pp. 865–937). Hoboken, NJ: Wiley.

Siegler, A. L. (2005). Home is where the hurt is: Developmental consequences of domestic conflict and violence on children and adolescents. In L. Gunsberg & P. Hymowitz (Eds.), *A handbook of divorce and custody: Forensic, developmental, and clinical perspectives* (pp. 61–80). Hillsdale, NJ: Analytic Press.

Siklos, S., & Kerns, K. A. (2004). Assessing multitasking in children with ADHD using a modified Six Elements Test. *Archives of Clinical Neuropsychology, 19,* 347–361.

Silbereisen, R. K., & Kracke, B. (1997). Self-reported maturational timing and adaptation in adolescence. In J. Schulenberg, J. L. Maggs, & K. Hurrelmann (Eds.), *Health risks and developmental transitions during adolescence* (pp. 85–109). New York: Cambridge University Press.

Silbereisen, R. K., Petersen, A. C., Albrecht, H. T., & Kracke, B. (1989). Maturational timing and the development of problem behavior: Longitudinal studies in adolescence. *The Journal of Early Adolescence, 9,* 247–268.

Silverman, P. R., & Klass, D. (1996). Introduction: What's the problem? In D. Klass, P. R. Silverman, & S. L. Nickman (Eds.), *Continuing bonds: New understandings of grief* (pp. 3–27). Washington, DC: Taylor & Francis.

Silverstein, M., Conroy, S. J., Wang, H., Giarrusso, R., & Bengtson, V. L. (2002). Reciprocity in parent-child relations over the adult life course. *Journals of Gerontology: Series B: Psychological Sciences and Social Sciences, 57B,* S3–S13.

Simes, M. R., & Berg, D. H. (2001). Surreptitious learning: Menarche and menstrual product advertisements. *Health Care for Women International, 22,* 455–469.

Simion, F., & Butterworth, G. (Eds.). (1998). *The development of sensory, motor, and cognitive capacities in early infancy: From perception to cognition.* Hove, England: Psychology Press/Erlbaum (UK), Taylor and Francis.

Simmons, R. G., & Blyth, D. A. (1987). *Moving into adolescence: The impact of pubertal change and school context.* Hawthorne, NY: Aldine.

Simmons, R. G., Carlton-Ford, S. L., & Blyth, D. A. (1987). Predicting how a child will cope with the transition to junior high school. In R. M. Lerner & T. T. Foch (Eds.), *Biological-psychosocial interactions in early adolescence* (pp. 325–375). Hillsdale, NJ: Erlbaum.

Simonton, D. K. (1997). Creative productivity: A predictive and explanatory model of career trajectories and landmarks. *Psychological Review, 104,* 66–89.

Simonton, D. K. (2002). Longitudinal changes in creativity. In D. K. Simonton (Ed.), *Great psychologists and their times: Scientific insights into psychology's history* (pp. 67–101). Washington, DC: American Psychological Association.

Simpson, J. A., Rholes, W. S., Oriña, M. M., & Grich, J. (2002). Working models of attachment, support giving, and support seeking in a stressful situation. *Personality and Social Psychology Bulletin, 28,* 598–608.

Sims, R. V., McGwin, G., Allman, R. M., Ball, K., & Owsley, C. (2000). Exploratory study of incident vehicle crashes among older drivers. *Journals of Gerontology: Series A: Biological Sciences and Medical Sciences, 55A,* M22-M27.

Singer, T., Verhaeghen, P., Ghisletta, P., Lindenberger, U., & Baltes, P. B. (2003). The fate of cognition in very old age: Six-year longitudinal findings in the Berlin Aging Study (BASE). *Psychology and Aging, 18,* 318–331.

Singg, S. (2003). Parents and the death of a child In C. D. Bryant (Ed.), *Handbook of death & dying* (pp. 880–884). Thousand Oaks, CA: Sage.

Singley, S., & Hynes, K. (2005). Transitions to parenthood: Work-family policies, gender, and the couple context. *Gender & Society, 19,* 376–397.

Sinnott, J. D. (1989). General systems theory: A rationale for the study of everyday memory. In L. W. Poon, D. C. Rubin, & B. A. Wilson (Eds.), *Everyday cognition in adulthood and late life* (pp. 59–70). New York: Cambridge University Press.

Sinnott, J. D. (1991). Limits to problem solving: Emotion, intention, goal clarity, health, and other factors in postformal thought. In J. D. Sinnott & J. C. Cavanaugh (Eds.), *Bridging paradigms: Positive development in adulthood and cognitive aging* (pp. 169–201). New York: Praeger.

Sinnott, J. D. (1998). *The development of logic in adulthood: Postformal thought and its applications.* New York: Plenum Press.

Sinnott, J. D. (2003). Postformal thought and adult development: Living in balance. In J. Demick & C. Andreoletti (Eds.), *Handbook of adult development* (pp. 221–238). New York: Kluwer/Plenum.

Sisk, C. L., & Foster, D. L. (2004). The neural basis of puberty and adolescence. *Nature Neuroscience, 7,* 1040–1042.

Skinner, B. F. (1960). *The behavior of organisms: An experimental analysis.* New York: Appleton-Century-Crofts.

Skinner, B. F. (1974). *About behaviorism.* New York: Knopf.

Skrzypek, S., Wehmeier, P. M., & Remschmidt, H. (2001). Body image assessment using body size estimation in recent studies on anorexia nervosa. A brief review. *European Child & Adolescent Psychiatry, 10,* 215–221.

Slade, L., & Ruffman, T. (2005). How language does (and does not) relate to theory of mind: A longitudinal study of syntax, semantics, working memory and false belief. *British Journal of Developmental Psychology, 23,* 117–141.

Slater, A. (2001). Visual perception. In G. Bremner & A. Fogel (Eds.), *Blackwell handbook of infant development* (pp. 5–34). Malden, MA: Blackwell.

Slater, A., Mattock, A., & Brown, E. (1990). Size constancy at birth: Newborn infants' responses to retinal and real size. *Journal of Experimental Child Psychology, 49,* 314–322.

Slater, A., Von der Schulenburg, C., Brown, E., Badenoch, M., Butterworth, G., Parsons, S., & Samuels, C. (1998). Newborn infants prefer attractive faces. *Infant Behavior & Development, 21,* 345–354.

Small, B. J., Hertzog, C., Hultsch, D. F., & Dixon, R. A. (2003). Stability and change in adult personality over 6 years: Findings from the Victoria Longitudinal Study. *Journals of Gerontology: Series B: Psychological Sciences and Social Sciences, 58B,* P166-P176.

Smetana, J. G., Campione-Barr, N., & Metzger, A. (2006). Adolescent development in interpersonal and societal contexts. *Annual Review of Psychology, 57,* 255–284.

Smetana, J. G., Daddis, C., & Chuang, S. S. (2003). "Clean your room!" A longitudinal investigation of adolescent-parent conflict and conflict resolution in middle-class African American families. *Journal of Adolescent Research, 18,* 631–650.

Smetana, J. G., Kochanska, G., & Chuang, S. (2000). Mothers' conceptions of everyday rules for young toddlers: A longitudinal investigation. *Merrill-Palmer Quarterly, 46,* 391–416.

Smith, C. L., & Rojewski, J. W. (1993). School-to-work transition: Alternatives for educational reform. *Youth & Society, 25,* 222–250.

Smith, L. B., Thelen, E., Titzer, R., & McLin, D. (1999). Knowing in the context of acting: The task dynamics of the A-not-B error. *Psychological Review, 106,* 235–260.

Smith, M. C. (1998). Sibling placement in foster care: An exploration of associated concurrent preschool-aged child functioning. *Children and Youth Services Review, 20,* 389–412.

Smith, M. E. (1926). An investigation of the development of the sentence and the extent of vocabulary in young children. *University of Iowa Studies: Child Welfare, 3,* 92.

Smith, P. K. (1982). Does play matter? Functional and evolutionary aspects of animal and human play. *Behavioral and Brain Sciences, 5,* 139–184.

Smith, P. K., Cowie, H., Olafsson, R. F., Liefooghe, A. P. D., Almeida, A., Araki, H., del Barrio, C., Costabile, A., Dekleva, B., Houndoumadi, A., Kim, K., Olaffson, R. P., Ortega, R., Pain, J., Pateraki, L., Schafer, M., Singer, M., Smorti, A., Toda, Y., Tomasson, H., & Wenxin, Z. (2002). Definitions of bullying: A comparison of terms used, and age and gender differences, in a fourteen-country international comparison. *Child Development, 73,* 1119–1133.

Smith, P. K., Morita, Y., Junger-Tas, J., Olweus, D., Catalano, R. F., & Slee, P. (Eds.). (1999). *The nature of school bullying: A cross-national perspective.* Florence, KY: Taylor & Frances/Routledge.

Smith, P. K., Smees, R., Pellegrini, A. D., & Menesini, E. (2002). Comparing pupil and teacher perceptions for playful fighting, serious fighting, and positive peer interaction. In J. L. Roopnarine (Ed.), *Conceptual, social-cognitive, and contextual issues in the fields of play* (pp. 235–245). Westport, CT: Ablex.

Smock, P. J., & Gupta, S. (2002). Cohabitation in contemporary North America. In A. Booth & A. C. Crouter (Eds.), *Just living together: Implications of cohabitation on families, children, and social policy* (pp. 53–84). Mahwah, NJ: Erlbaum.

Smock, P. J., Manning, W. D., & Porter, M. (2005). "Everything's there except money": How money shapes decisions to marry among cohabitors. *Journal of Marriage and Family, 67,* 680–696.

Smolucha, L., & Smolucha, F. (1998). The social origins of mind: Post-Piagetian perspectives on pretend play. In O. N. Saracho & B. Spodek (Eds.), *Multiple perspectives on play in early childhood education* (pp. 34–58). Albany, NY: State University of New York Press.

Snarey, J. R. (1985). Cross-cultural universality of social-moral development: A critical review of Kohlbergian research. *Psychological Bulletin, 97,* 202–232.

Snow, C. E. (1999). Social perspectives on the emergence of language. In B. MacWhinney (Ed.), *The emergence of language* (pp. 257–276). Mahwah, NJ: Erlbaum.

Snyder, K., & Bloom, J. D. (2004). Physician reporting of impaired drivers: A new trend in state law? *Journal of the American Academy of Psychiatry and the Law, 32,* 76–79.

Snyder, L. (1999). *Speaking our minds: Personal reflections from individuals with Alzheimer's.* New York: Freeman.

Soltis, J. (2004). The signal functions of early infant crying. *Behavioral and Brain Sciences, 27,* 443–490.

Song, Y., & Lu, H.-H. (2002). Early childhood poverty: A statistical profile. Retrieved January 13, 2006, from Columbia University, National Center for Children in Poverty (NCCP) Web site: http://www.nccp.org/pub_ecp02.html

Sood, B. G., Bailey, B. N., Covington, C., Sokol, R. J., Ager, J., Janisse, J., Hannigan, J. H., & Delaney-Black, V. (2005). Gender and alcohol moderate caregiver reported child behavior after prenatal cocaine. *Neurotoxicology and Teratology, 27,* 191–201.

Sossou, M.-A. (2002). Widowhood practices in West Africa: The silent victims. *International Journal of Social Welfare, 11,* 201–209.

Souza, P. E., & Hoyer, W. J. (1996). Age-related hearing loss: Implications for counseling. *Journal of Counseling & Development, 74,* 652–655.

Spitzer, D., Neufeld, A., Harrison, M., Hughes, K., & Stewart, M. (2003). Caregiving in transnational context: "My wings have been cut; where can I fly?" *Gender & Society, 17,* 267–286.

Spitzer, R. L. (2003). Can some gay men and lesbians change their sexual orientation? 200 participants reporting a change from homosexual to heterosexual orientation. *Archives of Sexual Behavior, 32,* 403–417.

Spronk, K. (2004). Good death and bad death in ancient Israel according to biblical lore. *Social Science & Medicine, 58,* 985–995.

Sroufe, L. A. (2000). Early relationships and the development of children. *Infant Mental Health Journal, 21,* 67–74.

Sroufe, L. A. (2002). From infant attachment to promotion of adolescent autonomy: Prospective, longitudinal data on the role of parents in development. In J. G. Borkowski, S. L. Ramey, & M. Bristol-Power (Eds.), *Parenting and the child's world: Influences on academic, intellectual, and social-emotional development* (pp. 187–202). Mahwah, NJ: Erlbaum.

Sroufe, L. A., Egeland, B., Carlson, E., & Collins, W. A. (2005). Placing early attachment experiences in developmental context: The Minnesota Longitudinal Study. In K. E. Grossmann, K. Grossmann, & E. Waters (Eds.), *Attachment from infancy to adulthood: The major longitudinal studies* (pp. 48–70). New York: Guilford Press.

St James-Roberts, I., & Conroy, S. (2005). Do pregnancy and childbirth adversities predict infant crying and colic? Findings and recommendations. *Neuroscience & Biobehavioral Reviews, 29,* 313–320.

Stahl, G. K., Miller, E. L., & Tung, R. L. (2002). Toward the boundaryless career: A closer look at the expatriate career concept and the perceived implications of an international assignment. *Journal of World Business, 37,* 216–227.

Stamatiadis, N. (1996). Gender effect on the accident patterns of elderly drivers. *Journal of Applied Gerontology, 15,* 8–22.

Stamatiadis, N., Agent, K. R., & Ridgeway, M. (2003). Driver license renewal for the elderly: A case study. *Journal of Applied Gerontology, 22,* 42–56.

Stams, G.-J. J. M., Juffer, F., & van IJzendoorn, M. H. (2002). Maternal sensitivity, infant attachment, and temperament in early childhood predict adjustment in middle childhood: The case of adopted children and their biologically unrelated parents. *Developmental Psychology, 38,* 806–821.

Stanford, E. P., & Usita, P. M. (2002). Retirement: Who is at risk? *Generations, 26*(2), 45–48.

Stark, P., & Hickson, L. (2004). Outcomes of hearing aid fitting for older people with hearing impairment and their significant others. *International Journal of Audiology, 43,* 390–398.

State of Oregon Department of Human Services. (n.d.). Death with dignity act. Retrieved October 17, 2006, from http://oregon.gov/DHS/ph/pas/

Stattin, H., & Kerr, M. (2000). Parental monitoring: A reinterpretation. *Child Development, 71,* 1072–1085.

Stattin, H., & Magnusson, D. (1990). *Pubertal maturation in female development.* Hillsdale, NJ: Erlbaum.

Steele, S., Joseph, R. M., & Tager-Flusberg, H. (2003). Brief report: Developmental change in theory of mind abilities in children with autism. *Journal of Autism and Developmental Disorders, 33,* 461–467.

Stein, J. H., & Reiser, L. W. (1994). A study of White middle-class adolescent boys' responses to "semenarche" (the first ejaculation). *Journal of Youth and Adolescence, 23,* 373–384.

Steinberg, L. (2001). We know some things: Parent-adolescent relationships in retrospect and prospect. *Journal of Research on Adolescence, 11,* 1–19.

Steinberg, L. (2004). Risk taking in adolescence: What changes, and why? In R. E. Dahl & L. P. Spear (Eds.), *Adolescent brain development: Vulnerabilities and opportunities* (Vol. 1021, pp. 51–58). New York: New York Academy of Sciences.

Steinberg, L. (2005). Cognitive and affective development in adolescence. *Trends in Cognitive Sciences, 9,* 69–74.

Steinberg, L., & Scott, E. S. (2003). Less guilty by reason of adolescence: Developmental immaturity, diminished responsibility, and the juvenile death penalty. *American Psychologist, 58,* 1009–1018.

Steinberg, L. D., & Hill, J. P. (1978). Patterns of family interaction as a function of age, the onset of puberty, and formal thinking. *Developmental Psychology, 14,* 683–684.

Stenberg, G. (2003). Effects of maternal inattentiveness on infant social referencing. *Infant and Child Development, 12,* 399–419.

Stephens, D., Vetter, N., & Lewis, P. (2003). Investigating lifestyle factors affecting hearing aid candidature in the elderly. *International Journal of Audiology, 42*(Suppl. 2), 2S33–32S38.

Sternberg, R. J. (1984). Toward a triarchic theory of human intelligence. *Behavioral and Brain Sciences, 7,* 269–315.

Sternberg, R. J. (1986). A triangular theory of love. *Psychological Review, 93,* 119–135.

Sternberg, R. J. (1988). Triangulating love. In R. J. Sternberg & M. L. Barnes (Eds.), *The psychology of love* (pp. 119–138). New Haven, CT: Yale University Press.

Sternberg, R. J. (1996). *Successful intelligence: How practical and creative intelligence determine success in life.* New York: Simon & Schuster.

Sternberg, R. J. (1997). The triarchic theory of intelligence. In D. P. Flanagan, J. L. Genshaft, & P. L. Harrison (Eds.), *Contemporary intellectual assessment: Theories, tests, and issues* (pp. 92–104). New York: Guilford Press.

Sternberg, R. J. (2004). A triangular theory of love. In H. T. Reis & C. E. Rusbult (Eds.), *Close relationships: Key readings* (pp. 213–227). Philadelphia: Taylor & Francis.

Sternberg, R. J., & Berg, C. A. (1992). *Intellectual development.* New York: Cambridge University Press.

Sternberg, R. J., & Grigorenko, E. L. (2000). Practical intelligence and its development. In R. Bar-On & J. D. A. Parker (Eds.), *The handbook of emotional intelligence: Theory, development, assessment, and application at home, school, and in the workplace* (pp. 215–243). San Francisco: Jossey-Bass.

Sternberg, R. J., Grigorenko, E. L., & Bundy, D. A. (2001). The predictive value of IQ. *Merrill-Palmer Quarterly, 47,* 1–41.

Sternberg, R. J., Grigorenko, E. L., & Kidd, K. K. (2005). Intelligence, race, and genetics. *American Psychologist, 60,* 46–59.

Sternberg, R. J., Torff, B., & Grigorenko, E. L. (1998). Teaching for successful intelligence raises school achievement. *Phi Delta Kappan, 79,* 667–669.

Stessman, J., Hammerman-Rozenberg, R., Maaravi, Y., & Cohen, A. (2002). Effects of exercise on ease in performing activities of daily living and instrumental activities of daily living from age 70 to 77: The Jerusalem Longitudinal Study. *Journal of the American Geriatrics Society, 50,* 1934–1938.

Stewart, A. J., Copeland, A. P., Chester, N. L., Malley, J. E., & Barenbaum, N. B. (1997). *Separating together: How divorce transforms families.* New York: Guilford Press.

Stewart, A. J., Ostrove, J. M., & Helson, R. (2001). Middle aging in women: Patterns of personality change from the 30s to the 50s. *Journal of Adult Development, 8,* 23–37.

Stewart, A. J., & Vandewater, E. A. (1998). The course of generativity. In D. P. McAdams & E. de St. Aubin (Eds.), *Generativity and adult development: How and why we care for the next generation* (pp. 75–100). Washington, DC: American Psychological Association.

Stewart, C., & Power, T. G. (2003). Ethnic, social class, and gender differences in adolescent drinking: Examining multiple aspects of consumption. *Journal of Adolescent Research, 18,* 575–598.

Stewart-Knox, B., Gardiner, K., & Wright, M. (2003). What is the problem with breast-feeding? A qualitative analysis of infant feeding perceptions. *Journal of Human Nutrition and Dietetics, 16,* 265–273.

Stice, E., & Shaw, H. (2004). Eating disorder prevention programs: A meta-analytic review. *Psychological Bulletin, 130,* 206–227.

Stice, E., & Whitenton, K. (2002). Risk factors for body dissatisfaction in adolescent girls: A longitudinal investigation. *Developmental Psychology, 38,* 669–678.

Stigler, J. W., & Hiebert, J. (1999). *The teaching gap: Best ideas from the world's teachers for improving education in the classroom.* New York: Free Press.

Stins, J. F., Tollenaar, M. S., Slaats-Willemse, D. I. E., Buitelaar, J. K., Swaab-Barneveld, H., Verhulst, F. C., Polderman, T. C., & Boomsma, D. I. (2005). Sustained attention and executive functioning performance in attention-deficit/hyperactivity disorder. *Child Neuropsychology, 11,* 285–294.

Stipek, D. J. (1996). Motivation and instruction. In D. C. Berliner & R. C. Calfee (Eds.), *Handbook of educational psychology* (pp. 85–113). New York: Macmillan Library Reference.

Stipek, D. J. (1997). Success in school—For a head start in life. In S. S. Luthar, J. A. Burack, D. Cicchetti, & J. R. Weisz (Eds.), *Developmental psychopathology: Perspectives on adjustment, risk, and disorder* (pp. 75–92). New York: Cambridge University Press.

Stone, M. R., & Brown, B. B. (1998). In the eye of the beholder: Adolescents' perceptions of peer crowd stereotypes. In R. E. Muuss & H. D. Porton (Eds.), *Adolescent behavior and society: A book of readings* (5th ed., pp. 158–169). New York: McGraw-Hill.

Stradmeijer, M., Bosch, J., Koops, W., & Seidell, J. (2000). Family functioning and psychosocial adjustment in overweight youngsters. *International Journal of Eating Disorders, 27,* 110–114.

Straus, M. A., & Donnelly, D. A. (1994). *Beating the devil out of them: Corporal punishment in American families.* New York: Lexington Books.

Straus, M. A., & Stewart, J. H. (1999). Corporal punishment by American parents: National data on prevalence, chronicity, severity, and duration, in relation to child and family characteristics. *Clinical Child and Family Psychology Review, 2,* 55–70.

Strauss, B. (2002). *Involuntary childlessness: Psychological assessment, counseling, and psychotherapy.* Seattle, WA: Hogrefe & Huber.

Strawbridge, W. J., Wallhagen, M. I., Shema, S. J., & Kaplan, G. A. (2000). Negative consequences of hearing impairment in old age: A longitudinal analysis. *Gerontologist, 40,* 320–326.

Streissguth, A. P., Sampson, P. D., Barr, H. M., Bookstein, F. L., & Olson, H. C. (1994). The effects of prenatal exposure to alcohol and tobacco: Contributions from the Seattle Longitudinal Prospective Study and implications for public policy. In H. L. Needleman & D. Bellinger (Eds.), *Prenatal exposure to toxicants: Developmental consequences* (pp. 148–183). Baltimore: Johns Hopkins University Press.

Striegel-Moore, R. H., Seeley, J. R., & Lewinsohn, P. M. (2003). Psychosocial adjustment in young adulthood of women who experienced an eating disorder during adolescence. *Journal of the American Academy of Child & Adolescent Psychiatry, 42,* 587–593.

Strong, T. H. (2000). *Expecting trouble: The myth of prenatal care in America.* New York: New York University Press.

Sturm, R. (2004). The economics of physical activity: Societal trends and rationales for interventions. *American Journal of Preventive Medicine,* 27(Suppl. 3), 126–135.

Subrahmanyam, K., Greenfield, P. M., & Tynes, B. (2004). Constructing sexuality and identity in an online teen chat room. *Journal of Applied Developmental Psychology, 25,* 651–666.

Sugisawa, H., Shibata, H., Hougham, G. W., Sugihara, Y., & Liang, J. (2002). The impact of social ties on depressive symptoms in U.S. and Japanese elderly. *Journal of Social Issues, 58,* 785–804.

Sullivan, A. M., Warren, A. G., Lakoma, M. D., Liaw, K. R., Hwang, D., & Block, S. D. (2004). End-of-life care in the curriculum: A national study of medical education deans. *Academic Medicine, 79,* 760–768.

Sullivan, H. S. (1953). *The interpersonal theory of psychiatry.* New York: Norton.

Sun, S. S., Schubert, C. M., Chumlea, W. C., Roche, A. F., Kulin, H. E., Lee, P. A., Himes, J. H., & Ryan, A. S. (2002). National estimates of the timing of sexual maturation and racial differences among US children. *Pediatrics, 110,* 911–919.

Suomi, S. J. (2004). How gene-environment interactions shape biobehavioral development: Lessons from studies with rhesus monkeys. *Research in Human Development, 1,* 205–222.

Super, C. M., & Harkness, S. (2003). The metaphors of development. *Human Development, 46,* 3–23.

Super, D. E. (1957). *The psychology of careers: An introduction to vocational development.* New York: Harper.

Surra, C. A., & Hughes, D. K. (1997). Commitment processes in accounts of the development of premarital relationships. *Journal of Marriage & the Family, 59,* 5–21.

Surra, C. A., Hughes, D. K., & Jacquet, S. E. (1999). The development of commitment to marriage: A phenomenological approach. In J. M. Adams & W. H. Jones (Eds.), *Handbook of interpersonal commitment and relationship stability* (pp. 125–148). Dordrecht, Netherlands: Kluwer Academic.

Sutcliffe, P. A., Bishop, D. V. M., & Houghton, S. (2006). Sensitivity of four subtests of the Test of Everyday Attention for Children (TEA-Ch) to stimulant medication in children with ADHD. *Educational Psychology, 26,* 325–337.

Suzuki, H. (2003). The Japanese way of death. In C. D. Bryant (Ed.), *Handbook of death & dying* (pp. 656–672). Thousand Oaks, CA: Sage.

Suzuki, L. K., & Greenfield, P. M. (2002). The construction of everyday sacrifice in Asian Americans and European Americans: The roles of ethnicity and acculturation. *Cross-Cultural Research: The Journal of Comparative Social Science, 36,* 200–228.

Swann, W. B., & Pittman, T. S. (1977). Initiating play activity of children: The moderating influence of verbal cues on intrinsic motivation. *Child Development, 48,* 1128–1132.

Swarr, A. E., & Richards, M. H. (1996). Longitudinal effects of adolescent girls' pubertal development, perceptions of pubertal timing, and parental relations on eating problems. *Developmental Psychology, 32,* 636–646.

Sweeney, M. M. (2002). Two decades of family change: The shifting economic foundations of marriage. *American Sociological Review, 67,* 132–147.

Szinovacz, M. E. (2003). Caring for a demented relative at home: Effects on parent-adolescent relationships and family dynamics. *Journal of Aging Studies, 17,* 445–472.

Talpade, M., & Talpade, S. (2001). Early puberty in African-American girls: Nutrition past and present. *Adolescence, 36,* 789–794.

Tamis-LeMonda, C. S., & Cabrera, N. (2002). *Handbook of father involvement: Multidisciplinary perspectives.* Mahwah, NJ: Erlbaum.

Tang, W.-R., Aaronson, L. S., & Forbes, S. A. (2004). Quality of life in hospice patients with terminal illness. *Western Journal of Nursing Research, 26,* 113–128.

Tangney, J. P. (1995). Recent advances in the empirical study of shame and guilt. *American Behavioral Scientist, 38,* 1132–1145.

Tangney, J. P. (1998). How does guilt differ from shame? In J. Bybee (Ed.), *Guilt and children* (pp. 1–17). San Diego, CA: Academic Press.

Tangney, J. P. (2003). Self-relevant emotions. In M. R. Leary & J. P. Tangney (Eds.), *Handbook of self and identity* (pp. 384–400). New York: Guilford Press.

Tanner, E. M., & Finn-Stevenson, M. (2002). Nutrition and brain development: Social policy implications. *American Journal of Orthopsychiatry, 72,* 182–193.

Tanner, J. M. (1955). *Growth at adolescence.* Oxford, UK: Blackwell.

Tanner, J. M. (1978). *Foetus into man: Physical growth from conception to maturity.* Cambridge, MA: Harvard University Press.

Tanner, J. M. (1990). *Foetus into man: Physical growth from conception to maturity* (Rev. and enl. ed.). Cambridge, MA: Harvard University Press.

Tanzi, R. E., & Parson, A. B. (2000). *Decoding darkness: The search for the genetic causes of Alzheimer's disease.* Cambridge, MA: Perseus.

Tardif, T., & Wellman, H. M. (2000). Acquisition of mental state language in Mandarin- and Cantonese-speaking children. *Developmental Psychology, 36,* 25–43.

Taylor, M. A., & Doverspike, D. (2003). Retirement planning. In G. A. Adams & T. A. Beehr (Eds.), *Retirement: Reasons, processes, and results* (pp. 53–82). New York: Springer.

Taylor, S. E., & Seeman, T. E. (1999). Psychosocial resources and the SES-health relationship. In N. E. Adler, M. Marmot, B. S. McEwen, & J. Stewart (Eds.), *Socioeconomic status and health in industrial nations: Social, psychological, and biological pathways* (pp. 210–225). New York: New York Academy of Sciences.

Terry, R. D. (2006). Alzheimer's disease and the aging brain. *Journal of Geriatric Psychiatry and Neurology, 19,* 125–128.

Teti, D. M., Sakin, J. W., Kucera, E., Corns, K. M., & Eiden, R. D. (1996). And baby makes four: Predictors of attachment security among preschool-age firstborns during the transition to siblinghood. *Child Development, 67,* 579–596.

Thapar, A., Fowler, T., Rice, F., Scourfield, J., van den Bree, M., Thomas, H., Harold, G., & Hay, D. (2003). Maternal smoking during pregnancy and attention deficit hyperactivity disorder symptoms in offspring. *American Journal of Psychiatry, 160,* 1985–1989.

Thelen, E., Corbetta, D., Kamm, K., Spencer, J. P., Schneider, K., & Zernicke, R. F. (1993). The transition to reaching: Mapping intention and intrinsic dynamics. *Child Development, 64,* 1058–1098.

Thiessen, E. D., Hill, E. A., & Saffran, J. R. (2005). Infant-directed speech facilitates word segmentation. *Infancy*, 7, 53–71.

Thoman, E. B., & Whitney, M. P. (1990). Behavioral states in infants: Individual differences and individual analyses. In J. Colombo & J. W. Fagen (Eds.), *Individual differences in infancy: Reliability, stability, prediction* (pp. 113–135). Hillsdale, NJ: Erlbaum.

Thomas, A., & Chess, S. (1977). *Temperament and development*. Oxford, England: Brunner/Mazel.

Thomas, A., Chess, S., & Birch, H. G. (1968). *Temperament and behavior disorders in children*. Oxford, England: New York University Press.

Thomas, C., Morris, S. M., & Clark, D. (2004). Place of death: Preferences among cancer patients and their carers. *Social Science & Medicine*, 58, 2431–2444.

Thomas, J. R., & French, K. E. (1985). Gender differences across age in motor performance: A meta-analysis. *Psychological Bulletin*, 98, 260–282.

Thome, M., & Skuladottir, A. (2005). Changes in sleep problems, parents distress and impact of sleep problems from infancy to preschool age for referred and unreferred children. *Scandinavian Journal of Caring Sciences*, 19, 86–94.

Thompson, C. A., Beauvais, L. L., & Lyness, K. S. (1999). When work-family benefits are not enough: The influence of work-family culture on benefit utilization, organizational attachment, and work-family conflict. *Journal of Vocational Behavior*, 54, 392–415.

Thompson, M., Grace, C. O. N., & Cohen, L. J. (2001). *Best friends, worst enemies: Understanding the social lives of children*. New York: Ballantine.

Thompson, R. A. (1999). Early attachment and later development. In J. Cassidy & P. R. Shaver (Eds.), *Handbook of attachment: Theory, research, and clinical applications* (pp. 265–286). New York: Guilford Press.

Thomson, E., & Colella, U. (1992). Cohabitation and marital stability: Quality or commitment. *Journal of Marriage and the Family*, 54, 259–267.

Thorne, B. (1993). *Gender play: Girls and boys in school*. New Brunswick, NJ: Rutgers University Press.

Thornton, A., & Young-DeMarco, L. (2001). Four decades of trends in attitudes toward family issues in the United States: The 1960s through the 1990s. *Journal of Marriage & the Family*, 63, 1009–1037.

Tilden, V. P., Tolle, S. W., Drach, L. L., & Perrin, N. A. (2004). Out-of-hospital death: Advance care planning, decedent symptoms, and caregiver burden. *Journal of the American Geriatrics Society*, 52, 532–539.

Timimi, S. (2004). A critique of the International Consensus Statement on ADHD. *Clinical Child and Family Psychology Review*, 7, 59–63.

Tinto, V. (1987). *Leaving college: Rethinking the causes and cures of student attrition*. Chicago: University of Chicago Press.

Tisserand, D. J., & Jolles, J. (2003). On the involvement of prefrontal networks in cognitive ageing. *Cortex*, 39, 1107–1128.

Tolman, D. L. (1999). Female adolescent sexuality in relational context: Beyond sexual decision making. In N. G. Johnson, M. C. Roberts, & J. Worell (Eds.), *Beyond appearance: A new look at adolescent girls* (pp. 227–246). Washington, DC: American Psychological Association.

Tolman, D. L., Spencer, R., Harmon, T., Rosen-Reynoso, M., & Striepe, M. (2004). Getting close, staying cool: Early adolescent boys' experiences with romantic relationships. In N. Way & J. Y. Chu (Eds.), *Adolescent boys: Exploring diverse cultures of boyhood* (pp. 235–255). New York: New York University Press.

Tomasello, M. (2001). Cultural transmission: A view from chimpanzees and human infants. *Journal of Cross-Cultural Psychology*, 32, 135–146.

Tomlinson, M., Cooper, P., & Murray, L. (2005). The mother-infant relationship and infant attachment in a South African peri-urban settlement. *Child Development*, 76, 1044–1054.

Tremblay, L., & Frigon, J.-Y. (2005). Precocious puberty in adolescent girls: A biomarker of later psychosocial adjustment problems. *Child Psychiatry & Human Development*, 36, 73–94.

Triandis, H. C. (1995). *Individualism & collectivism*. Boulder, CO: Westview Press.

Trickett, P. K., Kurtz, D. A., & Pizzigati, K. (2004). Resilient outcomes in abused and neglected children: Bases for strengths-based intervention and prevention policies. In K. I. Maton, C. J. Schellenbach, B. J. Leadbeater, & A. L. Solarz (Eds.), *Investing in children, youth, families, and communities: Strengths-based research and policy* (pp. 73–95). Washington, DC: American Psychological Association.

Troll, L. E. (1983). Grandparents: The family watchdog. In T. H. Brubaker (Ed.), *Family relationships in later life* (pp. 63–74). Beverly Hills, CA: Sage.

Troxel, W. M., & Matthews, K. A. (2004). What are the costs of marital conflict and dissolution to children's physical health? *Clinical Child and Family Psychology Review*, 7, 29–57.

Tucker, P., & Aron, A. (1993). Passionate love and marital satisfaction at key transition points in the family life cycle. *Journal of Social & Clinical Psychology*, 12, 135–147.

Tully, L. A., Arseneault, L., Caspi, A., Moffitt, T. E., & Morgan, J. (2004). Does maternal warmth moderate the effects of birth weight on twins' attention-deficit/hyperactivity disorder (ADHD) symptoms and low IQ? *Journal of Consulting and Clinical Psychology*, 72, 218–226.

Tulving, E. (1985). How many memory systems are there? *American Psychologist*, 40, 385–398.

Tulving, E., & Craik, F. I. M. (2000). *The Oxford handbook of memory*. New York: Oxford University Press.

Turcotte, P., & Bélanger, A. (1997). Moving in together: The formation of first common-law unions. *Canadian Social Trends*, 47, 7–11.

Turkheimer, E., Haley, A., Waldron, M., D'Onofrio, B., & Gottesman, I. I. (2003). Socioeconomic status modifies heritability of IQ in young children. *Psychological Science*, 14, 623–628.

Turkington, C., & Alper, M. M. (2001). *The encyclopedia of fertility and infertility*. New York: Facts On File.

Turner, L., Mermelstein, R., & Flay, B. (2004). Individual and contextual influences on adolescent smoking. In R. E. Dahl & L. P. Spear (Eds.), *Adolescent brain development: Vulnerabilities and opportunities* (Vol. 1021, pp. 175–197). New York: New York Academy of Sciences.

Turner, M., & Rack, J. (2004). *The study of dyslexia*. New York: Kluwer.

Turner, S., & Alborz, A. (2003). Academic attainments of children with Down's syndrome: A longitudinal study. *British Journal of Educational Psychology*, 73, 563–583.

2004 World Population Data Sheet. (2004). Retrieved January 13, 2006, from Population Reference Bureau Web site: http://www.prb.org/pdf04/04WorldData Sheet_Eng.pdf

U.S. Bureau of Labor Statistics. (2006). Current population survey. Retrieved July 12, 2006, from Bureau of Labor Statistics Web site: http://www.bls.gov/cps/

U.S. Department of Agriculture Food and Nutrition Service. (n.d.-a). Food stamp program: Frequently asked questions. Retrieved March 24, 2006, from http://www.fns.usda.gov/fsp/faqs.htm

U.S. Department of Agriculture Food and Nutrition Service. (n.d.-b). Women, infants and children: Frequently asked questions about WIC. Retrieved March 24, 2006, from http://www.fns.usda.gov/wic/FAQs/faq.htm

U.S. Department of Health and Human Services [USDHHS]. (2004). Prevalence of overweight among children and adolescents: United States, 1999–2002. Retrieved April 13, 2006, from Centers for Disease Control and Prevention Web site: http://www.cdc.gov/nchs/products/pubs/pubd/hestats/overwght99.htm

U.S. Department of Health and Human Services Administration for Children and Families. (2005). Head Start impact study: First year findings. Retrieved March 28, 2006, from http://www.acf.hhs.gov/programs/opre/hs/impact_study/reports/first_yr_finds/first_yr_finds.pdf

U.S. Department of Health and Human Services Administration for Children and Families [USDHHS]. (2002). Making a difference in the lives of infants and toddlers and their families: The impacts of Early Head Start: Executive summary. Retrieved March 28, 2006, from http://www.acf.hhs.gov/programs/opre/ehs/ehs_resrch/reports/impacts_exesum/impacts_execsum.pdf

Udry, J. R. (1990). Biosocial models of adolescent problem behaviors. Social Biology, 37, 1–10.

Udry, J. R. (2000). Biological limits of gender construction. American Sociological Review, 65, 443–457.

Udry, J. R., & Campbell, B. C. (1994). Getting started on sexual behavior. In A. S. Rossi (Ed.), Sexuality across the life course (pp. 187–207). Chicago: University of Chicago Press.

Ulbrich, P. M., Coyle, A. T., & Llabre, M. M. (1990). Involuntary childlessness and marital adjustment: His and hers. Journal of Sex & Marital Therapy, 16, 147–158.

Umbach, P. D., & Porter, S. R. (2002). How do academic departments impact student satisfaction? Understanding the contextual effects of departments. Research in Higher Education, 43, 209–234.

Umberson, D., & Gove, W. R. (1989). Parenthood and psychological well-being: Theory, measurement, and stage in the family life course. Journal of Family Issues, 10, 440–462.

Umeta, M., West, C. E., Verhoef, H., Haidar, J., & Hautvast, J. G. A. J. (2003). Factors associated with stunting in infants aged 5–11 months in the Dodota-Sire district, Rural Ethiopia. Journal of Nutrition, 133, 1064–1069.

UNICEF (United Nations Children's Fund). (2002b). The state of the world's children 2003. New York: Author.

United Nations Children's Fund. (2002a). Profiting from abuse (No. E.01.XX.14). New York: Author.

United Nations Development Programme. (2003). Human development report 2003: Millennium development goals: A compact among nations to end human poverty. New York: Oxford University Press.

United States General Accounting Office. (2003, March). Report to congressional requesters: Newborn screening: Characteristics of state programs (GAO-03-449). Washington, DC: Author.

Vaillant, G. E. (1977). Adaptation to life. Boston: Little, Brown.

van den Brink, C. L., Tijhuis, M., van den Bos, G. A. M., Giampaoli, S., Kivinen, P., Nissinen, A., & Kromhout, D. (2004). Effect of widowhood on disability onset in elderly men from three European countries. Journal of the American Geriatrics Society, 52, 353–358.

van der Geest, S. (2002). Respect and reciprocity: Care of elderly people in rural Ghana. Journal of Cross-Cultural Gerontology, 17, 3–31.

van Hoof, A. (1999a). The identity status approach: In need of fundamental revision and qualitative change. Developmental Review, 19, 622–647.

van Hoof, A. (1999b). The identity status field re-reviewed: An update of unresolved and neglected issues with a view on some alternative approaches. Developmental Review, 19, 497–556.

van IJzendoorn, M. H., & Sagi, A. (1999). Cross-cultural patterns of attachment: Universal and contextual dimensions. In J. Cassidy & P. R. Shaver (Eds.), Handbook of attachment: Theory, research, and clinical applications (pp. 713–734). New York: Guilford Press.

Vandermaas-Peeler, M., King, C., Clayton, A., Holt, M., Kurtz, K., Maestri, L., Morris, E., & Woody, E. (2002). Parental scaffolding during joint play with preschoolers. In J. L. Roopnarine (Ed.), Conceptual, social-cognitive, and contextual issues in the fields of play (pp. 165–181). Westport, CT: Ablex.

Vartanian, T. P., & McNamara, J. M. (2002). Older women in poverty: The impact of midlife factors. Journal of Marriage and Family, 64, 532–547.

Verbrugge, L. M. (1990). The twain meet: Empirical explanations of sex differences in health and mortality. In M. G. Ory & H. R. Warner (Eds.), Gender, health, and longevity: Multidisciplinary perspectives (pp. 159–199). New York: Springer.

Verwoerdt, A., Pfeiffer, E., & Wang, H. S. (1969). Sexual behavior in senescence. II. Patterns of sexual activity and interest. Geriatrics, 24, 137–154.

Volkmar, F. (2005). Editorial: Toward understanding the basis of ADHD. American Journal of Psychiatry, 162, 1043–1044.

von Bothmer, M. I. K., & Fridlund, B. (2005). Gender differences in health habits and in motivation for a healthy lifestyle among Swedish university students. Nursing & Health Sciences, 7, 107–118.

Von Raffler-Engel, W. (1994). The perception of the unborn across the cultures of the world. Seattle, WA: Hogrefe & Huber.

Vondracek, F. W., & Skorikov, V. B. (1997). Leisure, school, and work activity preferences and their role in vocational identity development. Career Development Quarterly, 45, 322–340.

Vygotsky, L. S. (1962). Thought and language (E. Hanfmann & G. Vakar, Eds. & Trans.). New York: MIT Press and Wiley. (Original work published 1934)

Vygotsky, L. S. (1978). Mind in society: The development of higher psychological processes. Cambridge, MA: Harvard University Press. (Original work published 1935)

Vygotsky, L. S. (1978). *Mind in society: The development of higher psychological processes* (M. Cole, V. John-Steiner, S. Scribner, & E. Souberman, Eds.). Cambridge, MA: Harvard University Press. (Original work published 1935)

Vygotsky, L. S. (1986). *Thought and language* (A. Kozulin, Ed., E. Hanfmann & G. Vakar, Trans., Revised ed.). Cambridge, MA: MIT Press. (Original work published 1934)

Wade, T. J., Cairney, J., & Pevalin, D. J. (2002). Emergence of gender differences in depression during adolescence: National panel results from three countries. *Journal of the American Academy of Child & Adolescent Psychiatry, 41,* 190–198.

Wadsworth, B. J. (1989). *Piaget's theory of cognitive and affective development* (4th ed.). New York: Longman.

Wadsworth, B. J. (1996). *Piaget's theory of cognitive and affective development: Foundations of constructivism* (5th ed.). White Plains, NY: Longman.

Wagner, R. K. (1997). Intelligence, training, and employment. *American Psychologist, 52,* 1059–1069.

Wagner, R. K., & Sternberg, R. J. (1984). Alternative conceptions of intelligence and their implications for education. *Review of Educational Research, 54,* 179–223.

Wagner, T. (2000). *How schools change: Lessons from three communities revisited* (2nd ed.). New York: RoutledgeFalmer.

Wagstaff, A., & Watanabe, N. (2000). *Socioeconomic inequalities in child malnutrition in the developing world* (Policy Research Working Paper No. 2434). Washington, DC: World Bank.

Waite, L. J., & Gallagher, M. (2000). *The case for marriage: Why married people are happier, healthier, and better off financially.* New York: Doubleday.

Walden, T., Lemerise, E., & Smith, M. C. (1999). Friendship and popularity in preschool classrooms. *Early Education and Development, 10,* 351–371.

Walker, E. F., Sabuwalla, Z., & Huot, R. (2004). Pubertal neuromaturation, stress sensitivity, and psychopathology. *Development and Psychopathology, 16,* 807–824.

Walker, G. C. (2003). Medical euthanasia. In C. D. Bryant (Ed.), *Handbook of death & dying* (pp. 405–423). Thousand Oaks, CA: Sage.

Wallhagen, M. I., Strawbridge, W. J., & Kaplan, G. A. (1996). Six-year impact of hearing impairment on psychosocial and physiologic functioning. *The Nurse Practitioner, 21,* 11–14.

Wallin, A. K., Gustafson, L., Sjögren, M., Wattmo, C., & Minthon, L. (2004). Five-year outcome of cholinergic treatment of Alzheimer's disease: Early response predicts prolonged time until nursing home placement, but does not alter life expectancy. *Dementia and Geriatric Cognitive Disorders, 18,* 197–206.

Walter, T. (2003, July 24). Historical and cultural variants on the good death. *BMJ, 327,* 218–220.

Wang, Q. (2004). The emergence of cultural self-constructs: Autobiographical memory and self-description in European American and Chinese children. *Developmental Psychology, 40,* 3–15.

Wapner, R., Thom, E., Simpson, J. L., Pergament, E., Silver, R., Filkins, K., Platt, L., Mahoney, M., Johnson, A., Hogge, W., Wilson, R., Mohide, P., Hershey, D., Krantz, D., Zachary, J., Snijders, R., Greene, N., Sabbagha, R., MacGregor, S., Hill, L., Gagnon, A., Hallahan, T., & Jackson, L. (2003). First-trimester screening for trisomies 21 and 18. *New England Journal of Medicine, 349,* 1405–1413.

Warden, D., & Mackinnon, S. (2003). Prosocial children, bullies and victims: An investigation of their sociometric status, empathy and social problem-solving strategies. *British Journal of Developmental Psychology, 21,* 367–385.

Warr, P., Butcher, V., Robertson, I., & Callinan, M. (2004). Older people's well-being as a function of employment, retirement, environmental characteristics and role preference. *British Journal of Psychology, 95,* 297–324.

Wass, H. (2004). A perspective on the current state of death education. *Death Studies, 28,* 289–308.

Waterman, A. S. (1999). Identity, the identity statuses, and identity status development: A contemporary statement. *Developmental Review, 19,* 591–621.

Waters, E., Merrick, S., Treboux, D., Crowell, J., & Albersheim, L. (2000). Attachment security in infancy and early adulthood: A twenty-year longitudinal study. *Child Development, 71,* 684–689.

Watson, J. B. (1930). *Behaviorism* (Revised ed.). New York: W. W. Norton.

Watson, J. B. (1998). *Behaviorism.* New Brunswick, NJ: Transaction. (Original work published 1924)

Watson, J. B. (with the assistance of Watson, R. R.). (1972). *Psychological care of infant and child.* New York: Arno Press. (Original work published 1928)

Webster-Stratton, C., & Lindsay, D. W. (1999). Social competence and conduct problems in young children: Issues in assessment. *Journal of Clinical Child Psychology, 28,* 25–43.

Wechsler, D. (1991). *Wechsler intelligence scale for children (WISC-III).* San Antonio, TX: The Psychological Corporation.

Weese-Mayer, D. E., Berry-Kravis, E. M., Zhou, L., Maher, B. S., Curran, M. E., Silvestri, J. M., & Marazita, M. L. (2004). Sudden infant death syndrome: Case-control frequency differences at genes pertinent to early autonomic nervous system embryologic development. *Pediatric Research, 56,* 391–395.

Weibel-Orlando, J. (1999). Powwow princess and gospelettes: Growing up in grandmother's world. In M. Schweitzer (Ed.), *Indian grandparenthood* (pp. 181–202). Albuquerque, NM: University of New Mexico Press.

Weigel, D. J., Bennett, K. K., & Ballard-Reisch, S. (2003). Family influences on commitment: Examining the family of origin correlates of relationship commitment attitudes. *Personal Relationships, 10,* 453–474.

Weinfield, N. S., Sroufe, L. A., & Egeland, B. (2000). Attachment from infancy to early adulthood in a high-risk sample: Continuity, discontinuity, and their correlates. *Child Development, 71,* 695–702.

Weinfield, N. S., Sroufe, L. A., Egeland, B., & Carlson, E. A. (1999). The nature of individual differences in infant-caregiver attachment. In J. Cassidy & P. R. Shaver (Eds.), *Handbook of attachment: Theory, research, and clinical applications* (pp. 68–88). New York: Guilford Press.

Weisfeld, G. (1997). Puberty rites as clues to the nature of human adolescence. *Cross-Cultural Research: The Journal of Comparative Social Science, 31,* 27–54.

Weisman, A. D. (1984). Denial and middle knowledge. In E. Schneidman (Ed.), *Death: Current perspectives* (pp. 452–469). Palo Alto, CA: Mayfield.

Weissman, M. M., Myers, J. K., Tischler, G. L., Holzer, C. E., 3rd, Leaf, P. J., Orvaschel, H., & Brody, J. A. (1985). Psychiatric disorders (DSM-III) and cognitive impairment among the elderly in a U.S. urban community. *Acta Psychiatrica Scandinavica, 71,* 366–379.

Welles, C. E. (2005). Breaking the silence surrounding female adolescent sexual desire. *Women & Therapy, 28,* 31–45.

Wellman, B. (1990). The place of kinfolk in personal community networks. *Marriage & Family Review, 15,* 195–228.

Weppelman, T. L., Bostow, A., Schiffer, R., Elbert-Perez, E., & Newman, R. S. (2003). Children's use of the prosodic characteristics of infant-directed speech. *Language & Communication, 23,* 63–80.

Werner, E. E., & Smith, R. S. (1982). *Vulnerable, but invincible: A longitudinal study of resilient children and youth.* New York: McGraw-Hill.

Werner, E. E., & Smith, R. S. (1992). *Overcoming the odds: High risk children from birth to adulthood.* Ithaca, NY: Cornell University Press.

Werth, B., & Tsiaras, A. (2002). *From conception to birth: A life unfolds.* New York: Doubleday.

Wertz, R. W., & Wertz, D. C. (1989). *Lying-in: A history of childbirth in America* (Expanded ed.). New Haven: Yale University Press.

Wetle, T. (1994). Individual preferences and advance directives. *Hastings Center Report, 24*(Suppl. 6), S5–8.

Whaley, A. L. (2000). Sociocultural differences in the developmental consequences of the use of physical discipline during childhood for African Americans. *Cultural Diversity & Ethnic Minority Psychology, 6,* 5–12.

Whitaker, D. J., Lutzker, J. R., & Shelley, G. A. (2005). Child maltreatment prevention priorities at the Centers for Disease Control and Prevention. *Child Maltreatment: Journal of the American Professional Society on the Abuse of Children, 10,* 245–259.

White, L., & Edwards, J. N. (1990). Emptying the nest and parental well-being: An analysis of national panel data. *American Sociological Review, 55,* 235–242.

White, N. R. (2002). "Not under my roof!" Young people's experience of home. *Youth & Society, 34,* 214–231.

White, S. H. (2000). Conceptual foundations of IQ testing. *Psychology, Public Policy, and Law, 6,* 33–43.

Whitebook, M., Howes, C., & Phillips, D. (1998). *Worthy work, unlivable wages: The national child care staffing study, 1988–1997.* Washington, DC: Center for the Child Care Workforce.

Whitehouse, P. J. (2003). Classification of the dementias. *Lancet, 361,* 1227.

Whiting, B. B., & Edwards, C. P. (1988). *Children of different worlds: The formation of social behavior.* Cambridge, MA: Harvard University Press.

Whiting, B. B., & Whiting, J. W. M. (1975). *Children of six cultures: A psycho-cultural analysis.* Cambridge, MA: Harvard University Press.

Wiegers, T. A., Keirse, M. J. N. C., van der Zee, J., & Berghs, G. A. H. (1996). Outcome of planned home and planned hospital births in low risk pregnancies: Prospective study in midwifery practices in the Netherlands. *BMJ, 313,* 1309–1313.

Wiener, J. M. (2003). An assessment of strategies for improving quality of care in nursing homes. *Gerontologist, 43,* 19–27.

Wiese, B. S., Freund, A. M., & Baltes, P. B. (2002). Subjective career success and emotional well-being: Longitudinal predictive power of selection, optimization and compensation. *Journal of Vocational Behavior, 60,* 321–335.

Wiesner, M., Kim, H. K., & Capaldi, D. M. (2005). Developmental trajectories of offending: Validation and prediction to young adult alcohol use, drug use, and depressive symptoms. *Development and Psychopathology, 17,* 251–270.

Wilcox, S., & Stefanick, M. L. (1999). Knowledge and perceived risk of major diseases in middle-aged and older women. *Health Psychology, 18,* 346–353.

Wiley, D., & Bortz, W. M., II. (1996). Sexuality and aging—Usual and successful. *Journals of Gerontology: Series A: Biological Sciences and Medical Sciences, 51A,* M142-M146.

Wilkinson, R. G. (1996). *Unhealthy societies: The afflictions of inequality.* New York: Routledge.

Wilks, C., & Melville, C. (1990). Grandparents in custody and access disputes. *Journal of Divorce, 13,* 1–14.

Willems, D. L., Hak, A., Visser, F., & Van der Wal, G. (2004). Thoughts of patients with advanced heart failure on dying. *Palliative Medicine, 18,* 564–572.

Williams, J., & Dayan, P. (2005). Dopamine, learning, and impulsivity: A biological account of attention-deficit/hyperactivity disorder. *Journal of Child and Adolescent Psychopharmacology, 15,* 160–179.

Williams, J. M., & Dunlop, L. C. (1999). Pubertal timing and self-reported delinquency among male adolescents. *Journal of Adolescence, 22,* 157–171.

Williams, W. M. (1998). Are we raising smarter children today? School- and home-related influences on IQ. In U. Neisser (Ed.), *The rising curve: Long-term gains in IQ and related measures* (pp. 125–154). Washington, DC: American Psychological Association.

Williamson, R. C., Rinehart, A. D., & Blank, T. O. (1992). *Early retirement: Promises and pitfalls.* New York: Insight Books/Plenum Press.

Willott, S., & Griffin, C. (2004). Redundant men: Constraints on identity change. *Journal of Community & Applied Social Psychology, 14,* 53–69.

Wilson, S. M., Ngige, L. W., & Trollinger, L. J. (2003). Connecting generations: Paths to Maasai and Kamba marriage in Kenya. In R. R. Hamon & B. B. Ingoldsby (Eds.), *Mate selection across cultures* (pp. 95–118). Thousand Oaks, CA: Sage.

Wimmer, H., & Perner, J. (1983). Beliefs about beliefs: Representation and constraining function of wrong beliefs in young children's understanding of deception. *Cognition, 13,* 103–128.

Wines, M. (2000, December 3). An ailing Russia lives a tough life that's getting shorter. *New York Times,* p. A1.

Winston, C. A. (2006). African American grandmothers parenting AIDS orphans: Grieving and coping. *Qualitative Social Work: Research and Practice, 5,* 33–43.

Wiseman, C. V., Sunday, S. R., & Becker, A. E. (2005). Impact of the media on adolescent body image. *Child and Adolescent Psychiatric Clinics of North America, 14,* 453–471.

Wolchik, S. A., Sandler, I. N., Winslow, E., & Smith-Daniels, V. (2005). Programs for promoting parenting of residential parents: Moving from efficacy to effectiveness. *Family Court Review, 43,* 65–80.

Wolfe, L. (2004). Should parents speak with a dying child about impending death? *New England Journal of Medicine, 351,* 1251–1253.

Wong, C.-Y., & Tang, C. S.-K. (2004). Coming out experiences and psychological distress of Chinese homosexual men in Hong Kong. *Archives of Sexual Behavior, 33,* 149–157.

Wong, E. H., Wiest, D. J., & Cusick, L. B. (2002). Perceptions of autonomy support, parent attachment, competence and self-worth as predictors of motivational orientation and academic achievement: An examination of sixth-and-ninth-grade regular education students. *Adolescence, 37,* 255–266.

Wood, D., Bruner, J. S., & Ross, G. (1976). The role of tutoring in problem solving. *Journal of Child Psychology and Psychiatry, 17,* 89–100.

Wood, W. R., & Williamson, J. B. (2003). Historical changes in the meaning of death in the western tradition. In C. D. Bryant (Ed.), *Handbook of death & dying* (pp. 14–23). Thousand Oaks, CA: Sage.

Woods, S., & Wolke, D. (2004). Direct and relational bullying among primary school children and academic achievement. *Journal of School Psychology, 42,* 135–155.

Worden, J. W. (1982). *Grief counseling and grief therapy: A handbook for the mental health practitioner.* New York: Springer.

World Health Organization [WHO]. (2003a). *Global strategy for infant and young child feeding.* Geneva, Switzerland: World Health Organization.

World Health Organization [WHO]. (2003b). *Kangaroo mother care: A practical guide.* Geneva, Switzerland: Dept. of Reproductive Health and Research, World Health Organization.

World Health Organization [WHO]. (2005). World health statistics 2005. Retrieved November 7, 2006, from http://www.who.int/healthinfo/statistics/whstatsdownloads/en/index.html

Worrell, F. C. (1997). Predicting successful or non-successful at-risk status using demographic risk factors. *High School Journal, 81,* 46–53.

Wu, T., Mendola, P., & Buck, G. M. (2002). Ethnic differences in the presence of secondary sex characteristics and menarche among US girls: The Third National Health and Nutrition Examination Survey, 1988–1994. *Pediatrics, 110,* 752–757.

Wynbrandt, J., & Ludman, M. D. (2000). *The encyclopedia of genetic disorders and birth defects* (2nd ed.). New York: Facts on File.

Xia, Y. R., & Zhou, Z. G. (2003). The transition of courtship, mate selection, and marriage in China. In R. R. Hamon & B. B. Ingoldsby (Eds.), *Mate selection across cultures* (pp. 231–246). Thousand Oaks: Sage.

Yabroff, K. R., Mandelblatt, J. S., & Ingham, J. (2004). The quality of medical care at the end-of-life in the USA: Existing barriers and examples of process and outcome measures. *Palliative Medicine, 18,* 202–216.

Yancey, G. A., & Yancey, S. W. (2002). *Just don't marry one: Interracial dating, marriage, and parenting.* Valley Forge, PA: Judson Press.

Yang, C.-K., Kim, J. K., Patel, S. R., & Lee, J.-H. (2005). Age-related changes in sleep/wake patterns among Korean teenagers. *Pediatrics, 115,* 250–256.

Yang, C. K., & Hahn, H. M. (2002). Cosleeping in young Korean children. *Journal of Developmental & Behavioral Pediatrics, 23,* 151–157.

Yates, M., & Youniss, J. (1998). Community service and political identity development in adolescence. *Journal of Social Issues, 54,* 495–512.

Yeh, C. J., Carter, R. T., & Pieterse, A. L. (2004). Cultural values and racial identity attitudes among Asian American students: An exploratory investigation. *Counseling and Values, 48,* 82–95.

Yeung, W. J., Linver, M. R., & Brooks-Gunn, J. (2002). How money matters for young children's development: Parental investment and family processes. *Child Development, 73,* 1861–1879.

Yogman, M. W., Cooley, J., & Kindlon, D. (1988). Fathers, infants, and toddlers: A developing relationship. In P. Bronstein & C. P. Cowan (Eds.), *Fatherhood today: Men's changing role in the family* (pp. 53–65). Oxford, England: Wiley.

Young, A. M., Stewart, A. J., & Miner-Rubino, K. (2001). Women's understandings of their own divorces: A developmental perspective. In D. P. McAdams, R. Josselson, & A. Lieblich (Eds.), *Turns in the road: Narrative studies of lives in transition* (pp. 203–226). Washington, DC: American Psychological Association.

Youngblade, L. M., & Belsky, J. (1992). Parent-child antecedents of 5-year-olds' close friendships: A longitudinal analysis. *Developmental Psychology, 28,* 700–713.

Youngblade, L. M., & Dunn, J. (1995). Individual differences in young children's pretend play with mother and sibling: Links to relationships and understanding of other people's feelings and beliefs. *Child Development, 66,* 1472–1492.

Youniss, J., & Ruth, A. J. (2002). Approaching policy for adolescent development in the 21st century. In J. T. Mortimer & R. W. Larson (Eds.), *The changing adolescent experience: Societal trends and the transition to adulthood* (pp. 250–271). New York: Cambridge University Press.

Yount, K. M., & Agree, E. M. (2004). The power of older women and men in Egyptian and Tunisian families. *Journal of Marriage and Family, 66,* 126–146.

Zacks, R., & Hasher, L. (1997). Cognitive gerontology and attentional inhibition: A reply to Burke and McDowd. *Journals of Gerontology: Series B: Psychological Sciences and Social Sciences, 52B,* P274-P283.

Zacks, R. T., Hasher, L., & Li, K. Z. H. (2000). Human memory. In F. I. M. Craik & T. A. Salthouse (Eds.), *The handbook of aging and cognition* (2nd ed., pp. 293–357). Mahwah, NJ: Erlbaum.

Zaichkowsky, L. D., & Larson, G. A. (1995). Physical, motor, and fitness development in children and adolescents. *Journal of Education, 177,* 55–79.

Zametkin, A. J., Zoon, C. K., Klein, H. W., & Munson, S. (2004). Psychiatric aspects of child and adolescent obesity: A review of the past 10 years. *Journal of the American Academy of Child & Adolescent Psychiatry, 43,* 134–150.

Zarit, S. H., Reever, K. E., & Bach-Peterson, J. (1980). Relatives of the impaired elderly: Correlates of feelings of burden. *Gerontologist, 20,* 649–655.

Zayas, L. H., Jankowski, K. R., & McKee, M. (2003). Prenatal and postpartum depression among low-income Dominican and Puerto Rican women. *Hispanic Journal of Behavioral Sciences, 25,* 370–385.

Zeigler, D. W., Wang, C. C., Yoast, R. A., Dickinson, B. D., McCaffree, M. A., Robinowitz, C. B., & Sterling, M. L. (2005). The neurocognitive effects of alcohol on adolescents and college students. *Preventive Medicine, 40,* 23–32.

Zelinski, E. M., & Burnight, K. P. (1997). Sixteen-year longitudinal and time lag changes in memory and cognition in older adults. *Psychology and Aging, 12,* 503–513.

Zelkowitz, P., Schinazi, J., Katofsky, L., Saucier, J. F., Valenzuela, M., Westreich, R., & Dayan, J. (2004). Factors associated with depression in pregnant immigrant women. *Transcultural Psychiatry, 41,* 445–464.

Zeller, M., Vannatta, K., Schafer, J., & Noll, R. B. (2003). Behavioral reputation: A cross-age perspective. *Developmental Psychology, 39,* 129–139.

Zeskind, P. S., & Barr, R. G. (1997). Acoustic characteristics of naturally occurring cries of infants with "colic." *Child Development, 68,* 394–403.

Zeskind, P. S., & Lester, B. M. (2001). Analysis of infant crying. In L. T. Singer & P. S. Zeskind (Eds.), *Biobehavioral assessment of the infant* (pp. 149–166). New York: Guilford Press.

Zeskind, P. S., & Marshall, T. R. (1988). The relation between variations in pitch and maternal perceptions of infant crying. *Child Development, 59,* 193–196.

Zhan, H. J. (2004). Socialization or social structure: Investigating predictors of attitudes toward filial responsibility among Chinese urban youth from one- and multiple-child families. *International Journal of Aging & Human Development, 59,* 105–124.

Zimprich, D., & Martin, M. (2002). Can longitudinal changes in processing speed explain longitudinal age changes in fluid intelligence? *Psychology and Aging, 17,* 690–695.

Zucker, A. N., Ostrove, J. M., & Stewart, A. J. (2002). College-educated women's personality development in adulthood: Perceptions and age differences. *Psychology and Aging, 17,* 236–244.

Zuckerman, M., Porac, J., Lathin, D., Smith, R., & Deci, E. L. (1978). On the importance of self-determination for intrinsically-motivated behavior. *Personality and Social Psychology Bulletin, 4,* 443–446.

Subject
Index